D0251626

Morocco

Anthony Ham

Alison Bing, Paul Clammer, Etain O'Carroll, Anthony Sattin

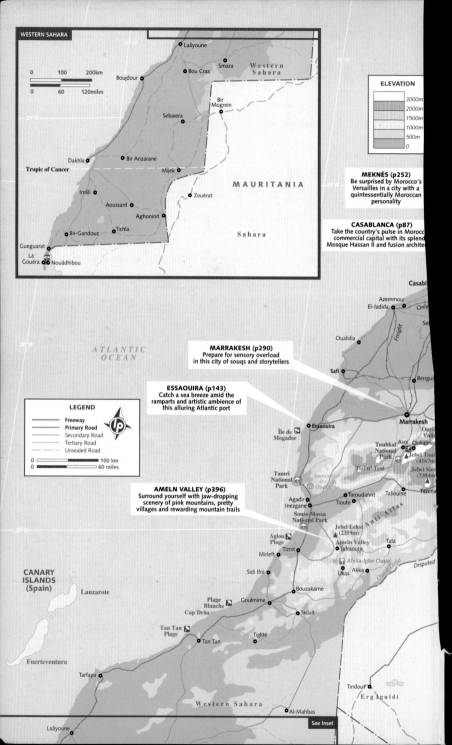

WESTERN SAHARA

Laâyoune
Smara
Bou Craa
Boujdour
Western Sahara
Bir Mogrein
Sebaiera
Dakhla
Bir Anzarane
Mijek
Tropic of Cancer
MAURITANIA
Imlili
Zouérat
Aoussard
Aghoninit
Tichla
Bir-Gandouz
Sahara
Gueguarat
La Gouéra
Nouâdhibou

ELEVATION

3000m
2000m
1500m
1000m
500m
0

MEKNÈS (p252)
Be surprised by Morocco's
Versailles in a city with a
quintessentially Moroccan
personality

CASABLANCA (p87)
Take the country's pulse in Morocco's
commercial capital with its splend...
Mosque Hassan II and fusion archite...

Casabl...

Azemmour
El-Jadida
Only...
Oualidia
Se...
Safi
Bengu...

ATLANTIC OCEAN

MARRAKESH (p290)
Prepare for sensory overload
in this city of souqs and storytellers

Marrakesh
Ouri...
Valle...
Toubkal
National
Park
Asg...
Oukaimed...
Jebel Tou...
4167m...
Tizi n' Test
Jebel Siro...
(3304m...

ESSAOUIRA (p143)
Catch a sea breeze amid the
ramparts and artistic ambience of
this alluring Atlantic port

Île de Mogador
Essaouira

LEGEND

Freeway
Primary Road
Secondary Road
Tertiary Road
Unsealed Road

0 —— 100 km
0 —— 60 miles

Tamri
National
Park
Immouzer
des Ida Ou...
Taroudannt
Taliouine
Tazena...
Agadir
Inezgane
Tioute
Souss-Massa
National Park
Jebel Leksi
(2359m)
Anti Atlas

AMELN VALLEY (p396)
Surround yourself with jaw-dropping
scenery of pink mountains, pretty
villages and rewarding mountain trails

Aglou
Plage
Tiznit
Ameln Valley
Tafraoute
Tata
Mirleft
Afella-Ighir Oasis
Disputed
Sidi Ifni
Ukas
Akka
Oued Drâa
Bouzakarne

CANARY
ISLANDS
(Spain)
Lanzarote

Plage
Blanche
Cap Drâa
Goulmime
Tadalt

Tan Tan
Plage
Tan Tan
Tiglite

Fuerteventura

Tarfaya

Tindouf
Erg Iguidi

Western Sahara
Al-Mahbas

Laâyoune

See Inset

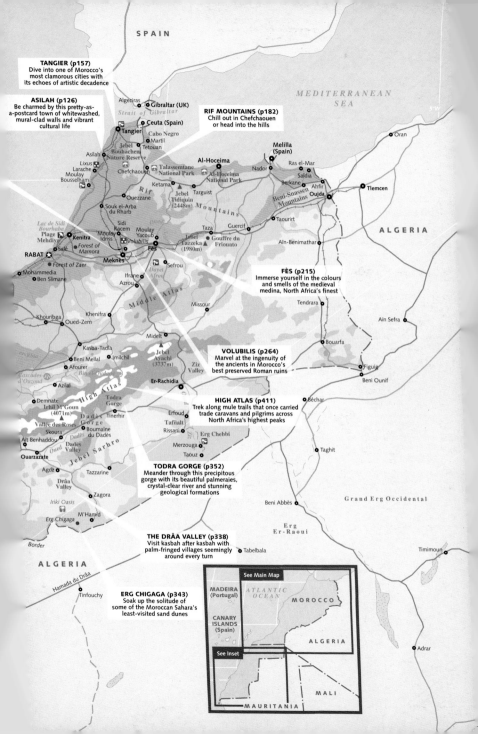

TANGIER (p157)
Dive into one of Morocco's most clamorous cities with its echoes of artistic decadence

ASILAH (p126)
Be charmed by this pretty-as-a-postcard town of whitewashed, mural-clad walls and vibrant cultural life

RIF MOUNTAINS (p182)
Chill out in Chefchaouen or head into the hills

FÈS (p215)
Immerse yourself in the colours and smells of the medieval medina, North Africa's finest

VOLUBILIS (p264)
Marvel at the ingenuity of the ancients in Morocco's best preserved Roman ruins

HIGH ATLAS (p411)
Trek along mule trails that once carried trade caravans and pilgrims across North Africa's highest peaks

TODRA GORGE (p352)
Meander through this precipitous gorge with its beautiful palmeraies, crystal-clear river and stunning geological formations

THE DRÂA VALLEY (p338)
Visit kasbah after kasbah with palm-fringed villages seemingly around every turn

ERG CHIGAGA (p343)
Soak up the solitude of some of the Moroccan Sahara's least-visited sand dunes

Destination Morocco

Welcome to one of the greatest shows on earth.

Morocco is sensory overload at its most intoxicating, from the scents and sounds that permeate the medinas of medieval Fès and magical Marrakesh to the astonishing sights of the infinitely varied Moroccan landscape.

Morocco has always been a crossroads of Africa, Europe and the Middle East and nowhere evokes this sense more than Tangier. The faded poster boy for Europe's presence – often decadent but sometimes creative – on Moroccan shores, Tangier is most people's introduction to the country. Turn south along Morocco's Atlantic coast and you'll be accompanied by a sea breeze that massages the ramparts of wonderful cities whose names – Essaouira, Casablanca, Asilah, Rabat – and atmosphere carry a strong whiff of African magic. Travel east along Morocco's Mediterranean coast and you'll be bidden into enchanted towns like Tetouan and Chefchaouen, and the mountains of the Rif.

An abundance of mountains stretches from the Rif, through the Middle Atlas and on into the extraordinary contours of the 1000km-long, over 4000m-tall High Atlas. This is a land custom-built for trekking and getting off-road as you follow quiet mountain trails amid mountain villages, fields of flowers and the homeland of the friendly Berber people.

And then, suddenly, everything changes. The mountains fissure into precipitous gorges, mud-brick kasbahs turn blood-red with the setting sun and the sense that one has stumbled into a fairytale takes hold. From rocky fortresses such as these, the Sahara announces its presence in Morocco with perfectly sculpted seas of sand.

At journey's end, the solitude of the Sahara is ideal for contemplating why it is that Morocco has such cachet. The answer is simple: There is no place on earth quite like this.

Explore the rooftop of North Africa by trekking in the High Atlas (p411)

OTHER HIGHLIGHTS

- Keep an eye out for Barbary apes (p428) while hiking through the Rif.
- Stroll Boulevard de la Corniche (p92), Casablanca's premier beachfront promenade.

Scale the steep streets of Chefchaouen (p189), one of the prettiest towns in the Rif

Dramatic Landscapes

Thread your way through the towering ochre cliffs of the Todra Gorge (p352)

DAVID WALL

Kasbahs and *ksour* (fortified strongholds) line the route to the Dadès Gorge (p348)

JOHN ELK III

OTHER HIGHLIGHTS

- Witness the wildflowers blooming in the springtime on the highland meadows of the Tichka plateau (p423).
- Wind the dramatic coastal road to Oued Laou (p197), a sleepy village of fishing boats and hidden coves.

Jagged peaks are snowbound all winter around Jebel Toubkal (p419)

MARK DAFFEY

Be mesmerised by summits of sand at Erg Chebbi (p362), most spectacular when viewed at sunrise or sunset.

MARK DAFFEY

Monuments, Mosques & Medersas

DOUG MCKINLAY

The *mihrab*, or prayer niche, points the direction to Mecca at the Ali ben Youssef Medersa (p298), Marrakesh

Marvel at the massive Hassan II Mosque (p91) in Casablanca, an architectural wonder

CAROL POLICH

Be awestruck by the legacy of ancient empires at the 2000-year-old Roman ruins of Volubilis (p264)

OTHER HIGHLIGHTS

▨ Visit Meknès (p252), the pint-sized imperial city that's still full of attractions.

▨ Walk from Volubilis to the holy town of Moulay Idriss (p266), an important pilgrimage site and resting place of Morocco's most revered saint.

CAROL POLICH

Medina Life

OLIVIER CIRENDINI

Women walk through the maze that is the medina of the old city, Fès el-Bali (p220)

JEFFREY BECOM

Streets glow unearthly blue in the famous Chefchaouen medina (p191), where Moroccan and Andalucian architecture meet

OTHER HIGHLIGHTS

- Ramble the 16th-century ramparts of El-Jadida's Cité Portugaise (p132).
- Tackle the tapas and sneak a siesta in the Spanish enclave of Ceuta (p176).

Dine under the stars at Djemaa el-Fna (295), centre of the Marrakshi universe

SARA-JANE CLELAND

Outdoors Morocco

VLADIMIR LIBA

Take in the views over the Dadès Valley (p348), sometimes called the 'Valley of a Thousand Kasbahs'

OTHER HIGHLIGHTS

- Go bird-watching or simply cruise the blue lagoon by boat at Merdja Zerga National Park (p122).
- Hit the surf and sand at Mirleft (p386), taking your pick of six gorgeous beaches.

Camel trek for hours, days or weeks into the dunes of the Sahara at Erg Chigaga (p343)

JOHN ELK III

Serious Shopping

Head south to the Souss to see the finest of Berber jewellery (p385)

OTHER HIGHLIGHTS

- Test your mettle haggling for a carpet – but be sure to do your homework (p60).
- Follow the walking tour (p304) through the labyrinth of shops and souqs in the Fès medina.

Stroll through the souqs of Marrakesh and see the traditional medicines, powders and potions at the apothecary stalls (p306) in Place Rahba Qedima

Don't miss market day at one of the Berber villages in the lush Aït Bou Goumez Valley (p343)

Culinary Morocco

DOUG MCKINLAY

Before stocking up on spices in the souqs, get hands-on hints with a cooking course (p306) in Marrakesh

OTHER HIGHLIGHTS

- Shuck your share of the world-famous oysters of Oualidia (p137).
- Escape the bustle of Marrakesh on a day trip to the dramatic Ourika Valley (p326), enjoying pristine views and fine dining.

The main event at a Moroccan *diffa* (feast) is hand-rolled couscous (p73)

OLIVIER CIRENDINI

DOUG MCKINLAY

Discover your sweet tooth at a souq stall, just don't spoil your dinner if you're planning to do the *diffa* (p74)

Contents

Regional Map Contents

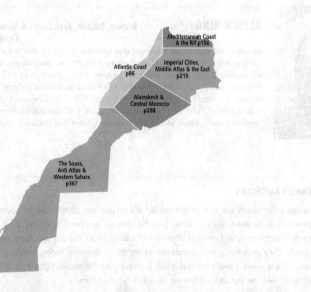

Mediterranean Coast & the Rif p156

Atlantic Coast p86

Imperial Cities, Middle Atlas & the East p215

Marrakesh & Central Morocco p288

The Souss, Anti Atlas & Western Sahara p367

The Authors

ANTHONY HAM
Coordinating Author, Getting Started, Itineraries, Snapshot, Directory

Anthony's Moroccan love affair began too many years ago to remember when he began dreaming of medieval medinas and the endless horizons of the Sahara. These contradictory passions continue to drive him on in search of the most intimate medina secrets, the most perfectly sculpted sand dunes and the contentment that always comes from drawing near around the Saharan campfire on a starry desert night. For most of the year, Anthony travels, writes and photographs his way around Africa and the Middle East from his base in Madrid, but finds himself called back to Morocco on a regular basis.

My Favourite Trip
Tangier (p157) has that gritty decadence of port cities throughout the world but its association with the Beat Generation writers gives it a whole new dimension. I can't miss **Chefchaouen** (p189), but, unable to wait any longer, I'd push on to **Fès** (p215), which is everything that I love about Morocco. A long bus ride across the soaring Atlas Mountains awaits to the sand seas of my imagination at **Erg Chebbi** (p362) and **Erg Chigaga** (p343) where I'd linger for as long as time allows before setting off in search of the kasbahs in the **Drâa Valley** (p338). **Aït Benhaddou** (p331) is always on my itinerary, before continuing on to **Marrakesh** (p290) – it's clichéd and overrun by tourists but there's no place like it on earth.

Tangier O
Chefchaouen O
O Fès
O Marrakesh
Aït Benhaddou O
Erg Chebbi
Drâa Valley O
O
Erg Chigaga

ALISON BING
History, Culture, Arts, Crafts & Architecture, Food & Drink

Alison's first crush was Sufi poet and whirling dervish honcho Rumi, after visiting his shrine in Turkey at age five. Though her own career as a dervish didn't quite pan out, she studied Islamic art, architecture and political economy at the American University in Cairo and Bryn Mawr College. She also earned a master's degree from the Fletcher School of Law and Diplomacy, a program of Tufts and Harvard Universities – diplomatic credentials she regularly undermines with opinionated art, food and culture commentary.

LONELY PLANET AUTHORS

Why is our travel information the best in the world? It's simple: our authors are independent, dedicated travellers. They don't research using just the internet or phone, and they don't take freebies in exchange for positive coverage. They travel widely, to all the popular spots and off the beaten track. They personally visit thousands of hotels, restaurants, cafés, bars, galleries, palaces, museums and more – and they take pride in getting all the details right, and telling it how it is. For more, see the authors section on www.lonelyplanet.com.

PAUL CLAMMER

Mediterranean Coast & The Rif (including Rif Trekking), Imperial Cities, Middle Atlas & the East, Transport, Health

As a student, Paul had his first solo backpacking experience when he took a bus from his Cambridgeshire home all the way to Casablanca. Morocco instantly enchanted him. After an interlude when he trained and worked as a molecular biologist, he returned years later working as a tour guide, trekking in the Atlas and trying not to lose passengers in the Fès medina. When he's not working on Lonely Planet guides to other parts of the Islamic world, Paul is happy to tell anyone who asks that Moroccan orange juice is the best in the world.

ETAIN O'CARROLL

Atlantic Coast

Hopping off the ferry in Tangier on her first, spur-of-the-moment trip to Morocco, Etain was prepared for the worst but was smitten instead by the sights, smells and scenery of this incredible country. Since then, she's spent innumerable hours drinking mint tea, haggling, warding off would-be husbands and reviving dead legs after marathon journeys squashed up beside the door of a grand taxi. She's travelled by bike, foot and camel to get to the far reaches of the country and still hasn't got over the need to go back. Etain works as a freelance travel writer and photographer for a variety of publishers.

ANTHONY SATTIN

Marrakesh & Central Morocco, The Souss, Anti Atlas & Western Sahara, Trekking, Language

Since his first visit as a teenager, Anthony has spent much of his adult life living in, travelling around or writing about North Africa and the Middle East. He is the author of several highly acclaimed books about Africa, including *The Pharaoh's Shadow*, in which he searched for Egypt's surviving ancient culture. His most recent book, *The Gates of Africa*, tells the history of early exploration in Africa and the search for Timbuktu. Now based in London, he is a regular contributor to the *Sunday Times*. As a broadcaster, Anthony has made both television and radio documentaries about Egypt. Described by one British newspaper as 'a cross between Indiana Jones and a John Buchan hero', he loves to divide his time between London and the further reaches of the Nile.

Getting Started

Morocco is Africa and the Middle East rolled into one and therefore comes with all the rewards and challenges of both. Far more than an easy add-on to a European journey, Morocco repays those who carefully prepare their trip by reading widely, both in print and on the net, and is best understood by those who understand that Morocco is at once frustrating and a deliciously overwhelming assault on the senses. You'll also need to plan your journey around the vagaries of climate and the moveable feast of Islamic holidays that can impact upon your time in Morocco. But above all, don't forget to dream, to spend time imagining the journey of a lifetime that Morocco could just provide.

WHEN TO GO

See climate charts on p447 for more information.

Morocco is at its best in spring (mid-March to May), when the country is lush and green, followed by autumn (September to November) when the heat of summer has eased.

At other times, don't underestimate the extremes of summer heat and winter, particularly in the High Atlas, where snowcapped peaks persist from November to July. If you are travelling in winter, head for the south, although be prepared for bitterly cold nights. Morocco's Mediterranean coast and Rif Mountains are frequently wet and cloudy in winter and early spring.

Apart from the weather, it is the timing of Ramadan, the traditional month of fasting and purification, which is another important consid-

---

DON'T LEAVE HOME WITHOUT...

- your ID card or passport and visa if required (p465)
- valid travel insurance (p456)
- driving licence, car documents and appropriate car insurance (p485) if driving
- loose-fitting cotton shirts and long skirts or trousers for women and men
- a universal washbasin plug or a tennis ball cut in half
- a compass to navigate the labyrinthine medinas
- a good tent, warm sleeping bag and sturdy walking boots if you plan on trekking (p406)
- some wet-weather gear, preferably Gore-Tex
- a torch
- earplugs for successful sleeping in the noisier cheap hotels
- a water bottle, purification tablets and a medical kit (p490) for longer stays
- an emergency supply of toilet paper
- a small (size-three) football – a great way to meet locals
- a sense of perspective – persistent shopkeepers are just trying to make a living and can actually be nice people
- patience – most things do run on time, but the timetable may be elusive to the uninitiated.

eration. During Ramadan some restaurants and cafés are closed during the day and general business hours are reduced (for more details see p455).

COSTS & MONEY

Morocco is probably more expensive than you thought. Once taking into account a few small tips, taxi fares, entry charges to museums, and with a willingness to stay in cheap hotels without respite, those carefully counting their dirhams could get by on Dh350 (US$40) per day. At the other end of the scale, if you intend to travel in style in cities like Marrakesh, expect your daily budget to increase dramatically – quality accommodation starts at Dh600, hovers around Dh1300 and then passes Dh3000 and keeps on going. Staying in an average-priced riad and enjoying quality restaurants will require a budget of at least Dh1000 a day per person. Outside the major cities most of the better accommodation tends to hover around Dh600.

A meal in a cheap restaurant costs as little as Dh30. In a midrange restaurant you'd pay up to Dh200 and in a more upmarket place it will cost around Dh300, including wine; in cities like Marrakesh you can pay up to Dh700 per person.

If you want to explore the country in your own car, average hire charges for a small car (Renault Clio) are Dh500 per day, with an additional Dh420 to fill up the tank with petrol (gas). Diesel is significantly cheaper (around Dh7 per litre) so it's best to hire a diesel car. For a 4WD you are looking at about Dh1430 per day, with driver.

There's not much difference in price between trains and buses – a bus ticket between Casablanca and Marrakesh costs Dh70, compared to Dh75.50 for a second-class train ticket. As a general rule, a 100km bus or train journey costs about Dh25.

HOW MUCH?

Pot of mint tea Dh5

Foreign newspaper Dh 30-35; weekend papers Dh70-80

Hammam Dh7-10

Petit-taxi ride Dh5-10

City bus ride Dh2-3

TRAVEL LITERATURE

The Caliph's House (Tahir Shah) A brilliant account of how a writer and filmmaker left behind London life to renovate the djinn-haunted former home of the caliph of Casablancan – overflowing with insight and Moroccan characters writ large.

Hideous Kinky (Esther Freud) A young hippie takes her children to Marrakesh to find herself and an alternative life. Famously made into a film starring Kate Winslet, Esther Freud's witty lightness-of-touch is even more engaging.

Morocco: In the Labyrinth of Dreams and Bazaars (Walter M Weiss) An ambitious journey through the contradictions of modern Morocco from its polyglot past to its modern liberal-conservative fault lines.

The Spider's House (Paul Bowles) Fès in the twilight of the French occupation is the arena for this political *tour de force* considered by many to be Bowles' finest. Daily Fès life, with its web-like complexities, provides a fascinating backdrop.

Street in Marrakech (Elizabeth Warnock Fernea) A peerless account that gets beneath the skin of beguiling Marrakesh, with fascinating portraits of city life and the struggles of a Western woman to fully enter the Moroccan world. Written in the 1980s, it still resonates.

Tangier: City of the Dream (Iain Finlayson) A highly readable account of the life of this 'seedy, salacious, decadent, degenerate' city with intriguing insights into the Beat Generation of writers including Paul Bowles, Truman Capote and Jack Kerouac.

Valley of the Casbahs: A Journey Across the Moroccan Sahara (Jeffrey Tayler) An epic modern-day camel journey from the Drâa Valley to the Atlantic, leaving behind tourist Morocco, with Berbers and a harsh desert terrain for company.

Zohra's Ladder: And Other Stories from Morocco (Pamela Windo) A lively window on the traveller's hard-love affair with Morocco, set against the vivid backdrop of Moroccan historical and social life.

TOP TENS

Our Favourite Festivals & Events

Moussems (festivals) honouring *marabouts* (local saints) are held all over the country throughout the year and some draw big crowds. Morocco also has a burgeoning selection of good international cultural events.

- Almond Blossom Festival (Tafraoute and around) February/March
- Festival du Desert (Er-Rachidia) May
- Moussem of Ben Aïssa (Meknès) May/June
- Gnaoua and World Music Festival (Essaouira) June
- Festival of World Sacred Music (Fès) June/July
- Festival International de Rabat (Rabat) June/July
- Marrakesh Popular Arts Festival (Marrakesh) July
- Festival of Casablanca (Casablanca) July
- International Cultural Festival (Asilah) July/August
- Marriage Festival (Imilchil) September

Must-see Moroccan Movies

Cinematic Morocco comes in many guises from hard-hitting social commentaries, usually the work of contemporary Moroccan film-makers, to Hollywood fantasy with its illusory idea of exotic North Africa.

- *Morocco* (1930) Director: Josef von Sternberg
- *Casablanca* (1942) Director: Michael Curtiz
- *The Man Who Knew Too Much* (1956) Director: Alfred Hitchcock
- *A Thousand and One Hands* (1972) Director: Souheil Ben Barka
- *El Chergui* (1974) Director: Moumem Smihi
- *Alyam Alyam* (1978) Director: Ahmed el Maanouni
- *Le Coiffeur du Quartier des Pauvres* (1982) Director: Mohamed Reggab
- *Badis* (1988) Director: Mohamed Aberrahman Tazi
- *Hideous Kinky* (1998) Director: Gilles MacKinnon
- *The Wind Horse* (2001) Director: Daoud Aoulad-Syad

Top Reads

If you're interested in further reading on Morocco, try some of the books we've detailed here. To track down hard-to-find books try the following online bookstores: www.amazon.com, www.stanfords.co.uk, www.thetravelbookshop.co.uk.

- *Morocco That Was* (1921) Walter Harris
- *In Morocco* (1927) Edith Wharton
- *The Sheltering Sky* (1949) Paul Bowles
- *The Voices of Marrakesh* (1967) Elias Canetti
- *The Conquest of Morocco* (1986) Douglas Porch
- *The Sand Child* (1987) Tahar Ben Jelloun
- *Tales of a Harem Girlhood* (1995) Fatima Mernissi
- *For Bread Alone* (2000) Mohamed Choukri
- *A Year in Marrakesh* (2002) Peter Mayne
- *Morocco: The Traveller's Companion* (2005) Margaret & Robert Bidwell

INTERNET RESOURCES

The Lonely Planet website (www.lonelyplanet.com) has up-to-date news and the Thorn Tree bulletin board, where you can post questions.

Al-Bab (www.al-bab.com/maroc) Also called The Moroccan Gateway, Al-Bab has excellent links, especially for current affairs, news and good books about Morocco.

Maghreb Arts (www.maghrebarts.ma in French) Up-to-the-minute coverage of theatre, film, music, festivals and media events in Morocco.

Office National des Chemins de Fer (www.oncf.ma in French) Official website of the Moroccan rail services with information on timetables and prices.

Tourism in Morocco (www.tourism-in-morocco.com/index_en.php) Morocco's official tourist information site; user-friendly, with guided tours, links and news.

Itineraries

CLASSIC ROUTES

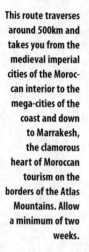

This route traverses around 500km and takes you from the medieval imperial cities of the Moroccan interior to the mega-cities of the coast and down to Marrakesh, the clamorous heart of Moroccan tourism on the borders of the Atlas Mountains. Allow a minimum of two weeks.

IMPERIAL CITIES   Two Weeks/Fès to Marrakesh

Immerse yourself in the cities once ruled by enlightened dynasties, who crossed the Strait of Gibraltar and pulled Europe out of its dark age. Begin in **Fès** (p215), venerable heart of Morocco's religious and cultural life, and see modern Morocco and its rich antecedent crowd for space in the extraordinary medina. **Meknès** (p252) is a name that resonates through Moroccan history, which finds lavish expression in the palace built by Sultan Moulay Ismail (1672–1727). **Volubilis** (p264), easily Morocco's best-preserved ancient city, stands testament to the astonishing breadth of the Roman Empire. Nearby **Moulay Idriss** (p266), home to the shrine of the founder of Morocco's first imperial dynasty, is a wonderful antidote to the clamour of the cities.

While **Rabat** (p103) lacks the prestige of Morocco's other cities, it's enjoying its third period as Morocco's imperial capital. A modern city of elegant French streets, its quiet, 12th-century medina hints at former imperial grandeur. Street-savvy **Casablanca** (p87), Morocco's principal port and most prosperous city, has an energy and anarchy rivalled only by **Marrakesh** (p290), that icon of today's Morocco, where centuries of souqs, street performers and imperial architecture have been perfected in an intoxicating mix.

MOROCCAN ODYSSEY   One Month/Imperial Cities & the South

With a month at your disposal and taking little time to rest, you can get a taste of the best Morocco has to offer, by journeying from the sea to the Sahara and back again. Fly in to **Casablanca** (p87) before heading to **Meknès** (p252) and **Fès** (p215).

From Meknès, leave behind the noise and hassles of the city and head directly south to the relatively under-visited Middle Atlas around **Azrou** (p269) where the Barbary apes are one of Moroccan wildlife's most mischievous sights. Pretty **Ifrane** (p267) also stands at the heart of some stunning mountain scenery and offers enticing possibilities for hiking in the lush countryside, although continuing south through **Midelt** (p272) is arguably even more scenic. The journey through the delightfully palm-and-*ksar* (fortified stronghold) terrain of the **Ziz Valley** (p355) is one of Morocco's most picturesque roads and carries you down towards **Merzouga** (p362), southwestern Morocco's gateway to the Sahara. Lorded over by towering dunes, it's an ideal spot to saddle up your camel and sleep under the stars amid Morocco's largest sand sea, the perfectly sculpted **Erg Chebbi** (p362).

Shadowing the High Atlas as you head southwest brings you to the sharp cleft of the **Todra Gorge** (p352). From here, you can travel through dramatic boulder-strewn valleys, full of nomad camps in spring time, into the **Dadès Gorge** (p348). If time allows, strike out from Boumalne du Dadès for some spectacular trekking around the **M'Goun Massif** (p424) before making for **Aït Benhaddou** (p331) which seems like an evocation of a fairytale.

En route to the coast, check into a luxurious riad in **Marrakesh** (p290), stay as long as you can, and then don't stop until you reach artsy **Essaouira** (p143).

The arc from cosmopolitan Casablanca to chic Essaouira involves a journey of around 1500km. En route, you'll pass through a microcosm of Moroccan landscapes, from coast to quiet mountain valleys to the solitude of Saharan sand dunes and back to the shores of the Atlantic. You'll need a month to make the most of this itinerary.

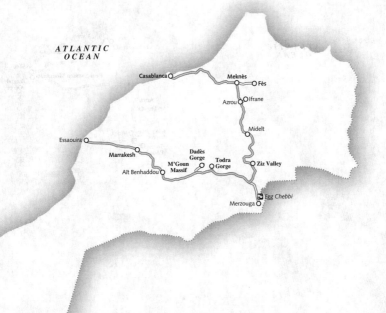

ROADS LESS TRAVELLED

HIDDEN MOROCCO

Three to Four Weeks/ Mediterranean Coast & Middle Atlas

From the Mediterranean Coast to Morocco's deep south, there are abundant opportunities for finding a Morocco that you may have all to yourself – with a few Moroccan friends, of course. Is **Chefchaouen** (p189) too much of a scene? Stay just long enough to organise a five-day trek via **Akchour** (p431) to the tiny fishing village of **Bou Ahmed** (p431); try and be here on Tuesday for the weekly souq. Continue east along the coast to **Al-Hoceima** (p199), gateway to the Al-Hoceima National Park and otherwise a place where fresh seafood and fine beaches offer a fine way to break up the journey. **Berkane** (p211) in Morocco's far northeast provides few reasons to linger, but it serves as an entry point to the **Beni-Sanssen Mountains** (p211) and the achingly beautiful and flower-filled **Zegzel Gorge** (p212).

Double back towards Meknès and then south into the Middle Atlas. Head to the quaint mountain town of **Azrou** (p269) to shop for Berber rugs and to organise a trek through the ancient cedar forests of the surrounding highlands. The Berber villages around **'Ain Leuh** (p271) in particular are how all the Atlas used to be. As you go further south, landscapes change from green to pink as you enter the Eastern High Atlas region around earth-toned **Midelt** (p272) and the nearby **Kasbah des Noyers** (p273). Spend two days trekking to the **Cirque Jaffar** (p274), and another two climbing to the summit, or hire a vehicle and visit the eerily beautiful **Gorges d'Aouli** (p274).

This journey from the Rif Mountains, along the coast to the mountains close to the Algerian border and back into the Middle Atlas covers around 900km. Three weeks is a minimum but a month allows more trekking time.

SERIOUS ABOUT THE SOUTH   Three Weeks/Agadir & The Souss

If the thought of sharing Marrakesh and tourist-oriented beachside restaurants with the hordes is not how you'd like to remember Morocco, consider an activity-filled exploration of the south, where your companions are more likely to be locals, the odd camel and the solitude of sweeping landscapes.

Agadir is few travellers' idea of paradise so escape south to tiny **Tafraoute** (p392) encircled by the beautiful **Ameln Valley** (p396) with its lush, green *palmeraies* (palm groves) and pink-hued houses. Hire a bike and camp by the painted rocks, spend three days climbing **Jebel Lekst** (p396), or trek through the **Aït Mansour gorges** (p395) where the beautiful scenery contrasts poignantly with the ancient slave routes that once passed this way. Stay in **Tiwadou** (p395) then journey overland to see the rock engravings at **Ukas** (p395) before returning to Tafraoute.

By now you've a taste for the Moroccan wilderness (not to mention enormous calf muscles), so head east to the magnificent rock engravings around **Tata** (p396) and **Akka** (p396), then down to **Erg Chigaga** (p343), dunes which see few tourists. Leave your vehicle in M'Hamid and find yourself a camel to lead you north into the kasbah-littered **Drâa valley** (p338).

At **Ouarzazate** (p332), go quad biking in the stony desert landscape famous for its film studios, then loop back through the saffron capital of **Taliouine** (p382) with a detour for a trekking reprise on the **Tichka Plateau** (p423). Forge on to **Taroudannt** (p378) with its red walls, backdrop of snow-capped peaks and hassle-free echoes of Marrakesh, before heading back to **Agadir** (p371) for the much-needed robust pampering of a hammam.

This journey through the picturesque peaks of the Atlas Mountains and down into the desert landscapes and kasbahs of the south requires at least three weeks and you'll probably need your own vehicle in some areas as public transport can be scarce. By the time you reach Agadir, you'll have covered around 1000km.

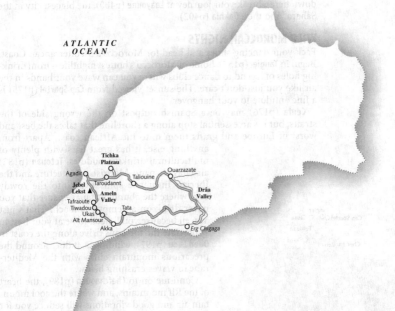

TAILORED TRIPS

ATLANTIC ADVENTURE

Morocco's Atlantic seaboard takes you from the clamour of the north to the deserted coastline of the south.

Take the ferry from Spain to **Tangier** (p157), at once a quintessentially Moroccan mosaic and a decadent outpost of Europe that feels more like Marseilles than Morocco. Catch the train south, first to artsy **Asilah** (p126), which is loaded with whitewashed charm and then on to **Casablanca** (p87) with its melange of Art Deco and skyscrapers. Follow Casa's suburbanites to **El-Jadida** (p132) then visit **Oualidia** (p137), a St Tropez lookalike grafted onto the African coast and arrayed around a perfect crescent lagoon. There are also safe surfing spots nearby. Further down the coast, **Essaouira** (p143) may have been discovered long ago, but its white-walled ramparts, bohemian beat and renovated riads have that special something that makes travellers stay longer than they planned. The peaceful beaches of **Diabat** (p154) and **Sidi Kaouki** (p154) are close at hand.

For family-friendly beaches head on to **Agadir** (p371) or escape the crowds further south in **Mirleft** (p386) or **Sidi Ifni** (p386), the last ports of call before the Western Sahara. If you're heading south to Mauritania (and there are few other reasons to come down here), break your journey at **Laâyoune** (p400), the biggest city in the Sahara, and then **Dakhla** (p402).

WILD MOROCCAN NIGHTS

Pack your dancing shoes and head for Morocco's Mediterranean Coast. Begin in **Tangier** (p157), home of Morocco's hottest nightlife – from drinking holes of legend to dance clubs where you can wave your hands in the air like you just don't care. The sunset viewed from **Cap Spartel** (p175) is a fine antidote to your hangover.

Ceuta (p176) may be a Spanish outpost on the wrong side of the straits, but it's an essential stop along a shoreline that takes the best and worst of Europe and grafts them onto the African coast. Apart from anything else, it has great bars with plenty of multicultural drinking buddies. **Tetouan** (p182) also has Hispano-Moorish architecture and the Iberian influence spills over into the rowdy bars where the abundant tapas ensure that you never drink on an empty stomach. That's just as well because you'll need to be at your best to appreciate the tortuous drive along the coast to **Oued Laou** (p197), winding as it does around the precarious mountain cliffs with the Mediterranean waves crashing below.

Continue on to **Chefchaouen** (p189), the heart of the Rif mountains, and where the cool mountain air and good vibrations will seduce you for as long as you let yourself be swept away.

WORLD HERITAGE SITES

Morocco has eight Unesco World Heritage-listed Sites (http://whc
.unesco.org) which provide some excellent focal points around which to
build your Moroccan journey.

The jewel in the crown is the vast, living, ramshackle museum that
is **Fès El-Bali** (p220) in Fès, the first Moroccan site to be inscribed on the
list in 1981. The splendour of the **Imperial City of Meknès** (p255), including the medina, have received official recogni-
tion to match the widespread view that this is
Morocco's Versailles. Nearby, the Roman city
of **Volubilis** (p264), with its astonishing mosaics
left *in situ*, suggests that this region has always
inspired world-class architects.

To the north, the splendid **Tetouan medina**
(p183) is not your ordinary Moroccan medina
due to the strong Andalusian overtones be-
queathed by Moorish architects escaping Spain
in the 16th century. From Tetouan, head for
the coast and down past Casablanca to **El-Jadida**
(p132) where the enchanting Portuguese port
yields many surprises, not least the remarkable underground cistern where Orson Welles
chose to film scenes in his 1954 classic *Othello*.
Continuing down the coast, the **Essaouira medina** (p145) is deservedly on
the list, as is the iconic **medina of Marrakesh** (p295). Of all the extraordinary
mud-brick architecture in Morocco's south, Unesco chose the **Ksar of Aït
Benhaddou** (p331) and it's hard to disagree with their choice.

A MOROCCAN CULINARY TOUR

Fès is a Moroccan culinary capital that travellers of all budgets can
enjoy, from the local *b'sara* (a butterbean and garlic soup) served at
stalls (p233) all over town to one of the sumptuous palace restaurants
like **Restaurant Laanibra** (p233). Marrakesh is a
feast in more ways than you can imagine but
you can learn how to make your own at **Souq
Cuisine** (p306) or **Chambres d'Amis** (p306), two
of many wonderful cooking schools in town.
As you continue south, saffron-scented Taliouine does more than produce saffron – at
the **Coopérative Souktana du Safran** (p382) there's
a saffron museum, saffron tasting and a saffron
shop. *Mechoui* (spit-roasted lamb) is a High
Atlas speciality so pause in Taroudannt at **Jnane
Soussia** (p381) before continuing on your way.
At Tamanar, 80km north of Agadir, make for
Coopérative Amal (p389), where they'll tell and
show you everything you need to know about
argan oil, which is unique to Morocco. Away to
the southeast, the villages of the **Ameln Valley** (p396) are known for their
food festivals; if you're here in late February, the **almond harvest** (p392)
around Tafraoute is a wonderfully food-focussed celebration, although
the delicious *amlou* (honey-and-almond paste made with argan oil) is
available year-round. For regional Moroccan specialties, see Been There,
Eaten That, on p75.

Snapshot

Morocco's polyglot identity may provide endless fascination and intrigue for travellers, but it lays bare many of the country's fault lines. The tension between conservative and liberal, secular and Islamic, modern and traditional elements of Moroccan society is at times creative but just as often deeply unsettling for ordinary Moroccans.

FAST FACTS

Population: 33.2 million

GDP per head: US$4200

GDP growth: 1.8%

Inflation: 2.1%

Unemployment rate: 20%

External debt: US$15.6 billion

Life expectancy at birth: 69.7 years

Adult literacy rate: 50.7%

Year Moroccan women won the right to vote: 1963

Internet users: 3.5 million

These tensions impact on all Moroccans, from the Berber nomad scratching a hard-won living from remote mountain fields to the king in his palace. All eyes remain on the latter, who watches over it all with a sometimes patrician, sometimes sophisticated goal of forging a modern country from deeply traditional roots, while the former watches with heroic, if not infinite, patience.

When Mohammed VI ascended the throne upon the death of his father, Hassan II, on 23 July 1999 (p40), there was an expectant and collective intake of breath across the country. Would the new king follow in his father's authoritarian footsteps? How would Mohammed VI balance the pressure from the conservative old guard that surrounded his father with the clamour for change coming from the country's increasingly youthful population?

The answer is that many Moroccans feel no closer to knowing the answers.

The female half of the Moroccan population has been encouraged by the king's 2004 Mudawanna reforms (p52) under which women were guaranteed rights to custody, divorce, property ownership and child support, while female literacy is on the rise. The king has also made human rights freedoms a showpiece of his rule and although much remains to be done, there has been progress. Many former political prisoners now have their freedom (and, in some cases, compensation), dissent in public is no longer the act of great bravery it once was, Berber languages are now taught in some schools and Morocco has held its first-ever municipal elections.

At a practical level, investment in new roads, the widespread introduction of electricity, the provision of better sanitation and a huge number of social housing developments are all improving the daily lives of average Moroccans.

For all these signs of progress, however, the Moroccan leadership's unstinting support for the US-led War on Terror has alienated many, pushing some Moroccans into the arms of the extremists who carried out the 2003 Casablanca and 2004 Madrid terrorist bombings. The government has responded in kind, shelving human rights protections and thereby drawing the battle-lines for a potential future conflict for the soul of Morocco.

At the same time, Morocco continues to risk alienating international opinion by refusing to yield on the stalemate that is the Western Sahara.

As important as these issues are, however, it is the persistent poverty in which most Moroccans live that dominates everyday discussion in Morocco and which could most shape Morocco's future. With almost a third of Morocco's people under 15 years of age, how the problems of high unemployment and the resulting alienation are resolved will determine whether the next generation of Moroccans continues to drift towards conservative Islam or onto boats taking them to Europe, or whether they are able to envisage a prosperous future for themselves in the new Morocco that has for so long been promised.

History

NOW SHOWING: ANCIENT HISTORY

Stand amid Morocco's striped canyons, rich fossil deposits and sweeping deserts, and there's no denying that a truly ancient history is on display here as in few other places on earth. Henri Matisse, Paul Klee, Winston Churchill and the many others who have captured this country in watercolours were not exaggerating: the shades of Moroccan soil really do range from sunbaked gold and orange to highly unlikely pinks, reds and violets. This artistry is the work of prehistoric mineral deposits stranded here when tectonic plates wrested Morocco apart from what is today Pennsylvania, which might explain the two regions' shared mineral content – not to mention an otherwise puzzling mutual fondness for pancakes and headcheese for breakfast.

Morocco has been covered not in sand but water for most of its billions of years of geological history, and travellers through the High Atlas Mountains and the Atlantic plains near Agadir are certain to see stands selling both real and bogus fossilised souvenirs of this aquatic past. Morocco is a kind of reverse-Atlantis, where the Atlas ranges, the Saharan steppes, fertile plains and entire civilisations gradually surfaced from a rugged seabed over a few thousand years of drought. The earliest evidence of human settlement here dates from 75,000 to 125,000 BC, when most of North Africa was covered in lush semitropical forest and stone tools were cutting-edge technology. But what the proto-Moroccan 'pebble people' really needed were radiators; the Ice Age wasn't kind to them, and left the country wide open for settlement when the weather finally began to improve around 5000 BC (and you thought English summers were gloomy).

According to local folklore, the Berbers were descended from the earth's first couple, who had 100 children. Imagine the nappies...

LIVE FREE OR DIE TRYING: THE BERBERS

The fertile land revealed after the great thaw proved to be a magnet for Near Eastern nomads, early ancestors of Morocco's Amazigh (plural Imazighen, loosely translated as 'free people') who may have been distant cousins of the ancient Egyptians. They were joined by Mediterranean anglers and Saharan horse-breeders around 2500 BC. In the High Atlas, Bronze Age petroglyphs from 1600 BC depict fishing, hunting, and horseback riding – a versatile combination of skills and cultures that would define this adaptable, resilient people. Phoenicians appear to have arrived around 800 BC and East Africans around 500 BC, and when the Romans arrived in the 4th century they didn't know quite what to make of this multicultural milieu. The Romans called the expanse of Morocco and Western Algeria 'Mauretania' and the indigenous people 'Berbers' meaning 'barbarians'. The term has recently been reclaimed and redeemed by the Berber Pride movement, but at the time it was taken as quite a slur.

The ensuing centuries were one long lesson for the Romans in minding their manners. First the Berbers backed Hannibal and the Carthaginians against Rome in a rather serious spat over Sicily known as the

For news and insight on Berber culture, history, and politics today, visit www.amazigh-voice.com, an online Berber Pride forum. Many articles are in English, with others in French and postings in transliterated Tamazight (written Berber).

TIMELINE

5000-2500 BC	800-500 BC
Saharan, Mediterranean and indigenous people make themselves at home in Morocco	Phoenicians and East Africans add to the mix in the Maghreb

Punic Wars (264–202 BC). Then in 49 BC, North African King Juba I supported renegade general Pompey's ill-fated power play against Julius Caesar (whose senators picked up where Pompey left off a few years later). Fed up with the persistently unruly Berbers, the new Roman emperor Caligula finally declared the end of Berber autonomy in the Maghreb (North Africa) in AD 40. Caligula had a reputation for brutality to uphold, and subjugated entire North African communities, dividing relatively egalitarian Berber clans into subservient classes of slaves, peasants, soldiers and Romanised aristocrats. But whereas the Vandals and Byzantines failed to oust the Romans from their home turf, Berbers in the Rif and the Atlas ultimately succeeded through a campaign of near-constant harassment – a tactic that would later put the squeeze on many an unpopular Moroccan sultan and is still favoured by certain carpet salesmen today.

Ultimately Rome was only able to gain a sure foothold in the region by crowning local favourite Juba II king of Mauretania. The enterprising young king married the daughter of Mark Antony and Cleopatra, supported scientific research and performing arts, and helped foster Moroccan industries still vital today: olive oil production from the region of Volubilis (near Meknès), vineyards on the Atlantic plains, and fishing along the coasts. During his reign from 25 BC to AD 23, Juba II turned his headquarters at Volubilis into a bustling metropolis of 20,000 mostly Berber residents – including one of Morocco's earliest Jewish communities, judging from religious artefacts found there. Today you can still see polychrome Roman mosaics cut in Italy and assembled by Volubilis artisans into a blushing Ariadne awoken by Bacchus and intricate Berber carpet patterns – a hint of the stunning *zellij* (fitted mosaic) masterworks to come under Moroccan dynastic rule.

WHEN PURPLE WAS PURE GOLD

The port that is today called Essaouira was hot property in ancient times, because it had one thing everyone wanted: the colour purple. Imperial purple couldn't be fabricated, and was the one colour strictly reserved for Roman royalty. This helps explain the exorbitant asking price, which according to Aristotle was 10 to 20 times its weight in gold. The natural dye came from the spiky murex marine snails that clung to the remote Purpuraire (Purple) Islands, as though that could save them from ancient Roman fashionistas.

Technically the Phoenicians were there first and discovered the stuff, but that didn't stop others angling for a piece of the purple action. Savvy King Juba II established a coastal dye works in the 1st century BC to perform the tricky task of extracting murex dye from the vein of the mollusc and kept his methods a closely guarded secret. The hue became wildly popular among royal celebrities of the day; Cleopatra loved the stuff so much that she dyed the sails of her royal barge purple to meet Mark Antony.

But the colour proved downright dangerous. Legend has it that Juba's son Ptolemy was murdered by Emperor Caligula for having the audacity to sport a purple robe – talk about a fashion victim. The bright, nonfading dye was never successfully produced commercially and the secret extraction methods were assumed lost in the the siege of Constantinople in 1453. But in Essaouira the stuff is mysteriously still available, for a price; the mysteries of the colour purple are still passed down from one generation of murex collectors to the next.

The Roman foothold in Mauretania slipped in the centuries after Juba II died, due to increasingly organised Berber rebellions inland and attacks on the Atlantic and Mediterranean coasts by the Vandals, Byzantines and Visigoths. But this new crop of marauding Europeans couldn't manage Mauretania either. Taking heavy hints from hostile Rif warriors, the Vandals quickly moved along from Tangier toward Algeria in AD 429. The Berbers also showed up Byzantine emperor Justinian, whose grand plans to extend the Holy Roman Empire into Mauretania in 533 were soon reduced to a modest presence in Essaouira, Tangier and Salé. Justinian's Holy Roman enterprise turned out to be an unholy mess of treaties with various Berber kingdoms, who played their imperial Byzantine connections like face cards in private high-stakes games. The history of Morocco would be defined by such strategic gamesmanship among the Berbers, whose overlapping, often contradictory alliances with various nations competing for control of their land helped make foreign dominion over Morocco a near-impossible enterprise for more than a millennium.

> Despite Roman demands that locals make sacrifices to Roman gods, many North Africans practiced Christianity right under Roman noses – St Augustine himself was a Berber convert.

THE POWER OF CONVICTION

By the early 7th century, the Berbers of Morocco were mostly worshipping their own indigenous deities, alongside Jewish Berbers and a smattering of local Christian converts. History might have continued thus, but for a middle-aged man thousands of miles away who'd had the good fortune to marry a wealthy widow, and yet found himself increasingly at odds with the elites of his Arabian Peninsula town of Mecca. This was no ordinary midlife crisis. Mohammed bin Abu Talib was his given name, but he would soon be recognised as the Prophet Mohammed for his revelation that there was only one God and that believers shared a common duty to submit to God's will. The polytheist ruling class of Mecca did not take kindly to this new religion that assigned them shared responsibilities and took away their minor deity status and kicked the Prophet out of town on 16 July AD 622.

> The most comprehensive Berber history in English is *The Berbers* by Michael Brett and Elizabeth Fentress. The authors leave no stone unturned, providing archaeological evidence to back up their historical insights.

This *Hejira* (exile) only served to spread the Prophet Mohammed's message more widely. By the Prophet's death in AD 632, Arab caliphs – religious leaders inspired and emboldened by his teachings – were carrying Islam east to Central Asia and west to North Africa. But infighting limited their reach in North Africa, and it took Umayyad Arab leader Uqba bin Nafi until 682 to reach the Atlantic shores of Morocco. According to legend, Uqba announced he would charge into the ocean, if God would only give him the signal. But the legendary Algerian Berber warrior Queen Al-Kahina would have none of Uqba's grandstanding and with her warriors soon forced Uqba to retreat back to Tunisia.

> Queen Al-Kahina had one distinct advantage over the Umayyads: second sight. The downside? She foretold her own death at the hands of her enemy.

Although an armed force failed to win the Berbers over to Islam, force of conviction gradually began to succeed. The egalitarian premise of Islam and its emphasis on duty, courage and the greater good of the group were compatible with many Berber beliefs, including clan loyalty broadly defined to include almost anyone descended from the Berber equivalent of Adam and Eve. Many Berbers willingly converted to Islam and not incidentally reaped the benefits of Umayyad overland trading routes that brought business their way. So although Uqba was killed by his Berber foes before he was able to establish a solid base in Morocco, by the 8th century his successors were able to pull off this feat largely through diplomatic means.

THE CONVICTION OF POWER

The admiration between the Berbers and the Arab Umayyads was not always mutual, however. While the Umayyads respected Jews and Christians as fellow believers in the word of a singular God, they had no compunction about compelling polytheist Berbers to pay special taxes and serve as infantry (read: cannon fodder). The Umayyads greatly admired Berber women for their beauty, but this wasn't necessarily advantageous; many were conscripted into Umayyad harems.

Even the Berbers who converted to Islam were forced to pay tribute to their Arab overlords – an entitlement that seemed contrary to Mohammed's teachings. A dissident school of Islamic thought called Kharijism critiqued the abuses of power of the Umayyads as a corruption of the faith, and called for a new moral leadership. In the mid-eighth century, insurrections erupted across North Africa. Armed only with slings, a special force of Berbers defeated the elite Umayyad guard. The Umayyads were soon cut off from Spain and Morocco, and the new local leaders took over an increasingly lucrative trade in silver from the Western Sahara, gold from Ghana and slaves from West Africa.

DYNASTIC DRAMAS

Looking back on early Berber kingdoms, the 14th-century historian Ibn Khuldun noted a pattern that would repeat throughout Moroccan dynastic history. A new leadership would arise determined to do right and make contributions to society as a whole – and contributions to the royal coffers, too. When the pursuit of power and royal comforts began to eclipse loftier aspirations, the powers that be would forfeit their claim to moral authority. A new leadership would arise determined to do right, and the cycle would begin all over again.

So it was with the Idrissids, Morocco's first great dynasty. A descendant of the Prophet Mohammed's daughter Fatima, Idriss I fled Arabia for Morocco in 786 after discovering ambitious Caliph Haroun er-Rashid's plan to murder his entire family. But Idriss didn't exactly keep a low profile. After being proclaimed an imam (religious leader) by the local Berbers, he unified much of northern Morocco in the name of Islam. Just a few days after he'd finally settled into his new capitol at Fès in 792, Haroun er-Rashid's minions finally tracked down and poisoned Idriss I. Yet death only increased Idriss I's influence; his body was discovered to be miraculously intact five centuries later, and his tomb in the hillside town of Moulay Idriss remains one of the holiest pilgrimage sites in Morocco.

His son Idriss II escaped Haroun's assassins, and extended Idrissid control across northern Morocco and well into Europe. In perhaps the first (but certainly not the last) royal approximation of democracy in Morocco, Idriss II's 13 sons shared power after their father's death. Together they expanded Idrissid principates into Spain and built the glorious mosques of Fès: the Kairaouine and the Andalous.

Some beauty secrets Berber women reportedly brought to Umayyad harems are still available in Morocco, including argan oil and *gommage* (scrub down) exfoliation – no harem initiation required.

Muqqadimah is the landmark account of early Moroccan and Berber history by Ibn Khuldun, renowned Arab historian at Kairaouine University in Fès. The man knew his history – six centuries later, scholars still reference his text.

788-829   1062

Islam takes root in Morocco under Idriss I and Idriss II with Fès as centre | Berber leader Yusuf bin Tachfin founds Marrakesh as a launching pad for Almoravid conquests of North Africa and Europe

WARRIORS UNVEILED: THE ALMORAVIDS

With religious leaders and scholars to help regulate trade, northern Morocco began to take shape as an economic entity under the Idrissids. But the south was another story. A dissident prophet emerged near Salé brandishing his own Berber version of the Quran, and established an apocryphal Islam called Barghawata that continued to be practiced among Berbers in the region for centuries. The military strongmen who were left in control of trading outposts in the Atlas Mountains and the Sahara demanded what they called 'alms' – bogus religious nomenclature that didn't fool anyone and stirred up resentments among the faithful.

From this desert discontent rose the Sanhaja, the pious Saharan Berber tribe that founded the Almoravid dynasty. While the Idrissid princes were distracted by disputes over control of Spain and Mediterranean Morocco, the Sanhaja swept into the South of Morocco from what is today Senegal and Mauritania. Tough doesn't do justice to the Sanhaja; they lived on camel's meat and milk instead of bread, wore wool in the scorching desert and abstained from wine, multiple wives and music. Their manly habit of wearing dark veils is still practiced today by the Tuareg, the legendary 'blue men' of the desert (and the many tourists who imitate them in camel-riding photo-ops). When these intimidating shrouded men, under the command of Yahya ibn Umar and his brother Abu Bakrrode, rode into Shiite and Barghawata outposts, they demolished brothels and musical instruments as well as their opponents. After Yahya was killed and Abu Bakr recalled to the Sahara to settle Sanhaja disputes in 1061, their cousin Yusuf bin Tachfin was left to run military operations from a camp site that would become Marrakesh the magnificent.

The Almoravids took awhile to warm up to their new capital – too many mountains and rival Berbers around and too few palm trees. To make themselves more at home, the Almoravids built a mud wall around Marrakesh 5m high and 19 km long, and set up the ingenious *khettara* underground irrigation system that still supports the Palmeraie, a vast palm grove outside of Marrakesh (and home away from home for celebrities including Paul McCartney and designer Jean-Paul Gaultier). When the Almoravids took over Fès in 1069, they outfitted the city with running water, hammams, mills and gardens. The Jewish and Andalusian communities in Fès thrived under bin Tachfin, a soft-spoken consummate diplomat and brilliant military strategist. His Spanish Muslim allies urged him to intercede against Christian and Muslim princes in Spain, complaining bitterly of extortion, attacks and debauchery. At the age of almost 80, bin Tachfin launched successful campaigns securing Almoravid control of Andalusia right up to the Barcelona city limits.

Yusuf bin Tachfin was a tough act to follow. Ali was his son by a Christian woman, and he shared his father's commitments to prayer and urban planning. But while the reclusive young idealist Ali was diligently working wonders with architecture and irrigation in Marrakesh, a new force was gathering the strength of an Atlas thunderstorm beyond the city walls: the Almohads.

Arabic spoken in France? It's nothing new. In the 8th century, Arab caliphates controlled a swath of Western Europe that ended 320km shy of Paris.

To spare his wife hardships in the Sahara, Abu Bakr divorced brilliant Berber beauty Zeinab and arranged her remarriage to Yusuf bin Tachfin. Now that's love.

A treasure trove of articles on Morocco past, present, and future can be found at www.al-bab .com/maroc. Subjects cover ancient history and traditional cuisine as well as human rights movements and gay and lesbian communities.

1147	1276
Almohads defeat the Almoravids and raze Marrakesh – only to rebuild it as their capital under Yacoub al-Mansour	With strategic military manoeuvres and even more strategic marriages, the Merenids oust the Almohads

STICKS & STONES: THE ALMOHADS

Almohad historians would later accuse Ali of two supposedly dangerous acts: leaving the women in charge and allowing Christians near drink. While the former was hardly a shortcoming – the mighty Bin Tachfin prized the counsel of his savvy wife Zeinab – there may be some merit in the latter. While Ali was in seclusion praying and fasting, court and military officials were left to carry on and carry on they did. Apparently, Almoravid Christian troops were all too conveniently stationed near the wine merchants of Marrakesh.

Morocco is only 13km away from Europe across the Strait of Gibraltar.

None of this sat well with Mohammed ibn Tumart, the Almohad spiritual leader who'd earned a reputation in Meknès and Salé as a ninja-style religious vigilante, using his walking stick to shatter wine jars, smash musical instruments and smack men and women with the audacity to walk down the street together. Ibn Tumart finally got himself banished from Marrakesh in the 1120s for knocking Ali's royal sister off her horse with his stick. But though Ibn Tumart died soon after, there was no keeping out the Almohads. They took over Fès after a nine-month siege in 1145, but reserved their righteous furore for Marrakesh two years later, razing the place to the ground and killing what was left of Ali's court (Ali died as he lived, quietly, in 1144). Their first projects included rebuilding the Koutoubia mosque – which Almoravid architects not up on their algebra had misaligned with Mecca – and adding the soaring stone minaret that epitomised the sublime geometry and refined ornament of Andalusian Islamic architecture.

A bloody power struggle ensued among sons of Ibn Tumart and the sons of his generals that wouldn't be settled definitively until 1185, when Abu Yusuf Yacoub, the young son of the Muslim governor of Seville and Valencia, rode south into Morocco and drove his foes into the desert. But he never left Spain either, and continued to win so many victories against the princes of Spain that he earned the moniker Al-Mansour, 'the victorious'. He modelled Seville's famous La Giralda after Marrakesh's Koutoubia Minaret, and reinvented Marrakesh as an Almohad capital and learning centre to rival Fès. Yacoub's urban planning prowess also made Fès arguably the most squeaky clean city of medieval times, with 93 hammams, 47 soap factories and 785 mosques with the customary ablutions facilities. Yacoub al-Mansour was also a patron of great thinkers, including Aristotle scholar Ibn Rashid – whose commentary would help spark a Renaissance among Italian philosophers – and Sufi master Sidi Bel-Abbes. Yacoub's enlightenment and admiration of architecture was apparently not all-encompassing; several synagogues were demolished under his rule.

Similar thinking (or lack thereof) prevailed in 12th-century Europe, where a hunt for heretics turned to officially sanctioned torture under the rather ironically named Pope Innocent IV. Bishop Bernard of Toledo seized Toledo's mosque, and rallied Spain's Castilian Christian kings in a crusade against their Muslim rulers. The Almohads were in no condition to fight back. When Yacoub's 16-year-old son was named Caliph, he was hardly up to the religious responsibilities that came with the title. He was far more interested in bullfighting, which was the Nintendo of the day, only considerably more dangerous; he was soon gored to death.

1415	1498
Prince Henry the Navigator of Portugal takes Ceuta, the first of many conquests of Moroccan seaports by the Portuguese and Spanish	Church Inquisitors give European Muslims and Jews a choice: conversion and persecution, or torture and death. Morocco, anyone?

Yacoub al-Mansour must've done pirouettes in his grave around 1230, when his next son tapped as Caliph, al-Mamun, allied with his Christian persecutors and turned on his fellow Almohads in a desperate attempt to hang onto his father's empire. This short-lived Caliph added the ultimate insult to Almohad injury when he climbed the Koutoubia *minbar* (pulpit) and announced that ibn Tumart wasn't a true Mahdi, or leader of the faithful; that title, he claimed, rightfully belonged to Jesus.

UNTIL DEATH DO US PART: THE MERENIDS

When Zenata Berbers from the Atlas invaded the Almohad capital of Marrakesh in 1269, the Almohad defeat was complete. The Zenata had already ousted the Almohads in Meknès, Salé, Fès and most of the Atlantic coast and won over several religious scholars with vows of moral leadership under a new Merenid dynasty. To advance their case, they undertook construction of a *medersa* (school of religious learning) in every major city they conquered, levying special taxes on Christian and Jewish communities for the purpose. In exchange, they allowed these communities to practice key trades and hired Christian mercenaries and Jewish policy advisors to help conduct the business of the Merenid state.

But this time, the new rulers faced a tough crowd not easily convinced by promises of piety. Fès revolted, the Castilian Christians held sway in Salé, and the Merenids eventually allied with Castilian princes against the Muslim rulers of Granada to shore up their Spanish interests. Once again, this proved not to be a winning strategy. By the 14th century, Muslim Spain was lost to the Christians and the Strait of Gibraltar was forfeit. During the Inquisition that followed under zealous Christian leadership, over one million Muslims and Jews would be terrorised and forcibly expelled from Spain.

Without military might or religious right to reinforce their imperial claims, the Merenids chose another time-tested method: marriage. In the 14th century, Merenid leaders cleverly co-opted their foes by marrying princesses from Granada and Tunis, and claimed Algiers, Tripoli and the strategic Mediterranean port of Ceuta. But the bonds of royal marriage were not rat-proof. When the bubonic plague struck Mediterranean North Africa in 1348, kingdoms crumbled.

Abu Inan, son of the Merenid leader Abu Hassan, glimpsed opportunity in the Black Death, and proclaimed himself the new ruler despite one minor glitch: his father was still alive. Abu Hassan hurried back from Tripoli to wrest control from his treacherous son in Marrakesh, but to no avail. Abu Inan buried his father in the royal Merenid necropolis outside Rabat in 1351, and was laid to rest nearby after he was strangled by one of his own advisors in 1358.

'What goes around, comes around' became a recurring theme among the Merenids. To cover his tracks, Abu Inan's killer went on a royal killing spree, until Merenid Abu Salim Ibrahim returned from Spain and dispatched the homicidal bureaucrat. Abu Salim's advisor sucked up to his boss by offering his sister in marriage, only to lop off Abu Salim's head after the wedding. He replaced Abu Salim with a Merenid patsy before thinking better of it and strangling the new sultan, too. This slippery advisor was assassinated by another Merenid, who was deposed a

Legend credits the Egyptian mongoose, or Pharaoh's Rat, with sparing southernmost Morocco from the plague. This local hero can be glimpsed skulking around the Souss at sunset.

Saadians take over; business booms and all that glitters actually is gold under Ahmed el-Mansour ed-Dahbi	The Saadian dynasty repels invading Portugal at the infamous Battle of Three Kings

SUGAR & SALT: JEWISH MOROCCO

Jewish history has been intertwined with Moroccan history since the 1st century AD. By this time, Jewish Berber communities were already established in Moroccan cities, culture and industry. Jewish communities excluded from vital trades in Europe played crucial roles in Morocco as farmers, metalworkers, dyers, glassblowers, bookbinders and cowboys. Often taxed when business went well for the ruling dynasty and not infrequently blamed when it didn't, Jewish Moroccans managed to flourish despite the caprices of royal rule.

Faced with the prospect of persecution, Inquisition and death in Europe in the 14th to 16th centuries, many European Jews fled to Morocco. Under the comparatively tolerant Merenids and Saadians, some rose to prominence as royal advisors and confidantes. In an act of enlightened self-interest truly remarkable for the time, these dynasties afforded Jewish communities some security, setting aside sections of Fès and Marrakesh as the first Jewish quarters, or *mellahs* – a name derived from salt, a key trading commodity. By day, Jewish merchants were free to trade alongside Christian and Muslim merchants in salt, sugar, gold and other goods brought across the Sahara; by night they were under official guard in their quarters. This protection was repaid many times over in taxes levied on Jewish and Christian businesses, and the royally flush Saadians clearly got the sweet end of the deal. The Mellahs of Fès and Marrakesh soon became overcrowded with European arrivals and other notable Mellahs were founded in Essaouira, Safi, Rabat and Meknès. The traditions of skilled handicrafts that flourished there continue to this day and the culinary influence of the Mellahs can be tasted throughout Morocco in tangy dishes with the signature salted, pickled ingredients of Moroccan Jewish cuisine.

In the 17th to 19th centuries, the Alawite policy toward Jewish Moroccans was one of give and take: on the one hand were opportunities as tradespeople, business leaders, officials and even ambassadors to England, Holland and Denmark in the 19th century; on the other were taxes, surveillance and periodic scapegoating. But in good times and bad, Jewish Moroccans remained a continuous presence. By 1948, some 250,000 to 300,000 Jewish Moroccans lived in Morocco. Many left after the founding of the states of Morocco and Israel and today only an estimated 8000 to 10,000 remain, mostly in Casablanca. A Jewish community centre in Casablanca was a bombing target in 2003, along with commercial facilities; the blasts left 33 dead and 100 wounded. Yet the community remains intact, and is even undergoing a modest renaissance under the current king. Jewish schools now receive state funding; a few Jewish expatriates have responded to a royal invitation to return and are contributing to the revival of Essaouira's Mellah; and like his Alawite forbearers, King Mohammed VI counts Jewish advisors among his confidantes. The future of the now largely ageing population is unclear, but the past makes this much seem certain: as long as a Jewish community remains in Morocco, they'll continue to make history.

scant few years later by yet another Merenid – and so it continued for 40 years, with new Merenid rulers declaring themselves with the regularity of parliamentary candidates. While the Merenids were thus engaged in Meknès and Fès, the upstart Portuguese took over coastal Morocco.

VICTORY IS SWEET: THE SAADIANS

Much of Portugal (including Lisbon) had been under Muslim rule during the 12th century and now the Portuguese were ready for payback – literally. The tiny, rugged kingdom needed steady supplies of food for its people and gold to fortify its growing empire; in other words, Portugal needed Morocco. But instead of trying to beat the Berbers at their own game – control over Saharan trade routes – the Portuguese went with tactics where

1659-66	1830
Alawites take control and build a new capital in Rabat with help from many a hapless conscripted labourer	France seizes the Algerian coast, putting increasing pressure on the Moroccan sultan to cede power

they had clear technical advantages: naval warfare and advanced firearms. By systematically capturing Moroccan ports along the Mediterranean and Atlantic coasts, Portuguese gunships were able to bypass the Berbers inland and head directly to West Africa for gold and slaves.

Once trade in the Sahara began to dry up, something had to be done. Entire inland communities were decimated and formerly flush Marrakesh was wracked with famine. The Beni Saad Berbers from the desolate Drâa Valley took up the fight against Portuguese, and a new dynasty was founded when they revived Marrakesh as their capital in 1525. With successive wins against European, Berber and Ottoman rivals, the Saadians were able to reinstate inland trade and supply such sought-after European commodities as gold, slaves, ivory, ostrich feathers and the must-have luxury for trendy European royals: sugar.

The Saadians satisfied European sugar cravings at a price that makes today's oil and cocaine cartels look like rank amateurs. With threats of full-scale invasion, the Saadians had no problem scaring up customers and suppliers. The most dangerous sugar-dealer of all was Saadian Sultan Ahmed al-Mansour ed-Dahbi, who earned his names al-Mansour (the Victorious) for defeating foes from Portugal to the Sudan, and ed-Dahbi (the Golden) for his success in bilking them. He used the proceeds to line his Badi Palace in Marrakesh floor to ceiling with gold and gems, inspiring his court jester to wisecrack: 'It'll make a beautiful ruin'. That joker wasn't kidding: after the Sultan died, his short-lived successor stripped the palace down to its mud-brick foundations, as it remains today. The Saadian legacy is most visible in their Marrakesh tombs, decked out for a decadent afterlife with painted Carrara marble and gold leaf. The Saadians died as they lived: dazzling beyond belief and a touch too rich for most tastes.

For the bigger picture of Morocco's role in African history, Edward William Bovill's *The Golden Trade of the Moors* traces shifting trade routes and power dynamics across the continent.

Although it's long been part of the Moroccan diet, sugar was so valuable in 16th-century Europe that royals could only afford it for special occasions.

PIRATES & POLITICS: THE EARLY ALAWITES

The Saadian empire dissolved in the 17th century like a sugar cube in hot water, and civil war prevailed until the Alawites came along. With illustrious ancestors from the Prophet Mohammed's family and descendents extending to the current King Mohammed VI, the Alawites were quite a change from the freewheeling Saadians and their anarchic legacy. But many Moroccans might have preferred anarchy to the second Alawite ruler, the dreaded Moulay Ismail (1672–1727). A despot whose idea of a good time included public disembowelments and amateur dentistry on courtiers who peeved him, Moulay Ismail was also a scholar, dad to hundreds of children and Mr. Popularity among his royal European peers. He lavishly feted guests at his royal palace in Meknès, built by conscripted Christian labourers. Rumour has it that when these decidedly nonunion construction workers finished the job, some were walled in alive (so much for a Christmas bonus). Moroccan legend is rife with such tales of Moulay Ismail, whose love of books supposedly inspired him to dispatch an army of Senegalese to Timbuktu to ransack its world-renowned library – apparently no-one dared suggest a library card. Grudge-bearing librarians will be gratified to hear that the 50,000- to70,000-strong Abid, or 'Black Guard', ran amok after Moulay Ismail's death and not one of his many children was able to succeed him.

Moulay Ismail was pen pals with England's James II and Louis XIV of France, and tried to convert the Sun King to Islam by mail.

1860	1906
If at first you don't succeed, try for seven centuries: Spain finally manages to occupy northern Morocco, with help from allies	The rather sneaky Act of Algeciras divvies up North Africa among European powers

THE PIRATE KINGS

Before Johnny Depp, Captain Hook, *The Pirates of Penzance* and many an unfortunate men's fashion statement, there were Barbary pirates. Many were Moriscos, Spanish Muslims who'd been forcibly converted and persecuted in Spain and hence had an added motivation to ally with the Dutch to fleece the Spaniards. But they didn't stop there. In the 17th century, Barbary pirates attacked Ireland, Wales, Iceland and even Newfoundland.

For years, pirates along the coasts of Portugal, Spain and Morocco had official license as privateers to settle scores with the Spanish – and score Spanish doubloons. This was the practice of Queen Elizabeth I, who allied with profiteers and the Saadians against her arch-nemesis King Phillip II of Spain. James I outlawed English privateering in 1603, but didn't seem to mind when his buddy Moulay Ismail aided and abetted the many British and Barbary pirates who harboured in the royal ports at Rabat and Salé.

Moulay Ismail's cut of the action grew from a percentage to more than half, until he decided to control pirate operations and keep the cargo and captives. Among his booty were a couple hundred British prisoners, giving rise to the tale of the shipwrecked Robinson Crusoe, captured by Barbary Corsairs (pirates). But the master pirate proved to be England, by filching the entire city of Tangier right out from under Moulay Ismail. So while British captives were stuck behind prison bars in Rabat, English and Moroccan ambassadors were smiling at one another through clenched teeth, artfully bickering about who had rightfully stolen what from whom first. The prisoners were released when England finally relinquished the port of Tangier in 1684 – but only after destroying the port, leaving Moulay Ismail with a pile of rubble and a shallow victory.

Prisoners of the Barbary pirates were typically held for ransom and often freed after a period of servitude, except for those who joined the pirates or the Moroccan government – a far better fate at that time than awaited French captives, who were generally doomed to a life plying the oars of slave galleys. When the Portuguese were forced out of Essaouira in the 17th century, the city was rebuilt by European captives under the leadership of a French profiteer and a freed British prisoner who'd converted to Islam. Today the only pirates to be found in Essaouira, Tangier, Rabat and Salé are the ones peddling bootleg CDs atop cardboard boxes.

The Alawite dynasty would struggle on until the 20th century, but the country often lapsed into lawlessness when rulers overstepped their bounds. Piracy and politics became key ways to get ahead in the 18th and 19th centuries – and the two were by no means mutually exclusive. By controlling key Moroccan seaports and playing European powers against one another, officials and outlaws alike found they could demand a cut of whatever goods were shipped through the Strait of Gibraltar and along the Atlantic coast. In the late 18th century, when Sidi Mohammed ben Abdullah ended the officially condoned piracy of his predecessors and nixed shady side deals with foreign powers, the financial results were disastrous. With added troubles of plague and drought, Morocco's Straits were truly dire.

Alawite trading partners included a youthful rogue nation calling itself the United States, which Morocco was the first country to officially recognise in 1777.

WITH FRIENDS LIKE THESE: EUROPEAN ENCROACHMENT

For all their successful European politicking, the Alawites had apparently forgotten a cardinal rule of Moroccan diplomacy: never neglect Berber alliances. Sultan Moulay Hassan tried to rally support among the Berbers of the High Atlas in the late 19th century, but by then it was too late. France had taken an active interest in Morocco around 1830, and allied with

1912	1921-26
Treaty of Fès hands Morocco to the misnamed French Protectorate, which mostly protects French interests at Moroccan taxpayer expense	Berber rebel Abd el-Krim leads resistance against the French and Spanish in the Rif War

Berbers across North Africa to fend off the Ottomans. After centuries of practice fighting Moroccans, Spain finally managed to occupy areas of Northern Morocco in 1860 – and not incidentally, generated lasting resentment for desecrating graveyards, mosques and other sacred sites in Melilla and Tetouan. While wily Queen Victoria entertained Moroccan dignitaries and pressed for Moroccan legal reforms, her emissaries were busy brokering deals with France and Spain. Order became increasingly difficult to maintain in Moroccan cities and in Berber mountain strongholds, and Moulay Hassan employed powerful Berber leaders to regain control – but accurately predicting Moulay Hassan's demise, some Berbers cut deals of their own with the Europeans.

By the time Moulay Hassan's teenage successor Sultan Moulay Abdelaziz pushed through historic antidiscrimination laws to impress Morocco's erstwhile allies, the Europeans had reached an understanding; while reforms were nice and all, what they really wanted were cheap goods. Europeans and Americans set up their own duty-free shop in Tangier, declaring it an 'international zone' where they were above the law and beyond tax collectors' reach. In 1880, France, Britain, Spain and the US met in Madrid and agreed amongst themselves that Morocco could retain nominal control over its territory – that is, as long as they enjoyed trade conditions so favourable as to sound distinctly colonial.

But the lure of prime North African real estate proved irresistible. By 1906, Britain had snapped up strategic waterfront property in Egypt and the Suez; France took the prize for sheer acreage from Algeria to West Africa; Italy landed Libya; Spain drew the short stick with the unruly Rif and a whole lot of desert. Germany was incensed at being left out of this arrangement and announced support for Morocco's independence, further inflaming tensions between Germany and other European powers that would culminate in WWI.

> Moroccan pirate harbours Ceuta, Melilla and Isla de Perejil were snapped up in the 19th century by Spain, which still (loosely) governs these smuggling hotspots.

> For a compelling account of anticolonial struggles against the French and Spanish in the Rif, read CR Pennell's *Country with a Government and a Flag: The Rif War in Morocco, 1921–1926.*

FRANCE OPENS A BRANCH OFFICE: THE PROTECTORATE

Whatever illusions of control Morocco's sultanate might've been clutching slipped away at the 1906 Conference of Algeciras, when control of Morocco's banks, customs and police force was handed over to France for 'protection'. The 1912 Treaty of Fès establishing Morocco as a French Protectorate made colonisation official and the French hand-picked a new sultan with about as much backbone as a sock puppet. More than 100,000 French administrators, outcasts and opportunists arrived in cities across Morocco to take up residence in French *nouvelle villes* (new cities). Résident-Général Louis Lyautey saw to it that France's new property was kitted out with all the mod cons: electricity, trains, roads, running water. No expense or effort was spared to make the new arrivals feel right at home – which made their presence all the more galling for Moroccans footing the bill through taxes and shouldering most of the labour besides.

Lyautey had already set up French colonial enterprises in Vietnam, Madagascar and Algeria, so he arrived in Morocco with the confidence of a CEO and a clear plan of action: break up the Berbers, ally with the Spanish when needed and keep business running by all means necessary. Once French-backed Sultan Yusuf died and his French-educated 18-year-old son Mohammed V became sultan, Lyautey expected that

> *Nouvelle villes* were designed as worlds apart from adjacent Moroccan medinas (historic city centres) with French schools, churches, villas and grand boulevards named after French generals.

1944-53	1955-56
Nationalists demand independence; Sultan Mohammed V concurs and is exiled for the unspeakable crime of independent thought	Independence is declared and exiled nationalist Mohammed V returns as king

French business in Morocco would carry on as usual; he hadn't counted on a fiery young nationalist as sultan, or the staunch independence of ordinary Moroccans. Mining strikes and union organising interfered with France's most profitable colonial businesses, and military attention was diverted to force Moroccans back into the mines.

Berbers had never accepted foreign dominion without a fight and they were not about to make an exception for the French. By 1921 the Rif was up in arms against the Spanish and French under the leadership of Ibn Abd al-Krim al-Khattabi. It took five years, 300,000 Spanish and French forces and two budding Fascists (Francisco Franco and Marshal Pétain) to capture Ibn Abd al-Krim and force him into exile. The French won a powerful ally when they named Berber warlord Thami el-Glaoui Pasha of Marrakesh, but they also made a lot of enemies. The title gave the Pasha implicit license to do as he pleased, which included mafia-style executions and extortion schemes, kidnapping women and children who struck his fancy and friendly games of golf at his Royal Golf Club with Ike Eisenhower and Winston Churchill. The Pasha forbade talk of independence under penalty of death, and conspired to exile Mohammed V from Morocco in 1953 – but as fate and perhaps karma would have it, Pasha Glaoui ended his days powerless, wracked with illness, and grovelling on his knees for King Mohammed V's forgiveness.

A ROUGH START: AFTER INDEPENDENCE

Although the French Protectorate of Morocco was nominally an ally of Vichy France and Germany in WWII, in 1942 independent-minded Casablanca hosted American forces staging the Allied North African campaign – hence the classic Humphrey Bogart film *Casablanca*. So when Morocco's renegade Istiqlal (Independence) party demanded freedom from French rule in 1944, the US and Britain were finally inclined to agree. Under increasing pressure from Moroccans and the Allies, France allowed Mohammed V to return from exile in 1955 and Morocco successfully negotiated its independence from France and Spain in 1956–58.

When Mohammed V died suddenly of heart failure in 1961, King Hassan II became the leader of the new nation. Faced with a shaky power base, an unstable economy and elections that revealed divides even among nationalists, Hassan II consolidated power by crackdowns on dissent and suspending parliament for a decade. With heavy borrowing to finance dam-building, urban development and an ever-expanding bureaucracy, Morocco was deep in debt by the 1970s. Attempts to assassinate the king underscored the need to do something, quickly, to turn things around – and then in 1973, the phosphate industry in the Spanish Sahara started to boom. Morocco staked its claim to the area and its lucrative phosphate reserves with the Green March, settling the area with Moroccans while greatly unsettling indigenous Saharawi people agitating for self-determination.

RENOVATIONS IN PROGRESS: MOROCCO TODAY

With a growing gap between the rich and the poor and a mounting tax bill to cover Morocco's military debt, Hassan II's suppression of dissent only fuelled further resentment among his subjects. By the 1980s, the

Lords of the Atlas by Gavin Maxwell tells the true story of the vertiginous rise and prayers-answered fall of notorious Pasha Glaoui's clan.

In *Stolen Lives: Twenty Years in a Desert Jail,* Malika Oufkir describes her demotion from court favourite under Mohammed V to Morocco's Most Wanted after her father's arrest for plotting to assassinate Hassan II.

1961	1962
Mohammed V dies suddenly; young Hassan II becomes king	Hassan II transforms Morocco from a traditional sultanate into a constitutional monarchy

MARCHING TO THE KING'S TUNE

Talk of 'Greater Morocco' began idly enough in the 1950s, but in the 1970s it became the official explanation for Morocco's annexation of phosphate-rich Spanish Sahara. But there was a snag: The Popular Front for the Liberation of the Sahara and the Rio di Oro (Polisario) declared the region independent. Putting his French legal training to work, Hassan II took up the matter with the International Court of Justice in the Hague in 1975, expecting the court would provide a resounding third-party endorsement for Morocco's claims. Instead the International Court of Justice (ICJ) considered a counter-claim for independence from the Polisario, and dispatched a fact-finding mission to Spanish Sahara.

The ICJ concluded that the ties to Morocco weren't strong enough to support Moroccan sovereignty over the region, and the Western Sahara was entitled to self-determination. In a highly creative interpretation of this court judgment, Hassan II declared that Morocco had won its case and ordered a celebratory 'peace march' of more than 350,000 Moroccans from Marrakesh into Western Sahara in 1975 – some never to return. This unarmed 'Green March' established Morocco's regional presence, which was soon fortified by military personnel and land mines and vehemently resisted by armed Polisario fighters.

The Green March is no longer the symbol of national pride it once was in Morocco. Even Morocco's allies remain divided over Western Sahara's claims to independence; in 2005, the contentious issue ended negotiations for a North African free trade zone. Phosphate profits have dwindled, due to falling prices, mining sabotage and spiralling costs for Moroccan military operations exceeding US$300 million annually by 1981. A truce was finally established in 1991, but the status of Western Sahara remains unresolved – a rallying cry for many Saharawi, and an awkward conversation nonstarter for many deeply ambivalent Moroccan taxpayers.

king's critics included journalists, trade unionists, women's rights activists, Marxists, Islamists, Berbers advocating recognition of their culture and language, and the working poor – in other words, a broad cross-section of Moroccan society.

The last straw for many came in 1981, when official Moroccan newspapers casually announced that the government had conceded to the International Monetary Fund to hike prices for staple foods. For the many Moroccans subsisting on the minimum wage, these increases meant that two-thirds of their income would be spent on a meagre diet of sardines, bread and tea. When trade unions organised protests of the measure, government reprisals were swift and brutal. Tanks rolled down the streets of Casablanca and hundreds were killed, at least a thousand wounded, and an estimated 5000 protesters arrested in a nationwide *laraf*, or roundup.

Far from dissuading dissent, the Casablanca Uprising galvanised support for government reform. Sustained pressure from human rights activists throughout the 1980s achieved unprecedented results in 1991, when Hassan II founded the Truth and Reconciliation Commission to investigate human rights abuses that occurred during his own reign – a first for a king.

In his very first public statement as king upon his father's death in 1999, Mohammed VI vowed to right the wrongs of the era known to Moroccans as the Black Years. Today Morocco's human rights record is arguably the cleanest in Africa and the Middle East, though still not

For a Saharawi perspective on the Western Sahara you won't find in officially sanctioned Moroccan newspapers, see http://wsahara.net.

When Morocco's Truth and Reconciliation Commission televised testimonies of victims of Moroccan human rights abuses in 2004-05, the shows became the most-watched in Moroccan TV history.

1975	**1981**
UN concludes Western Sahara is independent; Hassan II concludes otherwise, ordering the Green March to enforce Morocco's claim	Casablanca Uprising crushed by military, but demands for political reforms are not; many Moroccan dissidents are later exonerated

When Mohammed
VI married computer
engineer Salma Bennani
in 2002, the royal couple
became an icon for
modern Morocco – not to
mention countless Moroc-
can Internet café habitués
making kissy faces at one
another via webcam.

exactly spotless – repressive measures were revived after 9/11 and the
2003 Casablanca bombings, when the usual suspects were rounded up
and subjected to some of the very tactics under investigation by the Truth
and Reconciliation Commission. But since that time, the Commission
has helped cement human rights advances by awarding reparations to
9280 victims of the Black Years, and the new parliament elected in 2002
has implemented some promising reforms. Foremost among these are
Morocco's first-ever municipal elections, the introduction of Berber
languages in some state schools and the much-anticipated Mudawanna,
a legal code protecting women's rights to divorce and custody.

This is the state of modern Morocco today: home to rich and poor,
old and new, deep contradictions and the courage to confront them.
The European and American powers that ignored Morocco's reforms
in the 19th century seem to be taking notice in the 21st: Morocco has
signed free trade agreements with the EU and the US and gained status
as a non-NATO ally in 2004. Tourism is flourishing in this nation of
moderate climates and politics, and though tourism stretches available
resources, it also helps support a middle class emerging between royalty
and subsistence farmers. In cafés and petitions, protests and free-form
poetry, Moroccans are making their voices heard and staying true to their
Berber roots as 'the free people'.

1999	2002-04
Hassan II dies; all hail Mohammed VI	Historic reforms include parliamentary and municipal elections, plus Mudawanna legal code protecting women's rights

The Culture

Forget for a moment the glossy travel brochures about Marrakesh, movies filmed in the Moroccan Sahara, urban legends about decadent Tangier: as anyone who's been there will tell you, the best way to get to know Morocco is through Moroccans. So to introduce you to Morocco, meet Fatima, Driss and Amina, three characters who are composites of people you're likely to encounter on your travels. Each is representative of a segment of Moroccan society in some ways, and atypical in others; this chapter will describe how their experience maps onto Moroccan culture as a whole. Once you visit Morocco, you'll appreciate where these characters are coming from – and Moroccan culture, in all its diversity.

> Here's how to make friends and influence people in Morocco: shake hands and then touch your heart with your right hand. Good friends tack up to four air kisses onto a handshake. Don't clasp the other person's hand or shoulder with your left hand – in Morocco, that hand is generally reserved for the bathroom.

Meet Fatima

Fatima grew up working on a farm and made carpets for sale on the side, and still it paid barely enough to put bread on the family table – but now she has a steady income collecting argan nuts at a fair trade women's cooperative near Agadir. The few times she's been into town, she was surprised by how informal young people were towards their elders, though not offended – she thinks it's good for young people to think for themselves – and was truly shocked by the prices. She lives frugally, saving every dirham to help cover school fees for her five grandchildren. All her four children are married, and she always has stories and sweets for her grandchildren when they visit. Her arthritis is beginning to interfere with her work, though, and she worries about the family that now depends on her; her husband passed away a few years ago. She speaks Berber at home, can get by in Moroccan Arabic, and knows how to say 'hello' and 'welcome' in French and English to foreigners who sometimes visit the argan cooperative, but she doesn't read or write. Her dream is to make the pilgrimage to Mecca, *ensha'llah* (god willing).

Meet Driss

Six days a week, Driss wakes up at dawn to bike from his family's apartment to the riad where he works as assistant manager to arrange breakfast for riad guests. He isn't an early riser by nature, but doesn't mind as long as he gets a catnap and mint tea. He knows enough Portuguese and Italian to explain the breakfast menu to guests and speaks fluent Moroccan Arabic, French, good Spanish, passable English and classical Arabic (mostly from watching the news on Al-Jazeera) – with so many new languages, his native Berber language of Tashelhit is rusty. Driss's father owns a small *hanout* (corner grocery) and doesn't read or write that well himself, but insisted that Driss and his four siblings attend school. Driss takes a computer course on his day off and is saving the part of his salary that doesn't go to his family for a scooter, so that he can get home before 10pm. He's in no special rush to get married, but he figures his parents will start pressuring him now that he's 30. He doesn't want to marry a village girl – he'd rather have a girlfriend in the tourism industry, and see how things go from there.

Meet Amina

Amina is a 22-year-old computer-engineering student, and she'd like to work in the Moroccan government – maybe even the foreign service. Her dad works for the government, and they live in a newer residential neighbourhood in a suburb of Rabat. Amina hasn't been to France yet,

SOCIAL GRACES

Many visitors are surprised at how quickly friendships can be formed in Morocco, and often a little suspicious. True, carpet sellers aren't necessarily after your friendship when they offer you tea, and an unexpected introduction to your new Moroccan friend's single cousin could be even more awkward than your last internet date. If you find yourself in these situations, just claim an obligation elsewhere, smile, and leave – no hard feelings.

But notice how Moroccans behave with one another, and you'll see that friendly overtures are the norm here rather than a mere contrivance. People you meet only in passing are likely to remember you and greet you warmly the next day, and it's considered polite to stop and ask how they're doing. Greetings among friends can last 10 minutes in Morocco, as each person inquires after the other's happiness, wellbeing and family.

Moroccans are generous with their time, and extend courtesies that might seem to you like impositions, from walking you to your next destination to inviting you home for tea or dinner. Do not mistake these favours for services and offer a tip, which is likely to offend your Moroccan host. (At the risk of stating the obvious, anyone who demands payment not agreed upon in advance is *not* your friend.) Stop by the next day to say hello or bring sweets to dinner, and your new friend will be most appreciative.

but a couple of her relatives who live there are financing her education. They keep in touch through email in French and Moroccan Arabic, and she keeps up on world news in French, Arabic and English through the internet and watching satellite TV with her cousins. On weekends, she often goes to restaurants with friends as one big group. She doesn't drink alcohol personally, but some people she knows do, and she doesn't judge them for it. As far as dating goes, she met a guy in an internet chat room awhile back, but that was nothing serious. She hasn't yet met anyone she'd consider chatting with via webcam, though some of her friends do. She's not ready to settle down yet – there's too much else to do first.

LIFESTYLE
Family values

As different as they may seem, Fatima, Driss and Amina have one thing in common: a profound attachment to family. While they each have careers and ideas of their own, their aspirations and ambitions are tied in some way to family – which makes them each quintessentially Moroccan.

With the possible exception of the royal family (see Economy p46), status is gained in Morocco not so much by hoarding or displaying wealth but from sharing it with family, as Fatima and Driss do. Even major status symbols (like Driss' motor scooter and the satellite TV at Amina's house) are valued less as prized possessions than as commodities benefiting the family as a whole. This is beginning to change, as the emerging middle class Driss represents moves out of large family homes and into smaller apartments in the suburbs, and common property becomes less, well, common. But family connections remain paramount in Morocco, and remittances from Moroccans living abroad are essential to family back home.

Since family is such a focal point for Moroccans, you might expect related questions to come up in the course of conversation: Where is your family? Are you married, and do you have children? How is your family? What do they do? This might seem a little probing, or a roundabout way of finding out who you are and what interests you. But to Moroccans, questions about where you work or what you do in your spare time might seem odd as icebreakers, since what you do for a living or a hobby says less about you than what you do for your family.

Education

Next to family, education is the most important indicator of social status in Morocco. City-dwellers Driss and Amina both read and write, like 55.3% of Morocco's urban population. But while Driss is like most Moroccan men in this respect, Amina is in the minority of Moroccan women, 60% of whom were illiterate as of 2003. Moroccan girls account for almost two thirds of the half-a-million Moroccan kids under 15 who work instead of getting an education. But progress is being made, thanks to positive social pressure that has made education to age 14 an official mandate, dramatically reducing child labour. Today, less than one quarter of one percent of Moroccan boys aged 10 to 14 work – an achievement that tops Italy and 91 other countries besides, according to the International Labour Organization.

> To help keep kids in school:
>
> Make purchases only from adults.
>
> Don't give kids handouts – it teaches kids to beg, and shames their parents.
>
> Urge kids to study hard, even if you do sound like your own grandma.

Social Norms

As you'll probably notice in your travels through Morocco, behaviour that is considered unacceptable outdoors, in full public view – such as drinking alcohol, or making kissy faces at someone of the opposite sex – is often tolerated in the relative privacy of a restaurant terrace, a riad, or an internet café. In this context, Amina's views on drinking and internet dating are not so radical. While there are still laws on the books in Morocco restricting the sale of alcohol in view of a mosque, sex outside of marriage, homosexuality, and an especially ambiguous offence described as 'insulting the king's person' (as opposed to, say, his clothes?), enforcement of these laws is very rare. With proper discretion, there is plenty of latitude when it comes to socially acceptable behaviour.

> According to the International Labour Organization, Morocco has the third largest percentage of women working in the industrial sector – that's above the US at number 49, the UK at 52, and Australia in 62nd place.

Fashion, Moroccan-style

Many Moroccan men and women wear the jellaba, an ankle-length kaftan with a pointy hood and silk buttons or a zipper down the front. It's roomy, cosy and intended to be modest, though some of the psychedelic swirl-printed ones women wear may seem just as eye-catching as a miniskirt.

VISITORS: DRESSING TO IMPRESS

Since they've had contact with Europeans for the last couple of millennia and satellite TV for about a decade, Moroccans are not likely to be shocked by Western attire. If you pull a Lawrence of Arabia and don traditional garb and headgear, you'll probably get puzzled stares in Morocco, and possibly a smirk or two. After all, this is not Saudi Arabia, and who wears a scimitar to work anymore? A head covering is handy protection against sandstorms in the desert, but nobody expects you to wear a headscarf or Tuareg blue turban in town – and these days, even Tuaregs wear Adidas.

That said, your choice of attire still may be perceived as a sign of respect for yourself, your family and your hosts (or lack thereof). Mostly likely no-one will say anything to you if your clothing is on the skimpy side – but in this sociable society, nothing indicates disapproval like the cold shoulder. Some people will be embarrassed for you and the family that raised you, and either give you pitying glances or avoid eye contact altogether. So if you want to make your family look good, and don't want to miss out on some excellent company – especially among older Moroccans – do make a point to dress modestly.

For men and women alike, this means not wearing shorts and sleeveless tops. Even in trendy nightclubs, clingy clothing, short skirts, and low-cut and midriff tops could be construed as, ahem, the oldest kind of professional attire. Basically, anything you could wear to the supermarket back home without attracting attention should do the trick – but do consider the climate, which in globally warmed Morocco can range from desert-scorching to mountain-chilly.

Many younger Moroccans mix up their wardrobe, or wear pants and shirts exclusively. Urbanites like Amina and Driss might wear a chic hip-length tunic or buttoned shirt, jeans or ankle-length pants, and Moroccan slippers or trendy shoes. Logo T-shirts and trainers are all the rage lately – if copyright were enforced here, major Moroccan cities would be half-naked. Some women wear the hejab, or headscarf, and some don't, depending on the locale and the individual woman. Women in Casablanca are more likely to wear headscarves (colour-coordinated with their outfits, of course) than Marrakshis, who you'll see more often in tank tops and jeans than in veils exposing only the eyes. Women in rural areas working in the fields may not wear the veil or hejab, either.

ECONOMY
Economic Status

Fatima, Driss, and Amina would all be considered fortunate in Morocco, where the World Bank cites 19% of the population living below the poverty line, and unemployment tops 13%. In a country where 7% of the population makes less than US$2 a day and the average annual income is US$1520, adequate funds to feed a family are not a given – let alone funds for higher education, motor scooters and internet access. When asked where they dine out, many Moroccans will give you the same answer: they don't. Social security is provided by the family, not the government, and workers' compensation is nonexistent – but with pressure from activists and unions, some industries are establishing regulations and licensing to ensure workers' wellbeing.

While the gap between rich and poor is growing in Morocco, a new middle class is emerging between subsistence farmers and government bigwigs. Driss and Fatima belong to this class, even though they probably make less in a day than you do in an hour. Still, the economic class that's head, shoulders and tiaras above all others is the Moroccan royal family, whose wealth was recently estimated by a (now-estranged) royal family member at between US$4 billion and US$20 billion. In response, an officially sanctioned Moroccan magazine published the king's salary: about US$45,000 a month, or 'less than a Western CEO's salary' – no mention of whether that's before or after taxes.

Products & Prospects

Driss, Amina and Fatima's incomes come from foreign trade, tourism, remittances from relatives living abroad, and hard work – which is fairly representative for the country as a whole. With a boost from tourism and a growing Moroccan middle class, services are now the fastest-growing sector of the Moroccan economy at 42% of GDP in 2004. Another estimated 15% of GDP comes from industry, including leather goods, textiles and food processing, but mostly from phosphate mining in the Western Sahara (see Marching to the King's Tune p41). A whopping 40% of GDP comes from agriculture, primarily from citrus exports. Fishing is not the pivotal industry it once was, with low fish stocks in the Mediterranean. Hashish is still a key cash crop in Morocco, though periodic police crackdowns have made it more of a high-risk, export-only product.

So what does the economic future hold for our Moroccan friends, beyond farming and tourism? In short: sun, wind, water and dung. Drilling oil off the coast of Western Sahara has proved expensive and environmentally messy, and Morocco is now turning towards more

At unlicensed riads or guesthouses, workers are not guaranteed the minimum wage of Dh3.20 an hour – something to keep in mind when choosing your riad and when tipping riad staff.

In 2004 King Mohammed VI's household expenditures were 18 times that of Queen Elizabeth II's.

reliable energy sources. The pioneering nation is already harnessing wind power in the Rif, and has partnered with British Petroleum to supply solar energy to 20,000 households in villages outside Marrakesh.

The water situation is less promising. Due to the demands of a growing number of city dwellers, Moroccan water reserves are at a historic low, and existing water may be soon be redirected away from subsistence farmers in the Atlas to support growing urban centres. According to the Centre for Environmental Systems Research, Morocco ranks in the top 25 of nations under the most severe water stress, above the Sudan and Mexico.

There may be hope for farmers and their donkeys yet. Morocco is the world's largest exporter what is delicately referred to as 'crude fertiliser', and redirecting resources towards intensive dung collection could be the beginning of a shift away from the dangerous mining and processing of phosphates into chemical fertiliser – not to mention a whole new meaning for the term 'gross national product'.

Buying argan oil and other Moroccan products from fair trade cooperatives ensures a more stable living for farm workers such as Fatima, whose living otherwise depends on the caprices of field bosses, exporters and other middlemen.

POPULATION

For a millennia-old civilisation, Morocco sure looks young for its age. There's a reason for this, beyond all those hammams and salt scrubs: almost a third of Morocco's population is under 15. Back in 1971, when Moroccan child-mortality rates were high and life expectancy was low, Moroccan women had an average of 7.8 children. But with improved healthcare and young Moroccans like Driss and Amina increasingly delaying marriage for careers and dating, Morocco's baby boom is officially winding down. The average number of births per woman is now just above 2.7 and population growth overall has dipped below 1.6%. Less than 5% of Morocco's population of almost 33 million is over 65, and most of these are women – often working widows like Fatima.

But though Fatima lives in a village, her children probably live in a town or city. Given nationwide unemployment rates of 19% for Moroccans under age 25, young people raised in rural areas often move to cities to find work or pursue educational opportunities. This brain drain is unlikely to slow anytime soon, without new initiatives in public education and agricultural development that might keep rural Morocco's best and brightest closer to home.

Most Moroccans you'll meet are of Berber-Arab origin, but you'll also probably interact with some of Morocco's 100,000-plus foreign residents. The majority are French, and many work in the tourism trade – especially in Marrakesh, Morocco's number-one tourism destination and the new substitute for Tangier as the home-away-from-home for many expatriates.

To help Moroccans conserve water:

Opt for steamy hammams instead of long showers.

Choose a riad with a plunge pool instead of an Olympic one.

Skip water-guzzling golf courses and water theme parks.

RELIGION

Like nearly 99% of Moroccans today, Driss, Fatima and Amina are Muslim. Christian and Jewish communities have been established in Morocco for 1700 years or more, but in recent years their numbers have dwindled. Along with a few stray Protestants and Hindus, there are about 23,000 Catholics and 65 Catholic priests in the country, mostly in major urban centres. Emigration to France, Israel and the US has reduced Morocco's once-robust Jewish community to about 7000 to 7500, and the Jewish communities that once inhabited the historic *mellahs* (Jewish quarters) of Fès, Marrakesh, Safi, Essaouira and Meknès have relocated to Casablanca. (For more on this subject, see Sugar and Salt: Jewish Morocco p36.)

BERBER PRIDE & PREJUDICE

For at least 5000 years, Morocco has been inhabited by a people with Saharan, Mediterranean and Sub-Saharan African roots collectively known as the Amazigh, or 'free people'. True to their name, they successfully ousted the many armies who swaggered into Amazigh territory with a mind to claim it for themselves. The Romans certainly tried – for 250 years – and when they couldn't defeat their foes they badmouthed them, calling them 'Berbers', or Barbarians.

The name stuck: the invading Umayyad Arabs picked up the term, only to stand corrected by Amazigh warrior queen al-Kahina and her armies, who ran the Umayyads out of most of the Maghreb. If you can't beat them, join them, was the lesson learned by every major Moroccan dynasty after the Umayyads (see the History section for the occasionally gory details). Rulers often rose to power through armed force and religious conviction, but they stayed in power through treaties with Amazigh leaders, marriages to Amazigh princesses and adaptability to local Amazigh custom.

Still, certain prejudices persisted. Despite a rich tradition of poetry, music and art dating as far back as 5000 BC, the Amazigh were often misconstrued as uneducated by outsiders, because no standard written language had been consistently applied to their many distinct languages. Since the Quran was written in Arabic, Moroccan religious instruction was in Arabic, and a hybrid Moroccan Arabic dialect (Darija) emerged in cities as a way to communicate across the many Berber languages. The Protectorate established French as the official language of Morocco to make it easier to conduct (and hence control) business transactions and affairs of state. Complex Amazigh artistic symbolism and traditional medicine were dismissed as charming but irrelevant superstition by those not privy to the oral traditions accompanying them, and the educated classes were encouraged to distance themselves from their Berber roots. After Independence, Arabic became the official language, though French continues to be widely spoken among the elite.

But Amazigh languages and traditions have prevailed in Morocco, and the Berber Pride movement has recently reclaimed 'Berber' as a unifying term. More than 60% of Moroccans now call themselves Amazigh or Berber, and Berber languages are currently spoken by upwards of 12 to 15 million Moroccans. Tashelhit is the most common Berber language, and is widely spoken in central Morocco. You'll also hear Tarifit along the Rif, Tamazight in the Middle Atlas, and Tuareg in the Sahara. There's still no guarantee that Berbers on one side of a mountain will be able to understand those on the other, but a concerted effort is now being made to teach and speak a standard Northern Berber dialect (also called Tamazight).

With the backing of King Mohammed VI – who is part Berber himself – the ancient written Tifinagh alphabet has been recently revived as a national language, and is now being taught in some schools. Within the next decade, Berber will be taught in public schools across Morocco, along with the new Lingua Franca of trade and tourism: English.

About Islam

Soaring minarets, shimmering mosaics, intricate calligraphy, the muezzin's mesmerising call to prayer: much of what thrills visitors in Morocco today is inspired by Moroccans' deep and abiding faith in Islam. It all began in AD 610, when a middle-aged merchant from Mecca named Mohammed began to receive revelations that there was one God, and that believers shared a common responsibility to submit to God's will (for more background, see The Power of Conviction p31.) Based on the teachings of the Old and New Testaments, this new religion would be built on five pillars: *shahada*, the affirmation of faith in God and God's word entrusted to the Prophet Mohammed; *salat*, or prayer, ideally performed five times daily; *zakat* or charity, a moral obligation to give to those in need; *sawm*, the fasting practiced during the month of Ramadan; and *haj*, the pilgrimage to Mecca that is the culmination of lifelong faith for Muslims.

During Ramadan, believers are expected to abstain from sex, and nothing is supposed to pass their lips from sunup to sundown – including cigarette smoke. Right... cough, cough.

While all Muslims agree on these basic tenets received by the Prophet Mohammed, some doctrinal disagreements ensued after his death. The Umayyads challenged his son-in-law Ali's claim to the title of caliph or leader of the faithful. Despite the Umayyads' considerable conviction and military might, some Muslims continued to recognise only successors of Ali; today they are known as Shiites. But history seems to have sided with those who agreed with the Umayyad caliphate, whose Sunni Muslim practice is the mainstream today.

ISLAM IN MOROCCO

Like many Muslim countries, Morocco is mostly Sunni. There are four main schools of thought among the Sunnis emphasising different aspects of doctrine, and today the one most commonly followed in Morocco is the Maliki school. Historically this school has been less strict, with Maliki *qaid*s (judges) applying the Sharia'a, or religious code, according to local custom rather than the absolute letter of the law.

One local tradition to emerge over centuries of Islamic practice in Morocco is the custom of venerating *marabout*s, or saints. *Marabout*s are devout Muslims whose acts of devotion and professions of faith were so profound, their very presence is considered to confer *baraka*, or grace, even after their death. Moroccans go out of their way to visit *marabout*s' tombs and *zawiya*s (shrines) – and many claim that, like a spa for the soul, the right *zawiya* can fix anything from a broken heart to arthritis.

This practice of honouring *marabout*s is more in line with ancient Berber beliefs and Sufi mysticism than orthodox Islam, which generally discourages anything resembling idol worship. (For more background on Islam in Morocco, see The Conviction of Power p32) But visits to *zawiya*s are side trips for the many devout Moroccans who – like Fatima – spend a lifetime preparing and planning for the haj. Moroccans do not necessarily see a conflict between *baraka* and belief, or local customs and universal understanding.

SPORT
Football

Look no further for a rousing game of *koura* (football, aka soccer): you'll find a football skidding across virtually every patch of *piste* (hard-packed dirt) in Morocco. Opportunities for a game abound in public gardens, but do mind the cactus – and don't get too cocky if you're assigned to guard a seemingly scrawny preteen in a jersey. That jersey means you're in for a workout, if not public humiliation.

If you prefer other people to do the kicking for you, you'll find plenty of company among fellow football fans in 320 stadiums across Morocco. A ticket will only set you back a few dirhams, so you can invest in the roasted pumpkin and sunflower seeds that hyped-up fans chomp throughout the game. Offer some to your neighbour, and maybe your new friend will explain to you what people are yelling at the referee. Probably it's 'Seer al muk!' – loosely translatable as 'How can you face your mother?!'

Football-fan behaviour in Morocco is generally more genteel than, ahem, England, though it always helps if you're rooting for the same team as the people sitting next to you. Usually this is Morocco's own 'Lions of the Atlas', who often make it to the World Cup finals – otherwise, it's any team but Tunisia, Morocco's football archrival. Local teams to watch include Marrakesh's stellar Kawkab, Raja Casablanca, MAS Fez and

Consider yourself warned: the *zawiya* of Moulay Ismail in the Atlas Mountains outside Marrakesh is reputed to increase the fertility of women visitors.

Top this: nineteenth-century Swiss adventurer Isabelle Eberhardt disguised herself as a Berber man, joined a Sufi sect, smoked kif, operated as a triple agent, married an Algerian dissident, got exiled from North Africa by the French and wrote her memoir *The Oblivion Seekers* – all before 30.

Morocco's had a bad streak of luck; after losing its bid to host the 2006 World Cup to Germany, the Lions failed to make the 2006 World Cup, losing a qualifying match to – ouch! – Tunisia.

Rabat's Fath. Star players on these teams often get recruited for the Lions, and sometimes for teams in France, Spain and Germany.

Athletics

Think your workout routine is tough? Try comparing notes with Moroccan marathoners. Runners quite literally feel the burn each April in the annual Marathon du Sable, which lasts seven days and covers 238 miles of scorching Sahara – 78 of them in a single stretch. Once they're warmed up, runners hit their high in May with the high-altitude Berber Marathon through the Atlas Mountains.

With training like this, it's no wonder Moroccans have been giving Kenyan frontrunners a reason to watch their backs in international track events. Moroccan Nawal el-Moutawakel became the first Arab woman to win Olympic gold in 1984, when she nabbed the medal for the 400m hurdles. Middle-distance maverick Hicham el-Guerrouj became the first man to hold the world records for the mile and 1500m in 1999, and a national hero in Morocco when he took home Olympic gold for both the 1500m and 5000m events in 2004.

Even if you're no el-Moutawakel or el-Guerrouj yourself and aren't much for sandstorms and high-altitude nosebleeds, you can still enjoy a decent jog in Morocco. The annual Marrakesh Marathon in January gives sports fans a chance to run a lap around the city ramparts, through the Palmeraie, and back again. Then again, somebody has to cheer on the runners from the comfort of a café in the Djemaa el-Fna with a fresh-squeezed orange juice in hand…

Golf

Golf courses are both a royal pleasure and a royal nuisance in Morocco, and not just because of the killer sand traps. Morocco's first course, the Royal Golf Club, was built in the 1920s at considerable taxpayer expense outside Marrakesh by the notorious Pasha Glaoui (for more on the Pasha's golf game and other less savoury pursuits, see France Opens a Branch Office, p39). The Royal Moroccan Golf Federation was founded under King Hassan II, who built his own Royal Dar es-Salaam Golf Course near Rabat – again at taxpayer expense. Two notable private golf courses were recently built outside Marrakesh, with designs by noted golf course architects: Robert Trent Jones' tricky switchback course at the Palmeraie Golf Palace, and CB Robinson's Golf d'Amelkis course. Both are so chock full of water hazards, you'd never guess there was a drought afflicting villages nearby.

Yet another course is soon to tap into the local water supply outside Essaouira, which brings us to the modern golfer's dilemma: knowing how much of Morocco's scarce water resources it takes to keep a fairway green in the desert, is a decent game of golf an oxymoron in Morocco? A growing number of resorts are betting you'll tee up regardless here, as in many other parched parts of the world – but as a caddie might tell a golfer facing a double bogey, the next shot's your call.

EMIGRATION & IMMIGRATION

With all the recent reporting on the subject (see A Brisk Trade in Dreams, opposite), you've probably read about Moroccans swimming across the Gibraltar Straits to seek agricultural work in Spain – but that's not even half the story of migration in Morocco. With most of Morocco's population just now hitting puberty, competition is more fierce than ever for coveted spots in Morocco's state-supported universities. Those who do

Farida ben Lyzaid's film *A Door to the Sky* tells the story of an émigrée's return to Morocco, and her delicate balancing act between activism and tradition.

succeed face limited work opportunities after graduation, with unemployment rates approaching 20% for Moroccans under 25.

Given limited state resources to remedy this situation, Moroccans are turning to family for help. Moroccan residents and naturalised citizens in France, Germany, Spain and the US – whose combined remittances to family back home represent as much as 20% of GDP – are increasingly sponsoring family members to pursue studies and careers abroad. With its shrinking labour force and aging population, the US in particular has extended green cards to many of Morocco's top talents. Between 2003 and 2005, Morocco was among the top ten recipients of green cards.

But not all of those who head abroad for family reunification, studies and work will stay there. With the war on terror inflaming tensions and suspicions among their neighbours in the US and Europe, some Moroccan expatriates are opting for the VIP status they often enjoy in Morocco. The growing numbers of Moroccan expats returning to Morocco to live, retire or start businesses are becoming an upper-middle economic class of their own, since their euros and dollars have considerably more buying power than nontransferable dirhams.

European and American expatriates living in Morocco and working in tourism, who earn income in euros and pay expenses in dirhams, also enjoy a considerable economic advantage – and incur a certain amount of resentment, as well as accusations of not paying their fair share of taxes, as in colonial times (see With Friends Like These, p38). Some expatriates accuse locals in turn of narrow-mindedness, so take any generalisations you hear on either side with a hefty grain of Salé sea salt.

But in Morocco, cultural differences are not insurmountable – witness the many intercultural married couples you'll meet running riads, restaurants and other businesses in Morocco. The international trade that has defined Morocco for millennia shows no signs of stopping, and the

> Be sure to get a receipt for all your major travel expenses: riads, hotels, tours and major meals. This is your guarantee that proprietors are paying their fair share of taxes, which helps build schools and hospitals – that way, all Moroccans stand to benefit from your contributions to the local economy.

A BRISK TRADE IN DREAMS

Cashing in on hopes of a better life abroad is nothing new in Morocco – the practice dates back at least 100 years to the eminently corruptible American consul Felix Matthews, whose unofficial business in US immigration papers in Tangier boomed until his suspension from duty in 1877. The focal point of the profitable immigration trade has since shifted from Tangier to Ceuta and Melilla, two remaining Spanish enclaves in Morocco along the Strait of Gibraltar.

With funding from Spain and the EU, these two cities have recently constructed razor-wire barriers, at a cost of about €295 million and €33 million, respectively – not that this has deterred smugglers. Uninhabited islands off the coast of Morocco have long been used as ports for an international trade in Moroccan hashish, and cocaine en route from South America to Europe, often via the Spanish-owned Isla del Perejil (or Leila, as it's called in Morocco). Now smugglers are earning as much or more promising to lead undocumented immigrants along these stepping stones to Europe – and many are quite literally making a killing. Migrants are often expected swim for miles through the treacherous waters, or are simply abandoned in the Strait.

Such as they are, smugglers' services range from €300 to €3500 – that's as much as three years' income for the average Moroccan – but the human costs are much higher. According to recent human-rights reports, over a five-year period as many as 4000 North African migrants have died in the attempt to reach Spanish shores. Spanish and Moroccan authorities have also been charged with extreme measures to curb migration, including firing on unarmed migrants and dumping deportees in the desert. But given daunting unemployment rates, limited educational opportunities and the need to support their families, many young Moroccans in particular continue to take the risk, convinced that all they have left to lose is their lives.

Médecins Sans Frontierès and Amnesty International provide key services and support to Moroccan migrants stranded between borders without family, funds or legal protection. For more information, visit www.amnesty.org and www.doctorswithout borders.org.

cultural exchange it brings will continue to redefine the local landscape, like shifting winds on sand.

WOMEN IN MOROCCO

A generation or two ago, you might not have had a chance to meet Fatima or Amina. Most of the people you'd see out and about, going to school, socialising and conducting business in the souqs, were men. But while the public sphere was mostly a male domain, the private sphere belonged to women. Women have long been the backbone of Moroccan households – and traditionally performed most of the back-breaking domestic labour. In poorer rural households, women typically had the burden of animal husbandry and tending crops in addition to childcare, cooking, cleaning, and fetching water and kindling; in well-to-do urban households, girls as young as 10 were hired as indentured servants, isolated from their families and receiving little more than a place to sleep for their efforts. A woman had no guarantee of support after marriage, either: women abandoned by their husbands could lose their homes to their husband's family, and be left to fend for themselves and their children.

But thanks to the bold efforts made by many pioneering Moroccans, women like Fatima and Amina now have choices open to them that would have been unthinkable just a generation or two ago. As of 2004, Morocco's Mudawanna legal code guarantees women crucial rights to custody, divorce, property ownership and child support, among other protections. Positive social pressure has nearly eradicated the practice of hiring girls under 14 as domestic workers, and initiatives to eliminate illiteracy are giving girls a better start in life. Women have asserted their rights in the workplace, too, joining industrial unions and forming agricultural collectives (such as the Coopérative Amal, p389). The first Moroccan woman was elected to Parliament in 1993, and many more are on the ballot for municipal elections.

According to recent UNESCO findings, Morocco has the largest percentage of women internet users anywhere in the Arab world.

The modern Moroccan woman's outlook extends far beyond her front door, especially for urban and middle-class women with access to satellite television, cell phones and the internet. Women visitors may meet urban Moroccan women who are eager to chat, and compare life experiences and ideas about world events. Men visiting Morocco will have less opportunity to befriend Moroccan women, since male-female interactions are still somewhat stilted by social convention. But despite customs that typically limit male-female interactions to large group outings, you'll surely notice some jittery internet daters meeting in parks, cafés and via internet webcam.

Even for visitors who don't engage them in conversation, Moroccan women leave quite an impression, whipping past on their motor scooters, tunics and headscarves billowing in the breeze, or taking over a sidewalk on an arm-in-arm evening stroll. While their future may still be uncertain, this much seems clear: Moroccan women are on the move, and making their presence known.

Arts, Crafts & Architecture

Everyone who's been to Morocco knows about Slideshow Syndrome: close your eyes and the day replays before you, one unforgettable mental picture after the next. There's nothing wrong with your eyes: nothing could prepare those optic nerves for the sheer dazzle, number and variety of sensations supplied daily by Moroccan artists and artisans. This is a country that rewards sideways glances, and where closer looks become lifelong fascinations. If it's true that we normally only use 10% of our brains, Morocco gives the other 90% something to do for a change.

ARTS

LITERATURE

Morocco has an ancient literary tradition that has only been recently recognised as such, because much of it wasn't available in print. In Morocco, poetry and stories have traditionally been passed along by storytellers and singers and in manuscripts circulated from one person to the next. For a population that for the most part couldn't read or afford books, Morocco's oral tradition has helped keep shared legends and personal histories alive. Watch the storytellers, singers and scribes in Marrakesh's Djemaa el-Fna in action and you'll understand how Morocco's literary tradition has remained so vital and irrepressible – even with a longstanding policy of press censorship.

Hearing a Different Beat

The international spotlight first turned on Morocco's literary scene in the 1950s and '60s, when Beat Generation authors Paul and Jane Bowles took up residence in Tangier and began recording the stories of Moroccans they knew. From these efforts came Larb Layachi's *A Life Full of Holes* (written under the pseudonym Driss ben Hamed Charhadi) and Mohammed Mrabet's *Love with a Few Hairs*, and eventually Mohammed Choukri's *For Bread Alone*. Not surprisingly, these books are packed with sex, drugs and unexpected poetry, like a lot of Beat literature – but if anything, they're more streetwise, humorous and heartbreaking.

Coming up for Air

Encouraged by the outspoken 'Tangerine' authors, a Moroccan poet named Abdellatif Laâbi founded a poetry magazine called *Anfas/Souffles (Breaths)* in 1966, not in the anything-goes International Zone of Tangier but right in the royal capital of Rabat. What began as a journal soon became a movement of writers, painters and filmmakers heeding Laâbi's outcry against censorship: 'A la poubelle poème/A la poubelle rythme/A la poubelle silence' ('In the trash, poetry/In the trash, rhythm/In the trash, silence'). *Anfas/Souffles* published 21 more issues and raised many more, until the censors shut it down in 1972 and sent Laâbi to prison for eight years for 'crimes of opinion'.

But the literary expression the magazine equated to breathing has continued unabated. In 1975, *Anfas/Souffles* cofounder and self-proclaimed

Government censorship notwithstanding, the complete French text of *Anfas/Souffles* is now archived online at http://clicnet.swarthmore.edu/souffles/sommaire.html.

For current articles on Berber poetry, song and culture – and outspoken critiques of its suppression – visit www .emazighen.com.

'linguistic guerrilla' Mohammed Khaïr-Eddine published his confrontational *Ce Maroc!*, an anthology of revolutionary writings. A Souss Berber himself, Khaïr-Eddine also called for the recognition of Berber identity and culture in his 1984 *Legend and Life of Agoun'chich*, which has emerged as a rallying cry for today's Berber Pride movement (see p29).

Living to Tell

Still more daring and distinctive Moroccan voices have found their way into print over the past two decades, both at home and abroad. Among the most famous works to be published by Moroccans living in Morocco are *Dreams of Trespass: Tales of a Harem Girlhood* and *The Veil and the Male Elite: A Feminist Interpretation of Islam*, both by Fatima Mernissi, an outspoken feminist and professor at the University of Rabat. In Rabati author Leila Abouzeid's *The Year of the Elephant*, one woman's search for life after divorce becomes a metaphor for Morocco's search for true independence after colonialism. Inspired by *Anfas/Souffles*, Fès-born expatriate author Tahar ben Jelloun combined poetic devices and his training as a psychotherapist in his celebrated novel *The Sand Child*, the story of a girl raised as a boy by her father in Marrakesh, and won France's Prix Goncourt for his book *The Sacred Night*.

Catch up on the latest developments in Moroccan and Middle Eastern writing with author Laila Lalami's blog at www .moorishgirl.com, updated multiple times daily.

The past few years have brought increased attention to individual Moroccan writers and their dissenting opinions – an encouraging sign of openness under King Mohammed VI, and a positive reaction to a war on terror that seems dangerously all-encompassing. Several recent Moroccan novels have explored the promise and trauma of emigration, notably Mahi Binebine's harrowing *Welcome to Paradise* and Laila Lalami's celebrated *Hope and Other Dangerous Pursuits*. On the last page of her novel, Lalami's Moroccan protagonist Murad daydreams of the stories he's been told, and may yet live to tell: 'He thought about his father, who'd told stories to his children, and how they were almost forgotten today. Anas closed the cash register with a loud ring, but Murad hardly paid attention; he was already lost in the story he'd start writing tonight.'

CINEMA & TV

Until recently Morocco has been seen mostly as a stunning movie backdrop, easily upstaging the actors in such dubious cinematic achievements as *Alexander, Ishtar, Hideous Kinky, The Four Feathers, The Mummy*,

---

WATCH THIS SPACE

For the ultimate Moroccan movie-going experience, don't miss these cinemas:

■ Tangier Cinematheque, the 2005 reincarnation of Cinema Rif, the great movie palace of the 1930s. This landmark, nonprofit cinema screens international independent films and documentaries, hosts filmmakers' workshops and promises open-air screenings for 4000 in the Grand Socco.

■ Cinema Eden (Marrakesh) for all-male Bollywood sing-along audience participation that makes *The Rocky Horror Picture Show* seem tame.

■ Megarama (Casablanca), Morocco's first multiplex, shows Hollywood, Bollywood and Moroccan films on 14 screens. (Coming soon: more multiplexes in Agadir and Marrakesh.)

■ Le Colisée (Marrakesh) earned the honour of hosting the Marrakech International Film Festival (see boxed text opposite) as one of few Moroccan cinemas regularly screening independent Moroccan film and original-language foreign features.

STARS ALIGN OVER MARRAKESH

Now entering its sixth year, the Marrakech International Film Festival is a jet-set destination and a plucky contender in the overwhelmingly European and American festival circuit. So is the festival a showcase for international independent features, or films shot in or relating to Morocco, or postcolonial cinema? The answer appears to be D, all of the above, though the festival is not above appealing to Hollywood egos for a little added attention – recent festival guests include David Lynch, Martin Scorsese, Francis Ford Coppola and (moment of awkward silence, please) Colin Farrell.

Festival organisers seem determined to remain broad-minded, giving its award ceremonies the unpredictable edge missing from, say, the Oscars. In 2004, top honours in the Marrakech International Film festival went to *Sideways* – apparently, a film about wine *can* be a hit in a Muslim country. The year before that, the Gold Star went to *Gori Vatra*, about a Bosnian town putting on a happy democratic face for a visit from Bill Clinton, and in 2005 it went to Kyrgyzstan's *Saratan*, a farce about post-Soviet bureaucracy (now there's a redundancy).

But the hands-down audience favourites are always the movies that are screened in the open-air cinema set up in the Djemaa el-Fna. Struggling filmmakers, take note: your vaguely political tragicomedies may yet find an appreciative audience among the fire jugglers and snake charmers of Marrakesh.

Troy and *Sahara*. But while there's much to cringe about in Morocco's filmography, the country had golden moments on the silver screen in Hitchcock's *The Man Who Knew Too Much,* Orson Welles' *Othello* and David Lean's *Lawrence of Arabia*. Morocco has certainly proved its versatility with some big-name directors: it stunt-doubled for Somalia in Ridley Scott's *Black Hawk Down*, stood in for Tibet in Martin Scorsese's *Kundun* and stole the show right out from under John Malkovich by playing itself in Bernardo Bertolucci's *The Sheltering Sky*. And talk about hard-working – Morocco serves as the location for more than 1000 French, German and Italian productions each year.

The movies Morocco gets paid to help make are not necessarily the movies Moroccans pay to see. In 2005, more than a third of the movies shown on Morocco's 105 screens were Bollywood films. Moroccan cinemas have considerable economic incentives to screen Hollywood blockbusters instead of independent or homegrown African films: the main film distributor in Francophone Africa, African American Films (AFRAM), provides blockbusters for a cut of the box office, while other films must be rented.

But recently Moroccans are getting an opportunity to see films shot in Morocco that are actually by Moroccans and about Morocco. French-backed independent Moroccan films are also now showing in select cinemas and on satellite TV, and Franco-Moroccan films are now serious festival contenders. Franco-Moroccan director Leila Marrakchi was awarded 'Un Certain Regard' at the 2005 Cannes Film Festival for her first feature, *Marock*. Several celebrated neorealist Moroccan films have been making the film festival rounds lately, including Jilali Ferhati's *Mémoire en Détention (Memory in Detention)*, about an ex-con's attempts to track down relations of an inmate who lost his memory during his long detention, and Narjiss Nejjar's controversial *Les Yeux Secs (Cry No More)*, about a former prostitute who returns to her Berber village to stop her daughter from being drawn into the local flesh trade.

The Moroccan government is showing initiative, too. In the 1970s, Moroccan 'ciné-clubs' encouraged debates that weren't always welcomed by the government, and filmmakers were more often purged than funded.

None of the 1942 classic *Casablanca* was actually shot in Casablanca. It was filmed on a Hollywood backlot, and the Rick's Café Américain set was based on the historic El-Minzah hotel in Tangier (see p168). Here's looking at you, kid – just not too closely.

Impress your friends by springing for movie tickets in Morocco – just don't mention the average ticket costs less than US$2.

What's on TV today in
Morocco? Find out online
at www.2M.tv.

Throughout the 1980s most filmmakers kept a low profile, with notable exceptions including *Amok*, the 1980 anti-apartheid film by Moroccan director (and Pasolini's onetime assistant) Souheil ben Barka. But times and kings have changed: one of the most outspoken film critics of the 1970s, Moroccan filmmaker and former Canal Plus bigwig Noureddine Saïl, recently returned from France to head up the Centre Cinématographique Marocain and 2M, Morocco's household TV channel.

Under new leadership, Moroccan filmmakers shot 20 features and 30 short films in Morocco in 2005, and Moroccan television viewers saw a drastic change of programming from the usual Egyptian comedies, Syrian soap operas and MTV-style hit parades. In 2004 and 2005, Moroccan television went where no other state-run television had gone before, airing the haunting personal testimonies of political prisoners rounded up during Morocco's 'Black Years' under Hassan II (see A Rough Start, p40). Moroccans were riveted, and the televised reports were the highest-rating shows in Moroccan television history.

MUSIC
Any trip to Morocco comes with its own syncopated soundtrack: women tapping out a funky beat with tea glasses on brass trays, hawkers singing the praises of knock-off Armani right over the early evening *azan* (call to prayer), and the ubiquitous donkey-cart-drivers' chants of 'Balek!' – fair warning that since donkeys don't yield, you'd better, and quick. Shopkeepers start drumming their fingers not because they're impatient with you, but just to replay one of the many rhythms overheard in a day's work in the souqs. As if this weren't enough to get you humming maniacally, there's also the actual music. Sample the varieties below for a memory bank of Maghrebi music mashups any DJ would envy.

Classical Arab-Andalusian Music
Leaving aside the thorny question of where exactly it originated (you don't want to be the cause of the next centuries-long Spain-Morocco conflict, do you?), this music combines the flamenco-style strumming and heartstring-plucking drama of Spanish folk music with the finely calibrated stringed instruments, complex percussion and haunting half-tones of classical Arab music. Add poetic lyrics and the right singer and you may find that lump in your throat makes it hard to swallow your *bastilla* (multilayered pastry) at dinner. Listen for it at classical music fests, fine restaurants and concerts across Morocco; popular interpreters include Abdelkrim Rais and Amina Alaoui.

Gnaoua
Joyously bluesy with a rhythm you can't refuse, this music may send you into a trance – and that's just what it's meant to do. Gnaoua began among freed slaves in Marrakesh and Essaouira as a ritual of deliverance from slavery and into God's graces. As you watch the musicians work themselves into a state of ecstasy, with fezzes spinning and sudden back flips, their music may set you free, too.

Join the jubilant crowds watching in Marrakesh's Djemaa el-Fna, at the annual Gnaoua and World Music Festival in Essaouira, and at musical festivals across the country, and hear it on Peter Gabriel's Real World music label, too. Gnaoua *maâlems* (master musicians) include Abdeslam Alikkane and his Tyour Gnaoua, famed fusion musician Hassan Hakmoun, Indian-inflected Nass Marrakech and reggae-inspired Omar Hayat. Since Gnaoua are historically a brotherhood, traditionally there

---

NOW HEAR THIS: MOROCCAN MUSIC FESTIVALS

Dates and locations may vary, so check www.maghrebarts.ma/musique.html for updates.

- January: Fès Andalusian Music Festival
- April: Jazzablanca (Casablanca)
- May: Festival du Desert (Errachidia), Jazz aux Oudayas (Rabat), Tanjazz (Tangier)
- June: Festival of World Sacred Music (Fès), Gnaoua and World Music Festival (Essaouira)
- July: Marrakesh Popular Arts Festival
- August: Marriage Festival (Imilchil)
- September: Atlantic Andalusian Music Fest (Essaouira)

---

have been few women Gnaoua musicians – but with more Moroccan women singers picking up Gnaoua musical cues, this may yet change.

Berber Folk Music

There's plenty of other indigenous Moroccan music besides Gnaoua, thanks to the ancient Berber tradition of passing along songs and poetry from one generation to the next. You can't miss it at village *moussem*s (festivals in honour of a local saint), the Marrakesh Festival of Popular Arts and Imilchil's Marriage Festival, as well as weddings and other family celebrations.

> Hear Morocco's latest hits at Radio Casablanca online: www.maroc .net/newrc.

The most renowned Berber folk group is the Master Musicians of Joujouka, who famously inspired the Rolling Stones, Led Zeppelin and William S Burroughs, and collaborated with them on some truly experimental fusion. Lately the big names are women's, namely the all-women group B'net Marrakech, and the bold Najat Aatabou, who sings protest songs in Berber against restrictive traditional roles.

Rai

Technically it's Algerian, but Moroccans have adopted and adapted it as their own. Rai started in the '60s as a fusion of Algerian music with jazz and electric guitar. In the 1980s it got a little heavy on the synthesiser sound effects, but rai's getting its edge back with an infusion of Gnaoua, hip-hop and even rap. Morocco's leading rai musicians are Cheb Mimoun and Chaba Zahouniacan.

Pop Music

Like the rest of the Arab world, Moroccans listen to a lot of Egyptian music, but Moroccopop is gaining ground with boy bands like Sawt al-Atlas and Morocco's answer to the Spice Girls: Spice Ray. A generation of local DJs with cheeky names like Ramadan Special and DJ Al Intifada have mastered the art of the remix, and so have a few pop acts. Some of the more intriguing talents to emerge in recent years: British-Moroccan U-Cef, who mixes Arab pop and hip-hop with Gnaoua to slick electronica effect; Moroccan singer Aisha Kandisha, who finds and works a groove from rock, soul and Moroccan rhythms; and the, um, bluntly named Ganga Fusion, a band pounding out a groovy mix of salsa, Moroccan folk music, reggae and jazz.

THEATRE & DANCE

When Shakespeare wrote 'All the world's a stage', he must've had Morocco in mind. Every square, souq and sidewalk is action-packed, with students urgently whispering sweet nothings into mobile phones, shopkeepers wisecracking that you won't find better prices at an insane asylum, and passers-by pausing to supply the chorus on a ballad blasting out a boom box. But if you think this opening scene is exciting, wait until you see Morocco's main act: *halqa*, Moroccan street theatre.

Enter storytellers stage left to joust with thin air, and die countless fake deaths in imaginary battles worthy of Don Quixote. Look up, and you'll notice a human pyramid performing very carefully synchronised dance movements, as an acrobat steadies his nerves for a flying leap to the top. As sun sets, cross-dressing belly dancers twirl their hands to distract from their five-o'clock shadows – and with a glance and an inviting flick of a scarf, you could be the next on stage.

This event might take place around dusk on any warm weekend, in the main square of any sizable Moroccan town, but the best venue of all is Marrakesh's legendary Djemaa el-Fna. After a thousand-year run, the Djemaa was finally given its due in 2001 as UNESCO's first World Heritage Site for Oral Tradition. Morocco offers more formal performances in urban cultural centres and theatres, and Fès is now giving Marrakesh an annual run for the money with its new Festival Populaire de l'Art de la Halqa in April.

Dinner Theatre

Programmed folk entertainment can't always match the nightly improvised drama in the Djemaa. This is certainly true of *fantasias*, fauxfolkloric theatre-restaurant spectacles big on chaotic horseback charges, blaring musket salutes and other noisy displays thwarting any attempt to digest the cold grilled meats on offer. Some restaurants also offer a 'dinner spectacle', complete with women belly-dancers – not part of Morocco's dance tradition, but a Turkish import – Gnaoua gamely trying to compete with the clatter of dishes, and 'candle-dancers' balancing brass trays of lit candles on their heads like characters in a Dr Seuss book. For real entertainment value, all you need is a balmy evening, a seat at a café or restaurant with a view of the town square, and a handful of coins to show your appreciation for the talents on display.

VISUAL ART

The usual arts and crafts hierarchy is reversed in Morocco, where the craft tradition is ancient and revered, and visual art is something of a minor, more recent development. Ornament was meant to be spiritually uplifting, even sublime, while nonfunctional objects and representational images were construed as pointless – or worse, a form of vanity verging on idolatry, as it's perceived in Jewish traditions and many (though not all) Muslim cultures. No doubt you'll see shops selling paintings of veiled harem women with exaggerated eyelashes and ceramic figurines of scowling turbaned tough guys, but these belong to an old French tradition of Orientalism and are mostly made for export – they're not generally considered the finest art Morocco has to offer.

In the 1950s and '60s, folk artists in Essaouira and Tangier made painting and sculpture theirs by incorporating Berber symbols and locally found materials. Landscape painting also became a popular way to express pride of place in Essaouira and Asilah, and abstract painting became an important means of poetic expression in Rabat and Casablanca. Photography had no such luck, and is still mostly stuck in documentary mode in Morocco – unless you count all those retouched glamour shots of the king on display everywhere. Installation art seems like a natural extension of Morocco's elaborately built interior environments, and it's finally putting all that floor space at Moroccan cultural centres and art expos to good use.

No, that's not a musical rugby scrum: the *haidous* is a complex circle dance with musicians in the middle, often performed in celebration of the harvest.

No conversation about art in Morocco is complete until someone mentions Edward Said's *Orientalism*, the ground-breaking book about how European artists have pictured the Middle East, and how those ideas affected Middle Eastern self-image. Works dubbed 'Orientalist' are trying too hard to fit the 'exotic Moroccan' mould – not exactly a compliment.

Calligraphy

Calligraphy is the standout visual art form in Morocco, practised and perfected in Moroccan *medersa*s (Quranic schools) over the last thousand years. The Quran praises lines written with the *qalam*, or reed-handled pen, and it's easy to see why: it takes a steady hand and a light touch to use this fine-tipped brush pen, but it does make a glorious impression. Sometimes the elegant letters are so cleverly intertwined they're hard to read, even for very learned Moroccans, but most form an *aya*, or Quranic verse.

Take a look at a few antique Qurans in a Moroccan museum and you'll notice that the same text can have an incredibly different effect in another calligraphic style. One calligrapher might take up a whole page with a single word, while another might turn it into a flower, or fold and twist the letters origami-style into graphic patterns. The style most commonly used for Qurans is Naskh, a slanting cursive script introduced by the Umayyads (see The Power of Conviction p31). Cursive letters ingeniously interlaced to form a shape or dense design are hallmarks of the Thuluth style, while high-impact graphic lettering is the Kufic style from Iraq. You'll see three main kinds of Kufic calligraphy in Morocco: those letters that look like they've been tied by sailors are knotted Kufic; the ones bursting into bloom are foliate Kufic; and the angular ones that seem determined to prove the Pythagorean Theorem are square Kufic.

In Morocco, calligraphy isn't just in the Quran: it's on the tiled walls, in the stucco arches overhead, and quite literally coming out of the woodwork. You'll also see calligraphy on Moroccan dishes, jewellery and tea trays, usually containing a religious invocation that brings *baraka* (blessings) to all those who witness it. One current Moroccan trend is to paint calligraphy in henna on leather to create 'tattooed' leather paintings, candleholders and lampshades. But so far as getting permanent actual tattoos on your own skin, know that Muslims do not always take kindly to non-Muslims sporting religious inscriptions. If you really want to surround yourself with Morocco's most elevated art, you can always snap up some ceramics, jewellery, tiles or other objects transformed into *objets d'art* with Moroccan calligraphy.

You too can read Islamic calligraphy: vertical lines are usually consonants, smaller marks above and below are vowels, and that tall letter that looks like the letter 'l' is probably an *alif*, the first letter in 'Allah'.

To find out more about where those splendid traditional designs originated and learn to trace a few yourself, check out *The Splendour of Islamic Calligraphy* by Mohammed Sijelmassi and Khatibi Abdelkebir.

CRAFTS

For Moroccan artisans, each object is an opportunity to combine beauty with purpose, and if your purpose happens to be a beautiful birthday present, well, they might be able to help you out there, too. You'll encounter artisans working small wonders in the souqs without computer models or even an electrical outlet. The tools of the trade here are imagination, an eye for colour and form, and steady hands you'd trust to take out a tonsil. Most of the artisans you'll see in the souqs are men, but you're likely to glimpse women *maâlems* (master artisans) working behind the scenes knotting carpets in Middle Atlas villages, weaving textiles along the Southern coast and painting ceramics in Fès, Salé and Safi.

Maâlems with saintly patience or a devilish sense of humour may invite to try your hand at their craft, and you'll never know how many thumbs you have until you try to mimic the acute hand-eye coordination required to work that loom, leather awl or chisel. Now that you fully appreciate the craftsmanship, naturally you'll want to bring home a sample – those craftspeople sure are crafty, eh? Just don't forget to bargain a little (see Rules to Remember p461 for tips).

Answers to your every 'how'd they do that?' are on display at Marrakesh's state-run Ensemble Artisanal, where you can watch *maâlems* at work and purchase their handiwork at fixed (if somewhat stiff) prices.

ZELLIJ

DIYers know that tiling a bathroom isn't always easy: there are corners, mathematics and gloppy grout to consider. But if you think that's tricky, try *zellij*, Moroccan-style mosaic. Each *zellij* tile is individually sculpted in a precise geometric shape with a small hammer and screwdriver-sized chisel; a slip of the hammer or wrong angle on the chisel, and that perfectly proportioned eight-pointed star will go all lopsided. Each tile must be exactly the right colour and shape, so that it fits together perfectly with hundreds or thousands of others to create a consistent pattern that covers an entire wall, floor or fountain. It's the most mind-numbing jigsaw puzzle ever.

Since a fountain probably won't fit in your carry-on, you might consider a *zellij* mirror, picture frame or small tabletop instead; the asking price depends on the quality of the work involved. The best *zellij* is cut in small pieces that fit together so perfectly that the grout is barely visible between pieces, and the surface appears smooth and almost unbroken. If there are a variety of shapes involved, you can expect to pay more. True *zellij maâlem*s can create 360 different shapes, and each one can take weeks or even months to master.

*Zellij maâlem*s from Fès are generally considered the Nobel Prize winners of Moroccan mosaics, though the *maâlem*s of Marrakesh and Meknès are no slouches either. Cutting *zellij* into rounded shapes or thin strips is particularly challenging, so those narrow bands of Arabic calligraphy you'll see made entirely of *zellij* at Marrakesh's Ali ben Youssef Medersa (p299) are impressive indeed. Some of the most highly prized *zellij* has a slight lustre to the glaze, so that it turns to gold at sunset and in candlelight. The glitz-loving Saadians couldn't get enough, and took it to the grave with them in their Marrakesh tombs (see p300). Thanks to the current riad craze, Marrakshi *maâlem*s now have greater opportunities to practice and hone their craft than *maâlem*s in other towns, whose skills are mostly used for historical restoration. Meknès' *zellij*-makers are quick to point out that Morocco's mosaics tradition got its start nearby, in the Berber/Roman town of Volubilis (for more, see Live Free or Die Trying, p29). Still, many consider the trademark green, black and white *zellij* of Fès the pinnacle of refinement, and if you take a look at the *medersa*s in the medina (pp220-1), it's tough to argue.

CARPETS

If you manage to return from Morocco without a carpet, you may well congratulate yourself on being one of few travellers to have outsmarted the wiliest salespeople on the planet. Huzzah! But then it sets in: they've got piles of splendid, one-of-a-kind handmade carpets underfoot, and you've got your acrylic bathmat. Hmmm.

Moroccan carpets hook travellers almost every time because there's a right carpet for almost everyone – and if that sounds like something your mother once said to you about soul mates, it's not entirely a coincidence. Women in rural Morocco traditionally created carpets as part of their dowries, expressing their own personalities in exuberant colours and patterns, and weaving in symbols of their hopes for health and married life. Now carpets are mostly made as a way to supplement household income and are sold to middlemen who resell them at a hefty mark-up. Consider buying directly from a cooperative or rural roadside stand instead – the producer is more likely to get her fair share of the proceeds, you'll get a better deal, and you may meet the artisan who

Try your hand at *zellij* with *Moroccan Style: Mosaic Project Book* by Katrina Hall – might want to skip the caffeinated mint tea beforehand, though. Some things are best left to the professionals.

And you thought you got fleeced in the souqs: millions of Moroccan sheep produce about 12,000 tons of wool a year for Moroccan carpets and other textiles.

gave your new rug so much personality, it could never be mistaken for
a mere doormat.

Once you begin to look around at Moroccan carpets – casually of
course, betraying no sales interest until the last minute – you'll begin to
distinguish some key types:

- Rabati carpets – plush pile carpets in deep jewel tones, featuring an
  ornate central motif balanced by fine detail along the borders. Many
  of the patterns may remind you of a formal garden, though you may
  see some newer animal motifs and splashy modern abstract designs.
  Rabati carpets are highly prized, and could run you Dh2000 per sq-
  metre.

- *Hanbels*, or kilims – these flat-woven rugs with no pile manage to
  make up for a lack of cushiness with character. Chichaoua rugs are
  among the most striking with zigzags, diamond patterns, and hori-
  zontal stripes in yellow, black and white on a red background (about
  Dh700 per sq-metre). Some *hanbels* include Berber letters and aus-
  picious symbols such as the Evil Eye, Southern Cross and Berber
  fibule (brooch) in their weave. Ask the seller to explain them for
  you – whether it's folklore or fib, the carpet-seller's interpretation is
  sure to be intriguing.

- *Zanafi*, or *glaoua* – kilims and shag carpeting, together at last. Op-
  posites attract in these rugs, where sections of fluffy pile alternate
  with flat-woven stripes or borders. These are usually in the Dh1000 to
  Dh1750 per-sq-metre price bracket.

- *Shedwi* – flat-woven rugs with bold patterns in black wool on off-white
  so *au naturel*, you can still feel the lanolin between your fingers when
  you rub it. At as little as Dh400 for a smaller rug, they're impressive
  yet inexpensive gifts.

> The most reliable resource in English on Moroccan carpets is the (aptly named) *Moroccan Carpets*, by Brooke Pickering, W Russell Pickering, and Ralph Yohe. Packed with photos to help pinpoint the origins and style of any carpet that mysteriously followed you home…

TOP CARPET-BUYING TIPS

To avoid both carpet-buyer's remorse and non-carpet-buyer's remorse:

- Know your limits, namely how much blank wall and floor space you actually have, your
  airline's luggage weight limit, whether you're prepared to pay for shipping and duty (see
  Sending Mail p460 for details), and how much you want to spend on a wall hanging for Aunt
  Gladys.

- Tread cautiously with antique rugs. Prices are typically much higher for antique carpets.
  Genuine antiques can be hard to distinguish from rugs taken out back and stomped on
  awhile, so buyer beware.

- Inspect the knots. You'll be asked to pay more for carpets with a higher number of knots per
  sq metre or sq cm, which you'll begin to discern by examining the back of carpets to look
  for gaps between knots. Some carpets are washed in hot water to bind the wool together
  more tightly, like that time you put your cashmere cardigan in the dryer – but you can often
  distinguish these shrunken rugs by their misshapen, irregular borders.

- Get plenty of vegetables. Prices are often higher for carpets whose wool is coloured using
  vegetable dyes instead of synthetics (which tend to fade faster); you can usually tell these by
  their muted tones, and the carpet seller may be able to tell you what plant was used to make
  the dye.

- Enjoy the transaction. Be prepared to banter before you bargain, keep your sense of humour,
  come back tomorrow, and drink mint tea so sweet you'll want to brush your teeth twice. Besides fond memories, at the end of it all you should have a carpet that suits you – and quite
  possibly one for your Aunt Gladys.

MOROCCAN FASHION STATEMENTS

Love that Moroc-chic look? Start a new trend back home with these Moroccan fashion finds:

■ *Kaftan* – proof that a one-size-fits-all dress can be glamorous, with bell sleeves, embroidery around the neck and cuffs, and tiny knotted buttons all down the front.

■ *Jellaba* – the ultimate in quirky unisex, these pointy-hooded cloaks are worn by men and women alike.

■ *Hendira* – yes, apparently you can wear your woollen security blanket as outerwear.

■ *Burnous* – a short jacket that combines the pointy hood of the jellaba with the versatility of the *hendira* – ideal for rocking kasbahs or runways.

TEXTILES

Anything that isn't nailed down in Morocco is likely to be woven, sewn or embroidered – and even then, it might be upholstered. Moroccan women are the under-recognised *maâlem*s of Moroccan textiles, and the tradition they've established has recently helped attract emerging fashion enterprises and global brands like Custo Barcelona to Morocco. One third of all women are now employed in Morocco's growing industrial garment industry. But for something produced with individual flair and hands-on expertise, check out these traditional textile handicrafts.

■ 'Cactus silk' *('soie végétale')* is made from cactus fibres typically woven with cotton (or synthetic) threads of another colour to produce cloth with a spectacular sheen and a starchy crispness. In the south, striped cactus silk scarves, pillow covers, tablecloths and bedspreads have become so popular, they're being mass-produced – hand-woven cactus silk has a stiffer feel, tighter weave and slightly irregular edge. Hand-woven bedspreads run from Dh400 to Dh600, depending on size; scale down the price for smaller-scale items.

■ Embroidery ranges from simple Berber designs to minutely detailed *terz Fezzi*, the elaborate nature-inspired patterns stitched in blue upon white linen that women in Fès traditionally spent years mastering for their dowries…practice for the even-more-delicate art of mastering their husbands, perhaps? But the ladies of Salé also deserve their due for their striking embroidery in one or two bold colours along the borders of crisp white linen. Though you might not be able to bring yourself to wipe your mouth or nose on anything this spectacular, it makes a lovely pillow case or table runner – and clumsy dinner guests don't have to know why they're being served white wine with their steaks.

■ Handmade felt hats, slippers, coats, pillows bags or floor coverings really put wool through the wringer: it's dyed, boiled and literally beaten to a pulp. Instead of being woven or sewn, felt is usually formed into the intended shape on a mould and allowed to dry gradually to hold its shape. Felt makers are usually found in the wool souq in major cities, in case a bad hair day calls for a Fès fix (around Dh100 to Dh150) or a dapper beanie (Dh100 to Dh200).

LEATHERWORK

There's not much call for camel saddles anymore, but that hasn't stopped Moroccan leather artisans from plying their trade by hand, much as they have for centuries – only they're fashioning next season's It Bag with what looks like medieval dentistry tools. In closet-sized shops along winding alleys of the leather souqs, you might be surprised to see freshly tanned and dyed lime-green leather sculpted into fashion-forward square poufs

(Ottomans, Dh200 to Dh450 and up, depending on size, shape and quality), yellow pompoms carefully stitched onto stylish fuchsia kidskin gloves (Dh150 to Dh200), or shocking silver leather stretched and sewn into the ultimate glam-rock bedroom slippers (Dh80 to Dh150, depending on decoration). If you're in town for a couple of days, you might even commission an artisan to make you a custom-made lambskin leather jacket, jodhpurs or whatever else you might imagine in leather (ahem).

If it's an authenticity trip you're after, for men you'll prefer the traditional yellow *babouches* (pointy slippers) or 'Berber Adidas', slippers with soles made from recycled rubber tyres (usually Dh50 to Dh100). Women's *babouches* come in a broader range of colours and designs (as much as Dh200 for very fancy pairs), and you may see vats of vibrant dye used for them in tanneries in Fès. But as colourful as they may look from afar, the tanneries give off a putrid stench that only the glue-sniffers that tend to congregate around them can withstand – fair warning.

CERAMICS

If Moroccan ceramics don't convince you to upgrade from Tupperware, nothing will. Blue-and-white pottery from Fès might even top your grandmother's china as the new family heirloom. Though the colour scheme might remind you of a Ming vase, you'll be pleased to hear that it's nowhere near as expensive – a decorative tajine may run you Dh150 to Dh400, depending on size and decoration. As usual, antiques have their own price range, and it can be hard to tell the real deal from a fake with a convincing patina.

Different regions have their own colour schemes: Meknès ceramics tend to be green, Salé is strong on yellow and turquoise; Safi is polychrome. Small, relatively plain plates might cost as little as Dh20, but the larger, more intricate ones could cost Dh150 and as much as Dh500. Marrakesh doesn't have much of a ceramics tradition but has proved a quick study, with monochrome ceramics that emphasise geometric and whimsical forms instead of elaborate decoration. Salé is the modern ceramics centre to watch, with innovative geometric patterns and intricate dot-patterned dishes the Impressionists might envy.

BRASS, COPPER, AND SILVER

Tea is something of a performance art in Morocco, and it requires just the right props. As though tea poured from over your head weren't dramatic enough, gleaming brass teapots (Dh200 and up) and copper tea trays (Dh500 and up) are hammered by hand to catch the light and, engraved with calligraphy, convey *baraka* on all who partake. Pierced brass lamps (Dh150 and up) and tin lanterns (usually Dh50 to Dh100) create instant atmosphere – and if all else fails to impress, you might always brandish an antique inlaid dagger to serve your guests a sliver of cake.

Most 'silver' tea services are actually nickel silver, and should cost accordingly – about Dh50 to Dh200 for the teapot, and usually more for the tray (depending on size and design). Sterling will be marked with 925, and is often sold by weight rather than design – check the going world price for silver before you shop, watch those scales and calculate accordingly.

JEWELLERY

Not all that glitters is gold in Morocco, since Berbers traditionally believe gold to be the source of evil. (Wonder where they got that idea? See Victory is Sweet: the Saadians, p36). You may see some jewellers

Plain terracotta cooking tajines are oven safe, fine for stovetop cooking and cost less than Dh100. According to a recent *New York Times* review, newfangled tajines made by major European brands cost ten times that and don't cook as well.

The Art of the Islamic Tile, by Gerard Degeorge and Yves Porter, celebrates the splendours of ceramics across the Middle East, from Istanbul to Fès.

with magnifying glasses working a tricky bit of gold filigree, but most of what you see in the souqs is imported from India and Bali. Morocco's mining operations are more concerned with phosphates and oil than precious stones, but you will see semiprecious stones, including coral, agate, carnelian and amber.

Lots of the 'amber' you'll see in the souqs is plastic. The genuine article will have a faint incense smell when you light a match near it, and a slightly waxy feel.

The real gems of Moroccan jewellery craftsmanship don't necessarily glitter much at all. Moroccan silver is often ingeniously inlaid, engraved with good luck charms, or moulded into simple, striking shapes. For folkloric *fibules* (brooches) with modern minimalist impact, make a trip to the southern Atlantic coast, especially Tiznit. But Moroccan *maâlem*s don't need precious materials to create a thing of beauty. In the right hands, ancient fossils become cutting-edge pendants, and silk thread wrapped around copper wire makes a tiered necklace that demands to be taken clubbing.

WOODWORK

The most pleasingly aromatic area of the souq is the woodworker's area, with scents of orangewood, cedar, lemonwood and pine rising from the curls of wood carpeting the floors of master carvers' workshops. These are the *maâlem*s responsible for those ancient carved, brass-studded cedar doors you've been obsessively photographing (don't worry, everyone does it), and the carved cedar ceiling rafters and *muqarnas* (honeycomb-carved) domes in Moroccan palaces and *medersa*s that could drive MC Escher mad with their mind-boggling patterns. Tetouan, Meknès and Fès have the best reputations for carved wood ornament, but you'll see impressive woodworking in most Moroccan medinas.

Chronicle Books' *Arts and Crafts of Morocco* shows how all those historic details add up to one grand style.

You may not be able to take an entire building with you, but you might find carved wood architectural salvage at Bab el-Khemis in Marrakesh. For the gourmets on your gift list, hand-carved orangewood *harira* spoons (Dh5 to Dh8) are small ladles with long handles that make ideal tasting spoons. Cedar is used for most items, from carved jewellery boxes and picture frames to hefty carved chests sure to keep the moths at bay (priced according to size and ornament). The most admired objects of all are carved from thuja wood, knotty burl with a distinctive grain and appealing deep caramel colour. This wood is the root of a tree indigenous to the Essaouira region and now at risk of being admired to extinction, so consider buying from an artisans' collective more likely to practice responsible collection and reforesting.

ARCHITECTURE

Stubbed toes come with the territory in Morocco: with so much intriguing architecture to gawk at, you can't always watch where you're going. Some buildings are more memorable than others – like any developing country, there's a fair amount of makeshift housing and cheap concrete here – but it's the striking variation in architecture that keeps you wondering what could possibly be around the block and across that mountain range. Here's a sneak preview of what you'll find.

The only mosque non-Muslims are allowed to visit in Morocco is the Hassan II Mosque in Casablanca (see p91). It's the third-largest mosque in the world, so you certainly won't be cramping anyone's style.

IMPERIAL CENTRES

As thrillingly chaotic as Morocco's ancient imperial cities seem, there is a certain logic to their zoning that you can still discern today in Fès, Meknès and Marrakesh. At the centre of the medina (old city), you'll notice monumental mosques and labyrinthine souqs, twin symbols of the ruling power's higher aspiration and its worldly ambition. *Zawiyas* (saints' shrines closed to non-Muslims), public squares that are anything but square, domed hammams, fountains and communal ovens would all be found in this area, to meet the spiritual, social and physical needs of residents and traders alike.

In the midst of the souqs were *fuduq*s, courtyard compounds that housed workshops on the ground floor and rooming houses on the first. These multipurpose mud-brick buildings were the live-and-work lofts of medieval times, accommodating the city's industries and the workers required to keep them running. But some industries were inevitably stinkier than others – especially tanneries and animal husbandry – and these were usually relegated to the outskirts of town.

Naturally, the prime real estate in town was reserved for the royal palace and its fortified kasbah, tucked away securely within the ramparts amid lush gardens that seem miles away from the bustling souqs. The *mellah*, or Jewish quarter, would be positioned within reach of the kasbah guard and the ruling power's watchful eye. Not far from the palace would be some of the city's grander riads, courtyard mansions where families of royal relatives, advisors and rich merchants whiled away idle hours gossiping in *bhous* (seating nooks) around courtyards paved with *zellij* and filled with songbirds twittering in fruit trees. Not a bad setup, really, and one you can enjoy today as a guest in one of the many riad guesthouses in Marrakesh and Fès.

When imperial cities and the rest of Morocco came under colonial control, entirely new neighbourhoods were built outside the walls of the medina, complete with modern conveniences and modern architecture to impose a new visual order. Boulevards lined with trees and multistorey buildings with grand arcades and Mansard roofs must have come as quite a shock when they were initially introduced by the French and Spanish over a century ago – especially for Moroccan taxpayers who footed the construction bills, yet found themselves outside the colonial power structures represented by these 'nouvelles villes'. Even today the difference between Moroccan medinas and nouvelle villes is striking, and many of the neoclassical French façades and red-roofed Spanish villas seem out of place and ostentatious, even kitschy.

Casablanca is the exception to the rule, with local architectural features grafted onto whitewashed European edifices in a distinctive crossroads style that might be described as Islamic geometry meets Art Deco. Today you'll see elements of the Casablanca style all over Morocco – in architecture and in everyday life, Morocco is making a real effort to balance its indigenous traditions and global outlook.

DESERT OASES

Desert *ksour* (mud-brick castles) will take your breath away just as surely as a *hamseen* (hot desert wind) blowing in from the Sahara. Their locations are intimidating and spectacular: on a defensible incline, smack up against a rocky cliff, or rising majestically above the valley of a palm oasis. Cutting a fine figure against this backdrop and the unsmudged blue desert sky are metres-thick, straw-reinforced mud-brick fortifications, capped by zigzag *merlon* (crenellation). Centuries after they were built, the message they convey is as unmistakable as a stop sign: These rugged structures and the people who inhabit them are truly formidable. Only birds seem undaunted, making themselves at home in the holes left for wooden beam reinforcements.

Downtown Ouarzazate features a *ksar* (castle) carefully maintained and stage-managed as a film set location, but to get the full effect of

The next best thing to being there might just be *The Villas and Riads of Morocco*, by Corrine Verner, and Architectural Digest contributors Lisl and Landt Dennis' *Living in Morocco: Design from Casablanca to Marrakesh*. These splashy coffee-table books offer enough luxe design ideas to turn your flat into a royal retreat.

To see Moroccan gone modern, flip through the snazzy *Architecture du Maroc* magazine, published every two months – and if you read French, visit the website for more articles (alongside the inevitable real estate ads) at http://www.archimedia.ma.

this architecture in its natural setting, pay a visit to a *ksar* along the desolate Drâa Valley or the Dadès Valley (sometimes called 'Valley of a Thousand Kasbahs'). There you'll glimpse what many desert traders have before you: through those high wooden gates and beyond the stables lies a labyrinth of souqs and storehouses and perhaps the local *funduq*, where travellers of yore stayed the night (though you might prefer one of the desert camping locations or caravanserai hotels). You may see a public fountain or faucet, evidence of ingenious underground irrigation systems that sustained life within these walls through sieges from rival armies and clans.

Like a desert mirage, a *ksar* will play tricks with your sense of scale and distance with its odd combination of grandeur and intimacy. Looking toward the horizon from the *ksar* ramparts or oasis watchtowers, Timbuktu seems much closer than 52 days away by camel, as advertised by the famous weathered sign in Zagora – and in fact, the elegant mud-brick architecture of Mali and Senegal is a near relative of Morocco's *ksour*.

COASTAL TOWNS

Climb up onto a medina terrace to catch the sea breeze in Essaouira, Tangier, Asilah or Rabat, and you'll see a stark skyline of flat rooftops dotted by domes and soaring stone minarets. Blinding white walls, bright blue doors and keyhole archways: no wonder Morocco's coastal cities have transfixed artists and architects for centuries. The boldly elemental forms of coastal medinas may strike you as incredibly modern, but actually it's the other way around – Le Corbusier's International Style and the modernist movement it spawned was inspired by Mediterranean North African architecture.

Dramatic form follows defensive function in many of Morocco's fortified port towns. Strategically located along the Mediterranean and Atlantic sea routes that brought gold, slaves and sugar to Europe, Morocco's coastal towns have been the site of fierce international disputes for millennia – hence their heavy stone walls dotted by cannons, and crenellated ramparts that look like medieval European castles. The Romans, Vandals, Visigoths, Portuguese, Spanish and French all left behind traces of erstwhile occupations along Morocco's coasts, and Spain still claims the coastal towns of Ceuta and Melilla. It's a sore subject in Morocco, and the local architecture does nothing to resolve the conflict – those siding with Spain point out Andalusian elements, which Moroccans will certainly remind you developed under Almohad rule (for more on the subject, see Sticks and Stones, p34). But even if it hasn't always suited the political climate, coastal stone architecture has proved remarkably well adapted to the local climate, holding up much better in the salt air than concrete or wood.

Why'd they build it that way? Eight of the world's leading Islamic architectural scholars give you their best explanations in Architecture of the Islamic World: Its History and Social Meaning, *by Ersnt Grube, Oleg Grabar, et al.*

MOUNTAIN SETTLEMENTS

The villages that cling to the slopes of Morocco's Rif and Atlas Mountains are object lessons in tenacity. Follow zigzagging roads across mountain passes, and you'll see towns that seem timeless: low mud-brick houses and stables, ribbons of smoke rising from chimneys and communal ovens, and a plaza that draws farmers from the hills for market days and perhaps an annual *moussem*. Prehistoric rock carvings and other archaeological evidence of ancient settlements show that Berbers have lived along the Rif and High Atlas in remote villages like this for ages, despite the hardscrabble living afforded by high-altitude herding and terrace farming.

But don't be fooled by modest appearances or remote locations in Morocco. For centuries, mountain villages have drawn pilgrims from miles around to visit local *zawiya*s, and traders' caravans passed through with payloads destined to fetch fortunes in imperial cities. Villages in strategic locations along mountain passes served as strongholds in the Berbers' historic struggles against the encroachment of imperial and colonial powers on their turf (see p38).

Take the treacherous Tizi-n-Telouet pass toward the Drâa Valley, and you'll appreciate the daring of mud-brick mountain strongholds like Tamdaght and the picturesque Aït Benhaddou. The now-crumbling Telouet kasbah of notorious French collaborator Pasha Glaoui was once compared, by the *Times*' Walter Harris in his book *Morocco That Was*, to the Tower of London, but the mud-brick base wasn't intended to support so many stories. Set against the Atlas Mountains, the ruined structure still has Shakespearean overtones: towering ambitions come and go, yet these timeless mountains remain larger than life.

Food & Drink

Moroccan cuisine is the stuff of myth and legend – and sometimes sheer befuddlement, thanks to many seemingly indecipherable menus. Awkwardly phrased English and French menu descriptions often appear to require a special decoder ring, so visitors end up sticking to what they already know of Moroccan cuisine: couscous (see The Real Deal, p73) and tajines. Many other scrumptious Moroccan breakfast, lunch and dinner options are described in this chapter to take some of the mystery out of the menu, and help you explore your full range of dining options in Morocco.

Get adventurous with the menu in Morocco, and your tastebuds will thank you. Have no fear of the salad course, since these vegetable dishes are mostly cooked or peeled and among Morocco's finest culinary offerings. Entrées ominously described as 'spicy' on Moroccan menus are probably not overly hot or piquant – there could just be an extra pinch of delicate saffron or savoury-sweet cinnamon involved. Dessert is a temptation you won't want to resist, including flaky pastries rich with nuts and aromatic traces of orange flower water. In other words: come hungry.

Getting Fresh in Morocco

The foods you find in Morocco are likely to be fresh, locally grown and home-made, rather than shipped in from Brazil, microwaved and served semithawed. Most Moroccan produce is cultivated in small quantities the old-fashioned way, without GMOs, chemical pesticides or even mechanisation. These technologies are far too costly an investment for the average small-scale Moroccan farmer, as is organic certification and labelling – so though you may not see a label on it to this effect, most Moroccan produce you'll find in the markets is pesticide-free and GMO-free.

The splendid appearance, fragrance and flavour of Moroccan market produce will leave you with a permanent grudge against those wan, shrivelled items trying to pass themselves off as food at the supermarket. There's a reason for this: Moroccan produce is usually harvested by hand when ripe, and bought directly from farmers in the souqs. Follow the crowds of Moroccan grandmothers and restaurant sous-chefs to the carts and stalls offering the freshest produce. Here's what to look for on the menu and in the market, at its most ripe and delicious:

Spring Apricots, cherries, strawberries, kiwi, peaches.

Summer Watermelon, wild artichokes, tomatoes.

Autumn Figs, pomegranates, grapes.

Winter Oranges, mandarins, onions, beets, carrots, potatoes and other root vegetables.

Year-round Almonds, walnuts, bananas, squash, pumpkin, fava beans, green beans, lentils, eggplant, peppers, lemons (fresh and preserved).

Just be sure to peel, cook, or thoroughly wash produce before you eat it, since your stomach may not yet be accustomed to local microbes.

Playing Favourites

If there is one food you adore or a dish you detest, you might want to plan your visit to Morocco accordingly. Morocco offers an incredible bounty of produce, meats and fish, but these vary seasonally. The country's relative lack of infrastructure and hard currency can be advantageous to

---

Couldn't you just kill for fish sauce? The ancient Romans did: entire legions were dispatched to the Moroccan coast near Tangier to secure a steady supply of *garum*, a highly prized sauce made from pickled fish eggs.

Moroccan tap water is often potable, just not recommended for short-term visitors whose stomachs take time adjusting – so consider sticking to bottled mineral water for drinking and brushing teeth. The best local brands are Sidi Ali and sparkling Oulmes; others have a slightly chalky aftertaste.

visitors – hence the picturesque mountain villages that seem untouched by time, and the jackpot of dirhams you get for your euros – but this also makes importing produce tricky at best. This means that if you're visiting in the fall, you may have to enjoy fresh figs instead of kiwi fruit (not exactly a hardship).

When you consider your menu options, you'll also want to consider geography. Oualidia oysters may not be so fresh by the time they cross mountain passes to Ouarzazate, and Sefrou cherries can be hard to come by in Tiznit. So if your vacation plans include lavish seafood dinners, head for the coasts; vegetarians visiting desert regions should have a high tolerance for dates. For hints on where to find your favourite foods, see Local Treats below).

But Wait, There's More...

One final and important tip: pace yourself. Moroccan meals can be lengthy and generous, and might seem a bit excessive to an unyielding waistband. Take your time and drink plenty of water throughout your meal, especially with wine and in dry climates, instead of pounding a drink at the end. There are better ways to end a meal than dehydration and bloating – namely, a dessert *bastilla* (multilayered pastry) with toasted almonds, cinnamon and cream. Your Moroccan hosts may urge you on like a cheerleading squad in a pie-eating contest, but obey your instincts and quit when you're full with a heartfelt '*al hamdu lillah*!' ('Thanks to God!')

WHAT'S FOR AL-FTOUR (BREAKFAST)?

Even if your days back home begin with just coffee, it would be a culinary crime to skip breakfast in Morocco. Whether you grab yours on the go in the souqs or sit down to a leisurely repast, you are in for a treat. Breakfasts are rarely served before 9am in guesthouses and hotels, so early risers in immediate need of coffee will probably have to head to a café or hit the souqs.

Street Eats

Sidewalk cafés and kiosks put a local twist on Continental breakfast, with Moroccan pancakes and doughnuts, French pastries, coffee and mint tea. Follow your nose and rumbling stomach into the souqs, where you'll find tangy olives and local *jiben* (fresh goat's or cow's milk cheeses) to be devoured with fresh *khoobz*, Moroccan-style pita bread baked in a wood-fired oven until it's crusty on the outside, yet fluffy and light on the inside. *Khoobz* can be found wrapped in paper at any *hanout* (cupboard-sized corner shops found in every neighbourhood).

In Morocco, many foods are thought to have healing properties: cumin to soothe stomachs unsettled by Pasha's revenge, ginger to prevent motion sickness from long camel rides, galangal for enhanced bedroom antics. Here's to your health, and, um, enjoyment.

LOCAL TREATS

Agadir Oranges, lemons, argan oil.	**Meknès** Mint, olives, olive oil.
Casablanca Cactus fruit.	**Oualidia** Oysters.
Dades Edible rosebuds, rosewater.	**Rif** Walnuts, chestnuts, citrus, goat's
Doukkala Melons.	cheese.
Erfoud Dates.	**Safi** Shellfish.
Essaouira Fish, argan oil.	**Sebou** Shad, shad roe caviar.
Fès Wild artichokes, olive oil, oranges, orange-flower	**Sefrou** Cherries.
water, lemons.	**Souss** Almonds, lamb, dates.
Marrakesh Pomegranates.	**Tagoundaft** Honey.

In the souqs, you can't miss vendors with their carts piled high with fresh fruit, singing their own praises. They're right: you'll never know how high oranges can be stacked or how delicious freshly squeezed *aseer limoon* (orange juice) can be until you pay a visit to a Moroccan juice vendor's cart. Drink yours from a disposable cup or your own water bottle, because the vendor's glasses are rinsed and re-used dozens of times daily.

One savoury southern breakfast not to be missed is *bessara* – a steaming hot fava bean puree with cumin, olive oil, and a dash of paprika – best when mopped up with *khoobz* still warm from the communal oven right down the street. For a twist on the usual French breakfast pastries, try *rghaif* – flaky, dense Moroccan pastries like flattened croissants – usually served with warm honey or apricot jam. Protein fiends will enjoy *rghaif* stuffed with *khlii*, sundried strips of spiced beef like beef jerky. The truly adventurous can start their day with a rich stew of lamb's head or calves' feet, generously ladled into an enamel bowl from a huge vat precariously balanced on a makeshift Buddha gas burner.

Breakfast of Champions

As a guest in a Moroccan home, you'd be treated to the best of everything, and the best guesthouses scrupulously uphold this Moroccan tradition each morning. You'll eat like a Moroccan marathon runner, with some combination of the following to jumpstart your day:

Ahwa (Coffee) is one option, but also *café au lait*, *thé b'na na* (tea with mint) or *thé wa hleb* (tea with milk), *wa* (with) or *bla* (without) *sukur* (sugar).

Aseer limoon Orange juice.

Bayd (Eggs) in omelettes, cooked with a dash of *kamun* (freshly ground cumin) or *zataar* (cumin with sesame seeds).

Beghrir Moroccan pancakes with an airy, spongy texture like crumpets, with honey or jam.

French pastries Croissants, *pain au chocolat* and others.

Khoobz Usually served with butter and jam or olive oil and *zataar*.

Rghaif Flat, buttery Moroccan pastries.

Seasonal fruit (See Get Fresh in Morocco, p68).

Sfenj Moroccan doughnuts.

LET'S DO EL-GHDA (LUNCH)

Lunch is traditionally the biggest meal of the day in Morocco, followed by a nice nap through the heat of the day. The lunch hour here is really a three- to four-hour stretch from noon to 3.30 or 4pm, when most shops and facilities are closed, apart from a few places catering to tourists.

For speed eaters this may seem inconvenient, but especially in summer it's best to do as the locals do, and treat lunchtime as precious downtime. Take the opportunity to tuck into a tajine, served a la carte with crusty bread, or upgrade to a prix fixe, three-course lunch at a fancy

---

WHERE IN THE WORLD?

Can't quite place that taste? Here's where some of the distinctive flavours of modern Moroccan cuisine originate:

Essaouira Portuguese and Jewish origins.

Fès Andalucía (Spain) and Persia.

Marrakesh Senegal, France, Berber North Africa and Italy.

Tetouan Andalucía and Turkey.

ALL HAIL THE DADA

There's a reason why breakfasts at many Moroccan homes and guesthouses are so much better than in big hotels, and you'll find her presiding over the kitchen. *Dada*s, or cooks, used to spend their entire careers in the service of just one Moroccan family – sometimes a royal one. The royal *dada*s of yore were brought from as far away as Mali and Senegal, and rarely left the palace. But with increased competition for their services from guesthouses and a growing middle class, they are now free agents who command respect, real salaries and creative control.

At mealtimes, you might glimpse the *dada* cooking up royal feasts with whatever looked freshest in the market that morning, usually without a recipe or a measuring cup. If those dreamy figs poached in honeyed orange-flower water gave you a whole new reason to get up in the morning, ask to thank the *dada* personally – this is your chance for a brush with culinary greatness.

restaurant. Afterwards, you'll have a whole new appreciation for mint tea and afternoon naps.

Snak Attack

If you're still digesting your lavish guesthouse breakfast come lunchtime, try one of the many *snak*s (kiosks) and small restaurants offering lighter fare – just look for people clustered around sidewalk kiosks, or a sign or awning with the word *snak*. Many hardworking locals do not take afternoon siestas, and instead eat sandwiches on the go. At the risk of stating the obvious, always join the queue at the one thronged with locals: Moroccans are picky about their *snak*s, preferring the cleanest establishments that use the freshest ingredients.

Here's what you'll find on offer at a *snak*:

Brochettes Kebabs, rubbed with salt and spices, roasted on a spit, and served with *khoobz* and *harissa* (capsicum pepper sauce), cumin, and salt. Among the most popular varieties are lamb, chicken, *kefta* (spiced meatballs of ground lamb and/or beef) and the aggressively flavourful 'mixed meat' (usually lamb or beef plus heart and liver).

Merguez Hot, spicy, delicious homemade lamb sausage, not to be confused with *teyhan* (stuffed spleen) – *merguez* is usually reddish in color, while *teyhan* is pale.

Pizza Now found at upscale *snak*s catering to the worldly Moroccan middle class. Look for *snak*s boasting wood-fired ovens, and try tasty local versions with olives, onions, tomatoes and anchovies.

Shwarma Spiced lamb or chicken roasted on a spit and served with *tahina* (sesame sauce) or yogurt, with optional onions, salad, *harissa*, and a dash of *sumac* (a tart, purple spice; highly recommended).

Tajines The famous Moroccan stews cooked in conical earthenware pots that keep the meat unusually moist and tender. The basic tajines served at a roadside *snak* are usually made with just a few ingredients, pulled right off a camping stove or *kanun* (earthenware brazier), and plonked down on a ramshackle folding table. Don't let appearances fool you: these can be some of the best tajines you'll eat in Morocco. So pull up a stool and dig in, using your *khoobz* as your utensil (instead of rinsed-and-reused flatware).

The Moroccan Power Lunch

Some upscale Moroccan restaurants that serve an evening *diffa* (feast) to tourist hordes, serve a scaled-down menu at lunch, when wait staff are more relaxed, the clientele is more local and the meal is sometimes a fraction of the price you'd pay for dinner. You might miss the live music and inevitable bellydancing that would accompany your supper (but then again, you might not). Three courses may seem a bit much for lunch,

Dousing your tajine with *harissa* (capsicum pepper sauce), could stir up old rivalries in Morocco: it's more commonly done in Tunisia, Morocco's main North African rival in the kitchen and on the football field.

but don't be daunted: what this usually means is a delightful array of diminutive vegetable dishes, followed by a fluffy couscous and/or a small meat or chicken tajine, capped with the obligatory mint tea.

MEZZE (SALAD COURSE)

The salad course is a bonanza for vegetarians, with fresh bread and three to five small plates that might include lemony beet salad with chives, herbed potatoes, cumin-spiked chickpeas, a relish of roasted tomatoes and carmelised onions, pumpkin puree with cinnamon and honey, and roasted, spiced eggplant dip so rich it's often called 'aubergine caviar.'

ENTRÉES

The main course is usually a tajine and/or couscous – a quasi-religious experience in Morocco not to be missed (see The Real Deal, opposite). The most common tajine choices are *djuj mqalli bil hamd markd wa zeetoun* – chicken with preserved lemon and olives, zesty in flavour and velvety in texture; *kefta bil matisha wa bayd* – meatballs in a rich tomato sauce with a hint of heat from spices and topped with a sizzling egg; and *lehem bil berquq wa luz* – lamb with prunes and almonds served sliding off the bone into a saffron-onion sauce.

If you're in Morocco for a while, you may tire of the usual tajine options – until you come across one regional variation that makes all your sampling of chicken tajine with lemon and olives worthwhile. That's when you cross over from casual diner to true tajine connoisseur, and fully appreciate the passionate debates among Moroccans about such minutiae as the appropriate thickness of the lemon rind and brininess of the olives. Every region, city, restaurant and household has pronounced opinions you can actually taste in your tajine. No self-respecting Moroccan restaurant should ever serve you a tajine that's stringy, tasteless or overcooked. Vegetarians can sometimes, but not always, request a vegetable tajine instead; ingredients are bought fresh daily in small quantities, and the chef may not have factored vegetarians into the restaurant's purchases.

MECHOUI

The most powerful power lunch of all features *mechoui*, an entire lamb or calf stuffed with couscous and some combination of almonds (or other nuts) and prunes (or other dried fruit), which is basted with butter, garlic, cumin, paprika, and slow-roasted until it's ready to melt into the fire or your mouth, whichever comes first. Sometimes *mechoui* is accompanied by kebabs or *kwa*, grilled liver kebabs with cumin, salt and paprika. Do not attempt to operate heavy machinery or begin a whirlwind museum

---

BRIGHT, PLEASING FLAVOURS

What's in that dish that makes it so tasty? Probably one of four main kinds of stock, which you can distinguish by colour:

- light yellow *mqalli* is a base of saffron, oil and ginger
- golden *msharmal* has saffron, ginger and a dash of pepper
- orange or reddish *mhammar* includes paprika, cumin and butter
- *beige qadra* is made of seasoned clarified butter with vegetable stock, chickpeas and almonds.

THE REAL DEAL

Berbers call it *seksu*, *New York Times* food critic Craig Claiborne called it one of the dozen best dishes in the world, and when you're in Morocco, you can call couscous lunch. You know that yellowish stuff that comes in a box, with directions on the side instructing you to add boiling water and let stand for three minutes? That doesn't count. What Moroccans call couscous is a fine, pale, grain-sized hand-rolled pasta lightly steamed until toothsome and fluffy, served with a selection of vegetables and/or meat or fish in a delicately flavoured reduction of stock and spices.

Couscous isn't a simple side dish but rather the main event of a Moroccan meal, whether tricked out Casablanca-style with seven vegetables, heaped with lamb and vegetables in Fès, or served with tomatoes, fish and fresh herbs in Essaouira. Many delicious couscous dishes come without meat, including the pumpkin couscous of Marrakesh and a simple yet savoury High Atlas version with stewed onions, but scrupulous vegetarians will want to inquire in advance whether that hearty stock is indeed vegetarian. On occasion a couscous dish can be ordered à la carte, but usually it's a centrepiece of a multicourse lunch or celebratory *diffa* – and when you get a mouthful of the stuff done properly, you'll see why.

---

tour post-*mechoui*; no amount of post-prandial mint tea will make such exertions feasible without a nap.

DESSERT

At lunchtime, dessert is usually sweet mint tea served with almond cookies. You may not think you have room, but one bite of a dreamy *kaab al-ghazal* (crescent-shaped 'gazelle's horns' cookie stuffed with almond paste and laced with orange-flower water) will surely convince you otherwise.

SNACKTIME (5-ISH)

Miss the *mechoui* at lunch? Follow your nose and growling stomach to a street vendor for these treats:

- roasted corn fresh off the brazier
- roasted chick peas with salt and cumin
- sweet or salty roasted almonds
- roasted sunflower seeds and pumpkin seeds
- hard-boiled eggs with cumin
- sandwiches of brochettes or *merguez* sausage with cumin, salt and *harissa*
- *escargot* (snails) in hot, savoury broth, ladled into a tin bowl or cup.

Other popular late afternoon treats are coffee, mint tea, or ice cream at a café, or Moroccan or French sweets from your local patisserie.

A LATE L'ASHA (DINNER)

Dinner in Morocco doesn't usually start until around 9pm, after work and possibly a sunset stroll. Most Moroccans eat dinner at home (see Economic Status, p46), but you may notice young professionals, students and bachelors making a beeline for the local *snak* or pizzeria. In the winter, you'll see vendors crack open steaming vats of *harira*, a hearty soup with a base of tomatoes, onions, saffron and cilantro and often lamb meatballs, lentils or chickpeas. Dinner at home is probably *harira* and lunch leftovers, with the notable exception of Ramadan and other celebrations (see boxed text p74).

Majun are pastry balls rolled in sesame seeds and made of nuts, raisins and sometimes an extra-special ingredient: *kif*, or marijuana. Good to know before a cop orders you to put your hands up, and drop the dessert.

Special occasions in Morocco call for vintage *smen*, spiced clarified butter that is at least a year old. You won't find it spread on bread – it's saved up to make a rich, tasty *qadra* (sauce) for meat or vegetables.

Tax and tip are usually included in your bill at a Moroccan restaurant, but you can tack on 5% to 10% if the service is good.

Do the Diffa

With enough hard currency and room in your stomach, you might prefer Moroccan restaurant dining to *snak* fare for dinner. Most upscale Moroccan restaurants cater to tourists, serving an elaborate prix fixe Moroccan *diffa* (feast) in a palatial setting. This is not a dine-and-dash meal, but an evening's entertainment that often includes bellydancing, live music and wine or beer. It's a novel experience worth trying at least once; your best bets are listed in this book.

Fair warning about palace restaurants: your meal may come with a side order of kitsch. Many palace restaurants appear to have been decorated by a genie, complete with brass lamps, mirrors, tent fabric and cushions as far as the eye can see. Often it's the ambience you're paying for rather than the food, which can vary from exquisitely prepared regional specialties to mass-produced glop only a German tour group could love. Here's a rule of thumb: if the place is so cavernous that your voice echoes and there's a stage set up for a laser show, don't expect personalised service or authentic Moroccan fare.

Whether you're in for a *diffa* at a Moroccan home (lucky you), or a restaurant, your lavish dinner will include some combination of the following:

Mezze Up to five different small salads (though the most extravagant palace restaurants in Marrakesh and Fès boast seven to nine).

Briouat Buttery triangular or cigar-shaped pastry, stuffed with herbs and goat's cheese, savoury meats, or egg, then baked or fried.

Bastilla The justly famed savoury-sweet pie made of *warqa* (sheets of pastry even thinner than filo), painstakingly layered with pigeon or chicken cooked with caramelised onions, lemon, eggs and toasted sugared almonds, then dusted with cinnamon and sugar.

Couscous Made according to local custom (see The Real Deal, p73).

Tajine Often your choice of one of a couple of varieties.

Mechoui And/or some regional specialty (see Been There, Eaten That, opposite).

Dessert This may be a dessert *bastilla* (with fresh cream and toasted nuts), *briouat bil luz* (*briouat* filled with almond paste), *sfaa* (sweet cinnamon couscous with dried fruit and nuts, served with cream) or *kaab al-ghazal*.

EATING DURING RAMADAN

During Ramadan, most Moroccans observe the fast during the day, eating only before sunup and after sundown. Dinner is eaten later than usual – around 11 – and many wake up early for a filling breakfast before dawn. Another popular strategy is to stay up most of the night, sleep as late as possible, and stretch the afternoon nap into early evening. Adapt to the local schedule, and you may thoroughly enjoy the leisurely pace, late-night festivities and manic feasts of Ramadan.

Although you will not be expected to observe the fast, eating in public view is generally frowned upon. Hence many restaurants are closed during the day and around *Iftour*, the evening meal when the fast is broken. But with a little planning, there are plenty of workarounds: load up on snacks in the market to eat indoors, make arrangements for breakfast or lunch in the privacy of your guesthouse, and ask locals about a good place to enjoy *Iftour*.

Lftour comes with all the traditional Ramadan fixings: *harira* (a hearty soup with a base of tomatoes, onions, saffron and corriander leaves often accompanied by lamb meatballs, lentils or chickpeas), dates, milk, *shebbakia* (a sweet, coiled pastry that's guaranteed to shift your glucose levels into high gear), and *harsha* (buttery bread made of semolina and fried for maximum density). You may find that *harira* is offered free; even Moroccan McDonald's offers it as part of their special Ramadan Happy Meal. For more information on Ramadan and other religious holidays, see p455.

BEEN THERE, EATEN THAT

Eat your way across Morocco north to south with these outstanding regional dishes:

Casablanca *Seksu baydawi* (couscous with seven vegetables).

Chefchaouen *Djaj bil berquq* (chicken with prunes).

Essaouira *Hut Mqalli* (fish tajine with saffron, ginger and preserved lemons), *djej kadra toumiya* (chicken with almonds, onions and chickpeas in buttery saffron sauce).

Fès *Kennaria* (stew with wild thistle/artichoke, with or without meat), *hut bu'etob* (baked shad filled with almond-stuffed dates).

High Atlas *Mechoui* (slow-roasted stuffed lamb or beef).

Marrakesh *Bessara* (fava beans with cumin, paprika, olive oil, salt), *tangia* (crockpot stew of seasoned lamb, vegetables and onions cooked eight to twelve hours in a *hammam*, or sauna).

Meknès *Kamama* (lamb stewed with ginger, *smen*, saffron, cinnamon and sweet onions).

Southern Coast *Amelou* (almond paste with honey and argan nut oil).

Tangier Local variations on tapas and *paella* (Spanish dish made from rice, shellfish, chicken and vegetables).

DRINK UP

To wash your *diffa* down and stay hydrated, you'll need a good amount of liquid. Serving alcohol within many Moroccan medinas or within view of a mosque may be frowned upon, and liquor licences can cost an astronomical Dh20,000 – but many Moroccan guesthouses and restaurants get around these hurdles by offering booze in a low voice, and serving it out of sight indoors or on a terrace. So if you're in the mood for a beer and don't find it on the menu, you might want to ask the waiter in a low voice, speakeasy-style.

Day and night, don't forget to drink plenty of bottled water. Vying to quench your thirst are orange juice vendors loudly singing their own praises, and water vendors in fringed tajine-shaped hats clanging brass bowls together. If you want to take up these appealing offers, ask the vendors to pour right into your water bottle or a disposable cup – the glass cups and brass bowls are often reused, and seldom thoroughly washed.

When you're offered Moroccan mint tea, don't expect to bolt it and be on your way. Mint tea is the hallmark of Moroccan hospitality, and a sit-down affair that takes around half an hour. If you have the honour of pouring the tea, pour the first cup back in the teapot to help cool it and dissolve the sugar. Then starting from your right, pour each cup of tea from as high above the glass as you can without splashing. Your hosts will be most impressed.

Moroccan mint tea may be ubiquitous, but you can find a mean cup of coffee in Morocco too. Most of it is French-pressed, and delivers a caffeine wallop to propel you through the souqs and to the stratosphere.

MOROCCO TO GO

Want to fix Moroccan feasts at home? Consider a cooking course (the best ones are in Marrakesh; see p306 for details) and give your home kitchen a Moroccan makeover with these kitchen supplies:

Harira pot A deep ceramic pot with a lid to keep soup hot.

Mortar and pestle Used to crush herbs, garlic and spices.

Tajine slaoui The earthenware cooking tajine in basic terracotta (fancy painted ones are for presentation only).

Tbiqa A basket with a pointed lid for storing bread and pastries.

At a Moroccan home, it's considered polite to take your shoes off upon entry, always use your right hand in greeting and eating, and try at least a bite or two of everything.

When you're after something stronger than orange juice, Casa is a fine local pilsner beer, and Flag is a faintly herbal second-best. Admirable Moroccan white wines include Coquillages and Sémillant Blanc, and reliable reds include President, Beauvallon, Medallion Cabernet and Siroura S Syrah.

EAT YOUR WORDS

Begin your taste adventure by picking up some Moroccan food lingo – for pronunciation guide, see the language chapter (pp496-503).

Useful Phrases

Table for ..., please.	tabla dyal ... 'afak
Can I pay by credit card?	wash nkder nkhelles bel kaart kredee?
Can I see a menu please?	nazar na'raf lmaakla lli 'andkum?
I'm a vegetarian.	makanakoolsh llehem
What do you recommend?	shnoo tansaani nakul?
I'll try what she/he is having.	gha nzharrab shnoo kaatakul hiyya/huwwa
Without ..., please.	bla ..., 'afak
I'd like something to drink.	bgheet shi haazha nashrubha
I didn't order this.	tlabtsh had shshi

Please bring me...	llaa ykhalleek zheeb li ...
some water	shwiyya dyaal lmaa
some salt	shwiyya dyaal lmelha
some pepper	shwiyya dyaal lebzaar
some bread	shwiyya dyaal lkhoobz
a napkin	mandeel
a beer	birra
a glass/bottle of red/	kaas/qar'a dyal hmar/byad/roozi shshrab
white/rose wine	

This is...	Had shshi ...
brilliant	ldeed bezzef!
burnt	mahruqa
cold	barda
undercooked	ma taybash mazyan

Cheers! (To your health!)	bsaha!
The bill, please.	lahsaab, 'afak
Thank you.	shukran

Food glossary

MEAT

baqree	beef
farooj/dujaj	chicken
lehem	meat
kebda	liver
kelawwi	kidneys
lehem ghenmee	lamb
lehem jemil	camel

SEAFOOD

hut	fish
laangos	lobster
lamoori	cod
merla	whiting
qaimroon	shrimp
serdeen	sardines
shton	anchovies
sol	sole
ton	tuna

VEGETABLES & PULSES

'aads	lentils
batatas	potatoes
besla	onion
fasooliya	white beans
fegg'a	mushroom
khess	lettuce
khiyaar	cucumber
lbdanzhaal	aubergine
loobeeya	green beans
mataisha tamatim	tomato
qooq	artichoke
tooma	garlic
khoodar	vegetables
zeetoun	olives
zelbana bisila	peas

FRUIT

'eineb	grapes
banan/moz	banana
dellah	watermelon
fakiya	fruit
kermoos	figs
limoon	orange
meshmash	apricot
reman	pomegranate
teffah	apple
tmer	dates

OTHER FOODS

bayd	eggs
chorba	soup
filfil/lebzaar	pepper
fromaj/jiben	cheese
khoobz	bread
melha	salt
ships	chips
sukur	sugar
zabadee/laban/danoon	yoghurt
zebda	butter
zit	oil

Environment

THE LAND

Mention Morocco and you may soon be dreaming of layered sand dunes stretching to the horizon, but the Sahara is merely one of many seductive Moroccan landscapes. At some moment during your Moroccan sojourn you will almost certainly find yourself pressed to the window of a grand taxi, marvelling at the dramatic changes of the breathtaking vistas as they unfold. In short, Morocco's awesome fusion of rock, sand and sea is the most varied topography in North Africa, not to mention one of the most inspiring as well.

The diversity of climate, elevation, wildlife and population may be unexpected, but most startling of all is the synergy of the land and the Moroccan people, which come together to make a warm and starry Atlas night swell with the rhythm of folklore and tradition. This is a country where the significance of the land is a silent but universal understanding. Almost 55% of Moroccans live in rural areas and Morocco's landscapes can in no way be separated from the people who inhabit them.

Morocco's coastline runs for 1835km, which is almost as long as its land borders (2017.9km).

Coast & Waterways

Morocco's identity is powerfully shaped by its geography, and in particular its coastline that stretches from the relatively peaceful shoreline and sheltered coves of the Mediterranean to the remote, empty beaches buffeted by the trade winds of the Atlantic. Along its southwesterly march Morocco's Atlantic coast is punctuated by the raw and rocky beaches of Asilah, the beatnik coves of Essaouira and the commercialised boardwalks of Agadir. The experience of fronting onto so much open water has encouraged Moroccans down through the centuries to set out beyond their own shores, as well as fostering an openness to the people and trade that the sea has brought.

Outside Agadir on Morocco's Atlantic coast, goats perch in argan trees to snack on fruit, while farmers collect the seeds from their dung to press into oil.

Coastal weather is mild, with a tendency in the north to become cool and wet. Average daily temperatures range from 12°C in winter to 25°C in summer but the humidity is constant and makes drying laundry nearly impossible. The southern Atlantic and eastern Mediterranean coasts are noticeably more barren.

Morocco's rivers, which include the great Sebou, south of Fès, and the Oum er-Rbia, northeast of Khenitra, draw hikers in their droves, while these waterways also serves as critical sources of water for locals.

Mountains

The mountains of inland Morocco have always provided shelter for the self-contained Berbers and others who would escape (or rebel against) the invaders of Morocco.

Morocco unofficially exports up to 18,000kg of hashish to Europe each year and is by far Europe's major supplier of the drug.

In northern Morocco, the Rif Atlas Mountains form an arc of impenetrable limestone and sandstone, which rises steeply from the Mediterranean littoral to heights of about 2200m and protects coastal Morocco from the arid West African interior. The deep-green hues and lush pasture of the Rif surprise those who enter from Spain expecting endless, bone-coloured horizons. For the local population, mainly Tamazight Berbers, the fertile soil amounts to a happily expansive cultivation of kif (marijuana). Also concealed within these hills, especially notable around Taza, are largely unexplored caves and caverns (p279) whose shadowy, damp hollows beckon the fearless. The climate in the Rif can be unpredictable; summers are comfortably sunny but come October the temperature begins to fall as steeply as the land itself. When the merciless winter gives way around April and May, an intensive and humid rainy season begins.

The Middle Atlas is the Moroccan heartland, with a patchwork of farmland riven with quiet country roads. Running northeast to southwest from the Rif, the range soars to 3340m at its highest point. Agriculture drives the daily routine of the inhabitants of this interior territory, but travellers frequently fall in love with treasures like the magnificent Cascades d'Ouzoud (p322) and surrounding forests.

The low hills east of Agadir rise to form the gloriously precipitous High Atlas which tower over the villages of Marrakesh and reach the dizzy heights of Jebel Toubkal (p419), North Africa's highest summit (4167km). These High Atlas peaks, some sculpted red, others cloaked in moss and pine, nurture wheat, walnuts and almonds but do little to shield the blistering sun. The temperature is stifling in summer, easily exceeding 40°C. Where the High Atlas drops away to the southeast, deep and winding gorges give way to the Sahara.

Lastly, further south, the low and calloused Anti Atlas drops into the Sahara and protects the Souss Valley from the hot desert winds.

Desert

South of the Anti Atlas, the barren slopes, slashed with more gorges, trail off into the stony, almost trackless desert of the Western Sahara. This sparsely populated and unforgiving region is bounded to the east and south by Algeria and Mauritania.

Cresting the Middle Atlas in the Zagora region draws you down through the clustered palms of the chiselled Drâa Valley (p338) and into the desolate dunes known as Tinfou and Erg Chigaga. Southeast in Errachidia province are the saffron dunes of Merzouga, hunched and bowing as if in prayer. From their summit, you'll experience the dizzying sensation of staring down into the vertiginous eternity of the Sahara.

Even in winter the lowlands sizzle by day, with temperatures around 30°C, but the dry atmosphere lowers temperatures quickly in the evening and the nights can be frightfully cold, demanding layered clothing and good humour. The wild environment of the Moroccan deserts has also left its mark upon the people – the pace of life here is slower and the conversations are less garrulous, with every aspect of life dictated by the daytime heat and by the need to draw near around the campfire at night.

WILDLIFE

> God begot living things from water,
> Some of them creep, others crawl,
> and there are some who crouch.
> God creates what He wants.
> God is almighty in all things.
>
> *Quran, sura XXIV, verse 45*

Morocco's three ecological zones – coast, mountain and desert – host more than 40 different ecosystems that provide habitat for many endemic species. Unfortunately, the pressure upon these ecosystems from ever-more-sprawling urban areas and the encroachment of industrialisation

Sahara Overland (www .sahara-overland.com) is the most comprehensive site for do-it-yourself desert exploration; the travellers' forum is a mine of useful information.

Sahara: An Immense Ocean of Sand, by Paolo Novaresio and Gianni Guadalupi, has stunning Saharan images and informative text that'll have you dreaming of the desert.

Sahara: A Natural History, by Marq de Villiers and Sheila Hirtle, is a highly readable account of the Sahara's wildlife, its people and geographical history.

upon Morocco's wilderness has ensured that much of the country's iconic plant and animal life is endangered.

Animals

The Moroccan countryside teems with life, although you'll usually need to get away from well-travelled routes to catch a glimpse of the wildlife. For more information on bird-watching in Morocco, see p441.

COAST

The marine life along Morocco's Mediterranean coast has largely succumbed to or been driven elsewhere by growing human settlements and increasing sea-borne traffic. The less-populated Atlantic coast is still sufficiently free from an intensive human presence to enable porpoises and dolphins to prosper, along with abundant bird life. Important bird species include white-eyed gulls, Moroccan cormorants and sandwich terns found along the beaches.

DESERT

Despite its forbiddingly barren climate and terrain, the Sahara is home to a surprising variety of animal species, most notably the golden jackal, Berber skinks and sand vipers that prey on jerboas and sand rats. Concealed in the rocky terrain are spiny-tailed lizards, horned vipers and striped hyenas. Although few remain in Morocco, the fennec fox is one of the Sahara's emblematic species, with fur-soled feet to protect it from the scorching sands and enormous ears that give it a gremlin-like aspect. Like many desert species, it is largely nocturnal, active only in the cool of dusk and dawn.

MOUNTAINS

The sociable Barbary macaque (also known as the Barbary ape) is easily spotted making mischief in and around the forests of Azrou. Other mammals, rarely sighted, include mountain gazelles, red foxes and lynxes. Although outshone by the beautiful golden eagle, birds of this area include red crossbills, horned larks, acrobatic booted eagles, Egyptian vultures, and both black and red kites. Butterflies, too, are abundant, although you will probably only come across them in the

Sahara Conservation Fund (www.naturalsciences .be/cb/scf/index.htm), which is dedicated to preserving the wild creatures of the Sahara, has loads of useful links and information.

COLD-BLOODED CAPITALISM

Sadly, the easiest way to encounter Morocco's wildlife, particularly its reptiles, is in the anything-but-natural surrounds of a souq. Snake charmers, stalls selling various reptiles (or parts of reptiles) for use in folk medicine, and tortoise shells turned into decorative fire bellows or banjo-like musical instruments for souvenir-hungry tourists are common sights and, sadder still, common purchases made by tourists.

Take a close look at the snakes and you'll discover that their mouths are stitched closed, leaving tiny gaps for their tongues to flicker though. The snakes frequently develop fatal mouth infections and are unable to feed, requiring replacement by freshly caught specimens. As a result of the unceasing demand for tourist-charming snakes, numbers of Egyptian cobra have plummeted.

An estimated 10,000 tortoises are also killed annually for the tourist trade, which, when combined with large-scale habitat loss, helps explain why one of Morocco's tortoises (Testudo graeca graeca) is on the UN's Convention on the International Trade of Endangered Species list. Current legislation doesn't prohibit their sale (or the sale of their shells) within Morocco, but try to take an endangered tortoise out of the country and you'll be breaking the law.

LION KING

The last of the Barbary lions, a species indigenous to Morocco and formerly used in amphitheatres across the Roman Empire for disposing of Christians, died in captivity in the 1960s. The last wild specimen had been shot almost 40 years earlier.

Legend has it that the king of Morocco himself had been happily feeding wrongdoers to his personal collection of felines as late as 1914. The last dissident to meet this fate was apparently offered a short reprieve by the king, but instead retorted that, 'It's better to be eaten by lions than bitten by a dog', and was dispatched *tout de suite*.

The Parc Zoologique National in Rabat and Port Lympne in the UK, along with various other organisations, have established a small captive-breeding programme with the descendants of the king's man-eaters, now about 80% Barbary lion. This slow but genuine progress has naturalists dreaming of a release programme, although anecdotal evidence suggests that the move is unlikely to be popular among ordinary Moroccans.

---

spring. Species common to the area include the scarlet cardinal and bright-yellow Cleopatra.

ENDANGERED SPECIES

Like most countries in North Africa, Morocco has not distinguished itself with its protection of endangered species, with 18 endangered mammal species (a staggering 15% of the total) and 11 threatened bird species.

Along the coast, on a fertile strip of land between Agadir and Tiznit in the lagoon of Oued Massa, the last colony of the strikingly ugly bald ibis, once revered by the ancient Egyptians, retains a precarious foothold and remains under threat from Club Med-style resort development.

In mountainous regions, the Barbary leopard has been reduced to a small population (the last in North Africa), taking refuge in remote mountain redoubts.

In desert regions, the extremely shy addax antelope is in decline, even as it defies the desert's dictates, surviving its whole life without water when necessary, while the days of the Houbara bustard, which has been mercilessly hunted, are numbered.

Other endangered species include the occidental gerbil, tortoise, Barbary hyena, Barbary deer, Spanish imperial eagle, Mediterranean monk seal, Curvier's gazelle and damas gazelle.

The Saharan oryx (a white, horned antelope that gave birth to the unicorn legend) and Bubal hartebeest have sadly gone the way of the dodo, while the iconic Barbary lion with its abundant mane was last seen (and shot) in the Atlas Mountains in 1922.

For all Morocco's failures in wildlife conservation, there have been some notable successes. The dorcas gazelle and Barbary sheep have both taken a small step towards survival after active government programmes of protection.

www.barbarylion.com tells you everything you ever wanted to know about the Barbary lion, although we hope its effusive optimism is not misplaced.

Some 182 Moroccan plant species are considered endangered as a result of erosion and deforestation.

Plants

Morocco is particularly colourful in April and May when the country is briefly in bloom before the summer swelter. Highlights include irises, thyme, orchids, geraniums, cedar forests, oaks, thuja, pines, and, at higher altitudes, even juniper. But the more appetising of Morocco's plant life are its fruits and legumes, particularly abundant in the south due to the semi-tropical climate. While pomegranate and fig trees are found throughout the country, you'll find orange groves in Agadir, walnut trees in Marrakesh, almond trees in Ouarzazate and date palms in Zagora.

NATIONAL PARKS

Morocco's national parks are credited with saving the Barbary macaque, African marsh owl, Spanish festoon butterfly, fir tree and cork oak from extinction.

Morocco's record on environmental protection may be far from perfect, but the government has begun to set aside protected areas to arrest the alarming loss of habitat and the resulting disappearance of plant and animal species. Toubkal National Park in the Atlas Mountains was the first national park to be created in 1942, while Morocco's most impressive park, Souss-Massa National Park and Biological Reserve, was carved out in 1991 outside Agadir.

Evidence that Morocco is taking its environmental responsibilities seriously came in 2004 with the creation of four new national parks: Talassemtane (58,950 hectares) in the Rif; Al-Hoceima (48,460 hectares) in the Mediterranean, which protects outstanding coastal and marine habitats along the Mediterranean and one of the last outposts of osprey; Ifrane National Park (51,800 hectares) in the Middle Atlas, with cedar forests and Barbary macaques; and the Eastern High Atlas National Park (55,252 hectares). During this flurry of national park creation, the Tazekka National Park was also enlarged.

In all, Morocco has 12 fully fledged national parks, as well as 35 nature reserves, forest sanctuaries and other protected areas which are overseen by Morocco's Direction des Eaux et Forêts. The parks have also provided a sphere for research (including botanical inventories, bird censuses, primate studies and sediment analyses) into the region's biodiversity and the

NOTABLE NATIONAL PARKS

National park	Location	Features	Activities	Best time to visit
Toubkal National Park (p413)	near Marrakesh	highest peak in North Africa	hiking, climbing	May-Jun
Souss-Massa National Park (p375)	south of Agadir	coastal estuaries and forests: 275 species of birds, including endangered bald ibis, mammals & enclosed endangered species	hiking, bird-watching, wildlife-watching	Mar-Oct
Lac de Sidi Bourhaba (p121)	Mehdiya	lake & wetlands: 200 bird migratory species including marbled duck, marsh owl & flamingo	recreational swimming, hiking, bird-watching	Oct-Mar
Merdja Zerga National Park (p122)	Moulay Bousselham	lagoon habitats: 190 species of waterfowl, including African marsh owl, Andouin's gull, flamingo & crested coot	wildlife-watching	Dec-Jan
Talassemtane National Park (p432)	Chefchaouen	cedar & fir forests: Barbary macaque, fox, jackal & bat in the cedar forest	hiking, wildlife-watching	Jun-Sep
Bouarfa Wildlife Sanctuary (p284)	Bouarfa	red rock steppe	hiking, climbing	Apr-Oct
Tazzeka National Park (p279)	near Taza	oak forests & waterfalls	hiking	Jun-Sep

causes of habitat loss that could have implications for unprotected areas beyond the parks' boundaries. Lately, the international community has also shown interest; the Spanish and American Park Services have used Morocco's protected areas as a base for their own research into broader biodiversity issues.

But before you get too excited, remember this: less than 0.05% of Moroccan territory is protected.

Of the parks that do exist, the age-old tension between increasing tourist revenues from national parks and frustration over the parcelling of land and inattention to concerns like water shortages and health care means that support among local communities for the new protected areas is patchy at best. Though the parks' missions are perceived as valuable, there is a hushed undercurrent of disapproval over the government's priorities. The Ministries of Tourism and Agriculture temper this sentiment by reasoning that tourist activity means profits to fund future environmental programs – the very initiatives which will return plant and animal life to their original, more productive state, restore arable land and ultimately benefit the surrounding communities.

For all their problems, Morocco's national parks are becoming a major tourist draw card, particularly for the opportunities they present for recreational activities in pristine wilderness areas. Toubkal National Park, for example, encompasses North Africa's highest mountain range and has rich camping, hiking and climbing possibilities. As the parks' popularity grows, and with it Morocco's reputation as a venue for environmental tourism, the government has plans to make the parks self-supporting, mostly by charging admission.

The Al-Hoceima and Talassemtane parks in particular are examples of how far Moroccan nature conservation has come, integrating plans for promoting rural tourism and developing hiking routes. At the same time, the parks' authorities are working with local communities to allay their concerns and enable them to view the parks as a profitable alternative to kif cultivation.

ENVIRONMENTAL ISSUES

The interdependence of the people and the land is presenting environmental dilemmas that Moroccans live daily. Agriculture is as essential to the national economy (contributing between 21% and 30% of revenues) as it is to the lives of ordinary Moroccans, but the relationship is becoming increasingly frayed. With each year that passes, rural Moroccans find themselves more at the mercy of extreme and rising temperatures and unpredictable conditions that have the capacity to destroy a season's labour. Global warming has also stolen valuable snowfall from mountain regions whose rivers depend upon the melt; in the south, most rivers have been dry for at least 10 years and the subsequent burning of date palms and almond groves is nearly irreparable. Irresistible population pressures also result in more intensive farming practices and deforestation, while overgrazing is picking the land clean, thereby accumulating the pressures heaped upon the land by global environmental change. Desertification is the result, rendering crops defenceless against whipping sandstorms or torrential flooding. In the end, the ravaged villages confront a crisis in their food and water supplies: poor health and sanitation fester, land becomes unsuitable for farming and pristine environments are lost forever.

The sweeping savannah of old is a distant memory, thanks to serious miseducation and malpractice. The absence of hunting regulations, for example, caused the loss of predatory species like the Barbary lion and

Africa & the Middle East: A Continental Overview of Environmental Issues, by Kevin Hillstrom, contains an excellent exploration of North Africa's environmental past and future, focusing on how human populations impact upon the environment.

The North African Environment at Risk, by Will D Swearingen and Abdellatif Bencherifa (eds) can be hard to find but it's worth hunting down as it deals comprehensively with the regional causes of environmental degradation.

The Morocco page of the Ramsar Convention on Wetlands (www.ramsar.org/profile/pro files_morocco.htm) has a list of Morocco's most important and threatened wetlands

ENVIRONMENTALLY PISTE-OFF

The dire state of the Moroccan environment is something in which we are all implicated. An example of this is in the invasion of the desert by tourist 4WD vehicles in a process known as the 'Toyotarisation' of the Sahara. With their large wheels, 4WDs break up the surface of the desert, which is then scattered into the air by strong winds. By one estimate, the annual generation of dust has increased by 1000% in North Africa in last fifty years. And in case you thought that your 4WD tracks across the sands would soon be erased by the winds, remember that tracks from WWII vehicles are still visible in the Libyan desert five decades after the cessation of hostilities. Airborne dust is a primary cause of drought far more than it is a consequence of it, as it shields the earth's surface from sunlight and hinders cloud formation.

The consequences of our impatience in the desert extend far beyond Morocco and its desert communities. The stirred-up sand threatens to envelop the world in dust, with serious consequences for human health, coral reefs and climate change. Plankton on the surface of the world's oceans is also being smothered by sand, with devastating implications for marine life. Dust storms are increasingly common in cities like Madrid and the dust-laden winds threaten to transform 90% of Spain's Mediterranean regions into deserts. Once these deserts gain a European foothold, the process of desertification will be extremely difficult and costly to reverse. Sand from the Sahara has even reached as far away as Greenland, settling on icebergs and causing them to melt faster.

Exploring the desert by camel is infinitely more friendly to the environment, quite apart from the fact that it forces you to slow down to a desert pace, free from the intrusions of the modern world. It's also the best way to ensure that you leave behind nothing but easily erasable footprints in the sand.

resulted in a surplus of herbivores. Ambiguous grazing parameters also contributed to a severe loss of ground cover. The Moroccan forestry department reacted by employing methods intended for temperate forest climates, with disastrous results; in the Forest of Mamora near Rabat, broom was thinned from under the cork oaks, leading to serious soil erosion – the trees later died from dehydration. Fragile desert ecosystems are similarly imperilled. As the Sahara eats away at ever-growing tracts of southern Morocco, oases are left without natural defences and are in danger of drowning beneath the desert.

Plantation programmes are under way, some with international backing. Every year, two million fruit trees are distributed as the south fights to restore its palm groves. The Plan National de Replanter promised to meet the demand for timber by the year 2000, but it is criticised for planting rapidly growing trees – often foreign varieties – without considering suitability.

Pollution is another problem that threatens to choke Morocco's environment. Industrial waste is routinely released into the sea, soil and waterways, thereby contaminating water supplies used for drinking and irrigation. Morocco's cities alone produce an annual harvest of 2.4 million tonnes of solid waste, while the draining of coastal wetlands – which provide important habitats for endangered species – continues apace to address the rising demand and falling supply of water for irrigation.

The situation remains grave. One-third of Morocco's ecosystems are disappearing, 10% of vertebrates are endangered and each year 25,000 hectares of forest are lost. The Atlantic pistachio and wild olive have already perished. The Moroccan pine, thuja and Atlas cedar are seriously at risk. Argan, red juniper, holm oak, canary oak and tauzin oak are very degraded. Though dams have been constructed to divert water to these areas, this has lowered the water table, meaning that many ecosystems are no longer able to sustain animal life.

Visit www.wwf.us /about_wwf/where _we_work/africa/where /morocco/index.cfm, the Morocco page of the global environmental group World Wildlife Fund (WWF), which details conservation work underway in the country.

Atlantic Coast

شاطىء الأطلنطي

Miles of glorious sands peppered with small fishing villages, historic ports and fortified towns weave along Morocco's blustery Atlantic Coast, a region among the most prosperous and easy-going in the country. Throughout the ages, control of the coastal ports was imperative for both invading forces and local tribes hoping to expand their merchant empires. The Phoenicians, Romans, Portuguese and French all held sway here over the years and their legacy remains in the beautiful walled towns, wide city boulevards and relaxed attitude of this part of Morocco.

The Atlantic Coast is a region of contrasts and sweeps from pristine beachfront to urban sprawl around Rabat and Casablanca, the country's political and economic capitals respectively. A large chunk of Morocco's population lives in this area and the modern colonial-built cities are far more cosmopolitan than those of the interior, their Art Deco and neo-Moorish architecture, stylish cafés and liberal attitudes a far cry from traditional Morocco.

To the north and south, you'll find the fortified towns founded or occupied by European powers, low-key beach resorts and several nature reserves home to myriad birdlife. For travellers, the relaxed Portuguese towns of Asilah and Essaouira are highlights of the region, their growing international festivals drawing increasing numbers of visitors each year. Between them sweep miles of glorious, and often deserted, Atlantic beaches, and several world-class surf breaks.

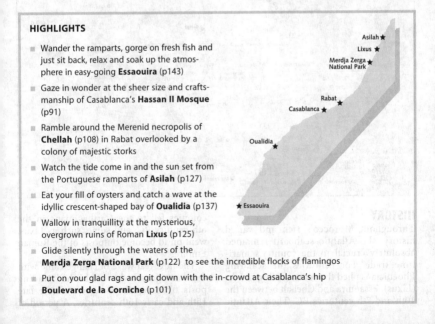

HIGHLIGHTS

- Wander the ramparts, gorge on fresh fish and just sit back, relax and soak up the atmosphere in easy-going **Essaouira** (p143)

- Gaze in wonder at the sheer size and craftsmanship of Casablanca's **Hassan II Mosque** (p91)

- Ramble around the Merenid necropolis of **Chellah** (p108) in Rabat overlooked by a colony of majestic storks

- Watch the tide come in and the sun set from the Portuguese ramparts of **Asilah** (p127)

- Eat your fill of oysters and catch a wave at the idyllic crescent-shaped bay of **Oualidia** (p137)

- Wallow in tranquillity at the mysterious, overgrown ruins of Roman **Lixus** (p125)

- Glide silently through the waters of the **Merdja Zerga National Park** (p122) to see the incredible flocks of flamingos

- Put on your glad rags and git down with the in-crowd at Casablanca's hip **Boulevard de la Corniche** (p101)

Asilah ★
Lixus ★
Merdja Zerga ★
National Park
Rabat ★
Casablanca ★
Oualidia ★
★ Essaouira

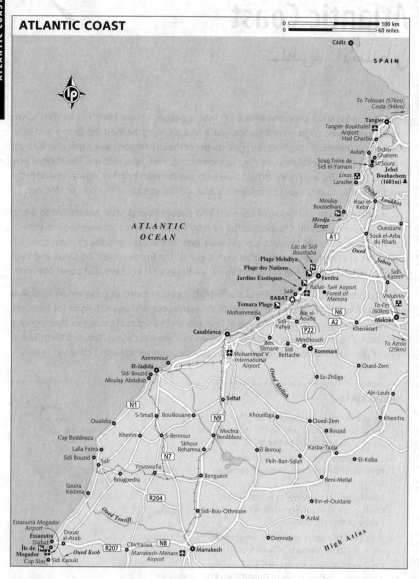

ATLANTIC COAST

0 ——— 100 km
0 ——— 60 miles

Cádiz

SPAIN

To Tetouan (57km);
Ceuta (94km)

Tangier
Tangier-Boukhalef
Airport
Had Gharbia
Asilah   Dchar
Chanem
Souq Tnine de   M'Soura
Sidi el-Yamani   Jebel
Lixus   Bouhachem
Larache   (1681m) ▲

Oued Loukkos

Moulay   Ksar el-
Bousselham   Kebir

Merdja   Ouezzane
Zerga   Souk el-Arba
du Rharb

*ATLANTIC
OCEAN*

A1   Oued Sebou

Lac de Sidi
Bourhaba   Sidi
Plage Mehdiya   Kacem
Plage des Nations
Jardins Exotiques   Kenitra   Volubilis
Salé   Rabat- Salé Airport
RABAT   Forest of   To Fès
Temara Plage   Mamora   (60km)
Mohammedia   Aïn el-   Meknès
Aouda   N6
Sidi-   A2   Khemisset
Yahya
Casablanca   Ben   P22
Slimane   Merchouch   To Azrou
Sidi   (25km)
Bettache   Rommani

Mohammed V   Ez-Zhiliga   Oued-Zem
Azemmour   International
Airport
El-Jadida   Aïn-Leuh
Sidi Bouzid   Oued Mellah
Moulay Abdallah   Settat

N1   Khouribga   Oued-Zem   Khenifra
S-Small   Boulâouane   N9
Oualidia   Boujad
Khemis   S-Bennour   Mechra
Cap Beddouza   Skhour   Benâbbou   Kasba-Tadla
Lalla Fatna   Rehamna   El Borouj
Sidi Bouzid   Safi   N7   Fkih-Ban-Salah   El-Ksiba
Youssoufia
Souira   Bouguedra   Benguérir   Beni-Mellal
Kedima
R204   Bin-el-Ouidane
Sidi-Bou-Othmane   Azilal
Essaouira Mogador   Oued Tensift
Airport
Essaouira   Douar   Demnate   *High Atlas*
Diabat   al-Arab
Île de   Chichaoua   N8
Mogador   R207   Oued Ksob   Marrakesh
Cap Sim   Sidi Kaouki   Marrakesh-Mênara
Airport

HISTORY

Throughout Morocco's rich and varied
history, the Atlantic seaboard remained
absolutely crucial to the country's maritime trade. For centuries the seafaring
Phoenicians plied the coast, settling in Liks
(Lixus), Essaouira and Chellah between the
10th and 7th centuries BC. Their Atlantic

colonies fell to the Carthaginians in the
6th century BC, and some, such as Lixus,
went on to become outposts of the Roman
Empire.

The next real wave of change came with
the Portuguese who established trading
posts from Asilah to Agadir in the late
15th and early 16th centuries. A period of

great prosperity followed, and as the ports were gradually recaptured by the Moroccans, the spoils from the trans-African caravan routes were shipped even further afield. With increasingly precious bounty on board, piracy became a lucrative trade. By the 18th century the Barbary Corsairs, pirates who mercilessly raided the European coastlines, terrorised the region and launched attacks as far afield as Cornwall in England. A ship's crew, who could be sold into slavery or held for ransom, were the most precious booty and over a million Europeans disappeared this way.

By the late 18th century the great European navies were busy bringing the region under control, while merchants began to open up new, and more stable, trade routes beyond the Mediterranean and Atlantic ports. Together, these two events forced the end of the golden era for the Moroccan coast.

Today, shipping is of major importance again and thanks to the huge industrial ports at Agadir and Safi, and thriving resorts up and down the coast, the region is the most prosperous of the whole country. It is here that you'll find the political capital, Rabat, and the country's economic hub, Casablanca; both cities that remain facing the sea.

CLIMATE

The climate of coastal Morocco is moderated by the ocean and is pleasant year-round. Winters are mild and moist, with average temperatures of 10 to 12°C. Spring temperatures are slightly higher and, although it rains frequently, wet weather is generally blown out to sea within a day. In summer you can expect highs of 25 to 27°C with ocean breezes, making the coast a welcome respite from the stifling heat of the interior. Throughout the year the Atlantic waters are chilly, and beaches are crowded in July and August only.

GETTING THERE & AWAY

Casablanca and Rabat are transport hubs for the region. Both are on the national train line with direct links to Tangier, Oujda, Fès, Meknès and Marrakesh and both have international airports, though Casablanca has a far greater number of international flights.

CASABLANCA (DAR EL-BAÏDA) الدار البيضاء

pop 3.8 million

Big, brash, restless and eager, Casablanca is Morocco's heaving metropolis. The city expanded rapidly during the early days of the French Protectorate and still attracts droves of the rural poor dreaming of a better lifestyle. Many have made it good and proudly flaunt their new-found wealth, while others languish in the grimy shantytowns in the city's sprawling suburbs.

Casa, as the city is popularly known, is a city of incredible contrasts. Despite its lack of headline attractions, it offers a unique insight into modern Morocco. In many ways, Casablanca represents the hopes and dreams of the country and once you've had your fill of Morocco's more traditional charms it can be a fascinating place to discover. Life here is far more cosmopolitan than in other parts of the country: designer sunglasses have replaced the veil, and men and women mix more easily, both on the beaches and in the hip bars and clubs around town.

More akin to southern European cities than to either Fès or Marrakesh, Casablanca is home to racing traffic and simmering social problems as well as wide boulevards, public parks, fountains and striking, colonial architecture. Imposing Hispano-Moorish buildings, and Art Deco and modernist gems line the streets – some stunningly restored and others fading into shameful disrepair. Their rundown façades stand in sharp contrast to Casablanca's modernist landmark: the enormous and incredibly ornate Hassan II Mosque.

HISTORY

Although the Phoenicians plied the coast and almost certainly traded in the area around present-day Casablanca, the earliest known settlers in the region were the Barghawata, a Berber tribe. The independent state they established at Anfa (now a suburb of Casablanca) in the 7th century was conquered by the Almohads in 1188, and then taken over by the Merenids 70 years later.

As the Merenid dynasty weakened in the early 15th century, the local tribespeople again took control, making the port a safe harbour for pirates and racketeers. By the second half of the 15th century the Anfa pirates had become such a serious threat to the Portuguese that 10,000 men and 50 ships were sent from Lisbon to subdue the unruly seamen. Anfa was sacked and left in ruins. However, the local tribes were undeterred and continued to terrorise the trade routes provoking a second attack by the Portuguese in 1515. Sixty years later the Portuguese arrived to stay, erecting fortifications and renaming the port Casa Branca (White House).

In 1755, a devastating earthquake destroyed Lisbon and severely damaged Casa Branca, forcing the Portuguese to abandon the colony. Although Sultan Sidi Mohammed ben Abdallah subsequently resettled and fortified the area, it never regained its former importance. By 1830 it was little more than a village of 600 inhabitants.

By the mid-1800s Europe was booming and turned to Morocco for increased supplies of grain and wool. The fertile plains around Casablanca were soon feeding the European markets, and agents and traders flocked to the city. Spanish merchants renamed the city Casablanca and by the beginning of the 20th century the French had secured permission to build an artificial harbour here.

The increased trade brought prosperity to the region, but the activities and influence of the Europeans also caused much resentment among the indigenous population. Violence erupted when European workers began to build a quarry railway across a Muslim cemetery in 1907 and the pro-colonialist French jumped at the chance to send troops to quell the dispute. A French warship and a company of marines soon arrived and bombarded the town.

Casablanca fell into fierce battle as French troops, tribes from the interior and locals fought for control. The French finally won the upper hand and gradually began the process of colonisation, dethroning the sultan and eventually declaring Morocco a French Protectorate in 1912.

The city began to boom and expanded rapidly. Under the first French resident-general, Louis Hubert Gonzalve Lyautey, a grand plan emerged to make Casablanca the economic centre of the new protectorate. His wide boulevards and modern city planning still survive and mark the city as eternally different from Morocco's imperial capitals. However, he underestimated the success of his own plans and the city grew far beyond his elaborate schemes. By the end of the Second World War Casablanca had a population of 700,000 and the suburbs were surrounded by heaving shantytowns.

Casablanca still has huge disparities of wealth and the shantytowns (see boxed text, p94) are easily visible on the train journey in from the airport. New migrants arrive daily and for every one that finds success many others continue to struggle.

ORIENTATION

Casablanca is a huge, modern city. The medina – the oldest part of town – is relatively small and sits in the north of the city close to the port. To the south of the medina is Place des Nations Unies, a large traffic junction that marks the heart of the city.

The city's main streets branch out from here: Ave des Forces Armées Royales (Ave des FAR), Ave Moulay Hassan I, Blvd Mohammed V and Blvd Houphouet Boigny. Ave Hassan II leads to Place Mohammed V, easily recognised by its grand Art Deco administrative buildings.

To the southeast is the Quartier Habous or *nouvelle medina* and to the west is Aïn

---

CASABLANCA IN...

24 hours

Start your day with breakfast at a city centre pavement café and watch businesslike Casa walk by. Visit the **Hassan II Mosque** (p91) and make your way back to town via the **medina** for lunch at **Café Maure** (p99) on the ramparts. Follow the **walking tour** (p93), taking in the best of Casa's Art Deco heritage, before making your way to the **Quartier Habous** (p92) for shopping and cakes the French-Moroccan way. Then treat yourself to stunning views over the ocean by dining at one of the **cliff-top restaurants** by Phare d'el-Hank (p99) before joining the city's pretty young things in the bars and clubs along **Boulevard de la Corniche** (p101).

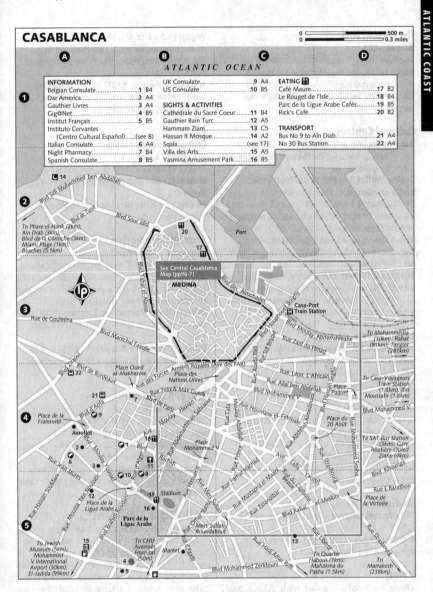

CASABLANCA

0 — 500 m
0 — 0.3 miles

ATLANTIC OCEAN

INFORMATION	
Belgian Consulate	1 B4
Dar America	2 A4
Gauthier Livres	3 A4
Gig@Net	4 B5
Institut Français	5 B5
Instituto Cervantes	
(Centro Cultural Español)	(see 8)
Italian Consulate	6 A4
Night Pharmacy	7 B4
Spanish Consulate	8 B5

UK Consulate	9 A4
US Consulate	10 B5

SIGHTS & ACTIVITIES	
Cathédrale du Sacré Coeur	11 B4
Gauthier Bain Turc	12 A5
Hammam Ziani	13 C5
Hassan II Mosque	14 A2
Sqala	(see 17)
Villa des Arts	15 A5
Yasmina Amusement Park	16 B5

EATING 🍴	
Café Maure	17 B2
Le Rouget de l'Isle	18 B4
Parc de la Ligue Arabe Cafés	19 B5
Rick's Café	20 B2

TRANSPORT	
Bus No 9 to Aïn Diab	21 A4
No 30 Bus Station	22 A4

Diab, the beachfront suburb home to up-market hotels and nightclubs.

The CTM bus station and Casa Port train station are in the centre of the city. Casa Voyageurs station is 2km east of the centre and the airport is 30km southeast of town. See Getting There & Away (p102) for more information.

Street Names

Casablanca's street names are slowly being changed and you'll probably see a few different names for one street. The French names are being replaced with Moroccan names but many older people and local street directories have yet to make the transition so be very specific when asking for directions.

INFORMATION

Bookshops

Gauthier Livres (Map p89; ☎ 022 264426; 12 Rue Moussa ben Nousseir) Books by French and Moroccan writers, as well as road maps.

Libraire Livre Servile (Map p96; Rue Tata) A small selection in a central location.

Cultural Centres

Dar America (Map p89; ☎ 022 221460; 10 Place Bel Air; ⏱ 8am-5pm Mon-Fri) The US information service and library; bring ID to get in.

Goethe Institut (Map p96; ☎ 022 200445; www .goethe.de in German; 11 Place du 16 Novembre; ⏱ 10am-noon & 3-6pm Tue-Sat) Conducts German classes and presents the occasional film screening and exhibition.

Institut Français (Map p89; ☎ 022 259870; www .ambafrance-ma.org in French; 121 Blvd Mohammed Zerktouni; ⏱ 9am-2.30pm Tue-Sat) Offers a good library, films, lectures and other events.

Instituto Cervantes (Centro Cultural Español; Map p96; ☎ 022 267337; www.cervantes.es in Spanish; 31 Rue d'Alger; ⏱ 10am-noon & 3-6pm Tue-Sat) Hosts film screenings and cultural events and has a library.

Emergency

Service d'Aide Médicale Urgente (SAMU; ☎ 022 252525) Private ambulance service.

SOS Médecins (☎ 022 444444; house call Dh310; ⏱ 24hr) Private doctors who make house calls.

Internet Access

EuroNet (Map p96; ☎ 022 265921; 51 Rue Tata; per hr Dh10; ⏱ 8.30am-11pm)

Fairnet (Map89; ☎ 022 482631; 25 Rue Zair Mers Sultan; per hr Dh8; ⏱ 8am-11pm)

Gig@net (Map p89; ☎ 022 484810; 140 Blvd Mohammed Zerktouni; per hr Dh10; ⏱ 24hr)

Medical Services

CHU Averroès Hospital (Hôpital Ibn Rochd; ☎ 022 224109)

Night Pharmacy (Map p89; cnr Place Oued al-Makhazine & Blvd d'Anfa; ⏱ 24hr)

Money

There are banks – most with ATMS and foreign exchange offices – on every street corner in Casablanca.

BMCE (Map p96; Hyatt Regency Hotel; ⏱ 9am-9pm) Good for after-hours and weekend services.

Crédit du Maroc (Map p96; ☎ 022 477255; 48 Blvd Mohammed V) Separate bureau de change that is very central; you can cash American Express (Amex) travellers cheques for free here.

Voyages Schwartz (Map p96; ☎ 022 222947; schwartz@mbox.azure.net; 112 Rue Prince Moulay Abdallah) The Amex representative (does not cash or sell travellers cheques).

Wafa Cash (Map p96; ☎ 022 208080; 15 Rue Idriss Lahrizi; ⏱ 8am-8pm Mon-Sat) Open longer hours, has an ATM and cashes travellers cheques.

Post

Central Market post office (Map p96; cnr Blvd Mohammed V & Rue Chaouia)

FedEx (☎ 022 541212; 313 Blvd Mohammed V)

Main post office (Map p96; cnr Blvd de Paris & Ave Hassan II)

Medina post office (Map p96; Place Ahmed el-Bidaoui) Near the youth hostel.

Tourist Information

The staff is polite but the tourist offices in Casablanca are of very little practical use. Try www.visitcasablanca.ma (in French) for information before you travel or ask the receptionist at your hotel for help.

Office National Marocain du Tourisme (ONMT; Map p96; ☎ 022 271177; 55 Rue Omar Slaoui; ⏱ 8.30am-4.30pm Mon-Fri)

Syndicat d'Initiative (Map p96; ☎ 022 221524; 98 Blvd Mohammed V; ⏱ 8.30am-4.30pm Mon-Sat, 9am-12.30pm Sun)

Travel Agencies

Carlson Wagonlit (Map p96; ☎ 022 203051; www .carlsonwagonlit.com; 60-62 Rue el-Araibi Jilali) A respected and widespread group of travel agencies.

Supratours (Map p89; ☎ 022 404289; Casa Voyageurs train station) Organises rail and bus connections.

Voyages Wasteels (Map p96; ☎ 022 314060; www .wasteels.fr; 26 Rue Léon L'Africain) A good place for cheap intercontinental rail tickets.

DANGERS & ANNOYANCES

Although Casablanca can feel pretty rough around the edges, it's relatively safe for tourists. However, there are huge disparities of wealth – as in any large city, you need to keep your wits about you. Travellers should take care when walking around the city centre at night and be extra vigilant in and around the old medina. Coming home late from a bar or club, it's best to take a taxi.

SIGHTS

Casablanca is Morocco's commercial hub and is more interested in big international business than the tourist dollar. For the traveller it can be a pretty workaday place to visit and for its size has a dearth of traditional tourist attractions. Apart from the incredible Hassan II Mosque, the city's main appeal is in strolling around its neighbourhoods: the Art Deco style of the city centre, the gentrified market district of the Quartier Habous and the beachfront views of the Corniche. You'll appreciate Casablanca more if you've seen other parts of Morocco first and can compare its cosmopolitan vibe to life in the rest of the country.

Hassan II Mosque

The brainchild and crowning achievement of King Hassan II, this phenomenal building is the world's third-largest mosque. It was built to commemorate the former king's 60th birthday and opened in 1993 giving Casablanca the heart and landmark it so sorely missed.

The **mosque** (Map p89) rises above the ocean on a rocky outcrop reclaimed from the sea, taking literally the verse from the Quran that states that God's throne was built upon the water. It's a vast building that can hold 25,000 worshippers within its structure and can accommodate a further 80,000 in the courtyards and squares around it.

The mosque was designed by the French architect Michel Pinseau and is topped by a soaring 210m-tall minaret, which shines a laser beam towards Mecca by night. In addition to this high-tech call to prayer, the mosque also has a centrally heated floor, electric doors, a retractable roof and a section of glass flooring allowing the faithful to see the Atlantic washing the rocks below.

Above all, though, it is the vast size and elaborate decoration of the prayer hall that is most striking. Large enough to house Paris' Notre Dame or Rome's St Peter's, it is blanketed in astonishing woodcarving, *zellij* (tilework) and stucco moulding. A huge team of master craftsmen was assembled to work on the mosque, delicately carving intricate patterns and designs in cedar from the Middle Atlas, marble from Agadir and granite from Tafraoute. Over 6000 traditional Moroccan artisans worked on the building over the course of its construction.

The project cost more than half a billion dollars and was paid for largely by public subscription. Although most Moroccans, particularly those from Casablanca, are very proud of their modern monument others believe this vast sum might have been better spent. In particular, resentment lingers among the slum dwellers who were evicted without compensation from the area around the mosque.

The Hassan II Mosque is one of the very few Islamic religious buildings open to non-Muslims. To see the interior you must take a **guided tour** (☎ 022 482886; adult/student/child Dh120/60/30; ☯ 9am, 10am, 11am & 2pm Sat-Thu). Visitors must be 'decently and respectfully dressed' and once inside you will be asked to remove your shoes. The hour-long tours are conducted in French, English, German and Spanish, and take in the prayer hall, ablution rooms and hammam. The latter is supposed to open for use by the public (including non-Muslims), but as yet no date has been set.

Although it is possible to walk to the mosque in about 20 minutes from Casa-Port train station, the road is busy with traffic and has few pedestrians. There have also been some isolated reports of muggings here. It's better to take a petit taxi from the town centre (around Dh10). Bus No 15 leaves from Place Oued al-Makhazine (Dh3.50).

Ancienne Medina

Casablanca's modest **medina** (p96) gives an idea of just how small the city was before the French embarked on their massive building programme. Even though it's the oldest part of the city, most of the buildings date from the 19th century and it lacks the medieval character of other city medinas.

Enter the medina from the northeast corner of the Place des Nations Unies near the restored **clock tower** (p96). The narrow lanes to the east are piled high with cheap shoes, high-sheen synthetic underwear and various household goods, while the rest of the medina remains largely residential. The old city's main Friday mosque is the **Chleuh Mosque** (p96) along Rue Chakab Arsalane.

On the north side of the medina, facing the port, you'll see the last remains of

Casablanca's 18th-century fortifications. Known as the **sqala**, the bastion offers panoramic views over the sea.

Quartier Habous (Nouvelle Medina)

The Quartier Habous, or *nouvelle medina*, is Morocco-lite – an idealised, almost toy-town version of a traditional medina, with neat little rows of streets and shop stalls. The district was built by the French in the 1930s as an attempted solution to the ongoing housing shortage. It marries the best features of traditional Moroccan architecture with modern facilities and French ideals – even the mosque fronts onto a strip of grassy lawn just like a village church.

For fans of the bustle and chaos of traditional markets, it may feel too sanitised to be authentic, but if you fancy some Moroccan character without the associated smells and hassle, it's got a decent selection of bazaars, craft shops, bakeries and cafés.

The **Royal Palace** (closed to the public) is to the north of the district, while to the south is the old **Mahakma du Pasha** (courts & reception hall; admission free; ☉ 8am-noon & 2-6pm Mon-Sat), which has more than 60 rooms decorated with sculpted wooden ceilings, stuccowork, wrought-iron railings and earthenware floors.

The Quartier Habous is located about 1km southeast of town. Take bus No 4 or 40 from Blvd de Paris, across from the post office.

Jewish Museum of Casablanca

Set in a beautiful villa surrounded by lush gardens, this is Casablanca's only **museum** (☎ 022 994940; 81 Rue Chasseur Jules Gros, Oasis; Dh20, with guide Dh30; ☉ 10am-5pm Mon-Fri) and the only Jewish museum to be found in the Islamic world. It demonstrates the history of the once-thriving Jewish community and its influence on modern Moroccan society.

The exhibits include historic artefacts such as documents, traditional clothing and ceremonial items and a vast collection of photographs featuring synagogues, *mellah* (Jewish Quarters) and other landmarks that remain from the 2000 years of Jewish civilisation in the region. The museum is in the suburb of Oasis, a 15-minute taxi ride (Dh20) from the city centre.

Villa des Arts

Located in a wonderful converted Art Deco building near the Parc de la Ligue Arabe, **Villa des Arts** (Map p89; ☎ 022 295087; 30 Blvd Brahim Roudani; admission Dh10; ☉ 9am-7pm Tue-Sat) is a gallery that rotates exhibitions of contemporary Moroccan and international art.

Aïn Diab

This affluent suburb runs along the Atlantic beachfront west of the centre and is home to the happening **Boulevard de la Corniche**. Lined with beach clubs, upmarket hotels, restaurants, bars and clubs, it is the entertainment hub of Casablanca and *the* place for young, chic professionals to see and be seen.

However, the promenade packed with walkers and joggers is really a potholed pavement. In between the busy beach clubs the view is spoiled by abandoned pleasure grounds and concrete swimming pools filled with construction rubbish.

The beach is still extremely popular, though, and the easiest way to find an empty strip of sand on which to spread your towel is to visit one of the beach clubs. The largest is **Miami Plage** (☎ 022 797133; adult/child Mon-Fri Dh55/20, Sat & Sun Dh60/30; ☉ 9am-7.30pm), which has basketball courts, beach umbrellas (Dh15), a swimming pool and a restaurant and bar.

Bus No 9 goes to Aïn Diab from Place Oued al-Makhazine. A taxi from the centre costs around Dh25 (Dh50 at night).

ACTIVITIES
Hammams

Sparklingly clean and decidedly modern, **Hammam Ziani** (Map p89; ☎ 022 319695; 59 Rue Abou Rakrak; Mon-Fri Dh40, Sat & Sun Dh50; ☉ 7am-10pm) offers massage, a Jacuzzi and also a juice bar, as well as the traditional steam room and *gommage* (being scrubbed by an attendant).

You'll find similar facilities at the brand new **Gauthier Bain Turc** (Map p89; ☎ 061 145926; 25 Rue Jean Jaures; Mon-Fri Dh50, Sat & Sun Dh60; ☉ 7am-10pm), where a scrub costs about Dh20 and a 30-minute massage Dh100.

For a more traditional experience, try the **Ancienne Medina Hammam** (Map p96; Place Ahmed el-Bidaoui; admission Dh7.50; ☉ 6am-noon for men, 1-10pm for women) near the youth hostel in the old medina.

WALKING TOUR

If you can see past the traffic, fumes and general chaos of central Casablanca, you'll discover the city's rich architectural heritage, a blend of French-colonial design and traditional Moroccan style known as Mauresque architecture. Developed in the 1930s and heavily influenced by the Art Deco movement, it embraced decorative details such as carved friezes, beautiful tile work and ornate wrought-iron balconies. Although some of the era's gems have been beautifully restored, others lie in shameful disrepair. This walking tour takes in the best Mauresque buildings and some other Casa treasures.

Start on the northwest edge of the Parc de la Ligue Arabe, where you can't miss the imposing **Cathédrale du Sacré Coeur (1)**, a massive white church that gracefully blends European style and traditional Moroccan influences. The cathedral was designed by Paul Tornon in 1930 and has been used as a school, theatre and cultural centre. It is due to be restored and its rundown interior is only open for special events.

From here, walk two blocks east to Place Mohammed V, the grand centrepiece of the French regeneration scheme. The vast square is surrounded by an impressive array of august administrative buildings, mostly designed by Robert Marrast and Henri Prost. The **ancienne préfecture (2**; old police headquarters), dating from 1930, dominates the south side of the square and is topped by a modernist clock tower.

The nearby **palais de justice (3**; law courts) was built in 1925. The huge main door and entrance was inspired by the Persian *iwan*, a vaulted hall that usually opens into the central court of the *medersa* (theological college) of a mosque.

Stroll across the grand square and admire the 1918 **main post office (4)**, a wonderful building fronted by arches and stone columns and decorated with bold mosaics. More in the style of traditional Moroccan architecture is the **Banque al-Maghrib (5)**, on Blvd de Paris. Fronted with decorative stonework, it was the last building constructed on the square.

From here, walk east on Rue Indriss Lahrizi, where impressive facades line both sides of the street. Pause to check out the prize piece, **La Princière Salon de Thé (6)**, easily recognised by the huge stone crown on the roofline. Turn right into Rue Mohammed Belloul to see **Hotel Guynemer (7**; p98), with its Art Deco panelling and then walk one block east and turn right down Rue Tahar Sebti, which is lined with colonial buildings.

Turn left into Rue Chaouia and look out for **Hotel Transatlantique (8**; p97), which dates

---

THE WALK AT A GLANCE

Start Parc de la Ligue Arabe, Blvd Rachidi
End Rue Prince Moulay Abdellah
Distance 3km
Duration 45 minutes

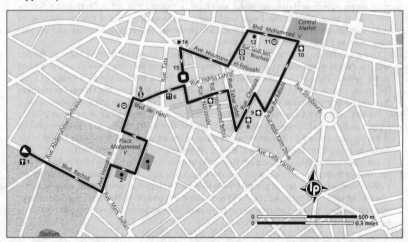

ATLANTIC COAST

from 1922 and has been beautifully restored. Just around the corner, the owners of the Transatlantique are in the process of restoring another gem, the **Hotel Volubilis (9)**.

Turn left up Rue Ibn Batouta and continue to the corner of Blvd Mohammed V. On your right is the derelict shell of the **Hôtel Lincoln (10)**, an Art Deco masterpiece built in 1916 and patiently awaiting a long-talked-about restoration.

Turn left into Blvd Mohammed V and look out for an array of wonderful facades along the south side of the street. The **post office (11)**, with its delicate, carved motifs, and the **Le Matin/Maroc Soir (12)** building, with its classic style, are two of the most impressive.

At the end of this block turn left into Rue Mohammed el-Qory to find the **Cinema Rialto (13; p100)**, a classic Art Deco building with some wonderful touches. Continue south to the junction with Ave Houmane el-Fetouaki and turn right to reach **Place 16 Novembre (14)**, which is home to an array of Art Deco buildings. Finally, continue to the south, along pedestrianised **Rue Prince Moulay Abdellah (15)**, where you'll find a selec-

tion of interesting façades with decorative doorways and ironwork.

For more information on Casablanca's architectural heritage look out for *Casablanca, Colonial Myths and Architectural Ventures* by Jean-Louis Cohen and Monique Eleb, or for francophones, *Casablanca – Portrait d'une Ville* by JM Zurfluh.

COURSES
Language
Casablanca has a multitude of language schools, almost all of which have French classes. However, many, including the Institut Français, only run semester-long courses. Some options for short-term lessons:

Centre International d'Étude de Langues (CIEL; Map pp96-7; ☎ 022 441959; ciel@menara.ma; 4th fl, 8 Blvd Khouribga, Place de la Victoire) Runs courses in a host of languages including classical Arabic.

École Assimil-Formation (Map pp96-7; ☎ 022 312567; 71 Rue Allah ben Abdellah) Offers private tuition in Arabic.

CASABLANCA FOR CHILDREN
Casablanca is a big, grimy city and your best bet when travelling with children is to retreat from the noise and traffic of the city

---

TIN TOWNS

In May 2003, Casablanca was rocked by a series of explosions that killed 45 people. Investigators blamed Salafia Jihadia, a loosely organised radical Islamic group whose founding members trained in Afghanistan. The bombers, however, were all young Moroccan men, many from Sidi Moumen, a desperately impoverished area on the outskirts of Casablanca.

Sidi Moumen is one Casablanca's most notorious slums, home to over 290,000 people and a place where poverty and unemployment are rife. It's estimated that 1/3 of Casablanca's population lives in areas like this. The illegal settlements on the outskirts of the city are made up of make-shift houses of cardboard, wood and corrugated iron, and are home to rural workers who have come to city in search of the big time.

Living conditions are desperate: the worst slums have no power, running water or sewage systems. People in these areas are socially alienated, despised by other Moroccans and ignored by the system. There is no public transport, literacy levels are low and there's no hope of a job. For young people with no sense of identity and no hope of affording the material possessions they see advertised around town, Islamic fundamentalism can seem an attractive alternative.

No-one outwardly supports the fundamentalists; Casablancans from all areas are at pains to explain that they condemned the 2003 bombings and that their city is one of the most tolerant in the Islamic world. Since the atrocities, a swarm of voluntary organisations have set up in the slums, teaching basic literacy and IT skills and attempting to improve conditions.

The government has also tried to alleviate problems by moving some slum residents into apartments but they complain that the new housing is too expensive and too small for extended families. Many feel it's a token gesture and unless the government addresses the underlying problems there will be no improvement in conditions. However, everyone hopes this will happen before the increasing anger and frustration boils over into support for a terrifying alternative.

centre. The beaches and **beach clubs** in Aïn Diab (p92) are the place to go. Along with swimming pools, slides and playgrounds, they have various sports courts and countless facilities. Staying at a hotel along the Blvd de la Corniche means you'll probably have your own swimming pool and won't have too far to walk for entertainment.

Back in town, Casa's biggest open space is the **Parc de la Ligue Arabe**. It's a good place for games and walks, and has a choice of small cafés and the **Yasmina amusement park** (Map p89; admission Dh150; 10am-7pm), with plenty of small-scale rides and fun-fair atmosphere.

TOURS

Both tourist offices (p90) offer a three-hour walking tour of the city (Dh450 for up to three people) that can be customised to suit the client's interests. **Olive Branch Tours** (Map p96; 022 220354; www.olivebranchtours.com; 35 Rue el-Oraïbi Jilali) offer a 'Grand Tour of Casablanca', which takes in the main squares in the ville nouvelle, the medina and the Mahakma du Pasha in Habous, as well as a stroll along the Corniche.

FESTIVALS & EVENTS

The city held the inaugural week-long **Festival of Casablanca** in July 2005, repeated the festivities in 2006 and plans to make it an annual event. The ambitious programme aims to bring the big players from the artistic, cultural, economic and political sectors together to promote cultural development in the city, and features a broad selection of music, cinema, street theatre and art.

SLEEPING

Most of Casablanca's hotels are in the centre of town with the exception of the youth hostel, which is in the medina, and the upmarket hotels along the Blvd de la Corniche. Hotels fill up fast during the summer months, particularly in August, so it's a good idea to make reservations in advance.

Budget

Casablanca's budget hotels are pretty basic. The medina hotels are invariably grotty and overpriced and don't offer good value compared with their ville nouvelle counterparts.

Youth Hostel (Map p96; 022 220551; fax 022 227677; 6 Place Ahmed el-Bidaoui; dm/d/tr incl breakfast Dh45/120/180, sheets Dh5; 8-10am & noon-11pm;) Clustered around a bright central lounge area, the rooms here are basic but well kept, with high ceilings and a lingering smell of damp in winter. It's not the place to party, but you'll get a good night's sleep and excellent hot showers in the morning. There's a small kitchen for guest use.

Hôtel Galia (Map p96; 022 481694; 19 Rue Ibn Batouta; s/d/tr Dh150/220/300, with shower Dh170/250/330) Tiled floors, plastic flowers, gold tasselled curtains and matching bedspreads adorn the rooms at the Galia, a top-notch budget option with excellent-value rooms and rather dubious taste in décor. Management is very friendly and helpful and it's in a very convenient location.

Hôtel Astrid (Map p96; 022 277803; hotelastrid@hotmail.com; 12 Rue 6 Novembre; s/d/tr Dh256/309/405) Tucked away on a quiet street south of the centre, the Astrid could offer the most elusive element of Casa's budget hotels – a good night's sleep. There's little traffic noise here and the spacious, well-kept rooms are all en suite. Each has a TV, telephone and frilly décor, and there's a friendly café downstairs.

Hôtel Noailles (Map p96; 022 202554; fax 022 220589; 22 Blvd du 11 Janvier; s/d Dh250/299) You'll get decent but characterless rooms at the Noailles, a spotlessly clean joint with a civilised bar/café on the first floor. All rooms have a TV and their own bathroom but the fittings and furnishings are pretty dated. Ask for a room facing the courtyard to get away from the street noise.

Hôtel Oued-Dahab (Map p96; 022 223866; oueddahab@yahoo.com; 17 Rue Mohamed Belloul; s/d Dh100/140, with bathroom Dh120/180) Frayed around the edges but cheap and clean, the Oued-Dahab has big, functional rooms right in the centre of town. It's run by the same family as the Hôtel Guynemer and is an extremely friendly place. Ask for a room facing inwards for a restful night's sleep.

Hôtel du Palais (Map p96; 022 276191; 68 Rue Farhat Hachad; s/d Dh80/120, with bathroom Dh140/240) At the lower end of this price range, this basic hotel makes a good choice, offering clean, spacious rooms with large windows. Although recently upgraded, it's still fairly spartan and can be noisy. A hot shower costs Dh10.

ATLANTIC COAST

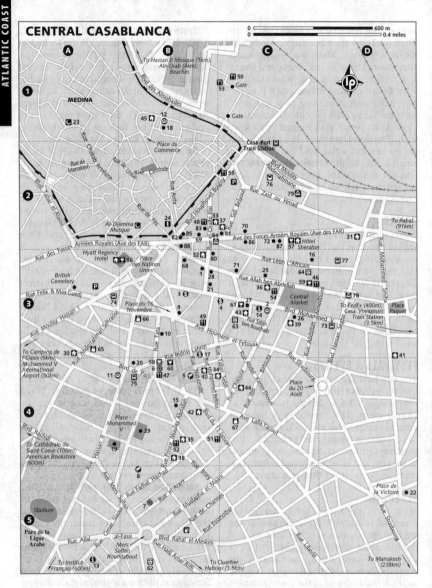

CENTRAL CASABLANCA

Hôtel des Negociants (Map p96; ☎ 022 314023; fax 022 314023; 116 Rue Allal ben Abdellah; s/d 105/145, with bathroom Dh168/207) Another decent option in the centre of town, this hotel has a selection of bright, clean rooms spread over four floors. It has little charm and only basic bathrooms, but it's a good deal for the price.

Hôtel Rialto (Map p96; ☎ 022 275122; 9 Rue Salah ben Bouchaib; s/d Dh100/120, with bathroom Dh140/160) A grand staircase leads up to a bright central courtyard at this conveniently located hotel. The rooms here have seen better days and the bathrooms are fairly ancient but it still retains a touch of its former class.

Hotel Foucauld (Map p96; ☎ 022 222666; 52 Rue el-Oraïbi Jilai; s/d Dh80/120, with bathroom Dh130/160) Incredible plasterwork decoration adorns the foyer at this simple hotel in the centre of town. The rooms aren't quite so grand and they can be noisy, but they're much bigger than average and have a certain faded charm lacking in a lot of newer hotels.

Hôtel du Centre (Map p96; ☎ 022 446180; 1 Rue Sidi Balyout; s/d Dh168/204) A good fall-back option in a very convenient location, this hotel offers faded en suite rooms with a fine line in time-warp décor. The place is spotless, though, and there are some nice Art Deco touches in the ancient lift and staircase balustrade.

Midrange

Casablanca has a good selection of mid-range accommodation scattered around the city centre. You'll also find some nice alternatives with ocean views and easy access to the beach along Blvd de la Corniche.

Hôtel Transatlantique (Map p96; ☎ 022 294551; www.transatcasa.com; 79 Rue Chaouia; s/d 620/740; ✿) Set in one of Casa's Art Deco gems, this 1922 hotel has buckets of neo-Moorish character. The grand scale, decorative plaster, spidery wrought iron and eclectic mix of knick-knacks, pictures and lamps give the Transatlantique a whiff of colonial-era decadence crossed with '70s retro. It has a lovely outdoor seating area and comfortable, but fairly plain, bedrooms. Avoid the 1st floor, as it gets the brunt of noise from the popular piano bar and nightclub.

Al-Mounia Hôtel (Map p96; ☎ 022 203211; al.mounia.hotel@menara.ma; 24 Blvd de Paris; s/d Dh512/600; ✿) Comfort rather than charm is the selling point at this international-style, four-star hotel. The spacious, modern rooms are tastefully decorated in neutral colours and are popular with business clients who frequent the nightclub, bar and restaurant on site. It's a good deal but you could be anywhere.

ATLANTIC COAST

Hôtel Métropole (Map p96; ☎ 022 301213; fax 022 305801; 89 Rue Mohammed Smiha; s/d Dh329/405) A dubious combination of deep red velour, gold brocade and plenty of tassels adorn the spacious rooms at this reliable three-star option. Although the styling may not be to your taste and the location a little inconvenient, the rooms are good value with decent furniture, en suite bathrooms and TVs.

Ibis Moussafir (☎ 022 401984; www.ibishotel.com; Blvd Bahmad, Place de la Gare Casa-Voyageurs; s/d Dh420/440; 🗷) If a comfortable room and reliable quality is more important than local character, the Ibis makes a good compromise. The rooms are modern and bright, if a little compact, and the location is handy for late night trains.

Hôtel Bellerive (☎ 022 797504; www.belleriv.com; 38 Blvd de La Corniche, Aïn Diab; s/d Dh471/620; 🗷) The lovely terrace, pool and garden make up for the dated, standard rooms at this small, family-run hotel. Many have ocean views, though, and it's cheaper than most along this waterfront strip. There's plenty of space and a playground, which makes it a good bet if you're travelling with children.

Hôtel de la Corniche (☎ 022 798181; fax 022 797467; Blvd de la Corniche, Aïn Diab; s/d Dh632/784; 🗷 🖳 🗷) Once bright, modern and businesslike but now sadly faded, the rooms at this hotel are a little overpriced. It offers excellent access to the beach, and has a great terrace overlooking the sea.

Hôtel le Littoral (☎ 022 797373; fax 022 797374; www.hotel-littoral.ma; Blvd de l'Océan Atlantique, Aïn Diab; s/d Dh699/850; 🗷 🗷) This cavernous, well-kept hotel is rather dark with rooms that were once the height of fashion but now look dangerously '80s. However, there are large balconies and wonderful views over the waterfront.

Top End

Casablanca has a glut of top-end hotels with all the major international chains represented in town. Most are along Ave des FAR, with a few others along the Blvd de la Corniche. For something less generic try one of the following:

Hôtel les Saisons (Map p96; ☎ 022 490901; www.hotellessaisonsmaroc.ma; 19 Rue el Oraïbi Jilali; s/d Dh 950/1200; 🗷 🖳) At the bottom end of this price range, this small hotel offers extremely comfortable, quiet rooms with all the usual facilities such as safe, minibar, satellite TV and direct dial phone. It's a more personal place than the larger international hotels and offers good value for money.

Hotel Farah (Map p96; ☎ 022 311212; www.goldentulipfarahcasablanca.com; 160 Ave des FAR; r Dh1600; 🗷 🖳 🗷) Revamped, renamed and re-branded, this huge four-star hotel offers top-notch facilities and amenities. The spacious rooms are tastefully decked out in contemporary style but with old-school details such as padded headboards and swag curtains. The hotel gets few Western tourists but has a fitness centre and spa, restaurants and bars.

Hôtel Riad Salam (☎ 022 391313; fax 022 391345; r Dh2325; 🗷 🗷) Although not as swish as it once was and with rather erratic service, the Riad Salam is still the top spot along the waterfront. The Moroccan-style, non-smoking rooms with low couches, woven rugs and decorative tiling are centred round the hotel's two swimming pools and landscaped terrace. It has a thalassotherapy centre, a health club and tennis courts, and substantial discounts in the off season.

EATING
Restaurants

Casablanca has a great selection of restaurants, and you can eat anything from excellent tajine to French pâté and Thai dumplings. However, seafood is the real local speciality and it's worth checking out the restaurants at the port or on the way to Aïn Diab for a culinary treat.

CENTRAL CASABLANCA

Taverne du Dauphin (Map p96; ☎ 022 221200; 115 Blvd Houphouet Boigny; menu Dh110, mains Dh70-90; ☺ Mon-Sat) A Casablanca institution, this traditional Provençal restaurant and bar has been serving up *fruits de mer* (seafood) since it opened in 1958. On first glance it's a humble, family-run place but one taste of the succulent grilled fish, fried calamari and *crevettes royales* (king prawns) will leave you smitten.

Restaurant al-Mounia (Map p96; ☎ 022 222669; 95 Rue Prince Moulay Abdallah; mains Dh110-140) Dine in style at this wonderfully traditional restaurant where you can choose to sit in the elegant Moroccan salon or the cool, leafy garden to enjoy the sumptuous Moroccan cuisine.There's a selection of salads worthy of any vegetarian restaurant and an array of exotic delicacies such as chicken *pastilla* (rich, savoury pie) and pigeon with raisins.

Brasserie la Bavaroise (Map p96; ☎ 022 311760; 129 Rue Allah ben Abdellah; mains Dh100-140) Savour the best of French cuisine at this upmarket brasserie where the locals like to hang out, see and be seen. It offers a rich selection of fine fish as well as French classics such as veal, steak and pheasant cooked to perfection.

Restaurant du Port de Peche (Map p96; ☎ 022 318561; Le Port de Pêche; mains Dh80-140) This smoky, rustic seafood restaurant is packed to the gills at lunch and dinner with happy diners

tucking in to fish freshly whipped from the sea. A nautical theme pervades the whole place and the simple grilled fish and tangy paella are some of the best in town.

Ostréa (Map p96; ☎ 022 441390; dozen oysters Dh74, mains Dh90-150; ☺ 11am-11pm) Across the road from Restaurant du Port de Peche is this more upmarket seafood restaurant specialising in Oualidia oysters and lobster.

Rick's Cafe (Map p96; ☎ 022 274207; 248 Blvd Sour Jdid; mains Dh60-150; ☺ noon-3.30pm, 6.30pm-1.30am) Cashing in on the Hollywood hit, this beautiful bar and restaurant serves up a taste of home for the nostalgic masses. Lamb chops, chilli, hamburgers and American breakfasts are all on tap. There's also an in-house pianist, a Sunday jazz session, wi-fi access and even souvenir T-shirts and mugs. It's hardly real-life Morocco, but is a good place for late night drinks.

Le Rouget de l'Isle (Map p89; ☎ 022 294740; 16 Rue Rouget de l'Isle; mains Dh110-130; ☺ closed Sat lunch & Sun) Sleek, stylish and renowned for its simple but delicious French food, Le Rouget is one of Casa's top spots. Set in a renovated 1930s villa, it is an elegant place filled with period furniture and contemporary artwork. The impeccable food is reasonably priced, though, and there's a beautiful garden. Book in advance.

Golden China (Map p96; ☎ 022 273526; 12 Rue el-Oraïbi Jilali; mains Dh45-90) Casa's top Chinese restaurant is a welcome break from tajine if you've been in Morocco for some time. It's an excellent choice for vegetarians with plenty of meat-free options on offer.

AÏN DIAB

The best of this neighbourhood's restaurants are clustered together on a cliff-top overlooking the crashing Atlantic waves near the El-Hank Lighthouse.

La Fibule (☎ 022 360641; Blvd de la Corniche, Phare El-Hank; meals around Dh250) Subtle lighting, warm colours and traditional décor give La Fibule a wonderfully inviting atmosphere. The food here is traditional Moroccan and Lebanese and is lovingly prepared and presented at low tables overlooking the ocean.

La Mer (☎ 022 363315; Blvd de la Corniche, Phare el-Hank; meals around Dh250) Right next door to La Fibule, and under the same management, this seafood restaurant is a more refined place with white linen and bone china replacing the ethnic vibe. The menu and

---

AUTHOR'S CHOICE

Café Maure (Map p89; ☎ 022 260960; Blvd des Almohades; mains Dh60-90; ☺ 10am-midnight, to 6pm in winter) Nestled in the ochre walls of the *sqala*, an 18th-century fortified bastion, this lovely restaurant is a tranquil escape from the city. Choose to sit in the rustic interior or the lovely garden surrounded by flower-draped trellises and enjoy the wonderfully relaxed atmosphere and friendly service. The menu favours seafood and salads, although meat dishes are also available, and the exotic fruit juices are simply sublime.

service is very French, bordering on stuffy, but the food is divine.

Mystic Garden (☎ 022 798877; 33 Blvd de la Corniche; Aïn Diab; mains Dh60-140; ✆ noon-3pm, 7pm-2am) Giant glass walls swathe this sleek, modern restaurant-cum-bar in light. It's an ultra cool hangout for Casa's well-heeled youth but the French and Asian fusion menu is well worth sampling. Dinner is accompanied by low-key sounds that morph into a full-on disco beat later in the evening, and for once on this strip the beer isn't astronomically priced.

Thai Gardens (☎ 022 797579; Ave de la Côte d'Emeraude, Anfa; meals Dh200) Slightly out of town in the affluent suburb of Anfa, but worth seeking out for its excellent Thai cuisine, this place is another top-notch option. The vast menu of Thai classics is a welcome break from Moroccan fare and makes a good choice for vegetarians.

A Ma Bretagne (☎ 022 362112; Sidi Abderrahman, Blvd de la Corniche; meals around Dh500; ✆ dinner only) Locally promoted as the best restaurant in Africa, this self-consciously cool establishment is all modern lines and masterclass food. Although seafood tops the bill here, you can opt for some other French delicacies, cooked by the *maître cuisinier* (master chef).

Cafés, Patisseries & Ice-cream Parlours

Pâtisserie de l'Opéra (Map p96; 50 Blvd du 11 Janvier; ✆ 6am-6pm Mon-Fri & 6am-1.30pm Sat & Sun) Drop in for breakfast and try getting by the counter at this bakery/café without giving in to one of the incredible cakes. It's a wonderfully relaxed place with a hidden seating area out the back.

Patisserie Bennis Habous (☎ 022 303025; 2 Rue Fkih el-Gabbas; ✆ 8am-8pm) One of the city's most famous and traditional patisseries, this place in the Quartier Habous is Casa's best spot for traditional Moroccan treats as well as made-to-order *pastillas*.

Palais des Glace (☎ 022 798013; Blvd de la Corniche, Aïn Diab; ✆ 7am-9pm) Famous across the city for its excellent ice cream, this is one of the city's oldest sweet-tooth stops, serving up delicious ice creams and sorbets for 125 years. Set across from the beach in Aïn Diab, it makes a glorious retreat on a fine day.

Hediard (☎ 022 797232; Résidence Jardin d'Anfa, Blvd Lido Route Côterie aïn Diab) Slick, new and popular with the young and beautiful, this café

in Aïn Diab serves a range of sumptuous cakes (Dh12 to Dh28) as well as light meals (Dh45 to Dh60) and deli-style sandwiches (Dh30 to Dh50).

Quick Eats

The best place for a quick, cheap meal is Rue Chaouia opposite the central market. The line of rotisseries, stalls and restaurants serving roast chicken, brochettes and sandwiches (Dh20 to Dh30) stays open until about 2am.

La Petite Perle (Map p96; ☎ 022 272849; 17-19 Ave Houmane el-Fetouaki; mains Dh22-45; ✆ 11.30am-3pm, 6-11pm) Popular with young professionals and a quiet break for women travelling alone, this spotless, modern café serves up a range of sandwiches, crêpes, pastas and pizzas as well as a great choice of breakfasts.

Epsom (Map p96; ☎ 022 220746; cnr Rue Tata & Mouftakar; mains Dh22-60) Almost always crowded and spilling customers onto the street-side seating, this friendly café serves a choice of grills and brochettes at bargain prices. It's a relaxed place with a very mixed clientele and hassle-free eating for women.

Snack Amine (Map p96; ☎ 022 541331; Rue Chaouia; mains Dh25-45; ✆ noon-2am) Tucked between the chicken rotisseries by the central market, Snack Amine serves up big plates of simple but tasty fried fish in a bright, rather soulless atmosphere.

Self-Catering

If you're planning a picnic on the beach, head for the **central market** (Map p96), which is located between Blvd Mohammed V and Rue Allah ben Abdellah. It's a fascinating place to just stroll and has a great selection of fresh produce and a couple of good delis.

DRINKING

Although there are plenty of classic French-style drinking dens in the centre of town, they are pretty much a male preserve and can be intimidating for women.

Cafés

Café Alba (Map p96; ☎ 022 227154; 59-61 Rue Indriss Lahrizi; ✆ 8am-1am) High ceilings, swish, modern furniture and subtle lighting mark this café out from the more traditional smoky joints around town. It's hassle-free downtime for women and a great place for watching Casa's up-and-coming.

Café Maure (Map p89; ☎ 022 260960; Blvd des Almohades; mains Dh60-80; ☒ 11am-1am) Another exception to the men-only rule, this lovely café is set behind the *sqala* (fortified bastion) in the medina wall. The flower-filled garden is quiet all afternoon and makes a great place for coffee or delicious juices.

Bars

Casablanca's bars can be pretty rough around the edges and generally attract a male-only clientele (plus prostitutes). In general, the bars in the larger hotels are more refined places to drink, especially for women.

La Bodéga (Map p96; ☎ 022 541842; 129 Rue Allah ben Abdellah; ☒ 12.30-3pm & 7pm-midnight) Hip, happening and loved by a mixed-aged group of Casablanca's finest, La Bodega is essentially a tapas bar where the music (everything from Salsa to Arabic pop) is loud and the alcohol flows freely. It's a fun place with a lively atmosphere and a packed dance floor after 10pm.

Petit Poucet (Map p96; Blvd Mohammed V; ☒ 9am-10pm) A die-hard relic of 1920s France, this strictly male-only bar was where Saint-Exupéry, the French author and aviator, used to spend time between mail flights across the Sahara. Today, the bar is pretty low key but is an authentic slice of old-time Casa life.

La Petite Roche (☎ 022 395748; Blvd de la Corniche, Phare El-Hank; ☒ 12.30-3pm & 7pm-midnight) With stunning views across to the Hassan II Mosque, this is another favourite Casa hangout. Littered with pillows thrown across low-level seating and lit by an army of candles, this place has a laid-back but exotic atmosphere. The clientele is not quite as self-consciously cool, or as unruly, as at La Bodéga and the restaurant downstairs serves good tapas, paella and seafood.

ENTERTAINMENT
Nightclubs

The beachfront suburb of Aïn Diab is the place to go for late-night drinking and dancing in Casa. However, hanging out with Casablanca's beautiful people for a night on the town doesn't come cheap. Expect to pay at least Dh100 to get in and as much again for drinks. Heavy-set bouncers guard the doors and practise tough crowd control – if you don't look the part, you won't be getting in.

The strip of disco joints along the beachfront ranges from cabaret-style bar-cum-restaurants such as **Balcon 33** (33 Blvd de la Corniche) to the pastel-coloured pop sensation **Candy Bar** (55 Blvd de la Corniche) and the catch-all **VIP club** (Rue des Dunes). **Joya** (☎ (10 Rue La Mer Jaune) and **Le Village** (11 Blvd de la Corniche) are two other popular haunts, the latter the only place with even a slightly gay-friendly atmosphere.

Other than Aïn Diab the only real options are the clubs at the large international hotels. They're pretty predictable places with little atmosphere but they attract plenty of business people and tourists. Try **Caesar** (Map p96; Hôtel Sheraton, 100 Ave des FAR) and **Black House** (Map p96; Hyatt Regency, Place des Nations Unies). Prostitutes work all of the clubs, men are always expected to pay for the drinks and women shouldn't expect hassle-free drinking anywhere.

Theatres

Complex Cultural Sidi Belyout (Map p96; 28 Rue Léon L'Africain; ☒ performances 9pm) This 200-seat theatre hosts plays (usually in Arabic) and the occasional music recital or dance performance. There is also a small exhibition space for paintings.

Cinema

Megarama (☎ 090 102020; www.megarama.info in French; Blvd de la Corniche; afternoon/evening shows Dh35/45) The plushest cinema in town, this huge new complex in Aïn Diab has four comfortable theatres that are usually packed.

Cinéma Lynx (Map p96; ☎ 022 220229; 50 Ave Mers Sultan; screen/balcony/std Dh30/35/55) A good option if you don't wish to trek out to Aïn Diab, this spacious and comfortable cinema has an excellent sound system.

Cinéma Rialto (Map p96; ☎ 022 487040; Rue Salah ben Bouchaib; Mon-Fri Dh25, Sat & Sun Dh30) This is a classic, cavernous Art Deco cinema with one theatre.

SHOPPING

Although not an artisan centre, Casablanca has a good choice of traditional crafts from around Morocco. The most pleasant place to shop is the picturesque Quartier Habous (p92), south of the centre. Merchants here do little to pressure you into their shops, so it's less of an ordeal than in other places.

However, the quality of crafts can be variable and hard bargaining is the order of the day.

If you'd rather avoid haggling altogether, head for the **Exposition Nationale d'Artisanat** (Map p96; ☎ 022 267064; 3 Ave Hassan II; ☒ 8.30am-12.30pm & 2.30-8pm), where you'll find three floors of high-quality, fixed-price crafts. For a good selection of traditional Arab and Berber music try **Disques GAM** (Map p96; ☎ 022 268954; 99 Rue Abderrahman Sehraoui) or **Le Comptoire Marocain de Distribution de Disques** (Map p96; ☎ 022 369153; 26 Ave Lalla Yacout).

GETTING THERE & AWAY
Air
Casablanca's **Mohammed V International Airport** (☎ 022 539040) is 30km southeast of the city on the Marrakesh road. Regular flights leave here for most countries in Western Europe, as well as to West Africa, Algeria, Tunisia, Egypt, the Middle East and North America. For a list of airlines with flights in and out of Casablanca see Transport (p469).

Internally, the vast majority of Royal Air Maroc's (RAM) flights go via Casablanca, so you can get to any destination directly from the city. For example, there are three to five flights daily to Agadir, Tangier and Ouarzazate.

Bus
The modern **CTM bus station** (Map p96; ☎ 022 541010; 23 Rue Léon L'Africain) is behind the Hôtel Farah. It's a pretty efficient place with a café and **left-luggage counter** (per 24hr Dh5; ☒ 6am-11.30pm). There are daily CTM departures to the following:

Destination (Dh)	Cost	Duration (hrs)	No of daily services
Agadir	160	9	10
El-Jadida	27	1½	6
Essaouira	120	7	3
Fès	90	5	12
Laâyoune	300	24	3
Marrakesh	70	4	9
Meknès	70	4	11
Rabat	25	1	11
Tangier	120	6	6
Taza	120	7½	6
Tetouan	120	7	3

There are also overnight buses to Ouarzazate (Dh135) and Er-Rachidia (Dh150) via Tinerhir, as well as one or two buses daily to Oujda (Dh170), Al-Hoceima (Dh150), Nador (Dh160), Taroudannt (Dh150) and Dakhla (Dh480). CTM also operates international buses to Belgium, France, Germany, Italy and Spain from Casablanca (see p474).

The modern **Gare Routière Ouled Ziane** (☎ 022 444470), 4km southeast of the centre, is the bus station for almost all non-CTM services. The main reason to trek out here is for services not covered by CTM, mainly Ouezzane (Dh50, nine daily) and Chefchaouen (Dh65, two daily). A taxi to the bus station will cost about Dh15, alternatively take bus No 10 from Blvd Mohammed V near the market.

Also on Route Ouled Ziane, but more than 1km closer to town, is the **SAT bus station** (☎ 022 444470). SAT runs national and international buses of a similar standard to CTM, but fares are slightly cheaper.

Car
Casablanca is littered with car rental agencies, many of them with offices around Ave des FAR, Blvd Mohammed V and at the airport.

Avis Casablanca (☎ 022 312424; 19 Ave des FAR); Mohammed V International Airport (☎ 022 539072)

Budget Casablanca (☎ 022 313124; Tours des Habous, Ave des FAR); Mohammed V International Airport (☎ 022 339157)

Europcar Casablanca (☎ 022 313737; Tours des Habous, Ave des FAR); Mohammed V International Airport (☎ 022 539161)

Hertz Casablanca (☎ 022 484710; 25 Rue el-Oraïbi Jilali); Mohammed V International Airport (☎ 022 339181)

National Casablanca (☎ 022 277141; 12 Rue el-Oraïbi Jilali); Mohammed V International Airport (☎ 022 539716)

Casablanca has horrendous parking problems and it's almost impossible to find a space in the city centre between 8am and 6pm. There is a guarded car park next to the British cemetery (per day/night Dh20) and another just off of Rue Tata (per hour Dh4).

The parking meters around the city centre charge Dh2 per hour (two hours maximum stay). They operate from 8am to noon and 2pm to 7pm daily, except on Sunday, public holidays and during festivals. Anywhere you park (except in a private lot), a guard will undoubtedly ask for a tip for watching your car. It is common practice to pay a few dirhams.

Taxi

Grands taxis to Rabat (Dh30), and some to Fès (Dh50 to Dh60), leave from Blvd Hassan Seghir, near the CTM bus station. However, the train is more convenient and comfortable.

Train

If your destination is on a train line, it's generally the best way to travel. Casablanca has five train stations, but only two are of interest to travellers.

All long-distance trains as well as trains to Mohammed V airport depart from **Casa-Voyageurs train station** (☎ 022 243818), 4km east of the city centre. Catch bus No 30 (Dh3.50), which runs along Blvd Mohammed V, or hop in a taxi and pay about Dh10 to get there.

Destinations include Marrakesh (Dh75.50, three hours, nine daily), Fès (Dh97, 4½ hours, nine daily) via Meknès (Dh81, 3½ hours), Oujda (Dh200, 10 hours, three daily) via Taza (Dh132.50, seven hours), Tangier (Dh117, 5¾ hours, three daily) and El-Jadida (Dh30, 1½ hours, five daily). For Safi (Dh85.50, 4½ hours, two daily) change at Benguérir.

The **Casa-Port train station** (Map p96; ☎ 022 223011) is a few hundred metres northeast of Place des Nations Unies. Although more convenient, trains from here only run to Rabat (Dh29.50, one hour) and Kenitra (Dh45).

GETTING AROUND
To/From the Airport

The easiest way to get from Mohammed V International Airport to Casablanca is by train (Dh30, 2nd class, 35 minutes). The trains are comfortable and reliable and they leave every hour from 6am to midnight. You can also continue to Rabat (Dh55) or Kenitra (Dh70), though you'll probably have a change of train at Casa-Voyageurs or Aïn Sebaa. The trains leave from below the ground floor of the airport terminal building.

From Casa-Voyageurs train station to the airport, trains go every hour from 5am to 10pm. A few additional trains go from Casa-Port.

A grand taxi between the airport and the city centre costs Dh250, though you

may be asked for Dh300 at unsocial hours. Some taxi drivers receive commissions if they bring clients to particular hotels. Know your destination before you get in and do not be persuaded to change it.

Bus

The local bus system is underfunded and very crowded; unless you're travelling alone and on a very limited budget a petit taxi is generally much easier. Buses cost Dh3.50 and stop at designated bus stops. The city bus system is about to be overhauled by French transport company RATP, the following routes are useful but numbers and routes may change in the restructure:

No 2 Blvd Mohammed V to Casa-Voyageurs train station.
No 4 Along Blvd de Paris and down Ave Lalla Yacout to Nouvelle Medina.
No 9 From Blvd d'Anfa to Aïn Diab and the beaches.
No 10 From Place de la Concorde, along Blvd Mohammed V to Gare Routière Ouled Ziane.
No 15 Northbound from Place Oued al-Makhazine to the Hassan II Mosque.
No 30 From Blvd Ziraoui to Casa-Voyageurs train station via Ave des FAR and Blvd Mohammed V.

Taxi

Casa's red petits taxis are excellent value and can generally get you to your destination far faster than any bus. You can hail one anywhere, or there's a petit taxi stand on Ave des FAR. The minimum fare is Dh7, but expect to pay Dh10 in or near the city centre. Most drivers use the meter without question, but if they refuse to, just get out of the cab. Prices rise by 50% after 8pm.

NORTH OF CASABLANCA

RABAT   الرباط
pop 1.7 million

Relaxed, well kept and very European, flag-waving Rabat is just as cosmopolitan as its economic big brother down the coast, but lacks the frantic pace and grimy feel of Casablanca. Its elegant tree-lined boulevards and imposing administrative buildings exude an unhurried, diplomatic kind of charm, making it a pleasant, if slightly pedestrian, place to visit.

However, this also makes it easy to negotiate and there's little of the hustle or hassle of the country's prime tourist centres about it. You'll be blissfully ignored on the streets and in the souqs, so you can discover the city's rich history at your own pace.

Although only the capital since 1956, Rabat was an important settlement in Phoenician, Roman, Almohad and Merenid times and the city is littered with interesting architectural remains. There is also a clutch of monuments and museums, and just across the estuary is the historic whitewashed city of Salé.

History

The fertile plains inland from Rabat drew settlers to the area as far back as the 8th century BC, but it was the Phoenicians and the Romans who successively took control of this section of the coast and set up outposts of their empires here.

The Roman settlement, Sala Colonia, was built along the river of the same name (today's Bou Regreg, the course of which has since altered), and like Volubilis, it lasted long after the empire's fall. It eventually became the seat of an independent Berber kingdom, but fell from favour during the first Moroccan dynasties and as its river port silted up, the town declined.

By the 10th century, the new town of Salé had sprung up on the north bank of the river. Its inhabitants, from the Zenata tribe, built a *ribat* (fortress-monastery) on the present site of Rabat's kasbah as a base for fighting a rival tribe south of the river.

The arrival of the Almohads in the 12th century saw the *ribat* rebuilt as a kasbah, a strategic jumping-off point for campaigns in Spain, where the dynasty was successfully returning Andalusia to Muslim rule.

Under Yacoub al-Mansour (the Victorious) Rabat enjoyed a brief heyday as the imperial capital, Ribat al-Fatah (Victory Fortress). Al-Mansour had extensive walls built, added the enormous Bab Oudaïa to the kasbah and began work on what was intended to be the greatest mosque in all of the Islamic West, if not in all of the Islamic world.

However, Al-Mansour's death in 1199 brought an end to these grandiose schemes, leaving the great Hassan Mosque (Le Tour Hassan) incomplete. The city soon lost all significance and it wasn't until the 17th century that Rabat's fortunes began to change.

As Muslim refugees arrived from Christian Spain, so did a band of Christian renegades, Moorish pirates, freebooters and multinational adventurers. Rabat and Salé became safe havens for the corsairs (merciless pirates whom English chroniclers called the Sallee Rovers) as they set about a brazen campaign.

The corsairs roved as far as the coast of America seeking Spanish gold, and to Cornwall, southern England, to capture Christian slave labour. The first Alawite sultans attempted to curtail their looting sprees, but no sultan ever really exercised control over the corsairs, who continued plundering European shipping until well into the 19th century.

Meanwhile, Sultan Mohammed ben Abdallah briefly made Rabat his capital at the end of the 18th century but the city soon fell back into obscurity. In 1956 France strategically abandoned the hornet's nest of political intrigue and unrest in the traditional capitals of Fès and Marrakesh, and opted to shift power to coastal Rabat, where supply and defence were more easily achieved. Since then, the city has remained the seat of government and home of the king.

Orientation

Ave Hassan II divides the medina from the ville nouvelle and follows the line of the medina walls to the Oued Bou Regreg. The river separates the twin cities of Rabat and Salé.

The city's main thoroughfare – the wide, palm-lined Ave Mohammed V – is where you'll find many hotels and the main administrative buildings. Most embassies cluster around Place Abraham Lincoln and Ave de Fès east of the centre; see Directory (p451) for addresses. Rabat Ville train station lies towards the southern end of Ave Mohammed V.

MAPS

Rabat is one of the few places where you can get a range of topographical Moroccan maps and town plans. The **Conservation & Topography Department** (☎ 037 708935; www .acfcc.gov.ma in French; Ave Hassan II; ⊗ 9-11.30am & 2.30-5.30pm Mon-Thu, 9-11am & 3-5.30pm Fri) houses a Cartography Division with a sales office. However, staff are sensitive about selling some maps; see p405.

The office is in a huge government complex 4km southwest of the city centre. To get there take bus No 52 from Ave Moulay Hassan towards the *gare routière* and get off at the Centre de Transfusion Sanguine. Turn right about 100m after the centre, and left after another 100m. The building (marked *Direction du Cardastre et de la Cartographie*) is 30m further on the right. The sales room is marked *Espace Carto*.

Information

BOOKSHOPS

American Bookshop (Map p106; cnr Rues Moulay Abdelhafid & Boujaad) A small but insightful collection of new books.

English Bookshop (Map p110; ☎ 037 706593; 7 Rue al-Yamama) Has second-hand English-language novels and magazines.

Librairie Kalila Wa Dimma (Map p110; ☎ 037 723106; 344 Ave Mohammed V) Carries a decent collection of trekking and travel guides (in French) to Morocco.

Librairie Livre Service (Map p110; ☎ 037 724495; 46 Ave Allal ben Abdallah; ⏱ 9am-noon & 3-8pm Mon-Sat) Among the best for Francophone readers; mainly aimed at students.

CULTURAL CENTRES

British Council (Map p110; ☎ 037 760836; www .britishcouncil.org.ma; 36 Rue Tanger; ⏱ 2-6pm Mon, 9.30am-12.15pm & 2.30-6pm Tue-Fri, 9.30am-1.45pm Sat) Offers a large library (with English papers) as well as a programme of lectures and exhibitions.

Goethe Institut (Map p110; ☎ 037 732650; www .goethe.de; 7 Rue Sana'a; ⏱ 10am-7pm Mon-Fri) Features a library, art and photography exhibitions and the cool Café Weimar (p114).

Instituto Cervantes (Map p110; ☎ 037 708738; 5 Zankat Madnine; ⏱ 9am-1pm & 3-6pm Mon-Fri)

Institut Français (Map p110; ☎ 037 701122; ifrabat@menara.ma; 2 Rue al-Yanboua; ⏱ 2.30-7pm Tue, 10am-noon Wed-Sat)

Instituto Italiano di Cultura (Map p106; ☎ 037 766826; 2 Ave Ahmed el-Yazidi; ⏱ 9am-noon Mon, Wed & Fri)

EMERGENCY

SAMU (☎ 037 737373) Private ambulance service.

SOS Médecins (☎ 037 202020; house call Dh310; ⏱ 24hr) Doctors on call.

INTERNET ACCESS

Librairie Livre Service (Map p110; ☎ 037 724495; 46 Ave Allal ben Abdallah; per hr Dh7; ⏱ 9am-noon & 3-8pm Mon-Sat)

Zerrad Net (Map p106; ☎ 037 686723; 68 Blvd al-Amir Fal Ould Omar, Agdal; per hr Dh8; ⏱ 8am-midnight)

LAUNDRY

Laverie Automatique (Map p106; ☎ 037 721869; 70 Blvd Fal Ould Ouemir; wash/dry per 7kg Dh27/18; ⏱ 9.30am-7.30pm)

MEDICAL SERVICES

Night Pharmacy (Map p110; Rue Moulay Rachid; ⏱ 9.30pm-7.30am) Town pharmacies open nights and weekends on a rotational basis; check the rota posted in French and Arabic in all pharmacy windows.

Polyclinique de Rabat (☎ 037 206161; 8 Rue de Tunis, Agdal)

MONEY

Numerous banks (with ATMs) are concentrated along Ave Mohammed V and the parallel Ave Allal ben Abdallah, including Banque Populaire.

BMCE (Map p110; Ave Mohammed V; ⏱ 8am-8pm Mon-Fri)

POST

DHL (Map p106; ☎ 037 779934; Ave de France, Agdal)

Main post office (Map p110; cnr Rue Soékarno & Ave Mohammed V)

TOURIST INFORMATION

Office National Marocain du Tourisme (ONMT; Map p106; ☎ 037 673756; visitmorocco@onmt.org.ma; cnr Rue Oued El Makhazine & Rue Zalaka, Agdal; ⏱ 8.30am-noon & 3-6.30pm Mon-Fri) Smiles and vacant faces await at this bureaucratic office. Take bus No 3 from the train station or take a taxi; the office is opposite 'Belle Vue' swimming pool.

TRAVEL AGENCIES

CAP Tours (Map p110; ☎ 037 733571; fax 037 731878; 7 Rue Damas) A good place for cheap flights to African destinations; also makes ferry reservations.

Carlson Wagonlit (Map p110; ☎ 037 709625; cwtrab@atlasnet.net.ma; 1 Ave Moulay Abdallah)

Sights
MEDINA

Rabat's walled medina (Map p110) is a rich mixture of spices, carpets, crafts, cheap shoes and bootlegged DVDs. It was built on an orderly grid in the 17th century and lacks a little of the more colourful character of the older medinas of the interior. However, it's a great place to roam with no aggressive selling and far more locals than tourists wandering the narrow streets.

ATLANTIC COAST

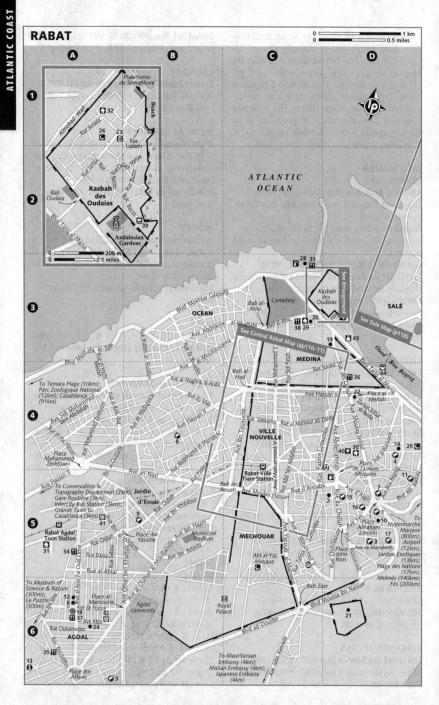

RABAT

INFORMATION			SIGHTS & ACTIVITIES			EATING 🍴		
Algerian Embassy	1	D5	Carpet Souq	19	D3	Borj Eddar	33	C3
American Bookshop	2	D5	Center for Cross-Cultural			Galapagos Café	34	A5
Belgian Embassy	3	D5	Learning	20	C3	Le Fuji	35	A6
British Embassy	4	D4	Chellah	21	D6	Le Ziryab	36	D4
Canadian Embassy	5	A6	Flea Market	22	D4	L'Entrecôte	37	A6
DHL	6	A6	Galérie d'Art Nouiga	23	A1	Restaurant de la Plage	(see 33)	
Dutch Embassy	7	D5	Institute for Language &			Restaurant Dinarjat	38	C3
French Consulate	8	B4	Communication Studies					
French Embassy	9	B5	(ICLS)	24	A6	DRINKING 🍷 🍸		
Instituto Italiano di			Le Tour Hassan	(see 25)		Café Maure	39	B2
Cultura	10	D5	Mausoleum of Mohammed V	25	D4	Le Purple	40	D4
Italian Embassy	11	D5	Mosque	26	A1			
Laverie			Musée des Oudaia	27	A2	ENTERTAINMENT 🎭		
Automatique	12	A6	Oudayas Surf Club	28	C3	5th Avenue	41	A5
ONMT	13	A6	Sala Colonia	(see 21)		XVIIéme	42	A6
Polyclinique de								
Rabat	14	D4	SLEEPING 🛏			SHOPPING 🛍		
Spanish Consulate	15	D5	Dar Al Batoul	29	C3	Ensemble Artisanal	43	D3
Tunisian Embassy	16	D5	Hôtel Yasmine	30	D4			
US Embassy	17	D5	Ibis Moussafir	31	A5	TRANSPORT		
Zerrad Net	18	A6	Riad Kasbah	32	A1	Rowboats to Salé	44	D4

The main market street is Rue Souika, which is lined with food and spice shops at the western end, then textiles and silverware as you head east. The **Souq as-Sebbat** (Jewellery Souq; Map p110) specialises in gaudy gold and begins roughly at Rue Bab Chellah. The **Grande Mosquée**, a 14th-century Merenid original much rebuilt in the intervening years, is just down this road to the right.

If you continue past the Rue des Consuls (so called because diplomats lived here until 1912), you'll come to the *mellah* where there is an interesting **flea market** (Map p106) which descends towards the river. Turning north along Rue des Consuls, you'll be surrounded by colourful carpets, leatherworks, *babouches* (leather slippers) and copper crafts. It's one of the more interesting areas of the medina for travellers, with many original diplomatic residencies still intact. After the **carpet souq** (Map p106) the street ends in an open area lined with craft shops, which was the setting for the slave auctions in the days of the Sallee Rovers. From here you can make your way up the hill to the kasbah.

KASBAH DES OUDAIAS
The **kasbah** (Map p106) occupies the oldest part of the city, the site of the original *ribat,* and commands powerful views over the river and ocean from its cliff-top perch. The kasbah is predominately residential and the narrow streets are lined with whitewashed houses – most of which were built by Mus-

lim refugees from Spain. It's a tranquil and picturesque place to wander and there's no need for a guide. Ignore anyone who advises you that the kasbah is 'forbidden'.

The most dramatic entry to the kasbah is through the enormous Almohad gate of **Bab Oudaia**, built in 1195. Its location, facing the heart of the city and just outside the original palace, made it more ceremonial than defensive and the gateway is elaborately decorated with a series of carved arches.

Inside the gateway, the main street, Rue Jamaa, runs straight through the kasbah. About 200m ahead on the left is the oldest **mosque** in Rabat, built in the 12th century and restored in the 18th. You'll also find a number of low-key tourist shops and a couple of art galleries, such as the **Galérie d'Art Nouiga**, along this street.

Opening out at the end of the street is a wide grassy area where the **Plateforme du Sémaphore** (Signal Platform) provides an incredible vista over the estuary and across to Salé. The elevated position provided an excellent defence against seagoing attackers negotiating the sandbanks below.

Returning from the Plateforme turn left down Rue Bazzo, a narrow winding street that leads down to the popular Café Maure (p114) and a side entrance to the formal **Andalusian Gardens** (☉ sunrise-sunset). The gardens, laid out by the French during the colonial period, occupy the palace grounds and make a wonderful shady retreat, popular with groups of Moroccan women.

The palace itself is a grand 17th-century affair built by Moulay Ismail. The building later became a *medersa*, and now houses the **Musée des Oudaia** (Map106; ☎ 037 731537; admission Dh10; ⊗ 9am-noon & 3-5pm Oct-Apr, to 6pm May-Sep), which exhibits an interesting collection of traditional musical instruments, clothing, ceramics and jewellery. The collections are on display in the reception rooms around the central courtyard but you can also visit the original palace hammam and mosque.

LE TOUR HASSAN & MAUSOLEUM OF MOHAMMED V

Towering above Oued Bou Regreg is Rabat's most famous landmark, **Le Tour Hassan** (Hassan Tower, Map p106). This enormous minaret was begun by the Almohad sultan Yacoub al-Mansour in 1195 and was intended to reach 60m, making it the largest and highest in the Muslim world. However, the sultan's grand plans were thwarted by his death four years later, and the tower was never completed. Abandoned at 44m, the beautifully designed and intricately carved tower still lords over the remains of the adjacent mosque. The mosque was destroyed by an earthquake in 1755, and today only a forest of shattered pillars testifies to the grandiosity of Al-Mansour's plans.

The cool marble **Mausoleum of Mohammed V** (Map p106; admission free; ⊗ sunrise-sunset), built in traditional Moroccan style, lies opposite the tower. The present king's father (the late Hassan II) and grandfather have been laid to rest here, surrounded by intensely patterned *zellij* mosaics from floor to ceiling. Visitors to the mausoleum must be respectfully dressed and can look down into the tomb from a gallery.

CHELLAH

Abandoned, crumbling and overgrown, the ancient Roman city of **Sala Colonia** and the Merenid necropolis of **Chellah** (Map106; cnr Ave Yacoub al-Mansour & Blvd Moussa ibn Nassair; admission adults/children Dh10/3; ⊗ 9am-5.30pm) are among Rabat's most peaceful and evocative sights.

The first people to settle on the grassy slopes above the river were the Phoenicians, but the town grew when the Romans took control in about AD40. The thriving city was one of the last remaining outposts of the Empire but it eventually fell to Berber rule. The city was abandoned in 1154 in favour of Salé but in the 14th century the Merenid sultan Abou al-Hassan Ali built a necropolis on top of the Roman site and surrounded it with the towers and defensive wall and that stand today.

The site is an extremely tranquil place to roam, its ruins overgrown by fruit trees and wild flowers. From the main gate, a path heads down through fragrant fig, olive and orange trees to a **viewing platform**, which overlooks the ruins of the Roman city. Making out the structures takes a bit of imagination, but the mystery is part of the magic of this place. A paths leads through the ruined remains of the triple-arched entrance known as the Arc de Triomphe, past the Jupiter Temple (to the left) and to the forum (at the end of the main road), while another goes to the octagonal Pool of the Nymph, part of the Roman system of water distribution.

Far easier to discern are the remains of the **Islamic complex**, with its elegant minaret now topped by a stork's nest. An incredible colony of storks has taken over the ruins, lording over the site from their tree-top nests. If you visit in spring, the clacking bills of the mating couples is a wonderful soundtrack to a visit.

Near the ruined minaret is the tomb of Abou al-Hassan Ali and his wife, complete with ornate *zellij* ornamentation. A small *medersa* is nearby, where the remains of pillars, students' cells and scalloped pools – as well as the blocked-off mihrab (prayer niche) – are still discernable.

As you leave the mosque complex, the path passes the **tombs** of several saints on the far right. To the left, the murky waters of a walled pool (marked 'bassin aux anguilles') still attract women who believe that feeding boiled eggs to the eels here brings fertility and easy childbirth.

ARCHAEOLOGY MUSEUM

Dusty and underfunded but fascinating to visit, the **Archaeology Museum** (Map p110; ☎ 037 701919; 23 Rue al-Brihi Parent; admission Dh10; ⊗ 9am-4.30pm Wed-Mon) gives a wonderful account of Morocco's ancient history.

Exhibits date back 350,000 years to the Stone Age and include artefacts from the oldest known civilisations. The highlight of the collection is the **Salle des Bronzes**, which displays ceramics, statuary and artefacts from the Roman settlements at Volubilis, Lixus and Chellah. Look out for the beautiful head of Juba II and the unforgiving realism of the bust of Cato the Younger – both found at Volubilis.

MUSEUM OF SCIENCE & NATURE
Squirreled away in the government administrative buildings is the **Museum of Science & Nature** (☎ 037 688705; Ministère l'Energie et des Mines, Rue Abou Marouane, Agdal; admission free; ☽ 8am-noon & 2.30-6.30pm Mon-Fri). The museum explains the history of the earth's geology but is most noted for the reconstructed skeleton of the giant dinosaur *Atlasaurus imelakei* (Giant Lizard of the Atlas) found in the High Atlas in 1979. The massive beast measured 15m long and roamed the earth 165 million years ago.

Activities
SURFING
You'll be in regal company at the **Oudayas Surf Club** (Map p106; ☎ 037 260683; fax 037 260684; 3 Plage des Oudayas; 90-min lesson surfboard/bodyboard Dh120/90, insurance Dh70) below the kasbah, where the king was a founding member. The club offers surf and body-boarding lessons on the beach in front of the club house, and tuition for more advanced learners at **Temara Plage**, 13km south of Rabat. Equipment is included in the price of lessons or is available for hire on its own.

Courses
LANGUAGE
Rabat is full of language schools but many only offer semester-long courses. The following schools offer short-term classes suitable for travellers.
Center for Cross-Cultural Learning (CCCL; Map p106; ☎ 037 202365; www.cccl-ma.com; Ave Laalou, 11 Zankat Hassani) Offers three-, six- and 12-week courses in classical Arabic, Moroccan Arabic and (in theory) Tamazight Berber, as well as special programmes for children.
Institute for Language & Communication Studies (Map p106; ☎ 037 675968; www.ilcs.ac.ma; 29 Rue Oukaimeden, Agdal) Offers intensive 60-hour courses as well as private tuition in French, Arabic and Moroccan Arabic.

Festivals & Events
Rabat hosts a number of festivals and events each year, including the **International Moroccan Music Competition** in March and the popular **Oudayas Jazz Festival** held in the last weekend of May. The biggest drawcard is the **Festival International de Rabat**, which attracts hoards of music lovers and film buffs to the capital for two weeks each summer. Big-name musical acts from all over Africa descend upon the city in late June and early July, and there are also traditional theatre performances and an annual film festival.

Rabat for Children
Hassle-free shopping in the souqs and the impressive kasbah make Rabat a pleasant place to visit with children. However, there are few specific attractions in the city for younger visitors. The best bet is to head out of town to the Parc Zoologique National (p120) and the Jardins Exotiques (p119) for child-size fun.

Sleeping
Most of Rabat's better accommodation options are in the nouvelle medina between Ave Mohammed V and Ave Abderrahman, while the old medina has a host of low-budget dives and a couple of upmarket riads. Rabat caters mainly for business travellers and has a disproportionate number of top-end hotels.

BUDGET
Although the medina is full of budget hotels, they're pretty basic and many lack any kind of creature comfort, including showers. The best medina options are listed here, otherwise pay the extra and head for the ville nouvelle.
Hôtel Splendid (Map p110; ☎ 037 723283; 8 Rue Ghazza; s/d Dh104/159, with bathroom Dh128/187) Slapbang in the heart of town, this hotel has spacious, bright rooms with high ceilings, big windows, cheerful colours and simple wooden furniture. Bathrooms are new and even rooms without bathrooms have a hot-water washbasin. The hotel is set around a pleasant courtyard with the quietest rooms facing inwards.
Hôtel Majestic (Map p110; ☎ 037 722997; www.hotelmajestic.ma; 121 Ave Hassan II; s/d Dh239/279) Another excellent option, though not as palatial as it sounds, this wonderfully modern place has bright rooms with sleek, new furniture and fittings. Some of the compact rooms overlook the medina and can

ATLANTIC COAST

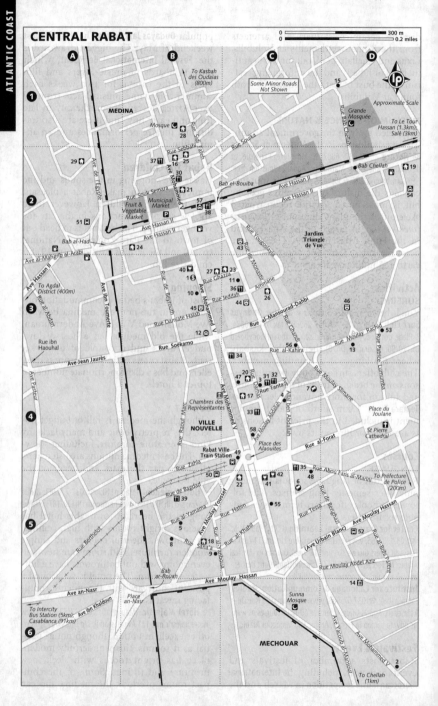

CENTRAL RABAT

0   300 m
0   0.2 miles

MEDINA

To Kasbah
des Oudaias
(800m)

Some Minor Roads
Not Shown

Approximate Scale

To Le Tour
Hassan (1.3km);
Salé (3km)

Grande
Mosquée

Rue Bab Chellah

Bab Chellah

Mosque
28

Rue Sidi Fateh

Rue Souika

29

Ave de l'Egypte

37   16   25
           30
           21

Rue Sebbahi

Rue Souk Semara

Fruit &
Vegetable
Market

Municipal
Market

57
38

Bab el-Bouiba

Ave Hassan II

Ave Hassan II

51

Ave Hassan II

Jardins
Triangle
de Vue

54

19

24

Ave Hassan II

Bab al-Had

Ave al-Maghrib al-Arabi

Ave Hassan II

To Agdal
District (400m)

Ave al-Abdari

40   27 23
   1   11
10   Rue Ghazza

Rue de Beyrouth

Rue de Monastir

Rue Youssoufeyia

43

Rue ibn
Haouhal

Ave Ibn Tournerte

45
Rue Damiate Halab
12

Rue Jeddah
44

36
26

Anninane

46

Rue al-Mansourad-Dahbi

Rue Chand

53
13

Rue Moulay Rachid

Rue Patrice Lumumba

Ave Jean Jaurès

Rue Soekarno

34

56
Rue al-Kahira

Ave Pasteur

47
20

3 31 32
17

Rue Tantan

7

Rue Moulay Slimane

Place du
Joulane

Ave Mohammed V

Chambres des
Représentants

33

58

Rue Mairi

**VILLE
NOUVELLE**

Allal ben Abdallah

Rue Moulay Abdallah

Place des
Alaouites

Rue al-Forat

St Pierre
Cathedral

St Pierre
Cathedral

Rabat Ville
Train Station

49

35
Rue Abou Faris al-Marini

To Préfecture
de Police
(200m)

Rue Zahla

50

22

42
41   48
6

Ave Mohammed V

Rue de Bagdad

39

Rue al-Yamama

Rue Hatim

5

Rue Tessa

Rue Berghazi

55

Rue Berthelot

8
18
9

Rue al-Sana'a

Rue Jamboia

Rue al-Khatib

Ave Moulay Youssef

Ave Moulay Hassan
(Ave Urbain Blanc)

52

Rue al-Bith Bayern

Rue Moulay Abdel Aziz

To Intercity
Bus Station (5km);
Casablanca (91km)

Bab
at-Rouah

Place
an-Nasr

Ave an-Nasr

Ave Ibn Khaldoun

Ave Moulay Hassan

14

Sunna
Mosque

Ave Yacoub al-Mansour

MECHOUAR

2

Ave Mohammed V

To Chellah
(1km)

15

be noisy, so it's best to forego the view and ask for a room at the back of the building.

Hôtel d'Orsay (Map p110; ☎ 037 701319; fax 037 708208; 11 Ave Moulay Youssef; s/d Dh211/264) Right by the train station and handy for late arrivals, this friendly hotel has 30 comfortable, bright rooms decorated with faded and curling tourist-board posters. All rooms have en suites, TVs and telephones. The rooms on the upper floors have balconies but overlook a noisy street.

Hôtel Dorhmi (Map p110; ☎ 037 723898; 313 Ave Mohammed V; s/d Dh80/120, hot showers Dh10) Immaculately kept, very friendly and keenly priced, this family-run hotel is the best of the medina options. The simple rooms are bright and tidy and surround a central courtyard on the first floor above the Banque Populaire.

Hôtel al-Maghrib al-Jadid (Map p110; ☎ 037 732207; 2 Rue Sebbahi; s/d Dh60/100, hot showers Dh7.50) Although the rooms at this hotel are fairly small and spartan, they are pristinely clean, and have shuttered windows that let in lots of light. You'll either love or hate the shocking pink walls but it's all part of the rather quirky character of this place. The friendly owners also run the identically styled and priced **Hotel Marrakech** (Map p110; ☎ 037 727703; 10 Rue Sebbahi) just down the road.

Hôtel la Paix (Map p110; ☎ 037 732031; 2 Rue Ghazza; s/d/tr Dh150/200/230) Big rooms with high ceilings and shuttered windows give an illusion of colonial-era grandeur at this once-charming hotel. The rooms are now a little faded and the bathrooms, though clean, could do with an overhaul.

Hotel Central (Map p110; ☎ 037 707356; 2 Rue Al-Basra; s/d 90/130, with bathrooms Dh120/170, hot showers Dh10) Opposite the imposing Balima and right in the heart of town, the Hotel Central has a good-value range of simple rooms. It's all a little past its best but remains a friendly place handy for everything in town.

Youth Hostel (Map p110; ☎ 037 725769; 43 Rue Marassa; dm HI members/non-members Dh45/50, hot showers Dh5; ☻ 8am-10.30pm, closed 10am-noon & 3-6.30pm Oct-Apr) Centred round a bright, traditional courtyard, this 48-bed youth hostel has plenty of rustic character but pretty basic facilities. The dorms are dark and dingy and the toilets are pretty grotty. Hot water is intermittent.

CAMPING
Camping de la Plage (Map p118; camping adult/child under 12 Dh15/8, plus per small tent/car/camper Dh18/15/30, power & water Dh15) Across the estuary by the beach in Salé, this walled camp site offers basic facilities and 24-hour security but little shade. A hot shower costs Dh10. Follow the signs from the bridge over the Oued Bou Regreg.

MIDRANGE

Rabat has a limited choice of midrange accommodation, most of it located on or just off Ave Mohammed V.

Hôtel Royal (Map p110; ☎ 037 721171; royal hotel@mtds.com; 1 Rue Jeddah Ammane; s/d Dh350/400) One of the best value choices in this price bracket, the Royal's tastefully renovated rooms are very comfortable, with polished wooden furniture and sparkling new bathrooms. Each has a balcony overlooking the park or street. Look out for the ancient telephone switchboard at reception.

Hôtel Yasmine (Map p110; ☎ 037 722018; fax 037 722100; cnr Zankat Marinyne & Mekka; s/d 359/467) Strong on traditional Moroccan style and popular with local business travellers, the public areas of this seemingly elegant hotel are all marble floors, *zellij* and leather furniture. The bedrooms are more mundane but they are tasteful and comfortable.

Hôtel Bouregreg (Map p110; ☎ 037 720445; fax 037 734002; cnr Rue Nador & Ave Hassan II; s/d Dh355/523; ✱) The Bouregreg has a range of rooms in dubious style veering from newly renovated fuddy-duddy to over-the-hill naff. Nevertheless, rooms are large and comfortable – if floral patterns, shiny fabrics and swag curtains don't put you off, it's a good deal. Bathrooms in the older rooms are in need of an overhaul.

Hôtel Balima (Map p110; ☎ 037 707755; fax 037 707 450; Ave Mohammed V; s/d Dh418/536) The grand dame of Rabat hotels has seen better days but slowly the rooms here are being renovated. Ask for a newer room or be prepared to put up with the time-warp furniture and fabrics. The hotel has a decent restaurant and nightclub and a glorious shady terrace facing Ave Mohammed V.

Hôtel Bélère (Map p110; ☎ 037 203301; fax 037 709801; 33 Ave Moulay Youssef; s/d Dh674/882; ✱ 🖳 🕸) This four-star hotel is a step up from the other options in this price range and offers small but extremely comfortable nonsmoking rooms with tasteful décor. It has a refined bar and restaurant and it's handy for the train station.

Ibis Moussafir (Map p106; ☎ 037 774919; fax 037 774903; 32-34 Rue Abderrahmanne El Ghafiki, Place de la Gare, Agdal; s/d Dh474/548; ✱) A reliable fall-back option, the Ibis has small, modern rooms with en suite bathroom and satellite TV. It's hardly loaded with character but offers consistent standards and friendly service.

TOP END

Rabat offers all the usual top international chain hotels but for something with a little more local flavour the options below offer ultra-chic style and service and a glimpse of the mystique of historic Rabat.

Riad Oudaya (Map p110; ☎ 037 702392; www .riadoudaya.com; 46 Rue Sidi Fateh; r/ste Dh1350/1650) Tucked away down an alleyway in the medina, this gorgeous guesthouse is a real hidden gem. The rooms are beautifully decorated with a wonderful blend of Moroccan style and Western comfort. Subtle lighting, open fires, balconies and the gentle gurgling of the fountain in the tiled courtyard below complete the romantic appeal. Meals here are sublime (see opposite).

Dar Al Batoul (Map p106; ☎ 037 727250; albatoul@menara.ma; 7 Derb Jirari; B&B d Dh1100) This 18th-century merchant's house has been transformed into a sumptuous small hotel with just eight beautiful rooms. Centred around a graceful columned courtyard and with each room individually styled, they are stunning combinations of rich fabrics, stained glass and intricate tile work. You might never want to leave.

Riad Kasbah (Map p106; ☎ 037 705247; www.riad oudaya.com; 49 Rue Zirara; s/d incl breakfast Dh880/980) Set in the heart of the kasbah away from the hubbub of the city, this sublimely peaceful guesthouse is a sister property to the Riad Oudaya. Although it's not quite as luxurious as Riad Oudaya this beautiful house has six rooms with elegant traditional décor and carved wooden doors.

Eating

Rabat has a wonderful choice of restaurants from cheap and cheerful hole-in-the-walls serving traditional tajines and couscous, to upmarket gourmet pads feeding the legions of politicians, dignitaries and visiting officials who come to the capital. Most of the more expensive restaurants are located in Rabat's affluent suburbs.

RESTAURANTS
Medina
Restaurant el-Bahia (Map p110; ☎ 037 734504; Ave Hassan II; mains Dh40-70; ☉ 6am-midnight, close 10.30pm in winter) Built into the outside of the medina walls and an excellent spot for people-watching, this laidback restaurant has the locals lapping up hearty Moroccan

fare. Choose to sit in the pavement terrace, in the shaded courtyard or upstairs in the traditional salon.

Restaurant de la Libération (Map p110; 256 Ave Mohammed V; mains Dh29) Cheap, cheerful and marginally more classy than the string of other eateries along this road (it's got plastic menus and tablecloths), this basic restaurant does a steady line in traditional favourites. Friday is couscous day when giant platters of the stuff are delivered to the eager masses.

Café de la Jeunesse (Map p110; 305 Ave Mohammed V; meals Dh20-30) Just down the road from the Libération and more a large hole-in-the-wall than a proper sit-down affair, this basic place is great for brochettes, sandwiches and tajines.

Le Ziryab (Map p106; ☎ 037 733636; 10 Zankat Ennajar; mains Dh90-140) This chic Moroccan restaurant is in a magnificent building just off Rue des Consuls. The blend of old world character and stylish contemporary design is also reflected in the excellent menu of interesting variations on tajine, couscous, *pastilla* and grilled meat and fish.

Riad Oudaya (Map p110; ☎ 037 702392; 46 Rue Sidi Fateh; lunch/dinner Dh220/330) This lovely restaurant squirreled away behind a wooden door in the depths of the medina is reason enough to come to Rabat. Set in a gorgeous riad, it dishes up gourmet five-course dinners featuring anything from juicy tajines or *pastilla* to stuffed calamari.

Restaurant Dinarjat (Map p106; ☎ 037 724239; 6 Rue Belgnaoui; mains around Dh150, bottle wine Dh80) A favourite with locals and visitors alike, this traditional Moroccan restaurant is set in a 17th-century house at the heart of the medina. It's wildly fanciful with Andalusian-style palace décor and belly dancers sashaying across the lush carpets. The food is traditional Moroccan with local specialities like *pastilla* on the menu. Book in advance.

Ville Nouvelle

La Mamma (Map p110; ☎ 037 707329; 6 Rue Tanta; mains Dh78-100) It doesn't look too much from the outside, but this modest little place serves some of the best pizza and pasta in town. The beamed ceilings and candlelit tables add a touch of romantic atmosphere and the wood-fired pizzas and grilled meats will leave you planning a return visit.

Tajine wa Tanja (Map p110; ☎ 037 729797; 9 Rue de Baghdad; mains Dh60-90; closed Sun) Down-to-earth Moroccan dishes are the speciality at this small, friendly restaurant near the train station. Choose from a range of wood-fired grills or tajines prepared to traditional recipes or make a special outing for the magnificent Friday couscous. It's a fairly quiet spot, and not so intimidating for women travelling alone.

Le Grand Comptoir (Map p110; ☎ 037 201514; 279 Ave Mohammed V; mains Dh95-135) Sleek, stylish and oozing the charms of an old-world Parisienne brasserie, this suave new restaurant and bar is wooing customers with its chic surroundings and classic French menu. Candelabras, giant palms and plenty of gilt mirrors adorn the grand salon while a pianist tinkles in the background. Go for the succulent steaks or be brave and try the *andouillette* (tripe sausage) or veal kidneys.

Le Petit Beur – Dar Tajine (Map p110; ☎ 037 731322; 8 Rue Damas; tajines Dh84, pastilla Dh66; closed Sun) This modest little place is renowned for its excellent Moroccan food, from succulent tajines to one of the best *pastillas* in town. It's a little sombre at lunchtime but livens up at night when the waiters double as musicians and play oud music to accompany your meal.

Outside the Centre

Le Fuji (Map p106; ☎ 037 673583; 2 Ave Mischliffen, Agdal; mains Dh80-120; closed Tues & Wed lunch) Simple, pared-back design and authentic Japanese dishes make this tranquil place a welcome break from the fanfare and traditional menus of other Rabat restaurants. Go for delicious sushi, sashimi or tempura or fill up on one of the colourful bento boxes. A good option for vegetarians.

L'Entrecôte (Map p106; ☎ 037 671108; 74 Blvd al-Amir Fal Ould Omar, Agdal; mains around Dh130) The menu and attitude at this upmarket restaurant in Agdal are very French but the dark woods and rough plaster are more reminiscent of Bavaria than Bordeaux. Steak, fish and game specialities dominate the classic French menu and to further confuse the ambience there's jazz or traditional Spanish music by night.

Restaurant de la Plage (Map p106; ☎ 037 202928; mains from Dh110) Overlooking the wide, sandy beach below the kasbah, this place specialises in fresh grilled fish and seafood.

Borj Eddar (Map p106; ☎ 037 701500; mains from Dh110; ☺ closed Oct-Apr) Alongside the Restaurant de la Plage, Borj Eddar serves a similar menu of seafood and grilled fish. There's little to choose between them: both have glass-fronted terraces overlooking the ocean.

CAFÉS, PATISSERIES & ICE-CREAM PARLOURS

Café Weimar (Map p110; ☎ 037 732650; 7 Rue Sana'a; pizza Dh55) This hip café in the Goethe Institut is where the young and beautiful hang out for cake and coffee. It also does a simple Mediterranean menu and is a good spot for Sunday brunch.

Pâtisserie Lina (Map p110; ☎ 037 707291; 45 Ave Allal ben Abdallah; ☺ 6.30am-9.25pm) Mountainous cakes in elaborate guises adorn the window displays at this traditional French patisserie. Come for breakfast and you may find yourself returning for an afternoon sugar fix just so you can try some more of the tantalising gateaux on display.

Pâtisserie Majestic (Map p110; cnr Rue Jeddah Ammane & Ave Allal ben Abdallah) There's slightly less fanfare at this patisserie but the cakes are just as good. It is conveniently located in the centre of town.

La Dolce Vita (Map p110; ☎ 037 707329; Rue Tanta; cones/tubs Dh7/12; ☺ 7.30am-1am) The Italian owners of La Mamma restaurant in Ville Nouvelle have expanded their empire to include this tiny, but oh-so-delectable, ice-cream parlour next door. Over 40 flavours of traditional, home-made Italian gelato are on offer, all of them rich, creamy and cold.

Galapagos Café (Map p106; ☎ 037 686879; 14 Blvd al-Amir Fal Ould Omar; snacks Dh25-45) This slick café with dark wood panelling, sleek contemporary furniture and floor-to-ceiling windows makes a good stop in Agdal. It's popular with young professionals for its ice cream, crêpes, panini, pizza and people-watching.

QUICK EATS

The best place for quick, cheap food in Rabat is on Ave Mohammed V just inside the medina gate. Here you'll find a slew of hole-in-the-wall joints dishing out tajines, brochettes, salads and chips for cheap and cheaper. You'll know the best ones by the queue of locals waiting patiently to be served.

Another good spot is around Rue Tanta in the ville nouvelle, where you'll find a selection of fast food joints serving everything from burgers and brochettes to pizza and panini.

SELF-CATERING

The medina is the best place to go for self-catering supplies. The indoor **fruit and vegetable market** (Map p110; Ave Hassan II) has a fantastic choice of fresh produce, dried fruits and nuts. You should be able to find everything else you need (including booze) at the surrounding stalls or along Rue Souika and near Bab el-Bouiba.

You'll find Western foodstuffs at the **Hypermarché Marjane** (☺ 7am-7pm) on the road to Salé.

Drinking

CAFÉS

Café Maure (Map p106; Kasbah des Oudaias; ☺ 9am-5.30pm) Sit back, relax and just gaze out over the estuary to Salé from this chilled little open-air café near the Andalusian Gardens. Mint tea is the thing here, accompanied by little almond biscuits delivered on silver trays. It's an easy place to pass time writing postcards and a relaxed venue for women.

Cafetéria du 7ème Art (Map p110; ☎ 037 733887; Ave Allal ben Abdallah) Set in the shady grounds of a cinema (opposite), this popular outdoor café attracts a mixed clientele of students and professionals. It's a relaxed place but the noise of passing traffic makes it less tranquil than the Café Maure.

BARS

Most Rabat bars are pretty intimidating for women but the more modern, popular joints are a safer bet for female travellers.

Le Purple (Map p106; ☎ 037 733680; 14 Rue Mekka; ☺ 7.30pm-1am) Slick, contemporary style, designer furniture and bright, sultry colours make this hip bar one of the hottest spots in the centre of town. It's a hang-out for the young and the beautiful and hosts a lively karaoke night on Sundays.

Le Puzzle (☎ 037 670030; 79 Ave ibn Sina, Agdal; bottle of beer Dh35; ☺ 7.30pm-1am, closed Sun lunch) Another hip-and-happening place is this bar and restaurant in Agdal, a favourite haunt of the suburban sophisticates. It's got a strange mix of traditional style and modern design but pulls in the punters with karaoke, live music and half-price beer.

Pachanga (Map p110; ☎ 037 262931; 10 Place des Alaouites; mains Dh80-100, bottle of beer Dh40-

50; ☺ 7.30pm-1am) This restaurant-bar is a strangely popular place with a canary-yellow colour scheme and cabaret-style setting. It's frequented by Rabat's in-crowd and has more of the ubiquitous karaoke on Tuesday, Thursday and Sunday nights.

Hôtel Balima (Map p110; ☎ 037 707755; Ave Mohammed V; ☺ 8am-11pm) Less self-conscious than the chic town bars and an excellent place to watch Rabat go by, the leafy terrace in front of the Balima is a great place to just see and be seen. It's a relaxed place for women and pleasantly cool on summer nights.

If you're in search of old-time local haunts rather than squeaky clean trend setters, try **Henry's Bar** (Map p110; Place des Alaouites) or **Bar de L'Alsace** (Map p110; Ave Mohammed V), both staunch male-only preserves where the smoke is thick and the alcohol neat. These two are open all day but close by about 10pm.

Entertainment

Rabat has a large international community and plenty of young, well-heeled and well-educated locals looking for entertainment so there's usually a good choice of events on offer. Check the French-language newspapers for listings.

NIGHTCLUBS

Rabat's nightlife is a lot more limited – and subdued – than Casablanca's but there's still a fairly good range of clubs to choose from. All the large hotels have their own discos, usually fairly standard fare, and there's a few try-hard theme clubs where you need plenty of booze to numb the décor. Expect to pay about Dh100 to get in and the same for drinks, and dress up or you won't even make it past the door.

Amnesia (Map p110; ☎ 037 701860; 18 Rue de Monastir; admission Mon-Fri Dh80, Sat & Sun Dh100, women free) The most popular club in downtown Rabat, this American-themed place (complete with a diner-style backroom) buzzes most nights of the week. The music is pretty standard chart pop but the young socialites who come here just lap it up.

XVIème (Map p106; ☎ 037 774844; 12 Ave Atlas, Agdal; cover Dh100-150) More upmarket, more stylish and more expensive, this urbane club in Agdal even requires reservations in advance. Rabat's finest socialities come here safe in the knowledge that the bouncers are intent on keeping out the riffraff. Put on

your fanciest clothes and visit an ATM before joining the queue at the door.

5th Avenue (Map p106; ☎ 037 775254; 4 Rue Bin al-Widane, Agdal; cover Dh100; ☺ Sat & Sun until 5am) Another American-themed bar, this one styled on a Moroccan impression of New York, it plays a better range of music than the others and features everything from hip-hop to techno to Middle Eastern.

CINEMA & THEATRE

Cinéma Renaissance (Map p110; ☎ 037 722168; Ave Mohammed V; orchestra/balcony Dh25/30) This large cinema complex on the main drag shows mainstream Hollywood flicks.

Cinéma du 7ème Art (Map p110; ☎ 037 733887; Ave Allal ben Abdallah; admission Dh15) A good bet for more local offerings and art-house films, this cinema shows mainly Moroccan, Middle Eastern and European films.

Théâtre Mohammed V (Map p110; ☎ 037 707300; Rue Moulay Rachid) Rabat's most prominent theatre hosts a wide variety of performances, from classical music and dance to the occasional light-hearted play (usually in Arabic).

Shopping

Rabat's great shopping secret is that the merchants here usually don't bother with the hard-sell tactics of their counterparts in more popular tourist towns. There's little pressure to buy, so you can stroll the stalls in relative peace, taking your time to choose crafts or gifts without feeling hustled or hassled. However, be aware that this also means there's less room for manoeuvre on price.

Rabat was traditionally an artisan centre and a wide range of handicrafts are still practised here, so the choice and quality of goods is generally high. Rue des Consuls in the medina is the best place to go, with more offerings along Blvd Tariq al-Marsa towards the kasbah. You'll find everything in this area from jewellery, silks and pottery to *zellij* and carved wooden furniture.

Weaving was one of the most important traditional crafts in Rabat, and the more formal, Islamic style (see p60) is still favoured. On Tuesday and Thursday mornings women descend from the villages to auction their carpets to local salesmen at the carpet souq off Rue des Consuls. Although tourists are not normally allowed in on the action, if you can begin negotiations you'll probably end up with a bargain.

For more formal shopping head to the **Ensemble Artisanal** (Map p106; ☎ 037 730507; Blvd Tariq al-Marsa; ◷ 9am-noon & 2.30-6.30pm), which sells a variety of carpets, pottery and furniture at fixed prices. For ceramics, your best bet is to head across to Salé to the Complexe des Potiers (p119).

Getting There & Away

AIR

Tiny **Rabat-Salé Airport** (☎ 037 808090), 10km northeast of town, has direct flights to Paris with **Royal Air Maroc** (RAM; Map p110; ☎ 037 709766; fax 037 723516; Ave Mohammed V) and **Air France** (Map p110; ☎ 037 707066; Ave Mohammed V). A grand taxi to the airport will cost about Dh100.

BUS

Rabat has two bus stations – the main **gare routière** (☎ 037 795816) where most buses depart and arrive and the less chaotic **CTM station** (☎ 037 281488). Both are inconveniently situated about 5km southwest of the city centre on the road to Casablanca. The main station has a **left-luggage service** (per item per day Dh5; ◷ 6am-11pm). To get to the town centre from either station, take bus No 30 (Dh3) or a petit taxi (Dh15).

Arriving by bus from the north, you may pass through central Rabat, so it's worth asking if you can be dropped off in town. Otherwise, you could save some time by alighting at Salé and taking a local bus (Dh3) or grand taxi (Dh3) into central Rabat.

CTM has buses to the following:

Destination	Cost (Dh)	Duration (hr)	Number of daily services
Agadir	170	12	3
Casablanca	25	1½	8
El-Jadida	52	3½	3
Er-Rachidia	125	10	1
Essaouira	15	8	3
Fès	58	3½	7
Marrakesh	100	5	3
Nador	130	9½	1
Oujda	130	9½	1
Safi	100	5½	3
Tangier	80	4½	5
Taroudannt	180	10	1
Tetouan	80	5	1
Tiznit	186	10½	2

The main bus station has 13 separate ticket windows, each one clearly marked by destination. You'll probably be picked up by a tout telling you which company has the most imminent departure long before you find the one you need, so just follow them to the window and buy a ticket.

There are six departures per day to Casablanca (Dh18) and Tangier (Dh60), and nine for Fès (Dh50), as well as services to numerous other destinations including Agadir (Dh120), Asilah (Dh50), Chefchaouen (Dh45), El-Jadida (Dh42), Marrakesh (Dh70) and Tetouan (Dh60). You can even get international services to Barcelona (Dh1070), Madrid (Dh645), and Paris (Dh1220).

CAR

Rabat has no shortage of local car rental agencies – most of which will offer cheaper rates than these international agencies:

Avis (Map p110; ☎ 037 769759; 7 Rue Abou Faris al-Marini)

Budget (Map p110; ☎ 037 705789; Rabat Ville train station, Ave Mohammed V)

Europcar (Map p110; ☎ 037 722328; 25 Rue Patrice Lumumba)

Hertz (Map p110; ☎ 037 709227; 46 Ave Mohammed V)

National (Map p110; ☎ 037 722731; cnr Rue al-Kahira & Rue Ghandi)

City centre parking restrictions apply from 8am to noon and 2pm to 7pm Monday to Saturday. Tickets (from meters) cost Dh2 for 48 minutes up to a maximum of Dh10 for 4 hours.

There's a convenient car park at the edge of the medina close to the junction of Ave Hassan II and Ave Mohammed V.

TAXI

Grands taxis leave for Casablanca (Dh27) from just outside the intercity bus station. Other grands taxis leave for Fès (Dh55), Meknès (Dh40) and Salé (Dh3.50) from a lot off Ave Hassan II behind the Hôtel Bouregreg.

TRAIN

Train is the most convenient way to arrive in Rabat, as **Rabat Ville train station** (Map p110; ☎ 037 736060) is right in the centre of town. Don't confuse this with Rabat Agdal train station to the west of the city. The station has a café, **left-luggage counter** (per item per day Dh10; ☺ 7am-10.30pm), bureau de change and ATM. **Budget** (☎ 037 705789) and **Supratours** (☎ 037 208062; ☺ 9am-12.30pm & 3-7pm Mon-Sat) also have offices here.

Trains run every 30 minutes from 6am to 10.30pm between Rabat Ville and Casa-Port train stations (Dh30) and Kenitra (Dh13.50, 30 minutes). Taking the train to Mohammed V Airport (Dh55) in Casa-blanca requires a change at Casa Voyageurs or at Aïn Sebaa.

On all long-distance routes there's always one late-night ordinaire train among the rapide services. Fares for the second-class rapide service include Fès (Dh72, 3½ hours, eight services daily) via Meknès (Dh56, 2½ hours), Oujda (Dh177, 10 hours, three serv-ices) via Taza (Dh108, six hours), Tangier (Dh90, 4½ hours, seven services) and Mar-rakesh (Dh101, 4½ hours, eight services).

Getting Around
BUS
Some useful bus routes (Dh3) are listed below:

Nos 2 & 4 Ave Moulay Hassan to Bab Zaer, for the Chellah.
No 3 Rabat Ville train station to Agdal.
No 16 Ave Moulay Hassan to Salé (get off after passing under the railway bridge).
Nos 17 & 30 From near Bab al-Had to Rabat's intercity bus station via the map office; No 17 goes on past the zoo to Temara Beach.
Nos 37 & 52 From the intercity bus station into central Rabat.

TAXI
Rabat's blue petits taxis are plentiful, cheap and quick. A ride around the centre of town will cost about Dh10. There's a petit taxi rank near the entrance of the medina on Ave Hassan II.

SALÉ   سلا
pop 400,000
A few hundred metres and half a world away, Salé is a walled city and strongly tra-ditional backwater on the far side of the Oued Bou Regreg estuary. In comparison to modern Rabat it seems forgotten by time. Little has changed over the centuries in this whitewashed city and women will find a sharp difference in attitudes towards them here in comparison to the liberalism of the capital. Outside the walls of the old city,

Salé is a sprawling modern dormitory town with little of interest for the traveller.

History
People began to settle in Salé in the 10th century and the town grew in importance as inhabitants of the older settlement at Sala Colonia began to move across the river to the new town. Warring among local tribes was still rampant at this stage and it was the Almohads who took control of the area in the 12th century, establishing neighbouring Rabat as a base for expeditions to Spain.

Spanish freebooters attacked in 1260; in response the Merenids fortified the town, building defensive walls and a canal to Bab Mrisa to allow safe access for shipping. The town began to flourish and established valuable trade links with Venice, Genoa, London and the Netherlands.

As trade thrived so too did piracy, and by the 16th century the twin towns had become home to the infamous pirate bands known as the Sallee Rovers (see the Rabat history section p104). Both cities prospered from the Sallee Rovers' pirate activities, and an influx of Muslim refugees from Spain in the 17th century only improved matters.

By the 19th century the pirates had been brought under control, Rabat had been made capital and Salé began to dwindle into relative obscurity.

Orientation & Information
Salé is best seen on a half-day trip from Rabat. The main entrance to the medina is Bab Bou Haja, on the southwestern wall, which opens onto Place Bab Khebaz. From here it's a short walk to the souqs to the northwest. The Grande Mosquée is 500m further northwest along Rue Ras ash-Shajara (also known as Rue de la Grande Mosquée) but it can be tricky finding your way through the narrow alleyways. Walk along the road that runs inside the city walls past Bab Bou Haja and Bab Malka for a more straightforward approach.

There are a few banks along Rue Fon-douk Abd el-Handi. To the south Bab Mrisa was once connected to the ocean by canal, allowing ships to float right into the city. It was here that Robinson Crusoe was brought into the town in Daniel Defoe's novel. The Complexe des Potiers is southeast of the medina on the road to Oulja.

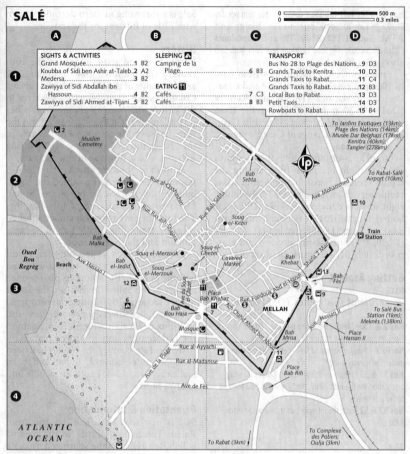

SALÉ

SIGHTS & ACTIVITIES		SLEEPING		TRANSPORT	
Grand Mosquée.........................1 B2		Camping de la		Bus No 28 to Plage des Nations...9 D3	
Koubba of Sidi ben Ashir at-Taleb.2 A2		Plage.........................6 B3		Grands Taxis to Kenitra............10 D2	
Medersa................................3 B2				Grands Taxis to Rabat.............11 C4	
Zawiyya of Sidi Abdallah ibn		EATING		Grands Taxis to Rabat............12 B3	
Hassoun............................4 B2		Cafés............................7 C3		Local Bus to Rabat................13 D3	
Zawiyya of Sidi Ahmed at-Tijani..5 B2		Cafés............................8 B3		Petit Taxis.........................14 D3	
				Rowboats to Rabat.................15 B4	

Sights

GRANDE MOSQUÉE & MEDERSA

Central to life in pious Salé and one of the oldest religious establishments in the country, the Grand Mosquée and *medersa* are superb examples of Merenid artistry. They were built in 1333 by Almohad Sultan Abu al-Hassan Ali. The mosque is closed to non-Muslims, but the **medersa** (admission Dh10; ⏰ 9am-noon & 2.30-6pm) is open as a museum. Similar to those in Fès or Meknès, it takes the form of a small courtyard surrounded by a gallery. The walls are blanketed in intricate decoration from the *zellij* base to the carved stucco and elegant cedar woodwork.

Small student cells surround the gallery on the upper floor, from where you can climb to the flat roof, which has excellent views of Salé and across to Rabat. The guardian who shows you around will expect a small tip.

SHRINES

To the rear of the Grande Mosquée is the **Zawiya of Sidi Abdallah ibn Hassoun**, the patron saint of Salé. This respected Sufi died in 1604 and is revered by Moroccan travellers in much the same way as St Christopher is among Christians.

An annual pilgrimage and procession in his honour makes its way through the streets of Salé on the eve of Mouloud (the Prophet's birthday, usually in late spring). On this day, local fishers dress themselves up in elaborate corsair costume, while others carry decorated wax sculptures and parade through the streets, ending up at the shrine of the *marabout*.

The Zawiya (shrine) of Sidi Abdallah ibn Hassoun is one of three shrines in Salé. The other two are the **Zawiya of Sidi Ahmed at-Tijani**, which is on the lane that runs between the mosque and *medersa*, and the white **Koubba of Sidi ben Ashir at-Taleb** (the Doctor), located in the cemetery northwest of the mosque.

SOUQS

From the Grande Mosquée, head back to the souqs via the Rue Ras ash-Shajara, a street lined with the houses built by wealthy merchants. Shaded by trees and unchanged for centuries, the **Souq el-Ghezel** (Wool Market), makes an interesting stop. Here, men and women haggle over the price and quality of rough white wool as it hangs from ancient scales suspended from a large tripod.

In the nearby **Souq el-Merzouk**, textiles, basketwork and jewellery are crafted and sold. The least interesting souq for travellers is the **Souq el-Kebir**, featuring second-hand clothing and household items.

Sleeping & Eating

Unless you are camping (see p111) there is little point in staying in Salé as there's a much better choice of accommodation in Rabat. There are plenty of hole-in-the-wall cafés in the souqs and surrounding streets, as well as in the area just south of Place Bab Khebaz.

Getting There & Away
BOAT

The most atmospheric way to reach Salé is to take one of the small rowboats (Dh1 per person) that cross the Oued Bou Regreg from just below the *mellah*. They operate all day, and leave when full.

BUS

Salé's main bus station is 1km east of the medina. If you're coming from Rabat take bus No 16 (Dh3) and get off after passing under the railway bridge. From here walk west to Bab Fès and the medina. You can pick up a bus (No 16 or 28) back to Rabat from Bab Fès.

TAXI

The easiest way to get to Salé medina from Rabat is to pick up a taxi close to the Hôtel Bou Regreg, on Ave Hassan II; ask for the Bab Bou Haja. From Salé there are departures from Bab el-Jedid and Bab Mrisa (Dh3 one way). Note that Salé's beige petits taxis are not permitted to cross into Rabat. Petits taxis are frequent, and there's a taxi stand at Bab Fès. Grands taxis for Kenitra leave from just north of the train station (Dh11).

TRAIN

Trains run to/from Rabat, but buses or grands taxis are probably the simplest options. Trains north to Kenitra run every 30 minutes (Dh13.50).

AROUND RABAT & SALÉ
Complexe des Potiers   مُجمّع الفخاريات

To shop for ceramics, see potters at work or just get an idea of what is on offer, head to the village of Oulja, 3km southeast of Salé. The modern **Complex des Potiers** (Pottery Cooperative; ☾ sunrise-sunset) here produces a huge variety of ceramics ranging from tajine dishes of every size and colour to platters, lamps, vases and domestic china.

The potters work at the back of the complex, bringing in clay from a rich seam in the surrounding hills (you'll see it on the left as you drive in), throwing and turning it on kick wheels, then glazing and firing the finished pieces in enormous kilns. A firing takes 15 hours and reaches 900°C. Fine domestic pottery is fired in gas kilns designed to reduce environmental degradation and air pollution, but more rustic pieces are still fired in kilns fuelled by twigs and leaves from nearby eucalyptus forests.

The centre also has a café and some workshops used by basket weavers and blacksmiths. To get here take a petit taxi from Salé (about Dh12) or catch bus No 35 or 53 (Dh3).

Jardins Exotiques   الحدائق الغريبة

The grand idyll of a French horticulturist, the **Jardins Exotiques** (adult/child Dh5/3; ☾ 8am-5.30pm) are a monument to one man's belief in a philosophical ideal: 'It is poetry that recreates lost paradises; science and technology alone are not enough', a plaque boldly proclaims by the entrance.

The elaborately themed gardens were created in 1951 by Marcel François and, though neglected over the years, are slowly being brought back to their former glory. Colour-coded paths lead through over-grown Brazilian rainforest, Polynesian jungle, Japanese pleasure grounds and an Andalusian garden. Pools, bridges, exotic flora, twisting paths and a general sense of discovery makes it a great place to bring children and a popular spot for courting couples.

The gardens are 13km north of Rabat on the road to Kenitra. Take bus No 28 from Ave Moulay Hassan in Rabat, or Bab Fès, the main gate at Salé medina.

Musée Dar Belghazi   متحف دار بلغازي

Three generations of the Belghazi family have amassed a vast collection of traditional Andalusian, Jewish Moroccan and Islamic arts and crafts, now on display at the **Musée Dar Belghazi** (☎ 037 822178; belghazi@maghrebnet. net.ma; admission Dh40; ☉ 8.30am-6pm), housed in an old country mansion.

Displays include 17th-century carpets, exquisitely carved wooden *minbars* (pulpits from a mosque), doors and ceilings dating from the 10th century, intricate gold and silver jewellery, exceptional pottery and embroidery from Fès, and miniature copies of the Quran.

The museum is 17km from Salé on the road to Kenitra. Take bus No 28 from Ave Moulay Hassan in Rabat or from the main gate of the Salé medina.

Beaches

The clean, sandy strip of beach at **Plage des Nations**, 17km north of Rabat, is a popular spot with local day trippers. It gets some serious wave action of interest to surfers but the currents can be dangerous for swimming. Above the beach, the **Hôtel Firdaous** (☎ 037 822131; fax 037 822143; s/d Dh460/600; 🏊) is a haven of retro glory with décor largely unchanged since the '70s. The rooms at this resort hotel are comfortable and have ocean views and new bathrooms. Book in advance for any chance of a room in summer.

To get to the beach, drive north as far as the Musée Dar Belghazi and turn left down a road known as Sidi Bouknadel. Bus No 28 from Rabat or Salé will drop you at

the turn off, from where it's a 2km walk to the beach.

There are other beautiful beaches closer to Rabat, such as the wild sandy stretches around **Temara Plage**, 13km south of the city. Popular with surfers and sunbathers alike, this beach can be reached on bus No 17 from Bab al-Had in Rabat.

Parc Zoologique National   حديقة الحيوانات الوطنية

Home to a sizeable collection of animals and several captive-breeding programmes, the impressive Temara **zoo** (adult/child Dh10/5, parking Dh3; ☉ 9.30am-6pm Mon-Sat, 9am-6pm Sun). Although the zoo is underfunded and underappreciated, most of the enclosures are spacious and clean, and the it's well known internationally for its big cats, including lions that are 80% Barbary in their genetic make-up. At over 50 hectares it is a vast place and makes a good outing for children.

The zoo is 9km south of Rabat on the road to Temara. Bus No 17 leaves just outside Bab al-Had and takes about 20 minutes to reach the zoo. Get off at the stop just past Prince Moulay Abdallah sports stadium and walk a few hundred metres east.

Forest of Zaer   غابة زائر

If you have your own transport it's possible to do a picturesque driving loop through the Forest of Zaer (Forêt des Zaers), south of Rabat. Although suffering from some environmental degradation, the area is still rich in cork-oak and eucalyptus.

Take the P22 about 30km south of Rabat to the little village of **Aïn el-Aouda**. Continue on for another 10km before taking the tiny S216 to **Merchouch**, signposted to the right. At Merchouch, bear right again onto the S106 towards **Sidi Bettache** and **Ben Slimane**, which takes you through green valleys and impressive gorges. Alternatively, take the S208 north from Sidi Bettache to **Sidi-Yahya**, a favoured spot with birdwatchers.

KENITRA   القنيطرة
pop 374,000

Although there's little to detain you in Kenitra, this easy-going port town is the access point for a couple of worthwhile attractions in the surrounding area, including the beach and kasbah at Mehdiya and the lake at Sidi Bourhaba.

Kenitra's main street is Ave Mohammed V, where you'll find almost everything you need including banks and an internet café.

If you're stuck in Kenitra overnight, the **Hôtel d'Europe** (☎ 037 371450; 63 Ave Mohammed Diouri; s/d Dh208/245) is your best bet. It's clean and simple with good-value en suite rooms. Slightly more upmarket is the **Hôtel Mamora** (☎ 037 371775; fax 037 371446; Ave Hassan II: s/d Dh322/391; 🖫), where the rooms are larger and more businesslike.

The most popular lunch spot in town is the American-themed **El-Dorado** (64 Ave Mohammed Diouri; burgers from Dh22, steak & chips Dh46), which serves a limited menu of fast food. Alternatively, try the more modern **Cactus** (☎ 037 377242; 44 Ave Mohammed Diouri; mains Dh30-60) for pizza, pasta and sandwiches, or **La Sangria** (☎ 037 371450; 63 Ave Mohammed Diouri; mains Dh22-40) for a combination of Italian and Moroccan dishes.

Kenitra is on the train line with frequent connections to Rabat (Dh13.50), Casablanca (Dh40.50), Fès (Dh60.50) and Meknès (Dh44) and less regular services to Tangier (Dh78) and Asilah (Dh65). Kenitra station is on Ave Mohammed Diouri about 500m south of the main drag. When arriving, get off here, not at Kenitra Medina.

The main bus station is at the eastern end of Ave Mohammed V, while **CTM** (☎ 037 376238) has a depot in the town centre. Buses depart for Souk el-Arba du Rharb (Dh15), Larache (Dh30), Chefchaouen (Dh38), Tangier (Dh50) and Tetouan (Dh48) from both stations.

Grands taxis to Souk el-Arba du Rharb (Dh20) leave from the bus station; grands taxis to Rabat (Dh12) leave from a block south of McDonald's.

AROUND KENITRA
Plage Mehdiya   شط المهديّة

This windswept stretch of sand 7km west of Kenitra is popular with surfers, boogie-boarders and beachcombers. It gets busy with day-trippers in summer but is deserted for the rest of the year.

Apart from the beach itself the main sight here is the impressive **kasbah**, high on a bluff above the sea. The peaceful ruins date mostly from the time of Moulay Ismail, although everyone from the Carthaginians to the US Marines occupied the site at some time over the years. It's a pleasant

place to wander and has good views from the upper terraces. From just north of the kasbah you can take a path down to the coastal road and daily **fish market**.

Mehdiya has a selection of basic accommodation including a simple **Youth Hostel** (Auberge de Jeunesse; ☎ 037 388212; Villa No 6, Lotissement Amria; dm Dh30). Alternatively there's decent camping at **Camping International** (☎ 060 663125; camping per person Dh15, plus per tent/car/caravan Dh10/10/20), a cluster of holiday-camp-style bungalows at the **Complexe Touristique** (bungalows incl breakfast Dh500; 🖫). All of these places open in summer only.

A strip of grill bars and cheap cafés line the beach road but for something more substantial try **L'Étoile du Gharb** (☎ 037 388035; mains Dh70-90; ⏲ 7am-10pm Sep-May, 24hr Jun-Aug), a stylish place with a good selection of seafood and grills, or **Café Restaurant Belle Vue** (☎ 037 388953; mains Dh50-80), overlooking the port, for simply prepared seafood.

To get to Mehdiya from Kenitra take bus No 9, which goes to the main village and kasbah, or No 15, which follows the lower beach road. Both of these buses (Dh3) and grands taxis (Dh4) leave from the corner of Rue du Souk el-Baladia and Ave Mohammed Diouri.

Lac de Sidi Bourhaba   بحيرة سيدي بورهابة

The beautiful freshwater Lac de Sidi Bourhaba, a protected nature reserve, is just inland from Plage Mehdiya. Surrounded by forested hills laced with walking trails, it's a scenic spot for gentle hiking but more famous internationally as a refuelling stop for thousands of birds migrating between Europe and sub-Saharan Africa.

The lake, surrounding scrub and marsh provide some of the best bird-watching in the country, especially between October and March. More than 200 species of birds have been seen here and many choose to winter or nest here – among them a number of rare or endangered species. This is one of the last places on earth where you can still see large numbers of marbled duck, distinguished by the dark patch around their eyes. Other birds to look out for include the beautiful marsh owl (seen most often at dusk), the crested coot, black-shouldered kite and greater flamingo.

The simple **information centre** (☎ 037 747209 or ☎ 060 383331; www.spana.org.ma in French; ☯ noon-4pm Sat & Sun) on the northern side of the lake is useful but has limited opening hours.

To get to the lake follow the signposts from the beach road to Plage Mehdiya, 300m past the Café Restaurant Belle Vue. If you're on foot, the lake is a 3.3km walk from the turn-off.

MOULAY BOUSSELHAM مولاي بوسلهام

The sleepy fishing village of Moulay Bousselham is a tranquil place, home to a magnificent beach, incredibly friendly people and an internationally important wildfowl reserve. Beyond this there is little to do except take in the glorious views and relax.

In summer the village becomes a low-key resort but outside the high season it is practically deserted. Although increasingly popular with novice surfers, the crashing waves and strong currents here can be dangerous for swimmers.

Moulay Bousselham is named after a 10th-century Egyptian saint who is commemorated in one of the *koubbas* (shrines) that line the slope down to the sea. You'll find everything you need along the one main street, including a bank, post office, pharmacy and a couple of internet cafés (Dh8 per hour).

Sights & Activities
MERDJA ZERGA NATIONAL PARK
One of the greatest pleasures of a trip to Moulay Bousselham, even for the most unenthusiastic of twitchers, is a boat trip on the Merdja Zerga (Blue Lagoon). This 7000-hectare national park attracts thousands of migrant birds, including wildfowl, waders and flamingos in huge numbers, making it one of Morocco's prime bird-watching habitats.

Although the largest flocks are present from December to January, you'll find herons, flamingos, ibises, spoonbills, plovers and egrets here as late as March or April. The calm lagoon is also a good place to see slender-billed and Audouin's gulls, and the African marsh owl. Shelducks, teals, and numerous terns are frequently seen, as are marsh harriers and peregrine falcons.

Boat trips to see the greater flamingos and other birds in the lagoon are easily arranged if you wander down to the small beach where the boats are moored. Prices depend on how far you have to travel to see the birds (expect to pay about Dh150 to 250) but the cheapest option is to travel with the local boatmen, who have been trained to guide tourists around the lagoon. **Mansoury el Boukhary** is a recommended option run by partners Khalil (☎ 063 095358) and Mansour (☎ 063 093794).

There is also one officially recognised guide, **Hassan Dalil** (☎ 068 434110; half day Dh200, motorboat per hr Dh50), who can also be contacted at the Café Milano. The café keeps a bird log, which is updated by birders from all over the world. Trips can also be arranged through La Maison des Oiseaux and Villanora (see below).

Boats generally accommodate a maximum of five people and trips go from around dawn until noon or from 3pm to dusk. The best time for bird activity in the lagoon is just after dawn.

Hardcore bird-watchers may also want to explore **Merdja Khaloufa**, an attractive lake about 8km east of Moulay Bousselham, which offers good viewing of a variety of wintering wildfowl.

Sleeping & Eating
Villanora (☎ 037 432071; s/d incl breakfast Dh200/400) Set in a charming house with glorious ocean views, this little B&B has a few cosy rooms (with shared bath) where you can fall asleep to the sound of crashing waves. It's a family affair, run by a British brother and sister who can also organise half-day birding trips to the lagoon for Dh100 per person. Villanora is at the far northern end of town about 2km from the main street and it's essential to book in advance.

La Maison des Oiseaux (☎ 037 432543; http://moulay.bousselham.free.fr; half board per person Dh300) This small, friendly guesthouse is set in a lovely garden and has eight simple but beautifully styled traditional rooms. There's a seminar room upstairs for visiting school groups and birding excursions can be arranged for Dh200 to Dh250 for 2½ hours. The guesthouse is hidden down a maze of sandy lanes to the left as you drive into town. Ask for directions.

Hôtel Le Lagon (☎ 037 432650; fax 037 432649; d Dh250; ☒) This faded hotel's saving grace is that each room comes with a spacious terrace overlooking the stunning lagoon below. The rooms themselves are big, bright and clean but well past their best and in dire need of updating.

There are two camp sites in town: **Camping Flamants-Loisirs** (☎ 037 432539; http://flamants-loisirs.ifrance.com in French; camping per person Dh15, plus per caravan/car/tent Dh50, bungalows Dh240-330; 🈺), a large place that's aging badly, and the slightly run-down but beautifully situated **Camping Caravaning International** (☎ 037 777226; tent/car/caravan Dh10/20/30 plus per adult/child Dh12/6).

The road down to the seafront is lined with cafés and restaurants serving up platters of grilled fish and tajines (Dh45 to Dh60). The modest **Restaurant l'Ocean** (☎ 037 432256) is one of the locals' favourites. The incredibly helpful staff can also help to arrange renting a basic **apartment** (Sep-May Dh200, Jun-Aug Dh300-500), which sleeps up to six people. During the summer months they fill up quickly, so it's best to call and reserve in advance.

Getting There & Away

Moulay Bousselham is about 40km due south of Larache. To get here by public transport you'll need to make your way to the little town of Souk el-Arba du Rharb, from where there are frequent grands taxis (Dh13) and a few buses (Dh8) to Moulay Bousselham. You can get to Souk el-Arba du Rharb by grand taxi from Kenitra or Larache (Dh25) and Rabat (Dh35). The town also has a train station with daily trains in either direction.

LARACHE   العرائش

Low-key, little visited and genuinely friendly, Larache is an underappreciated place with the languid charm of a town long forgotten. The main tourist attraction here is the overgrown ruins of ancient Lixus to the north, but the tumble-down medina, Spanish architecture and laidback attitude gives the town itself an unmistakable allure.

Larache was occupied by the Spanish for most of the 17th century and became the main port of the Spanish protectorate in 1911. Today, whitewashed houses with blue doors and window frames make up the bulk of the town, which centres round Place de la Libération, a typical example of colonial Spanish urban planning. The church, market, hotels and bars reveal the strength of the Spanish influence here, and although the town is not as quaint as Asilah, it gets far fewer visitors and none of the hustle of its more famous neighbour.

In the evening, Larache comes alive as everyone takes to the streets for the *paseo*, or 'evening stroll'. The cafés fill up as the locals drink coffee, play cards and chew over the days events and by 10pm the streets are again deserted.

Information

The banks cluster at the northern end of Blvd Mohammed V; most accept cash and travellers cheques, and have ATMs. For internet access try **Cyber Space** (☎ 039 914141; Rue 2 Mars; per hr Dh5-8; ⏳ 24hr) or **Marnet** (☎ 039 916884; Ave Mohammed ben Abdallah; per hr Dh8; ⏳ 10am-midnight Sat-Thu, 3pm-midnight Fri).

Sights
MUSÉE ARCHÉOLOGIQUE

Housed in a former Merenid palace, and often closed, the tiny **archaeological museum** (admission Dh10; ⏳ 10am-noon & 3.30-5.30pm Tue-Sat) has a limited but interesting collection of artefacts, mostly from the nearby Roman ruins of Lixus (p125). If you can get in, the displays include ceramics and utensils from Phoenician and Roman times with explanations in Arabic and French. Look out for the arms of Charles V above the main door.

OLD TOWN

Perched on the cliff-top overlooking the ocean are the ruins of the **kasbah** (Qebibat), a 16th-century fortress built by the Portuguese and now in a state of serious disrepair. Head south from here to the old cobbled **medina**, through **Bab al-Khemis**, a large, unmistakable Hispano-Moorish arch on Place de la Libération. You come immediately into a colonnaded market square, the bustling **Zoco de la Alcaiceria**, which was built by the Spaniards during their first occupation of Larache in the 17th century. South of the square, through the medina, is the **Casbah de la Cigogne** (Fortress of the Storks), a 17th-century fortification built by the Spaniards under Philip III. Unfortunately, the building is not open to visitors.

To the west of town, the old Spanish cemetery is the final resting place of French writer Jean Genet (1910–1986). If the gate

ATLANTIC COAST

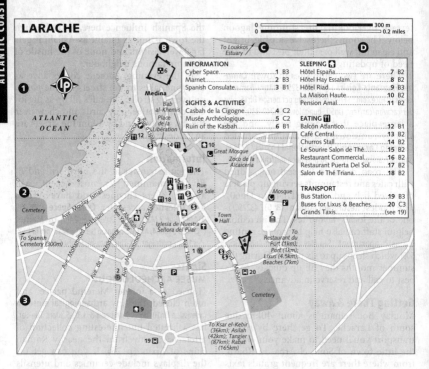

LARACHE

INFORMATION	
Cyber Space	1 B3
Marnet	2 B3
Spanish Consulate	3 B1

SIGHTS & ACTIVITIES	
Casbah de la Cigogne	4 C2
Musée Archéologique	5 C2
Ruin of the Kasbah	6 B1

SLEEPING	
Hôtel España	7 B2
Hôtel Hay Essalam	8 B2
Hôtel Riad	9 B3
La Maison Haute	10 B2
Pension Amal	11 B2

EATING	
Balcón Atlantico	12 B1
Café Central	13 B2
Churros Stall	14 B2
Le Sourire Salon de Thé	15 B2
Restaurant Commercial	16 B2
Restaurant Puerta Del Sol	17 B2
Salon de Thé Triana	18 B2

TRANSPORT	
Bus Station	19 B3
Buses for Lixus & Beaches	20 C3
Grands Taxis	(see 19)

is not open, ring the bell on the right and the caretaker will let you in. A small tip is expected for showing you to the grave.

BEACHES

Larache has a small strip of sand below the town but the best beach is 7km north across the Loukkos Estuary. To get there take the hourly No 4 bus (Dh5; June to August). Out of season the No 5 bus will drop you at the turn-off just before Lixus (Dh3), from where it's a 3km walk to the beach. Both buses leave from opposite the Casbah de la Cigogne.

Sleeping

Larache has a decent selection of accommodation, most of which is clustered along the streets just south of the Place de la Libération.

Pension Amal (☎ 039 912788; 10 Rue Abdallah ben Yassine; s Dh40, d Dh60-70) Dirt cheap, immaculately kept and extremely friendly, this little pension has basic rooms with shared facilities. A hot shower is Dh6. If you've any interest in music, the owner will jump at the

chance to get out his guitar and put on an impromptu performance in the evening.

Hôtel Hay Essalam (☎ 039 916822; 9 Ave Hassan II; s/d Dh90/140, with bathroom Dh116/166) Big, bright, functional rooms with new bathrooms are on offer at this good-value central hotel. Although a little musty, the rooms are clean and have satellite TV and tasteful wooden furniture. However, management is pretty indifferent and won't win any prizes for friendliness or effort.

Hôtel España (☎ 039 913195; hotelespana2@yahoo .fr; 6 Ave Hassan II; s/d Dh204/243) A relic of colonial times, this once-grand hotel is now suffering from a lack of investment and the rooms are sadly faded. Although clean, the décor and bathrooms fittings are dated and the thin glazing means street noise can be a problem. Ask for a room on the second floor with a view over the square.

Hôtel Riad (☎ 039 912626; Ave Mohammed ben Abdallah; s/d incl breakfast Dh239/314; ☒) This grand old 19th-century mansion is set in landscaped gardens just south of the centre and offers comfortable rooms and plenty of child-friendly activities. Although a little shabby, it's an atmospheric place with tennis courts, bicycle hire, a pool and its own pizzeria.

La Maison Haute (☎ 065 344888; www.lamaison haute.com; 6 Derb ben Thami; r Mar-Jun & Sep-Nov Dh320-430, Jul-Sep & public holidays Dh370-520) The top accommodation choice in Larache, this wonderfully restored Hispano-Moorish house has a choice of six charming rooms with modern bathrooms. Bright colours, stained-glass windows and mosaic floors give this place a feeling of simplicity, warmth and tradition, while the roof terrace boasts incredible views of the ocean and market square.

Eating

Eating out in Larache is cheap and cheerful with plenty of little places around Place de la Libération and the Zoco de la Alcaiceria serving simple but substantial meals. The Spanish influence lingers on in the *churros* (a kind of doughnut) stall on the main square.

Restaurant Commercial (☎ 061 682420; Place de la Libération; mains Dh20; ⏰ noon-9.30pm) The locals' favourite, this basic place on the main square does a roaring trade in simple soup, brochettes and fried fish. It's ultra-cheap, is packed with happy diners every night and is a great place for people watching.

Restaurant du Port (☎ 039 417463; Larache Port; mains Dh40; ⏰ 10am-5pm & 7-11pm) Out of town by the port, but worth the trip, this slightly more upmarket place specialises in fresh seafood cooked simply but to perfection.

Restaurant Puerta Del Sol (☎ 039 913641; Rue de Salé; mains Dh20-30; ⏰ noon-9pm) For more seafood and a choice of Moroccan dishes, this no-nonsense place is another good bet. It's popular but a little quieter than the Commercial.

Balcón Atlantico (☎ 039 910110; Rue de Casablanca; pizza Dh30-40, crepes Dh10-15; ⏰ 6am-10pm) Overlooking the beach and the nicest spot in town for a relaxed breakfast or simple lunch, this bright, bustling café has plenty of outdoor seating and passable pizzas.

For a quick breakfast or ice cream your best options are the **Salon de Thé Triana** (☎ 039 500913; Ave Mohammed ben Abdallah), which also serves decent pizza (Dh26 to Dh40) in summer, or, just off the square, **Le Sourire Salon de Thé** (Ave Hassan II; ⏰ 6am-10pm). The **Café Central** (Place de la Libération; ⏰ 6am-midnight) is a strictly

male preserve but a wonderful relic of the days of the Spanish protectorate.

Getting There & Away

The bus station is south of the town centre on Rue du Caire.

CTM buses include services to Casablanca (Dh100, four hours, three daily) via Kenitra (Dh40, two hours) and Rabat (Dh70, three hours); Fès (Dh65, four hours, three daily) via Meknès (Dh45, three hours); Tangier (Dh25, 2½ hours, four daily); Tiznit (Dh272) via Marrakesh (Dh152, eight hours) and Agadir (Dh200, 12 hours).

Cheaper non-CTM buses also cover these destinations as well as Ouezzane (Dh20), Tetouan (Dh20) and Kenitra (Dh30) and are generally more frequent.

Grands taxis run from outside the bus station to Ksar el-Kebir (Dh12) and occasionally to Asilah (Dh15) and Tangier (Dh30).

LIXUS   الاوكوس

Set on a hill overlooking the Loukkos Estuary are the Roman ruins of **Lixus** (admission free), a rather mysterious and neglected site that is one of the oldest inhabited places in the country. Only about a quarter of the ancient city has been excavated but the visible ruins, though badly damaged and overgrown, are impressive. Although not as extensive or as well excavated as Volubilis (see p264), the location, size and serenity of Lixus give it a lingering sense of gravitas and with a little imagination you can picture just how grand and important this city once was.

The site is not enclosed, so you're at liberty to wander around on your own. Few visitors make it here outside the summer months, and in winter your only companions will be the wind and the odd goat quietly grazing. Although some unemployed locals may offer their services as a guide, it's not really necessary and their knowledge of the site is often pretty sketchy.

History

Megalithic stones found in the vicinity of Lixus suggest that the site was originally inhabited by a sun-worshipping people with knowledge of astronomy and mathematics. However, little more is known about the prehistoric society who inhabited the area long before the Phoenicians set up the colony Liks here in about 1000 BC. According to Pliny the Elder, it was here that Hercules picked the golden apples of the Garden of Hesperides, thus completing the 11th of his 12 labours.

In the 6th century BC the Phoenician Atlantic colonies fell to the Carthaginians. Lixus remained a trading post, principally in gold, ivory and slaves and, by AD 42, had entered the Roman Empire. Its primary exports soon changed to salt, olives, wine and *garum* (an aromatic fish paste) and its merchants also grew rich from the export of wild animals for use in the empire's amphitheatres.

The colony at Lixus rapidly declined as the Romans withdrew from North Africa, and was abandoned completely with the collapse of the Roman Empire sometime in the 5th century AD. Later, the site became known to Muslims as Tuchummus.

Sights

The main gate to Lixus is in the green railings that border the Larache–Tangier road. Inside the railings to the left are the remains of the *garum* factories, where fish was salted and the prized paste produced. A gravel path leads up the hill from the gate past a number of minor ruins to the **public baths** and **amphitheatre**. The amphitheatre provides impressive views of the surrounding countryside and makes a wonderful place just to sit and relax.

Most mosaics from the site were removed and are now on display at the archaeology museum in Tetouan (see p185). The Grand Temple mosaics depicting Helios, Mars and Rhea, the three Graces, and Venus with Adonis are all there. The only remaining mosaic at Lixus is that of **Oceanus** (the Greek Sea God). Unfortunately, it's been exposed both to the elements and to local vandalism, so is in rough shape.

Continue up the path to the main assembly of buildings, which straddle the crest of the hill. From here there are incredible views down over the Loukkos Estuary and salt fields below. The civic buildings, additional public baths and original city ramparts are here, while to the south is the striking citadel, a flurry of closely packed ruins standing stark against the sky. Al-

though most of the antiquities are in an advanced state of decay, you should be able to make out the main temple and associated sanctuaries, an oratory, more public baths and the remains of the city walls.

Getting There & Away

Lixus is approximately 4.5km north of Larache on the road to Tangier. To get there take bus No 4 or 5 from outside the Casbah de la Cigogne (Dh3). A petit taxi costs about Dh20 one way.

ASILAH أصيلا

The bijou resort town of Asilah has become the firm favourite on the traveller's trail of the North Atlantic coast. It's a wonderful introduction to Morocco, especially if you're straight off the boat from Tangier, and a far easier place to negotiate than its northerly neighbour. There's a good choice of hotels, plenty of restaurants and a lively arts scene with lots of little galleries and an annual International Cultural Festival.

The small medina is fast being gentrified by affluent Moroccans and Europeans and its narrow streets are now squeaky clean. A legion of tourist-oriented facilities spill out onto the surrounding streets and in midsummer the town is overrun with tourists, the beaches are packed and the touts come out in force. Visit out of season to appreciate the old-world charm of this lovely whitewashed town at its best.

History

Asilah has had a turbulent history as a small-but-strategic port since it began life as the Carthaginian settlement of Zilis. During the Punic Wars the people backed Carthage, and when the region fell to the Romans, the locals were shipped to Spain and replaced with Iberians. From then on, Asilah was inexorably linked with the Spanish and their numerous battles for territory.

As Christianity conquered the forces of Islam on the Iberian peninsula in the 14th and 15th centuries, Asilah felt the knock-on effects. The Portuguese captured the port in 1471 and built the walls that still surround the medina, and in 1578 King Dom Sebastian of Portugal embarked on an ill-fated crusade from Asilah. He was killed and Portugal (and its Moroccan possessions) passed into the hands of the Spanish.

Nine years later Asilah was captured by the Moroccans, who lost the port to the Spanish. It was then recaptured by Moulay Ismail in 1691. In the 19th century, continued piracy prompted Austria and then Spain to send in their navies to bombard the town. Its most famous renegade was Er-Raissouli (p128), one of the most colourful bandits ever produced by the wild Rif Mountains. Early in the 20th century, Er-Raissouli used Asilah as his base, becoming the bane of the European powers when the Spain made Asilah part of its protectorate in 1911.

Information

Place Mohammed V is crowded with banks, including BMCE and Banque Populaire, both of which will change cash and travellers cheques and have ATMs.

Internet access is available at **Pyramide Net** (Ave Hassan II; per hr Dh8; ☯ 9am-midnight).

There are a couple of pharmacies in town including **Pharmacie l'Océan** (Place Zellaka) and **Pharmacie Loukili** (Ave Mohammed V).

Dangers & Annoyances

As tourism has increased so too has the number of touts operating in Asilah. Offers of luxurious accommodation at rock-bottom prices usually turn out to be basic rooms with simple sleeping mats in the depths of the medina. More worryingly, tourists are increasingly being offered kif in Asilah but it's often part of an elaborate scam to fleece you of your money (see drugs, p448).

Sights & Activities

CENTRE DE HASSAN II RENCONTRES INTERNATIONALES

This modern cultural centre just inside the medina walls displays a revolving exhibition of international painting and sculpture in its **gallery** (☎ 039 417065; foundationdassilah@yahoo .fr; admission free; ☯ 8.30am-12.30pm & 2.30-7pm) and at times, in the nearby **El-Kamra Tower**, a renovated Portuguese fortification on Place Abdellah Guennoun.

The centre is also the main focus for the annual **International Cultural Festival** held in August, when artists, musicians, performers and thousands of spectators descend upon the town. Numerous workshops and public art demonstrations, concerts, exhibitions and events are held throughout the month with a strong Spanish and Islamic slant. A three-day horse festival (including a Moroccan *fantasia* or musket-firing cavalry charge) takes place towards the end of the festival.

The festival began in 1978 and has become the main catalyst for Asilah's regeneration. However, critics complain that the festival is too highbrow for local residents to participate in, that the influx of tourists has increased property prices and rental rates beyond what local people can afford, and that the narrow emphasis on the festival means that there is little effort to create year-round employment for local people.

RAMPARTS & MEDINA

Asilah's largely residential medina is surrounded by sturdy stone fortifications built by the Portuguese in the 15th century, and it is these walls, flanked by palm trees, that have become the town's landmark.

The medina and ramparts have been largely restored in recent years and the narrow streets lined by whitewashed houses are well worth a wander. Although the

RASCALLY ER-RAISSOULI

Feared bandit, kidnapper and general troublemaker, Moulay Ahmed ben Mohammed er-Raissouli (or Raisuni) was one of Asilah's most legendary inhabitants. He started life as a petty crook in the mountains but saw no problem in bumping off unwilling victims and was soon renowned as a merciless murderer and feared right across the region.

Internationally, Er-Raissouli was best known for kidnapping Westerners. He and his band held various luminaries to ransom, including Greek-American billionaire Ion Perdicaris, who was ransomed in 1904 for US$70,000.

In an attempt to control the unruly outlaw, consecutive sultans appointed him to various political positions including governor of Asilah and later Tangier. However, Er-Raissouli continued with his wicked ways, amassing great wealth in whatever way he could. He held considerable sway over the Rif tribes and the Spanish funded his arms in the hope of keeping order in the mountains, but er-Raissouli often used them against his benefactors.

The Spaniards eventually forced Er-Raissouli to flee Asilah after WWI, but he continued to wreak havoc in the Rif hinterland until 1925, when the Rif rebel Abd al-Krim arrested him and accused him of being too closely linked with the Spanish.

In Asilah, **Raissouli's palace** (Palais de Raissouli, also known as the Palace of Culture) still stands as a testament to the sumptuous life this scoundrel led at the height of his power. The building includes a main reception room with a glass-fronted terrace overlooking the sea, from where Er-Raissouli forced convicted murderers to jump to their deaths onto the rocks 30m below. The palace is now open only for cultural events and workshops though if you can find the caretaker you may be able to persuade him to let you in.

restoration work has left the medina very sanitised, the ornate wrought-iron window guards and colourful murals (painted each year during the festival) give it a very photogenic quality. Craftsmen and artists have opened workshops along the main streets and invite passers-by in to see them work.

Access to the ramparts is limited. The southwestern bastion is the best spot for views over the ocean and is a popular spot at sunset. It also offers a peek into the nearby **Koubba of Sidi Mamsur** (which is otherwise closed to non-Muslims) and the **Mujaheddin Graveyard**.

The southern entrance to the medina, **Bab Homar**, is topped by the much-eroded Portuguese royal coat of arms. There are a few old cannons just inside the medina's seaward wall, but they are cut off from the walkway below and can only be seen from a distance. The medina is busiest on Thursdays, Asilah's main market day.

BEACHES

Asilah's main beach, flanked by camp sites and hotels, stretches north from town. It's a wide sweep of golden sand and although pleasant in low season, the crowds and noise from the nearby road make it less appealing in summer. For more peace and quiet head 3km south of Asilah to **Paradise Beach**, a gorgeous, pristine spot that really does live up to its name. It's a pleasant walk along the coast or, alternatively, hop on one of the horse-drawn carriages that ply this route in summer.

HAMMAM

The best place for a good scrub is the **Bain Maure** (Ave de la Liberté; admission Dh6; ☺ 5-11am & 7pm-midnight for men, 11am-7pm for women), a hammam close to the police station.

Sleeping

Asilah has a choice of decent but uninspiring accommodation options, all of it in the new part of town. Touts meeting the buses or trains offer basic accommodation in the medina for about Dh50. It's usually a large room sleeping up to seven people on thin mattresses on the floor. During the high season (Easter week & July to September) the town is flooded with visitors so it's advisable to book well in advance.

BUDGET

Asilah has a limited choice of budget hotels, most of which are ageing badly.

Hôtel Sahara (☎ 039 417185; 9 Rue Tarfaya; s/d Dh98/126, hot showers Dh5) By far Asilah's best budget option, this small, immaculately kept hotel offers simple rooms set around an open courtyard. Patterned tiles and potted plants adorn the lovely entrance, and the compact rooms, though fairly spartan, are comfortable and well maintained. Some have tiny windows, so it may be worth checking more than one. The sparkling shared toilets and showers are all brand new and scrubbed till they gleam.

Hôtel Belle Vue (☎ 039 417747; Rue Hassan ben Tabit; d low/high season Dh100/200) Friendly and functional, this small hotel has rather nondescript but well-kept rooms with dated décor and spotless shared facilities. A few rooms have their own bathroom (Dh50 extra) and balconies.

Hôtel Marhaba (☎ 039 417144; Place Zellaka; s/d Dh60/80, Jul-Aug 80/150) Right in the centre of town but fading badly, the friendly Marhaba offers clean but well-worn rooms with aging furniture and colourful blankets. The shared facilities are ancient but there's a nice roof terrace overlooking the medina.

There are a number of camp sites along the beach north of town with only basic washing facilities:

Camping Echrigui (☎ 039 417182; camping per person Dh15, plus per tent/car/caravan/camper Dh10/10/20/20, r low/high season Dh100/200)

Camping as-Saada (☎ 039 417317; camping per person Dh15, plus per tent/car/caravan/camper Dh10/10/20/20, electricity Dh15, r low/high season Dh100/120)

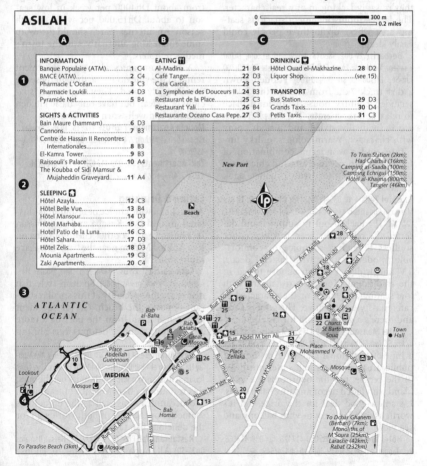

MIDRANGE & TOP END

Hôtel Patio de la Luna (☎ 039 416074; 12 Place Zellaka; s/d Dh300/450) The only accommodation option in Asilah with any local character is this intimate, Spanish-run place secluded behind an unassuming door on the main drag. The simple, rustic rooms have wooden furniture, woven blankets and tiled bathrooms and are set around a lovely leafy patio. It's very popular, so book ahead.

Hôtel Azayla (☎ 039 416717; e-elhaddad@menara .ma; 20 Rue ibn Rochd; s/d Dh296/346, Jul-Sep Dh380/380) Big, bright, comfy and well-equipped, the rooms here are a really good deal. The bathrooms are new, the décor is tasteful and the giant windows bathe the rooms in light, but you could be almost anywhere, as they're sadly lacking in any real character. The larger rooms include a spacious seating area where up to three people could easily sleep.

Berbari (☎ 062 588013; www.berbari.com; Dchar Ghanem, Cercle de Tnine Sidi El Yamani; d/ste Dh260-300 Jun-Sep Dh300-60, ste Dh480-700) Hidden down a dirt track 7km from Asilah, this lovely secluded country house is an ideal place to relax and recuperate. The simple rooms are individually styled and just dripping with character. Warm colours, quirky furniture, and a wonderful combination of traditional Moroccan crafts and chic European style make them truly original. Book in advance.

Hôtel Zelis (☎ 039 417069; fax 039 417098; 10 Ave Mansour Eddahabi; s/d Dh400/483, Jul-Sep Dh521/604; ✂ ☲ ▯) Packed out in summer and deserted the rest of the year, this big, rather soulless hotel has a choice of comfortable, modern rooms with tasteful décor, TV and fridge. You can choose to eat in the traditional Moroccan restaurant with low seating and tables or the characterless cafeteria-style alternative. The pool is good and there's a games room for children.

Hôtel Mansour (☎ 039 417390; www.hotelmansour .fr.fm; 56 Ave Mohammed V; s/d Dh180/220) You'll get a hint of traditional character in the tiled public areas at this small hotel northeast of the centre, but the bedrooms are fairly bland with faded décor and tiny bathrooms. It's still a good deal for the price, but it's worth asking for a room with balcony and sea view.

Hôtel al-Khaima (☎ 039 417428; fax 039 417566; Rue Tanger; s/d Dh364/439, Jul-Sep Dh474/549; ☲) Just north of town by the beach, this three-star, 110-room resort is a big, brash place with everything from tennis courts to minigolf and disco on offer. The spacious rooms are comfortable enough with wooden furniture and tiled floors (and no TVs) but those overlooking the pool are much quieter than the roadside rooms.

Houses & Apartments

A host of properties in Asilah's medina have been bought up by foreigners or wealthy Moroccans and reconstructed as slick holiday homes. There are some wonderful three- and four-bedroom houses available with stunning décor and all the comforts you can imagine. Prices range from about Dh4000 per week in low season to about Dh15,000 per week in high season. An internet search should throw up some interesting alternatives to the town's mediocre hotels.

A few companies also offer apartment rental in the ville nouvelle, though these are usually fairly dated. They're generally spacious and clean but have only basic kitchen facilities and well-worn furnishings.

Mounia Apartments (☎ 039 417815; 14 Rue Moulay Hassan ben el-Mehdi; 2/4-person apt Dh250/350, Jul-Aug 450/600)

Zaki Apartments (☎ 039 417497; 14 Rue Imam al-Assili; 2/4/7-person apt Dh250/400/500)

Eating & Drinking

Asilah has a wide choice of restaurants clustered around Bab Kasaba and Ave Hassan II. There are a few other cheap options on Rue Ahmed M'dem near the banks on Place Mohammed V.

Casa García (☎ 039 417465; 51 Rue Moulay Hassan ben el-Mehdi; mains Dh80) Spanish-style fish dishes are the speciality at this small restaurant opposite the beach. Go for succulent grilled fish fresh from the port or a more adventurous menu of octopus, eels, shrimp and barnacles.

Restaurant de la Place (☎ 039 417326; 7 Ave Moulay Hassan ben el-Mehdi; mains Dh40-80) Friendly, less formal and more varied than its neighbours, this restaurant offers a choice of traditional Moroccan dishes as well as the ubiquitous seafood. For the best of both worlds go for the delicious fish tajine.

Restaurant Yali (☎ 071 043277; Ave Hassan II; mains Dh25-50) Although there's little to choose between them, this is one of the most popular of the string of restaurants along the medina walls. It serves up a good selection of fish, seafood and traditional Moroccan staples.

Restaurante Oceano Casa Pepe (☎ 039 417395; 8 Place Zellaka; mains Dh80-100) Black-tied waiters lure in the punters from the street at this slightly more formal dining option, where fresh seafood tops the bill. Spanish wine, low lighting and soft music make it a more refined atmosphere but the food is arguably the same as elsewhere in town.

Al-Madina (Place Abdellah Guennoun; mains Dh30-45) The main attraction of this simple little café in the medina is its sunny seating area in the square in front of El-Kamra Tower. It's a great place to sip a coffee or have a snack from the simple, Moroccan menu.

La Symphonie des Douceurs II (☎ 039 416633; 26 Place Zellaka) The best place for breakfast or an afternoon sugar fix is this French-style patisserie, where you can devour pastries and ice cream in very civilised surroundings. It's popular with tourists and young couples.

Café Tanger (52 Ave Mohammed V) If the Symphonie is too chichi for you, head for this café north of the square where the predominantly male clientele sip coffee, suck their teeth and watch over the world.

Asilah has little in the way of drinking dens; you could try the bar at the Hôtel Ouad el-Makhazine (Ave Melilla) or the small liquor shop next to the Hôtel Marhaba near Bab Kasaba.

Getting There & Away
BUS
Asilah is 46km south of Tangier and has good bus connections to most towns. The tiny bus station is on Ave de la Liberté, where CTM has a ticket office. Ticket prices are about 10% less in low season.

CTM has services to Casablanca (Dh70, 4½ hours) via Rabat (Dh60, 3½ hours), Fès (Dh65, 4½ hours) via Meknès (Dh55, 3½ hours), Nador (Dh190), Oujda (Dh190), Tangier (Dh10, one hour) and Tiznit (Dh300) via Marrakesh (Dh200, nine hours) and Agadir (Dh275, 13 hours). A number of south-bound services (both CTM and non-CTM) stop at Larache. It's a good idea to book long distance buses in advance as they tend to fill up in Tangier.

Cheaper non-CTM buses to Tangier and Casablanca leave roughly every half hour, from 6.30am to 8pm. There are also plenty of services to Meknès, Fès, Tetouan and Ouezzane. Just wait until a bus pulls in and hope there's a seat available.

CAR
There is **guarded parking** (overnight Dh10, per 24 hr Dh15) outside Bab al-Baha (Sea Gate), near the port.

TAXI
Grands taxis to Tangier (Dh15) and Larache (Dh15) depart when full from Ave Moulay Ismail, across from the mosque. Tangier's airport is only 26km north of here, so taking a taxi from Asilah (Dh160) may save you spending a lot of time and energy in Tangier. The petit taxi stand is at Place Mohammed V.

TRAIN
The train station is 2km north of Asilah, but a bus (Dh3) generally meets trains and drops passengers at Place Mohammed V and Bab Homar. Three trains run daily to Rabat (Dh77, 3½ hours) and Casablanca (Dh101, 4½ hours), one to Meknès (Dh66, three hours) and Fès (Dh81, four hours) and six daily to Tangier (Dh14, 45 minutes). One overnight train goes direct to Marrakesh (Dh174, nine hours), but this train originates (and fills up) in Tangier, so you may want to buy your ticket in advance.

AROUND ASILAH
The mysterious **Monoliths of M'Soura** make an interesting half-day trip from Asilah if you've got time to spare. The prehistoric site consists of a large stone circle (it's actually an ellipse) consisting of about 175 stones, thought to have originally surrounded a burial mound. Although many of the stones have fallen or been broken, the circle is still impressive, its strange presence heightened by the desolation of its location. The tallest stone reaches about 5.5m in height and is known as *El-Uted* (The Pointer).

The stone circle is about 25km (by road) southeast of Asilah. To get there you'll need a sturdy vehicle. Head for the village of Souq Tnine de Sidi el-Yamani, off highway R417, which branches east off the main Tangier to Rabat road. Veer left in the village and follow a poorly maintained, unsealed track 6km north to the site. It can be difficult to find so you may want to ask for directions or hire a guide in the village.

Another interesting trip from Asilah is a visit to the lively Sunday market in the village of **Had Gharbia** 16km north of town off the road to Tangier.

SOUTH OF CASABLANCA

EL-JADIDA   الجديدة
pop 144,000

A rather faded but easy-going town, El-Jadida is overwhelmed in summer by holidaying Moroccans attracted by the wide sandy beach, tree-lined boulevards and relaxed attitude. For the rest of the year it's a quiet, workaday place with genuinely friendly locals and no hassle.

The city's major attraction is the fortified Cité Portugaise (Portuguese city), a well-preserved relic of rambling lanes and sturdy ramparts dating from the 16th century. Mazagan, as El-Jadida was known, was the principal Portuguese port, built along with other coastal fortresses to protect their burgeoning caravels travelling to the Indies and China.

The city was renamed El-Jadida (the New) in the 19th-century and eventually lost its importance as a port to Casablanca and Safi. Today El-Jadida awaits a long-promised injection of funds to spruce up its historic buildings and remodel the waterfront to lure even greater numbers of tourists.

History
In 1513 the Portuguese founded Mazagan on the site of an old Almohad fortress, quickly developing it into their main Moroccan trading centre. They managed to hold on to the town until 1769, when, following a siege by Sultan Sidi Mohammed ben Abdallah, they were forced to evacuate the fortress. As they left they mined the ramparts, blowing the fort and a good part of the besieging army to pieces.

Although the fortress ruins were rebuilt in 1820 by Sultan Moulay Abd ar-Rahman, new settlers preferred to live outside the city walls and the town began to expand. The fort lay largely empty until the mid-19th century when Portuguese

merchants returned and recolonised the narrow winding streets. A large and influential Jewish community became established here and grew rich on trade with the interior. Unlike most other Moroccan cities, there was no *mellah*; the Jews mixed with the general populace and an attitude of easy tolerance was established in the city.

Nowadays, tourism, sardine fishing and a prosperous agricultural hinterland make contemporary El-Jadida a growing commercial centre.

Orientation
El-Jadida sits on the eastern coast of a large promontory jutting north into the Atlantic. (Although the map appears to be orientated incorrectly, this is only due to the city's location on the promontory.)

The town's focal point is Place Mohammed V, home to the post office, banks, tourist office and several hotels. The Cité Portugaise and the main market area lie a short walk to the north.

The bus station is about 1km south down Ave Mohammed V, and El-Jadida's train station is another 3km further south on the Marrakesh road.

Information
INTERNET ACCESS
@Kiltec (☎ 023 350487; 1st fl, 62 Place Hansali; per hr Dh6; ☯ 9am-11pm, closed Friday lunchtime for prayer)
Internet du Centre (26 Blvd Mohammed VI; per hr Dh5; ☯ 8am-11pm Mon-Sat, 10.30am-5pm Sun) A small centre with fewer computers.

MEDICAL SERVICES
Clinique Les Palmiers (☎ 023 393939; Rte de Casablanca) Has a 24-hour emergency service
Night Pharmacy (just off Blvd Mohammed VI; ☯ 8am-noon & 2.30-11pm)

MONEY
There are numerous banks in the centre of town including BMCE, BMCI and Bank al-Maghrib; most have ATMs.

POST
Main post office (Place Mohammed V; ☯ 8.30am-noon & 2.30-6.30pm Mon-Thu, 8.30-11am & 3-6.30pm Fri)

TOURIST OFFICE
Syndicat d'Initiative (33 Place Mohammed V; ☯ 9am-noon & 3-6pm closed Wed) Welcoming, knowledgeable

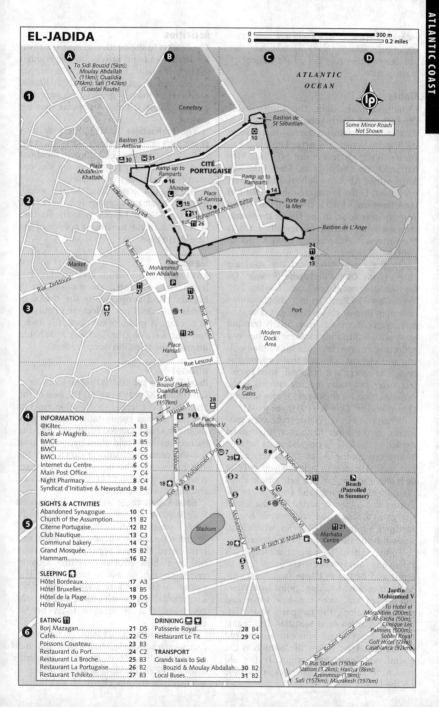

EL-JADIDA

ATLANTIC COAST

and helpful, this tourist office is a rarity in Morocco – it's actually useful. Although it has no maps or brochures, the staff can answer all your questions and help to arrange apartment rental.

Sights

El-Jadida's main sight, the unmistakable **Cité Portugaise** (Portuguese city), is a compact maze of twisting streets, surrounded by brawny ochre ramparts. The main entrance to the fortress is just off Place Mohammed ben Abdallah and leads into Rue Mohammed Ahchemi Bahbai. Immediately on the left is the Portuguese-built **Church of the Assumption**, which is closed to the public. Almost next door, to the left, is the **Grande Mosquée**, whose minaret originally acted as the fortress' lighthouse and has a unique pentagonal shape.

On the main street past the souvenir shops is the **Citerne Portugaise** (Portuguese Cistern; Rue Mohammed Ahchemi Bahbai; admission Dh10; 9am-1pm & 3-6.30pm), an incredible, vaulted cistern lit by a single shaft of light. The subterranean cistern is a spectacularly tranquil spot, with a thin film of water on the floor reflecting a mirror image of the vaulted ceiling and elegant columns that support the roof. The cistern was originally used to collect water, but today is more famous as the eerie location for the dramatic riot scene in Orson Welles' *Othello* (1954; see p148).

When you exit the cistern take a few moments in the foyer to look at the model depicting the Cité Portugaise in its heyday, before continuing down the street to the ramparts. Directly in front of you is **Porte de la Mer**, the original sea gate where ships discharged their cargo and from where the Portuguese finally departed. To the left of the gate, through the archway, is one of the town's communal bakeries, where local women bring their bread to be cooked.

To the right of the sea gate, a ramp leads up to the windy ramparts (open 9am to 6pm) and **Bastion de L'Ange** (southeast corner), an excellent vantage point with views out to sea and over the new town and port. Walk along the ramparts to the left to reach **Bastion de St Sébastian** (northeast corner), from where you can see the old Jewish cemetery. Below the bastion is the abandoned **Synagogue** (originally the old prison) with its Star of David clearly visible on the façade.

Activities

The **beaches** to the north and south of town are fairly clean and safe, enjoyable enough in the low season, but packed with tourists in July and August. The beach at **Hauzia**, northeast of town is generally quieter and more pleasant. It's also a popular spot for surfing.

The **Club Nautique** (☎ 023 373509; Port de Jadida) at the port rents out sailing skiffs, caravels, zodiacs or windsurfing equipment for about Dh60 to Dh100 per person per session; you need to bring your own wetsuit.

For a good scrub head to the small, friendly **hammam** (admission Dh7; 7am-6pm women only, 6-10.30pm men only) near the Bastion St Antoine in the northwest corner of the Cité Portugaise.

Sleeping

Most visiting Moroccans own holiday chalets or stay in rented accommodation in El-Jadida and consequently the choice of hotels here does not reflect its popularity as a resort. A group of new hotels is under construction along the Corniche and should improve the selection once finished.

BUDGET

Hôtel Bordeaux (☎ 023 373921; 47 Rue Moulay Ahmed Tahiri; s/d Dh80/100, hot showers Dh5) The best of the cheapies, this friendly, good-value hotel in the medina has comfortable but compact rooms around a covered courtyard. En suite bathrooms have cold showers, you'll have use the communal shower downstairs for any hot water. The hotel is down a narrow, twisting laneway but is well signposted from Rue ben Tachfine.

Hôtel Royal (☎ 023 341100; 108 Ave Mohammed V; s/d Dh100/140, with bathroom Dh140/240) Slightly more upmarket, this large hotel has big, bright rooms with cheap furnishings and retro-fitted showers separated from your bed by a sheet of glass panelling. Quality varies, though, so ask to see several. The public areas are more stylish with trickling fountains, colourful tiling and a lovely courtyard that becomes a lively bar at night.

Hôtel Bruxelles (☎ 023 342072; 40 Rue Ibn Khaldoun; s/d with bathroom Dh75/140) Rather old and dowdy, the Bruxelles is set in what was once a lovely 1930s building and still retains a touch of its former charm. It's definitely well past its best and not the friendliest spot in town but the rooms are clean and there's secure parking in the garage next door (Dh10).

Hôtel de la Plage (☎ 023 342648; 30 Ave Mohammed VI; s/d/tr Dh60/70/85) This seafront hotel has a selection of spacious, but fairly basic rooms. It's clean and well kept but the furnishings are worn and the plumbing in the shared bathrooms is ancient. A shower costs Dh5.

MIDRANGE & TOP END

Sofitel Royal Golf Hotel (☎ 023 379100; www.accor hotels.com; d from Dh1000; ☒ ☒) This secluded hotel, set around a large pool in the midst of the manicured golf course, is 7km northeast of town and the top spot for miles around. The comfortable colonial-style rooms, traditional restaurant and air of refinement are certainly attractive but you're totally insulated from the real world here.

Hotel el Morabitine (☎ 023 379430; cnr Av Mohammed VI & Ave Ennakhil; www.elmorabitine-hotel .com; s/d Dh250/350, Jun-Sep Dh345/490; ☒ ☒) This 114-room hotel near the waterfront has big, bright comfortable rooms with modern furniture and fittings and good service. It's more Western business hotel than charming bolthole but has a decent restaurant and bar and a great pool.

Eating

El-Jadida has a handful of reasonable restaurants and a thriving café culture.

Borj Mazagan (☎ 023 343435; 4th fl, Marhaba Centre, 54 Ave Mohammed V; mains Dh60-100; ☒ 7am-midnight) Slick, stylish and trying hard to be hip, this friendly café and restaurant is popular with professionals and El-Jadida's up-and-coming young things. Sleek modern furniture, floor-to-ceiling windows and an international menu featuring home-made pasta, wood-fired pizzas and succulent steaks mean it's an ideal place to just feel anonymous once more. It's not licensed but is fantastic for breakfast (Dh18 to Dh28) or luscious afternoon cake on what is easily El-Jadida's finest terrace.

Restaurante du Port (☎ 023 342579; Port du Jadida; mains Dh60-70; ☒ closed Sun evening) Ignore the building and just head upstairs for excellent views over the port and ramparts from one of El-Jadida's best restaurants. Unsurprisingly the focus here is fish and seafood, cooked simply but well. The atmosphere

is pretty mellow making it a comfortable spot for women – and joy of joys – it's licensed.

Poissons Cousteau (☎ 067 899191; 6 Ave Nabeul; mains Dh25-40) Despite the rather characterless new building and the wall-to-wall white tiles, this is the firm local favourite for gargantuan plates of fried fish. It's a no-nonsense affair but by the time you make it through the fish, bread and sauces you'll be grinning like a local.

Restaurante La Portugaise (☎ 063 037480; Rue Mohammed Ahchemi Bahbai; mains Dh25-48) Just inside the walls of the old city, this characterful little place serves up a decent menu of good value fish, chicken and tajine dishes. It's a quiet spot outside high season but lively when the tourists roll into town.

Restaurant Tchikito (4 Rue Mohammed Smiha; mixed fish platter Dh25-30) This hole in the wall just off Place Hansali pulls in the crowds for, you guessed it, fried fish, served here with a fiery chilli sauce. It's pretty basic with plastic furniture and no cutlery but it's always packed.

Restaurante La Broche (Place Hansali; mains Dh35-45) Another cheap and cheerful option, this basic café on Place Hansali offers a wide choice of Moroccan and international fare, from tajine to fresh fish and paella. It's a friendly, family-run place with plenty of pavement tables for people-watching.

If you want to self-cater, the **market** (Rue Zerktouni) is a short walk west of the Cité Portuguese, and has plenty of fruit and veg stalls and small grocery shops.

Drinking

Ave Nabeul, on the seafront, is in the process of being redeveloped and should be home to a new selection of cafés once finished.

Patisserie Royale (☎ 061 878354; Place Mohammed V; ☒ 6am-8pm) A good spot for breakfast or a quiet coffee, the Royale is an old-style kind of joint where you can blend into the woodwork or chat to the locals without feeling under any pressure.

Al-Bacha (☎ 023 354621; Blvd Mohammed VI; breakfast Dh18, ice cream Dh25) Slightly out of town, this large, popular café overlooking the public gardens is the place to go for ice cream. It's a civilised place frequented by women and families and makes a good break from the male preserves in the town centre.

Restaurant Le Tit (☎ 023 343908; 2 Ave Al-Jamia El-Arabi; mains Dh45-90; ☺ 9am-midnight) More a drinker's den than a fine dining location, this place still serves up decent nosh from a short international menu. It's not somewhere women are likely to feel comfortable alone and you'll find the hard-core drinkers here from early morning till late at night.

Getting There & Away

BUS

The bus station is a 10-minute walk southeast of town on Ave Mohammed V. It has a **left-luggage counter** (per 24hr Dh5; ☺ 7am-9pm) but you'll need to show ID.

CTM runs services to and from Casablanca (Dh27, 1½ hours, four daily). There are also services to Oualidia (Dh22, 1½ hours, three daily), Safi (Dh43, 2½ hours, six daily) and Essaouira (Dh70, 4½ hours, one daily).

Cheaper local buses go to all the same destinations as well as Rabat (Dh35, four hours, 12 daily) and Marrakesh (Dh35, four hours, hourly). In summer, buses to Casablanca (Dh19) and Marrakesh should be booked at least one day ahead.

Bus Nos 2, for Sidi Bouzid (Dh2.10), and 6, for Moulay Abdallah (Dh4), leave from just north of the Cité Portugaise.

TAXI

Grands taxis for Azemmour (Dh6) and Casablanca (Dh35) leave from the side street next to the long-distance bus station. Taxis to Oualidia (Dh25) and Safi (Dh55) depart from a junction on the road to Sidi Bouzid. You'll need to take a petit taxi (Dh5) to get there. The grand taxi rank for Sidi Bouzid (Dh4) and Moulay Abdallah (Dh5) is beside the local bus station north of the Cité Portugaise.

TRAIN

El-Jadida **train station** (☎ 023 352824) is located 4km south of town. There are five services a day to and from Casablanca (Dh30, one hour). A petit taxi to the centre costs around Dh10. For timetable details ask at the tourist office.

AROUND EL-JADIDA

Sidi Bouzid & Moulay Abdellah

The thriving beach resort of Sidi Bouzid is just 5km southwest of El-Jadida. It's a popular spot with sunbathers and surfers and outside July and August makes an enjoyable half-day excursion or an overnight stop on the route south.

Six kilometres further on, the small fishing village of Moulay Abdallah sits within the ruins of a 12th-century fortress, built by the Almohad Sultan Abdel Moumen. Although there's little to see today, the village comes alive each August (generally the second week) when thousands of pilgrims gather for a *moussem* (festival) to venerate the saint. If you're in the area, it's well worth dropping by for the dramatic demonstrations of horsemanship known as *fantasias*.

If you want to stay overnight in Sidi Bouzid, your best bet is the Spanish-style **Club Hacienda** (☎ 023 348954; apt Nov-Feb from Dh500, Jul & Aug from Dh800; ⛱), a timeshare resort where you can rent vacant apartments. It's set in well-tended gardens but the complex has gone downhill in recent years.

The town's top restaurant is **Le Requin Blue** (☎ 023 348067; set menus from Dh110), a popular destination for El-Jadida's lunch set. It serves excellent fish dishes on tiered terraces overlooking the beach.

Local bus No 2 runs from El-Jadida to Sidi Bouzid (Dh2.10) every hour. Bus No 6 links Moulay Abdallah with El-Jadida (Dh4), via Sidi Bouzid, though it's quicker and more comfortable to travel by grand taxi (Dh6).

Azemmour

The little-visited and underappreciated town of Azemmour sits picturesquely on the banks of the Oum er-Rbia River. It's a sleepy backwater with a languid charm, a sturdy Portuguese medina and some wonderful accommodation options – a great place to hole up and while away a few days overlooking the river.

Azemmour has several banks, a pharmacy and internet access at **Capsys** (off Place du Souk; per hr Dh5).

The main sight is the medina, an ochrewalled town of narrow winding streets and whitewashed houses. Unlike Asilah, to the north, it is completely unadorned for the tourist market and gives an authentic insight into life in modern Morocco. You can get up onto the **ramparts** near Place du Souk or via some steps at the northeastern corner of the medina. Walk along the walls to see **Dar el Baroud** (the Powder House) a Portuguese gunpowder store of which only the tower remains. To the north of the medina is the *mellah* and further on you'll get wonderful views over the river.

Azemmour has two wonderful accommodation options. The more traditional is the **Riad Azama** (☎ 023 347516; www.riad azama.com in French; 17 Impasse Ben Tahar; d Dh450-750) an incredible old house complete with original carved woodwork and charming rooms surrounding a lovely courtyard. The carved, painted ceilings here are some of the finest you'll see anywhere in the country and the rooftop terrace has great views of the medina. Totally different but equally special, **L'Oum Errebia** (☎ 023 347071; www.azemmour-hotel.com; 25 Impasse Chtouka; d Dh350-700) seamlessly blends traditional Moroccan style with chic modern design. The simple rooms are really lovely and the large lounge, complete with open fire and grand piano, acts as a modern art gallery displaying the work of international artists. It has a large terrace overlooking the river and communal meals (Dh150) are served at the big dining-room table.

Otherwise, the best bet for food is across the bridge and up the hill (where you'll get a great view back to town) at the **Restaurant Panorama** (☎ 023 358968; Sidi Ali; mains Dh30-80), which has a lovely garden at the back. The menu features *kefta* (spiced meatballs of minced lamb and/or beef), brochettes, fish and chicken and you can get a cold beer to wash it all down.

At Hauzia beach, 7km from town, **Restaurant La Perle** (☎ 023 347905; mains Dh40-80) is another good bet for simple meals overlooking the beach.

A grand taxi to/from El-Jadida costs Dh6.

OUALIDIA الوالدية
pop 4000

There's little to do in Oualidia other than sit back, relax, admire the views and pile on the pounds. It's a gem of a little resort, set on an idyllic, crescent-shaped lagoon fringed with golden sands and sheltered from the crashing Atlantic waves by a rocky breakwater. The people are incredibly friendly, the accommodation is good, the food superb and the atmosphere very chilled.

Visited out of season it is gorgeously tranquil, and one of the finest spots to relax on the Moroccan coast. Unfortunately, the little town is thronged with visitors in the summer months. New apartment blocks and hotels are being built and the pace of development threatens to destroy the tranquil charm of this stunning location. Visit now while it's still got some character.

Orientation & Information

The village sits on either side of the main road on an escarpment above the lagoon. Most hotels and restaurants are along the road to the beach (1km) – follow signs down beside the post office. You'll find a bank, CTM office and **internet café** (per hr Dh5; ☺ 8am-midnight) here, and a Saturday souq when people from surrounding villages come to town to sell their wares.

Sights & Activities

The town is named after the Saadian Sultan el-Oulalid, who built the atmospherically crumbling **kasbah** on the bluff overlooking the lagoon in 1634. The kasbah was built to defend the harbour in the sheltered waters below and offers great views over the lagoon and ocean. The lagoon also attracted Morocco's royalty and the grand villa on the water's edge was once the **summer palace** of Mohammed V.

The safe, calm waters of the lagoon are perfect for **swimming**, **sailing** and **fishing**, while the wide, sandy beach on either side of the breakwater is good for **windsurfing** and surfing. Signposted left off the road to the beach is **Surfland** (☎ 023 366110; ☺ Apr–mid-Nov) a well-organised surf school offering surfing lessons for children (Dh200) and adults (Dh250) as well as **kitesurfing** tuition in low season.

Oualidia is famous in food circles for its **oyster beds**, which produce about 200 tonnes of oysters annually. You can visit oyster farm No7 at Maison de l'Ostréa II (see p138) to see how it all works.

To explore the countryside around Oualidia you can hire mountain bikes (Dh100 per half day) and scooters (Dh200 per half day) from **Oualidia Maroc Adventure** (☎ 061 157743) on the main drag. South of Oualidia the coast road becomes ever-more dramatic, passing through green grazing lands that end at precipitous sea cliffs. Along this stretch there are a series of completely deserted sandy beaches of which Cap Beddouza, 33km from Oualidia, is one of the most scenic.

Sleeping & Eating

Oualidia has a good choice of accommodation options and plenty of gourmet food. All the hotels have their own restaurants and there are some slightly cheaper places lining the road down to the beach. For bargain meals there is a selection of cheap eateries on the main road in the village. The most atmospheric option is simply to stroll down to the beach after 4pm when the fishermen pull up and fry their catch for anyone who is interested. Expect to pay about Dh30 for a large fish and Dh50 for crab.

Hotel Thalassa (☎ 023 366050; r Dh100-150, Jun-Sep Dh150-200) The only hotel on the main drag, this place is better than you might expect with bright, airy rooms tastefully decked out in a modern style. The bathrooms are a little dated but if you're travelling in a group the large rooms with seating areas (where up to three others can sleep) are a steal. The restaurant serves a decent selection of traditional dishes and pizza (mains Dh35-60).

Camping Les Sables d'Or (☎ 066 122932; camp sites from Dh25 plus per person Dh3.50) Campers should head for this well-maintained site on the road down to the beach. It doesn't have a lot of shade, but is within a stone's throw of the sand. A hot shower costs Dh6.

Hôtel-Restaurant L'Initiale (☎ 023 366246; linitiale@menara.ma; s/d Dh300/400, Jun-Sep Dh400/500) Keen new owners, an excellent location and some lovely rooms make this small hotel a real gem. Warm orange walls, new furnishings and fittings, spotless bathrooms and tiny balconies give the rooms a real sense of style. The licensed restaurant is one of the best in town and serves a wide selection of delicious dishes. Set menus start at Dh90.

Surfland (☎ 022 276324; fax 022 265054; full-board child/adult Dh220/270) Big marquee-like tents double as communal bedrooms at this small centre, which caters mainly for groups of children in summer. Smaller, two-person tents are also available and meals are served in the large main tent where things can get a bit hectic when it's crowded. The shower and toilet facilities are spotless.

Motel A l'Araignée Gourmande (☎ 023 366447; fax 023 366144; s/d Dh200/300, Jun-Sep Dh246/280) Al-though a little faded and in need of some investment, this friendly hotel is still a good deal with spacious, comfortable rooms. The bathrooms could do with modernising and the towels are as hard as rocks, but if you bag a room at the back the views of the lagoon from your large balcony will make up for it all. The restaurant downstairs serves up a feast of incredible seafood with set menus ranging from Dh110 to Dh250.

Maison de l'Ostréa II (☎ 023 366324; www.ilove -casablanca.com/ostrea; Parc à Huîtres No7; d Dh600-750) Set right on the edge of the lagoon by the oyster beds, this modern hotel has five sparkling but businesslike rooms with plenty of facilities but little charm. The attached restaurant is understandably popular with an upmarket clientele and has a lovely terrace overlooking the lagoon (meals including wine Dh200 to Dh250). For a more relaxed meal pick up some bread and a lemon in town, buy your oysters (per dozen Dh30 to Dh85) from the little stall on site and sit on the shady benches to dine.

By the time you read this Oualidia's new five-star boutique hotel **La Sultana** (☎ 024 388008; www.lasultanaoualidia.com in French; Parc à Huîtres No3; B&B d Dh2100-4200 ste Dh3800-4750; ☒ closed mid-Jan–mid-Feb; ☒ ☐) will have opened. It's a seriously luxurious place: just 11 rooms with private Jacuzzi and terrace overlooking the lagoon. There's a choice of three restaurants (set menu Dh200 to Dh350), an indoor-outdoor pool and a spa – all set in gorgeous landscaped gardens.

If you'd like to stay a little longer, you can rent **apartments** and villas through www .oualidia.net (in French; studios from Dh300 per night) or try the owner of the L'Initiale who has a six-bed place available for Dh800 to Dh1200 per night.

Getting There & Away

Local buses and grands taxis run at irregular times to El-Jadida (bus/taxi Dh16/25) or Safi (bus/taxi Dh16/20); they leave from near the post office on the main road. CTM also has an office here and has a daily bus (Dh17) in either direction.

SAFI   آسفي

pop 415,000

A thriving port and industrial centre, Safi is quite a pleasant town if you can ignore the giant phosphate plant that mars the view of the seafront and concentrate instead on the relaxed atmosphere, tree-lined boulevards and whitewashed villas. Few foreign tourists make it here but it's well worth a visit to see the imposing Portuguese fort, the walled and fortified medina and the giant pottery works that take over a whole city quarter. The other main draw is the beaches. Renowned for their impressive surf, the immaculate sands north of town were the location for the 2006 Billabong Challenge and are said to have some of the finest waves in the world. South of town the landscape is largely industrial and of little interest to visitors.

History

Safi's natural harbour was known to the Phoenicians and the Romans, but it was the Almohads who founded a permanent settlement here in the 12th century. The town grew into an important religious and cultural centre, and was home to a Portuguese trading post by 1481. The Portuguese took control of the city in 1508, building the monumental Qasr al-Bahr fortress, but their time here was short-lived and they abandoned it just 33 years later.

In the 16th century Safi grew wealthy from the trade in copper and sugar, and became the principal port for Marrakesh. European merchants and agents flocked to the city, but when the port at Essaouira was rebuilt in the 18th century, trade was diverted and Safi was largely forgotten.

Safi's real revival came in the 20th century when the fishing fleet expanded and huge industrial complexes were built to process the 30,000 tonnes of sardines caught annually. A major phosphate-processing complex was established south of the town and the city began to expand rapidly. Today, Safi is one of Morocco's largest ports.

Orientation

The fortress, medina and the bulk of cheaper hotels and restaurants are in the lower town, on or around Place de l'Indépendance. The 'new' town – up on the hill to the east – is home to the city's administrative buildings, the more expensive hotels and the smarter cafés. At its centre is Place Mohammed V, occupied for some reason by a giant tajine pot.

Safi's bus and train stations are roughly 1km south of the town centre.

Information

INTERNET ACCESS
Club Salma (Rue de R'bat; per hr Dh5; 9am-12.30pm & 2.30-8pm) A basic place with slow connections and terrible music.
Cyber Club Lascala (Ave Sidi Mohammed Abdallah; per hr Dh5; ☼ 8am-midnight) Fantastic games den, full of pool tables (Dh5 per game) and heaving with students.

MONEY
There are plenty of banks and ATMs clustered around Place de l'Indépendance and Place Driss Ben Nacer.

POST
Main post office (Ave Sidi Mohammed Abdallah)
Post office (Place de l'Indépendance)

TOURIST INFORMATION
Syndicat d'Initiative (Rue de la Liberté; ☼ 9am-noon & 3-7pm) Hardly worth the trip for the dust-encrusted brochures and only the possibility of a staff presence. Try www.safi-ville.com for more information.

Sights

QASR AL-BAHR & THE MEDINA
Restored in 1963 and in impressively good nick, the **Qasr al-Bahr** (admission Dh10; ☼ 8.30am-noon & 2.30-6pm) lords over the crashing waves of the Atlantic on the rocky waterfront. The fortress, known as the 'Castle on the Sea', was built to enforce Portuguese authority, house the town governor and protect the port.

From the central courtyard, where there are a number of old Spanish and Dutch cannons dating from the early 17th century, you can climb the ramp to the southwest bastion, where there are good views down the coast. To the right of the entrance is the prison tower. Prisoners were kept in the basement before being killed or shipped as slaves, but you can climb to the top for views across the medina. To the left of the entrance is the tomb of the soldier who remained to light the explosives and destroy the fort as the Portuguese abandoned the city.

The entrance to the fort is via an underpass opposite the Hotel Majestic. Bring a torch (flashlight) if you have one, as the stairs in the towers are dark.

Across the street from the Qasr al-Bahr lies the walled **medina**. The main street, Rue du Souq, runs northeast from Bab Lamaasa, and you'll find most of the souqs, stalls, jewellery, clothing and food in this area.

ATLANTIC COAST

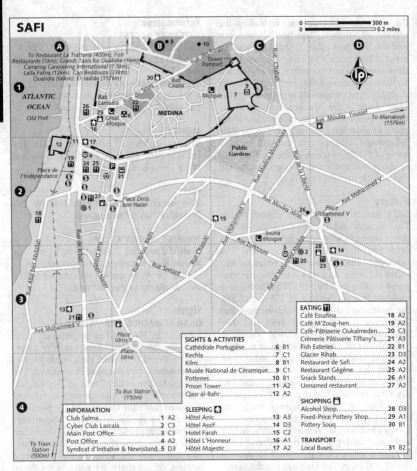

SIGHTS & ACTIVITIES
Cathédrale Portugaise	6	B1
Kechla	7	C1
Kilns	8	B1
Musée National de Céramique	9	C1
Potteries	10	B1
Prison Tower	11	A2
Qasr al-Bahr	12	A2

INFORMATION
Club Salma	1	A2
Cyber Club Lascala	2	C3
Main Post Office	3	C3
Post Office	4	A2
Syndicat d'Initiative & Newsstand	5	D3

SLEEPING
Hôtel Anis	13	A3
Hôtel Assif	14	D3
Hotel Farah	15	C2
Hôtel L'Honneur	16	A1
Hôtel Majestic	17	A2

EATING
Café Essafina	18	A2
Café M'Zoug-hen	19	A2
Café-Pâtisserie Oukaïmeden	20	C3
Crèmerie Pâtisserie Tiffany's	21	A3
Fish Eateries	22	B1
Glacier Rihab	23	D3
Restaurant de Safi	24	A2
Restaurant Gégène	25	A2
Snack Stands	26	A1
Unnamed restaurant	27	A2

SHOPPING
Alcohol Shop	28	D3
Fixed-Price Pottery Shop	29	A1
Pottery Souq	30	B1

TRANSPORT
Local Buses	31	B2

To the right of this street, down a twisting alley are the remains of the so-called **Cathédrale Portugaise** (admission Dh10; ☑ 8am-noon & 2.30-6pm), which would have become Safi's cathedral had the Portuguese remained. As it turned out, they stayed only long enough to complete the choir and now just one vaulted hall is all that's left.

Dominating the eastern end of the medina is the Kechla, a massive defensive structure with ramps, gunnery platforms and living quarters. It was used as a prison until 1990 but now houses the recently restored **Musée National de Céramique** (admission Dh10; ☑ 8.30am-6pm Wed-Mon). Exhibits include pottery from Safi, Fès and Meknès, and some contemporary pieces by local artists.

Climb up to the roof for great views over the medina and pottery works.

COLLINE DES POTIERS
Outside Bab Chaba, on the hill opposite the gate, you can't miss the earthen kilns and chimneys of the **Colline des Potiers** (Potters' Hill). The skills used here are predominantly traditional and you can wander around the cooperatives and see the potters at work. Apart from seeing the ancient wood-fired kilns in action, you can watch the artisans moulding clay, hand-painting complex designs and glazing. Some potters devote themselves entirely to the production of the green tiles that top many important buildings throughout the country,

while others manufacture bowls, platters, vases, and other decorative ceramics. If a potter invites you in to watch him at work, you'll be expected to give a small tip or buy an item or two from the shop.

Courses

If you're aged between 18 and 30 and interested in studying Moroccan Arabic, the Safi-based **Jeunesse des Chantiers Marocains** (☎ 024 621090; http://perso.menara.ma/youthcamps; internationalcamps@yahoo.com) offers three- to four-week courses with 18 hours of tuition per week. This nonprofit group is aimed at promoting cultural tourism and participants stay with local families and take part in cultural events learning about traditional food, culture and music. The association also runs week-long traditional pottery-making and painting courses.

Sleeping

Safi's budget hotels are pretty grim and if you can afford it, this is the place to spend a little more than usual. The cheapest places are around the port end of Rue du Souq and along Rue de R'bat and none of them are great choices for women. Safi is popular with Moroccan tourists and hotels get very busy in August so book ahead.

BUDGET

Hôtel Majestic (☎ 024 464011; fax 024 462490; Place de l'Indépendance; s/d/tr Dh40/80/120) Better than it looks from the outside and as cheap as chips, this is the best of the medina options although it can be quite noisy. The rooms are basic and have shared bathrooms (hot shower Dh5), but everything is clean and well-kept and you might even get a view of the ocean.

Hôtel Anis (☎ 024 463078; fax 024 462329; Rue de R'bat; s/d Dh135/159; apt 2/4 person Dh304/488) A hefty step up in price but not in quality, the Anis is a stylistically challenged place with a fascination for plastic flowers and pictures of farm animals. The rooms, with their brass lamps and red velour covers, are tame by comparison. Each has its own old, but clean, bathroom and there's limited onsite parking (Dh10).

Hôtel L'Honneur (☎ 061 709436; Rue du Souq; s/d Dh30/60) Basic rooms surround a tiled court-yard at this family-run place just inside the medina. It's a no-frills, functional place

with shared bathrooms (hot shower Dh5) and little charm but you can't beat the rock-bottom prices.

Camping Caravaning International (☎ 024 463816; camping per person Dh15, plus per tent/car Dh10/10; 🔊) This decent municipal site 2km north of town has its own pool and clean facilities (hot showers Dh10). A metered petit taxi will cost around Dh10 from the centre, or take bus No 4 (Dh2.50) from Rue Driss Ben Nacer.

MIDRANGE & TOP END

Hôtel Assif (☎ 024 622311; www.hotel-assif.ma; Rue de la Liberté; s/d with shower Dh185/237, with bath Dh237/290; 🖭) Comfortable, slightly faded rooms with en suite bathrooms and small balconies are available at this reliable, three-star hotel. Unless you really want a soak, it's not worth paying the extra for a bath as you'll still get a decent-sized bathroom with shower. Although the rooms aren't anything exciting, they're a big step up from the Anis.

Hôtel Farah (☎ 024 464299; www.goldentulipfarah safi.com; Ave Zerktouni; s/d/ste Dh514/728/1500; 🖭 🔊) The best hotel and the best value in Safi, the recently renovated Farah is a bargain for what you get. The large rooms are stylishly decked out in pale neutrals and have everything from sparkling new bathrooms to anti-allergy duvets and fully stocked minibars. The staff is incredibly eager to please and the views from the pool terrace are some of the best in town. There's a fitness room, hammam, two restaurants (set menu Dh170), a pizzeria and nightclub. In any other Moroccan town it'd cost at least twice the price.

Eating

RESTARANTS

Restaurant Gégène (☎ 024 463369; 11 Rue de la Marne; mains Dh60-80; ⊙ closed Sun) Soft music, low lighting, tasteful décor and a damn fine menu make this place one of the top spots in town. It has a wide choice of dishes from lamb tajine to Oualidia oysters and even pizza, and is also licensed.

Restaurant La Trattoria (☎ 024 620959; 2 Rue l'Aouinate; meals Dh200, fish Dh150; ⊙ closed Sun) Run by the same management as Gégène, but more upmarket, La Trattoria is a lovely place with a relaxed ambience and surprisingly good Italian food. The menu has a full range of pizzas and pasta as well as a good choice of fish and seafood.

Restaurant de Safi (Rue de la Maraine; meals Dh30) This no-frills choice where you can fill up on traditional Moroccan dishes has a decent selection of good-value meals. Brochettes, tajine or fish come with chips, salad and bread or go for the chunky *harira* (lentil soup).

CAFÉS, PATISSERIES & ICE-CREAM PARLOURS

The best cafés are up in the new town where **Café-Pâtisserie Oukaïmeden** (Ave Sidi Mohammed Abdallah) is the top spot for breakfast. It's a relaxed place, popular with women and the adjoining patisserie does excellent cakes. For ice cream, head to **Glacier Rihab** (Rue de la Liberté) near place Mohammed V.

In the old town, Place de l'Indépendance is the centre of the coffee-drinking universe. Chilled **Café M'Zoug-hen** (Place de L'Indépendance) is a decent breakfast venue, while **Café Essafina** (Rue Allal ben Abdallah), a short walk southwest along the cliffs, is a good late afternoon spot where you can watch the sun set over the ocean – and the industrial complex. For sugary treats **Crémerie Pâtisserie Tiffany's** (Rue de R'bat) is the place to go.

QUICK EATS

Fish and seafood, and in particular sardines, are a speciality in Safi. The best place to sample them is at the **open-air fish restaurants** on the hill at the *rond-point de Sidi Bouzid* (the Sidi Bouzid roundabout). Establish the price before ordering as fish is charged by the weight, or order the fish special – a plate of fish served with bread and a spicy tomato sauce for Dh35. A petit taxi to get there costs about Dh10.

A good alternative in town are the little **fish eateries** in the lanes near the Cathédrale Portugaise. A meal of fresh fish with chips, salads and drinks costs about Dh20. In the evening you'll find a few snack stands set up at the port end of Rue du Souq. Offerings include tiny bowls of snails (Dh5).

For something slightly more formal try another locals' favourite, the small **unnamed restaurant** (Ave Moulay Idriss; meals Dh35; 10am-late) near the Crédit du Maroc bank. It's brilliantly decorated with plastic flowers and a blow-up whale and has fresh fruit and veg piled artistically outside the door. It serves decent helpings of brochettes and tajines, both served with chips, salad and bread.

Shopping

Safi is an excellent place to buy pottery of all types. To get a feel for prices visit the **fixed-price pottery shop** (open 9am to 8pm) on the right-hand side of Rue du Souq as your enter the medina from Bab Lamaasa. To the left, towards the eastern end of the same street, you'll find the colourful **pottery souq**. There's little pressure to buy here, so it's easy to stroll around and take a good look at what is available. Just outside Bab Chaba, a string of pottery showrooms line Rue des Forgerons and are worth a look before seeing what is available at the potteries themselves (p140).

Getting There & Away

BUS

Most of the **CTM** (☎ 024 622140) buses stopping in Safi originate elsewhere, so consider booking at least a day in advance. CTM has one daily service to Agadir (Dh90, five hours) and others to Casablanca (Dh75, four hours, seven daily), El-Jadida (Dh45, two hours, four daily) and Essaouira (Dh41, two hours, two daily).

Other operators run daily departures to the same destinations as well as to Oualidia (Dh20, one hour, one daily) and Tiznit (Dh90, six hours, one daily).

TAXI

There are grands taxis to Marrakesh (Dh50) and Essaouira (Dh50), among other destinations, which leave from the parking lot beside the bus station. The rank for Oualidia (Dh20) and El-Jadida (Dh45) is a good kilometre north of town on the El-Jadida road.

TRAIN

There are two services from Safi **train station** (☎ 024 462176; Rue de R'bat) for Benguérir, where you change for services to Rabat (Dh104, 5½ hours), Casablanca (Dh75, 4½ hours), Fès (Dh172, 8½ hours) and Marrakesh (Dh55, three hours). They depart at 5.50am and 3.50pm; there are return trains to Safi at noon and 8pm.

Getting Around

Both the **bus station** (Ave Président Kennedy) and the **train station** (Rue de R'bat) are quite a distance south from the centre of town. A metered petit taxi from either will cost around

Dh7. Local buses operate from just north of Place Driss ben Nacer.

AROUND SAFI

The wonderfully wild coastline north of Safi makes a great drive with its dramatic cliffs sheltering gorgeous sandy coves. The first stop is the headland of Sidi Bouzid, where you'll get a great view back over town. It's a good spot for lunch at the popular fish restaurant **Le Refuge** (☎ 024 464354; Route Sidi Bouzid; set menu Dh150; ✆ closed Mon).

Driving further on, you'll hit some un-developed beaches that are up-and-coming surf spots and home to one of the longest tubular right handers in the world. Professionals such as Gary Elkerton, Tom Carroll and Jeff Hackman come here to train and in 2006 the Billabong Challenge was held here. At 12km from Safi, sheltered **Lalla Fatna** is one of the nicest spots on this stretch. Take a left by the Lalla Fatna café down a series of hairpin bends to the sands beneath the cliffs. Further on you'll reach the headland and lighthouse at **Cap Beddouza** (23km), where there's a wonderful wide sandy beach.

In summer (May to September) Bus No 15 runs along this route from Rue Driss ben Nacer.

ESSAOUIRA الصويرة
pop 69,000

The laid-back attitude, plum accommodation, bracing sea breezes and picture-postcard ramparts make Essaouira (pronounced esa-wera) a firm favourite on the traveller's trail. It's the kind of place where you'll sigh deeply and relax enough to shrug off your guarded attitude and just soak up the atmosphere.

Essaouira is an increasingly chic place, a beautiful 18th-century port town with a gentrified but authentically scruffy medina, a chilled out, artsy atmosphere and a growing reputation as Morocco's finest resort. Artists, musicians, craftsmen and film-makers have all fallen for its charms, its fortified walls, turrets and colonnades hiding a maze of narrow streets lined with white-washed houses, workshops, art galleries and renovated riads offering affordable luxury on almost every budget. While the strong coastal wind, known locally as the *alizee*, has made it Morocco's best-known wind-surfing centre.

Essaouira's true strength, however, lies in the fact that tourism has not totally taken over the town. The port remains a hive of activity with fishermen and boat builders getting on with daily life much as it has been for centuries, and the medina is as important for locals as it is popular with tourists.

In winter Essaouira is idyllic, and for most of the rest of the year it remains one of Morocco's most refreshing and captivating towns. In summer hard-core travellers will find its subtle charms saccharine-sweet as busloads of tourists coo over the piles of spices, naïf art, and wood-turned bowls. If you plan to visit in July or August, book accommodation well in advance and be prepared for the crowds.

History

Although the fortifications seen in Essaouira today date from the 18th century, the port has had a long and glittering career, favoured over the years as a safe harbour, wealthy trade centre and hippie hangout.

The Phoenicians founded the settlement of *Migdol,* meaning watchtower, here around the 7th century BC and the rocky offshore islands soon supported a large population who extracted a much-prized purple dye from a local mollusc, the murex.

In the late 15th century the Portuguese swept through town, renamed it Mogador, and established a trade and military post here. By 1541, they had lost control to the Saadians, the port fell from favour and trade diverted to Agadir. Although trade returned to Mogador when political power shifted to the Alawites, the town never fully recovered.

In order to revive the port's fortunes, Sultan Sidi Mohammed ben Abdallah hired a French architect, Théodore Cornut, in 1765 to create a city suitable for foreign trade. The combination of Moroccan and European styles pleased the Sultan, who renamed the town Essaouira, meaning 'well designed'. The port soon became a vital link for trade between Timbuktu and Europe, a place where the trade in gold, salt, ivory, and ostrich feathers was carefully monitored, taxed and controlled by the 2000 imperial soldiers who manned the ramparts.

By 1912 the French had established their protectorate, changed the town's name back to Mogador and diverted trade to Casablanca, Tangier and Agadir. It was only with independence in 1956 that the sleepy backwater again became Essaouira. The town enjoyed a brief hippie fling in the late '60s and early '70s after a much talked-about visit by Jimi Hendrix but has seen much change in the last decade. The traditional industries of fishing and crafts-making have been outpaced by the income garnered from the steadily increasing numbers of tourists coming to town.

Dangers & Annoyances

Essaouira is a very safe, relaxed tourist town but you should be on your guard in the backstreets of the *mellah* after dark. Although much cleaned up in recent years, it was the traditional hangout for drug dealers and junkies and is the least salubrious part of town. The area in question lies east of l'Lunétoile and north of Ave Zerktouni.

Orientation

Almost everything you'll need in Essaouira is in the old walled town, around the port or along the seafront, a pretty compact area that is easy to navigate.

The main thoroughfare in the walled town is Ave de l'Istiqlal, which becomes Ave Zerktouni as you head towards Bab Doukkala to the northeast. At the southwestern end is the main square, Place Moulay Hassan. Beyond the square is the port, fish market and the bastion of Skala du Port.

Intersecting the main thoroughfare is Rue Mohammed el-Qory, which runs from Bab Marrakesh in the southeast to near Bab Al-Bahr in the northwest, changing into Rue Abdelaziz el-Fechtaly and then into Rue d'Oujda along the way. Parallel to this is another busy street, Rue Lattarine, merging into Rue Laâlouj.

The bus station and grands taxis are 1km northeast in a fairly raggedy part of town.

MAPS

The tourist office sells a useful map of town (Dh15) and an interesting guidebook *Essaouira – La Séductrice* (Essaouira – The Enchantress; in French; Dh35), which has information on everything from local history and arts to traditional music, festivals

and architecture. Another good buy (though not always available locally) is *Essaouira de Bab en Bab: Promenades* by Hammad Berrada (Publiday-Multidia 2002), a wonderful book of walking tours. It provides details (in French) of eight different walks, accompanied by descriptive text, photographs and comprehensive maps of the medina.

Information

BOOKSHOPS

Galerie Aida (☎ 024 476290; 2 Rue de la Skala) Stocks a selection of books in European languages.

Jack's Kiosk (☎ 024 475538; 1 Place Moulay Hassan) Sells foreign-language newspapers and magazines along with some English, French and German books. You can also rent apartments here (see p151).

CULTURAL CENTRES

Alliance Franco-Marocaine (☎ 024 472593; afme@menara.ma; Derb Lâalaouj, 9 Rue Mohammed Diouri; ☿ 9am-12.30pm & 2.30-6.30pm Mon-Fri) Offers semester-long French classes and eight-week Arabic classes as well as regular films and cultural events.

EMERGENCIES

Medical Emergencies (☎ 024 475716)
Police (☎ 024 784880; Rue du Caire)

INTERNET ACCESS

There are internet cafés all over town. Most open from 9am to 11pm and charge Dh10 per hour.

Hicham Net (5 Rue Abdelaziz el-Fechtaly)
Mogador Informatique (5 Ave de l'Istiqlal)
Salsabil News (8 Rue de Caire)

LAUNDRY

Laverie Automatique (Ave al-Aqaba, Ville Nouvelle; wash/dry Dh25/15; ☿ 9am-7pm) There's a small self-service laundry in the new town. Walk southeast on Blvd de l'Hopital for 300m and turn left into Ave al-Aqaba. The laundrette is on the right 400m ahead.

MEDICAL SERVICES

Hospital (☎ 024 475716; Blvd de l'Hopital)
Pharmacie la Kasbah (☎ 024 475151; 12-14 Rue Allal ben Abdellah)

MONEY

There are several banks with ATMs around Place Moulay Hassan and along the main road leading northeast to Bab Doukkala. Most are good for foreign-exchange and credit-card cash advances.

POST

Main post office (Ave el-Moukaouama; ✆ 8.30am-12.15pm & 2.30-6.30pm Mon-Thu, 8.30-11.30am & 3-6.30pm Fri, 8.30-11.30am Sat)
Post office (Rue Laâlouj; ✆ 8.30am-12.15pm & 2.30-6.30pm Mon-Thu, 8.30-11.30am & 3-6.30pm Fri)

TOURIST INFORMATION

Syndicat d'Initiative (☎ 024 783532; www.essaouira.com; 10 Rue du Caire; ✆ 9am-noon & 3-6.30pm Mon-Fri) This helpful tourist office has lots of information and advice for travellers, and noticeboards with information on events and activities around town.

Sights

Although there are few formal sights in Essaouira, it's a wonderful place for rambling. The medina, souqs, ramparts, port and beach are perfect for leisurely discovery interspersed with relaxed lunches and unhurried coffee or ice cream.

MEDINA & PORT

Essaouira's walled medina was added to Unesco's World Heritage list in 2001, its well-preserved, late 18th-century fortified layout a prime example of European military architecture in North Africa. For the visitor, the mellow atmosphere, narrow winding streets lined with colourful shops, whitewashed houses and heavy old wooden doors make it a wonderful place to stroll.

The dramatic, wave-lashed ramparts that surround the medina are a great place to get an overview of the labyrinth of streets. The ramparts were famously used in the opening scene of Orson Welles' *Othello* for a panoramic shot where Iago is suspended in a cage above the rocks and sea. The easiest place to access the ramparts is at **Skala de la Ville**, the impressive sea bastion built along the cliffs. A collection of European brass cannons from the 18th and 19th centuries line the walkway here and you'll also get great views out to sea and wonderful sunsets.

Down by the harbour, the **Skala du Port** (adult/child Dh10/3; ✆ 8.30am-noon & 2.30-6pm) offers more cannons and fantastic picturesque views over the fishing port and the Île de Mogador. Looking back at the walled medina from here, through a curtain of swirling seagulls, you'll get the same evocative picture that is used on nearly all official literature.

The large working port is a bustling place with plenty of activity throughout the day. Along with the flurry of boats, nets being repaired and the day's catch being landed you can see traditional wooden boats being made here. It's also worth visiting the **fish auction** (✆ 3-5pm Mon-Sat), which takes place in the market hall just outside the port gates.

ÎLE DE MOGADOR & ELEANORA'S FALCONS

Used in Phoenician and Roman times for the production of Tyrian purple dye, and once known as the Îles Purpuraires (Purple Isles), the Île de Mogador is actually two islands and several tiny islets. A massive fortification, a mosque and a disused prison are all that is left of what was once a thriving settlement, and today the uninhabited islands are a sanctuary for Eleanora's falcons.

These elegant birds of prey come here to breed from April to October before making their incredible return journey south to Madagascar. The falcons can easily be seen through binoculars from Essaouira beach, with the best viewing in the early evening. Another viewing place (though not recommended in the evening if you're alone) is south of town, about 1km or so beyond the lighthouse, on the shore by the mouth of the river.

The islands are strictly off limits in breeding season but you can arrange a private boat trip at other times. You need to obtain a permit (free) from the port office before seeking out one of the small fishing boats at the port and negotiating the price of the trip. It shouldn't cost more than Dh300.

There is also an organised boat trip, **Promenade en Mer** (☎ 024 474618; Port du Peche; adult/child Dh80/40; ✆ 10.30am & 11.30am, 3pm, 4.15pm & 5.30pm) around the islands, but bad sailing conditions can delay departures or leave you stranded at sea unable to escape relentless folk music.

MUSEUM

Essaouira's recently refurbished **museum** (☎ 024 475300; Rue Laâlouj; adult/child Dh10/3; ✆ 8.30am-noon & 2.30-6.30pm Wed-Mon) has a small but interesting collection of jewellery, costumes, weapons, musical instruments and carpets of the region. There's a section explaining the signs and symbols used by local craftspeople and some interesting

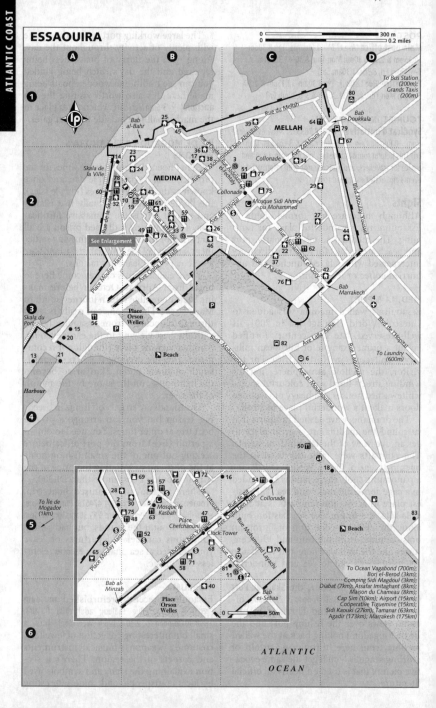

ESSAOUIRA

0   300 m
0   0.2 miles

To Bus Station
(200m);
Grands Taxis
(200m)

Bab
al-Bahr

Bab
Doukkala

MELLAH

Rue du Mellah

Rue de l'Oued Medjiba ben Abdallah

Skala de
la Ville

MEDINA

Collonade

Collonade

Mosque Sidi Ahmed
ou Mohammed

Skala du
Port

See Enlargement

Place
Orson
Welles

Place Moulay Hassan

Ave Oqba ben Nafii

Beach

Bab
Marrakech

Bab
es-Sebaa

Harbour

To Île de
Mogador
(1km)

Mosque le
Kasbah

Place
Chefchaouni

Clock Tower

Place Moulay Hassan

Rue de Tetouan

Rue de Rif

Ave Oqba ben Nafii

Rue Mohammed Lavachi

Collonade

Beach

Rue Abdallah ben Yacine

Rue de Caire

Bab al-
Minzah

Place
Orson
Welles

0   50m

To Ocean Vagabond (700m);
Borj el-Berod (3km);
Comping Sidi Magdoul (3km);
Diabat (7km); Assafar Imitaghant (8km);
Maison du Chameau (8km);
Cap Sim (10km); Airport (15km);
Cooperative Tiguemine (15km);
Sidi Kaouki (27km); Tamanar (63km);
Agadir (173km); Marrakesh (175km)

ATLANTIC

OCEAN

ATLANTIC COAST

photographs of Essaouira at the turn of the century.

Activities

BEACH & WATERSPORTS

Essaouira's wide, sandy beach is a wonderful place for walking, but the strong winds and currents mean it's not so good for sunbathing or swimming. Footballers, windsurfers and kitesurfers take over the town end of the beach, while fiercely competitive horse and camel owners ply the sands further on. They can be quite insistent, so be firm if you've no interest in taking a ride – and bargain hard if you do.

If you're walking, head south, across the Ksob River (which is impassable at high tide), to see the ruins of the Borj el-Berod, an old fortress and pavilion partially covered in sand. Local legend has it that this was the original inspiration for the Jimi Hendrix classic 'Castles Made of Sand'; however, the song was released a year before he visited. From here you can walk inland to the village of Diabat (p154) or

continue along the sands for about 8km to the sand dunes of Cap Sim.

A number of outlets rent watersports equipment and offer instruction along the beach. **Magic Fun Afrika** (☎ 024 473856; www .magicfunafrika.com; Blvd Mohammed V; ⏰ 9am-6pm daily Mar-Dec) rents windsurfing equipment (Dh150 per hour) and surfboards (Dh60 per hour). It also offers kitesurfing (from Dh250 per hour) and kayaking (Dh100 per hour, Dh330 per day). Six-hour surfing courses cost Dh1100, 10-hour kitesurfing courses cost Dh2300.

Further along the beach, **Océan Vagabond** (☎ 024 783934; www.oceanvagabond.com in French) rents surfboards (three days Dh500) and gives two-hour surfing lessons (Dh350). It also offers kitesurfing lessons (six hours Dh1850) and rental (three days Dh1200), and windsurfing lessons (one hour/six hours Dh500/1200) and rental (per hour Dh50).

HAMMAMS

There are plenty of small hammams hidden about town; one of the oldest is the newly

ATLANTIC COAST

restored **Hammam Lalla Mira** (☎ 024 475046; 14 Rue d'Algerie; hammam Dh15, gommage Dh60 ☉ 8.30am-10pm). This lovely place is heated by solar energy and, although aimed at tourists, has a wonderful traditional interior.

Another good place to break a first sweat is the **Hammam Mounia** (☎ 024 784247; www .lallamira.ma; Rue Oum Rabii; gommage Dh65; ☉ 12.30-6.15pm women only, 6.30-10.30pm men only), off Ave Sidi Mohammed ben Abdallah. For a more traditional and local experience try the women-only **Hammam de la Kasbah** (7 Rue de Marrakesh; admission Dh5).

RIDING

For something more serious than the horse and camel rides on the beach, several companies offer cross-country trekking and multi-day rides in the countryside around Essaouira. Tailor-made horse trips can be arranged through Ranch de Diabat (p154), which also offers riding lessons for adults and children, while **Abouda Safar** (☎ 028 271258, 062 743497; www.abouda-safar.com) offers an eight-day trek around the region or half-day/full-day (Dh250/400) local treks.

For camel riding the best place to go is the **Maison du Chameau** (☎ 024 785962; maisonduchameau@yahoo.fr; Douar Al Arab; r low/high Dh270/320), a remote guesthouse that is home to eight *mehari*s (white Sudanese racing camels). The guesthouse offers week-long camel-riding courses, shorter excursions and a selection of wonderfully peaceful rooms decked out in vibrant fuchsia-pink and electric-blue.

Festivals & Events

Essaouira has three major festivals that draw hoards of performers and spectators to town.

Printemps Musical des Alizés (May) A small music festival featuring classical music and opera.

Gnaoua and World Music Festival (3rd weekend Jun) A four-day musical extravaganza featuring international, national and local performers as well as a series of art exhibitions.

Festival des Atlantiques Andalouises (late Sept) An eclectic mix of Andalusian music, art and dance by local and international performers.

Sleeping

Accommodation in Essaouira isn't cheap but there's a wonderful selection of properties to choose from at all price levels. Most hotels and riads are within the walls of the medina, so everything you need is within walking distance. In summer book ahead or at least arrive early in the day to find a room.

BUDGET

The choice of budget accommodation in Essaouira is well above the usual Moroccan standard. Not only will you find a place where the bathrooms won't scare you: you'll probably get a character-laden room and terrace as well.

Le Grand Large (☎ 024 472866; www.riadlegrand large.com; 2 Rue Oum-Rabia; s/d/t Dh290/390/490) After the simple whitewash and muted colours of many riads in town, Le Grand Large is a riot of colour with pink, green and blue walls, bright throws on cast-iron beds and

---

ORSON WELLES' OTHELLO

In recent years Essaouira has become a popular spot as a film location appearing in Ridley Scott's *Kingdom of Heaven* (2005) and Oliver Stone's epic *Alexander* (2004). However, Orson Welles had discovered the little port's cinematic qualities decades previously and came here to film much of his adaptation of Shakespeare's *Othello* (1952), what many consider his most dazzling visual work. He also used locations in Safi and El-Jadida, including the atmospheric Citerne Portugaise (see p134).

The film's production was beset by problems and took three years to complete. Welles had to leave the set regularly to traipse around Europe in search of money to finance the project, and during the course of the film he went through at least four Desdemonas (including his fiancée, who then had an affair with one of the crew). Despite all this *Othello* won the Grand Prix (now Palme d'Or) at Cannes in 1952.

At the time of Welles' death, *Othello* was the only one of his films he owned. In 1992 it was restored by his daughter and re-released to huge acclaim. At an open-air screening of the film in Essaouira, a square on the seafront was officially renamed Place Orson Welles in his honour.

AUTHORS CHOICE

Riad Nakhla (☎ /fax 024 474940; www
.essaouiranet.com/riad-nakhla; 2 Rue Agadir; s/d
Dh200/300) For budget travellers who have
endured countless nights in grotty hotels,
the Riad Nakhla is a revelation. The stone
columns and fountain trickling in the
courtyard immediately make you feel like
you're somewhere much more expensive,
and the bedrooms, though simple enough,
are immaculately kept. Shuttered windows,
colourful bedspreads and great bathrooms
give the rooms some local character, and if
you're planning a night in, you'll even get a
TV. Breakfast on the stunning roof terrace
is another treat. All in all, it's an incredible
bargain at this price.

buckets of character. It's a friendly, cheerful
place with an excellent restaurant (mains
Dh65 to Dh140) serving steaks, homemade
pasta and pizza (Dh45 to Dh70).

Maison Mounia (☎ 024 472988; www.maisonmou
nia.com; 2 Re Laâlouj; B&B d/ste Dh400/600) Right in
the centre of the medina, this large house
has a variety of rooms with carved and inlaid furniture, fantastically tiled bathrooms –
some with incredible baths – and open fires
in almost every room. Some rooms are better
than others, though, so ask to see a few.

Hôtel Les Matins Bleus (☎ 024 785363; www.les
-matins-bleus.com; 22 Rue de Drâa; s/d/ste Dh250/380/660,
Jun-Sep Dh270/420/840) Hidden down a dead end,
this charming hotel has bright, traditionally
styled rooms surrounding a central courtyard painted in cheerful colours. The rooms
all have plain white walls, cheerful local
fabrics and spotless bathrooms. Breakfast is
served on the sheltered terrace from where
you'll get good views over the medina.

Hôtel Souiri (☎ /fax 024 475339; souirir@menara
.ma; 37 Rue Lattarine; B&B s/d Dh120/150, with bathroom
from Dh180/250, 4-bed apt Dh450) Perfectly placed
and well kept, this central hotel has a range
of rooms varying from small singles with
over-the-top stencilled paintwork to a
rooftop apartment complete with seating
area, kitchen and terrace.

Dar Afram (☎ 024 785657; www.dar-afram.com; 10 Rue
Sidi Magdoul; s/d Dh100/200-300, Jun–Sep Dh150/300-400)
This extremely friendly guesthouse has simple, spotless rooms with shared bathrooms
and a funky vibe. The Aussie-Moroccan

owners are musicians and an impromptu session often follows the evening meals shared
around a communal table. It also has a lovely
tiled hammam and a bar and restaurant are
planned for the rooftop terrace.

L'Lunétoile (☎ /fax 024 474689; suehunt21@yahoo
.com; 191 Ave Sidi Mohammed ben Abdallah; B&B
s Dh300-550, d Dh300-650) Lovingly restored and
sprinkled with stars and moons, this 200-
year-old riad offers great privacy with just
two rooms on each floor. The bright, simple rooms come with lovely bathrooms, a
shared kitchen on each floor and a wonderful roof terrace with ocean views.

Dar el-Qdima (☎ 024 473858; www.essaouiranet
.com/dar-el-qdima/index.htm; 4 Rue Malek Ben Rahal;
s/d Dh200/350, Jun-Sep Dh250/450) This lovely old
house in the medina has plenty of character in the public rooms and lots of original
features. The bedrooms are simpler, with
plain white walls, functional furniture and
mosaic bathrooms. It's a good deal but a
little dark and not as cosy as others in this
price bracket.

Hôtel Smara (☎ 024 475655; 26 Rue de la Skala; s/d
Dh66/96, d with sea view Dh156) Popular because it's
cheap, the Smara has none of the character
of Essaouira's other budget choices offering
decent but soulless rooms with shared bathroom. In winter it's worth paying the extra
for those with a sea view as others can be
cold and damp. The roof terrace overlooking the ocean has one of the best views in
town. Book ahead or arrive early.

Résidence Hôtel Al-Arboussas (☎ 024 472610;
arboussas@hotmail.com; 24 Impasse Rue Laâlouj; B&B s/d
Dh250/350) Simple rooms decked out in yellow and blue surround a central courtyard
at this rather plain but comfortable hotel in
the centre of the old town. Wrought-iron
furniture and potted plants add a hint of
style. There are only nine rooms so you'll
need to reserve in advance.

Camping Sidi Magdoul (☎ 024 472196; per
person/tent/car/camping place Dh12/15/10/20, per cara-
van/electricity Dh15/15) About 3km from town
near the lighthouse on the Agadir road, this
well-maintained camp site has only simple
facilities including hot showers (Dh5).

MIDRANGE

If you can afford midrange accommodation prices, you'll be spoilt for choice in
Essaouira. Each place is more charming
than the next and becomes a real retreat

ATLANTIC COAST

from the world once you've had enough of the souqs and the stall owners.

Lalla Mira (☎ 024 475046; 14 Rue d'Algerie; www .lallamira.ma; s/d/ste Dh436/692/920; 🖳) This gorgeous little place claims to be Morocco's first eco-hotel and has a selection of simple rooms with ochre *tadelakt* (smooth-polished lime) walls, wrought-iron furniture, natural fabrics and solar-powered underfloor heating. The anti-allergy beds, onsite hammam (see p147) and cheerful restaurant (mains Dh90 to Dh120) serving a good selection of vegetarian food are all nice touches.

La Casa del Mar (☎ 024 475091; www.lacasa-delmar .com; 35 Rue D'Oujda; B&B s/d Dh650/750) This guesthouse seamlessly blends contemporary design with traditional style and creates a stunning yet simple atmosphere where you can sit back, relax and just soak up the atmosphere. Retire to your room, join the other guests for a communal Moroccan meal or Spanish paella (Dh150), arrange a home visit from a masseur or henna-artist or just watch the sunset from the seafront terrace.

Hôtel Villa Bagdad (☎ 024 472023; www.villa-bag dad.com; 12-14 Rue de Bagdad; B&B d Dh550-650, ste Dh1000) The theatrical décor, grand salons, decorative plasterwork, bold tiling and collection of old photographs, masks, animal skins and saddle bags give this former *caid's* (local chief's) palace the air of a sumptuous colonial drawing room. The bedrooms are more restrained but equally quirky and a steal at this price. The area may feel a little uncomfortable for women at night and there are reports that service here is a bit pot luck.

Casa Lila (☎ 024 475525; www.riad-casalila.com; 94 Rue Mohammed el-Qory; d/ste Dh750/1200) An oasis of calm, this glorious little place is all restful hues and natural materials. A subtle palette of blues, purples and soft pinks runs through this lovely riad with plenty of original carved woods and traditional tiling blending with the wrought iron, soft linens and *tadelakt* (smooth, lustrous lime plaster) bathrooms with their chrome or copper baths.

Dar Adul (☎ 024 473910; www.dar-adul.com; 63 Rue Touahen; s Dh500-700 d Dh550-750) This lovingly restored house has a wonderful choice of cosy rooms with subtle lighting, beautiful furniture, restrained colour schemes and plenty of little touches that make it feel like a home rather than a hotel. The staff is incredibly friendly – you'll feel more like family than a paying guest by the time you leave.

Dar Liouba (☎ 024 476297; www.darliouba.com; 28 Impasse Moulay Ismail; s Dh500-1200, d Dh600-1300, Jun-Sep Dh700-1500) This beautiful, light-filled former imam's house has a choice of elegant rooms surrounding an unusual octagonal atrium. It's an extremely tranquil place with simple Islamic arches, cedar-wood screens and plasterwork details in the whitewashed bedrooms. Stylish fabrics add a splash of colour to each room and the bathrooms are new and traditionally tiled.

Dar Loulema (☎ 024 475346; www.darloulema.com; 2 Rue Souss; d/ste Dh750/1100) Another stylish 18th-century riad with whitewashed walls, Moroccan fabrics and chic décor, this place is very popular so make sure you book ahead. The sleek, simple rooms blur the line between Moorish decadence and modern minimalism creating a peaceful yet sultry ambiance that's perfect as a romantic getaway.

Dar Ness (☎ 024 476804; www.darness-essaouira .com; 1 Rue Khalid ben Oualid; B&B s Dh550, d Dh590-690) Another stunning option, Dar Ness has nine spacious, elegant rooms each of which takes up a complete side of the house. The décor is traditional but stylishly restrained with white walls and only touches of colour introduced in the fabrics and the lovely *tadelakt* bathrooms.

Riad Émeraude (☎ 024 473494; www.essaouira hotel.com in French; 228 Rue Chbanate; s/d B&B Dh340/440) This gorgeous little place opens up from a stunning central courtyard with stone arches and tiled floors to 12 charming rooms bathed in light. Elegantly simple with brilliant white linens, minimalist local touches and splashes of blues or yellow, these rooms offer incredible value for money.

Dar Al-Bahar (☎ 024 476831; www.daralbahar .com; 1 Rue Touahen; d Dh450-550) The rooms at the Al-Bahar are elegantly simple, with plain white walls, wrought-iron furniture and a contrasting touch of blue, pink, green or yellow in the traditional bedspreads and curtains. Local artworks adorn the walls and the views from the terrace overlooking the ocean are magnificent.

Dar Nafoura (☎ 024 472855; www.darnafoura .com; 30 Rue Ibn Khaldoun; s/d/ste Dh380/490/630) This lovely riad has a selection of whitewashed rooms with warm orange, deep blue or rich purple fabrics, simple furniture and lovely bathrooms. It's not as snazzy as some of the others but an excellent deal for the price.

Apartments & Riads

Essaouira has a great selection of apartments and riads to rent, most done up in impeccable style. If you're travelling as a family or in a group, they can be an affordable and flexible option. Prices range from about Dh500 per night for a one-bed apartment up to Dh3000 per night for the grand three-bedroomed former British consulate.

The two best places to look are **Jack's Apartments** (☎ 024 475538; www.essaouira.com/apartments) and **Karimo** (☎ 024 474500; www.karimo.net; Place Moulay Hassan). Otherwise try www.riadselection.com, www.villasetvisagesdumaroc.com or do an internet search to find options from independent letters. It's essential to book rental accommodation well in advance, up to several months ahead if you hope to find anything available during the high season.

TOP END

Riad Mimouna (☎ 024 785753; www.riad-mimouna.com; 62 Rue d'Oujda; s Dh700-1050, d Dh850-1200, ste Dh1500-1900; 🖳) This stunning new hotel offers incredible value at the lower end of this price range. The grand Moorish design has bucket loads of character with sumptuous carved thuya ceilings, plush carpets, the whiff of incense as you walk into your room and glorious sea views. It also has a fantastic roof terrace, a hammam and a subtly lit restaurant (menu Dh160).

Madada (☎ 024 475512; www.madada.com; 5 Rue Youssef el-Fassi; Dh1000-1500; 🔀) Sleek, stylish and very, very slick, Madada offers luxurious contemporary-styled rooms in a traditional house. Ivory and sand *tadelakt*, pared-back minimalism, designer furniture, neutral colours and a profound sense of calm run throughout. The spacious, bright rooms have subtle décor, brass hand basins, private terraces and rosewood furniture.

Palais Heure Bleue (☎ 024 474222; www.heure-bleue.com; 2 Rue Ibn Batouta; d/ste Dh2200/3900; 🔀 🖳 🖳) A decided hush falls as you walk through the doors of the Heure Bleue, Essaouira's top hotel. This swish pile has everything you could ever want from a rooftop swimming pool to its own private cinema and billiards room. Chic European style and colonial charm meet in the lounge, where a grand piano sits beneath trophy heads from a long forgotten hunting trip, and in the bedrooms where zebra prints, dark woods and marble counter tops vie for attention.

Eating

RESTAURANTS

Essaouira is packed with cafés and restaurants so there's no difficulty finding somewhere to eat. However, standards vary substantially from place to place. Along with the following recommendations most hotels and guesthouses also have restaurants with respectable food.

Medina

Chez Françoise (☎ 086 164087; 1 Rue Hommane el-Fatouaki; lunch set menu Dh60; 🕑 closed Sun) An excellent choice for a light, healthy meal, this pared-back little place offers a choice of savoury tarts served with three tangy salads. It has simple, well-made food and is a glorious find after a diet of tajine and *kefta*.

Restaurante Les Chandeliers (☎ 024 476450; 14 Rue Laâlouj; mains Dh60-90) This popular place opposite the museum has an atmospheric setting in a historic town house with candle-lit tables and an interesting menu of French and Moroccan fare. You can get anything here from a fine *magret du canard* (duck breast) to cheap and cheerful pizza.

Riad Al-Baraka (☎ 024 473561; 113 Rue Mohammed el-Qory; mains Dh45-95, set menu Dh90-130; 🕑 noon-3pm & 6.30pm-late Mon-Sat) Set in a former Jewish school, this hip place has several dining rooms and a bar set around a large courtyard shaded by a huge fig tree. The food is mainly Moroccan with some Middle Eastern and Jewish influences, the décor unconsciously cool, and there's live music by local bands at weekends.

Le 5 (☎ 024 784726; 5 Rue Youssef el-Fassi; menu Dh150; 🕑 7-11pm Wed-Mon & noon-3pm Sat & Sun) Deep-purple seating, warm stone arches and giant lampshades dominate this slick newcomer on the Essaouira restaurant scene. It's currently *the* place to see and be seen in town and serves a good choice of international and Moroccan dishes.

Restaurant Ferdaous (☎ 024 473655; 27 Rue Abdesslam Lebadi; mains Dh50, set menu Dh75) Don't be put off by the grimy backstreet this place is on – it's still one of the best spots in town for traditional Moroccan food. The seasonal menu offers an innovative take on traditional recipes and the low tables and padded seating make it feel like the real McCoy.

Les Trois Portes (☎ 068 864963; 34 Rue Lattarine; mains Dh40-60) Stone arches, tiled tables and a constant stream of happy customers make this cheerful little place one of the most popular joints in town. Run by a group of jovial sisters, it's warm and friendly with a full range of pizzas and pastas.

Restaurant Les Alizés (☎ 024 476819; 26 Rue de la Skala; set menu Dh75) Favoured by locals and tourists alike, this tiled and vaulted little place is generally packed with punters enjoying typical Moroccan fare at low tables. The candle-lit atmosphere, no-nonsense food and large portions make it great value for money.

Restaurant El-Minzah (☎ 024 475308; 3 Ave Oqba ben Nafii; mains Dh50-120, set menus from Dh95) Choose to sit on the outside terrace or in the elegant dining room inside at this popular place facing the ramparts. The menu features a good selection of international dishes and there's lively Gnaoua music here on Saturday nights.

Beach-front

Ocean Vagabond (☎ 024 783934; Blvd Mohammed V; mains Dh60-80) Although a good walk from town, this simple little café is the best of the beach-front offerings. It serves a decent but limited range of sandwiches, pizza, pasta and salads and has plenty of comfy seats in the sand from where the kids can run free.

Côté Plage (☎ 024 479000; Blvd Mohammed V; mains Dh150) Part of the looming Sofitel across the road, this beach-front café has a nice decked area where you can sit beneath the shade of giant white umbrellas. You can nibble on tapas (Dh35) as you look out over the ocean for the afternoon or arrive on Sunday for the all-day barbecue.

CAFÉS, PÂTISSERIES & ICE-CREAM PARLOURS

Taros Café (☎ 024 476407; 2 Rue de la Skala; ☿ 8am-11pm Mon-Sat) The roof terrace at the Taros is a wonderful place for afternoon tea or for quiet evening drinks lit by giant Moroccan lamps. The salons in this beautifully restored house are lined with art works and although the restaurant (mains Dh70 to Dh120) is a bit hit-and-miss for food it has live music and belly dancing most nights.

Café d'Horloge (Place Chefchaouni) Set on the attractive square beneath the clock tower, this popular café is an excellent choice for a breakfast of *amlou* (a spread made of local argan oil, almond and honey) and crepes or bread (Dh25). It's away from the hoards of

people on the main café drag and a good choice for a quiet coffee or snack.

Gelateria Dolce Freddo (Place Moulay Hassan) With more than 30 varieties of authentic Italian ice cream on offer, you'll find it hard to resist temptation at this little place on the main square. It's just Dh5 a scoop and the best you'll find in town.

For morning croissants or an afternoon pastry the best places to go are **Pâtisserie Driss** (which has a hidden seating area) and **Café Faid**, both near Place Moulay Hassan.

QUICK EATS

One of Essaouira's best food experiences is the **outdoor fish grills** that line the port end of Place Moulay Hassan. Just choose what you want to eat from the colourful displays of fresh fish and seafood at each grill, agree on a price (expect to pay about Dh40 for lunch) and wait for it to be cooked on the spot.

Alternatively, you can visit the **fish souq** just off Ave de l'Istiqlal, buy some of the day's catch and take it to one of the grill stands in the southern corner. It'll come back cooked and served with bread and salad for Dh25.

There are plenty of snack stands and hole-in-the-wall type places along Ave Sidi Mohammed ben Abdallah, Ave Zerktouni and just inside Bab Doukkala. On Place Moulay Hassan, three sandwich stands sell excellent baguettes stuffed with meat, salad and just about anything else for around Dh15.

Another great spot for lunch is **Mareblú** (☎ 067 646438; 2 Rue Sidi Ali Ben Abdallah; meals Dh30; ☿ 9am-3pm, closed Wed), a tiny, incredibly popular place that serves up bowls of steaming Italian pastas.

Drinking

Despite its popularity as a tourist destination, Essaouira isn't the hottest place for nightlife. To warm up for an evening out, you could visit the alcohol shop near Bab Doukkala and take your drinks to your hotel terrace to watch the sun go down. Alternatively, try the terrace at the **Café Restaurant Bab Laachour** (Place Moulay Hassan).

BARS

One of the most atmospheric terraces in town is at the **Taros Café** (☎ 024 476407; 2 Rue du Skala; ☿ 8am-11pm Mon-Sat), where you can sip your drinks under giant lamps and huddle round your table to fend off the wind whipping up from the sea.

For something more sultry, the hip bar and restaurant **Le Patio** (☎ 024 474166; 28 Rue Moulay Rachid; ⏱ 5.30-11pm Tue-Sun) is a candlelit den with blood-red furnishings and a black mirror ball. You'll need to buy some tapas (Dh35) to just sit and drink or you might even be tempted by the whiff of grilled fish coming from the canopied restaurant (mains Dh85 to Dh150).

For live music and a chilled atmosphere head to **Riad al-Baraka** (☎ 024 473561; 113 Rue Mohammed el-Qory; ⏱ 6.30pm-late Mon-Sat), where the best local bands play at weekends.

Shopping

Essaouira is well known for its woodwork and you can visit the string of **woodcarving workshops** near the Skala de la Ville. The exquisite marquetry work on sale is made from local fragrant thuya wood, which is now an endangered species. Although the products are beautiful and sold at excellent prices, buying anything made from thuya threatens the last remaining stands of trees by increasing demand and therefore encouraging illegal logging. For a guilt-free conscience look for crafts made from other woods instead.

Essaouira's other great product is its raffia work, made from the fibres of the doum palm. For the most stylish designs, try **Rafia Craft** (☎ 024 783632; 82 Rue d'Agadir), which sells much of its line to European outlets. Shops selling rugs, skin lamps, jewellery and brassware are found all over town. Carpet sellers tend to cluster on the laneways between Place Chefchaouni and Place Moulay Hassan. For fixed-price shopping try the **Coopérative Artisanal des Marqueteurs** (6 Rue Khalid ibn Oualid).

For herbal Viagra, Berber lipstick, cures for baldness and exotic spices, the **spice souq** is the place to go. The jovial traders will try and draw you in with their more eccentric wares but the best buys are the aromatic spice blends for tajine, fish and chicken. You can also buy argan oil products here as well as the traditional *amlou* (about Dh40 per bottle). Nearby is the fish souq, an interesting place to wander even if you're not buying, and across Ave de l'Istiqlal is the **jewellery souq**, a small area of jewellery shops with everything from heavy Berber beads to gaudy gold.

Essaouira also has a reputation as an artists' hub and several galleries around town sell works by local painters. It's a mixed bag of talent and you may need to look in all of them before finding something you like. **Galeries Damgaard** (☎ 024 784446; Rue Oqba ben Nafi) is one of the most famous in town and features the work of local artists. Nearby, the **Association Tilal des Arts Plastiques** (☎ 024 475424; 4 Rue de Caire; admission free) and **Espace Othello** (☎ 024 475095; 9 Rue Mohammed Layachi; ⏱ 9am-1pm & 3-8pm) feature up-and-coming artists. Another place to look for art work is the **Taros Café** (2 Rue du Skala), which hosts exhibitions and sells crafts.

Surfers in need of wax, board shorts or distressed T-shirts should head for **Gipsy Surfer** (☎ 02 153295; Rue de Tetouan) or **No Work Team** (☎ 024 475272; 2 Rue de la Skala & 7 Bis Rue Houman el-Fatouaki).

Getting There & Away

AIR

Direct flights to Casablanca and Paris leave from **Aéroport de Mogador** (☎ 024 476709; Route d'Agadir), 15km south of town, though the schedule can be unreliable.

BUS

The **bus station** (☎ 024 784764) is about 400m northeast of the medina, an easy walk during the day but better in a petit taxi (Dh6) if you're arriving/leaving late at night. The **left-luggage** (Dh5 per item) office here is open 24 hours.

CTM has two buses daily for Safi (Dh40, 2½ hours), El-Jadida (Dh78, four hours), and Casablanca (Dh110, six hours), and one to Marrakesh (Dh50, 2½ hours). The bus to Agadir (Dh60, three hours) continues to Inezgane (Dh65). It's best to book a day in advance for long-distance services.

Other companies run cheaper and more frequent buses to the same destinations as well as Taroudannt (Dh60, six hours), Tan Tan (Dh110, six hours) and Rabat (Dh80, six hours).

Supratours (☎ 024 475317), the ONCF subsidiary, runs buses to Marrakesh train station (Dh60, 2½ hours, four daily) to connect with trains to Casablanca. You should book several days in advance for this service, particularly in summer.

Local bus No 5 to Diabat (Dh4) and Sidi Kaouki (Dh6) leaves from Blvd Moulay Youssef outside Bab Doukkala. There are about eight services a day.

ATLANTIC COAST

TAXI
The grand taxi rank lies immediately west of the bus station. The fare to Agadir (or Inezgane) is Dh75.

Getting Around
To get to the airport take bus No 5 (Dh6, 15 minutes) or a petit taxi (Dh100). The blue petits taxis are also a good idea for getting to and from the bus station (Dh6) but they can't enter the medina. If you're happy to walk but don't want to carry your bags, there are plenty of enterprising men with luggage carts who will wheel your bags directly to your hotel (about Dh20).

For a more atmospheric, but touristy, view of town, you can take a tour in a horse-drawn carriage or calèche. You'll find them just outside Bab Doukkala (Dh60 per hour).

You can hire bikes for Dh80 per day from **Résidence Shahrazed** (☎ 024 472977; 1 Rue Youssef el-Fassi) and **Résidence Hôtel Al-Aroussas** (☎ 024 472610; 24 Impasse Rue Laâlouj).

Cars can be hired from **Wind Car** (☎ /fax 024 472804; Rue Princesse Lalla Amina) for around Dh400 per day. **Avis** (☎ 024 474926) also has an office at the airport.

AROUND ESSAOUIRA
If you have your own transport, it's worth taking a trip to one of the small women's cooperatives around Essaouira that sell argan products, natural cosmetics and food stuffs. Try **Assafar Imitaghant** (☎ 061 553586) 8km from town on the road to Marrakesh or the **Coóperative Tiguemine** (☎ 024 790110) 7km further on. The tourist office has a full list of places to visit. Best of all, travel south to the village of Tamanar to see the whole process at the **Coopérative Amal** (see boxed text p389).

Diabat
ديابات
The sleepy Berber village of Diabat, just south of Essaouira, was once a dope-smoking colony made popular with hippies after a visit by Jimi Hendrix in the early '70s. Today it's a quiet place awaiting funding for the development of a 'tourist complex' on the beach.

The main reason to visit is to hire a horse or join a trekking tour at **Ranch de Diabat** (☎ 062 297203; www.ranchdediabat.com in French). You can take a lesson, ride along the beach or sign up for a multi-day trip through the surrounding countryside (3 days/6 days Dh3500/6000).

If you want to stay in Diabat, your best bet is the rustic **Auberge Tangaro** (☎ 024 784784; www.auberge-tangaro.com; d half board per person Dh700-900), a remote old house in a serene location. The rooms here are chic but spartan, each has its own open fire and is lit by candlelight (there's no electricity on the property). The hearty communal evening meals are good and romantically lit by candelabra.

To get to Diabat drive south on the coast road to Agadir and turn right just after the bridge about 7km out of town. Alternatively, local bus No 5 leaves from outside Bab Marrakech (Dh4, every two hours).

Sidi Kaouki
سيدي كاوكي
The constant blustery winds, wild beach and decent accommodation at Sidi Kaouki are fast turning it into one of Morocco's top windsurfing and surfing spots. It's not for the faint-hearted and the waters here can be dangerous for inexperienced surfers.

A clutch of guesthouses and small stalls serving tajine, seafood and snacks stretch along the beachfront. You can rent a horse (half-hour/hour Dh70/120) and ride along the long stretch of beach, or try your hand at mono-gliding (per hour Dh90) at **VHM** (Village Hôtel Meziane; ☎ 024 475035; ⏰ 10am-6pm) at the far end of the beach. The centre also has a restaurant (mains Dh30 to Dh55).

For overnight stays try **Auberge de la Plage** (☎ 024 476600; www.kaouki.com; B&B d Dh260-390, Dh360-540 with bathroom), where the big, bright rooms are individually styled with white walls and colourful fabrics ranging from subtle natural colours to deep reds, blues and greens. It has a wonderful roof terrace and meals on request (half-board Dh100 extra).

Alternatively, try the swish new apartments at **Windy Kaouki** (☎ 024 472279; www.wind-y-kaouki.com; apt Dh650-1050). Although they're fairly plain from the outside, these are wonderful rooms displaying a modern take on traditional Moroccan décor, with warm colours, open fires and balconies with sea views. The apartments sleep between two and four people and there's a restaurant serving traditional dishes and wood-fired pizzas.

Sidi Kaouki is about 27km south of Essaouira. Bus No 5 (Dh6) leaves from outside Bab Marrakech every two hours.

Mediterranean Coast & the Rif

شاطىء البحر المتوسط والريف البحري

Bounded by the red crags of the Rif Mountains and the crashing waves of the Mediterranean, northern Morocco has kept its charms well hidden from outsiders and remains one of the least-visited parts of the country.

The cosmopolitan hustle of Tangier has been attracting the curious, the criminal and the artistic for decades, and has acted as a gateway between Africa and Europe for far longer. Travelling east, the coast is a rocky jumble of wild and beautiful cliffs that only occasionally calm into sandy coves and picturesque fishing ports. Also along this stretch of coast are the enclaves of Ceuta and Melilla, the last vestiges of Spain's African empire. In the early 20th century they formed part of Spanish Morocco, and even today the region reflects the influence of its northern neighbour across the Mediterranean in cuisine, architecture and language.

Inland are the old colonial capital of Tetouan and the relaxing town of Chefchaouen – a long-hidden gem on the backpacker trail that's now moving closer to the tourist spotlight. The surrounding Rif abounds with trekking opportunities, and even the less energetic will get a kick from the mountain-crest rides through the rugged surrounds. This region, long-neglected by the government in Rabat, is the centre of kif (marijuana) cultivation.

The mountains gave rise to the tough Berber tribes, whose independent streak, which kept the Spanish at arm's length, continues to this day. But their proud hospitality is a boon for visiting travellers, who may feel they have discovered their own secret corner of Morocco.

HIGHLIGHTS

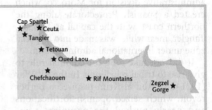

- Look for the ghosts of Henri Matisse, Paul Bowles and William Burroughs in cosmopolitan **Tangier** (p157)

- Relax in the supremely chilled-out blue medina of **Chefchaouen** (p189), high in the Rif Mountains

- Hike through the **Rif Mountains** (p192) exploring tiny mountain villages with sweeping views

- Check out the old medina and unique Hispano-Moorish architecture of **Tetouan** (p182)

- Watch the sunset over the Atlantic from the grotto of **Cap Spartel** (p175)

- Take a siesta and a change of pace in the Spanish enclave of **Ceuta** (p176)

- Drive through the stunning **Zegzel Gorge** (p212), tucked in the Beni-Snassen mountains

- Explore the winding coast road to **Oued Laou** (p197), with its steep dramatic cliffs and unexpected sandy coves

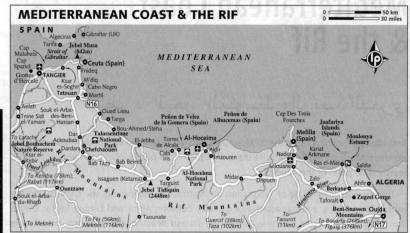

History

Due to its location just across the Strait of Gibraltar, Mediterranean Morocco has long been subject to European influences, especially from Portugal and Spain. During the 15th century, every port on the Mediterranean fell under the control of the Portuguese, with the exception of Melilla, which was Spanish. These Iberian players were finally pushed out of Morocco in the 16th century, but not for good.

In the 19th century, Morocco was again carved up by European powers, and Spain landed 90,000 troops at Melilla. France and Spain soon came to agreement on a territorial-administrative division for Morocco, which created a Spanish Protectorate along the northern coast, with the capital at Tetouan. Tangier, meanwhile, was made into a special zone under international administration.

It did not take long for colonial rule to give rise to tribal rebellions. In the Rif War (1921–26), Abd al-Krim inspired a Berber revolt, which seized Spanish fortifications and nearly pushed the occupiers completely out of the north. Although a combined French and Spanish force eventually quashed the rebellion, the European occupiers were never able to completely subdue the rowdy Rif rebels.

Spain finally withdrew from northern Morocco in 1956, after years of independence movements and nationalist uprisings. The exceptions, of course, are the Spanish enclaves of Ceuta and Melilla, to which Spain

claims a historical right. In any case, the whole region still maintains a strong Spanish flavour, from the language preferences (Spanish is spoken much more widely than French) and culinary influences to the Spanish tourists who flock here every summer.

Climate

Weather in this mountainous, coastal region is generally mild, with a tendency toward cool and wet. Average daily temperatures range from 12°C in winter to 25°C in summer. This region has more rainfall than other parts of the country. Weather can be cloudy and rainy for days on end, as the clouds get trapped in the mountains. Only the summer months – especially July and August – are dry.

Getting There & Away

Tangier is easily the most convenient gateway into this region, as it is well connected by ferry to Europe and then by rail to the cities along the Atlantic coast. Several other cities along the coast, including Ceuta, Melilla, Nador and Al-Hoceima, also have ferry connections to Spain. If you are making your way to the region from the south, Chefchaouen is accessible by road from Fès, Meknès and Rabat.

Getting Around

The area comprising the Mediterranean Coast and the Rif is more difficult to get around than some other parts of Morocco.

With the exception of Tangier, this region is not connected by the train line, so travellers are dependent on buses and cars. Roads here weave and wind around the Rif mountains, so routes never seem to be as direct as they could be, and many feel the lack of investment and maintenance. Reaching some of the smaller coastal resorts can require long waits for grands taxis to fill – or hiring a vehicle yourself.

WEST MEDITERRANEAN COAST شاطىء البحر المتوسط

TANGIER طنجة
pop 650,000

More than any other city, Tangier has been Morocco's face to the world for more years than anyone cares to remember. Its strategic location on the narrow strait that separates Africa from Europe has been coveted and controlled by a seemingly endless procession of empires and kingdoms. The Phoenicians, Romans, Visigoths, Portuguese, British and Spanish: Tangier has seen them all come and go, absorbing a little from each conqueror before blithely getting back to doing what it has always done best – making money. Its most recent occupants prior to Moroccan independence came in a shotgun marriage between the western powers who controlled the port via a dubious international council for half the 20th century. Today, Tangier is like an ageing libertine propped up languidly at a bar, having seen it all.

International Tangier was both a resort for the millionaire jet set and a bolt hole for artists, currency speculators, beatniks and prostitutes. Everyone from Elizabeth Taylor to author William Burroughs came here, revelling in a climate where seemingly nothing was forbidden and anything – or anyone – could be bought for a price.

Independence brought incorporation into Morocco, and the city was cleaned up and began to lose much of its zing. The beatniks went home and the high-fliers moved elsewhere. Government neglect left the place a dreary port, and, as world economics moved on, people-trafficking and

drug smuggling moved in. The remaining tourists came on day-trips from Spain and, faced with a barrage of street hustlers, left quickly, unlikely to return in a rush.

Recent years have seen an upswing in Tangier's fortunes. Rabat has poured huge funds into the economic development of the area, matched with infrastructural investment from the EU. Trade with Europe is booming, and the outskirts of Tangier increasingly resemble a huge industrial zone.

Visitors to Tangier quickly learn that business is what makes the city's heart beat. Everyone, from the street boys selling cigarettes up, is on the make. There's been a crackdown (with some efficiency) on the hustlers that have ruined many a tourist's day, but the place isn't entirely hassle free. Those arriving on the ferry from Spain will do well to remind themselves that they've crossed to another continent. Despite Tangier's cosmopolitan airs, Europe this isn't.

Many people shoot through Tangier quickly, finding even a short taste too much. It's a city that takes some getting to know, but rewards in spades those who take the time. The culture is vibrant and the streets lively. Hardly truly Moroccan, nor European, nor even African, Tangier is a heady mix of all three. It defies categorisation, which is precisely why it is so appealing.

History

Tangier has been coveted for millennia as a strategic site commanding the Strait of Gibraltar; its port has been one of the most contested in the Mediterranean. The area was settled by the ancient Greeks and Phoenicians, for whom it was a trading base.

These early days are shrouded in myth. Paradise on earth, the Garden of the Hesperides, supposedly lay nearby. It was here that Hercules slew the giant Antaeus and fathered a child, Sophax, by the giant's widow, Tinge, who provided the city's original name, Tingis.

Little is known about Tangier's early history. It was the capital of the Roman province of Mauretania Tingitana before the Vandals attacked from Spain in AD 429. Whether the Vandals actually occupied the city is not recorded. The Byzantines took an erratic interest in the port, but for the most part they contented themselves with their strongly fortified outpost at Ceuta.

PAUL BOWLES IN TANGIER

Perhaps the best-known foreign writer who lived in and wrote about Morocco was the controversial American author Paul Bowles, who died in Tangier in 1999 aged 88. A highly respected author in his own right, he also did more than anyone else to introduce Moroccan authors to English-speaking audiences.

Bowles was born in New York in 1910. Somewhat directionless after leaving school, he spent time travelling in Europe and associating with influential artists and intellectuals. In 1931, on Gertrude Stein's rather off-beam advice, he stopped writing and went briefly to Tangier – a trip which would have a huge impact on his later years. Bowles devoted the next 15 years to music composition and criticism. In 1938 he married Jane Sydney Auer, but they were never a conventional couple – he was an ambivalent bisexual and she was an active lesbian.

After WWII Paul returned with Jane to Tangier, which he would call home for the rest of his life. Here he was at the centre of a lively creative circle, which included the likes of Allen Ginsberg and William Burroughs. He also returned to creative writing.

During the 1950s Bowles began taping, transcribing and translating stories by Moroccan authors, in particular Driss ben Hamed Charhadi (also known by the pseudonym Larb Layachi) and Mohammed Mrabet. He was also an important early recorder of Moroccan folk music.

Thanks to Bernado Bertolucci's 1990 film, Bowles' best known book is *The Sheltering Sky* (1949), a bleak and powerful story of an innocent American couple who arrive in North Africa shortly after WWII and try to put their relationship back together. His other works include *Let It Come Down* (1952), a thriller set in Tangier; *The Spider's House*, set in 1950s Fès; and two excellent collections of travel tales: *Their Heads Are Green* (1963) and *Points in Time* (1982). *A Distant Episode: the Selected Stories* is a good compilation of Bowles' short stories.

There is a definite dark undercurrent to some of Bowles' writing, which is almost gothic at times. His autobiography *Without Stopping* (nicknamed Without Telling) sheds a little light on a few dark corners of his life.

The Arabs arrived in 705. Once they had established their supremacy over the indigenous Berber tribes, they passed Tangier between various factions before it eventually came under Almohad rule in 1149.

The Portuguese captured Tangier on their second attempt in 1471, only to give it to the British 200 years later as a wedding gift for Charles II. The English diarist Samuel Pepys worked here briefly, famously describing Tangier as the 'excrescence of the earth'.

Moulay Ismail besieged Tangier in 1679, causing Britain to abandon it, but not before destroying the port and much of the city. The Moroccans remained in control until the mid-19th century.

At this time, North Africa once again piqued the interest of European powers. While the rest of Morocco was divided between France and Spain, Tangier's strategic location meant that imperial rivalry eventually deemed it an 'international zone'. Technically ruled by a representative of the Moroccan sultan, the city was in reality controlled by the resident diplomatic agents of France, Spain, Britain, Portugal, Sweden, Holland, Belgium, Italy and the USA.

Each of the controlling powers maintained its own banks, currency and post offices, and took a share in the policing of the city. Banks, in particular, made fortunes out of manipulating the currency markets. Tangier was to remain an international zone until a few months after Morocco's independence in 1956, when it was reunited with the rest of the country (although it was some years before all its economic and financial privileges were removed).

Tangier's anomalous status made it a haven for freebooters, hedonists, exiles and paedophiles. Rich westerners flocked to the city, making it one of the Mediterranean's most fashionable resorts. Gays were attracted by its sexual freedoms, while artists and writers came in search of artistic inspiration and cheap drugs.

The American Beat writers became particularly associated with Tangier – Alan Ginsberg and Jack Kerouac passed through, as did William Burroughs, who spent much of the 1950s here, christening it 'Interzone', a city where everything was permitted and nothing was forbidden. Paul Bowles settled here, becoming Tangier's most celebrated international resident (see box, opposite).

The Interzone days lasted into the 1960s, when the Moroccan authorities clamped down hard on the brothels and the gay bars. Tangier today is now a busy industrial port, although whiffs of its former notoriety linger in the sea air when the sun goes down.

Orientation

Tangier's small medina climbs up the hill to the northeast of the city, while the ville nouvelle surrounds it to the west, south and southeast. The large, central square known as the Grand Socco (officially renamed Place du 9 Avril 1947) provides the link between the medina and the ville nouvelle. Rue as-Siaghin leads northeast off the Grand Socco to the medina's tiny central square, the Petit Socco (also known as Socco Chico, and officially as Place Souq ad-Dakhil).

From Petit Socco, leaving the medina's southern gate brings you out near the end of Ave d'Espagne. The CTM bus station is around the corner, along with the entrance to the port – the ferry terminal is a further 500m walk from the gates.

Three hundred metres south of the Grand Socco, Place de France, Blvd Pasteur and the northern end of Blvd Mohammed V constitute the heart of the ville nouvelle. Here you'll find the main post office, banks and many of the restaurants, bars and hotels. A further 1.5km south at the junction of Rue du Prince Héritier and Ave Louis van Beethoven is Place Jamia el-Arabia, where the main bus station and grand taxi rank are located.

Ave des FAR stretches southeast along the coast from the medina. Hotels, cafés and nightclubs line this strip overlooking the Bay of Tangier. Tanger Ville train station is a few blocks inland off this road in the southeast of the city.

IN SEARCH OF A BETTER LIFE

Each year Spanish authorities intercept nearly 20,000 would-be immigrants trying to make it to Spain by sea. Many are Moroccan, but most come from south of the Sahara hoping to find their way to Europe. Moroccans tend to be deported immediately but some others who make it across are allowed to stay and will slip into the black economy, as Spanish law doesn't allow police to expel people whose identity and nationality they are unable to prove.

The would-be immigrants have brought a new complexion to Tangier, Casablanca and Rabat. Many cheap hotels are booked out on a semi-permanent basis by West African migrants, or *camarades* as they call themselves. All are waiting for the chance to make their break for Europe, widely considered to be the promised land.

Traditionally, hopefuls were trafficked in tiny zodiac inflatables across the Strait of Gibraltar, one of the busiest sea lanes in the world, and it became a sick local joke that there were no pedalos left to hire along the city's long stretch of beach. Under intense pressure from Spain, the Moroccan authorities largely closed this route, so many west Africans turned their attention to the vulnerable Spanish enclaves of Ceuta and Melilla. In late 2005 several hundred *camarades* stormed the fence at Melilla. The Moroccan army patrolling the border responded with lethal force, and mass arrests by the government led to 500 migrants being literally dumped back on the edge of the Sahara. The height of the razor-wire–topped fences surrounding Ceuta and Melilla has since been doubled to around 6m.

Following an extended clampdown by the Moroccan authorities, a new route further south opened in 2006, from Mauritania to the Canaries. The overloaded canoe-like pirogues are prone to swamping by waves, and Spanish authorities estimate that, in the first three month of 2006, around 1000 would-be immigrants drowned on this route.

With people-trafficking now a multi-million dollar industry, this unhappy trade shows no signs of subsiding. From the Petit Socco, in Tangier's heart, to Nouâdhibou in Mauritania, desperate hopefuls continue to pay out for the hazardous crossing. Many are willing to sign themselves into virtual slavery in order to get into Europe, where they then have a huge debt to pay. Given sub-Saharan Africa's chronic problems, for some the lure of Europe is too strong, or their desperation is too deep, to find any other alternative.

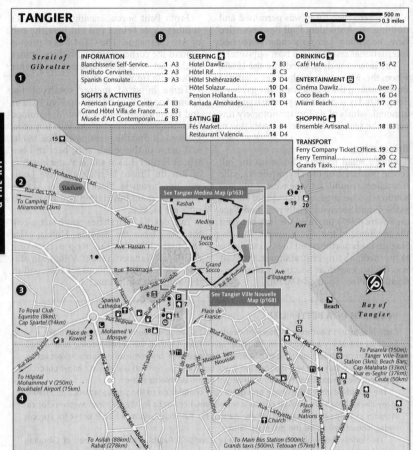

TANGIER

INFORMATION	
Blanchisserie Self-Service..........**1** A3	
Instituto Cervantes...................**2** A3	
Spanish Consulate....................**3** A3	
SIGHTS & ACTIVITIES	
American Language Center **4** B3	
Grand Hôtel Villa de France.....**5** B3	
Musée d'Art Contemporain.....**6** B3	
SLEEPING	
Hotel Dawliz...........................**7** B3	
Hôtel Rif................................**8** C3	
Hôtel Shéhérazade...................**9** D4	
Hôtel Solazur.........................**10** D4	
Pension Hollanda....................**11** B3	
Ramada Almohades.................**12** D4	
EATING	
Fés Market............................**13** B4	
Restaurant Valencia...............**14** D4	
DRINKING	
Café Hafa..............................**15** A2	
ENTERTAINMENT	
Cinéma Dawliz..................(see 7)	
Coco Beach **16** D4	
Miami Beach.........................**17** C3	
SHOPPING	
Ensemble Artisanal................**18** B3	
TRANSPORT	
Ferry Company Ticket Offices.**19** C2	
Ferry Terminal.......................**20** C2	
Grands Taxis.........................**21** C2	

Information
BOOKSHOPS
Librairie des Colonnes (Map p168; ☎ 039 936955; 54 Blvd Pasteur) Tangier's best bookshop, with a modest selection of English-language books.

CULTURAL CENTRES
Galerie Delacroix (Map p168; 86 Rue de la Liberté; admission free; ☑ 10am-1pm & 4-9pm Tue-Sun) Contemporary art gallery operated by the Institut Français.
Institut Français (Map p168; ☎ 039 941054; info@iftanger.ma; 41 Rue Hassan ibn Ouazzane; ☑ 8.30am-noon & 2.30-7pm Tue-Sat) Offers a full programme of films, concerts, theatre and other cultural events in French.
Instituto Cervantes (Map p160; ☎ 039 932001; www.tanger.cervantes.es in Arabic & Spanish; 99 Blvd Sidi

Mohammed ben Abdallah; ☑ 10am-1pm & 3-7.30pm Mon-Fri, 10am-1pm Sat) Spanish library with a varied collection of material on Tangier.

EMERGENCY
Emergency Service (☎ 039 373737; ☑ 24hr)

INTERNET ACCESS
Cyber Café Adam (Map p168; Rue ibn Rochd; per hr Dh10; ☑ 9.30-3.30am) Serves hot and cold drinks.
Espace Net (Map p168; 16 Ave Mexique; per hr Dh10; ☑ 9.30am-midnight)
Maroc Telecom Internet (Map p168; cnr Blvd Pasteur & Rue du Prince Moulay Abdallah; per hr Dh10; ☑ 9am-midnight) Internet on 1st floor.
Pigier Internet (Map p168; cnr Rue Khalid ibn Oualid & Blvd Pasteur; per hr Dh10; ☑ 10am-10pm)

LAUNDRY
Blanchisserie Self-Service (Map p160; 99 Ave Hassan II)
Pressing Détroit (Map p168; 10 Rue el-Jarraoui)

LEFT LUGGAGE
Consigne (Map p163; cnr Rue Dar Dbagh & Rue du Portugal) A convenient place to leave your luggage for the day. At the southeast entrance to the medina.

MEDICAL SERVICES
Clinique du Croissant Rouge (Map p168; Red Cross Clinic; ☎ 039 946976; 6 Rue al-Mansour Dahabi)
Hôpital Mohammed V (☎ 039 930856; Rue Val Fleurie) On the road to the airport.
Pharmacy Anegax (Map p163; Rue as-Siaghin)
Pharmacy El Yousr (Map p168; Blvd Mohammed V)

MONEY
Blvds Pasteur and Mohammed V are lined with numerous banks with ATMs and *bureau de change* counters. Outside of working hours, try the exchange bureaus in the big hotels.
Banque Marocaine du Commerce Extérieur (BMCE; Map p168; Blvd Pasteur; ☾ 9am-1pm & 3-7pm Mon-Fri, 10am-1pm & 4-7pm Sat & Sun) One of several on this stretch of the road.

POST
Main post office (Map p168; Blvd Mohammed V) Post restante is at the counter furthest to the right; parcel post is on the south side of the building.

TOURIST INFORMATION
ONMT (Délégation Régionale du Tourisme; Map p168; ☎ 039 948050; fax 039 948661; 29 Blvd Pasteur; ☾ 8.30am-noon & 2.30-6.30pm Mon-Fri)

TRAVEL AGENCIES
The following all sell ferry, as well as flight, tickets.
Carlson Wagonlit (Map p168; ☎ 039 331024; 91 Rue de la Liberté)
Hispamaroc (Map p168; ☎ 039 932178; hispamaroc@mamnet.net.ma; 2 Rue el-Jabha el-Ouatania)
Med Travel (Map p168; ☎ 039 935875; fax 039 932118; 3 Rue ibn Rochd)
Voyages Schwartz (Map p168; ☎ 039 374837; fax 039 930159; 54 Blvd Pasteur) Amex agent.

Dangers & Annoyances
Tangier's dangers are as nothing compared to the Interzone days, but the city still carries a poor reputation for hustlers and petty thieves. Touts and *faux guides* (unofficial or informal guides), who usually have just a few hours to make their money from the day-trippers from Algeciras, can be persistent. The situation has improved considerably in recent years, but it's still a place to keep your wits about you. Solo women may be subject to hassle after about 10pm, and will probably seek to avoid the port area after dark. Male travellers may become quickly tired with furtive offers of hash from shady-looking young men. If you do have problems with a shopkeeper, unofficial guide or anyone else, and have a fair cause for complaint, contact the **Brigade Touristique** (Tourist Police; Map p163; Ave des FAR, Tangier Port).

ARRIVING BY BOAT
The hordes of touts that would descend in packs on unwary travellers have largely disappeared from Tangier's port, but you're still likely to be greeted by a few multilingual 'guides'. They can be especially tiresome if this is your introduction to Morocco (and your first trip outside Europe). The best way to deal with this is to look blasé, claim that you already know the city and politely decline any offers of assistance. Smile and keep moving. It helps to know exactly where you're going, so you can jump quickly into a cab if necessary. A petit taxi into the centre will cost around Dh10 and a grand taxi around Dh30 between all passengers. Remember to change money on the boat to pay the fare. Tackling anywhere unfamiliar after dark is always more traumatic, so try to arrive early in the day and, above all, with a good sense of humour.

DEPARTING BY BOAT
If you're catching the ferry *from* Tangier and arrive at the port on foot, you'll be approached by touts intent on getting you into one or other of the numerous ticket offices and travel agencies along Ave d'Espagne. To minimise the hassle, you might buy your ticket in advance or take a taxi to the terminal building. In any case, be sure to pick up an exit form with your ticket. The scribes who distribute them at the port will expect a tip for their 'assistance' filling out the form. Allow a good 90 minutes before your boat sails to get tickets and make your way through passport control.

MEDITERRANEAN COAST & THE RIF

SCAMS

Tangier's scammers can be inventive. You might be approached by Moroccans claiming to have met you the previous day in Algeciras or on the ferry; their intention is usually nothing more than to take you to their cousin's shop or hotel. The same applies on the train from Tangier: over-friendly 'students' who are actually touting for hotels in Fès or Marrakesh. Trains also attract a few real con-artist teams – a friendly, well-dressed man comes to the rescue when you are being harassed by a nasty, aggressive hustler. The two are actually partners: having established your trust, your 'saviour' tries to lure you to his authentic village, a Berber celebration or a bargain hotel. Asilah is a popular disembarkation point for these con artists.

Sights

MEDINA

The gateway to the medina is the **Grand Socco** (Map p163), once as full of life as Place Djemaa el-Fna in Marrakesh. Its official name, Place du 9 Avril 1947, refers to the date that Mohammed V first publicly allied himself to the cause of Moroccan independence. The square was being rebuilt and gentrified during research, so it's hard to know if its soul will survive. The best we may hope for is that the terrible traffic surrounding the square is tamed.

From here, enter the medina by Rue Semmarine through a gate surrounded by Riffian women selling fruit and vegetables. This is Rue as-Siaghin. This was once Tangier's main gold market (a fair number of jewellery stores remain). South of here was the *mellah* (old Jewish quarter).

Heading downhill, you soon pass the lovely Spanish **Church of the Immaculate Conception** (Map p163) on your right, built in 1880 when Spaniards comprised one-fifth of Tangier's population. A few doors down, at No 41, is the old **residence of the naib** (sultan's agent; Map p163), who was the point of contact between the Moroccan leader and European legations until 1923. Inside is a small courtyard filled with orange trees. Another reminder of international Tangier is the huge painted sign for the British Bank of West Africa on a nearby wall. Continue downhill to emerge onto the Petit Socco.

Gone are the days when William S Burroughs could cheerfully write of the endless stream of louche offers from young boys and men around the **Petit Socco**. Nowadays, the busy little square is a great place to linger over a mint tea, watch the world go by and contemplate its colourful past. And sleaze remains close to the surface: you'll have plenty of offers of 'something special, my friend' and several of the cheap pensions overlooking the square still double as brothels.

From the Petit Socco, Rue Jemaa el-Kebir (formerly Rue de la Marine) leads east past the **Grande Mosquée** (Map p163). It is said to have been the site of a Roman temple, and at one time housed a church built by the Portuguese. A little further on you reach a **scenic overlook** over the port.

Returning to the Petit Socco, Rue des Almohades (formerly Rue des Chrétiens) takes you north, past some very determined shopkeepers, to join Rue M Torres. From here, stick to the wider streets and continue uphill and you should eventually emerge near a little, white domed building that contains the **tomb of Sidi Hosni** (Map p163). Nearby is the **Sidi Hosni Palace** (Map p163), where Barbara Hutton, the Woolworth heiress, lived and gave some of her grandest parties.

KASBAH

The kasbah sits on the highest point of the city, behind stout walls. Coming from the medina, enter through Bab el-Aassa, the southeastern gate, to find **Dar el-Makhzen Museum** (Map p163; ☎ 039 932097; admission Dh10; ◷ 9am-12.30pm & 3-5.30pm Wed-Mon, closed Fri afternoon), the former sultan's palace, which now houses a worthwhile collection of Moroccan arts.

The palace was built by Moulay Ismail in the 17th century and enlarged by later sultans, including Moulay Hafid, who lived here with his four wives and 40 concubines until 1912. The private apartments – arranged around an inner courtyard – contain beautiful examples of carved wood ceilings and doors, *zellij* (tilework) and *muqarnas* (plasterwork).

Displayed in the salons are wonderful examples of Moroccan crafts, including musical instruments, Fès pottery, Berber kilims, Chefchaouen embroidery, leatherwork, metalwork and weapons. The small archaeological collection comes mostly from

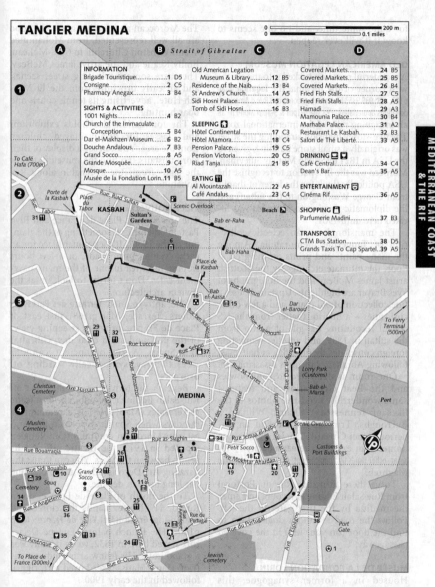

TANGIER MEDINA

MEDITERRANEAN COAST & THE RIF

Volubilis, including the well-preserved Roman mosaic, *Voyage of Venus*. Before leaving, take a stroll around the Andalusian-style **Sultan's Gardens**. The central fountain and citrus and pomegranate trees provide welcome shade.

In the 1950s the kasbah was the setting for a legendary café called **1001 Nights** (Map p163), which was established by Brion Gysin, the artist who introduce the cut-up writing technique to William Burroughs. The café was famous for its house band of trance musicians – the Master Musicians of Jajouka – who later released a record produced by the Rolling Stones' Brian Jones. The café has been closed for renovations for quite some time, and no one seems to know if it will ever reopen.

OLD AMERICAN LEGATION MUSEUM

A wonderful museum tucked into the south-west corner of the medina, the **legation** (Map p163; ☎ 039 935317; www.legation.org; 8 Rue d'Amerique; donations appreciated; ☺ 10am-1pm & 3-5pm Mon-Fri) is an intriguing relic of the international zone. The five-storey mansion straddling the street was originally a small stone building, given to the USA in 1821 by Sultan Moulay Suleyman. Morocco was the first nation to recognise the USA politically (look for the letter of thanks from George Washington to the sultan) and the diplomatic mission to Morocco was located here until 1961.

The mansion hosts an eclectic collection of Tangerine memorabilia. Among the many paints and prints on the ground floor, the intimate etchings by the Scottish artist James McBeay and the lithographs of Yves Brayer are highlights. Upstairs houses a fine collection of old maps, and a few other curiosities – a hilarious letter from the US consul recounting his gift of a lion from the sultan in 1839, and another requesting foreign consulates fly their flag at half-mast following Abraham Lincoln's assassination.

One room is dedicated to Paul Bowles and the Beat Generation and features some wonderfully evocative photos of the likes of Tennessee Williams, William S Burroughs, Truman Capote and an imperious Noel Coward. The legation is also home to an excellent **research library** (☺ Thu & Sat, other times by appointment) focusing on the Maghreb.

To get here turn into Rue du Portugal from Rue Salah Eddine el-Ayoubi and enter the medina by the first gate on the left. Follow the road around a dogleg turn to find the door (on your left) in the covered passageway.

MUSÉE DE LA FONDATION LORIN

Housed in a former synagogue, this **museum** (Map p163; ☎ 039 930306; lorin@wanadoo.net.ma; 44 Rue Touahine; admission free, donations appreciated; ☺ 11am-1pm & 3.30-7.30pm Sun-Fri) is a gem of a place if you're interested in Tangier's 20th-century history. A peaceful large room houses an engaging collection of photographs, newspaper cuttings and posters of Tangier from 1890 to the 1960s.

The Moroccan and foreign great and good are all well represented, from Mohammed V and Winston Churchill to Caid McLean, Emily Keane and the artist James McBeay. There are some fascinating street scenes, and an early brochure from the El Minzah Hotel, advertising its tennis courts and boar hunting.

The foundation also holds exhibitions and classes for disadvantaged children from the area. You can see a display of their work upstairs. To find the museum, follow the signs from Rue as-Siaghin along Rue Touahine.

VILLE NOUVELLE

The area around Place de France and Blvd Pasteur still hints at something of the glamour of the 1930s. It's a popular place for an early evening promenade, or a few hours sipping mint tea in one of the many pavement cafés. Don't forget to look up at the Riviera architecture.

The aptly named **Terrasse des Paresseux** (Idlers' Terrace; Map p168), just east of Place de France, provides sweeping views of the port and, on a clear day, Gibraltar and Spain. A set of ancient cannons faces the bay, symbolically warding off usurpers.

Beneath the terrace, in a side street off Rue Salah Eddine el-Ayoubi, the **Gran Teatro de Cervantes** (Map p168) is a remnant of the days when Spaniards formed the largest non-Moroccan community in Tangier. Opened in 1913, the theatre enjoyed its zenith between the wars. You can't miss the dazzling Art Deco façade, but the building has long been in decline.

To the north of Place de France, down Rue de la Liberté, stands the closed and crumbling **Grand Hôtel Villa de France** (Map p160). The French painter Eugène Delacroix stayed here in 1832, when it really was a grand hotel. His fellow artist and compatriot, Henri Matisse (see boxed text, right), followed in the early 1900s.

ST ANDREW'S CHURCH

A small English church existed in Tangier as far back as the 1660s, when England occupied the city for a 20-year period. The present church, **St Andrew's** (Map p163; Rue d'Angleterre; admission free, donations welcome; ☺ 9.30am-12.30pm & 2.30-6pm; services 8.30am Wed &

Sun, 11am Sun), was built in 1894 on ground donated by Sultan Moulay al-Hassan and consecrated in 1905. You might recognise it from Matisse's rendition (a copy of which hangs inside). The church is a beautiful white Anglo-Moorish building, with a carved cedar ceiling and the Lord's Prayer in Arabic around the chancel arch. You may have to find the caretaker to unlock the door; he can also give enthusiastic tours.

The graveyard contains equally colourful characters. The imposing tombstone just outside the main south door is that of Caid McLean, a military adviser to the sultans, who died in 1920. McLean was at one time imprisoned and held to ransom by the Rif bandit Er-Raissouli. Also buried here is Walter Harris who, as the local correspondent of the *Times* of London, chronicled Tangier's goings-on at the turn of the 19th century. The shady cemetery is a peaceful escape from the chaos on the street.

Legend has it that the Grande Mosquée was built after a rich Arab Gulf sheikh sailing past Tangier noticed that St Andrew's spire overshadowed all the city's minarets. Shocked, he financed the Grande Mosquée. The spire now plays second fiddle to the new minaret.

MUSÉE D'ART CONTEMPORAIN
Housed in the former British consulate, this **Musée d'Art Contemporain** (Contemporary Art Museum; Map p160; 2 Rue d'Angleterre; admission

Dh10; 9-11.30am & 3-6pm Wed-Mon) displays examples of Moroccan art, mainly from the 1980s and early '90s. Given the Islamic injunction against figurative art, the paintings tend towards the abstract. Notable exhibits include the exuberant colours of Fatima Hassan and the African styles of Mohammed Hamid.

BEACHES
The beaches of Tangier are decent for a seaside stroll or an afternoon aperitif, but not for swimming or surfing. The sand itself is clean enough for a city beach and still manages to attract beachcombers, football-playing kids and the odd courting couple. A stroll in the sea breeze is a good way to clear the air if Tangier's hustlers have been over-attentive. Football matches take place here at weekends and in the evening, and the beach bars strung along the sand can be fun. Besides bars, these places also have changing cabins, showers and deckchairs. The much-reduced European gay population still frequents certain bars; women will feel extremely exposed sunning themselves here. It's also not a great place for an evening stroll: muggings aren't unknown.

Activities
HAMMAMS
Douche Andalous (Map p163; Rue Sebou; admission Dh8; 9am-11pm) Traditional hammam for women only.

A PAINTER'S PARADISE
Of the many artists who have passed through Tangier, one of the most famous is the French impressionist and leading light of the early 20th-century Fauvist movement, Henri Matisse (1869–1954). His two visits to the city, in the spring of 1912 and again the following winter, had a profound influence on his work. He called Tangier a 'painter's paradise'.

Inspired by the luminous North African light and the colour and harmony found in traditional Moroccan art, Matisse completed some 20 canvases and dozens of sketches during his time in Tangier. In them he honed the qualities that define his mature work: bold abstract lines, two-dimensional shapes and vibrant, expressive – as opposed to natural – colours.

Matisse mainly looked to the daily life of the medina for his themes. He produced several striking portraits of Zohra, a local prostitute, and a wonderful painting of a strong-featured Rifian woman sitting legs akimbo against an azure sky.

However, it is Matisse's renditions of the city that really strike a chord. Two of the most evocative are *Vue sur la Baie de Tanger* (View of the Bay of Tangier) and *La Porte de la Kasbah* (Entrance to the Kasbah). Both are relatively subdued in their use of colour, but in *Paysage Vu d'une Fenêtre* (Window at Tangier) the artist hits full stride. The painting shows the view from his window in the Grand Hôtel Villa de France, looking out over St Andrew's Church, with its squat tower, to the kasbah beyond. The overriding colour is a pure, sizzling Mediterranean blue.

El Minzah Wellness (Map p168; ☎ 039 935885; www .elminzah.com; 85 Rue de la Liberté; admission Dh150) Pamper yourself at this luxury spa with exercise facilities, sauna and Jacuzzi, as well as a whole range of massage and therapeutic treatments.

HORSE RIDING

Along the road to Cap Spartel, the **Royal Club Equestre** (☎ 039 934384; Rte Boubana Tanger; per hr Dh110; ☺ 8am-noon & 2-6pm, closed Mon) is set in the midst of forested hills, a pleasant place to explore on horseback. All riders must be accompanied by a guide, which is included in the price of the horse hire.

Courses

American Language Center (Map p160; ☎ 039 933616; 1 Rue M'sallah) Offers courses or may be able to arrange private tuition (about Dh120 per hour).

Institut Français (Map p168; ☎ 039 941054; www .iftanger.ma in French; 41 Rue Hassan ibn Ouazzane) Sometimes offers semester-long language courses.

Festivals & Events

The French-language newspaper *Les Nouvelles du Nord* is good for listings of events, along with the website www.maghrebarts .ma (in French).

Salon de Livre (Map p168; ☎ 039 941054; Institut Français, 41 Rue Hassan ibn Ouazzane) Annual book festival every January with Moroccan writers and foreign authors who write about Morocco.

International Festival of Amateur Theatre (☎ 039 930306) Traditionally held every May, a week-long event that brings Arabic- and French-speaking theatre groups to the Cinéma Rif (Map p163) on the Grand Socco.

TANJAzz (www.tanjazz.com in French) Usually held in the last week of May, this ever-popular festival hosts concerts by local and international jazz musicians, sometimes snaring the big names in the field.

Sleeping

Tangier's sleeping options cater to all budgets and styles, spanning the spectrum from the ultracheap pensions near the port to the chic hotels along the oceanfront. Most of Tangier's budget accommodation is clustered around the medina and close to the port gate. They're cheap but only occasionally cheerful, so it can pay to hunt around. In addition to those listed below, you can find plenty of choice in the streets around Ave Mokhtar Ahardan, and in the lanes running uphill from the Hôtel Biarritz. For midrange and above, it's always worth asking for a low-season discount if you're visiting outside the summer months.

MEDINA
Budget

With a few exceptions, the hotels in the medina are extremely basic, offering little more than a bed and shared bathroom facilities (squat toilets), although some do have hot water (for a small extra charge).

Hôtel Continental (Map p163; ☎ 039 931024; hcontinental@iam.net.ma; 36 Rue Dar el-Baroud; s/d incl breakfast Dh310/396) Something of a Tangerine institution, the Hôtel Continental is the pick of the bunch in the medina. Overlooking the port with a charming eccentricity, rooms are well-sized, with bathrooms and TV. It's busy in summer, so advance booking is recommended. Although the drinks are vastly over-priced, the terrace is great for views and imagining you're a character in a Paul Bowles novel (scenes in *The Sheltering Sky* were filmed here).

Pension Victoria (Map p163; ☎ 039 931299; 22 Ave Mokhtar Ahardan; s/d Dh50/100) This place is a bit dusty and worn, but perfectly serviceable for the price. Most rooms are set around a cool interior courtyard, but a few have good sea views, which make them a real budget bargain. Hot showers cost Dh10. A decent canteen restaurant is next door.

Hôtel Mamora (Map p163; ☎ 039 934105; 19 Ave Mokhtar Ahardan; s/d from Dh225/255) With attached bathrooms and good-quality rooms, the Mamora is another decent option in the medina if you're looking for an extra bit of comfort; it is run well and kept in good order. The rooms overlooking the green-tiled roof of the Grande Mosquée are certainly picturesque, but early morning wake-up calls are guaranteed.

Pension Palace (Map p163; ☎ 039 936128; 2 Ave Mokhtar Aharden; s/d Dh50/100, d with shower Dh120) Not quite the palace you'd hoped for, this is still another decent choice of the many cheapies off Petit Socco. Rooms are as basic as you'd expect for the price. Hot showers are promised, but the seats on the toilets could do with fixing. The foliage-filled courtyard adds some character.

VILLE NOUVELLE
Budget

Many of the unrated hotels and pensions along Rue Salah Eddine el-Ayoubi and Ave d'Espagne are little better than the cheapies in the medina. This area can be dodgy at night, and mightn't be a good choice for women travelling alone.

Hôtel Biarritz (Map p168; ☎ 039 932473; 102-4 Ave d'Espagne; s/d Dh150/200) This old place holds its age well – all rooms have showers and are nicely furnished (some have balconies), more than comfy enough to lay your head. The 1940s glazed tile staircase adds a bit of character, plus there's a bar and handy restaurant.

Hôtel el-Muniria (Map p168; ☎ 039 935337; 1 Rue Magellan; s/d Dh130/150) One for fans of the Beats – Ginsberg, Burroughs and Kerouac all stayed here (*The Naked Lunch* was supposedly written here), and the hotel has been coasting on that reputation ever since. Rooms are clean if a little shabby, and the management seems curiously disinterested in its guest. Get a room with a sea view to blow some fresh air into the place.

Youth Hostel (Map p168; ☎ 039 946127; 8 Rue al-Antaki; dm with/without HI card Dh30/40; ⏰ 8-10am, noon-3pm & 6-11pm) Tangier's youth hostel is just off Ave d'Espagne, close to an area with plenty of bars. It's fair value as Moroccan youth hostels go – clean enough but a bit tired. A hot shower costs Dh5.

Hôtel ibn Batouta (Map p168; ☎ 039 939311; postmaster@ibn-batouta.com; 8 Rue Magellan; s/d Dh150/200, with bathroom Dh200/250) Perched on the steep lane opposite the El-Muniria, this is another Interzone hangover. Rooms in the main building come with bathroom; ironically those without around the terrace feel nicer – airy with views to the sea, but hot in summer. The roof café adds value.

Hôtel de Paris (Map p168; ☎ 039 931877; 42 Blvd Pasteur; s/d Dh160/220, high season Dh331/371) This reliable choice in the heart of the ville nouvelle has a classy, old-world aura in its elegant lobby. Rooms have showers but not toilets, and are all good, clean and modern, although those overlooking Blvd Pasteur could potentially be a bit noisy. The management is friendly and helpful.

Pension Hollanda (Map p160; ☎ 039 937838; 139 Rue de Hollande; s/d Dh100/150) Tucked away in a quiet street a short walk from Place de Franc, this friendly pension has sparkling clean whitewashed rooms. All have sinks; doubles come with a shower. Hot water can be an issue – reception may ask you to give notice so that the water heater goes on.

Hôtel el-Djenina (Map p168; ☎ 039 922244; eld-jenina_hotel@caramail.com; 8 Rue al-Antaki; s/d from Dh271/318) This excellent hotel is making a serious bid for being a midrange option for those on tighter budgets. Bright, clean and modern, rooms come with bathroom, TV and the occasional balcony looking out to the sea. It has a restaurant and bar.

Camping Miramonte (☎ 039 937133; camping per adult/child Dh20/15, plus per tent/car/caravan Dh20/15/25; 🚐) A 2km walk or taxi ride west from the city centre, this hillside camp site with its lush gardens can make the hustle of Tangier miraculously melt away. Facilities are adequate (hot showers Dh10, electricity Dh10), with a small restaurant/café overlooking the bay.

Midrange

Nicer hotels line the Ave des FAR, offering spectacular views over the Bay of Tangier and close proximity to the attractions of the city, with a couple of options right in the centre.

Hôtel Rembrandt (Map p168; ☎ 039 937870; rembrandt@menara.ma; Blvd Mohammed V; s/d Dh427/564; 🌐 🚐) The Rembrandt is a reliable midrange choice in the heart of the ville nouvelle. Rooms are comfortable and modern, with only the plastic 'marble' bathrooms striking an odd note. Service is efficient. The green garden café is a tranquil spot to relax.

Hôtel Dawliz (Map p160; ☎ 039 333337; www.ledawliz.com in French; 42 Rue Hollande; s/d Dh570/780, high season Dh710/910; 🌐 🚐) This complex offers four-star comforts and unbeatable views of

---

THE AUTHOR'S CHOICE

Riad Tanja (Map p163; ☎ 039 333538; www.riadtanja.com; Rue du Portugal, Escalier Américain; r Dh800-1000; 🌐) On the edge of the medina, the Tanja combines as much modern Spain as traditional riad in a very stylish mix. Rooms are exceedingly comfortable, and decorated with myriad paintings and prints that speak of Tangier's artistic heritage. Some look over the city while the terrace (with excellent restaurant, serving alcohol) offers grand views over the strait to Spain. The riad is well signed from the stepped gate to the medina on Rue Portugal.

MEDITERRANEAN COAST
& THE RIF

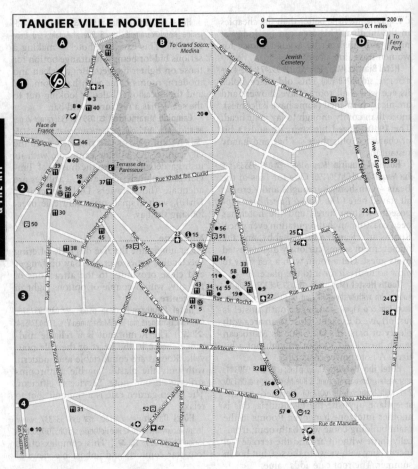

TANGIER VILLE NOUVELLE

the medina and the Bay of Tangier – which helps make up for its unexciting décor. Rooms have the expected facilities (the fridge is a nice touch). The hotel complex has several shops, restaurants and an ATM.

Hôtel Shéhérazade (Map p160; ☎ 039 940803; fax 039 940801; Ave des FAR; s/d Dh536/618; ☒) Of all the midrange places on this stretch of road, the Shéhérazade probably offers the best sea views, even if not all the rooms match its competitors. Rooms are plain but comfortable, with satellite TV and telephone.

Ramada Almohades (Map p160; ☎ 039 940755; www.ramadahotels.com; 43 Ave des FAR; s/d Dh659/808, high season Dh780/1010; ☒ ☒) This international chain does what you'd expect, pro-

vide high-quality, comfortable and spacious rooms, with all mod cons. But for the great views over the bay, you could almost be anywhere in the world.

Hôtel Solazur (Map p160; ☎ 039 940164; fax 039 945286; Ave des FAR; s/d Dh642/774; ☒) The Solazur is similar to the Ramada, without the familiarity of a Western chain; nonetheless, it offers comfortable if nondescript rooms with all the standard four-star amenities. And the lobby has a cool, trompe l'oeil stairwell. Again, views from the rooms facing the ocean are fantastic.

Top End
El-Minzah (Map p168; ☎ 039 935885; www.elminzah .com; 85 Rue de la Liberté; s/d incl breakfast from Dh1200/

1500, high season from Dh1500/1800; ⛔ 🚫) The classiest five-star hotel in Tangier proper is this landmark, a beautifully maintained period piece from the 1930s. Rooms are sumptuous, and while taking a drink in Caid's Bar (see p172) you might even get a hint of the days of WWII, when the hotel was a nest of secret agents, mercenaries and dodgy dealings of every kind. Nowadays of course the hotel is much more genteel, offering a fitness centre, spa, pleasant gardens and even a baby-sitting service. Whatever would the spies think?

Hôtel Rif (Map p160; ☎ 039 941766; Ave d'Espagne; r from Dh1000; ⛔) This grand old place has sat on Tangier's seafront for an age – Churchill used to favour it back in the day – but in recent years had fallen into benign neglect. The renovation was in full swing when we visited, in anticipation of a royal reopening, and it was looking a treat. Expect modern classy interiors with sea views, bar and restaurant, and a pool tucked into a grotto.

Eating
RESTAURANTS
Medina
Marhaba Palace (Map p163; ☎ 039 937927; Rue de la Kasbah; meals from Dh120) Tangier's medina may be small, but it can still manage palace restaurants like the best of them. This garden house is lovingly decorated in traditional style, with music and folkloric shows thrown into the cost of your meal. Set meals follow the classic pattern of soup, salad, tajine or couscous plus dessert, cooked and presented well.

Hamadi (Map p163; ☎ 039 934514; 2 Rue de la Kasbah; mains Dh40-60) Another traditionally styled place just outside the medina walls. The surroundings are sumptuous, and live music accompanies your Moroccan meal (the *pastilla* is good). However, you might struggle to hear the musicians when the place is overwhelmed by tour groups at lunchtimes – come back in the evening when the day-trippers have gone back to Spain. Prices exclude 10% tax.

Mamounia Palace (Map p163; ☎ 039 935099; 4 Rue as-Siaghin; set menus Dh100; ⏰ 9am-10pm) Although the salon's decoration is textbook Morocco, 'palace' seems too grand a title for this restaurant, just inside the Grand Socco entrance to the medina. Set menus are the order of the day, and those traditional musicians continue to strum their ouds for added dining ambience. A hefty 15% service charge is added to all bills.

Café Andalus (Map p163; 7 Rue du Commerce; salad Dh5, mains from Dh25) Much more of a local's place, the tiny Andalus dishes out cheap and tasty plates of fish, brochettes and bowls of soup. Definitely not a palace, but none the worse for it.

Restaurant Le Kasbah (Map p163; ☎ 067 118847; 7 Rue Gzenaya; set menus Dh40-80; ⏰ 11am-10pm)

Another decent local dining hall, very much in the hole-in-the-wall vein. Soups, tajines, brochettes, fish – they're all there, in good portions and simple surroundings.

Ville Nouvelle

Casa de España (Map p168; ☎ 039 947359; 11 Rue el-Jebha el-Ouatania; mains from Dh60, lunch set menu Dh60) Buzzing with Spanish expats, local businessmen and the occasional tourist, this joint is as lively as they come. Snappily dressed waiters serve up classic Spanish dishes, with some wonderful specials like lamb with summer fruits. Wash it down with a bottle of wine; it's good value even with extra tax added to all bills.

Restaurant Valencia (Map p160; ☎ 039 945146; 6 Ave Youssef ben Tachfine; mains Dh50-70; ☒ closed Tue) This excellent spot just off the waterfront is a perennial favourite, and always seems busy. The décor hints at the captain's table, and the menus are suitably seafaring. Have a look at the catch of the day on offer in the chiller as you walk in, then enjoy a cold beer while waiting for your meal.

Agadir (Map p168; ☎ 068 827696; 21 Rue du Prince Héritier; mains Dh32-40, set menu Dh48) The interior is thoroughly unassuming, but the checked tablecloths, red wine and Gallic crooning in the background give this place more than a hint of French bistro. Meals are good and hearty, with the free use of fresh herbs raising the succulent tajines to a level above the usual fare. Prices exclude a 10% tax.

Restaurant el-Korsan (Map p168; ☎ 039 935885; El-Minzah Hotel, 85 Rue de la Liberté; mains around Dh130)

THE AUTHOR'S CHOICE

Restaurant Populaire Saveur (Map p168; ☎ 039 336326; 2 Escalier Waller; set menus Dh150; ☒ closed Fri) This attractive and welcoming little fish restaurant down the steps from Rue de la Liberté serves excellent, filling set menus. It's as rustic as you could imagine – quaint decoration and rough-hewn wooden cutlery. The food is delicious, though, with steaming fish soup, and plenty of grilled fish. Dessert is typically sticky *seffa* (sweet couscous), all washed down with the house fruit-juice cocktail – your glass continually refreshed. Not just a meal, a whole experience.

One of Tangier's top restaurants, a chic and classy place inside the El-Minzah. You might want to dress a little smarter than normal when eating here. Well-presented Moroccan classics are served to the soft playing of live musicians, and often traditional dancing later in the evening. It's not cheap, but the ambience is worth it.

Anna e Paolo (Map p168; ☎ 039 944617; 77 Rue du Prince Héritier; mains from Dh65) You might think you are in Roma when you are seated at a tiny candlelit table with a red-checked cloth, sipping your *rosso*. It's both quaint and very romantic, with Italian fare as good as your mamma makes it.

San Remo (Map p168; ☎ 039 938451; 15 Rue Ahmed Chaouki; pizzas around Dh50, mains around Dh100) This place is also strong on Italian food, with hefty doses of Spanish and French cuisine thrown in for good measure.

Le Pagode (Map p168; ☎ 039 938086; Rue al-Boussiri; mains from Dh70) If you're tired of tajines and pasta, this place might just refresh your palate. The menu is familiar from Chinese takeaways the world over, with plenty of noodles, sweet and sour, and black-bean sauce on offer. It makes a nice change, but the ambience is a little lacking.

Africa (Map p168; 83 Rue Salah Eddine el-Ayoubi; soups Dh10, mains from Dh35, set menu Dh50; ☒ 10am-11pm) An unpretentious place on a side road leading up to the Grand Socco, Africa dishes up good Moroccan standards quickly and without fuss. Alcohol is served.

Rubis Grill (Map p168; ☎ 039 931443; 3 Rue ibn Rochd; mains Dh70-80) This bar and grill is heavy on the meat and fish in good, tasty portions. If you only want a quick bite, you can sit at the bar and enjoy tapas over a cold beer.

CAFÉS, PATISSERIES & ICE-CREAM PARLOURS

Dolcy's Café (Map p168; Blvd Pasteur; breakfast from Dh15; ☒ 6am-10pm; ☒) At the southern tip of Blvd Pasteur, this is a large café popular with both men and women, with clean, modern décor and friendly service. A good choice for breakfast, before the heat of the sun scorches the outside seating area.

Pâtisserie La Española (Map p168; 97 Rue de la Liberté; ☒ 8am-10pm) A heavily mirrored tea room, this café simultaneously manages to be quiet and dainty – perhaps it's the pretty arrangements of cakes and pastries tempting people off the street. Everyone seems to come here – locals and foreigners, business-men and courting couples.

Al Mountazah (Map p163; Grand Socco; 🕑 7am-10pm) You can't beat this rooftop perch for observing the activity on the Grand Socco: sip your morning coffee and watch the square come alive from the great terrace. The whole place was under renovation when we most recently visited.

La Giralda (Map p168; 1st fl, 5 Blvd Pasteur; break-fast from Dh12; 🕑 6am-10pm; 🔀) While huge windows give fantastic views over the Ter-rasse des Paresseux and to the sea, they are double-glazed to keep out the noise of the street, lending an air of calm elegance. The plush furniture and intricately carved ceiling add to the luxury. Young, rich and beautiful Tangerines adore this chic café.

Salon de Thé Liberté (Map p163; 47 Rue de la Lib-erté; 🕑 6.30am-10pm) Neatly decorated in dark wood, with a garden at the back, this place is also a restaurant serving up reliable Mo-roccan and international dishes. It excels as a café, though, with its wide front windows opening to let the air in, where you can sit and watch the street at work and play.

Porte du Nord (Map p168; cnr Rue ibn Rochd & Rue du Prince Moulay Abdallah; breakfast from Dh18; 🕑 6.30am-10pm) A grand and classy patisserie, this place works hard to maintain its airs and graces. Ideal for an elegantly poured mint tea and other refined pastimes.

Café Champs Élysées (Map p168; 6 Blvd Moham-med V; breakfast from Dh18; 🕑 6am-10pm) If Porte du Nord is elegant, this café is downright sumptuous, complete with chandeliers and red velour. The lack of a dress code is the big surprise. Great sticky pastries.

QUICK EATS

In the medina there's a host of cheap eating possibilities around the Petit Socco and Ave Mokhtar Ahardan, with rotisserie chicken, sandwiches and brochettes all on offer. In the ville nouvelle, try the streets imme-diately south of Place de France; they are flush with fast-food outlets, sandwich bars and fish counters.

Fried Fish Stalls (Map p163; Rue Salah Eddine el-Ayoubi; soup Dh3, fish from Dh15) Several cheap hole-in-the-wall places huddle here looking onto the Grand Socco. They're as basic as can be, but serve out generous portions of fried sardines and the like with chips, salad, a hunk of bread and a squeeze of lemon.

Quick, filling and exceedingly tasty. Similar stalls sit near the steps at Rue Dar Dbagh.

Safarine (Map p168; Blvd Pasteur; sandwiches Dh17-22, pizzas Dh35-70) A bright, clean fast-food joint popular with couples. The pizzas and *shwarma* are good, or you might linger longer over the lasagne and pasta.

Fast Food Brahim Abdelmalik (Map p168; 16 Ave Mexique; sandwiches Dh15-18) You can't go wrong here with half a baguette filled with *kefta* (seasoned minced lamb) and salad to eat on the hoof.

Mix Max (Map p168; 6 Ave du Prince Héritier; meals Dh20-45; 🕑 noon-11pm) One of the newer and trendier fast-food joints, with burgers and the like served with generous portions of chips and salad.

SELF-CATERING

The covered markets (Map p163) south of the Grand Socco are the best place for fresh produce, with Riffian women in traditional hats selling fruit, vegetables and delicious creamy goats cheese. Fès market (Map p160), to the west of the city centre, is good for imported cheese and other treats.

Casa Pepé (Map p168; 9 Rue ibn Rochd; 🕑 8am-10.30pm) One of several general stores in this area. You can stock up at the good delica-tessen here, and buy dry goods and booze.

Drinking

CAFÉS

Tangier's cafés have long been a crucial in-gredient of the city's intellectual life, inspir-ing artists, poets and philosophers (amateur and professional alike) for decades. Places listed below are dedicated primarily to the weighty themes of caffeine and conversa-tion. For pastries, you're better to check out those listed under Eating (opposite).

Café de Paris (Map p168; Place de France; 🕑 6am-11pm) An ageing *grande dame* of Tangier coffee society spilling out onto the pave-ment of Place de France, this is the most famous of the coffee establishments along Blvd Pasteur. Overwhelmingly male Mo-roccans and expats gather here over strong coffee and mint tea to thrash out the issues of the day.

Café Hafa (Map p160; Ave Mohammed Tazi; 🕑 10am-8pm) With its shady terrace overlooking the strait, you could easily lose an afternoon lazing in this café. Paul Bowles and the Roll-ing Stones came here to smoke hashish, and the indolent air still lingers among the locals who hang out here to enjoy the view and a game of backgammon.

Café Central (Map p163; Petit Socco; ◷ 6am-11pm) A place for people-watching on Petit Socco, or possibly trying a little cut-up poetry in honour of William Burroughs – this was one of his favourite cafés. Today it's not much more than a regular Moroccan coffeehouse, but is still good for surveying the passing world, although women travellers may find themselves equally surveyed.

BARS

Given its recent hedonistic past, it's no surprise that the drinking scene is firmly entrenched in Tangerine culture. It's equally no surprise that bars are home to the male of the species, although there are a few more-Westernised places where women can take a drink.

Caid's Bar (Map p168; El-Minzah, 85 Rue de la Liberté; wine from Dh20; ◷ 10am-midnight) Long the establishment's drinking hole of choice, this bar is a classy relic of the grand days of international Tangier, and photos of the famous and infamous who've preceded you adorn the walls. The bar is snug, with a decent selection of wines, spirits and beers, plus appetisers if you're after finger food. Women are more than welcome.

Dean's Bar (Map p163; 2 Rue Amérique du Sud; ◷ 9am-11pm) Hardly a Westerner of any repute has failed to prop up this bar at some time. Founded in 1937, it's a bit dowdy now, though ceiling fans and B&W photos retain the colonial air. Now firmly a locals' drinking hole, it's worth investigating for its historical links, but don't expect heads to go unturned when you walk in.

Tanger Inn (Map p168; Hôtel el- Muniria, 1 Rue Magellan; beer Dh10; ◷ 10.30pm-1am, to 3am Fri & Sat) This tiny, kitsch pub is one of the last reminders of the Interzone days. Ginsberg's photo hangs on the wall and Burroughs used to prop up the bar, but it can be hard to detect their ghosts if the barman slams his favourite gangsta rap on at maximum volume. It's better late at night, but take care, as the area can be dodgy after dark.

Negresco (Map p168; 20 Ave Mexique; ◷ 11am-3pm & 7-11pm) With more of a European air than most Tangier bars, this pub draws a mixed local and foreign crowd. The adjacent restaurant means a good bar menu for food,

with draught beer and spirits satisfying more essential needs.

London's Pub (Map p168; ☎ 039 942094; 15 Rue al-Mansour Dahabi; draught beer from Dh20; ◷ 6.30pm-1am) A Tangerine dream of Olde England, this theme pub has a reassuringly long wooden-and-brass bar, and a good host of beers that try to deceive you into thinking you're within earshot of the chimes of Big Ben. It almost succeeds. A bar singer belts out a song or two, but sadly not 'Roll out the barrel'.

The Pub (Map p168; ☎ 039 934789; 2 Rue Sorolla; beer Dh18; ◷ 7pm-12.30am Mon-Sat) As the name suggests, this place gets down to brass tacks – more cod-English décor, warm and cosy with reasonable bar food.

Entertainment
NIGHTCLUBS

Tangier's clubbing scene picks up in the summer, when Europeans arrive on the ferries and get the urge to dance until the small hours. Cover charges are typically Dh100, with drinks three times the normal bar price.

Regine's (Map p168; 8 Rue al-Mansour Dahabi; ◷ 11.30pm-3am Mon-Sat) A large club popular with young and trendy Tangerines, Regine's spins a bit of everything from rai to Europop to house.

Pasarela (Ave des FAR; ◷ 8pm-3am Mon-Sat, happy hour 8-11pm Sep-Jun) This Canadian-owned seaside venue is a large complex with several bars, an attractive garden and an outdoor swimming pool. Music is mostly Western and fairly up to the minute, with live bands adding to the mix at the height of summer.

Morocco Palace (Map p168; Rue du Prince Moulay Abdallah; ◷ 9pm-4am Mon-Sat) A purely Moroccan interpretation of the nightclub experience, with traditional décor and mostly Arabic pop. Moroccan dancers put on a floor show and rev the place up – it's a little tacky perhaps, but it seems to work and is tremendous fun on a good night.

GAY VENUES

Tangier was hugely popular with British homosexuals before legalisation in 1967, but today's gay scene is a mere shadow. **Scotts Nightclub** (Map p168; Rue al-Moutanabi; Dh100; ◷ 11pm-2am) is one of the few places retaining a gay reputation, along with the Tanger

Inn (opposite) on weekends. Get to both late in the hour.

As anyone who has read William Burroughs knows, the cafés near the Petit Socco – particularly Café Central – were an infamous gay hang-out during the Interzone period. Nowadays, however, bars along the beach, such as Miami Beach and Coco Beach (Map p160), are a better bet, especially in summer.

CINEMAS

Cinéma Dawliz (Map p160; ☎ 039 333151; 42 Rue Hollande; admission Dh20; ✷) has two upmarket screens showing a mixture of Bollywood and Hollywood films. Another option is **Cinéma Paris** (Map p168; Rue de Fès; admission Dh15).

Shopping

Shop carefully in Tangier – many places sell cheap goods aimed squarely at the day-tripping market, with variable quality and inflated prices. Get off the main streets in the medina for better deals and, as always, look and haggle patiently.

Ensemble Artisanal (Map p160; cnr Rue Belgique & Rue M'sallah; ✷ 8.30am-noon & 2.30-7pm) The government-backed arts-and-crafts centre always makes a good first stop to get an idea of the range and quality of crafts available,

and to watch the artisans at work, with no pressure to buy. Prices are fixed.

Parfumerie Madini (Map p163; 14 Rue Sebou; Map p000; 5 Blvd Pasteur; ✷ closed Fri) This is the place for sweet smells – the Madini family has been distilling essential oils for some 14 generations and they claim to be able to perfectly reproduce any scent you care to give them, with a little time. The range of perfumes and essences on sale is literally intoxicating.

Getting There & Away

AIR

Royal Air Maroc (RAM; Map p168; ☎ 039 379503; fax 039 932681; 1 Place de France) flies twice daily from Tangier to Casablanca (Dh1145, 50 minutes), daily direct to Malaga (Spain), and twice weekly direct to London Heathrow and Paris Orly. There's also a weekly flight to Amsterdam.

British Airways (☎ 039 935877; 83 Rue de la Liberté) flies to London Heathrow at least twice a week, and **Iberia** (Map p168; ☎ 039 936178; 33 Blvd Pasteur) flies to Madrid daily. For more information on international flights, see p469.

BOAT

If you're heading to Spain or Gibraltar by boat, you can buy tickets from the company ticket booths outside the ferry terminal

---

IBN BATTUTA

The world might be more familiar with Marco Polo, but his travels pale in comparison with his Moroccan rival. Ibn Battuta was the greatest traveller of the medieval ages, covering most of the known world and, unlike the Venetian, there's no dispute as to whether he actually made his trips or not.

Born in 1304 in the bustling port city of Tangier, Ibn Battuta, son of an Islamic judge, spent 30 years crisscrossing the Muslim world from one end to the other. 'I left Tangier, my birthplace, on the 2nd of Rajab in the year 725 (14 June 1325)…I decided to leave behind my friends, men and women, and abandoned my home as birds leave the nest…'. And so Ibn Battuta set off on his first journey to Egypt.

On his initial trip, after crossing North Africa and visiting Syria, he made his first pilgrimage to Mecca in 1326. He went there again the following year, after travelling to Mosul in Iraq and Esfahan, Shiráz and Tabriz in Iran. In subsequent years he explored the east coast of Egypt, the Arabian coast and the Gulf before heading to Constantinople and circling the Black Sea. He spent seven years at the court of the sultan in Delhi, India, before heading south, in 1342, for the Maldives and then east to Sumatra. He supposedly ended up in Peking (now Beijing) at one point but here his accounts seem shaky at best. Later travels included the Sudan, Niger, Mali and Muslim Spain.

Finally, and thankfully, in his later years Ibn Battuta dictated his adventures. The manuscript now lies in the Bibliothèque Nationale in Paris. The Arabist writer Tim Mackintosh Smith has edited the recently reissued *Travels of Ibn Battutah*, and written two volumes of his own travels following in the footsteps of his hero – *Travels with a Tangerine* and *The Hall of a Thousand Columns* – required reading for all fans of this master traveller.

building (Map p160), in the terminal itself, or from virtually any travel agency around town. The main destination is the Spanish port of Algeciras. There are also less frequent services to Tarifa and Málaga (Spain), Gibraltar and Sète (France). For more details see p477.

There is a strip of foreign-exchange booths and a couple of ATMs outside the terminal building, and grand taxi stop. A left-luggage office (p161) is just outside the port gates.

BUS – CTM

The **CTM station** (Map p163; ☎ 039 931172) is conveniently beside the port gate. All CTM's international and long-distance buses depart from and arrive here.

CTM has four daily departures for Casablanca (Dh120, six hours) from 11am to midnight. They all stop at Rabat (Dh90, 4½ hours), and some also go via Kenitra (Dh67, 3½ hours). One bus departs for Marrakesh (Dh175, 10 hours), travelling on to Agadir (Dh245, 14 hours) and Tiznit (Dh275, 15½ hours). Four buses go to Fès (Dh95, six hours); most of these stop at Asilah (Dh16, one hour), Larache (Dh30, 2½ hours) and Meknès (Dh80, five hours). One bus goes to Ouezzane (Dh50, four hours) via Tetouan (Dh15, one hour) and Chefchaouen (Dh35, three hours). There is one evening departure for Oujda (Dh180, 11 hours).

BUS – OTHER COMPANIES

Cheaper bus companies operate from the **main bus station** (gare routière; ☎ 039 946928; Place Jamia el-Arabia), about 2km to the south of the city centre – the distinctly un-Moroccan-looking minarets are a useful nearby landmark. There are regular departures for all the destinations mentioned above, plus services to Al-Hoceima (Dh85, 10 hours), local destinations and Fnideq (Dh20, 1½ hours) – a small town 3km from the Ceuta border.

The main bus station can be busy, but pretty hassle-free. It has a **left-luggage facility** (per item per 24hr Dh5; ⏰ 5.30am-midnight). A metered petit taxi to/from the town centre will cost around Dh8.

CAR

Tangier car rental agencies:
Amine Car (Map p168; ☎ 039 944050; fax 039 325835; 43 Blvd Mohammed V)

Avis (Map p168; ☎ 039 933031; 54 Blvd Pasteur)
Budget (Map p168; ☎ 039 948060; fax 039 948060; 7 Rue du Prince Moulay Abdallah)
Hertz (Map p168; ☎ 039 322210; fax 039 322165; 36 Blvd Mohammed V)

A reasonably secure and convenient **car park** (Map p160; 42 Rue Hollande; per hr Dh2, per night Dh15, per 24hr Dh25) is next to the Dawliz complex.

TAXI

You can get grands taxis to places outside Tangier from a lot next to the main bus station. The most common destinations are Tetouan (Dh30, one hour), Asilah (Dh15, 30 minutes), Larache (Dh30, one hour). For Ceuta, travel to Fnideq (Dh30, one hour), 3km from the border. There are no direct taxis to the border (Bab Sebta) from Tangier.

Grands taxis to Tetouan frequently wait for arriving trains at Tanger Ville train station, providing a convenient through-connection.

TRAIN

Tanger Ville, the swish new train station 3km southeast of the centre, is hassle free, but keep your guard on the train itself (see Dangers & Annoyances, p162). Note that the **left luggage office** (per item Dh10; ⏰ 7am-1pm & 2-9.30pm) only accepts locked bags. A petit taxi to/from Tangier centre should cost around Dh10.

Four trains depart daily from Tanger Ville. One morning and one afternoon service go to Casa-Voyageurs in Casablanca (Dh117, 5½ hours); a midday service travels via Meknès (Dh80, four hours) to Fès (Dh96, five hours); and a night service (with couchettes) goes all the way to Marrakesh. All these trains pass through Sidi Kacem, where you can get connections south to Marrakesh or east to Oujda.

The overnight train to Marrakesh takes about 10 hours and costs Dh274/193 for 1st/2nd class with a couchette and Dh213/143 without. The same overnight service from Marrakesh arrives in Tangier in time to catch the morning ferries to Spain if you're shooting straight through. The overnight trains sell out, so buy your ticket in advance to be on the safe side.

Getting Around
TO/FROM THE AIRPORT

The tiny **Boukhalef Airport** (☎ 039 393720) lies 15km southeast of the city in the Ibn Batouta district. No direct bus service exists between the airport and city centre, so take a cream-coloured grand taxi to/from Tangier (Dh70). The main road between Asilah and Tangier passes the airport, useful if you're coming from further south.

BUS

Buses aren't really necessary for getting around Tangier, but there are a couple of potentially useful services (run by the Autasa company).

Bus No 13 runs from the train station via Ave des FAR to the port gate, while Bus No 17 links the train station and the main bus station. Tickets cost Dh3.

TAXI

Distinguishable by their ultramarine colour with a yellow stripe down the side, petits taxis do standard journeys around town for Dh7 to Dh10; they charge 50% more at night.

AROUND TANGIER
Cap Spartel   رأس سبارطيل

Just 14km west of Tangier lies Cap Spartel, the northwestern extremity of Africa's Atlantic coast, marked by a lighthouse and fish restaurant. It's a dramatic drive from Tangier through La Montagne, an exclusive suburb of royal palaces and villas, and over the pine-covered headland. The beaches to the south are clean and quiet outside the summer season.

If you're keen on birds, the area around Cap Spartel is a great place for watching flocks of birds migrating to Europe in late March to early April, or returning to Africa from Europe in October. The most impressive of the migrant species are the large raptors such as the black kites and booted eagles, but white storks also make the trip, along with more than 200 other species.

Below Cap Spartel, the beach **Plage Robinson** stretches off to the south. It's a lovely place for a bracing walk. Five kilometres along here you reach the **Grottes d'Hercule** (admission Dh10), next to Le Mirage hotel. Mythically, these caves were the dwelling place for

Hercules when he mightily separated Europe from Africa. Since the 1920s these caves have been quarried for millstones, worked by prostitutes and used as a venue for private parties by rich celebrities from Tangier. It's worth paying the small entrance fee for a much-photographed view of the Atlantic from one of the openings. The caves have long been something of a tourist attraction and are surrounded by a mass of souvenir stalls and café-restaurants offering cheap fish tajines.

SLEEPING & EATING

Le Mirage (☎ 039 333332; www.lemirage-tanger.com; d from Dh1380, May-Nov from Dh1800; ⚑ ⚑ ⚑) This is one of the finest hotels in the Tangier area, with a dramatic location perched on the cliff beside the grotto. From the sunny terrace, well-manicured lawns sweep down to a private beach. Rooms are exquisite, as the price suggests. Non-guests can get a taste of the opulence in the immaculate restaurant (meals from Dh200).

Robinson Plage (☎ 039 338152; www.robinson -tanger.com in French; 2-/4-person bungalows Dh330/520, May-Nov Dh380/600; ⚑) In a more comfortable price-bracket, the bungalows at this mid-range place make a pleasant alternative. They're a little old-fashioned, but you'll be spending most of your time enjoying the fine views over the Atlantic, and the nearby sandy beach.

Camping Achakkar (☎ 039 333840; camping per person Dh20, plus per tent/car/camper Dh20/10/45) Inland from the grotto, this shady site has clean facilities, but no hot water (electricity Dh25). It has a café with simple meals and a shop that stocks essentials.

Restaurant Cap Spartel (☎ 039 933722; Cap Spartel Rd; salads Dh40-60, mains from Dh70) This seafood restaurant next to the lighthouse is a good place for a meal; lucky, as there isn't a lot of competition.

GETTING THERE & AWAY

Grands taxis are the best way of getting to Cap Spartel. A one-way charter should cost around Dh50, and slightly more than double for a round trip including waiting time. Taxis leave from the rank in front of St Andrew's Church in Tangier. Petits taxis are reluctant to make the trip one way only – the price isn't much different to a grand taxi.

Cap Malabata & Ksar es-Seghir

و القصر اسصغير
ر رأس ملاباطا

Cap Malabata, 8km northeast of Tangier, has more fine beaches and a curious Gothic folly, **Château Malabata** (closed to the public), and the **lighthouse**. Both are outclassed by the magnificent views of Tangier and the strait. Bus Nos 15 and 16 come here from the city (Dh4, 20 minutes).

Ksar es-Seghir, 25km further around the coast, is a small fishing port still largely surrounded by high Portuguese walls and dominated by the remains of a castle. It's a very picturesque place, worthy of a day trip from Tangier, and its pristine beaches attract locals in the summer. There's a handful of decent café-restaurants near the beach. A couple of buses a day (Dh10, 45 minutes) go here from Tangier's main bus station.

Road to Ceuta

If you have your own transport, the drive from Ksar es-Seghir along the wild and hilly coast road to Fnideq and Ceuta is a highly scenic route to Tetouan and Chefchaouen from Tangier, although it will add a couple of hours to the trip.

The road climbs up to Jebel Musa. Like Cap Spartel to the west, in spring or autumn this is a great place to watch migrating birds. These birds use the thermal currents that rise up from the Jebel Musa and Gibraltar peaks to reach a good height before crossing the strait between Africa and Europe.

CEUTA (SEBTA)

سبتة

pop 75,000

Jutting out east into the Mediterranean, the peninsula that is Ceuta covers just 20 sq km and has been a Spanish enclave since 1640, meaning you cross an international border to get here. If you've been spending time in Morocco, Spanish Ceuta's relaxed, well-kept city centre with bars and cafés and Andalucian atmosphere provide a sharp contrast to the other side of the border.

Despite being in the EU, Ceuta is still recognisably African. Between a quarter and third of the population are of Rif Berber origin, giving the enclave a fascinating Iberian-African mix. This interplay of cultures has been put to the test in recent years, particularly following the Madrid bombings of 2004. In spring 2006, youths set fire

to several mosques in Ceuta, after a number of Ceuta-born Muslims were arrested on the Spanish mainland on terror charges.

The Spanish military dominates both on the peninsula, along with a dash of duty-free shopping and more than a hint of shady cross-border commerce. Although Spanish citizens get huge tax breaks for living in Ceuta (and Melilla), the enclave's uncertain economic future has led some to migrate to the Spanish mainland. It remains to be seen how the EU Free Trade Agreement, under which trade barriers are set to be abolished by 2012, will affect Ceuta once the profit in smuggled goods disappears. Nevertheless, considerable amounts of money are being invested in the enclave, not least by Spanish shipping lines that operate high-speed catamarans across the strait.

Ceuta is a popular entry point to Morocco for those seeking to avoid the adrenaline of Tangier (and fill up on duty-free fuel to boot), but it's a worthy stop in its own right. Those with a little Morocco fatigue might also enjoy its charms while recharging batteries – you'll just have to remind your wallet that you're on more expensive European soil.

History

Ceuta's earliest history dates to antiquity, when two heroes of Greek mythology – Hercules and Ulysses – supposedly passed through. More certainly, Ceuta served as one of the Roman Empire's coastal bases and in fact its Arabic name, Sebta, stems from the Latin *Septem*.

After a brief stint under the control of the Byzantine Empire, the city of Ceuta was taken in AD 931 by the Arab Umayyad rulers of Muslim Spain – the basis for Spain's claim of historical rights to the land. For the next 500 years, however, this city at the tip of Africa was like a prized possession, fought over and ruled successively by Spanish princes, Moroccan sultans and Portuguese kings. Things began to settle down when Portugal and Spain united under one crown in 1580, and Ceuta passed to Spain by default. When the two countries split in 1640, Ceuta remained Spanish, as it has ever since.

There have been surprisingly few rumblings about Moroccan rights to the enclave, notwithstanding an incident in 2002 (see boxed text, p179). But the importance of maintaining good relations, especially as Spain becomes an increasingly significant partner, seems to outweigh Morocco's political interest in Ceuta.

Orientation

Most of the hotels, restaurants and offices of interest are on the narrow spit of land linking the peninsula to the mainland. The Plaza de Africa, unmistakable with its giant cathedral, dominates the city centre. The port and ferry terminal are a short walk to the northwest. The border is 2km to the south along the Avenida Martinez Catena.

Information

To phone Ceuta from outside Spain, dial ☎ 0034. Remember that Ceuta is two hours ahead of Morocco during summer and one hour ahead at other times, and that most businesses are closed on Sunday.

INTERNET ACCESS

Cyber Ceuta (☎ 956 512303; Paseo Colón; per hr €2.50; 🕑 11am-2pm & 5-10pm Mon-Sat, 5-11pm Sun)
Indy Net Café (6 Isabel Cabral; per hr €3; 🕑 10am-10pm)

MEDICAL SERVICES

Hospital de la Cruz Roja (☎ 956 528400; 🕑 24hr) East of the fishing port.

MONEY

Euros are used for all transactions in Ceuta. ATMs are plentiful; outside banking hours you can change money at the more expensive hotels. There are informal moneychangers on both sides of the border, although it's technically illegal to take dirham out of Morocco. Branches of BMCE and Banque Populaire on the Moroccan side change cash only.
Banco Unicaja (Plaza Ruiz; 🕑 8.30am-2pm)
Caja Madrid (cnr Calle Real & Plaza de los Reyes; 🕑 8.30am-2pm)

POST

Main post office (correos y telégrafos; Plaza de España; 🕑 8.30am-8.30pm Mon-Fri, 9.30am-2pm Sat)

TOURIST INFORMATION

Tourist office (www.ceuta.es in Spanish) Avenida Muelle Cañonero Dato (☎ 956 501401; fax 956 507746; 🕑 9am-3pm Mon-Fri) Very friendly and efficient, with good maps and brochures; Estacion Marítima (☎ 956 506275; 🕑 9am-9pm); Plaza de Africa (☎ 956 528146; 🕑 9am-9pm Mon-Fri, 10am-2pm & 5-7pm Sat & Sun)

SURVIVAL SPANISH

Hello/Goodbye
   ¡Hola!/¡Adios!

Yes/No
   Sí/No

Please/Thankyou
   Por favor/Gracias

Where is ...?
   ¿Dónde está ...?

hotel
   hotel

guesthouse
   pensión

camping
   camping

Do you have any rooms available?
   ¿Tiene habitaciones libres?

a single room
   una habitación individual

a double room
   una habitación doble

How much is it?
   ¿Cuánto cuesta?

What time does the next ... leave?
   ¿A qué hora sale/llega el próximo ...?

boat
   barca

bus
   autobús

I'd like a ...
   Quisiera un ...

one-way ticket
   billete sencillo

return ticket
   billete de ida y vuelta

beer
   cerveza

sandwich
   bocadillo

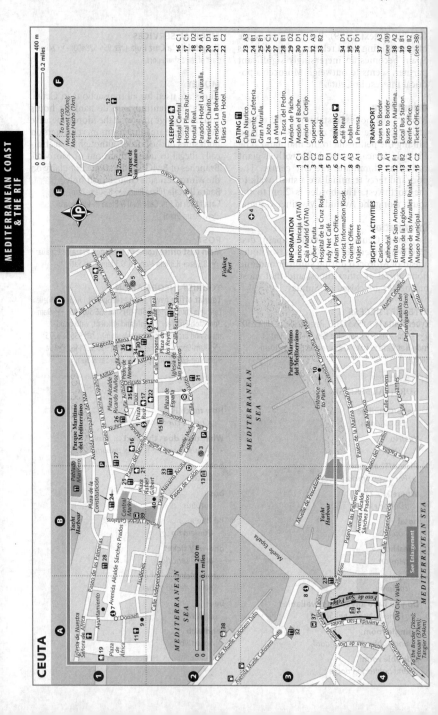

CEUTA

INFORMATION
Banco Unicaja (ATM)	1 C1
Caja Madrid (ATM)	2 D2
Cyber Ceuta	3 C2
Hospital de la Cruz Roja	4 E3
Indy Net Café	5 D1
Main Post Office	6 C2
Tourist Information Kiosk	7 A1
Tourist Office	8 A3
Viajes Eiders	9 A1

SIGHTS & ACTIVITIES
Casino	10 C3
Cathedral	11 A1
Ermita de San Antonio	12 F1
Museo de la Legión	13 B2
Museo de los Murallas Reales	14 A4
Museo Municipal	15 C2

SLEEPING
Hostal Central	16 C1
Hostal Plaza Ruiz	17 C1
Hostal Real	18 D2
Parador Hotel La Muralla	19 A1
Pensión Charito	20 D1
Pensión La Bohemia	21 B1
Ulises Gran Hotel	22 C2

EATING
Club Nautico	23 A3
El Puente Cafetería	24 B1
Gran Muralla	25 B1
La Jota	26 C1
La Marina	27 C1
La Tasca del Pedro	28 B1
Mesón de Pacho	29 D2
Mesón el Bache	30 D1
Mesón el Cortijo	31 C2
Supersol	32 A3
Supersol	33 B2

DRINKING
Café Real	34 D1
Dublin	35 C1
La Prensa	36 D1

TRANSPORT
Buses to Border	37 A3
Buses to Border	(see 39)
Estacion Marítima	38 A2
Local Bus Station	39 B1
Renfe Office	40 A4
Ticket Offices	(see 38)

GET A PIECE OF THE ROCK

It would have been one of the most bizarre wars in recent times. In July 2002, half a dozen Moroccan soldiers raised the Moroccan flag on an uninhabited lump of rock – nominally under Spanish control – less than 200m off the Moroccan coast. Six days later they were ousted by Spanish troops, which Morocco promptly denounced as an act of war.

The situation was saved from deteriorating further by massive pressure from the USA. Under the resulting settlement both sides agreed to return to the status quo.

The island, known to the Spanish as Illa de Perejil (Parsley Isle) and to the Moroccans as Leïla, has long been a bone of contention between the two countries. It has been under Spanish control since the 17th century. But a 1912 French-Spanish treaty defining the boundaries of the Spanish protectorate failed to mention the island – thus the source of the tension a century later.

The rock, little bigger than a football pitch, was just a symbol of difficulties in Morocco's relationship with Spain. Fishing rights, marijuana smuggling and oil prospecting off the Canary Islands have all caused trouble in recent years, plus the ever-increasing problems of illegal African immigrants trying to reach mainland Europe through Morocco. The action over Illa de Perejil closely followed talks between the UK and Spain over Gibraltar's future, possibly prompting Rabat to remind the world about Ceuta and Melilla.

Thankfully, cooperation rather than antagonism has been the theme in bilateral relations since the incident. In the wake of the 2003 Casablanca bombings and those in Madrid a year later, these neighbours have realised the advantages of joining forces and working together towards mutual goals.

TRAVEL AGENCIES

Avenida Muelle Cañonero Dato and the approach to the estación marítima are lined with agencies selling ferry tickets to Algeciras.

Viajes Eideres (☎ /fax 956 524656; eidere@teleline.es; Plaza de Africa)

Dangers & Annoyances

Many people enter Morocco via Ceuta to avoid the hassle of Tangier, but the Ceuta–Morocco border is not completely hustler-free – some travel all the way from Tetouan especially to meet the ferry disembarkations. Watch out for suspiciously over-friendly ferry passengers.

Sights & Activities

Ceuta's history is marked by the **Ruta Monumenta**, a series of excellent information boards in English and Spanish outside key buildings and monuments.

CITY WALLS

The impressive remnants of the **city walls** (☎ 956 511770; Avenida González Tablas; admission incl gallery free; ☑ 10am-2pm & 5-8pm) are probably Ceuta's most interesting historical sight. They've been beautifully restored to their 16th-century glory, with information boards in English telling the gripping story of the plague and famine that accompanied Moulay Ismail's ultimately unsuccessful 33-year siege of Ceuta, which began in 1694. In the walls is the **Museo de los Muralles Reales**, a gallery that houses temporary art exhibitions. Squeezed out of the fort's unforgiving architecture, it's a beautifully designed space, worth visiting irrespective of what's on show.

MUSEO MUNICIPAL

Ceuta's main **museum** (☎ 956 517398; 30 Paseo del Revellín; admission free; ☑ 10am-2pm & 5-8pm Mon-Fri, 10am-2pm Sat mid-Sep–May, 10am-2pm & 7-9pm Mon-Fri, 10am-2pm Sat Jun–mid-Sep) has a small collection showing the peninsula's history in artefacts from the Stone Age to the arrival of the Spanish in the 16th century. The Phoenician and Roman periods are the highlight, with ceramics and amphorae, but unfortunately all labels are in Spanish.

MUSEO DE LA LEGIÓN

This intriguing **museum** (☎ 606 733566; Paseo de Colón; admission free, donations appreciated; ☑ 10am-1.30pm & 4-6pm Mon-Fri, 4-6pm Sat & Sun) is dedicated to and run by the Spanish Legion, an army unit set up in 1920 that played a pivotal role in Franco's republican army at the beginning of the Spanish Civil War, as well as the Rif War against local Berbers. Memorabilia marks campaigns up to the

MEDITERRANEAN COAST & THE RIF

recent Bosnian War, and guided tours in English are available.

PENINSULA

A walk around the peninsula reveals a bit more of the history and mystery that makes Ceuta what it is. The peninsula, northeast of town, is topped by Monte Hacho, said by some to be the southern Pillar of Hercules (Jebel Musa, west of Ceuta, is the other contender; Gibraltar being the northern pillar). The summit is crowned by **Fortaleza de Hacho**, a fort first built by the Byzantines and added to since by the Moroccans, Portuguese and Spanish. Now occupied by the army, it is out of bounds.

On the northern slopes of Monte Hacho stands the yellow-and-white **Ermita de San Antonio**. This convent, originally built in the 17th century and reconstructed in the 1960s, is the venue for a large festival held annually on 13 June to mark St Anthony's day. At any time of year, however, it's worth coming up here for the magnificent views over Ceuta and north to Gibraltar. To find the convent, follow the main road clockwise around the peninsula 2.5km to Parque de San Amaro and a small zoo. Take one of the paths leading up steeply into a bowl of hills, and veering eastwards, and you should come out on a lane below the convent.

Back down at the main road, after another kilometre northeast you reach a colossal brutalist **monument honouring Franco** and the 1936 uprising that marked the start of the Spanish Civil War.

Castillo del Desnarigado (☎ 956 511770; admission free; ☼ 11am-2pm Sat & Sun) is a small fort on the southeastern tip of the peninsula. It now houses a small military museum.

PARQUE MARÍTIMO DEL MEDITERRÁNEO

Designed by the Catalonian architect César Manrique, the **Parque Marítimo del Mediterráneo** (Maritime Park; ☎ 956 517792; adult/child high season €6/3; ☼ 11am-8pm & 9pm-1am) is a huge complex on the seafront. It opened in 1995, complete with manufactured beach, landscaped pools and waterfalls, bridges, sculptures and even a mock castle. It is a great stop for families with children. More adult diversions include several restaurants and bars and a **casino** (☼ 9pm-4am Sun-Thu, 9pm-6am Fri & Sat).

Sleeping

Ceuta isn't overrun with sleeping options, so if you're arriving late in the day an advance reservation can be a good idea.

BUDGET

Most cheap places are *pensiónes* or *casas de huéspedes* (guesthouses), some of which are identifiable only by the large blue-and-white 'CH' plaque.

Pensión La Bohemia (☎ 956 510615; 16 Paseo de Revellín; r €30) A charming and spotless little place above a shopping arcade, with potted plants, shiny tile floors and a surfeit of pictures of Marilyn Monroe. Bathrooms are shared, with plenty of hot water. The rooms are also fresh and clean and there are piping-hot communal showers.

Hostal Real (☎ 956 511449; fax 956 512166; 1 Calle Real; r €30; 🖫) Not quite as cosy as La Bohemia, but still with good, clean rooms, this guesthouse has the added bonus of on-site laundry facilities – and a popcorn machine in the lobby.

Pensión Charito (☎ 956 513982; pcharito@terra.es; 1st fl, 5 Calle Arrabal; s/d €15/20) This place is poorly signed – its the green and cream building with the almost imperceptible 'CH' plaque. Looking a little aged, the inside is clean and homely with hot showers and a small, well-equipped kitchen.

MIDRANGE & TOP END

Hostal Central (☎ 956 516716; www.hostalesceuta .com; Paseo del Revellín; s/d €40/56; 🖫) This good-value, centrally located two-star hotel is the next step up from a pension, but has the same cosy charm. Bright rooms are small but spotless, and all come with bathroom and fridge. Low-season discounts can tip this place into the budget bracket.

Hostal Plaza Ruiz (☎ 956 516733; www.hostales ceuta.com; 3 Plaza Ruiz; s/d from €40/56; 🖫) Sister hotel to the Central, this place has a similar, welcoming style. Rooms are airy (some overlook the plaza) with nice pine furniture. Bathrooms and fridges are standard. Good discounts apply in low season.

Ulises Gran Hotel (☎ 956 514540; fax 956 514546; 5 Calle Camoens; s/d incl breakfast €52/83; 🖫 🖳) Falling one short of its four-star aspirations, the Ulises is nevertheless a fine, well-appointed place to stay. Rooms with balconies have views of the sea, and the recently refurbished lobby gives the whole place a lift.

Parador Hotel La Muralla (☎ 956 514940; ceuta@ parador.es; 15 Plaza de Africa; s/d from € 65/90; 🅿 ⌨) Ceuta's top address is this grand four-star hotel on the main square. It is mostly a 1970s creation, although some rooms occupy converted munitions stores lining the Foso de San Felipe. Rooms are spacious and comfortable, although the décor is often a little tired. Balconies overlook a pleasant garden overflowing with palm trees.

Eating

RESTAURANTS

In addition to the places listed here, the Pablado Marinero (Seamen's Village) beside the yacht harbour is home to a number of reliable, though not outstanding, restaurants ranging from Italian to burger places. Most restaurants and bars are closed on Sundays unless noted.

La Marina (☎ 956 514007; 1 Alférez Bayton; mains €10-12, set menu €8; 🕙 closed Sunday) This smart, friendly restaurant is often crowded at lunch time. It specialises in fish dishes, but also does a great value three-course set menu of the chicken/fish and chips variety.

Gran Muralla (☎ 956 517625; Plaza de la Constitution; mains from €5) If your tastebuds have had enough Spanish (or Moroccan) food, this Chinese restaurant will serve up something quite different. The menu has a wide range of Chinese standards, and portions are hearty. Window tables have views over the plaza and out to sea.

La Tasca del Pedro (☎ 956 510473; 3 Avenida Alcalde Sánchez Prados; mains €5-10; 🕙 closed Sunday) Small, friendly and popular with the locals, this restaurant has a good range of seafood, Spanish and simple Italian dishes.

Club Nautico (☎ 956 514440; Calle Edrisis; set menu from €7) This simple restaurant has a nice location overlooking the yacht harbour. The three-course *menú del diá* (daily set menu) is a popular choice, while the luscious fish dishes will set you back the same amount on their own.

CAFÉS & ICE-CREAM PARLOURS

La Jota (6 Calle Méndez Nuñez; breakfast €1.80, tapas €0.60) With a delightful array of cakes and ice creams, this little joint also does decent tapas; you can have full meals in the adjoining restaurant. A good place to start – or end – a day of exploring the city.

El Puente Cafeteria (Plaza de la Constitution; breakfast/sandwiches from €1.50) Opening out onto a plaza made for people-watching, El Puente is a trendy and modern café-bar with great sandwiches. It's an ideal stop for breakfast. It gets hugely busy, so work hard to catch the eyes of the staff.

TAPAS BARS

The best place to look for tapas bars is in the streets behind the post office and around Millán Astray to the north of Calle Camoens. In addition to tapas, they all serve more substantial *raciones* (a larger helping of tapas) and *bocadillos* (sandwiches).

Mesón el Bache (☎ 956 516642; Sargento Mena Algeciras; tapas €1.20, bocadillos €3; 🕙 dinner) Plenty of seating space and a printed menu (albeit in Spanish) make this less like the real thing, but still a great place to devour some tapas.

Mesón de Pacho (☎ 956 513138; 7 Calle Beatriz de Silva; tapas €0.75, raciones from €5; 🕙 dinner) Each drink comes with a plate of tapas. This place is very homely and welcoming, but tends to get crowded. Other dishes, like burgers and omelettes, are also available.

Mesón el Cortijo (☎ 956 511983; 14 Calle Cervantes; tapas from €1, baguettes from €2.75, raciones from €3; 🕙 dinner) This slightly more upmarket choice is still very welcoming with its friendly atmosphere and tempting counter display.

SELF-CATERING

The **Supersol supermarket** (Avenida Muelle Cañonero Dato) is the best place to stock up on essentials and treats alike; there's a smaller branch in the city centre on Dean Navarro Acuña.

Drinking

The tapas bars and cafés above are all good to while away a few hours with a drink. Those below have less focus on food. They're a far cry from the men-only establishments of Morocco.

Café Real (☎ 956 510393; Millán Astray; 🕙 3.30pm-4am) This very sophisticated coffee lounge features comfy chairs, subdued music and Art Deco touches. It's an excellent place for a coffee, brandy or ice cream (or all three) at almost any time of day or night.

Dublin (Delgado Serrano; beer from €2.50; 🕙 3pm to 3am) Styled as an Irish tavern, this straight-down-the-line pub is dark and loud. But you can escape to the tables on the little square outside.

La Prensa (Pedro de Meneses; beer €2; ☿ 10pm-3am Thu-Sat) This no-frills dive is the most popular of several small bars spilling out onto this pedestrian street. La Prensa packs in the locals till the wee hours.

Getting There & Away
MOROCCO
On the Moroccan side of the border, you must collect, fill in and present a yellow card at the passport window and, if you have a car, a green one at the vehicle registration window (ignore the touts who try to sell you these free cards). If you're driving a hire car, you will be required to show proof of authorisation to take the vehicle out of the country.

There is a large grand taxi lot next to Moroccan border control. Departures are plentiful to Tetouan (Dh30, 40 minutes), from where you can pick up onward transport. Taxis to Chefchaouen or Tangier are rare, and you'll most likely have to bargain hard to hire a vehicle yourself (Chefchaouen 300Dh, 90 minutes; Tangier 180Dh, one hour). A good alternative is to take a grand taxi to Fnideq (Dh5, 10 minutes), just south of the border, from where transport to Tangier is more frequent (Dh30, one hour).

Coming the other way, buses and some grands taxis terminate in Fnideq, so check if your transport goes to the actual border at Bab Sebta, or get dropped at the junction (a 1km walk to the border). Although the border is open 24 hours, there's little in the way of public transport between about 7pm and 5am.

MAINLAND SPAIN
The **estación marítima** (ferry terminal; Calle Muelle Cañonero Dato) is west of the town centre. There are several daily high-speed ferries to Algeciras (p477). Much flashier (and far more expensive) is to take the helicopter service **Helicopteros del Sureste** (Málaga airport ☎ 95204 870; www.helisureste.com) from Ceuta to Málaga Airport.

You can purchase train tickets to European destinations at the **Renfe office** (☎ 956 511317; 17 Plaza Rafael Gilbert), or at a travel agent. Several agencies in the ferry terminal also sell Enatcar (the main Spanish coach company) bus tickets.

Getting Around
Bus 7 runs up to the border (*frontera*) every 10 minutes or so from Plaza de la Constitución (€0.60). If you arrive by ferry and want to head straight for the border, there's a bus stop on Avenida González Tablas opposite the entrance to the ramparts. There's also a taxi rank outside the terminal building.

If you have your own vehicle, street parking is restricted to a maximum of two hours (€1) during the day. If you are staying longer, use the **car park** (per hr €0.50, per 12hr €4) on Calle Ingenieros or near the Pablado Marinero.

THE RIF MOUNTAINS جبل اريف

TETOUAN تطوان
pop 320,000
Tetouan is quite unlike anywhere else in the Rif, or even Morocco. For more than 40 years, from 1912 to 1956, it was the capital of the Spanish Protectorate, bequeathing it a unique Hispano-Moorish atmosphere. The neat medina – a Unesco World Heritage site – sits hard against the modern Spanish part of town, with its whitewashed buildings and high shuttered windows. The spectacular backdrop of the Rif Mountains is ever present, making it easy to forget that the coast is just a few kilometres away.

Tetouan is popular with Spanish visitors from Tangier and, given its history, the town's inhabitants still speak Spanish in preference to French as a second language. Don't be surprised if street directions are given to a *calle* or *avenida* instead of a *rue*. Unfortunately, the day-trippers appear to attract more than their fair share of hustlers and chancers, who congregate around Tetouan's dimly lit subterranean bus station. It's not the best introduction to the town, but, once away from here, you should find Tetouan a friendly and laid-back town.

History
Tetouan's ancient predecessor is Tamuda, a Mauritanian city that was founded in the 3rd century BC, but destroyed in the 1st cen-

tury AD following a local revolt. In Tamuda's place, the Romans built a fortified camp, the unremarkable remnants of which are visible about 5km from the modern town.

In the 14th century the Merenids established the town of Tetouan as a base from which to control rebellious Rif tribes, but it was destroyed by Henry III of Castille in 1399.

In the 15th and 16th centuries, Muslim and Jewish refugees from Granada, who were led initially by Sidi Ali al-Mandari, re-occupied this area between the mountains and the sea. Tetouan prospered, due in part to the skills new arrivals brought, and also to the thriving pirate activity on the water. The Spanish put an end to local piracy by blockading Tetouan's port at Martil. Unfortunately, this move caused legitimate trade to suffer too.

Moulay Ismail built Tetouan's defensive walls in the 17th century, and the town's trade links with Spain improved and developed. At the turn of the 20th century, Spanish forces occupied Tetouan for three years, claiming it was a punitive campaign against Rif tribes aimed at protecting Ceuta. This short stint foreshadowed later events. In 1913 the Spanish made Tetouan the capital of their protectorate, which was abandoned only in 1956 when Morocco regained independence.

Orientation

The ville nouvelle is centred on Place Moulay el-Mehdi and the pedestrian stretch of Ave Mohammed V, which runs east to the vast Place Hassan II. Around here you'll find the hotels, banks, most of the restaurants and cafés and the bus station. The entrance to the medina is off the grand Place Hassan II, flanked on the north side by the Royal Palace. From a compact centre the town sprawls along the hillside and down into the valley.

Information

BOOKSHOPS

Librairie Alcaraz Papeterie Generale (Ave Mohammed V) Stocks a few books on Morocco in French and Spanish, as well as foreign-language press – occasionally in English.

CULTURAL CENTRES

Institut Français (☎ 039 961212; institutfrancais@if tetouan.ma; 13 Rue Chakib Arsalane; ☯ 8am–noon &

3–6pm Tue-Fri) Puts on an interesting programme of films, concerts and exhibitions, as well as operating a library and café.

INTERNET ACCESS

Cyber Primo (☎ 039 963271; 1st fl, 6 Place Moulay el-Mehdi; per hr Dh10; ☯ 9am–11pm)
Remote Studios (☎ 039 711172; 13 Ave Mohammed V; per hr Dh9; ☯ 24hr)

MEDICAL SERVICES

Clinique du Croissant Rouge (Red Cross Clinic; ☎ 039 962020; Place al-Hamama, Quartier Scolaire)
Dépot de Médicaments d'Urgence (☎ 039 965902; 7 Ave al-Wamda; ☯ 10pm-9am) Night pharmacy.
Main hospital (☎ 039 972430; Martil Rd) About 2km out of town.

MONEY

There are plenty of banks with ATMs along Ave Mohammed V.
BMCE foreign exchange office (Place Moulay el-Mehdi; ☯ 10am-2pm & 4-8pm) Change cash and travellers cheques outside regular banking hours.

POST

Post office (Place Moulay el-Mehdi)

TOURIST INFORMATION

ONMT (Délégation Régionale du Tourisme; ☎ 039 961915; fax 039 961914; 30 Ave Mohammed V; ☯ 8.30am-noon & 2.30-6.30pm Mon-Thu, 8.30-11am & 3-6.30pm Fri)

TRAVEL AGENCIES

Royal Air Maroc (RAM; ☎ 039 961577; 5 Ave Mohammed V)
Voyages Hispamaroc (☎ 039 964224; fax 039 963821; Ave Mohammed V)

Sights

MEDINA

Surrounded by three mosques and four modern minarets, not to mention the Royal Palace, Place Hassan II links the medina to the ville nouvelle. The square forms the heart of the old town and has traditionally served as a meeting place. It is ringed with small cafés that are prime spots for people-watching. The main entrance to the medina is Bab er-Rouah (Gate of the Winds), which leads off from the square's southeast corner.

The medina is an industrious, bustling place; it's quite unlike the great medinas

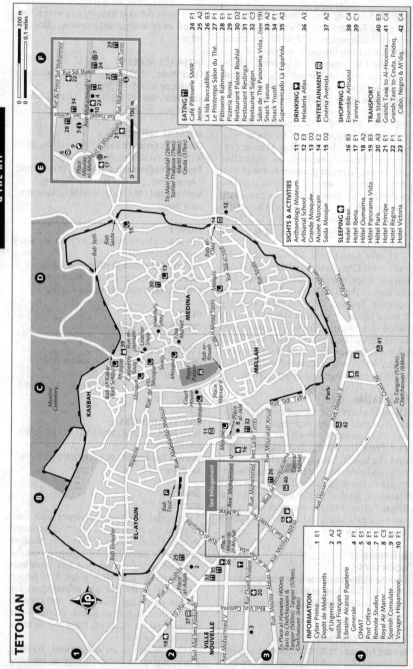

TETOUAN

MEDITERRANEAN COAST & THE RIF

INFORMATION	
Cyber Primo................................	1 E1
Dépôt de Médicaments	
d'Urgence...............................	2 A2
Institut Français..........................	3 A3
Librairie Alcaraz Papeterie	
Generale................................	4 F1
ONMT.....................................	5 E1
Post Office................................	6 E1
Remote Studios..........................	7 F1
Royal Air Maroc..........................	8 C3
Spanish Consulate.......................	9 E1
Voyages Hispamaroc....................	10 F1

SIGHTS & ACTIVITIES	
Archaeology Museum...................	11 C2
Artisanal School..........................	12 E3
Grande Mosquee.........................	13 D2
Musee Marocain..........................	14 E2
Saida Mosque.............................	15 D2

SLEEPING	
Hotel Bilbao...............................	16 B3
Hotel Iberia...............................	17 E1
Hôtel Oumaima..........................	18 A2
Hôtel Panorama Vista..................	19 B3
Hôtel Paris.................................	20 A3
Hôtel Príncipe............................	21 E1
Hôtel Regina..............................	22 F1
Hôtel Victoria............................	23 F1

EATING	
Café Pâtisserie SMIR....................	24 F1
Jenin..	25 A2
La Isla Boccadillos.......................	26 B3
Le Printemps Salon du Thé...........	27 F1
Pâtisserie Rahmouni....................	28 E1
Pizzeria Roma............................	29 F1
Restaurant Palace Bouhlal............	30 D2
Restaurant Restinga....................	31 F1
Restaurant Saigon......................	32 C3
Salon de The Panorama Vista...(see 19)	
Snack Taouss..............................	33 A2
Snack Yousfi..............................	34 F1
Supermercado La Española............	35 A2

DRINKING	
Heladería Atlas...........................	36 A3

ENTERTAINMENT	
Cinéma Avenida..........................	37 A2

SHOPPING	
Ensemble Artisanal......................	38 C4
Tannery.....................................	39 C1

TRANSPORT	
Bus Station................................	40 B3
Grands Taxis to Al-Hoceima..........	41 C4
Grands Taxis to Ceuta, Fnideq,	
Cabo, Negro & M'diq.................	42 C4

further south, as the Spaniards had a hand in some of the building in the 19th century, and most of its inhabitants, from the 16th century on, were refugees from what had been Muslim Spain, including a sizeable Jewish population who built the *mellah* (Jewish quarter) south of Place Hassan II. There are some 40 mosques within the medina, of which the **Grande Mosquée** and **Saidi Mosque**, both northeast of Place Hassan II, are the most impressive. As is customary, non-Muslims are not allowed to enter the mosques.

Bab el-Okla is the oldest gate. This southeastern corner of the medina was historically an upmarket neighbourhood. Some of the fancy houses built by the city's residents in the 19th century still remain; one or two have been turned into carpet showrooms.

MUSÉE MAROCAIN

This **ethnographic museum** (Musée Ethnographique; admission Dh10; ☼ 9.30am-noon & 3.30-6.30pm Mon-Fri) off Calle Garnata is worth a visit, if only for a peek inside the bastion in the town wall, where it is housed. Cannons are still in place in the garden, and the terrace is sometimes open, offering incredible views of the Rif Mountains. Unfortunately, the museum is frequently closed outside the summer months.

The museum contains the requisite collection of traditional clothing, musical instruments, antique jewellery, carpets, arms and household implements. Keep an eye out for the gold embroidered Jewish wedding robes with gold thread, and the highly elaborate iron doorknockers and keyhole covers. All of the captions are in French and Arabic.

To find the museum, you'll need to take the lane heading south just inside Bab el-Okla, then the left fork at the first junction, and the entrance is immediately on your left.

ARTISANAL SCHOOL

Opposite Bab el-Okla is the **artisanal school** (☎ 039 972721; admission Dh10; ☼ 8am-noon & 2.30-5.30pm Mon-Thu & Sat), where children learn traditional arts and crafts. The school is only for boys, who study the intricate art of carving plaster, bronzework and *zellij*, among other crafts.

The school, founded in 1928 by the Spanish to preserve traditional Moroccan

craftsmanship, has around 40 pupils between eight and 16 years old. It can take up to eight years to perfect many of the necessary techniques; the first couple of years of learning *zellij* are given over to learning and drawing the intricate designs before even touching a mosaic.

Tours show the classrooms, the palatial exhibition room where the work of pupils and masters is displayed (but not for sale) and the peaceful courtyard garden.

ARCHAEOLOGY MUSEUM

Tetouan has an unexpectedly good **archaeology museum** (Ave al-Jazaer; admission Dh10; ☼ 8.30am-noon & 2.30-6.30pm Mon-Fri). Andalucian culture is well represented, particularly mosaics and gravestones, but the highlight is the Roman collection from the ruins at Lixus (p125) on the Atlantic Coast.

A striking mosaic of the Three Graces from Lixus greets visitors as they enter. A room on the ground floor houses more artefacts from Lixus, including a good collection of Roman coins, some bronze statuettes and two mosaics depicting Venus and Adonis, and Mars and Rhea (the mother of Romulus and Remus).

Sleeping

Tetouan has a decent range of cheap, basic pensions, although choices for midrange and top-end accommodation are a lot thinner. Most are located around Place Moulay el-Mehdi or just off Ave Mohammed V.

BUDGET

Hotel Regina (☎ 039 962113; 8 Rue Sidi Mandri; s/d Dh145/168) One of the larger budget choices, the Regina initially feels a bit dowdy, but the whitewashed walls and crazy 1970s fabrics give the place a lift. While the attached bathrooms are sometimes a little tired, there's plenty of hot water making it great value for the price.

Hotel Victoria (☎ 039 965015; 23 Ave Mohammed V; s/d/tr Dh50/80/120) Small but nicely formed, the Victoria gives guests a warm welcome. Rooms are simple but comfortable, and the shared bathrooms are scrubbed spotlessly clean. With just a clutch of rooms, it's worth booking ahead at busy times of year.

Hotel Bilbao (☎ 039 944114; 7 Ave Mohammed V; s/d 55/70) Virtually on Place al-Jala, this is a reliable cheapie with surprisingly big rooms, many with wrought-iron balconies. That rooms come with showers is also a big selling point. Be on your best behaviour, though – feisty chambermaids rule the hotel with a rod of iron.

Hotel Iberia (☎ 039 963679; 5 Place Moulay el-Mehdi; s/d/tr Dh50/80/120) Set above the BMCE bank, this pension has just a handful of clean, cell-like rooms with shared bathrooms (hot showers cost Dh10). It's all quite tidy and friendly, although the echoing walls can make it quite noisy at times, particularly as the owner's family lives in the hotel.

Hotel Príncipe (☎ 066 553820; 20 Rue Youssef ben Tachfine; s/d Dh60/70, with shower Dh70/100) Upstairs from a boisterous and very masculine café, this place has several floors of rooms, all of which are clean enough but very basic. Furniture is worn; paint is peeling; staff are accommodating. Pay extra for a room with a shower.

The nearest camp site is at Martil, about 8km northeast of Tetouan (p188). There are also several sites on the coast road between Martil and the Ceuta border.

MIDRANGE

Hôtel Panorama Vista (☎ 039 964970; Rue Moulay Abbas; s/d incl breakfast from Dh236/322; 🔲) This three-star hotel is a rare piece of class in the centre of Tetouan, and more than lives up to its name. Rooms are immaculate, and the best have dramatic views over the Rif Mountains. The 1st-floor café is incredibly popular with young couples as well as for business meetings.

Hôtel Oumaima (☎ 039 943473; 10 Rue 10 Mai; s/d Dh205/206) Just up from Place al-Adala you'll find this reliable two-star option. Undeniably aged, rooms are airy with decent furniture, all with bathrooms and satellite TV. The café downstairs does a decent breakfast (Dh32).

Hôtel Paris (☎ 039 966750; 31 Rue Chakib Arsalane; s/d Dh205/246) This dependable if uninspiring hotel sums up the lack of midrange choice in Tetouan. Rooms are clean, but bathrooms are small. The whole impression is rather dull, but it's good enough in a pinch.

TOP END

Sofitel Thalassa (☎ 039 971234; www.accorhotels.com; Marina Smir, Route de Sebta; r from Dh1400, high season Dh2600; 🔲 🔳) The best accommodation in the Tetouan area, the Thalassa sits on its own sandy beach, in whitewashed Spanish colonial grandeur. All rooms overlook the Mediterranean, with their own balconies and all the facilities you'd expect from this top-end international chain.

Eating
RESTAURANTS

Tetouan has a surprising lack of decent restaurants.

Restaurant Restinga (21 Ave Mohammed V; fish dishes from Dh40; 🕙 noon-2.30pm & 7-9.30pm) Easily Tetouan's top dining spot is the vine-covered courtyard of this charming restaurant, with the abundance of fish and seafood on the menu a reminder of the town's proximity to the coast. As the only restaurant serving alcohol, it's always busy – something the management takes advantage of by automatically adding a 10% service charge to the bill. There's a small inside seating area for inclement weather.

Restaurant Palace Bouhlal (☎ 039 998797; 48 Jamaa Kebir; set menu Dh100; 🕙 10am-4pm) The only palace restaurant in Tetouan is popular with Spanish tour groups, so reservations are essential. The palace is suitably sumptuous: plush carpets, gurgling fountains and rose petals. Live folk music accompanies the classically Moroccan four-course meal: soup, salad, brochettes, couscous and tajines. Follow the lane north around the Grande Mosquée and look for signs directing you down a tiny alley; you may need to get directions.

Pizzeria Roma (☎ 039 713140; 8 Rue Mohammed ben Larbi Torres; pizzas from Dh35, burgers Dh20, salads Dh15-25) This pizzeria has a bright, fast-food-style interior, while the scooter outside services the home-delivery business. The food here is good with several vegetarian options to satisfy the stomach, while the wood oven gives the place a pleasing aroma (the false fireplace is fooling no one!).

Restaurant Saigon (2 Rue Mohammed ben Larbi Torres; fish dishes Dh22-55) Grilled fish, plus a few Moroccan standards, rather than anything Vietnamese, is the order of the day at Saigon. The food is excellent, and it can heave at lunch time, so make sure you head upstairs to grab a table away from the throng.

CAFÉS & PATISSERIES

Café Pâtisserie SMIR (☎ 039 961734; 17 Ave Mohammed V; ☼ 5am-10pm) On a corner in the heart of the pedestrian way, SMIR is a popular place for a coffee or pastry. There are two options: the tables strung along the pavement to watch the world go by, or the quiet seating area upstairs, which is notable for the groups of women it often attracts.

Le Printemps Salon du Thé (☎ 039 710016; 16 Rue Sidi Mandri; ☼ 6am-10pm) A good breakfast option, Le Printemps has a large interior, with a slightly upscale feel, seemingly designed for losing hours over the newspapers.

Salon de Thé Panorama Vista (☎ 039 964970; fax 039 964969; Hôtel Panorama Vista, Ave Moulay Abbas) Tetouan's trendiest café, this hotel café has quite glorious views over the Rif Mountains. It's always busy, but, even if you don't manage to grab a window seat, the salon is a lovely place wherever you sit. Waiters work hard, and you'll need to do the same to grab their attention.

Pâtisserie Rahmouni (10 Rue Youssef ben Tachfine; ☼ 6am-10pm) Ask a local where to get the best pastries in Tetouan, and they'll probably send you here. The Rahmouni family has a high reputation for its sticky delights, which have the punters queuing deep at breakfast time. Get a juice or coffee to go with your croissant at the stand-up bar at the back.

Jenin (☎ 039 962246; 8 Rue al-Ouahda; ☼ 5.30am-9pm) The fancy, modern interior of this café makes it a popular with courting couples and groups of young women, a world away from the smoky male cafés on the same block.

QUICK EATS

In keeping with the Spanish influence, *bocadillos* are the order of the day if you fancy a sandwich.

Snack Yousfi (Rue Youseff ben Tachfine; sandwiches from Dh16; ☼ 10am-midnight) Fill up on a sandwich here for lunch and you might not be hungry again until breakfast. Baguettes are stuffed to overflowing with various fillings, topped out with salad and a handful of chips. Great value.

La Isla Boccadillos (19 Rue Mourakah Anual; sandwiches from Dh12; ☼ 10am-10pm) One of the cheapest places in town to sate your appetite is this snack bar just outside the bus station offering a variety of sandwiches, *kofta* (mincemeat and spices grilled on a skewer) and salads with rice.

Snack Taouss (3 Rue 10 Mai; burgers Dh12-25; ☼ 7am-10pm) Known for its burgers and chips, this little snack bar also does decent, inexpensive pizzas, salads, *harira* (lentil soup) and the like. There's a small seating area upstairs (handy if you're waiting for a pizza), or you can eat on the hoof.

SELF-CATERING

There's loads of fresh fruit and veg for sale in the medina on the road leading east to Bab el-Okla. The central market (closed Friday) by the bus station puts on a good display, with fish brought in from the coast. **Supermercado La Española** (Rue 10 Mai) next to Heladería Atlas sells alcohol and other staples.

Drinking

As is the Moroccan norm, Tetouan's drinking establishments are firmly in the male sphere. The more welcoming cafés are listed under Eating (left); for a drop of the hard stuff, head for the dark and smoky bars along Rue 10 Mai, northwest of Place Moulay el-Mehdi. Restaurant Restinga also serves alcohol in a more genial atmosphere.

Heladería Atlas (Rue 10 Mai; juice Dh4-18) This place is great for a refreshing vitamin C fix, squeezing and mixing up a great selection of juices and smoothies. There is no seating area: slug it back and keep moving.

Entertainment

If you are looking for some evening diversion in town, about the only option is to catch a flick at **Cinéma Avenida** (Place al-Adala; Dh15-30). Films are usually in Spanish.

Shopping

Ensemble Artisanal (Ave Hassan II) Tetouan is home to the country's first government-sponsored emporium, founded in 1970, which now boasts some 60 craftspeople working as a part of the cooperative. The ensemble is a hive of activity, with carpet weavers, leatherworkers, jewellers and woodworkers all plying their trades – most welcome the opportunity to show off the techniques of their craft. Prices are fixed.

Tetouan's medina has the usual mix of craft shops and showrooms for the souvenir hunter. Wood and leatherwork are the local specialities; for the latter go straight to the source at the small **tannery** (Bab M'Kabar) in the north of the medina. Unique to the Rif are the eye-catching *mendeels* (hand-woven, brightly coloured striped cloths), worn by farmers. The best place to buy them is from the women on the tiny square to the northeast of Bab er-Rouah.

Getting There & Away

BUS

All buses depart from the **bus station** (cnr Rue Sidi Mandri & Rue Moulay Abbas), which is rather dark and seedy, despite its convenient location. It does have a **left luggage office** (per item Dh5; ⏲ 24hr).

CTM (☎ 039 961688) has buses to Tangier (Dh15, 1¼ hours, once daily); Casablanca (Dh110, six to seven hours, twice daily) via Rabat (Dh85, four to five hours); and Chefchaouen (Dh20, 1½ hours, three daily). Some of the Chefchaouen buses continue via Ouezzane (Dh36, three hours) to Fès (Dh80, 5½ hours). Buses for Nador (Dh110, 11 hours, twice daily) pass through Al-Hoceima (Dh78, seven hours).

There are regular non-CTM departures for all these destinations and more, including daily services to Oujda (Dh145, 11 hours), Larache (Dh30, two hours), Meknès (Dh62, five hours) and Marrakesh (Dh145, 11 hours).

Local buses for Martil (Dh4, 25 minutes), M'diq (Dh8, one hour), Fnideq (Dh10, 1¼ hours) and other local destinations also leave from here.

TAXI

Grands taxis to Fnideq (for Ceuta; Dh28, 30 minutes), Martil (Dh4, 15 minutes), Cabo Negro and M'diq (Dh5, 20 minutes) leave from Ave Hassan II, southeast of the bus station. Occasional grands taxis to Al-Hoceima (Dh150, five hours) wait on a dusty lot 100m further east behind the distinctive green-and-white building (once a railway station).

The taxi rank on Place al-Hamama, 2km west of central Tetouan, is the place to pick up grands taxis to Chefchaouen (Dh30, one hour) and Tangier (Dh25, one hour). If you are arriving from either of these places, the taxi driver may drop you closer to the town centre.

Getting Around

Petits taxis are canary yellow but don't have meters; a ride around town should be about Dh8 to Dh10. If you have your own vehicle, you can keep your car at the guarded **car park** (Bab Tout; per 4hr daytime Dh8, per night Dh8).

AROUND TETOUAN

Martil   مارتيل

About 8km northeast of Tetouan is the beach town of Martil, where the Rif Mountains tumble down into the sea. Its port was once a haven for corsairs, whose piracy swelled the Tetouan's coffers, but nowadays it makes its money as a summer getaway. Out of season it can almost be desolate, but the place throngs in July and August, with crowds enjoying walks along the corniche and the many waterfront cafés.

SLEEPING & EATING

As Martil is so close to Tetouan, there's hardly any need to stay here, but there are still a couple of decent possibilities, most notably if you have a tent or are in a camper van.

Camping al-Boustane (☎ 039 688822; fax 039 689682; Corniche; camping per person D10, plus per tent /car/camper van Dh10/10/20) This camp site has excellent facilities for its size (electricity Dh10), even down to a couple of sheep to keep the grass neatly clipped. It's well-signed, 200m back from the Corniche at the western end of town.

Hotel Estrella del Mar (☎ 039 979058; Ave Moulay al-Hassan; s/d Dh240/310) Distinctive with its whitewashed front and geometric blue windows, the Estrella is Martil's best sleeping option. The rooms are comfortable, especially those with balconies overlooking the sea. Outside summer, prices drop by 30%.

Cheap eats cluster around the bus station. For something better, try **Restaurant Scampis** (☎ 039 979120; Ave Rabat; mains Dh40-80), one street behind the corniche. It has good fish dishes in a friendly bistro setting and serves alcohol. **La Vitamin de la Mer** (☎ 062 865544; Ave Miramar; meals from around Dh100) is also worth a visit, claiming to do the best seafood in the region.

GETTING THERE & AWAY

Local buses to Tetouan (Dh4, 25 minutes) leave from the bus station near the water tower at the south end of the beach. You'll find grands taxis (Dh4, 15 minutes) near the big new mosque.

Cabo Negro & M'diq

الرأس الاسود و مضيق

About 5km up the coast from Martil, the headland of Cabo Negro (Ras Aswad in Arabic) juts out into the Mediterranean and is clearly visible from Martil. Tucked in the lee of its north side is the small fishing port of M'diq. Fishing is the lifeblood of this small community: hassles are few and the pace of life is slow.

The corniche, with its old Spanish church at its easternmost point, is popular for promenading. The whole area was being re-modelled when we visited, pedestrianising many of the other streets. The beach, more seashell than sand, sweeps north, where it is taken over by the discos and bars of tourist resorts at Restinga-Smir.

SLEEPING & EATING

M'diq's sleeping options tend to cater to the summer tourist trade and ignore the lower end of the price bracket. Ask for discounts outside the summer months. There's a string of cafés and cheap eateries along the M'diq seafront.

Hotel Narijiss (☎ 039 975841; Ave Lalla Nezha; s/d Dh150/250; ☒) This decent hotel is 200m up the hill rising from the seafront to the Tetouan road. It's a bit nondescript, but rooms have bathrooms and satellite TV, and there's a café tucked outside.

Hôtel Playa (☎ 039 975166; 24 Rte de Sebta; r incl breakfast Dh250; ☒) On the seafront, the Playa has modern, comfortable rooms from the tourist-class mould. There's a restaurant on the 1st floor with good seafood options (and breakfast in the morning).

La Sirena Restaurant (seafood dishes from Dh35) Set virtually on the beach, this place has a good selection of fish dishes. You can eat with your toes in the sand, or shelter from the elements on the 1st floor according to the season.

Royal Yachting Club de M'diq (☎ 039 663887; meals from Dh90, alcohol served) This classy place down by the port is a private club, so you'll have to ask nicely to eat there, though this isn't usually a problem.

GETTING THERE & AWAY

Grands taxis and buses travelling between Tetouan and Fnideq (3km short of the bor-der with Ceuta) pass through M'diq. Grands taxis to Tetouan (Dh5, 20 minutes) depart from a stand near the Narijiss Hotel. Those for the border (Dh10) gather on the north side of town beside the Banque Populaire.

CHEFCHAOUEN

شفشاون

pop 45,000

Set beneath the striking peaks of the Rif Mountains, Chefchaouen has long been charming travellers. One of the pretti-est towns in Morocco, its old medina is a delight of Moroccan and Andalucian in-fluence with red-tiled roofs, bright-blue buildings, and narrow lanes converging on a delightful square. Backpackers, many drawn by the easy availability of kif, will find plenty of good budget accommodation, but Chefchaouen has now started to attract higher-spending visitors too, spurring the opening of a clutch of boutique hotels in-spired by the riads of Marrakesh and Fès.

Chefchaouen is the sort of place where a two-night stay can easily slip into a week. The air is cool and clear, and those with energy enough to leave the street cafés will find some lovely day walks – and longer treks – offering inspiring mountain views.

History

Old habits die hard, which is why locals often refer to Chefchaouen by its original name, Chaouen, meaning 'peaks', refer-ring to the surrounding mountains. Under Spanish occupation the spelling changed to Xaouen and in 1975 the town was renamed Chefchaouen ('Look at the Peaks'). These days, the names are used interchangeably.

Moulay Ali ben Rachid founded Chaouen in 1471 as a base for Riffian Berber tribes to launch attacks on the Portuguese in Ceuta. The town prospered and grew consider-ably with the arrival of Muslim and Jewish refugees escaping persecution in Granada in 1494. It was these refugees who built the whitewashed houses, with tiny balconies, tiled roofs and patios (often with a citrus tree in the centre), which give the town its distinctive Hispanic flavour. The pale-blue wash now so typical was only introduced in the 1930s by the Jewish refugees – previ-ously windows and doors had been painted green, a traditional Muslim colour.

The town remained isolated, and almost xenophobic, until occupied by Spanish troops in 1920. In fact, prior to the Spanish occupation Christians were forbidden and

CHEFCHAOUEN

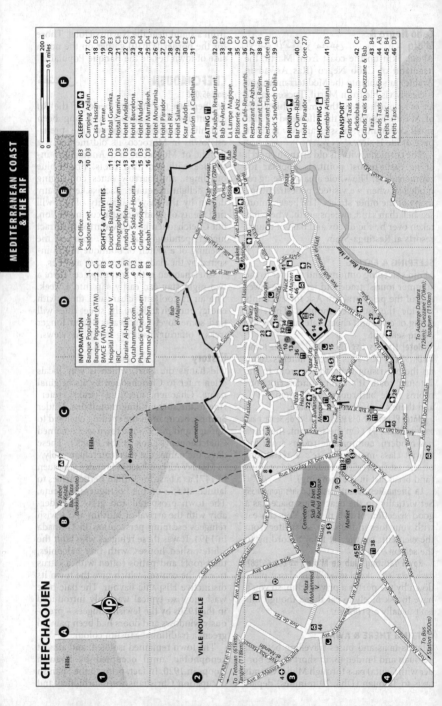

entered on pain of death. Two daredevils managed to sneak in: the French adventurer Charles Foucauld in 1883 and, five years later, the British wanderer and journalist Walter Harris (disguised as a Jew).

When the Spaniards arrived they were surprised to hear the Jewish inhabitants still speaking a variant of medieval Castilian. The Spanish were briefly thrown out of Chefchaouen by Abd al-Krim during the Rif War in the 1920s, but they soon returned to stay until independence in 1956.

Orientation

Although the medina retains the feel of a mountain village, Chefchaouen has grown into a modern town. Centred on Plaza Uta el-Hammam, the medina occupies the eastern half of the town centre, with its main entrance on its western side at Bab el-Ain. From here, Ave Hassan II stretches west to Plaza Mohammed V, making up the principal route of the ville nouvelle. The majority of hotels and restaurants are in the medina, while administrative offices and such are in the ville nouvelle. The bus station is a 1km hike southwest of the town centre.

Information

BOOKSHOPS
Librairie Al-Nahj (☎ 039 986945; Ave Hassan II) Has a reasonable selection of international newspapers and magazines.

INTERNET ACCESS
Institut Raouachid pour l'Information et le Commerce (IRIC; Ave Hassan II; per hr Dh10; ☼ 9am-midnight)
Outahammam.com (Place el-Majzen; per hr Dh10; ☼ 9am-midnight)
Saadoune.net (Plaza Uta el-Hammam; per hr Dh10; ☼ 10am-midnight)

MEDICAL SERVICES
Hospital Mohammed V (☎ 039 986228; Ave al-Massira al-Khadra)
Pharmacy Alhambra (Rue Moulay Ali ben Rachid)
Pharmacie Chefchaouen (Ave Moulay Driss)

MONEY
There are no ATMS in the medina.
Banque Populaire medina (Plaza Uta el-Hammam; ☼ 9.30am-1pm & 3.30-9pm) Actually keeps erratic hours; ville nouvelle (Ave Hassan II)
BMCE (Ave Hassan II)

POST
Post office (Ave Hassan II)

Sights & Activities

MEDINA
Chefchaouen's medina is one of the loveliest in Morocco. Small and uncrowded, it's easy to explore, with enough winding paths to keep you diverted, but compact enough that you'll never quite get lost. Most of the buildings are painted a blinding blue-white, giving the whole place a clean, fresh look, while the terracotta pantiles on many buildings add an Andalucian flavour.

The heart of the medina is the shady, cobbled **Plaza Uta el-Hammam**, dominated by the red-hued walls of the kasbah (below) and the striking Grande Mosquée. Noteworthy for its unusual octagonal tower, the **Grande Mosquée** was built in the 15th century by the son of the town's founder, Ali ben Rachid. It is closed to non-Muslims. The mosque also has a striking terracotta-tiled roof, best seen from the tower of the kasbah.

The square is lined with cafés, which are blissfully relaxing places from which to watch the world go by, or for recuperating after a hard day's trekking (or shopping). Just off the northeast corner of the square is the **Funduq Chfichu**, an ancient accommodation and stabling block, long used by pilgrims and travellers and still full on market days.

KASBAH
The **kasbah** (☎ 039 986343; admission incl museum & galerie Dh10; ☼ 9am-1pm & 3-6.30pm Wed-Mon) was built by Moulay Ali ben Rachid. In the 17th century, Moulay Ismail restored the structure to defend the town against unruly Berber tribes, as well as against outsiders such as the Spaniards. For a time in the 1920s Abd al-Krim had his headquarters here.

The walls enclose a peaceful, blooming garden. To the left is a modest **ethnographic museum** containing a collection of antique weapons, musical instruments, carpets and some photos of townspeople in traditional Berber attire and views of old Chefchaouen – the views of Plaza Uta el-Hammam in the 1920s and the pre-restoration kasbah are fascinating.

On the right are the gloomy prison cells (with rusting chains) and the kasbah's tower. Beautifully restored, it affords

MEDITERRANEAN COAST & THE RIF

wonderful views over the town. Also in the grounds is the **Galerie Saïda al-Hourra**, used for temporary art exhibitions.

RUINED MOSQUE

Heading northeast from Place el-Majzen, all roads lead to Bab al-Ansar, the eastern medina gate. Just below the gate, you'll see women gathering to do their washing in the fast running Ras el-Maa river, which pours out of the mountains above the town. From here, it's a 2km walk to a ruined mosque overlooking the town. It was built by the Spanish, but abandoned during the Rif War in the 1920s. The views of Chefchaouen from here are truly gorgeous. The mosque is popular with picnicking locals on Fridays, and lads smoking kif at other times – they're friendly enough, but solo females might not appreciate the attention.

HAMMAMS

A traditional, rather than touristy, hammam is **Douches Barakat** (shower Dh6, hammam Dh8; ☺ men 8am-noon, women noon-8pm).

TREKKING

The Rif Mountains, bordering the Moroccan coast for about 200km, rarely reach more than 1800m, but these are the highest peaks in northern Morocco. The hillsides are green and magnificent. Cedars dominate the hillsides close to Chefchaouen, while forests of pine and holm oak grow on the higher slopes. Trekking opportunities here are good enough to draw even the most sloth-like backpacker away from the cafés and roof terraces of Chefchaouen, if only for a few hours. See p428 for further information.

Towering high above Chefchaouen, **Jebel el-Kelaâ** (1616m) is an inviting peak and can be easily climbed in one day. See boxed text, below, for details.

Tours

Chefchaouen doesn't have a tourist office. The president of the **Association des Guides du Tourisme** (☎ 062 113917; guiderando@yahoo.fr; half-day tour Dh120), Abdeslam Mouden, can arrange guided tours of the medina and advise on trekking. He can also be reached through the Hotel Parador.

Festivals & Events

The active cultural association **Rif el-Andalus** (☎ 039 986800) organises various events, including a big open-air art exhibition in July. Paintings by local artists are displayed around town, including at the Galerie Saïda al-Hourra at the kasbah. Every June there's also a small, slightly ad hoc, festival of Andalucian music.

Sleeping

Chefchaouen has a fair range of accommodation. It can be very cold in winter and few hotels have heating – ask for extra blankets or bring a sleeping bag.

CLIMBING JEBEL EL-KELAÂ

Looming over Chefchaouen at 1616m, Jebel el-Kelaâ might initially appear a daunting peak, but with an early start and a packed lunch, it can easily be climbed in a day if you're in reasonably good shape.

The hike starts from behind Camping Azilane, following the 4WD track that takes you to the hamlet of Aïn Tissimlane. Rocks painted with a yellow and white stripe indicate that you're on the right path. The initial hour is relatively steep as you climb above the trees to get your first views over Chefchaouen, before cutting into the mountains along the steady *piste*. You should reach Aïn Tissimlane within a couple of hours of setting out, after which the path climbs and zigzags steeply through great boulders for nearly an hour to a pass. Turn west along the track, which leads to the saddle of the mountain, from where you can make the final push to the summit. There's a rough path, although you'll need to scramble in places. The peak is attained relatively quickly, and your exertions are rewarded with the most sublime views over this part of the Rif.

It's straightforward and quick to descend by the same route. Alternatively, you can head north from the saddle on a path that takes you to a cluster of villages on the other side of the mountain. One of these villages, El-Kelaâ, has 16th-century grain stores, and a mosque with a leaning minaret. From here, a number of simple tracks will take you back to Chefchaouen in a couple of hours.

Chefchaouen struggles to meet demand for upscale options, and although new places are slowly coming on tap, it's advisable to book in advance outside winter.

MEDINA
Budget

Most of the budget options are in the medina. The best of these are cheerful, tiled places with interior courtyards and superb roof terraces. Facilities are mostly shared, but toilets are generally Western-style and hot showers are often included in the price.

Hotel Mouritania (☎ 039 986184; 15 Rue Qadi Alami; s/d Dh45/70) For budget value, you'll have to go a long way to beat the Mouritania. Rooms are simple as anything, but there's the obligatory roof terrace and a comfy courtyard lounge that's ideal for meeting other travellers. Staff are helpful, and the breakfasts (Dh15) are great too.

Hostal Yasmina (☎ 039 883118; yasmina45@hotmail .com; 12 Rue Zaida al-Horra; r per person Dh60) For the price bracket, this place sparkles. Rooms are bright and clean, there's lots of hot water in the showers and a great roof terrace. It feels like a bargain, and as it doesn't have many rooms it can fill up quickly.

Pensión La Castellana (☎ 039 986295; 4 Sidi el-Bouhali; r per person Dh75) A well-established budget option, its rooms are boxy, and the price possibly reflects its popularity with travellers rather than the standard of the accommodation. Still, there's a roof terrace and the showers are hot, so this will presumably remain a backpacker's favourite for some time yet.

Hotel Barcelona (☎ 039 988506; 12 Rue Targui; r per person Dh50, d with bathroom Dh300) A friendly budget option in bright Chefchaouen blue. Fixtures and fittings are pretty basic, but there was some extensive renovation in progress when we visited, which could make this hostel with its great roof terrace a real bargain.

Hostal Guernika (☎ 039 987434; 49 Calle Ibn Askar; r Dh140, with shower Dh180) It's hard to say if this hostel is run by the cheerful Spanish couple that owns it, or by the dogs and cats who lounge on the downstairs sofas. Just east of the main square, it has a good selection of welcoming and simply decorated rooms, several with bathrooms (shared facilities are spotless). The roof terrace with gorgeous views is the icing on the cake.

Hotel Andaluz (☎ 039 986034; 1 Rue Sidi Salem; r per person Dh50) Popular with the shoestringers, the Andaluz has a selection of rooms clustered around a courtyard, although the lack of external windows makes many a bit gloomy. It plays better in the colder months, when you can grab a title from the book exchange and curl up in front of the log fire.

Midrange & Top End

Ksar Aladdin (☎ 065 406464; Rue Rauachid; r Dh450 ☒) One of the newest guesthouses on the block, Ksar Aladdin rates high on the score-card. Plush rooms are beautifully decorated with dark wood and bright colours against strikingly painted walls. Even the bathroom fittings are quirkily individual. The best options come with romantic bedrooms for surveying the medina and hills. Made for spinning Sheherezade-tales before bedtime.

Dar Terrae (☎ 039 987598; darterrae@hotmail.com; Ave Hassan I; r incl breakfast Dh250-450) Dar Terrae feels like an escape from the outside world: the cheerfully painted rooms are individually decorated with their own bathroom and fireplace, all hidden up and down a tumble of stairs and odd corners. Three terraces add to the hideaway factor. The Italian owners prepare a fantastic breakfast spread every day, and other meals on request. It's poorly signed – if in doubt ask for the 'Hotel Italiano'.

Casa Hassan (☎ 039 986153; www.casahassan.com; 22 Rue Targui; s/d/tr with half board from Dh450/600/750; ☒) A long-established upmarket choice, this guesthouse has more than a hint of the Arabian Nights about it. Rooms are individually decorated, with carved wooden doors, beds tucked into coves, colourful, tiled bathrooms and locally woven rugs, all stylish and comfortable. The terrace is set for elegant lounging, and the cosy Restaurant Tissemlal finishes the whole thing nicely.

Hotel Parador (☎ 039 986136; parador@iam.net .ma; Place el-Majzen; s/d Dh349/436, May-Sep Dh398/ 498; ☒) An ageing four-star (look for the 1930s brochure framed in the lobby), the Parador has consistently comfortable tourist-class options. Some rooms are on the cramped side, but perks include a good restaurant and one of Chefchaouen's few bars.

MEDITERRANEAN COAST
& THE RIF

AROUND THE MEDINA
Budget

There's another cluster of budget hotels on Ave Hassan II, which runs south of the medina alongside the old city walls. These places are a step up from the pensions in the medina, in that they offer private bathrooms and have restaurants on site. They also offer great Rif views from one side of the building.

Hotel Rif (☎ 039 986982; hotelrif@caramail.com; 29 Rue Hassan II; s/d incl breakfast Dh150/180, with bathroom & breakfast Dh180/240; 🗙) Just below the medina walls, it has some good rooms with great views, and adequate rooms without. A little on the nondescript side, it's nevertheless popular with tour groups, so advance booking is a good idea. The restaurant has the bonus of an alcohol licence.

Hotel Marrakesh (☎ 039 987774; Ave Hassan II; s/d Dh140/250, with shower Dh200/300) Set downhill from the action, the Marrakesh is a hotel with a bit of soul. Bright blue rooms invite the fresh air in, and if you need more of it then the roof terrace offers fine views over the valley. Breakfast and dinner are available in the attached restaurant.

Hotel Salam (☎ 039 986239; 39 Ave Hassan II; s/d/tr Dh80/120/180) Another out-of-medina experience, the Salam is a decent enough choice, maybe in want of a little character. Shared facilities are adequate, but sinks in all rooms are a bonus. The ground floor café opens onto a pleasant balcony-cum-terrace.

Camping Azilane (☎ 039 986979; camping per adult Dh15, plus per tent/car/campervan Dh15/20/35) A shady setting with great views makes this site popular, even if it is a stiff 20-minute walk from the medina. A small restaurant opens during the summer, and a shop sells some essentials, but otherwise facilities are pretty basic (hot showers Dh10).

Midrange & Top End

Auberge Dardara (☎ 061 150503; www.dardara.com in French; Rte Nationale 2; s/tw/d Mon-Fri Dh330/440/540, Sat & Sun Dh370/490/590; 🗙 🗙) At Dardara Junction, 11km southwest of Chefchaouen, this fully refurbished guesthouse with lush gardens is a truly lovely hideaway if you have your own transport. Traditionally decorated rooms – each with bathroom and fireplace – are charming, but it's the little touches that stand out: paintings by local artists, and local honey and olive oil for sale

at the front desk. There's a great restaurant, and you can also arrange horse-trekking (Dh100 for four hours).

Hotel Madrid (☎ 039 987497; Ave Hassan II; s/d from Dh253/380; 🗙) The Hotel Madrid has a slightly musty air and an old-fashioned line in floral European-Moroccan décor. All of which makes the rooms such a pleasant surprise: positively cosy with wrought-iron canopy beds and well-appointed bathrooms packed with complimentary toiletries.

Eating
RESTAURANTS

Plaza Café-Restaurants (Plaza Uta el-Hammam; breakfast from Dh15, mains from Dh25; ⏰ 8am-11pm) A popular eating option in Chefchaouen is to choose one of about a dozen café-restaurants on the main square. Menus are virtually identical – continental breakfasts, soups and salads, tajines and seafood – but the food is generally pretty good, and they have the best ambience in town.

La Lampe Magique (☎ 065 406464; Rue Targui; mains from Dh45, set menu Dh75) This magical place overlooking Plaza Uta el-Hammam serves delicious Moroccan staples in a grand setting. Three floors include a laid-back lounge, a more formal dining area, and a roof-top terrace that is open to the stars. Painted blue walls bring Chefchaouen's charm inside, while brick floors and dark wooden tables enhance the local flavour. The food – featuring favourites like lamb tajine with prunes and some great cooked salads – is delicious, but this place is really about atmosphere.

Restaurant Tissemlal (☎ 039 986153; 22 Rue Targui; set menu Dh60) The restaurant inside the Casa Hassan is another sure-fire bet for a fine meal in enchanting surroundings. Always hospitable, this place is especially welcoming on a chilly evening, when a fire roars and warms the bones. The open kitchen is another draw, allowing guests to see the chefs at work. The menu includes the Moroccan standards with a few twists. Don't miss the fresh goat-cheese salad, a local Rif speciality.

Al-Kasbah Restaurant (off Plaza Uta el-Hammam; set menu Dh60) This place has a great flavour, with its central dining area and series of secluded booths decked out as Berber tents. Well-cooked Moroccan standards are the order of the day (individual courses can also be ordered), plus a paella that's worth the extra wait. Eat quickly though, as dishes tend to appear while you're still finishing the previous course.

Restaurant al-Azhar (Ave Moulay Driss; mains from Dh25; ☽ 8am-9pm) Tucked in by the steps down from the post office, this local place does a roaring trade, attracting workers and families in equal measure. Tajines and the like are all on offer; a better option is to check out the fish counter out front and order a huge seafood platter (Dh50).

Restaurant Les Raisins (☎ 039 988641; 7 Rue Sidi Sifri; tajines Dh20, set menu from Dh40; ☽ 7am-9pm) Slightly out of the way in the ville nouvelle, Les Raisins is a perennial favourite with locals and tourists alike. It's particularly well regarded for its couscous. Late, lazy lunches are the best, with the front terrace catching the afternoon sun.

CAFÉS, PATISSERIES & ICE-CREAM PARLOURS

Unsurprisingly, it's hard to get past the cafés on Plaza Uta el-Hammam for a long juice or a relaxing mint tea. From mid-afternoon, hawkers do the rounds of the cafés carrying trays laden with sticky pastries for sale. In the back rooms, local men play cards and smoke kif – worth a look, although women won't feel particularly welcome.

Bab el-Ansar Café (Bab el-Ansar) This café has a great location overlooking Oued Ras el Mar and out of the medina. Three terraces tumble down the hill, keeping the waiters good and fit. Views are particularly nice in the late afternoon, with the sun catching the mountains opposite.

Pâtisserie Aziz (Ave Hassan II) For a great selection of pastries, make your way here. They squeeze a mean juice, and make good coffee too, for a quick breakfast on the hoof.

Snack Sandwich Dahlia (Rue Jarrazin; light meals Dh10) The tiny square near Hotel Andaluz is a delightful spot for a quick lunch, and this snack bar fits the bill. Dahlia will prepare you a hamburger or omelette with salad and warm bread to munch under the shady vines.

SELF-CATERING

The market off Ave Hassan II is excellent for fresh fish, meat, fruit and vegetables, and particularly throngs on Monday and Thursday, when people come from outside Chefchaouen to sell produce.

Several local specialities are worth checking out, particularly the fragrant mountain honey and soft ewe's cheese – both served up at breakfast. Add fresh *dial makla* (a type of bread) and you have all the ingredients for a heavenly picnic.

Drinking

At the edge of kif country, Chefchaouen isn't big on drinking. There's just one, very masculine, bar, **Bar Oum-Rabiá** (Ave Hassan II; ☽ 10am-10pm). Alternatives are the **Hotel Parador Bar** (☽ 2-11pm), although it's a bit soulless and the drinks are expensive, or the restaurant at the Hotel Rif.

Shopping

Chefchaouen remains an artisan centre and, as such, an excellent place to shop – especially for woven rugs and blankets in bright primary colours. Many shops have looms in situ, so you can see the blankets being made. Previously silk was the material of choice: the mulberry trees in Plaza Uta el-Hammam are a legacy of these times. Most of the weaving nowadays is with wool, one of the area's biggest products.

A fair smattering of tourist shops are located around the focal points of Uta el-Hammam and Place el-Majzen. It's also worth stopping at the **Ensemble Artisinal** (Place el-Majzen), if only for the sake of comparison.

Getting There & Away

BUS

Many bus services from Chefchaouen originate elsewhere, so are often full on arrival. Where possible, buy your ticket a day in advance to secure your seat. The bus station is 1.5km southwest of the town centre at the far end of Ave Mohammed V (Dh10 in a petit taxi from Place el-Majzen). CTM and all other buses use the same station.

CTM (☎ 039 988769) has four services passing through Chefchaouen: two afternoon buses to Fès (Dh60, four hours) via Ouezzane (Dh20, 1½ hours); one afternoon bus to Tangier (Dh35, three hours) via Tetouan (Dh20, 1½ hours); and one early morning service to Nador (Dh100, nine hours) via Al-Hoceima (Dh65, six hours).

Other companies run a number of cheaper services starting in Chefchaouen. These include frequent buses to Tetouan

---

KIF IN THE RIF

The smoking of kif is an ancient tradition in northern Morocco. (The word stems from the Arabic word for pleasure.) In the Rif Mountains, from Chefchaouen to Ketama and beyond, its cultivation is widespread; some villages grow nothing else. One theory claims that the Rif is the source of the Western slang term 'reefer'.

Hashish, which is essentially compressed kif, is a stronger, modern (1960s) invention developed for export. While an old goatherd in the mountains may break out his kif pipe should you stop to chat, hashish is favoured by younger, more Westernised Riffians.

The Rif is one of the most economically deprived areas of Morocco, and kif has become the mainstay of the economy, flourishing with the aid of a blind eye from the authorities. In recent years though, pressure from the US and particularly the EU – now Morocco's major trading partner – has led to a less favourable opinion of this illicit activity. International aid programmes have started to target ecological and cultural tourism as sectors of development, although a day riding on the poor roads in the mountains shows the high levels of continued investment needed just to bring the local infrastructure up to scratch.

In 2004 the production of kif was technically made illegal and farmers can now actually be prosecuted. In practice, only a few prosecutions have been brought, and the discreet possession and use of kif is still largely tolerated. Some travellers get away with buying small quantities for personal use. However, never travel in possession of kif and mistrust all dealers – many double as police informers.

(Dh15, 1½ hours), several of which continue to Tangier (Dh27, three hours). There are also departures for Casablanca (Dh70, six hours) via Rabat (Dh55, five hours). For Meknès (Dh50, five hours), through services from Tetouan stop in Chefchaouen. All of the southbound buses stop in Ouezzane (Dh18, 1½ hours). There's a daily departure for Oued Laou (Dh18, two hours).

TAXI

Grands taxis north leave from just below Plaza Mohammed V. Most just run to Tetouan (Dh30, one hour), where you must change for Tangier or Ceuta – direct taxis are rare. From Ave Allal ben Abdallah you can catch a grand taxi to Dar Ackoubaa (Dh15, 20 minutes), the junction for Oued Laou.

Grands taxis headed south gather below the central market. Catch one to Ouezzane (Dh30, 75 minutes), where you can pick up onward transport to Fès and Meknès. There is very little transport heading east to the coast. The best option is to take a grand taxi to Dardara junction (Dh8, 15 minutes) or Bab Taza (Dh15, 30 minutes) and hope for the best from there.

Getting Around

Blue petits taxis congregate on Place el-Majzen and near the market. They're unmetered; most fares shouldn't top Dh10.

The safe and convenient Hotel Parador **car park** (Place el-Majzen; per night Dh10) can be used by non-guests.

OUEZZANE وزان

pop 53,000

Lying in rolling hills at the southern edge of the Rif, Ouezzane is another town that attracted Andalucian refugees, many of them Jewish, in the 15th century. They left a few Spanish touches, although as a busy modern commercial centre, the town lacks the charm of Chefchaouen. Wool and olive oil are the mainstays of the economy, and Ouezzane holds a large market every Thursday.

There's a touch of holiness amid the commerce. A *zawiya* (fraternity based around a saint's mausoleum) is dedicated to the memory of Moulay Abdallah ben Brahim, the 18th-century Sufi leader, a descendant of the Prophet Mohammed and ancestor of the present sherif of Ouezzane. He is celebrated with a *moussem* (festival) in late March. Another famous descendent was Sherif Si Absellam, who in the late 19th century scandalised polite society by divorcing his wives to marry an English woman, Emily Keane (who is buried at St Andrews church in Tangier – see p164).

Jews make an annual pilgrimage in early May to visit the tomb of Rabbi Amrane ben Diwan, an Andalucian 'miracle worker' who died in about 1780. His tomb is 9km northwest of Ouezzane off the Rabat road, in the Jewish cemetery of Azjem.

Orientation

The centre of Ouezzane is Place de l'Indépendence, a vast square (actually a triangle) sitting between the medina to the south and west and the ville nouvelle to the north and east. Useful landmarks are clearly visible to the south of the square: the minarets of the Mosque of the Zawiya (also known, appropriately, as the Green Mosque) and, beyond it, the Moulay Abdallah Sherif Mosque.

Sleeping & Eating

Ouezzane is not the most hospitable place in terms of accommodation options. You have a choice of two very basic but adequate hotels, and a few others that are less respectable.

Hôtel Bouhlal (☎ 037 907154; Hay el-Haddadine Qu; s/d/tr Dh80/94/126) Easily Ouezzane's best sleeping option, this small hotel on a side street northeast of the Mosque of the Zawiya is uncluttered, spic-and-span rooms. Shared bathrooms have squat toilets; there's also a small roof terrace with views. Staff can rustle up a decent breakfast with a little warning.

Grand Hôtel (☎ 037 907096; Place de l'Indépendence; s/d/tr Dh60/70/100) Despite the gloomy exterior, rooms here are slightly better than you'd expect, although they're still pretty basic. Shared bathrooms have cold showers and squat toilets. There's a small café on the terrace for tea and some simple grills.

Place de l'Indépendence also has a couple of other grubby hotels if budgets are tight and you're feeling brave.

Numerous cafés and snack stands are on the southwest side of the square, while cheap sandwiches and brochettes are sold at the bus station. **Restaurant des Négociants** (Place de l'Indépendence) on the west side of the square is popular with Ouezzane's men, for drinks and simple snacks.

Getting There & Away

BUS

Two dusty lots on Rue de la Marche Verte, 50m northwest of the main square, function as the bus station and grand-taxi stand. Get an early start when trying to leave Ouezzane, as there are virtually no buses after 5pm.

CTM has two buses daily to Fès (Dh40, two hours) and one to Tetouan (Dh35, three hours) via Chefchaouen (Dh20, 1½ hours). There are frequent non-CTM buses before 5pm to Meknès (Dh30), Fès (Dh30), Tetouan (Dh30), Chefchaouen (Dh15), Kenitra (Dh23, 2½ hours), Casablanca (Dh50, five hours) and Tangier (Dh45, four hours). Most non-CTM buses for Chefchaouen actually stop at Dardara junction, on the main road, from where you can pick up a grand taxi (Dh8) for the final 10km into town.

TAXI

There are regular grands taxis to Chefchaouen (Dh30, 75 minutes) and Fès (Dh60, 2½ hours). For longer-distance destinations (such as Rabat or Tangier) you may have to take a taxi to Souk el-Arba-du-Rharb (Dh20, 45 minutes) or Ksar el-Kebir (Dh25, one hour), and change.

NORTH & EAST OF CHEFCHAOUEN

Oued Laou   وادِ لاو

With the feel of an overgrown fishing village, Oued Laou stretches lazily along a wide sandy beach with the charm of an undiscovered paradise. The wide bay is a rarity along this stretch of the coast, but the mountains are never far away, making the town's location particularly attractive.

There's little to do in Oued Laou apart from take the air and watch the fishing boats haul up on the beach. It's a great place to catch your breath.

SLEEPING & EATING

Hôtel Restaurant Oued Laou (☎ 039 972855; Blvd Massira; d from Dh120) There's just one decent hotel in town, and it's here, 200m north of the octagonal mosque, on the beach. Rooms are bright and clean, and the showers are hot. The restaurant is also Oued Laou's best eating option – the seafood unsurprisingly scores highly.

Camping Oued Laou (☎ 039 670895; camping per person Dh15, plus per tent/car/caravan Dh10/15/30) Also near the mosque is the camp site. It's a secure site, but the amenities aren't great and could do with a bit of attention.

GETTING THERE & AWAY

If you're driving from Chefchaouen turn off the main Tetouan road at Dar Ackoubaa, 11km north of Chefchaouen. It's

MEDITERRANEAN COAST & THE RIF

a wonderful drive past the large hydro-electric dam and through rolling hills and the stunning Laou Gorge. Coming from Tetouan, S608 hugs the dramatic coastline for 140km all the way to El-Jebha.

Three buses a day connect Tetouan and Oued Laou (Dh21, two hours). There's also one bus from Chefchaouen (Dh18, 90 minutes), which continues along the coast to El-Jebha (Dh25, five hours); the return service leaves El-Jebha early in the morning. However, at Oued Laou it dumps you out by the souq, leaving you a 45-minute walk or Dh5 grand-taxi ride to town.

Grands taxis run from beside the mosque in Oued Laou to Tetouan (Dh30, one hour) via Dar Ackoubaa (Dh15, 20 minutes), where you can pick up a passing taxi for Chefchaouen.

Targa to El-Jebha

This stretch of the coast is very dramatic, and is as far off the beaten track as you're likely to get in the north. On the edge of kif country, tourists are virtually unheard of.

Seventeen kilometres southeast of Oued Laou, **Targa** is a little village with an illustrious history of piracy. High atop an outcrop of black rock, a stone fort overlooks the village, built during the Spanish protectorate. The 13th century mosque, associated with a local saint, speaks of older traditions.

About 18km southeast of Targa, in the wide valley of Oued Bouchia, are the twin villages of **Steha** (an administrative centre) and **Bou-Ahmed**. Set back from the coast, the latter is the end point for a long-distance trek from Chefchaouen (see p432). There's an interesting souq every Tuesday.

From here the road follows the coast on a splendid roller-coaster ride to the blue and white town of **El-Jebha**, 52km to the southeast. The rugged coastline here forms a number of breathtaking and secluded bays – worth exploring if you have your own transport. Each Tuesday, the local souq draws Rif farmers from the surrounding villages. El-Jebha is the last stop before the road climbs up through the Rif to Issaguen.

Issaguen (Ketama)   دازكان
pop 5000

Heading southeast out of Chefchaouen, the road N2 plunges into the heart of the Rif, running about 150km along the back-bone of the mountains. As it climbs out of Chefchaouen, it traverses forests of cork oak and majestic pine. The small town of Bab Berret marks the unofficial entry point to kif country – note the huge stacks of chemical fertiliser for the crop on sale in the markets.

Issaguen, known locally (and on many maps) as Ketama, appears unexpectedly from the middle of the pine forests. It's little more than an over-grown road junction and has a scruffy, frontier feel – which comes as no surprise when you learn that this is the centre of kif cultivation and smuggling.

To the southeast, Jebel Tidiquin (2448m), the highest peak in the Rif Mountains, dominates the skyline.

DANGERS & ANNOYANCES

The Ketama area is one of the biggest hash-ish producing areas in the world. You'll see whole hillsides planted with marijuana, especially north towards the coast. There are plenty of police roadblocks in evidence, but despite the best efforts of Rabat, many local gendarmes turn a blind eye to the huge trade beneath their noses. Hassle for foreigners at roadblocks is now the exception rather than the norm. As you'll stand out from the crowd, you should be extremely circumspect about accepting offers of kif.

More frustrating are the roads, whose often terrible state reflects years of neglect of this poor and unloved part of the country. Endless twists and turns make the going even slower, and there are few petrol stations.

SLEEPING & EATING

Issaguen is not somewhere you'd choose to spend the night. **Hotel Tidighine** (☎ 067 255171; s/d Dh223/252) is the only sensible option, off the main road near the CMH petrol station. That said, don't expect too much – it's overpriced and badly maintained.

There are a few cafés on the main road than can offer simple food and a bed out back, but they're pretty seedy.

GETTING THERE & AWAY

There is no bus station in Issaguen. Passing buses simply stop on the main road by the T-junction (next to the petrol station). The main destinations from here are Tetouan (Dh44, five hours, around six daily) via Chefchaouen (Dh38, three hours), Al-

Hoceima (Dh36, three hours, at least nine daily) and Fès (Dh42, four hours, seven daily).

Almost all grands taxis are for local transport only. Occasional grands taxis leave for Al-Hoceima (Dh45) and Tetouan (Dh75), otherwise you're looking at hiring *collectif*.

AL-HOCEIMA
pop 113,000

Picturesque Al-Hoceima is set above a bay at one of the rare points along the coast where the Rif drops away and makes a little room for beaches. Founded by the Spanish as Villa Sanjuro, it has a very modern feel – the wide highways are something of a shock if you've been bumping your way through the Rif. In summer, it's popular with Moroccan holiday-makers, and Spaniards taking the seasonal ferry from Almería and Malaga.

The town was built as a garrison to keep an eye on the unruly Berbers after the Rif Wars in the early 20th century. However, during the 1920s the Rif rebel Abd al-Krim had one of his main bases only 10km away, at Ajdir, which shows how tenuous Spain's hold over this part of its protectorate was after 1912.

Moroccan independence brought the name-change of Al-Hoceima, but the Spanish influence remains strong in language, architecture and business. Al-Hoceima's many émigrés are ploughing money into apartment blocks and fancy new villas, giving the impression of something of a boomtown.

Orientation
Set around a quiet Mediterranean bay, Plage Quemado is the main city beach, dominated by the large Hôtel Quemado. Uphill and inland, Place de la Marche Verte is the main town square. From here, Blvd Mohammed V runs south and is the main location for banks, hotels and restaurants. East of this boulevard and south of the beach you will find the remnants of the old Spanish town centre. Here, the budget hotels and eateries, as well as the transport hubs, are clustered around Place du Rif. The fishing port and commercial port are about 300m northeast of the centre.

Apart from Plage Quemado, there are a few quieter beaches further east. From some vantage points you can see the Spanish-controlled islet of Peñon de Alhucemas: it may look pretty from a distance, but it has served mainly as a prison and military base.

Information
INTERNET ACCESS
Cyber Club On-line (103 Blvd Mohammed V; per hr Dh8; 10am-2pm & 4pm-midnight)
Internet al-Kods (Place de la Marche Verte; per hr Dh6; 12pm-midnight)

MEDICAL SERVICES
Pharmacie Nouvelle (Calle Moulay Idriss Alkbar)

MONEY
Blvd Mohammed V has several banks with ATMs, including branches of BMCE, BMCI and Banque Populaire.

POST
Post office (Calle Moulay Idriss Alkbar)

TOURIST INFORMATION
ONMT (Délégation Régionale du Tourisme; ☎ 039 981185; Ave Tariq ibn Ziad; 8.30am-noon & 2.30-6.30pm Mon-Thu, 8.30-11.30am & 3-6.30pm Fri)

TRAVEL AGENCIES
All sell ferry tickets from Al-Hoceima in season, and from Nador year-round.
Chafarinas Tours (☎ 039 840202; 109 Blvd Mohammed V)
Ketama Voyages (☎ /fax 039 982772; 146 Blvd Mohammed V)

Sights & Activities
BEACHES
A pretty steep-sided bay protects the town beach, **Plage Quemado**. The beach is clean enough, but the seaside resort atmosphere is marred by the port to the north and the massive buildings towering on the cliffs to the south.

Better are the pristine, white sandy beaches that lie 5km south of town at **Cala Bonita**, **Plage Isly** and **Plage Asfiha**. The best way to reach these beaches is by grand taxi. For the entire taxi, reckon on about Dh49 to Cala Bonita and Dh72 to Plage Asfiha. Local buses to Ajdir and Imzouren, which pass the turn-offs for these beaches (Dh2 to Dh3), leave from beside the Mobil petrol station at the south end of Blvd Mohammed V.

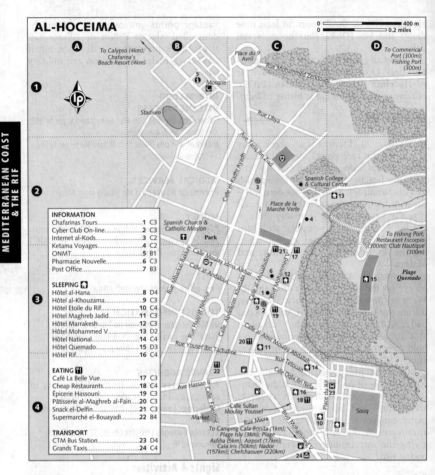

AL-HOCEIMA

INFORMATION
Chafarinas Tours.....................1 C3
Cyber Club On-line..................2 C3
Internet al-Kods.......................3 C2
Ketama Voyages.......................4 C2
ONMT.....................................5 B1
Pharmacie Nouvelle..................6 C3
Post Office...............................7 B3

SLEEPING
Hôtel al-Hana..........................8 D4
Hôtel al-Khouzama...................9 C3
Hôtel Etoile du Rif.................10 C4
Hôtel Maghreb Jadid..............11 C3
Hôtel Marrakesh.....................12 C3
Hôtel Mohammed V...............13 D2
Hôtel National.......................14 C4
Hôtel Quemado......................15 D3
Hôtel Rif..............................16 C4

EATING
Café La Belle Vue..................17 C3
Cheap Restaurants.................18 C4
Épicerie Hassouni..................19 C3
Pâtisserie al-Maghreb al-Fain...20 C3
Snack el-Delfin......................21 C3
Supermarché el-Bouayadi.......22 B4

TRANSPORT
CTM Bus Station....................23 D4
Grands Taxis.........................24 C4

Sleeping

BUDGET

The streets between the Place du Rif and the souq are packed with ultra-cheap hotels. Some are pretty dingy, so look around before committing.

Hôtel Etoile du Rif (☎ 039 840848; Place du Rif; s/d/tr Dh159/185/239) As much an Art-Deco traffic island as a hotel, the Etoile is undoubtedly Al-Hoceima's bargain. Spotless rooms have bathrooms and satellite TV, and most have a balcony too. There's a handy café downstairs, and the hotel could hardly be better placed for buses. Excellent value.

Hôtel Marrakesh (☎ 068 105918; 106 Blvd Mohammed V; s/d Dh170/195) This place on the main drag is strangely laid out, so the rooms vary

a lot. They're serviceable at best, with attached bathroom – a little tatty but you could still make yourself at home here.

Hôtel al-Hana (☎ 039 981642; 17 Calle Imzouren; s/d/tr Dh50/60/75) At the lower end of this price range, this simple but immaculate hotel is tucked into the tiny streets east of Place du Rif. All facilities are shared, including the clean squat toilets (hot showers cost Dh10). It's well kept and the restaurant is not bad.

Hôtel Rif (☎ 039 982268; 13 Rue Moulay Youssef; s/d Dh40/80) If your budget is really maxed-out, you'll end up here. It's simple stuff, with shared bathrooms (cold showers and squat toilets), but you do get your own sink. Female travellers mightn't feel comfy here.

MEDITERRANEAN COAST & THE RIF

Camping Cala Bonita (☎ 064 006492; sites Dh50) About 1km south of town, the camp site is well-signed off the Nador road, and has a lovely location on the bay. It's a little cramped, though, and cold showers are the extent of the facilities. Each camp site takes up to four people.

MIDRANGE & TOP END

Hôtel al-Khouzama (☎ /fax 039 985669; Calle al-Andalous; s/d Dh265/325; ⊠) Just off Blvd Mohammed V, this three-star hotel is a long-time favourite for business travellers, and is suitably comfortable, with spacious rooms (though those facing away from the street are a bit dark). All come with bathroom and satellite TV, and the guys at reception are friendly and helpful.

Hôtel National (☎ 039 982681; fax 039 981123; 23 Rue Tetouan; s/d Dh265/325; ⊠) The sister-hotel to the Al-Khouzama offers pretty much identical facilities, but with a slightly more modern feel. The décor is certainly nicer.

Hôtel Maghreb Jadid (☎ 039 982504; fax 039 982505; 56 Blvd Mohammed V; s/d Dh264/333; ⊠) This is a reliable standby if the other hotels in this price range are booked, although the lobby seems a little over-grand for the quality of accommodation. Rooms are spacious; most have enclosed balconies, and bathrooms in need of updating.

Hôtel Mohammed V (☎ 039 982233; fax 039 983314; off Place de la Marche Verte; s/d Dh352/466; ⊠) Once Al-Hoceima's top option, this hotel occupies a series of low-rise concrete blocks perched above Plage Quemado – modern and bland. Rooms are comfortable enough and come with balconies giving lovely views over the bay. The view is shared by the complex's restaurant, bar and terrace.

Hôtel Quemado (☎ 039 982233; fax 039 983314; Plage Quemado; s/d Dh411/457) In summer only, the management of Hôtel Mohammed V opens this resort-type hotel right on the city beach. Rooms are bright white and airy, filled with beach breezes. They are fully equipped with tile bathrooms, TVs and views of the sea.

Eating
RESTAURANTS

Cheap restaurants cluster around Place du Rif, serving up filling tajines, brochettes and a bit of seafood to the bus station crowd from about Dh25 per head.

Restaurant Escorpio (☎ 039 984410; Port d'Al-Hoceima; fish mains Dh60-90) One of two good fish restaurants inside the fishing port gates. There's a great choice from the catch of the day, best eaten on the upstairs terrace, from where you can keep an eye on the happenings in the harbour.

Club Nautique (☎ 039 981461; Port d'Al-Hoceima; fish mains Dh60-90) As you come along the seafront, you can't miss this attractive spot, just before the port gates. This is the place to come if you want an alcoholic drink with your meal (or just an alcoholic drink). It has another great range of local fish dishes.

Snack el-Delfin (cnr Place de la Marche Verte; sandwiches from Dh17, pizzas from Dh35) This is a modern takeaway joint, with a few tables for eating-in, and clean steel and chrome fittings. The sandwiches are huge, and are best accompanied by one of the delicious salads.

CAFÉS & PATISSERIES

Café La Belle Vue (Blvd Mohammed V) This café gets its name from the terrace at the back overlooking the bay. There's an open-air 'family' terrace upstairs, which women travellers may appreciate more. La Belle Vue is one of several similar cafés on this stretch of Mohammed V with great views.

Pâtisserie al-Maghreb al-Fain (Blvd Mohammed V) If your sweet tooth needs some affection, this patisserie has the best selection around. The interior is a bit male-dominated, but there are tables outside where you can watch the world go by.

SELF-CATERING

Many small general food stores are dotted around town, including **Épicerie Hassouni** (Blvd Mohammed V) and **Supermarché el-Bouayadi** (Calle Abdelkrim Khattabi).

Drinking

All of the cafés mentioned under Eating (above) serve pastries and snacks, but they are also popular spots for locals to get their mint-tea fix.

Hôtel Mohammed V (☎ 039 982233; fax 039 983314; Place de la Marche Verte) This has an inviting bar, particularly as the terrace has some excellent views over Plage Quemado. A beer here will set you back Dh20.

Club Nautique (Port d'Al-Hoceima; beer Dh15) A more atmospheric option, and the bar here usually attracts quite a crowd.

RUMBLINGS OF DISCONTENT

On 24 February 2004, a massive earthquake hit the Al-Hoceima area. Despite it registering 6.4 on the Richter scale, the city itself did not suffer extensive physical damage, although many villages in the surrounding region were devastated. Huts of mud and earth without proper foundations couldn't withstand the shock and collapsed on their owners. The earthquake killed 564 people and left many thousands homeless. Place de la Marche Verte in Al-Hoceima became an impromptu tent city for survivors.

The quake revealed more serious fault lines in this part of Morocco, as the victims were largely Rif farmers of Berber descent, one of the most impoverished communities in the country. There has traditionally been little love lost between the region and the central government. Under the Spanish Protectorate, the Riffians fought a long campaign for their own independence, succeeding in kicking out the foreigners for much of the 1920s. They repeated their performance during the struggle for independence, only to find themselves excluded from government when freedom arrived. Following a rebellious uprising in 1958, the region has been largely regarded by Rabat as a backwater to be neglected.

Underdevelopment allowed local kif cultivation to flower into the huge criminal concern it is today. Belatedly, the government has started to recognise its failings, which were brought into sharp relief when riots broke out in response to the tardy earthquake relief effort in 2004. Mohammed VI (whose mother is Berber) has begun to pay the region more attention, and the EU has become involved, addressing infrastructure problems in an attempt to integrate the Rif more closely with the rest of Morocco. Expanded school-building programmes and agricultural projects have all been kicked off, although the region still remains politically under-represented at the highest levels. And as you bump through the Rif along the worst roads in the country, you'll understand the need for the frustrations of the local population to be addressed as quickly as possible.

Entertainment

Calypso (☎ 039 841601; Plage Tala Youssef; admission Dh80) This nightclub at Chafarina's beach resort 4km north of Al-Hoceima is the only option if you're carrying your dancing shoes; a lively place in the summer months.

Getting There & Away

AIR

RAM has a weekly flight to Amsterdam (Wednesdays) but, curiously, no service to Casablanca. A taxi to the airport, 17km southeast of the city, costs Dh100.

BOAT

From June to September, Trasmediterránea and Comanav each run a daily ferry from Almería in Spain. Fares are around Dh320 one way (five hours). Out of season the best alternative is a ferry between Almería and Nador (157km east of Al-Hoceima).

BUS

All the bus companies have offices around Place du Rif. **CTM** (☎ 039 982273) runs twice daily buses to Nador (Dh40, three hours) and four to Tetouan (Dh78, seven hours)

via Chefchaouen (Dh65, six hours). There's also one evening departure for Casablanca (Dh160, 11½ hours) via Taza (Dh60, four hours), Fès (Dh90, six hours), Meknès (Dh105, 7½ hours) and Rabat (Dh140, 10 hours). This bus is timed to arrive in Taza in time to connect with the night train headed for Marrakesh.

Several small companies also serve the aforementioned destinations. There are at least three buses a day to Tetouan and Tangier (Dh80, nine hours). These stop in Chefchaouen only if there's enough demand. Otherwise, they'll drop you on the main road at Dardara, from where you can share a grand taxi into Chefchaouen (Dh8, 15 minutes). Heading east, there are also a couple of buses a day to Nador (Dh39, three hours) and Oujda (Dh58, seven hours).

TAXI

Grands taxis line up on the road at the southern end of Blvd Mohammed V. The most popular destinations are Taza (Dh60, 2½ hours) and Nador (Dh55, 2½ hours), although occasional taxis do go to Fès (Dh120).

AROUND AL-HOCEIMA
Cala Iris & Torres
de Alcala   كالا إيريس و نهر الكالا

Worth the expedition to get here, Cala Iris has one of the finest beaches on this stretch of the coast, 50km west of Al-Hoceima. The road here is very attractive, through the rust-coloured foothills of the Rif. The beach itself is of superb white sand, and if you visit outside the summer months it's quite possible that you'll have the whole place to yourself.

Cala Iris has a small fishing port but not much else. There are a couple of very basic shops at Torres de Alcala, 5km east. Three semi-ruined Spanish towers stand sentinel over this village, set back from a shingle beach caught between two rocky headlands.

Five-hundred metres before the fishing port, **Camping Cala Iris** (☎ 039 808064; camping Dh50-60, bungalow from Dh300) is well tended, if a little exposed. The sites get more expensive the closer they are to the sea. The few basic bungalows tend to be booked year-round by long-term residents. Facilities include cold showers and a restaurant that operates in summer.

The **Restaurant du Port** (meals Dh45-50), just outside the port gate, is also open in summer only. Some small beach cafés at Torres serve drinks and simple meals. You can also camp here.

Without your own transport, you'll need to hire a grand taxi in Al-Hoceima to get to Cala Iris. In summer there may be enough people to share one, otherwise expect to pay Dh130 one-way.

EAST MEDITERRANEAN COAST

MELILLA   مليلية
pop 65,000

Melilla is the smaller of the two enclaves that mark the last vestiges of Spain's African empire. It's less affluent than its sister, Ceuta, but with a third of its inhabitants being of Rif Berber origin, as well as significant Jewish and even Hindu minorities, it has an atmosphere all of its own – neither quite Europe nor Africa. The centre of Melilla is a delight with its modernist architecture and quiet gardens.

In recent years, Melilla has been pushing hard to develop itself as an alternative Spanish tourist destination, but for now its economy relies heavily on its free-trade agreement with Morocco (due to be abolished in 2012), which supports both official and contraband trade between the two countries. A sizeable Spanish army garrison also provides much-needed injections of hard cash.

Relations between Muslims (worst hit by unemployment) and the rest of the inhabitants are strained. The ill feeling bubbled over into violent protests in the 1980s when new citizenship laws threatened to leave many Muslims in limbo without proper papers. Many Spaniards fear both being outnumbered by the Muslim community and a possible push from Rabat for the enclave to be returned to Morocco. This seems unlikely: Melilla's Berbers historically owe little or no allegiance to the Moroccan crown and prefer the tangible benefits of EU citizenry that the enclave provides. They do remain politically marginalised, however, given Melilla's pro-Franco past, its autonomous government (and representative in the Madrid parliament) is firmly right-of-centre.

History
The port and peninsula of Melilla (originally known as Russadir) have been inhabited for more than 2000 years. The Phoenicians and Romans both counted it among their network of Mediterranean coastal bases. After the departure of the Romans, the city fell into obscurity until it was captured by Abd ar-Rahman III of Cordoba.

In 1496 it was taken by a Spanish raiding party and has remained in Spain's hands ever since, although Abd al-Krim's rebels came close to taking the town during the Rif War in 1921. It was from here that Franco launched the Spanish Civil War in 1936.

Melilla's excellently preserved medieval fortress gives the city a lingering fascination. Right up until the end of the 19th century virtually all of Melilla was contained within these massive defensive walls.

Orientation
The old town, Melilla La Vieja, was built on a tiny peninsula that juts into the Mediterranean Sea. The passenger ferry port is immediately east of here, while the new town stretches out to the west.

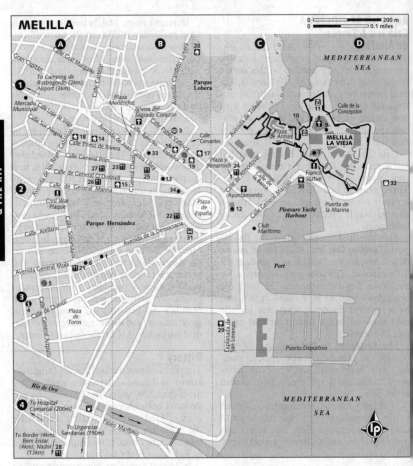

MELILLA

Plaza de España lies at the heart of the 'new' town. Most of the hotels, banks and restaurants are located in the grid of streets leading to the northwest of the plaza. The frontier with Morocco is 4km south, over the trickle of effluent known as the Río de Oro.

Information

To phone Melilla from outside Spain, dial ☎ 0034. Melilla is two hours ahead of Morocco during summer and one hour ahead at other times. Many shops and businesses are closed on Monday.

INTERNET ACCESS

Fon-Net (Calle Ejército Español; per hr €1.50; ⏰ 9am-2pm & 5-10pm)

Telefonica (Calle General Aizpuru; per hr €1.50; ⏰ 9am-2.15pm & 4-11pm)

MEDICAL SERVICES

Urgencias Sanitarias (☎ 956 674400; 40 Alvaro de Bazan; ⏰ 5pm-9am Mon-Sat, 24hr Sun & public holidays) Night pharmacy.

Hospital Comarcal (☎ 956 670000) South side of Río de Oro.

MONEY

As in mainland Spain, euros are used for all transactions in Melilla. You'll find several banks (with ATMs) around Avenida de Juan Carlos I Rey. Most will buy or sell dirham at an inferior rate to across the border – it's just as easy to use the Moroccan dealers hanging around the ferry port, or those at the land border.

On the Moroccan side of the border you can change cash at the Crédit du Maroc. There's also a Banque Populaire with an ATM 200m further into Morocco; walk straight ahead to the crossroads and it's on your left on the road to the port.

POST
Main post office (Correos y telégrafos; Calle Pablo Valescá; ✆ 8.30am-8.30pm Mon-Fri, 9.30am-1pm Sat)

TOURIST INFORMATION
Oficina del Turismo (☎ 956 675444; www.melilla turismo.com; 21 Calle Fortuny, Palicio de Congresos y Exposiciones; ✆ 8am-2.45pm & 4.30-8.30pm Mon-Fri) Many hotels also carry the tourist brochure 'Melilla', which has a useful map and town directory.

TRAVEL AGENCIES
Will sell plane and ferry tickets.
Andalucía Travel (☎ 956 670730; fax 956 676598; 11 Avenida de la Democracia)
Viajes Melisur (☎ 956 673595; fax 956 673678; 13 Avenida de la Democracia)

Sights & Activities
MELILLA LA VIEJA (OLD MELILLA)
Perched over the Mediterranean, Melilla la Vieja is a prime example of the fortress strongholds that the Portuguese and (in this case) the Spaniards built along the Moroccan littoral during the 16th and 17th centuries. Much of it has been painstakingly restored in recent years. The main entrance to the fortress is **Puerta de la Marina** (Calle General Macías), fronted by a statue of Franco.

You come out into an enclosed square, in the north wall of which is a pair of 15th-century water cisterns, **Aljibes de las Peñuelas**

(admission €1.20; ✆ 10am-2pm & 5-9.30pm Tue-Sat, 10am-2pm Sun Apr-Sep, 10am-2pm & 4.30-8.30pm Tue-Sat, 10am-2pm Sun Oct-Mar). The price of entry also allows access to Las Cuevas del Conventico.

The small **Museo de Arqueología e Historia de Melilla** (☎ 952 681339; Plaza Pedro de Estopiñán; admission free; ✆ 10am-1.30pm & 4-8.30pm Tue-Sat, 10am-2pm Sun) has a collection of historical and architectural drawings, Phoenician and Roman ceramics and coins, and numerous models and archaeological finds. The terrace alone is worth visiting for its fantastic views overlooking the city.

The Calle de la Concepción continues up to the baroque **Iglesia de la Concepción** and, just below it, the entrance to **Las Cuevas del Conventico** (☎ 952 680929; admission €1.20; ✆ 10.30am-1.30pm & 4.30-8pm Tue-Sat, 10.30am-2pm Sun). A short film and guided tour (both in Spanish) detail the history of the caves and tunnels that lead to the cliff face. The Phoenicians first excavated the tunnels; later occupiers took turns enlarging them and they now extend over three levels. They are meticulously maintained and well lit, which sadly eliminates much of their mystery.

Near the Iglesia de la Concepción, the **Museo Militar** (admission free; ✆ 10am-2pm Tue-Sun) is perched high over the Mediterranean. Its two small rooms are stuffed full of exhibits from the Spanish military in Melilla: regimental flags, medals, a motley collection of weapons and the obligatory bust of Franco.

NEW TOWN
Construction of the new part of town, west of the fortress, began at the end of the 19th century. Laid out by Gaudí-disciple Don Enrique Nieto, Melilla is considered by some to be Spain's 'second modernist city',

MEDITERRANEAN COAST
& THE RIF

after Barcelona. The highlight is Plaza de España, with the lovely facade of the **Palacio de la Asamblea** facing Parque Hernández.

Melilla's role in modern Spanish history isn't forgotten. The **Statue Grande Libre** (Avenida de Juan Carlos I Rey) marks 7 July 1936, when Franco began the campaign against the government in Madrid. With a soldier and lion backed by a Fascist eagle, it feels like a throwback to another, uncomfortable age.

Sleeping

BUDGET

There's no mistaking the difference between Europe and Morocco when you're looking for a place to stay. There are no bargains to be had and many places fill up quickly. Prices rise by around 15% during peak periods.

Hostal Residencia Cazaza (☎ 956 684648; 6 Calle Primo de Rivera; s/d €23/35) A decent-value pension, the Cazaza has eleven smallish, high-ceilinged rooms, with TVs, bathtubs and balconies. Management is friendly.

Hostal Residencia Parque (☎ 956 682143; 15 Calle de Marina; s/d €20/40) This popular pension overlooks Parque Hernández. Rooms are small but clean and bright, with TV and bathroom. Advance booking advised.

Hostal Residencia Rioja (☎ 956 682709; 10 Calle Ejército Español; s/d €19/22) The last of the trio of good cheap options. Don't be put off by the gloomy and uninspiring entrance. Rooms are a little tired but well-kept; they only have washbasins, and share one toilet and one shower.

Camping de Rostrogordo (☎ 956 685262; camping per adult €4, plus per tent/car/camper van €4/5/6) With the cramped streets of Melilla, this is a decent option if you have a vehicle, 2km north of town. It's well run with good facilities; prices take a 15% hike in summer.

MIDRANGE & TOP END

Parador de Melilla (☎ 956 684940; Avenida Cándido Lobera; r €97; 🍴 🏊) From the outside, Melilla's top hotel looks as if it's covered with strange sci-fi towers. Inside there are large, grand rooms, with shiny fittings and lots of marble. The best have balconies, with great views of the sea.

Hotel Rusadir (☎ 956 681240; hotelrusadir@wanadoo.es; 5 Calle Pablo Vallescá; s/d incl breakfast €65/81; 🍴) This three-star hotel looks unassuming but quite plush when you get inside.

Rooms are very well turned out, with TV, minibars and balconies. The restaurant, recommended for its buffet breakfast, puts out a pretty impressive spread.

Hotel Nacional (☎ 956 684540; fax 956 684481; 10 Calle Primo de Rivera; s/d €32/51; 🍴) More expensive and less intimate, this hotel offers similar amenities to the Parque and Cazaza. The compact rooms, with quaint iron furniture and modern bathrooms, can be quite snug, but those facing inside are dark and glum, so get one looking to the street.

Hotel Anfora (☎ 956 683340; fax 956 683344; 8 Calle Pablo Vallescá; s/d incl breakfast €37/59; 🅿 🍴) This rather dour two-star hotel offers standard-fare rooms with TVs, fridges and balconies. The highlight is the roof terrace, offering vistas of Melilla La Vieja and the sea beyond.

Eating

Many of Melilla's restaurants are associated with hotels (try the Rusadir or the Parador), but there are plenty of bars and cafés around Avenida de Juan Carlos I Rey offering sustenance. Further afield, the Paseo Marítimo is also worth exploring.

RESTAURANTS

Antony Pizza Factory (☎ 956 684320; Avenida de la Democracia; pizza €4-6, pasta from €5.50) Less factory than cosy brasserie, its staff still works hard to dish out heavily loaded pizzas and some rich pasta sauces. Popular with Melilla's young, it has a sunken snug area for quiet dining.

Cafetería Nuevo California (11 Avenida de Juan Carlos I Rey; mains €2-5; 🕐 7-2am Mon-Sat) This modern cafeteria with a small outdoor terrace has a wide-ranging menu and friendly waiters eager to help your clumsy Spanish along. The sandwiches and pasta are particularly good, all washed down with a cold *cerveza* (beer).

CAFÉS

Café Central (Plaza de España; breakfast from €2, sandwiches from €1.50; 🕐 7am-1pm & 4-10pm) Next to the park, this is a busy breakfast spot, with great coffee, pastries and cooked items. The inside can sometimes be a bit smoky, but there's a seating area outside. Clocks set to various time zones remind you of the hour at home.

Café Rossy (5 Calle General Prim; sandwiches from €1.50; 🕐 7am-1pm & 4.30-10pm) Another reliable place to grab a quick eat or while away an hour with a book and a coffee. The *bocadillos* are a perfect lunchtime snack – enjoy the ham ones now before you head into Morocco.

Café Toga (Plaza y Benarroch; sandwiches €1.80) This small bar in the lee of a grand church dishes out *cañas*, tapas and sandwiches throughout the day.

TAPAS BARS

La Onubense (5 Calle Pareja; tapas from €0.75; ☼ noon-3pm & 7pm-midnight Mon-Sat) With its rough-hewn wood furniture and unpolished décor, this place looks like the quintessential tapas bar. The house speciality is spicy *bollito de Pringá* (meatball) and other classic tapas delicacies.

La Cervecería (Calle de General O'Donnell; tapas from €1; ☼ 12.30-4pm & 8.30pm-midnight) Classier than the Onubense across the street, La Cervecería is decorated in Gaudíesque fashion by the Melillan architect Carlos Baeza.

SELF-CATERING

There are plenty of small grocery shops in the streets around Parque Hernández. For the complete supermarket experience, go to **Supersol** (Calle General Polavieja; ☼ 10am-10pm, closed Sunday) on the road to the frontier.

Drinking

As well as these bars, the tapas places (above) are good drinking holes.

La Pérgola (Calle General Marcías; ☼ 3-11pm) This café-bar on the pleasure-yacht harbour is an exceedingly pleasant place for a drink in the late afternoon, particularly on its wide sunny terrace on the waterfront.

El Galeón (☎ 952 695525; Hotel Melilla Puerto, Explanada de San Lorenzo; ☼ 5pm-midnight) With its long wooden bar and brass fixtures, the classy bar inside the Melilla Puerto follows the hotel's nautical theme. Don't dress too scruffily here, but apart from that it's a relaxed place to enjoy tapas and a few drinks.

Getting There & Away

AIR

Direct daily flights are operated by **Iberia** (☎ 902 400500; 2 Calle Cándido Lobera) to Granada, Málaga, Madrid and Almería (see p469). The airport is a €6.5 ride from town (3km).

CAR

Melilla is a duty-free zone, so if you're driving it's worth filling up here. Petrol is about one-third cheaper than in Morocco or Spain.

MOROCCO

To get to the border, you'll need to catch local bus 2 (marked 'Aforos'), which runs between Plaza de España and the Beni Enzar border post (€0.60) every 30 minutes from 7.30am to 11pm. From where the buses stop, it's about 50m to Spanish customs and another 200m to Moroccan customs.

Before entering Morocco, fill in a white form and get your passport stamped at the booth. Touts may approach trying to charge you for these forms, or ask a fee to fill them out for you. If you're driving into Morocco, remember to retain the green customs slip, which you must present when you (and your vehicle) leave the country. Large queues of vehicles entering Morocco are frequent and time-consuming; procedures for foot passengers are quick and easy.

On the Moroccan side of the border, bus 19 (usually unmarked) runs hourly to Nador (Dh23, 25 minutes). Frequent grands taxis (Dh5, 15 minutes) to Nador are tucked away on a lot to the right of this crossroad.

When *leaving* Morocco, fill in a yellow form and get your passport stamped. Some nationalities require visas to enter Spain: if they don't stop you here, they will when you try to move on to the mainland. Bus 43 goes to Plaza España (€0.60).

OTHER DESTINATIONS

Ferry and hydrofoil services out of Melilla are operated by **Trasmediterránea** (☎ 956 690 902; Plaza de España; ☼ 9am-1pm & 5-7pm Mon-Fri, 9am-noon Sat). Tickets are also available for purchase at the **estación marítima** (Ferry port; ☎ 956 681633). There are daily ferries to Málaga and Almería (see p477).

Getting Around

The centre of Melilla is compact and easy to walk around. Buses ply the route between Plaza de España and the border. The local **taxi service** (☎ 956 683621) is also useful. A taxi from town to the airport or the border costs around €8.

NADOR

الناظور

pop 120,000

Set on the broad lagoon of Sebkha Bou Areq, Nador is a sprawling city just 13km along the coast from Melilla. It's of primary interest for its transport links to Melilla and the Spanish mainland, which have given the place a slightly Iberian flavour, and if you've arrived in Morocco from the Spanish enclave, it's a relaxed introduction the country.

Commerce is the lifeblood of Nador, and cross-border trade thrives, on both official and unofficial levels. Fishing is the other mainstay, and the town's restaurants serve up great seafood.

Orientation

The centre of Nador is built on a strict grid system. The main north-south axis is Ave Hassan II, with the main bus station and taxi stand at its southern end. It is bisected by the promenade Ave Mohammed V, which runs east to west from the waterfront to the town hall. The needle-thin minaret of the Grande Mosquée is a useful landmark.

Information

Credit Maroc (64 Ave Mohammed V) One of several banks on Mohammed V with foreign exchange services and ATM.

Ketama Voyages (☎ 036 606191; ketama-nador@iam .net.ma; 56 Ave Mohammed) Sells ferry tickets to Almería.

Navigation Net (Ave Mohammed V; per hr Dh8; ☻ 3-11pm) Internet café.

Pharmacy al-Farabi (Ave Mohammed V)

Tourist Office (☎ 356 330348; 88 Rue ibn Rochd; ☻ 8.30am-noon & 2.30-6.30pm Mon-Fri)

Sleeping

There's no shortage of hotels of all classes in Nador. The cheaper places are near the bus and grand taxi stations.

Hôtel Mediterranée (☎ 036 606495; fax 036 606611; Ave Youssef ibn Tachfine; s/d Dh229/280) This comfortable hotel is excellent value, and Nador's best deal. The wooden furniture gives the place a homely feel, bathroom fixtures are good and the location is within a sniff of a sea breeze. The restaurant is worth a visit for non-guests (right).

Hôtel Ismail (☎ 036 332653; 34 Ave Sidi Mohammed; s/d Dh224/281) Next to the Supratours office, this is another good-value place with clean, comfy rooms with attached bathroom. There's a café at the entrance, where you need to search for the occasionally errant desk staff.

Hôtel Ryad (☎ 036 607717; hotelryad@hotmail.com; Ave Mohammed V; s/d Dh360/480; 🕸) This recently redone three-star hotel (the gloss-paint fumes nearly floored us) keeps a little Moroccan flavour in its décor, while presenting modern, plush rooms. Those on the top floor have views over the lagoon. The hotel bar is the best place in town for a drink.

Hôtel Rif (☎ 036 606535; fax 036 333384; Ave Youssef ibn Tachfine; s/d Dh554/778; 🕸 🖳) A large blue and white building pushing into the lagoon, the Rif is Nador's old flagship hotel. The rooms are light and airy, if a little old-fashioned, but the place is well-run and welcoming.

Hôtel Mansour Ed-Dahabi (☎ 036 606583; 105 Rue Marrakech; s/d Dh360/420) A pleasant central location and quiet atmosphere are the advantages of this three-star hotel. It's a bit bland but the rooms are comfortable and fully equipped. Off-season discounts here can be generous.

Hôtel Geranio (☎ 036 602828; 16 Rue No 20; Dh160/188) Just away from the chaos of the bus station, street-side rooms here can be noisy. Clean rooms come with tiny bathrooms. There's a ground-floor cafeteria serving the travelling crowds.

Hôtel ibn Khaldoun (☎ 036 607042; 91 Rue ibn Rochd; s/d Dh58/75, with bathroom Dh58/95). A solidly reliable budget option, you get no frills here, but the rooms are clean and functional. Get one with a bathroom rather than using the smelly shared facilities.

Hôtel Nador (☎ 036 606071; 49 Rue 22; s/d Dh50/70) A real cheapie near the bus station, this is down a quiet side street. It's fair, if grubby, for the price.

Eating & Drinking

Fish is the order of the day in Nador.

Restaurante Mediterranée (☎ 036 609494; Ave Youssef ibn Tachfine; dishes from Dh65; ☻ noon-3pm, 7-10pm) The Hôtel Mediterranée's restaurant is a swish dining room, with prompt service and a good menu. Unsurprisingly, fish dominates proceedings, with some tasty grilled dishes, and *crevettes au pil-pil* (sizzling garlicky prawns).

Restaurante Meramar (☎ 061 148282; 29 Rue Marrakech; meals around Dh100; ☻ noon-10pm)

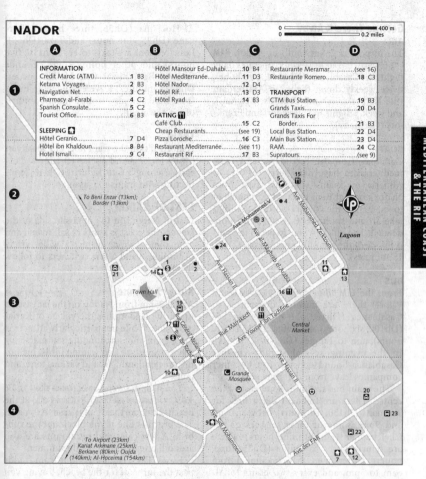

NADOR

INFORMATION
Credit Maroc (ATM)..................1 B3
Ketama Voyages.......................2 B3
Navigation Net.........................3 C2
Pharmacy al-Farabi..................4 C2
Spanish Consulate....................5 C2
Tourist Office............................6 B3

SLEEPING
Hôtel Geranio...........................7 D4
Hôtel ibn Khaldoun..................8 B4
Hotel Ismail..............................9 C4

Hôtel Mansour Ed-Dahabi.......10 B4
Hôtel Mediterranée.................11 D3
Hôtel Nador.............................12 D4
Hôtel Rif..................................13 D3
Hôtel Ryad...............................14 B3

EATING
Café Club.................................15 C2
Cheap Restaurants...............(see 19)
Pizza Loroche..........................16 C3
Restaurant Mediterranée......(see 11)
Restaurant Rif..........................17 B3

Restaurante Meramar.............(see 16)
Restaurante Romero................18 C3

TRANSPORT
CTM Bus Station......................19 B3
Grands Taxis.............................20 D4
Grands Taxis For
 Border...................................21 B3
Local Bus Station......................22 D4
Main Bus Station......................23 D4
RAM...24 C2
Supratours............................(see 9)

To Beni Enzar (13km);
Border (13km)

Lagoon

Town Hall

Central Market

Grande Mosquée

To Airport (23km);
Kariat Arkmane (25km);
Berkane (80km); Oujda
(140km); Al-Hoceima (154km)

MEDITERRANEAN COAST
& THE RIF

Brightly lit, this restaurant likes nothing more than serving up giant seafood platters, with everything from mussels to squid to a net full of fish, and salad, a drink and dessert thrown in for the price (Dh100). A single portion is big enough for two.

Restaurante Romero (☎ 036 332777; 50 Ave Youssef ibn Tachfine; meals around Dh60) Offering similar fare to the Meramar, this is another good seafood option. Pick out your fish from the chiller cabinet at the front.

Restaurant Rif (☎ 036 322315; 45 Rue ibn Rochd; meals Dh100) With decorations at the rustic end of bistro-style, this quaint restaurant is excellent for a leisurely meal. Hearty set meals of fish or meat are freshly prepared

and nicely presented. The next-door snack bar is open all day long (8am–11pm) for sandwiches (Dh5 to Dh10) and the like.

Pizza Loroche (☎ 066 055605; 30 Ave Al Maghreb el-Arabia; pizzas Dh20-36; ☺ 10am-10pm) If you're tiring of fish, this pizzeria may refresh your palate. They have crunchy thin crusts and all the usual toppings. Burgers, spaghetti and lasagne are also on the menu.

There are numerous cheap eats around the CTM bus station, serving up quick and tasty brochettes, sandwiches and tajines.

Ave Mohammed V is the place for a lazy coffee – street cafés line the road, under pleasant shady orange trees. At the far end, jutting into the lagoon, **Café Club** (☺ 6am-11pm) is a good breakfast option.

Getting There & Away

AIR

The airport is 23km south of Nador. **RAM** (☎ 056 606337; 45 Ave Mohammed V) operates daily flights to Casablanca (Dh1344, one hour), twice weekly direct flights to Amsterdam (the Netherlands) and Brussels (Belgium), and weekly flights to Düsseldorf and Frankfurt (Germany).

BOAT

Comanav, Comarit, Ferrimaroc and Trasmediterránea have daily ferry services for Almería, on Spain's southeast coast, from Nador's port at Beni Enzar (13km north of town, beside the Melilla border). Sailings take around six hours (see p477 for more details). The quickest way to get to the port is in one of the plentiful grands taxis (DH5, 15 minutes).

BUS

From the **CTM office** (☎ 056 600136; Rue Général Meziane) there are evening departures to Casablanca (Dh180, 11 hours) via Fès (Dh100, six hours) and Rabat (Dh155, nine hours), and to Tangier (Dh180, 12 hours). In the evening several slightly cheaper Casablanca-bound coaches run by other companies leave from the same area.

The main bus station is southeast of the centre. There are frequent departures for Tetouan (Dh130, 10 hours) between 9am and 9pm. Some of these services go via Chefchaouen (Dh130, nine hours). There are hourly buses to Oujda (Dh25, three hours) via Berkane (Dh16, one hour) from 6am to 5pm, and every two hours to Al-Hoceima (Dh35, three hours) throughout the day. Buses also leave for Fès (Dh74, seven hours) every 30 minutes or so in the morning.

Other useful services include buses to Ras el-Mar (Dh15, two hours) three times daily, and Saïdia (Dh22, two hours). Buses leave every hour between 7am and 7pm for Beni Enzar (the Melilla border) from outside the main bus station (Dh3, 25 minutes). In theory it's bus 19 but in practice they're usually unnumbered.

TAXI

The huge grand taxi lot next to the main bus station serves plenty of destinations including Oujda (Dh50, three hours),

Al-Hoceima (Dh55, three hours), Berkane (Dh25, one hour) and Taza (Dh55). Less frequent are taxis to Fès (Dh110, five hours) and other points south. Grands taxis to Beni Enzar (the Melilla border; Dh5, 15 minutes) leave every few minutes from here and also from a junction north of the town hall.

TRAIN

Nador isn't on the train line, but **Supratours** (☎ 056 607262; Ave Sidi Mohammed) runs a daily early evening bus to Taourirt (Dh 40), connecting with trains to Casablanca.

EAST OF NADOR

East of Nador, on the opposite side of the lagoon, the coast is a mix of salt marsh and sand dunes, which attract a wide-variety of birdlife – and a few twitchers to follow them.

Kariat Arkmane قرية أركمانه

About 25km from Nador, on the far eastern tip of the lagoon, lies the village of Kariat Arkmane. While not particularly attractive, the lagoon and surrounding salt marsh attract various sea and wading birds, including greater flamingos and various terns and gulls.

You'll find a very basic **camp site** (☎ 036 360241; camping per site Dh50; ☀ summer only) at the beach 2km northeast of Kariat Arkmane. The beach is fine if you block out the rubbish. A few cafés and restaurants are also around, often closed outside summer.

Buses (Dh5) run every hour from Nador past the turn-off for the beach, leaving you a 1km walk. The alternative is to hire a grand taxi (Dh36), but make it clear you want to go right to the beach.

Ras el-Mar (Cap de l'Eau) رأس المار

Further west lies Ras el-Mar, where the vast beach is a popular weekend spot with Moroccan families during summer and day-trippers from Melilla. A walk up to the lighthouse at the headland provides a view of the Spanish-owned Jaafariya Islands. Lying just off the coast (but inaccessible from Morocco), these tiny islands are said to support the Mediterranean's largest seabird colony, plus a handful of highly endangered Mediterranean monk seals. Populations of Audouin's gull breed on the islands and osprey nest in the coastal cliffs nearby – these fish-eating raptors are hugely impressive in flight. West of Ras el-Mar, the Moulouya Estuary is also very rich in birdlife.

The little fishing town of Ras el-Mar has a pleasant beach and a little bustle on weekends. Accommodation is limited to **Camping Ras el Mar** (camping per site Dh50). There is a cluster of quick and cheap restaurants around the port gate, serving up tasty grilled fish throughout the day.

To get here, catch a bus from Nador (Dh15, 20 minutes) or a grand taxi from Berkane (Dh10, 15 minutes).

BERKANE   بركان
pop 80,000

Berkane is a large, modern town about 80km southeast of Nador on the road to Oujda. It's most useful to travellers as a junction town and as a base for exploring the Beni-Snassen Mountains, which is an easy day trip.

The town is easy to navigate as it's stretched along Blvd Mohammed V, which leads from the green and white Grande Mosquée in the west past a large roundabout (marked with a stylised orange tree at its centre) nearly a kilometre away – you'll find the post office and plenty of ATMs here. Halfway between is the main square, with the shady Café du Jardin and CTM station on the south side and a CMH petrol station opposite.

Sleeping & Eating

Blvd Mohammed V and the surrounding streets have the standard slew of simple restaurants and cafés, particularly around the bus and grands taxi stands. You'll also find the hotels strung out along this road.

Hotel Zaki (☎ 036 613743; 27 Rte d'Oujda; s/d incl breakfast Dh340/413; ✹) This three-star hotel is 400m east of the main roundabout. Pretty rooms are individually decorated, each with its own style, and with private bathroom and TV. It has a good café and a pizzeria/restaurant serving up tasty meals. The carpets on the stairs are an accident waiting to happen, though.

Hotel Mounir (☎ 036 611867; 54 Blvd Mohammed V; r per person Dh50-70) This reasonable cheapie is next to the Grande Mosquée. You get a clean, self-contained room with hot shower, and an early morning wake-up call from the muezzin.

Restaurant el-Guerrouj (☎ 061 854332; meals Dh20-25; ✹ 11am-10pm) Has great tajines. Its owner, Hassan, is something of a local celebrity, as he's the brother of Olympic athlete Hicham el-Guerrouj.

Café du Jardin (Blvd Mohammed V) On the main square, this place is good for liquid refreshment.

Getting There & Away

Berkane's bus and taxi stands are scattered all over town. The **CTM office** (☎ 056 613992) is next to Café Laetizia on the west side of the main square. There is just one early evening departure for Fès (Dh100, six hours), Meknès (Dh115, 7½ hours), Rabat (Dh155, 10 hours) and Casablanca (Dh180, 11 hours).

Most other long-distance buses gather in the streets behind the CMH petrol station. As well as departures for the aforementioned destinations, there are hourly buses to Oujda (Dh11, one hour). Another useful service is the early morning bus to Beni Mellal (Dh155, 12 hours) via Ifrane (Dh95, seven hours) and Azrou (Dh110, 11 hours). Through buses to Nador (Dh18, one hour), which run hourly until mid-afternoon, stop immediately behind the petrol station.

Local buses for Taforalt (Dh8, 30 minutes) depart from beside Hotel Mounir twice a day, while grands taxis for Taforalt (Dh10, 25 minutes) and Nador (Dh25, one hour) use the lot on the opposite side of the road, between the Shell petrol station and the bridge.

Grands taxis for Oujda (Dh17; one hour) leave from near the bus station. To get one for Saïdia (Dh8, 15 minutes) or Ras el-Mar (Dh8, 15 minutes) head for the rank beside the 'orange tree' roundabout at the eastern end of Blvd Mohammed V.

AROUND BERKANE

South of Berkane, the scenic Beni-Snassen Mountains form an outrider to the main Rif chain. A small hill village 20km southwest of Berkane, **Taforalt** (Tafoughat), is the only nearby population centre. The S403 cuts across the range from just west of Nador through Taforalt to join the main Taza–Oujda road. A certain amount of public transport runs along here, but if you want to explore the heart of this area you will need plenty of time or your own transport.

The region's main highlight is the pretty **Zegzel Gorge**, really a series of gorges, which starts about 10km northeast of Taforalt. A road follows the gorge, winding down through orchards and past wild roses and oleander until the mountains end abruptly 5km or so north of Berkane.

On the way down, about 10km from Taforalt, you can't miss the gaping mouth of **La Grotte de Chameau**. This vast cave system, complete with stalagmites (one of which supposedly resembles a camel), stalactites and hot springs, is no longer open to the public – unless you can track down the *guardien* (attendant) and persuade him to unlock the gate.

Continuing down the gorge, the source of the **Charaâ River** provides a worthwhile detour. Follow signs to the tiny hamlet of Zegzel, 2km up a side road. At the end there's a popular picnic spot near where the river gushes out of the cliff. Not far from here, a ridge road cuts east to

Oujda. You'll need a 4WD vehicle, a good map, and an early start.

The gorge makes a very enjoyable half-day's outing from Berkane. If you don't have your own vehicle, the easiest option is to hire a grand taxi for the round trip. The minimum fare will be in the region of Dh200 for two hours, although not all drivers will be willing to take their vehicles along the poor roads near Zegzel.

A cheaper alternative is to walk down: take a bus or grand taxi heading for Taforalt and ask to be dropped off at the turning. Two buses each morning make the journey to Taforalt from Berkane (Dh8, 30 minutes), with return services in the afternoons. Grands taxis, most frequent on market days (Wednesday and Sunday), cost Dh10.

SAÏDIA السعيدية
pop 3000

The wide sandy beach at Saïdia marks the limits of the Moroccan coast – Algeria lies just around the next headland (although the border remains closed). The town is popular with Moroccan holidaymakers during the

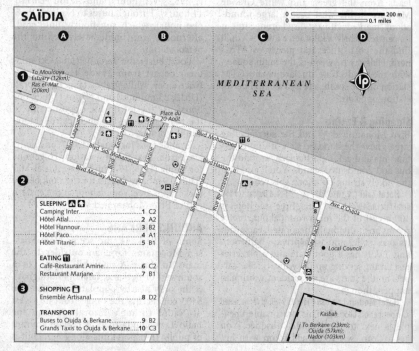

SAÏDIA

0 —————— 200 m
0 —————— 0.1 miles

MEDITERRANEAN SEA

SLEEPING
Camping Inter......................................1 C2
Hôtel Atlal...2 A2
Hôtel Hannour....................................3 B2
Hôtel Paco...4 A1
Hôtel Titanic......................................5 B1

EATING
Café-Restaurant Amine........................6 C2
Restaurant Marjane.............................7 B1

SHOPPING
Ensemble Artisanal.............................8 D2

TRANSPORT
Buses to Oujda & Berkane....................9 B2
Grands Taxis to Oujda & Berkane.........10 C3

To Moulouya Estuary (12km);
Ras el-Maz (20km)

Place du 20 Août

Blvd Laayoune
Blvd Zerkouni
Rue Khrout
Rue Zegzel
Blvd Sidi Mohammed
Pte El Anatanie
Blvd Moulay Abdallah
Blvd es-Samaia
Rue Ibn Inzarene
Blvd Mohammed V
Blvd Hassan II
Ave d'Oujda
Ave Moulay Rachid

Local Council

Kasbah
To Berkane (23km);
Oujda (57km);
Nador (103km)

summer and on weekends, but very quiet (and slightly forlorn) during the rest of the year. The seafood and long walks on the beach are Saïdia's best attractions. A small **Ensemble Artisanal** (Ave Moulay Rachid) serves the tourist trade with local handicrafts.

Sleeping & Eating

The following hotels are open year-round; calling ahead in high season (mid-June to early September) is recommended.

Hôtel Hannour (☎ 036 625115; Place du 20 Août; s/d Dh150/200; 🍴) Offering good value in the budget bracket, the Hannour has comfy self-contained rooms, some of which manage to squeeze out a sea view over the square. The café downstairs is a handy refreshment option.

Hôtel Atlal (☎ 036 625021; atlalben@menara .ma; 44 Blvd Hassan II; s/d Dh341/415; 🍴) The best midrange option in town, the Atlal has spacious rooms with large bathrooms, all well-appointed and very comfortable. The restaurant is a classy place to eat, and has a decent wine rack.

Hôtel Titanic (☎ 036 624071; Blvd Mohammed V; s/d Dh300/350) A blue-and-cream building on the seafront, the Titanic can't be beaten for sea views. Rooms are fresh, bright and breezy, those with balconies being the pick. The café out front is good for lazing the hours away in.

Hôtel Paco (☎ 036 625110; Blvd Hassan II; s/d Dh150/ 200) This is a reasonable cheapie, with basic rooms and small attached bathrooms. The bar next to reception is lively.

Camping Inter (☎ 036 624182; camping per site Dh35, plus per adult Dh5) The only site open year-round is very central (one block from the sea), shady and well kept. Facilities are excellent – it is, in fact, the best budget accommodation option.

The seafront is lined with fish restaurants and pizza parlours, many of which close up outside summer. **Café Restaurant Amine** (Blvd Mohammed V; mains from Dh30) and **Restaurant Marjane** (2 Blvd Zerktouni; mains Dh40-80) are good year-round options, as is the restaurant at the Hôtel Atlal.

Getting There & Away

Saïdia is most easily reached by grand taxi from Berkane (Dh8, 15 minutes) or Oujda (Dh22, one hour). There are also occasional taxis from Nador (Dh22). Except in summer, buses are few and far between. There are two a day for Oujda (Dh12), and one to Nador (Dh16). Both travel via Berkane.

Imperial Cities, Middle Atlas & the East

الأطلس المتوسط والشرق ىرهش روتاريمإ

From green hills and wooded mountains to historic cities and holy shrines – plus the odd desert oasis or two – this region lays claim to being the most diverse in the country.

Ancient Fès is the grandest of Morocco's imperial cities, with a warren of streets burrowing through its medieval medina that all travellers should get lost in at least once. The splendid palaces and Quranic schools continue in nearby Meknès, the second of the old imperial capitals. The region's importance as a political centre echoes still further through history at the holy town of Moulay Idriss and the ruins of the Roman city of Volubilis. All this is set among fertile rolling countryside planted heavily with olive groves that have been crucial to the area's economy, both ancient and modern.

Heading south, the land rises into the cedar forests of the Middle Atlas. Looking as much European as African, it's no surprise that trekking and skiiing are popular here, although seeing the occasional troop of monkeys will remind you which continent you're really on.

The region is also guardian of strategic routes into Morocco that have played important roles in the country's history. The town of Taza is flanked by the Rif to the north and Middle Atlas to the south, a strategic pass that also leads to the Algerian border, still closed due to troubled regional politics. Further south still, the land becomes increasingly parched until you reach the frontier oasis of Figuig, stuck in the sand and literally the end of the road.

HIGHLIGHTS

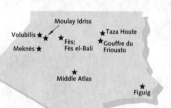

- Lose yourself in the maze-like medina of **Fès el-Bali** (p220)
- Haggle for your life with the potters, tanners and carpet sellers of **Fès** (opposite)
- Admire the 2000-year-old mosaics of the Roman ruins at **Volubilis** (p264)
- Take a horse-drawn carriage through **Meknès** to the Mausoleum of Moulay Ismail, Morocco's greatest ruler (p252)
- Make a pilgrimage to the holy town of **Moulay Idriss** (p266)
- Hike in the cedar forests of the **Middle Atlas**, looking for Barbary apes (p269)
- Dive into the endlessly deep caverns of **Gouffre du Friouato** (p279)
- Travel to the end of the desert road and the sleepy oasis of **Figuig** (p285)

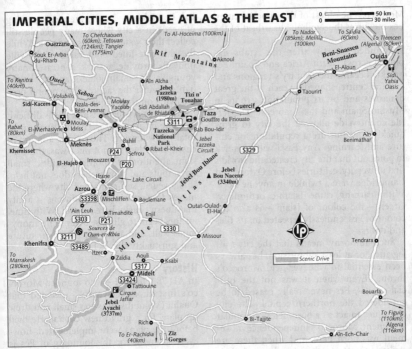

IMPERIAL CITIES, MIDDLE ATLAS & THE EAST

CLIMATE

The climate of this region varies widely between the mountainous area to the south and the dry flatlands of the valley (formed between the Middle Atlas and Rif Mountains) to the north and east. Around Fès and Meknès and in the east, summers are scorching hot, with temperatures averaging around 30°C in July and August. Levels of rainfall in the summer are miniscule, mimicking the climate of the desert further south. During the rest of the year, the climate is not as harsh. Winter and spring are pleasantly mild, and it rains enough to keep the countryside green.

The region comprising the Middle Atlas, by contrast, exhibits a typical mountain climate. The winters are generally cold and snowy, while the summers are cool and pleasant. For this reason, the mountains provide a popular retreat for the residents of Fès and Meknès who want to escape the heat in summer, or take advantage of the snow to ski in winter. Springtime is lush with wildflowers, but cold and wet in the mountains; snow often covers the highest peaks as late as June.

GETTING THERE & AWAY

The train line connects the region's major cities to the coast, with direct links from Tangier, Rabat and Casablanca. There are also direct flights from Europe – primarily Paris and London – to Fès, and from Paris to Oujda.

GETTING AROUND

The train line runs east through Meknès, Fès and Taza all the way to Oujda. Travelling around the mountainous Middle Atlas, however, requires catching a bus or hiring a grand taxi.

IMPERIAL CITIES

FÈS   فاس

pop 1 million

Marrakesh may currently be the queen bee of Moroccan tourism, and the foreign diplomats might place their embassies in Rabat, but the citizens of Fès go to bed every night, as they have done for centuries, knowing that their city is the *real* centre of

Morocco. The oldest of the imperial cities, Fès measures the symbolic heartbeat of the country.

Founded shortly after the Arabs exploded across North Africa and Spain, Fès quickly became the country's religious and cultural centre, shaped by each of the great dynasties and by its population's roots in Muslim Spain and the Arab east. The fertile countryside allowed the city to grow quickly, and nurture a reputation for culture and learning. Any Fassi will be quick to point out that the city created the world's first university, centuries before Oxford and Cambridge were a twinkle in anyone's eye. With learning came Islamic orthodoxy. Green – the colour of Islam – is also the colour of Fès, endlessly repeated on its tiles and doors.

Such authority means that the city's allegiance, or at least submission, has always been essential to whoever held Morocco's throne. Even when it was not the official capital, Fès never really ceased to be considered the northern capital. The city continues to act as a barometer of popular sentiment: Morocco's independence movement was born here, and when there are strikes or protests, they are always at their most vociferous in Fès.

The medina of Fès el-Bali (Old Fès) is the largest living Islamic medieval city in the world. Nothing quite prepares you for your first visit, which can truly be an assault on the senses. Its narrow winding alleys and covered bazaars are crammed with shops, restaurants, workshops, mosques, *medersas* (theological colleges) and extensive dye pits and tanneries, a riot of sights, sounds and smells. Donkeys and mules remain the main mode of transport and, but for the mobile phones and satellite dishes on the skyline, you could be forgiven for wondering which century you've accidentally slipped into.

But 21st-century Fès is groaning at its 9th-century seams and, in places, literally falling apart. Despite its designation as a World Heritage site, investment has been slow to follow. While the Moroccan government has created incentives for businesses and private interests to return to the medina and to preserve the artistic history there, in 2006 the city authorities were discussing plans for a scenic cable car ride from the nearby hills and a monorail to Bab Bou Jeloud – hardly the most pressing of needs in a city where many people still collect their water from a standpipe. While the chic café-lined boulevards of the ville nouvelle provide a stark contrast, many young Fassis remain jobless, and the bright lights disguise the sad lot of the poorer people living on the periphery.

For the short-term visitor, Fès is difficult to come to grips with. The medina can be totally bewildering. Though the amount of hassle is far less than it once was, the constant attention of unofficial guides, small boys, touts and shopkeepers does not help. It is a veiled, self-contained city where life moves to centuries-old traditions – a city that doesn't easily bare its soul. With time, visitors begin to glimpse behind the anonymous walls and appreciate the rich culture and spirituality that is Fès.

History

In AD 789, Idriss I – who founded Morocco's first imperial dynasty – decided that Oualili (Volubilis) was too small and drew up plans for a grand new capital. He died before the plans were implemented, however, so credit for the founding of Fès is often awarded to his son, Idriss II, who carried out the will of his father. The memory of Idriss II is perpetuated in his *zawiya* (religious fraternity based around a shrine) in the heart of Fès el-Bali.

By 809, Fès was well established. Its name is believed to come from the Arabic word for axe; one tale relates that a golden pickaxe was unearthed here at the start of construction.

The city started as a modest Berber town, but then 8000 families fleeing Al-Andalus settled the east bank of the Oued Fès. They were later joined by Arab families from Kairouan (Qayrawan) in modern-day Tunisia, who took over the west bank, creating the Kairaouine quarter. Both brought their own heritages, forming a solid foundation for future religious, cultural and architectural richness. Idriss II's heirs split the kingdom, but Fès continued to enjoy peace and prosperity until the 10th century.

Over the next centuries, the fortunes of Fès rose and fell with the dynasties. Civil war and famine – incited by Berber invasions – were relieved only by the rise of the Almoravids. When that dynasty fell from power around

1154, they fled Fès and destroyed the city walls as they went. Only when the succeeding Almohad dynasty was assured of the Fassis' loyalty were the walls replaced – large sections still date from this period.

Fès continued to be a crucial crossroads, wielding intellectual rather than political influence. With the Kairaouine Mosque and University already well established, it was *the* centre of learning and culture in an empire stretching from Spain to Senegal. It recovered its political status only much later, with the arrival of the Merenid dynasty around 1250.

The archaeological legacy of the Merenids is still evident today – credited with their exquisite *medersas* as well as the building of the self-contained Fès el-Jdid (New Fès). As the Merenids collapsed, successive battling dynasties were unable to retain power for any notable period, although sultans often resided in Fès in their attempt to maintain control over the north.

During the 19th century, as central power crumbled and European interference increased, the distinction between Marrakesh and Fès diminished with both effectively serving as capitals of a fragmented country. Fès retained its status as the 'moral' capital. It was here, on 30 March 1912, that the treaty introducing the French and Spanish protectorates over Morocco was signed. Less than three weeks later, rioting and virtual revolt against the new masters served as a reminder of the city's volatility.

The French may have moved the political capital to Rabat, but Fès remains a constituency to be reckoned with. The Istiqlal (Independence) Party of Allal al-Fassi was established here; many of the impulses towards ejecting the French originated here; and the city was the scene of violent strikes and riots in the 1980s.

As one of Morocco's most traditional cities, Fès is generally regarded with a certain amount of awe, perhaps tinged with jealousy, by the rest of the country. Indeed, a disproportionate share of Morocco's intellectual and economic elite hail from here and it's a widely held belief (especially among Fassis) that anyone born in Fès medina is more religious, cultured, artistic and refined.

Fassi womenfolk, also considered to be the country's most elegant and its most gifted cooks, are much sought after as wives.

When the news came out that Mohammed VI's new bride was from Fès, the locals were not in the least surprised.

Orientation

Fès can be neatly divided into three distinct parts: Fès el-Bali (the core of the medina) in the east; Fès el-Jdid (containing the *mellah* – Jewish quarter – and Royal Palace) in the centre; and the ville nouvelle, the administrative area constructed by the French, to the southwest. Nowadays, the city's expanding population has filled out the ville nouvelle and has spread to the hillsides to the north and south.

Fès el-Bali is the area most interesting to visitors. The main entrance is Bab Bou Jeloud in the northwest corner. The ville nouvelle is laid out in typical French colonial style with wide, tree-lined boulevards, squares and parks. Blvd Mohammed V – interrupted by Place Mohammed V – runs north-south and bisects the main road Ave Hassan II. Most restaurants and midrange hotels, as well as the post office and banks are along these streets.

Frequent local buses connect the ville nouvelle with the medina (Dh3, 10 minutes) via Ave de la Liberté, with two routes then splitting to run north and south along the old city walls, past either Bab el-Jedid or Bab el-Mahrouk. It is also possible to walk between the two – following Blvd Moulay Youssef from Ave Hassan II will take you there via the *mellah* and Royal Palace (Dar el-Makhzen). Allow about 30 minutes from Place Florence to Bab Bou Jeloud.

MAPS

Fez from Bab to Bab: Walks in the Medina by Hammad Berrada is a great book of walking tours in the Fès medina. It details 11 different walks, allowing readers to discover otherwise unknown corners and courtyards amidst this labyrinth. *Fès: Guide des Circuits Touristiques Thèmatiques* accompanies (in French) the self-guided walking tours marked throughout the medina; an English translation is due to be published in late 2006.

Information
BOOKSHOPS

Librarie Fikr al-Moasser (Map p232; 15 Rue du 16 Novembre) Stocks a small range of foreign-language titles, including travel guides and coffee-table books.

FÈS

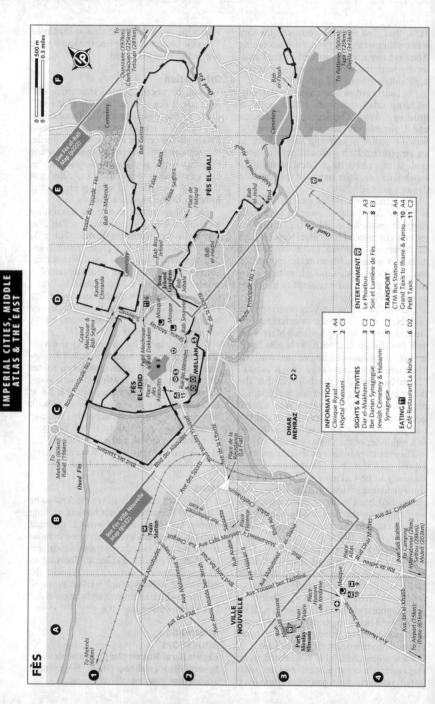

INFORMATION
Clinique Ryad........................1 A4
Hôpital Ghassani....................2 C3

SIGHTS & ACTIVITIES
Dar el-Makhzen......................3 C2
Ibn Danan Synagogue..............4 C2
Jewish Cemetery & Habarim
Synagogue..........................5 C2

EATING
Café Restaurant La Noria.........6 D2

ENTERTAINMENT
Le Phoebus..........................7 A3
Son et Lumière de Fès.............8 E3

TRANSPORT
CTM Bus Station....................9 A4
Grand Taxis to Ifrane & Azrou...10 A4
Petit Taxis..........................11 C2

CULTURAL CENTRES

Institut Français (Map p232; ☎ 035 623921; inst
.francais.fes@casanet.net.ma; 33 Rue Loukili) Organises
a packed programme of films, concerts, exhibitions and
plays; its reference library also contains a good collection of
French books on Fès.

INTERNET ACCESS

Cyber Club (Map p232; Blvd Mohammed V; per hr Dh6;
🕑 9am-10pm)
London Cyber (Map pp222-3; Ave de la Liberté; per hr
Dh10; 🕑 10am-10pm)
Teleboutique Cyber Club (Map p232; Blvd Mohammed V; per hr Dh7; 🕑 9am-11pm) Above téléboutique
on corner

LAUNDRY

Laundry (Map pp222-3; Place de l'Istiqlal)

MEDICAL SERVICES

Clinique Ryad (Map p218; ☎ 055 960000; 2 Rue
Benzakour, Place Hussein de Jordainie)
Hôpital Ghassani (Map p218; ☎ 055 622777) One
of the city's biggest hospitals; located east of the ville
nouvelle in the Dhar Mehraz district.
Night Pharmacy (Map p232; ☎ 055 623493; Blvd
Moulay Youssef; 🕑 9pm-6am) Located in the north of
the ville nouvelle; staffed by a doctor and a
pharmacist.

MONEY

There are plenty of banks (with ATMs) in the
ville nouvelle along Blvd Mohammed V, virtually all offering foreign exchange. There's

not much happening in the medina, with this
useful exception:
Société Générale (Map pp222-3; Ave des Français;
🕑 8.45am-noon & 2.45-6pm Mon-Thu, 8.45-11am Fri,
8.45am-noon Sat) Immediately outside Bab Bou Jeloud,
changes cash and travellers cheques.

POST

Main post office (Map p232; cnr Ave Hassan II & Blvd
Mohammed V) Poste restante is at the far left; the parcels
office is through a separate door.
Post office (Map pp222-3; Place de l'Istiqlal) Located in
the medina.

TOURIST INFORMATION

Syndicat d'Initiative (Map p232; ☎ 035 623460; fax
035 654370; Place Mohammed V)
Tourist Office (Map p232; ☎ 055 623460; fax 055
654370; Place de la Résistance; 🕑 8.30am-noon & 2.30-
6.30pm Mon-Thu, 8.30-11.30am & 3-6.30pm Fri)

TRAVEL AGENCIES

Carlson Wagonlit (Map p232; ☎ 035 622958; fax
035 624436) Behind Central Market; useful for flights and
ferries.

Dangers & Annoyances

Fès has long been notorious for its *faux guides*
(unofficial guides) and carpet shop hustlers,
all after their slice of the tourist dirham.
Faux guides tend to congregate around Bab
Bou Jeloud, the main western entrance to
the medina. With the addition of touts for
hotels and restaurants, entering here can

THE LIFE OF A *FAUX GUIDE*

Anas is 17. He is the oldest of four siblings. Until he was 13 he did well at school and hoped
to go to university one day. His world turned upside down when his father died unexpectedly,
and Anas was thrust into being the head of his household. To support his mother and family, he
dropped out of school and tried to find work with the tourists visiting Fès' medina.

Like many others before him, Anas hung around Bab Bou Jeloud trying to find tourists he
could guide to carpet and handicrafts shops, in hope of a little commission, picking up some
of the patter of the official guides, and pointing out the names of streets and fountains along
the way. On a good day he could earn Dh100 or so, but the police were a constant worry. He
has never spent a night in jail (unlike several of his *faux guide* friends), but he's had his knuckles
rapped plenty of times – and his day's earnings confiscated.

When the tourist numbers died down in the winter, Anas tried a brief stint working at the tanneries but it was a tough job for a small boy, carrying heavy wet skins for less than Dh40 a day. He
left after a few months, worrying that the chemicals in the dye pits were affecting his health.

Anas has now moved to Chefchaouen, where he touts for a handicrafts shop and has a casual
line in selling kif to backpackers. The money isn't as good as in Fès, but he says it's worth it to
no longer get hassled by the police. He'd eventually like to finish school, but earning to help
support his family will remain his number-one priority for the foreseeable future.

sometimes feel like running a gauntlet, but the situation improves once you're inside. A Brigade Touristique of plain-clothed policemen patrolling the medina has cracked down on *faux guides*, but high unemployment forces many to persist. See the boxed text, p219, for one guide's story.

Even many official guides will suggest visitors turn their tour into a shopping trip, and the pressure to buy can be immense. Fès' carpet shops are notorious, and the carpet sellers are masters of their game. If you really don't want to buy, it may be best not to enter the shop at all: once the parade of beautiful rugs begins, even the hardest-minded of tourists can be convinced to buy something they didn't really want (honeyed words suggesting that you could always sell the carpet later on eBay at vast profit should be treated with extreme scepticism). It's also worth remembering that, any time you enter a shop with a guide, the price of the goods immediately goes up to cover their commission. Shopping in Fès needn't be a battle – indeed it's best treated as a game – but it's worth being prepared.

The touts who used to hang about Fès train station to pick up custom have now taken to boarding trains to Fès, often at Sidi Kacem junction. Be particularly aware of overly friendly young men approaching you claiming to be students or teachers returning to Fès – they'll often have 'brothers' who have hotels, carpet shops or similar.

Sights
FÈS EL-BALI (OLD FÈS)
Thanks to the surrounding cemeteries and the enlightened siting of the ville nouvelle, nothing has been built immediately outside the old walls of Fès el-Bali. Within lies an incredible maze of twisting alleys, blind turns and hidden souqs. Navigation can be confusing and getting lost at some stage is a certainty, but this is part of the medina's charm: you never quite know what discovery lies around the next corner. A handy tip is to note the 'main' streets that eventually lead to a gate or landmark – just follow the general flow of people. Ask shopkeepers for directions, or you can fall back on the eager kids happy to rescue confused foreigners for a dirham or two.

Bab Bou Jeloud is the main entrance to the old city, with two main streets descend-ing into the medina's heart. On your left as you enter is Talaa Kebira (Big Slope), with Talaa Seghira (Little Slope) on your right. Both converge near Place an-Nejjarine, continuing to the Kairaouine Mosque. From here, it's uphill to reach the northern gates.

While major mosques and *medersas* are detailed below, they are only a small part of the charm of the old city. By giving yourself up to a little random exploration, the true character of Fès reveals itself. Look out for hanging camels' heads announcing a specialist butcher, and women filling bottles from the local fountains. Following your nose will lead you to children carrying trays of loaves to be baked in the local bakery, or a café selling glasses of spiced Berber coffee. All the while listen out for the mule driver's cry '*balak!*' (look out!) to warn of the approach of a heavily laden pack animal. The animals wear special shoes made of car tyres to help their hoofs grip, and the rooftops of the medina may be festooned with satellite dishes, but in many ways life has remained little changed here for hundreds of years.

Kairaouine Mosque
If Fès is the spiritual capital of Morocco, this mosque (Map pp222–3) is its true heart. Built in 859 by refugees from Tunisia, and rebuilt in the 12th century, it can accommodate up to 20,000 people at prayer. The mosque is in fact so large that it can be difficult to actually see: over the centuries the streets and houses of the Kairaouine quarter have encroached on the building so much to disguise its true shape. As non-Muslims are forbidden to enter, you'll have to suffice with glimpses of its seemingly endless columns from the gates on Talaa Kebira and Place as-Seffarine. Better still is to take the view from any vantage point over Old Fès: the huge green pyramidal roof and minaret immediately announce their presence to the faithful.

Medersa Bou Inania
Located 150m east of Bab Bou Jeloud, the **Medersa Bou Inania** (Map pp222–3; admission Dh10; 8am-5pm) is said to be the finest of Fès' theological colleges constructed by the Merenids. It was built by the Merenid sultan Bou Inan between 1350 and 1357. The *zellij* (tilework), *muqarna* (plasterwork) and

woodcarving are amazingly elaborate, and views from the roof are also impressive.

Different from other theological colleges you may have seen already, this *medersa* contains an elaborate mosque complete with a minaret. *Medersa*s usually have some form of prayer hall, referred to as a *masjid*, but it's normally of modest dimensions, perhaps with a simple *mihrab* (niche indicating the direction of Mecca). Some explain that the Medersa Bou Inania required a larger-scale mosque because there was none other nearby at the time. The *medersa* closes to non-Muslims during prayer times.

Unfortunately, the *medersa* remains closed for renovation for some time.

Medersa el-Attarine

Founded by Abu Said in 1325 in the heart of the medina, the **Medersa el-Attarine** (Map pp222-3; admission Dh10; 8.30am-1pm & 2.30-5pm) was designed as a separate annexe to the Kairaouine Mosque. Halls for teaching and a modest *masjid* flank the central courtyard. Displaying the traditional patterns of Merenid artisanship, the *zellij* base, stuccowork and cedar wood at the top of the walls and on the ceiling are every bit as elegant as the artistry of the Medersa Bou Inania.

Nejjarine Museum of Wooden Arts & Crafts

Opened in 1998, this **museum** (Map pp222-3; 035 740580; Place an-Nejjarine; admission Dh20; 10am-5pm; photography forbidden) is in a wonderfully restored *funduq* – a caravanserai for travelling merchants who stored and sold their goods below and took lodgings on the floors above. Centred on a courtyard, the rooms are given over to displays of traditional artefacts from craftsmen's tools, chunky prayer beads and Berber locks, chests and musical instruments (compare the traditional wedding furniture with the modern glitzy chairs outside in Place an-Nejjarine). Everything is beautifully presented, although the stunning building gives the exhibits a run for their money. The rooftop café has great views over the medina.

Dar Batha Museum

In a century-old Hispano-Moorish palace, the **Dar Batha Museum** (Museum of Moroccan Arts & Crafts; Map pp222-3; 035 634116; Place de l'Istiqlal; admission Dh10; 8.30am-noon & 2.30-6pm Wed-Mon) houses an excellent collection of traditional Moroccan arts and crafts. Historical and artistic artefacts include fine woodcarving, *zellij* and sculpted plaster, much of it from the city's ruined or decaying *medersas*. It also has some fine Fassi embroidery, colourful Berber carpets and antique instruments.

The highlight of the museum is the superb ceramic collection dating from the 14th century to the present. These are some fantastic examples of the famous blue pottery of Fès. The cobalt glaze responsible for the colour is developed from a special process discovered in the 10th century. The explanations are in Arabic and French only.

The museum's Andalucian-style garden offers temporary respite from the bustle and noise of the medina.

Belghazi Museum

The private **Belghazi Museum** (Map pp222-3; 035 741178; 19 Derb Elgorba; admission Dh20; 9am-6.30pm), owned by the family of the same name, contains a collection that almost rivals that of the Dar Batha Museum. The 17th-century palace in which it is housed provides a perfect backdrop for the exquisite carpets, jewellery, weapons and wedding chests on display. Much of this stuff is actually for sale if the price is right.

The palace also contains a shady courtyard café and a fancier (touristy) restaurant. Though buried in the guts of the medina, the museum is well signposted from the Kairaouine Mosque and Place as-Seffarine.

Tanneries

The tanneries of Fès (Map pp222-3) are one the city's most iconic sights (and smells). Head east or northeast of Place as-Seffarine and take the left fork after about 50m, you'll soon pick up the unmistakeable waft of skin and dye that will guide you into the heart of the leather district.

It's not possible to get in amongst the tanning pits themselves, but there are plenty of vantage points from the streets that line them, all occupied (with typical Fassi ingenuity) by leather shops. Each shop has a terrace that allows you to look over the action. Try to get here in the morning when the pits are awash with coloured dye. Salesmen will happily give an explanation of the

FÈS EL-BALI

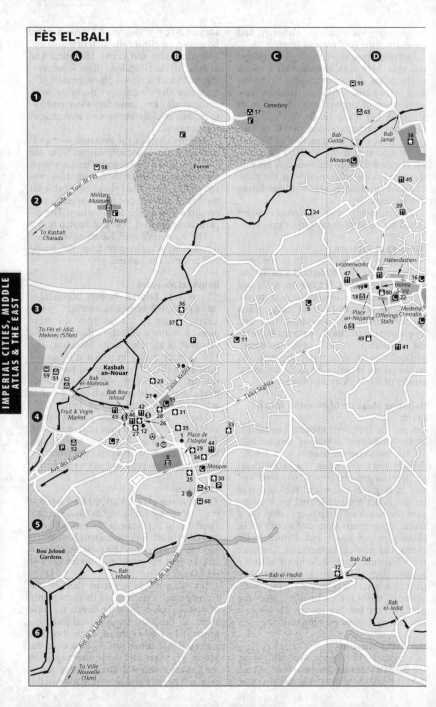

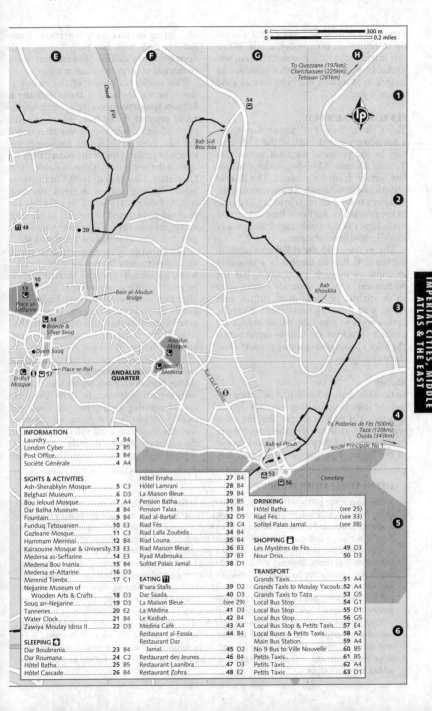

IMPERIAL CITIES, MIDDLE ATLAS & THE EAST

INFORMATION

Laundry	1 B4
London Cyber	2 B5
Post Office	3 B4
Société Générale	4 A4

SIGHTS & ACTIVITIES

Ash-Sherabliyin Mosque	5 C3
Belghazi Museum	6 D3
Bou Jeloud Mosque	7 A4
Dar Batha Museum	8 B4
Fountain	9 B4
Funduq Tetouanien	10 E3
Gazleane Mosque	11 C3
Hammam Mernissi	12 B4
Kairaouine Mosque & University	13 E3
Medersa as-Seffarine	14 E3
Medersa Bou Inania	15 B4
Medersa el-Attarine	16 D3
Merenid Tombs	17 C1
Nejjarine Museum of Wooden Arts & Crafts	18 D3
Souq an-Nejjarine	19 E2
Tanneries	20 E2
Water Clock	21 B4
Zawiya Moulay Idriss II	22 D3

SLEEPING

Dar Bouânania	23 B4
Dar Roumana	24 C2
Hôtel Batha	25 B5
Hôtel Cascade	26 B4
Hôtel Erraha	27 B4
Hôtel Lamrani	28 B4
La Maison Bleue	29 B4
Pension Batha	30 B5
Pension Talaa	31 B4
Riad al-Bartal	32 D5
Riad Fès	33 C4
Riad Lalla Zoubida	34 B4
Riad Louna	35 B4
Riad Maison Bleue	36 B3
Ryad Mabrouka	37 B3
Sofitel Palais Jamaï	38 D1

EATING

B'sara Stalls	39 D2
Dar Saada	40 D3
La Maison Bleue	(see 29)
La Médina	41 B4
Le Kasbah	42 B4
Médina Café	43 A4
Restaurant al-Fassia	44 B4
Restaurant Dar Jamaï	45 D2
Restaurant des Jeunes	46 B4
Restaurant Laanibra	47 C3
Restaurant Zohra	48 E2

DRINKING

Hôtel Batha	(see 25)
Riad Fès	(see 33)
Sofitel Palais Jamaï	(see 38)

SHOPPING

Les Mystères de Fès	49 D3
Nour Driss	50 D3

TRANSPORT

Grands Taxis	51 A4
Grands Taxis to Moulay Yacoub	52 A4
Grands Taxis to Taza	53 G5
Local Bus Stop	54 G1
Local Bus Stop	55 D1
Local Bus Stop	56 G5
Local Bus Stop & Petits Taxis	57 E4
Local Buses & Petits Taxis	58 A2
Main Bus Station	59 A4
No 9 Bus to Ville Nouvelle	60 B5
Petits Taxis	61 B5
Petits Taxis	62 A4
Petits Taxis	63 D1

processes involved and will expect a small tip in return or, even better, a sale. While this might feel a little commercialised, you probably won't find a better selection of leather in Morocco, and prices are as good as you'll get.

FÈS EL-JDID (NEW FÈS)

These days, 'New Fès' seems something a misnomer: it was built in the 13th century by the paranoid Merenid sultan Abu Youssef Yacoub (1258–86), seeking to isolate himself from his subjects. The district was packed with his mercenaries from Syria, and even today half of its area is given over to the grounds of the Royal Palace. Its other main legacy is the architectural evidence of its early Jewish inhabitants.

The entrance to **Dar el-Makhzen** (Royal Palace; Map p218; Place des Alaouites) is a stunning example of modern restoration, but the 80 hectares of palace grounds are not open to the public. Visitors must suffice with viewing its stunning brass doors. Note the lemon trees to one side – tour guides are prone to plucking the fruit to demonstrate the juice's astringent cleaning properties on the palace gates.

Mellah

In the 14th century Fès el-Jdid became a refuge for Jews, thus creating a *mellah* (Jewish quarter). The records suggest that the move was orchestrated to offer the Jews greater protection. And they did enjoy the favour of the sultan, repaying him with their loyalty during conflict. Very few Jewish families live here now, but their houses, with open balconies looking onto the streets, are in marked contrast to Muslim styles.

The southwest corner of the *mellah* is home to the fascinating **Jewish Cemetery & Habarim Synagogue** (Map p218; admission free, donations welcomed; 7am-7pm), where the sea of blindingly white tombs stretches down the hill; those in dedicated enclosures are tombs of rabbis. One of the oldest, high up against the north wall, is that of Rabbi Vidal Hasserfaty, who died in 1600. On the slope below, the large tomb with green trimming is that of the martyr Solica. In 1834 this 14-year-old girl refused to convert to Islam or accept the advances of the Governor of Tangier and subsequently had her throat slit.

The Habarim Synagogue, at the far end of the cemetery, now houses a museum with a whole mishmash of articles, including some poignant photos and postcards, left behind after the Jewish exodus. Genealogists with family ties to Fès are welcome to access the detailed records that have been researched here. If the museum is locked, the gatekeeper will open it for you.

The gatekeeper can direct you to the nearby **Ibn Danan Synagogue** (Map p218; admission free, donations welcomed), which was restored with the aid of Unesco in 1999. There are no set opening times, but someone will usually let you in and point out the main features, including a mikvah (ritual bath) in the basement. **Rue des Mérinides** (Map p218) is lined with houses distinguished by their

---

LIFE IN THE LEATHER DISTRICT

Tanneries provide perhaps the greatest illustration of how resolutely some parts of Morocco have clung to practices developed in medieval times. Moroccan leather, and more particularly the Fassi leather produced in Fès, has for centuries been highly prized as among the finest in the world. One type of leather, a soft goatskin used mainly in bookbinding, is simply known as 'morocco'.

It's claimed that tanning leather in Morocco goes back several millennia, and little has changed since medieval times. Donkeys still labour through the narrow street carrying skins to dye pits, which still constructed to traditional designs (with the addition of modern ceramic tiles). Tanners are organised according to ancient guild principles, with workers typically born into the job. Unfortunately, health and safety principles are similarly old-fashioned, and health problems among the workers, who are knee-deep in chemicals all day, are not uncommon.

Rank odours abound at the tanneries, and the delicate tourist who comes to view the work will often be offered a sprig of mint to hold to their nose to take the edge off the pong (rain also dampens the smell). Major components in processing the skins are pigeon shit and cow urine (for potassium) with ash; more delicate ingredients such as indigo, saffron and poppy are added later for colour.

WHAT THE MELLAH...?

The word *mellah* (from the Arabic word for salt) refers to the area of Fès el-Jdid where the city's Jewish population was transferred under the Merenids. Some say it was watered by a salty tributary of the Oued Fès, whereas others describe something more along the lines of a salty swamp. More likely is the Jews' traditional dominance in the important salt trade. Whatever the reason, the word eventually took on the same meaning in Morocco as 'ghetto' in Europe: the Jewish quarter.

---

wooden and wrought-iron balconies, and by their stuccowork.

NORTH OF THE MEDINA

Viewed from the surrounding hills, Fès' jumbled buildings merge into a palette of white-flecked sandstone. Only here and there do the green-tiled roofs of the mosques and *medersas* provide a hint of colour. For one of the best panoramas of the city, head up to **Borj Nord** (Map pp222–3). Like its counterpart on the southern hills (Borj Sud), Borj Nord was built by Sultan Ahmed al-Mansour in the late 16th century to monitor the potentially disloyal populace of Fès.

Further up, the **Merenid tombs** (Map pp222–3) are dramatic in their advanced state of ruin, although little remains of their fine original decoration. The views over Fès are spectacular and well worth the climb. Look for the black smoke in the southern part of the city, marking the potteries. It's best at dusk as the lights come on and the muezzins' prayer calls echo round the valley, although it's best not to hang around after dark.

Activities

HAMMAMS

The medina is rife with hammams – the **Hammam Mernissi** (Map pp222-3; Talaa Seghira; admission/massage Dh7/30; ☾ men 8.30pm-1am, women 11am-8.30pm) is both convenient and for-eigner-friendly.

Walking Tour: 'Mazing Medina

This route (Map p226) takes you from Bab Bou Jeloud to the Kairaouine Mosque, then north to the Sofitel Palais Jamaï. It could take a few hours or all day, depending on the number of distractions.

Unlike much of the rest of the city walls and gates, the main entry, **Bab Bou Jeloud (1)**, is a recent addition, built in 1913. Pass through it and you come upon a hive of activity. Though the touts and *faux guides* can be daunting when you first arrive, the cafés here are actually an incredible vantage point for observing the medina's goings-on.

Take the first left in front of Le Kasbah, and then right, heading down Talaa Kebira towards the minaret of the **Medersa Bou Inania (2)**, which represents the Merenid building style at its most perfect.

Opposite the entrance to the *medersa* is a famous 14th-century **water clock (3)** designed by a clockmaker and part-time magician. Regrettably it has been covered up for restoration for years – apparently they just don't have the magic (or money) to finish the work. Continue downhill on Talaa Kebira for about 150m to a fountain, tucked around a corner on your left, and a little further on to the **Gazleane Mosque (4)**, one of 350 mosques in the medina.

About 400m from the Medersa Bou Inania, as you go around an unmistakable dogleg, you'll catch sight of the pretty, green-tiled minaret of the **Ash-Sherabliyin Mosque (5)** (named after the slipper-makers who can still be found working in this area) straight ahead.

Still heading downhill, past the shoe sellers and a group of leatherworkers, about 230m from the Gazleane mosque, look out for a right turn and a sign indicating the entrance to a tiny tree-filled square known as the **henna souq (6**; see Berber Body Art, p352) – if you reach the Dar Saada restaurant, you'll know you've gone too far. Nowadays there are more stalls here selling blue Fès pottery than henna, which Moroccan women use to decorate their hands and feet for events such as weddings.

Exiting the henna souq the same way you entered, head south with your back to Dar Saada. After roughly 50m a right turn brings you into **Place an-Nejjarine (7)**, a larger square

IMPERIAL CITIES, MIDDLE ATLAS & THE EAST

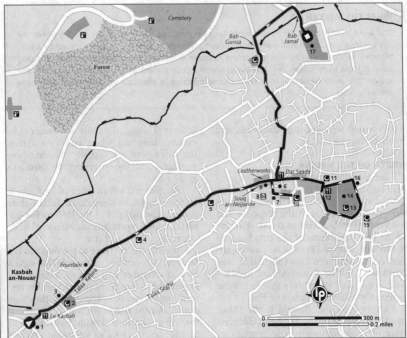

IMPERIAL CITIES, MIDDLE
ATLAS & THE EAST

THE WALK AT A GLANCE

Start Bab Bou Jeloud
End Palais Jamaï
Distance 3km
Duration two to three hours

dominated by one of the city's most beautiful fountains and a most impressive *funduq* (hotel) – now beautifully restored and transformed into the **Nejjarine Museum of Wooden Arts & Crafts (8)**. The lanes immediately north of the museum form part of the **Souq an-Nejjarine (9)** (Carpenters Souq), where you'll see craftsmen putting finishing touches to glittering thrones used in wedding ceremonies.

From Place an-Nejjarine, continue southwards and turn left almost immediately down a lane, ducking under the bar that prevents the passage of mules and donkeys. The lane leads between stalls piled high with candles and other offerings, to the entrance of **Zawiya Moulay Idriss II (10)**. You may peer into the bright, tiled interior, but you cannot enter. Moulay Idriss II

is highly revered – to Fassis this is the heart of their city.

Afterwards, the simplest thing is to backtrack to Dar Saada on Talaa Kebira. Follow the lane east – over a slight hummock and past haberdashers' stalls – until it ends at a T-intersection about 100m later, where you'll find the **Medersa el-Attarine (11)**.

On emerging from the *medersa*, turn left (south). After you've passed the **Pâtisserie Kortouba (12)** – a handy pit stop – the shops come to a sudden end at the walls of the great **Kairaouine Mosque & University (13)** (pronounced Qay-ra-win). The university claims to be the world's oldest and is surpassed only by Al-Azhar in Cairo as a centre of Muslim learning. Among its many luminaries was the pre-eminent historian Ibn Khaldun, and you may catch a sight of his successors hurrying to lessons.

As you proceed along the university walls anticlockwise, the sound of metalworkers leads you into another small and attractive square, **Place as-Seffarine (14)** (Brass-makers Square). The air rings with the sound of metalwork. Look out for the huge pans and plates that are hired out for wedding parties. With the university walls (and the entrance to its library) still on your left, there is the small **Medersa as-Seffarine (15)**, with a studded cedar door, on the square's east side. Built in 1280, it is the oldest *medersa* in Fès, but is in an advanced state of disrepair.

Still following the mosque walls anticlockwise (now heading north) keep a lookout on the right for the 14th-century **Funduq Tetouanien (16)**, with its rickety wooden galleries. Originally the preserve of businessmen from Tetouan, it served for centuries as a hotel and warehouse for travelling merchants.

If you continue around the Kairaouine, you'll pass its ornate north door before arriving back where you started beside the patisserie. From here you can retrace your steps uphill to Bab Bou Jeloud.

Alternatively, return only as far as Dar Saada, then turn north to reach Bab Guissa in the northern medina. Stick to the wider streets and you'll reach a little square with a disused cinema on its north side. Take the lane heading northwest and keep going up – you'll pass plenty of donkeys carrying sacks from the local cement merchant.

As you near Bab Guissa you can easily see the late 19th-century **Sofitel Palais Jamaï (17)**. What is now a luxury hotel was built by Sidi Mohammed ben Arib al-Jamaï, the grand vizier to Moulay al-Hassan I. Set in well-watered gardens, the former palace is a wonderful place to rest and admire the view. You can catch a petit taxi from Bab Guissa, or local buses 10 (to the ville nouvelle) or 12 (to Bab Bou Jeloud).

Courses

At **DMG Arabophon** (☎ 035 603475; www.arabicstudy .com; one-month intensive Dh3600) each intensive program offers 60 hours of training, available in all levels of modern standard Arabic. The centre also runs shorter courses aimed at travellers: a half-day 'Curious Explorer' (Dh250) and a one-week 'Serious Explorer' (Dh600) providing a basic grounding in etiquette, pronunciation and a few essential phrases. DMG also offers courses in Tamazight Berber.

The **Arabic Language Institute** (☎ 035 624850; www.alif-fes.com; 3-/6-week course Dh4900/8900), offers longer courses aimed at foreigners, and can assist in finding accommodation for students in apartments or with local families. Lessons are held at the **American Language Center** (Map p232; ☎ 035 624850; 2 Rue Ahmed Hiba)

Tours

The Fès authorities have recently woken up to the difficulties tourists have in navigating the medina, and have introduced a series of well-signed self-guided walks through the old city. There are five to choose from, each highlighting different aspects of traditional Fès:

Dark blue Monuments & Souqs
Green Andalucian Palaces & Gardens
Orange Fès Jdid
Pale blue Andalucian Riviera
Purple Artisanal Crafts tour

THE FOUNTAINS OF FÈS

As in any desert culture, water is a highly valued commodity in Morocco. In the past, complicated and ingenious engineering works were carried out to ensure its supply. Even today, life still often revolves around the fountain or village well.

It was largely the Almoravid (1061–1147) and Almohad (1147–1248) dynasties that were the great water engineers. To supply water to their cities they diverted rivers, created lakes and constructed vast canal systems. In Marrakesh underground canals built at this time still channel water to mosques, houses and dozens of fountains.

Fountain construction, however, reached its peak in imperial Fès. There are said to be well over 60 public fountains (*seqqâya*) inside the medina. Along with the hammam, they are usually located near the neighbourhood mosque. Many were paid for by princes and wealthy merchants.

Some of these fountains are simple basins against a wall. The majority are beautifully decorative structures of coloured tiles, often under a canopy of intricately carved wood. One of the finest is the an-Nejjarine fountain. Built in the 18th century, it features *zellij* (tilework) and stucco that form patterns as delicate as lacework. The fountain of Dar Jamaï in Meknès is another glorious example.

IMPERIAL CITIES, MIDDLE
ATLAS & THE EAST

FÈS SACRED MUSIC FESTIVAL

Every June the **Fès Festival of World Sacred Music** (☎ 055 740535; www.fesfestival.com) brings together music groups and artists from all corners of the globe, and has become an established favourite on the world music festival circuit. Based on the pluralism of Moroccan Sufism, the festival has attracted big international stars such as Ravi Shankar, Youssou N'Dour and Salif Keita. Concerts are held in a variety of venues, including the Batha Museum, the square outside Bab Bou Jeloud and even Volubilis. While the big names are a draw, equally fascinating are the more intimate concerts held by Morocco's various tariqas (Sufi orders). Fringe events include art exhibitions, films and talks at literary cafés. In 2001 the festival was praised by the United Nations as a major event promoting dialogue between civilizations.

The head-height signs are easy to follow, showing the direction of the next major landmark, and there are excellent English information boards at regular intervals.

An alternative is to hire a guide. As well as pointing out incredible architecture and clandestine corners, guides can answer cultural questions, help overcome language barriers, and – perhaps most importantly – ward off other would-be guides. A full-day tour with an official guide costs Dh200 to Dh250 – always ask to see identification.

The quality of guides can vary considerably, so communication is very important to ensure that you get the best out of the experience. If you're not interested in shopping, say so firmly at the outset, although be aware that the Fès guide who won't take a tourist to a single shop probably hasn't been born yet. If possible, get a recommendation for a guide from other travellers; alternatively arrange one through the tourist office, Syndicat d'Initiative or the larger hotels.

For those short of time, the tourist office offers panoramic tours of Fès, taking in all the best viewpoints of the city, including Borj Nord and Borj Sud, and the potteries. A 45-minute tour costs Dh200.

Sleeping

There are two main considerations when choosing a hotel in Fès: whether to immerse yourself in the colour and chaos of the medina, or get a little distance by staying in the ville nouvelle where your money tends to go further. Whichever your preference, there's something for all budgets, from simple pensions to opulent riad guesthouses as gorgeous as anything Marrakesh has to offer.

MEDINA
Budget

Many of the ultracheapies cluster around Bab Bou Jeloud in Fès el-Bali. They're pretty basic, and cold showers might have you exploring the local hammams. The area is a hang-out for faux guides; prepare for some hassle on arrival. Check where the nearest minaret is – the call to prayer is an unescapable early wake-up call in the medina. Many places charge more in the summer.

Dar Bouânania (Map pp222-3; ☎ 035 637282; 21 Derb be Salem; s/d Dh200/250, with shower Dh250/300) Fès has long lacked any riad-style budget accommodation, so this new hotel makes a welcome appearance on the scene. Well-signed off Talaa Kebira, it's very much a traditional Moroccan house, with lovely zellij and stucco courtyard, a series of nicely decorated bedrooms over several floors, and small roof terrace. For the price it's a real bargain; call in advance during summer.

Pension Talaa (Map pp222-3; ☎ 035 633359; pacohicham@hotmail.com; 14 Talaa Seghira; s/d Dh75/100) Right in the middle of the action, this place has just four small, clean rooms, with shared bathroom facilities in wooden cubicles. It's all quite spartan, but compensated for by the friendly welcome.

Pension Batha (Map pp222-3; ☎ 035 741150; 8 Sidi Lkhayat; s/d incl breakfast Dh110/145) You'll do a lot of stair-climbing in this tall thin building, to reach a cluster of simple, decent rooms. Its family-run nature gives the pension a friendly atmosphere, and there's a nice roof terrace to chill out on. Not to be confused with the nearby Hôtel Batha.

Hôtel Cascade (Map pp222-3; ☎ 035 638442; 26 Rue Serrajine; s/d Dh60/120) This place has been a backpacker's favourite as long as we've been visiting Morocco, noted for its central location and roof terraces with unbeatable views. That said, these days it's pretty battered and grubby, and the shared facilities could use a more frequent mopping. Adequate for the price.

Hôtel Lamrani (Map pp222-3; ☎ 035 634411; Talaa Seghira; r Dh150-200) Another place with a great location, just away from the hustle of Bab Bou Jeloud. Rooms are of a good size, and bathrooms are clean with hot showers. If only the management weren't so grumpy, this would be fantastic.

Hôtel Erraha (Map pp222-3; ☎ 035 633226; Place Bou Jeloud; s/d Dh50/80) Just outside Bab Bou Jeloud, this cheapie has large airy rooms and a roof terrace. Murals give the place a bit of a lift. As with many places in this bracket, the shared bathroom facilities reflect the price tag. A hot shower will cost you Dh10.

Midrange

Midrange options in the medina are thin on the ground, with most riads edging into the top-end bracket. A few, though, offer simpler rooms at manageable prices.

Hôtel Batha (Map pp222-3; ☎ 035 741077; fax 035 741078; Place Batha; s/d incl breakfast Dh327/452; 🅿 🖭) Great value on the edge of the medina, this old favourite is a mix of the reasonably modern with the traditionally decorated. Rooms come with sunken baths, although hot water can occasionally be erratic. The whitewashed courtyard is a wonderful, cool refuge from the city heat – as is the pool.

Riad Lalla Zoubida (Map pp222-3; ☎ 035 635053; www.riad-lallazoubida.com; 23 Rue Salaj; r/ste Dh500/800) This is the owner's childhood home and the seven rooms and suites on offer here are lovingly turned out, decorated with colourful fabrics, brass and woodwork. The smallest is positively cosy, and even the largest is on the homely side of grand. The pleasant courtyard and roof terrace add to the relaxed air.

Riad Louna (Map pp222-3; ☎ 035 741985; www.riad louna.com; 24 Derb Serraj; r incl breakfast Dh650-750) This traditional house – built in 1389 – is small but perfectly formed. There are three elegant suites and three smaller rooms set around a lovely, plant-filled courtyard, all done up in traditional Moroccan fashion. The roof terrace has been converted into an elegant dining salon, with small outside seating area. It's down several narrow lanes: look hard for the tiny signs pointing the way.

Riad al-Bartal (Map pp222-3; ☎ 035 637053; www.riadalbartal.com; 21 Rue Sournas; r/ste incl breakfast Dh750/1250; 🖭) Another small jewel-box of a riad, the Al-Bartal has six rooms around a courtyard, all finished with traditional craftsmanship and an eye for detail, plus the all-important roof terrace. It's just off Bab Ziat, and there's parking in a nearby garage.

Top End

Riad Fès (Map pp222-3; ☎ 035 741012; www.riadfes.com; 5 Derb ibn Slimane; r/ste incl breakfast from Dh1800/3000; 🖭 🖳) This labyrinthine riad blends ancient and modern with impressive panache. The older section shows off the best of traditional décor, while the newer quarters wouldn't look out of place in a Parisian boutique hotel yet remain unmistakably Moroccan. It has a trendy bar, restaurant, hammam and a plethora of terraces, and an elevator makes this place uniquely convenient for disabled or elderly travellers.

La Maison Bleue (Map pp222-3; ☎ 035 636052; www.maisonbleue.com; 2 Place de l'Istiqlal; r/ste from Dh1900/2800; 🖭) Right on Place Batha. Opening the door at the end of the tiled entrance passage reveals a luxurious cocoon hidden within. It's all tumbling rooms, staircases and mini-terraces, lavishly decorated, and with excellent personal service. All this, plus a restaurant that's regarded as one of the best in the medina.

Riad Maison Bleue (Map pp222-3; ☎ 035 741873; www.maisonbleue.com; 33 Derb el Mitter, Talaa Kebira; s/d from Dh1700/1900; 🅿 🖭 🖳) A larger annexe to La Maison Bleue is a five-minute walk

---

THE AUTHOR'S CHOICE

Dar Roumana (Map pp222-3; ☎ 035 741637; 30 Derb el Amer, Zkak Roumane; www.darroumana .com; r Dh700-1200; 🖭 🖳) Many riads claim to have the best views of Fès medina, but this beautiful house might just take the prize. There are only five rooms, all immaculate and subtly decorated to show off the painstaking restoration process that brought the building back to life, plus some modern touches like wi-fi throughout. The roof terrace is a gorgeous place for breakfast, or a drink over dinner – you may even get to lend a hand in the kitchen as the owner (a cordon bleu chef) offers Moroccan cookery lessons, with shopping expeditions in the souqs. Best reached via Bab Guissa.

IMPERIAL CITIES, MIDDLE
ATLAS & THE EAST

from Talaa Kebira, and is even more deluxe. Eleven unique suites are set around the Andalucian-style courtyard, which is dominated by fragrant orange trees and a plunge pool. The terrace – where you can relax after a meal in the private restaurant, or after some pampering in the spa – has good views to Borj Nord.

Ryad Mabrouka (Map pp222-3; ☎ 035 636345; www .ryadmabrouka.com; r Dh1150-1300, ste Dh1600; ✗ ⊠ ⊛) Now firmly established on the riad scene is this meticulously restored, Arab-Andalucian townhouse. The courtyard, with its stucco, magnificent cedar doors, babbling fountain and mosaics, opens onto a pleasant garden of flowers and trees. There are seven rooms, decked out with tiled floors and Berber fabrics. Enjoy a simple breakfast or an all-out Moroccan feast on the veranda overlooking the medina.

Sofitel Palais Jamaï (Map pp222-3; ☎ 035 634331; www.sofitel.com; Bab Guissa; s/d incl breakfast from Dh2490/2680; ✗ ⊠ ⊛) Once the pleasure dome of a late-19th-century vizier to the sultan, this grand hotel is set in Andalucian gardens overlooking the medina. While parts of it have lost their character through bland international decoration, rooms in the older section are still quite lovely (and attract the higher price tag). Nonguests should still visit to enjoy a sunset drink on the terrace.

VILLE NOUVELLE
Many hotels in the ville nouvelle happily span the categories given below, often offering midrange service at budget prices, so it pays to look around. Rooms are generally better value for your dirham here than in the medina.

Budget
Youth Hostel (Map p232; ☎ 035 624085; 18 Rue Abdeslam Serghini, 55; ⊗ 8-10am, noon-3pm & 6-10pm) Easily one of the better youth hostels in Morocco, the Fès branch is well looked after, and right in the centre of the ville nouvelle. Tidy rooms and facilities (including Western-style toilets) are superbly clean. If you're not a Youth Hostelling International (YHI) member, there's a Dh5 surcharge. Cold showers mean that that you should look to hammams – particularly in winter.

Hôtel Lamdaghri (Map p232; ☎ 035 620310; 10 Rue Abbase El-Msaadi; s/d Dh150/190) A great-value place just off the action on Mohammed V, the Lamdaghri has compact and fresh rooms, nicely maintained. Rooms come with hot showers, toilets are shared. Just watch out they don't put you on the top floor – it's a tall building with an awful lot of stairs.

Hôtel Central (Map p232; ☎ 035 622335; 50 Rue Brahim Roudani; s/d Dh150/180) The Central has had a lick of paint and a brush up since we last visited and is all the better for it. The lobby is bright and welcoming, and the airy whitewashed rooms make everything cleaner. Good value; a discount is usually given for the couple of rooms lacking a shower.

Hôtel Royal (Map p232; ☎ 035 624656; 36 Rue du Soudan; s/d with shower Dh100/130) Well-placed near Place Florence, this is one of the more reliable and popular budget options. A few of the bathrooms are a bit clunky (hot water in mornings only), but rooms are large and many come with balconies.

Hôtel Kairouan (Map p232; ☎ 035 623590; 84 Rue du Soudan; s/d Dh65/120, with bathroom Dh120/150) Dark corridors make this hotel feel more claustrophobic than it really is, but the welcome is warm, rooms are decent and even those with shared bathrooms get their own sink.

Hôtel Splendid (Map p232; ☎ 035 622148; splendid@iam.net.ma; 9 Rue Abdelkarim el-Khattabi; s/d Dh282/337; ✗ ⊛) A step up in the budget bracket, this place should really be a three-star. The rooms are large and comfortable, with modern amenities, TV and bathroom. Even better are the inviting pool, bar and restaurant (the breakfasts are excellent value).

Hôtel de la Paix Map p232; (☎ 035 625072; www .hotellapaixfes.com in French; 44 Ave Hassan II; s/d Dh285/365; ✗) Cast from the bland tourist class mould, this place is nevertheless good value for the money. Rooms are solidly comfortable, with TV and bathroom; there's also a bar and a good restaurant.

Hôtel Olympic (Map p232; ☎ 035 932682; fax 055 932665; cnr Blvd Mohammed V & Rue 3; s/d incl breakfast Dh240/289; ✗) A handy choice near the central market. Rooms are nondescript but comfortable, equipped with bathroom, TV, phone and stylish brass bedsteads. Its central location means it's often heavily booked, so call in advance.

Hôtel Perla (Map p232; ☎ 035 943641; www.hotel perlamaroc.com; 15 Rue de la Jordannie; s/d Dh307/384; ✗)

A stone's throw from the train station, this is another good tourist-class hotel. Rooms are compact and modern, and the service is reliable. Reassuringly unexciting.

Camping International (☎ 035 731439; fax 035 731554; camping per person Dh40, plus per tent/car/caravan Dh30/30/40; ☒) Set about 4km south of the centre, towards the airport and just off Rte de Sefrou, Fès' best camp site isn't ideally placed, but makes up for it with good facilities. Sites are well kept, along with the shower blocks and kitchens – if you don't feel like cooking there's a restaurant and bar on site too. Bus 38 from Place Atlas in the southwest of the city runs past the camp site.

Midrange

Hôtel Mounia (Map p232; ☎ 035 624838; www.hotel mouniafes.ma in French; 60 Blvd Zerktouni; s/d incl breakfast from Dh4246/536; ☒) A *zellij* lobby guides you into this modern and classy hotel. Rooms are bright and tidy, with satellite TV. The restaurant is good, and there's a smokier bar with plenty of water pipes. Staff are exceedingly helpful. Popular with tour groups. Good discounts are often available.

Hôtel Sofia (Map p232; ☎ 035 624265; fax 035 626478; 3 Rue Arabi Saoudite; s/d/tr Dh450/600/850; ☒ ☒) It's not that the Sofia is characterless, rather it just feels about 20 years out of date. It offers decent price comforts verging on the four-star, with good service, two restaurants and an 'English pub'. As such its pretty good value, but the management could do with investing in a new calendar.

Grand Hôtel de Fès (Map p232; ☎ 035 932026; grandhotel@fesnet.net.ma; 12 Blvd Chefchaouni, cnr Blvd Mohammed V; s/d Dh364/456; ☒) A top address during the French Protectorate, the Grand works hard to keep up its standards and holds its own against more modern rivals. The lobby is old-fashioned but elegant. Large rooms have high ceilings and stucco walls. They are simple, but spotless, with good bathrooms.

Hôtel Ibis Moussafir (Map p232; ☎ 055 651902; www.ibishotel.com; Ave des Almohades, Place de la Gare; s/d incl breakfast Dh413/556; ☒ ☒) There are no surprises on offer at this chain hotel, just exactly what you'd expect: reliable service and good amenities, less than a minute's walk from the train station. A good enough option, but one without even a hint of Morocco about it.

Top End

Hôtel Menzeh Zalagh (Map p232; ☎ 035 625531; menzeh.zalagh@fesnet.net.ma; 10 Rue Mohammed Diouri; s/d incl breakfast Dh900/1200; ☒ ☒) This four-star hotel has a great location, stretched along a low ridge in a sinuous wave with amazing views across to Fès el-Bali, yet convenient to the centre. Rooms are full of modern comforts with a splash of traditional Moroccan décor, and many come with balconies. Nonguests can use the pool for Dh60.

Hotel Menzeh Fes (Map p232; ☎ 035 943849; menzeh.zalagh@fesnet.net.ma; 28 Rue Abdessalam Serghini; s/d incl breakfast Dh900/1200; ☒ ☒) Sister hotel to the Zalagh up the road, this offers virtually identical facilities, albeit with slightly smaller rooms. Not all rooms look across the old city, so ask when checking in; otherwise you'll be left just enjoying the view from the glass elevator on the side of the building.

Crown Palace Fes (Map p232; ☎ 035 948000; www .crownpalacefez.com; 85 Ave des FAR; s/d from Dh1600/ 1900; ☒ ☒ ☒) This is the height of luxury hotels as far as the ville nouvelle goes, easily cruising for its five stars. Marrying tradition and modernity with lavish but tasteful décor, natural light and spacious interiors characterise the rooms. Three restaurants and as many bars offer a bewildering choice of refreshment options, all of which can be burned off in the gym and pool, or sweated out in the hammam.

Eating
RESTAURANTS

Restaurants in the medina can be roughly divided into two categories: regular eating houses and glitzy 'palace restaurants'. The latter offer extravagant meals in lavish surroundings, often accompanied by live music and even stage shows (which can be very much the sort of thing you'll either love or hate). Many palace restaurants just offer set menus, with the added bonus of serving alcohol (plus a 10% service tax). Many riads also run excellent restaurants that are open to nonguests.

Medina

Médina Café (Map pp222-3; ☎ 035 633430; 6 Derb Mernissi Bab Bou Jeloud; mains Dh70-100; ☻ 8am-10pm) Just outside Bab Bou Jeloud, this small restaurant is an oasis of serenity, decorated in a traditional yet restrained

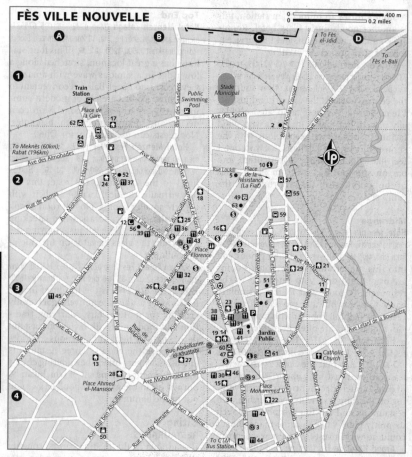

FÈS VILLE NOUVELLE

manner, with fine attention to detail. During the day its a good place to visit for a quick bite or a fruit juice; in the evening the best of Moroccan fare is on offer – the lamb tajine with dried figs and apricots is a real winner, while the plates of couscous are big enough for two.

Le Kasbah (Map pp222-3; Rue Serrajine; mains Dh40, set menu Dh70) On several floors opposite the cheap hotels at Bab Bou Jeloud, this restaurant occupies a prime spot: the top floor looks out over the medina. The food is good, standard Moroccan fare, with the four-course menu being particularly good value. Be warned if you just pop with a thirst, though – drinks attract a surcharge if you're not eating.

Restaurant Zohra (Map pp222-3; ☎ 055 637699; 3 Derb Ain Nass Blida; set menus Dh70-90) Tucked away in the backstreets north of the Kairaouine Mosque, this simple little place is well regarded for its home cooking and warm family welcome. You'll undoubtedly have to ask for directions, but it's worth the expedition.

La Maison Bleue (Map pp222-3; ☎ 035 636052; 2 Place de l'Istiqlal; set menu incl drinks guests/nonguests Dh500/550; ☽ dinner) Reservations are necessary at this elegant riad restaurant. The setting is intimate and romantic, with diners serenaded by an oud player (replaced by livelier Gnawa song and dance at the end of the evening). Set menus run along traditional lines – salads, tajines and the like – but the preparation and presentation are a definite cut above most other places. Alcohol is served.

Restaurant Dar Jamaï (Map pp222-3; ☎ 035 635685; 14 Funduq Lihoudi Zenjfour; set menu Dh100) Relatively modest among palace restaurants, this small place is slightly off the tourist track just below the Sofitel Palais Jamaï. The setting is a nicely restored house, whose restrained décor allows the delicious food to shine. Some will find the lack of live entertainment a bonus.

Dar Saada (Map pp222-3; ☎ 035 637370; 21 Souq el-Attarine; mains from Dh100; set menus Dh135-200; ☻ lunch) Right on Talaa Kebira, this is as much a good landmark as a great place to eat. The surroundings are lavish and the food particularly good – among the best in the medina. House specialities include a great lamb tajine with almonds. It's worth calling before dining as some items must be ordered in advance.

Restaurant Laanibra (Map pp222-3; ☎ 035 741009; 61 Ain Lkhail; set menus Dh120-400) This is a sumptuously decorated 14th-century palace, with all the craftsmanship you'd expect to find in a riad, with side alcoves forming a series of private dining areas. The menu shows equal care and attention. The rich *pastilla* (a rich, savoury-sweet chicken or pigeon pie made with fine pastry) is a favourite, difficult to finish if you've loaded up on starters (veg-

etarians will love the cooked salads). This place is open for lunch year-round, but for dinner only in summer.

Restaurant al-Fassia (Map pp222-3; ☎ 035 637314; 21 Rue Salaj; mains from Dh70, set menus Dh250-500; ☒) This huge, fancy place, the mother of palace restaurants, is famous across Fès for its elaborate evening floorshow (8pm, Dh50 surcharge). The spectacle includes no less than 10 numbers, ranging from folk music to a traditional wedding ceremony to the obligatory belly dancing. There's food, too. Follow the signs east from Place de l'Istiqlal.

La Médina (Map pp222-3; ☎ 035 635857; 13 Derb el-Hammam; set menus Dh120-150) This place is

---

THE AUTHOR'S CHOICE

B'sara Stalls (Map pp222-3; soup Dh3) You shouldn't leave town without sampling *b'sara*, a Fassi speciality. This butterbean and garlic soup is served out of hole-in-the-wall places throughout the medina – our favourites are in the Acherbine area. Look for the big cauldrons facing the street, and a guy serving great ladle-fulls into rough pottery bowls. Delicious with an extra dash of olive oil and a hunk of bread, *b'sara* is perfect fuel for exploring the city.

IMPERIAL CITIES, MIDDLE ATLAS & THE EAST

relatively modest (with no entertainment), but it is known for its excellent food: the *pastilla* is rated among the best in Fès. The menu selection is wide and service is excellent – the place heaves with tour groups in the summer. Follow the signs from Talaa Seghira to the southwest of the Nejjarine Museum.

Ville Nouvelle

Restaurant le Chamonix (Map p232; ☎ 035 626638; 5 Rue Moukhtar Soussi; set menu Dh52; ☺ 10am-10pm) It doesn't look like much, but the service here is friendly (the maître d' has been here for years) and the menu reliable, tasty and inexpensive. All sorts are on offer, from tajines to pizza, with the bonus of some outside seating – rare in the ville nouvelle.

Chez Vittorio (Map p232; ☎ 035 624730; 21 Rue Brahim Roudani; mains from Dh80, salads from Dh30, pizza or pasta from Dh50) This dependable favourite covers the rustic Italian restaurant angle well, right down to the candles and checked cloths. Pizzas, pasta and steaks are all good value and, while the initial service is a bit casual, your meal tends to arrive in a trice. You can also enjoy a glass of wine with your meal.

Restaurant Marrakech (Map p232; ☎ 035 930876; 11 Rue Omar el-Mokhtar; mains from Dh55) A recent makeover has added hugely to this place's charm – red plastered walls and dark furniture, with a cushion-strewn salon at the back. But the menu's variety continues to be its strength, offering delights such as chicken tajine with apple and olive, or lamb with aubergine and peppers. Delicious food in lovely surroundings.

La Médaille (Map p232; ☎ 055 620183; 24 Rue Laarbi al-Kaghat; mains Dh70-90; set menus Dh110-150; ☺ closed Sun dinner) This French-Moroccan place is unique for the Sephardic influence on the menu. Try the *saucisse merguez* (lamb sausage) or the *saucisse de foie* (liver sausage) – you won't find them anywhere else. Seats at the front of house are preferable, as the rear is a smoky bar that's more canteen than restaurant (alcohol is served, naturally).

Restaurant Zagora (Map p232; ☎ 035 940686; 5 Blvd Mohammed V; mains Dh80-100, set menus Dh120 & Dh140) Just off the southern end of Mohammed V, this classy restaurant is popular with tour groups and locals alike. The wine list is probably the most extensive in the ville

nouvelle and the menu is equally broad, although the pleasant setting (complete with oud player) means that both food and drink attract a sizeable surcharge.

Vesuvio (Map p232; ☎ 035 930747; 9 Rue Abi Hayane Taouhidi; pasta from Dh60, mains from Dh90) A new place near the Crown Palace Hotel, this Italian-style restaurant has a great ambience – low lighting, exposed brick walls and beams, and the smell of a wood-fired oven. Pasta dishes are generously sized, and the steaks are tasty and excellent. The want of an alcohol licence is the smallest of drawbacks.

Casa Nostra (Map p232; ☎ 055 932841; 16 Rue Arabie Saoudite; mains around Dh80, pizza or pasta from Dh35) Popular with the young and trendy of Fès, this bright restaurant has an informal, bistro-style atmosphere. It offers mainly Italian food, with a few Spanish classics thrown in for good measure.

La Cheminée (Map p232; ☎ 055 624902; 6 Ave Lalla Asmaa; mains Dh70-90; ☺ closed Sat lunch; ❄) Very civilised and incredibly French, this little brasserie remains popular for its first-rate cuisine and upscale atmosphere. Service is formal with waiters wearing bow ties – you might almost wish you'd brought your own. The menu is classic French, with just a hint of Morocco. Sip your wine with panache, please.

CAFÉS, PATISSERIES & ICE-CREAM PARLOURS

The ville nouvelle is packed with cafés and patisseries, especially along Blvd Mohammed V and Ave Hassan II. Buy some croissants or cakes, then settle down at an outdoor table and watch the day unfold. In the medina, many of the restaurants around Bab Bou Jeloud double as cafés, otherwise hole-in-the-wall places are the order of the day.

Crémerie Skali (Map p232; Blvd Mohammed V; breakfast around Dh20; ☺ 6am-10pm) With a good corner location, this is an ideal stop for breakfast – one that's popular with office workers and families alike. As well as pastries and juice, it can rustle up some mean scrambled eggs.

Florence (1 Ave Lalla Meryem; ☺ 7am-9.30pm) While quite a few of the outdoor cafés in the ville nouvelle are male-dominated, women should feel quite comfortable here. The terrace seating to watch the passing day is preferable to the slightly worn interior.

Sandwiches and the like are available in addition to sticky sweets.

Café Restaurant la Noria (Map p218; Fès el-Jdid; mains Dh40-60, salads Dh20; ☾ 7am-9pm) Something a little different for Fès, this café is tucked away in the Bou Jeloud Gardens next to an old waterwheel – a delightful retreat from the bustle of the city. In addition to drinks and juices, there's a simple dining menu if you're peckish.

Gelatitalia (Map p232; 3 Rue de la Lybie; gelato per scoop Dh6) Offering cool remedies on a hot summer's day, this ice creamery west of Place Florence has locals and tourists alike queuing out the door for its gelato. The authentic Italian-style ice cream comes in 15 toothsome flavours.

Café Renaissance (Map p232; Blvd Mohammed V; juices from Dh6; ☾ 8am-midnight) Another quick pastry option on Mohammed V, the juices here will make you linger. Choose a *panache* (Dh12) – a blend of orange, apple, banana and whatever else they've got on the counter. A mouthwatering mix, almost a meal in itself.

QUICK EATS

The cheap and cheerful restaurants and snack stands just inside Bab Bou Jeloud are among the most popular places to eat in the medina, especially as they provide prime seats to watch the passing cavalcade in and out of the medina. Elsewhere, look out for tiny cell-like places grilling brochettes or cooking huge bowls of *b'sara* (see p233). In the ville nouvelle, there are a few cheap eats on or just off Blvd Mohammed V, especially around the central market. You'll also find a good choice of sandwich places around Place Florence.

Restaurant des Jeunes (Map pp222-3; 20 Rue Serrajine; mains Dh25-30, set menu Dh35; ☾ 10am-10pm) One of the many popular hang-outs close to Bab Bou Jeloud is next to the Hôtel Cascade. It's basic, cheap and quick, with brochettes, sandwiches and the like.

Restaurant Bajelloul (Map p232; Rue Arabie Saoudite; meals around Dh30; ☾ noon-midnight) This simple little place that is popular with the locals has a good selection of meat, including liver and various sausages, which is grilled while you watch and served with salad and bread.

Pizza Milano (Map p232; 11 Ave Lalla Meryem; pizza Dh35-70, shwarma Dh35; ☾ 10am-10pm) It's not just pizzas: there's plenty of rotisserie chicken, grilled fish and *shwarma* (spicy lamb strips in pita bread) on offer here – and in the neighbouring three or four similar outfits.

Al-Khozama (Map p232; 23 Ave Mohammed es-Slaoui; set menu Dh60, sandwiches Dh15-20; ☾ 7am-11pm) The draw to this restaurant near Place Mohammed V is the indoor terrace – a comfortable, quiet place for women. There are no surprises on the menu, but the food's tasty and comes in decent portions.

Restaurant Pizza Mamia (Map p232; Place Florence; salads Dh20, pizzas from Dh25; ☾ 7am-11pm) Compact and cosy, this places serves good and quick pizzas from a wood-fired oven, plus salads, burgers and other fast-food options. Popular with families and young couples.

SELF-CATERING

For fresh fruit and vegies, spices, nuts, olives or a parcel of delicious dates, you can't beat the ville nouvelle's **central market** (Map p232; Blvd Mohammed V; ☾ 8.30am-2.30pm). It also has a couple of good cheese stalls and there are alcohol shops around the outside.

In the medina, fresh produce abounds – start at the fresh fruit stalls at the top of Talaa Kebira and work your way down from there (the squeamish might care to avert their eyes as they pass the butchers' stalls, with rows of sheep and cow heads). Vendors will call out at you to offer their freshest dates and olives.

Drinking
CAFÉS

The wide pavements of Ave Hassan II and Blvd Mohammed V are prime spots for whiling away the afternoon with a pot of mint tea or a cup of coffee. There's a host of cafés to choose from, but women will find themselves vastly outnumbered by Moroccan males – better to sit on the pavement seats than in the smoky interiors. See also cafés listed under Patisseries & Ice-Cream Parlours (opposite).

L'Entente (Map p232; 83 Blvd Mohammed V; ☾ 6am-9pm) This is a classic example of a Moroccan city café. Well located on Place Mohammed V, you can't beat it for people-watching though women may find they are the ones being observed. Take your pick from this or any of the half-dozen similar places on this stretch of avenue.

IMPERIAL CITIES, MIDDLE ATLAS & THE EAST

Café Pâtisserie New Peacock (Map p232; ☎ 055 941187; 29 Ave Mohammed es-Slaoui; ☒ 7am-11pm) More relaxed and definitely more stylish, this café set back from Place Mohammed V is airier than the places along the main drag. Its popularity with Moroccan women is a selling point for female travellers, but all will enjoy the juices and pastries.

BARS

Bars are easy to come across in the ville nouvelle, but they're almost exclusively seedy, smoky places, where men are men and women are prostitutes. Hotel bars offer more congenial surroundings. In the medina, drinking options are reduced to the more expensive hotels. All tend to wind up around 11pm.

Riad Fès (Map pp222-3; 5 Derb ibn Slimane) The classiest place for a drink in the whole city, the courtyard bar of Riad Fès is a delight. Stucco columns catch the light reflected off the central pool, and soft music plays while you sit at the glass bar or slump into the cushions. Open to the elements, it's a little cold in winter, but fashionably cool in summer.

Sofitel Palais Jamaï (Map pp222-3; Bab Guissa) A great place for a sundowner, the Palais Jamaï has a great terrace looking out across old Fès: an ideal way to finish up a day in the medina.

Pub Cala Iris (Map p232; 26 Ave Hassan II) In the ville nouvelle, this English-style pub is certainly a male enclave, but you can escape upstairs to the less seedy (but more expensive) bar.

Hôtel Batha (Map pp222-3; Place Batha) This hotel bar in the medina is a good bet, with a wide courtyard to relax in, or a snug interior for cooler nights.

Hôtel Mounia (Map p232; 60 Blvd Zerktouni; ☒ happy hour 7-8pm) One of the better hotel bars in the ville nouvelle. You can also enjoy a *sheesha* (waterpipe) here with your drink.

Entertainment

Son et Lumière de Fès (Map p218; Sound & Lights of Fès; ☎ 035 763652; Borj Sud; admission Dh100; ☒ 9.30pm May-Aug; 7.15pm Mar, Apr, Sep & Nov) This sound and light show recounts – in 45 minutes – 12 centuries of history, from the founding of the first Moroccan dynasty by Moulay Idriss up until the present. Tickets are available at the tourist office, Syndicat d'Initiative or at the larger hotels.

NIGHTCLUBS

Many of the larger hotels have nightclubs or discos. Most are open from 11pm to 3am Tuesday to Sunday. Entry generally costs about Dh100, which includes one drink. Prices for additional drinks are around Dh50–100. Arrive late and dress smartly – the beautiful people of Fès are likely to be out in force.

Hôtel Menzeh Zalagh (Map p232; ☎ 055 932234; 10 Rue Mohammed Diouri) One of the more popular hotel nightclubs, even if it does strike you as little more than a glorified bar with a glitter ball. It's good for throwing a few poses nonetheless.

Le Phoebus (Map p218; Jnan Palace, Ave Ahmed Chaouki) The trendiest club in town is at this five-star hotel. It's all a bit cool, even if the tunes – a hefty dose of Europop – don't always hit the mark. Things liven up when they're playing rai.

CINEMAS

L'Empire Cinema (Map p232; 60 Ave Hassan II; tickets Dh20-25) Screenings are heavy on Bollywood and Hong Kong beat 'em ups.

Shopping

Fès is and always has been the artisanal capital of Morocco. The choice of crafts is wide, quality is high, and prices are competitive, so take your time to shop around. As usual, it's best to seek out the little shops off the main tourist routes (principally Talaa Kebira and Talaa Seghira in Fès al-Bali).

In the medina, there are many well-restored riads and *funduq*s that have been converted into carpet showrooms. While they certainly offer a great opportunity to sit with a mint tea in spectacular surroundings and look at some fabulous rugs, the hard sell is like no other place in Morocco. You can pick up some wonderful pieces, but also pay over the odds for factory-made rubbish. See also p219 to help prepare you for the Fès carpet shopping experience.

Ensemble Artisanal (Map p232; Ave Allah ben Abdullah; ☒ 9am-noon & 2.30-6.30pm) Slightly out of the way in the ville nouvelle, the state-run Ensemble Artisanal is as always a decent place to get a feel for quality and price, as well as seeing artisans at work in a no-pressure environment. Prices are fixed.

(Continued on page 249)

CHRISTINE OSBORNE

Locals meet on the ramparts in front of Essaouira's medina (p145)

Family caravan on the beach at Agadir (p368)

IZZET KERIBAR

Mausoleum of Moulay Ismail (p255), Meknès

People outside Bab el-Mahrouk, gateway to Fès el-Bali (p220)

Granary at Heri es-Souani (p257), Meknès

Carved cedarwood door, Hassan II Mosque (p91), Casablanca

Doorways in Essaouira (p143)

Pavillion at Jardin Ménara (p303), Marrakesh

Jardin Majorelle (p303), Marrakesh

Cacti garden and Museum of Islamic Art in Jardin Majorelle (p303), Marrakesh

DOUG MCKINLAY

Hammam at Riad Farnatchi (p310), Marrakesh

DOUG MCKINLAY

Dar Cherifa literary café (p315), Marrakesh

242

Snake charmer, Djemaa el-Fna (p297),
Marrakesh

Gnaoui dancers, Djemaa el-Fna (p297)

Dusk at Djemaa el-Fna (p295)

CHRISTOPHER WOOD

Decorative pillar, Aït Benhaddou (p331)

Zellij (mosaic tilework) detail, Hassan II Mosque (p91)

JOHN ELK III

Zellij fountain, Musée de Marrakech (p299)

DOUG MCKINLAY

DAMIEN SIMONIS

Zellij detail, Saadian Tombs (p300)

CHRISTOPHER WOOD

Midelt (p272), between the Middle and High Atlas

Mountain village above the town of Setti Fatma (p327), Ourika Valley

DOUG MCKINLAY

CHRISTOPHER WOOD

Terraced fields near Tizi n'Tichka (p330)

Traditional doorway, Chefchaouen (p189)

MARK DAFFEY

SARA-JANE CLELAND

Houses in Tafraoute (p392), Ameln Valley

CHRISTINE OSBORNE

Tuareg man from near Goulmime (p389)
wearing customary blue clothing

Woman's hands with henna tattoos (p352)

CHRISTIAN ASLUND

Alley scene in the kasbah (p300), Marrakesh

DOUG MCKINLAY

DOUG MCKINLAY

Medina (p295), Marrakesh

Berber nomads in the desert near M'Hamid (p343)

SARA-JANE CLELAND

SARA-JANE CLELAND

Man wearing a traditional flowing garment, the jellaba (p45)

MARK DA

Desert at Erg Chebbi (p362)

Road to Tizi n'Tichka (p330), High Atlas

JOHN ELK III

(Continued from page 236)

Les Potteries de Fès (Bab el-Ftouh) An attraction in itself, this is the home of the famous Fassi pottery. You can see the entire production process, from pot-throwing to the painstaking hand painting and laying out of *zellij* – it's a joy to behold. The potteries are about 500m east of Bab el-Ftouh, an easy trip in a petit taxi – look for the plumes of black smoke produced by olive pits, which burn at the right temperature for firing the clay. The shop has the best range of pottery in the city, and you can even commission a mosaic fountain to be shipped home for you.

Les Mystères de Fès (Map p232; 53 Derb bin Lemssari) This place has something of the Aladdin's cave about it. Near the Belghazi Museum, it's stuffed to the gills with jewellery, furniture, pots and trinkets. They're all antiques of course – some pieces are genuinely old, others produced just the week before.

Nour Driss (Map p232; 15 Moulay Driss) Just one of a handful of equally decent shops around the henna souq, specialising in all kinds of perfumed oils, scents and spices. Enthusiastic salesmen will demonstrate the joys of kohl makeup, ambergris scent and a thousand other mixtures to spice up your cooking or love life in equal measure.

Getting There & Away

AIR
Fès airport (☎ 035 674712) is 15km south of the city, at Saïss. **RAM** (Map p232; ☎ 035 625516; 54 Ave Hassan II) operates daily flights to Casablanca (one way Dh945, 45 minutes) and flights to Paris five times a week. British Airways flies to London three times a week (via Marrakesh).

BUS
CTM
The main bus station for **CTM buses** (☎ 035 732992) is near Place Atlas in the southern ville nouvelle (Map p218). Make sure you check which one you are departing from beforehand. In high season it's a good idea to buy tickets in advance, particularly to Tangier, Marrakesh and Chefchaouen.

CTM runs seven buses a day to Casablanca (Dh90, five hours) via Rabat (Dh60, 3½ hours) between 6.30am and 4.30pm, and six buses to Meknès (Dh18, one hour) between 8.30am and 8.30pm. Buses for Marrakesh (Dh150, nine hours) run twice daily (morning and evening).

Heading north and east, there are three buses for Tangier (Dh80, six hours), three for Chefchaouen (Dh60, four hours), two for Tetouan (Dh80, five hours), one for Al-Hoceima (Dh90, six hours), two for Nador (Dh80, six hours), and a daily service for Oujda (Dh100, six hours).

International services to Spain and France (both three times a week) also depart from the CTM bus station.

Other Companies
Non-CTM buses depart from the **main bus station** (Map pp222–3; ☎ 035 636032) outside Bab el-Mahrouk. Fares are slightly less than CTM and reservations can be made for popular routes. It has a **left-luggage facility** (per item Dh5, ☉ 6am-midnight). At least six buses run daily to Casablanca, Chefchaouen, Er-Rachidia, Marrakesh, Meknès, Oujda, Rabat, Tangier and Tetouan. Less frequent buses go to Rissani (Dh120, 10 hours), Ouarzazate (Dh142, 14 hours) and Tinerhir (Dh108, 10 hours).

Locally, there are frequent departures to Azrou (Dh22, two hours), Ifrane (Dh16, 1¾ hours), Moulay Yacoub (Dh9, 30 minutes), Sefrou (Dh12, one hour), Taza (Dh30, two hours, hourly) and Ouezzane (Dh30, three hours, twice daily).

CAR
The following are among the car rental agencies in Fès:
Avis (Map p232; ☎ 035 626969; avisozz@iam.net.ma; 50 Blvd Abdallah Chefchaouni)
Budget (Map p232; ☎ 035 940092; fax 035 940091; Blvd Lalla Asmaa)
Europcar (Map p232; ☎ 035 626545; fax 035 626451; 45 Ave Hassan II)
Goldcar (Map p232; ☎ 035 620495; Rue Abdelkarim el-Khattabi)
Hertz (Map p232; ☎ /fax 035 622812; Ave Lalla Meryem)

There are car parks in several locations near the medina: just south of Place l'Istiqal, on Ave des Français outside Bab Bou Jeloud, and inside the medina wall north of Talaa Kebira. In the ville nouvelle is a guarded car park in front of the central market.

TAXI
There are several grand taxi ranks dotted around town. Taxis for Meknès (Dh14) and

Rabat (Dh55) leave from in front of the main bus station (outside Bab el-Mahrouk) and from near the train station. Taxis for Taza (Dh33) depart from near Bab el-Ftouh, the medina's southeastern gate. Those going to Moulay Yacoub (Dh8) leave from the open ground to the west of Bab Bou Jeloud. The rank for Sefrou (Dh10) is located just below Place de la Résistance in the ville nouvelle. Azrou (Dh25) and Ifrane (Dh21) taxis wait at a parking lot to the west of the CTM bus station in the south of the ville nouvelle.

TRAIN

The **train station** (Map p232; ☎ 035 930333) is in the ville nouvelle, a 10-minute walk north-west of Place Florence. To take advantage of the **left-luggage office** (per item Dh10; ☯ 6am-8pm), bags must be locked or padlocked.

Trains depart every two hours between 7am and 5pm to Casablanca (Dh97, 4¼ hours), via Rabat (Dh72, 3½ hours) and Meknès (Dh17, one hour). There are two additional overnight trains. Five direct trains go to Marrakesh (Dh71, eight hours) and one goes to Tangier (Dh96, five hours). Direct trains for Oujda (Dh107, six hours) via Taza (Dh38, two hours) leave three times daily.

Getting Around
TO/FROM THE AIRPORT

There is a regular bus service (bus 16) between the airport and the train station (Dh3, 25 minutes), with departures every half-hour or so. Grands taxis from any stand charge a set fare of Dh120.

BUS

Fès has a reliable local bus service. At certain times of day, however, the buses are like sardine cans and are notorious for pickpockets. The standard fare is Dh2.50. Some useful routes:

No 2 Bab Smarine (Fès el-Jdid) via Ave Hassan II (ville nouvelle) to Hay Hussein.

No 9 Place Atlas via Blvd Abdallah Chefchaouni (both in the ville nouvelle) to near the Dar Batha Museum (Fès el-Bali); the bus returns via Place de la Résistance, Ave Hassan II and Ave des FAR.

No 10 Train station via Bab Guissa (northern Fès el-Bali) to Bab Sidi Bou Jida (northeastern Fès el-Bali).

No 12 Bab Bou Jeloud via Bab Guissa to Bab el-Ftouh (all in Fès el-Bali).

No 18 Bab el-Ftouh to Dar Batha Museum (both in Fès el-Bali).

No 19 Train station via Ave Hassan II (both in ville nouvelle) and Bab el-Jdid (southern Fès el-Bali) to Place er-Rsif (central Fès el-Bali).

No 47 Train station to Bab Bou Jeloud (Fès el-Bali).

TAXI

Drivers of the red petits taxis generally use their meters without any fuss. Expect to pay about Dh10 from the train or CTM station to Bab Bou Jeloud. As usual, there is a 50% surcharge at night. You'll find taxi ranks outside all the gates of the medina. Only grands taxis go out to the airport (see left).

AROUND FÈS
Sefrou ﺻﻔﺮﻭ
pop 40,000

The small Berber town of Sefrou, just 30km southeast of Fès, is a quaint, picturesque place situated on the edge of the Middle Atlas mountains. It has a small but interesting medina, which once hosted one of Morocco's largest Jewish communities (as many as 8000 people, according to some accounts), and it was here that Moulay Idriss II lived while overseeing the building of Fès. It's an easy day trip from Fès, but there aren't many options if you want to spend the night.

INFORMATION

BMCE (Blvd Mohammed V) Has an ATM.

Club Internet Ibn Battouta (Off Blvd Mohammed V; per hr Dh7; ☯ 9am-midnight)

Pharmacie de Sefrou (Blvd Mohammed V; ☯ 8am-8pm Mon-Sat)

Main post office (Blvd Mohammed V)

Post office (Rte de Fès)

SIGHTS & ACTIVITIES

Sefrou's medina is a manageable place to get around, especially compared to Fès. The Oued Aggaï flows through its centre, opening the place up and giving it more of an airy feeling than many old medinas. The best point of entry is the northerly **Bab el-Maqam**. Follow the main flow of people downhill to the southeast and pass two mosques. Cross over the river and continue up the main shopping street to where the road splits: straight ahead takes you to Bab Merba, in the medina's southern wall, next to another mosque; the right fork brings you to the beginning of the **mellah**, which stretches from here northwest along the river. Although its Jewish population has gone, the district still retains a few distinctive wooden-galleried houses and lanes so narrow two people can only just pass. In its heyday, the mellah was so dark and crowded that street lamps had to be lit even in the middle of the day. Just south of Bab Merba is a **synagogue**, which is now closed.

A 1.5km walk west of town are the **Cascades**, a modest waterfall, with a small café that's only open in summer. Follow the signs from Ave Moulay Hassan around **Al-Qala'** (a semifortified village) and along the river's lush valley.

Sefrou is a sleepy place on the whole. However, things liven up on Thursday (market day) and in early June when the annual **Cherry Festival** fills the streets for three days of folk music, parades and sports events, culminating with the crowning of the Cherry Queen.

SLEEPING

Hôtel Sidi Lahcen el-Youssi (☎ 035 683428; Rue Sidi Ali Bousserghine; s/d Dh162/200; ☒) Situated in a very quiet part of town, this complex has decent rooms with attached bathrooms (and some with balcony), a restaurant and occasionally absent staff. Ask about discounts if you're visiting out of season.

Hôtel Frenaie (☎ 035 661027; Rte de Fès; s/d Dh80/120) This is the best cheapie in town, with pretty simple but clean rooms. There are shared bathrooms (squat toilets; hot showers Dh10), but all rooms have a sink. Staff are friendly, and there's a convenient café at the front of the building.

EATING

There is a decent choice of snack stands around the covered market and inside Bab Merba.

Restaurant Café Oumnia (☎ 055 660679; Ave Massira al-Khadka; set menu Dh50; ☒ 8am-10pm) This is Sefrou's one and only restaurant, near the post office. Set on two levels, with clean and bright restaurant décor, its daily three-course set menu is good value.

There's a string of cafés and a bar along Blvd Mohammed V, all fairly masculine places to drink coffee. For pastries, try **Café de la Marche Verte** (Ave Hassan II; ☒ 7am-9pm), with its terrace overlooking Bab Merba.

SEFROU

```
0                    200 m
0                    0.1 miles
```

INFORMATION	
BMCE	1 B3
Club Internet Ibn Battouta	2 C3
Pharmacie de Sefrou	3 B3
Main Post Office	4 B3
Post Office	5 B1

SIGHTS & ACTIVITIES	
Mosque	6 C2
Mosque	7 C2
Mosque	8 C2
Synagogue	9 C2

SLEEPING	
Hôtel Frenaie	10 B1
Hôtel Sidi Lahcen el-Youssi	11 B3

EATING	
Café de la Marche Verte	12 B2
Cafés & Bar	13 B3
Restaurant Café Oumnia	14 B3
Snack Stands	15 C2
Snack Stands	16 C2

SHOPPING	
Ensemble Artisanal	(see 5)

TRANSPORT	
Buses to Fès	17 B1
Grands Taxis	18 B1
Grands Taxis	19 B1

SHOPPING

You might snap up a bargain at the market held every Thursday; otherwise try **Ensemble Artisanal** (Rte de Fès), which offers the usual selection of rugs, pots, clothes and leather at fixed prices.

GETTING THERE & AWAY

Regular buses (Dh7, 40 minutes) and grands taxis (Dh10, 30 minutes) run between Sefrou and Place de la Résistance in Fès. For Azrou, take a grand taxi to Immouzzer (Dh12) and change.

Bhalil

بهاليل

pop 1500

This curious village is 5km from Sefrou, and worth a visit if you have your own transport. It contains a number of troglodyte houses (cave dwellings) built into the picturesque mountainside and picked out in pastel hues of pink, yellow and blue. Some go so far as to utilise caves for the primary room of the house. The result is a cool, spacious room – usually used as a salon – while bedrooms and private areas are built above. One resident is an official guide, and can easily be found for a tour – he'll almost certainly welcome you into his own cave home.

MEKNÈS

مكناس

pop 680,000

Morocco's third imperial city is often overlooked by tourist itineraries – its proximity to Fès rather works against it. But Meknès is worth getting to know. Quieter and smaller than its grand neighbour, it's also more laid-back, less hassle and no less full of attractions. Meknès has all the winding narrow medina streets and grand buildings that it warrants as a one-time capital of the Moroccan sultanate, but it wears these attractions in a rather understated manner. Sultan Moulay Ismail, the architect of Meknès' glory days, might be a little disgruntled at the city's current modesty, but visitors will find much to be enchanted by.

Encircled by the rich plains below the Middle Atlas, Meknès is blessed with a hinterland abundant with cereals, olives, wine, citrus fruit and other agricultural products that remain the city's economic backbone. In the midst of this agricultural region sit the Roman ruins at Volubilis and the hilltop tomb of Moulay Idriss, two of the country's most significant historic sites.

History

The Berber tribe of the Meknassis (hence the name Meknès) first settled here in the 10th century AD. Under the Almohads and Merenids, Meknès medina was expanded and some of the city's oldest remaining monuments were built.

It wasn't until the 17th century that Meknès really came into its own. The founder of the Alawite dynasty, Moulay ar-Rashid, died in 1672. His successor and brother, Moulay Ismail, made Meknès his capital, from where he would reign for 55 years.

Ismail endowed the city with 25km of imposing walls with monumental gates and an enormous palace complex that was never completed. That he could devote the time and resources to construction was partly due to his uncommon success in subduing all opposition in Morocco and keeping foreign meddlers at bay, mainly because of his notorious Black Guard (see p254).

Ismail's death in 1727 also struck the death knoll for Meknès. The town resumed its role as a backwater, as his grandson Mohammed III (1757–90) moved to Marrakesh. The 1755 earthquake that devastated Lisbon also dealt Meknès a heavy blow. As so often happened in Morocco, its monuments were subsequently stripped in order to be added to buildings elsewhere. It's only been in the past few decades, as tourist potential has become obvious, that any serious restoration attempts have taken place.

In 1912 the arrival of the protectorate revived Meknès as the French made it their military headquarters. The army was accompanied by French farmers who settled on the fertile land nearby. After independence most properties were recovered by the Moroccan government and leased to local farmers.

Orientation

The valley of the (usually dry) Oued Bou Fekrane neatly divides the old medina in the west and the French-built ville nouvelle in the east. Ave Moulay Ismail connects them, then becomes the principal route of the ville nouvelle, where its name changes to Ave Hassan II.

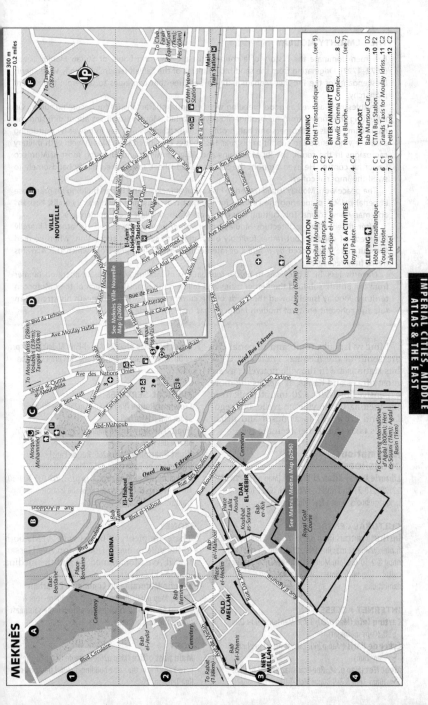

MEKNÈS

0 ——— 300 m
0 ——— 0.2 miles

IMPERIAL CITIES, MIDDLE & THE EAST

INFORMATION
Hôpital Moulay Ismail................1 D3
Institut Français........................2 C2
Polyclinique el-Menzah............3 C1

SIGHTS & ACTIVITIES
Royal Palace.............................4 C4

SLEEPING
Hôtel Transatlantique................5 C1
Youth Hostel............................6 C1
Zaki Hôtel................................7 D3

DRINKING
Hôtel Transatlantique................(see 5)

ENTERTAINMENT
Dawliz Cinema Complex............8 C2
Nuit Blanche.............................(see 7)

TRANSPORT
Bab Mansour Car......................9 D2
CTM Bus Station......................10 F2
Grands Taxis for Moulay Idriss...11 C1
Petits Taxis..............................12 C2

THE ALMIGHTY MOULAY

Few men dominate the history of a country like the towering figure of Sultan Moulay Ismail (1672–1727). Originating from the sand-blown plains of the Tafilalt region, his family were sherifs (descendants of the Prophet Mohammed) – a pedigree that continues to underpin the current monarchy.

Ruthlessness as well as good breeding were essential characteristics for becoming sultan. On inheriting the throne from his brother Moulay ar-Rashid, Moulay Ismail set about diffusing the rival claims of his 83 brothers and half-brothers, celebrating his first day in power by murdering all those who refused to submit to his rule. His politics continued their bloody vein with military campaigns in the south, the Rif Mountains and Algerian hinterland, bringing most of Morocco under his control. He even brought the Salé corsairs to heel, taxing their piracy handsomely to swell the imperial coffers.

The peace won, Moulay Ismail retired to his capital at Meknès and began building his grandiose imperial palace, plundering the country for the best materials, and building city walls, kasbahs and many new towns. This cultural flowering was Morocco's last great golden age.

After violence and architecture, Moulay Ismail's other love was love itself. He fathered literally hundreds of children, but rather foolishly did nothing to secure his succession. When he died the sultanate was rocked by a series of internecine power struggles, from which the Alawites never fully recovered.

Nevertheless, his legacy was to be the foundations of modern Morocco. He liberated Tangier from the British, subdued the Berber tribes and relieved the Spanish of much of their Moroccan territory. Moulay Ismail sowed the seeds of the current monarchy and beneath his strong-arm rule the coherent entity of modern Morocco was first glimpsed.

Moulay Ismail's tomb and imperial city are south of the medina. Train and CTM bus stations are in the ville nouvelle, as are most offices and banks, as well as the more expensive hotels. It's a 20-minute walk from the medina to the ville nouvelle, but regular (and crowded) local buses and urban grands taxis shuttle between the two.

Information

BOOKSHOPS

Librairie Dar al-Kitab al-Watani (Map p260; ☎ 035 521280; 10-21 Blvd Allal ben Abdallah) Good for French-language books, with a few English titles.

CULTURAL CENTRES

Institut Français (Map p253; ☎ 035 515851; inst. fr.mek@aim.net.ma; Rue Ferhat Hachad; ☻ 8.30am-noon & 2.30-6.30pm Mon-Sat) The centre of Meknès' cultural life, with films, plays, concerts and exhibitions.

INTERNET ACCESS

Carting Info (Map p260; 3 Rue Menton; per hr Dh8 ; ☻ 8.30am-midnight)

Cyber de Paris (Map p260; Zankat Accra; per hr Dh8; ☻ 9am-2am)

Meet Net (Map p256; Rue Rouamazine; per hr Dh8; ☻ 10am-1pm & 3-9.30pm Mon-Sat)

Quick Net (Map p260; 28 Rue el-Emir Abdelkander; per hr Dh10; ☻ 10am-10pm) Hot and cold drinks also on offer.

MEDICAL SERVICES

Croissant Rouge (Red Cross; Map260; Rue de Paris) South of the town hall.

Hôpital Moulay Ismail (Map p253; ☎ 035 522805; off Ave des FAR)

Night Pharmacy (Map p260; Rue de Paris)

Pharmacy el-Fath (Map p256; Place el-Hedim)

Polyclinique el-Menzah (Map p253; ☎ 035 400330; 10-12 Ave des Nations Unies) Near the Institut Français.

MONEY

There are plenty of banks with ATMs both in the ville nouvelle (mainly on Ave Hassan II and Ave Mohammed V) and the medina (Rue Sekkakine).

Banque Marocaine du Commerce Extérieur (BMCE; Map p260; 98 Ave des FAR; ☻ 10am-1pm & 4-7pm) An after-hours exchange office on the southeast side of the ville nouvelle.

POST

Main post office (Map p260; Place de l'Istiqlal) The parcel office is in the same building, around the corner on Rue Tetouan.

Post office (Map p256; Rue Dar Smen) Located in the medina.

TOURIST INFORMATION
Délégation Régionale du Tourisme (Map p260; ☎ 055 524426; fax 055 516046; Place de l'Istiqlal; ✆ 8.30am-noon & 2.30-6.30pm Mon-Thu, 8-11.30am & 3-6.30pm Fri) Limited tourist information and pamphlets

TRAVEL AGENCIES
Carlson Wagonlit (Map p260; ☎ 055 521995; 1 Rue Ghana) A source for air, ferry and coach tickets.
RAM (Map p260; ☎ 055 520963; 7 Ave Mohammed V) Handles tickets for all major airlines.

Sights
MEDINA
The heart of Meknès medina is Place el-Hedim, the large square facing Bab el-Mansour. Built by Moulay Ismail and originally used for royal announcements and public executions, it's a good place to sit and watch the world go by – kids playing football, hawkers selling miracle cures, and promenading families. The western side of the square is edged by an excellent covered produce market (see p262) and catches the spill-over from the souqs to the north.

To the south, the impressive monumental gateway of Bab el-Mansour leads into Moulay Ismail's imperial city. The narrow streets of the old *mellah* are in the west of the medina.

Dar Jamaï Museum
Overlooking Place el-Hedim is Dar Jamaï, a palace built in 1882 by the powerful Jamaï family, two of whom were viziers to Sultan Moulay al-Hassan I. When the sultan died in 1894, in keeping with the fickle political atmosphere of the Moroccan court, the Jamaï family fell into disgrace. They lost everything, including the palace, which was passed on to the powerful Al-Glaoui family. In 1912 the French commandeered the palace for a military hospital.

Since 1920 the palace has housed the Administration des Beaux Arts and one of Morocco's best **museums** (Map p256 ☎ 055 530863; Place el-Hedim; admission Dh10; ✆ 9am-noon & 3-6.30pm Wed-Mon). As usual, the museum building is as interesting as the exhibits, which rotate on a seasonal basis. Exhibits include traditional ceramics, jewellery,

rugs, textiles, embroidery and woodwork. The *koubba* (domed sanctuary) upstairs is furnished as a traditional salon complete with luxurious rugs and cushions. The museum also has a fine collection of antique carpets, representing various styles from different regions of Morocco.

The exhibits are well constructed; explanations are in French, Arabic and sometimes English. The museum's Andalucian garden and courtyard are shady, peaceful spots amid overgrown orange trees.

Grande Mosquée & Medersa Bou Inania
Opposite the Grande Mosquée, the **Medersa Bou Inania** (Map p256; Rue Najjarine; admission Dh10; ✆ 9am-noon & 3-6pm) is typical of the exquisite interior design that distinguishes Merenid monuments. It was completed in 1358 by Bou Inan, after whom a more lavish *medersa* in Fès is also named. This *medersa* is a good display of the classic Moroccan decorative styles – the *zellij* base, delicate stucco midriff and carved olivewood ceiling.

Students aged eight to 10 years once lived two to a cell on the ground floor, while older students and teachers lived on the 1st floor. You can climb onto the roof for views of the green-tiled roof and minaret of the Grande Mosquée nearby, but the *medersa* is otherwise closed to non-Muslims.

IMPERIAL CITY
Bab el-Mansour
The focus of Place el-Hedim is the huge gate of Bab el-Mansour, the grandest of all imperial Moroccan gateways. The gate is well preserved with lavish (if faded) *zellij* and inscriptions across the top. It was completed by Moulay Ismail's son, Moulay Abdallah, in 1732. You can't walk through the *bab* itself – which is opened only on grand occasions – but instead have to make do with a side gate to the left.

Mausoleum of Moulay Ismail
Diagonally opposite the Koubbat as-Sufara' is the **resting place** (Map p256; admission free, donations welcomed; ✆ 8.30am-noon & 2-6pm Sat-Thu) of the sultan who made Meknès his capital in the 17th century. Moulay Ismail's stature as one of Morocco's greatest rulers means that non-Muslim visitors are welcomed into the sanctuary (although they may not approach the tomb itself). The austere and peaceful

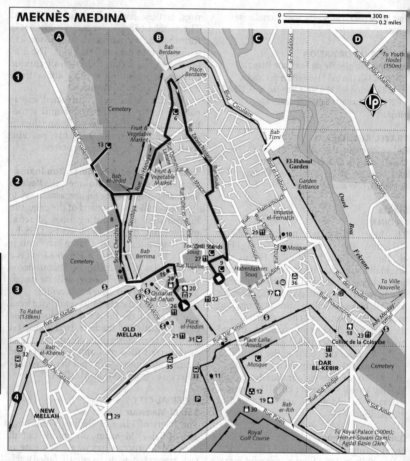

MEKNÈS MEDINA

courtyards are a contrast to the more lavish tomb hall, a showcase of the best of Moroccan craftsmanship.

Koubbat as-Sufara'

South of Bab el-Mansour lies the *mechouar* (parade ground), now known as Place Lalla Aouda, where Moulay Ismail inspected his famed Black Guard. After bringing 16,000 slaves from sub-Saharan Africa, Moulay Ismail guaranteed the continued existence of his elite units by providing the soldiers with women and raising their offspring for service in the guard. By the time of his death, the Black Guard had expanded tenfold. Its successes were many, ranging from quelling internal rebellions, to chasing European powers out of northern Morocco, to disposing of the Ottoman Turk threat from Algeria.

Following the road around to the right, you'll find an expanse of grass and a small building, the **Koubbat as-Sufara'** (Map p256; admission Dh10; ⏱ 9am-noon & 3-6pm), once the reception hall for foreign ambassadors. Beside the entrance, you will notice the shafts that descend into a vast crypt. This dark and slightly spooky network of rooms was used for food storage, although tour guides will delight in recounting the (erroneous) story that it was used as a dungeon for the Christian slaves who provided labour for Moulay Ismail's building spree. Bring a torch.

INFORMATION	Okchen Market.......15 B3	Restaurant Zitouna.......25 C2
BMCE.......1 B3	Spices, Herbs & Nuts Souq.......16 B3	Sandwich Stands.......26 B3
Meet Net.......2 D3		Snack Bounana.......27 B3
Pharmacy el-Fath.......3 B3	**SLEEPING**	
Post Office.......4 C3	Hôtel Regina.......17 C3	**SHOPPING**
	Maison d'Hôtes Riad.......(see 24)	Carpet Shops.......28 B3
SIGHTS & ACTIVITIES	Maroc Hôtel.......18 D3	Centre Artisinale.......29 B4
Bab el-Mansour.......5 C3	Palais Didi.......19 C4	Pottery stalls.......(see 21)
Berdaine Mosque.......6 B1	Ryad Bahia.......20 B3	Souvenir Shops.......30 C4
Dar Jamaï Museum.......7 B3		
Flea Market.......8 B2	**EATING**	**TRANSPORT**
Grande Mosquée.......9 C3	Covered Market.......21 B3	Calèches.......31 B3
Hammam Zitouna.......10 C2	Dar Sultana.......(see 20)	Grands Taxis.......32 A4
Koubbat as-Sufara'.......11 C4	Restaurant Mille et Une Nuits.......22 C3	Local Buses.......33 B4
Mausoleum of Moulay Ismail.......12 C4		Main Bus Station.......34 A4
Mausoleum of Sidi ben Aïssa.......13 A2	Restaurant Oumnia.......23 D3	Petits Taxis.......35 B4
Medersa Bou Inania.......14 C3	Restaurant Riad.......24 D4	Petits Taxis.......36 C3

Heri es-Souani & Agdal Basin

Nearly 2km southeast of the mausoleum, Moulay Ismail's immense granaries and stables, **Heri es-Souani** (admission Dh10; 9am-noon & 3-6.30pm), were ingeniously designed. Tiny windows, massive walls and a system of underfloor water channels kept the temperatures cool and air circulating. The building provided stabling and food for an incredible 12,000 horses, and Moulay Ismail regarded it as one of his finest architectural projects.

The roof fell in long ago, but the first few vaults have been restored. They're impressive, but overly lit to rob them of much of their ambience – seek out the darker, more atmospheric, corners. Those beyond stand in partial ruin, row upon row across a huge area.

Immediately north of the granaries and stables lies an enormous stone-lined lake, the **Agdal Basin**. Fed by a complex system of irrigation channels some 25km long, it served as both a reservoir for the sultan's gardens and a pleasure lake.

In summer it's a long hot walk here from Moulay Ismail's mausoleum, so you might want to catch a taxi or calèche (horse-drawn carriage). If you do decide to walk, follow the road from the mausoleum south between the high walls, past the main entrance of the Royal Palace (no visitors) and a camp site, to find the entrance straight ahead.

Activities

Club Farah d'Équitation (035 548844, 061 134951; www.clubfarah.com; Rte de Fès; adult/child per hr Dh125/75) It offers hourly lessons, day trips in the region and longer horse-riding treks around Morocco – book in advance. It's 7km out of Meknès at Dkhissa village (ask for the Swiss woman with the horses if you get lost).

Hammam Zitouna (Map p256; Rue Djemma Zitouna; admission Dh10; men 7am-noon, women 12.30-8pm) A traditional hammam in the heart of the medina.

Walking Tour: Saunter through the Souqs

The walk described here is marked on the Meknès medina map (Map p256). The easiest route into the souqs is through the arch to the left of the Dar Jamaï Museum on the north side of Place el-Hedim. Plunge in and head northwards, and you will quickly find yourself amid souvenir stalls and carpet shops.

As you walk, notice the *qissariat* (covered markets) off to either side. A couple of these are devoted to textiles and carpets, which are noisily auctioned off on Sunday mornings. **Okchen Market**, in the last *qissaria* on the left before you reach the T-junction with Rue Najjarine, specialises in fine embroidery.

Turning right on Rue Najjarine takes you to the **Grande Mosquée** and **Medersa Bou Inania**. For now though, turn left on Rue Najjarine, passing stalls with *babouches* (leather slippers) in multicoloured rows. Just before you hit Rue Sekkakine, look out on the left for **Qissariat ad-Dahab**, the jewellery souq.

Exit the medina via Bab Berrima and follow the lane north, hugging the outside of the city wall. You'll pass a colourful **souq**, selling

THE WALK AT A GLANCE

Start Place el-Hedim
End Grande Mosquée
Distance 1km
Duration two hours

IMPERIAL CITIES, MIDDLE ATLAS & THE EAST

spices, herbs and nuts, and a lively **flea market**. On the other side of the lane, workshops turn out gigantic bakers' 'paddles', used for scooping bread out of the ovens.

Beyond them you'll find workers busily stuffing mattresses. A left turn here takes you northwest to the newly restored **mausoleum of Sidi ben Aïssa** (closed to non-Muslims). Sidi ben Aïssa gave rise to one of the more extreme religious fraternities in Morocco. His followers gather here in July from all over Morocco and further afield.

A right turn by the mattress stuffers leads back into the medina via Bab el-Jedid, the arch that shelters a couple of musical instrument shops. Turning left up Rue el-Hanaya, through a small **fruit and vegetable market**, you will eventually arrive at the **Berdaine Mosque** and, just beyond it, the city's northernmost gate, Bab Berdaine.

From here you can wend your way back down Rue Zaouia Nasseria (which becomes Rue Souika), passing tailors and the odd carpet showroom. With luck you'll emerge near the Grande Mosquée.

Tours

Compared to Fès and Marrakesh, the Meknès medina is fairly easy to navigate. If you are short of time, or if you wish to gain some local insight, book an official guide through the tourist office for Dh250 for a day. Calèche rides of this imperial city with a guide are easy to pick up from around the Mausoleum of Moulay Ismail – expect to pay around Dh120 for a couple of hours.

Festivals & Events

One of the largest *moussem*s (festivals in honour of saints) in Morocco takes place in May/June at the mausoleum of Sidi ben Aïssa, outside the medina walls. Once devotees would cheerfully digest anything from glass to snakes; nowadays, although you'll still come across the entranced, you'll only see the hardcore stuff in photos displayed around town. Still, it's a busy festival with *fantasia*s (musket-firing cavalry charges), fairs and the usual singing and dancing.

Sleeping

Most of the accommodation is located in the ville nouvelle, with the exception of a cluster of ultrabudget options and a few exquisite new riads.

MEDINA

Most of Meknès' cheapies cluster along along Rue Dar Smen and Rue Rouamzine in the old city. In the high season and during festivals, they can fill up quickly. To be on the safe side, get here early in the day or reserve a room.

Budget

Maroc Hôtel (Map p256; ☎ 035 530075; 7 Rue Rouamzine; s/d Dh60/120) Despite the inauspicious exterior, this is a budget gem. Friendly and quiet, rooms (with sinks) are freshly painted, and the shared bathrooms are clean. The great terrace and courtyard filled with orange trees add to the ambience.

Hôtel Regina (Map p256; ☎ 035 530280; 19 Rue Dar Smen; s/d/tr Dh60/90/120) The beds may sag a bit and the air is sometimes a little dusty and tired, but this is still a decent place for the money. The central courtyard opens the place up and wards off claustrophobia. Basic but adequate. Hot showers are available for Dh5.

Camping International d'Agdal (☎ 035 551828; camping per adult/child Dh17/12, plus per tent/car/caravan/camper Dh10/17/17/20) Barely 50m from Heri es-Souani, heading towards the Royal Palace (but poorly signed), this camp site has a great location and an attractive shady site. Hot showers are Dh7 and electricity Dh15. Facilities are well-maintained, and it has a small shop, café and restaurant.

Midrange & Top End

Maison d'Hôtes Riad (Map p256; ☎ 035 530542; www .riadMeknès.com in French; 79 Ksar Chaacha, Dar el-Kabir; r incl breakfast Dh500-800; ✖) Meknès' first riad is located amidst the ruins of the Palais Ksar Chaacha, the 17th-century imperial residence of Moulay Ismail. There are just six rooms, each individually and tastefully decorated in traditional style. There's an excellent restaurant on the ground floor, and small plunge pool. Follow the signs from Rue Sidi Nedjaror Bab er-Rih.

Ryad Bahia (Map p256; ☎ 035 554541; www.ryad -bahia.com; Derb Sekkaya, Tiberbarine; r incl breakfast Dh500-800; ✖) This charming little riad is just a stone's throw from Place el-Hedim. The alley entrance opens onto a courtyard, which also hosts a great restaurant. Stairs lead off in all directions to quaint, pretty rooms that have been carefully restored and decorated with fine attention to detail, from the bathroom fittings to the plush rugs. Breakfast can be taken on the roof terrace.

Palais Didi (Map p256; ☎ 035 558590; www.palais didi.com; 7 Dar el-Kbira; r/ste incl breakfast Dh1200/1500; 🖭 🗶) Didi is the fancy older sister to the other riads in the Meknès medina, and easily the largest. Five sumptuous suites and five romantic rooms are set around a sleek marble-tiled courtyard. Each is different, but they're all decked out with antique furniture in the luxurious rooms and deep tubs in the zellij bathrooms. There's a restaurant opening out onto the roof terrace giving great dining views over the Imperial City, worth visiting even if you're not staying here.

VILLE NOUVELLE
The ville nouvelle also has some decent budget options, as well as more expensive establishments. Among them is a clutch of places, notably those with popular bars, which are little more than brothels. Phone ahead to avoid being stuck with one of these.

Budget
Youth Hostel (Map p253; ☎ /fax 035 524698; Rue ben Nafi; dm incl breakfast Dh50; ⏰ 8am-10pm Sep-Jun, 8am-midnight Jul & Aug) In a quiet residential area, the youth hostel has dorms clustered around a shady courtyard. There's a small café, a communal kitchen and pretty simple bathroom facilities (hot showers Dh5). A YHI membership card is mandatory.

Hôtel Majestic (Map p260; ☎ 035 522035; 19 Ave Mohammed V; s/d Dh136/178, with bathroom Dh214/241) Built in the 1930s, this grand old lady carries her age well. There's a good mix of rooms (all have sinks) and there's plenty of character to go around, plus a peaceful patio and panoramic roof terrace. The managers are helpful and breakfast is included in the price.

Hôtel Palace (Map p260; ☎ 035 400468; fax 055 401431; 11 Rue Ghana; s/d Dh176/220) Looking very dour from the street, this hotel turns out to be surprisingly good value: large airy rooms with attached bathrooms, many with balcony. The mezzanine sofas give an extra option for chilling out.

Hôtel Ouislane (Map p260; ☎ 035 524828; 54 Rue Allal ben Abdallah; s/d Dh195/227) Another decent and clean option at the higher end of the budget bracket, the Ouislane has large airy rooms with attached bathrooms. It doesn't

set the world alight, but for the prices it's reasonable value.

Hôtel Touring (Map p260; ☎ 035 522351; 34 Blvd Allal ben Abdallah; s/d Dh65/90, with shower Dh85/100) This is a clean, if slightly austere, budget option. But for the price you can't really complain, as rooms generally come with bathrooms and (mostly) hot water. Some of the beds are ridiculously squashy and made for inducing backache.

Hôtel Toubkal (Map p260; ☎ 035 522218; 49 Ave Mohammed V; s/d Dh70/120) A real shoestring option this one. The comfy sofas in the lobby are the plushest feature, and give a slightly misleading impression. The rooms upstairs are compact and basic, let down by grubby bathrooms (squat toilets; hot showers Dh10).

Hôtel Excelsior (Map p260; ☎ 035 521900; 57 Ave des FAR; s/d Dh70/95, with shower Dh120/140) Nobody can complain this hotel does not have character, with its splashy floral fabrics and coloured bathroom fixtures. The place is clean – even the shared, Western-style toilet – but female travellers might find the place a little seedy.

Midrange & Top End
Hôtel de Nice (Map p260; ☎ 035 520318; nice _hotel@menara.ma; cnr Rue Accra & Rue Antserapé; s/d Dh318/386; 🗶) A brand new place, this hotel seems to be aiming for something a little higher than its price tag suggests. It pulls it off with aplomb – nicely decorated and well-sized rooms, with a bar and restaurant and good service. Get there before they decide to put the prices up.

Hôtel Akouas (Map p260; ☎ 035 515967; 27 Rue Emir Abdelkader; s/d Dh310/375; 🗶 🗨) This friendly, family-run three-star has a little more local colour than its rivals. Rooms, while not huge, are modern, comfortable and very fairly priced. The place also has a decent restaurant and a popular nightclub.

Hôtel Bab Mansour (Map p260; ☎ 035 525239; fax 055 510741; 38 Rue el-Emir Abdelkader; s/d Dh342/447; 🗶) It's a fine line between tasteful and characterless and, while comfortable enough, the Bab Mansour never quite seems to develop much of a personality – except in the shockingly bright bathroom suites. But it's well-run, with everything you'd expect in a tourist-class hotel.

Hôtel Rif (Map p260; ☎ 035 522591; fax 035 524428; Rue Accra; s/d Dh412/523; 🗶 🗨) From the outside, this hotel appears as a concrete-chocolate

MEKNÈS VILLE NOUVELLE

INFORMATION		
BMCE Main Branch	1	D4
Carlson Wagonlit	(see 26)	
Carting Info	2	B4
Croissant Rouge	3	B3
Cyber de Paris	4	B3
Délégation Régionale du Tourisme	5	A3
Librairie Dar al-Kitab al-Watani	6	B3
Main Post Office	7	A3
Night Pharmacy	(see 3)	
Quick Net	8	D4
RAM	9	B2

SLEEPING		
Hôtel Akouas	10	D4
Hôtel Bab Mansour	11	D4
Hôtel de Nice	12	B3
Hôtel Excelsior	13	D4
Hôtel Majestic	14	C3
Hôtel Ouislane	15	C4
Hôtel Palace	16	A3
Hôtel Rif	17	A3
Hôtel Toubkal	18	D4
Hôtel Touring	19	C3

EATING		
Le Dauphin	20	B2
Le Pub	21	B3
Les Palmiers d'Aziza	22	C2
Marhaba Restaurant	23	C3
Mo Di Niro	24	A3
Pâtisserie Agadir	25	A2
Pâtisserie Glacier Florence	26	A3
Pizzeria le Four	27	C3
Restaurant Gambrinus	28	A2
Restaurant Pizza Roma	29	B3
Supermarché Jinane	30	B2

DRINKING		
Alpha 56	31	C3
Café Opera	32	B2
Café Tulipe	33	C2

ENTERTAINMENT		
La Bahia	(see 17)	

TRANSPORT		
Centre-Est	34	B2

confection and, while the lobby area (with handy ATM) looks fresh, the plain rooms betray its 1970s origins. The funky pool has a splash of class, although as it's overlooked by the bar, it isn't the most female-friendly place for a dip.

Hôtel Transatlantique (Map p253; ☎ 035 525050; transat@iam.net.ma; Rue el-Merinyne; s/d Dh580/730; 🅿 🏊) A model of business-traveller modernism, the Transatlantique is unlikely to win any beauty contests. Rooms are plain but comfy; look instead to the large grounds with lovely gardens, tennis courts, pool and terrace café and you'll enjoy your stay more.

Zaki Hôtel (Map p253; ☎ 035 514146; Blvd Al Massira, Rte 21; s/d Dh1200/1400; 🅿 🏊) A slight trek from

town, the Zaki is Meknès' swankiest modern hotel, with ornate *zellij* and stucco in the lobby, and landscaped grounds. Rooms contain all the modern creature comforts you'd expect for the price, with the décor adding a twist of Moroccan flavour.

Eating

RESTAURANTS

Medina

Dar Sultana (Map p256; ☎ 035 535720; Derb Sekkaya, Tiberbarine; mains from Dh60) A small but perfectly formed restaurant in a converted medina house, Dar Sultan is perfect for romantic dining. Nicely decorated with henna paintings and fabrics (the tent canopy over the courtyard gives an intimate atmosphere),

IMPERIAL CITIES, MIDDLE ATLAS & THE EAST

the food is equally delightful – try the great spread of cooked Moroccan salads. Only the wine glasses on the table disappointed us, as no alcohol is served.

Restaurant Riad (Map p256; ☎ 055 530542; 79 Ksar Chaacha; set menus Dh110 & Dh160) While all the riads in the Meknès medina have lovely restaurants, this is probably the pick of the bunch. Set around a lush green courtyard, it's a great place to relax, and while the menu of salads, tajines and couscous is simple, it's all delicious and served with care and attention.

Restaurant Oumnia (Map p256; ☎ 035 533938; 8 Ain Fouki Rouamzine; set menu Dh65; ☺ 7am-10pm) This informal restaurant is inside a family home, just off the main drag of the Meknès medina, giving diners a warm welcome. There's just a three-course set menu, but it's a real winner, with delicious *harira* (lentil soup), salads and a choice of several tajines of the day.

Restaurant Mille et Une Nuits (Map p256; ☎ 035 559002; off Place el-Hedim; mains Dh45-85) Another converted medina house, this restaurant works hard to capture the spirit of its name. You'll find all the Moroccan standards and classics on a reasonably priced menu.

Restaurant Zitouna (Map p256; ☎ 055 530281; 44 Rue Djemma Zitouna; set menus from Dh110) In the heart of the medina, this grand establishment offers the same palatial restaurant style you'd find in Fès. Its ornate covered courtyard is done up with *zellij* and stucco, with several small salons for more restrained dining. Traditional Moroccan dishes are the order of the day, with *pastilla* (rich pidgeon or chicken pie) being something of a house speciality.

Ville Nouvelle

Le Pub (Map p260; ☎ 035 524247; 20 Blvd Allal ben Abdallah; mains Dh75-110; ☺ 11am-midnight) Something of a newcomer to the Meknès dining scene, Le Pub will give your tastebuds a lift if you're feeling tajine fatigue. The menu is firmly continental, with some good steaks and a few more unusual dishes like crab ravioli. The décor reflects the more upscale price menu, and you can wash everything down with a bottle of red from the local vineyards.

Le Dauphin (Map p260; ☎ 035 523423; 5 Ave Mohammed V; mains Dh75-90, set menu Dh130) It might have an uninspiring exterior, but the French dining room and lovely garden give this restaurant one of the nicest dining settings in town. The menu is fairly international, with notably good seafood. Alcohol is served.

Pizzeria le Four (Map p260; ☎ 035 520857; 1 Rue Atlas; pizzas Dh38-49, mains Dh65-85) The dark timber and whitewashed walls lend a suitably Italian atmosphere to this popular pizzeria. The pizzas are great, served up on wooden platters, and there's a decent selection of meat dishes, pasta and some good salads. Alcohol is served, but don't let that dull your senses to the cheeky 14% tax.

Restaurant Gambrinus (Map p260; ☎ 035 520258; Zankat Omar ibn Ass; mains around Dh50, set menu Dh70) A good place for Moroccan food in colourful surroundings in the ville nouvelle, which feels like something of a surprise when you discover that the original Gambrinus was a Czech immigrant in 1914. It's perennially popular with locals, who come for the good range of tajines.

CAFÉS, PATISSERIES & ICE-CREAM PARLOURS

When choosing sticky pastries in Meknès, don't overlook the *marakchia* – the local take on an éclair, full of cream and covered with gooey chocolate. Sticky but delicious! While the patisseries below are in the Ville Nouvelle, you can also get good pastries in the covered market on Place el-Hedim (see p262).

Les Palmiers d'Aziza (Map p260; 9 Rue de Tarfaya; ☺ 6am-midnight) While the fancy cakes and mouthwatering cookies are attractive, the draw here is the sunny, flowering garden, where tables are topped with umbrellas and a cooling fountain gurgles. It is the most pleasant place in Meknès for repose – for women and men alike.

Pâtisserie Glacier Florence (Map p260; Rue Ghana; set breakfast Dh12; ☺ 6.30am-7.30pm) A good place for a pastry breakfast on the hoof, washed down with a glug of coffee or a healthy fruit juice.

Pâtisserie Agadir (Map p260; cnr Ave Hassan II & Rue Antserapé; ☺ 8am-8pm) This place doesn't have a sign, but it's easily spotted by its piles of sticky pastries. Another good takeaway option, or a quick juice and sugar refill.

QUICK EATS

Sandwich stands (Map p256; Place el-Hedim; sandwiches around Dh20; ☺ 7am-10pm) This cluster of snack stands on the northwest corner of Place el-Hedim is ideal for a lunchtime snack, which can easily stretch into an afternoon of people-watching on the square. There's a wide range of grilled meat fillings, all topped out with generous handfuls of salad.

Snack Bounana (Map p256; Rue Najjarine; meals Dh40-45; ☺ 11am-10pm) A popular pit stop on the souq trail is in the square near the *medersa*. The setting, on the square with its green vines, is half the attraction – a chilled respite from the haggling and finagling with shop owners.

Marhaba Restaurant (Map p260; 23 Ave Mohammed V; tajines Dh25; ☺ noon-9pm) 'Never beaten on price' should be this place's proud motto. More a canteen than restaurant, it packs in everyone from lunchtime workers to gangs of schoolgirls. Food is cheap and tasty – a bowl of harira and a plateful of *makoda* (fried potato patties) will fill you up and still give change from Dh10. Superb.

Mo Di Niro (Map p260; 14 Rue Antserapé; pizzas from Dh30, burgers Dh15-20; ☺ noon-3pm & 5-10.30pm Tue-Sun) If Western-style fast food is what you're after, this hip, nonsmoking joint is the place to be. Pizzas, burgers, salads and plenty of chips top the menu.

Restaurant Pizza Roma (Map p260; Rue Accra; mains from Dh20) Although the names suggest that pizzas are the speciality here, you could do far worse than load up on a filling plate of rotisserie chicken with rice and chips. An unassuming place, it's popular with female diners.

SELF-CATERING
Covered Market (Map p256; Place el-Hedim) This is *the* place in Meknès to get fresh produce, and is virtually a tourist attraction in itself, with its beautifully arranged pyramids of sugary sweet delicacies, dates and nuts, olives and preserved lemons in glistening piles. There's also good-quality fruit and veg here, as well as meat – the faint-hearted may choose to avoid the automated chicken-plucking machines at the rear of the hall.

Central Market (Map p260; Ave Hassan II) A good place to shop in the ville nouvelle, with a variety of fresh food stalls, alcohol shops and various imported foodstuffs.

Supermarché Jinane (Map p260; cnr Ave Mohammed V & Rue de Paris; ☺ 7.30am-10pm) A large supermarket stocked with the all the essentials.

Drinking
CAFÉS
The ville nouvelle is the place to go for relaxed café culture, especially on and around Ave Mohammed V. Those below are female-friendly as far as Moroccan cafés go.

Café Tulipe (Map p260; Rue de Tarfaya) Just off the main road, the Tulipe has a large shady terrace and modern interior, one of the most pleasant cafés to kill an hour or two.

Café Opera (Map p260; 7 Ave Mohammed V) Airy and old-fashioned, this grand café is a classic – among the most popular for Moroccan men to sip their mint tea. Sitting outside people watching is a great breakfast pastime.

Alpha 56 (Map p260; Ave Mohammed V) Popular with the young and trendy, this place has a good selection of pastries. The downstairs can be a little smoky, in which case you can retreat to the salon upstairs.

BARS
Meknès certainly isn't lacking in bars, all in the ville nouvelle and largely grouped around Blvd Allal ben Abdallah. Many are pretty seedy affairs, designed for serious drinking and smoking, with women not at all welcomed.

Le Pub (Map p260; 20 Blvd Allal ben Abdallah; mains Dh75-110; ☺ 11am-midnight) This place is a notable exception, and unusual in having female bar staff. The closest you can get to a modern western bar – slump in a comfy chair, drink at the bar itself, or head downstairs to smoke a *sheesha* and catch some live music on weekends.

Hôtel Transatlantique (Map p253; Rue el-Merinyne) The safest options for women are often hotel bars – the most attractive of which is the outdoor terrace at the Transatlantique. Come at sunset for a breathtaking view and an exceedingly civilised experience.

La Coupole (Map p260; 2 Ave Hassan II) This restaurant bar is a lively place with a good atmosphere for a drink or three, although women may feel a little out of place.

Entertainment
NIGHTCLUBS
The most popular nightclubs are all in hotels. Things usually get going around midnight, on weekends.

La Bahia (Map p260; Hôtel Rif, Zankat Accra; admission incl 1 drink Dh50; ☺ show 9.30pm) Features an early-evening spectacle à la *1001 Nights*.

Nuit Blanche (Map p253; Zaki Hôtel, Blvd Al Massira, Rte 21; admission Dh100) Nice terrace café. Three floors, with everything from raï to Britney.

CINEMAS

Dawliz Cinema Complex (Map p253; ☎ 055 516552; Ave Moulay Ismail; admission Dh20-30) The best cinema in town with several modern, comfortable theatres, as well as billiards and a nice terrace café.

Shopping

While the souqs of Meknès aren't as extensive as those of Fès or Marrakesh, the lack of hassle makes them a great place to potter around looking for souvenirs. For details, see Walking Tour: Saunter through the Souqs, p257.

As always, the government-run **Centre Artisanale** (Map p256; Ave Zine el-Abidine Riad; 9am-1pm & 3-7pm Mon-Sat) is the place to go if you want to get an idea of what to look for and how much to spend. Quality is high but prices are fixed. Other shops are located just outside the Mausoleum of Moulay Ismail. There are also some good **pottery stalls** (Map p256) set up on the western side of Place el-Hedim.

Getting There & Away

BUS

The **CTM bus station** (Map p253; ☎ 035 522585; Ave des FAR) is about 300m east of the junction with Ave Mohammed V. The main bus station (Map p256) lies just outside Bab el-Khemis, west of the medina. It has a left-luggage office and the usual snack stands.

CTM departures include: Casablanca (Dh75, four hours, six daily) via Rabat (Dh45, 2½ hours, six daily), Fès and Marrakesh (Dh135, eight hours, daily), Tangier (Dh80, five hours, three daily), Oujda (Dh108, six hours, two daily) via Taza (Dh53, three hours), Er-Rachidia (Dh95, six hours, daily), and three buses to Nador (Dh110, six hours).

Slightly cheaper than CTM, other buses are available from the numbered windows in the main bus station:

No 5 Rabat and Casablanca (hourly 6am to 3pm)

No 6 Tangier (hourly 5am to 4pm), Tetouan (six daily), Chefchaouen (three daily), Ouezzane (five daily)

No 7 Fès (hourly 5am to 6pm), Taza (six daily), Oujda (hourly 4am to 11.30pm), Nador (five daily)

No 8 Moulay Idriss (hourly 8am to 6pm)

No 9 Marrakesh (seven daily)

TAXI

The principal grand taxi rank (Map p256) is a dirt lot next to the bus station at Bab el-Khemis. There are regular departures to Sidi Kacem (Dh12), Fès (Dh18, one hour), Ifrane (Dh20, one hour), Azrou (Dh23, one hour) and Rabat (Dh40, 90 minutes). Taxis leave less frequently for Ouezzane (Dh55, 90 minutes) and Taza (Dh70, 2½ hours). Grands taxis for Moulay Idriss (Dh10, 20 minutes) leave from opposite the Institut Français (Map p253) – this is also the place to organise round trips to Volubilis.

TRAIN

Although Meknès has two train stations, head for the more convenient **El-Amir Abdelkader** (Map p260; ☎ 035 522763), two blocks east of Ave Mohammed V. There are nine daily trains to Fès (Dh17, one hour), three of which continue to Taza (Dh55, 3½ hours) and Oujda (Dh124, 6½ hours). Eight go to Casablanca (Dh81, 3½ hours) via Rabat (Dh56, 2¼ hours). There are five direct services to Marrakesh (Dh154, seven hours). For Tangier, take a westbound train and change at Sidi Kacem (Dh80, four hours, depending on the connection).

Getting Around

BUS

Overcrowded city buses ply the route between the medina and ville nouvelle. The most useful are bus 2 (Bab el-Mansour to Blvd Allal ben Abdallah, returning to the medina along Ave Mohammed V) and bus 7 (Bab el-Mansour to the CTM bus station). Tickets are Dh2.

CAR

Two reliable car hire companies:

Bab Mansour Car (Map p253; ☎ /fax 055 526631; 8 Rue Idriss II)

Centre-Est (Map p260; ☎ 055 523455; 8 Rue Pasteur)

There's a handy car park just southwest of Bab el-Mansour, and another in the ville nouvelle near the intersection of Ave Idriss II and Ave des FAR.

TAXI

Urban grands taxis (silver-coloured Mercedes-Benz with black roofs) link the ville nouvelle and the medina, charging Dh2.50

per seat or Dh15 for the whole taxi. Pale-blue petits taxis use the meter: from El-Amir Abdelkader train station to the medina expect to pay around Dh8.

A more touristy way to get around the medina is by calèche, available for hire on Place el-Hedim and outside the Mausoleum of Moulay Ismail. They charge around Dh60 per hour.

AROUND MEKNÈS
Volubilis (Oualili)
وليلي

The Roman ruins of Volubilis sit in the midst of a fertile plan about 33km north of Meknès. The city is the best preserved archaeological site in Morocco and was declared a Unesco World Heritage site in 1997. Its most amazing features are its many beautiful mosaics preserved *in situ*.

Volubilis can easily be combined with nearby Moulay Idriss to make a fantastic day trip from Meknès.

HISTORY
Excavations indicate that the site was originally settled by Carthaginian traders in the 3rd century BC. One of the Roman Empire's most remote outposts, Volubilis was annexed in about AD 40. According to some historians, Rome imposed strict controls on what could, and could not, be produced in its North African possessions, according to the needs of the empire. One result was massive deforestation and the large-scale planting of wheat around Volubilis. At its peak, it is estimated that the city housed up to 20,000 people. The site's most impressive monuments were built in the 2nd and 3rd centuries AD, including the triumphal arch, capitol, baths and basilica.

As the neighbouring Berber tribes began to reassert themselves, so the Romans abandoned Volubilis around AD 280. Nevertheless, the city's population of Berbers, Greeks, Jews and Syrians continued to speak Latin right up until the arrival of Islam. Moulay Idriss found sanctuary here in the 8th century, before moving his capital to Fès. Volubilis continued to be inhabited until the 18th century, when its marble was plundered for Moulay Ismail's palaces in Meknès, and its buildings were

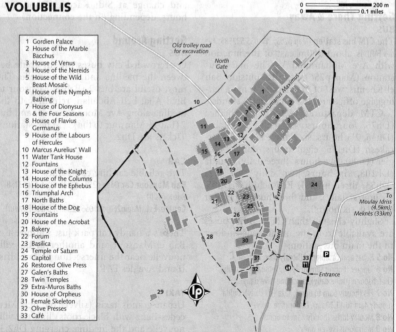

VOLUBILIS

0 — 200 m
0 — 0.1 miles

1 Gordien Palace
2 House of the Marble Bacchus
3 House of Venus
4 House of the Nereids
5 House of the Wild Beast Mosaic
6 House of the Nymphs Bathing
7 House of Dionysus & the Four Seasons
8 House of Flavius Germanus
9 House of the Labours of Hercules
10 Marcus Aurelius' Wall
11 Water Tank House
12 Fountains
13 House of the Knight
14 House of the Columns
15 House of the Ephebus
16 Triumphal Arch
17 North Baths
18 House of the Dog
19 Fountains
20 House of the Acrobat
21 Bakery
22 Forum
23 Basilica
24 Temple of Saturn
25 Capitol
26 Restored Olive Press
27 Galen's Baths
28 Twin Temples
29 Extra-Muros Baths
30 House of Orpheus
31 Female Skeleton
32 Olive Presses
33 Café

Old trolley road for excavation

North Gate

Decumanus Maximus

Fertassa

Oued

To Moulay Idriss (4.5km); Meknès (33km)

P

Entrance

finally felled by the Lisbon earthquake of 1722.

INFORMATION

Less than half of the 40-hectare **site** (admission Dh20, parking Dh5; ☉ 8am-sunset) has been excavated, and archaeologists continue to make the occasional exciting discovery, mostly now on display in the archaeology museum in Rabat (see p108). Notable by its absence is any sign of an amphitheatre.

Although parts of certain buildings are roped off, you are free to wander the site at will. Bar a couple of vague signboards, there's little in the way of signposting or information on what you're actually seeing. It's well worth considering taking a guide, especially if you're pressed for time. If you prefer to wander on your own, allow at least two hours to see the essentials, up to a full day for the real enthusiast.

In the heat of a summer day, the sun can be incredibly fierce at Volubilis, so bring a hat and plenty of water. Spring is the ideal season, when wildflowers blossom amid the abandoned stones, and the surrounding fields are at their greenest. The best time to visit is either first thing in the morning or late afternoon, when you're more likely to have the place to yourself, with just the guardian's donkey grazing among the ruins. At dusk, when the last rays of the sun light the ancient columns, Volubilis is at its most magical.

Guides

Official guides in Fès and Meknès are knowledgeable about this site, and most will be happy to accompany you for their normal daily rate. Alternatively, the guides that hang around the entrance conduct good one-hour tours for around Dh120. Most speak decent enough English to explain the site in detail.

SIGHTS

The better-known monuments are in the northern part of the site, although it's more convenient to start in the south. Once over the Oued Fertassa, the path leads onto the ridge and through the residential quarter. Although the least remarkable part of the site, the **olive presses** here indicate the economic basis of ancient Volubilis, much as the plentiful olive groves in the surrounding

area do today. Near the presses, the remains of a **female skeleton** (thought to be Muslim as she was buried facing Mecca) are entombed in one of the walls; she's now protected by an iron sheet.

Next to the House of Orpheus are the remains of **Galen's Baths**. Although much broken, they clearly show the highly developed underfloor heating used to heat this Roman hammam. Opposite the steam room are the communal toilets – where citizens could go about their business and have a chat at the same time.

The capitol, basilica and 1300-sq-metre forum are, typically, built on a high point. The **capitol**, dedicated to the trilogy of Jupiter, Juno and Minerva, dates back to AD 218; the **basilica** and **forum** lie immediately to its north. The reconstructed columns of the basilica are usually topped with storks' nests – an iconic Volubilis image if the birds are nesting at the time of your visit. Around the forum is a series of plinths carved with Latin inscriptions that would have supported statues of the great and good. Keep your eyes out for the carved stone drain-hole cover – an understated example of Roman civil engineering

Further north again, on the left just before the triumphal arch, are a couple more roped-off **mosaics**. One, in the **House of the Acrobat**, depicts an athlete being presented with a trophy for winning a desultor race, a competition in which the rider had to dismount and jump back on his horse as it raced along.

The marble **Triumphal Arch** was built in AD 217 in honour of Emperor Caracalla and his mother, Julia Domna. The arch, which was originally topped with a bronze chariot, was reconstructed in the 1930s, and the mistakes made then were rectified in the 1960s. The hillock to the east provides a splendid view over the entire site.

From the arch, the ceremonial road, **Decumanus Maximus**, stretches up the slope to the northeast. The houses lining it on either side contain the best mosaics on the site. The first on the far side of the arch is known as the **House of the Ephebus** and contains a fine mosaic of Bacchus in a chariot drawn by panthers.

Next along, the **House of the Columns** is so named because of the columns around the interior court – note their differing styles, which include spirals. Adjacent to this is the **House of the Knight** with its incomplete mosaic of Bacchus and Ariadne. The naked Ariadne has suffered somewhat from the attentions of admirers – or Muslim iconoclasts.

In the next couple of houses are excellent mosaics entitled the **Labours of Hercules** and **Nymphs Bathing**. The former is almost a circular comic strip, recounting the Twelve Labours. Several of Hercules' heroic feats were reputed to have occurred in Morocco, making him a popular figure at the time.

The best mosaics are saved until last. Cross the Decumanus Maximus and head for the lone cypress tree, which marks the **House of Venus**. There are two particularly fine mosaics here, appropriately with semi-romantic themes. The first is the **Abduction of Hylas by the Nymphs**, an erotic composition showing Hercules' lover Hylas being lured away from his duty by two beautiful nymphs. The second mosaic is **Diana Bathing**. The goddess was glimpsed in her bath by the hunter Acteon, who she turned into a stag as punishment. Acteon can be seen sprouting horns, about to be chased by his own pack of hounds – the fate of mythical peeping toms everywhere. A third mosaic from this house, of Venus in the waves, can be seen in the Tangier museum (p162).

GETTING THERE & AWAY

The simplest and quickest way to get here from Meknès is to hire a grand taxi for the return trip. A half-day outing should cost Dh350, with a couple of hours at the site and a stop at Moulay Idriss.

The cheaper alternative is to take a shared grand taxi from near Meknès' Institut Français to Moulay Idriss (Dh10) and then hire a grand taxi to take you to Volubilis (Dh36). If the weather isn't too hot, it's a lovely 45-minute walk between Moulay Idriss and Volubilis. Don't leave getting back to Moulay Idriss til too late in the afternoon or you could be stranded. There are no buses to Volubilis.

Moulay Idriss   مولاي ادريس

Moulay Idriss, about 4.5km from Volubilis, is named for Morocco's most revered saint, a great-grandson of the Prophet Mohammed and the founder of the country's first real dynasty.

Moulay Idriss fled Mecca in the late 8th century AD in the face of persecution at the hands of the recently installed Abbasid caliphate, which was based in Baghdad. Idriss settled at Volubilis, where he converted the locals to Islam, and made himself their leader. From there he went on to establish Morocco's first imperial dynasty.

The picturesque whitewashed town of Moulay Idriss, nestled in a cradle of verdant mountains, is one of the country's most important pilgrimage sites. The place has been open to non-Muslims for the past 70 years or so. The embargo of non-Muslims staying overnight in the town has recently been lifted, but mosques and shrines are still off-limits. Saturday is market day – the liveliest time to be in Moulay Idriss and the easiest day to get here.

SIGHTS

Although this twin-hill town is a veritable maze of narrow lanes and dead ends, it is not hard to find the few points of interest. The first is the **Mausoleum of Moulay Idriss**, the object of veneration and the reason for the country's greatest annual *moussem* in late August. An important pilgrimage for many, including the royals, it is accompanied by *fantasias*, markets, singing and dancing.

From the main road (where buses and grands taxis arrive), head uphill and bear right where the road forks. You'll quickly find yourself on a wide square, lined with cafés and cheap food stands – a great place to sit and watch the pace of life. At the top of the square is the entrance to the mausoleum via a three-arched gateway at the top of some steps, surrounded by shops selling religious goods to pilgrims. Not far inside there's a barrier, beyond which non-Muslims cannot pass. Moulay Ismail created this pilgrimage site by building the mausoleum and moving the body of Moulay Idriss, in a successful attempt to rally the support of the faithful. It's said locally that five pilgrimages here equals one haj to Mecca.

From here, head up into the maze of streets to find your way to a couple of vantage points that give good panoramic views of the mausoleum, the town and the surrounding country. Plenty of guides will offer their services – you can get an informative, entertaining tour for as little as Dh30.

If you don't feel like being guided, head back to the fork and take the road heading uphill, signposted to the Municipalité. Near the top of the hill, just before the Agfa photo shop, take the cobbled street to the right. As you climb up you'll notice the only **cylindrical minaret** in Morocco. The green tiles spell out in stylised script the standard Muslim refrain: *la illah illa Allah* (there is no god but Allah). At the top ask a local for the **grande terrasse** or **petite terrasse**. These terraces provide vantage points high above the mausoleum and most of the town.

SLEEPING & EATING

The main battery of cheap eateries and cafés is in the main street above the bus station.

Maison d'Hôte Slima (☎ 035 544793; near Les Trois Boules d'Or; s/d Dh100/200) The first hotel to open to take advantage of non-Muslims being allowed to stay in Moulay Idriss has got off on the right foot with this great budget option. The paint was still wet when we visited, with clean bright rooms (all with shower and toilet) and enthusiastic management. You can get breakfast here for Dh30. Head uphill from the Mausoleum following the signs to the View Panoramique – you can't miss it.

Les Trois Boules d'Or (View Panoramique, meals from Dh25; ☺ closes late afternoon) This café-restaurant has the best views over Moulay Idriss, and is a good place to finish your walking tour, with a mint tea or cold drink, although the eating options can be a bit limited.

Restaurant Baraka (☎ 035 544184; 22 Aïn Smen-Khiber; mains Dh60-70; ☺ lunch only) The town's only proper restaurant caters mainly to large tour groups – when a coach turns up, you'll understand why there are so many waiters lolling aimlessly around. Portions are huge and filling, with the couscous with fruit topping the menu.

The cheap food stands around the main square are all good for a quick snack.

GETTING THERE & AWAY

Grands taxis (Dh10, 20 minutes) to Moulay Idriss leave Meknès from outside the Institut Français, and buses (Dh6) leave from the Meknès bus station every hour from 8am to 6pm. Note that it can be extremely difficult to get out of Moulay Idriss after about 3pm.

If you have your own transport, you might consider continuing to Fès via Nzala-des-Béni-Ammar, or to Meknès via the village of El-Merhasiyne. Both routes have wonderful views and eventually join back up with the main roads. As the road surfaces are very rough, these drives are really only possible in summer unless you have a 4WD.

MIDDLE ATLAS
الأطلس المتوسط

IFRANE   إفران
pop 10,000

As your vehicle pulls into Ifrane, where plains start to rise up into the Middle Atlas, you could be forgiven a momentary double take. Are we in... Switzerland? It certainly doesn't feel like anywhere else in Morocco.

The French built Ifrane in the 1930s, deliberately trying to recreate an alpine-style resort. It has neat red-roofed houses, blooming flowerbeds and lake-studded parks, all kept impeccably tidy. It bursts with activity in the winter, when the affluent flock here to ski, and the hoi polloi come for the pure fun of throwing snowballs at each other. Outside the holiday season, Ifrane's population is boosted by the rich, trendy students of the town's prestigious Al-Akhawayn University.

Orientation

The main road from Meknès is called Blvd Mohammed V as it runs through Ifrane from west to east. This is where you will find the bus station, west of the centre, and the tourist office, at the intersection with Ave des Tilluels. Most of the cafés and hotels are clustered in the centre along two parallel roads a 10-minute walk to the south, Rue de la Cascade and Ave de la Poste. East of the centre, they intersect with Ave Hassan II, the main road out of town to the north (and to Fès).

Information

BMCE (Ave de la Marche Verte) One of several banks with ATMs on this road.
Pharmacie Mischliffen (Rue de la Cascade)
Post office (Ave de la Poste)
Tourist Office (☎ 035 566821; fax 035 566822; Ave Prince Moulay Abdallah; ☺ 8.30am-noon & 2.30-6.30pm Mon-Fri)

Sights

The campus of Al-Akhawayn University is at the northern end of town, a squeaky-clean showcase of Moroccan education. It was founded in 1995 by Morocco's King Hassan II and King Fahd of Saudi Arabia and includes in its lofty aims the promotion of tolerance between faiths. For now, only the rich and beautiful need apply – the car parks are full of flash cars, and the air trills with the most fashionable of mobile-phone ringtones. Lessons in English are based on the American system and there are US staff and exchange students. You can wander into the well-kept grounds – weekday afternoons are the best, as there are plenty of students who are usually willing to show you around.

Ifrane's other landmark is the **stone lion** that sits on a patch of grass near the Hôtel Chamonix. It was carved by a German soldier during WWII, when Ifrane was used briefly as a prisoner of war camp. Having your picture taken with the lion is something of a ritual for day-trippers.

Sleeping

Hotel prices in Ifrane reflect the town's affluence.

Hôtel Perce-Neige (☎ 035 566404; fax 035 567746; Rue des Asphodelles; s/d Dh343/437) Ifrane's prettiest accommodation option is about 200m southeast of the centre. The rooms could be a bit bigger, but they're very comfortable and come with satellite TV and bathrooms. The licensed restaurant is a good dining option (set menus Dh120). The shop in the lobby often sells paintings by local artists.

Hôtel Chamonix (☎ 035 566028; fax 035 566826; Ave de la Marche Verte; s/d with half board Dh410/550) This three-star is well maintained and centrally located. Rooms are bright and clean, with attached bathrooms, if a little bland. There's a decent restaurant and bar (which turns into a nightclub on weekends), and the hotel can rent out ski equipment.

Hôtel les Tilleuls (☎ 035 566658; fax 035 566079; cnr Ave des Tilluels & Rue de la Cascade; s/d from Dh260/320) The cheapest hotel in Ifrane is this old, comfortable institution. It's a bit tired and could do with a spring clean. If you want to escape your room you can head for the 'tequila bar'.

Hôtel Mischliffen (☎ 035 566607; www.concorde-hotels.com; 🅿 🔲) Set in pine and oak forests overlooking Ifrane from the north, this oversized ski lodge was closed for extensive renovations when we visited. Last time around it claimed to be five stars, and the rework should bring plenty of comfort, as well as doubling the hotel's capacity. Expect rates to start at around Dh700/900 for a single/double.

If you wish to camp, the leafy **camp site** (Blvd Mohammed V; camping per person Dh7, plus per car/tent/camper Dh8/15/30; 🕑 closed winter) is just west of the bus station.

Eating

Several cafés and cheap eats cluster around the bus station area, where you'll also find the market for fresh produce.

Rendez-vous des Skiers (Ave de la Marche Verte; mains around Dh60; 🕑 10am-10pm) Near the Hôtel Chamonix, this is a good, no-nonsense sort of a place. The menu is standard Moroccan, but the restaurant prides itself on its Fès soup, and local Middle Atlas trout cooked in a variety of ways, all tasty.

Cookie Craque (☎ 055 567171; Ave des Tilleuls; pizza Dh50-60, crêpes Dh24-40; 🕑 7am-midnight) This wildly popular café has a wonderful choice of sweets, savouries and ice cream to take away or eat in. The toasted sandwiches and filled crêpes are the biggest draw, although there are plenty of more substantial meals on the menu. In winter, get in quick to nab the seats by the log fire.

Café Restaurant la Rose (☎ 055 566215; 7 Rue de la Cascade; mains around Dh45, set menu Dh70) The attractive La Rose offers an excellent-value set menu. Always busy with day-trippers, this is another place that's good for dining on the local trout.

Le Crouistillant (Rue de la Cascade) More of a straight café, Le Crouistillant is a good place for a caffeine refill and a sticky pastry or two, opposite Café Restaurant La Rose. If you use the toilets, take some spare change to tip the vigilant cleaning staff.

Getting There & Away

The main bus and grand taxi stations are next to the market, west of the town centre.

Each morning, CTM buses leave for Marrakesh (Dh125, eight hours) via Beni Mellal (Dh60, four hours), and for Casablanca (Dh95, 4½ hours) via Meknès (Dh24, one hour) and Rabat (Dh65, 3½ hours).

Non-CTM buses are more frequent. There are hourly buses to Fès (Dh15, one hour) and Azrou (Dh6, 25 minutes). Less frequent are services to Beni Mellal (Dh52, four hours), Marrakesh (Dh95, eight hours) and Midelt (Dh38, 3½ hours).

There are plentiful grands taxis to Fès (Dh20), Meknès (Dh22) and Midelt (Dh50), as well as Azrou (Dh5).

LAKE CIRCUIT (ROUTE DES LACS)

A pretty diversion north of Ifrane is the lake circuit around **Dayet Aoua**. Signposted off the main Fès road 17km north of Ifrane, the route winds for 60km through the lake country between the P24 and P20. If you don't have your own vehicle, hiring a grand taxi in Ifrane for a tour of a couple of hours should cost around Dh250. That said, the joy of the area is to get out and walk along the lake shore and enjoy the tranquillity of the scenery. This is an area made for mountain bikers.

Dayet Aoua is surrounded by woodlands, and the whole area is notably rich in birdlife. Keep an eye out in particular for raptors, including booted eagles, black and red kites and harriers. The lake itself attracts significant numbers of ducks and waders, including crested coot, woodpeckers, tree creepers and nuthatches, which flit among the trees around the southeastern end of the lake.

The lake is a popular picnic destination for families at the weekend, but during the week you'll get the place largely to yourself. Beyond Dayet Aoua, the road loops east and then south, skirting past Dayet Ifrah and the even smaller lake of Dayet Hachlat. The road is decent, but is liable to be snowbound in winter.

If you want to linger longer, there are two good sleeping options at Dayet Aoua. Advance reservations for both are recommended during holiday periods.

An attractive French-run chalet sitting on the northern shore of the lake, **Hôtel Restaurant Chalet du Lac** (☎ /fax 035 663197; s/d with half board Dh330/570) has simple rooms with shared facilities, but the restaurant (mains Dh80 to Dh100, set menu Dh190) is the big draw, a reason in itself to make it out here. The four-course menu is a great splurge for lunch, followed by a walk around the lake to burn it off.

Le Gîte Dayet Aoua (☎ 035 604880; www.gite -dayetaoua.com in French; r incl breakfast from Dh300, s/ d with half board Dh350/540; mains Dh60-70) This is another appealingly rustic and quiet place east of Dayet Aoua. There are five pretty rooms, all with showers and hot water, and a cheerful licensed dining room serving wholesome country cooking. Prices vary greatly according to occupancy and meals. The *gîte* is also a great source of local information for hiking, and can hire out tents (Dh50), guides (Dh250) and horses (Dh300) if you're tempted to really get exploring (all prices per day).

AZROU   آزرو

pop 50,000

Travelling south from Fès to the cheerful Berber town of Azrou you really find yourself starting to head deeper into the Middle Atlas. Its cooler climes support plentiful pine and cedar forests, making it a relaxing spot to wind down if you've had too much of big cities.

Azrou hosts one of the region's largest weekly souqs, and is particularly known for its Berber carpets, so timing your visit for market day (Tuesday) is a good idea. There's not much else to do in town, although a museum of the Middle Atlas was under construction when we recently visited. If you're feeling energetic, the surrounding countryside has some tempting day walks that take in the mountain air and great views. You might even spot a few of the local Barbary apes.

Orientation

Azrou (Great Rock) takes its name from the outcrop marking the town's western boundary. The big new Ennour mosque in front of it provides another handy landmark. The bus station and taxi stands lie to the north, and some cafés and banks are further north along Blvd Hassan II. Other hotels, banks and eateries are southeast of here on and around Place Mohammed V.

Information

BMCE (Place Mohammed V) Bureau de change and ATM.
Cyber Abridn (Place Mohammed V; per hr Dh6; ☽ 9am-midnight)
Cyber Kawtar (Bus station; per hr Dh6; ☽ 9am-midnight)
Pharmacie Sakhra (Place Mohammed V)
Post office (Blvd Prince Héritier Sidi Mohammed)

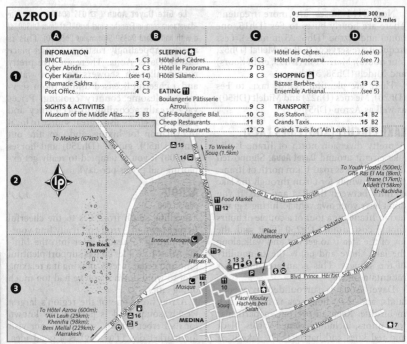

AZROU

INFORMATION	
BMCE..1 C3	
Cyber Abridn....................................2 C3	
Cyber Kawtar..............................(see 14)	
Pharmacie Sakhra..........................3 C3	
Post Office.......................................4 C3	

SIGHTS & ACTIVITIES	
Museum of the Middle Atlas......5 B3	

SLEEPING	
Hôtel des Cèdres............................6 C3	
Hôtel le Panorama..........................7 D3	
Hôtel Salame...................................8 C3	

EATING	
Boulangerie Pâtisserie	
Azrou..9 C3	
Café-Boulangerie Bilal................10 C3	
Cheap Restaurants........................11 B3	
Cheap Restaurants........................12 C2	

Hôtel des Cèdres.........................(see 6)	
Hôtel le Panorama.......................(see 7)	

SHOPPING	
Bazaar Berbère.............................13 C3	
Ensemble Artisanal....................(see 5)	

TRANSPORT	
Bus Station....................................14 B2	
Grands Taxis..................................15 B2	
Grands Taxis for 'Ain Leuh.........16 B3	

Sleeping

For its size, Azrou has a surprising number of sleeping options.

Hôtel Salame (☎ 035 562562; salame_hotel@ yahoo.fr; Place Moulay Hachem ben Salah; s/d Dh50/100) Hidden behind an inauspicious front, this hotel is a pleasant surprise. Small, cute rooms are nicely presented with a smattering of traditional Berber decoration, and you will be made welcome by the friendly staff. Shared bathrooms are spotless, with 24 hour hot showers (Dh10).

Hôtel des Cèdres (☎ 035 562326; Place Mohammed V; s/d/tr Dh75/104/161) The front of house is a large and slightly masculine café, but rooms upstairs are a little more welcoming, decent-sized and clean – a few have balconies looking to the mountains. Bathroom facilities are shared and adequate (hot showers Dh10).

Hôtel le Panorama (☎ 035 562010; www.hotel panorama.web.com; s/d Dh280/342) Built in grand alpine-chalet style, Azrou's most comfortable hotel is in a quiet wooded spot a short walk northeast of town. Staff are friendly and efficient. Rooms are compact and modern, with private bathrooms and balconies.

Hôtel Azrou (☎ 035 562116; Rte de Khenifra; s/d with shower Dh91/117, with shower & toilet Dh140/168) A decent midrange place on the south side of town, this is a good, laidback choice. It has comfy rooms – plus a bar, restaurant and ivy-covered terrace. If you fancy a game, the staff are the local *petanque* champions.

Youth Hostel (☎ 035 563733; dm Dh20) The youth hostel is about 500m east of town, set back slightly from the road. The facilities are pretty basic with cold showers (what did you expect for Dh20?), and you need a YHI membership card to check in.

Gîte Ras El Ma (Gîte de Charme; ☎ 035 560008; http://giterasalma.ifrance.com in French; r per person incl half board Dh200) About 8km north of Azrou on the Ifrane road, this guesthouse is run with loving care by its husband-and-wife owners. Rooms are attractive, with slightly rustic decoration. It's an ideal base for day walks in the region, from which you can return at the end of the day for a communal meal in the traditionally decorated salon, in front of a log fire.

Eating

The best cheap eats are in three main areas – strung along Blvd Moulay Abdelkader south of the bus station, and clustered around Place Hassan II and Place Moulay Hachem ben Salah. You can find all the trusty favourites here – rotisserie chicken, brochettes and steaming bowls of *harira*. You should be able to fill up for around Dh25.

Hôtel le Panorama (☎ 035 562010; set menu Dh130) This midrange hotel offers Azrou's nicest dining surroundings. As well as the usual tajines and the like, the menu also contains local river trout, pan-grilled and served up with rice or fried potatoes. Alcohol is served.

Hôtel des Cèdres (☎ /fax 035 562326; Place Mohammed V; mains around Dh50) This hotel has an attached restaurant, with a good range of tajines. Rabbit and prune tajine is an unusual, but tasty, local recipe.

Café Boulangerie Bilal (Place Mohammed V) A large café with good sandwich and pastry options, plus fruit juices and the occasional ice cream for the hot weather.

Boulangerie Pâtisserie Azrou (Place Hassan II) This café is another smarter option, with a quiet seating area upstairs, which women might appreciate.

Shopping

The weekly souq is held on Tuesday about 1.5km northeast of town. Here you'll witness Berber women from the surrounding villages haggling with dealers over the flat-weave carpets, as well as fresh produce and other market goods. Take care if it's been raining though, as the souq area can easily turn into a muddy quagmire. At other times, you'll find carpets and handicrafts aplenty in the stores around Place Mohammed V and in the medina.

Bazaar Berbère (7 Place Mohammed V; ☺ 10am-6pm) This is one of several shops along this stretch of road with a good selection of Middle Atlas rugs, including those of the seminomadic Beni M'Guild Berbers.

Ensemble Artisanal (Blvd Mohammed V; ☺ 8.30am-noon & 2.30-6.30pm) Here you'll find more Berber rugs, plus some interesting carved cedar and juniper wood. The planned Museum of the Middle Atlas will be next door.

Getting There & Away

Azrou is a crossroads, with one axis heading northwest to southeast from Meknès to Er-Rachidia, and the other northeast to Fès and southwest to Marrakesh.

BUS

CTM (☎ 035 562002) offers daily departures from the bus station on Blvd Moulay Abdelkader to Beni Mellal (Dh55, three hours), Casablanca (Dh100, six hours), Fès (Dh27, two hours), Marrakesh (Dh125, seven hours) and Meknès (Dh25, 1½ hours).

Other slightly cheaper companies have frequent daily departures to Fès (Dh18),

---

WALKS IN THE AZROU AREA

Azrou sits on the edge of some of the prettiest parts of the Middle Atlas – ideal for throwing a few things in your daypack and setting out for a hike. The area is known for its Barbary apes (see p428), and you might be lucky enough to spot a troupe foraging in the woods. To reach the best walking spots, however, you'll need some wheels to get yourself started.

'Ain Leuh is a pretty village 25km southwest of Azrou. The drive here is through thick cedar forest, so you might just be tempted to stop your vehicle anywhere and hit the trail. Instead, take in the large Wednesday weekly souq (the best day to get public transport), which attracts market-goers from around the region, particularly from the seminomadic Beni M'Guild tribe. It's a pleasant climb through the rough streets of flat-roofed houses to a waterfall in the hills above.

Around 20km south of 'Ain Leuh, an even more picturesque walk leads to the waterfalls at the **Sources de l'Oum-er-Rbia**. Leave the road at **Lac Ouiouane** and follow the path down past a number of farmhouses to a small valley, where a bridge crosses the Rbia river. From here, it's about a 15-minute walk to the gorge where several dozen springs break out of the rocks to form a series of waterfalls. There are a couple of cafés where you can take a rest.

It's possible to incorporate the above into a much longer circuit trek of up to six days from 'Ain Leuh. **Moulay Abdellah Lahrizi** (☎ 062 190889; lahrizi37@yahoo.co.uk) of the Association des Guides in Azrou can help organise logistics and guides.

Meknès (Dh16), Ifrane (Dh5), Midelt (Dh30) and Er-Rachidia (Dh70).

TAXI

The grand taxi lot is down a stepped path below the bus station. Regular taxis go to Fès (Dh25, one hour), Meknès (Dh26, one hour), Khenifra (Dh24, one hour), Ifrane (Dh8, 10 minutes) and Midelt (Dh40, 90 minutes). Those for 'Ain Leuh (Dh12, 20 minutes) wait beside the Shell petrol station on the main road out to the southwest.

MIDELT   ميدلت
pop 35,000

Although an unassuming sort of place, Midelt could make a good argument for being the centre of Morocco. It sits in a no-man's land between the north and the south, stuck between the Middle and the High Atlas. Coming from the north in particular, the landscape seems dry and barren but it offers some breathtaking views, especially of the Eastern High Atlas which seem to rise out of nowhere. But few people are likely to stop and listen to

Midelt's argument, as it's the sort of place you zoom through on the way to somewhere else.

For those who do stop (and it's a handy break between Fès or Meknès and Er-Rachidia and the south) Midelt can make a good base for some off-piste exploring, most notably the mountain Jebel Ayachi, which can be climbed without technical experience.

Midelt consists of little more than one main street (Ave Mohammed V in the north, which becomes Ave Hassan II to the south), a modest souq and a number of oversized restaurants, which cater to the tourist buses whistling through on their way south.

Information

BMCI (Ave Hassan II) One of several banks with ATMs on this street.

Complexe Touristique Timnay Inter-Cultures

(☎ 035 360188; timnay@iam.net.ma; Rte de Zaidia) The best source of information – including trekking guides and 4WD rental – in the Eastern High Atlas, about 20km north of Midelt.

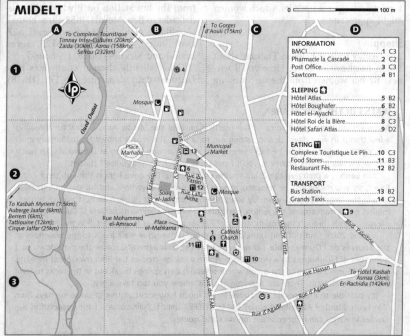

MIDELT

0 ———————— 100 m

To Complexe Touristique Timnay Inter-Cultures (20km); Zaïda (30km); Azrou (158km); Sefrou (232km)

To Gorges d'Aouli (15km)

Mosque

Oued Outoul

Place Marhaba

Mosque

Ave Mohammed V

Ave Zayane Zammouri

Municipal Market

Rue ibn Yassin

Souq el-Jadid

Rue Lalla Aicha

Rue Mohammed el-Amraoui

Place el-Mahkama

Catholic Church

Ave de la Marche Verte

Blvd Palestine

Ave Hassan II

Rue d'Agadir

Ave des FAR

To Kasbah Myriem (1.5km); Auberge Jaafar (6km); Berrem (6km); Tattiouine (12km); Cirque Jaffar (25km)

To Hôtel Kasbah Asmaa (3km); Er-Rachidia (142km)

INFORMATION	
BMCI	1 C3
Pharmacie la Cascade	2 C2
Post Office	3 C3
Sawtcom	4 B1

SLEEPING	
Hôtel Atlas	5 B2
Hôtel Boughafer	6 B2
Hôtel el-Ayachi	7 C3
Hôtel Roi de la Bière	8 C3
Hôtel Safari Atlas	9 D2

EATING	
Complexe Touristique Le Pin	10 C3
Food Stores	11 B3
Restaurant Fès	12 B2

TRANSPORT	
Bus Station	13 B2
Grands Taxis	14 C2

Pharmacie la Cascade (☎ 055 360877; ☼ 8.30am-8pm)

Post office (off Ave Hassan II) South of the centre.

Sawtcom (Rue Ezzerqutouni; per hr Dh6; ☼ 8am-midnight) Internet access.

Sights

KASBAH MYRIEM

If you're in the mood for carpets, this **workshop** (☎ 035 582443; ☼ 8am-noon & 2-5.30pm Mon-Thu & Sat), about 1.5km out of town, is worth a look. Run by Franciscan nuns as a charitable organisation, it assists local Berber women to develop their trades of embroidery and weaving. The workshop provides looms and materials, as well as a simple place to work. Local Berber girls – aged 15 or so – come here in order to learn these skills from more experienced women. Literacy lessons are also offered to the girls. The works are for sale; prices are high, but so is the quality. Follow the signs from the main road, then enter behind the clinic. The workshop is also known as the Atelier de Tissages et Borderie.

While you are here, you may wish to peek into the **monastery** (☼ services 7.15am daily & 10am Sun), which is home to five Franciscan monks. The grounds and chapel are a peaceful place to collect your thoughts. Ring the bell at the gate to the right of the workshop.

KASBAH DES NOYERS

The village of **Berrem**, 6km west of Midelt, is also known as the Kasbah des Noyers for its ancient walnut trees shading the environs. There's not much going on here, but the quaint village – with its colourful mosque and ancient earthen walls – makes a good destination for a day-hike from Midelt. As you wander along the narrow, dusty paths and hear the call of the imam, you will wonder if you have walked 6km across the terrain or 500 years through time. Follow the main path through the kasbah to the scenic overlook of the **Gorges des Berrem**. The Auberge Jaafar (below) is about 500m past the village. Hiring a grand taxi from Midelt costs about Dh30.

Sleeping

Auberge Jaafar (☎ 035 583415; fax 055 583514; Berrem; r Dh225; ☒) This lovely kasbah-style complex is about 6km west of Midelt, just past the village of Berrem. Ideally you need a vehicle to get here, but you might not want to leave once you've checked in. Charming rooms are set up around tiled terraces and blooming courtyards. All facilities are shared, but everything is clean and well run. Order during the day if you're going to eat in. The hotel can also organise local excursion.

Hôtel Atlas (☎ 035 582938; 3 Rue Mohammed el-Amraoui; s/d Dh60/90) This tiny pension is something of a gem, run by a friendly Berber family who keep the place shipshape. Rooms are predictably simple, but spotless, as are the shared bathrooms with squat toilets (hot showers Dh10). There's a nice terrace, where you can fill up on home-cooked food.

Hôtel Roi de la Bière (☎ /fax 035 582675; 1 Ave des FAR; s/d/tr Dh100/150/200, with bathroom Dh120/200/300) Despite the name, there's a disappointing lack of the amber nectar here. Still, rooms are decent, the showers are hot, and there's a handy restaurant.

Hôtel Safari Atlas (☎ 035 580069; safariatlas _hotel@yahoo.fr; 118 Blvd Palestine; s/d/tr incl breakfast Dh192/241/274) East of the centre is this relatively new midrange hotel with tidy, spacious rooms, all with private bathrooms, wooden furniture and televisions. The décor hints at traditional. The hotel also rents out 4WDs for excursions in the region.

Hôtel Boughafer (☎ 035 583099; hotel_cafe _restau_boughafer@yahoo.fr; 7 Ave Mohammed V; s/d Dh50/80, with shower Dh84/138, with shower & toilet Dh164/208) Over three floors, this hotel tries to be all things to all budgets, from comfy rooms with wood furniture and Western bathrooms on the 1st floor, to more basic and darker rooms on the top floor. All of the rooms are clean, however, and the restaurant and roof terrace are added benefits.

Hôtel el-Ayachi (☎ 035 582161; hotelayachi@ caramail.com; Rue d'Agadir; s/d Dh279/340) One of Midelt's older hotels, as described by its 1950s exterior, the Ayachi lives off the tour groups. Rooms are a bit shabby, along with the slightly musty bathrooms.

Hôtel Kasbah Asmaa (☎ 035 580405; fax 055 583945; s/d Dh300/350; ☒ ☒) About 3km south of Midelt, this hotel is hard to miss – the kasbah-styled exterior announces that you're on the road south. Another tour group staple, it has comfy modern rooms and an inviting pool at the bottom of the property, far away from the rooms so as not to be overlooked. The licensed restaurant, contained in several traditionally decorated salons, is worth eating at for nonguests.

Complexe Touristique Timnay Inter-Cultures (☎ 035 360188; timnay@iam.net.ma; Rte de Zaïdia; camping per person Dh18, plus per tent/car/camper Dh15/15/25, bungalows per person Dh50-80, Berber tents per person Dh25, homestay per person Dh70; ▣) About 20km north of Midelt, this centre is a joint Moroccan-Belgian venture aimed at developing local tourism. Accommodation is simple – it works best with your own tent – but the Camping Timnay (as it's known locally) is a great base for exploring the region, as you can organise treks and guides from here. For the evenings, there's a restaurant and bar. To get here, take a grand taxi headed for Zaïdia and ask the driver to let you out at Timnay.

Eating

As usual, cheap eats and snacks are plentiful in the area around the bus station, where there's also a produce market. The general stores opposite Hôtel Roi de la Bière are good for provisions.

Restaurant Fès (☎ 062 057754; Rue Lalla Aicha; set menu Dh70) Serving up hearty portions of traditional cooking, this place is ever-popular. The menu never seems to change – salad or soup, tajine and fruit – and is always simple but fresh. The vegetarian tajine is rare in not seeming to contain any lurking bits of meat.

Complexe Touristique le Pin (☎ 035 583550; Ave Hassan II; mains Dh50-60, buffet Dh70; ☯ noon-5pm all year & 7-10pm Apr-Aug) This large restaurant draws the coach groups (beware the lunchtime crush), but you can easily escape them in the garden, and the large turnover of covers ensures fresh meals, all served in generous portions.

Getting There & Away

Midelt's bus station is off Ave Mohammed V. CTM services mostly run at night. There's an evening departure to Casablanca (Dh110, seven hours) via Rabat (Dh85, 6½ hours), and to Rissani (Dh70, five hours) via Er-Rachidia (Dh40, 2½ hours) and Erfoud (Dh55, 4½ hours). There are also night-time services for Azrou (Dh40, 90 minutes), Meknès (Dh60, four hours) and Fès (Dh70, five hours).

Other buses cover the same routes at more sociable hours for slightly less, as well as servicing Sefrou (Dh40, four hours). Fès (Dh55, five hours) is serviced by six departures throughout the day.

AROUND MIDELT

Midelt's location on the cusp of the Eastern High Atlas makes it a great base for exploring. Off the main routes, roads are rough piste, with many only really negotiable between May and October and even then only by 4WD. It's heaven for mountain bikers, as well as ideal hiking country. Complexe Touristique Timnay Inter-Cultures and Safari Atlas in Midelt will rent you a 4WD (with driver) for around Dh1000 – good value if there's a group of you.

Cirque Jaffar

The Cirque Jaffar winds through the foothills of Jebel Ayachi, 25km southwest of Midelt. It's a rough piste, and regular cars will grumble on the route in all seasons but the height of summer. The scenery is wonderful though – the dramatic crests of the Atlas, carpeted in places with cedar forest, and studded with tiny Berber mountain villages. Take the Zaïdia road for about 10km from Midelt, and turn off at the signpost for the village of Aït Oum Gam. Then follow the signs to Matkan Tounfit. After that the route loops back through Tattiouine and on to route S3424 back to Midelt. Allow a day for the whole 80km circuit. The Complexe Touristique Timnay Inter-Cultures offers this day trip for Dh300 per person including meals.

If walking is more your thing, and you have a tent, it's possible to strike out from Timnay to the Cirque Jaffar on foot. A two-day round trip gives a good taste of the area. From Timnay you can walk to the village of Sidi Amar, which is surrounded by apple orchards and is particularly colourful during the souq each Wednesday. Camp further along at Jaffar, located in the valley in the centre of the spectacular circle. On day two, return to the Timnay complex via the impressive river gorges. A guide isn't strictly necessary, but can be organised via the Complexe Touristique Timnay Inter-Cultures. An equally good companion is the guidebook *Grand Atlas Traverse* by Michael Peyron.

Gorges d'Aouli

An interesting road trip takes you 15km northeast of Midelt along the S317 road to the **Gorges d'Aouli**. A series of cliffs carved

CLIMBING JEBEL AYACHI

The highest mountain in the eastern High Atlas, Jebel Ayachi (3737m) is more a massif than a single peak, stretching along a 45km ridge southwest of Midelt. Its size offers a host of trekking opportunities, not least an ascent of Ichichi n'Boukhlib, the highest peak.

The best time to tackle Jebel Ayachi is April to May or September to November, although you should be aware that snow can persist above 3400m well into July. From Midelt, take a grand taxi to the village of Tattiouine, from where you start the climb. It's a tiring but nontechnical ascent achievable in a single day. There's a simple mountain bivouac at the summit, although you'll obviously need to bring your own supplies.

A guide is definitely a good idea. The best place to arrange one is through the Complexe Touristique Timnay Inter-Cultures (p272) north of Midelt. The daily rate is around Dh250. An alternative, if you're up to the arranging, is to hire a mule and driver in Tattiouine.

by the Moulaya, they were until recently mined extensively for lead, copper and silver. The abandoned workings can be clearly seen – many halfway up the cliff face – although the mine entrances themselves are blocked off for safety reasons. Nevertheless, the place exudes a slightly creepy ghost-town feel, especially with the dipping sun at the end of the day. Further along the road, the small village of **Aouli** sits against the spectacular backdrop of the river gorge. This would be a great stretch to explore by mountain bike (the road deteriorates to rough piste at some points); a round trip by grand taxi from Midelt should cost no more than Dh200.

THE EAST

TAZA
تازة

pop 210,000

Although Taza has played an important part in Moroccan history, you wouldn't necessarily know it on first impressions. It comes across as a quiet provincial town, with its sprawling layout giving it a slightly abandoned air. But, if you climb the crumbling fortifications of Taza Haute, the panoramic views of the Rif to the north and the Middle Atlas to the south are breathtaking. Taza also provides a handy base for exploring the eastern Middle Atlas, including Gouffre du Friouato – one of the most incredible open caverns in the world – and Tazzeka National Park.

History

The fortified citadel of Taza is built on the edge of an escarpment overlooking the only feasible pass between the Rif Mountains and the Middle Atlas. It has been important throughout Morocco's history as a garrison town from which to exert control over the country's eastern extremities.

The Tizi n'Touahar, as the pass is known, was the traditional invasion route for armies moving west from Tunisia and Algeria. This is, in fact, where the Romans and the Arabs entered Morocco. The town itself was the base from which the Almohads, Merenids and Alawites swept down into Fès to conquer lowland Morocco and establish their dynasties.

All Moroccan sultans had a hand in fortifying Taza. Nevertheless, their control over the area was always tenuous because the fiercely independent and rebellious local tribes continually exploited any weakness in the central power in order to overrun the city. Never was this more so than in the first years of the 20th century, when 'El-Rogui' (the Pretender to the Sultan's Throne) Bou Hamra, held sway over most of northeastern Morocco.

The French occupied Taza in 1914 and made it the main base from which they fought the prolonged rebellion by the tribes of the Rif Mountains and Middle Atlas.

Orientation

If you arrive by train or bus, you are likely to find yourself on the main Fès to Oujda road, a short taxi ride north of Place de l'Indépendance. This square is the heart of the ville nouvelle and the site of the banks, main post office and most hotels and restaurants, as well as the CTM bus station.

The medina, usually referred to as Taza Haute (Upper Taza), occupies the hill 2km to the south. Local buses (Dh2) and

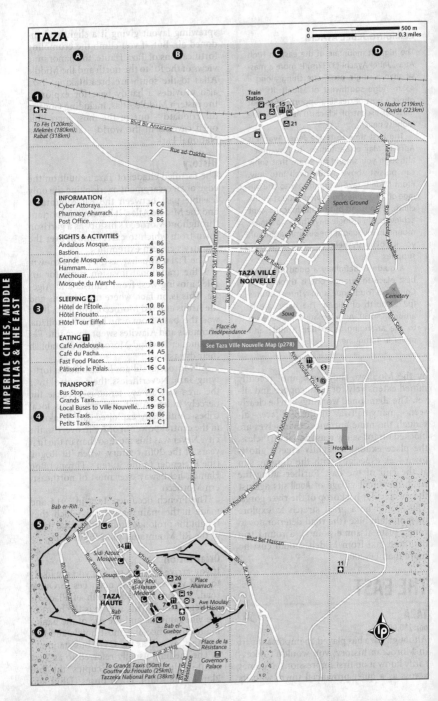

TAZA

0 ———— 500 m
0 ———— 0.3 miles

To Fès (120km);
Meknès (180km);
Rabat (318km)

Blvd Bir Anzarane

To Nador (219km);
Oujda (223km)

Rue ad-Dakhla

Train
Station

Sports Ground

TAZA VILLE
NOUVELLE

Souq

Place de
l'Indépendance

See Taza Ville Nouvelle Map (p278)

Cemetery

Hospital

Bab er-Rih

Sidi Azout
Mosque

Souqs

Bou Abu
al-Hassan
Medersa

TAZA
HAUTE

Bab
Titi

Bab el-
Guebor

Place
Aharrach

Ave Moulay
el-Hassan

Place de la
Résistance

Governor's
Palace

To Grands Taxis (50m) for
Gouffre du Friouato (25km);
Tazzeka National Park (38km)

INFORMATION	
Cyber Attoraya	1 C4
Pharmacy Aharrach	2 B6
Post Office	3 B6

SIGHTS & ACTIVITIES	
Andalous Mosque	4 B6
Bastion	5 B6
Grande Mosquée	6 A5
Hammam	7 B6
Mechouar	8 B6
Mosquée du Marché	9 B5

SLEEPING	
Hôtel de l'Étoile	10 B6
Hôtel Friouato	11 D5
Hôtel Tour Eiffel	12 A1

EATING	
Café Andalousia	13 B6
Café du Pacha	14 A5
Fast Food Places	15 C1
Pâtisserie le Palais	16 C4

TRANSPORT	
Bus Stop	17 C1
Grands Taxis	18 C1
Local Buses to Ville Nouvelle	19 B6
Petits Taxis	20 B6
Petits Taxis	21 C1

sky-blue petits taxis (Dh5) run regularly between the ville nouvelle and Place Aharrach in the medina.

Information

BMCI (Map p278; Place de l'Indépendance) Has an ATM.
Cyber Attoraya (Map p276; Rue Allal ben Abdallah; per hr Dh5; 24hr)
Guillaume Tell Cybercafé (Map p278; Place de l'Indépendance; per hr Dh5; 9am-10pm)
Main post office (Map p278; off Rue de Marché)
Pharmacy Aharrach (Map p276; Place Aharrach)
Post office (Map p276; Ave Moulay el-Hassan) In the medina.

Sights & Activities

The partially ruined **medina walls**, around 3km in circumference, are a legacy from when Taza served briefly as the Almohad capital in the 12th century. The **bastion** (Map p276) – where the walls jut out to the east of the medina – was added 400 years later by the Saadians. The most interesting section of wall is around **Bab er-Rih** (Gate of the Wind; Map p276), from where there are superb views over the surrounding countryside. Look southwest to the wooded slopes of Jebel Tazzeka in the Middle Atlas, and then to the Rif in the north, and it's easy to see the strategic significance of Taza's location.

Not far from Bab er-Rih is the **Grande Mosquée** (Map p276), which the Almohads began building in 1135; the Merenids added to it in the 13th century. Non-Muslims are not allowed to enter, and it's difficult to get much of an impression from the outside of the building. From here the main thoroughfare wriggles its way southeast to the far end of the medina. Keep your eye out for occasional examples of richly decorated doorways and windows high up in the walls, guarded by old, carved cedar screens.

The **souqs** and **qissariat** start around the Mosquée du Marché (Map p276), offering mats and carpets woven by the Beni Ouarain tribe in the surrounding mountains. It's a great chance to observe the workings of a typical Berber market. At the end of the main street, close to the **mechouar**, is the **Andalous Mosque** (Map p276), constructed in the 12th century.

There is also a **hammam** (Map p276; Place Aharrach; Dh8; 5am-noon & 7pm-midnight men only, noon-7pm women only) in the medina.

Sleeping

Taza isn't overrun by hotels. Some of the cheaper places are a bit grubby – an excellent excuse to head for the hammam in the medina.

Hôtel Dauphiné (Map p278; ☎ 035 673567; Place de l'Indépendance; s/d Dh125/155) Right on the central square, this spick and span hotel is the best of the budget choices. Rooms at the front have balconies, and all are airy with generously sized bathrooms. Staff are amenable, and there's a decent bar and restaurant on site.

Hôtel Guillaume Tell (Map p278; ☎ 035 672347; Place de l'Indépendance; s/d Dh50/70) This cheapie has a great location, although the off-street entrance is round a few corners and up a few stairs. For the price you wouldn't expect much, but rooms are pretty decent, with sinks. Only the slightly grimy shared bathrooms let it down.

Hôtel de l'Étoile (Map p276; ☎ 035 270179; 39 Ave Moulay el-Hassan; s/d Dh44/68) If you want to be in the thick of it in the medina, this Spanish-run pension is opposite the post office. Rooms are tiny but have sinks; those on the top look out onto the medina. Head for the hammam if you don't like cold showers.

Hôtel Tour Eiffel (Map p276; ☎ 035 671562; Blvd Bir Anzarane; s/d Dh278/350;) The name is chosen well: this is Taza's tallest hotel by some distance. Everything here feels brand new, well kept and comfy, and the rooms on the top floor have dramatic views to the mountains. The house restaurant is also worth more than a look.

Hôtel Friouato (Map p276; ☎ 035 672593; fax 055 672244; Blvd Bel Hassan; s/d Dh260/295;) Stuck somewhat out on a limb between the medina and the ville nouvelle, the Friouato is nevertheless a fair choice if you're after a bit of comfort and a pool to have a dip in. All the three-star amenities are there, including a bar and restaurant – lucky, given its far-flung location away from anywhere else to eat.

Eating

While there are no real restaurants in the medina, there are numerous small stands where you can pick up a snack, and there is plenty of fresh produce in the souqs. You'll find market stalls selling food supplies around the Mosquée du Marché, and grocery stores along Ave Mohammed V. If you're waiting for onward transport and are

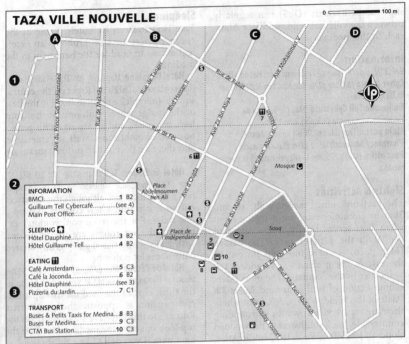

TAZA VILLE NOUVELLE

0 —————— 100 m

INFORMATION
BMCI...**1** B2
Guillaum Tell Cybercafé............(see 4)
Main Post Office.....................**2** C3

SLEEPING
Hôtel Dauphiné.....................**3** B2
Hôtel Guillaume Tell...............**4** B2

EATING
Café Amsterdam **5** C3
Café la Joconda......................**6** B2
Hôtel Dauphiné.....................(see 3)
Pizzeria du Jardin....................**7** C1

TRANSPORT
Buses & Petits Taxis for Medina...**8** B3
Buses for Medina....................**9** B2
CTM Bus Station.....................**10** C3

in need of sustenance, there's a whole row of fast-food places where the buses stop on the Fès–Oujda road (Blvd Bir Anzarane).

Hôtel Dauphiné (Map p278; ☎ 035 673567; Place de l'Indépendance; meals Dh80) Probably Taza's best restaurant (although to be fair there's not much competition), the Dauphine offers the usual range of Moroccan standards, plus a few fish continental dishes thrown in. It's pretty tasty and efficiently served, but the big dining room could use a little atmosphere.

Pizzeria du Jardin (Map p278; 44 Rue Sultan Abou el-Hassan; mains Dh35-40; ☺ noon-1am) This is a friendly place serving a few tajines, pizzas and fast-food options – try the grilled cutlets. It's busy in the evenings but dead in the afternoon, when the cook sometimes goes home for a nap, leaving you with a long wait if you're hungry.

Café Amsterdam (Map p278; Ave Moulay Youssef) This is a great breakfast stop. There's no outside seating, but the interior is crisply decorated, and there's an excellent selection of sticky pastries to go with your coffee and juice.

Café la Joconda (Map p278; Ave d'Oujda) This is another good modern café that's not threatened by the concept of female customers.

Pâtisserie le Palais (Map p276; 65 Blvd Allal ben Abdullah) The pastries available here are considered by many to be the best in Taza.

Café du Pacha (Map p276; Khalaq Torris) This serves as a basic coffee-stop but it does have a good vine-covered terrace with sweeping views of the town and countryside

Café Andalousia (Map p276; Place Aharrach) Nice cafe overlooking the main medina square.

Getting There & Away

BUS

There are no bus services originating in Taza, but plenty pass through on their way between Oujda and points west of Taza such as Fès, Tangier and Casablanca.

The **CTM office** (Map p278; ☎ 055 673037; Place de l'Indépendance) is located in the ville nouvelle. There's a morning departure for Casablanca (Dh120, eight hours), stopping at Fès (Dh38, two hours), Meknès (Dh53, 2½ hours) and Rabat (Dh91, 6½ hours). Two overnight buses leave for Tangier (Dh128, eight hours). There are also morning services for Oujda (Dh55, 3½ hours) and Nador (Dh45, 2½ hours).

All other buses servicing these same destinations stop on the Fès-to-Oujda road next to the grand taxi lot. It's all a bit random, so turn up early and ask around as to what's expected – and jump in a grand taxi if the wait seems too long.

TAXI

Most grands taxis leave from the main Fès-to-Oujda road, near the train station. They depart fairly regularly for Fès (Dh38, two hours). Less frequently, taxis head for Oujda (Dh65, 3½ hours) and Al-Hoceima (Dh60, 2½ hours). Grands taxis to the Gouffre du Friouato (Dh12) leave from a lot to the south of the medina.

TRAIN

Taza's location on the train line makes rail the best transport option. Four trains run to Fès (Dh38, two hours), two of which continue to Meknès (Dh45, three hours), Rabat (Dh108, six hours) and Casablanca (Dh133, seven hours), and there's one service to Tangier (Dh131, eight hours). In the opposite direction, three trains go to Oujda (Dh72, three hours).

AROUND TAZA
Jebel Tazzeka Circuit

The circuit around Jebel Tazzeka, southwest of Taza, makes an appealing day trip. It takes in the Cascades de Ras el-Oued at the edge of Tazzeka National Park, Daïa Chiker, the cave systems of Gouffre du Friouato and the gorges of the Oued Zireg. Though the road (S311) is sealed the whole way, it's very narrow and twisty in parts, with plenty of blind corners from which grands taxis can unexpectedly speed out.

The road is too quiet to hitch easily. If you don't have a vehicle, expect to pay around Dh500 for a grand taxi for the day from Taza, although a few direct grands taxis to the Gouffre du Friouato can sometime be found near the medina.

THE FIRST LEG

The first stop is the **Cascades de Ras el-Oued**, 10km from Taza. They're at the their grandest in the early spring, flushed with rain and snow melt – by the end of summer the flow is just a trickle. Just above the waterfalls is the village of **Ras el-Mar**, where there's a small café with great mountain views. The entry to **Tazzeka National Park** is also near here; a good place for walks among the oak forests.

Leaving the waterfalls, continue along the right fork onto the plateau and up to a small pass. On your left you'll see the strange depression of the **Daïa Chiker**, a dry lake bed. In early spring, however, a shallow lake often forms as a result of a geological curiosity associated with fault lines in the calciferous rock structure.

GOUFFRE DU FRIOUATO

Further along, 25km from Taza, the **Gouffre du Friouato** (☎ 067 640626; admission Dh3, guide Dh100, torch Dh100; ☉ 8am-6pm) is well signposted, up a very steep road. The cavern is the main attraction of this circuit and it's well worth coming up here simply to look into its gaping mouth.

At over 20m wide and 150m deep, it is said to be the deepest cavern in the whole of North Africa, and the cave system is possibly the most extensive. It was first investigated in 1935 and has only been partially explored to date.

Access is via 520 precipitous steps (with handrails) that lead you all the way to the floor of the cavern (it's a quite strenuous climb back up). At the bottom, you can squeeze through a hole to start exploring the fascinating chambers that are found 200 more steps below. It's dark and dirty and eerily beautiful. The most spectacular chambers, full of extraordinary formations, are the **Salle de Lixus** and the **Salle de Draperies** – allow at least 2½ hours there and back. Speleologists have explored to a depth of 300m, but they believe more caves are another 500m below.

The admission fee allows you to enter as far as the cavern mouth. Beyond that, you are strongly advised to take a guide. The *guardien* for over 25 years, Mostapha Lachhab, will take you further and deeper into the caves for around Dh200. A torch, good shoes and warm clothes are recommended, but leave your claustrophia in the outside world. Treat the caves with caution and respect, and be prepared for a scramble.

BACK TO TAZA

Beyond the Gouffre du Friouato, the road begins to climb again into coniferous forests past **Bab Bou-Idir**. Abandoned for much of the year, this village comes alive in summer when holiday-makers fill its camp site and tiled alpine-style houses. This is a good base if you wish to do some day hikes in the area. There's a national park information office, open in summer, and marked trails commencing in the village.

About 8km past Bab Bou-Idir, a rough track branches off to the right 9km up to **Jebel Tazzeka** (1980m). A piste goes to the summit, and it's a tough climb. At the top there's a TV relay station (4WDs can get up here), and really great panoramic views out to both the Rif and the Middle Atlas.

The main road continues for another 38km to join the main Fès-to-Taza road at Sidi Abdallah de Rhiata. On the way you will wind around hairpin bends through some dense woodland and then down through the pretty gorges of the **Oued Zireg**. From the intersection at Sidi Abdallah de Rhiata, you can take the main highway back east to Taza, pausing at **Tizi n'Touahar** on the way for more views.

OUJDA وجدة
pop 880,000

The largest city in eastern Morocco, Oujda is a lively modern place, free of much of the hassle of other Moroccan cities. Despite few genuine attractions for the traveller, it's a relaxed place in which to catch your breath after heading down from the Rif Mountains or taking the long look south to Figuig and the Sahara. As the terminus of the train line, it had good links to the rest of the country and is close enough to the Mediterranean to make a trip to the seaside an easy prospect.

Oujda grew – and then suffered – due to its proximity to the Algerian border. A brisk cross-border trade swelled the local economy, which then crashed on the closure of the Algerian border in 1995. Some smuggling persists (notably in petrol), but the numerous hotels thrown up when the border trade was at its peak in the early 1990s have greatly suffered. Oujda has an important university, which makes a huge contribution to the city's intellectual life.

History

The site of Oujda has long been important as it lies on the main axis connecting Morocco with the rest of North Africa (the Romans built a road through here). Like Taza,

it occupied a key position in controlling the east and was often seen as a vital stepping stone for armies aiming to seize control of the heartland around Fès.

The town was founded by the Meghraoua tribe in the 10th century and remained independent until the Almohads overran it in the 11th century. Later, under the Merenids, Algerian rulers based in Tlemcen took the town on several occasions, and then in the 17th century it fell under the sway of the Ottoman in Algiers.

Moulay Ismail put an end to this in 1687, and Oujda remained in Moroccan hands until 1907 when French forces in Algeria crossed the frontier and occupied the town in one of a series of similar 'incidents'. The protectorate was still five years away, but the sultan was powerless to stop it.

The French soon expanded Oujda, which has since swelled in size as provincial capital and in its role as the main gateway for commerce with Algeria. Its industrial economy rests on mining, particularly zinc, which is found further to the south.

Orientation

Although it's quite large, only the centre of Oujda is of any interest to travellers. The main street is Blvd Mohammed V, along or near which you'll find banks, offices, hotels and restaurants. The medina lies east of here, at the southern end of the street.

About a five-minute walk to the west of the medina along Blvd Zerktouni lies Oujda train station. A further 15 minutes to the southwest, across Oued Nachef, is the main *gare routière* (bus station).

Information
CULTURAL CENTRES
Institut Français (Map p282; ☎ 056 684404; ifooujda@maroc-oriental.com; 3 Rue de Berkane; ☽ 8.45am-noon & 1.45-6.30pm Tue-Sat) Concerts, lecture and films, with occasional exhibitions by local artists.

INTERNET ACCESS
@IphaNet (Map p282; Blvd Mohammed V; per hr Dh5; ☽ 9am-11.30pm) Big screens and swivel chairs.

MEDICAL SERVICES
Hôpital el-Farabi (Map p281; ☎ 036 682705; Ave Idriss el-Akbar)
Pharmacie Mouslime (Map p282; Blvd Mohammed V)

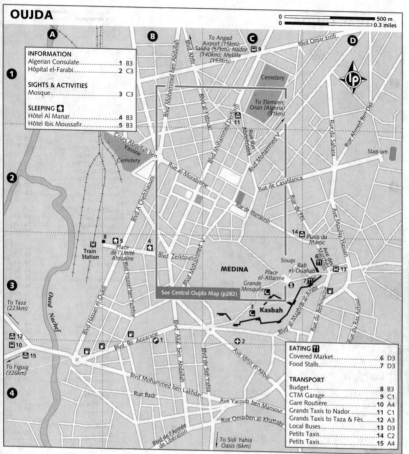

OUJDA

See Central Oujda Map (p282)

See Central Oujda Map (p282)

IMPERIAL CITIES, MIDDLE ATLAS & THE EAST

MONEY

Most banks – with ATMs – are located along Blvd Mohammed V in the medina and around Place du 16 Août near the town hall.

Western Union (Map p282; Blvd Mohammed V; 8am-noon & 2-6pm Mon-Thu, 8-11.30am & 2.30-6.30pm Fri, 9am-12.30pm Sat) Has a *bureau de change* where you can change cash outside banking hours.

POST

Main post office (Map p282; Blvd Mohammed V)

TOURIST INFORMATION

Tourist Office (Map p282; ☎ 036 685631; fax 036 689089; Place du 16 Août; 8.30am-noon & 2.30-6.30pm Mon-Fri)

TRAVEL AGENCIES

Carlson Wagonlit (Map p282; ☎ 036 682520; fax 036 681968; Blvd Mohammed V) For ferry and air tickets.
Maroc Voyages (Map p282; ☎ 036 683993; fax 036 708710; 110 Blvd Allal ben Abdallah)

Sights

While Oujda's **medina** (Map p282) isn't that large, it stills warrants a little exploration. The eastern gate, **Bab el-Ouahab** (Gate of Heads; Map p281), is the best place to enter, through the old city walls. The gruesome name is derived from the old habit of hanging the heads of criminals here, which persisted until the French Protectorate. This area of the medina is chock-full of food stalls (Oujda olives are very well

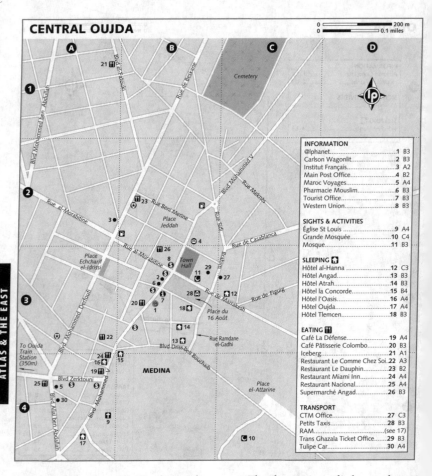

CENTRAL OUJDA

INFORMATION	
@lphanet	1 B3
Carlson Wagonlit	2 B3
Institut Français	3 A2
Main Post Office	4 B2
Maroc Voyages	5 A4
Pharmacie Mouslim	6 B3
Tourist Office	7 B3
Western Union	8 B3

SIGHTS & ACTIVITIES	
Église St Louis	9 A4
Grande Mosquée	10 C4
Mosque	11 B3

SLEEPING	
Hôtel al-Hanna	12 C3
Hôtel Angad	13 B3
Hôtel Atrah	14 B3
Hôtel la Concorde	15 B4
Hôtel l'Oasis	16 A4
Hôtel Oujda	17 A4
Hôtel Tlemcen	18 B3

EATING	
Café La Défense	19 A4
Café Pâtisserie Colombo	20 B3
Iceberg	21 A1
Restaurant Le Comme Chez Soi	22 A3
Restaurant Le Dauphin	23 B2
Restaurant Miami Inn	24 A4
Restaurant Nacional	25 A4
Supermarché Angad	26 B3

TRANSPORT	
CTM Office	27 C3
Petits Taxis	28 B3
RAM	(see 17)
Trans Ghazala Ticket Office	29 B3
Tulipe Car	30 A4

IMPERIAL CITIES, MIDDLE ATLAS & THE EAST

regarded) and street cafés. Bustling without being overwhelming, it's a great slice of tradition and modernity. From **Place el-Attarine**, head north through the souqs past the 14th-century Grande Mosquée built by the Merenids, eventually popping out near Place du 16 Août – the centre of the ville nouvelle.

Sleeping
BUDGET
Hôtel Angad (Map p282; ☎ 036 691451; Rue Ramdane el-Gadhi; s/d Dh90/140, high season Dh161/194) The top pick of the budget hotels is a surprisingly affordable two-star. Rooms are just about essentially furnished, with large bathroom and TV, everything you need for a good

rest. The downstairs café does a decent breakfast.

Hôtel la Concorde (Map p282; ☎ 036 682328; 57 Blvd Mohammed V; s/d Dh177/206) The cavernous entrance is gloomy and unappealing, but rooms here are handy and functional; it has the air of a midrange hotel fallen on harder times – not unusual in Oujda.

Hôtel Atrah (Map p282; ☎ 036 686533; off Rue Ramdane el-Gadhi; s/d Dh113/178) The tiles and plasterwork in the lobby lend some traditional Moroccan flavour here. Self-contained rooms are a bit boxy, but otherwise this is a good budget choice.

Hôtel Tlemcen (Map p282; ☎ 036 700384; 26 Rue Ramdane el-Gadhi; r per person Dh60) This friendly little place offers excellent value, and has an exceedingly grand-looking lobby for the price of the rooms. Quarters are small but bright, with bathrooms and TV.

Hôtel al-Hanna (Map p282; ☎ 036 686003; 132 Rue de Marrakesh; s/d Dh57/77, with bathroom Dh77/93) This is a good-value place, with airy rooms, many with balconies. All rooms have their own sink, but it's worth paying the extra for an attached bathroom – the shared (squat) toilets are a bit whiffy.

MIDRANGE & TOP END

Hôtel Al Manar (Map p281; ☎ 056 688855; 50 Blvd Zerktouni; s/d Dh300/400; ✦) It has everything you'd expect from a business-class hotel: clean, comfortable rooms with all mod cons, and a complete charisma bypass. No surprises, but no disappointments either.

Hôtel Oujda (Map p282; ☎ 036 684093; fax 036 685064; Blvd Mohammed V; s/d Dh260/327; ✦ ✦) According to the décor, this hotel's clock stopped in the early 1970s – there's a 'space age' lobby and funky bathroom tiles. Still, everything works, it's all comfy enough and the staff are eager to please. The restaurant offers lovely views of the nearby square and Église St Louis.

Hôtel Ibis Moussafir (Map p281; ☎ 036 688202; www.ibishotel.com; Blvd Abdella Chefchaouni; s/d incl breakfast Dh472/584; ✦ ✦) All the up-to-the-minute facilities and comfortable rooms you'd expect from this international hotel chain. Straight off the peg, it has exactly the same layout as the Ibis in Fès.

Eating
RESTAURANTS

Restaurant Nacional (Map p281; ☎ 036 703257; 107 Blvd Allal ben Abdallah; meals from Dh25) This busy place practically has them queuing out of the door at lunchtimes. The small downstairs fills quickly, so try the larger salon up top. There's the usual tajines and huge salads, plus some delicious cutlets and meat dishes (some varying according to the day of the week).

Restaurant le Comme Chez Soi (Map p281; ☎ 036 686079; 8 Rue Sijilmassa; mains from Dh80) This is Oujda's top dining option, all liveried waiters and neatly pressed tablecloths. The menu is heavily French, divided more or less equally between meat and fish dishes, with some good soups and salads. Alcohol is served.

Restaurant le Dauphin (Map p281; ☎ 035 686145; 38 Rue de Berkane; mains Dh75-100) Oujda is surprisingly close to the Mediterranean, and

this restaurant takes full advantage, offering seafood and more seafood. Catch of the day determines the menu, but you won't want for choice as the selection is huge. The surroundings are pleasant, and a bottle of wine adds to the ambience.

CAFÉS, PATISSERIES & ICE-CREAM PARLOURS

Blvd Mohammed V is lined with pavement cafés, offering mint tea, pastries and people-watching. A couple of our favourites are **Café Pâtisserie Colombo** (Map p282; Blvd Mohammed V; ⏲ 7am-10pm) and **Café la Défense** (Map p282; Blvd Mohammed V; breakfast Dh12; ⏲ 6am-10pm). Oujda's best ice cream can be found at **Iceberg** (Map p282; 51 Blvd el-Fatouki; per scoop Dh3; ⏲ 6am-9.30pm Sat-Thu, 6am-noon & 1-9.30pm Fri).

QUICK EATS

Two main areas stand out for street food. There are plenty of kebabs and other quick snacks around Rue de Marrakesh; alternatively the stalls inside Bab el-Ouahab in the medina are a good option. Boiled sheep heads, deep-fried intestines and very large bags of snails are all on offer, plus a few more mundane options like soup and omelettes.

Restaurant Miami Inn (Map p282; 67 Blvd Mohammed V; meals around Dh30) This fast-food place serves the standard salads and rotisserie chicken and chips. It's cheap, fast and popular with the locals.

SELF-CATERING

For those in search of picnic fodder, fresh fruit and veg is on offer in the covered market to the north of Bab el-Ouahab. **Supermarché Angad** (Map p282; off Place Jeddah; ⏲ 7.30am-noon & 3-8.30pm) also stocks a fair selection of imported goodies and packaged goods.

Getting There & Away
AIR

Oujda's **Angad Airport** (☎ 036 683261) is 15km north of the town, and 400m east of the road to Ahfir and Saïdia. Grand taxi fares are set at Dh120, but any bus to Nador, Berkane, Saïdia etc can drop you on the main road for a few dirham.

RAM (Map p282; ☎ 036 683909; 45 Blvd Mohammed V) has two daily flights to Casablanca (Dh1350, 75 minutes). RAM also operates weekly direct flights to Brussels, Amsterdam and Marseilles, and five flights a week to Paris.

BUS

East of the town hall, the small **CTM office** (Map p282; ☎ 036 682047; Rue Sidi Brahim) sells tickets for its two daily buses: Casablanca (Dh180, 11 hours) via Taza (Dh55, 3½ hours), Fès (Dh100, 4½ hours), Meknès (Dh115, five hours) and Rabat (Dh155, 9½ hours); and Tangier (Dh180, 12½ hours) also via Taza, Fès and Meknès. The buses leave in the evening from the CTM garage further north on Blvd Omar Errifi.

SAT and Trans Ghazala operate from the *gare routière*. Between them they run five daily services to Casablanca via Fès, Meknès and Rabat. You can buy tickets for these services at the **Trans Ghazala ticket office** (Map p282; ☎ 036 685387; Rue Sidi Brahim), opposite CTM, or at the *gare routière*.

Numerous other companies with ticket offices in the bus station offer frequent departures for Taza, Fès and Meknès as well as Berkane (Dh11, one hour) and Nador (Dh25, three hours). There are two buses a day (more in summer) to Saïdia (Dh12, 1½ hours), and four to Al-Hoceima (Dh58, five hours). There are also two daily buses to Tangier (Dh130, 14 hours) via Chefchaouen (Dh110, 11 hours) and Tetouan (Dh120, 12 hours). Buses leave for Bouarfa (Dh50, five hours) and Figuig (Dh68, seven hours) until mid-afternoon.

CAR

The following rental agencies can be found in Oujda:

Avis (☎ 036 701616; fax 036 703922) At Angad Airport.

Budget (Map p281; ☎ 036 681011; fax 036 681013) At the train station.

Tulipe Car (Map p282; ☎ /fax 036 683861; Résidence Le Paris, Blvd Allal ben Abdallah)

TAXI

Grands taxis to Taza (Dh65, 3½ hours) leave regularly from outside the main *gare routière*. You'll need to change here if you're continuing to Fès. Grands taxis heading north to Nador (Dh50, three hours), Saïdia (Dh22, one hour) and Berkane (Dh17, one hour) congregate to the north of town near the junction of Rue ibn Abdelmalek and Blvd Mohammed Derfoufi.

TRAIN

Oujda's **train station** (Map p281; ☎ 056 686737), at the west end of Blvd Zerktouni, has a **left-luggage counter** (per item per day Dh10, ☺ 6am-9pm). There are three daily direct departures for Casablanca (Dh200, 10 hours) and one for Tangier (via Sidi Kacem, Dh200, 11 hours). All these trains stop at Taza (Dh62, 3½ hours), Fès (Dh107, six hours) and Meknès (Dh124, 6½ hours).

TO ALGERIA

There are no plans to reopen the border with Algeria. In previous years, buses and grands taxis ran to the border throughout the day, and onto the town of Tlemcen. In the unlikely event of diplomatic breakthroughs, expect these to be up and running very quickly.

AROUND OUJDA

Sidi Yahia Oasis   واحة سيدي يحيى

The oasis of Sidi Yahia, 6km south of Oujda, is venerated by Moroccan Muslims, Jews and Christians alike as being the last resting place of Sidi Yahia Ben Younes who, according to local tradition, is none other than John the Baptist.

For most of the year it's a disappointingly scruffy place that's little more than a satellite town for Oujda, all urban sprawl and litter. But every September (dates vary according to the lunar calendar), thousands of pilgrims flock here for a week-long *moussem*. It is one of the bigger celebrations of this type in the country, complete with a *fantasia*, and is worth making a detour for. The trees around the shrine (closed to non-Muslims) are festooned with rags, tied to receive blessings – a throwback to pre-Islamic fertility beliefs.

To get to Sidi Yahia, take bus 1 (Dh3) from outside Bab el-Ouahab in Oujda. A petit taxi should cost around Dh18.

BOUARFA   بوعرفة

It's a long and hot 376km trip south from Oujda to Figuig. The road is good, but the views of dusty scrub and desert quickly become monotonous. This was once a busy stretch of highway, but with the border closure it's a sensitive area, and there are plenty of checkpoints with bored gendarmes killing time by pulling over vehicles.

The administrative and garrison town of Bouarfa is the biggest place you'll pass through en route to Figuig. A minor transport hub for the southeastern corner of Morocco, it's a useful spot to refuel, stretch your legs and find somewhere to eat.

There are a couple of adequate hotels if you get stranded. The **Hôtel Tamlalt** (☎ 026 798799; Blvd Massira; d Dh60) is a simple rock-bottom option: each spartan room has a bed and little else. There are no showers, but there's a hammam around the corner. The hotel is on the main street about 100m south of the bus station.

You could be forgiven for thinking the **Hôtel Climat du Maroc** (☎ 036 796382; Blvd Hassan II; d/ste Dh372/480; ✗ ☒) was a desert mirage, as its facilities are unexpectedly good for such an out-of-the-way location. Plush rooms have attached bathroom and satellite TV, and a pool to cool off in. The restaurant is quiet and slow to serve, but probably the best option in town.

The area around the bus station has the usual assortment of places offering brochettes, rotisserie chicken and the like. **Restaurant Elwafa** (Blvd Hassan II; meals Dh20) near the Hôtel Climat du Maroc, is a good seated option, with tajines and couscous. **Café Amsterdam** (cnr Blvd Mohammed V & Blvd Hassan II) has pastries for breakfast.

Around eight buses a day link Bouarfa to Oujda (Dh50, five hours), with about half as many going south to Figuig (Dh22, two hours). There's a daily morning bus to Er-Rachidia (Dh54, five hours), where you can pick up transport to Marrakesh and onward destinations.

Grands taxis seem reluctant to head far outside Bouarfa; you may have to hire a whole taxi to get to Oujda or Er-Rachidia (both around Dh600) or Figuig (Dh280).

FIGUIG
فجيج

pop 15,000

There's no mistaking that Figuig (Fig-*eeg*) is the end of the road. Its 200,000 date palms, fed by artesian wells, almost spread into Algeria, just 2km away at the nearest point. Like Oujda, Figuig used to be a busy border post between the two countries (as well as a historic way station for pilgrims travelling to Mecca), but now it sleeps its days away, only labouring into action for the autumn date harvest.

Figuig is made up of seven communities, whose main activity in the past was fighting over water resources and grazing rights. Nowadays the blood feuds have ended and Figuig looks fairly modern, with returning migrants investing in new concrete houses at the expense of the crumbling old kasbahs.

For some, Figuig's somnolent air will be its biggest attraction. There's no passing traffic – you have to make a real effort to get here – and life more or less matches the pace of the donkey cart and bicycle. As a place to unwind, it has its charms and, when the heat of the day isn't too oppressive, you can venture out to explore the *ksars* (fortified settlements) of the local villages.

Orientation & Information

The main road from Bouarfa runs roughly north-south through the oasis and – in theory – on to Beni Ounif, on the Algerian side of the frontier.

The town's petrol station, bus station, two hotels and post office are lined up along this main road, Blvd Hassan II.

Banque Populaire, Figuig's sole bank, has an ATM and exchange facilities, while **Figuig Net** (per hr Dh10) plugs the town into the web.

Where the road passes the second of the two hotels, Hôtel Figuig, it drops downhill towards what is known as the 'lower town' – the basin of palms that makes up the oldest part of Figuig. This ridge provides a handy landmark as well as good views over the *palmeraie* (oasis-like area).

Sights & Activities

The parched landscape of Figuig is dotted with seven *ksars* that make up the town, all the same ochre colour as the earth they're made from. Each settlement controls an area of *palmeraie* and its all-important supply of water. In the past, feuding families would divert these water channels to wash around the foundations of their enemy's kasbah, hoping that the walls would eventually collapse.

The largest and most rewarding of the *ksars* is **Zenaga**, which stretches south below the ridge splitting the oasis. Numerous paths follow the irrigation channels through the palm trees and past neatly tended vegetable gardens. Then suddenly you're in among a warren of covered passages. As you tunnel between the houses, look out for some marvellous, ancient wooden doors; and watch out – sometimes you may find yourself in someone's backyard.

The crumbling state of many of the *ksars* enables you to see their clever construction: palm tree trunks plastered with pisé, and ceilings made of palm fronds. It's cool and dark and often eerily quiet. Occasionally you may meet married women swathed in white robes from head to toe, with the startling exception of one uncovered eye. It's very easy to get lost. Village children will happily guide you for a few dirham, or you can arrange a more formal half-day tour through the Figuig Hotel.

In the upper part of town, to the west of the main road, **Ksar el-Oudahir** is home to a lovely octagonal minaret built in the 11th century. It's known, for obvious reasons, as the *sawmann al-hajaria*, the 'tower of stone'.

There's a souq every Wednesday in the lower town, with some pretty local textiles and embroidery. There's also a very sleepy **Ensemble Artisanal** (Blvd Hassan II; ☼ 4-8pm), across the public gardens from the post office.

Sleeping & Eating

Figuig has just two hotels, patiently waiting for better and busier days.

Figuig Hotel (☎ 036 899309; camping per person Dh35, s/d Dh160/190; ☙) This is the more up-market option, though you can also camp here. It has good views across the *palmeraie* and into Algeria. It's very reasonable value, with cool and comfy rooms and attached bathrooms. It's pool is something of a lifesaver at the end of a long, dusty ride. There's a restaurant (meals around Dh40–70), but order in advance to give staff a chance to nip to the market.

Hôtel el-Meliasse (☎ 036 899062; Blvd Hassan II; r per person Dh60) Next to the Shell garage 500m north of the bus station, this place is far more basic than the Figuig. It has large rooms and the facilities are adequate. Although the hot showers are a good touch, they're often a little superfluous in the climate.

Figuig's eating options are equally limited. Apart from the Figuig Hotel, your best bet is the **Café des Palmeraie** (Blvd Hassan II), opposite the bus station. Staff can rustle up a basic omelette, brochettes and chips. **Café Oasis** (Blvd Hassan II), in the public gardens by the post office, is a better option for coffee and a snack.

Getting There & Away

BUS

Arriving in Figuig, buses stop at the 'bus station' – little more than a junction and three ticket offices – at the north end of town. They then continue on to the lower town; if you're staying at the Figuig Hotel, ask the driver to drop you off.

Always try to check out transport options the day before travelling. There are just a couple of buses a day to Oujda (Dh70, seven hours) in the early morning, via Bouarfa (Dh22, two hours). There are more direct buses to Bouarfa itself – get the earliest possible connection if you want to transit and catch onward transport to Er-Rachidia.

TO ALGERIA

The border with Algeria is closed, but, should it reopen, it's 3km from Figuig to Moroccan customs, another 1km to Algerian customs and a further 3km to the first Algerian town, Beni Ounif.

Marrakesh & Central Morocco

مراكش و وسط مراكش

Few would dispute that the central region is Morocco's most exciting, romantic and popular, with its biggest attraction at its heart: Marrakesh. Founded nearly 1000 years ago, it is one of the great cities of the Maghreb, and home to its most venerated Islamic monument, the Koutoubia Mosque. Its spectacular setting against the snow-capped High Atlas Mountains lingers long in the minds of most travellers, and the famous Djemaa el-Fna square provides perhaps the greatest open-air spectacle in the world.

Just an hour away is a very different scene: the High Atlas foothills of the Ourika Valley and the wilder territory around Jebel Toubkal, rarely visited except by Berber shepherds and their animals, now see increasing numbers of trekkers and visitors seeking beauty and serenity.

Beyond the High Atlas lie the first touches of the Sahara, a vast, arid landscape cut by the lush valleys of the Dadès, Drâa and Ziz rivers. Thick with *palmeraies* (palm groves) and overlooked by imposing red-earth kasbahs, these valleys have all the allure of a desert fantasy. While the magnificent Dadès and Todra gorges offer good walking opportunities, more serious trekking possibilities are higher up, around North Africa's highest mountain, Jebel Toubkal, and among the jagged blue-black peaks of Jebel Sarhro. For a very different experience, head to the far southeast and the alluring Saharan sand dunes of Merzouga or Erg Chigaga, which provide the perfect pink-hued curtain call to this extraordinary region.

HIGHLIGHTS

- Jostle with the crowds in **Djemaa el-Fna** (p297) in Marrakesh – an eye-popping microcosm of traditional Morocco
- Join the young and beautiful on one of the new beaches outside **Marrakesh** (p304) and go dancing at the hippest joints in town (p317)
- Enjoy lunch and a stroll in the lush **Ourika Valley** (p326) or admire the High Atlas from the terrace of the **Kasbah du Toubkal** (p328)
- Wish upon every *ksar* (fort) in the huge kasbah complex of **Aït Benhaddou** (p331), to bring a long and fruitful life
- Take a camel trek and sleep beneath the stars at the spectacular dunes of **Erg Chigaga** (p343)
- Walk through Morocco's Shangri-la, the stunning **Aït Bou Goumez Valley** (p323) with ancient villages melting into the rock formations, and some of the friendliest people in Morocco
- Wonder at the stunning, 300m-high ochre-coloured cliffs of **Todra Gorge** (p352)
- Drive through the scenic **Drâa** (p338) and **Dadès** (p348) valleys
- Listen to the belching camels and Berber drums create the sounds of **Merzouga** (p362), or watch the changing colours of the nearby Erg Chebbi dunes and stunning night skies steal the show

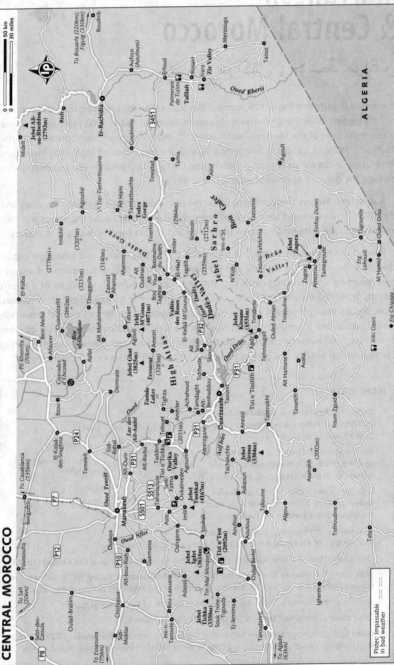

CENTRAL MOROCCO

HISTORY

Originally the domain of Berber tribes of the High Atlas, the history and politics of Central Morocco were irrevocably changed with the establishment of Marrakesh in 1062. The city was founded by the Almoravids (of Arab ethnicity) as the capital of their growing empire, and the Berbers were gradually driven up into the isolated valleys of the High Atlas, where they remain to this day. The city flourished for more than a century, but when the Merenid Sultans moved the capital to Fès in the 13th century it became no more than a provincial backwater.

Under Saadian rule (1524--1668) the tide turned, particularly under Ahmed al-Mansour, who earned the epithet 'ed Dahbi', the Golden One, for himself and the city, after his army took control of Timbuktu. Marrakesh grew rich and powerful as Ahmed took control of the lucrative caravan trade between the Sahara and sub-Sahara and the Atlantic coast. The slaves, gold, ivory and other exquisite luxury goods that returned from Mali and Niger, and the motley band of tribal traders attracted by the profits of the caravans, did much to establish the '1001 Nights' oriental mystique that still lingers over Marrakesh.

The glory faded with Ahmed's death and the Golden City went into a long decline. But the opulent legend lived on and was revived in the court of the infamous Thami el-Glaoui, the last pasha of Marrakesh (1912–56), the 'Lord of the Atlas', the uncrowned king of the South and one of the richest men in the world. A Berber of the Glaoua tribe, el-Glaoui did more than anyone else to cultivate the mystique of Marrakesh. A supporter of colonial rule, which he used to bolster his own regional power, his cruelty and connoisseurship were legendary. Together with his brother el-Mandani, the pasha was responsible for building many of the grand kasbahs of the south. His violent downfall at Independence (1956) brought to an end the great and terrible age of Moroccan sultans.

CLIMATE

With a geography ranging from desert dunes and rocky plains to mountains rising more than 4000m above sea level, the climate of Central Morocco is one of extremes, from bitterly cold High Atlas winters that start in September and last into June, to sweltering deserts that will have you sweating your socks off in the summer.

Spring and autumn are the best times to explore, with temperatures averaging 20–25°C. April is traditionally sandstorm season in the desert, when wind speeds of only 10km/h start to pick up the fine sand and dust, and whisk it across the plains. Storms usually last three to four days, during which time desert travel is inadvisable. If travelling in the desert during this period, allow a few extra days there to ensure that you actually get to see the dunes, rather than just a face full of sand.

LANGUAGE

In the High Atlas the predominant language is the Berber dialect of Tashelheit (with some pockets of Tamazight). Elsewhere Moroccan Arabic and French are universally spoken.

GETTING THERE & AWAY

Marrakesh is the transport hub of the region, well supplied by train, bus and air links. Direct international flights, now including low-cost airlines such as Easyjet and Atlas Blue from London and Atlas Blue from Brussels, fly directly into Marrakesh airport, while daily services from Casablanca offer a host of travel options.

Royal Air Maroc (RAM) also runs daily flights from Casablanca to Ouarzazate – although these tend to cater for film crews and local residents rather than tourists, all of whom will want to stop over in Marrakesh at some point. However, you could consider flying directly out of Ouarzazate on one of the two weekly flights to Paris.

A direct three-hour rail service from Casablanca links Marrakesh to the major cities in the north. Supratours bus services continue on to Essaouira, Agadir and right down south to Laâyoune and Dakhla. Similar services are offered by CTM and other local bus companies, although these tend to be more crowded and less comfortable.

GETTING AROUND

Except for the line from Casablanca to Marrakesh, there are no rail links in Central Morocco. CTM and a host of local bus companies provide a relatively slow but adequate service. Shared grands taxis are an alternative. There are now good sealed roads to every destination featured in this chapter. Desert travellers will need to hire either a 4WD (around Dh1200 to 1400 per day) or camels (Dh350 to 380 per person per day) for that ultimate experience at the sand dunes of Chigaga and Chebbi.

MARRAKESH

pop 1,091,540

Capital of the south and the epicentre of Moroccan tourism, Marrakesh is changing fast. Once the hub of camel caravans from the south, the oasis was the finest city many traders had ever seen. Marrakesh remains exotic but it is no longer the remote, dusty, down-at-heels city of the 1970s and '80s. Just as Moroccans craved modern housing, Europeans arrived dreaming of old houses in the heart of the medina (old town). This happy exchange has transformed the place, bringing money and work to a city that lives off its looks and its wits.

The looks are still there, as the first glimpse of its 16km-long time-worn ramparts confirm. And some things have remained – the Djemaa el-Fna and the area around it remains the beating heart of the city, the greatest souq in the south, whose ebbs and flows retain something of the transitory atmosphere that must have lingered around those first nomad campfires. But a new city is growing up around it, a playground for Europeans who want the exoticism of staying in a riad in the medina, but also want to hang around the Parisian-styled cafés in Guéliz and the new 'beach-style' swimming pools, or head up to the mountains for a day and party all night.

None of this has changed the essence of the place, yet: the heat, the dust, the Berbers, the mud-brick ramparts and all those other things that go into making Marrakesh so uniquely African and Moroccan are still there.

HISTORY

Founded in 1062 by the Almoravid sultan Yusuf bin Tachfin, Marrakesh became one of the Islamic world's most important artistic and cultural centres. Using much of the wealth plundered during the Almoravid conquest of Spain, Youssef extended and beautified the city.

The city's first golden age, however, was under Youssef's son Ali, born to a Christian slave mother. As well as palaces, mosques and baths, Ali commissioned construction of the extensive khettara (underground irrigation canals), which still supply Marrakesh's gardens with water from the High Atlas.

Sadly, much was razed by the Almohads in 1147, although the walls and the gateway to Ali's vast palace were spared. The city was rebuilt shortly afterwards and artisans from Andalucía were responsible for much of its construction. Marrakesh was to remain the capital of Morocco until the collapse of the Almohad dynasty in 1269, when the conquering Merenids moved the capital to Fès.

With the rise to power of the Saadians in the 16th century, Marrakesh again became the capital. One of the more outstanding of the Saadian sultans, Ahmed al-Mansour, the Golden One because of his riches, left his mark with the exquisite El-Badi Palace and the Saadian tombs.

With the accession to power of the Alawites, the capital moved to Meknès, but Marrakesh was too strategically important to be ignored. So, while Moulay Ismail was responsible for plundering the El-Badi Palace for building materials, his successor, Sidi Mohammed ben Abdallah, found he needed to pour resources into rebuilding the city walls, kasbah, palaces, mosques and mechouars (royal parade grounds), as well as creating new gardens (such as the Jardin Ménara).

By the 19th century, Marrakesh had been long in decline, although it regained some prestige in 1873 when Moulay al-Hassan I was crowned there. Then, under the French Protectorate, the ville nouvelle was laid out and the medina revitalised and resettled.

And now another Moroccan king is in the process of transforming Marrakesh: the current young monarch has announced ambitious plans to boost tourism to the city over the next decade. Many hotel complexes are being built among the olive groves, large developments of villas line the road in from the airport, shops spring up in the new industrial zone and, in a city where it used to be hard to find a drink, nightclubs now throb through the night packed with party people dancing to music from guest DJs. Meanwhile, in the medina the old houses are being revived, museums are being opened, and riads and restaurants are thriving as another golden age dawns.

ORIENTATION

The medina and the ville nouvelle of Marrakesh are roughly the same size. It takes 30 minutes to walk from the centre of the ville nouvelle to Djemaa el-Fna, the main square in the heart of the old city; you may want to use public transport between the two.

The main areas of the ville nouvelle are Guéliz and Hivernage. The latter is home to the majority of midrange and luxury hotels. In Guéliz you'll find the bulk of offices, restaurants, cafés and shops, plus a few hotels, clustered on or near the main thoroughfare, Ave Mohammed V. The train station lies southwest of Guéliz, following Ave Hassan II from the central Place du 16 Novembre. The main bus station is near Bab Doukkala; it's roughly a 10-minute walk northeast of this same square, and about 20 minutes from Djemaa el-Fna.

Most budget hotels are clustered in the narrow streets and alleys south of Djemaa el-Fna. The souqs and principal religious buildings lie to the north and the palaces to the south. To the southwest rises the city's most prominent landmark, the minaret of the Koutoubia Mosque.

Guides

You don't really need a guide in the medina if you have time on hand, as one of the great pleasures is to get lost. However if time is limited or if this is your first time into the warren of a North African medina, there are benefits to having a guide: you will get to where you want to be, and it will save you from the advances of *faux guides* (unofficial guides). Official guides can be booked for Dh 200/300 for a half/full day at the tourist offices (p295) and in bigger hotels. Entry to the monuments, taxi rides and so forth are extra. Most travel agencies can also arrange guides (see Tours, p307).

If you have serious shopping in mind, you can book a private shopping tour with Laetitia Trouillet (☎ 074 217228; www.lalla.fr), a resident French fashion designer with fluent English, who for Dh3000 per day including car and driver, for two or three people, takes you from flea markets to hidden showrooms, and then on to the souqs where she bargains better than the locals.

INFORMATION
Bookshops

International newspapers can be bought from stands around town, notably those

---

MARRAKESH IN...

Two Days

Start the day on the terrace of **Café-Restaurant Argana** (p314) and make your way to the **Ali ben Youssef Medersa** (p298) and the **Musée de Marrakech** (p299). Head for **Dar el-Bacha** (p300) and plunge into the labyrinthine **souqs** (p304). Have lunch in the shade at **Café Arabe** (p317). Back in the **Djemaa el-Fna** (p297) take in the full spectacle, before indulging in an epic evening meal at **Le Tobsil** (p313). The next day concentrate on the **mellah** (p300) and visit the city's most famous palace, the **Palais el-Badi** (p300), the **Saadian Tombs** (p300) and the **Museum of Moroccan Arts** (p302). Later in the afternoon head for the ville nouvelle and relax in the tranquillity of the **Jardin Majorelle** (p303). Return to the medina, watch the sun set on the terrace of **Kosybar** (p317) and finish up with an utterly memorable meal in **Djemaa el-Fna** (p297).

Four Days

Follow the two day itinerary, and on the third day head out on an easy day-trip to the **Kasbah du Toubkal** (p328) where you can have lunch and take in the spectacular mountain scenery. In the evening go to heaven and back at **Dar Moha** (p314) around a glittering pool. Finish in style, strutting your stuff at **Pacha** (p317). On the fourth day go **cycling** (p304) in the Palmeraie, after which you can rest your weary limbs in the steamy comfort of one of Marrakesh's wonderful **hammams** (p304).

MARRAKESH

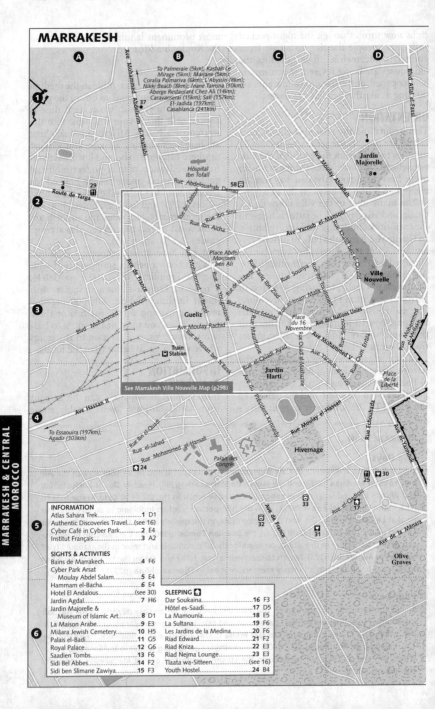

To Palmeraie (5km); Kasbah Le
Mirage (5km); Marjane (5km);
Coralia Palmariva (6km); L'Abyssin (8km);
Nikki Beach (8km); Jnane Tamsna (10km);
Aberge Restaurant Chez Ali (14km);
Caravanserai (15km); Safi (157km);
El-Jadida (197km);
Casablanca (241km)

To Essaouira (197km);
Agadir (303km)

See Marrakesh Ville Nouvelle Map (p298)

**MARRAKESH & CENTRAL
MOROCCO**

INFORMATION
Atlas Sahara Trek	1 D1
Authentic Discoveries Travel	(see 16)
Cyber Café in Cyber Park	2 E4
Institut Français	3 A2

SIGHTS & ACTIVITIES
Bains de Marrakech	4 F6
Cyber Park Arsat Moulay Abdel Salam	5 E4
Hammam el-Bacha	6 E4
Hotel El Andalous	(see 30)
Jardin Agdal	7 H6
Jardin Majorelle & Museum of Islamic Art	8 D1
La Maison Arabe	9 E3
Miâara Jewish Cemetery	10 H5
Palais el-Badi	11 G5
Royal Palace	12 G6
Saadien Tombs	13 F6
Sidi Bel Abbes	14 F2
Sidi ben Slimane Zawiya	15 F3

SLEEPING
Dar Soukaina	16 F3
Hôtel es-Saadi	17 D5
La Mamounia	18 E5
La Sultana	19 F6
Les Jardins de la Medina	20 F6
Riad Edward	21 F2
Riad Kniza	22 E3
Riad Nejma Lounge	23 E3
Tlaata wa-Sitteen	(see 16)
Youth Hostel	24 B4

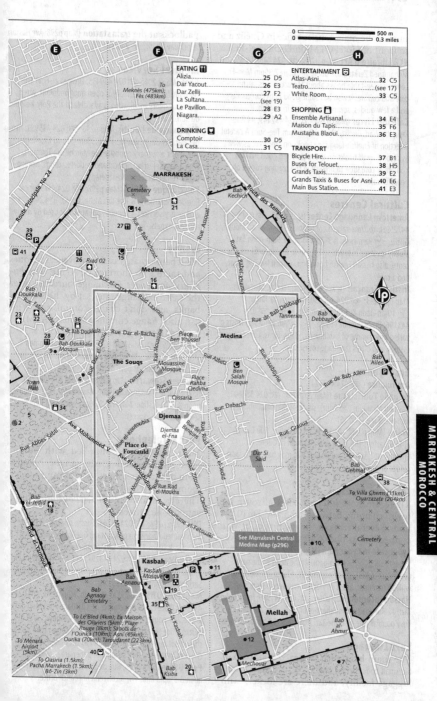

0   500 m
0   0.3 miles

EATING 🍴
Alizia...25 D5
Dar Yacout...................................26 E3
Dar Zellij.....................................27 F2
La Sultana..............................(see 19)
Le Pavillon..................................28 E3
Niagara.......................................29 A2

DRINKING 🍷
Comptoir.....................................30 D5
La Casa.......................................31 C5

ENTERTAINMENT 🎭
Atlas-Asni....................................32 C5
Teatro...................................(see 17)
White Room.................................33 C5

SHOPPING 🛍
Ensemble Artisanal........................34 E4
Maison du Tapis...........................35 F6
Mustapha Blaoui...........................36 E3

TRANSPORT
Bicycle Hire..................................37 B1
Buses for Telouet..........................38 H5
Grands Taxis................................39 E2
Grands Taxis & Buses for Asni........40 E6
Main Bus Station...........................41 E3

To
Meknès (475km);
Fès (483km)

MARRAKESH

Cemetery

Route Principale No 24

Bab
Kechich

Route des Remparts

Rue Assouel

Medina

Riad 02

Rue de Bab Taghzout

Rue-el-Caza Rue Riad Laarous

Bab
Doukkala

Rue de Bab Khemis

Rue de Bab Debbagh

Tanneries

Bab
Debbagh

Rue Fatima Zohra

Rue de Bab Doukkala

Rue Dar el-Bacha

Place
ben Youssef

Medina

Bab
Ailen

Rue de Bab Ailen

Bab Doukkala
Mosque

The Souqs

Rue Dar el-Glaoui

Rue Mouassine

Mouassine
Mosque

Rue Azbet

Rue Issebtyine

Rue de Bab Ailen

Town
Hall

Rue Sidi el-Yamani

Rue El
Ksour

Place
Rahba
Qedima

Ben
Salah
Mosque

Qissaria

Rue Dabachi

Djemaa

Djemaa
el-Fna

Rue el-Koutoubia

Rue des
Banques

Rue Graoua

Rue Bâ Ahmad

Place de
Foucauld

Ave Mohammed V

Rue Moulay Ismail

Rue de Bab Agnaou

Rue Riad Zitoun el-Jedid

Rue Riad Zitoun el-Qedim

Dar Si
Said

Bab
Gehmat

Ave el-Mouahidine

Bab
el-Jedid

Blvd el-Yarmouk

Rue Sidi Mimoun

Rue Riad
el-Moukha

Ave Houmane el-Fétouaki

To Villa Chems (11km);
Ouarzazate (204km)

See Marrakesh Central
Medina Map (p296)

Cemetery

Kasbah

Kasbah
Mosque

Bab
Agnaou

Rue de la Kasbah

Bab Agnaou
Cemetery

To Le'Bled (4km); La Maison
des Oliviers (5km); Plage
Rouge (8km); Sabots de
l'Ourika (10km); Asni (45km);
Ourika (70km); Taroudannt (223km)

Mellah

Bab
al-Ahmar

To Ménara
Airport
(5km)

To Oasiria (1.5km);
Pacha Marrakech (1.5km);
Bô-Zin (3km)

Bab
Ksiba

Mechouar

Rue Abbes Sebti

Ave Mohammed V

MARRAKESH & CENTRAL
MOROCCO

outside the main tourist office in Guéliz and in front of Hôtel CTM on Djemaa el-Fna.

ACR Libraire d'Art (Map p298; ☎ 024 446792; 55 Blvd Mohammed Zerktouni, Guéliz; ☼ 8am-7.30pm Mon-Fri) Lovely coffee-table books about Moroccan arts, architecture and culture. It also has some good books on cookery and a few guides, some of which are in English.

Café des Livres (Map p298; ☎ 024 432149; 44 Rue Tariq ibn Ziad, Guéliz; ☼ 9.30am-9pm Tue-Sun) A careful selection of English-language books on Morocco, as well as second-hand books on the region and good fiction. You are encouraged to browse in the reading corner or peaceful café.

Cultural Centres

American Language Center (Map p298; ☎ 024 447259; http://marrakesh.aca.org.ma; 3 Impasse du Moulin, Guéliz; ☼ 9am-noon & 3-7pm Mon-Fri, 9am-noon Sat) Mainly involved in teaching English to Arabic speakers, the centre also has an English bookshop, a small lending library and a café.

Institut Français (www.ifm.ma in French; Marrakesh Map pp292-3; ☎ 024 446930; Route de la Targa; ☼ 10am-noon & 3-6pm Mon-Sat; Medina ☎ 024 443196; Place Djemaa el-Fna; ☼ 3-7pm Mon-Sat) Hosts a varied programme of exhibitions, plays, films, concerts and events, and offers language courses.

Emergency

Ambulance (☎ 024 443724)

Brigade Touristique (Map pp292-3; ☎ 024 384601; Rue Sidi Mimoun; ☼ 24hr), south of the Koutoubia Mosque. **Fire** (☎ 15)

Police (Map p298; ☎ 19; Hôtel de Police, Rue Ouadi el-Makhazine) The main police station in Guéliz. Effective at resolving arguments you may have with local guides or drivers.

Internet Access

There are now internet cafés all over the town, charging between Dh5 and Dh10 per hour. Several riads in the medina offer Wifi connection, as does Café des Livres (above).

Cyber Café in Cyber Park (Map pp292-3; Ave Mohammed V; per hr Dh5; ☼ 9.30am-8pm) At the heart of the new Cyber Park (p303) is, not surprisingly, a large internet centre with 15 terminals, a fast connection and very helpful staff.

Hassan Internet (Map p296; ☎ 024 441989; Immeuble Tazi, 12 Rue Riad el Moukha; per hr Dh8; ☼ 7am-1am) A busy popular café near the Tazi Hotel with 12 fast terminals.

Left Luggage

The main **bus station** (Map pp292-3; Bab Doukkala; big/small bags per day Dh8/5; ☼ 24hrs) has a left-luggage facility, and there are lockers with

padlocks at the **train station** (Map p298; Ave Hassan II; per day Dh10; ☼ 24hrs).

Medical Services

Phar (Map p296; ☎ 024 430415; Djemaa el-Fna) This centrally located pharmacy is open until midnight, after that emergency medication is available at the Polyclinique du Sud.

Pharmacie de l'Unité (Map p298; ☎ 024 435982; Ave des Nations Unies, Guéliz; ☼ 8.30am-11pm) Excellent late-night pharmacy opposite the Marché Ibn Toumert, with a vast selection of local and imported drugs, homeopathic remedies and aromatherapy.

Polyclinique du Sud (Map p298; ☎ 024 447999; cnr Rue de Yougoslavie & Rue Ibn Aicha, Guéliz; ☼ 24hr emergency service) A popular, private clinic used by many resident expats.

Money

Most banks change cash or travellers cheques and there's no shortage of ATMs. The *bureaux de change* (exchange bureaus) offer the same exchange rate (set by the state) as banks, and don't charge commission. You can also change currency at many ATMs.

Crédit du Maroc (☼ 8.45am-1pm & 3-6.45pm Mon-Sat) Ville nouvelle Map p298; 215 Ave Mohammed V; Medina Map p296; Rue de Bab Agnaou) Offers after-hours exchange facilities at both of these branches.

Voyages Schwartz (Map p298; ☎ 024 437469; 2nd fl, Immeuble Moutawakil, 1 Rue Mauritanie; ☼ 8.30am-noon & 2.30-6.30pm Mon-Fri, 8.30am-noon Sat) Represents American Express.

Post & Telephone

Marrakesh is well supplied with public card phones, and cards can be bought from post offices, news vendors and *tabacs* (combined tobacconist and newsagency). The city is also full of *téléboutiques* (private phone offices).

DHL (Map p298; ☎ 024 437647; www.dhl.com; 113 Ave Mohammed Abdelkrim el-Khattabi, Guéliz; ☼ 8am-6pm Mon-Fri, 8.30am-12.20pm Sat) International courier service.

FedEx (Map p298; ☎ 024 448257; 113 Ave Abdelkrim el-Khattabi, Guéliz; ☼ 8am-6.30pm Mon-Fri, 8am-12.15pm Sat) International courier service.

Main Post Office (Barid al-Maghrib; Map p298; ☎ 024 431963; Place du 16 Novembre; ☼ 8.30am-2pm Mon-Sat) In the ville nouvelle, poste restante is at window 3 and the parcel office (Ave Hassan II) is around the corner (parcels should not be wrapped beforehand as they need to be checked at the counter; string and paper are provided).

Post Office (Map p296; Rue de Bab Agnaou; ☼ 8am-noon & 3-6pm Mon-Fri) A convenient branch office.

Toilets

There are no clean official public toilets in Marrakesh. If you're caught short, you'll find that the toilets in Les Terrasses de l'Alhambra (p314) are clean, or otherwise stop for a quick juice at the Café des Épices (p315). In Guéliz are dozens of swanky cafés where you can easily nip to the loo.

Tourist Information

Office National Marocain du Tourisme (ONMT; Map p298; ☎ 024 436131; Place Abdel Moumen ben Ali, Guéliz; ☒ 8.30am-noon & 2.30-6.30pm Mon-Fri, 9am-noon & 3-6pm Sat) The main regional tourist office with willing staff but unhelpful ONMT glossy brochures.
Syndicat d'Initiative (Map p298; ☎ 024 430886; 176 Ave Mohammed V; ☒ 8.30am-12.30pm & 2.30-6.30pm Mon-Fri, 9am-noon Sat) More basic information about the city.

Travel Agencies

The bulk of the travel agencies have offices on or near Ave Mohammed V, west of Place du 16 Novembre in Guéliz.

Atlas Voyages (Map p298; ☎ 024 430333; www .atlasvoyages.com in French; 131 Ave Mohammed V)
Destination-Evasion (Map p298; ☎ 024 447375; www.destination-evasion.com in French; Villa El Borj, Rue Khaled ben Oualid) Specialises in tailored tours around Morocco, particularly to the south. Books flights, transport and accommodation, as well as organised tours.
Menara Tours (Map p298; ☎ 024 446654; 41 Rue de Yougoslavie) Books flights, transport and organised tours, and is the only registered agent for British Airways.

SIGHTS

All the monuments in Marrakesh are located within the vast **medina** walls (a 16km circuit) and will take at least a couple of days to get around. At the core of the medina lies **Djemaa el-Fna**, the most overwhelming experience in town, and to its north the warren of lanes that constitute the **souqs** (see p304). Shopping seems to be the main occupation in this area, but if you have the stamina, just wander off the main drags and discover day-to-day life in the medina's food markets and more residential areas. After a hectic day in the medina, many people find themselves drawn to gentile **Guéliz** with its hip cafés, 1930s architecture and boutique-style shops.

The Koutoubia

Dominating the Marrakshi landscape, southwest of Djemaa el-Fna, is that most famous and most venerated monument, the **Koutoubia** (Map pp292-3; Ave Mohammed V; closed to visitors). Its 70m tall minaret, nearly double the height of its precursor at Córdoba, is visible for miles in all directions. The word 'minaret' originates from the Arabic *al-manar*, which means both lighthouse and minaret. At dusk, in the fading crimson light of evening, the resounding call to prayer that echoes across the city has a powerful emotive effect.

Built by the Almohad Sultan Yakoub el-Mansour (1184–99), on the site of a previous

---

THE ULTIMATE BANQUET

As the sun sets, the beat of the Djemaa el-Fna gets turned up and the square disappears in a cloud of smoke. The snail soup is steaming, the kebabs and *merguez* (sausages) are smoking on the grills, and it all smells delicious. Friendly chefs woo passers-by with promises of fresh produce and free mint tea. Don't be afraid to talk back: the banter is part of the fun. Squeeze in at the communal table. No sooner have you ordered than the food arrives.

Most stalls in the square serve brochettes of chicken, beef or *kefta* (meat balls) with chips (five for Dh20 to Dh25), couscous with vegetables and meat (Dh 25) and a variety of traditional tajines (Dh25). Look out for the stall selling *harira* (Dh3), a thick soup of meat, chick peas, tomatoes and lentils served with dates and honey cakes, and *tanjia Marrakshiya* (Dh 20), beef cooked in an earthenware pot with *smen* (clarified butter). For something more exotic try out *berbouch* (snail soup, Dh10). Or sheep's head: the hair is singed off in a fire, then the head is cleaned in hot water and stewed with chickpeas. It is quite a delicacy – everything is eaten but the eyes.

Large copper urns contain *hunja* (Dh2), a spicy cinnamon tea, which traditionally comes with spicy-sweet cakes (Dh2.50) known as *sellou*, similar to gingerbread.

The hubbub at the food stalls is pure entertainment, but the real dessert is the show unfolding around the square, as musicians, magicians, acrobats, storytellers, fortune tellers and snake charmers take the stage.

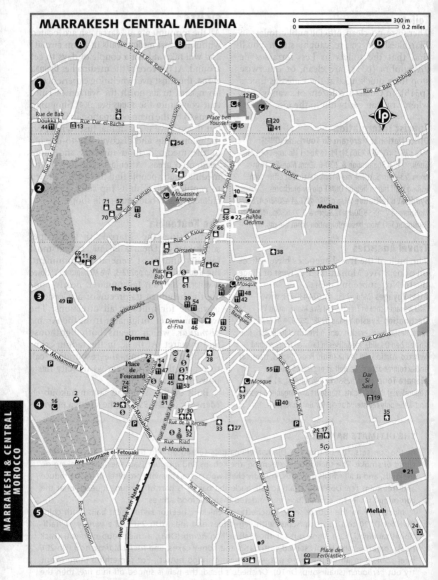

MARRAKESH CENTRAL MEDINA

11th-century Almoravid mosque, this is the oldest and best preserved of the Almohad's three most famous minarets – the others being the Tour Hassan in Rabat (p108) and the Giralda in Seville (Spain). It is also a classic example of Moroccan-Andalucian architecture; its features are mirrored in many other minarets throughout the coun-

try, none of which can match the Koutoubia for sheer size.

When first built, the Koutoubia was covered with painted plaster and brilliantly coloured *zellij* (tilework), but this decoration has all disappeared. What can still be seen, however, are the decorative panels, which are different on each face and practi-

INFORMATION
Crédit du Maroc (ATM & Bureau de Change)	1	B4
French Consulate	2	A4
Hassan Internet	3	B4
Parcel Office	(see 6)	
Pharmacie de Garde	4	B4
Police Station	5	C4
Post Office	6	B4

SIGHTS & ACTIVITIES
Ali ben Youssef Medersa	7	C1
Ali ben Youssef Mosque	8	C1
Apothecary Stalls	9	C5
Criée Berbère (Carpet Souq)	10	C2
Dar Attajmil	11	A3
Dar Bellarj	12	C1
Dar Si Said	(see 19)	
Dar el-Bacha	13	A1
Institut Français	14	B4
Koubba Ba'adyin	15	C1
Koutoubia Mosque	16	A4
Maison Tiskiwin	17	C4
Mouassine Fountain	18	B2
Museum of Moroccan Arts	19	D4
Musée de Marrakesh	20	C1
Palais de la Bahia	21	D5
Place Rahba Qedima	22	C2
Souq Cuisine	23	C2
Synagogue	24	D5

SLEEPING
Dar al Sultan	25	C4
Hôtel Central Palace	26	B4
Hôtel Chellah	27	C4
Hôtel CTM	28	B4
Hôtel de Foucauld	29	A4
Hôtel Gallia	30	B4
Hôtel Sherazade	31	C4
Hôtel Souria	32	B4
Jnane Mogador Hôtel	33	B4
Marrakech Medina	34	A1
Riad Akka	35	D4
Riad Eden	36	C5
Riad Hôtel Assia	37	B4
Riad Magi	38	C3

EATING
Café-Restaurant Argana	39	B3
Casa Lalla	40	C4
Chez Abdelhay	41	C1
Chez Chegrouni	42	C3
Dar Cherifa	43	B2
Dar Moha	44	A1
Fast Food al-Ahbab	45	B4
Food Stalls	46	B3
Hôtel Ali	47	B4
Le Marrakchi	48	C3
Le Tobsil	49	A3
Les Terrasses de L'Alhambra	50	B3
Mabrouka	51	B4

Market
Market	52	B3
Pâtisserie des Princes	53	B4
Qissaria Food Stalls	54	B3
Ryad Tamsna	55	C4

DRINKING
Café Arabe	56	B2
Café Bougainvillea	57	A2
Café des Épices	58	B2
Juice Stands	59	B3
Kosybar	60	C5

SHOPPING
Akbar Delights	61	B3
Au Fil d'Or	62	B3
Aya's	63	C5
Beldi	64	B3
Belhadj	65	B3
Chez Brahim	66	B2
Fnac Berbère	67	B3
Kifkif	68	A3
Kulchi	69	A3
La Maison du Kaftan	70	B2
Ministerio del Gusto	71	A2
Souk Sebbaghine (Dyers Souq)	72	B2
Zenbougue	(see 68)	

TRANSPORT
Caléche Stand	73	B4
Local Buses	74	A4

cally constitute a textbook of early Islamic design.

The name (from *kutubiyyin,* Arabic for booksellers) is the only echo of the large booksellers' market that once existed here. Nowadays, the area around the mosque is a favourite place for an evening stroll. You can walk around the flowered gardens and piazza to the west where excavations have revealed traces of the earlier Almoravid mosque, which had to be knocked down as it did not align with Mecca.

Djemaa el-Fna

The focal point of Marrakesh is **Djemaa el-Fna** (Map p296), a huge square in the medina, and the backdrop for one of the world's greatest spectacles. According to the author Paul Bowles, without it Marrakesh would be just another Moroccan city. 'La place' (the square) as it's called here, is where it all happens. This magical place can be overwhelming at first, but you'll find yourself returning to it time after time.

Although it can be lively at any hour of day, Djemaa el-Fna comes into its own at dusk (see boxed text, p295) when the curtain goes up on rows of open-air food stalls infusing the immediate area with mouth-watering aromas. Jugglers, storytellers, snake charmers, musicians, occasional acrobats and benign lunatics consume the remaining space, each surrounded by jostling spectators who listen and watch intently, or fall about laughing before moving on to the next act. Naturally, tourists are soon cajoled into joining in and to paying a few dirham for the show.

In between the groups of spectators, diners, shoppers and tourists weave the occasional hustler, pickpocket, knick-knack seller, hashish dealer and glue-sniffing kid. On the outer edges are the juice stalls with their kerosene lanterns ablaze. Beyond them, hunched on the ground with their eye-catching wares spread before them, herbalists sit poised to prescribe a potion for whatever ails you. Later at night, with fewer visitors around, musicians from the Derkaoua and Gnaoua spiritual brotherhoods start playing their strong hypnotic music on drums, flutes and *ginbris* (two- or three-string guitars).

Many believe that it is the tourists who fuel the activity in Djemaa el-Fna, but at night the vast majority of the crowd is local: few tourists would understand the tales of marvels or lunacies that the storytellers recount. It should not be surprising to

MARRAKESH & CENTRAL MOROCCO

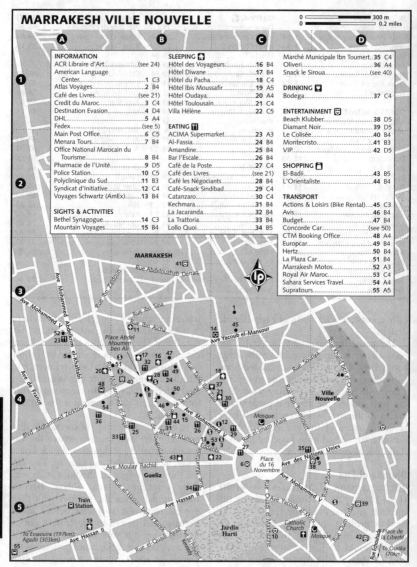

MARRAKESH VILLE NOUVELLE

0 — 300 m
0 — 0.2 miles

INFORMATION
ACR Libraire d'Art....................(see 24)
American Language
Center....................................**1** C3
Atlas Voyages.............................**2** B4
Café des Livres.......................(see 21)
Credit du Maroc.........................**3** C4
Destination Evasion.....................**4** D4
DHL...**5** A4
Fedex.......................................(see 5)
Main Post Office.........................**6** C5
Menara Tours.............................**7** B4
Office National Marocain du
Tourisme.................................**8** B4
Pharmacie de l'Unité....................**9** D5
Police Station...........................**10** C5
Polyclinique du Sud.....................**11** B3
Syndicat d'Initiative...................**12** B4
Voyages Schwartz (AmEx).............**13** B4

SIGHTS & ACTIVITIES
Bethel Synagogue.......................**14** C3
Mountain Voyages.......................**15** B4

SLEEPING
Hôtel des Voyageurs....................**16** B4
Hôtel Diwane.............................**17** B4
Hôtel du Pacha...........................**18** C4
Hôtel Ibis Moussafir....................**19** A5
Hôtel Oudaya.............................**20** A4
Hôtel Toulousain.........................**21** C4
Villa Hélène..............................**22** C5

EATING
ACIMA Supermarket.....................**23** A3
Al-Fassia..................................**24** B4
Amandine.................................**25** B4
Bar l'Escale...............................**26** B4
Café de la Poste.........................**27** C4
Café des Livres.......................(see 21)
Café les Négociants.....................**28** B4
Café-Snack Sindibad....................**29** C4
Catanzaro.................................**30** C4
Kechmara.................................**31** B4
La Jacaranda.............................**32** B4
La Trattoria...............................**33** B4
Lollo Quoi.................................**34** B5

Marché Municipale Ibn Toumert..**35** C4
Oliveri......................................**36** A4
Snack le Siroua......................(see 40)

DRINKING
Bodega.....................................**37** C4

ENTERTAINMENT
Beach Klubber...........................**38** D5
Diamant Noir.............................**39** D5
Le Colisée.................................**40** B4
Montecristo...............................**41** B3
VIP..**42** D5

SHOPPING
El-Badii....................................**43** B5
L'Orientaliste.............................**44** B4

TRANSPORT
Actions & Loisirs (Bike Rental)....**45** C3
Avis...**46** B4
Budget.....................................**47** B4
Concorde Car........................(see 50)
CTM Booking Office....................**48** A4
Europcar...................................**49** B4
Hertz.......................................**50** B4
La Plaza Car..............................**51** B4
Marrakesh Motos.......................**52** A3
Royal Air Maroc.........................**53** C4
Sahara Services Travel.................**54** A4
Supratours...............................**55** A5

MARRAKESH

Rue Abdelouahab Derraq

Ave Mohammed V Abdelkrim el-Khattabi

Ave Mohammed V Abdelkrim el-Khattabi

Rue Ibn Zaidoun

Rue Ibn Sina

Rue Ibn Aicha

Place Abdel
Moumen
ben Ali

Rue Souriya

Ave Yacoub el-Mansour

Ville
Nouvelle

Rue Khalid ben el-Ouald

Rue de la Liberté

Ave de France

Rue Mohammed el-Beqal

Ave Mohammed V

Rue Tariq ben Ziad

Blvd. Mohammed Zerktouni

Rue de Yougoslavie

Blvd el-Mansour Eddahbi

Mosque

Rue el-Imam Malik

Ave Moulay Rachid

Rue Mauritania

Rue Ibn Toumert

Guéliz

Place
du 16
Novembre

Ave des Nations Unies

Ave Mohammed V

Rue Zebou

Rue Sebou

Ave Hassan II

Train
Station

Rue el-Hassan ben N'Batek

Ave Hassan II

Rue el Ouad Ayad

Ave Oued el-Makhzine

Jardin
Harti

Catholic
Church

Mosque

Rue Echouhada

Place de
la Liberté

To Essaouira (197km);
Agadir (303km)

To Ourika
(70km)

discover that in 2001 Unesco declared the square a World Heritage site, as 'a masterpiece of the oral and intangible heritage of humanity'.

Once you've wandered the square, take a balcony seat in a rooftop café or restaurant to absorb the spectacle at a more relaxing distance.

Ali ben Youssef Mosque & Medersa

The largest of the mosques inside the medina is the **Ali ben Youssef Mosque** (Map pp292-3), which marks the intellectual and religious heart of the medina and is closed to non-Muslims. First built in the second half of the 12th century by the Almoravid sultan of the same name, it is the oldest surviving mosque in Marrakesh, although it was almost completely rebuilt in the 19th century in the Merenid style, in response to popular demand.

Next to the mosque is the **Ali ben Youssef Medersa** (Map pp292–3; ☎ 024 441893; Place ben Youssef; admission Dh40, ⏱ 9am-6pm winter, 9am-7pm in summer). A ticket for joint admission to the *medersa* (theological college), Koubba Ba'adiyn and Musée de Marrakech is only Dh60. After a long and painstaking restoration, the *medersa* is again a peaceful and meditative place with some absolutely stunning examples of stucco decoration. The most valuable treasure of the *medersa*, a 10th-century marble basin which used to adorn the courtyard, has now been moved to the Dar Si Said Museum (p302).

The *medersa* was founded by the Merenid Sultan Abu Hassan in the 14th century, and restored in 1564 by the Saadians who made it the largest theological college in the Maghreb and a rival to the important Medersa Bou Inania in Fès (p220). Follow the mosque walls around to the left, and you'll come to the entrance on your right.

Enter down a dark corridor and turn right into the splendid courtyard centred around a white marble ablution basin. Like the other great Merenid *medersa*s open to non-Muslims, the courtyard has intricate stucco decoration combined with a *zellij* base and crowned by carved cedar. A magnificent portal gives way to the prayer room.

Upstairs are 132 students' cells, tiny and bare in stark contrast to the rich Andalucian decoration elsewhere in the *medersa*. It's hard to imagine how, as is claimed, they crammed as many as 900 people into these rooms!

To be viewed in conjunction with the *medersa* is the **Koubba Ba'adiyn** (Map p296; Place ben Youssef; admission Dh15, ⏱ 9am-7pm), signposted opposite. Although modest in appearance and size, the *koubba* (sanctuary or shrine) is interesting for the fact that it pre-dates the *medersa* and is the only example of Almoravid Marrakesh that wasn't destroyed by the zealous Almohads who succeeded them.

Built in the early 12th century, probably as an ablutions block for the mosque, it is a small but elegant display of Muslim decorative invention – fine arabesque designs, ziggurat merlons and complex octagonal

ribbed vaulting – much of which was used here for the first time, but has since become very familiar.

With these three exceptions, all the mosques and working *medersa*s in Marrakesh are closed to non-Muslims.

Musée de Marrakech

Inaugurated in 1997, the **Musée de Marrakech** (Map p296; ☎ 024 390911; www.museedemarrakech.ma in French; Place ben Youssef; admission Dh40, ⏱ 9am-7pm) is housed in a beautifully restored 19th-century palace, Dar Mnebhi. For Dh60 you can get a joint ticket for admission to the museum, Medersa ben Youssef and Koubba Ba'adiyn.

The original home of Mehdi Mnebhi, a highly regarded defence minister to Moulay Abdelaziz (1894–1908), the decaying palace was bought by dedicated patron of the arts Omar Benjelloun, who set about restoring it. Inside, an orgy of stalactite stuccowork drips from the ceiling and combines with a mind-boggling excess of *zellij*. Not only does the house have a glorious central courtyard with fountains, around which galleries display artworks, it also allows the visitor an insight into household features such as the original hammam – although those on the scale of this example obviously belonged only to the wealthiest of Marrakshi grandees.

Temporary exhibitions cover both traditional and contemporary Moroccan arts. The museum also hosts the occasional concert or theatrical event.

Outside there is a pleasant and tranquil courtyard café and a small bookshop selling a selection of art books, posters and postcards.

Dar Bellarj

An old caravanserai near the Medersa ben Youssef, with a stork hospital (*bellarj* is Arabic for stork) on its top floor, was beautifully restored by the Dar Bellarj Foundation and turned into a cultural centre, **Dar Bellarj** (Map pp292–3; ☎ 024 444555; 9 Toulalat Zaouiat Lahdar; Dh15; ⏱ 9am-1.30pm & 2.30-6pm). The elegant architecture makes a perfect backdrop for temporary exhibitions of contemporary Moroccan art. The peaceful courtyard, where mint tea is offered free with admission, is a good place to relax after shopping in the souqs.

Dar el-Bacha

The former palace of the notorious Pasha Thami el-Glaoui (see p289), **Dar el-Bacha** (Map pp292-3; 1 Rue Dar el-Bacha) has been under restoration for a few years, but at least part of it should be open to the public by the end of 2006 as a Museum of Islamic Arts. The entry is on rue Sar el-Batha. The museum will house the large collection of Patti Birch, a wealthy American who has devoted herself to history and arts, has been involved in the Metropolitan and Guggenheim museums in New York, and now lives in Marrakesh.

Kasbah & Mellah

South of the main medina area is the **kasbah** (Royal Quarter; Map pp292-3) and, east of it, the **mellah** (the Jewish quarter; Map pp292-3). The kasbah contains the ruins of the Palais el-Badi, the tombs of the Saadian princes and the current royal palace (closed to visitors).

The *mellah*, to the east, is still home to some of Marrakesh's 238 remaining Jews. Saadian Sultan Abdullah el-Ghalib moved the Jews into this secure quarter beside the royal palace, surrounded by walls and entered by just two gates, in 1558. The royal family appreciated the talents of the Jewish community of jewellers, bankers and traders who spoke many languages. The *mellah* still looks different from the rest of the city and its local cemetery, the **miâara** (Map pp292-3), is an eerie sight: brilliant white tombs stretching into the distance.

The main entrance to the *mellah* is off Place des Ferblantiers through the *qissaria* (covered market). If you want to visit any of the small synagogues you'll need a local guide. The oldest **synagogue** (Map pp292-3) on Rue Talmud Torah is still in use.

PALAIS EL-BADI

The most famous of the city's palaces is the now-ruined **Palais el-Badi** (Map pp292-3; Place des Ferblantiers; admission palace/Koutoubia minbar Dh10/20; 8.30-noon & 2.30-6pm), south of Djemaa el-Fna. Built by Ahmed al-Mansour between 1578 and 1602, it was reputed to be one of the most beautiful palaces in the world and well deserved its name, the Incomparable.

What you can see today is only a fraction of the whole as the private palaces and apartments of courtiers and family are now incorporated in the current royal palace,

Dar el-Makhzen. All that is left are the towering pisé walls taken over by stork nests, and the staggering scale to give an impression of its former splendour.

After entering the palace you proceed into the vast 130m-long central court with, at its centre, a 90m-long pool surrounded by sunken orange groves and flower gardens. The large structure to the west is the Koubba al-Khamsiniyya, which was used as a reception hall on state occasions and was named for its 50 marble columns. Proceed south and you'll find yourself in a confusing maze of underground corridors, storerooms and dungeons – a torch (flashlight) will come in handy. A pavilion in the southeastern corner houses a 12th-century treasure, the beautifully restored *minbar* (pulpit) from the Koutoubia (p295) that inspired so many Arab and Andalucian poets.

The enormous cost of building the palace was met largely from the ransom of Portuguese nobles following their disastrous defeat at the hands of the Saadians in 1578 in the Battle of the Three Kings, a victory that earned the Saadian ruler the epithet 'al-Mansour' (the Victorious). The building work itself, carried out by the best craftsmen of the age, took over 20 years to complete, with marble pillars paid for by their weight in sugar, and gold leaf to cover the walls, brought along the newly captured caravan routes from Timbuktu. Unfortunately, the quality and luxury of the palace did not escape the plundering hand of Alaouite Moulay Ismail, who spent a further 12 years stripping the palace bare.

The easiest way to get to the palace is to take Ave Houmane el-Fetouaki southeast from the Koutoubia Mosque to Place des Ferblantiers, where the ramparts begin, and you'll see a large gate. Go through this and turn right. The entrance and ticket booth are straight ahead.

Used as the main venue for the Marrakesh Festival of Popular Arts in July (see p307) and the International Film Festival (see p307), the ruins provide an atmospheric arena, when myriad lights reflect off the water-filled pools and the aroma of orange-blossom lingers in the evening air.

SAADIAN TOMBS

Long hidden from intrusive eyes, the area of the **Saadian Tombs** (Map pp292-3; Rue de la Kasbah; admission Dh10; 8.30-11.45am & 2.30-5.45pm), along-side the Kasbah Mosque, were originally the privileged burial place of the sherif, the descendants of the Prophet Mohammed.

The ornate tombs that can be seen today are the resting places of Saadian princes, most notably Ahmed al-Mansour. Unlike the Palais el-Badi, another of Al-Mansour's projects, the tombs escaped Moulay Ismail's depredations – possibly he was supersti-tious about plundering the dead. Instead he sealed up the entrance to the tombs, which were not rediscovered until the early 20th century. As a result, they still convey some of the opulence and superb artistry that must also have been lavished on the palace.

The tombs were not 'rediscovered' until 1917 when General Lyautey, his curiosity awakened by an aerial survey of the area, ordered a passageway to be made to the tombs. They have since been restored.

A high corridor leads into the peaceful and splendid cemetery, where 66 Saadians are buried inside the *koubbas*, including Al-Mansour, his successors and their closest family members. More than 100 are bur-ied in the gardens outside the buildings. At the entrance of the main *koubba* is a Prayer Hall supported by four pillars, where mainly children are buried. The central Hall of the Twelve Columns is one of the finest examples of Moroccan-Andalucian deco-rative art. Among the columns of Italian marble and under the gilded sculpted dome are the tombs of Ahmed al-Mansour, his son and grandson, as well as 33 others. The elegant second mausoleum, set further in, houses the tomb of Al-Mansour's father Mohammed ech-Cheikh and his mother, Lalla Messaouda.

The tombs are signposted down a nar-row alleyway at the southern edge of the Kasbah Mosque. The entry fee allows you to wander around at will – it doesn't take long. If you prefer, a guide will accompany you and explain what you are looking at. A tip (Dh10 to Dh20) will be expected. To avoid the coach tours the best time to visit is in the early morning or evening.

The tombs were originally connected to the nearby Palais el-Badi and the authorities responsible for them are preparing plans to open a new passage between the two.

Rue Riad Zitoun el-Jedid
PALAIS DE LA BAHIA

The **Palais de la Bahia** (Map pp292-3; ☎ 024 389564; Rue Riad Zitoun el-Jedid; admission Dh10; 8.30-11.45am & 2.30-5.45pm Sat-Thu, 8.30-11.30am & 3-5.45pm Fri), the 'Brilliant', is the perfect antidote to the simplicity of the nearby el-Badi (see oppos-ite). Built by two grand viziers, a father and his son, Si Ahmed ben Musa (also known as Bou-Ahmed), its splendour so much aroused the envy of the ruling sultan, Abdel

---

THE HOLY SEVEN

Popular belief has it that *es-sebti*, the seven patron saints of Marrakesh, are merely sleeping and that one day they will wake and resume their good works. Every year pilgrims come to Marrakesh for a *ziara* (pilgrimage) when, over a week, they visit a different saint's tomb each day. In the past, when travel to the holy cities of Mecca and Medina was impossibly arduous from western-most Morocco, a pilgrimage to all seven tombs was considered, in popular folklore, a suitable equivalent. The *ziara* started at the shrine of Sidi Lyad, then moved to Sidi Youssef ben Ali, Sidi Abd el-Aziz, Sidi el-Ghawzani, Sidi Es-Suhayi and Sidi ben Slimane al-Jazuli (**Sidi ben Slimane Zawiya**; Map pp292-3) before finishing at the most important one of all, **Sidi bel Abbès** (Map pp292-3). You can't enter these shrines, but even from outside you can appreciate the strength of continuing belief when you witness the daily distribution of food and alms to the poor and blind beggars who linger around the shrine of Sidi bel Abbès.

Gnaoui religious brotherhoods also hold the number seven sacred. They believe in the seven *mlouk* (spirits) that inhabit the air, the water, the forests and other specific places. Each spirit is distinguished by a colour: white, black, blue, green, yellow, red and one that is all these colours. A group of young Gnaoua musicians from the medina has for the first time recorded an entire *lila*, a night of trance and possession, and has brought out the first of seven CDs dedicated to the spirit of the invisible, represented by the colour black. The CD *Marrakech Undermoon: The Black Album* is available at Kifkif (p305) or www.kamarstudios.com.

Aziz, that he had the palace looted on the day Si Ahmed ben Musa died.

The rambling rooms, elaborate reception halls, living quarters, pleasure garden, fountains and numerous secluded shady courtyards were built towards the end of the 19th century, and housed Bou-Ahmed's family and retinue of four wives, 24 concubines and countless children.

The Bahia exemplifies the priority of privacy in Muslim architecture. You will often find that the multiple doorways linking various parts of the palace are placed so that you often can't see much past the open doorway, creating the impression of a series of separate and unconnected zones within the whole. The place may lack architectural cohesion, but this in no way detracts from its visual appeal.

You can only visit part of the palace, as some of it is still used by the royal family and maintenance staff. Follow the arrows through a series of rooms, among them the vizier's sleeping quarters (he had separate ones for snoozing during the day and evening) and various courtyards set aside for his wives and concubines. The four wives merited a room each around a courtyard. Sleeping quarters for the rather more numerous concubines were gathered around a (separate) courtyard.

To get there (orientation is easiest from the Palais el-Badi), take the road heading northeast from Place des Ferblantiers and you'll soon come to the entrance on your right.

DAR SI SAID
Further north of Palais de la Bahia and again off to the right from Rue Riad Zitoun el-Jedid (it's signposted) is **Dar Si Said** (Map pp292-3; ☎ 024 389564; Riad Zitoun el-Jedid; admission Dh20; ☑ 9-12.15pm & 3-6.15pm Wed-Mon), which now houses the **Museum of Moroccan Arts**, and is well worth a visit.

Si Said, Bou-Ahmed's brother, built his town house at about the same time as the grand vizier's Palais de la Bahia (p301) was constructed. While the Bahia is all about show and size, this much smaller house is finer and more impressive in decoration. Today the museum houses an exceptional collection of arts, including jewellery from the High Atlas, the Anti Atlas and the extreme south; carpets from the Haouz and the High Atlas; oil lamps from Tarou-

dannt; blue pottery from Safi; green pottery from Tamegroute; and leatherwork from Marrakesh.

As you enter, you will see a series of doors typical of the richer High Atlas and Anti Atlas houses. At the end of this corridor is the oldest exhibit in the museum: a marble basin dating back to the 10th century and brought to Marrakesh by Ali ben Youssef from Córdoba (Spain), then an epicentre of art and culture.

Next up are some charming medieval precursors of the Ferris wheel for tiny tots, which were used in local *moussem*s (festivals honouring local saints) right up until the 1960s.

The central garden and courtyard is flanked by rooms housing displays of heavy southern jewellery in silver, traditional women's garments, household goods, old muskets and daggers.

All explanations are in Arabic and French only.

MAISON TISKIWIN
En route to the Dar Si Said is **Maison Tiskiwin** (Map pp292-3; ☎ 024 389192; 8 Rue de la Bahia; adult/child Dh15/10; ☑ 9.30am-12.30pm & 3.30-5.30pm), the house of Bert Flint, a Dutch art lecturer and long-time resident of Morocco.

Flint opened his house, where he still lives and works, and his amazing collection to the public as a small but delightful museum. His passionate mission is to expose Marrakesh and Morocco's African roots. His permanent exhibition is set up as a journey from Marrakesh to Timbuktu and back, featuring a well-explained and rich collection of basketwork, textiles, woodwork, carpets and exotic jewellery arranged by area or tribe. Cosy lounge areas and delicious cooking smells are reminders that you're in a home, and a pleasant retreat.

Gardens
Marrakesh has more gardens than any other Moroccan city, offering the perfect escape from the hubbub of the souqs and the traffic, or just some shade from the heat of the afternoon sun. The municipality, with the help of landscapers, botanists and ecologists are working hard to restore and lay out more gardens. As well as those described here, the rose gardens of the Koutoubia mosque (p295) and at La Mamounia

(p312) offer cool respite near the Djemaa el-Fna. American ethno-botanist Gary Martin laid out a superb ecological garden at the Jnane Tamsna (p312) in the Palmeraie, with scented plants, vegetables, olive groves and date palms.

CYBER PARK ARSAT MOULAY ABDEL SALAM

The 18th-century gardens of the Alawite prince and poet Moulay Abdel Salam were given a 21st-century overhaul by the Fondation Mohammed VI for the Protection of the Environment in conjunction with Maroc Télécom. The eight-hectare garden (Map pp292–3) was partly restored to its former glory as an orchard and olive grove, and is partly a contemporary garden with grasses and flowers, water features, a cyber café at its centre and a show room for new technology. The shaded alleys in the groves are perfect to cool down, while the wider lanes offer good people-watching from the benches.

JARDIN MAJORELLE & MUSEUM OF ISLAMIC ART

Owned by the Pierre Bergé–Yves Saint-Laurent Foundation, the exotic sub-tropical **Jardin Majorelle & Museum of Islamic Art** (Map pp292-3; www.jardinmajorelle.com; admission gardens/ museum Dh30/15; 8am-7pm Jun-Sep, 8am-6pm rest of year) provides a haven away from the hectic pace outside. The garden was designed by the French painter Jacques Majorelle, who lived here from 1922 to 1962. In among the cooling water features, the cacti, bamboo, majestic palm trees and cascades of bougainvillaea, is an electric-blue villa, now housing a small museum. It contains one of those Moroccan collections you'd love to scoop up and take home, including Berber and Tuareg jewellery and textiles, carpets, wedding curtains and cobalt-blue pottery from Fès – all labelled in Arabic and French. Another room is dedicated to Majorelle's work.

JARDIN MÉNARA

About 2km southwest from the Koutoubia Mosque is the **Jardin Ménara** (Ave de la Ménara; Dh10; 8.30am-11.45 & 2.30-5.45pm), laid out in the 12th century by the Almohads. Popular with Marrakshis, it is a peaceful place to escape the summer heat and bustle of the city.

The centrepiece of what is basically a more organised continuation of the olive groves immediately to the east is a large, still pool backed by a pavilion built in 1869 (you'll see photos of it in all the tourist literature). Now open to the public, with a wonderful view of the pool from its balcony, this was once the exclusive preserve of sultans and high ministers.

JARDIN AGDAL

Stretching for several kilometres south of the royal palace, the **Jardin Agdal** (Map pp292-3; admission free; 8.30am-5.30pm), the original Almohad gardens, were laid out in 1156–57, extending over some 16 hectares. The vegetation is more varied here than in the Jardin Ménara and there are several pavilions.

ENDANGERED SPECIES

Nearly 1.6 million people live in the southern oases, over 5% of the country's total population, but their homeland is under serious threat due to the continuing drought, desertification, urbanisation and the Bayoud disease, a fungus that kills palm trees. In the last hundred years more than two-thirds of the southern palm groves have disappeared and the date harvest has dropped by 35%. Tourism has played a significant role in this, as too many water pumps have been installed to provide hotels, swimming pools and golf courses, and there is a lot of waste.

The Fondation Mohammed VI pour la Protection de l'Environment (the King's Foundation for the Protection of the Environment; www.fm6e.org in French) together with international organisations, is working hard to find a solution to this problem. Several projects are currently under way to preserve the *palmeraie*. In Marrakesh, for instance, 300,000 new palm trees will be planted, and the old trees will be properly cared for. Elsewhere efforts are being made to waste less water, to protect the culture and traditions typical of the oases, to promote eco-tourism and to create an awareness of the importance of the oases. Plans are also underway for Morocco's first eco-museum in the Palmeraie in Marrakesh. See also Palm Tree Trafficking, p346.

To get here (a bicycle would be ideal), take the path that runs south from the southwestern corner of the *mechouar* in front of the royal palace.

ACTIVITIES
Cycling
Bicycle rental is readily available in Marrakesh from most budget hotels around the Djemaa el-Fna or at the large hotels along Ave Mohammed Abdelkrim el-Khattabi in the ville nouvelle. The going rate is Dh70–80 per day. The best bikes for rent are available from **Actions & Loisirs** (Map p298; ☎ 024 430931; apt 4, 1 Ave Yacoub el-Mansour, Guéliz; 2hrs/half day Dh140/350). The circuit around the Palmeraie, the ritzy, palm-shaded district 5km northwest of the centre, is a pleasant place to ride away from the traffic. The olive trees of La Menara also provide a shady route for cyclists. For longer adventures, **D&O** (☎ 024 421996; www.dandoadventures.com) organise both road and mountain cycling trips, for one day or longer, out of Marrakesh, using quality imported bikes.

Hammams
Every month sees the opening of a new hammam or spa in Marrakesh but for a traditional, authentic experience that won't break the bank, head for an old-fashioned roughing-up at **Hammam el-Bacha** (Map pp292-3; 20 Rue Fatima Zohra, medina; admission Dh 7 & massage Dh50; ☉ men 7am-1pm, women 1-9pm). A cleaner more upmarket bath can be had at the **Hammam Menara** (Quartier es-Saada, medina; admission Dh 60 & massage Dh60; ☉ men 10am-9pm Tue, Thu, Sat, women 10am-9pm Mon, Wed, Fri, Sun), but for ultimate indulgence try the exquisite traditional hammam at **La Maison Arabe** (Map pp292-3; ☎ 024 387010; www.lamaisonarabe.com; 1 Derb Assehbe, Bab Doukkala, medina; hammam Dh 200 plus massage per hr Dh500), or **Bains de Marrakech** (Map pp292-3; ☎ 024 381428; www.lesbainsdemarrakech.com; 2 Derb Sedra, Bab Agnaou, medina; body scrub in hammam Dh 150 & massage from Dh200), a luxurious complex of baths including a hammam, with a wide range of exotic spa treatments, such as a Zen massage with chocolate.

Swimming
Many riads have a tiny plunge pool but that does not quite do the trick. In some hotels you can use the pool if you have lunch, among them **El Andalous** (Map pp292-3; ☎ 024

PINK CITY: GAY & LESBIAN MARRAKESH
The aptly named 'pink city' has replaced Tangier as the southern Mediterranean destination of choice for gay and lesbian travellers. Most clubs are gay-friendly; there's a happening same-sex scene at Diamant Noir (p318), Beach Klubber (p318) and the **VIP** (Map p298; ☎ 068 168999; Place de la Liberté, Guéliz). Many riads are run by same-sex couples, and many more actively cater to gay and lesbian travellers. The key word that appears often on riad websites is 'discreet'.

448226; Ave du President Kennedy, Hivernage; admission adult/child incl buffet lunch Dh150/75; ☉ 8.30am-6.30pm), **Coralia Palmariva** (☎ 024 329036; Palmeraie; admission incl lunch or dinner Dh 200) and **Jnane Tamsna** (☎ 024 329423; www.jnanetamsna.com; Douar Abiad, Palmeraie; admission incl organic three-course lunch with wine Dh 350).

The latest trend is the opening of 'beach clubs' (bar-restaurant with swimming pools, sometimes also with sand) on the outskirts of Marrakesh. The largest one is **Plage Rouge** (☎ 024 378086; www.lacompagniedescomptoirs.com; 10km on Ourika Rd off E6; admission Dh 140) with a sandy beach, sunbeds (included in admission price), a fantastic 80m x 40m pool, bars and gourmet restaurant, run by Michelin-starred chefs. During the day you can lunch, sunbathe, swim and show off your new bikini (or buy one if you want), while at night it is a restaurant-bar-nightclub. Young tanned bodies also hang out at the trendy **Nikki Beach** (☎ 024 301010; Golf Palace Hotel, Palmeraie; admission Dh200; ☉ 9am-7pm), not a pool for children. **Oasiria** (☎ 024 380438; 4km on Amizmiz Rd, Cherifa, admission whole day adult/child Mon-Fri Dh160/80, Sat & Sun Dh180/100; ☉ 10am-6pm, closed winter) is the largest water park in North Africa, set in a vast garden with a wave pool measuring 5000 cu metres, plus lagoons, a river, a beach and several restaurants.

WALKING TOUR
The lively, noisy, colourful, ever-expanding, overwhelming, sometimes smelly and always totally fascinating **souqs** (☉ 8.30am-8pm, many shops closed Fri) are the throbbing heart of Marrakesh's medina. The great shopping labyrinth is relatively compact, but it is a full-on experience – shop till you drop can be taken quite literally here.

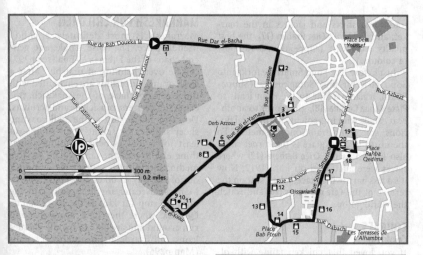

The walking tour takes in the quieter and often more interesting shopping lanes, through the Mouassine quarter where some of the funkier dealers and designers have set up shop, and ends through the busy main Souq Smarrine in the wonderfully atmospheric square of Rahba Kedima.

Start at **Dar el-Bacha** (**1**; p300) and follow Rue Dar el-Bacha with interesting antique shops showcasing stunning jewellery, estate agents selling riads and several untouched caravanserais full of workshops further along the street. Walk through the passage under a house, and take a right on Rue Mouassine. You can stop for a drink on the terrace of **Café Arabe** (**2**; p317) or continue along to the end of the street. Take a left past the **Mouassine Fountain** (**3**) into the **Souq des Sebbaghine** (**4**), the Dyers' Souq, where freshly dyed wool is draped between shops to dry. The right fork leads through workshops where felt is made: at the end take a left and then left again with weavers of straw baskets and woodworkers. Return to the fountain, walk straight past the **Mouassine Mosque** (**5**) where you can only glimpse at the courtyard, and continue along Rue Sidi el-Yamani. Take a right into Derb Azzouz, the first alley to the right after **Café Bougainvillea** (**6**), and follow the zigzagging alley for 150m to the wildest shop in town, **Ministerio del Gusto** (**7**) an art gallery that also sells wacky furniture and vintage clothes, in a riad turned psychedelic African temple. Return to Rue Sidi el-Yamani and take a

THE WALK AT A GLANCE

Start Dar el-Bacha
End Place Rahba Qedima
Distance 1.5-2km
Duration 3 hours or all day

right, past **La Maison du Kaftan** (**8**) with every kaftan you could ever dream up, until after 500m you reach Rue el-Ksour on the left. Turn off and find **Kulchi** (**9**), with funky kaftans and accessories. Further along, **Kifkif** (**10**) has great accessories and T-shirts, and next door **ZenBougie** (**11**) sells gorgeous candles. Continue along the street with several other interesting shops until you hit the tiny bookshop **FNAC Berbère** (**12**) on Rue Mouassine, which has interesting if pricey art books. Take a right, past **Beldi** (**13**) who makes haute couture traditional clothes, until the Place Bab Ftouh. To the right is a *funduq* (merchants' inn) with **Belhadj** (**14**) on the 1st floor, a small shop filled to the brim with Berber jewellery, semiprecious stones and Tuareg amulets at reasonable prices. On the other side of the square, **Akbar Delights** (**15**) is a swanky boutique with elegant Moroccan shirts and dresses embroidered in Kashmir. Continue left to the crossroads with the crowded Souq Smarrine, lined with textile shops and souvenir stalls, interspersed with big-name carpet sellers and antiques dealers. Turn left and find at No 10 **Au Fil d'Or** (**16**), with the finest traditional shirts and jackets in the market, and at No 82 **Chez Brahim (17)**, the best quality *babouches* (slippers) in a rainbow of colours.

Just before Rue Souq Smarrine forks into Souq el-Kebir and Souq Smata (Slipper Souq), a narrow lane to the right leads to **Place Rahba Qedima (18)**, given over to apothecary stalls with ingredients for magical potions, spices and traditional cosmetics. To the north of the square is the carpet souq, also known as the **Criée Berbère (19)** where slaves were auctioned off until 1912. Now it's a less harrowing place; take a seat on the terrace of the **Café des Épices (20)** and watch the world go by.

COURSES
Cooking

If you loved that chicken tajine with olives and lemon, you can learn to cook it yourself. Many riads in the medina organise sessions with their cook, where you can learn to cook a basic tajine or couscous. The **Souk Cuisine** (Map pp292-3; ☎ 073 804955; www.soukcuisine.com; Zniquat Rahba, 5 Derb Tahtah, Medina; per day incl meal & wine Dh350) organises wonderful hands-on cooking classes either in its own kitchen, or for groups of six or more at the beautiful riad **Chambres d'Amis** (www.chambresdamis.com) in the medina. Sessions are led by two Moroccan women who usually cook for Moroccan weddings. Participants are fully involved in the cooking of several Moroccan dishes, and eat the meal at the end. Those who like can go food shopping with the proprietor.

Other cookery workshops are available at the gorgeous **Jnane Tamsna** (☎ 024 329423; www.jnanetamsna.com; Douar Abiad, Palmeraie; course including meal Dh450) where you cook with organic produce from the garden, **Dar Attajmil** (Map pp292-3; ☎ 024 426966, 064 235954 www.darattajmil.com; 23, Rue Laksour, medina; courses incl meal Dh500) and from Dh500 per person at **La Maison Arabe** (Map pp292-3; ☎ 024 387010; www.lamaisonarabe.com; 1 Derb Assehbe, Bab Doukkala, medina).

Languages

The Institut Français (p294) offers an intensive French course during July (Dh850), as well as Moroccan dialect (Dh1600) and French (Dh850) during term time. Private classes in French and Arabic are available at any time (Dh250 per hour).

MARRAKESH FOR CHILDREN

Marrakesh is most definitely a child-friendly place. The noise, smoke and general chaos of the Djemaa el-Fna (see p297) can be overwhelming at first but, after a fresh orange juice, kids are enchanted with the exotic spectacle of the snake charmers, water carriers, musicians and acrobats. Don't forget to stop at the stall roasting sheep's heads or selling snail soup – at least for a look – before finding something else to feed the family. The car-free medina too is much appreciated, but duck out of the way of bikes and donkey carts. Many stalls cater for little ones, but the ultimate stop for kids is the Place Rahba Qedima, where they have some space to run around and are able to handle chameleons and lizards at the apothecary stalls (Map p296).

When they start complaining about tired feet, flag down a horse-drawn carriage (see p321) or hop on a double-decker of Marrakech-Tour (opposite) for a tour around town. Riding bikes (see p304) or swimming, particularly at the **Oasiria** (see p304) are a few more ways to get your kids moving. A camel ride is also popular. Camels usually camp out in the Palmeraie; a 15-minute traipse-about is Dh30 to Dh50. **Kasbah Le Mirage** (☎ 024 314444; Ouahat Sidi Brahim, Palmeraie) organises 90-minute dromedary rides through the Palmeraie with pancakes at the end for Dh290. Marrakesh also has a wide choice of stables but the **Sabots de l'Ourika** (☎ 060 031110; www.sabots-ourika.com in French; Km11 Ourika Rd; 1-/3-hr walk Dh200/500) specialises in one- to three-hour walks in the countryside.

When evening rolls around, kids will be thrilled by the folkloric show at the **al-Menara Reflets & Merveilles** (☎ 024 439580; admission Dh250-400, under 12 free, with dinner Dh 400-550; ☽ 9pm Mon-Sat). Each night the Jardin Ménara (see p303) becomes the stage for a fantastical sound-and-light show, complete with 50 singers, dancers and acrobats.

One last note on accommodation: if you have noisy tots it may not be a good idea to stay in a riad (see p309) in the medina. Plunge pools and stairs are hazardous enough, but most of all there is little space to run and the sound really echoes around the house. Opt for a larger hotel with a garden in Hivernage or the Palmeraie.

TOURS

Finding one's way around Marrakesh hardly requires a guide, but some local expertise can't hurt to locate and explain the *medersas*, mosques and museums that are deep in the heart of the medina. Most riad guesthouses and hotels offer day trips or can suggest a guide, and official guides can be booked through the tourist office. (For more about guides to Marrakesh, see p291). The agencies listed here offer city tours, as well as tours out of the city, which are very useful if time is an issue or if you want to hook up with other travellers. (For dedicated Trekking agencies see p441).

Authentic Discoveries (Map pp292-3; ☎ 024 436905; www.authenticdiscoveries.com; Résidence Palm House B, Rue Imam Ali, Guéliz) Specialises in sustainable tourism. Working hand-in-hand with local communities (non-government organisations – NGOs – and social and cultural associations), itineraries are tailored to fit every budget, from Dh300 per person per day. A portion of this income is then redistributed to the organisations the company works with.

Diversity Excursions (☎ 024 329423; www.diversity-excursions.co.uk) In-depth tours inside and outside Marrakesh are organised by the Global Diversity Foundation and led by Moroccan experts on the culture, history, botany and ecology of the region. Might include visits to private gardens, one of the Foundation's projects, restored monuments in the medina, or an oasis further south.

Marrakech-Tour (☎ 024 339637; www.marrakech -tour.com in Spanish & French; adult/child 24hr ticket Dh130/65, 48hr Dh200/100; ⏱ every 30 mins) See the sites of Marrakesh from the open top of a double-decker bus and hop on and off where you like. The multilingual 'Marrakesh Monumental' tour takes in the medina and

Guéliz (80 mins), and the 'Marrakesh Romantique' heads for the Palmeraie.

Mountain Voyage (Map p298; ☎ 024 421996; www .mountain-voyage.com; 2nd floor, Immeuble El-Batoul, 5 Ave Mohammed V, Guéliz) This very experienced British-owned company organises tailor-made trips in and around Marrakesh. Also owns the Kasbah du Toubkal (p328) and keenly promotes better understanding of Moroccan people and culture.

FESTIVALS & EVENTS

Grand Prix de Hassan II Marathon This annual road race in January finishes at Djemaa el-Fna.

Festival of Folklore (☎ 024 446114; www.maghreb arts.ma in French) Held in July. See Festival of Folklore boxed text, below.

Rencontres Musicales de Marrakech (☎ 066 10 27 29; www.maghrebarts.ma in French) An annual music festival in September, bringing together musical and artistic traditions from Morocco and elsewhere that belong to the local oral heritage. Free concerts, lectures and an international conference. Events held at Palais de Bahia, Jardin Agdal and on a large screen on Djemaa el-Fna.

International Film Festival (☎ 024 420200; www .festival-marrakech.com) A week-long festival each autumn (September–October) that showcases Arab and African cinema, as well as films by directors from Europe, India, the US and elsewhere. See p54.

SLEEPING

Marrakesh has it all: you can sleep anywhere from the funkiest fleapit to the most amazing palace straight out of your Orientalist Hollywood fantasy. In fact the choice is so tremendous that it can be hard to decide. The first decision to make is where you want to be: in a quiet medina back street, or in the ville nouvelle, where most

FESTIVAL OF FOLKLORE

Now more than 40 years old, the Marrakesh Festival of Popular Arts (formerly the Festival of Folklore) is a unique celebration of Berber culture. The all-singing, folk-dancing extravaganza – which takes place every year in June or July in the grounds of the magnificent Palais el-Badi – features many of the country's best performers.

Each year the festival takes a different theme, such as wedding ceremonies or war rituals. Troupes from all over Morocco perform their songs and dance, reflecting the country's wide variety of ethnic groups and their specific traditions and culture. There are Berbers and Guedra, but it is often the Gnaoui, with their sub-Saharan origins, who steal the show. Using lutes, drums, castanets, shells and beads, they produce a hypnotic sound that builds to a crescendo. The music inspires them to break into tremendous acrobatic displays.

Besides the performances, various groups host exhibitions, theme nights and academic meetings. The festival is also an excellent opportunity to witness the famous *fantasia,* a charge of Berber horsemen, which takes place each sunset outside the ramparts near Bab el-Jdid.

MARRAKESH & CENTRAL MOROCCO

of the larger, chain-style hotels come with gardens and pools. Many people opt for both, and stay a few days in one of Marrakesh's wonderful riad hotels (see boxed text, opposite), then head for the tranquillity of the Palmeraie or Ourika Valley. Whatever you choose, sleeping in Marrakesh comes at a fast-rising price, and is more expensive than anywhere else in Morocco.

Riads are all the rage, and the combination of a beautifully converted courtyard house – complete with style magazine décor, hammam, excellent service and delicious home-cooked meals on the rooftop – and the popular melee of the medina is unbeatable, and worth saving your pennies for, although there are riads for all budgets. For short stays or families with small kids, where noise is an issue, and space and a pool are more of a priority, the new town is the place to be and certainly has its own charm after the intensity of the medina.

Medina
BUDGET

There are dozens of budget hotels in the lanes immediately south of Djemaa el-Fna. Many have rooms around cheerful little courtyards, and roof terraces to soak up the sun and views. Apart from that, their degree of cleanliness and the shower situation, there's often not much to choose between them. As they are small, the best ones fill up really quickly, so it's worth calling ahead. Some will let you sleep on the terrace for around Dh30 to Dh50 if you're really stuck.

Hôtel Gallia (Map p296; ☎ 024 445913; fax 044 444853; 30 Rue de la Recette; s/d Dh270/420; ⊠) This is a delightful budget hotel in a quiet backstreet near the Djemaa el-Fna, run by the same French family since 1929. The 20 pleasant rooms are located around two lovely courtyards and the entire place is scrubbed from top to toe daily. Most rooms have air-con, while the central heating is welcome in winter. The breakfast is excellent. Needless to say, you'll need to book (by fax only) weeks if not months in advance.

Jnane Mogador Hôtel (Map p296; ☎ 024 426323; www.jnanemogador.com; Derb Sidi Bouloukat, 116 Riad Zitoun el-Qedim; s/d/q Dh290/380/520) A wonderfully restored 19th-century riad, this place is constructed around an elegant central courtyard complete with tinkling fountain, grand marble staircase, a hammam and attractive

rooms decorated in Moroccan style. With 17 rooms the riad is surprisingly large and, at this price, surprisingly good value, but word has got out and it fills up quickly.

Hôtel Sherazade (Map p296; ☎ /fax 044 429305; www.hotelsherazade.com; 3 Derb Djamaa, Riad Zitoun el-Qedim; s/d Dh160/210, s with bathroom Dh210-510, d with bathroom Dh260-610, mini-apt d Dh460) Centrally located but very quiet, this riad is decorated in traditional style with a sea of *zellij* tiling. Run by a friendly Moroccan-German couple, this is on a par with the Hôtel Gallia and reservations are strongly recommended here as well.

Riad Hôtel Assia (Map p296; ☎ 024 391285; www .hotel-assia-marrakech.com; 33 Rue de la Recette; s/d/tr/ q incl breakfast Dh250/360/550/650, ⊠) The staff at this riad, next door to the Gallia, are friendly and helpful. The small but comfortable rooms, with bathrooms and TV, are decorated in traditional style with *zellij* tiling and local woodwork. It has superb views from the roof terrace over the Koutoubia and the Atlas Mountains.

Hôtel Chellah (Map p296; ☎ 024 442977; Derb Skaya, Rue Riad Zitoun el-Qedim; s/d/tr Dh80/130/180) Chellah is a relaxed and tranquil hotel – a nice place to chill out – with nine small rooms and clean communal bathrooms (hot showers Dh15), around a courtyard with orange trees, and some great Moroccan salons. It's also outside the main budget-hotel epicentre.

Hôtel Souria (Map p296; ☎ 024 426757; 17 Rue de la Recette; s/d Dh120/160) This popular and charming budget hotel has 10 simple, very well-kept rooms round a courtyard full of plants. The roof terrace is decorated with a patchwork of tiles and has great views over the rooftops of the medina. It fills up really quickly.

Hôtel de Foucauld (Map p296; ☎ 024 440806; Ave El Mouahidine; s/d Dh180/230; ⊠) This large budget hotel near the Djemaa el-Fna has clean and spacious rooms, each with an ensuite bathroom. It's popular with walking tour groups who all storm out after a chaotic buffet breakfast (Dh25).

Hôtel Central Palace (Map p296; ☎ 024 440235; hotelcentralpalace@hotmail.com; 59 Derb Sidi Bouloukat; d Dh150, with shower/bath Dh 200/300) A good budget option, the Central Palace has 40 clean rooms in an old house with a large central courtyard and fountain. Very centrally located, it is never empty because it offers good value accommodation.

Hôtel CTM (Map p296; ☎ 024 442325; Djemaa el-Fna; s/d/tr Dh68/104/158, with bathroom Dh100/150/200) Something of an institution, this hotel is in the thick of things, right on the Place, with unbeatable views from the roof and from the (noisy) front rooms, though most rooms open onto an unspectacular courtyard. The communal facilities have definitely seen better days. Parking is available for Dh25 to Dh35.

MIDRANGE

Dar Al Sultan (Map pp292-3; ☎ 071 083608; www .daralsultan.com; 26 Derb el-Arsa, Riad Zitoun Jdid; d incl breakfast Dh890-1200; 🖳 🖳) Dar Al Sultan is a very simple but stunning riad with just three rooms. The traditional architecture, *zellij* and carved wood have been preserved, but the simplicity and minimalism of the décor enhances the beauty of the modern cubic spaces. The atmosphere and charming owner make this place a haven of tranquillity in the heart of the souq. Rates go up to Dh1500 during Christmas holidays.

Riad Nejma Lounge (Map pp292-3; ☎ 024 382341; www.riad-nejmalounge.com; 45 Derb Sidi M'Hamed el-Haj, Bab Doukkala; d incl breakfast Dh300-600; 🖳 🖳) This is one of the coolest riads in town, at cool prices (rates rise up to Dh900 over Christmas). The French owners have painted it all very white, with bright colours in the details and blood-red carpets. With lots of palms

and exotic plants and a groovy roof terrace, this very laid-back house attracts the young 'lounge' crowd.

Dar Soukaina (Map pp292-3; ☎ 024 376055; www .darsoukaina.com; 19 Derb el-Ferrane, Riad Laârouss; s/d/tr incl breakfast Dh760/860/1010) Traditional Dar Soukaina has been lovingly restored to retain all its quirky features, not least the tiny doors and low ceilings. Beautifully whitewashed with a lilac trim, it's a peaceful and tranquil haven with orange trees in the courtyard and helpful staff.

Riad Akka (Map p296; ☎ 024 375767; www.riad -akka.com; 65 Derb Lahbib Magni, Riad Zitoun el-Jdid; d incl breakfast Dh800-1300; 🖳 🖳) *Akka* means the last oasis before the caravan hits the desert, and this is a quiet and delightful place to stay. The stylish décor is an interpretation of traditional Moroccan style elements, but the French owner-architect has created a different and very modern space. Rooms are decorated with sensual chocolate-brown *tadelakt* (polished limewash) and lots of oranges and reds. There is a great roof terrace and a delicious Moroccan breakfast.

Riad Eden (Map pp292-3; ☎ 078 447628; www.riad eden-marrakesh.com; 25 Derb Jdid, Riad Zitoun el-Qedim; d incl breakfast Dh490-1090, ste Dh790-1390; 🖳) Six colourful bedrooms named after local fruits are centred around a bright courtyard with palm trees. A lovely small Moroccan salon provides a cosy reading corner, there is

---

RIAD FEVER

A riad is a traditional house set around a garden courtyard. Many Europeans (and a few Moroccans) have restored these often-crumbling buildings to their former glory. Officially there are now 600 stylish guesthouses in the medina, most of them in the Top End or Midrange price bracket – and only Allah knows how many go unregistered. All serve traditional Moroccan breakfasts with fresh orange juice, pancakes and croissants, and many provide meals on request – often very good meals at that. Staying in a riad is like staying in wealthy friend's home: there are usually only a few rooms, and it has the advantage that, while you are right in the thick of it, the house is usually tranquil. Many of the upmarket riads, such as Riad Farnatchi (p310) are total flights of Oriental fantasy, where everyone is treated like royalty. If you can, treat yourself to a night in one: you won't regret it.

Riads are also available as weekly rentals. Rates start at around Dh5000/8000 per week for four/eight people, though for a really classy abode you're looking at Dh30,000 or more. Agencies to contact include **Marrakech Medina** (☎ 024 442448; www.marrakech-medina.com in French), **Marrakech Riads** (☎ 024 426463; www.marrakech-riads.net) or **Riads au Maroc** (☎ 024 431900; www .riadomaroc.com).

It's worth noting that many riads are tucked away down unmarked alleys in the depths of the medina. This is part of their magic, but it can make them difficult to find on first arrival. To be on the safe side, ask for directions when you book, or get someone to meet you at a nearby landmark.

sunbathing on the roof, and the French chef and his Moroccan staff prepare wonderful gourmet meals.

Riad W (☎ 065 367936; www.riadw.com; 41 Derb Boutouil, Qennaria; d incl breakfast Dh900-1200, ste Dh1500; ✗ ▣) Riad W has kept the basic architectural structure of the Moorish riad, but it plays with the volumes and light to give it a very contemporary feel. The furnishings have deliberately been kept simple to avoid the mad mix of styles seen in so many converted medina houses. Dinner is available for residents, by the big fireplace in winter or on the rooftop in summer.

Riad Magi (Map p296; ☎ /fax 024 426688; 79 Derb Moulay Abdelkader, Derb Debbachi; d incl breakfast Dh800-900 ✗) Another beautifully finished riad, Riad Magi comes with six individual rooms ranging from pale aquamarine blues to citrus yellow. Rooms are arranged around a cheerful blue-and-yellow courtyard complete with burgeoning lemon trees, and the affable manager speaks fluent English.

Dar Hanane (Map pp292-3; ☎ 024 377737; www.dar -hanane.com; 9 Derb Lalla Azzouna; tr incl breakfast Dh880-1320, ste Dh1100-1650) This unusually spacious riad with good-sized rooms, is luxurious but simply decorated in muted tones to bring out the best from the architecture. The house, near the Medersa ben Youssef, exudes an almost Zenic tranquillity, and the service is friendly and perfect.

Riad O2 (Map pp292-3; ☎ 024 377227; www.riado2 .com; 97 Derb Semmaria, Sidi Ben Slimane, Sidi Ahmed Soussi, Zaouia; d incl breakfast Dh500-1000, ste Dh900-1200; ✗ ▣) This is a large riad, lovingly restored with almost monastic simplicity, as the architecture says it all. After a hectic day in the medina you can come home and relax in the small pool, or steam away in the hammam. Bedrooms are equally pleasant, decorated in a fusion of modern Western and traditional Moroccan style, in particular the Chewing Gum Room, and all come with *tadelakt* bathrooms.

TOP END

Riad Edward (Map pp292-3; ☎ 024 389797/061 252328; www.riyadedward.com; 10 Derb Marestane, Zaouia Abbassia, Bab Taghzoute; ▣ incl breakfast Dh1200, ste Dh1750; ✗ ▣) Formerly the home of relatives of the royal family, this is a very large riad with a large tiled courtyard and a swimming pool in the shade of a 100-year-old cypress tree. The rambling house was carefully restored and has a very authentic feel, with each room very different from the other, but all full of pictures and books, with lots of different levels and terraces, as well as private little corners to relax. It takes a few hours to get the fires of the wonderful old hammam burning, so warn the housekeeper in advance.

Riad Farnatchi (Map pp292-3; ☎ 024 384910; www .riadfarnatchi.com; 2 Derb el-Farnatchi, Qa'at Benahid; ste incl breakfast Dh3100-4600 ✗ ▣) The five superbly luxurious suites here are each very different, but all have as many comforts as a person can reasonably demand, and then some. Use of the hammam is free for residents, service is exceptional and the manager is one of those 'can do' people who can organise almost anything you fancy.

Riad Kniza (Map pp292-3; ☎ 024 376942; www.riad kniza.com; 34 Derb l'Hôtel Bab Doukala; d incl breakfast Dh2000-2200, ste Dh2750-3200; ✗) Most of Mar-

---

THE AUTHOR'S CHOICE

Tlaata wa Sitteen (Map pp292-3; ☎ 024 383026; www.tlaatawasitteen.com; 63 Derb el-Ferrane, Riad Laarous; d incl breakfast Dh400, ste Dh500) Formerly known as Dar Bleue, this was one of the medina's best kept secrets. Also one of its most authentic riads. Rooms are comfortable and simple yet stylish, with no unnecessary frills. The spacious shared bathrooms are decorated in *tadelakt*. Delicious couscous or tajines are prepared at night for whoever wants to stay in, often shared by the proprietor and his friends. The ambiance is very laid-back, and quite often turns into a joyful party. Family friendly. Book ahead.

Riad Tchaï'kana Map pp292-3; ☎ /fax 024 284587; www.tchaikana.com; 25 Derb el-Ferrane, Azbest; d incl breakfast Dh700-900, ste Dh1300-1500; ✗) This gorgeous riad is at the end of a dark alley behind the Musée de Marrakech, with three rooms and two large suites round a large and wonderfully atmospheric courtyard, magical under the stars. The rooms are spacious and simple but very tastefully decorated with local finds. It is a hard place to leave in the morning, but the friendly Belgian owners know the city really well, and are keen for you to enjoy it as much as they do.

rakesh's luxury hotels are backed or run by foreigners, but the Kniza is Moroccan through and through, from the family house of the proprietor, a celebrity guide and antique dealer, and the antique decorations to the efficient staff and the generous welcome. The seven rooms are spacious and sumptuous and a pool and spa were under construction at the time of writing.

La Sultana (Map pp292-3; ☎ 024 388008; www.lasul tanamarrakech.com in French; Rue de la Kasbah, Kasbah; d incl breakfast Dh2561, ste from Dh3579; 🖭 🖳) La Sultana is a dream palace where all your wishes come true, with 11 luxurious rooms and 10 suites and a full-blown spa, hidden behind a totally unremarkable façade. The over-the-top Oriental fantasy décor blends Moroccan style with elements from further east. The wonderful shops and restaurant are open to nonresidents, but not the cute basement bar with a window onto the good-sized swimming pool.

Les Jardins de la Medina (Map pp292-3; ☎ 024 381851; www.lesjardinsdelamedina.com; 21 Derb Chtouka; d Dh1650-1950, ste Dh1950-2250; 🖭 🖳) Hidden behind spotless white walls is a lovely, lushly planted garden with a bright blue pool in the centre. With 36 rooms, this is a small hotel that has preserved the intimacy of a riad whilst offering superb facilities, including a hammam and spa with a bewildering array of spa treatments. The Thai restaurant is a welcome relief after one too many tajines.

Ville Nouvelle

BUDGET

The ville nouvelle is a bit short of cheap hotels. The few that do exist can be found around Ave Mohammed V, west of Place du 16 Novembre.

Youth Hostel (Map pp292-3; ☎ 024 447713; Rue Mohammed el-Hansali, Quartier Industriel; dm incl breakfast Dh60) This youth hostel is spotlessly clean and boasts a kitchen and hot showers (Dh6). But there is an 11.30pm curfew and, even though it is quiet, it is a long way from the action in the medina. You'll need your Hostelling International (HI) card.

Hôtel du Pacha (Map p298; ☎ 024 431327; fax 024 431326; 33 Rue de la Liberté; s/d Dh275/360; 🖭) Built in 1934, there's a nicely faded colonial air to the Pacha's louvred shutters, high ceilings and generous bathrooms. The lobby, dripping with stucco, and a cool central

courtyard provide local flavour. The rooms are nothing fancy, but most come with air-con and some with a small balcony.

Hôtel Toulousain (Map p298; ☎ 024 430033; www .geocities.com/hotel_toulousain; 44 Rue Tariq ibn Ziad; s/d incl breakfast Dh110/160, with bathroom Dh150/190) This is a nice quiet place arranged around two slightly shabby courtyards, one of them home to a venerable banana palm. Rooms on the 1st floor are more airy. It has limited parking.

Hôtel des Voyageurs (Map p298; ☎ 024 447218; 40 Blvd Mohammed Zerktouni; s/d Dh110/160, with shower Dh130/175) It's a beautiful building, albeit a bit frayed. The rooms, some with balconies, are simply furnished with Berber blankets and are reasonably sized.

MIDRANGE

The bulk of the midrange hotels are in Guéliz or in the quieter and more leafy Hivernage area. Most of the larger hotels with swimming pools in this category are usually cheaper when booked as part of a package including flights.

Villa Hélène (Map p298; ☎ 024 431681; www.villa -helene.com; 89 Ave Moulay Rachid, Guéliz; 2- to 4-person apt Dh 950-1150; 🖭 🖳) This very tranquil and stylish 1930s villa with three small flats, behind the big post office, is set in a lush garden with an amazing variety of flowers and plants. The French owners clearly fell in love with the fine Art Deco architecture in Guéliz, and fitted out their villa with period furnishings mixed with Berber rugs, a winning combination.

Hôtel Diwane (Map p298; ☎ 024 432216; www .diwane-hotel.com in French; 24 Rue de Yougoslavie; s/d/ ste Dh600/750/1100; 🖭 🖳) A big, flash, flag-waving hotel in the centre of Guéliz with all modern amenities. The large pool in its secluded patio is a particular feature and rooms are decorated with the same flag-waving verve and lots of red.

Hôtel Oudaya (Map p298; ☎ 024 448512; www.ou daya.ma; 147 Rue Mohammed el-Beqal; s/d/tr incl breakfast Dh380/500/690, ste from Dh720; 🖭 🖳) Much favoured by tour groups, the Oudaya provides very comfortable modern accommodation with shiny marble bathrooms. There is also an attractive, private swimming pool surrounded by bougainvillea-draped walls.

Hôtel Ibis Moussafir (Map p298; ☎ 024 435929; www.ibishotel.com; Ave Hassan II; s/d incl breakfast Dh380/ 440; 🖭 🖳) The Ibis Moussafir offers good three-star accommodation, and its location is particularly handy if you arrive on a late train. It's modern, comfortable and reliable, with a smallish pool set in a peaceful garden with willow trees and birds. The breakfast buffet is generous.

TOP END

The ville nouvelle is well supplied with four- and five-star hotels aimed largely at tour groups and conference delegates. The newer places are clustered along Ave de France (near the Palais des Congrès) and further out of town on the road to Casablanca.

La Mamounia (Map pp292-3; ☎ 024 444409; www .mamounia.com; Ave Houmane el-Fetouaki; d Dh2300-4300 ste Dh3300-14000; 🏊 🖳) The *grand dame* of Marrakesh hotels, the Mamounia has seen them all, from Winston Churchill (who came for the climate and to indulge a passion for painting) and Eric von Stroheim to the current king, Mohammed VI. The hotel was undergoing renovation at the time of writing to bring it on a par with other luxurious riad hotels in town. From 10am to 4pm the hotel generally opens its doors to the riff-raff, allowing them (well, us) to wander the cool lobby and stunning old gardens. Sneakers and shorts are not allowed; 'bouncers' in fezzes enforce the dress code at the door.

Hôtel es-Saadi (Map pp292-3; ☎ 024 448811; www.es saadi.com; Ave el-Qadissia; d from Dh1500, ste from Dh2800; 🏊 🖳) Hardly in the same league, the es-Saadi, in the Hivernage area, is a charming old-style hotel with impeccably polite staff and efficient services. Though bland, the rooms are spacious and well appointed and the large pool (complete with orange loungers) and refreshing gardens are wonderful to return to after a day in the medina. The hotel also has a casino and a popular night club.

Palmeraie & Outskirts of Marrakesh

Many of the hotels that open in the Palmeraie or within a 30-minute drive from Marrakesh are pure luxury. The drive into town is easy – a taxi is called – but rather costly (Dh60 to Dh100). The ideal combination would be to stay in a riad in the medina for a few days, then have a few days of luxurious bliss away from it all.

MIDRANGE

Le Bled (☎ 024 385939; www.lebled-marrakech.com in French; Douar Coucou, Oasis Hassan II Taselnatet; r incl break-

fast Dh1200, ste Dh600; 🏊 🖳) Le Bled is a modern Moroccan riad with three elegant rooms and four suites decorated in bright colours that accentuate the green of the surrounding countryside, orchard and vegetable gardens. Farm animals make it even more authentic. It has a good-size pool and an excellent restaurant, open to nonresidents.

La Maison des Oliviers (☎ 024 375405/061 291946; www.lamaisondesoliviers.com in French; Douar Lagouacem, Tassoultante, 6km Ourika Rd; d Dh850-1260; 🏊 🖳) This is three modern villas designed as a riad, with 20 spacious and airy rooms called suites, are set in a 5-hectare park surrounded by countryside. The two restaurants serve excellent food, Moroccan and Mediterranean. Breakfasts are DH60 and there's a very good Moroccan lunch buffet on Saturday and Sunday for Dh180 (kids free). Guests can use the hammam or attend regular courses from cooking to astronomy and Egyptian hieroglyphics.

Villa Chems (☎ 024 331467; www.villa-chems.com in French; 63 Lotissement el-Hamra, Amerchich, Quartier el-Ksour; d incl breakfast Dh450-800, q/ste Dh700-850; 🏊 🖳) Villa Chems has simple, well-kept bedrooms in a wonderful new house built close to Moroccan traditions. The welcoming French host is passionate about Morocco, which shows from his villa, but he is also a wonderful raconteur at the dinner table. The food is excellent, too.

TOP END

Jnane Tamsna (☎ 024 329423; www.jnanetamsna.com; Douar Abiad, Palmeraie; d incl breakfast from Dh2200, ste from Dh3700; 🏊 🖳) In this little oasis within the Palmeraie, the scent of rosemary wafts towards you when you arrive. Luxurious comfort with large and wonderfully cosy, beautifully furnished rooms set in several villas, each with their own pool. There's a lush organic garden with local plants and vegetable gardens to provide for the restaurant – no water-devouring grass! The service is informal but efficient, and the organic food is superb. The sort of place you won't want to leave.

Caravanserai (☎ 024 300302; www.caravanserai .com; 264 Ouled Ben Rahmoun; s incl breakfast Dh650-1300, d incl breakfast Dh1300-2600, ste from Dh1800-4200; 🏊 🖳) This is the countryside but not as you know it. The Caravanserai is a very sophisticated version of a large village house with 17 rooms and suites, some with private pool. The pink walls, simple rustic furnishings, the superb central heated pool set in delightful gardens and the excellent management make it a tranquil place to hang out for a few days.

EATING

There is more to Marrakesh's restaurants than couscous and tajine – yes, even good sushi and a fiery red Thai curry have arrived in town! As the well-heeled from all over the world have fallen head over heels for the Red City, the choice in good dining is increasingly diverse, but also increasingly expensive. Locals are complaining that, apart from a few stalwarts, it has become unaffordable to eat out well. The cheapest and most exotic eateries in town remain the food stalls on Djemaa el-Fna, piled high with fresh meats and salads, goats' heads and steaming snail soup (see The Ultimate Banquet p295). A good second bet if you are staying in a riad is to have dinner at home, cooked by the woman of the house.

Restaurants

Both in the medina and the ville nouvelle there is a good range of restaurants. The medina palaces offer a set menu at a fixed price – an extensive traditional Moroccan feast before which you'd be advised to fast all day – but trendy places are opening up in every corner of the old city. The ville nouvelle also has old-fashioned, reasonably priced Italian and French restaurants, as well as ultrahip fusion joints. Increasingly, restaurants are opening in the countryside outside Marrakesh (see opposite), offering lunch by the pool, or dinner before clubbing.

MEDINA

Le Tobsil (Map pp292-3; ☎ 024 444052; 22 Derb Abdellah ben Hessaien, Bab Ksour; set menu incl drinks Dh600; ☼ dinner Wed-Mon) Intimate and elegant, this French-owned place is downright classy. Service is impeccable, though perhaps less formal than at some of the other venues. Some foodies consider Le Tobsil to be the best restaurant in Marrakesh.

Casa Lalla (Map p296; ☎ 024 429757; www.casalalla .com; 16 Derb Jamaa, off Riad Zitoun el-Qedim; set menu Dh350; ☼ 7-11pm Tue-Sun) The Michelin-starred chef runs this small unlicensed restaurant in his guesthouse, delights in shopping in the market every morning and prepares a set

six-course menu of beautifully presented delicacies, a fusion of Moroccan and French *haute cuisine*. You need to book well in advance, bring your own wine (no corkage) and arrive on time: you risk being refused entry if only 15 minutes late.

Dar Zellij (Map pp292-3; ☎ 024 382627; 1 Kaasour Sidi Ben Slimane, Bab Taghzout; meals Dh250-350; ☼ dinner Wed-Mon) Superb 17th-century riad with a courtyard of orange trees, traditional Moroccan salons with carved cedarwood ceilings and a rooftop terrace with views over the medina. The food is just as traditional, but looks even better. The Moroccan owner serves dishes quite hard to find elsewhere, such as lamb tajine with fresh figs, and *trid*, pigeon wrapped in a pancake. Keep a space for tea and heavenly homemade pastries.

La Sultana (Map pp292-3; ☎ 024 388008; set menu Dh400-500; ☼ lunch & dinner) The food is as refined, sumptuous and exotic as the setting, a happy fusion of French with traditional Moroccan, using only the freshest seasonal ingredients. Have a romantic dinner under the stars overlooking the Saadian Tombs or sit in the warm patio in winter. For nonresidents, dinner is by reservation only.

Fondouk (Map pp292-3; ☎ 024 378190; meals Dh200-250; ☼ noon-4pm & 7pm-midnight Tue-Sun) Very trendy, colourful Gothic décor in a large riad with a delightful roof terrace, perfect for drinks at sunset or lunch on a not too hot day. The food is a mix of French and Moroccan, but can be hit or miss: some days it's great, on others it takes forever and is practically inedible. Stick to the basics or have a bottle of wine with salads, under the stars.

Le Marrakchi (Map p296; ☎ 024 443377; www .lemarrakchi.com; cnr Djemaa el-Fna & Rue des Banques; meals Dh150-250, set menu Dh250-350; ☼ 11.30am-11pm) A good, safe option for a couscous with a view. The sweeping views over the square and the city, particularly from the 2nd floor, are wonderful. The food is good, and comes with a belly dancer later in the evening.

Dar Yacout (Map pp292-3; ☎ 024 382929; 79 Sidi Ahmed Soussi; set menu incl aperitifs & wine Dh700; ☼ dinner Tue-Sun) Frequented by the royal family, Yacout is one of the city's grandest palace restaurants. Designed by American architect Bill Willis, it's an extraordinary place, complete with illuminated terrace, a pool and a beautiful fountain. The food doesn't quite live up to the surroundings but is served with great panache.

Le Pavillon (Map pp292-3; ☎ 024 387040; 47 Derb Zaouia, Bab Doukkala; meals Dh250-350; ⊙ dinner Wed-Mon) Set up like a riad around a courtyard with a huge tree, this gorgeous French restaurant is far from traditional when it comes to cuisine. The menu changes regularly, written on a board, but specialities include lobster and scallop of foie gras, all livened up by a jolly jazz band. Book in advance.

Les Terrasses de L'Alhambra (Map p296; Djemaa el-Fna; meals Dh100-150; ⊙ 8am-11pm) The view of the square from the balcony is superb, but patrons sitting inside will also enjoy tasteful, traditional décor – carved cedar ceilings, tiled tables and a very fancy toilet. Salads and pizza are good options for veggies, but the menu also offers more traditional Moroccan fare. A perfect place to lunch or stop for a mint tea.

Ryad Tamsna (Map p296; ☎ 024 385272; 23 Derb Zanka Daika; meals Dh 180-250; ⊙ noon-midnight) Achingly stylish, Tamsna is one of the trendiest 'little-known' spots for a light lunch or dinner. The innovative menu offers a welcome break from tajine: freshly made soups, salads and pastas, as well as some wonderful desserts. Don't skip mint tea on the roof terrace after your meal.

Café-Restaurant Argana (Map p296; ☎ 024 445350; 1 & 2 Djemaa el-Fna; set menus Dh90-140) Overlooking Djemaa el-Fna's frenzied chaos, Argana is a good place to try some local delicacies such as *pastilla* (Dh85 to Dh90) and *tanzhiya* (slow-cooked stew; Dh90). They also serve speedy lunchtime tajine. Pick up a pastry or ice cream from the café downstairs as you leave.

VILLE NOUVELLE

The majority of restaurants in the ville nouvelle serve international cuisine, but you can also sample some fine Moroccan fare in this European oasis. All of these places serve alcohol.

Kechmara (Map p298; ☎ 024 434060; 3 Rue de La Liberté, Guéliz; set menu Dh80-120; ✗) Carefully chosen contemporary décor, good music all day and night, beautiful staff and, most importantly, this is one of the few trendy places that does not charge the world for excellent and well-presented Moroccan-Mediterranean food. Hugely popular with local residents, both for lunch and dinner. Great rooftop terrace.

Al-Fassia (Map p298; ☎ 024 434060; 55 Blvd Mohammed Zerktouni, Guéliz; mains around Dh120-160; ⊙ noon-2.30 & 7.30-11pm; ✗) A reminder that the ville nouvelle is still in Morocco, Al-Fassia serves some of the best local cuisine in town. Specialities need to be ordered in advance, but there is plenty to choose from the à la carte menu, and beware: portions are pretty big. Unusually, the place is run by a women's cooperative, and only women work here. All dressed as *dadas*, these women traditionally looked after the kids and cooked for wealthy families. Book ahead.

Catanzaro (Map p298; ☎ 024 433731; 42 Rue Tariq Ibn Ziad, Guéliz; pizzas or pasta Dh50-70, mains Dh80-120; ⊙ noon-2.30pm & 7.30-11pm Mon-Sat; ✗) This little Italian trattoria has earned a loyal following and locals queue to get in at weekends. The menu contains no surprises – a range of fish and meat dishes as well as excellent pizzas, pasta, salads and so forth – but the quality is consistently high.

THE AUTHOR'S CHOICE

Chez Chegrouni (Map p296; ☎ 065 474615; 4-6 Djemaa el-Fna; salads Dh10-15, mains Dh35-50; ⊙ 8am-11pm) Known for its excellent tajines (considered by many to be the best in the city), this little restaurant is almost always crowded. Whether you choose lemon chicken with olives or lamb with prunes, it will arrive steaming hot and delectably tender. Squeeze into a table on the terrace for an unbeatable people-watching spot right on Djemaa el-Fna, or head up for the quieter rooftop seating with a view.

Dar Moha (Map pp292-3; ☎ 024 386400; www.darmoha.ma; 81 Rue Dar el-Bacha; set menu lunch Dh220, dinner excl drinks Dh420; ⊙ noon-3, 7.30-late Tue-Sun; ✗) The chef learned his trade in Switzerland, but since returning to Marrakesh he has applied himself to creating a modern Moroccan cuisine – tajines with a twist. Flavours are exquisite and dishes are delivered with panache. The setting is a beautiful villa with garden and swimming pool, formerly the home of French fashion designer Pierre Balmain. Musicians complete the scene, playing calming Andalucian music.

Lolo Quoi (Map p298; ☎ 072 569864; 82 Ave Hassan II, Guéliz; mains Dh80-180; ⏰ 7pm-1am; ✘) Lolo Quoi serves delicious and inventive Italian-French dishes, served by good-looking staff with lots of panache. It calls itself a 'restaurant familial', but the trendy décor with gold leaf and poems on the wall, and the 1970s French pop music, make this a popular hang out for hip Marrakshis and their beautiful friends.

Alizia (Map pp292-3; ☎ 024 438360/076 516295; cnr Rue Ahmed Chouhada Chawki, Hivernage; pizzas from Dh50, mains Dh100-150; ⏰ noon-2.30pm & 7-11pm; ✘) This very pleasant Italian-Moroccan restaurant with terrace is popular with the Marrakesh old-timers. There's a lot of fish on the menu, as well as delicious wood-oven baked pizzas and some Marrakshi specialities like *tanzhiya*. Keep a space for the dessert as there is a great choice.

Café de la Poste (Map p298; ☎ 024 433038; Ave Mohammed V; starters Dh75-120, mains Dh95-150; ⏰ 8am-1pm; ✘) From the outside this café-bar-restaurant, just behind the central post office, looks like an old colonial hang out, but it's all new, and one of the hippest places to meet for lunch or a drink before going clubbing. The food, fusion Moroccan-Mediterranean with a hint of Asia, is excellent, but portions are small and expensive.

Bô-Zin (☎ 024 388012; www.bo-zin.com; Douar Lahma, 3.5km Route de l'Ourika; meals Dh220-280; ⏰ 8pm-1am; ✘) Bô-Zin is a hot nightspot with lots of different rooms and atmospheres as well as a cool garden in summer, full of beautiful people who come to see and be seen. The waiting staff are gorgeous, the music usually good but very loud, depending on the DJ, and it always feels as if a party is about to happen (and often does). Oh and the food… It is officially a restaurant serving fusion food, and the cooking here is good, but not great – that's not really why you come.

Niagara (Map pp292-3; ☎ 024 449775; 31 Centre Commercial En-Nakhil, Route de Targa; pizzas Dh40-50, mains Dh50-80; ⏰ noon-2.15pm &7.15-11pm Tue-Sun; ✘) Large Marrakshi families flock to this hugely popular old-time restaurant with some of the best pizzas in town, baked in a wood fire. The menu is large and not a tajine in sight, with pastas, meat and fish dishes all very reasonably priced.

La Trattoria (Map p298; ☎ 024 432641; 179 Rue Mohammed el-Beqal, Guéliz; mains Dh100-250; ⏰ 7.30-11.30pm ✘) Enter through iron gates into a beautifully restored 1920s mansion, where a country-house party is often in full swing. A small pool and open wintertime fires add to the ambiance. The Italian cuisine on the menu is top-notch; it's advisable to book.

La Jacaranda (Map p298; ☎ 024 447215; 32 Blvd Mohammed Zerktouni, Guéliz; lunch/dinner set menus from Dh85/180, beef/fish fondues Dh170/180; ⏰ noon-3pm & 6.30-11pm; ✘) Very small and very French, La Jacaranda is nondescript on the outside, all white cloths and gleaming tableware on the inside. It is one of the city's top restaurants, serving such classics as tripe, preserved duck and foie gras as well as plenty of fish. The lunch menus are particularly good value.

Cafés, Patisseries & Ice-Cream Parlours

Djemaa el-Fna is surrounded by cafés offering various vistas of the square. By day, street-level terraces provide a front-row view of the activity. In the evening, head up to the rooftop terraces for a grandstand view of the spectacle unfolding below. Ave Mohammed V in the ville nouvelle is the other part of town that attracts a people-watching crowd of caffeine addicts.

MEDINA

Café des Épices (Map pp292-3; ☎ 024 391770; Place Rahba Qedima; breakfast Dh25, sandwich or salad Dh 25-30; ⏰ 8am-10pm) This is the best place in the medina to people-watch, or while away the time over a pot of mint tea or a fresh orange juice, while listening to a cool beat. The young Moroccans who run this place, are true medina boys, always up for a good time or a chat. Sit on the terrace on the lively square or watch the sunset over the city from the upper terraces. There is a Wifi connection and a limited, delicious lunch menu.

Dar Cherifa (Map pp292-3; ☎ 024 426463; 8 Derb Cherfa Lakbir, Mouassine; set menu Dh140-150; ⏰ 8.30am-6pm) A splendid riad transformed into an attractive literary café, Dar Cherifa has a library filled with books on Morocco to browse and a space for exhibitions and the occasional concert. Admire the bleached carved wood, the paintings and the rose petals strewn all over the floor whilst sipping a mint tea with Moroccan pastries.

Pâtisserie des Princes (Map p296; ☎ 024 443033; 32 Rue de Bab Agnaou; ⏰ 5am-11.30pm; ✘) This is one of the city's most famous patisseries, and with good reason. The seductive array of local delicacies, cakes and ice creams will sate any sweet tooth. The small café at the back is a welcome respite for women, or anyone in search of a quiet coffee.

VILLE NOUVELLE

Café des Livres (Map p298; ☎ 024 432149; 44 Rue Tariq ibn Ziad, Guéliz; breakfast Dh40, dishes Dh55-75, Sun brunch Dh85; 9.30am-9pm Tue-Sun) This bookshop-cum-tearoom is an oasis of tranquillity where you can browse through books while munching on an excellent sandwich, salad or slice of homemade cake. The menu makes for a great brunch or lunch. Excellent wi-fi connection.

Amandine (Map p298; ☎ 024 449612; 177 Rue Mohammed el-Beqal, Guéliz; breakfast Dh40-50; 6am-11pm) An elegant patisserie with a mouth-watering display of fine French pastries and ice cream, hugely popular with the expat crowd. There's a more intimate café for coffee, mint tea, fresh juices and breakfast next door.

Café les Négociants (Map p298; ☎ 024 435762; 110 Ave Mohammed V; 6am-11pm) Sitting on the wide Parisian-style terrace, one has the feeling that this is the centre of the universe (and it is, in terms of the ville nouvelle). It's a wonderful place for men to sit and watch the world go by.

Oliveri (Map p298; ☎ 024 448913; 9 Blvd el-Mansour Eddahbi; ice cream concoctions from Dh10; 7am-10pm;) For over 50 years this place has been scooping out ice cream, made from the freshest ingredients and seasonal fruits. Escape the heat on the street in the time-warp ice-cream parlour, complete with wrought-iron furniture and mirrored walls.

Quick Eats

MEDINA

At lunch time, before the stalls on Djemaa el-Fna get going, much of the same fare is available in the *qissaria* on the north side of the square. Here several vendors sharing a central kitchen whip up meals – such as *tanzhiya*, fried fish or lemon chicken and french fries – for under Dh40.

Chez Abdelhay (Map pp292-3; ☎ 071 157821; 46 Rue el-Baroudiyenne; meals Dh25-40; 8am-8pm) This great eatery near the ben Youssef medersa, specialising in grills, Moroccan salads and *harira*, has tables outside.

Fast Food al-Ahbab (Map p296; Rue de Bab Agnaou; salads Dh15-25, sandwiches Dh20-30; 7am-11pm) Almost always crowded, this sandwich shop

specialises in *shwarma* (spit-grilled meat or chicken). Tables on the terrace are close to the constant movement on the pedestrian thoroughfare Rue de Bab Agnaou, but that does not seem to deter the patrons.

Mabrouka (Map p296; ☎ 024 442426; Rue de Bab Agnaou; mains Dh40-60; 6am-midnight) Next to the historic theatre by the same name, this modern pizzeria and ice-cream parlour also offers the Moroccan standbys. An enclosed balcony overlooks the bustle of Rue de Bab Agnaou below.

Hôtel Ali (Map p296; ☎ 024 444979; Rue Moulay Ismail; set menus from Dh60, buffet guests/nonguests Dh60/70; dinner) The all-you-can-eat buffet attracts hungry travellers who binge on couscous, salads, fruit and desserts, including lots of options for vegetarians. This is a great place to meet other travellers if you are not staying at the hotel.

VILLE NOUVELLE

For bottom-rung local food, head for a group of hole-in-the-wall places on Rue ibn Aicha, where a solid meal of rotisserie chicken or brochettes (skewered meat), french fries and salad will cost around Dh35 to Dh50.

Bar l'Escale (Map p298; ☎ 024 433447; Rue de Mauritanie; mains Dh30-70; 11am-10.30pm) A simple eatery that has been running since 1947, specialising in good grills, which all come with chips and a tomato salad.

Café-Snack Sindibad (Map p298; 3 Ave Mohammed V; mains Dh25-35; 6am-11pm) This popular snack shop may look down-at-heel, but the food is as tasty as it is cheap. Try the *tanzhiya* with either lemons or prunes.

Snack Le Siroua (Map p298; ☎ 024 430174; 22 Blvd Mohammed Zerktouni; breakfast Dh18, mains Dh30-40, set menus Dh50; 4.30am-midnight) Typically Moroccan dishes like salads and tajine are good value, and the environment is pleasantly retro. The clientele, however, is exclusively male, which might deter female travellers. You can finish off the meal in the next door *glacerie* (ice-cream parlour), one of the city's best.

Self-Catering

For fresh produce, dried fruits and nuts, the new Marché Municipale Ibn Toumert, off Ave Mohammed V, or the market on the east side of Djemaa el-Fna have a great selection. The souqs are also filled with food stalls. For staples such as cheese, cereal and alcohol (often difficult to find elsewhere), a few markets in the ville nouvelle are useful, otherwise head for the supermarkets, **ACIMA supermarket** (Map p298; 109 Ave Mohammed Abdelkrim el-Khattabi, Guéliz) and **Aswak Assalam** (Map p298; Ave du 11 Janvier, Bab Doukkala) or the huge shop **Marjane** (Casablanca road), 4km out of town.

DRINKING

The number-one spot for a cheap and delicious drink is right on Djemaa el-Fna, where fresh-squeezed orange juice is only Dh3. The juice stands are open all day and much of the night for a thirst-quenching, refreshing treat. A word to the wise: ask the man to squeeze it right in front of you, as sometimes they add water and sugar to the already squeezed juice in the bottle.

Bars

As elsewhere in Morocco, the traditional bars in Marrakesh are mostly dire, beer- and male-oriented places. The new trendy upscale bars however are OK for women, particularly if you are not alone. Most of the women will be Western, but Moroccan girls do increasingly go out on the town together. Many bars also serve food and may turn into party places later at night, such as Le Foundouk (p313), Bô-Zin and Café de la Poste (p315).

Kosybar (Map pp292-3; ☎ 024 380324; http://kozi bar.tripod.com; 47 Place des Ferblantiers, Medina; ☺ noon-1am; ☒) The Kosybar combines three different venues within one riad near the *mellah*. The ground floor is a piano bar, the first floor a Moroccan salon and, best of all, the gorgeous terrace overlooks the medina and storks nesting on the city walls. The food ranges from sushi to Moroccan and is OK, but this is most interesting as a place to drink, as it has one of the largest selections of local and imported wines, as well as a properly maintained cigar humidor.

Café Arabe (Map p296; ☎ 024 429728; 184 Rue el-Mouassine, Medina; ☺ 10am-midnight; ☒) Another bar-tearoom-restaurant in a large riad in the medina, perfect for a sunset drink or a light meal with a beer. The décor is funky Moroccan, with a large courtyard and more intimate salons inside, while the terrace commands great views over the medina.

Comptoir (Map pp292-3; ☎ 024 437702; Rue Echouhada, Hivernage; ☺ 8pm-1am ☒) Couples

come at their peril: more relationships break up here than anywhere else in town. Although there is a restaurant downstairs, it is the flash lounge upstairs that draws the modish Moroccans and trendy tourists of all genders. The bar is very hip, complete with fancy cocktails and prices to match. A nightly show features a bevy of belly dancers (one who balances candles on her head!).

L'Abyssin (☎ 024 328584; www.palaisrhoul.com; Palais Rhoul, Dar Tounsi, Palmeraie, Route de Fès; ☺ 8-11pm Tue, noon-3.30pm & 8-11pm Wed-Sun; ☒) A summer garden restaurant and, most of all, ultracool lounge club at the back of the bling-bling Palais Rhoul villa hotel and spa. It's all very white, with staff dressed in white, white candles and white fluffy sofas. The food, however, is Mediterranean and Moroccan.

Bodega (Map p298; ☎ 024 433141; 23 Rue de la Liberté; ☺ 7pm-1am ☒) This wildly popular spot is unique in Marrakesh for its raucous crowd and unassuming atmosphere. Music is a mix of Latin, Arabic and good old-fashioned rock-and-roll. *Cervezas* (beers) and *mojitos* (rum cocktails) are reasonably priced, and tapas (Dh40 to Dh50) are available if you get the munchies.

La Casa (Map pp292-3; ☎ 024 448226; Ave du Président Kennedy; ☺ 7.30pm-4am ☒) Located in the Hôtel el-Andalous, La Casa is a fun tapas bar with reasonable food. It also has a dance floor, which may or may not be active depending on the night. Music is loud and a groovy mix of Latin and Arabic.

ENTERTAINMENT
Nightclubs

Marrakesh no longer sleeps and nightlife is fast becoming one of its attractions. Most of the hottest clubs are in the ville nouvelle, or in a new zone outside the city. Admissions range from Dh150 to Dh300 including the first drink. Each drink thereafter costs at least Dh50. Dress smartly and remember most places don't get going till after midnight or 1am. For out-of-town clubs like Pacha, remember that a taxi back can be really expensive.

Pacha (Map pp292-3; ☎ 024 388405; www.pachamarrakech.com; Complexe Pacha Marrakech, Blvd Mohammed VI; admission Mon-Fri before/after 10pm free/Dh150, Sat & Sun Dh300; ☺ 8pm-5am) Pacha Ibiza has arrived on the Marrakesh scene with two restaurants (open for lunch and dinner, with very good food), several bars and lounge areas and

A RISING PROBLEM

There is a dark side to the increase in tourism and the freedom of the riads. Sex tourism, and particularly paedophilia, is a growing problem, especially in Marrakesh and Agadir. Officially guests are not allowed to take anyone to their room but, until recently, if you paid a tip no-one cared who came or went. Then word got out that some riad owners were involved in sex tourism and others were allowing pornographic films to be shot in their rooms. The problem has become so large that the Governor of Marrakesh has clamped down on this, particularly on paedophilia. Zero tolerance is the policy and new laws were passed, allowing foreigners to be arrested and tried in Morocco. Arrests have been made and the campaign has had some success, but the problem continues. If you witness child prostitution or a paedophile in action, get in touch with the organisation Touche Pas à Mon Enfant (Hands off my Child; ☎ 070 410364; www.touchepasamonenfant.org), who are prepared to take direct action, and have already had several people arrested *in situ*.

a huge club that attracts '*le tout Marra-kech*'. Famous guest DJs are flown in, and at weekends up to 3000 people can crowd the place.

Montecristo (Map p298; ☎ 024 439031; 20 Rue Ibn Aicha; admission free with drink purchase; ⏰ 8pm-2am) For a night on the town in Marrakesh, this Latin club/salsa bar should be the first stop after drinks. The crowd is good-looking, there are quite a few prostitutes around, and they know how to dance. If you can't beat the heat on the dance floor, head up to the gorgeous roof terrace for a water pipe or a cocktail.

Beach Klubber (Map p298; ☎ 024 422877; www .beachclubber.com; Ave des Nations Unies; admission free with drink purchase; ⏰ 7.30pm-1am) The original Beach Klubber is in St Tropez, but the Marrakesh branch, opposite the Gendarmerie Centrale, is just as popular with young Marrakshis. The décor is decadent purple, strewn with cushions, and when it all heats up too much there is a fab roof terrace on which to shoot the breeze.

Teatro (Map pp292-3; ☎ 024 448811; Hôtel es Saadi, Rue Quadissia; admission Dh150; ⏰ 11.30pm-5am) Converted from an old theatre, this high-end club pulses to a techno beat. The dance floor is on the former stage – very appropriate for the ladies who now strut their stuff there. The house, emptied of its seats, serves as the bar area.

White Room (Map pp292-3; ☎ 060 595540; Hôtel Royal Mirage, Rue de Paris, Hivernage; admission Dh100; ⏰ 10pm-dawn) Yes, it is a big white room, but the music is the opposite of minimal, house DJs and the occasional guest DJ spinning an eclectic but very groovy mix of contemporary Arab dance tracks, techno beats, 1980s new wave and salsa.

Diamant Noir (Map p298; ☎ 024 434351; Hôtel Marrakech, Ave Mohammed V; admission from Dh80; ⏰ 10pm-4am) Although it is sometimes described as seedy, the 'Black Diamond' is still popular for its three bars, the dark dance floor and the very latest in hip-hop-happening music. It is one of the few clubs with any gay scene.

Atlas-Asni (Map p298; ☎ 024 447051; Hôtel Atlas, 101 Ave de France; admission Dh150; ⏰ midnight-4am) Dark and exotic, Atlas-Asni is a great spot for late-night dancing. The crowd and music are predominantly Arabic. It's a great place to see young Marrakshis let loose and get their groove on.

Cinema

The plushest cinema in town is **Le Colisée** (Map p298; ☎ 024 448893; Blvd Mohammed Zerktouni; stall/balcony Mon Dh15/25, Tue-Sun Dh25/35; ⏰ 3pm, 7pm & 9.30pm) in the ville nouvelle. Both sound and comfort are excellent. For a good selection of French and sometimes Moroccan films check out the program at the Institut Français (see p294).

SHOPPING

Marrakesh is a shopper's paradise, a city full of skilled artisans producing quality products in wood, leather, wool, metal, bone, brass and silver. It is also a city with more than its fair share of tat. The skill is in knowing how to sift the gold from the dross.

To get a feeling for the quality of merchandise it is always good to start at the government-run **Ensemble Artisanal** (Map pp292-3; Ave Mohammed V; ⏰ 8.30am-7.30pm daily), in the ville nouvelle. There are various other fixed-price craft shops along Ave Mohammed V. With a firm idea of prices in mind you may then feel up to tackling the souqs (see Walking Tour: The Souqs, p304), but be prepared to haggle hard. It's worth checking out some of the hotel boutiques like Jnane Tamsna (p312), and La Sultana (p311), which stock local designers you don't find in the souqs. There are also stylish boutiques at Comptoir (p317) and Ryad Tamsna (p314), which also exhibit some of the better modern artwork available. If you have something particular in mind and you can't find it, you could always hire a personal shopper (see p291).

The following shops are in the local residents' little black book, as they are different, sometimes funky and a change from what you find in the souqs.

Mustapha Blaoui (Map pp292-3; ☎ 024 385240; 142-4 Bab Doukkala; ☾ 9am-8pm) Knock on the huge, unmarked door and enter an Aladdin's cave – this is the best warehouse in town and the source of many of those chic riad furnishings. If you have certain specifications, the owner can get anything made up in one of his many workshops.

Aya's (Map pp292-3; ☎ 024 383428; www.ilove-marrakesh.com/ayas; 11 Bis Derb Jdid Bab Mellah; ☾ 9am-1.30pm & 3.30-8pm) This tiny boutique is a well-kept secret among local residents. It has gorgeous, very wearable clothes in wool, silk and cotton, based on traditional Moroccan designs and handmade by the finest tailors, who also do made-to-measure. Also stocks great accessories by local designers. The shop is in the little alley beside the restaurant Douiria near the place des Ferblantiers.

L'Orientaliste (Map p298; ☎ 024 434074; 11& 15 Rue de la Liberté, Guéliz; ☾ 10am-12.30pm & 3-7.30pm Mon-Sat, 10am-12.30pm Sun) This is a small boutique shop and a huge basement full of *objets d'art*, some modern and some antique. There are all sorts of nice knick-knacks, which make better-than-average holiday souvenirs.

Belhadj (Map p296; ☎ 024 441258; 1st fl, 22-23 Souq Funduq Ouazarzi, Bab Ftouh; ☾ 10am-7pm) Tiny shop filled to the brim with silver Berber jewellery, beads and necklaces from all over Africa, as well as jewellery made in semi-precious stones by the owner himself, who is obsessed with and very knowledgeable about beads. He is fair in his prices, and not interested in serious bargaining.

El-Badii (Map p298; ☎ 024 431693; 54 Ave Moulay Rachid, Guéliz; ☾ 9am-7pm) A stunning collection of fine antiques, rare embroideries, museum-piece ceramics and a hall of carpets in the basement. The haunt of celebrities, this shop has top-of-the-range stuff but some of the carpet prices are surprisingly reasonable and the proprietors are knowledgeable and free with advice.

Au Fil d'Or (Map p296; ☎ 024 445919; 10 Souq Semmarine, Medina; ☾ 9am-1pm & 2.30-7.30pm Mon-Thu, 9am-1pm Sat & Sun) Unlike the open stalls and shops around it in the tourist souq, curtains prevent you looking into this fine shop selling the best quality *babouches*, exquisite handmade shirts and traditional jackets, for men and women.

GETTING THERE & AWAY
Air
Six kilometres southwest of town is **Ménara airport** (☎ 024 447865 flight information). The airport has an **information desk** (☾ 8am-6pm) in the check-in hall and there are some banks where you can exchange currency.

RAM (Royal Air Morocco; Map p298; ☎ 024 436205; www.royalairmaroc.com; 197 Ave Mohammed V, Guéliz; ☾ 8.30am-12.20pm & 2.30-7pm) has several flights daily to and from Casablanca (from Dh850, 40 minutes), where you can pick up connections, as well as a direct weekly flight to Agadir (from Dh720, 35 minutes). It is advisable to reconfirm your flight with their 24-hour **call centre** (☎ 090 000800).

RAM also operates direct international flights to Geneva (three hours) once a week; London (3½ hours) at least once a week; and daily flights to Paris (3¼ hours). **Atlas Blue** (☎ 082 009090; www.atlas-blue.com; Ménara Airport), the sister company of RAM, has cheap flights to Marrakesh from London, Paris, Amsterdam and many other European cities. Other carriers include **British Airways** (☎ 024 448951; www.ba.com; Ménara Airport), with at least five flights a week to London, and Air France, which flies to Paris at least once a day. **Easyjet** (www.easyjet.com) has just started flights from London to Marrakesh.

Bus
The main **bus station** (Map pp292-3; ☎ 024 433933; Bab Doukkala), where the majority of buses arrive and depart, is just outside the city walls, a 20-minute walk or roughly Dh5 to Dh10 taxi ride from Djemaa el-Fna. The main building is big with many booths covering all sorts of local and long-distance destinations.

BUS TIMETABLE

Destination	Price (Dh)	Duration (hr)	Departures	Window (number)
Beni Mellal	40	3	7 daily	1
Rabat	80	5-6	half-hourly 5am-midnight	2
via Casablanca	45-50	4	(as for Rabat)	2
Tangier	120-150	11	8am	2
Asni (for Jebel Toubkal)	12	1½	4 daily	3
Safi	30	3	7 daily, 4.30am-2pm	4
El-Jadida	37	4½	hourly 5am-4pm	5
Ouarzazate	65	4	8 daily, 4.30am-9pm	6
Tinerhir	99	10	5.30am, 10am, 11am & 3.30pm	6
Boumalne du Dadès	80	(as for Tinerhir)		6
Er-Rachidia	125	10	10am	6
Essaouira	35	3	9 daily 4am-5pm	7
Taroudannt	60	7	10am, 12.30pm & 9pm	17
Azilal	44	3	8.30am, 12.30pm & 3.30pm	18
Demnate	24	2	9 daily, 6am-6.30pm	18
Agadir	from 70	4	hourly 5am-10pm	19
Erfoud	160	10	3.45pm	19
M'Hamid	120	8	8.30am, 8.15pm & 10pm	29
via Zagora	95	8	(as for M'Hamid)	29
Tata	130	10	9.30am	29

The majority of buses leave between 4am and 7pm. It's advisable to get tickets for early-morning departures the day before as some booths aren't open first thing.

The bus station also has **left-luggage facilities** (small/big bag per day Dh5/8; ☼ 24hr), cafés, disgusting toilets and touts.

A number of companies run buses to Fès (from Dh120, 8½ hours, at least six daily) and Meknès (from Dh110, six hours, at least three daily).

Buses to Asni (Dh10) also leave from a dirt patch on the southern side of the medina outside Bab er-Rob. There's at least one bus a day to Telouet (Dh45, four hours) at 3pm from beside Bab Gehmat in the medina's southwest wall.

CTM (Map pp292-3; Window 10, Bab Doukkala bus station; ☎ 024 434402) operates daily buses to Fès (Dh150, 8½ hours, one daily) via Beni Mellal (Dh60, 2½ hours), Ouarzazate (Dh70, four hours, one daily), and Tan Tan (Dh175, six hours, five daily) via Tiznit (Dh108, five hours). There are also daily services to Agadir (Dh80, four hours, nine daily), Casablanca (Dh80, fours hours, three daily) and Laâyoune (Dh285, 14 hours, four daily). CTM services to Essaouira (Dh60, three

hours) fill up quickly so it is best to purchase your ticket the day before.

Tickets can also be bought at the **CTM Office** (Map p298; ☎ 024 448328; Blvd Mohammed Zerktouni, Guéliz). This is also the arrival and departure point for their international buses, including Paris (from Dh900, 48 hours) and Madrid (from Dh800, 36 hours), on Tuesday, Wednesday and Saturday.

Supratours (Map p298; ☎ 024 435525) is west of the train station. You can catch a bus from here to Agadir (Dh85, four hours, five daily), Dakhla (Dh400, 25 hours, one daily), Essaouira (Dh60, 2½ hours, three daily), Laâyoune (Dh285, 15 hours, two daily) and Tan Tan (Dh175, 10 hours, two daily).

Car

Local car rental companies often offer more competitive deals than international operators, with quoted rates starting at around Dh400 per day with unlimited mileage, cheaper if you take it for a minimum of three days. However, you should be able to negotiate a 10% to 20% discount normally and even more in the low season (October to mid-December and mid-January to the end of February). It'll cost you Dh700 to Dh1000 per day for a 4WD or, if you want to enjoy the landscape and don't feel like driving south or in the mountains, **Sahara Services Travel** (Map p298; ☎ 024 420673, 061 776766; www .saharaservicestravel.com; Apt 38 Immeuble Mouttasali, 88-90 Blvd Mohammed Zerktouni) has 4WD Toyota Landcruisers with driver (Dh1300 per day, all inclusive) or a small minibus (for 9 or 13 people, Dh 1250 per day). Car-rental agencies in Marrakesh include the following:

Avis (www.avis.com; Ave Mohammed V Map p298; ☎ 024 432525;137 Ave Mohammed V; Airport ☎ 024 431265)

Budget (www.budgetrentacar.com; Blvd Mohammed Zerktouni Map p298; ☎ 024 431180; 68 Blvd Mohammed Zerktouni; Airport (☎ 024 438875)

Concorde Car (Map p298; ☎ 024 431116; http://con cordecar.ifrance.com; 154 Ave Mohammed V)

Europcar (www.europcar.com; Blvd Mohammed Zerktouni (Map p298; ☎ 024 431228; 63 Blvd Mohammed Zerk-touni; Airport (☎ 024 437718)

Hertz (www.hertz.com; Ave Mohammed V (Map p298; ☎ 024 431394; 154 Ave Mohammed V; Airport (☎ 024 447230)

La Plaza Car (Map p298; ☎ 024 421801;www.laplaza car.com; Immeuble 141, 23 Rue Mohammed el-Beqal)

Taxi

Standard grands taxis to destinations in the High Atlas, including Asni (Dh18), Ijoukak (Dh28), Ourigane (Dh25) and Setti Fatma (Dh22) depart from outside Bab er-Rob near the royal palace.

Those serving destinations further afield gather on a dirt lot to the north of the main bus station. Destinations include Agadir (Dh100), Azilal (Dh70), Beni Mellal (Dh100), Demnate (Dh50), Essaouira (Dh100), Ouarzazate (Dh80) and Taroudannt (Dh100).

Train

From the **train station** (Map p298; ☎ 024 447768, 090 203040 information only; www.oncf.org.ma; cnr Ave Hassan II & Blvd Mohammed VI, Guéliz) you can take a taxi or city bus (bus 3, 8, 10 or 14, among others; Dh3) into the centre.

There are numerous trains to Casablanca (2nd-class rapide, Dh76, three hours, nine daily) and Rabat (Dh101, four hours).

There are direct trains to Fès (Dh171, eight hours, eight daily) via Meknès (Dh154, seven hours), and Safi (Dh25, 4½ hours, two daily; change at Benguérir). Overnight trains to Tangier (Dh188) leave once daily; if you want a couchette you pay a supplement of Dh100, it's advisable to book it at least two days in advance.

GETTING AROUND
To/From the Airport

A petit taxi to Marrakesh from the airport (6km) should be no more than Dh60, but you may have difficulty convincing the driver of this. As with any taxi trip, the taxi should use the meter to determine the price: this may require a bit of a fight. Alternatively, bus 11 runs irregularly to Djemaa el-Fna.

Bus

Local buses (Map p296; ☎ 024 3433933; all fares Dh3) run from Place de Foucauld, near Djemaa el-Fna, to the following destinations:

Nos 1 & 20 Ave Mohammed V, Guéliz

Nos 3 & 10 Bab Doukkala gare routière, main post office, train station, Douar Laskar

No 8 Bab Doukkala gare routière, main post office, train station, Douar Laskar

No 11 Ave Ménara, airport

No 14 Train station

Calèches

These horse-drawn carriages are a pleasant way to get around, if you avoid the rush hours (8am, midday and 5.30-7.30pm), and can work out cheaper than a taxi. The official fares are Dh15 for a straightforward one-way trip within the medina walls and Dh25 outside. Otherwise, it's Dh100 an hour for pottering around the sights. If you're interested in a bit of horse-drawn romance or you want to do the 1½-hour tour of the ramparts, you'll find calèches lined up on the north side of Place de Foucault.

Car & Motorcycle

The Marrakesh medina is more driver-friendly than many cities' old towns, but there are still places where the streets are too narrow to drive. Djemaa el-Fna is off-limits to cars, as are the smallest streets immediately north and south of the square. There are often parking places near the gates and entrances to the medina.

Parking is not as difficult as it seems, as long as you are willing to pay. Most hotels in the ville nouvelle offer parking. In town you can park on the street but will have to pay Dh10 to the attendant (locals pay Dh2 in

MARRAKESH & C MOROCC

the day and Dh 5 at night, but tourists will rarely get away with that). There are public parking lots near the Koutoubia Mosque and just south of Place de Foucauld on Ave el-Mouahidine: expect to pay Dh20/40 per day/24 hours.

For travel on two wheels, **Marrakesh Motos** (Map p298; ☎ 024 448359, 061 316413; 31 Ave Mohammed Abdelkrim el-Khattabi; ☼ 9am-10pm), about 2km out of the town centre on the Casablanca road, just beyond the Goodyear garage, rents out scooters and 125cc motorcycles for Dh250 to Dh300 per day.

Taxi

The creamy-beige petits taxis around town charge Dh5 to Dh15 per journey. They're all supposed to use their meters, but you may need to insist, especially coming from the train station or airport. If your party numbers more than three you must take a grand taxi, which requires some negotiation.

EAST OF MARRAKESH

With all its marvels, Marrakesh is a full-on experience. It's undeniably fun but equally noisy, dusty, overwhelming and pretty exhausting. Anyone with a day or two to spare should get out of town, take a trip into the countryside or into the mountains, and check out the contrasting attractions of the lush Aït Bou Goumez Valley and the sparkling waterfalls known as the Cascades d'Ouzoud.

DEMNATE دمنات

If you are headed to the Cascades d'Ouzoud it might be worth stopping at Demnate, particularly on Sunday, the day of the weekly market famous for its excellent olives and varnished pottery. Overlooking a valley of olive groves, Demnate is a bustling walled town. Once you've come this far, it's worth detouring another 6km to the east to Imi-n-Ifri, a natural bridge over a gorge. It's possible to clamber down into the gorge and pass under this curious formation. There is a café overlooking the gorge and the seasonal *gîte d'étape* (trekkers' hostel) **Kasbah Imi-n-Ifri** (☎ 062 105168; s/d Dh150/240, d per person Dh90; ☼ Jun-Sep). Minibuses leave when full from the far end of Demnate (Dh5); it costs around Dh40 one way for a grand taxi.

About 7km further, there are dinosaur footprints at the 2 hectare excavation site of Iroutane. Four kilometres before Demnate (2km off the main road) is the pottery centre of Boughrart.

The best place for lunch is **Café d'Ouzoud** (☎ 023 456087; Ave Mohammed V), a couple of hundred metres before the main gate into Demnate.

Grands taxis to Marrakesh (Dh50) and Azilal (Dh30) leave from the main gate. Buses leave for Marrakesh (Dh25) every couple of hours until 6pm from the bus station (take the road to the right before entering the main town gate).

CASCADES D'OUZOUD شلالات د ت أزوض

About 167km northeast of Marrakesh are Morocco's most spectacular waterfalls; they're well worth the effort of getting there. If you have a car, it's an easy day trip.

The waterfalls are a popular attraction for both tourists and Moroccans, particularly on weekends and in the summer, but it is not too crowded yet. The Oued Ouzoud (Ouzoud river; *ouzoud* is Berber for olives, and refers to the cultivation of olive trees in the area) drops spectacularly some 110m, in three tiered falls, into the canyon of Oued el-Abid. The view from above is powerful, particularly after a few rainy days but, to enjoy the spectacle fully, it pays to walk down and get sprayed with the mist of the tumbling water. Further down river there are several icy pools to cool down in. The site is at its best from March to the end of June, when there is most water, but young Moroccans love to camp here in the summer. The falls are in the shade all morning, but catch the sun in the afternoon when you can clearly see rainbows.

To reach the falls walk past the riad (see opposite) towards the edge of the precipice, where various paths all head down to the falls. Locals might try to 'guide' you for a few dirham but it is easy to find your own way down. At the bottom, a line of souvenir stalls leads to boats that ferry across the river (Dh15 to Dh20), where another path leads back up to the village, lined with cafés and stalls. Along the path families of Barbary apes amuse the tourists and beg for food, but a signpost advises not to feed them.

If you are down for the day, you can go for a walk following the course of the

river. An easier walk is to the picturesque
Berber village of Tanaghmelt, by following
the path by the lower pools up past a farm-
house, and then up to the slopes for about
1.5km. Otherwise, for a longer walk, follow
the course of the river to caves (two hours)
and the Gorges of Oued el-Abid (another
two hours). As you continue downstream
there are small, clean pools offering a great
opportunity for a swim. For longer walks
stay for the night in Ouzoud and the hotel
can organise a route and guides.

Interspersed between the souvenir stands
on the tiers surrounding the falls are several
cafés with shady campsites. Facilities are
basic but popular with young Moroccans
and Europeans. There are a few basic hotels,
which also set up treks in the area.

The **Riad Cascades d'Ouzoud** (☎ 023 459658;
www.ouzoud.com; s/d/tr Dh470/630/830) is tastefully decorated – think rustic chic – with a
roof terrace where you can have breakfast
(Dh40) with scenic views. It's definitely the
best place to stay. The enthusiastic owner
is happy to arrange trekking as well as ab-
seiling down dry canyons, kayaking, river-
sliding and even water-skiing on Lake Ben
el-Ouidane.

Chalal (☎ /fax 023 459660, 072 384791; s/d Dh170
200) is a simple hotel run by a family who
used to be nomads, with cosy and clean
rooms with communal bathrooms, and a
huge Berber tent set up as a dormitory.
They are very friendly and helpful if you
want to discover the region.

Getting There & Away
From Marrakesh, it's easiest to get transport direct to Azilal, from where grands
taxis run when full to Ouzoud (Dh15 per
person, or Dh200 for the whole taxi, return). Don't leave it past 4pm to try to begin
your trip back to to Azilal.

AZILAL   أزيلال
This quiet administrative centre is mainly
of interest to travellers as an accommodation and transport hub for the Cascades
d'Ouzoud and the Aït Bou Goumez Valley.

The **Délégation du Tourisme** (☎ 023 458722;
Ave Hassan II; 9am-noon & 3-6pm Mon-Fri), near the
Hôtel Assounfou, has a useful notice board.
Also nearby is **Cyber Itri Internet** (per hr Dh8;
 10am-2pm & 4-11.30pm), and the **Banque Popu-
laire** (Ave Hassan II), which has a cash machine.

Further along is a Crédit Agricole. Market
day is Thursday.

Hôtel Assounfou (☎ 023 459220; fax 023 458442;
s/d Dh150/300), on the main road, offers the
most comfortable accommodation with
carpeted and heated rooms with lukewarm
showers. Otherwise try **Hôtel Dadès** (☎ 023
458245; hoteldades@yahoo.fr; Ave Hassan II; s/d with
shower Dh130/150), or **Hôtel Souss** (☎ 023 458917;
d Dh70), with spacious and clean rooms (hot
showers Dh5). The best place to eat is the
nearby Ibnou Ziad Restaurant.

Buses run between Azilal and Marrakesh (Dh60, two to six daily). There are
three or four bus services to Beni Mellal
(Dh35). Plenty of grands taxis run from
the taxi lot behind Marrakesh's bus station to Azilal (Dh60) and, less frequently,
from Azilal to Demnate (Dh30) and Beni
Mellal (Dh35).

The drive between Azilal and Afourer,
which brings you to the main Marrakesh-
to-Beni Mellal road, is a treat, especially
the views of the lake formed by the Bin
el-Ouidane Dam. This single dam produces
over 25% of Morocco's electricity.

AÏT BOU GOUMEZ
VALLEY   وادي عيت بو غومز
They call it 'the Happy Valley' and when
you get there you will understand why:
there is a touch of Shangri-la about this
lush and unusually beautiful valley to the
southwest of Beni Mellal, beyond Azilal.
In part the Aït Bou Goumez Valley, feels
remote because it is. A year-round road link
was only opened in 2001, before which the
valley was snowbound for four months a
year. Even now you'll find that the road is
rarely busy.

For trekkers the valley provides access
to walks up into the M'Goun massif (see
p424).

The valley is peppered with a network
of *gîtes d'étape*, opening up a rare range
of opportunities for walkers without a tent
as well as for visitors who want to stay a
while.

The main village in the valley is **Tabant**,
which has shops selling some essentials,
two basic cafés and a busy Sunday market.
East of the village is the Centre de Formation aux Métiers de la Montagne, the main
school for mountain guides, although there
is no *bureau des guides* here.

The only real sight in the valley is the **marabout of Sidi Moussa**. The shrine, which sits on top of an eye-catching pyramid-shaped hill, 150m above the valley floor, is still resorted to by women who need help acquiring a husband or having children. But the real attraction of the valley is not these buildings but the joy of being in so peaceful a place and seeing this landscape – the rich fertility of the valley floor and terraced hillsides – and the Berber villages, which seem to have grown out of the mud and rock on which they sit. The views over the valley from the shrine, and from the *agadir* (fortified granary) on the adjacent hill, are spectacular.

Sleeping

There are several *gîtes d'étape* in and around Agouti village, including **Chez Daoud** (☎ 062 105183, dm Dh50), a short walk down from the road, beside barley fields, with rudimentary washing facilities. Up on the road, **Flilou** (☎ 024 343796; tamsilt@menara.ma; dm/d Dh50/150) has clean dorms and considerably more expensive doubles in a neat Berber house with spotless washing facilities. In Tabant, the *gîte* of **Aït Oliqdim Mohamed** (☎ 023 459326; dm Dh50) is clean, has cold showers and serves a delicious tajine if warned in advance. Of three *gîtes* in the nearby village of Ikhf-n-Ighir, that of **Outagloute Benassar** (☎ 023 459175; dm Dh50) has clean dorm rooms, outside toilets and a selection of maps and books.

The only place that stands out in the valley is the delightful **Dar Itrane** (☎ 024 31 39 01 Marrakesh booking office; www.atlas-sahara-trek.com; s/d half board Dh340/500; meals Dh70). Located in Imelghas village, Dar Itrane is the successful result of a French-Berber collaboration. A wonderful pisé auberge with comfortable whitewashed rooms in an astonishingly pretty location, it is a centre for trekking and the manager is an excellent host and guide.

Getting There & Away

Minibuses run from Azilal to Tabant (Dh35, three hours) in the morning when full, from near the central mosque. You can sometimes find a grand taxi for Dh50 per seat. There are plenty of trucks that head to Azilal on Thursday for its Friday market.

ZAOUIAT AHANSAL   زاوية أهنسال

With a 4WD it's possible to continue over the rough *piste* and 2629m Tizi 'Tirghist to Zaouiat Ahansal and from there continue north to Ouaouizarht (wah-ri-zat), which has a hotel and a Wednesday market, and Beni Mellal. There are trucks from Tabant to Zaouiat Ahansal on Sunday. Regular minivans run between Zaouiat Ahansal and Aït Mohammed (Dh40) and less frequently to Ouaouizarht via Tilougguite.

Accommodation is available in Zaouiat Ahansal at the *gîte d'étape* of **Sidi Ahmed Amahdar** (☎ 023 459393; Dh35). There are more *gîtes* in the surrounding villages of Agoudim, Amezrai and Taghia, the latter being two hours' walk upstream. Market day in Zaouiat Ahansal is Monday.

Specialist trekking agencies lead trips to explore nearby Aqa n'Tazart and Taghia Gorges and the sheer rock faces of the La Cathédrale du Rocher, a climber's delight.

BENI MELLAL
pop 500,000

About 200km northeast of Marrakesh you may find yourself passing Beni Mellal if you are headed into the Middle or High Atlas. Thanks to the nearby dam of Bin el-Ouidane, Beni Mellal has grown rich in recent years. The city has expanded dramatically, and is of no great interest to visitors, except as a handy stopover on the Marrakesh-Fès road.

From the bus station it's a 10-minute walk uphill to the main street in the centre, Ave Mohammed V. For the medina, cross the small square and head left for Place de la Liberté. The huge Tuesday market, sprawling all the way up the hill from the bus station to Ave Mohammed V, gathers villagers and farmers of the rich agricultural Tadla plain. Beni Mellal reputedly has the best oranges in Morocco.

The **tourist office** (☎ 023 488663; Ave Hassan II) is just south of Ave Mohammed V. There are heaps of banks, most with ATMs and money-changing facilities, including the Banque Populaire opposite the bus station. **Hansali 2000 Internet** (Rue Tarik ibn Ziad; per hr Dh8) is in the medina opposite Hôtel es-Saada).

The kasbah in the medina is of little interest, but a walk up into the hills south of the town leads to the smaller kasbah of Ras el-Aïn and the nearby spring, Aïn Asserdoun, set within gardens.

Sleeping & Eating

There are plenty of hotels in town, including a useful cluster located opposite the bus station. The best restaurants are those in the Hôtel Ouzoud and Hôtel de Paris (which is popular with tour groups). Plenty of local cheap eats can be found along Ave Mohammed V and in the old medina.

Hôtel Al-Bassatine (☎ 023 482247; fax 023 486806; Route de Fkih ben Salah; s/d Dh330/420; ❄ ☎) Heading northwest out of town on the P21 is this comfortable large hotel used by tour groups, overlooking orange and olive groves. The food is not great, so head into town for dinner.

Hôtel es-Saada (☎ 023 482991; 129 Rue Tarik ibn Ziad; s/d/tr Dh50/90/125) Just off Ave Mohammed V and close to the medina, it has small, clean rooms and a public shower (Dh7) downstairs. The management is friendly and helpful.

Hôtel Ain Asserdoun (☎ 023 483493; Ave des FAR; s/d Dh100/150) This is a nice option five minutes' walk from Zidania up the hill towards town. Rooms are clean and spacious and most come with a balcony and ensuite bathroom.

Hôtel de Paris (☎ 023 482245; hotel_paris@menara.ma; Rue ibn Sina; s/d Dh200/290) Recently renovated, this hotel is clean and comfortable, but has very little character. Tour groups crowd the restaurant for the lunch buffet (Dh100).

Hôtel Ouzoud (☎ 023 483752; www.sogatour.com; Km3 Route de Marrakech; s/d Dh750/950; ❄ ☎) A modern four-star hotel that is part of the Sogatour chain, this hotel has spacious, comfortable rooms and a magnificent garden. Check out the website for special offers.

Restaurant Tawada (Ave Mohammed V; mains Dh45-60) Tawada is a reliable favourite, much cheaper than the Ouzoud and Paris hotels. It serves up grills and excellent tajines.

Safa-Glace (Rue Chouki II; mains Dh35-55) Away from brochettes and tajines, join the local youngsters at Safa-Glace for a good pizza, and ice cream for dessert.

Getting There & Away

CTM buses leave from the main bus station once a day for Fès (Dh76, six hours) and Marrakesh (Dh60, 3½ hours). Cheaper and more frequent local buses cover the same routes, and also go to El-Jadida, Er-Rachidia, Essaouira, Meknès, Nador and Safi. Local buses leave three or four times a day for Azilal (Dh35) and Demnate (Dh38) as well.

Grands taxis leave from a lot behind the bus station for Azilal (Dh35) and Ouaouizarht (Dh18).

IMILCHIL

In the heart of the Middle Atlas, the small village of Imilchil, just another gorgeous Berber village for most of the year, is particularly known for its September *moussem*. This is a huge trade fair where the Berber families stock up and gather before the first snow returns them to their isolation and, most famously of all, where young Berbers come to find someone to marry. Though a lot more touristy than it once was, it is still a major event attracting merchants, singers and dancers, as well as would-be brides and grooms. It's very colourful with the flirtatious girls in their striped woollen cloaks and elaborate jewellery and the strutting boys in their flowing white jellabas. The dates of the three-day festival, from Friday to Sunday in the third or fourth week of September are posted at tourist offices throughout the country and there are many organised tours from the large cities. Since the new paved road from Rich to Imilchil, the number of tourists has risen dramatically, and thousands are now bussed in – and with that comes a large number of hustlers and *faux guides*, as well as souvenir stalls.

During the festival the area is covered in tented accommodation; otherwise, there are two basic hotels, a few simple refuge-style places and several café/restaurants.

To get to Imilchil from Marrakesh, head northeast by bus or a series of grands taxis to Kasba Tadla. From there you need to get another grand taxi to El-Ksiba. From El-Ksiba there is a daily bus to Aghbala. The turn-off for Imilchil is near Tizi n'Isly, about 10km before Aghbala. From there, the 61km of what was until recently a rough *piste*, now a newly surfaced road, leads south to Imilchil. Around here there are a few grands taxis or souq lorries for transport – market days in Imilchil are Friday and Sunday.

If you have plenty of time, it's also possible to get to Imilchil (a breathtaking 160km by souq lorry or 4WD) from Boumalne du Dadès or Tinerhir. Minivans leave Imilchil for Tinerhir (Dh40 to Dh45) on Saturday. The road from Rich, on the Er-Rachidia-Midelt road, to Imilchil is now surfaced too.

SOUTH OF MARRAKESH

OURIKA VALLEY واد‍ة اوريكة

The Ourika is one of the more beautiful and dramatic of the valleys that run down from the High Atlas and its proximity to Marrakesh (45 minutes by car) makes it a great day out. The valley sides tower precipitously above the mass of emerald green fields on the valley floor. In summer, when Marrakesh swelters in the sun, this is one of the places Marrakshis come to camp or picnic beside the cooling water.

The valley, lying east of Jebel Toubkal, is popular with skiers in winter and trekkers in spring and summer. The main towns are the ski resort of Oukaïmeden, which is busiest during the snow season from November-to-April, and the fast-growing village of Setti Fatma further east. But the main attraction is the valley itself and the mountains that overlook it, still sufficiently pristine for Morocco's popular sparkling mineral water to be drawn from the Lalla Haya source near the hamlet of Oulmes.

In winter the valley is threatened by flash floods, which have caused tremendous damage. The worst of these, in August 1995, resulted in the loss of hundreds of lives.

The **Centre d'Informations Touristique Ourika** (☎ 068 465545), in the village of Tnine, 33km from Marrakesh as you head to Ourika, is operated by a local NGO and provides information and a map of attractions in the valley. These include potteries, watermills, a salt mine and quarries. A good country souq is held in Tnine each Monday. Also here is **Dar Atif** (☎ /fax024 444490, 077 519971; http://daratif.qdo.org; d incl breakfast Dh300-350, ste Dh600), a terracotta house surrounded by trees and flowers, which makes a good base for walks in the countryside.

Approximately 8km further on, there is a sign for the very pleasant **Timalizene** (☎ 024 439909 after sunset; www.timalizene.com in French; r per person half board Dh400), both a beautiful garden and a *chambre d'Hôte (bed and breakfast)*. Reached by bridge across the river, the Timalizene is wonderful place to relax in a beautifully kept garden (garden visit Dh15), with the prospect of a warm welcome and a good lunch (Dh100, booking recommended). Each Tuesday and Thursday, Timalizene also arranges day trips from Marrakesh (Dh300 per person), leaving the city at 9.20am and including a three-hour walk, lunch, garden visit and return to the city. Make a reservation the previous day between 8am and 10am (☎ 024 439909 or 063 564 56).

Above the village, perched on a ridge, the **Kasbah Timalizen** (024 384855, 061 252328) is currently being turned into a high-end retreat by the owner of the Riad Edward (see p310). Due to open in spring 2007, it will have 18 rooms, a pool, tennis courts and a spa.

About 45km from Marrakesh is the very pleasant **Auberge le Maquis** (☎ 024 484531; www.le-maquis.com in French; half board per person Dh380). The surrounding views are marvellous and le Maquis is particularly good for families, with board games, bunk beds and kids' menus. Children aged under 12 get half board for the cost of the food only. The auberge arranges treks to the Yaggour plateau with its prehistoric carvings.

Oukaïmeden اوكيمدين

Although it is best known as a ski resort, Oukaïmeden (elevation 2650m) also makes a good trekking base. Out of the snow season, you can explore the immediate vicinity in search of rock carvings. A useful book for this is *Gravures Rupestres du Haut Atlas* by Susan Searight and Danièle Hourbette. The Club Alpin Français (CAF) offers good trekking advice.

Oukaïmeden is Morocco's only ski resort. It boasts seven runs from nursery to black, six tows and the highest ski lift in Africa (3243m). But conditions are very variable and even in the peak ski season, February to April, there is no guarantee of snow. If there is skiing, then gear, passes and lessons are all available in town at prices that will be a pleasant surprise to anyone who has skied in Europe or the US.

It's a concrete eyesore amidst the beauty of the mountains, but the four-star **Hotel Kenzi Louka** (☎ 024 319080, fax 024 319088; www.kenzi-hotels.com; s/d Dh750/900; 🅿 🌊) has a following, more for its facilities, including a hammam and swimming pool, than for the good-sized but tired ensuite rooms. Still the best in town. Breakfast is available for Dh90.

CAF refuge (☎ 024319036; www.cafmaroc.co.ma; CAF or HI members/nonmembers adult per person Dh95/140) is a well-run place with dormitory beds, a few private rooms, hot showers, a bar-restaurant (Dh15 for breakfast) and a well-equipped kitchen. You'll need your own sleeping bag. They sell a selection of French trekking and mountaineering guidebooks. The **Hôtel de L'Angour, Chez Juju** (☎ 024 319005; fax 024 319006; full board s/d Dh390/680) has old-fashioned rooms, with slightly crummy showers in the corner of the room and communal toilets. The bar-restaurant is good.

Out of season there is little or no transport to Oukaïmeden, although you can charter a grand taxi (Dh350 to Dh400 return from Marrakesh). Otherwise, take a Setti Fatma or Aghbalou-bound bus or grand taxi (Dh25) and try hitching up the mountain.

Setti Fatma   ستي فتما

This village, 24km south of the Oukaïmeden turn-off, sits high up the Ourika Valley road and has become the centre of tourism in the valley. Originally two separate villages, Asagour and Ilkhrie, Setti Fatma is also the site of an important four-day *moussem* in August when a fair and market are set up at the Koubba of Setti Fatma.

Most people come to relax by the river or eat at one of the many restaurants, but there is good walking locally, with seven waterfalls hidden in a side valley across the river.

The village also makes a good starting point for treks further afield (see p421). Beware *faux guides* and consult your hotel or the **bureau des guides** (☎ /fax 024 426113) some 200m beyond the Hôtel Asgaour, who can arrange guides and muleteers. There are fine day or multiday hikes east to Tourcht, north to Imi n'Taddert, or to Anammer and Tizi n'Oucheg in the Aït Oucheg Valley. The *bureau des guides* can offer advice on these hikes and also on three-day trips up to the Yaggour Plateau, involving sleeping at shepherds' huts at Amddouz.

A cut above most places in the village, **Hôtel Restaurant La Perle D'Ourika** (☎ 061 567239; d Dh180) is still pretty basic, although serving good solid Moroccan cooking (set meals Dh80).

One of the best options in Setti Fatma is **Hôtel Asgaour** (☎ 066 416419; s/d/tr Dh60/70/100), offering a warm welcome to simple rooms with communal showers. The good restaurant downstairs serves excellent tajines for Dh80.

Run by a French couple, **Dar Piano** (☎ 024 484842; www.darpiano.com; s/d/tr/q 200/250/300/400; breakfast Dh40; ☺ June-August) has an interesting mix of France and Morocco in both the décor and its good cooking. This small house has good views over the valley, though rooms on the roadside can be noisier. Enjoy the log fire in winter.

The location of **Le Noyer** (☎ 066 720641) isn't the best, across the road from the river, but the crowds of Moroccans who come here for lunch are a clear sign that this is some of the best – and keenest priced – cooking in Setti Fatma, with set menus from Dh45 to Dh100. Dining is on the terrace or, in winter, around the large fire.

There are many other café-restaurants on both side of the river, many with better location than cooking. Some of them offer accommodation of variable standards.

Grands taxis to Setti Fatma leave frequently all day from Bab er-Rob in Marrakesh (Dh20) and there are less-frequent minibuses (Dh10 to Dh15). Transport returns when full.

JEBEL TOUBKAL

The highest mountain in North Africa is also one of the favourite destinations for people heading out of Marrakesh for the day. Travellers looking for some serious multiday walking should look at the Toubkal walks described in Trekking (p411). But if you want to escape the hustle and pollution of Marrakesh and breathe some clean mountain air for a day, or just have lunch with snow-capped mountains as a backdrop, Toubkal and the villages that sit at its feet make a great destination.

Asni

At the junction of the Marrakesh–Taroudannt road and the road that leads up the Mizane Valley to Imlil and Jebel Toubkal, Asni has long been a meeting point. Before the road to Toubkal was paved, it boasted the best hotel in the immediate area, the Grand Hôtel du Toubkal, which was closed and looking for a buyer at the time of writing. Most days the only reason to stop is to change bus or taxi, but on Saturday Asni holds one of the largest souqs in this part of the Atlas Mountains, where producers bring fruit, vegetables and livestock to sell. The number of travellers visiting the souq has also encouraged others to bring jewellery, rugs and other souvenirs.

The road winds up the west side of the Mizane Valley which, although not as pristine as others in the High Atlas, has still retained much of its beauty, particularly in spring when the fruit trees are in blossom. The old mule track still runs along part of the east side and makes a good walk. Several villages along the valley now cater to travellers' needs and there are several notable eating and sleeping options along the road.

Imlil   إمليل

The paved road ends at the village of Imlil (elevation 1740m), which sits astride the Mizane Valley, a five-hour trek from the base of Jebel Toubkal. As well as being the most popular trailhead in Morocco and well-equipped with guides, stores and muleteers, Imlil has also become a popular destination for a day or a night out from Marrakesh, partly thanks to the success of the Kasbah du Toubkal. There isn't much to see in Imlil beyond the beauty and drama of the surrounding High Atlas, best appreciated in the company of a guide from the excellent **bureau des guides** (☎ /fax 024 485626).

SLEEPING & EATING

Imlil has come a long way from the days when it only served climbers heading to the peaks and it now sees a growing number of day- or night-trippers from Marrakesh. The majority of hotels and restaurants in the village are very basic, providing little more than a bed (often without linens), a tajine and a shower, warm if you are lucky. But several notable and more expensive places have opened outside the village, a trend that looks set to continue. Prices tend to increase by about 15% in the highest season, between April and October.

Budget

Dar Adrar (☎ 070 726809, http://toubkl.guide.free.fr /gite; s/d incl breakfast Dh60/110, half board per person Dh100) A lovely place at the top of Imlil, Dar Adrar is run by one of the star guides of the Atlas, Mohamed Aztat, and has great views, peaceful rooms with hot showers and an in-house hammam (Dh30 per person, book two hours ahead).

Café-Hotel Soleil (☎ /fax 024 485622; d with/without bathroom incl breakfast Dh200/150; half board per person Dh150/200) The rooms here are spartan but clean, some with beds, others with mattresses on the floor. Showers are hot. The café-restaurant (breakfast Dh25, lunch/dinner Dh60) on the terrace overlooking the river is among the village's most pleasant places for a meal.

Hôtel Etoile de Toubkal (☎ 024 485618; s/d/tr Dh100/140/200, d with bathroom Dh230) Overlooking the parking at the village entrance, the reasonable rooms each have a balcony and some have a bathroom. There is a decent restaurant on the ground floor and the management also owns Adrar Adventure next door: useful if you need to rent equipment, but we recommend organising treks through the *bureau de guides*.

Hôtel el-Aïne (☎ 024 485625; rooftop beds Dh25, r per person Dh40) This hotel has bright, comfortable rooms, hot showers and squat toilets are clustered around a tranquil courtyard with an old walnut tree. Below the hotel, Café de la Source serves reasonable food.

Hotel Café Aksoual (☎ 024 485612; s/d/tr/q Dh70/ 80/100/120) Aksoual, across from the CAF Refuge, has grown into one of the larger hotels in town, with clean comfortable rooms and hot showers. Breakfast is Dh20.

CAF Refuge (☎ 024 485612; dm CAF/HI members Dh30/45, nonmembers Dh60) CAF is a climbers' hostel now in general use, with dorm-style accommodation and cooking facilities. Show your Lonely Planet guidebook to get the HI rate.

Auberge Chez Ait Idar Mohammed (☎ 024 485616; www.geocities.com/imaitidar in French; d per person with/without bath incl breakfast Dh120/50, per person half board Dh160/80) Along the road to Ouaneskra, this is a simple and friendly place with kitchen facilities.

Atlas Gîte Imlil (Chez Jean Pierre; ☎ /fax 024 485609; d with half board Dh150; ☺ mid Feb-end Oct) Here you will find four simple, clean rooms with communal bathrooms, cosy sitting areas, and a recommended bar and restaurant, serving Moroccan food with a hint of Burgundy. Good for lunch (Dh80) on the covered terrace, if you book ahead.

Midrange & Top End

Kasbah du Toubkal (☎ 024 485611; 061 343337; www.kasbahdutoubkal.com; incl breakfast d Dh1400-2100, tr Dh1750-2450, ste Dh2700-4000) The spectacular former summerhouse of the local ruler, the kasbah sits 60m above Imlil and has stunning views of the mountains. UK travel company Discover Ltd has restored and developed it along environmentally sustainable lines and involved people from Imlil in the project. The eight luxurious double rooms and three suites have been decorated with the utmost care and the kasbah has a library, traditional hammam (two hours' notice required), open fires, board games and attentive staff. Dorm space is on mezzanine floors in three comfortable Moroccan-style salons (three-person room Dh1100, per person from Dh350). Meals here are excellent (Dh180 to Dh250). The kasbah is so popular that a 'minimum two night' policy is often in force. The same people run Dar Toubkal, an 'overflow' house below the kasbah (four-person room Dh900, double with bathroom Dh1000).

Toubkal Lodge (d incl breakfast Dh2000) The latest project from the Kasbah du Toubkal is this three-bedroom house in a Berber village in the adjacent Azzadene valley. Spectacular views, central heating and marble bathrooms make this the most luxurious trekking lodge in the country. A four- to six-hour trek from the Kasbah, it offers the possibility of trekking in style. Book through Kasbah du Toubkal.

Dar al-Abir (☎ 024 484757, 067 413056; www.al -abir.com in French; d half board Dh400) The house of a Franco-Berber couple, in a village a couple of miles along the Mizane Valley from Asni, its four rooms are simple, in keeping with the surroundings. The Moroccan cooking is notable, and a good alternative to the Kasbah du Toubkal as a lunch stop (Dh80 to Dh130). The owners also run a rural art space, Al Arkam, and arrange treks to it and other villages.

GETTING THERE & AWAY

The Toubkal area of the High Atlas is just over 60km south of Marrakesh, from where you'll glimpse the snowcapped peaks in winter and spring. Frequent local buses (Dh10, 1½ hours) and grands taxis (Dh15, one hour) leave south of Bab er-Rob in Marrakesh (south of the medina) to the village of Asni, 47km south of Marrakesh. (The road continues over the Tizi n'Test to Taroudannt and then on to Agadir.) Local minibuses and occasional taxis then travel the final 17km between Asni and Imlil (Dh15 to Dh20, one hour).

The dirt road to Imlil is poor, but the scenery is spectacular as the road climbs steadily up into the fertile Mizane Valley. If you're lucky the journey from Marrakesh to Imlil will take 2½ hours.

TO THE TIZI N'TEST

Heading south towards Taroudannt is one of the most spectacular (and spectacularly scary) drives in Morocco as the road weaves its way up through the High Atlas, over the Tizi n'Test at 2092m, then down onto the Souss plain.

The views are often breathtaking from numerous points along the way, but if you are driving be aware that, as well as the many s-bends, you may have to grapple with fast-changing weather. Heavy cloud and mist often cut visibility to near zero at the top of the pass and snow often blocks it in winter. Check conditions before leaving.

Along the way you might consider stopping at the pretty town of Ouirgane, 15km south of Asni, which has some of the best accommodation in this part of the mountains. If you are driving, the mosque at the village of **Tin Mal** is worth a detour. The village is on the right of the road, coming from Marrakesh, just past a couple of kasbahs (you can't miss the one on the left, perched on a rocky outcrop).

The Almohad-era mosque was built in 1156 in honour of Mohammed ibn Tumart, the dynasty's austere 'founding father' and spiritual inspiration. It is still used for Friday prayers, but is one of the few mosques open to non-Muslims and on other days the guardian will be happy to show you around (a tip is expected). The soft, rose-coloured pink building towering above the valley contains some beautifully decorated archways. Inside the immense doors, the prayer hall has a feeling of great tranquillity and openness.

A Foreign Legionnaires' stop that has been run by the same French family for more than sixty years. **Au Sanglier Qui Fume** (☎ /fax 044 485 707; www.ausanglierquifume.com; Route de Taroudannt, 61km; s incl breakfast/half board Dh325/415, d incl breakfast/half board Dh415/595, d ste half board Dh675-805; 🏊) is a charming old-fashioned hotel offering 25 rustic rooms with fireplaces and en-suite bathrooms. Three dining rooms serve Franco-Moroccan cooking. Tour groups eat here in season. It hires out mountain bikes

(Dh100 per day), and can arrange horse riding through the plush nearby resort La Roserie (Dh150/700 per hour/day).

Near the souq in the centre of the village and 150m off the main road, **Chez Momo** (☎ 044 485704; www.aubergemomo.com in French; Route de Taroudannt, 62km; d/ste half board Dh550/680; ☒) is a charming *maison d'hôte* (small hotel) with just six cosy rooms, a lovely garden and pool, and terrace seating. Suites have their own fireplaces. Reservations are recommended. Expect a 30% price increase in European summer and autumn breaks.

Grands taxis (Dh20 per person) run to Ouirgane frequently from Bab er-Rob in Marrakesh.

TO THE TIZI N'TICHKA

Higher than the Tizi n'Test to the west, the Tizi n'Tichka is an easier road that spectacularly connects Marrakesh with the pre-Sahara oases. During the winter months check with the **Gendarmerie of the Col du Tichka** (☎ 024890615) whether the pass is open. Being caught on the pass in snow can be dangerous: several tourists died in their car in 2005.

About 50km southeast of Marrakesh, the N9 to Ouarzazate crosses the Oued Zat at Aït Ourir (Le Coq Hardi, a hotel and restaurant of long standing, sits by the bridge). If you have a 4WD or don't mind a five-hour walk, there is a lovely *gîte d'étape*, totally remote and deep in the valley of the Oued Zat.

The spectacular **Tigmi Atlas** (☎ 061 245238; fax 024 376054; Douar Ansa, Tighrouine; half board per person Dh190) was built totally in local style by the villagers as part of a sustainable development project. It is surrounded by walnut trees and you can get lunch here for Dh75 if you book in advance. This small walking centre belongs to Authentic Discoveries (see p307) and has two dorms that each sleep six people. It's a great place for getting closer to the local people and for hikes in this stunning region.

Soon after Aït Ourir, the road climbs towards the village of Taddert. Around here you'll see oak trees, walnut groves and oleander bushes. Past Taddert, the road climbs even steeper and the landscape is stripped of its bright green mantle. Once over the pass, however, a remarkable, totally different scene is unveiled: the lunar landscape of the Anti Atlas and the desert beyond.

Halfway between the turn-off for Telouet and Aït Benhaddou is **I Rocha** (☎ 067 737002; www.irocha.com; Tisseldi, Ighrem N'Oudal; d half board per person Dh320; ☒), a wonderful guesthouse with panoramic views from its terrace over the lush river valley. Food is great (lunch Dh100), prepared by the French owner and Moroccan cooks. Cookery classes are available for Dh350 per person per day. The pool and rooms are simply beautiful and the atmosphere is like staying with friends. It's the kind of place where people come for a day and end up staying for a week. There are many superb walks in the neighbourhood which the hosts, one of whom was born and bred in the village and is a geologist, are happy to organise. Options include the Aït Oaziz Valley, the Flint Oasis and natural springs in the neighbourhood, all far from the tourist trail.

Telouet   تلوات

Telouet was an important stop on the main caravan route to Mali and the town is dominated by a superb crumbling **kasbah** (admission by donation, Dh5 to Dh10) that once served as a palatial residence and headquarters of the powerful Glaoui tribe. Until independence in 1956, Thami el Glaoui was the most powerful man in the south and one of the richest men in the country. This kasbah, one of his follies, is in ruin but the caretaker will let you visit the fantastically ornate central hall and reception rooms.

Those with a 4WD or mountain bike (or the lucky ones with a couple of days to spare on foot) could follow the 36km of rough *piste* south from Telouet, following the Ouadi Ounila through Anmiter and Tamdaght, to Aït Benhaddou. Most hotels in Telouet, including the Auberge and Hôtel Le Pin, can arrange guides and mules for the walk for around Dh250 to Dh300 per day. There is accommodation in Anmiter, 11km from Telouet, a beautifully preserved fortified village, or at the **gîte** (☎ 024 445499) of the brothers Bouchahoud at Tighza, 10km north of Anmiter in the Ounila Valley. They are excellent mountain guides, who organise interesting hikes in the region. Further on are other basic *gîtes*.

SLEEPING & EATING

Auberge Telouet (Chez Ahmed; ☎ /fax 024 890717; www.telouet.com; mattresses in salon Dh30, d with/with-

MARRAKESH & CENTRAL MOROCCO

out toilet Dh150/100) In a prime position at the turn-off to the kasbah, this place is very popular with tour groups. There is a pleasant Berber-tented eating area across the road (meals from Dh60). The new block has plusher rooms with communal hot showers and a terrace with fine views, and there are also three small houses for longer stays.

Auberge Lion D'Or (☎ 024 888507; mattress on roof Dh25, s/d incl breakfast Dh50/80) This is a small auberge with just three double rooms and communal hot showers. All rooms are very neat and tidy with simple pine beds and a perfect location, right on the doorstep of the kasbah (great views of it from the roof terrace).

Restaurant Telouet Palace (☎ 024 890714; mains Dh40) In the central square, this is a decent place for lunch, as is the Auberge de Telouet. All serve up the standard local omelette *berbère* – a thick tomato omelette cooked in a tajine dish with olives and spices (Dh30).

GETTING THERE & AWAY
From the N9 Marrakesh-Ouarzazate Road, the turn-off to Telouet is a few kilometres beyond the pass (watch out in winter, as the narrow road can be blocked by snow). There's a daily bus from Bab Gehmat in Marrakesh (Dh42), which returns to Marrakesh at 7am. A bus leaves Ouarzazate at noon, also returning at 7am (Dh30 to Dh35). The bus terminus is actually at Anmiter, 11km from Telouet, so you can get on or off the bus there as well.

AÏT BENHADDOU   آيت بنحدو
Aït Benhaddou, 32km from Ouarzazate, is one of the most exotic and best-preserved kasbahs in the entire Atlas region. This is hardly surprising, since it has had money poured into it as a result of being used for scenes in many films, notably *Lawrence of Arabia*, *Jesus of Nazareth* (for which much of the village was rebuilt) and, more recently, *Gladiator*. The kasbah's fame may endure on film but its population has dwindled in recent years. Thought to have been founded by the Almoravids (11th century) to control the caravan route from Telouet to Ouarzazate, it is now under Unesco protection.

From the Hôtel la Kasbah, head down past the souvenir stalls and you'll see the kasbah on the other side of the largely dried-up Oued Ounila. A couple of locals make a few dirham by showing you their houses, and

you'll probably have to pay around Dh5 to gain entry through one of these to the kasbah. In the upper reaches of the kasbah is a ruined fortified granary with magnificent views of the surrounding *palmeraie* and, beyond, the unforgiving *hammada* (stony desert).

A further 7km from Aït Benhaddou along the tarmac road stands the **Tamdaght kasbah** (admission Dh10), yet another Glaoui fortification, topped by storks' nests. Not as spectacular as Aït Benhaddou, it is comparatively little visited. However, on our last visit it was the setting for an Italian version of the reality-TV series *Big Brother*, so things are changing. Pay your entry fee to the caretaker. From Tamdaght you'll need a 4WD to continue north to Telouet.

Sleeping & Eating
Dar Mouna (☎ 024 843054; www.darmouna.com; s/d incl breakfast Dh350/600, s/d half board Dh450/750 ste incl breakfast/half board Dh650/850; ❂ ❊) This charming *pisé* guesthouse boasts a swimming pool, and spectacular views over the kasbah. It's the best place to stay, with comfortable rooms, tastefully decorated with local finds, and the atmosphere is really friendly. It offers meals from Dh100: dinner on the terrace overlooking the kasbah is a treat!

Complexe Touristique la Kasbah (☎ 024 890302; hotellakasbah@yahoo.fr; s/d incl breakfast Dh210/360, half board Dh270/440; ❂ ❊) This is a large comfortable hotel, which receives most of the tourists in Aït Benhaddou due to its extensive facilities (including a shop that sells film and stamps) and views over the kasbah. David Lean stayed here during the filming of *Lawrence of Arabia*. The Kasbah Restaurant across the road is now an annexe with some cheaper rooms (single/double Dh80/140). Nonguests can use the pool for Dh40.

Defat Kasbah (☎ 024 888020; fax 024 883787; camping per person Dh15, camper van Dh25, mattresses on roof Dh30, d with/without bathroom Dh140/100, ste Dh300; ❊) This beautiful budget place, 3km towards Tamdaght, is run by a charming French-Moroccan couple and has a range of nicely decorated, very clean rooms. There's a fine swimming pool, and a bar and restaurant. Nonguests can use the pool for Dh25.

Auberge Baraka (☎ 024 890305; fax 024 886273; mattresses on terrace Dh20, s/d Dh90/150) Baraka has very simple, clean and tidy ensuite rooms, a good Moroccan restaurant (set menu Dh70) and is slap-bang in the middle of town.

Auberge Café Restaurant Kasbah du Jardin
(☎ 024 888019; fax 024 884494; d/tr Dh70/90) This is
very basic but peaceful place at the far end
of town. The rooms are a steal at the price
but the inner building has the aesthetic
charm of a concrete barn. The manager can
arrange mules (Dh120 per day) if you want
to hike north to Telouet.

Kasbah Ellouze (☎ 024 890459, 067 965483; www
.kasbahellouze.com; Tamdaght, 7km n of Aït Benhaddou;
s/d incl breakfast Dh360/400; with bathroom Dh550/600)
A newly built kasbah in the traditional
style, Ellouze has terraces overlooking the
almond orchards (*louz* is Arabic for almonds) and the old kasbah. It serves lunch
(Dh100) and dinner (Dh120) and offers a
very peaceful atmosphere along with possibilities for walks through the groves or to
several rarely visited villages and kasbahs
in the region, like the *Kasbah des Juifs* (Kasbah of the Jews).

Getting There & Away
To get here from Ouarzazate, take the main
road towards Marrakesh as far as the signposted turn-off (22km); Aït Benhaddou is
another 9km down a bitumen road.

Grands taxis run from outside Ouarzazate bus station when full (Dh20 per person)
and from the turn-off (Dh50 for the taxi).
Chartering a grand taxi from Ouarzazate
will cost between Dh250 and Dh350 for half
a day. Minibuses run from Tamdaght to
Ouarzazate in the morning when full.

Cycling from Ouarzazate takes around
three hours.

OUARZAZATE   ورزازت
pop 57,000
Ouarzazate (war-zazat) at the confluence of
the Atlas, Drâa and Dadès valleys, has always
been strategically important, evidenced by
the huge Taourirt kasbah at its heart. Like so
many other places, the town really only came
into being in the 1920s when the French
made it an administrative centre and garrison town, which it remains today.

At first glance the sleepy modern town is
far from the exotic destination one has in
mind when conjuring the Sahara, but the
times they are changing! So far Ouarzazate
has been synonymous with package tourism, as charter flights fly directly into European cities into the nearby airport. However,
stimulated by King Mohammed VI, who is

very keen to develop tourism in the south
of Morocco, it is slowly developing from a
stopover en route to the south into a desert
destination in its own right.

Recent years have seen heavy investment
and promotion by the Ministry of Tourism,
and equally important was the economic
boost provided by the wealthy film studios
nearby. As a result, the town is going more
upmarket, and there are now a host of activity companies based in Ouarzazate, from
quad- and motor-biking to camel and walking treks, all of them taking advantage of the
fantastic desert countryside and the proximity of the Atlas, Drâa and Dadès valleys.

Ouarzazate is far south but it can be bitterly cold in winter, as the icy winds often
whip down off the snow-covered High Atlas
and may continue to do so well into spring.

Information
EMERGENCY
Police (☎ 190; Ave Mohammed V)

INTERNET ACCESS
Info Ouar (per hr Dh8) Around the corner from Hôtel Amlal.
Ouarzazate Web (Ave Mohammed V; per hr Dh8)
Centrally located and professionally run.

LAUNDRY
Lavanderie (Rue du Marché; ☽ 9am-noon & 2-8pm)
Near Hôtel Amlal, has modern washers (Dh30) and dryers
(Dh20).

MEDICAL SERVICES
Hôspital Bougafer (☎ 024 882444; Ave Mohammed
V) Public hospital east of the tourist office.
Kabinet Kabir (☎ 024 885276) More reliable private
clinic used by resident expatriates.
Night Pharmacy (☎ 024 882490; Ave Mohammed V)

MONEY
There are plenty of banks on the northern
end of Ave Mohammed V, all with ATMs.
Banque Populaire (Ave Moulay Rachid; ☽ 8.30-
11.30am & 2.30-4.30pm Mon-Fri, 3-6pm Sat, 9am-1pm Sun)
Crédit du Maroc (cnr Ave Mohammed V & Ave Bir
Anzaran) At the western end of town, does cash advances
on your credit card.

POST & TELEPHONE
There are numerous téléboutiques in the centre.
Main post office (Ave Mohammed V; Mon-Fri 8.30am-
noon & 2.30-6pm, Sat 8.30am-noon) Postal services and a
direct-dial international phone.

TOURIST INFORMATION

Délégation Régionale du Tourisme (ONMT; ☎ 024 882485; fax 024 885290; Ave Mohammed V; ✆ 8.30am-4.30pm daily) Unusually helpful tourist office.

TRAVEL AGENCIES

Many of the budget hotels, as well as the *faux guides* hanging out around town, offer excursions heading to the gorges and to the south. However, as there are many scams going on it pays to be wary of these offers, and it is recommended to go with a licensed guide as used by the following agencies.

Daya Travels (☎ /fax 024 887707; dayatravels@ hotmail.com; Ave Mohammed V) The best place to hire mountain bikes (half/full day Dh60/80). The owners speak Dutch and English, offer information and free maps on local route options and also organise 4WD trips.

Desert Dream (☎ 024 885343/068 961796; www .sahara-desert-dream.com; 4 Blvd Al-Mansour ed-Dahbi) Friendly owners can organise excursions to the desert or the gorges by 4WD or camel, or walking, using the best local guides and transport, all at fixed rates. Located opposite the Berbère Palace hotel.

Désert et Montagne (☎ 024 854949; www .desert-montagne.ma in French; Douar Talmasla, Tarmigt) Excellent walking or 4WD adventure trips in the High Atlas (particularly the Sarhro and Siroua mountains), desert trips of three to 15 days, and longer trips following the caravan routes (up to 60 days). The first of Morocco's four female mountain guides leads fascinating trips designed for women and families, to meet Berber women in the mountains and treks along nomads' transhumance routes. Operates from Dar Daïf (see p336).

Ksour Voyages (☎ 024 882840; www.ksour-voyages .com; Place du 3 Mars) Books flights and organises a wide variety of trips in the region from mountain hikes to desert camps. Also rents mountain bikes by the day.

Sights

The only real 'sight' in Ouarzazate itself is the **Taourirt Kasbah** (Dh10; ✆ 8am-6.30pm), the largest Glaoui kasbah in the area. During the 1930s it housed numerous members of the Glaoui dynasty, along with hundreds of their servants and workers. Unesco has carefully restored small sections of the building although still only one third of it is visitable. The Glaoui 'palace' consists of courtyards, living quarters, reception rooms and the like.

You don't really need a guide to explore the alleys but finding specific sights is difficult. Nonetheless, it is interesting enough just to wander down these narrow lanes.

It's also possible to walk all the way down to the Al-Mansour ed-Dahabi Dam, the waters of which now encircle a highly photogenic kasbah.

Another good place to visit is the **Atlas Film Corporation Studios** (☎ 024 882212/23; www .atlastudios.com; adult/concession Dh30/15; ✆ 8.30-11.50am & 2.30-5.50pm, guided tours every 30-40 min), a popular excursion with kids. It was the first of now several film studios in Ouarzazate, and you get shown around the sets and props of the famous movies filmed here (see boxed text, below). It is 5km west of town on the Marrakesh road, but easily accessible on the yellow STUDID bus (see p338).

HOLLYWOOD IN THE DESERT

King Mohammed VI loves the movies, and is keen to promote Morocco, particularly the south, as a location shoot. Ouarzazate is the country's film centre, and many productions, including *The Sheltering Sky*, *Gladiator*, *Mummy I & II*, *The Last Temptation of Christ*, *Asterix*, *Sahara* and *Kingdom of Heaven* have been shot in the area. Filming of the historical epic *Alexander the Great* in Morocco in 2003 attracted over US$60 million in foreign investment. There are now several film studios around Ouarzazate, although the only one open to the public is Atlas Studios (above) and then only if no film is being shot. On the tour you can see the Tibetan monastery built for Scorcese's *Kundun*, the plane used in *Jewel of the Nile* and the Egyptian sets used for *Asterix*. The North Africa Horse show (see p334) repeats stunts that they did, with horses and dromedaries, for the big productions.

There are sometimes parts as extras available during shooting – Hollywood hopefuls should check hotel noticeboards and American Language Centers.

The **International Film Festival** (www.festival-marrakech.com) takes place every year in Marrakesh, but there are several other festivals in Morocco. For more information check with the **Morocco Cinema Center** (☎ 037 289200; www.ccm.ma)..

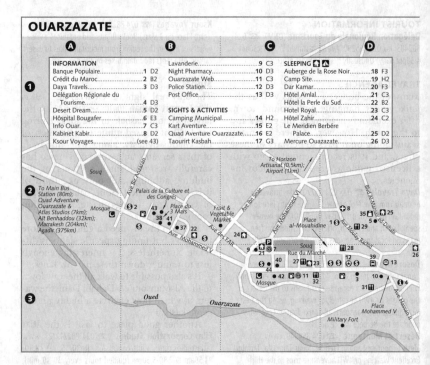

OUARZAZATE

INFORMATION	Lavanderie..................................9 C3	**SLEEPING**
Banque Populaire...................1 D2	Night Pharmacy.......................10 D3	Auberge de la Rose Noir.........18 F3
Crédit du Maroc......................2 B2	Ouarzazate Web.......................11 C3	Camp Site................................19 H2
Daya Travels...........................3 D3	Police Station..........................12 D3	Dar Kamar...............................20 F3
Délégation Régionale du	Post Office...............................13 D3	Hôtel Amlal.............................21 C3
Tourisme..............................4 D3		Hôtel la Perle du Sud.............22 B2
Desert Dream..........................5 D2	**SIGHTS & ACTIVITIES**	Hotel Royal..............................23 C3
Hôspital Bougafer...................6 E3	Camping Municipal..................14 H2	Hôtel Zahir..............................24 C2
Info Ouar................................7 C3	Kart Aventure..........................15 E2	Le Meridien Berbère
Kabinet Kabir..........................8 D2	Quad Aventure Ouarzazate....16 E2	Palace..................................25 D2
Ksour Voyages.................(see 43)	Taourirt Kasbah.......................17 G3	Mercure Ouarzazate...............26 D3

Activities

As an activity centre, Ouarzazate has many reliable companies running a variety of excursions. **Quad Aventure Ouarzazate** (☎ 024 884024; 17 Ave Moulay Rachid), offers quad biking around the local *pistes* and *palmeraies* for Dh1200 per person a day, while **Kart Aventure** (☎ 024 886374; www.kart-adventure.com; 18 Ave Moulay Rachid) offers similar excursions at similar prices to Skoura and Aït Benhaddou. Quad Aventure also hires out mountain bikes (Dh160 per day), which is a great way to do some of your own exploring.

For professionally guided off-*piste* motorbike tours throughout southern Morocco contact British-run **Wilderness Wheels** (☎ 024 888128; www.wildernesswheels.com; 44 Hay al-Qods, half/whole day Dh800/1400, 2 days Dh3500) just off Ave Mohammed V. Prices include well-maintained bikes and complete riding gear. The company can also arrange for tours to start in Marrakesh from its Marrakesh office (☎ 024 330443).

North Africa Horse (☎ 024 886689/061 168472; joelpro@hotmail.com; Route de Skoura, opp Golf Royal; show incl drink/meal Dh300/500), located 20km from Ouarzazate, arranges stunts with horses and dromedaries from Mali in the big Hollywood productions. It now has a horse show for tourists, which includes a Moroccan-style *fantasia*, as well as famous scenes the proprietors performed in Hollywood blockbusters such as *Kingdom of Heaven*, *Gladiator* and *Alexander the Great*. It also organises five- to six-day horse and camel trips.

Festivals & Events

Within Ouarzazate itself, the *moussem* of Sidi Daoud is held in August.

Marathon des Sables (www.saharamarathon.co.uk) A seven-day foot race in March/April, across the desert. Originates and finishes in Ouarzazate.

Sleeping

BUDGET

Ouarzazate's budget hotels do fill up, so it is worth booking ahead if you are going to arrive late.

Hôtel Zaghro (☎ 024 854135; hotelrestaurantzaghro@yahoo.fr; Rte de Zagora, 1.5km; d with/without TV & air-con Dh250/150; ❄ ☎) Across the Oued Ouarzazate is the very reasonable, com-

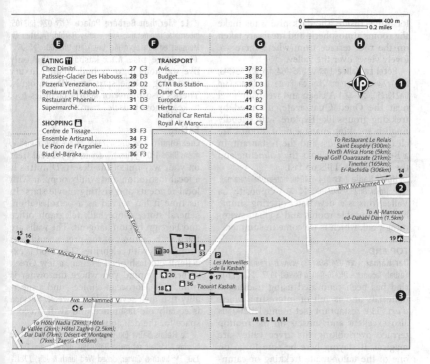

EATING 🍴
Chez Dimitri.............................**27** C3
Patissier-Glacier Des Habouss....**28** D3
Pizzeria Venezziano.................**29** D2
Restaurant la Kasbah................**30** F3
Restaurant Phoenix..................**31** D3
Supermarché...........................**32** C3

SHOPPING 🛍
Centre de Tissage....................**33** F3
Ensemble Artisanal..................**34** F3
Le Paon de l'Arganier..............**35** D2
Riad el-Baraka........................**36** F3

TRANSPORT
Avis..**37** B2
Budget....................................**38** B2
CTM Bus Station.......................**39** D3
Dune Car.................................**40** C3
Europcar.................................**41** B2
Hertz......................................**42** C3
National Car Rental..................**43** B2
Royal Air Maroc.......................**44** C3

fortable and quite charming Hôtel Saghro. It has ensuite rooms and a pool in its central patio, making it excellent value for money. Breakfast costs Dh30 and dinner Dh80. The only drawback is its distance from the centre.

Hôtel Amlal (☎ 024 884030; fax 024 884600; hotel_amlal@yahoo.fr; 24 Rue du Marché; s/d/tr/q Dh200/250/300/350; 🅿) A block north of Ave Mohammed V, Hôtel Amlal is modern, clean and good value, and the comfortable rooms have proper bathrooms. Breakfast is Dh20, and there's parking out the front.

Hôtel Zahir (☎ 024 885740; Ave al-Mouahidine; s/d/tr/ste Dh142/195/250/300) Northwest of the market, this is a friendly place and has spotless rooms with bathrooms. A suite for four to six people comes with TV and heating. The hotel has a restaurant and café.

Hôtel Royal (☎ 024 890042; 24 Ave Mohammed V; s/d/tr Dh46/82/103, with bathroom Dh80/122/163) This is the best of the cheaper hotels in town in the most central location. There is a range of rooms with or without bathroom, or with just a shower, but all are clean and well kept. The rooms on the street side

are quite noisy. Pleasant terrace with fresh juices, good coffee and pizza (Dh 45) and tajines (Dh40).

Camping Municipal (☎ 024 888322; camping per person Dh15 plus per car/site Dh8) This camp site is signposted next to the 'Tourist Complex' (basically a zoo and swimming pool) off the main road out of town towards Tinerhir, about 3km from the bus station. There is some shade, electricity costs Dh10, the bathrooms are OK and it's tranquil beside the Oued Ouarzazate. It has a basic restaurant.

MIDRANGE
Hôtel la Perle du Sud (☎ 024 888640; www.laperle dusud.com; 39/40 Ave Mohammed V; d with shower/bath Dh495/528, ste Dh742-1062; 🅇 🅡) Perle du Sud is a very natty modern hotel with great-value accommodation and an attractive, secluded oasis-style pool. Brick floors, *tataoui* (woven reeds or palm stems) ceilings and *zellij* bathrooms bring a touch of local colour.

Auberge de la Rose Noir (☎ /fax 024 886067; Quartier de la Mosquée, Hay Taourirt; s Dh300, d Dh500-800) One of only two options inside the glorious kasbah, the Rose Noir is embedded in the

MARRAKESH & CENTRAL MOROCCO

local life. Inside, the dark pisé walls make the rooms atmospheric and meals are taken on the roof terrace from where there are lovely views over the valley.

Hôtel La Vallée (☎ 024 854034; fax 024 854043; zaid172@caramail.com; 2km on Route de Zagora; s/d Dh210/250, 🔀 🔳 🔳) A clean and well-run hotel near the Oued Ouarzazate, it's used by trekking groups like Explore, with friendly English-speaking management. Rooms are clean and spacious, and the restaurant, in a Berber tent, overlooks the *palmeraie* and the mountains. Fills up fast.

Hôtel Nadia (☎ 024 854940; hotelnadia@caramail. com; s/d/tr Dh280/360/390; 🔀 🔳 🔳) Opposite La Vallée, this is a new hotel offering simple but comfortable rooms and a small swimming pool, which is welcome in summer.

TOP END

Dar Kamar (☎ 024 888733; www.darkamar.com; 45 Kasbah Taourirt; s Dh770-940, d Dh960-1177; 🔀) This riad has been renovated using traditional materials and is full of interesting *objets d'art*. The restaurant (set menu Dh200) is also excellent and sunsets on the rooftop terrace overlooking the river valley are magical. If staying here be sure to go on one of the tailor-made trekking or camping excursions using what they call their 'mobile rooms'.

Dar Daïf (☎ 044 854232; www.dardaif.ma in French; d incl breakfast Dh370-680, ste Dh1000-1400; 🔀 🔳 🔳) A sensitively restored kasbah right on the edge of the *palmeraie* near the ruined Kasbah des Cigognes, this pisé construction climbs over several levels, with a traditional internal courtyard and lots of homely touches. It's popular with families who can lose themselves in the jigsaw-like interior. Hammam is free, but dinner is compulsory at adults/children Dh180/100. To get here, head 1.5km along the road to Zagora and take a left turn at the sign. Follow signs for a further 3km off-*piste*. Reservations are recommended.

Mercure Ouarzazate (☎ 024 899100; www.mercure.com; Ave Moulay Rachid; s/d incl breakfast Dh765/980; 🔀 🔳 🔳) A totally modern four-star hotel, with 68 rooms overlooking the mountains and the town, this is the trendiest hotel in town, incorporating contemporary design with traditional Moroccan wood and stonework. The restaurant serves Moroccan and international cuisine and there's also a hammam, swimming pool and tennis court.

Le Meridien Berbère Palace (☎ 024 883105; mberpala@iam.net.ma; Ave Moulay Rachid, Quartier El-Mansour ed-Dahabi; d incl breakfast Dh2000; 🔀 🔳) This large pisé *faux*-kasbah is the only five-star hotel in town, built to offer luxury to visiting movie stars and film moguls. There's also plenty of sports facilities too, to keep those muscles trim.

Eating

Chez Dimitri (☎ 024 887346; 22 Ave Mohammed V; mains Dh80-130; 🕙 lunch & dinner; 🔀) A real treat on your way out of the desert, Dimitri's is a local institution and wildly popular with local residents and visiting movie stars. In its time it has served as a petrol station, general store, dance hall, telegraph office and Foreign Legion hangout. The walls are filled with pictures of the present and past proprietors with celebrities. The food is excellent: old-fashioned French, a few Greek dishes to remind you where the owner is from, plus Moroccan choices, and a speciality fish dish several days a week. Service is equally old-fashioned and swift. Keep a space for the delicious deserts.

Le Relais Saint Exupéry (☎ 024 887779; 13 Blvd Moulay Abdallah; set menu Dh80-190, dinner mains Dh90-130; 🕙 lunch & dinner, closed Wed lunch & July) Delicious French-run restaurant serving good French food and equally fine Moroccan specialities in an intimate dining room full of old aviation pictures devoted to the *Little Prince* and its creator, Antoine de St Exupéry. The *pastilla* with seafood, the trout with almonds, the saffron bread, sorbets and delicious chocolates with coffee may have you wondering if you're really in the desert.

Restaurant Phoenix (☎ 024 888313; mains Dh70) Something completely different, behind L'Hôtel de Ville, the tastefully decorated Phoenix serves up freshly made Italian pasta to the hordes of Italian technicians working at the film studios. There are plenty of good options for vegetarians.

Patisserie-Glacier des Habouss (Rue du Marché; 🕙 6am-10pm) This is the best bakery/tea room/ice-cream parlour in town, with good bread, baguettes, croissants and Moroccan pastries as well as juices, ice cream and coffee. Another institution.

Pizzeria Venezziano (☎ 024 887676; Ave Moulay Rachid; pizzas Dh30-45) A bright, good-value place, Venezziano serves decent pizzas, continental dishes like *foie provençale* (calf's liver with tomato and aubergine sauce, Dh30) and *jus panache* (Dh15), a mix of apple, almond, bananas, dates and raisins.

Restaurant la Kasbah (☎ 024 882033; Ave Mohammed V; mains Dh60-80, set menus Dh100) With a pleasant and strategic spot overlooking the Taourirt Kasbah, this restaurant is inevitably popular with exhausted sightseers.

The **Supermarché** on Ave Mohammed V carries an excellent range of alcohol, local and imported foods, and toiletries. Fresh cheese, meat and vegetables can be found at the daily central market on Rue du Marché.

Shopping

Opposite the entrance to the kasbah is the **Ensemble Artisanal** (☺ 9am-noon & 3-6.30pm), with stone carvings, pottery and woollen carpets woven by the region's Ouzguita Berbers. Nearby, opposite the kasbah, is the **Coopérative de Tissage** (Weaving Cooperative; ☎ 024 884057; Ave Mohammed V), where *hanbels* (locally woven carpets) are made and sold. It is also a good idea to have a wander in the streets of the kasbah as an out-of-the-way shop like **Riad el-Baraka** (☎ 024 887055), near Place du Marriage, has interesting finds at reasonable prices.

Le Paon de l'Arganier (☎ 024 884197; 5 Blvd Laayounne), opposite the Berbère Palace hotel, has a very different selection of goodies, mostly produced by women cooperatives around the country, including beauty products based on organic argan oil, and hand-dyed linen and tablecloths in cotton damask, or *sabra* (an artificial silk made from a local cactus) from Sidi Ifni.

On the north side of town, **Horizon Artisanat** (☎ 024 882415; 181 Ave de la Victoire; ☺ 9am-6pm Mon-Fri) is a great shop selling handmade pottery, metalwork and carpets produced by the local Horizon Association, which works to integrate disabled children and adults into the community.

Getting There & Away

AIR

Two kilometres north of town is **Taourirt airport** (☎ 024 882383). **RAM** (☎ 024 885102; 1 Ave Mohammed V) has a daily morning flight direct to Casablanca (from Dh900, one hour). On Friday and Monday there is a flight to Paris via Casablanca, and there are regular charter flights from Belgium, France and

Germany. There is no bus into town, but a taxi should cost Dh30 to Dh50.

BUS

The most convenient way to arrive is with **CTM** (☎ 024 882427; Blvd Mohammed V), as its station is bang in the centre of town near the post office. It has buses to Marrakesh (Dh65, five hours, three daily) and Casablanca (Dh135, 8½ hours, one daily).

At the main bus station, 1.5km northwest of the town centre, Trans-Ghazala has buses to Marrakesh (Dh55, four to five hours, six daily) and Satas has a bus to Er-Rachidia (Dh65, six hours) at 11am. There are frequent departures to Agadir (Dh95, four to five hours, six daily), Boumalne du Dadès (Dh25, five daily) and Taroudannt (Dh65, five hours, five daily); one of these goes via Tazenakht (Dh20), Foum Zguid (Dh35, four hours) and Tata (Dh45, five hours). Services also go to M'Hamid (Dh60, seven hours, four daily) via Zagora (Dh35, four hours).

CAR

Since the Drâa Valley route down to Zagora and beyond to M'Hamid is such a spectacular and interesting journey, it's worth considering hiring a car (from Dh250 per day) before you leave Ouarzazate. With your own vehicle, you'll be able to stop wherever you like to explore the many *ksaour* or take photographs.

In a bus or shared taxi you'll simply speed through all these places, catch only fleeting glimpses and probably arrive in Zagora feeling disappointed. Most of the car rental agencies are on Ave Mohammed V and Place du 3 Mars. Prices are pretty low, particularly in the local agencies, but check out the car before leaving. Ouarzazate agencies include:

Avis (☎ 024 888000; www.avis.com; cnr Ave Mohammed V & Place du 3 Mars)

Budget (www.budget.com; Ave Mohammed V ☎ 024 884202; airport ☎ 024 888152) A particularly reliable and friendly agency.

Dune Car (☎ 024 887391; fax 024 884901; Ave Mohammed V) Reliable and much cheaper than the international agencies. Also has 4WDs.

Europcar/InterRent (☎ 024 882035; www.europcar.com; Place du 3 Mars)

Hertz (☎ 024 882084; www.hertz.com; 33 Ave Mohammed V)

National Car Rental (☎ 024 885244; Place du 3 Mars)

TAXI

Taxis leave from outside the main bus station to Agdz (Dh25), Aït Benhaddou (Dh20), Boumalne du Dadès (Dh35), Marrakesh (Dh80 to Dh100), Skoura (Dh12), Tinerhir (Dh50) and Zagora (Dh60).

Getting Around

Shared petits taxis run up and down Ave Mohammed V for the flat rate of Dh5 per person (based on three people sharing). Grands taxis do the same but can take more people, and charge more: always discuss the price before getting in.

The yellow STUDID bus (Dh3) runs a half-hourly service up and down Ave Mohammed V.

DRÂA VALLEY وادة درعة

From Ouarzazate the N9 continues southeast along the magical Drâa Valley, a ribbon of technicoloured *palmeraies,* orchards, kasbahs and stunning Berber villages. The longest river in Morocco, the Drâa originates in the High Atlas before reaching the Atlantic at Cap Drâa, just north of Tan Tan. In reality, the waters generally seep away into the desert. The richest section of the valley lies between Agdz and Zagora, a stretch of about 95km. Beyond that, a minor road takes you a further 96km south to the village of M'Hamid, just 40km short of the Algerian border.

The drive to Zagora takes three to four hours. If you have a 4WD you can take the even more scenic route on the *piste* that runs parallel to the road and the river, from Tamnougalt to Zagora.

AGDZ اكدز

About 20km southeast of the 1660m Tizi n'Tinififft, Agdz (ag-a-dez), dominated by the weird-looking Jebel Kissane, is little more than a one-road town with a beautiful *palmeraie,* a Thursday souq and kasbah. Several shops along the main thoroughfare sell the typical saffron-coloured carpets from Tazenakht, a carpet-weaving centre on the road to Taliouine.

At the Ouarzazate end of town, the pleasant **Kissane Hôtel** (☎ 024 843044; kissane@iam.net .ma; s/d/tr Dh190/300/390;), offers comfortable rooms, some with balconies overlooking

the mountain. The hotel has a good Moroccan restaurant (meals Dh90) and a pool.

There are two cheapies on the main square, Place de la Marche Verte. Choose between the run-down **Hôtel Restaurant Drâa** (☎ 024 843153; s/d Dh35/70) with big, simple rooms with hot showers, and the slightly better **Hôtel des Palmiers** (☎ 024 843127; s/d Dh70/95), with brighter but mostly windowless rooms (Dh110 if you want a window facing the street). Past the town's kasbah is the attractive **Kasbah Caïd Ali** (☎ 024 843640; www .casbah-caidali.net; Rue Hassan II; d Dh160;), part of which is still inhabited by the original family. The simple rooms are really comfortable and offer excellent value. Meals are served (breakfast Dh20; set menu Dh65 to Dh85). This is a good base for walks in the nearby mountains and countryside. In the garden, in the shade of the palm trees, is also a camp site (Dh50 per tent).

CTM and several other buses stop here en route between Ouarzazate and Zagora, though you are not guaranteed a seat. Otherwise, occasional grands taxis go to Ouarzazate (Dh23) and Zagora (Dh25).

AGDZ TO ZAGORA

With your own transport it is possible to break this trip with a visit to the beautiful and really dramatic *ksour* (fortified strongholds or castles) at **Tamnougalt** (admission Dh 10; guide compulsory Dh50-100). To reach Tamnougalt turn left off the main road, 5km past Agdz, and then 3km down a bumpy *piste*. **Chez Yacob** (☎ 024 843394/066 104305; www.chezyacob.com; Route de Zagora, Agdz; half board per person Dh250) next door to the main *ksar*, 4km from Agdz, is a wonderful, tranquil auberge with five simple but very cosy rooms, with clean, shared bathrooms, and a large terrace overlooking the kasbah and the *palmeraie*. Set menu meals are Dh80. This is another good base for hikes in the surrounding countryside. Nearby in the *palmeraie* is the friendly **Kasbah Itrane** (☎ /fax024 843614; merrsana@g.mail.com; Route de Zagora, Agdz; per person half board with/without bathroom Dh220/200;) with less character, but clean rooms in a beautiful garden with swimming pool, and a set menu for Dh80.

There are other kasbahs along the main road at Timiderte, Kasbah Said Arabi at Ouled Atman, and Tinzouline, which has a great souq on Monday. About 10km before Tinzouline you'll see a string of local children frantically trying to sell boxes of dates to passing motorists. The *boufeggou* variety of dates that grow in this area are particularly sweet. About 30km before Zagora, at Tansikht, is an old watchtower and fine lookout over the *palmeraie*, signposted 'Oasis Du Drâa'.

With a 4WD there are several excursions you could make along the far (north) side of the Drâa. These are signposted (*'circuits touristiques'*) from the road. From Tamnougalt you can continue on a dirt road, parallel to the Drâa, that leads through villages, fields and fantastic vistas of the river, to Zagora.

ZAGORA   زاكورة
pop 34,851

The modern town of Zagora is largely a recent creation, a French colonial administrative post, although the oasis has always been inhabited. It was from here that the Saadians launched their expedition to conquer Timbuktu in 1591. The now famous, somewhat battered sign still reads 'Tombouctou 52 jours' (by camel caravan), although it took the Saadian army 135 days to get there.

The modern town, dominated by Jebel Zagora, has little obvious character, but it has all the travel agencies and some of the older hotels, and it is a good base to organise treks in the region. It feels very much like a border town, fighting back the encroaching desert with its lush *palmeraie*, and it does have its moments, particularly when a dust storm blows up out of the desert and the light becomes totally surreal.

More atmospheric, however, and with a good range of accommodation, is Amezrou, across the Oued Drâa, about 3km south of the centre, but now part of Zagora.

Zagora has a large market on Wednesday and Sunday, with fruit (dates are the big commodity around here), vegetables, herbs, hardware, handicrafts, sheep, goats and donkeys.

The *moussem* of Moulay Abdelkader Jilali takes place at the same time as Moulid (see p455), and it brings the town to life.

Information

Banks including **Banque Populaire** and **BMCE** are on Blvd Mohammed V. All have ATMs, and are open during normal banking hours.

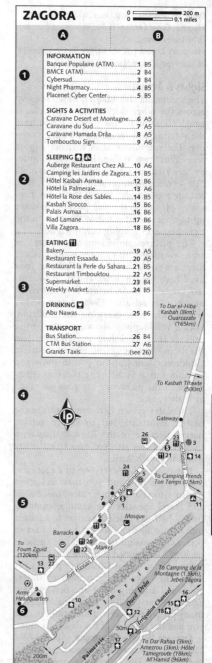

ZAGORA

0 —— 200 m
0 —— 0.1 miles

INFORMATION
Banque Populaire (ATM)..........1 B5
BMCE (ATM)...........................2 B4
Cybersud...............................3 B4
Night Pharmacy.....................4 B5
Placenet Cyber Center............5 B5

SIGHTS & ACTIVITIES
Caravane Desert et Montagne.....6 A5
Caravane du Sud....................7 A5
Caravane Hamada Drâa............8 A5
Tombouctou Sign....................9 A6

SLEEPING
Auberge Restaurant Chez Ali....10 A6
Camping les Jardins de Zagora...11 B5
Hôtel Kasbah Asmaa................12 B6
Hôtel la Palmeraie..................13 B6
Hôtel la Rose des Sables..........14 B5
Kasbah Sirocco......................15 B6
Palais Asmaa.........................16 B6
Riad Lamane.........................17 B6
Villa Zagora..........................18 B6

EATING
Bakery.................................19 A5
Restaurant Essaada.................20 A5
Restaurant la Perle du Sahara....21 B5
Restaurant Timbouktou............22 A5
Supermarket..........................23 B4
Weekly Market.......................24 B5

DRINKING
Abu Nawas............................25 B6

TRANSPORT
Bus Station............................26 B4
CTM Bus Station.....................27 A6
Grands Taxis.....................(see 26)

To Dar el-Hiba
Kasbah (8km);
Ouarzazate
(165km)

To Kasbah Titawte
(500km)

Gateway

To Camping Prends
Ton Temps (0.5km)

Mosque

Barracks

To
Foum Zguid
(120km)

Market

Army
Headquarters

To Camping de la
Montagne (1.5km);
Jebel Zagora

To Dar Rahaa (3km);
Amezrou (3km); Hôtel
Tamegroute (18km);
M'Hamid (96km)

Ave Hassan

Blvd Mohammed V

Oued Drâa

Irrigation Channel

Palmeraie

Cybersud (Ave Hassan II; per hour Dh10) Internet access.

Placenet Cyber Center (95 Blvd Mohammed V; per hr Dh10) Internet access.

Pharmacy Zagora (☎ 024 847195; Blvd Mohammed V; h8.30am-1pm &3-8pm Mon-Fri, 8.30am-1pm Sat)

Sights & Activities

The spectacular **Jebel Zagora**, which rises up across the other side of the river Drâa, is worth climbing for the views – if you have the stamina and set off early in the morning. The round-trip walk to Jebel Zagora takes about two to three hours (45 minutes by car). Halfway up are the faint ruins of an 11th-century Almoravid fortress to explore, but the modern-day fort at the summit remains off-limits. It's also possible to drive up to a viewpoint – follow the *piste* to the right beyond Camping la Montagne.

The picturesque village of **Amezrou** has an interesting 17th-century *mellah*, where there are still a few silver workshops. Jews lived here for centuries and used to control the silver trade, before they moved en masse to Israel after 1948. A few Berber silversmiths now carry on the tradition. Locals will happily show you the entire process (one workshop is signposted) in the hope that you will buy something. Children might leap on you to show you around, but it is all quite pleasant. Elsewhere in the *palmeraie* life goes on much as it always has.

The dates grown here are reputedly the best in Morocco, but times are getting harder because of the Bayoud disease, a fungus that has attacked and killed many palms in North Africa.

It may seem like everyone in Zagora has a camel for hire and you may feel some pressure to take a camel ride. Most hotels and travel agencies can arrange anything from a half-day ride on a camel to a longer trek of two to three weeks. For an idea of prices and possibilities, check out agencies on Blvd Mohammed V before you commit. Prices start at about Dh300 per person per day – check whether you need to supply your own drinking water and bedding, exactly how far you'll be travelling and how many people will sleep at the camp, in case you had the solitude of the desert in mind.

Caravane Dèsert et Montagne (☎ 024 846898, 066 122312; www.caravanedesertetmontagne.com; 112 Blvd Mohammed V) is a reliable agency that can tailor programmes according to special interests. Other reliable agencies are **Caravane Hamada Drâa** (☎ /fax 024 846031; www.hamadadraa.com in French; Blvd Mohammed V), which has English-speaking guides, and **Caravane du Sud** (☎ 024 847569; www.caravanedusud.2zagora.com; Blvd Mohammed V).

Sleeping

BUDGET

Auberge Restaurant Chez Ali (☎ /fax 024 846258; chez_ali@hotmail.com; s/d Dh70/120, with shower Dh100/200) This is a real oasis in the middle of this dusty desert – four impeccably clean rooms and four cosy Berber tents in a luxuriant garden. Home-cooked food (set menu Dh80) can be eaten while gazing at the greenery of the garden. The auberge can arrange reliable camel treks for Dh350 per person per day. Book ahead. To get there turn south off Blvd Mohammed V, just before the western gate, and take the second street to the left.

Hôtel la Palmeraie (☎ 024 847008; fax 024 847878; Blvd Mohammed V; s/d Dh90/130, with bathroom Dh90/180, with bathroom & air-con Dh120/210; 🖳 🖳) A large one-star place, this is popular with budget tour groups for its good-value rooms. The main attractions are the pool, restaurant and bar. It's possible to sleep in the Berber tent by the pool for Dh40.

Hôtel la Rose des Sables (☎ 024 847274; Ave Allal Ben Abdallah; s/d Dh50/60, with bathroom Dh60/90) This is the best budget option, with clean and comfortable rooms and friendly management. It also has a popular restaurant (set menu Dh60).

Camping

Zagora has several camp sites but the following, all with some form of shade, are recommended.

Camping les Jardins de Zagora (☎ 024 846971/ 068 961701; Amezrou; camping for 2 incl tent & car Dh50; d Dh150) Next door to the hotel Ksar Tinzouline, this is a clean camp site, full of flowers and in the shade of palm trees, overlooking Jebel Zagora. Communal bathrooms are very clean. Also available are two simple rooms with private bathroom, and beds in small Berber tents with electricity (Dh 40 per person). The hostess cooks delicious tajines to order (set menu Dh80).

Camping de la Montagne (☎ 024 847578; Amezrou; camping per person Dh10 plus Dh5 per tent) Camp at the foot of Jebel Zagora. Follow the sign to the left after La Fibule. Cold drinks are available but hot showers are free but there's no electricity. The manager arranges camel trips (Dh300 per day) and keeps his camels at the camp site for you to inspect.

Camping Prends Ton Temps (☎ 024 846543/067 596877; http://campingauberge.skyblog.com in French; Hay El-Mansour ed-Dahabi; camping per person Dh10 plus per tent Dh5, hut per person Dh30, hut with shower & toilet s/d Dh80/100, fixed tent s/d Dh40/60) This is a very clean and shady camp site with a variety of accommodation. You can pitch your own tent or sleep in one of theirs. Breakfast (Dh15) and good simple meals available (Dh60).

MIDRANGE

Kasbah Tifawte (☎ 024 848843/067 596241; www .tifawte.com; mattresses on terrace Dh50, half board Dh350, with air-con Dh500; ☒) Hidden in a quiet back street, this hotel overlooks the *palmeraie* and the mountain. The kasbah-style building has five traditional rooms, all unique and stylishly decorated but with the advantage of modern bathrooms, and some with air-con. The kohl-eyed owner was one of the first official guides in the south and is incredibly knowledgeable about the region and its history. He arranges trips in the area by camel or 4WD, as well as an overnight in a fixed desert camp with dinner and music (Dh350 per person).

Dar Raha (☎ /fax 024 846993; darraha_zagora@ yahoo.fr; Amezrou; d incl breakfast Dh350-500) 'Raha' means rest and that is what you find here. Five rooms in a beautiful old pisé kasbah in the heart of Amezrou village. Meals are available for Dh100 to Dh150. The friendly French and Moroccan owners offer insights into village life and encourage their guests to discover local history and culture. They can arrange visits to craftsmen in their workshops and trekking with well-informed guides.

Kasbah Sirocco (☎ 024 846125; sayrriko@menara.ma; Amezrou; s/d incl breakfast Dh316/412; ☒ ☒) Sirocco has simple but very cosy rooms decorated with colourful local textiles. Great views from the balcony over the *palmeraie*, and excellent French-Moroccan cooking. The hotel offers a whole range of excursions (quads, camel treks, camping and trekking).

Hôtel Kasbah Asmaa (☎ 024 847599; ksbasmaa@ iam.net.ma; tents per person Dh50, s/d incl breakfast Dh300/500, half board Dh450/700; ☒ ☒) A pleasant two-star hotel designed to resemble a Berber *ksar*, this place has a lovely garden and pool, as well as an outdoor tea salon and a good restaurant. The old-block rooms around an interior courtyard vary greatly. Cheaper beds are available in the tents set up in the garden.

Kasbah Dar El-Hiba (☎ /fax 024 847805; Ksar Tissergate 8km before Zagora; half board per person with/without air-con Dh250/200; ☒ ☒) Renovated old kasbahs with simple rooms on several floors, overlooking the nearby *ksar* and *palmeraie*. The garden has two air-conditioned rooms with bathroom, and meals are served (Dh70).

TOP END

Villa Zagora (☎ 024 846093; www.mavillaausahara .com; Amezrou; d incl breakfast Dh500; ☒ ☒) Only just in the top-end price bracket, this is undoubtedly the most charming place to stay in Zagora. The comfortable guesthouse has just five stylish and delightful rooms with beautiful paintings and mosquito nets, and very friendly staff. In winter dinner is served by a roaring fireplace, in summer you sit on the terrace with great views over the mountain and the palms (meals around Dh120).

Riad Lamane (☎ 024 848388; www.riadlamane.com; Amezrou; s/d half board Dh700/1200, May-Oct Dh500-800; ☒ ☒) In the middle of the *palmeraie*, this comfortable hotel has spacious and beautifully decorated rooms, although nowhere near as polished as riads in Marrakesh, set in a large tranquil garden. Take the track by La Fibule along the irrigation canal and you will find it on your right after about 200m (it is not well signed so it may be best to phone).

Palais Asmaa (☎ 024 847491; www.palais-asmaa .com in French; Amezrou; s/d incl breakfast Dh510/710, s/d half board Dh600/900; ☒ ☒) This vast mock kasbah is the most upmarket hotel in town, a favourite with package tours. The 90 rooms are relatively small but very clean, with good views, and all offer a good standard of comfort. There's a great pool in the garden and several restaurants.

Eating

All hotels have their own restaurants serving Moroccan dishes. Offering much the same are a few popular restaurants, including Restaurant Essaada, Restaurant la Perle du Sahara and Restaurant Timbouktou, all along Blvd Mohammed V.

Hôtels Palais Asmaa, Riad Lamane and la Palmeraie all have good licensed restaurants. For more pleasant or cosy surroundings, head to the outdoor restaurants at the hotels Kasbah Sirocco, Kasbah Tifawte or Dar Raha (but call ahead). A three-course meal with wine or beer will cost upwards of Dh100. For a drink head for the pleasant Abou Nawas in the garden of the run-down colonial style hotel La Fibule du Draa, or to the bar of the Palais Asmaa.

There's fresh produce at the main entry to the market, a supermarket at the northern end of town with limited supplies (no alcohol) and a bakery.

Getting There & Away

AIR

At the time of writing, King Mohammed VI had announced, as part of his plan to develop the south of Morocco, that he will open the new Zagora airport to domestic and international flights at the end of 2006 or early 2007.

BUS

The **CTM bus station** (☎ 024 847327) is at the southwestern end of Blvd Mohammed V, and the main bus and grand taxi lot is at the northern end. There's a daily CTM bus to Ouarzazate (Dh40, four hours) at 7pm, which continues on to Marrakesh (Dh90) and Casablanca (Dh160).

Other companies have at least one run a day (either morning or around 9pm) to Boumalne du Dadès (Dh70), Casablanca (Dh170), Erfoud (Dh80), Er-Rachidia (Dh110), Marrakesh (Dh80, two daily), Ouarzazate (Dh40) and Rabat (Dh160). There are buses to Rissani (Dh75) via N'Kob (Dh 20) and Tazzarine (Dh30) three times a week. A bus passes through headed to M'Hamid (Dh20, two hours) at 7.30am. More frequent minibuses run to M'Hamid (Dh25) throughout the day when full.

TAXI

Grands taxis are more regular early in the morning. Destinations include Agdz (Dh28, 1½ hours), Ouarzazate (Dh58, three hours), M' Hamid (Dh25, 1½ hours), Tazzarine (Dh42, 2½ hours) and N'Kob (Dh34, 1½ hours).

SOUTH OF ZAGORA

Tamegroute تامكروت

About 18km south from Zagora, is Tamegroute. From the 11th century the town was an important religious and educational centre whose influence was felt throughout the Drâa region and into the desert beyond. In the 17th century Abou Abdallah ben Mohammed Naceur founded a branch of the Naciri brotherhood here. The Naciri believe that Islam can only be understood through serious Quranic scholarship, hence the importance of libraries.

Tamegroute consists of a series of interconnected *ksour,* at the centre of which is the green-roofed **Zawiya Naciriya**. This *zawiya* (religious fraternity) consists of a mosque, a *medersa* for Quranic scholars, the tomb of its founder and a famous library.

The library (signposted on the main road as 'Librairie Coranique') houses a magnificent collection of illustrated religious texts, dictionaries and astrological works, some of them on gazelle hides. The oldest date back to the 13th century. Most are shelved behind glass doors, but others are displayed in glass cases.

Visitors are allowed into the outer sanctuary and the library in the morning and late afternoon (it's generally closed from noon to 3pm). You'll be expected to leave a donation for the upkeep of the place. The *zawiya* (off-limits to non-Muslims) remains a pilgrimage site for people needing charity and hoping to be cured of their ills.

There are several small pottery factories on the left just past the *zawiya* as you head towards M'Hamid, worth a look for their distinctive green glazed products. Tamegroute has a Saturday souq.

The **Auberge-Restaurant-Camping Jnane Dar Diafa** (☎ 024 840622/061 348149; www.jnanedar.ch in German; s/d Dh125/170; s/d/tr/ste with bathroom from Dh200/250/320/600) is a friendly place to stop for the night (breakfast Dh20 to Dh35) or for lunch (set menu Dh100). It's a traditional building with a range of comfortable rooms and a great tranquil garden. The food is really good too, prepared with vegetables from the garden.

Tinfou Dunes كتبا

About 5km south of Tamegroute you can get your first glimpse of Saharan sand dunes. If you've never seen a sandy desert and do not intend to go further past M'Hamid or Merzouga, Tinfou is a pleasant spot to take a breather and enjoy a tiny taste of the desert. The dunes, which are small, do get a bit trampled on busy days, though.

Le Repos du Sable (☎ /fax 024 848566; s/d Dh100/140; 🏊) If you are not too worried about comfort or cleanliness, then this is a great place to stay. A couple of Moroccan painters built this kasbah-style hotel in pisé, around a beautiful courtyard-gallery. Their first son now runs the place, while the second one organises camel treks. Spartan rooms but great atmosphere.

Kasbah Sahara Sky (☎ 024 848562; www.hotelsah ara.com; s/d/tr Dh325/390/550) This comfortable three-star hotel has well-appointed rooms and a good observatory (www.saharasky .com) on the roof where stargazing is the order of the night. There's also a fully licensed restaurant, plus a snooker table and a hammam. Excursions to the Erg Chigaga can easily be arranged from here (Dh350 per person per day).

Tinfou to M'Hamid

Most people who come to Zagora try to make it to the end of the road at M'Hamid, about 96km to the south via the village of Tagounite and the dramatic Tizi Beni Selmane. Tagounite has petrol, several cafés and the *ksar* of Oulad Driss makes a picturesque stop before the final 5km run into M'Hamid. There's a little private-house museum here (donations welcome) with a small collection of tools and objects illustrating the traditional way of life.

M'Hamid   المحاميد
pop 3000

The oasis of M'Hamid is the end of the road, the goal of the long trip south. It used to be an important marketplace for the trans-Saharan trade, and the town's many different ethnicities, Blue Men, Harratine, Berber, Chorfa and Beni M'Hamed, bear witness to that. M'Hamid Jdid, the modern town, is the typical one-street administrative centre with a mosque, a few restaurants, small hotels, craft shops and a Monday market. The old town M'Hamid Bali, 3km away across the Oued Drâa, has an impressive and very well preserved kasbah.

Until a few years ago tension between Morocco and Algeria kept tourists away

from M'Hamid, but now this sleepy town is safe and perfectly set up as a base for excursions into the desert. In fact, the dunes near M'Hamid, like Erg Chigaga, are arguably as spectacular as Merzouga's (see p362), but with fewer hustlers and *faux guides*, and so far also without the crowds.

Desert treks can be organised from Zagora, Ouarzazate or even Marrakesh, but you can book in M'Hamid and deal directly with the local people. Most overnight camel treks (from Dh350 per person) end up in Erg Lehoudi (Dunes of the Jews), a section of 100m-high dunes 10km north of town. If you have a sturdy vehicle, preferably a 4WD, you can drive out there along a *piste* leading here from the main road 18km before M'Hamid, but it is advisable to take a guide. There are now several bivouacs around the dunes, used by the travel agencies.

Erg Chigaga, a spectacular 40km stretch of 300m Saharan dunes, 56km from M'Hamid, is a more ambitious trip. These are the sand dunes of Hollywood movies, and definitely worth the extra time and expense. A return camel trip takes five days or a week (from Dh380 per day) and is highly recommended.

Otherwise you'll need to shell out for a 4WD, which costs around Dh1200, plus another Dh220 for the camp.

Other possible destinations include the Iriki oasis, which isn't far from Erg Chigaga, or some of the smaller dunes at Mesouria, 8km from M'Hamid. Adventurers might also consider the epic 12-day camel trip to Foum Zguid.

Sahara Services (☎ 061 776766; www.saharaserv ices.info) on the main street of M'Hamid is a reliable and professional agency who organises camel and 4WD trips, from one night to a week or more in the dunes. The camp in Erg Chigaga has comfortable Berber tents and even hot showers (with water heated by a wood burner). Prices start at Dh380 per person for a sunset tour on camels.

SLEEPING & EATING

Most accommodation in M'Hamid is very basic as the majority of people who come here want to spend their nights under the stars in the desert – by far the most attractive option! But things are changing and the first more upmarket hotel opened early in 2006.

MARRAKESH & CENTRAL MOROCCO

Dar Azawad (☎ 024 848730, 061 247018; www.dar azawad.com; Douar Ouled Driss s/d incl breakfast Dh550/800; 🅿 🅿) Just at the entrance of M'Hamid, this comfortable new hotel has 13 air-con rooms, each stylishly decorated with Marrakshi *tadelakt*. In the garden are several tents (half board Dh 350 per person) with shared bathrooms. A hammam and spa were under construction at time of research. There's a restaurant (set menu Dh100) and a good shop with more upmarket crafts.

Hôtel-Restaurant les Dunes d'Or (☎ 024 848009; s/d incl breakfast Dh40/70; central square) This small hotel, right next door to (and owned by) Sahara Services, has three simple but clean rooms, and a good restaurant (meals Dh65) with a terrace where you can watch the world, or camels and 4WDs, go by.

Jnane le Pacha (☎ 024 848696; www.jnane -lepacha.com; Bounou, M'Hamid El-Ghizlane; d tent incl breakfast Dh340, ste Dh1040; 🅿) Luxury, colourful tent camp set in a garden, and four suites in the pisé kasbah. There is a western-style and a Moroccan tent restaurant (set menu Dh80).

Camping Hammada du Drâa (☎ 024 848080; camping per person Dh15 plus per car Dh20, Berber tents per person Dh50) This is a respectable camp site with clean communal facilities.

GETTING THERE & AWAY

There's a daily CTM bus at 4.30pm to Zagora (Dh20, two hours), Ouarzazate (Dh60, seven hours), Marrakesh (Dh120, 11 to 13 hours) and Casablanca (Dh194 15 hours). Private buses to Marrakesh (via Zagora and Ouarzazate) leave at around 7am and 2pm (Dh110, 15 hours).

ZAGORA TO RISSANI

The roads that encircle the stark mass of the Jebel Sarhro make it possible to complete a loop from Ouarzazate, heading to Zagora, then Rissani and returning via the Todra and Dadès gorges (or the other way, of course). There are two routes from Zagora to Rissani. The shorter leads from south of Zagora (on the Tamegroute road) up towards Tazzarine. The easier but slightly longer route heads 98km back up the Drâa Valley before turning off (by Restaurant la Gazelle) towards Tazzarine. This route has the advantage of taking in the kasbah-filled village of N'Kob.

Grands taxis run between Tazzarine and Ouarzazate (Dh60); between Tazzarine and

Alnif (Dh20); and Alnif and Rissani (Dh25). So if you are not driving you can cobble together transport. There is also a bus between Rissani and Zagora via Alnif, Tazzarine and N'Kob on Tuesday, Friday and Sunday. Local minibuses run daily between Alnif and Rissani (Dh25) and between Tazzarine and Zagora, normally leaving early in the morning, and only when they are full (so if you are in a hurry, you may want to pay for several seats).

If you are driving, there are Ziz petrol stations along the way, but they sometimes run out of fuel. A full tank should easily see you through from Zagora to Rissani.

N'Kob, Tazzarine & Alnif   نيكوب تزارين و النيف

The road south of Jebel Sarhro used to see little traffic until recently, which might explain why N'Kob still feels like a sleepy, traditional village, in spite of being home to more kasbahs than any other village in Morocco and having a colourful Sunday market. There are a staggering 45 kasbahs here, two of which have been transformed into fun places to stay or just to visit. The village is now well set up as a base for trekking trips north into the Jebel Sarhro region (see p434), with a **Bureau des Guides** (☎ 067 487 509) on the main street. Some of the hotels listed here can also arrange treks into the mountains. If you have a 4WD you can follow the main *piste* north, through the heart of the Sarhro to Ikniouln and Boumalne du Dadès.

Beyond N'Kob, Tazzarine (150km from Rissani) is a scruffy crossroads town where the roads from Zagora and Agdz meet. There are internet cafés and a petrol station. Just before town is a dramatic defile and small *palmeraie*. From here it is possible to visit rock engravings (25km away) and fossil sites (18km away).

Beyond Tazzarine, the oasis town of Alnif is located in the heart of the Maidir basin, one of Morocco's richest seams of fossils, particularly of trilobites, the ancestors of crabs. There are plenty of fossils for sale along the roadsides here, but beware of fakes: many of these are sculptured out of stone or glued together. The genuine article, for sale at fixed prices, is available at **Ihmadi Trilobites Center** (☎ 055 884116, 066 221593; trilobites@caramail.com; Alnif). The owner is a geologist of considerable experience and knowledge, who also acts as a guide (Dh150 for the afternoon) for trips to local fossil sites.

The main road continues 100km or so across the hammada to Rissani. A rough *piste* branches north for 47km to the main Ouarzazate to Er-Rachidia road near Tinerhir. You can get information on the route (and also a photocopied map) from the Ihmadi Trilobites Center.

SLEEPING & EATING

Ksar Jenna (☎ 024 839790; www.ksarjenna.com; N'Kob; half board per person Dh1100; ✗ ⭐) A couple of kilometres out of N'Kob on the Ouarzazate road, this light-filled villa with seven large rooms and spacious bathrooms decorated in a Mediterranean-Moroccan style makes a great antidote to kasbah fatigue. Meals can be served in the flower-filled garden or in the elegant house.

Kasbah Imdoukal (☎ 024 839798; www.kasbah imdoukal.com in French; N'Kob; s/d/tr Dh600/700/900; ✗ ⭐) The most luxurious kasbah in N'Kob, Imdoukal has been decorated using local materials but with modern bathrooms and a welcome pool, and a sun terrace with views of the mountains.

Kasbah Baha Baha (☎ 024 838463; www.bahabaha .com in French; N'Kob; s/d/tr Berber tents Dh80/150/210, s/d/tr Dh200/300/400, s/d with shower Dh250/350; ⭐) This sensitively restored kasbah has traditionally decorated rooms, but no water facilities or heating in the main building. The Baha Baha is now such a 'sight' that nonguests are charged Dh10 to visit a small ethnographical museum in the courtyard.

Auberge Restaurant Enakhil (☎ 024 839719; N'Kob; s/d/tr Dh90/130/160) A new place on the edge of N'Kob, this has great views onto the village and Jebel Saghro. Simple rooms, a nice garden and big welcome make this the best budget option in town. It'll also arrange excursions in the area and treks into the Saghro.

Bougafer Hôtel (☎ 024 839169; Tazzarine; d half board per person Dh250) Tazzarine's best has good clean rooms and a decent restaurant and is linked to the Village Touristique Bougafer.

Village Touristique Bougafer (☎ 024 839005; Tazzarine; camping per person Dh15 plus per caravan Dh35, half board s/d Dh310/580; ✗ ⭐) Bougafer is a huge coach-tour place with a pool (Dh60 for nonguests) and restaurant (set meals Dh120).

DADÈS VALLEY & THE GORGES سهول داداس والمضايق

Heading roughly east from Ouarzazate, the Dadès Valley threads its course between the mountains of the High Atlas to the north and the rugged Jebel Sarhro range to the south. The biggest oases and the line of kasbahs that give this extremely popular route its nickname, Valley of a Thousand Kasbahs, begin just before the town of Skoura.

Further along the valley, the beautiful Dadès and Todra gorges, also lined with *palmeraies*, cut back up into the High Atlas. From here rough *pistes* lead all the way over to the Middle Atlas.

SKOURA سكورة

The first town east of Ouarzazate (39km), Skoura is often visited as a day trip, but is a great place to spend a night or two. The *palmeraie* here contains some impressive kasbahs, which makes it a good place to explore on foot or, even better, mountain bike, out of the midday sun. You can walk to the most accessible of the old kasbahs, the **Kasbah Amerdihl** (admission by donation Dh10), owned by the Nasser family, a few hundred metres from Kasbah Aït Ben Moro. Give your entry contributions to the caretaker.

Skoura has a growing choice of accommodation, of which the newcomer **Les Jardins de Skoura** (☎ 024 852324; www.lesjardinsdeskoura.com; d/tr half board Dh800/950, suites d/tr/q 1100/1250/1400; ⭐), hidden deep in the *palmeraie*, is one of the best. A beautifully executed retreat of five rooms and three suites, with a pool and hammam, developed out of an old mill using local materials. Chic and comfortable.

Coming from Ouarzazate, 7km before Skoura, **Chez Talout** (☎ 062 498283; s/d per person half/full board Dh150/210) makes a great stopover either for lunch (Dh60) or overnight in the simple rooms. The terrace has wonderful views of the *palmeraie* and mountains. It also offers the possibility of outings on foot, horse and mountain bike.

The long-established **Kasbah Aït ben Moro** (☎ 024 852116; hotelbenmoro@yahoo.fr; s/d/tr half board Dh700/1000/1350) is a well restored 18th-century kasbah on the main road. Rooms,

PALM TREE TRAFFICKING

Palm trees are very fashionable and instantly exotic. They are the cherry on the icing for foreigners doing up their riad in Marrakesh, as well as for Moroccans who have moved out of the medina and want to fill the garden of their new villa. Nobody has the patience to wait 15 to 20 years for a palm tree to rise majestically above their property, so they pay high prices to buy adult trees.

As if the oases didn't suffer enough (see Endangered Species, p303), the traffic of palm trees to the big cities is the latest and probably the last blow. The impoverished oasis people are happy to receive the cash, even though the deal is not fair. In Skoura, for instance, a farmer was paid Dh70 to Dh100 for a 25- to 30-year-old palm tree, which was then sold in Marrakesh or Casa for Dh6000. What's more, it's mostly the non-fruit-bearing male trees that get pulled out so, if the trafficking continues at the current rate, there may be no more male trees in Skoura by 2008. The Save Skoura organisation is trying to stop the process. For more information, contact martinecabarez@men ara.ma or anikoboehler@mac.com.

with Berber rugs and *tataoui* ceilings, are naturally dark, cool in summer and heated in winter. There are panoramic views of the *palmeraie* and the Atlas from the roof terrace, which serves meals (Dh150).

Further into the *palmeraie*, **Sawadi** (☎ 024 852341; www.sawadi.ma; s/d in small house half board Dh750/1150, up to 7 people in large house Dh2300-3850; 🏊) has three traditional houses on a large farm. There are no chemicals in the pool, and there's homegrown organic food.

Among several budget *gîtes d'étape*, **Chez Famille Ben Moro** (☎ 068 763521; s/d half board Dh150/200) has seven basic rooms and hot showers, just past (but not connected with) the Kasbah Aït Ben Moro.

There are regular but infrequent buses from Ouarzazate and Tinerhir (Dh10), but a grand taxi from Ouarzazate (Dh12) is a better option.

EL-KELAÂ M'GOUNA   قلعة مكونة

Although it takes its name from the nearby M'Goun mountain, the small town of El-Kelaâ (or Qalaa't) M'Gouna, 50km from Sk-

oura, is famous for roses. The town depends on their cultivation and on the production of rosewater. There are differing stories as to the origin of the roses: some say they are Persian, brought back by Mecca pilgrims, others that French colonists imported them from Syria in the 1930s. Wherever they came from, the roses now nestle among hedgerows and are not immediately visible, but their harvest is celebrated in May with a colourful and sweet-smelling rose festival.

You can buy almost any rose product, from cream and soap to rosewater, in a number of shops in town, but beware of synthetic products made in Casablanca. Market day is Wednesday.

There is a long tradition of dagger making in the area, particularly in the village of Azlag. This has been exploited by the **Cooperative Artisan du Poignards Azlag,** on the main road at the eastern edge of town, where ceremonial daggers sell from Dh200 to several thousand dirham. Expect a hard sell.

For those who have access to decent transport, a 40km meander through the Vallée des Roses makes a pleasant loop north of El-Kelaâ M'Gouna. In spring the entire area is completely awash with pink Persian roses and it's a stunning place for walking. For more information on trekking in the M'Goun massif see p424. The **bureau des guides** (☎ 061 796101, 062 132192) is 1km west of town.

Sleeping

Kasbah Itran (☎ /fax 024 837103; www.kasbahitran .com; half board s Dh150-300, d Dh210-360) A small, stylish kasbah 4km north of town, the Itran has stunning views over the M'Goun river to the nearby Ang Ksar and Kasbah des Glaouis. The food is excellent and the welcome extremely friendly. The hotel offers a range of hiking programs (two people trekking for two nights in the M'Goun, for instance, costs Dh800 per person including guide, transport and food). Minivans from town run past the kasbah en route to the village of Torbis (Dh5).

Hôtel Rose M'Gouna (☎ 024 836336; fax 024 836007; s/d Dh250/320; 🏊) The four-star rating is a little generous, but this concrete-block house overlooking town does have great views, a pool and the only bar in town.

Hôtel du Grand Atlas (☎ 024 836838; Ave Mohammed V; s/d/tr Dh45/80/90) The Grand is a misnomer, cheap and friendly is more to the point. Rooms and washing facilities are basic, but there is a hammam (Dh8) and a popular café/restaurant, a cut above most of the town's basic cafés. The hotel has good contacts with guides.

Eating

Most café-restaurants in the centre of town will prepare some very basic fare. One of the best is the restaurant of the **Hôtel du Grand Atlas** (Ave Mohammed V) where a standard meal of soup, tajine, dessert and tea costs Dh80.

Coming from Ouarzazate, 6km before El-Kelaâ M'Gouna, stop at **Rosa d'Amaskina** (☎ 024 836913) for lunch or a drink and to enjoy the wonderful view over the river and valley, though the hotel rooms look tired. Menus from Dh98 to Dh137.

Getting There & Away

Buses run between Ouarzazate and Tinerhir and beyond, but are often full. You can catch a grand taxi to Ouarzazate (Dh25), Skoura (Dh10), Boumalne du Dadès (Dh7) and Tinerhir (Dh8).

BOUMALNE DU DADÈS بوملنه داده

The Dadès Valley road forks 24km northeast of El-Kelaâ M'Gouna: the left branch leads up the stunning Dadès Gorge, while the main road continues over the river to the hillside town of Boumalne du Dadès.

Though you may want to press on up to the gorge, Boumalne du Dadès itself is a pleasant, laid-back place and has a reasonable choice of accommodation. Market day is Wednesday.

The **Banque Populaire** (Ave Mohammed V) changes money and has an ATM. On the same street there's internet access at **Taziri Net** (per hr Dh6; ☺ 8.30am-11.30pm). Treks can be arranged through some hotels, but the best option is to contact **Hamou Aït Lhou** (☎ 067 593292; hamou57@voila.fr), the only guide present at the Bureau des Guides, who has vast experience of the south and is equipped to lead a wide range of trips on foot or VTT. To explore the surrounding area on your own, you can hire bicycles from **Chez Youssef** (☎ 067 690214; Ave Mohammed V; bike hire per day Dh100), just behind the bus station.

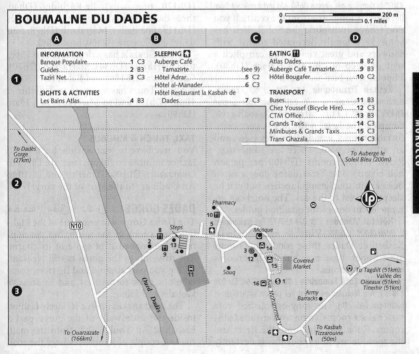

The hammada and grassy plains immediately south of Boumalne du Dadès offer some rewarding bird-watching opportunities. Take the *piste* leading off the main road beyond town south towards the village of Tagdilt and Vallée des Oiseaux (Valley of the Birds) to look for larks, wheat-ears, sandgrouse, buzzards and eagle owls. The manager of the Auberge le Soleil Bleu is a keen ornithologist and can give details of the latest spottings.

The town hammam, **Les Bains Atlas** (8am-8pm; Dh5), down the steep stairs beside the CTM office, serves men and women.

Sleeping

Hôtel Restaurant la Kasbah de Dades (024 830041; fax 024 831308; kasbahdedades@yahoo.fr; s/d/tr Dh150/180/220) Formerly the Chems, this place has changed its name, but not its friendly nature, nor its great location overlooking the valley. Rooms and bathrooms are clean and modern and there's a pleasant restaurant and terrace café. Very popular with tour groups.

Auberge le Soleil Bleu (024 830163; fax 024 830394; camping per person Dh50, s/d incl breakfast from Dh150/200) A long hike from the centre if you don't have transport, the Soleil Bleu has some very loudly decorated rooms with showers and great views. You can pitch a tent or sleep on the roof terrace (Dh30). Popular with bird-watchers.

Kasbah Tizzarouine (024 830690; kasbah. tizzarouine@menara.ma; s/d half board per person Dh450/300;) This attractive kasbah-style complex, the best in town, has very comfortable rooms, wonderful valley views and an attractive pool. There are some troglodyte double rooms (Dh400 per person half board). The Tizzarouine does a rapid business in tour-group lunches, but can be sleepy the rest of the day. The hotel can arrange excursions with qualified guides.

Hôtel al-Manader (024 830172; Ave Mohammed V; s/d/tr Dh120/150/180) Virtually next door to La Kasbah de Dades, these good value rooms are cheaper, have new ensuite bathrooms and nice balconies.

Auberge Café Tamazirte (068 886564; fax 024 830131; Ave Mohammed V; s/d per person with/without bathroom Dh50/40) The long-established café now has six rooms, some with ensuite bathrooms. Rooms looking onto the street and the mosque are noisy, but this is currently the best budget option with a good restaurant downstairs.

Hôtel Adrar (024 830765; Ave Mohammed V; s/d/tr Dh60/120/180) Cheap, central and basic, the Adrar makes a good budget stopover en route to the hills.

Eating

For cheap eats, the restaurants below Hôtel Adrar and the nearby Hôtel Bougafer both serve a filling meal of tajine or brochettes with salad and a drink for about Dh35 to Dh45. **Auberge Café Tamazirte** (068 886564; Ave Mohammed V; mains Dh35-60), further down the main street, has the advantage of a 1st-floor terrace and is a popular local eatery. Opposite, with a nice shaded terrace, is the similarly popular **Atlas Dades** (Ave Mohammed V; mains Dh30 to Dh45). The restaurants of the Hôtel al-Manader and the Hôtel Restaurant la Kasbah de Dades both have good menus (Dh65 and Dh76) and great views.

Getting There & Away

BUS

Tramesa has daily departures for Casablanca (Dh170, one daily), Er-Rachidia (Dh40, three daily), Erfoud (Dh60, two daily), Fès (Dh118, one daily), Marrakesh (Dh78, four daily) and Zagora (Dh60, one daily).

Trans Ghazala has a departure at 6.15pm for Ouarzazate (Dh34), Marrakesh (Dh70), Casablanca (Dh150) and Rabat (Dh180).

Supra Tours has a service to Tinerhir at 10pm (Dh15) and to Marrakesh at 6.15am (Dh90).

TAXI, TRUCK & MINIBUS

You may have to wait a while for a grand taxi or minibus to fill up; fares are Dh40 to Ouarzazate, Dh10 to Tinerhir and Dh10 to Aït Oudinar (to the start of the gorge).

DADÈS GORGE مخنف ا مفيق ا دادس

The Dadès Gorge was once one of the highlights of a tour in the south, but development has robbed it of some of its charm. The drive up to the gorge is still pleasant, taking you past almond and fig trees, some fabulous rock formations and impressive kasbahs and *ksour*.

The road snakes up in a leisurely fashion inside the wide walls of the gorge past a kasbah at Aït Youl, 6.5km from the main road. A couple of kilometres later the road crosses an *oued* (river bed); this valley offers a trekking route to El-Kelaâ M'Gouna.

After another 5km and over a small pass, the hidden Sidi Boubar Gorge (Gorge de Miguirne) joins from the right. The small gorge has springs and rock pools and makes a good half-day hike, part of which requires some wading. Another 4km brings you to a weird collection of rock formations. Further on, the village of Aït Oudinar has a few shops and a Sunday souq. Here the gorge narrows abruptly and the river flows right beside the road.

These first wider stretches of valley are increasingly built up, but about 2km beyond Aït Oudinar the road winds up inside the main canyon in a series of hairpin bends. When the road eventually flattens out again you leave the best of the scenery behind you.

The road is sealed all the way to Msemrir (63km), beyond which you will definitely need a 4WD, especially for the *piste* that leads east and then south down into the Todra Gorge. Many of the *pistes* are impassable in winter or after heavy rain and even in good weather are extremely rough. The driving here is slow.

If you have plenty of time, you could easily spend several days pottering about in the gorge, watching nomads bring goats down the cliffs to the river or fossicking for fossils. There are some challenging walks up into some of the smaller gorges west and east of the Oued Dadès, some of which lead up to nomad pastures. There's a good trail heading northwest, which begins just across the river from the cluster of hotels at 28km from Boumalne du Dadès.

A more ambitious journey would be to travel north from Msemrir into the heart of the High Atlas and beyond to Imilchil. It's a long way, but it's feasible (there is a slow but regular and reliable market circuit of trucks and minivans). Market day in Msemrir is Saturday.

Most hotels in the gorge and in Boumalne du Dadès can put you in touch with hiking guides (from Dh150 to Dh200 per day) and many offer 4WD trips to the Todra Gorge. You can also hire bicycles (Dh70 per day).

Sleeping & Eating
The choice of places to stay in the gorge is growing rapidly, and most of what's on offer is good value. Nearly all will let you

sleep in the salon or on the terrace (even in summer you may need a sleeping bag) for around Dh25, or camp by the river for around Dh10.

Most hotels offer half-board rates and dinner is often accompanied or followed by Berber music. There is little in the way of shops in the gorge so, if you want to self-cater, you will need to bring supplies from Boumalne or Ouarzazate.

The kilometre markings here refer to the number of kilometres into the gorge from Boumalne du Dadès.

Chez Pierre (☎ 024 830267; http://chezpierre.ifrance .com; 27km; half board per person Dh550; ⊠) Stylish, elegant and comfortable, this is simply the best hotel in the gorge. The pisé kasbah and its flowering terraces cling to the slopes of the gorge in an impossible balancing act. The airy rooftop pool and sun decks have precipitous views of the gorge and the restaurant is justifiably famous.

Auberge des Gorges du Dadès (☎ 024 831719; www.aubergeaitoudinar.com; 25.5km; camping per person Dh15, s/d Dh170/240) Overlooking the river and with a pleasantly shaded camping area, the Auberge has nicely decorated ensuite rooms, the best being on the 2nd floor. The trek leader speaks English, French and Spanish and has more than 23 years' experience.

Auberge Tissadrine (☎ /fax 024 831745; 27km; mattress on terrace or in salon Dh25, r s/d/tr Dh150/170/ 180) Nicely sited over the river, the 13 rooms were being updated at the time of our visit and should have new bathrooms and electric heating, some with balconies.

Hôtel la Gazelle du Dadès (☎ 024 831753; 28km; mattress on floor Dh20, s/d Dh90/120, half board per person Dh130) The 16 neat rooms, all simply decorated with Berber bedcovers, are good value, especially the ones at the front with views of the gorge. Hot showers and communal toilets are spotless.

Hôtel la Kasbah de la Vallée (☎ /fax 024 831717; 28km; mattresses on roof/salon Dh15, half-board per person Dh150) Warmly recommended by readers, the Kasbah offers clean, bright rooms with clean linen. The owner is licensed to organise tours, including guided day hikes and 4WD trips to Todra. The hotel rents mountain-bikes (Dh100 per day).

Hôtel le Vieux Chateau du Dadès (☎ 024 831261; fax 024 830221; 27km; half board per person s/d/tr Dh180/ 150/130) Tidy rooms (a few with balconies), across the road from the river. Good information on local excursions. The hotel also has a very pleasant terrace restaurant.

Café Mirguirne (14km; mattresses on terrace Dh20, d with/without view Dh100/80) A basic place lower down the gorge, with a terrace overlooking the valley, this place makes a good base for exploring the nearby Sidi Boubar Gorge.

Hôtel Berbère de la Montagne (☎ /fax 024 830228; 34km; camping Dh15 per tent plus per person Dh15; r half board per person with/without bathroom Dh280/150) Just beyond the most dramatic stretch of the gorge, it has neat well-kept rooms and a garden for camping.

In Msemrir there is a choice of two basic hotels, the cheerful **Hôtel El-Ouarda** (☎ 024 831609; r per person Dh60) and the **Café Agdal** (r per person Dh60).

Getting There & Away

Grands taxis and minibuses run up the gorge from Boumalne and charge Dh15 per person to the cluster of hotels in the middle of the gorge (Kasbah de la Vallée, Tissadrine, Vieux Chateau) and Dh30 to Msemrir. You can ask to be dropped at your chosen hotel. To return, simply wait by the road and flag down a passing vehicle. Hiring a taxi for a half-day trip into the gorge should cost around Dh200.

Alternatively, you could get up to the gorge by a combination of hitching and walking. The energetic could combine the Dadès and Todra gorges by crossing between the two (a two- to three-day walk); otherwise you'll have to hire a 4WD.

Minibuses run fairly frequently up to Msemrir; the last one back to Boumalne leaves around 4pm. Trucks go Saturdays to Tamtattouchte and Aït Haini, which continue on the next day to Imilchil. There's accommodation in Tamtattouchte (see p353) but none in Aït Haini (souq on Thursday).

TINERHIR تنر هير

There is little to delay you in this bustling mining town, some 51km northeast of Boumalne du Dadès, but it has a range of hotels and therefore makes a very useful stopover for the gorges.

There are several banks with ATMs in the west of town, including BMCE and Crédit du Maroc. **Tichka Internet** (per hr Dh10), is next to the Hôtel de l'Avenir. **Maison Berbere** (☎ 024 834359) has two shops in the back streets behind the mosque, heavy on carpets and jewellery.

The old town is immediately southeast of the modern centre and has a souq and interesting old *ksar*. Off the Erfoud road, 15km east and southeast of town, are some lush *palmeraies* dotted with kasbahs and crisscrossed by *pistes* that are well worth exploring. You can hire bikes at several places, including **Ali VTT** (☎ 024 834359; per day Dh100).

An enormous souq is held about 2.5km west of the centre on Monday. A smaller livestock souq is held in town on Saturday.

Sleeping

BUDGET

Hôtel Restaurant les Gorges (☎ 024 834800; www .lesgorges.tk in French; Ave Mohamed V; s/d/tr Dh100/100/ 130, with bathroom Dh150/150/195) The best of the budgets, the hotel is a little way from the centre of town, but has good rooms, solar-powered hot water, electric heaters, some of the best food in town and great views of Sarhro from the terrace.

Hôtel el-Houda (☎ 024 833280, 061 776619; 11 rue Moulay Ismail; s/d Dh45/80, with bathroom Dh80/120) A quiet hotel just off Ave Hassan II with hot showers and decorated in some loud colours: crazy wallpaper and bright bedspreads. The charming management organise rock climbing in the gorges and cycle hire (per day Dh100).

Hôtel de l'Avenir (☎ /fax 024 834599; s/d/tr Dh50/ 120/150) Near the market, this is a popular place. The ten pleasant, clean rooms are arranged around the sociable restaurant area. Trekking and mountain-bike hire can also be organised here.

Hôtel l'Oasis (☎ 024 833670; Ave Mohammed V; s/d Dh50/80, with bathroom Dh120/160) Another reliable budget option l'Oasis has some ensuite rooms, many with balconies, though rooms can be noisy (the Total petrol station is next door). The rooftop restaurant is popular for its good food and great views.

MIDRANGE & TOP END

Kasbah Lamrani (☎ 024 835017; www.kasbah-lam rani.com in French; s/d half board Dh487/574; 🖭 🔊) A privately run *faux*-kasbah built in a kitsch Disneyesque fashion, with a good pool, Lamrani has bright ensuite rooms, which are well equipped and have satellite TV and air-con. The hotel is opposite the Monday souq, 2.5km west of town.

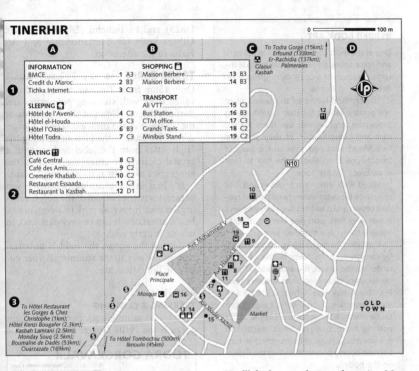

TINERHIR

0 —————— 100 m

INFORMATION
BMCE..1 A3
Credit du Maroc...........................2 B3
Tichka Internet.............................3 C3

SLEEPING
Hôtel de l'Avenir..........................4 C3
Hôtel el-Houda.............................5 C3
Hôtel l'Oasis.................................6 B3
Hôtel Todra..................................7 C3

EATING
Café Central.................................8 C3
Café des Amis...............................9 C2
Cremerie Khabab........................10 C2
Restaurant Essaada....................11 C3
Restaurant la Kasbah..................12 D1

SHOPPING
Maison Berbere...........................13 B3
Maison Berbere...........................14 B3

TRANSPORT
Ali VTT..15 C3
Bus Station.................................16 B3
CTM office..................................17 C3
Grands Taxis...............................18 C2
Minibus Stand.............................19 C2

To Todra Gorge (15km);
Erfound (133km);
Er-Rachidia (137km);
Glaoui Palmeraies
Kasbah

N10

Place Principale

Mosque

Market

OLD TOWN

Ave Mohammed V
Ave Hassan II
Ave Moulay Rachid

To Hôtel Restaurant
les Gorges & Chez
Christophe (1km);
Hôtel Kenzi Bougafer (2.3km);
Kasbah Lamrani (2.5km);
Monday Souq (2.5km);
Boumalne de Dadès (53km);
Ouarzazate (169km)

To Hôtel Tomboctou (500m);
Iknouln (45km)

Hôtel Tomboctou (☎ 024 834604; www.hoteltom
boctou.com; 126 Ave Bir Anzarane; s/d/tr incl breakfast Dh355/
470/600, half board Dh430/620/825; ☒) Tinerhir's
most characterful hotel is this kasbah, built
in 1944 for the local sheikh. Rooms tend to
be small and dark and service is irregular, so
you are paying for the kasbah 'experience'
rather than the room. There's a pool and a
very mediocre restaurant. Mountain trekking and bicycle trips can be organised.

Hôtel Todra (☎ 024 834249; fax 024 834565; Ave
Hassan II; s/d Dh50/100, with bathroom Dh209/252) Right
in the thick of it, between the taxi and bus
stations, the Todra has some character
with plenty of ageing. There's a pleasant
balcony terrace and a bar and restaurant.
Opt for either the cheapest or most expensive rooms; the midrange rooms don't have
any windows.

Eating
Several simple restaurants line Ave Hassan
II, including Café des Amis, which serves
excellent brochettes. Café Central, Restaurant Essaada and the Hôtel Alqods all serve
simple Moroccan dishes.

You'll find more choices along Ave Mohammed V. Cremerie Khabab is a good
simple place for a cheap breakfast.

Slightly fancier are **Restaurant la Kasbah**
(☎ 024 834471) and the restaurant at Hôtel
l'Oasis, both of which offer three-course
meals for Dh80 to Dh90. The restaurant
l'Avenir (in the same building, but not
connected to the hotel) serves good grills
and salads. Some of the best meals in town
are served at **Chez Christophe** (Ave Mohammed V),
the restaurant of Hôtel Les Gorges (mains
Dh40 to Dh60, meals Dh80).

The only restaurants in Tinerhir licensed
to serve alcohol are the overpriced restaurants of the Hôtel Kenzi Bougafer (dinner
around Dh180).

Getting There & Away
BUS
In the centre of town, buses leave from the
Place Principale, off Ave Mohammed V.

El Fath buses run to Marrakesh (Dh89,
five daily) via Ouarzazate (Dh40), and to
Casablanca (Dh145, departs 3pm), Erfoud
(Dh30, departures 6am, 8.30am and 3pm),

MARRAKESH & CENTRAL
MOROCCO

BERBER BODY ART

One of the most common sights in the herb and spice souqs throughout Morocco is the large pyramids of a deep, olive-green powder known as henna.

The crushed leaves of the henna plant are greatly valued for their health-giving properties, and women use them for the care and beautification of their skin and hair. Mixed with egg, milk or the pulp of fruit, henna is applied to the hair to lend it a vibrant reddish tone.

Mixed with lemon juice, cloves and rose or orange blossom water, henna stains reddish brown and is used to decorate women's hands and feet, pumped out in intricate designs through a modified syringe.

The latest henna fashion, driven largely by foreigners, is for black henna. In order to darken the henna, the artist adds chemical substances, among them the very toxic PPD black hair dye, which is banned in most countries. In the worst cases it can cause death, although most people suffer nothing more than an allergic reaction to it, sometimes chemical burns, which in turn become oozing blisters branding the design on the body.

Black 'henna' should be avoided at all cost, particularly for kids, with whom the new tattoos are really popular. Always insist on natural henna. For more information on the traditions and techniques of henna, as well as some gruesome pictures of the worst effects of black henna, visit www .hennapage.com.

Meknès (Dh105, six daily), Rissani (Dh35, departs 6am) and Zagora (Dh70, departs 1pm). Anything westbound will drop you in Boumalne du Dadès (Dh10).

CTM has a couple of buses that pass through Tinerhir on their way east and west but seats are scarce.

TAXI & MINIVAN

Grands taxis to Ouarzazate (Dh45) and Er-Rachidia (Dh40) leave from the eastern end of the gardens. This is also the place to hunt for a ride (taxis, lorries or pick-up trucks) up to the Todra Gorge (Dh7) and beyond.

An 8am minivan runs to Tamtattouchte (Dh15 to Dh20) and Aït Haini (Dh20 to

Dh25) and to Imilchil (Dh30 to Dh35). Others leave for Tamtattouchte and Aït Haini in the afternoon.

TODRA GORGE مخنف ا مفيق ا تودرغة

Only 15km from Tinerhir, at the end of a valley thick with stunning *palmeraies* and Berber villages, is one of the highlights of the south, the magnificent Todra Gorge. A massive fault in the plateau dividing the High Atlas from the Jebel Sarhro, with a crystal-clear river emerging from it, the gorge rises to 300m at its narrowest point.

It's best in the morning, when the sun penetrates to the bottom of the gorge, turning the rock from rose pink to a deep ochre. In the afternoon it can be very dark and, in winter, bitterly cold.

Beyond the gorge, the road is now tarmac all the way to the stunning Berber village of Tamtattouchte.

Activities
TREKKING & CLIMBING

About a 30-minute walk beyond the main gorge is the Petite Gorge. There are some

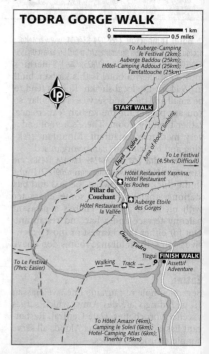

TODRA GORGE WALK

0 ——————— 1 km
0 ——————— 0.5 miles

To Auberge-Camping
le Festival (2km);
Auberge Baddou (25km);
Hôtel-Camping Addoud (25km);
Tamtattouche (25km)

START WALK

Oued Todra

Area of Rock Climbing

To Le Festival
(4.5hrs; Difficult)

Hôtel Restaurant Yasmina;
Hôtel Restaurant
les Roches

Pillar du
Couchant

Hôtel Restaurant
la Vallée

Auberge Etoile
des Gorges

Oued Todra

Tizgui FINISH WALK

To Le Festival
(7hrs; Easier)   Walking Track

Assettif
Adventure

To Hôtel Amazir (4km);
Camping le Soleil (6km);
Hotel-Camping Atlas (6km);
Tinerhir (15km)

FROM GORGE TO GORGE

The 42km from Tamtattouchte to the Dadès Gorge should only be attempted by 4WD during the summer months (May to September). The five-hour journey is bone-shakingly tough but traverses a stunning landscape of twisted hills, and the boulder-strewn valley of Tizgui n'Ouadda.

In May the tents of nomadic Berber tribes (many of whom have homes in Aït Hani) dot the valley floor, grazing large herds of sheep. And if you stop it is not uncommon for women to invite you to their tent for tea, intensely curious about foreign visitors.

About midway you crest the 2639m-high Tizi n'Uguent Zegsaoun before a bone-rattling descent to Msemrir.

The crossing is prone to flash floods in the early spring and you should always seek up-to-date advice on the state of the *piste* before setting off. The turning for the *piste* is just after Tamtattouchte, just below the auberge on the top of the hill. The track is very difficult to follow and a local guide is recommended.

nice day hikes around here, one of the best starting by the Auberge-Camping Le Festival, 2km after the Petite Gorge.

A more strenuous hike would be to walk a three-hour loop from north of the gorge to Tizgui, south of the gorge. The walk starts after leaving the main gorge (Map p352); as the road heads right (northeast), take the track leading up the hill to the left (southwest). It's well defined for most of the route, as it is used by donkeys and mules. Head to the pass and from there ascend southeast to the next pass. You can deviate off the main route to look over the rim of the gorge but be careful, as the winds get mighty powerful up there. From the second pass descend to the beautiful village of Tizgui, from where you can walk back through the *palmeraies* to the gorge.

There are many ruined kasbahs in the *palmeraies* to the south of here, and photographic opportunities abound. You could walk back to Tinerhir through the *palmeraies* in three or four hours.

Climbing is becoming increasingly popular on the vertical rock face of the gorge. There are some sublime routes here (French

grade 5), some of them bolted. Pillar du Couchant, near the entrance to the gorge, offers classic long climbs; the Petite Gorge is better for novice climbers with some good short routes. Most hotels can provide further information, but the guides with the most experience predominantly speak Spanish.

Assettif Aventure (☎ 024 895090; www.assettif .org in French), located 700m before the gorge, arranges treks and horse riding (day trip Dh350) and hires out bikes (per day Dh100) and mountaineering equipment. You can also do an overnight horse trek with guide and food for Dh800. Advance booking is recommended, especially at busy periods.

A network of difficult *pistes* links the sporadic villages here in the High and Middle Atlas, many of which are snowbound in winter. The two most popular trips are the rough *pistes* west to the Dadès Gorge (see the boxed text, left) and north to Imilchil. You'll need a 4WD for either trip.

Sleeping & Eating

Auberge-Camping Le Festival (☎ 061 267251, 073 494307; aubergelefestival@yahoo.fr; per person half board s Dh300, d with/without shower Dh230/210, camping/camper van per person Dh25) Right in the heart of the gorge, this wonderful stone auberge has breezy light rooms with fantastic views, furnished with wrought-iron beds and spotless white linens. The charming owner, who built the house, speaks French, Spanish and English and can arrange trekking and climbing. He will lead walks for Dh150 a day. Meals are very reasonable (around Dh35 to Dh55).

Hôtel Amazir (☎ 024 895109; s/d half board Dh370/ 490) On a bend in the road at the southern end of the gorge, 5km before you enter, is the attractive and stone-built Amazir. Rooms are comfortable and bright (try for a balcony) and there's a lovely terrace restaurant by the riverside.

Hôtel Restaurant Yasmina (☎ 024 895118; www .todragorge.com; s/d/tr half board Dh220/300/480) A fantastic location beside the ford and beneath the sheer rock walls at the heart of the gorge, the Yasmina has fairly small functional rooms and a good terrace restaurant (set menu Dh70 to Dh100) to take in the views. Because of its location, it is overrun by tour groups during the day.

Hôtel Restaurant les Roches (☎ 024 895134; www.hotellesroches.free.fr; s/d/tr incl breakfast Dh150/

200/275) This restaurant is next door to Yasmina, although not quite as good and suffers just as much from daytime crowds. There are also bikes available for hire (per day Dh100).

Hôtel Restaurant la Vallée (☎ 024 895126; s/d/tr incl breakfast Dh70/80/125, with bathroom 150/200/250) With a brilliant location on the river, before the Yasmina, this simple hotel has 11 rooms, some newly renovated, some looking tired. Those on the 2nd floor have lovely views of the gorge. Plenty of nice touches, checked tablecloths, fabric wall-hangings and clean communal facilities. It can provide information on trekking.

Auberge Etoile des Gorges (☎ 024 895045; fax 024 832151; mattress on terrace/salon Dh20/30, s/d/tr Dh40/60/80, with bathroom Dh60/80/100) A good, friendly budget option, this has simple rooms, some with basic showers heated by solar panels. There's a comfortable terrace restaurant (three-course meals Dh55 to Dh70).

Along the road to the gorge, about 9km from Tinerhir, is a line of camp sites, all with basic rooms but benefiting from a gorgeous setting amid the *palmeraie*. One of the best and friendliest is **Camping le Soleil** (☎ 024 895111; camping per person Dh15 plus per tent/car/camper van Dh12/12/20, d with/without bathroom Dh240/120), which is also the first site you come to. Facilities include a good restaurant, clean hot showers, shady sites and a washing machine (per load Dh20). Also recommended is **Hôtel-Camping Atlas** (☎ 024 895046; per person/tent/car/camper van Dh10/15/15/20; s/d/tr Dh100/120/180). Hot showers are included in the fee.

Since the road to the top of the gorge was paved, accommodation choices in Tamtattouchte have improved and alongside the shockingly pink, long-established **Auberge Baddou** (☎ 072 521 389, www.auberger-baddou.com; with bathroom s Dh50-100, d Dh100-200, tr Dh 200-300; camping/sleeping in nomad tent per person Dh20/30) are newcomers such as **Les Amis** (☎ 070 234374, amistamt@yahoo.fr; camping/camper van Dh10/30, d/tr half board per person Dh200). One of the most interesting projects (it was still under construction at the time of our visit) is **Hôtel-Camping Addoud** (☎ 066 193368; oudorjousef@caramail.com; per person half board Dh150, camping per person Dh30) on a rise above the village with wonderful views, with an apartment, ensuite doubles with electric panel heaters and ensuite bathrooms and with an exposed camp site (hot showers included in price).

Getting There & Away

See p350 for transport to the gorge.

Headed northwards, transit minivans run most days from Tinerhir to Aït Haini (market day Thursday). From here, however, you'll have to hitch. A sealed road now runs all the way to Aït Hani (planned to extend to Imilchil) beyond which the *piste* continues over the Tizi Tirherhouzine to Agoudal (the highest village en route) and Imilchil, just over 100km from the gorge. There is accommodation in Tamtattouchte and a simple auberges/camp sites in Agoudal.

GOULMIMA
غولميما

Goulmima is the centre of Berber culture and, although there isn't much to see, it makes a more interesting stopover than Er-Rachidia, despite limited sleeping options. Market days are Tuesday, Thursday and Saturday. Most facilities, including ATMs, internet and cafés can be found along the main street.

The main attraction is the labyrinthine **Ksar Aït Goulmima**. Unlike many *ksour* and kasbahs in the region, this walled village is still home to several hundred people. A guide can lead you to the 500-year-old mosque and through the Jewish *mellah* into the *palmeraie*.

To get to the *ksar* turn left at the main roundabout coming from Er-Rachidia, before you reach the main town. After 500m you pass the excellent Maison d'Hôtes les Palmiers. After another 800m is the turnoff left to the youth hostel; the *ksar* is straight on.

The peaceful converted home of a French-Moroccan couple **Maison d'Hôtes Les Palmiers** (☎ /fax 035 784004; d with/without bathroom Dh240/200, half board Dh220 per person) sits in a mature garden on the edge of the *palmeraie*. Rooms are spacious, spotless and heated in winter. Children aged under four stay free and it's half price for those aged four to 15. The food, mostly Moroccan, is fabulous (dinner Dh90). Trekking information and guides for the *ksar* are available.

In another converted family home, but this time in true Moroccan style, the **Youth Hostel** (☎ 066 908442; www.aub.ht.st in French; Hay Othmane Secteur 3, No 4 Ksar Goulmima; dorm/d per person Dh50/100, camping per person Dh30) is stuffed full of patterns and knick-knacks. It has a couple of double rooms and several larger ones, shared showers, often with hot water, and a kitchen. Meals are available – breakfast Dh20, other meals Dh60. You can camp in the large garden, part of the *palmeraie*.

In the centre of town, on the main street, **Hôtel Gheriz** (☎ 035 783167; s/d Dh70/100) is a decent, clean place in the centre of the town. Rooms come with bathrooms and hot water.

Grands taxis run from town when full to Er-Rachidia and Tinerhir.

ZIZ VALLEY & THE TAFILALT

وادة زيز و تافلالت

The Ziz river brings life to this barren landscape, running past the small town of Rich and carving out a valley that continues south beyond Merzouga. The road to Er-Rachidia is spectacular. The main highlight are the Ziz Gorges, stretching from the French-built Tunnel du Légionnaire, 20km south of Rich. This magnificent route through palm-fringed towns also passes several *ksour* and a series of dams, including the Barrage Hassan Adakhil, its turquoise blue water visible from the main highway.

Beyond Er-Rachidia the road heads past the fertile Source Bleue de Meski before heading deep into the desert and rolling dunes of Merzouga.

The Tafilalt was one of the last areas to succumb to French control under the protectorate, its tribes putting up sporadic resistance until 1932. Two years later Morocco was officially considered 'pacified'. To make sure this state of affairs did not change, Erfoud was built as an administrative and garrison town to keep a watchful eye on the Tafilalt tribes.

ER-RACHIDIA

الراشيدية

At the crossroads of important north-south and east-west routes across Morocco, Er-Rachidia (named after the first Alawite leader, Moulay ar-Rashid) was built by the French as a military outpost. The modern town still has this administrative character and a fairly large army garrison is still stationed there.

Er-Rachidia is unexciting but has useful amenities. It is also a convenient place to break your journey if you're heading north to Midelt and Meknès or south to Merzouga. Each May it is transformed by music and dancing during the annual **Festival du Desert** (www.festivaldudesert.ma), which began in 2003 under the patronage of the King and now attracts performers from around the Sahara.

Market days are Sunday, Tuesday and Thursday.

Information

There are at least four banks in town, including a **BMCE** (Place Moulay Hassan) and a Banque Populaire near the main street heading out to Erfoud, both of which have ATMs.

Cyber Challenge Internet (Rue Sidi Bou Abdallah; per hr Dh8; ☉ 9.30am-8pm) is on a 2nd floor, near the covered market.

Mars Travel Agency (☎ 035 571007; Ave Moulay Ali Cherif) is the only car-hire place in the region with small cars starting at Dh500 per day.

The Douche Bain Sidi Ammi is opposite the bus station. There's another hammam by the main mosque.

Sleeping

Hôtel Kenzi Rissani (☎ 035 572186; www.kenzi-hotels .com in French; Route d'Erfoud; s/d Dh600/750; ✹ ⓡ) Just across the Ziz bridge, this sprawling four-star place lacks atmosphere, but is friendly and offers the best facilities with air conditioning and a big pool (nonresidents Dh70). Mint green corridors lead to peach-coloured rooms with huge picture windows. The pleasant licensed restaurant overlooks the pool.

Hôtel Errachidia (☎ 035 570453; hotelerrachidia@ yahoo.fr; 31 Rue Ibn Battuta; s/d/tr Dh250/320/400; ✹) This is one of the best and most woman-friendly hotels in town. Don't be fooled by the setting, right behind the bus station (handy for early or late arrivals), or the ugly concrete exterior. Inside are neat, cheerful rooms with yellow linen and sparkling white bathrooms. Note that only three of the 21 rooms have air-con.

Auberge Tinit (☎ 035 791759; fax 035 791811; tinit_auberge2000@yahoo.fr; Route de Goulmima; s/d Dh300/400; ✹ ⓡ) Er-Rachidia's newest accommodation, some 3km out of town, the 16-room Tinit is a good midrange hotel

with pisé walls and plenty of local touches. The restaurant serves Moroccan standards and a pool was being constructed at the time of our visit.

Hôtel M'Daghra (☎ 035 574047; fax 055 574049; 92 Rue M'Daghra; s/d/tr Dh148/182/244) On a busy street leading to the market, this is another reliable option. Comfortable, clean rooms come with hot showers and some have a balcony.

Hôtel Al Ansar (☎ 035 573919; 31 Rue Ibn Battuta; s/d/tr Dh50/70/90) A good, clean option, close to the bus station, Al Ansar's exterior rooms with balconies are best, though they can be noisy. There are shared hot showers.

Hôtel de l'Oasis (☎ 035 572519; fax 035 570126; Rue Sidi Bou Abdallah; s/d Dh125/148) At 28 years old this one-star option is showing its age, with shabby furnishings and small rooms. Still, it's cleanish, has some new bathrooms and is cheap.

Eating

The most salubrious and expensive place for a sit-down meal is the restaurant of the Hôtel Kenzi Rissani, where a Dh120 dinner

is served by black-tie waiters and alcohol is on the menu. **Restaurant Imilchil** (☎ 035 572123; Ave Moulay Ali Cherif), with a big terrace opposite the covered market, is very popular and serves good tajines (Dh60). In much the same league is the busy **Restaurant Lipton** (Ave Moulay Ali Cherif).

Restaurant Ben Allal (Route D'Erfoud) is a pleasant open-air place serving up rotisserie chicken (Dh50) and pizzas (Dh55) and with a patisserie attached for dessert.

You can get a range of vegetables and other food for picnics, or to eat at stalls, in the covered market.

Getting There & Away
BUS

All buses operate out of the central **bus station** (Rue M'Daghra). **CTM** (☎ 035 572024) has daily departures to Rabat/Casablanca (Dh140/ 170, about 10/11 hours, one daily), Fès (Dh105, 8½ hours, one daily) and Meknès (Dh95, eight hours, two daily).

Private buses run to Fès (Dh85, five daily), Marrakesh (Dh125, four daily), Ouarzazate (Dh55, three daily), Rissani

(Dh18, nine daily) via Erfoud (Dh15) and Zagora (Dh100, one daily).

TAXI
Most grands taxis depart from a lot located about three blocks northeast of the main bus station. The main destinations include Azrou (Dh80, five hours), Erfoud (Dh20, one hour), Fès (Dh110, 6½ hours), Meknès (Dh100, six hours), Tinerhir (Dh40, two hours), Rissani (Dh25) and Merzouga (Dh50).

AROUND ER-RACHIDIA
Source Bleue de Meski   عين مسكي الزرقاء
The source, about 17km southeast of Er-Rachidia, is a wonderful natural spring spilling into a swimming pool.

On weekends, heat-plagued locals from Er-Rachidia flock here in droves; otherwise, it's pretty quiet. It's a swimming stop (Dh5, free for campers) that's well recommended for the hot and sweaty traveller passing by.

Women should note that there is the usual crowd of Moroccan men ready to ogle while you swim.

If you really like the place, you can stay longer at the pleasant **Camping Source Bleue de Meski** (camping per person Dh10, plus per tent/car Dh10/20). There's a café-restaurant and a few souvenir shops.

From the camping area there is a nice hike to the deserted Ksar Meski on the far side of the *oued*.

The spring is about 1km west of the main road and signposted. Public buses travel from Er-Rachidia to a terminal just above the spring between 7am and 9pm (Dh3). Alternatively any bus or grand taxi to Erfoud or Aufous (also spelled Aoufouss) can drop you off at the turn-off. When leaving, you should be able to flag down a grand taxi or hitch from the main road.

If you are driving south to Erfoud, there are great photo opportunities of the Ziz *palmeraies* just north of Aufous. The road drops down from the desert plateau. Down in this *palmeraie* is the **Maison d'Hôtes Zouala** (☎ /fax 035 578182; http://labrisenet.free.fr/maison _zouala in French; km30 on the Er-Rachidia-Erfoud road; half board per person Dh250), a peaceful hideaway with ensuite and shared bathrooms, a great place to stop for a rest and some home cooking (they bake their own bread).

Nearby, at the edge of the *palmeraie*, the town of **Aufous** makes a good stopping point en route for the south. As well as useful services – food, petrol and phone – there are some brilliant pisé buildings on the edge of the palm groves and an impressive ruin of a kasbah above. There is a souq on Thursday.

ERFOUD   ارفود
pop 24000
Erfoud is a fairly quiet place, noted for its dates. Before the road was laid to Merzouga, this was the main base for tourists, which explains why there are so many hotels. It still makes an alternative, and less hassled staging point for desert excursions to Erg Chebbi, but most travellers prefer to stay at the base of the dunes in and around Merzouga.

If you are driving, you may be approached in Erfoud by people offering to guide you to Merzouga. Now that there is tarmac all the way, this is not necessary, although unwary travellers are still falling for the scam.

Information
There are several banks in town but only the **BMCE** (Ave Moulay Ismail) has an ATM.

Of the many internet places in the centre of town, **Cyber.Net Tafilalet** (100 Ave Mohammed V; 9am-midnight) currently has the fastest connection. Dh10 per hour is the standard.

Sights & Activities
Hammams for men and women are located behind Hôtel Sable d'Or.

Erfoud is full of shiny black fossilised marble, which is quarried nearby in the desert. You can watch it being cut at **Manar Marbre**, the marble factory between the town and Kasbah Tizimi. The **Museum of Fossils & Minerals** (☎ 061 425927/068 757563; brahimtahiri@hotmail.com; donation expected Dh25; 8am-7pm) 3km on the Rissani road, has a massive store of fossils, some arranged as a museum; some, of course, for sale. You may also be shown the workshop where fossils are extracted from the rock.

Just 5km north of Erfoud is the impressive **Ksar M'Aadid**, well worth a look if you have your own transport.

In October Erfoud has an increasingly well-attended date festival, with dancing and music.

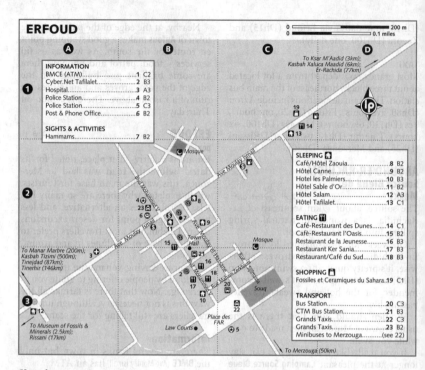

ERFOUD

INFORMATION
BMCE (ATM)............................1	C2
Cyber.Net Tafilalet...................2	B3
Hospital....................................3	A3
Police Station...........................4	B2
Police Station...........................5	C3
Post & Phone Office................6	B2

SIGHTS & ACTIVITIES
Hammams.................................7	B2

SLEEPING
Café/Hôtel Zaouia....................8	B2
Hôtel Canne..............................9	B2
Hotel les Palmiers...................10	B3
Hôtel Sable d'Or......................11	B2
Hôtel Salam............................12	A3
Hôtel Tafilalet........................13	C1

EATING
Café-Restaurant des Dunes.......14	C1
Café-Restaurant l'Oasis.............15	B2
Restaurant de la Jeunesse........16	B3
Restaurant Ker Sania................17	B3
Restaurant/Café du Sud...........18	B3

SHOPPING
Fossiles et Ceramiques du Sahara.19	C1

TRANSPORT
Bus Station.............................20	C3
CTM Bus Station.....................21	B3
Grands Taxis..........................22	C3
Grands Taxis..........................23	B3
Minibuses to Merzouga...........(see 22)	

To Ksar M'Aadid (3km);
Kasbah Xaluca Maadid (6km);
Er-Rachida (77km)

To Manar Marbre (200m);
Kasbah Tizimi (500m);
Tinejdad (87km);
Tinerhir (146km)

To Museum of Fossils &
Minerals (2.5km);
Rissani (17km)

To Merzouga (50km)

Sleeping

BUDGET

Hôtel Canne (☎ 035 578695; fax 035 578696; 85 Ave Moulay el-Hassan; s/d/tr Dh150/180/240; ✷) This is a great, centrally-located women-friendly budget option with female receptionists (unusual for Morocco) who keep the place spick-and-span Decorative features include pink shower curtains and turquoise bedding, and a large TV in the lounge.

Hôtel les Palmiers (☎ 035 578894; hassane_hotel@yahoo.fr; 36 Ave Mohammed V; s/d/tr Dh60/80/120) Centrally located opposite Restaurant/Café du Sud and other popular eating places, the Palmiers has good clean rooms with showers in the rooms (WC on the landing).

Hôtel Sable d'Or (☎ 035 576348; Ave Mohammed V; s/d/tr Dh150/170) A variety of comfortable rooms with ensuite bathrooms, some with views of pine trees outside, are on offer here. The café/restaurant downstairs has nice open-air seating.

Café/Hôtel Zaouia (☎ 068 758768; Ave Moulay Ismail; s/d Dh50/100) Zouuia has several clean, bright and excellent-value rooms above the café, with shared hot showers.

MIDRANGE & TOP END

Kasbah Xaluca Maadid (☎ 035 578450; www.xalucamaadid.com; half board per person s/d Dh880/625, royal ste Dh2900; ✷ ☎) This is a wildly opulent *faux*-kasbah 6km north of Erfoud. Much attention has been paid to the extravagant décor of the spacious rooms, from sinks made from fossilised marble to lights set inside crystals. The hotel has a fleet of quad bikes and can also arrange every imaginable excursion into the surrounding *palmeraies* and visits to the dunes of Erg Chebbi.

Kasbah Tizimi (☎ 035 576179; www.kasbahtizimi .com; s/d Dh550; ☎) A bustling hotel, Tizimi is popular with guides and groups and is built in traditional kasbah style. The hotel has nice gardens and comfortable, if over-styled rooms, with bathrooms. It has a restaurant (menu Dh132), pool (nonguests Dh35) and bar.

Hôtel Salam (☎ 035 576665; fax 035 576426; ☎) With its pool, gardens, bar and sauna, this has long been a favourite of 4WD drivers, but at the time of our visit it was closed due to industrial action.

Eating

Don't miss the chance to try the local speciality *kalia*, minced mutton with tomato, peppers, egg, onion and 44 spices (no, you can't count them) served in a tajine.

Restaurant/Café du Sud (19 Ave Mohammed V; mains Dh30-50) Next to the Hôtel Ziz, this is one of the most popular local eateries. The *kalia* (Dh30) is excellent and a local pizza known as *madfouna* (Dh45) is available if you order in advance.

Café-Restaurant des Dunes (☎ 035 576793; Ave Moulay Ismail; meals Dh60) The door is plastered with tour and rally stickers, but you won't find large groups here as it only has four tables inside, a few more out on the terrace. *Kalia* is good and only Dh25. The same family owns the top-end Kasbah Zaluca Maadid and, at the time of our visit, was building a large new upmarket restaurant across the road.

Restaurant Ker Sania (☎ 035 578539; 36 Ave Mohammed V; meals Dh90) A civilised place, with B&W photos on the wall and classical music on the stereo, the menu here is strong on *pastilla* (Dh50).

Two other popular places are **Restaurant de la Jeunesse** (Ave Mohammed V; mains Dh25-50) and **Café-Restaurant l'Oasis** (Ave Mohammed V; mains Dh30-45), both of which serve solid Moroccan dishes for reasonable prices.

For a more sophisticated meal, you will need to try the restaurants of the top-end hotels, the best of these being in the Kasbah Tizimi. Expect to pay Dh150 to Dh200 for a meal.

The souq at the southern end of town sells fresh produce and some of the town's brilliant dates.

Shopping

You can buy pieces of fossilised marble in several shops around town, among them **Fossiles et Ceramiques du Sahara**, across the road from the Café Restaurant des Dunes. The Museum of Fossils & Minerals (p357) has fossils for sale.

Getting There & Away

BUS

The **CTM station** (☎ 035 576886; Ave Mohammed V) runs a single service to Fès (Dh124, seven hours) via Er-Rachidia (Dh22, 1¼ hours), Midelt (Dh59, five hours) and Meknès (Dh109, 6½ hours).

Other busses leave from Place des FAR. There are services to Tinerhir at 8.30am (Dh40), to Ouarzazate (Dh80, 3pm) and Fès (Dh97, three daily).

A local bus runs to Zagora at 9am (Dh75, six hours) via Rissani, Alnif and Tazzarine at 8.30am on Sunday, Tuesday and Thursday. Minibuses shuttle between Erfoud and Rissani (Dh4, 30 minutes).

A minivan runs at least once a day to Merzouga (Dh15 to Dh20) at around 1pm from the parking lot in Place des FAR. The driver might try to steer you towards whichever auberge pays commission so stand by your guns if you have a particular place in mind. Minibuses can drop you off at any auberge en route.

TAXI

Grands taxis are, as a rule, a more reliable bet. Some leave from Place des FAR and others from opposite the post office for Rissani (Dh6) and Er-Rachidia (Dh20) and Tinerhir (Dh50). Since the road was laid to Merzouga, the price of hiring a 4WD and driver, formerly the only certain way of getting over the *piste*, has dropped. **Association Tamounte** (☎ 035 577523; 5 Ave Moulay Ismail) rents car and driver for Dh450 a day, plus the cost of diesel.

RISSANI   الريصاني

Many visitors are tempted to pass straight through the small town of Rissani, but those who stay are well rewarded for it has long been an important meeting place. This is where the Ziz river is finally overwhelmed by stone and sand and where caravans from the Sahel used to unload some of their gold and slaves.

It was from Rissani that the Filali (ancestors of the Alawite dynasty that rules today) swept north to supplant the Saadians as the ruling dynasty in Morocco. It did not happen overnight; the founder of the dynasty, Moulay Ali ash-Sharif, began expanding his power in the early 17th century in a series of small wars with neighbouring tribes, and the campaign was continued by his sons. The conquest of Morocco was completed by his successor, Moulay ar-Rashid, who was recognised as sultan in 1668. Moulay ar-Rashid's brother and successor, the deranged and violent Moulay Ismail, later became the uncontested ruler of Morocco,

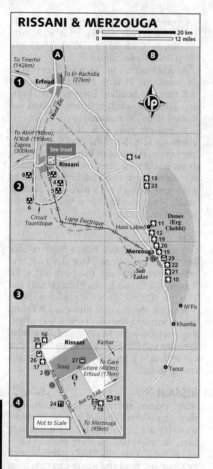

There is a Banque Populaire with an ATM opposite the souq.

Circuit Touristique

For a tour of Rissani's famed *palmeraie* and a glimpse of life as it is lived on the edge of the desert, try this 21km loop (Map p360) along a circuit south of Rissani, some of it on bumpy roads, which also takes you past several ruined *ksour* and the scant ruins of the fabled city of Sijilmassa.

From Rissani's centre head north from the souq then follow the main road west. About 2km to the southeast is the **Zawiya Moulay Ali ash-Sharif** (closed to non-Muslims), the founder of the Alawite dynasty that still rules Morocco today. Nearby and worth a look are the 19th-century ruins of the **Ksar Aber**, which was formerly housed the dynasty's disgraced or unwanted members.

and emphasised his power by abandoning Marrakesh and establishing a new capital at Meknès.

The centre of Rissani is quite small and manageable and still has a significant *ksar* at its heart. Travellers will find most of their practical needs satisfied along the northern edge of the souq, which becomes a bustling hive of activity every Sunday, Tuesday and Thursday.

Information

There is a post and phone office at the northern end of the medina walls. **Info Keys Cyber Club** (per hr Dh5), one of several internet places, is about 50m north of Hôtel Restaurant Panorama.

About 1km or so further on is the **Ksar Oulad Abdelhalim**, built around 1900 for Sultan Moulay Hassan's elder brother. There is still a substantial amount of beautiful decoration remaining, enough to suggest that its claim to be the 'Alhambra of the Tafilalt' wasn't entirely fanciful.

The road continues past another group of *ksars*, some of which are still inhabited by members of the Filali. There are good views from **Ksar Tinheras**.

You come to the ruins of **Sijilmassa** just before you reach Rissani. This was the capital of a virtually independent Islamic principality adhering to the Shiite 'heresy' (see About Islam, p48) in the early days of the Arab conquest of North Africa.

Sijilmassa's foundation is lost in myth – some say AD 757 – but certainly by the end of the 8th century it was playing a key role as a staging post for trans-Saharan trade. Caravans of up to 20,000 camels crossed the sands to the remote desert salt mines of Taodeni and Tagahaza (in modern-day Mali), then continued to Niger and Ghana, where a pound of Saharan salt was traded for an ounce of African gold. The return trip brought gold, ostrich feathers, ebony, ivory, salt and slaves back to Sijilmassa and the oases of the Tafilalt.

However, the inevitable internal feuding led to the collapse of the fabled city in the 14th century and Sijilmassa is now a ruin with little to indicate its past glories beyond two decorated gateways and a few other partially standing structures.

There are other *ksour* in the region including Ksar al-Beidha, Ksar Haroun and several *ksour* on the road to Mezguida, but you'll need a guide's help in locating them.

A very dusty collection of old pots from recent excavations and some comprehensive information (in French only) on the area can be found in the small **museum** (admission free; ☺ 9am-4pm Mon-Fri) of the Research Centre for Alawite Culture (Centre d'Études et de Recherches Alaouites) located on the north side of the central square in Rissani.

Sleeping & Eating

Most tourists stay in Erfoud or Merzouga and as a result accommodation in Rissani is very limited and the standards mostly poor.

Hôtel Kasbah Asmaa (☎ 035 774083; fax 035 575494; asmaabivouac@yahoo.fr; s/d Dh257/334, d half board per room Dh574; ⚲) The rooms are nothing special and the hotel sits on the main road, but this friendly place, about 3km along the road to Erfoud, is still Rissani's best. The gardens are wonderful and the swimming pool is a draw on hot days. It can also organise quad outings and trips into the Merzouga dunes.

RISSANI ROGUES

Traditionally the domain of tough and wily tribes, it is hardly surprising that the depressed town of Rissani continues a healthy tradition of rogues and charlatans.

Touts and *faux guides* lurk around the bus station waiting to ensnare unsuspecting travellers to embark on a 4WD excursion to Merzouga, for a long time claiming that the sealed road to Merzouga was nowhere near finished. When that ploy lost its effectiveness a concerted effort was made to obscure or vandalise road signs so that travellers would not be able to find the road south without some assistance.

More serious, however, is the boycotting of certain hotels in Merzouga. Groups of travellers have repeatedly complained that their Rissani 'guides' have refused to take them to the hotels of their choice, preferring to deposit them at auberges that pay the 'guides' commission. On a note closer to home, one particular individual has taken to advertising himself as an official Lonely Planet guide. However, readers should take note that Lonely Planet does not officially endorse any local guide or business.

The flip side of the coin is, of course, poverty. Both Rissani and Erfoud previously lived off the business of escorting travellers south to Erg Chebbi. The new paved road, which runs as far as Taouz, beyond Merzouga means that travellers can now make their own way to the dunes. This has had a big impact on the local economy, but hasn't stopped the rogues: when we passed through to research this edition, we were told that the road to Merzouga was still unpaved.

Hôtel Sijilmassa (☎ /fax 035 575042; Place al-Massira al-Khadra; s Dh80, d Dh140-160) The ensuite rooms here are clean and comfortable, but can be damp. There are great views from the rooftop terrace. The restaurant in the basement is gloomy but serves some of the more reliable food in town (set menus from Dh60).

Hôtel Restaurant Panorama (☎ 035 774093, 066 351836; panoramahotel2000@yahoo.fr; mattress on roof Dh25, s/d/tr Dh40/60/120) You couldn't be more central than here, just on the eastern side of the market and upstairs from the *camionette* stop, but the rooms are tired and the washing facilities very grotty. Definitely not recommended for women travelling alone. There is a good terrace restaurant (meals Dh40) and the hotel rents mountain bikes (Dh60 per day), which are particularly useful for exploring the *circuit touristique*.

Restaurant Café Merzouga (41 Rue Moulay Ali Cherif; breakfast Dh15, set menu Dh40) This is the best place in town for food by a long way. The *kalia* is great, as are the *madfouna*, which will feed four (Dh80). The owners are very friendly.

At the time of our visit a new hotel and restaurant, Dar Lamrani, was almost ready to open. Owned by the same family as the rug and jewellery shop, it is beside the Maison Berbere and has six ensuite rooms on the 1st floor, two twins with communal facilities on the 2nd and two dining rooms on the ground floor.

Shopping

If you have time on your hands, Rissani has a few carpet and jewellery shops with some interesting stock, including the highly-respected **Maison Berbère** (☎ 061 348011), beyond Hotel Restau Panorama, opposite the entrance to the souq. On market days it is also worth looking around the souq for a solid-quality jellaba or burnous, plus crafts and the occasional old jewellery.

Getting There & Away

Buses leave from the new *gare routière* 400m from the square, on the road to Erfoud. There are services to Fès, (Dh100, two daily, 13 hours) via Meknès (Dh100, nine hours), and Marrakesh (Dh140, one daily, 10 hours), plus an evening run to Casablanca (Dh138, one daily, 15 hours). Buses run on Sunday, Tuesday and Thursday to Zagora (five hours) and on Saturday, Monday and Wednesday to Tinerhir (Dh34, six hours). There are six buses a day to Er-Rachidia (Dh18, three hours) via Erfoud.

CTM (☎ 066 367006; Place de la Marche Verte) has an office in the centre of town, and runs one bus a day at 8pm to Fès/Meknès (Dh135/125, eight–nine hours) via Er-Rachidia (Dh25, 1½ hours).

Grands taxis run frequently from opposite the Hôtel Sijilmassa to Erfoud (Dh7), Er-Rachidia (Dh25), Tinerhir (Dh55), Merzouga (Dh12) and occasionally to Taouz (Dh20).

You can also reach Merzouga by *camionette* (minivan), which leaves hourly from outside the Hôtel Restaurant Panorama (Dh10).

ERG CHEBBI, MERZOUGA & HASSI LABIED

One local legend has it that Erg Chebbi was God's way of punishing a local wealthy family who didn't offer hospitality to a poor woman and her son and were buried under the sand. Erg Chebbi is Morocco's only genuine Saharan *erg*, an impressive, drifting chain of sand dunes that can reach 160m and seem to have escaped from the much larger dune field across the nearby border in Algeria. The *erg* is a magical landscape, which deserves much more than the sunrise or sunset glimpse many visitors give it. The dunes are a scene of constant change and fascination as sunlight transforms them from pink to gold to red. The largest dunes are near to the villages of Merzouga and Hassi Labied. At night, you only have to walk a little way into the sand, away from the light, to appreciate the immense clarity of the desert sky and the brilliance of its stars.

For bird-watchers, this is perhaps the best area in Morocco for spotting many desert species, including desert sparrows, Egyptian nightjars, desert warblers, fulvous babblers and blue-cheeked bee-eaters. Sometimes in spring (dependent on rainfall) a shallow lake appears northwest of Merzouga, near the Auberge Yasmina, attracting flocks of pink flamingos and other water birds.

Merzouga, some 50km south of Erfoud is a tiny village, but does have *téléboutiques*, general stores, a mechanic and, of course, a couple of carpet shops. It also has an internet place, **Merzouga.net** (8am-midnight, Dh8 per hour). Even smaller Hassi Labied has the **Dépôt Nomade**, a former desert caravan trading centre turned carpet shop.

These villages have become the focus of fast-expanding tourism in the area and have a reputation for some of the worst hassle in Morocco. You are likely to be approached on arrival by people selling rooms in hotels and, later, by others selling excursions into the dunes. Things are now so bad here, especially during low season, that touts and hoteliers have been known to stop cars on the road coming from Rissani in an attempt to drum up business. You have been warned.

Most hotels offer excursions into the dunes and it's here that they make their money. Asking prices can be high. At the time of our visit, they ranged from Dh80 to Dh200 for a couple of hours' sunrise or, more usual, sunset camel trek. Overnight trips, including a bed in a Berber tent, dinner and breakfast range from Dh300 to Dh650 per person. Outings in a 4WD are more expensive, up to Dh1200 per day for a car taking up to five passengers. Several things should be checked before you agree a price – and definitely before you hand over money. The cheaper treks often congregate in the same spot, so if you have a romantic notion of being alone in the dunes under the stars, you need to find an outfit with a separate camp or set up a longer trip.

MERZOUGA FLOODS

Rain in the desert might sound like tea in the Sahara, but it is no laughing matter. Spring often brings rain to the Moroccan south and the sudden flash floods have long caused problems for locals and visitors, because the ground is so hard it does not absorb the water. But no-one was expecting the rains that fell at the end of May 2006. Over a period of three days, and during one particular storm, heavy rains caused such severe flooding that it cut the road, caused the death of at least six people, brought down 300 of the 2000 houses and seems to have destroyed at least a dozen of Merzouga's hotels. Some people are calling it the worst rain in more than a century. The stories of hardship and tragedy will long be told.

When fixing a price, be sure to ask how far you will be travelling and whether bottled water is included. Either way, it's well worth bringing water with you, as it is a pricey commodity in the desert! A sleeping bag can be useful as nights can be surprisingly cold. You should also know before leaving whether you have any language in common with the people leading you into the desert.

Sleeping & Eating

A string of camps and auberges, most built in similar kasbah style, flank the western side of Erg Chebbi for many miles to the north and south of the villages of Merzouga and Hassi Labied. Most offer half-board options, which isn't a bad thing as there aren't many stand-alone restaurants. In many of these places you can sleep on a mattress on the roof, in the salon or in a Berber tent for between Dh20 and Dh30 per person. Almost all have views of the dunes, and some form of sand toy (snowboard, skis etc) and/or bicycles.

Many are reached along a series of *pistes* that run east off the tarmac road. Because of the distances involved – Hassi Labied is 5km from Merzouga, and some of the hotels listed here are far beyond that – it is worth making sure hotels have space before you check them out and, if you are travelling by taxi, that your driver understands where you want to go.

HASSI LABIED

This tiny village, 5km north of Merzouga and some way off the tarmac road, has a good range of accommodation.

Kasbah Mohajut (☎ 066 039185; fax 035 578428; mohamezan@yahoo.fr; s/d/ste half board per person Dh210/160/220) This is a delightful, small kasbah with two courtyards and only eight rooms, all soothingly decorated in terracotta and two-colour *zellij*, and with nice attention to details, including old doors, Berber rugs and wrought-iron fittings. Great value for money (including reductions for children) and repeatedly recommended by readers.

Kasbah Tomboctou (☎ 035 577091; fax 035 578449; www.xaluca.com; s/d/tr/ste half board per person Dh475/355/355; ❄) A big, noisy, popular place in an excellent location at the foot of the dunes, with very friendly management and lots of excursions on offer. Rooms are large, well equipped and decorated in *tadelakt*: communal facilities are spotless and the family, who also run the Xaluca Maadad in Erfoud, is contagiously friendly. Currently in the process of expanding to include more rooms and a hammam.

Dar el Janoub (☎ /fax 035 577852; www.darel janoub.com; s/d/tr with bathroom incl breakfast per person Dh580/480/380; ☒ ☎) Hassi Labied's smartest auberge has 17 pastel-painted rooms and four suites, all fully equipped. The pool could be a major deciding factor if you are visiting in the heat.

Auberge Camping Sahara (☎ 035 577039; s half board Dh110, d/tr/ste half board with bathroom Dh140/170/250; terrace/camping per person Dh20) Basic but spotless rooms and Turkish toilets in a friendly Tuareg-run place backing right onto the dunes at the southernmost end of the village. The auberge organises excursions and will even help you buy your complete Tuareg outfit in the market.

Auberge Camping l'Oasis (☎ /fax 035 577321; s/d with bathroom Dh100/120) Another pleasant hotel arranged around a courtyard is l'Oasis with a good restaurant and efficient service. Simple rooms are a bit boxy; the more expensive ones come with tiled bathrooms.

Kasbah Panorama (☎ /fax 062 085573; www.kasbahpanorama.com; s/d/tr Dh160 per person half board, tents Dh25 per person) No missing this place of a dozen basic rooms as it sits on a rise above Hassi Labied on the way to Merzouga. It lives up to its name – the views are panoramic and you can see the dunes from some of the beds.

Maison Merzouga (☎ 035 577299; fax 035 578428; s/d half-board Dh360/540) Unlike places nearer the dunes, this eight-room Berber house does little more than offer you a place to eat and sleep. Like everyone else in the Merzouga area, management can arrange excursions, but what they do best is offer a friendly welcome to their village house.

MERZOUGA

Most places are south of the scruffy village.

Ksar Sania, Chez Francoise (☎ 035 577414; www.ksarsania.com; per person camping/half board in Berber tents Dh25/175, s/d/tr half board per person Dh400/300/270, luxury d per person Dh400, ste per person Dh450; ☒ ☎) This delightful and stylish French-run midrange option at the foot of the dunes has domed buildings and nicely furnished

rooms (some with air-con) all with pictures and individual bedspreads. Excellent food is served in a lovely restaurant area (set menu Dh100). A favourite.

Chez Julia (☎ 070 181360; s/d/tr Dh130/160/200) A lovely auberge in the heart of Merzouga, Chez Julia offers nine spotlessly clean, simply furnished rooms in blues and yellow. The Moroccan ladies who run the place can cook up a storm of delicious Moroccan meals (Dh100; breakfast Dh38). Very popular and fills up fast.

Auberge la Tradition (☎ 070 039244; 150 per person half board) Another would-be kasbah, this place has simple ensuite rooms in a quiet location near the Ksar Sania and the foot of the dunes.

Some of the cheapest places are grouped together,and include **Auberge Camping Africa** (d Dh80) and **Lac du Sahara** (d Dh80), with basic rooms and camping space. These places have skis, snowboards and boogie boards for use on the dunes free of charge.

NORTH OF HASSI LABIED

Auberge Kasbah Derkaoua (☎ /fax 035 577140; www.aubergederkaoua.com in French; half board per person Dh500; ☒ closed Jan some of Jun-Aug; ☒ ☎) The furthest north of the auberges (one of the first signs when coming from Rissani), Kasbah Derkaoua is a world of its own, as befits a former Sufi centre. Its walled compound is full of greenery, which shades a series of very comfortable chalets decorated in calming desert colours. It is extremely popular with families and organises some excellent excursions by camel, horse and 4WD. The food is a delicious combination of French and Moroccan and is served beneath the starlit sky if weather permits. The owner also runs a highly recommended tented camp.

Riad Maria (☎ 062 232647; fax 035 576560; www.riadmaria.com; s/d/ste half board per person Dh900/600/1400; ☒ closed 10 Jun-10 Aug) A remarkable top-end lodge in a great location, Riad Maria is run by an Italian couple. Rooms are decorated in a modern style and could be more exciting, but the facilities are worth the price, including a pool and hammam, and the Italian and Moroccan food is to die for.

Auberge Camping Yasmina (☎ 035 576783/061 351667; yasminadesert@yahoo.fr; per person half-board Dh250, Berber tents per person half-board Dh200) Set amid the drifting sand, this a good option, with a fine location at the northernmost end of the dunes. The auberge sits on the edge of a lake, which is dry most of the year but usually fills in spring, a great time for bird-watching. Rooms have ensuites, there's excellent Berber food and the possibility of camping or sleeping on the roof.

Getting There & Away
Thankfully, the sealed road now continues all the way to Merzouga and 25km beyond it to Taouz, releasing unsuspecting travellers from the clutches of *faux guides*.

Most hotels are located at least 1km off the road at the base of the dunes. However, they are all accessible by car. The *pistes* can be rough and there is a possibility, albeit remote, of getting stuck in sand, so make sure you have plenty of water for emergencies and a mobile phone.

Without your own transport you'll have to rely on grands taxis or on the minivans that run from Merzouga to Rissani and Erfoud and back. All minibuses will pick up or drop off in Hassi Labied – your auberge can make arrangements. Minivans run from Merzouga between 7.30am and 9.30am.

Grands taxis leave from Merzouga centre, opposite the Café des Dunes, heading north to Rissani (Dh12) and south to the end of the road at Taouz (Dh10).

TAOUZ
Come to Taouz if you want to know what it feels like to be at the end of the road. The only sight in this desolate village, beyond the pull of the surrounding desert with its rocks, minerals and dinosaur remains, is **Casa Taouz**, a house beyond the village. At the time of writing, it was offering tea and occasionally food, but perhaps by now also beds.

The village of Khamlia, between Merzouga and Taouz, is referred to locally as 'the village of the blacks'. Its inhabitants were originally slaves brought from south of the Sahara who have settled here. The place looks unexceptional, but is home to several Gnaoua musicians, the best known being Les Pigeons du Sable: some of their music is available on CD in Europe and they perform here on occasions, as well as at the annual Festival du Desert (see p355). Ask at their house (marked by a banner) for details.

If you have a 4WD, there are several places to stay in the desert around Taouz. Signposts along the road include their GPS locations.

The Souss, Anti Atlas & Western Sahara

سو الأطلس الصغير و الصحراء الغربيّة

Cross the High Atlas to find a very different Morocco in the south. The dramatic changes of landscape are one thing, but the Souss and the Anti Atlas regions are also the most culturally distinct region of Morocco. Fiercely independent Chleuh tribes and desert nomads make up the majority of the population. Quite notable is the absence of the hassle often inescapable further north. Here the open spaces and rugged mountains have softened the sharp edges of the people, while the inhospitable environment has nurtured a legendary hospitality.

From Agadir, principal port of the south and Morocco's premier beach resort, the coast sweeps southwest for 300km, past the Art Deco splendours of Sidi Ifni, to the tiny town of Tarfaya, just north of the Western Sahara. In between are beaches galore, stunning wild coastlines and prime bird-watching opportunities. Inland the scenery of the Anti Atlas varies from the contorted slopes of Jebel Bani and the prehistoric rock carvings of the Akka oasis to the brooding, black slopes of Jebel Sarhro and the peaceful and idyllic Ameln Valley.

Further south stretch the disputed deserts of the Western Sahara. It's a vast, desolate and lightly populated tract of hammada (stony desert), characterised by free-spirited Saharawis (desert tribes), fishing communities and industrious Moroccans, watched over by the ever-present security forces. Beyond that is the desert proper and the Mauritanian border.

HIGHLIGHTS

- Ride killer waves or eat grilled fish looking at the ocean at Morocco's top surfing spot of **Taghazout** (p377)
- Watch the sun set over surreal shipwrecks rising out of the sea on **Tarfaya beach** (p399)
- Get your boots dusty around **Tata** (p396) and explore prehistoric rock engravings
- Hang loose in **Mirleft** (p386), the coolest spot in the south with six fabulous beaches
- Lose yourself among the pink-hued rock faces and lush green *palmeraies* of the peaceful **Ameln Valley** (p393)
- Trek or drive through the foothills of the **Anti Atlas** (p382), concertinaed like *millefeuille*
- Chill out at **Villa Mandala** (p376), Aourir, and engage with like-minded travellers and local projects
- Travel to the end of the road in the **Western Sahara** (p397) along the treacherous Cape Boujdour

Aourir ★
Ameln Valley ★
Mirleft ★ ★ ★★ Tata
Anti Atlas
Tarfaya ★
★ Western Sahara

THE SOUSS, ANTI ATLAS & WESTERN SAHARA

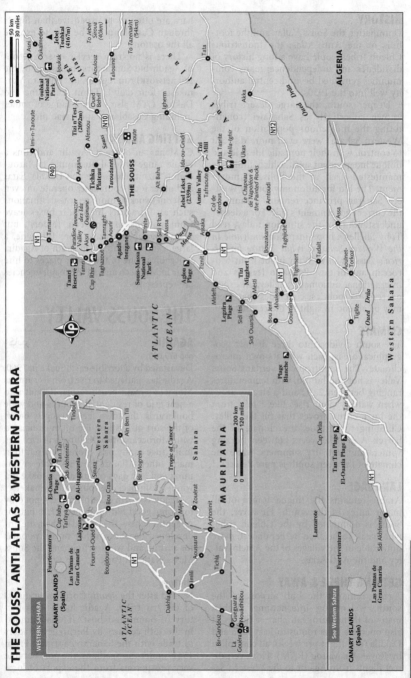

HISTORY

Dominating the Souss Valley and the foothills of the Anti Atlas, the industrious Chleuh tribespeople have a long history of dissidence and independence; many communities remained beyond central authority well into the 1930s.

Deeper south, the large desert tribes known collectively as Saharawi (constituting the indigenous population of the Western Sahara) were even more difficult to control, with their nomadic lifestyle and unique independent spirit, which ultimately manifested itself in the Polisario movement. The bid for autonomy for the Western Saharan province remains a thorn in the current government's side. For a deeper understanding of the situation today, read Toby Shelley's hope-inspiring *Endgame in the Western Sahara: What Future for Africa's Last Colony?* With input from Moroccan authorities, Polisario leaders and international diplomats, Shelley, an expert on resource politics, concludes that there may be an end in sight to the conflict.

CLIMATE

The south divides into three distinct geographical areas, each with its own microclimate. The semitropical, verdant Souss Valley is hot and humid, with temperatures ranging between 22°C and a steamy 38°C, when water vapour rises like a mist from the huge citrus groves that fill the valley. Climbing to altitude, the climate of the barren Anti Atlas veers between freezing winters and hot, dry summers, while the climate of the deep south is pure desert.

LANGUAGE

Arabic remains the lingua franca of all major cities in the south. However, the Souss is dominated by the Chleuh tribes who speak Tachelait, a Berber dialect, more noticeable in the villages of the Ameln Valley and the Anti Atlas.

GETTING THERE & AWAY

Agadir remains the hub airport of the south, welcoming international flights, many of them European charter flights. It also operates local routes to Laâyoune and Dakhla (one flight per week), all controlled by Royal Air Maroc (RAM). However, direct flights from Agadir to the Western Sa-

hara are often more expensive than flights through Casablanca, so be sure to explore all the options.

There is no train service operating out of Agadir but Supratours (buses run by the rail network) run regular, fast buses to Marrakesh (four daily), Tiznit, Laâyoune and Dakhla. CTM also offers a range of routes including Casablanca and Essaouira.

GETTING AROUND

CTM has an office in Agadir and runs a whole range of local bus routes to Taroudannt, Tiznit, Laâyoune and Dakhla. Satas and other local companies operate an even wider network to more remote destinations such as Tafraoute. In Agadir buses leave from stations in Nouveau Talborjt, but many local buses leave from Inezgane, a large transport hub 13km south of Agadir.

Agadir is one of the better places to hire a car in Morocco and all the major agencies are represented.

THE SOUSS VALLEY

AGADIR　　　　اكادير
pop 679,000

Devastated by a terrible earthquake in 1960, Agadir has managed to rise from its ruins as Morocco's main beach resort. Rebuilt into a neat grid of residential suburbs and wide boulevards, the town feels strangely bereft of the sort of bustling life often associated with Moroccan cities. Its lure, however, lies in its huge sandy bay, more sheltered than many other Atlantic beaches. Safe swimming and 300 days of sun a year make it a winner with package-tour holidaymakers.

Agadir is worth a couple of days, not only for some good old-fashioned R&R, but for its gentle sights – the ruined kasbah, the undeveloped beaches further north, popular for surfing and windsurfing, and the Souss Massa National Park.

History

Named after the *agadir* (fortified granary) of the Irir tribe, Agadir has a long history of boom and bust. It was founded in the 15th century by Portuguese traders to trade with the Saharan caravans. From 1541, under the Saadians, the port became very prosperous from the export of local sugar, cotton and saltpetre, and the products of the Saharan trade. This prosperity ended abruptly when the Alawite Sultan Sidi Mohammed diverted the trade north to Essaouira, and Agadir sank into total obscurity.

Subsequent French colonisation began to see the redevelopment of Agadir, but the devastating earthquake on 29 February 1960, which killed some 18,000 people, resulted in an apocalyptic aftermath of death and disease. Unable to disinter many of the bodies, the authorities decided to leave them and the ruined city where they had fallen. The entire town and its deceased inhabitants were buried, forming the mound now known as Old Talborjt, north of the modern city.

Since the earthquake Agadir has developed into a lucrative fishing port, with one of the largest catches of sardines in the world. It continues to grow as Morocco's top beach resort, and the development of a luxury marina complex is promising an even better economic future.

Orientation

Agadir's bus stations and most of the budget hotels are in Nouveau Talborjt (New Talborjt) in the northeast of the town. From here it's about a 15-minute walk down to Blvd du 20 Août, the main strip, which is lined with cafés, restaurants and big hotels. Most of the shops and offices, including the main post office, are along Ave du Prince Moulay Abdallah and Blvd Hassan II.

Information

BOOKSHOPS

Newsstands along Blvd Hassan II, particularly near the junction with Ave des Forces Armées Royals (FAR) have a good selection of international papers (usually a day or two late) and magazines.

Crown English Bookshop (Map p370; Immeuble A, Ave Sidi Mohammed) Just off Ave Sidi Mohammed, near the Tourist Office, this small shop sells second-hand English books as well as new books on Morocco.

EMERGENCY

Most large hotels can recommend reliable English-speaking doctors.

Ambulance (☎ 15)

Police (☎ 19; Rue du 18 Novembre)

INTERNET ACCESS

There are dozens of internet places, all charging up to Dh10 per hour.

Futurenet (Map p372; Ave du 29 Février, Talborjt; per hr Dh8).

Internet Swiss (Map p370; Blvd Hassan II; per hr Dh10; ☟ 9am-11pm) The busiest, most conveniently located cybercafé.

MEDICAL SERVICES

The Syndicat d'Initiative posts a list of doctors and pharmacies on its door.

Clinique al-Massira (Map p370; ☎ 028 843238; Ave du 29 Février)

Night Pharmacy (Map p370; ☎ 028 820349; Ave Sidi Mohammed) In the basement of the town hall, next to post office.

MONEY

Most banks have ATMs, and there are exchange booths and ATMs at the airport. Large hotels change cash and travellers cheques. These banks have exchange offices.

Banque Populaire (Map p370; Blvd Hassan II)

Wafa Bank (Map p370; Blvd Hassan II)

POST

Main post office (Map p370; Ave Sidi Mohammed; ☟ 8.30am-6.30pm Mon-Fri, 8.30am-noon Sat)

TOURIST INFORMATION

Délégation Régionale du Tourisme (ONMT; Map p370; ☎ 028 846377; fax 028 846378; Immeuble Iguenouane, Ave Mohammed V; ☟ 8.30am-noon & 2.30-6.30pm Mon-Thu, 8.30-11.30am & 3-6.30pm Fri) The best place for local and regional information.

Information booth (☎ 028 839077; Al-Massira airport; ☟ 8.30am-noon & 2.30-6.30pm).

Syndicat d'Initiative (Map p370; ☎ 028 840307; Ave Mohammed V; ☟ 9am-noon & 3-6.30pm) Useful for the list of doctors and pharmacies.

TRAVEL AGENCIES

Carlson Wagonlit (Map p370; ☎ 028 841528; 26 Ave des FAR) Represents all major airlines.

Sights

The ruined old **kasbah** (Map p370), on a hill 7km to the northwest of the town, commands good views over the port. It was built in 1540 by the Saadian Sultan Mohammed ech-Cheikh, and restored and regarrisoned in 1752 by the Alawite Sultan Moulay Abdallah, who was responsible

AGADIR

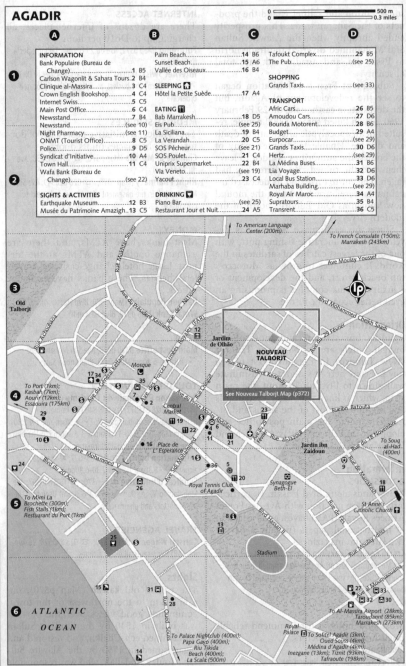

INFORMATION			Palm Beach.....................14 B6		Tafoukt Complex................25 B5
Bank Populaire (Bureau de			Sunset Beach..................15 A6		The Pub...........................(see 25)
Change).............................1 B5			Vallée des Oiseaux..........16 B4		
Carlson Wagonlit & Sahara Tours.2 B4					**SHOPPING**
Clinique al-Massira...............3 C4			**SLEEPING**		Grands Taxis...................(see 33)
Crown English Bookshop........4 C4			Hôtel la Petite Suède........17 A4		
Internet Swiss......................5 C5					**TRANSPORT**
Main Post Office...................6 C4			**EATING**		Afric Cars.........................26 B5
Newsstand...........................7 B4			Bab Marrakesh................18 D5		Amoudou Cars..................27 D6
Newsstand........................(see 10)			Eis Pub..........................(see 25)		Bourida Motorent.............28 B6
Night Pharmacy.................(see 11)			La Siciliana.....................19 B4		Budget.............................29 A4
ONMT (Tourist Office)...........8 C5			La Verandah....................20 C5		Eurpocar........................(see 29)
Police.................................9 D5			SOS Pécheur...................(see 21)		Grands Taxis.....................30 D6
Syndicat d'Initiative.............10 A4			SOS Poulet......................21 C4		Hertz.............................(see 29)
Town Hall.........................11 C4			Uniprix Supermarket..........22 B4		La Médina Buses...............31 B6
Wafa Bank (Bureau de			Via Veneto......................(see 19)		Lia Voyage.......................32 D6
Change)..........................(see 22)			Yacout...........................23 C4		Local Bus Station...............33 D6
					Marhaba Building..............(see 29)
SIGHTS & ACTIVITIES			**DRINKING**		Royal Air Maroc.................34 A4
Earthquake Museum............12 B3			Piano Bar.......................(see 25)		Supratours.......................35 B4
Musée du Patrimoine Amazigh..13 C5			Restaurant Jour et Nuit......24 A5		Transrent.........................36 C5

for the demise of Agadir as a trade depot. Abandoned to the inhabitants of Agadir, the garrison provided housing for nearly 300 people, and traces of these dwellings can still be made out.

The grassy area below the kasbah, **Ancienne Talborjt** (Map p370), covers the remains of Agadir's medina and constitutes a mass grave for all those who died in the 1960 earthquake. The walk up to the kasbah is long and hot: get a taxi up (Dh12 to Dh15) and walk back down. After a visit to the kasbah it is worth dropping in at the **port** (Map p370), where you'll find some real Moroccan atmosphere.

The small **Musée du Patrimoine Amazigh** (Map p370; Passage Aït Souss, Blvd Hassan II; admission Dh10; ☺ 9.30am-7.30pm Mon-Sat) has a good display of Berber artefacts, which explain the traditional life and culture of the Berbers of the region. Nearby is the **Vallée des Oiseaux** (Valley of the Birds; Map p370; adult/child Dh5/3; ☺ 9.30am-12.30pm & 2.30-6pm), a shaded children's playground, with an aviary and zoo, created in the dry riverbed that runs down from Blvd Hassan II south to Blvd du 20 Août.

Equally refreshing is **Jardim de Olhão** (Map p370; Ave du Président Kennedy; admission free; ☺ 8am-6.30pm), a cool, relaxing spot that marks the twinning of Agadir with the Portuguese town of Olhão. In the southwest corner there's a small **museum** (Map p370; admission free; ☺ 9am-12.30pm & 3-7pm Tue-Sat) dedicated to the 1960 earthquake. It displays some interesting photos of old Agadir.

Four kilometres south of Agadir, Coco Polizzi, an Italian architect born in Rabat, has created the **La Médina d'Agadir** (☎ 028 280253; www.medinapolizzi.com in French; Aghroud Ben Sergao; adult/child Dh40/20; ☺ 8.30am-6.30pm), an idealised Berber village, built using traditional techniques and materials, with workshops for 30 independent artisans. A café-restaurant provides refreshments. Shuttle buses (adult/child Dh60/30) come out here from the kiosk on Agadir's Blvd du 20 Août, calling at several hotels on the way.

Activities

THE BEACH

The glory of Agadir is its crescent **beach**, which usually remains unruffled when the Atlantic winds are blustering elsewhere. It's very clean and during peak periods (June to September) is patrolled by lifeguards (there is a strong undertow) and police.

The beach is mostly hassle-free, but single females or families will have a more relaxed time at one of the private beaches (Dh20 for a deckchair and umbrella) such as **Sunset Beach** or **Palm Beach** (Map p370) – which also has showers, toilets and a kids' play area.

Most of the larger hotels, and surf clubs on the beach, rent out windsurfing equipment (Dh120 per hour), jet skis (Dh300 for 20 minutes), bodyboards (Dh60 per hour) and surfboards (Dh120 per hour).

HAMMAMS

There are a few hammams in Nouveau Talborjt, including **Hammam Salam** (Map p372; 12 Rue de Tarfaya; from Dh10) and very spruce, women-only **Hammam Talborjt** (Map p372; Rue de Tarfaya; from Dh10) just south of Ave du Président Kennedy.

Many big hotels have more luxurious hammams where you can pamper yourself from Dh80.

Sleeping

High season in Agadir constitutes Easter (March to April), summer and the Christmas period, when European holidaymakers fly out on package tours. During these months get into town early in the day (or book ahead) to be sure of a room. Midrange and top-end hotels offer substantial discounts during low season, but prices for budget hotels remain pretty much constant throughout the year.

BUDGET

Most of the budget hotels are in Nouveau Talborjt. The all-night bus activity and prostitution ensures that most hotel receptions here are open 24 hours so, if you've already booked a room, don't worry about arriving late.

Hôtel Tiznine (Map p372; ☎ 028 843925; 3 Rue Drarga; s/d Dh90/120, with shower Dh120/150) Exceptionally clean and tidy hostel with 12 immaculate rooms, arranged around a green-and-white tiled courtyard with geraniums. The showers and toilets are spotless, and the manager speaks good English.

Hôtel Diaf (Map p372; ☎ 028 825851, 061 200719; Rue Allal ben Abdallah; s with/without bathroom Dh100/70, d with/without bathroom Dh130/100) Comfortable budget option with clean rooms, some with ensuite bathrooms.

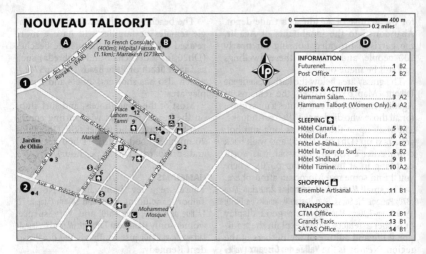

Hôtel Canaria (Map p372; ☎ 028 846727; Place Lahcen Tamri; s/d Dh80/100) One of the better crash pads near the bus offices, overlooking the same pleasant square as the midrange el-Bahia. The rooms are a notch above basic, with pine furniture and potted plants around the upstairs courtyard.

MIDRANGE
Hôtel La Tour du Sud (Map p372; ☎ 028 822694; Ave du Président Kennedy; s/d Dh189/225) Formerly the Hotel de Paris, this two-star hotel is a good option with bright and clean ensuite rooms in traditional style, gathered around two courtyards shaded by ficus trees.

Hôtel La Petite Suède (Map p370; ☎ 028 840779; fax 028 840057; cnr Blvd Hassan II & Ave du Général Kettani; s/d/tr Dh160/244/333) Simple but perfectly located hotel, five minutes' walk from the beach, with very good and friendly service. The street-side rooms have large balconies, but the inside rooms are quieter.

Hôtel el-Bahia (Map p372; ☎ 028 823954, fax 028 824515; Rue el-Mehdi ben Toumert; s/d Dh130/160, with bathroom & terrace Dh207/237) This is a good choice in Nouveau Talborjt, with friendly management and 27 attractively modernised rooms equipped with a phone and satellite TV.

Hôtel Sindibad (Map p372; ☎ 028 823477; fax 028 842474; Place Lahcen Tamri; d Dh283-308; ☒) Popular midrange option, with smart rooms, all with TV, phone and a tiny balcony overlooking the square. It also has a bar, restaurant, money-changing facilities (cash only), a small rooftop pool and sun terraces.

TOP END
Most luxury hotels along the seafront cater to package tours, but most of them offer deals on their published rates, so be sure to ask.

Riu Tikida Beach (☎ 028 845400; resabeach@tikidahotels.co.ma; Chemins des Dunes; s/d from Dh1125/1600; ☒ ☐ ☒) Simply the best of the beach hotels with a tasteful low-rise building sitting amid landscaped gardens with direct beach access. Rooms are set around internal courtyards, and there is a thalassotherapy spa on site and Agadir's most popular nightclub.

Sofitel Agadir (Map p370; ☎ 037 262727; www.sofitel.com; Baie des Palmiers, Ben Sergao; s/d from Dh750/900; ☒ ☒) Luxurious hotel, built like a low-rise kasbah with 240 rooms, an excellent thalassotherapy spa, a hammam, several swimming pools and restaurants, as well as night-time entertainment. Good value.

Eating
Agadir is packed with eating places, but most tend to stop serving food by 10pm, though some stay open later for drinks.

RESTAURANTS
La Scala (☎ 028 846773; Rue du Oued Souss; meal with wine Dh350) Excellent Moroccan restaurant, popular with wealthy Moroccans, Arab tourists and Westerners, which makes for a pleasantly cosmopolitan atmosphere. The food is elegant and fresh, and beautifully presented. Book ahead.

Bab Marrakesh (Map p370; ☎ 028 826144; Rue de Massa; tajine for 2 Dh90, couscous Dh60, sandwich Dh25-35) Near Souq al-Had, this is the real thing, far removed from the tourist traps near the beach. Highly regarded by locals, it serves authentic Moroccan food at authentic prices.

Mimi La Brochette (☎ 028 840387; Rue de la Plage; mains Dh70-95) Up at the north end of the beach, Mimi's kitchen reflects her mixed origins – Jewish, French and Spanish – and the cooking is a treat. The menu features everything from brochettes and pasta to smoked eel and ducks' gizzards – they go down a treat with raspberry sauce. There's great music here, too.

Restaurant Du Port (Yacht Club) (☎ 028 843708; meal Dh200) Excellent fish restaurant inside the fishing port. Enter the port, after the harbour police office take the first street to the right, and then immediately left – take a passport just in case!

Via Veneto (Map p370; ☎ 028 841467; Blvd Hassan II; mains Dh90) Small, intimate trattoria that serves the best Italian fare in town, including excellent pizzas baked in a wood oven and a great selection of fish.

La Siciliana (Map p370; ☎ 028 820973; Blvd Hassan II; pizzas around Dh50) A bustling little trattoria, this hits the spot with a long list of good wood-fired pizzas.

CAFÉS

There are plenty of cafés where you can relax from the rigours of Agadir beach life or ease into the day with coffee and pastries.

Yacout (Map p370; Ave du 29 Février) With its shaded garden and delicious Moroccan-Western pastries, Yacout wins hands down as *the* breakfast spot. Later in the day it serves sandwiches, Moroccan sweets and ice-cream cakes to die for.

La Verandah (Map p370; Blvd Hassan II) Opposite the Royal Tennis Club, and very popular with Agadir's smart set, this Parisian-style café has a seductive array of sweet and savoury treats.

Eis Pub (Map p370; Centre Commercial Tafoukt, Blvd du 20 Août; ice cream Dh20-55) Creates concoctions wicked enough to satisfy the most discerning ice-cream connoisseur.

QUICK EATS

The cheap snack bars in Nouveau Talborjt and around the bus stations are open after

hours. **SOS Poulet** and **SOS Pecheur** (Map p370; Ave du Prince Moulay Abdallah), serve tasty rotisserie chickens (half chicken Dh60) and fried fish (Dh30 to Dh40).

For ultra-fresh fish, head to the port, where the dozens of **fish stalls** (Map p370; meals around Dh50) offer the most lively lunch in town, or try a superb fish tajine (Dh15) at the stalls at Souq al-Had.

SELF-CATERING

The large **Uniprix supermarket** (Map p370; Blvd Hassan II) sells everything from cheese and biscuits to beer, wine and spirits. At the **Souq al-Had** (☼ Tue-Sun), you can buy fresh fruit and veg from the Souss Valley. It's liveliest on Saturday and Sunday.

Drinking

Sunset Beach and Palm Beach have good beach cafés, and the latter stays open till 1am in summer. The majority of bars have happy hours between about 5pm and 8pm each night, or offer karaoke or crooning entertainers – the standards are often questionable.

To get in the mood, watch the sunset at the popular beachfront **Restaurant Jour et Nuit** (Map p370; ☎ 028 840610; Rue de la Plage; ☼ 24hr), which gets seedy as the night wears on, or try **Piano Bar** (Map p370; Tafoukt Complex; Blvd du 20 Août), with a real pianist under the palm trees and some of Agadir's cheapest beers. In the same complex is also the Irish bar, The Pub.

Entertainment

Agadir has a decent range of clubs, mostly scattered along Blvd du 20 Août, or attached to the big hotels.

As the bars start to close around 1am, Moroccans and tourists move to the hotel discos. Entry ranges from Dh50 to Dh150 during weekends, including a drink. During the low season, tourists are often allowed in free of charge and clubs close around 2am.

Papa Gayo (Map p370; Riu Tikida Beach; Chemins des Dunes; admission Dh120; ☼ 10pm-4am) Agadir's most popular nightclub and well regarded even in fairly respectable Moroccan circles. Dance the night away and chill on the beach.

Palace (Dorint Atlantic Palace; Chemins des Dunes; admission Dh150; ☼ 11pm-5am) Ultra-cool – and rich – Moroccans and Saudis on holiday strut their stuff at the Palace – it gets going around 3am.

Shopping

Most of the souvenirs on offer in Agadir are trucked in from other parts of the country and tend to be of low quality. **Uniprix supermarket** (Map p370; Blvd Hassan II) sells handicrafts at fixed prices. For some Moroccan atmosphere head to **Souq al-Had** (☉ Tue-Sun) in the southeastern suburbs, with souvenirs, household goods and a second-hand items area outside the western gate. Better-quality crafts are available at the **Ensemble Artisanal** (Map p372; Ave du 29 Février; ☉ 9am-1pm & 3-7pm Mon-Sat).

Getting There & Away

AIR

Al-Massira Airport (Map p370; ☎ 028 839122), 28km southeast of Agadir, is the destination for many European charter flights. British Airways (www.ba.com) has one flight a week to Agadir from London Gatwick. There are banks with exchange booths and ATMs, car-hire offices, a tourist information office and a couple of restaurants.

Royal Air Maroc (RAM; Map p370; ☎ 028 840793; www.royalairmaroc.com; Ave du Général Kettani) has daily flights to Casablanca and Paris, as well as weekly services to Dakhla, Marrakesh and several European capitals.

Regional Air Lines (☎ 028 839339) operates daily services to Casablanca and Las Palmas in the Canary Islands, and flies to Laâyoune on weekdays (1¾ hours) and Dakhla on Thursday only (1¾ hours).

BUS

Although a good number of buses serve Agadir, it is quite possible you'll end up in the nearby transport hub of the region, Inezgane (13km south) – check before you buy your ticket. Plenty of grands taxis (Dh5) and local buses (Dh3) take you from there to Agadir or back.

For the moment buses stop at their respective company offices along Rue Yacoub el-Mansour in Nouveau Talborjt, but they will all move to the new *gare routière* (main bus station) on Rue Chair al-Hamra Mohammed ben Brahim, past the Souq el-Had, once it is finished.

CTM (Map p372; ☎ 028 822077) has buses to Casablanca (Dh160, nine hours, six daily).

The 10.30pm continues to Rabat (Dh175, 10 hours, two daily). There are also departures for Marrakesh (Dh70, four hours, seven daily), Essaouira (Dh50, four hours, one daily), Safi (Dh80, six hours, one daily) and El-Jadida (Dh110, nine hours, one daily).

Satas (Map p372; ☎ 028 842470) and other smaller companies have buses serving the same destinations.

Supratours (Map p370; ☎ 028 841207; 10 Rue des Orangiers) has fast services to Marrakesh train station (Dh80, four hours, several daily), Tiznit (Dh25, four hours, one daily), Laâyoune (Dh200, 11 hours) and Dakhla (Dh330, 21 hours). It's a good idea to buy your ticket in advance.

CAR & MOTORCYCLE

Some very good deals on car and motorcycle hire are to be found in Agadir. It is worth checking out the local agencies along Blvd Hassan II, where prices start at around Dh300 per day for the smallest car, but there's always room for haggling. Immeuble Marhaba, at the west end of Ave Mohammed V, has numerous rental offices.

Afric Cars (Map p370; ☎ 028 40922; Ave Mohammed V)
Amoudou (Map p370; ☎ 028 848222; cnr Blvd Hassan II & Ave El-Moqaouama)
Avis (Map p370; ☎ airport 028 839244, office 028 841755; www.avis.com; Ave Hassan II)
Budget (Map p370; ☎ airport 028 839101, office 028 848222; www.budget.com; Immeuble Marhaba, Ave Mohammed V)
Hertz (Map p370; ☎ airport 028 839071, office 028 840939; www.hertz.com; Immeuble Marhaba, Ave Mohammed V)

You'll find scooters for rent at **Bourida Motorent** (Map p370; ☎ 061 719437; Blvd du 20 Août) and at **Transrent** (Map p370; ☎ 028 843378; Blvd Hassan II), which also rents out motorcycles; scooters cost from Dh50/200 per hour/day and motorcycles from Dh300 per day.

TAXI

The main grand taxi rank is located at the south end of Rue de Fès. There is a smaller grand taxi rank on Rue Yacoub el-Mansour in Nouveau Talborjt. The most frequent destinations are Inezgane (Dh5), Taroudannt (Dh32), Essaouira (Dh70) and Marrakesh (Dh90).

Getting Around

TO/FROM THE AIRPORT

A comfortable shuttle bus connects the airport with the city. Tickets can be bought at the airport or at **Lia Voyage** (☎ 028 822139; www .almassirabus.com; Blvd Hassan II; adult/child Dh60/30). Nine buses depart from the airport between 8.30am and 12.30am, and there are six buses a day from Hotel Sahara on Ave Mohammed V between 4.30am and 4.30pm. Otherwise take a grand taxi between the airport and Agadir, which costs Dh200 during the day/ night and takes up to six people.

Bus 22 leaves from outside the airport (about 500m straight out on the road) to Inezgane (Dh5) every 40 minutes or so until about 8.30pm. In Inezgane you can change to bus 20, 24 or 28 for Agadir (Dh3), or take a grand taxi (Dh5).

BUS

The main local bus station is next to the grand taxi rank at the southern end of town. Buses 5 and 6 run every 10 minutes or so to Inezgane (Dh3). Ratag buses 12 and 14 go to Taghazout (Dh5).

TAXI

Orange petits taxis run around town. Prices are worked out by meter, so ask for it to be switched on.

AROUND AGADIR

Inezgane   إنزكان

One of the biggest transport hubs for the whole region, Inezgane is 13km south of Agadir. It's not a tourist destination at all, but some travellers enjoy stopping off here for that very reason. There's a vast fresh-produce market across from the combined bus station and grand taxi lot – Tuesday is the main souq day.

Should you need to stay overnight, there's a clutch of cheap hotels around the bus station.

Hôtel Louz (☎ 028 331990; fax 028 331842; Ave Mokhtar Soussi; s/d Dh80/130, with shower Dh120/160) Cheerful, modern rooms, if a bit boxy, with bathroom and small salons. It also has a TV lounge and a restaurant.

Hôtel-Restaurant La Pergola (☎ 028 271803; lapergola@menara.ma; Km 8 Rte d'Agadir; s/d Dh194/226) Comfortable bungalows set in a garden full of flowers. The restaurant (breakfast Dh24; set menu Dh115) is old-fashioned French

with some Moroccan specialities, all very comforting after a long bus journey.

You'll also find dozens of cheap cafés and restaurants around the main square and outside the market.

There are plenty of buses going in all possible directions. The bus station is just off the Agadir–Tiznit road. The CTM and Supratours offices are on either side of Ave Mokhtar Soussi.

Loads of grands taxis to Essaouira (Dh50, three hours), Tiznit (Dh20, two hours) and Taroudannt (Dh20, 2½ hours) also gather here, as well as less regular taxis for Goulmime (Dh50, 4½ hours) and Tan Tan (Dh90, six hours).

Adding to the organised chaos are regular local buses (Dh3) and grands taxis (Dh5) to Agadir and Al-Massira airport (bus 22).

SOUSS-MASSA NATIONAL PARK   منتزه سو ماسه الوطني

Souss-Massa is Morocco's most important national park. Stretching south from Agadir for 70km off the main highway, it has a spectacular and wild landscape, made up of cliffs, sand dunes, farmland, coastal steppes and forests. The park is very popular with bird-watchers, but it is also a great place for walking. The best times to visit are March to April, and October to November.

During the winter, ospreys and large flocks of pochard and other ducks are commonly seen, as well as greater flamingos, but the biggest attraction is the population of bald ibises. These birds, revered in ancient Egypt and once widespread in Central Europe, North Africa and the Middle East, are now an endangered species. At Souss-Massa there are four vital breeding colonies with 85 closely monitored pairs. The breeding grounds are off limits, but you can spot the ibises around Oued Massa or at the mouth of the Tamri river (see p377).

Among the species of mammal present are the jackal, red fox, wild cat, genet and Eurasian wild boar. A large fenced area in the north of the park contains species that have now disappeared from the south like Dorcas gazelles, addaxes, red-necked ostriches and scimitar horned oryxes. The **Souss-Massa National Park headquarters** (☎ 028 333880) are at Oued Souss, 800m off the main Agadir–Inezgane highway, past Golf des Dunes.

THE SOUSS, ANTI ATLAS & WESTERN SAHARA

Oued Massa   لويد مصا

Some 58km south of Agadir there's a second entrance to the park near the village of Massa, signposted from the main highway. Properly trained guides (Dh100 to Dh150), as well as donkey rides for kids, can be booked at the forestry warden's office beside the car park. A track leads along the river to the estuary mouth (3km) and the village of Sidi R'bat.

Some of the species to be seen in the vast reed beds of the Oued Massa include the black-bellied sandgrouse, bald and glossy ibis, marbled duck, crane, little crake, warbler, black-headed bush shrike, brown-throated sand martin, flamingo and even Bonelli's eagle. Note that it is forbidden to leave the track.

The tiny village of Sidi R'bat has two claims to fame. Supposedly this is where the biblical Jonah was vomited up by a whale, and also where Uqba bin Nafi, the first Arab conqueror of Morocco (in the 7th century), rode his horse triumphantly into the sea. Spectacularly located right on the gorgeous beach and in the middle of the park is **Ksar Massa** (☎ 061 280319; www.ksarmassa.com; Sidi R'bat, Oued Massa; s/d incl breakfast Dh1120/1440, full board per person Dh1170; 🍴 🖭). This wonderful guesthouse, with bright colour washes and luxuriously spacious rooms and suites, is the perfect place to unwind completely. Management can also arrange guided trips into the park, and in summer you can sleep in a tent for four people (Dh500 per person, including breakfast). To get there follow the signposts from Massa.

Getting There & Away

From Agadir, 4WD tours head into the park, but both Oued Massa and Oued Souss are perfectly accessible by 2WD (or grand taxi). The Gab bus 17 runs from Inezgane to Massa (Dh10) every 30 minutes or so, from where it is about an hour's walk to Oued Massa and the park headquarters. For Oued Souss and the park headquarters, take bus 40 from any bus stop on Ave Mohamed V in Agadir.

NORTH OF AGADIR

Most of the beaches closer to Agadir have been colonised by Europeans who have built their winter villas here. King Fahd

of Saudi Arabia has a palace here and funded the building of the road along this stretch.

If you're looking for surf and less crowded beaches, then head further north, where there are beautiful sandy coves every few kilometres.

Local bus 12 from Agadir bus station (with a stop outside the Sheraton) runs up the coast to Taghazout (Dh5) and beyond. The daily buses between Essaouira and Agadir also stop here.

Aourir & Tamraght   طمرات و اورير

Known collectively as Banana Village because of the large banana groves that surround them, Aourir and Tamraght lie some 12km and 15km north of Agadir, respectively. They share Banana Beach, a good beach for beginning surfers.

Hôtel Littoral (☎ 028 314726; fax 048 314357; s/d incl breakfast Dh205/300) is on the main road in Aourir and has 20 spacious and airy rooms

---

AUTHOR'S CHOICE

Villa Mandala (☎ 028 314773; www.villa -mandala.com; Aourir; d incl breakfast Dh690) Despite its unprepossessing location, close to the town of Aourir, Villa Mandala is a haven of convivial company and inspiring community projects.

Having established the villa in 1999 with the aim of helping women travel safely in Morocco, the tireless Regina Tongola, originally a Swiss body therapist, has turned her enthusiasm to some grass-roots projects. She has set up a crafts commune, where Moroccan craftspeople are able to practise, preserve and develop their skills alongside interested European artisans.

The villa on the beach, with five airy rooms, makes a great and interesting base for travellers, both women and men, to wind down. Meals are taken communally and guests are free to wander the house, even the kitchen, where they can see how local dishes are prepared. There is an in-house hammam (Dh100), but a female staff member can also take you to the hammam in town (Dh250). The villa also organises body therapy and psychotherapy sessions. Guests are encouraged to engage with the local community and with the artists.

with immaculate bathrooms. Rooms at the back are much quieter.

In Tamraght, in the midst of numerous surf spots, is the villa of **Surf Marokko** (☎ 068 395124; www.surfmarokko.de), five minutes' walk from the beach. A week's accommodation including meals costs around Dh2600 to Dh3800. Add Dh400 to hire all the gear. **Mamy Salerno Surf Dynamic Loisir** (☎ 028 314655;fax 028 314654; Tamraght; 1hr lesson per person Dh100) is also popular with the surfing crowd, offering board rental and lessons.

Taghazout   تاغزوت

Six kilometres further on is this laid-back fishing village, once famous for its calamari and hippies – but this superb beach is now increasingly popular with surfers. The serious guys get to spots such as Killer Point, La Source and Anka Point to the north, while beginners try out the appropriately named Hash Point at the northern end of the village. The best surf is from September until May.

The beachfront villa of **Surf Maroc** (☎ 028 200368, in UK 00 44 1794 322 709; www.surfmaroc.co.uk) is run by passionate British surfers and offers the opportunity to fall asleep listening to waves breaking. Breakfast is served on a sweeping terrace from where you can check the surf. Packages including airport transfers, one week's accommodation with half board and surf guiding, start from Dh3800 per person. Equipment hire is Dh150 and a two-hour coaching session Dh230.

Otherwise, try **Résidence Amouage** (☎ 028 200006; d Dh350), with simple self-catering rooms, or the very basic **camp site** (camping per adult Dh5 plus per tent/car/camper van Dh10/5/15) overlooking the southern beach (hot showers Dh10).

There are plenty of good eateries here, many of them visited by weekending Agadiris, including the delightful **Sable d'Or**, on the main road 400m south of Taghazout with steps down to the beach, which specialises in seafood (meals around Dh150). Equally pleasant is **Panorama** (breakfast Dh18, tajine Dh40) at the south end of the beach, which does great fish. Several cheaper restaurants in the village serve simple grilled fish with salads.

Further North

To get to the more unspoiled beaches, continue northwards. You'll find a few attractive spots either side of **Cap Rhir**, a 1200m

wave-dashed promotory (easily identified by its shipwreck). The surf spot known as Boilers, a reef break, is just south of the lighthouse.

About 12km north of Cap Rhir the road turns inland to **Tamri**. The lagoon is the most reliable and easily accessible site for spotting the very rare bald ibis – there's even a Bald Ibis Café here. Other birds you may see include Audouin's gulls, Barbary falcons, Lanner falcons and passerines. For surfers, it's worth continuing another 4km north to find an excellent beach break.

IMMOUZZER DES IDA OUTANANE   ايموزار ادو اوتنان

This thoroughly recommended side trip takes you about 60km northeast of Agadir, into the High Atlas foothills. On the way you pass through the aptly named **Paradise Valley**, an oleander- and palm-lined gorge, and a popular picnic and swimming spot.

The famous cascades of Immouzzer flow most strongly between February and August – at other times they're reduced to little more than a trickle. There is a cool plunge pool and second waterfall nearby. Any villager will be glad to take you there, telling you along the way how Jimi Hendrix is responsible for the peace/love symbol carved in the rock. Immouzzer, even without water pressure, is a delightful place to hang around for a few days, and walk.

In spring the white almond blossom rules, there is a honey harvest (including a festival) in July/August, and around late November you may be lucky enough to witness the olive harvest, when villagers climb up into the trees to shake the olives from the branches. Thursday is souq day.

Sleeping & Eating

Hôtel Tifrit (☎ 028 826044; Paradise Valley; s/d with half board Dh250/390; ☷) Set right by the river, this family-run auberge is about halfway along the road to Immouzzer from the coastal turn-off. Functional rooms come with clean shared bathrooms. The hotel has a pleasant terrace on to the river, and serves good Moroccan meals.

Auberge à la Bonne Franquette (☎ 028 823191; www.labonnefranquette-maroc.com in French; half board per person from Dh350) In the village of Aksri, 15km from Immouzzer, is a surprising place to find tasty and reasonably priced French fare (meals around Dh100). There are five cosy ensuite rooms around a courtyard. From here you can work off that lunch with a walk through the palm groves.

Hôtel des Cascades (☎ 028 826016; www.cascades -hotel.com in French; s/d Dh462/572; ☒) Just east of Immouzzer, this hotel occupies a wonderful location perched high above the valley. The large rooms (the best ones are on the 3rd floor) come with a west-facing terrace or balcony. It is set amid a riotous garden and there are tennis courts and a good restaurant (set menu Dh180). A path leads down through the olive groves to the cascades and there's other excellent walking around – ask in the hotel for suggestions.

Auberge Le Panoramic (☎ 028 826041; meals Dh25-100) This pleasant restaurant serves good Moroccan food on a terrace with a great view over the waterfalls. The rooms are simple and clean (s/d half board Dh250/350).

Getting There & Away

A very unreliable local bus runs from Agadir bus station to Immouzzer (Dh20, two hours), but unfortunately it doesn't run if there are not enough people. Also, you'll have to wait until the following morning for the unreliable bus back. A better option would be to share a grand taxi (Dh25). The best day to get there is Thursday, which is market day. Many hotels and travel agencies in Agadir offer coach tours to Immouzzer.

TAROUDANNT تارودانت

pop 70,000

Hidden by magnificent red-mud walls and with the snowcapped peaks of the High Atlas beckoning beyond, Taroudannt appears a touch mysterious at first. It is, however, every inch a market town, where the produce of the rich and fertile Souss Valley is traded.

The town's souqs are well worth a browse, more laid-back than Marrakesh, but with an atmosphere of activity that is missing in Agadir. This makes it a very worthwhile day trip (it is only 80km from Agadir) and an excellent base for travellers interested in trekking up into the little-explored western High Atlas (see p434).

Some 53km east of Taroudannt is the turning for the Tizi n'Test road (see p329), one of the most spectacular and perilous passes in the country, leading you across the High Atlas and on to Marrakesh.

History

The Almoravids took Taroudannt in 1056, at the beginning of their conquest of Morocco. In the 16th century the newly emerging Saadians made it their capital for about 20 years. Later they moved on to Marrakesh, but not before the Souss Valley, in which the city stands, had been developed into the country's most important producer of sugar cane, cotton, rice and indigo – valuable items on the trans-Saharan trade routes. The Saadians constructed the old part of town and the kasbah; most of the rest dates from the 18th century.

When in 1687 the city opposed the rule of Moulay Ismail, it was thoroughly sacked and all its inhabitants massacred – only the ramparts remained.

Taroudannt was to remain a centre of intrigue and sedition against the central government well into the 20th century, and indeed played host to the Idrissid El-Hiba, a southern chief who attempted to rebel after the Treaty of Fès (which introduced French Protectorate rule) was signed in 1912.

Orientation

Unlike many southern Moroccan towns, Taroudannt was never chosen as a French administrative or military centre, so it has no 'European' quarter.

The cheaper hotels are all on or near the two central squares: Place al-Alaouyine (more often called by its former Berber name, Place Assarag) and Place an-Nasr (formerly Talmoqlate). You'll find banks, restaurants and a small post office clustered in this area.

Most of the buses and grands taxis terminate just outside the medina's southern gate, Bab Zorgane.

Information

There are three banks with ATMs on Place al-Alaouyine (Banque Populaire, BMCE and BMCI), and all have exchange facilities and accept travellers cheques. BMCE also does cash advances.

Club Roudana (Ave Bir Zaran; per hr Dh8) Internet access.

Hospital (Ave Moulay Rachid) By the kasbah.

Main post office (Rue du 20 Août) Off Ave Hassan II, to the east of the kasbah.

Night pharmacy (Ave Prince Héritier Sidi Mohammed)

Wafanet (Ave Mohammed V; per hr Dh8) Internet access.

TAROUDANNT

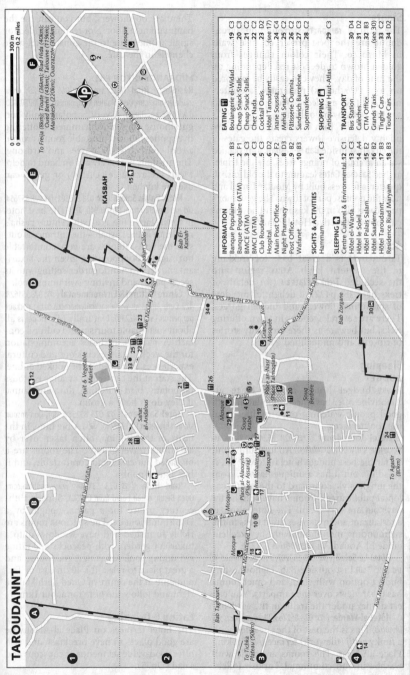

To Freija (8km); Tioute (36km); Riad Hida (40km);
Oued Berhil (43km); Taliouine (119km);
Marrakesh (220km); Ouarzazate (300km)

KASBAH

Bab El-
Kasbah

Saadian Gates

Fruit & Vegetable
Market

Sahat
al-Andalous

Souq
Arabe

Souq
Berbère

Bab Zorgane

Place al-Nasr
(Place Talmoqlate)

Ave Bir Zaran

Place al-Alaouyine
(Place Assarag)

Rue du 20 Août

Bab Zorgane

Bab Taghount

To Tichka
Plateau (50km)

To Agadir
(80km)

INFORMATION	
Banque Populaire.....................	1 B3
Banque Populaire (ATM)............	2 F1
BMCE (ATM)............................	3 C3
BMCI (ATM).............................	4 C3
Club Roudani...........................	5 C3
Hospital..................................	6 D2
Main Post Office.......................	7 F2
Night Pharmacy.......................	8 D3
Post Office..............................	9 B2
Wafanet..................................	10 B3

SIGHTS & ACTIVITIES	
Hammam.................................	11 C3

SLEEPING	
Centre Culturel & Environmental...	12 C1
Hôtel el-Warda........................	13 C3
Hôtel le Soleil..........................	14 A4
Hôtel Palais Salam....................	15 E2
Hôtel Saadiens.........................	16 B2
Hôtel Taroudannt.....................	17 B3
Residence Riad Maryam............	18 B3

EATING	
Boulangerie el-Widad................	19 C3
Cheap Snack Stalls....................	20 C3
Cheap Snack Stalls....................	21 C2
Chez Nada..............................	22 C2
Cocktail Oasis..........................	23 C2
Hôtel Taroudannt....................	(see 17)
Inane Soussia..........................	24 C4
Mehdi Snack...........................	25 C2
Pâtisserie Oumnia.....................	26 C2
Sandwich Barcelone..................	27 C2
Supermarket............................	28 C2

SHOPPING	
Antiquaire Haut-Atlas...............	29 C3

TRANSPORT	
Bus Station..............................	30 D4
Calèches.................................	31 D2
CTM Office..............................	32 B3
Grands Taxis............................	(see 30)
Tinghir Cars.............................	33 C2
Toute Cars..............................	34 D2

0   300 m
0   0.2 miles

Sights

The 5km of **ramparts** surrounding Taroudannt are the best-preserved pisé walls in Morocco. Their colour changes from golden brown to deepest red depending on the time of day. They can easily be explored on foot (1½ hours) preferably late afternoon, or take a *calèche* (see opposite) and see the walls by moonlight.

Built in the 16th and 17th century, five mighty defensive towers create the gates of the city. Just inside **Bab el-Kasbah**, approached via an avenue of orange trees, are the triple-arched **Saadian Gates** leading to the old kasbah quarter, a fortress built by Moulay Ismail and now the poorest part of town. The governor's palace was also in the kasbah and now forms part of the attractive Hôtel Palais Salam.

Activities

Taroudannt is a great base for trekking in the western High Atlas region and the secluded **Tichka Plateau** (for details of treks here see p422), a delightful meadow of springtime flowers and hidden gorges. There are several agencies in town offering treks, but beware as there are many stories of rip-offs and unqualified guides.

Sleeping

BUDGET

Most budget hotels around Place al-Alaouyine offer basic accommodation with good people-watching opportunities from the roof terraces.

Hôtel Taroudannt (☎ 028 852416; Place al-Alaouyine; s/d/tr Dh120/140/160) An institution and by far the best budget hotel in town. Yes, it is fading, but it has a unique flavour, from the jungle-style courtyard to the faintly colonial public areas. Rooms have seen better days but are very clean. The hotel also has a restaurant and organises great treks in the surrounding mountains with the excellent guide El Aouad Ali (☎ 066 637972).

Hôtel Le Soleil (☎ 028 551707; Ave Mohammed V; s/d Dh95/140) Just outside Bab Taghount, this budget option with clean and quiet rooms has great views over the ramparts. You can eat dinner under the trellis in the garden.

Hôtel el-Warda (☎ 028 852763; Place an-Nasr; s/d Dh40/60) This is the best of the cheapies, with a funky *zellij* (tilework) terrace overlooking Place an-Nasr. The rooms are basic with washbasin and communal Turkish toilets.

There are no showers, but you can use the hammam next door. Not recommended for single women due to the constant all-male clientele in the café.

MIDRANGE & TOP END

Résidence Riad Maryam (☎ 066 127285; www.riadmaryam.fr.fm; Derb Maalen Mohammed; s/d Dh250/400, d with shower Dh600) A very popular family-run guesthouse off Ave Mohammed V offering five spotless and comfortable rooms around a cool courtyard full of trees and birdsong. The gracious host is always on hand to help. Meals are available (Dh150) or guests can use the kitchen.

Hôtel Palais Salam (☎ 028 852501; fax 028 852654; s/d incl breakfast from Dh700/940; 🏊) The best hotel in town started life as a 19th-century pasha's residence in the kasbah – the entrance is outside the walls. Rooms are very comfortable but slightly disappointing given the luxuriant and very romantic garden setting with its secret patios and inviting swimming pool.

Centre Culturel & Environmental (☎ 028 551628; 422 Derb Afferdou; www.naturallymorocco.co.uk; package per person 1 wk UK£215). Naturally Morocco is all about sustainable tourism and cultural contact. A package includes accommodation for the week, meals, excursions and cultural experiences, and needs to be booked online. The staff at the centre can arrange ecotours on botany, bird-watching, flora and fauna, if they don't have a group.

Hôtel Saadiens (☎ 028 852589; Borj Oumansour; s/d incl breakfast Dh180/240; 🏊) A big hotel in the heart of the medina, often taken over by adventure travel groups. The rooms are a bit faded but clean and comfortable, and it has a great pool.

Riad Hida (☎ 028 531044; www.riadhida.com; Oued Berhil; d half board from Dh750). Superb 19th-century palace for a pasha, bought by a Danish millionaire. The spacious rooms are richly furnished and have windows onto a luxuriant garden, with peacocks and a fine swimming pool. Amazingly good value, and a great place to relax. It's 40km east of Taroudannt: at the centre of Oued Berhil take a right and follow the *piste* for about 1km.

Eating & Drinking

The hotel terraces on Place al-Alaouyine are good places to have breakfast, and also offer good-value set menus of couscous and salad (Dh75).

RESTAURANTS

Jnane Soussia (☎ 028 854980; set menu Dh75; 🌙 dinner; 🍴 🏊) Delightful restaurant, outside Bab Zorgane, with tented seating areas set around a large pool, in a garden adjacent to the ramparts. The house specialities are a mouthwatering *mechoui* (whole roast lamb) and pigeon *pastilla,* which have to be ordered in advance, but everything is good.

Chez Nada (☎ 028 851726; Ave Moulay Rachid; set menu Dh70) West of Bab al-Kasbah, this is a quiet modern place, famous for its excellent and good-value tajines. If you can, get a table on the terrace with views over the surrounding flower-filled gardens.

Hôtel Taroudannt (☎ 028 852416; 3-/4-course menus Dh70/90) This licensed hotel restaurant is good for an old-fashioned dinner. Go Moroccan or, if you've had one tajine too many, choose a French classic, but keep it simple as it can be a bit hit and miss.

QUICK EATS

The best place to look for cheap eateries is around Place an-Nasr and north along Ave Bir Zaran, where you find the usual tajine, *harira* (lentil soup) and salads.

Mehdi Snack (off Ave Moulay Rachid; set menu Dh25-45) Run by the same family, and just behind Chez Nada, this is a good snack bar with cheap burgers, salads and fried sardines.

Cocktail Oasis (3 Ave Moulay Rachid; small/large juice Dh7/10) Run by a cheerful chap surrounded by piles of fruit, which he juices into an amazing range of cocktails. Ideal for cooling down on hot sticky days.

Sandwich Barcelone (Place al-Alaouyine; sandwich with chips Dh15) Small sandwich bar serving up satisfyingly fat baguettes stuffed with *kefta* (seasoned minced lamb), chips and salad.

Boulangerie el-Widad (Ave Prince Héritier Sidi Mohammed) and **Pâtisserie Oumnia** (Ave Bir Zaran) have a wide selection of Moroccan cookies.

SELF-CATERING

Putting together a picnic is not a problem in Taroudannt – the markets are brimming with fresh produce. In addition to stalls in the souqs, there's a dedicated fruit and vegetable market at the northern end of Ave Bir Zaran. The supermarket to its southwest stocks a limited selection of yogurts and cheese.

Shopping

Taroudannt is the central Chleuh city of the Souss, so it is a good place to look for the good-quality silver jewellery for which this tribe is renowned. The jewellery is influenced by both the tribes of the Sahara and the Jews; the latter formed a significant part of the community until the late 1960s.

Bab Taghount is the easiest way into the pleasant medina. South of Place an-Nasr is the **Souq Berbère** with fresh vegetables, spices, pottery and baskets. The main souq, **Souq Arabe**, east of Place al-Alaouyine, is where you find antique and souvenir shops hidden in the quiet streets. Look out for the **Antiquaire Haut-Atlas** (☎ 028 852145; 36-37 Souq Smata, Souq Arabe), a favourite of European connoisseurs, with a huge collection of carpets, fabulous jewellery and antique pottery. This serious dealer drives a hard bargain, but the quality is amazing.

A large souq on Sunday morning, just outside Bab al-Khemis, brings in people from the whole region.

Getting There & Away

BUS

CTM (office; Hotel Les Arcades, Place al-Alaouyine) has the most reliable buses, with one departure per day for Casablanca (Dh150, 10 hours) via Marrakesh (Dh90, six hours).

Other companies run services throughout the day to both these cities as well as to Agadir (Dh20, 2½ hour), Inezgane (Dh18, 2½ hours) and Ouarzazate (Dh75, five hours). There's one bus to Tata (Dh70, five hours).

All buses leave from the main bus station outside Bab Zorgane.

CAR

Local agencies **Tinghir Cars** (☎ 028 850810; Ave Moulay Rachid Ferk Lahbab) and **Tioute Cars** (Ave Prince Héritier Sidi Mohammed) hire out small cars from Dh400 per day.

TAXI

Taroudannt's grands taxis also gather at the bus station outside Bab Zorgane. The main destinations are Inezgane, and sometimes Agadir (Dh25) and Marrakesh (Dh85).

Getting Around

You can tour the ramparts in a *calèche.* The *calèches* gather just inside Bab al-Kasbah, on Place al-Alaouyine and other prominent

TAROUDANNT-TATA-TIZNIT CIRCUIT

Driving south from Taroudannt on the 7011 you pass through the extraordinary tortured mountains of the Anti Atlas. Some 33km out of town, the road starts to wind its way out of the Souss Valley, with marvellous views back over the plain framed by the snow-capped High Atlas. Approaching the midway town of Igherm you enter a bizarre landscape of wrenched and folded mountains, the concertinaed slopes of Jebel Bani, which offer more great photo opportunities.

About 55km south of Igherm there is a turning west off-*piste* (4WD only) towards the valley of Tazegzaoute from where 4WDs can continue on to Tafraoute. The valley itself is green and secluded and great for walking. Back on the main road, you head directly south for Tata (p396) on the Saharan plains.

From Tata a sealed road, the 7084, heads west through Akka where, with a guide, you can hunt out the rock engravings. Further on at Bouzakarne you turn right on to the P30 for Tiznit.

A worthwhile side excursion (although only to be contemplated if you have time on your hands) is to Amtoudi and the 12th-century *agadir* (fortified granary) of Id-Aïssa, 37km northeast of the village of Taghjicht. The 800-year-old *agadir* is precariously perched high above the village of Amtoudi. The local caretaker will take you up on foot or by donkey, and give you an excellent guided tour; there's no fee, but a donation is appreciated.

There are no facilities in Amtoudi, but you can camp by the river nearby, or park your camper van (Dh40) in the concrete compound that passes for a camp site. If you order in advance, you can get basic meals here or in the village.

At Tiznit continue west to Aglou Plage, Mirleft or Sidi Ifni for a breath of fresh Atlantic air after this hot and dusty trip.

---

spots. A one-way trip around town costs Dh15 to Dh20, while one-hour tours are Dh50 or more depending on your bargaining skills.

TALIOUINE تالوين

The straggling village of Taliouine, halfway between Taroudannt and Ouarzazate, is dominated by the impressive Glaoui kasbah. It is disintegrating fast, but the best part of it is still inhabited by the families who are descendants of the servants of the Glaoui. A caretaker can show you around.

Taliouine is the centre for saffron, sold at the **Coopérative Souktana du Safran** (7.30am-1.30pm & 2-8pm), which has a small museum, saffron tasting and shop. Top-quality saffron here is around Dh15 per gram, cheaper from the vendors along the road. It takes about 140 to 230 flowers to produce one gram of the most expensive spice in the world.

The village comes to life during the Monday souq, behind the kasbah.

With a few nice hotels, Taliouine is becoming a popular trekking centre for the nearby **Jebel Siroua** (see p434), which offers some of the finest walking in the Anti Atlas.

The N10 road east from Taroudannt to Taliouine is less dramatic than the Tizi n'Test, but it provides a good alternative if you are heading to Ouarzazate. The road north of Taliouine crosses a beautiful and immense landscape, to join the main Marrakesh–Ouarzazate road near the turn-off to Aït Benhaddou.

Auberge Souktana (028 534075; souktana@menara.ma; s/d with shower Dh150/200, s/d bungalow Dh95/140, bed in standing tent Dh80) Wonderful family-run auberge 1km east of the village on the main road, with recently modernised rooms, four small bungalows with basin, and you can pitch your tent in the garden (Dh40). The English- and French-speaking hosts can provide a wealth of information on the region, and are excellent guides, who organise tent and mule hire for Jebel Siroua treks. Reservations strongly recommended in trekking season.

Auberge le Safran (/fax 028 534046, 068 394223; www.auberge-safran.fr.fm in French; d/q with shower Dh120/260) Slightly closer to the village centre, this is another hive of trekking activity. Simple but pretty rooms, hot water and hearty meals are available, as well as well-organised treks.

Hotel Ibn Toumerte (028 534125; fax 028 534126; s/d/ste Dh382/475/750;) Right next to the kasbah, this big modern hotel has little character but offers the most comfortable rooms in town, with great views. Meals cost Dh169.

Buses pass through Taliouine from both Ouarzazate and Taroudannt, but there are not always seats available. Your best chance is to wait at the main bus stop in town. Grands taxis head west to Oued Berhil, where you can change for Taroudannt, and east to Tazenakht (Dh20), where you can change for Ouarzazate (Dh27).

TIZNIT تزنيت

pop 53,600

In an arid corner of the Souss Valley at the end of the Anti Atlas, Tiznit is an old medina town with a modern crust. Sultan Moulay al-Hassan (1873–94) built thick walls around 12 existing kasbahs to mark Tiznit as a trade centre in the south. It remains the provincial capital, a central point between the coastal towns and the Anti Atlas, and it is the last large town before the Western Sahara.

History

In 1881 Sultan Moulay Al-Hassan chose Tiznit as a base from which to assert his authority over the rebellious Berber tribes. As in Taroudannt, Jewish silversmiths were moved into the town, establishing its reputation as a centre for silver.

However Tiznit remained embroiled in local sedition, becoming a base for the resistance against the 1912 treaty that turned Morocco into a French and Spanish protectorate. The resistance was led by El-Hiba, the 'Blue Sultan' from Mauritania, who was regarded as a saint and even credited with performing miracles.

El-Hiba proclaimed himself sultan at Tiznit's mosque in 1912, and succeeded in uniting the Tuareg and the tribes of the Anti Atlas in a vain effort to dislodge the French. Ejected from Tiznit, and at one point forced to move to Taroudannt, El-Hiba pursued a campaign of resistance against the French until his death in 1919.

Orientation

Within the medina, Place al-Méchouar is where you'll find the jewellery souq, most buses and the cheap hotels. Outside the main gate, Bab Méchouar, is the main

grand taxi rank, the main post office, banks, restaurants and a food market.

The campsite and midrange to top-end hotels can be found to the south of the medina.

Information

Banks in Tiznit include **BMCE** (Ave Mohammed V), **BMCI** (Ave du 20 Août) and **Banque Populaire** (Ave du 20 Août), all of which have ATMs.

The main **post office** (Ave du 20 Août) and a smaller branch in the medina are open the usual hours.

Sights & Activities

The sleepy medina is a fun place to wander around, as is the just-as-sleepy jewellery souq, where you can try to strike a bargain.

The minaret at the **Grande Mosquée** (Great Mosque) is reminiscent of those found in Mali. Souls of the departed supposedly use the perches sticking out of its mud walls to help them in their climb to paradise.

Nearby is the now-dry **Source Bleue**, the original town spring. Legend has it that a woman of ill repute, Lalla Zninia, stopped to rest here at what was then plain desert. She spent the next three days repenting her wicked ways and God was so impressed with her fervour that he showed forgiveness by having a spring gush beneath her feet. Her name was thus given to the village that preceded Moulay al-Hassan's 19th-century fortress town.

It's possible to climb onto sections of the 5km-long city walls, which have 29 towers and nine gates. From **Bab Targua**, for instance, you get a great view over the lush *palmeraie*, where there is another natural spring, used as a laundry by local women.

Things liven up considerably on Thursday, which is market day.

Sleeping

Many budget hotels are right on Place al-Méchouar, but lone women may find the area a bit off-putting late at night.

Hôtel des Touristes (☎ 028 862018; Place al-Méchouar; s/d Dh50/90) This place boasts immaculate rooms and a charming host, who has made this a very homely place. It is safe for women and the hot showers are free.

Hôtel Atlas (☎ 028 862060; Place al-Méchouar; s/d Dh50/90) Popular budget option with clean rooms and a laid-back atmosphere. No hot water, but a roof terrace and a good restaurant (set menu Dh100).

Hôtel Aït Maten (☎ 028 601790; 64 Place al-Méchouar; s/d/tr Dh40/60/80) This place has very simple rooms with iron bedsteads above a lively restaurant. Those at the front have washbasins and good views of the square, and that's about it.

Hôtel de Paris (☎ 028 862865; fax 601395; Ave Hassan II; s/d/tr Dh138/164/221) The pink frilly bedspreads are not to everyone's taste, but this midrange hotel offers comfortable and good-value ensuite rooms, and has one of the best restaurants in town.

Hôtel du Soleil (☎ 028 600289; fax 048 862259; Rte de Tafraoute; s/d Dh80/100) This modern hotel

has spotless, good-value rooms with ensuite bathrooms. Slightly out of town and with a very male-oriented 24-hour bar downstairs.

Hôtel Idou Tiznit (☎ 028 600333; www.idoutiznit .com in French; Ave Hassan II; s/d half board Dh475/750; 🅿 ⌨) From the grand marble lobby to the tasteful bedrooms, marble-tiled bathrooms and protected pool terrace, this is an opulent hotel for modest Tiznit, equipped with all creature comforts.

Eating

Most of the budget hotels on the main square have cafés offering food. The most popular are at Hôtel Atlas and the slightly more upmarket Hôtel de Paris.

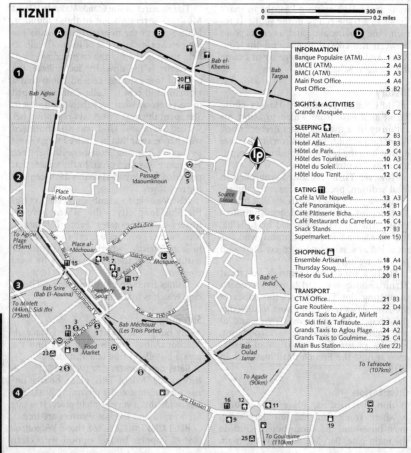

TIZNIT

INFORMATION	
Banque Populaire (ATM)	1 A3
BMCE (ATM)	2 A4
BMCI (ATM)	3 A3
Main Post Office	4 A4
Post Office	5 B2

SIGHTS & ACTIVITIES	
Grande Mosquée	6 C2

SLEEPING 🛏	
Hôtel Aït Maten	7 B3
Hotel Atlas	8 B3
Hôtel de Paris	9 C4
Hôtel des Touristes	10 A3
Hôtel du Soleil	11 C4
Hôtel Idou Tiznit	12 C4

EATING 🍴	
Café la Ville Nouvelle	13 A3
Café Panoramique	14 B1
Café Pâtisserie Bicha	15 A3
Café Restaurant du Carrefour	16 C4
Snack Stands	17 B3
Supermarket	(see 15)

SHOPPING 🛍	
Ensemble Artisanal	18 A4
Thursday Souq	19 D4
Trésor du Sud	20 B1

TRANSPORT	
CTM Office	21 B3
Gare Routière	22 D4
Grands Taxis to Agadir, Mirleft Sidi Ifni & Tafraoute	23 A4
Grands Taxis to Aglou Plage	24 A2
Grands Taxis to Goulmime	25 C4
Main Bus Station	(see 22)

BERBER JEWELLERY

The traditional assemblage of necklaces made in the southern oasis valleys is striking, with some of the more exquisite featuring talismans of silver, pink coral, amazonite, amber, Czech glass and West African ebony beads.

Berber jewellery, always made of silver (gold was considered evil), serves a much wider purpose than simple adornment: identifying clan, symbolising wealth, reflecting cultural traditions and acting as a source of supernatural and religious power to protect the wearer from the evil eye.

A woman will receive jewellery from her mother until she marries. Her future husband will commission pieces made by his mother or sister and these will be kept by her as dowry and added to throughout her life. Necklaces are important, but she will also have bracelets, *fibulas* (elaborate brooches, often triangular, used for fastening garments), anklets, earrings and headdresses. Some pieces will be worn every day, while the finest will be saved for occasions such as festivals, pilgrimages and funerals.

The protective, medicinal and magical properties of jewellery are extremely important. The necklaces contain charms bought from magicians or holy men, which offer protection against the evil eye, disease, accidents and difficulties in childbirth.

Silver is believed to cure rheumatism; coral symbolises fertility and is thought to have curative powers; amber is worn as a symbol of wealth and to protect against sorcery (it's also considered an aphrodisiac and a cure for colds); amazonite and carnelian stones are used in divining fortunes; and shells traded from East Africa symbolise fertility.

Talismans feature stylised motifs of animals, sun, moon and stars, all of which are believed to have supernatural powers. A common symbol to ward off the evil eye is the hand of Fatima, the daughter of the prophet Mohammed. Any depiction of the hand (which represents human creative power and dominance) or of the number five is believed to have the same effect as metaphorically poking fingers into the evil eye with the words *khamsa fi ainek* (five in your eye).

A number of snack stands along Rue Bain Maure offer acceptable sandwiches for around Dh10.

Café Restaurant du Carrefour (Ave Hassan II; set menu Dh80; ⚅) This modern and rather stylish little place offers well prepared Moroccan dishes, salads and grills. Excellent fresh juices and delicious breakfasts, including bread dipped in *hambou* (grilled almonds crushed with argan oil). Ideal for hot, sticky days, it has a chilled drinking water fountain and air-con.

Café Panoramique (27 Bab el-Khemis; tajines Dh50-60) Lively café-restaurant decorated with *zellij* tiles. The roof terrace is pleasant for evening tea and looks over Bab el-Khemis and the old farms beyond.

Café La Ville Nouvelle (Ave du 20 Août; mains Dh25-55) The attractive restaurant serves the classic salads, brochettes and couscous, while the popular downstairs café is the best place for coffee and patisseries.

If you want food for a picnic, head for the **market** (Ave du 20 Août), or the supermarket next to Café Pâtisserie Bicha, which sells cheese and imported goodies.

Shopping

With its long history of silversmiths, the jewellery souq is reputed to have some of the best stuff in the south. Jewellery is made in Tiznit, but also bought to be traded for tribal jewellery in the Saharan regions further south. Get an idea of the prevailing prices before you buy and be prepared to bargain.

A good port of call is **Trésor du Sud** (☎ 028 862885; 27 Bab al-Khemis), which only deals in hallmarked solid silver. You can see a craftsman at work here and browse through the neatly laid out stock.

The **Ensemble Artisanal** (Ave du 20 Août; ⊗ 8.30am-1pm & 2.30-8.30pm), opposite the main post office, covers the full range of local crafts.

Getting There & Away

BUS

All buses leave from the main bus station just off the Tafraoute road, past the Thursday souq. CTM tickets are also available from the CTM office in town. CTM has buses for Agadir (Dh26, two hours, two daily),

Casablanca (Dh161, 10 hours, two daily), Marrakesh (Dh96, five hours, one daily) and Tan Tan (Dh64, five hours, 3 daily).

Other companies run daily buses to the above destinations plus Sidi Ifni (Dh20, 1½ hours), Tafraoute (Dh25, three hours) and Tata (Dh70, 6½ hours).

TAXI

Grands taxis to Sidi Ifni (Dh20), Mirleft (Dh13), Agadir (Dh23) and occasionally Tafraoute (Dh35) leave from the main grand taxi rank, opposite the post office in the western part of town.

Goulmime-bound grands taxis (Dh30) wait at a stand just south of the Hôtel Idou Tiznit roundabout. For Aglou Plage (Dh5) they leave from a junction on Ave Hassan II.

AROUND TIZNIT
Aglou Plage   اكلو بلاج

Aglou Plage, 15km from Tiznit, is a long, deserted beach with good surf, but the strong undertow makes it dangerous for swimming most of the time. When Atlantic winds start blustering, it's a wild and woolly sort of place. It is a great place to escape from Tiznit, for a long walk and an excellent lunch at **Hotel Aglou Beach** (☎ 028 866196; Aglou beach@hotmail.com; set menu Dh120), which also makes for a comfortable night's stay (s/d Dh177/250, sea view supplement Dh60).

Grands taxis come out here from Tiznit (Dh5).

MIRLEFT   ميرلفت
pop 6500

An exceptionally picturesque coast road connects Aglou Plage with Mirleft, 40km southwest of Tiznit. Popular with artists, musicians and backpackers returning from some serious desert bashing, Mirleft with its totally undeveloped beach and sandy main street (with post office but no bank) is the perfect place to chill out.

If at first the place seems uninspiring, the gentle bustle soon becomes contagious. A social morning coffee is followed by a trip to the beach – choose from Fish Beach, Camping Beach, Coquillage Beach, Aftas Beach, Plage Sauvage and Marabout's Beach, the last being the most dramatic with its *marabout's* (saint's) tomb and savage-looking

rocks. And as if that is not enough, Mirleft is blessed with several blissful little hotels, by far the best accommodation along this stretch of coast, that organise all sort of activities from surf and fishing trips to desert excursions.

Hôtel Resto Abertih (☎ 028 710304, 072 225872; www.abertih.com; d without bathroom Dh200-240, with bathroom Dh260-300) The gorgeous blue and yellow cubist guesthouse has 11 simple beach-style rooms and an atmospheric bar and restaurant. The proprietor is happy to help organise fishing trips (Dh50 to Dh100), surfing or paragliding.

Hôtel Atlas (☎ 028 719309; www.atlas-mirleft .com in French; s/d incl breakfast Dh150/180, with shower Dh180/260; 🖳) In the same vein is Hotel Atlas, with a great 1st-floor street-side balcony – fantastic in the early evenings. Vibrant aquamarines, yellows, terracottas and blues splash colour throughout the 17 rooms. There is also a huge roof terrace with sofas and cushions for summertime barbecues and music. Set-menu meals are Dh100. The hotel organises surf classes (from Dh100), fishing trips (Dh50 to Dh100) and desert trips by 4WD (from Dh600).

Les 3 Chameaux (☎ 028 719187; www.3chameaux .com; d/ste half board Dh600/1200; 🐾) High on the hill in a renovated military fort, this is a lovely guesthouse with fabulous views over the village to the sea beyond. Whitewashed wood and terracotta urns make for subdued and relaxed surroundings.

Apart from the excellent restaurants at the above hotels, a number of cafés on the main street serve up some of the tonnes of fresh fish that end up here.

Local buses and grands taxis between Tiznit and Sidi Ifni stop in Mirleft.

SIDI IFNI   سيدي إفني
pop 20,600

The eerily empty outpost of Sidi Ifni, with its fabulous decaying Spanish Art Deco architecture, often shrouded in Atlantic mists in July and August, is a haunting reminder of Spanish imperial ambitions. At the heart of what was the Spanish Sahara, Sidi Ifni was once a base for slave-trading operations and later a large exporter of fish to the Spanish mainland.

Returned to Moroccan control in 1969, the splendid esplanade and *calles* (streets) feel as if the Spanish didn't leave that long

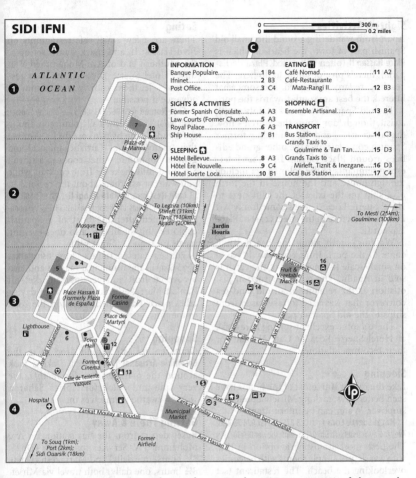

SIDI IFNI

0 ———————— 300 m
0 ———————— 0.2 miles

INFORMATION		EATING 🍴	
Banque Populaire.....................1 B4		Café Nomad............................11 A2	
Ifninet...................................2 B3		Café-Restaurante	
Post Office.............................3 C4		Mata-Rangi II.....................12 B3	
SIGHTS & ACTIVITIES		SHOPPING 🛍	
Former Spanish Consulate...........4 A3		Ensemble Artisanal..................13 B4	
Law Courts (Former Church).......5 A3			
Royal Palace...........................6 A3		TRANSPORT	
Ship House.............................7 B1		Bus Station............................14 C3	
		Grands Taxis to	
SLEEPING 🛏		Goulmime & Tan Tan...........15 D3	
Hôtel Bellevue........................8 A3		Grands Taxis to	
Hôtel Ère Nouvelle...................9 C4		Mirleft, Tiznit & Inezgane.....16 D3	
Hôtel Suerte Loca...................10 B1		Local Bus Station....................17 C4	

ATLANTIC OCEAN

Plaza de la Marina

To Legzira (10km);
Mirleft (31km);
Tiznit (110km);
Agadir (200km)

To Mesti (25km);
Goulmime (100km)

Mosque

Jardin Houria

Zankat Marrakesh
Fruit & Vegetable Market

Place Hassan II
(Formerly Plaza de España)

Former Casino

Place des Martyrs

Lighthouse

Town Hall

Former Cinema

Calle de Teniente Vazquez

Hospital

Zankat Moulay al-Boudali

Municipal Market

Former Airfield

Calle de Gomara

Calle de Oviedo

Ave Sidi Mohammed ben Abdallah

Ave Hassan II

Zankat Moulay Ismail

To Souq (1km);
Port (2km);
Sidi Ouarsik (18km)

---

ago. However, the town's unhurried pace of life attracts a surprising number of visitors, and is becoming an increasingly popular base for surfing and paragliding.

History

After the Spanish-Moroccan war of 1859, which Morocco lost, Spain obtained the enclave of Sidi Ifni (which they christened Santa Cruz del Mar Pequeña) by treaty. Quite what they were going to do with it seems to have been a question in a lot of Spanish minds, because they did not take full possession until 1934. In fact, most of Sidi Ifni dates from the 1930s and features an eclectic mix of faded Art Deco and traditional Moroccan styles.

By the 1950s some 60% of the town's population was Spanish, but under pressure from the UN, Spain agreed to cede the enclave back to Morocco in 1969. Ifni still celebrates 'Independence Day' (30 June) with a 10-day festival held on the abandoned airfield.

Information

Sidi Ifni has just one bank, **Banque Populaire** (Ave Mohammed V) with a currency exchange and ATM. The nearby **post office** (Ave Mohammed V) still has a letter box outside marked 'Correos'. Internet is available at **Ifninet** (Ave Hassan II; per hr Dh8), just off Place Hassan II. For information on the town, check out the website: www .geocities.com/ifnirocks.

Sights & Activities

Apart from wandering around the small old Spanish part of town, the heart of which is **Place Hassan II** (often still called Plaza de España), there's precious little to do here. The beaches are largely deserted, and somewhat littered; the best are south towards the port.

The old Spanish town is certainly worth a visit, though: don't miss the church – now the law courts – and the crumbling former Spanish consulate, nor the other grand edifices around Place Hassan II. Other interesting remnants of the colonial era include the lighthouse and the house in the form of a ship on the edge of the cliff next to Hôtel Suerte Loca. There's some funky Art Deco architecture in the streets east of Place Hassan II.

Walking south along the beach you'll come to the port. Ifni's economy is based on small-scale fishing; most of the catch is sold in Agadir. The odd construction just offshore is the remains of an old land-sea conveyor that was used to take cargo from ships to the old Spanish port.

There's some excellent surfing here – ask at Hôtel Suerte Loca or Café Nomad for their recommendations.

Sleeping

Like the rest of Ifni, most of the hotels have seen better days, making Mirleft a preferred stopover. Water can be intermittent.

Hôtel Suerte Loca (☎ 028 875350; fax 028 780003; Ave Moulay Youssef; s/d Dh70/105, with shower Dh130/190) The best, most atmospheric option in Ifni, with a variety of simple rooms with balconies overlooking the beach. The restaurant (set menu Dh56) is very popular for its French, Spanish and Moroccan cuisine, including paella. The friendly, English-speaking owners provide information about surf spots or hiking, and organise local excursions.

Hôtel Bellevue (☎ 028 875072; fax 028 780499; Place Hassan II; s/d Dh89/110, with bathroom Dh149/184) There is good sunset viewing from the top terrace, a really noisy bar and a good restaurant (set menu Dh80), as well as several categories of clean rooms with great views (shower Dh10). *Langouste* (lobster) is often on the menu from Dh600 for two.

Hôtel Ère Nouvelle (☎ 028 875298; 5 Ave Sidi Mohammed ben Abdallah; s/d Dh30/50) Best cheapie with respectable rooms (go for the brighter top floor), a terrace and a decent restaurant.

Eating

There are a few small café-restaurants on Blvd Hassan II, and snack stands set up at the southern end of Ave Mohammed V at dusk. Hôtel Suerte Loca has the best restaurant – let them know you're coming in advance if possible.

Café Nomad (☎ 062 173308; 5 Ave Moulay Youssef; meals Dh75) This is Ifni's all-round top dining spot, and it's run by two cool dudes. Among their many talents – artistic, musical and general bonhomie – they cook up a storm. Sip on a milkshake or fruit cocktail while you wait, or ask them about the region.

Café Restaurant Mata-Rangi II (☎ 063 508561; Ave Hassan II; mains Dh48-55, breakfast Dh14; ❤ noon-3pm) Named after the boat of a Spanish explorer, this small café also does evening meals on request. Great value.

For self-caterers there's a busy **fish market** (❤ 5-8pm) in the municipal market and also a covered fruit and vegetable market off Zankat Marrakesh. Sunday is souq day; it takes place 1km out of town on the road to the port.

Shopping

Crafts enthusiasts should drop in to the **Ensemble Artisanal** (Ave Hassan II). Take a look around the markets, too, for *mlahfa*, the very fine and colourful fabrics Saharan women swathe themselves in.

Getting There & Away

Buses depart from the bus station on Ave Mohammed V. Services for Agadir (Dh25, 3½ hours, one daily) and Marrakesh (Dh90, 8½ hours, one daily) both travel via Mirleft (Dh10, 30 minutes) and Tiznit (Dh15, 1½ hours). The local bus to Legzira costs Dh3 and leaves from the local bus station. Grands taxis, which leave from the bus station northeast of the town, to Tiznit, Goulmime (both Dh20), and to Mirleft (Dh10). There are irregular grands taxis to Agadir (Dh45).

AROUND SIDI IFNI

You can make several excursions into the countryside from Sidi Ifni. Walk 18km south along a coastal track to **Sidi Ouarsik**, a fishing village with a great beach.

Legzira, 10km north of Ifni, is even better, with a superb secluded bay with excellent sand and two dramatic natural **stone arches** reaching over the sea. The **Auberge Legzira**

THE NEW OLIVE OIL

The Haha Coast north of Agadir, and the Souss Valley are home to the argan tree *(Argania spinosa)*, a slow-growing thorn tree similar to the olive. Unique to the southwest of Morocco, the sparse forests of argan have recently been recognised by Unesco as a Biosphere Reserve. The argan tree is very resistant to heat and can survive in temperatures up to 50°C, so it is an essential tool in the fight against desertification in southern Morocco.

The tree has also become vital to the local economy, providing firewood and fodder for the goats – who actually climb among its branches – and oil for humans, extracted from the nuts. In spring, Berber women harvest the fruits and traditionally feed them to goats, whose digestive systems dissolve the tough elastic coating on the shell. The nuts are then recovered from the goats' dung, and the kernels are split, lightly toasted, pulped and pressed. To produce just one litre of oil takes 30kg of nuts and 15 hours of really hard labour, solely done by women. In a recent change to this tradition, some co-operatives have decided to cut the goats out of the process and are handpicking fruits from the trees to produce a more subtle-tasting oil. You can see this whole process in a guided tour at the **Coopérative Amal** (☎ 024 788141; www.targanine.com in French; Tamanar; admission free; ☉ 8am-7pm Mon-Fri), 80km north of Agadir, whose organic oil won the 2001 Slow Food Award. For centuries the Berbers have used argan oil to heal scars and relieve rheumatic pain. Modern research has also confirmed the oil's virtue in reducing cholesterol and helping to prevent arteriosclerosis. European beauty salons have caught on to the oil's beneficial properties and are now offering treatments containing argan oil, as the high vitamin E content makes it a great anti-wrinkle cream.

Argan oil's culinary qualities are less well known, although the oil is slowly reaching the dining tables of the great and good in New York, Paris and London. Its deliciously distinct rich and sweet nutty flavour works wonders as a salad dressing, or added to grilled vegetables or tajine. The oil mixed with ground almonds and honey makes the Berber delicacy *amlou*, believed to be an efficient aphrodisiac.

The oil doesn't come cheap, but should be bought from a reputable shop or co-operative; roadside vendors sell it cheaper but often adulterated with vegetable oils.

(☎ /fax 028 780457; s/d Dh150/300) provides good meals (tajine for two Dh80) and a bed for the night. A cheaper lunch can be had at **Snack Les Amies** (☎ 028 875510; menu Dh35)

At Mesti, a Berber village some 25km south of Ifni on the Goulmime road, it's well worth visiting the **Tafyoucht Cooperative** (☎ 028 867252; ☉ 7am-noon & 2-6pm). This women's cooperative produces oil and suchlike from the versatile argan tree (see above).

GOULMIME

pop 96,000

Hard to believe that dusty derelict Goulmime (or Guelmim) was once the 'Gateway of the Sahara'. The town sprang up as a border town between the agricultural region of the Souss and the nomadic desert to the south, and was an important trading place on the caravan routes.

In its heyday, Tuareg, the so-called 'blue men' came in from the desert to buy and sell camels at the weekly souq. In the evenings, the women would perform the mesmerising *guedra* dance to the beat of drums of the same name. Nowadays you might only get a taste of this during the week-long *moussem* and camel fair held here in July or August (the dates change).

The only tourist sight in town is the Palace of Caid Dahman (admission free), in the street behind Hotel de la Jeunesse on Blvd Mohammed V. The rather unremarkable ruins of the palace are about a hundred years old.

The sleepy pace of the town is disturbed only once a week, when coach loads of day-trippers from Agadir descend for the Saturday-morning souq, a few kilometres outside town on the road to Tan Tan. There is plenty of fruit there, and some overpriced souvenirs, but most day-trippers leave sorely disappointed.

Information

Place Bir Anazarane is the centre of town and that is where you'll find the post office and a bank. The main bus and grand taxi stations are about 1km north of here along Ave Abaynou.

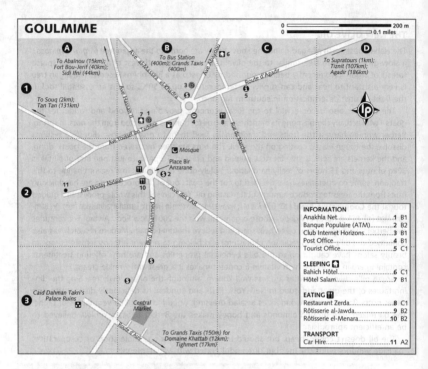

GOULMIME

0 — 200 m
0 — 0.1 miles

To Abaïnou (15km);
Fort Bou-Jerif (40km);
Sidi Ifni (44km)

Ave al-Massira el-Khadra

To Bus Station
(400m); Grands Taxis
(400m)

Route d'Agadir

To Supratours (1km);
Tiznit (107km);
Agadir (186km)

To Souq (2km);
Tan Tan (131km)

Ave Hassan II

Ave Youssef ibn Tachfine

Ave Abaynou

Rue du Marché

Mosque

Place Bir
Anzarane

Ave Moulay Abdalah

Ave des FAR

Bd Mohammed V

Caid Dahman Takri's
Palace Ruins

Central
Market

Route d'Asrir

To Grands Taxis (150m) for
Domaine Khattab (12km);
Tighmert (17km);

INFORMATION
Anakhla Net...........................1 B1
Banque Populaire (ATM)..........2 B2
Club Internet Horizons............3 B1
Post Office.............................4 B1
Tourist Office.........................5 C1

SLEEPING
Bahich Hôtel..........................6 C1
Hôtel Salam...........................7 B1

EATING
Restaurant Zerda....................8 C1
Rôtisserie al-Jawda.................9 B2
Rôtisserie el-Menara.............10 B2

TRANSPORT
Car Hire...............................11 A2

The **Tourist Office** (☎ 028 872911; 3 Résidence Sahara, Agadir Rd; ☯ Mon-Fri 9am-noon & 2.30-6pm) offers basic information on the town and trips further south.

Internet access is available at **Anakhla Net** (Ave Youssef ibn Tachfine), next to Hôtel Salam, and **Club Internet Horizons** (Ave Abaynou). Hourly rates are Dh8.

Sleeping

Accommodation in Goulmime is basic and most cheapies can be tricky for women, full as they are of trans-Saharan tradesmen.

Hôtel Salam (☎ 028 872057; fax 048 770912; Route de Tan Tan; s/d Dh109/141) An old hotel but Goulmime's best, with large and clean rooms around a courtyard, a good restaurant and rooms and the town's only bar.

Bahich Hotel (☎ 028 772178; www.geocities.com/hotelbahich in French; 31 Ave Abaynou; s/d/tr Dh75/180/200) Cosy and cheerful rooms decorated by a local artist, around a bright patio. There's a roof terrace and meals are available on request.

Domaine Khattab (☎ 061 176411; fax 028 873150; Km 12 Route d'Assa; camping per site Dh40 plus per tent Dh25, bungalow s/d Dh150/200) With rooms and

camping, this 20-hectare working farm with a tiny zoo, is a little paradise for kids. Set menu meals are available (Dh65). Bathroom facilities are spotless, and you can have a hot shower by candlelight (Dh10). The friendly owner organises treks in the region

Fort Bou-Jerif www.fortboujerif.com; camping per site Dh20 plus per tent Dh33, half board per person hotel with/motel without bathroom Dh385/220) A wonderful oasis of civilisation in the desert about 40km northwest of Goulmime (the last 9km is rough *piste*). Built near a ruined French Foreign Legion fort, it has motel/hotel-style doubles, plenty of camping space and an excellent restaurant (menu Dh165), where you can try a camel tajine. It's run by a French couple who offer 4WD trips to Plage Blanche, a little-visited and unspoiled stretch of beach 40km west of Bou-Jerif.

Eating

The best place to eat is at Hôtel Salam, but there are a few good rotisseries on Place Bir Anzarane – it's a toss-up between **Rôtisserie** al-Jawda and **Rôtisserie el-Menara**, meals at around Dh30. The signless **Restaurant Zerda** (Ave 20 Août; small/large tajine Dh40/60), with tajines lined up outside, has great tajines.

Getting There & Away
BUS
Opposite the main bus station, **CTM** (☎ 028 873855) has a bus for Marrakesh (Dh125, seven hours) via Tiznit (Dh35, two hours, one daily) and Agadir (Dh65, four hours, one daily). There is a daily departure to Tan Tan (Dh39, 1½ hours), Laâyoune (Dh142, seven hours) and Dakhla (Dh280, 15 hours).

Other companies, including Supratours and Satas, serve the same destinations.

TAXI
You can catch grands taxis to Abaïnou (Dh7), Sidi Ifni (Dh20), Tiznit (Dh50), Tan Tan (Dh40), Inezgane (Dh50) and Laâyoune (Dh130) from beside the bus station. For a grand taxi to Tighmert (Dh7), head southeast of town on the Asrir road.

TAN TAN   طانطان
pop 50,000
South of Goulmime, across the dry Oued Drâa, you enter the cauldron of the Sahara proper. The 125km of desert highway to Tan Tan is impressive for its bleak emptiness and harsh *hammada* (flat, stony desert).

You could probably drive through the main street of Tan Tan and not realise you had missed most of the town, which spreads south of the highway (known as Ave Hassan II within the town boundaries). The majority of the inhabitants are nomads who settled here, and blue robes are a big feature. The army and police presence is also noticeable, due to the disputed status of the Western Sahara.

The town had its moment, as the departure point for the Green March (see Marching to the King's Tune, p41) in 1975, but now there's nothing much to do in Tan Tan. A *moussem* takes place in September. The souq is on Sunday, 1½km south of town.

Tan Tan Plage, also known as Al-Ouatia, 28km south of Tan Tan, is a large, usually windswept beach with a few hotels and guesthouses.

Information
Banque Populaire (Ave Mohammed V).
BMCE (Ave Hassan II) Has an ATM, next to the Shell petrol station.
El-Hagounia Internet (Ave Hassan II; per hr Dh8)
Main post office (Ave Hassan II) To the east of town.
Mondial Internet (Ave Hassan II; per hr Dh8)

Sleeping & Eating
Hôtel Sable d'Or (☎ /fax 028 878069; Ave Hassan II; s/d Dh150/200) Tan Tan's best hotel by a long chalk. The enormous rooms here come with comfy beds, TV and hot showers. There's also a popular café terrace and a rather bleak restaurant (meals Dh80).

Hôtel Al-Aoubour (☎ 028 877594; 51 Ave Hassan II; s/d Dh60/90) With its duck-egg blue corridors and well-scrubbed communal facilities, it's not a bad choice for those who are just stopping over as it is well placed for both CTM and Supratours buses.

Villa Océan (☎ 028 879660, 060 943366; villaocean@menara.net; Blvd de la Plage, Tan Tan Plage; s/d Dh150/220, fixed tent per person Dh70, camping per tent Dh6) This is a delightful guesthouse with spacious and airy rooms overlooking the ocean, and clean bathrooms – a good value option with friendly French owners. The grilled fish is served straight from the sea (meals Dh80).

Hôtel Tafoukt (☎ 028 877031; 98 Place de la Marche Verte; s/d Dh35/65) Best cheapie with reasonable and clean rooms on the bus-station square (not advisable for solo women travellers) south of the centre. Hot showers Dh10.

Hôtel Dakar (☎ 028 877245; Place de la Marche Verte; s/d Dh40/50, with shower Dh90/100) The rooms aren't as smart as the exterior might suggest. Those right up top are brighter; some have ensuite bathrooms.

There are dozens of cheap restaurants on Ave Hassan II, Ave Mohammed V and around the Place de la Marche Verte. To sip a mint tea, or for breakfast, head back up the hill to **Pâtisserie Le Jardin** (Ave Mohammed V).

Getting There & Away
BUS
CTM (Ave Hassan II) buses depart nightly for Laâyoune (Dh100, 4½ hours) and Dakhla (Dh238, 14 hours) and there's another departure for Goulmime (Dh34, 1½ hours), Tiznit (Dh64, 3½ hours) and Agadir (Dh85, 4½ hours).

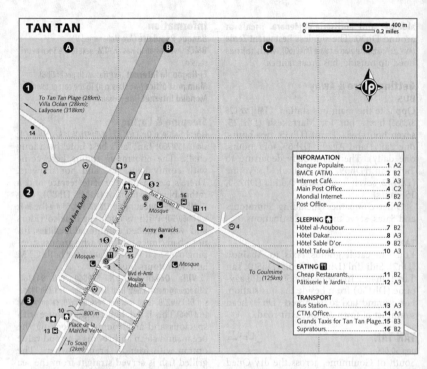

TAN TAN

0 — 400 m
0 — 0.2 miles

To Tan Tan Plage (28km);
Villa Océan (28km);
Laâyoune (318km)

Oued ben Kheīl

Ave Mohammed V

Ave Hassan II

Mosque

Army Barracks

Mosque

Mosque

blvd el-Amir
Moulay
Abdallah

Ave Mohammed V

To Goulmime
(125km)

Ave Moukaouma

Place de la
Marche Verte

To Souq
(2km)

INFORMATION	
Banque Populaire..................1	A2
BMCE (ATM).........................2	B2
Internet Café.......................3	A3
Main Post Office...................4	C2
Mondial Internet..................5	B2
Post Office..........................6	A2
SLEEPING	
Hôtel al-Aoubour..................7	B2
Hôtel Dakar.........................8	A3
Hôtel Sable D'or...................9	B2
Hôtel Tafoukt.....................10	A3
EATING	
Cheap Restaurants...............11	B2
Pâtisserie le Jardin..............12	A3
TRANSPORT	
Bus Station........................13	A3
CTM Office.........................14	A1
Grands Taxis for Tan Tan Plage..15	B3
Supratours.........................16	B2

Further east, **Supratours** (Ave Hassan II) operates similar services at similar prices.

Other, cheaper companies, all serving the same destinations, use the main bus station 500m south of the centre.

TAXI

You can catch grands taxis headed for Laâyoune (Dh85), Goulmime (Dh37) and occasionally Tarfaya (Dh60), Tiznit (Dh80) or Inezgane (Dh100), at the bus-station square. Grands taxis to Tan Tan Plage (Dh12) leave from the top of Blvd el-Amir Moulay Abdallah.

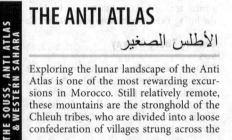

THE ANTI ATLAS
الأطلس الصغير

Exploring the lunar landscape of the Anti Atlas is one of the most rewarding excursions in Morocco. Still relatively remote, these mountains are the stronghold of the Chleuh tribes, who are divided into a loose confederation of villages strung across the

barren mountains and far beyond the reach of any central authority. The region was only finally pacified by the French in the 1930s.

Moulded by the demanding landscape of granite boulders and red lava flows, the Chleuh have always been devoted to their farms in the lush oasis valleys, with some of the country's most beautiful *palmeraies*.

TAFRAOUTE   تافراوت
pop 5000

Nestled in the enchanting Ameln Valley is the village of Tafraoute, surrounded on all sides by mountainous boulders. Despite its unassuming appearance the area is actually quite prosperous due to the hard-earned cash sent home by relatives working in the big cities or abroad.

It is a pleasant and relaxed base for exploring the region.

In late February/early March the villages around Tafraoute celebrate the almond harvest with all-night singing and dancing; the festivities move from village to village and therefore last several days. A lively souq takes place near Hôtel Salama from Monday evening through to Wednesday.

Information

BMCE (behind the post office)
Banque Populaire (Place Mohammed V; ☻ Wed)
Internet café (per hr Dh12) On the Tazekka road. Internet is also available at Hôtel Les Amandiers.
Post office (Place Mohammed V) Has pay phones outside.

Activities

CYCLING

The best way to get around the beautiful villages of the Ameln Valley is by walking or cycling. Bikes can be rented from Abid, next to Hôtel Salama, or from the shop **Artisanat du Coin** (per day Dh60). You can also rent mountain bikes or book a mountain-biking trip from **Tafraoute Aventure** (☎ 061 387173) and **Au Coin des Nomades** (☎ 061 627921).

HAMMAMS

Tafraoute is an excellent place for a completely authentic hammam experience as most houses here still lack water. There are three hammams in the town, but locals prefer the old one, just behind the mar-

ket. Second choice is the one off the main roundabout. All cost Dh10.

TREKKING

The area around Tafraoute is great for trekking. Several companies and mountain guides offer mountain-biking and trekking trips either up Jebel Lekst (2359m) or along the palm-filled gorges of Aït Mansour, leading towards the bald expanses of the southern Anti Atlas (see p432).

Both **Au Coin des Nomades** (☎ 061 627921) and **Maison Touareg** (☎ 061 387173, Rte de Tazekka) are good sources of information and maps for both trekking and rock climbing in the area.

Sleeping

Hôtel Les Amandiers (☎ 028 800088; hotellesaman diers@menara.ma; s/d from Dh307/414; ☒ ☒) Sitting on the crest of the hill overlooking the town is Tafraoute's top hotel, in every sense. The kasbah-style hotel has spacious ensuite rooms and a pool with spectacular views, as well as a bar and restaurant (set menu Dh120).

Hôtel Salama (☎ 028 800026; s/d with bathroom Dh115/150; ☒) This hotel has some Moroccan flavour, large, comfortable rooms, great

TIZNIT–TAFRAOUTE–AGADIR CIRCUIT

The village of Tafraoute, tucked away in the Ameln Valley, can be reached by good road from either Tiznit (107km) or Agadir (198km). Although the trip is best done with your own car, it is possible by public transport.

From Tiznit, the road east to Tafraoute starts off ordinarily enough across gentle farming country, until it reaches Oued Assaka. From here it winds up into the mountains, which in the late afternoon light take on every hue imaginable – from soft pinks and mauves to golden browns. (Afternoon bus departures from Tiznit coincide with this light show.)

Sprinkled about the hills are precarious Berber pisé (mud brick) villages, surrounded by the cultivated terraces that are worked all through the day – mostly by women.

At 1100m you cross the stunning Col de Kerdous and from here you hardly lose altitude for the remainder of the run into Tafraoute.

The **Hôtel Kerdous** (☎ 028 862063; fax 028 600315; per person incl breakfast Dh350; ☒ ☒) is perched in a former kasbah right on the pass. There are extraordinary views on all sides, but especially towards Tiznit. It's worth stopping here for a drink or meal just for the outlook.

The route to Agadir is just as fascinating. Leaving Tafraoute the road passes through the eastern half of the Ameln Valley and over Tizi Mlil before doubling back on itself for the trip northwest to Agadir. The land is generally much gentler and more heavily cultivated on this run, but the road passes through plenty of villages, sometimes in the most unlikely places.

The most remarkable of these is the Tizergane kasbah, perched on a solitary hilltop beside the road, about 50km from Tafraoute near the turning to Ida-ou-Gnidif. It's currently being restored (there's a collection box for donations), but a quick wander round the ancient Berber construction is a step back in time.

From there the road descends to Aït Baha, where it flattens out for the final stretch to Agadir.

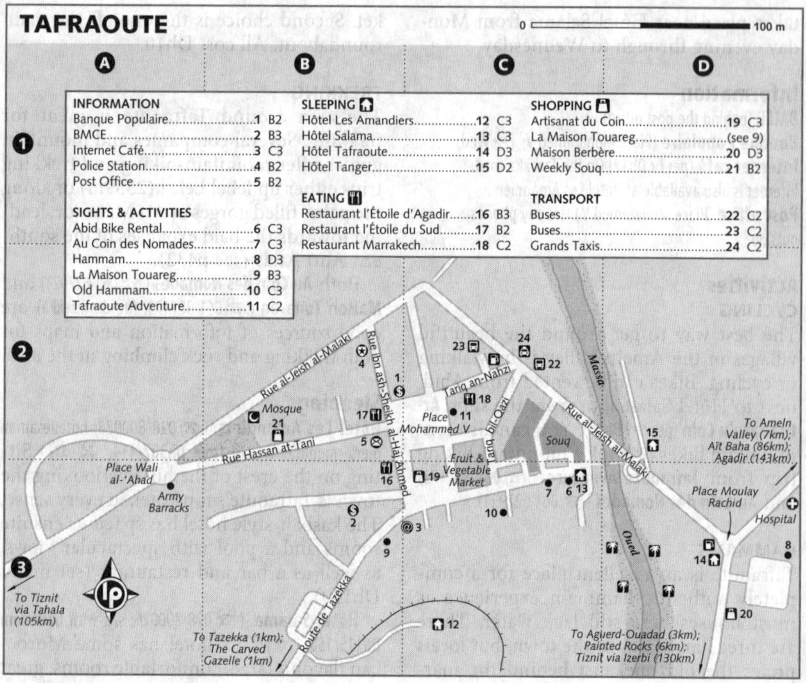
TAFRAOUTE
0 100 m
A B C D
1 2 3
INFORMATION
Banque Populaire 1 B2
BMCE 2 B3
Internet Café 3 C3
Police Station 4 B2
Post Office 5 B2
SIGHTS & ACTIVITIES
Abid Bike Rental 6 C3
Au Coin des Nomades 7 C3
Hammam 8 D3
La Maison Touareg 9 B3
Old Hammam 10 C3
Tafraoute Adventure 11 C2
SLEEPING
Hôtel Les Amandiers 12 C3
Hôtel Salama 13 C3
Hôtel Tafraoute 14 D3
Hôtel Tanger 15 D2
EATING
Restaurant l'Étoile d'Agadir 16 B3
Restaurant l'Étoile du Sud 17 B2
Restaurant Marrakech 18 C2
SHOPPING
Artisanat du Coin 19 C3
La Maison Touareg (see 9)
Maison Berbère 20 D3
Weekly Souq 21 B2
TRANSPORT
Buses 22 C2
Buses 23 C2
Grands Taxis 24 C2
Rue al-Jeish al-Malaki
Rue Ibn ash-Sheikh al-Haj Ahmed
Tariq an-Nahzi
Tariq bil-Qazi
Rue Hassan at-Tani
Mosque
Place Mohammed V
Fruit & Vegetable Market
Souq
Massa
Oued
Place Wali al-'Ahad
Army Barracks
Place Moulay Rachid
Hospital
To Ameln Valley (7km); Aït Baha (86km); Agadir (143km)
To Tiznit via Tahala (105km)
To Tazekka (1km); The Carved Gazelle (1km)
Route de Tazekka
To Aguerd-Ouadad (3km); Painted Rocks (6km); Tiznit via Izerbi (130km)

views from the terrace and a teahouse overlooking the market square.

Hôtel Tafraout (☎ 028 800060; Place Moulay Rachid; s/d Dh70/100) The best of the cheap hotels, with cosy and clean rooms, and a very welcoming owner. Half board is obligatory in summer at Dh200 for two.

Hôtel Tanger (☎ 067 033073; r per person Dh25) Very basic rooms, but friendly. You can eat on the roof (Dh20 to Dh60) as long as the wind is blowing the right way from the *oued* (river).

Eating

Apart from the hotel restaurants, Tafraoute has a few good local places to eat.

Restaurant L'Étoile d'Agadir (☎ 028 800268; Place de la Marche Verte; meals around Dh35; 8am-6pm) Locals swear by this place for its succulent tajines, all beautifully presented. This is also *the* place to ease into the day.

Restaurant L'Étoile du Sud (☎ 028 800038; set menu Dh80) An excellent set menu is served in a rather kitsch Bedouin-style tent, but the place is often taken over by tour groups, particularly at lunch time. Still, you can take your own wine along and the lamb tajine is commendable.

Restaurant Marrakech (Rue Tariq an-Nakhzi; couscous Dh25) A cheap, family-run restaurant on the road up from the bus station. It attracts a local crowd and knocks up a mean couscous.

Plenty of small food stores sell cheese and basic picnic supplies to supplement the fruit and veg available in the market.

Shopping

Tafraoute has several slipper shops around the market area selling the traditional leather slippers (yellow for men, red for women; Dh90 or more for top quality). Look out, too, for people selling local argan and olive oil.

Buying a carpet here is less pressurised than in Marrakesh. The two main outlets are **Maison Touareg** (Rte Tazekka) and **Maison Berbère** (Rte Aguerd-Oudad). Alternatively you can also pick Berber carpets up from small dealers at the weekly **souq**.

Artisanat du Coin (Sharia ibn ash-Sheikh al-Haj Ahmed), near the post office, specialises in

Berber jewellery and other portable knick-knacks.

Getting There & Away

BUS

Buses depart from outside the various company offices on Sharia al-Jeish al-Malaki.

Trans Balady runs buses to Agadir (Dh40, four hours, four daily): the 2pm and 6.30pm departures go via Tiznit (Dh25, three hours); the 6pm bus takes you through Aït Baha (Dh20, 2½ hours). Other companies serve these same destinations as well as Casablanca (Dh120, 14 hours, five daily) and Marrakesh (Dh90, seven hours, four daily).

CAR

You can hire a 4WD with a driver from Maison Touareg or Tafraout Aventure, which will set you back about Dh1200 per day plus fuel (about Dh300 for a whole day's driving).

TAXI

The occasional grand taxi goes to Tiznit in the morning (Dh45) from Sharia al-Jeish al-Malaki. Otherwise, station wagons and Land Rovers do the rounds of various villages in the area, mostly on market days. They hang around the post office square and near the Afriquia Petrol Station. The going rate to the Ameln Valley is Dh5 per person.

AROUND TAFRAOUTE

Before setting off to explore the region, arm yourself with *Tafraout in Colours* (Dh15), a basic map available at hotels, shops and restaurants in Tafraoute.

Rock Carvings

The area around Tafraoute has some easily accessible examples of prehistoric rock engravings. The closest is the **Gazelle**, at the edge of the village of Tazekka. The easiest way to walk here is to take the road past the BMCE and the sports ground, then follow a footpath southwest through the palm groves. After about 15 minutes you reach the edge of the village. From here on you'll need a local to help you locate the gazelle, a simple engraving on the top face of a fallen block.

To find the other engravings at **Tirn-matmat**, you need to go further west to-wards Aït Omar (on Rte 7148). Just before the village, an unmarked *piste,* opposite a well, leads to Tirnmatmat, where you will find the *gravures* (engravings) along the riverbed (the local kids will lead you there, or engage a guide from Tafraoute). The village sits in a lovely spot and there is good walking in all directions.

Le Châpeau de Napoléon & the Painted Rocks

The village of Aguerd-Oudad, 3km south of Tafraoute, makes for a nice stroll. On the way you pass the unmistakable rock formation known as Le Chapeau de Napoléon (Napoleon's Hat).

Take the signposted track through the village to the square, where there's a mosque. Veer right and left to get around the mosque, then follow the *piste,* power lines and river out into the flat countryside. After 1.5km you'll spot some pale-blue rocks to your left, the Pierres Bleues (Painted Rocks) – the work of Belgian artist Jean Verame.

Verame spray-painted the smooth, rounded boulders in shades of blue and red in 1984 and, although the rocks have a faded air, they remain impressive against the landscape. On a bike or driving you can follow a *piste* signposted off the new Tiznit Rd and then walk for 10 minutes.

Afella-Ighir

South of Tafraoute is the pretty oasis of Afella-Ighir. You could get there in a 4WD but it's preferable to drive part of the way, then leave the car and continue on foot or mountain bike. Alternatively make your base the village of Tiwadou, which has the simple **Auberge Sahnoun** (☎ /fax 028 800547; half board per person Dh120) run by an excellent and very knowledgeable mountain guide who can, of course, organise treks in his region.

Leave Tafraoute on the new road past Aguerd-Oudad, turning left 3km south of the village, and travel roughly 19km over a mountain pass (snowed over in winter) through Tlata Tasrirte to the start of the dramatic Aït Mansour gorges. The surfaced road continues south to the village of Aït Mansour at the bottom of the gorge where the river runs across the road, marking the start of the Afella-Ighir oasis. From here

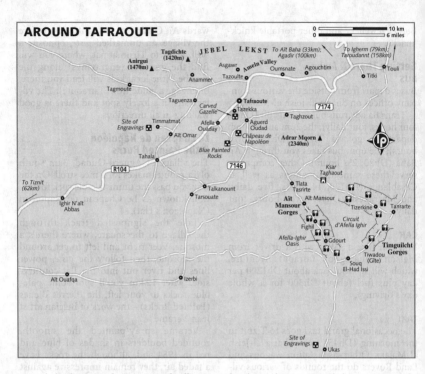

AROUND TAFRAOUTE

a track leads through a string of villages for about 10km to Souq el-Had Issi (30km from Tafraoute), a rather depressing town that has exploded with newly arrived workers for the nearby gold mine, Minas de Akka. From Souq el-Had Issi you can loop round 25km through the Timguilcht gorges and back up to Tlata Tasrite. Another option is to head 12km south to Ukas to see some impressive rock carvings, although you probably need a guide to find them.

On market days grands taxis sometimes go out to villages around this area, but otherwise you'll probably have to hire the whole taxi.

AMELN VALLEY & JEBEL LEKST جبل لكست و اميلن وادي

Tafraoute lies in a basin, largely surrounded by craggy gold-pink rocks and cliffs. To the northwest lies one such ridge, on the other side of which runs the Ameln Valley. North of the valley is **Jebel Lekst** (2359m). From Tafraoute you can make out a rock formation in this range that resembles a lion's face. Villagers will jokingly tell you

that he is there to guard the women while their husbands are away working.

The Agadir road takes you to the valley, which is lined by picturesque Berber villages. Four kilometres out of Tafraoute, the road forks with the right branch turning east up the valley towards Agadir. Another few kilometres on from there is **Oumesnate**. Follow a signpost off to the left along a short *piste* and a footpath for the **Maison Traditionelle** (admission Dh10; ☼ 8.30-sunset). This three-storey house (some 400 years old) has been opened to the public by its owner, who was blinded as a young man, to explain about traditional life. His son will give you a tour for which they expect a small consideration – it's worth every dirham.

For trekking in Jebel Lekst and the Ameln Valley, see p432.

TATA طاطا
pop 40,000
Situated on the Saharan plain at the foot of Jebel Bani, Tata was an oasis settlement along the trade route from Zagora to Tan Tan. Close to the Algerian border, the small

modern town has a garrison feel, dominated as it is by the military fort on the hill above.

The *palmeraie* is well worth exploring as is the old kasbah, now restored into Dar Infiane (see boxed text below) with a small museum.

Tata is a great base for some off-the-beaten-track excursions, such as Akka oasis, desert camping and the rock engravings at Oum el-Alek, Tircht and Aït Herbil, considered to be the finest in Morocco. Information is available from the tourist office at the **Maison du Patrimoine Tataoui** (☎ 072 130395; Ave Mohammed V) on the main road, or, if you are lucky enough to be staying at Dar Infiane, the staff can arrange any number of fantastic excursions.

You'll find a post office and Banque Populaire (with an ATM) just off the main road, as well as the **Délégation de Tourisme** (Tourist office; ☎ 028 802076, 076 002699) with helpful staff.

Sleeping & Eating

Along Ave Mohammed V are several basic hotels, at around Dh40 per person.

Les Relais des Sables (☎ 028 802301; fax 028 802300; s/d Dh217/264, ste Dh414; ☒ ☒) A popular group-oriented hotel with the most comfortable accommodation in town. It has a bar and a licensed restaurant, and rooms are arranged around flowery courtyards. It is worth the extra dirham even though the cheaper rooms (with bathroom) are a bit poky.

Hôtel Renaissance (☎ 028 802225; fax 028 802042; Ave Mohammed V; d/ste Dh140/320; ☒) This big hotel is on both sides of the road, with the older part on one side and an annexe with comfortable minisuites on the other. There is a good licensed restaurant.

Café Restaurante el-Amal (Ave Mohammed V; mains Dh50) In an attractive spot next to the camp site, you can get a good square meal here of tajine or brochette.

Getting There & Away

Buses and taxis collect on Place Massira, one block east of Ave Mohammed V. A Satas bus leaves at every other day for Agadir (Dh80, eight hours, three daily) via Tiznit (Dh60, 6½ hours). Other companies operate departures to Marrakesh (Dh120, one daily), Agadir via Tiznit or Taroudannt (Dh70, five hours, one daily) and Goulmime (Dh60, six hours, one daily).

Grands taxis ply the routes to Tiznit (Dh100), Taroudannt (Dh70), Agadir (Dh90) and Goulmime (Dh80).

WESTERN SAHARA
الصحراء الغربيّة

Few travellers venture beyond Goulmime into what Moroccans call the Saharan provinces, the still-disputed territory of the Western Sahara. This area largely comprises the former Spanish colonies of Spanish Sahara and part of Tarfaya. Travelling through here, one does marvel at the dispute. The towns are merely administrative centres, and the road cuts through a vast area of *hammada* – featureless, arid, inhospitable and uninviting.

Despite the 1991 ceasefire in the Polisario-backed war, the desert is still occupied by the Moroccan military. But, apart from the endless police roadblocks, going south to Dakhla is now a routine affair.

One of the consequences of the area's tax-free status is that petrol here costs a couple of dirham less per litre than in the rest of the

---

AUTHOR'S CHOICE

Dar Infiane (☎ /fax 028 802408; www.dar infiane.com; s/d incl breakfast Dh600/900; ☒) Buried deep in the *palmeraie* is Tata's old kasbah, turned into an extraordinary guest house by architect Latifa Maali and owner Patrick Simon. For nearly three years Latifa has worked tirelessly to renovate the crumbling kasbah. The carpet-strewn central courtyard took eight months in itself and since then they have added six rooms and a fabulous terrace pool, which looks out over Tata's 20,000 palm trees.

The excursions from Dar Infiane are also carefully crafted. Arrange for Patrick's light aircraft to fly you over the green veins of the southern oases, go with Latifa to the local markets or visit the rock engravings with knowledgeable guides. In the evening return to Dar Infiane and sit out on the rooftop terrace in the magical still of the Sahara night.

country. The first of the Atlas Sahara petrol stations is just south of Tarfaya.

HISTORY

Despite its windswept desolation, the Western Sahara has a long and violent history. Islamic missionaries started to spread Islam among the Zenata and Sanhaja Berber tribes in the 7th century, but it was only in the 13th century when a second wave of Arab settlers, the Maqil from Yemen, migrated to the desert that the whole region was Arabised.

By the 19th century the desert had new overlords again: the Spanish, who grabbed the Western Sahara and renamed it Rio de Oro, even though it had neither water nor gold. In reality, until 1934 it was Sheikh Ma El-Ainin and his son El-Hiba who controlled the desert and the nomadic tribes. After that, an uneasy colonial peace prevailed until Moroccan independence in 1957, when new nationalist fervour contributed to the establishment of the Polisario Front and the guerilla war against the Spanish.

When it was abandoned by Spain in 1975, Morocco and Mauritania both raised claims to the desert region, but Mauritania soon bailed out. In November 1975 King Hassan II orchestrated the Green March – 350,000 Moroccans marched south to stake Morocco's historical claims to the Western Sahara (see Marching to the King's Tune, p41).

In the following years 100,000 Moroccan troops were poured in to stamp out resistance. When the Polisario lost the support of Algeria and Libya, it soon became clear that Rabat had the upper hand. The UN brokered a cease-fire in 1991, but the promised referendum, in which the Saharawis could choose between independence and integration with Morocco, has yet to materialise.

Ever since, Morocco has strengthened its hold on the territory, pouring money into infrastructure projects, particularly offshore oil exploration, and attracting Moroccans from the north to live here tax-free. The debate is still open but, to all intents and purposes, Morocco seems to have succeeded in its claim to the territory.

For the most up-to-date information on the Western Sahara, or the Saharawi Arab Democratic Republic (as they officially call themselves), log on to www.un.org, www .wsahara.net or www.arso.org.

CLIMATE

Beyond the foothills of the Anti Atlas lies an arid hinterland starved of moisture. Here temperatures can exceed 45°C during the day and plunge to 0°C at night, while an annual rainfall of less than 125mm a year gives a suffocating aridity hovering between 5% and 30% – dry enough to mummify corpses. March to April sandstorms also plague the desert, making driving inadvisable. (The desert wind is known locally as the *chergui, irifi* or *sirocco*.)

Remember, it is important to carry a good supply of water. In winter it is also essential to carry a warm sleeping bag and some warm clothing as desert nights can be bitterly cold.

DANGERS & ANNOYANCES

In both Laâyoune and Dakhla you will be more aware of the military and police, both of whom remain sensitive to photography around military installations.

Similarly, they will not take too kindly to the photographing of the depressing refugee camps in both cities, where many Saharawis still live. The busy red-light district in Dakhla, opposite the military headquarters and barracks, is also off-limits to Westerners.

If you are crossing the border into Mauritania, you will need to engage a local guide (on the insistence of the Mauritanian authorities) to negotiate the off-*piste* road to Nouâdhibou due to the very real danger of landmines.

LANGUAGE

In the Western Sahara, Arabic and French are spoken almost universally. As a previous Spanish Protectorate, the more common second language was, until recently, Spanish, a habit that lingers on with the older generation. English is also spoken, due to the UN presence.

GETTING THERE & AWAY

There is no officially designated border between Morocco and the Western Sahara, and Morocco treats the region as an integrated part of the country.

Laâyoune is served by regular flights from Casablanca. More infrequent flights from Agadir and Dakhla are also available. There is a small airport at Dakhla, which operates one flight a week to Agadir and a few more to Casablanca.

There is talk of running buses to the border from Dakhla, but for now you need to arrange good 4WD transport. Take plenty of water and food (enough for two days), and allow at least six hours to cover the 380km. Hôtel Erraha in Dakhla is the best local source of information regarding the border. Jeep drivers can be found hanging out near the Dakhla checkpoint, and in the Hôtel Sahara, and charge around Dh500 to Dh600 per person for border crossings. During the winter season (November to March) overland trucks may consider giving you a lift.

Once you arrive at the border you will need to go through two customs points, one on the Moroccan side and the other in Mauritania.

It is possible to have a Mauritanian visa issued in Casablanca, but you are strongly advised to get one before arriving in Africa.

See p476 for more on crossing into Mauritania.

GETTING AROUND

Supratours and CTM both operate buses to Laâyoune and Dakhla, although Supratours provides the faster and more efficient service.

TAN TAN TO TARFAYA

The 225km drive from Tan Tan to Tarfaya takes you across a monotonous stretch of desert highway. The road is good and the traffic relatively light.

Along the route you'll see anglers' huts perched on the cliff tops (many of these anglers sell their catch by the roadside) and, further south, herds of camels wandering slowly through the *hammada*. Sidi Akhfennir, 110km further on, is a good place to stop, either at one of the garages or at a café serving grilled fish straight from the sea.

If you want to hang around longer, the **Auberge Pêche et Loisirs** (☎ 061 211983; http://peche.sudmaroc.free.fr in French; per person Dh300) has clean and comfortable rooms, and organises fishing trips on the nearby Naïla Lagoon or ocean.

The tiny fishing port of Tarfaya was the second-largest town in the Spanish-controlled zone of the same name. The Spanish left behind a stronghold set out amid the breakers, known appropriately as Casa Mar (house in the sea). A monument on the beachfront is dedicated to the French pilot and writer Antoine de Saint-Exupéry, who found inspiration here for the story of *The Little Prince*, featuring a pilot lost in the desert. While he was stationed here, as a pilot for the French airmail service between

---

THE CRUELLEST JOURNEY

On 28 August 1815 the US brig *Commerce*, captained by James Riley, was passing through the narrow straits between the Canary Islands and the treacherous Cape Boujdour bound for the Cape Verde islands. Strong winds and low visibility due to fog caused a fatal error in navigation that stranded the ship in the rocky waters of Cape Boujdour, one of the navigable world's most treacherous places.

The 12 *Commerce* sailors, wrecked below the precipitous cliff of the Western Sahara, were taken prisoner by desert nomads and faced the nightmarish prospect of slavery. Among almost unimaginable desert sufferings, the sailors faced hunger, thirst and brutality, survived on little more than snails, urine, and camel's milk and blood, during a 1200km trek across the desert to redeem their freedom in Essaouira.

At the time the Western Sahara was very little known and James Riley, one of the survivors, became an unwilling explorer and ethnographer. His sensational memoir was published in 1817 at a time when most of the US still tolerated slavery. Among the readers electrified by his account was a young Abraham Lincoln, who would later cite Riley's *Sufferings in Africa*, along with the Bible and *Aesop's Fables*, as one of the books that had most influenced him.

Driving down the coast of Western Sahara, particularly from Tan Tan to Tarfaya and near Cape Boujdour, the eerie shipwrecks, still visible in the surf, serve as a ghostly reminder of Riley's and many other unfortunate sailors' sufferings.

The gripping story of Riley's shipwreck is provided in Dean King's *Skeletons on the Zahara*.

Toulouse and Dakar, he wrote another book, *Southern Mail*.

The area just north of Tarfaya is extremely scenic, with wild, untouched Atlantic beaches and a series of surreal shipwrecks, clearly visible from the road, rising from the waters.

LAÂYOUNE (AL-'UYUN) العيون

pop 200,000

Built by the Spanish to administer the local phosphate mines at Bou Craa, Laâyoune is now the principal city of the Western Sahara. Little evidence of the Spanish presence remains as Morocco has poured more than US$1 billion into its development. With a population of mostly outsiders, tempted here by government projects, tax-free goods and healthy wages, Laâyoune remains a government centre and a military garrison.

Laâyoune doesn't have an awful lot to see, although the atmosphere is odd enough to make a stay of a day or two worthwhile. In any case, whether you're heading north or south, the distances involved are such that you'll almost have no choice but to sleep over for at least a night.

Orientation

The town's showpiece is the vast Place du Méchouar (where bored youths hang about at night), but there is no obvious centre. The post office, banks and most hotels are along either Blvd Hassan II or Blvd de Mekka.

Buses mostly gather at offices towards the southern end of Blvd de Mekka. Grand taxi stations are scattered about town.

Information

There are several banks with ATMs and exchange facilities near the intersection of Blvd Hassan II and Blvd Mohammed V, including Banque Populaire, BCM and Wafa.

Banque Populaire (Place Dchira)

BMCE (Place Hassan II) Has another branch at Place Dchira.

Délégation Régionale du Tourisme (ONMT; ☎ 028 891694; Ave de l'Islam; 🕑 9am-noon & 2.30-6.30pm Mon-Fri) Few handouts, but the staff are anxious to please.

Post office (Place Hassan II; 🕑 8.30am-noon & 2.30-6.30pm Sat-Thu, 8.30-11.30am & 3-6.30pm Fri) Also has public phones with international connection. There is a smaller (post only) branch on Place Dchira.

Sahar@Network (Blvd de Mekka; per hr Dh10) Internet access.

Telephone W@dernet (Blvd de Mekka; per hr Dh8) Internet access.

Sights & Activities

Laâyoune may lack sights, but the atmosphere – still very much that of an occupied town – is interesting enough. The original Spanish town runs along the riverbed Saquia el-Hamra over which presides the startling **Spanish cathedral**, (now closed) on Ave Hassan II, with its huge rounded white dome mimicking the local architecture.

To the southwest of the cathedral is the bustling **Souq Djemal**, the liveliest area of Laâyoune with plenty of street life and some of the best food stalls in town, a far cry from the monuments of officialdom uphill at the grand Place du Méchouar such as the **Palais de Congrès** or the new **Grande Mosquée** (Moulay Abdel Aziz Mosque; Blvd Moulay Youssef).

Then there are the kilometres of dunes, clearly visible from several vantage points in and around the city, spreading north and west of Laâyoune. To get in among them, take a 4WD off the road to Tarfaya (local travel agents can organise trips). To the north of town are a few coastal lagoons with prolific bird life.

Sleeping

There is a strong UN presence in Laâyoune so it is advisable to ring ahead and book for the better hotels. Unsurprisingly, good accommodation in this desert outpost is relatively expensive by Moroccan standards.

BUDGET

Hôtel Jodesa (☎ 028 992064; fax 048 893784; 223 Blvd de Mekka; s/d Dh100/144, with shower Dh144/155) North of Place Dchira, this modern hotel has reasonably spacious rooms with a bit of style, some of them ensuite. It's friendly, too.

Hôtel Sidi Ifni (☎ 028 893488; 12 Rue Sanhaja, Souq ez-Zaj; s/d Dh35/55) By far the best of the real cheapies,this place is very local in flavour. Showers here use cold, salty bore-water – luckily there are public showers opposite.

Hôtel As-Smara (130 Ave Salem Bila, Souq Djemal; s/d Dh55/75) Very basic and cleanish rooms, but centrally located in the lively Souq Djemal quarter.

MIDRANGE & TOP END

Hôtel Parador (☎ 028 892814; fax 028 890962; Ave de l'Islam; s/d Dh1100/1400; ❄ 🏊) Built in the

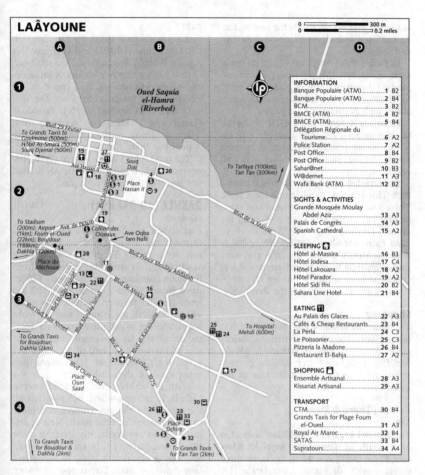

LAÂYOUNE

1960s in hacienda style around courtyard gardens, it has a faintly colonial bar and a good but rather expensive restaurant (set menu Dh180). The rooms are equipped with all the creature comforts you'd expect and small terraces.

Sahara Line Hotel (☎ 028 995454; fax 028 990155; Blvd el-Kairaouane; s/d/tr Dh399/506/614; ✕) A reliable three-star option. Swish, carpeted air-conditioned rooms have fridge, bathrooms and TV. There's a restaurant on the top floor (breakfast Dh50), but no bar.

Hôtel Lakouara (☎ 028 893378; hotellak_1@menara.ma; Ave Hassan II; s/d Dh300/400) A modern two-star hotel much used by the UN, with decent-sized rooms, all with ensuite bathrooms and satellite TV. Lacking in character

perhaps, but it is comfortable and functional, and overlooks the attractive cathedral.

Hôtel Al-Massira (☎ 028 994848; fax 028 890962; Blvd de Mekka; s/d Dh1000/1300; ✕ ✦) Often booked up by the UN, this is a comfortable modern hotel with cool courtyards, a good restaurant and a welcome pool.

Eating

There are many cafés and simple restaurants around Place Dchira, where Dh20 should get you a filling meal. More lively food stalls can be found at the Souk Djemal.

The hotel restaurants at the Massira and the Parador offer more upmarket meals.

Le Poissonier (☎ 028 993262, 061 235795; 183 Blvd de Mekka; meals Dh40-70) Apart from the restaurants at the top-end hotels, this is the best restaurant in town, specialising in lobster, fresh fish and seafood.

La Perla (☎ 028 991191, 061 995383; 187 Blvd de Mekka; set menu Dh100) Mainly fresh fish and seafood on the menu, including lobster (Dh300 to Dh400), but there are also Spanish specialities such as paella and gazpacho.

Pizzaria la Madone (☎ 028 993252; 141 Ave Chahid Bouchraya; pizzas Dh30-50) A cosy place to eat with a brisk takeaway trade. Thin-crust pizzas, *harira*, salads, omelettes – it's all excellent.

Restaurant el-Bahja (Blvd Mohammed V; set menu Dh20) This is where locals come for a feast. There's no menu, so just see what's on offer, or you can get a sandwich and salad for around Dh10.

Au Palais des Glaces (☎ 028 980476; Blvd de Mekka; breakfast Dh10-17) A modern and very European-style tearoom, patisserie and ice-cream parlour, with the best ice creams in town. A good place to start the day, too.

Shopping

The **Ensemble Artisanal** (Ave Okba bin Nafa) has domed workshops for local artisans, mainly silversmiths. The **Kissariat Artisanal** (Blvd Moulay Youssef) is a slightly better stocked government crafts centre on the far side of the square.

Getting There & Away

AIR

The **Hassan I Airport** (☎ 028 893346) is located 2km south of Laâyoune. **Royal Air Maroc** (RAM; ☎ 028 894071; Place Dchira) operates three direct weekly flights to Casablanca (1½ hours) and one to Dakhla (one hour). **Regional Air Lines** (in Casablanca ☎ 022 538080) has flights to Agadir (1¼ hours).

BUS

CTM (Blvd de Mekka) has a morning bus to Dakhla (Dh141, seven hours, one daily) and services to Agadir (Dh190, 10½ hours, three daily) via Tan Tan (Dh100, three hours) and Goulmime (Dh140, 6½ hours, three daily).

Supratours (Place Oum Essad) has two daily buses to Marrakesh (Dh250, 16 hours), and one to Dakhla (Dh141, nine hours).

Satas (Blvd de Mekka) will get you to Tiznit (Dh130, nine hours, two daily), Agadir (Dh160, two daily), Dakhla (Dh140, one daily) and Tan Tan (Dh80, two daily).

TAXI

Catch grands taxis north to Tan Tan (Dh 75), Goulmime (Dh105) and Inezgane (for Agadir; Dh160) from a rank 2km southeast of the centre along Ave Mekka. A local red-and-white petit taxi will take you there for Dh5 or so; ask the driver for Place Tan Tan.

Grands taxis heading south to Boujdour (Dh60) and Dakhla (Dh150) leave from 'Place Boujdour' in the southern suburbs. A petit taxi there also costs about Dh4.

The taxi lot for Foum el-Oued (Dh6), the nearest beach, is more conveniently located just south of the Great Mosque.

DAKHLA (AD-DAKHLA)   الداخلة
pop 40,000

Established by the Spanish in 1844 and formerly called Villa Cisneros, Dakhla lies just north of the Tropic of Cancer on a sandy peninsula stretching out 40km from the main coastline. It's a very lonely 520km drive from Laâyoune (more than 1000km from Agadir) through endless *hammada*, and only worth the effort if you are making an attempt to get into Mauritania. Having driven this far, you might imagine that you will arrive at the end of the earth, but surprisingly Dakhla feels less remote than many towns in the south.

With its whitewashed, arcaded streets, Dakhla is rather soulless but pleasant all the same, and the government continues to pour money into the town. New apartment blocks are constantly stretching the town boundaries, roads are being paved and a huge new port is home to Morocco's largest fishing fleet. Day-trippers arriving by boat from the nearby Canary Islands scuttle through town looking for Moroccan exotica.

The old **Spanish lighthouse** at Point Durnford is good for some fantastic views.

Orientation & Information

Dakhla is reasonably easy to get around, with the bus offices, central post office and most hotels and cafés situated around the old central market.

The **tourist office** (☎ 028 898228; 1 Rue Tiris; ☽ 8.30am-noon & 2.30-6.30pm Mon-Fri) is up a side street to the east of the CTM office.

Dakhla has a number of banks with ATMs, including **BMCE** (Ave el-Walaa) and **Crédit du Maroc** (Ave Mohammed V) on the road running along the seafront. You'll also find internet cafés dotted around town charging Dh10 per hour.

There are plenty of mechanics, mostly in the newer part of town to the southwest, who can service vehicles before a long trek south.

Sleeping & Eating

Hôtel Aigue (☎ 028 897395; Ave Sidi Ahmed Laaroussi; s/d Dh50/60) Peach paintwork, hot water and standards of cleanliness above the norm make this one of Dakhla's better budget deals. It lies south of the CTM office.

Sahara Regency (☎ 028 931555; www.sahara regency.com; Ave al-Walae; s/d/tr incl breakfast Dh600/800/900; 🕸 🖳) Totally modern four-star resort hotel, 100m from the gorgeous bay of Dakhla. The colourful spacious rooms have all modern amenities, and all kinds of water sports including fishing and kitesurfing are available. The hotel has no less than three bars and a rooftop restaurant.

Hôtel Erraha (☎ /fax 028 898811; Ave Beuchekroune; s/d Dh167/200) This spic-and-span hotel boasts 24-hour hot water and spacious rooms, some with kitchenettes. The only downside is its location about 1km southwest of the centre, near the new Edderhem Mosque.

Hôtel Doumss (☎ 028 898046; fax 028 898045; Ave el-Walaa; s/d Dh230/280) Large rooms have bathrooms and balconies, but are pretty functional. To find it, head north to the water tower and keep going for another 200m.

In addition to cheap eateries around the market, there's a good Spanish restaurant,

Casa Luis (☎ 028 898193; 14 Ave Mohammed V; meal around Dh70), where you can enjoy an excellent octopus salad and decent paella.

Dakhla trendies, and just about any foreigners in town, congregate under the pergolas at the **Café Restaurant Samarkand** (☎ 028 898316; Ave Mohammed V; mains Dh40-70). Fairylights, mock gaslights and stone lions are what pass for posh down here. Despite a lengthy menu, the choice narrows down to salads, fish and omelettes – but it's all good. It can usually stretch to coffee and croissants.

The uninspiring bar at Hôtel Doumss closes at 7pm, but you can buy alcohol to take away. The bars at the Sahara Regency are open until a wild 10pm.

Getting There & Away

Aéroport Dakhla (☎ 028 897049) is just west of town; a petit taxi to a hotel costs Dh4, although most are within walking distance. **RAM** (☎ 028 897049; Ave des PTT) operates three flights a week to Casablanca, one of them stopping in Agadir and two in Laâyoune. **Regional Airlines** (☎ 082 000080) have four flights a week to Casablanca, three to Laâyoune, two to Las Palmas in the Canaries, and one to Agadir.

CTM (Blvd 4 Mars), **Supratours** (Ave Mohammed V), and **Satas** (Blvd de Walae) have daily services to Laâyoune (Dh141, eight hours), Tan Tan (Dh238, 14 hours) and Agadir (Dh320, 19 hours); tickets should be booked ahead.

Grands taxis for Laâyoune (Dh150) leave from an area called Al-Messira at the southwest end of town.

Trekking

You don't have to be an experienced trekker to get out and about in the mountains nor to discover that this is one of the most exciting and rewarding things you can do in Morocco. The country is blessed with some of the world's most dramatic and beautiful mountains, many of which only see a handful of travellers every year; others remain totally unexplored by foreigners. With such a variety of terrain on offer there is something for everyone, from leisurely strolls through the cedar forests of the Middle Atlas to gruelling climbs up the steep, rocky slopes of the High Atlas.

Morocco's broad range of climates is a blessing for trekkers. When December snows make Jebel Toubkal (4167m), North Africa's highest peak, impossible to trek, Jebel Sarhro, on the southern side of the Atlas and at the edge of the Sahara, is passable. At the same time, when the summer sun makes the Rif too hot to trek, it also melts the snow off Toubkal, enticing crowds up to the summit.

Not every trekking area or mountain range is covered in this chapter. Instead we have selected some of what we think are the most exciting and interesting walks in a country overendowed with walking possibilities. Some are obvious – the ascent of Toubkal, for instance. Others, such as the M'Goun walk, are less so, but no less extraordinary.

Trekking in Morocco is growing in popularity, and even without using an agency you shouldn't have much difficulty in finding a guide, essential for getting the most out of visiting Berber villages, and for hiring mules, which will make walking all the more fun.

HIGHLIGHTS

- Admire the blue skies, red rocks and green valleys of the **High Atlas** (p411)

- Reach the summit of **Jebel Toubkal** (p419), the highest mountain in North Africa

- Track the Barbary apes through the cedar forests of the **Rif** and **Middle Atlas** (p428)

- Wade through springtime flowers on the remote **Tichka Plateau** (p423)

- Test your stamina with a hard trek in the **Jebel Sarhro** (p434) and be rewarded with some of the most rugged and stunning scenery in Morocco

- Get away from the crowds in the remote **M'Goun Massif** (p424) and be inspired by its spectacular valleys

★ Rif Mountains

★ Middle Atlas

★ Eastern High Atlas

★ High Atlas

★ M'Goun Massif

Jebel Toubkal ★   ★ Jebel Sarhro

★ Tichka Plateau

GETTING STARTED

MAPS

Morocco is covered by 1:100,000 and 1:50,000 topographical map series. However, some of the 1:50,000 series are unavailable to the public (the coverage of the Jebel Sarhro, Eastern High Atlas and Middle Atlas is patchy). Due to the restrictions placed upon map purchases, travellers exploring wide areas are advised to stick to the 1:100,000 series. The Soviet military also made 1:100,000 maps of Morocco and although marked in Cyrillic script these are as topographically accurate as any.

Division de la Cartographie (☎ 037 295034; fax 037 230830; Ave Hassan II, Rabat; www.acfcc.gov.ma in French; ☽ 9am-3.30pm Mon-Fri), of the Moroccan Survey stocks a range of topographical Moroccan maps and town plans, many prepared by the French IGN. Staff can be touchy about selling maps, particularly to regions they consider to be sensitive. For some of these, you may need to make a written request (in French), explaining who you are and why you want the maps. A panel meets on Friday, so you'll get a decision on Friday afternoon or (more likely) Monday morning. Most maps cost Dh70 a sheet. You must bring your passport for ID.

If you get no joy in Rabat, you may find maps of the Toubkal area, the M'Goun Massif and Jebel Sarhro in shops in Marrakech, Imlil and elsewhere. Photocopies of maps of some parts of the High Atlas are sometimes available at the reception of **Hôtel Ali** (☎ 024 444979; www.hotel-ali.hostel-marrakech.co.uk; Rue Moulay Ismail) in Marrakesh, at the marked-up price of Dh140 or more.

Several sources in the UK may be able to supply maps. **Stanfords** (☎ 020-7836 1321; www.stanfords.co.uk) has one of the world's largest collections of maps for sale. At the time of writing, they only had the four-sheet, 1:100,000 Toubkal map, but others are sometimes available. The map room of the **Royal Geographical Society** (☎ 020-7591 3050; www.rgs.org; 1 Kensington Gore, London SW7 2AR) has a considerable collection of maps of Morocco and is open to the public. Some maps can also be ordered online.

You can buy West Col's *Mgoun Massif* map at several online sites including, at the time of writing, on Amazon (www.amazon

INTERNATIONAL SPECIALIST TRAVEL MAP AND BOOKSHOPS

Au Vieux Campeur (☎ 01 53 10 48 27; www.au-vieux-campeur.fr in French; 2 Rue de Latran, Paris, France and branches)

Map Link (☎ 805-692 6777; www.maplink.com; Unit 5, 30 S La Patera Lane, Santa Barbara, CA 93117, USA)

Map Shop (☎ 016-8459 3146; www.themapshop.co.uk; 15 High St, Upton upon Severn, Worcestershire, UK)

Mapland (☎ 03-9670 4383; www.mapland.com.au; 372 Little Bourke St, Melbourne, Australia)

Rand McNally (☎ 847-329 8100; www.randmcnally.com; 8255 N Central Park, Skokie, IL 60076, USA)

Stanfords (☎ 020-7836 1321; www.stanfords.co.uk; 12-14 Long Acre, Covent Garden, London, UK)

.co.uk). This and the complete range of Soviet maps, some of which you can download, are available from **Omnimap** (www.omnimap.com).

Another trusted source for maps and information is **Atlas Mountains Information Services** (☎ /fax 015-92 87 3546; 26 Kirkcaldy Rd, Burntisland, Fife, Scotland KY3 9HQ), run by Hamish Brown, a specialist author, lecturer, photographer and guide for the Atlas who has been travelling in Morocco for more than forty years. He's often away leading treks, so you are advised to contact him well in advance, preferably by fax.

BOOKS

The Moroccan tourist office, Office National Marocain du Tourisme (ONMT), publishes an extremely useful booklet called *Morocco: Mountain and Desert Tourism* (2005). A French edition should also be available. The booklet has a good introduction to trekking in Morocco and then lists car hire, bureaux des guides, tourist offices, lists of *gîtes d'étape* (trekkers' hostels), huts, refuges, camp sites, souq days and other useful information. You should be able to pick them up at the office of the Association of Guides in Imlil, at the ONMT office in Marrakesh or in other major cities, or at Moroccan tourist offices overseas.

Some trekking guidebooks are listed in the boxed text. The ONMT and the publishing house Edisud/Belvisi also publish *Gravures Rupestres du Haut Atlas*, which looks at the rock art of Plateau du Yagour, northeast of

Setti Fatma, and *Randonnées Pédestres Dans le Massif du Mgoun*. These are only sporadically available at tourist offices, in bookshops in Rabat and Marrakesh, the Club Alpin France (CAF) and at the refuge in Oukaïmeden, but should be available online.

CLUBS

The Fédération Royale Marocaine de Ski et de Montagne (Royal Moroccan Ski & Mountaineering Federation) (☎ 022 203798/fax 022 474979; Le Min-istère de la Jeunesse et Sport, Parc de la Ligue Arabe, PO Box 15899, Casablanca; frmsm@hotmail.com) runs three basic refuges (see p409) and can provide information for trekkers.

Club Alpin Français (CAF; ☎ 022 270090; www .cafmaroc.co.ma in French; 50 Blvd Moulay Abderrahman,

Quartier Beauséjour, Casablanca) operates key ref-uges in the Toubkal area, particularly those in Imlil, Oukaïmeden and on Toubkal (see p409). The club website is a good source of trekking information, including links to recommended guides.

ORGANISED TREKS

For details of foreign and Moroccan op-erators offering trekking tours in Morocco, see p441.

CLOTHING & EQUIPMENT

Strong, well-broken-in walking boots are the key to happy trekking whatever the season, as is a waterproof and windproof outer layer – it's amazing how quickly the

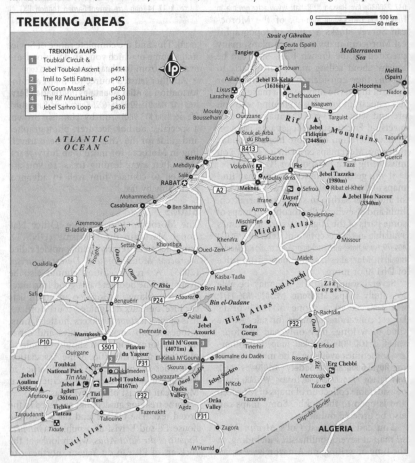

TREKKING AREAS

TREKKING MAPS		
1	Toubkal Circuit & Jebel Toubkal Ascent	p414
2	Imlil to Setti Fatma	p421
3	M'Goun Massif	p426
4	The Rif Mountains	p430
5	Jebel Sarhro Loop	p436

0 — 100 km
0 — 60 miles

Strait of Gibraltar
Ceuta (Spain)
Mediterranean Sea
Tangier
Tetouan
Melilla (Spain)
Asilah
Jebel El-Kelaâ (1616m) ▲ 4
Al-Hoceima
Nador
Lixus
Chefchaouen
Larache
Issaguen
Targuist
Moulay Bousselham
Ouezzane
Rif
Jebel Tidiquin (2448m) ▲
Taourirt
Mountains
Taza
Guercif
ATLANTIC OCEAN
Souk el-Arba du Rharb
R413
Kenitra
Sidi-Kacem
Mehdiya
Volubilis
Fes
Jebel Tazzeka (1980m) ▲
Salé
Moulay Idriss
Sefrou
Ribat el-Kheir
RABAT
A2
Meknès
Jebel Bou Naceur (3340m) ▲
Mohammedia
Ifrane
Dayet Afrou
Casablanca
Ben Slimane
Azrou
Boulemane
Azemmour
Mischliffen
El-Jadida
Only
Middle Atlas
Missour
Oued
Settat
Khouribga
Khenifra
Midelt
Oualidia
P8
P7
er-Rbia
Kasba-Tadla
P24
Beni Mellal
Jebel Ayachi
Ziz Gorges
Safi
Benguérir
Bin el-Oudane
High Atlas
Er-Rachidia
Azilal ▲
Todra Gorge
P32
Oued
Marrakesh
Jebel Azourki ▲
P10
Demnate
Irhil M'Goun (4071m) ▲ 3
Tinerhir
Erfoud
Ouirgane
S501
Plateau du Yagour
El-Kelaâ M'Gouna
Boumalne du Dadès
Rissani
Ziz
Erg Chebbi
Toubkal National Park
Asni
P31
Skoura
Ouarzazate
Merzouga
Taouz
Tin Mal
Oukaïmeden
Jebel Toubkal (4167m) ▲ 1
Jebel Sarhro
Jebel Aoulime (3555m) ▲
Jebel Igdet (3616m) ▲
Tizi n'Test
Dadès Valley
N'Kob
Tazzarine
Oued Dadès
Afensou
Tichka Plateau
Tizi n'Test
P32
Agdz
Drâa Valley
Taroudannt
Taliouine
Tazenakht
P31
Disputed Border
Tioute
Anti Atlas
Zagora
ALGERIA
M'Hamid

TOP TREKKING GUIDEBOOKS

- *Great Atlas Traverse* by Michael Peyron. Peyron lived in Morocco for decades and his two-volume paperback work is the definitive text (volume one covers the Toubkal region) for the great traverse. Less useful for the casual trekker.

- *Le Massif du Toubkal* (Edisud/Belvisi) by Jean Dresch & Jacques de Lépiney; published in French, it is primarily of use to mountaineers concentrating on the high peaks around Toubkal.

- *Trekking in the Atlas Mountains: Toubkal, Mgoun Massif and Jebel Sahro* by Karl Smith. A guide from the walkers' guidebook publisher Cicerone, intended for experienced trekkers, with route descriptions and a weatherproof cover, but minimal mapping.

- *Trekking in the Moroccan Atlas* by Richard Knight. The most recent guide, with coverage of Jebel Sarhro and Jebel Siroua, and detailed sketch maps of each part of the route. Likely to be the most useful of all for inexperienced trekkers, although also the bulkiest..

---

weather can change. Light, baggy, cotton trousers and long-sleeved shirts are best in summer (June to August), but prepare for very cold weather during winter (November to March) wherever you trek in the country. Outside the height of summer pack warm clothing, a woollen hat and gloves for trekking in the High Atlas. In summer, even at 1800m, it's cold enough at night to require a fleece or jumper. At the same time, you will need a sunhat, sunglasses and quality sunscreen year-round.

The key decision to make, when planning a route, is whether or not to sleep in tents. A good tent opens up endless trekking possibilities, but you don't necessarily have to bring your own, as most tour operators will rent one. It is also possible to rent them from some guides and from trailheads such as Imlil. If you would rather not camp, in most regions you can choose to stay in villages, either in *gîtes d'étape* or *chez l'habitant* (in someone's home). In both of these and especially in remote areas, rooms may not even have a mattress on the floor, although in places such as Imlil they often come with beds.

Whether you are camping or staying in houses, from September to early April a four-season sleeping bag is essential for the High Atlas and Jebel Sarhro – temperatures as low as -10°C are not unknown at this time. In lower mountain ranges, even in high summer, a bag comfortable at 0°C is recommended. A thick sleeping mat or thin foam mattress is a good idea since the ground is extremely rocky. These can usually be supplied by guides.

If you want to go above 3000m between November and May, you will need to have experience in winter mountaineering and be equipped with crampons, ice axes, snow shovels and other essential equipment. Again, this equipment is available for hire through most tour operators or in Imlil.

Many *gîtes* have cooking facilities, but you may want to bring a stove if you are camping. Multifuel stoves that burn anything from aviation fuel to diesel are ideal. Methylated spirits is very hard to get hold of, but kerosene is available. Pierce-type butane gas canisters are available, but are not recommended because of environmental reasons. Your guide will be able to advise you on this.

Bring a basic medical kit and a supply of water purification tablets or a mechanical purifier – all water should be treated unless you take it from the very source.

If you are combining trekking with visits to urban areas, consider storing extra luggage before your trek. Most hotels will allow you to leave luggage, sometimes for a small fee. Train stations in larger cities have secure left-luggage facilities, although many of these offices will only accept luggage that is locked, so make sure you have a lock for your suitcase.

GUIDES

We strongly recommend that you hire a guide even if you are an experienced trekker. If you have considerable experience reading maps in mountain regions, you may not need a guide from a navigational point of view, but you should seriously consider

TREKKING

HAPPY FEET

You will notice as you travel around the mountains of Morocco that many Berbers manage to walk up and down mountains in sandals. How do they do it? Practice makes perfect and they have had a lifetime to achieve this happy state. Should you copy them? Not if you want to carry on walking. The most common difficulty that people experience on a trek is with their feet, usually with blisters from ill-fitting boots. If you are planning on doing more than strolling across a valley, you will be greatly enhancing your pleasure by buying a pair of properly fitted, waterproof (preferably Gore-Tex) boots that have been broken in. Even then you may get blisters. Many trekkers carry 'second skin', a plastic layer that can be put over blisters and usually stops them hurting. Happy feet makes for a happy walker.

engaging one anyway. Why? If for no other reason than to be your translator, your chaperone (*faux guides* won't come near you if you are with a guide), deal-getter and vocal guidebook. A good guide will also enhance your cultural experience. For one thing, they will know people throughout the area, which will undoubtedly result in invitations for tea and food, and richer experiences of Berber life. And then, if something were to go wrong, a local guide will be the quickest route to getting help. Every year foreigners die in the Moroccan mountains, sometimes in freak storms that strike at unlikely times. Their chances of survival would invariably have increased with the presence of a guide. So however confident you feel, we recommend that you never walk into the mountains unguided.

Choosing a guide can be a problem. Remember that a flash-looking, English-speaking *faux guide* from Marrakesh is no substitute for a gnarly old local mountain guide who knows the area like the back of his hand. All official guides carry photo identity cards. Guides should be authorised by the Fédération Royale Marocaine de Ski et Montagne or l'Association Nationale des Guides et Accompagnateurs en Montagne du Maroc. They should be credited as *guide de montagne* (mountain guide),

which requires study for at least six months at the Centre de Formation aux Métiers de Montagne, a school for mountain guides at Tabant in the Aït Bou Goumez valley. Note that *accompagnateurs* (escorts) will have had only one week's training and not insured to lead a trip into the mountains. It is also worth pointing out that someone credited as a *guide de tourisme* (tourist guide) is also not qualified to lead treks.

Official mountain guides, who can always show an identity card as proof of their status, have been trained in mountain craft, including first aid. In times of uncertain weather or in an emergency, they will be infinitely more efficient than a cheaper guide lacking proper training who you picked up along the way. If a guide you are thinking of engaging is reluctant to show his photo card, it probably means they either don't have one or it has expired (they should be renewed every three years).

There are more than four hundred accredited mountain guides working in Morocco and many of them can be found through the *bureaux des guides* (guide offices) in Imlil, Setti Fatma, Azilal, Tabant (Aït Bou Goumez Valley) and El-Kelaâ M'Gouna.

Some *guides de montagne* will have additional training in rock climbing, canyoning and mountaineering. All guides speak French and some also speak English, Spanish or German. In the past few years several young Moroccan women have succeeded in breaking into the previously all-male world of mountain guiding, but their services are in high demand.

At the time of writing, the minimum rate for official guides was Dh250 per day (per group, not per person). This rate can vary according to season and location. Rates do not include food and accommodation expenses. Guides generally get free accommodation in refuges and *gîtes*, but you may be asked to cover expenses for meals. If you embark on a linear route you'll also be expected to pay for the return journey of the guide.

Negotiate all fees before departure and count on giving at least a 10% tip at the end, unless you have been very unhappy with the service. If your guide is organising your trip (rather than a tour operator), be sure to go through all aspects of the trek ahead of time, including discussing where each day will start and end, whether tents will be shared (most guides have a tent or sleeping bag), how many mules will be hired, who will be cooking (if there are enough of you, the guide may insist on hiring a cook, usually at Dh100 a day), food preferences, water provision and the division of food and equipment between the group.

MULES

Mules (and the odd donkey) are widely used in Morocco for transporting goods through the mountains, and you can easily hire one to carry your gear. If you are relying on heavy local supplies, or are in a large group, hiring a mule (which can carry the gear of four people) makes especially good sense. As a rough guide, mules can carry up to 120kg, although, if the route is very steep or demanding, the muleteer may insist upon carrying less. He will have the well-being of his meal-ticket in mind, although Moroccans are rarely sentimental about their pack animals.

Some trekking routes are not suitable for mules, although detours (for the mule) are often possible. If high passes are covered in snow, porters may have to be used instead of mules (one porter can carry up to 18kg). A mule and muleteer usually charge a standard Dh100 per day.

As with guides, if you embark on a linear route you'll also be expected to pay for the return journey of the muleteer.

ON THE TREK

ACCOMMODATION

The bulk of trekking accommodation in the High and Middle Atlas are *gîtes*. In the Rif and little-walked Anti Atlas, *gîtes* are uncommon, and accommodation is more often in local homes or in tents.

Gîtes provide basic accommodation, often offering little more than a foam mattress in an empty room, or on a roof terrace or balcony. They have basic bathrooms and toilets, although the better ones will have hot showers. Given notice, the proprietor can rustle up a tajine. The official rate is set at Dh30 per person per night, but prices can vary according to season and location. Meals are extra (usually Dh30 to Dh50 per person), as are hot showers (usually Dh10 to

Dh15 per shower). The more upscale, privately owned *gîtes* charge as much as Dh100 for accommodation and the same for meals, while one new luxury lodge charges €200 a night for a double room (see p328).

CAF has five refuges in the Toubkal/ Oukaïmeden area, and officially bookings should be made in advance through the **Oukaïmeden Refuge** (☎ 024 319036; ouka@cafmaroc.co.ma). However, in practice you can usually find out if space is available at the other refuges in the Toubkal region by asking in Imlil. Be warned, though, that refuges are often packed in July and August. Members of CAF and other affiliated and recognised alpine organisations (eg the Alpine Club in the UK) get the cheapest price for a bed, followed by HI members. Children aged between five and 15 years get a 50% reduction.

The Fédération Royale Marocaine de Ski et de Montagne (Royal Moroccan Ski & Mountaineering Federation) has refuges (per person Dh50, Dh20 breakfast) at Oukaïmeden (well maintained and comfortable) and in the Jebel Bou Iblane (less comfortable, but with a guardian) in the Middle Atlas, 60km south of Taza. Their refuge at Ain Aflafal, on the southern face of Irhil M'Goun, was abandoned and it is now a summer shop selling water and soft drinks.

FOOD

Other than powdered milk, a range of dried fruit and sachets of soup, dehydrated rations are not widely available in Morocco, though hypermarkets in major cities are well stocked. If you intend to rely on local foods, then prepare yourself for a diet of biscuits, tuna or sardines, bread, olives, dates and processed cheese. By taking a mule you have the option to take bulkier, heavier (and more satisfying) local foodstuffs, including ingredients for tajines.

Bread, eggs, vegetables and some basic supplies (eg tea and tinned tuna) may be available in some mountain villages, but don't count on it. Meals can be also arranged in some villages (Dh30 per person is standard), especially at *gîtes* and refuges, although they usually need to be ordered in advance. Again, do not rely on local suppliers as your only source of food unless you have made previous arrangements.

Change money in the nearest major town and ensure that you have plenty of small notes. If you do get stuck, euro notes may be accepted.

RESPONSIBLE TREKKING

Morocco's potential as a walking destination has been only lightly tapped, so many remote regions are extremely susceptible to the cultural and environmental impact of tourism. Many travellers return home warmed and heartened by the hospitality of the Berber people, but as the number of visitors increases so does the pressure on the inhabitants. In response, travellers should adopt an appropriate code of behaviour.

Cross-Cultural Considerations

Dress code is a very important issue, especially among the remote hill peoples, who, however friendly and experienced, remain conservative in their habits. In villages travellers should wear buttoned shirts or T-shirts and not sleeveless vests, which villagers use as underwear. Above all, trousers should be worn rather than shorts. This applies equally to men and women. The importance of dress in the villages cannot be overemphasised (as many a frustrated and embarrassed trekking tour leader will affirm). However much you might disagree with this conservatism, respecting local traditions will bring greater rewards, not least by way of contact, hospitality and assistance.

Invitations for tea and offers of food are common in the mountains. By taking a guide, who may have friends in many villages, you'll open yourself to even more offers of genuine hospitality. While these offers are unconditional, it is worth bearing in mind that the mountain economy is one of basic subsistence farming. No-one has large supplies and in outlying villages there may be no surplus food. Being able to offer your hosts some Chinese gunpowder tea and some sugar (preferably in cones) is a very welcome gesture. Dried fruits are also appreciated, as is a taste of any imported food you may have. For this reason, it is important to be generous when buying provisions for yourself and guides.

In remote areas, people along the way will often ask for medicine, from a disinfectant and bandages, to painkillers or cream for dry skin (which many children

---

WORDS TO TREK BY

The following words will be helpful while trekking in Morocco – '(A)' indicates Arabic, '(B)' indicates Berber. Other useful Arabic and Berber words can be found in the Glossary p504.

adfel (B) – snow
adrar (B) – mountain (plural *idraren*)
afella (B) – summit
agdal (B) – pasture (also *aougdal*)
aghbalu (B) – water spring
'ain (A) – water spring
aman (B) – water
anzar (B) – rain
argaz (B) – man
asserdoun (B) – mule
assif (B) – watercourse, river
azaghar (B) – plane, plateau (also *izwghar*)
azib (B) – seasonal shelter for shepherds
brhel (A) – mule
châba (B) – ravine
iferd (B) – lake
ifri (B) – cave
jebel (A) – mountain or hill
kerkour (B) – cairn
taddart (B) – house
talat (B) – dried-up ravine or watercourse
tamada (B) – lake
tigm (B) – house
tizi (B) – mountain pass

---

have). Always make sure that the guide explains them what to do with what you offer, how and how often to take it.

For considerations on alcohol, taking photos and giving gifts to children see the boxed text p445.

Environmental Considerations
RUBBISH

Carry out all your rubbish; never bury it or burn it (Western-style packaging never burns well). Your guide may be happy to bag up all your rubbish then hurl it over a cliff, but that approach is simply unsustainable, especially given that more and more people are now trekking in Morocco. So if you have carried it in, then you should carry it out. Minimise the waste you'll carry out by taking minimal packaging and by repackaging provisions into reusable containers when appropriate. If you want to make a gesture, think about making an effort to carry out rubbish left by others.

Don't rely on bought water in plastic bottles. Disposal of these bottles is creating a major problem in Morocco. Use iodine drops or purification tablets with locally sourced water.

HUMAN WASTE DISPOSAL

Contamination of water sources by human faeces can lead to the transmission of hepatitis, typhoid and intestinal parasites. This is a particular problem in more populated trekking areas.

Where there is a toilet, it is a good idea to use it; where there is none, bury your waste. Dig a small hole 15cm (six inches) deep and at least 100m from any watercourse – something important to remember, given how many trekking routes follow rivers and streams. Consider carrying a lightweight trowel for this purpose: in the arid Atlas Mountains, digging without one can be difficult. Cover the waste with soil and a rock. Use toilet paper sparingly, burn it when possible or bury it with the waste. In snow dig down to the soil; otherwise, your waste will be exposed when the snow melts.

WASHING

Don't use detergents or toothpaste in or near watercourses, even if they are biodegradable. For personal washing use biodegradable soap and wash at least 50m away from any watercourse. Disperse the waste water widely to allow the soil to filter it fully before it finally makes its way back to the watercourse. Use a scourer, sand or snow to wash cooking utensils rather than detergent. Again, make sure you're at least 50m from any watercourse.

EROSION

Hillsides and mountain slopes, especially at high altitudes, are prone to erosion. Stick to existing tracks and avoid short cuts that bypass a switchback. If you blaze a new trail straight down a slope, it will turn into a watercourse with the next heavy rainfall, eventually causing soil loss and deep scarring.

LOW-IMPACT COOKING & CAMPING

Don't depend on open fires for cooking. As you will see on your walk, the cutting of wood for fires in Morocco has caused widespread deforestation. Ideally, cook on a lightweight multifuel or kerosene stove and avoid those powered by disposable butane gas canisters. If you do make a fire, ensure it is fully extinguished after use by spreading the embers and dousing them with water. A fire is only truly safe to leave when you can comfortably place your hand in it.

Vegetation at high altitude is highly sensitive. When camping minimise your impact on the environment by not removing or disturbing the vegetation around your camp site. In order to avoid aggravating the persistent and serious problem of overgrazing in many of the regions, sufficient fodder (barley) for all baggage mules and donkeys should be brought in. It is a good idea to enquire carefully about this before setting off.

THE HIGH ATLAS

الأطلس الكبير

The highest mountain range in North Africa is a trekker's paradise. The High Atlas runs diagonally across Morocco, from the Atlantic coast northeast of Agadir all the way to northern Algeria. Running for almost 1000km, the range includes several summits higher than 4000m and more than 400 above 3000m. This makes a spectacular setting for walks and offers the possibility of bagging a few summits as you go. The Toubkal region contains all the highest peaks and is the most frequently visited area of the High Atlas, partly because it is only two hours from Marrakesh and easily accessible by public transport.

The Berbers call the High Atlas Idraren Draren (Mountains of Mountains) and their presence here will be one of the most memorable aspects of a walk. Although wild and harsh, the area has long been inhabited by Berbers, whose flat-roofed, earthen villages seem to have grown out of the mountainsides, above terraced gardens and orchards of walnuts and fruit trees.

The first road, up the Tizi n'Test, was only cut through this remote region in the early 20th century. Before then, the only way to travel was via the well-worn mule trails that crisscross the mountains and once carried trade caravans and pilgrims between the Sahara and the northern plains. Walking along

TREKKING

them now often gives the sense of stepping back into an earlier time.

WILDLIFE

Spectacularly rugged and sparsely vegetated, these mountains contain terraced cliffs, enormous escarpments, deep gorges and flat-topped summits. Where the rock is exposed you can see a thick sequence of sedimentary and volcanic rocks, most often Jurassic limestone, cut through by layers of granite. The oldest rocks are the 610-million-year-old granites and granodiorites of the Ourika region (near Setti Fatma). Some minor glaciation also took place around 45,000 years ago.

The slopes and valleys have been transformed over centuries by the work of Berber farmers, who have cut terraces high up on the steep mountainsides and irrigated them with ingenious systems of small channels, called *targa* in Berber, which bring water from rivers and streams.

In spite of the harsh climate, icy in winter and scalding in summer, the Atlas Mountains are extremely fertile and productive. The lower valleys are full of almond and apricot orchards, as well as carob, quince, pomegranate, apple, cherry and fig trees. Vegetable plots include potatoes, carrots, turnips, onions, lentils and beans. In October much of the terraces is ploughed for a winter crop of barley, which is harvested in late May or June. Walnuts are also a major crop in higher villages, and are harvested in late September.

Overgrazing, agriculture and the collection of wood for fuel has had a tremendous impact on the High Atlas and much of its indigenous vegetation has disappeared. In the subalpine zone (2400m to 3200m) you'll see thickets of Spanish juniper *(Juniperus thurifer)*. These thick, gnarled trees are often blasted into extraordinary shapes by the wind, their exposed roots clinging like fingers to the rock. Higher up, the main sight is 'hedgehog plants', spiny, domed bushes that burst into flower for a short time in the spring. Wild herbs including lavender, rosemary and thyme are common – you will smell them underfoot as you walk.

Big mammals are not common in the High Atlas, though mouflons (mountain sheep with big horns), wild boars and gazelles are found in some areas. Other wildlife includes Moorish geckos, Iberian wall lizards and painted frogs. Small snakes are quite common, but will usually be dealt with by guides before you get a chance to look at them closely.

Birds of the subalpine zone include Moussier's redstarts, crimson-winged finches and, in wooded areas, Levaillant's green woodpeckers. Crows are omnipresent, and you'll sometimes catch a glimpse of majestic raptors such as lammergeiers, Egyptian vultures and golden eagles.

PLANNING
When to Trek

You can trek throughout the year in the High Atlas, but different seasons offer some very different experiences. Above 2000m, temperatures often drop below freezing between November and May, when snow covers the higher peaks and passes. Only lower-valley walking is possible during this season, unless you are prepared to bring ropes and crampons. Late April to late June is one of the ideal times to visit because in April and May the alpine flowers will be in bloom and by June, when Marrakesh is already simmering, daytime temperatures are usually pleasantly warm.

Midsummer guarantees long daylight hours and snow-free passes (though not always a snow-free Toubkal), but in the lower valleys temperatures can be extremely hot and water nonexistent. Rivers have maximum flow in autumn (November) and in late spring (April or May), after the winter snows have melted. Though many rivers are reduced to a trickle by midsummer, the area can still be subject to flash flooding in summer after tremendous thunderstorms, something to bear in mind when deciding where to camp. Despite the heat, July and August are the busiest months for visitors to Marrakesh and the High Atlas: trekking at this time can be wonderful, but is best done early morning and later in the afternoon, leaving plenty of time for a shady lunch and rest in between.

Guides & Mules

Imlil is by far the best place to engage a guide and hire a mule if necessary. There is a **bureau des guides** (☎ /fax 024 485626) on the village square, which has a list of official guides, complete with mugshots, which eliminates the risk of impostors. Guides work in rotation, so if you have specific needs try to organise a guide in advance. Of the 60 official guides based in the Toubkal area, only 10 or so may be in Imlil at any one time. Some of the more successful guides are also attached to the Kasbah du Toubkal and can be contacted through Aztat Treks and Discover (see p441).

It's rarely a problem to organise mules, usually done once a guide has been hired and with his help. Trekkers should be aware that mules have problems crossing Tizi n'Ouanoums, east of Lac d'Ifni, or Tizi n'Taddate, between the Toubkal and Tazaghart refuges. As the mules will have to take lengthy detours, you may need to carry one day's kit and food. Talk this through with your guide and muleteer. Allow a day or so to hire a guide and make the required trekking arrangements.

Accommodation

Imlil is the most convenient and best-equipped trailhead for the High Atlas and Toubkal. For accommodation and eating in Imlil see p328.

Three kilometres above Imlil, and now also accessible by a drivable *piste* (track), **Aroumd** (or Armed), at 1960m, is a growing village surrounded by orchards and terraced fields at the beginning of a broad valley that leads up towards Toubkal. Several trekking companies use Aroumd as a base for group treks around the Toubkal area and, with four *gîtes*, it makes a good stop on the Toubkal ascent.

Gîte Atlas Toubkal (☎ 024 485664, 068 882764; dm with half board Dh60) In the middle of the village, this large multi-storey place is run by veteran mountain guide Mohamed Id Balaïd's efficient and friendly family. Facilities are clean (hot shower Dh10) and the rooms are relatively comfortable.

Les Roches Armed/Chez Lahcen (no phone; dorm Dh30 per person; meals on request) At the top of the village, it's a steep climb with luggage to get here, but worth it for the mountain views. Rooms are neat and recently redecorated, with mattresses. A hot shower costs Dh10. New rooms were under construction at the time of writing.

Hôtel Armed (☎ 024 485745; idbelaid@menara.ma; s/d 80/100) Run by one of longest-established tour operators in the High Atlas, this hotel-restaurant sits across the valley, with views of Aroumd village and the mountains. It has basic rooms with mattresses, hot showers, a panoramic terrace and good solid Moroccan cooking in the restaurant. Highly recommended for family tours.

Camping-Auberge Atlas Toubkal/Chez Omar le Rouge (☎ 024 485750/066 936488; omar_le_rouge@hotmail.com; per person dm Dh30, camping per tent Dh15) Near Hotel Armed, the Atlas Toubkal has 10 basic rooms with mattresses and communal facilities, including hot showers (Dh10). There is also a basic camp site across the *piste*, with the possibility of using the showers. New rooms were under construction at the time of writing.

TOUBKAL CIRCUIT VIA LAC D'IFNI
جولة جبل توبقال
عبردحيرة إفني

You get the best of both worlds on this circuit: the majestic peaks and fabulous views of the Jebel Toubkal and a fascinating glimpse into Berber life in some remote High Atlas villages. You will need tents and camping gear for this particular route, though with short detours you could use basic village accommodation and mountain refuges, a good option early or late in the season, when temperatures can plummet.

The trek is fairly strenuous so you might want to include an extra rest day, or consider the options for making the trek a little shorter. Indeed, if the following seems

---

THE TREK AT A GLANCE

Duration seven to nine days
Distance 60.2km
Standard medium to hard
Start/Finish Imlil village
Highest Point Jebel Toubkal (4167m)
Nearest Large Town Marrakesh
Accommodation camping, village *gîtes* and mountain refuges
Public Transport yes
Summary Easily accessible from Marrakesh, this circuit around (and up) Jebel Toubkal passes through a variety of landscapes, ranging from lush, cultivated valleys and Berber villages to forbidding peaks and bleak high passes. This is a demanding trek, with long, gruelling climbs over rocky terrain. A guide is highly recommended, fitness essential.

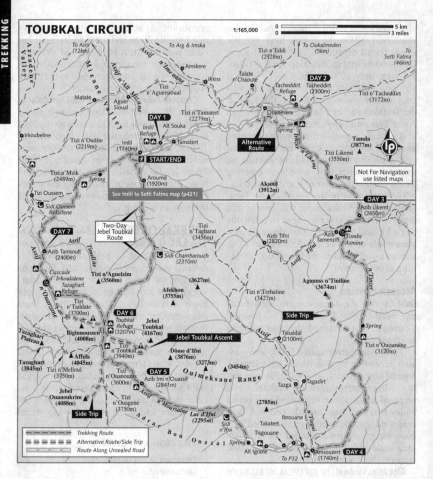

too much, there is always the simple and popular two-day ascent of Toubkal from Imlil (see p419).

Most of the route is above 2000m, with several high passes over 3000m. The ascent of Jebel Toubkal takes place on the sixth day, allowing five days of acclimatisation to altitude, which can be an issue over 3000m. The circuit detailed below is best done in late spring or summer. Numerous other trekking routes emanate from this outline.

Planning

The best place to organise this trek is in Imlil (p328). The walk described requires seven days, but the circuit can be shortened or lengthened. From Azib Likemt, for in-

stance, you could head west to Sidi Chamharouch via Tizi n'Tagharat (3465m), which would make a three-day circuit from Imlil (spending the second night at Azib Tifni). Alternatively, you could save two days by skipping the trek over Tizi n'Taddate to the Tazaghart refuge after you've ascended Toubkal. There are options for extending the trek, either by peak-bagging or exploring side routes, such as the Tazaghart plateau. Mountain guides can customise routes to suit time, ability and conditions.

Maps

The 1:50,000 sheet map *Jebel Toubkal* covers the whole Toubkal Circuit and is sometimes available through the Bureau des Guides in Imlil. Occasionally you can get hold of the clearer and more accurate 1994 edition.

The four-sheet 1:100,000 topographical *Toubkal Massif Walking Map*, which also covers the circuit, is produced by the Division de la Cartographie (Moroccan Survey) and can usually be obtained from their office in Rabat or from Stanfords in London (for both see p405).

The government-produced 1:100,000 *Cartes des Randonnées dans le Massif du Toubkal* marks trekking routes but is less useful because it includes less topographical detail.

Day 1: Imlil to Tacheddirt
3½ to 4½ hours/9.5km/560m ascent

For much of this relatively gentle first day, the route follows the 4WD track that links **Imlil** (1740m) to the village of **Ouaneskra**, 2km west of Tacheddirt (2300m).

Follow the track up through the centre of Imlil and take the left-hand fork over the river, **Assif n'Aït Mizane**. The *piste* climbs gently eastwards through fields of barley and orchards of walnuts, apple and cherry trees before zigzagging up to **Aït Souka**.

After an hour or so, just past a stream known as Talat n'Aït Souka, a fairly well defined but rocky path heads east, skirting the village of Tamatert. The rocky path continues eastwards for about 15 minutes, passing through a small pine grove and crossing the road. It then climbs steeply northeast to the pass, **Tizi n'Tamatert** (2279m). The walk up takes 30 to 45 minutes. At the pass is Bivi Thé, a weather-beaten tin shed which sells soft drinks and mint tea when there is enough business. To the northeast there are great views of **Tizi n'Eddi** (2928m), the pass that leads to the ski resort of Oukaïmeden, and **Tizi n'Tacheddirt** (3172m), northeast of which is the beautiful **Ourika Valley**.

The path rejoins the dirt road at Tizi n'Tamatert, from where it's an easy 45-minute walk to the village of Ouaneskra. All along this stretch you will be treated to great views across the valley to the neat Berber houses and lush terraces of Talate n'Chaoute, Tamguist and Ouaneskra.

A little before reaching Ouaneskra, the path divides. The mule track to the right traverses the southern side of the valley. This is a short cut to the best camping place,

near the track and close to **Irhzer n'Likemt**, a stream and reliable water source. This is the starting place for the next day's climb.

If you would rather take the longer route via Ouaneskra and Tacheddirt, then take the northern side of the valley after crossing Tizi n'Tamatert. There are three *gîtes* in Ouaneskra, and a pleasant little restaurant, so it is tempting to stop here for the night. But the second day's walk is fairly long, so it's best to have lunch here and then carry on. The village of **Tacheddirt** is 2km further along the well-defined mule trail or by the 4WD road that runs along the north side of the slope. In Tacheddirt, 23 people can sleep at the basic **CAF refuge** (dm CAF/HI members Dh26/39, nonmembers Dh52). You may also be able to stay *chez l'habitant* in the house of the refuge *gardien* (attendant) and elsewhere in the village (Dh30).

From Tacheddirt, the track then loops south to the camp site near Irhzer n'Likemt.

Day 2: Tacheddirt to Azib Likemt
five to six hours/9km/1200m ascent/900m descent

There is a lot of climbing on this day, but the rewards are all around you. From Tacheddirt you can either head straight down and across the **Assif n'Imenane** and then up past the camp site, or wind around the head of the valley on a more gentle route to the start of the climb. Either way, you will want to leave Tacheddirt as early as possible to make the two- to three-hour walk up to **Tizi Likemt** (3550m). Though the majority of the walk should be shaded, it's still a hard climb, especially for the 'unaclimbatised'. Half way up it gets steeper and then turns into a very steep scree slope towards the top. The doyen of Atlas climbers Michael Peyron calls this 'the grandfather of all Atlas scree slopes'. He also points out that skiers would be challenged to manage skiing down it when the snow falls.

Close to the camp site, a well-defined rocky path heads up the centre of the gully on the east side of the river bed (though it crosses over twice). It climbs for about 50 minutes before bearing left (southeast) up to the col (pass). From the top of the Tizi Likemt there are great views of jagged peaks and verdant valleys, up to Oukaïmeden and, on clear days, as far as Jebel Toubkal.

The path leading down the other side (southeast) is quite rocky. You'll pass a semipermanent water source on the left after 30 minutes, and the first of the irrigated pastures above **Azib Likemt** after another hour. An *azib* is a summer settlement and Azib Likemt (2650m) is occupied from the first week of May usually to the last week of October, during which time local people grow crops on the irrigated terraces and fatten their cattle in lush summer pastures. Their rudimentary stone dwellings, the well-worked terraces and sheer natural beauty of the valley provide an amazing vista.

You may be offered shelter or a place to pitch your tent in Azib Likemt, but if not then walk through the terraces down to the **Assif Tifni**, cross the river, turn right and then walk upstream to a group of large boulders, where you'll find some flat ground close to the river to pitch your tent.

Day 3: Azib Likemt to Amsouzert
six to 7½ hours/15.2km/470m ascent/1380m descent

This direct route south to **Amsouzert** is less demanding than yesterday's walk and is packed with contrasts, from precipitous valleys to stunning peaks and some good ridge walking too.

From Azib Likemt, the well-worn trail leads south from behind the camp site, up the mountainside and into the tremendous gorge formed by **Assif n'Tinzer**. Well above the river's eastern bank, the trail snakes above what at certain times of the year is the thundering **Tombe Asmine waterfall** and an alternative camp site before descending close to the river. Follow the river for about two hours, past stunning cliffs and through wide pastures, until an obvious track leads up the side of the valley to **Tizi n'Ououraïne** (3120m; also known as Tizi n'Ouaraï).

From here you are treated to some brilliant views of the eastern face of Toubkal, **Dôme d'Ifni** (3876m) and the rest of the jagged Toubkal massif. By way of contrast, **Agounss n'Tiniline** (3674m), 90 minutes away to the northwest, and other lesser peaks and ridges to the east are softer and rounded. (There's huge potential for sustained ridge walking or a long circuit back to Azib Likemt from Tizi n'Ououraïne.)

Continue over the col, where the trail traverses around the head of the valley to a spur and the crossroads of trails. Heading southwest, a trail leads down the ridge to **Tagadirt** (after 50m there's a fantastic viewpoint looking south to **Jebel Siroua**), but turn left (southeast) and follow the mule track south. Traverse around the head of another valley and then along the side of a spur, finally gaining the ridge after about 90 minutes. **Lac d'Ifni** is visible to the west. After a further 15 minutes, just before two pointed outcrops, the path forks. Turn right and continue descending slowly southwards to a large cairn (another good viewpoint). Descend southwest, then west down the end of the spur to arrive in Amsouzert (1740m) in 30 minutes.

Amsouzert is a relatively large, prosperous village (with one mosque and half a handful of satellite dishes at last count), spread on both sides of the river. If you're planning a rest day, this is an excellent place to take it. Next to the school you'll find an outdoor teashop shaded by an enormous walnut tree. You may be able to **camp** (per tent Dh20) here or else stay at **Gîte Himmi Omar** (dm Dh30, tajine Dh30) or at the same family's new *gîte* just a little further down the road.

Above the village, just below the track to Lac d'Ifni, is **Hotel Igroute** (dm Dh40-50).

There are a number of small shops in Amsouzert, and a couple of cafés near the village school, just west of the river. There's also early morning transport to the Taroudannt to Ouarzazate N10 road, with connections to Marrakesh and Ouarzazate. About 3km south of Amsouzert is another village called Imlil (not to be confused with the Imlil trailhead on the northern side of the range), which hosts a weekly souq each Wednesday.

SIDE TRIP: AGOUNSS N'TINILINE
From Tizi n'Ououraïne the easiest side trip is the straightforward 1½-hour trek up to **Agounss n'Tiniline** (3674m), which lies to the northwest. The summit is reached after crossing a number of lesser peaks, and it affords tremendous views of the Toubkal ridge.

Day 4: Amsouzert to Azib Imi n'Ouassif
5½ to six hours/10.5km/1100m ascent

Unfortunately for those with mules, your beasts of burden will not be able to make it more than 2km west of Lac d'Ifni. The muleteer will have to take the animal around to the Toubkal Refuge via Sidi Chamharouch, which means you will have to carry your necessary kit to **Azib Imi n'Ouassif**, over **Tizi n'Ouanoums** (3600m) to Toubkal Refuge. But there are consolations, among them Lac d'Ifni, the largest lake in the Atlas and a welcome contrast to the barren landscape of the approach.

From Amsouzert follow the level, well-used 4WD track that continues northwest towards Lac d'Ifni above the north side of the river. The path takes you through the villages of **Ibrouane**, **Takatert** and **Tisgouane** before reaching **Aït Igrane**, where there's a couple of cafés and, should you need it, basic accommodation at **Gîte Belaïde** (dm Dh30). There is also a shady camp site (Dh30) on a flat, stony site just beyond the Café Toubkal, with a rudimentary shower (cold) and toilet block.

Follow the 4WD track along the riverbed northwest out of Aït Igrane. Pick up the narrow rocky mule path at the end of the river valley, where the vegetation ends abruptly and the 4WD track crosses the river (there's a spring to the north) then turns sharp left. The mule path then leads around the north side of Lac d'Ifni (2295m), across an incredibly sharp, rocky, barren and inhospitable terrain. The climb is steep at first, but there is relief as it descends to the northeastern corner of Lac d'Ifni, a surprisingly large, and very inviting expanse of still, green water. The walk to the lake should take two to three hours. After you have seen the lake, but before you reach the shore, you will pass somewhere marked as a café. No coffee here, but if it is attended you should be able to buy water and soft drinks and, if no one else has ordered before you, a tajine.

On the small beach on the northern shore are a few stone shelters where you can seek shade – they make a good, if at times fly-filled, spot for a lakeside lunch. The ground is rocky and there is no vegetation to speak of, but the lake is safe – and very refreshing – to swim in.

Every October, villagers from the surrounding area gather at Lac d'Ifni for a three-day *moussem* (festival) in honour of a local *marabout* (saint), whose tomb sits in splendid isolation high above the southeastern corner of the lake. A track leads around from the northeast shore of the lake up to the tomb. At other times, anglers come to fish for the lake's celebrated trout.

From the northwestern side of the lake the track crosses the wide, dry part of Lac d'Ifni and then makes a long snaking trudge of more than 1km towards **Tizi n'Ouanoums**. Once clear of the lake, the path climbs through a rocky gorge, keeping to the south side of the river. It's a hot, sweaty climb in the afternoon sun, but relieved somewhat by the cooling sound of running water. About 3.5km from the lake, you'll reach **Azib Imi n'Ouassif** (2841m; marked on the 1:100,000 map by altitude only), situated at a crossing of dramatic gorges. Beyond this point the path climbs steeply to Tizi n'Ouanoums. There are some small waterfalls (freezing even in the height of summer) nearby. You'll find several flat but rocky areas for pitching tents, as well as natural shelters in the surrounding cliffs, which local shepherds have probably used for centuries.

Day 5: Azib Imi n'Ouassif to Toubkal Refuge
three to four hours/4km/759m ascent/393m descent

The path to Tizi n'Ouanoums (3600m) is immediately to the northwest of the camp site, leading up into a particularly rocky, rugged landscape. It's a steep, demanding climb for pretty much the entire way, but the views from the top over **Assif n'Moursaïne**, which is hemmed in by the jagged ridges of **Adrar bou Ouzzal** and **Ouimeksane**, are spectacular. The path crosses the river several times after leaving the camp, and the col is reached after 1½ to two hours (a stone shelter and water source is an hour away). Even in midsummer it's likely to be cold and blustery at the top, and with a fair bit of snow in shady crevices.

Coming down the other side, there's lots of treacherous loose rock and snow until July. From here you can see Jebel Toubkal and, to the west, the path up to **Tizi n'Melloul** (3850m). After the descent the track levels out and heads due north to the Toubkal refuge (3207m), which is about two hours from Tizi n'Ouanoums.

Toubkal Refuge (☎ 061 695463; camping per person Dh6, plus per tent Dh12, dm CAF members/HI members/nonmembers May-Oct Dh80/100/130, Nov-Apr Dh40/60/80), formerly known as Neltner, was totally rebuilt in 1999 and can now accommodate more than 80 people, although even this is sometimes insufficient to meet summer demand and a new hut was under construction at the time of writing. The refuge has hot showers (Dh10, residents only), flush toilets, a kitchen (Dh7 per hour for gas) and a generator. Meals are available and there's a small shop selling chocolate, cola, biscuits and other limited supplies. Bring your own bedding. The warden has a rather unreliable mobile (cell) phone, though, so it's best to make a reservation through the **Oukaïmeden Refuge** (☎ 024 319036; ouka@cafmaroc.co.ma).

You can also camp downstream from the refuge or pick a spot 20 minutes south of the refuge on a flat area of pasture. The latter is preferable, but you won't have access to the refuge's facilities.

Assuming you reach the refuge before lunch, there are a number of trekking options to keep you busy in the afternoon, including the three- or four-hour descent to Imlil, if you don't want to climb Jebel Toubkal. You might tackle the tough climb up and over Tizi n'Taddate to the Tazaghart refuge, which lies at the head of the Azzadene Valley, or ascend Jebel Ouanoukrim, which is best attempted straight after descending from Tizi n'Ouanoums. However, the best option (especially if you've got three days of trekking ahead of you) is to rest all afternoon to prepare for the climb up Jebel Toubkal the following morning (see pp419-21).

If you intend to complete the Toubkal circuit with your mules via the Tazaghart refuge, you should send your mules ahead on the day that you climb Toubkal. However, you might consider releasing your mules once you've been resupplied at the Toubkal refuge, or even at Lac d'Ifni, as with two high passes ahead that mules cannot climb, and with supplies run down, this may be the wiser course of action. You will have to pay for the time it takes your mules and muleteers to return to Imlil.

SIDE TRIP: JEBEL OUANOUKRIM ASCENT
The final stages of the circuit are fairly demanding, but if you still have itchy feet it's possible to spend the afternoon climbing Jebel Ouanoukrim (4088m, five to six hours return), the second-highest mountain in the region.

To do this, after descending from Tizi n'Ouanoums, turn left as you hit the river and head south up the valley. As ever, it is a good idea to take a guide, or at least get

some advice before setting off for this peak. Take the valley path back beyond the turn-off to Tizi n'Ouanoums and continue to climb up to Tizi n'Ouagene (3750m); from there follow the ridge to the summit.

Day 6: Toubkal Refuge to Azib Tamsoult
5½ to six hours/6km/493m ascent/1300m descent
From the refuge pick up the mule track that heads northwest then gently climbs north across the slope. Pass the first jagged, narrow gully; then, from a position high above a stream, turn left along a ridge west into the second valley. Initially keep to the southern side of the gully. The rough trail soon switches to the northern side and the route becomes rougher, requiring considerable scrambling.

After about 80 minutes, and having passed a couple of flat areas and a spring, you'll reach a wide and rather difficult scree slope: it's an unpleasant climb with a heavy pack. Follow the rough, zigzagging trail up to a small cliff face to the northeast, then turn left and traverse across to the rocky and exposed **Tizi n'Taddate** (3700m). To the left of the col is **Biginoussen** (4008m), while straight ahead the trail traverses the head of **Assif n'Timellite** to another col. (This area is covered in snow until mid-June, sometimes even later.) From this second col is a steep, tricky descent down the northern side of the narrow, rocky gully. Some scrambling is required for the first hour, until the cliffs part, leaving a simple descent to 3000m and the small but homy **CAF Tazaghart Refuge** (☎ 067 852754 or via the CAF Chalet in Oukaïmeden 024 319036; dm CAF/HI members Dh36/54, nonmembers Dh72), which sits beside a stunning waterfall.

An alternative route has recently been opened between the Toubkal and Tazaghart refuges. From the Toubkal refuge, head down the mule trail for about 15 minutes. You will come to a fork near a small rounded wall, used as a sheepfold. Turn left, westwards, up the zigzagging mule path, which will bring you after two hours to **Tizi n'Aguelzim** (3560m). There are amazing views on all sides at the pass: east to the Toubkal summit, northeast to the Imlil valley, northwest to Azzadene and west to the Tazaghart plateau. From here the track drops down in some 72 hairpins bends, at the bottom of which it crosses a stream.

Twenty minutes further on, at a fork, take the left hand track, and again 15 minutes later. Here the track leads uphill for around 10 minutes to the Tazaghart refuge.

Booking at the refuge is made complicated by the fact that the *gardien* is based in Tizi Oussem. You need to phone ahead, or else try passing a message to him via the muleteers or shepherds who pass. This will be easier if you are coming from the north. You'll probably find the place closed unless you've made a reservation. There are mattresses for 22 people, gaslights and a basic kitchen (there is a charge for using their gas). Campers can pitch tents beside the refuge, or on flat ground above the falls.

The refuge is mostly used by climbers drawn to the cliffs of Tazaghart, whose summit (3845m) is accessible to trekkers, who also have the chance to explore the wonderful **Tazaghart plateau** to the west.

Tizi n'Melloul (3850m), southeast of Tazaghart refuge, not only offers a harder route to and from the Toubkal Refuge, but also provides access to **Afella** (4045m), to the southeast of the pass, and to the jagged ridge leading north to Biginoussen.

The route down to **Azib Tamsoult** (2400m) is straightforward. Shortly after passing the impressive **Cascades d'Irhoulidene**, vegetation and tree cover increase. A five-minute walk from the base of the falls brings you to a pleasant wooded area, ideal for camping. To reach the village walk north for 10 to 15 minutes.

Day 7: Azib Tamsoult to Imlil

4½ to five hours/6km/89m ascent/749m descent

If you have made good time and you have the legs, you could continue down to Imlil at the end of day six. From the vegetable patches of Azib Tamsoult, with the **Assif n'Ouarzane** down to the left, a mule track traversing the forested slopes of the valley is visible to the north. Head towards it through the village and over the stream, and stay on it, avoiding left forks into the valley.

Climbing slightly and heading steadily northeast, with **Tizi Oussem** due west, you arrive at **Tizi n'Mzik** (2489m), where there's a possible camp site. Imlil is a 90-minute descent along a well-worn mule track; there's a spring to the right of the trail after 20 minutes.

JEBEL TOUBKAL ASCENT
تساق جبل توبقال

North Africa's highest mountain is something of a crowd puller and every year, summer and winter, hundreds of people come to climb the big one. Part of the reason for its popularity is that Jebel Toubkal is more of a challenging walk rather than a climb, and anyone in good physical condition can get to the summit. Mountain runners can jog up from Imlil in a few hours, while overnighters from Marrakesh will take longer to plod up in trainers. Although the ascent isn't technically difficult, it can be made something more of a challenge by Toubkal's notoriously extreme climate and its long, steep slopes of brooding deep-brown, red and almost black volcanic scree. The other issue here can be altitude sickness: at 4167m, Jebel Toubkal is high enough to make this a possibility, which means you should factor in sufficient time to ascend slowly and steadily.

The route described here is the standard walk undertaken by most visitors to Jebel Toubkal, but there are plenty of variations. An ascent of Toubkal can be combined with satellite peaks, and many (very fit) people squeeze in an ascent of Ouanoukrim (4088m) as well. Alternatively, the ascent

---

THE TREK AT A GLANCE

Duration two days
Distance 22km
Standard medium to hard
Start/Finish Imlil village
Highest Point Jebel Toubkal (4167m)
Nearest Large Town Marrakesh
Accommodation camping and mountain refuges
Public Transport yes
Summary The ascent of Jebel Toubkal is the most popular walk in the High Atlas. The views are magnificent. The route is straightforward and, outside winter and spring, usually easily achieved without mountaineering experience or a guide. However, it should not be taken lightly as the trek up the scree slope is hard, trekkers can be struck down with altitude sickness and the mountain's climate can be extreme: there can be snow even in June.

can be made more leisurely by spending a night en route between Imlil and the Toubkal refuge, either camping or lodging the night at Sidi Chamharouch.

Maps

The same maps are recommended for the ascent as for the Toubkal Circuit (see p414).

Day 1: Imlil to Toubkal Refuge
four to six hours/10km/1467m ascent

Toubkal rears above you when leaving the trailhead at Imlil (see p328). Try for a departure as early as possible for the walk up to the Toubkal refuge. It's not a particularly steep climb, but it is uphill all the way, there is little shade once past Aroumd and it can be very tiring, especially if you haven't done any previous warm-up walks or spent time acclimatising. Follow the dirt track that leads through Imlil towards **Aroumd** (Armed). At the top of the village, a mule track on your left wends its way steeply through barley fields and apple and walnut trees and past the imposing Kasbah du Toubkal (see p328). Beyond the kasbah the path zigzags steeply upwards to rejoin the road at Aroumd, where the broad valley floor is hemmed in by towering slopes.

Once past Aroumd, heading up the valley, cross the broad, stony valley floor. On the other side follow the well-defined mule trail, which climbs up to a very large rock (you can see this from the valley floor) above the eastern side of the Assif Reraya, which leads to the hamlet and *marabout* of Sidi Chamharouch. The origins of **Sidi Chamharouch** (2310m) may be pre-Islamic, but the *marabout* is now a place of pilgrimage for Muslims, so not everyone travelling this way is going to the summit. The number of pilgrims and peak-baggers has given birth to a hamlet, a cluster of stalls just under halfway between Imlil and the Toubkal refuge selling soft drinks, some food and sometimes jewellery and souvenirs. Just beyond the *marabout*, which is off bounds to non-Muslims, and to the left of the track, there are a couple of nice cascades and pools which make a great place to have lunch, with shade in the overhang of the rocks.

After crossing the river by the bridge at Sidi Chamharouch, the rocky path veers away from the river for a couple of kilo-

metres and zigzags above the valley floor. It then levels off a bit, before rejoining the course of the river. The refuge (p417) is visible for a good hour or so before you reach it, situated immediately below the western flank of Jebel Toubkal.

Day 2: The Ascent
six hours/12km/960m ascent & descent

There is usually an air of excitement at the refuge as trekkers consider the prospects ahead. Two cwms (valleys formed by past glacial activity) run down the western flank of Toubkal, divided by the west-northwest ridge, which leads down from the summit. The southern cwm is the more usual route, and starts immediately below the refuge. Set off as early as possible to avoid climbing in the sun – there is no shade apart from the rocks – and be sure to have more than enough water and snacks. Warm clothing is also essential as a strong, bitter wind often blows across the summit.

If you have come up on a one-day trek from Imlil you may not be properly acclimatised, which means that altitude sickness is a real possibility. Be sure to walk at a steady, slow pace. If you do experience more than mild symptoms (serious symptoms may include a severe headache or vomiting) you should descend immediately. However tempting, do not lie down to sleep for a while on the slope.

The southern cwm track starts behind the refuge, where you need to cross the river and head eastwards to the clearly visible scree slope. Start to climb on the well-defined path that moves to the left of the slope. Cross the 'field' of boulders and then follow the straightforward path that zigzags up to **Tizi n'Toubkal** (3940m), straight ahead on the skyline. From there the path turns left (northeast) and follows the ridge to the summit (4167m). Provided there is no heat haze, you should be rewarded by superb views in all directions, especially early in the morning. Allow 2½ to 3½ hours to reach the top, depending on your fitness and weather conditions.

Stick to the same route coming down, bearing left when the refuge comes into view. The descent to the refuge should only take an hour or two, after which you can return directly to Aroumd or Imlil. If you are planning on spending a second night at the refuge, you could come down the longer route via the *Ihibi sud*, or south circuit. It is a straightforward two- to three-hour walk down to the refuge.

IMLIL TO SETTI FATMA إمليل إلى ستي فاطمة

Instead of the highest peaks of the highest mountains of the High Atlas, this walk provides variety and a taste of just about everything that the mountains have to offer: high, windswept passes, wild and rocky landscapes and lush valleys that support a way of life that seems to have changed little in centuries. The route crosses a widely varied terrain and passes through a dozen or more Berber villages, some of which have yet to be connected with electricity. What's more, the trailhead is only two hours from Marrakesh and is easily accessible by public transport.

Planning

This walk can be done comfortably in three days and could feasibly be completed in two by a very fit walker, although they might prefer taking in some of the many possible side trips and variations, especially around Timichi. If you're planning a longer stay, you'll need to bring extra supplies. This area of the High Atlas is covered by the 1:100,000 *Oukaïmeden-Toubkal* government survey sheet.

Setti Fatma has a **bureau des guides** (☎ /fax 024 426113), several small hotels (with hot showers) and plenty of cafés; see p327.

THE TREK AT A GLANCE

Duration three days
Distance 30km
Standard easy to medium
Start Imlil village
Finish Setti Fatma
Highest Point Tizi n'Tacheddirt (3172m)
Nearest Large Town Marrakesh
Accommodation camping and *gîtes*
Public Transport yes
Summary A superb and relatively leisurely three-day walk through some of the most spectacular country in the High Atlas. The route leads over only one rocky high pass, which is followed by a long descent into the upper Ourika Valley, a heavily cultivated area where countless green terraces and shady walnut groves cascade down the steep mountain sides.

Buses and grands taxis (Dh20) travel pretty frequently between Setti Fatma and Bab er-Rob in Marrakesh (67km).

Day 1: Imlil to Ouaneskra
three to 3½ hours/7km/560m ascent
The first section of this trek is almost the same route as for the first day of the Toubkal Circuit (see p415), walking out of the trailhead and into the mountains. Once at **Tizi n'Tamatert** (2279m), it's an easy 45-minute walk to the village of **Ouaneskra** along a track that gives lovely views across the valley.

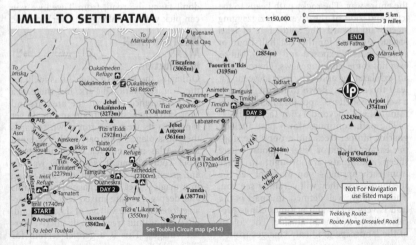

IMLIL TO SETTI FATMA   1:150,000   0 — 5 km / 0 — 3 miles

TREKKING

Ouaneskra now has three well-run **gîtes** (per person Dh30, meals Dh30, hot shower Dh10). You will pass the first one just before you cross the river, outside the village. The other two are at either end of the village. Where you stay will probably depend upon whom your guide has family connections with.

If you have walked to Ouaneskra in the morning, you could spend the afternoon in the **Imenane Valley**, which stretches from Ouaneskra and Tacheddirt northwest towards Asni. As the land is fertile and well watered and therefore heavily cultivated, the valley is dotted with Berber villages.

Alternatively, you could make a head start on the next day's walk by continuing another 2km to **Tacheddirt** (2300m), following the new road as it veers off to the right before Ouaneskra and crossing the Amagdoul plateau, which in summer is a popular place to bivouac. In Tacheddirt there is a **CAF refuge** (dm CAF/HI members Dh26/39, nonmembers Dh52) and the possibility of staying *chez l'habitant* in the house of the runner from the refuge (Dh30).

Day 2: Ouaneskra to Timichi
six to seven hours/12km/900m ascent/1300m descent
Follow the well-used mule path out of Ouaneskra and on to the village of Tacheddirt, which is surrounded by huge swathes of beautifully terraced fields. On the far side of the village the track begins to climb steadily up some 850m to **Tizi n'Tacheddirt** (3172m), with the pass ahead of you visible the entire way. The rocky path keeps to the left-hand side of the riverbed, zigzagging steeply up towards the south face of **Jebel Angour** (3616m) for the last half-hour or so. The pass is exposed and windy, but as ever has some stunning views. There is then an exhilarating and very long descent (at least three hours) down to **Timichi**. There is a welcome sheltered spot for lunch some 30 minutes' walk beyond Tizi n'Tacheddirt.

The path continues down past ancient, gnarled juniper trees and around the sloping eastern flank of Jebel Angour, where sheep and goats are brought to graze from early spring – you may not see the shepherds, but they will certainly see you. Though fairly well defined, this part of the trail is very rocky and at times clings precariously to the mountainside. The colour of the landscape gradually changes from a pale coffee colour to red and then to green. Finally, the cascading terraces of **Iabassene** village come into view. Head now for the huge old walnut tree that stands guard outside the village, and then follow the path that leads past the village houses. The path veers northeast from here and Timichi is just another 2km further on.

There are two places to stay, a **gîte** (dm Dh30) in Iabassene and another in Timichi. The Timichi **gîte** (dm Dh30) is outside the village proper, on the south side of the river, and has a great terrace from which to watch village activities. Basic meals are usually available at both places.

Day 3: Timichi to Setti Fatma
four to 4½ hours/11km/370m descent
Cross the river bed and turn right to follow the long, easy trail that runs east, high above the valley full of cornfields and walnut groves and passing through Tiourdiou, Tadrart and a string of other small villages: Tiwediwe, Anfli and Tadrart. There are fantastic, bird's-eye views down onto the intricate irrigation channels and village terraces. In late May and early June many of these terraces are crammed with golden barley, ready for summer harvest. As the valley gradually opens out, the path climbs higher, clinging to the bare mountain sides.

As the path becomes increasingly rocky, at Tadrart you might prefer to follow the dirt road, which will bring you into **Setti Fatma** (p327) in an hour and a half. If you don't fancy the road, from Tiwediwe you can pick your way along the river's course.

WESTERN HIGH ATLAS
الأطلس الكبير الغربي
Introduction
Officially, the Western High Atlas includes the Toubkal National Park, but there is a great difference between the area around Morocco's highest mountain and the lower ranges to its west that run down towards the Souss plains. This part of the Western High Atlas may not reach the heights of Jebel Toubkal, but it is generally warmer and greener and can still offer great walking in a magical area where jagged mountains and deep gorges are mixed with considerable forests, fertile valleys of date, almond, olive and walnut trees, and distinctive Berber villages. This is a gentler terrain for

trekking that still offers some challenges and plenty of rewards.

Highlights

The gem here is the Tichka plateau, a bewitching area of highland meadows that is particularly delightful in spring, when they are covered in wild flowers. Although much of the walking here is less demanding than in the Toubkal area, the Tichka is still cut through with hidden gorges, thick with forests, edged with peaks and studded with stunning Berber villages.

Information

This area has some of the most remote walking Morocco has to offer. Some of the villages are very cut off and will not have seen the number of foreigners who pass through the villages of the Toubkal area or even the M'Goun.

While being off the beaten track is its strength, it also presents difficulties. There are, for instance, very few places to stay here, no official refuges, and almost no hotels outside the two bases, Taliouine and, nearer Taroudannt, Tioute (see p382), although there is a delightful riad-style place now in Afensou and it is possible to stay in houses in other mountain villages. For most treks in this area you will need to carry camping equipment as well as all your necessary supplies. Although there are Berber villages up in the mountains, travellers cannot rely on finding food, water or anything else.

While these issues can be problems for visiting trekkers, they are not for the local experts, so, as ever, we recommend you travel with a guide. Alternatively, consult the UK-based **Atlas Mountain Information Service** (☎ /fax 00 44 1592-873546; 26 Kirkcaldy Rd, Burntisland, Fife, Scotland KY3 9HQ). As well as being able to offer advice and make recommendations, they are also experts at running treks right across the plateau.

The best map for this area is the 1:100,000 *Tizi n'Test* and *Igli*, available from the Division de la Cartographie in Rabat or try www.omnimap.com and Hotel Ali in Marrakesh.

Guides & Mules

There is no *bureau des guides* in Taroudannt or any of the other towns that you might visit this area. If you are not travelling with an organised tour, you can arrange a trek with guides from the *bureau des guides* in Imlil (☎ /fax 024 485626).

As elsewhere in the mountains of Morocco, mules and muleteers are usually easy to find and happy to travel, usually with a day's notice. Your guide will be able to arrange this.

Routes

If you don't want to camp then your options are limited, but using Afensou as a trailhead (and taking advantage of its hotel), you can make several varied circular day walks – to Imoulas, for instance, which has a Sunday souq and is a 9km round trip. You can also make a two-day trek out of Afensou to the village of Zawyat Tafilalt, where you can sleep in village houses, returning the next day via Tazoudot.

The Tichka plateau can be crossed in a leisurely week on a route that starts at Afensou and could run like this: Day 1, walk to Tazoudot and sleep *chez l'habitant*; Day 2, walk to Imamarn, then up the Medlawa Valley to the plateau, where you camp; Day 3, crossing the plateau and camp; Day 4, you could spend the day peak bagging by walking up Jebel Amendach (3382m); Day 5, descend from the plateau down the spectacular Nfis Gorge, camping near the village of Imi n'Oksar; Day 6, walk down to Souq Sebt Talnakant, from where you should find transport out, especially after the weekly Saturday market.

The Tichka plateau is riven by the Oued Nfis, which can be followed all the way to Imlil and then on to Jebel Toubkal. This is a long trek (12 days), but five or six days will get you to Tin Mal and the Tizi n'Test road.

Transport

You can get into the west of the range via **Imi n'Tanoute**, **Timesgadiouine** or **Argana**, on the Agadir-to-Marrakesh road, and also from **Taroudannt** to the south.

If you come from the west, you can get along the dirt roads to **Afensou** (not to be mistaken with another village of the same name to the south) on transport heading for the nearby mines or, on Wednesday, heading for the Thursday souq. **Souq Sebt Talnakant**, which is closer to Timesgadiouine and Argana, is an alternative, more westerly, trailhead. Transports head up there on Friday for the Saturday souq.

Heading south from Taroudannt things are a little easier, as *camionettes* (pick-up trucks) ply the route beside the Oued Ouaar up to **Tasguint** and **Imoulas** (with a Sunday souq) and up to **Tagmout** and **Souk Tnine-Tigouga** (with a Monday souq).

CENTRAL HIGH ATLAS – M'GOUN MASSIF
الأطلس الك - جبل المكون

While the crowds flock to Jebel Toubkal, attracted by its 'highest mountain' tag and proximity to Marrakesh, a growing number of trekkers are moving over to the central High Atlas and the **M'Goun Massif**. The M'Goun offers great scope for trekkers, arguably more so than the Toubkal as it is remote and, so far, relatively unexploited. There is just as much drama here as around Toubkal: sedimentary rock forms, dramatic ridges and escarpments, and erosion has carved some tremendous gorges displaying deep-red and orange walls. These gorges are one of the highlights of the area and some can be walked and/or waded through (they're sometimes waist deep with water), making for a memorable, not to say chilling, experience. One of the great pleasures of this walk is the chance of following one river up to its source, crossing the mountain and then following another river down into its valley.

Planning

MAPS
The 1:100,000 survey sheets *Azilal, Zawyat Ahannsal, Qalat M'Gouna* and *Skoura* cover all of the major trekking areas. The government also produces the 1:100,000 *Carte des Randonnées de Zaouiat Ahancal* map, which covers everywhere from Agouti in the east to Zaouiat Ahansal in the west, but its scope is of limited use for most trekkers.

More easily found and more useful is West Col Productions' 1:100,000 *Mgoun Massif* (occasionally available in Morocco, but otherwise usually stocked by Stanfords, www.stanfords.co.uk and Omnimap, www.omnimap.com), which, although devoid of contours, is a good trail reference and useful for planning.

The German-produced *Kultur Trekking im Zentralen Hohen Atlas* shows the trek from Aït Bou Goumez to El-Kelaâ M'Gouna, and usefully marks and grades the many *gîtes* throughout the range.

Randonnées Pédestres Dans le Massif du M'Goun is a French trekking guidebook to the region, usually available in major Moroccan cities.

EQUIPMENT & SUPPLIES
All basic food supplies (meat, fruit, vegetables and bottled water) are available in Tabant. For anything else, including gas canisters, the hypermarket in Marrakesh is the best bet; otherwise, petrol, diesel and kerosene can be bought in Azilal.

Bottled water is widely available, but purifying locally sourced water is a more responsible alternative (see Rubbish, p410).

There is no *gîte* in Rougoult, but there is excellent camping beside the river. Your guide should be able to arrange tents. But if not, you will need to spend the night in Sebt Aït Bou Wlli, making the second day walk much longer.

If you are walking in spring and perhaps at other times of the year, a stick or trekking pole will be useful to help vault over the many streams and to balance as you skip stones across rivers. If the river is high you may need to wade and, as the riverbed is too stony to walk barefoot, you may need plastic or waterproof sandals, or be prepared to get your boots wet.

GUIDES & MULES
Perhaps because the Centre de Formation aux Métiers de Montagne, the guide school, is in Tabant, many guides have good knowledge of the M'Goun. The nearest **bureau des guides** is in Azilal (☎ 023 459430), but guides from the Dadès and Sarhro area to the south and from further west in Imlil and in Marrakesh are all likely to have the knowledge and the enthusiasm to lead a trip through the M'Goun.

All guides can sort out local muleteers and mules for you.

THE M'GOUN TRAVERSE
سلسلة جبال المكون

The M'Goun Massif contains some of Morocco's highest peaks and toughest trekking, but this particular walk is designed for all grades of trekkers, including families – children will enjoy riding the mules on the steeper section or through the rivers. The landscape is incredibly varied, with lush valleys and bare

---

THE TREK AT A GLANCE

Duration four days

Distance 57km

Standard medium

Start Agouti

Finish Aït Alla

Highest Point Tizi n'Rougoult (2860m)

Accommodation camping and gîtes

Public Transport yes

Summary A walk that will suit most grades of trekkers, even younger ones, this one runs through the heart of the M'Goun. There is one long day of walking, but this varied trek crosses some stunning mountain landscapes, passes through river gorges, leads up one river and down another into valleys blessed by beauty and fertility.

---

rock walls. Some of the Berber architecture styles you will see are found only in this valley, Yemen and Afghanistan.

Arrival Day

If you have come from Marrakesh the chances are you will be longing to stretch your legs. If you have camping equipment, you could start the first day's walk by strolling down the valley to Agerssif, where there is an ideal camping spot beside the river, shaded by walnut trees, just near the bridge. Alternatively, you could make the hour-long walk along the quiet road from Agouti to Tabant, where you can stock up at the shops and where there is a basic café. If you have walked to Tabant, then continue on to the *marabout* and *agadir* (fortified communal granary) of Sidi Moussa, which sits on top of an unmistakable pyramid-shaped hill northwest of the village. Sidi Moussa is said to be effective in helping girls marry and bear children. The Aït Bou Goumez Valley (p323) is so beautiful here, especially in spring, and the views from the *marabout* so stunning that you will soon forget the long and winding drive to get here.

There are several **gîtes** in Agouti and neighbouring Talsnant village, the quietest being **Chez Daoud** (☎ 062 105183, Dh50), a short walk down from the road, beside barley fields, with rudimentary washing facilities. **Flilou** (☎ 024 343796; tamsilt@menara.ma; dorm/d Dh50/150), on the road, has clean dorms and considerably more expensive doubles in a

neat Berber house with spotless washing facilities.

Day 1: Agouti to Rougoult

Six to seven hours/17km/326m descent/ascent

Agouti sits at the head of the Aït Bou Goumez Valley and the walk out of the village along the road has delightful views of the Happy Valley, the reasons for its name soon becoming obvious. After a leisurely hour and a half, a *piste* leads off left down from the road. A little further on there is a choice of following the *piste* or taking a steeper, shorter path that zigzags down into the valley, rejoining the *piste* at the village of **Agerssif** (1489m), which you should reach in under three hours from Agouti. Agerssif sits at the confluence of the Lakhdar and Bou Goumez Rivers, where there is a bridge. The river here is a good place to rest and a great spot to camp.

The Lakhdar Valley narrows considerably as the *piste*, wide enough to be used by vehicles, climbs its south side. A half an hour or so upstream is the picturesque village of **Taghoulit** (1519m), surrounded by juniper trees, and with a simple *gîte* (per person Dh30). The *piste* continues up the gorge and then out into the broadening and more fertile upper valley, until it reaches **Sebt Aït Bou Wlli**, (pronounced Ait Bouli) a sizeable village above the river, with a school (marked by flags), a Saturday market and, since 2005, with electricity. The **Gîte d'Etape Adrar** (☎ 023 458479; per person Dh30) is on the main *piste* and if you don't want to camp this is one option, the other being a homestay in Rougoult.

Several valleys meet at this village: Jebel Rat heads straight up on another good walk past the village of Abachkou to Jebel Rat (3797m). Our *piste* heads left, south, the valley becoming ever more beautiful as it winds up above wheat and barley fields, juniper, wild fig and almond trees. The village of **Tazouggart**, on the opposite side of the valley, marks a more-than-halfway point between Sebt Aït Bou Wlli and the day's end. From here, the landscape becomes ever more fantastic, with a hint of Shangri-la about it, until after two to 2½ hours you reach **Rougoult** (1893m). There is excellent camping just below the village beside the Tifra River. If you don't want to camp, there is the possibility of staying **chez l'habitant** (per person Dh30) in village houses, though you will need to ask around to see who has space.

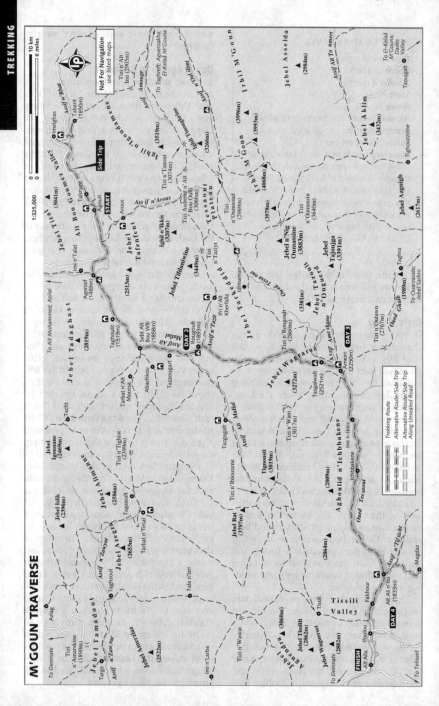

Day 2: Rougoult to Amezri
Six to seven hours/14km/600m descent/970m ascent

For two hours, the morning walk follows the Tifra, the stony path crisscrossing the river. There are terraces wherever there is space on the banks, although in places the valley is simply too narrow to cultivate. As it climbs, so the landscape becomes more barren. The mule path is well-trodden and although it occasionally is forced to climb above gorges, it does follow the course of the river, roughly due south.

The source of the Tifra, no more than a trickle at the best of times, sits just below the pass of **Tizi n'Rougoult** (2860m). At this point, even the juniper trees are below you and only alpine plants and bushes above. From the broad saddle beneath the pass, a path leads left (east) to a ridge that climbs to over 3500m. The Rougoult pass is well worn, straight ahead. From the pass, the summit of Ighil M'Goun – at 4068m just under 100m lower than Jebel Toubkal – is due east. Ahead of you there are long views across the southern M'Goun Massif and, more immediately, across the **Tessaout River**, a vast primordial scene that looks as though it has just been formed, the mountain slopes showing great gashes of rust, green and grey rocks.

From the Rougoult pass, the mule path is clearly marked, winding down in front of you and arriving after two hours at the first village, **Tasgaïwalt**. From here, keeping the river to your left, in all likeliness being followed by curious village children looking for entertainment, it is a gentle walk – 40 minutes, though you could easily spend longer – along the track to the village of **Amezri** (2250m). The 24-bed (mattress) **Gîte d'Etape Agnid Mohamed** (per person Dh30, breakfast Dh15, meals Dh35) has several large sleeping rooms, some of which look down onto the valley, a rudimentary shower and toilets, and the possibility of camping (around Dh10).

Day 3: Amezri to Aït Ali n'Ito
6 hours/18km/427m descent/150m ascent

The third day is one of gentle pleasures as the path follows the Tessaout River, shelving gently from 2250m to 1833m. The valley is hemmed in by some impressive cliffs, particularly by the Ichbbakene escarpment, which rises a sheer 1000m above the river.

The river has little or no fish since a large flood flushed them out a few years back, but it does irrigate some exceptionally fertile farmland which the Berbers, here of the Aït Atta tribe, use to grow a range of seasonal crops. In the spring, the valleys are carpeted with wild flowers, while the fruit and nut trees add their blossom to the spectacle. In this part of its course, the Tessaout flows more or less due west and is fed by a series of smaller streams that bring melted snow off the higher mountains.

At several places along the day's walk, the path crosses the river. For much of the year, it should be possible to hop over stones. But in spring, when the valley is at its most beautiful, the river may be too high and you may have to wade, as at the village of **Imi n'Ikkis**, some 5km from Amezri. The village is no more than a cluster of houses, but does have a shop (no sign) that usually stocks water and soft drinks, may also have the lurid green plastic shoes villagers wear to wade in the rivers, and occasionally has some tinned food.

As the path passes beneath the larger village of **Ichbbakene**, an hour and a half further downstream and backed by the sheer escarpment, you will see the significant building of the Hotel Edare. Built by a villager who worked in France, it was not operating at the time of our visit.

Two and a half hours further on, having crossed the river at several places, the path narrows and squeezes itself beneath the stone and mud houses of the village of Aït Hamza. At the bottom of the village is a working **water mill**. Powered by water diverted from the river, it's used to grind the annual wheat crop. Another hour of delightful walking leads to the village of Aït Ali n'Ito. The **Gîte d'Etape Assounfou** (☎ 066 075060,024 385747;fax 024 385744; per person Dh30; breakfast Dh20) is one of the best in the region, with great views over the valley, not to mention hot showers (Dh10), a boutique and electricity.

If you have time, there is a good side trip to the village of **Magdaz**, a three-hour round trip to the south of Aït Ali n'Ito, but well worth the effort as this is one of the most beautiful villages in the Atlas Mountains. Apart from the beauty of the place, check out the village's extraordinary architecture, where tower-houses have been built in steps using stone and wood, a technique only known here, in Fakhour (see tomorrow's walk), Yemen and Afghanistan.

Day 4: Aït Ali n'Ito to Aït Alla
2½ to 3 hours/8km/150m descent

A dirt road leads alongside the river on a gentle walk down to the end of the trek. Occasionally the route does climb a little before it reaches the beautiful little village of **Fakhour**, where the houses climb up the hillside and noted for its *agadir*, which can be visited. There's no entry fee, but the *gardien* should be tipped (Dh10 would be welcomed).

Less than an hour beyond Fakhour, the village of Ifoulou sits on a bend of the river and the road. This village seems to sleep for most of the week, there being little other than a drinks stand open, but on Monday it is the site for a large souq, when villagers from along the valleys come to trade and talk. Half an hour beyond the village, the *piste* joins the main Demnate-Skoura road by the new road bridge over the Tessaout River, below the village of Aït Alla. From here it should be possible to find transport in either direction, although there is no certainty as to how long you will need to wait.

THE RIF MOUNTAINS جبل اريف

The Rif Mountains, the first and lowest of the wave of mountain ranges that ripple south through Morocco, are perfect trekking country, which makes it all the more curious that so few people come here to walk. This is a shame, as the region is blessed with magnificent ranges, gorges and valleys, clothed in forests of cedar, cork oak and fir. Well watered by the Mediterranean climate, the Rif are the greenest mountains in Morocco, and springtime, with its riot of wildflowers, can be a particularly delightful time to walk here.

Some people may be put off walking in the Rif due to the area's notoriety as an area of drug production. It's a largely unfounded fear. Although kif (marijuana) production takes up over three quarters of cultivatable land east of Chefchaouen, there's little reason for trekkers to feel threatened, especially if they take a guide – villagers will be genuinely interested and surprised to see you. The trek detailed here, setting out from Chefchaouen, is well trodden and unproblematic in this respect.

The Rif Mountains rarely top more than 2500m in height, with most treks rarely venturing over 2000m, so altitude sickness isn't the worry it can be in other parts of Morocco.

WILDLIFE

The Rif's climate and proximity to Europe endows it with a Mediterranean climate – the area closely resembles the sierras of southern Spain. Cedars make up the majority of tree species, including a rare local species *Abies maroccana*, a variant of the Spanish cedar that is only found above 1500m. It's a relict of an older, cooler period in Morocco's history. In addition, cork oak, holm pine and wild olive dot the limestone mountains. The stony land is hard to cultivate and thin in nutrients; deforestation is an issue here as in other parts of Morocco.

BARBARY APES

Barbary apes (*Macaca sylvanus*), famous as the only non-human primate found in Europe (in Gibraltar) are resident in Morocco's Rif and Middle Atlas, with a range that extends across into Algeria. Their name is something of a misnomer as they are a species of macaque (a monkey) rather than ape – their virtually absent tail is responsible for their colloquial name.

Northern Morocco's cedar and oak forests are perfect Barbary ape country. They live in large social groups of up to 30 monkeys, foraging on the ground for seeds and fruit, picking out tasty caterpillars and bulbs in the spring, but making do with tree needles and bark in the winter months. The most terrestrial of macaques, they generally only retreat to the safety of the trees to sleep or at the sight of potential trouble – including the approach of humans.

Barbary apes are matrilineal, meaning that group hierarchy is determined by an individual's relation to the dominant female. Unusually among macaques, males take an active role in raising their offspring, spending much of their day carrying and grooming their young; male parental skills are highly selected for by females when choosing their mates.

Locals may tell you that there are wolves in the mountains, but you shouldn't believe the stories – the closest you'll get is spotting a red fox or feral dog near a village. Wild boar are also native, but have a retiring nature that makes them hard to spot. The Rif's most famous mammals are the Barbary apes (known locally as *mgou*), whose range extends south into the Middle Atlas.

You'll have better luck with birdlife. Raptors easily spotted wheeling on thermals include black-shouldered kites, golden eagles and long-legged buzzards. Ravens can also be seen against the limestone cliffs.

Scorpions present a small risk in the Rif, although less so than further south. Be wary of the red scorpion; stings are extremely painful. The venomous *fer à cheval* viper (named for the horseshoe-like mark on its head) is more likely to flee from you than vice versa.

PLANNING

You can trek year-round in the Rif Mountains, though it can be bitterly cold between November and March, when snow is common. It rains frequently between late September and June, while during high summer it is fiercely hot, even on the peaks, and some water sources dry up.

Trekking is relatively undeveloped in the Rif, but in many villages there are simple *gîtes* where it's possible to sleep for the night. Otherwise, a tent is extremely worthwhile. A decent sleeping bag is essential whatever the season, as is a light waterproof jacket – rain showers are common. Most treks originate in Chefchaouen, where it's possible to get food and fuel supplies.

Trekking guides can be organised through Abdeslam Moude, the head of the **Association des Guides du Tourisme** (☎ 062 113917; guiderando@yahoo.fr; ½day tour Dh120) in Chefchaouen. There's no office, so contact him direct. The Association charges Dh250 per day for a guide, and Dh170 for *gîte* accommodation including dinner and breakfast. It's also possible to arrange gîtes in person during the trek, this is slightly cheaper but can be a risk if the *gardien* isn't around – not uncommon at quieter, colder times of year.

Mules can be arranged to carry your luggage – not a bad idea if you're camping. They're more expensive than in other parts of Morocco (around Dh200 per day including muleteer) and must be organised in advance. During August to October, mules can be hard to organise as they're used for the kif harvest, and prices increase accordingly.

From the government 1:50,000 topographical series, survey sheets *Chaouen* and *Bab Taza* cover the Chefchaouen-to-Bab Taza trek.

CHEFCHAOUEN TO BAB TAZA   شفشاون إلى باب تازة

This straightforward trek is a great introduction to kif country and the Rif Mountains. Starting from Chefchaouen, it takes in some spectacular scenery, including the geologically improbably God's Bridge, a natural stone arc spanning the Oued Farda. The trek also gives the opportunity to spot troupes of Barbary apes as you skirt the edge of Talassemtane National Park.

Although we've listed the trek as five days, there are plenty of ways to shorten the distance or duration. If pushed for time it's straightforward to arrange transport from Akchour back to Chefchaouen at the end of day two. Transport isn't too hard to find in Akchour, or you can arrange for a grand taxi from Chefchaouen to pick you up at a specified time. Alternatively, simply hike back along an alternative route.

Day 1: Chefchaouen to Afeska
5½ to 6½ hours/14.5km/1200m ascent/600m descent

The first day starts on the 4WD track behind Camping Azilane (see Map190), with

---

THE TREK AT A GLANCE

Duration four to five days
Distance 56km
Standard medium
Start Chefchaouen
Finish Bab Taza
Highest Point Sfiha Telj Pass (approx 1800m)
Accommodation camping and gîtes
Public Transport yes
Summary Worth resisting the laidback charms of Chefchaouen for, this relatively undemanding trek takes in some spectacular mountain scenery and tiny Riffian villages, forest, gorges and weird geology.

TREKKING

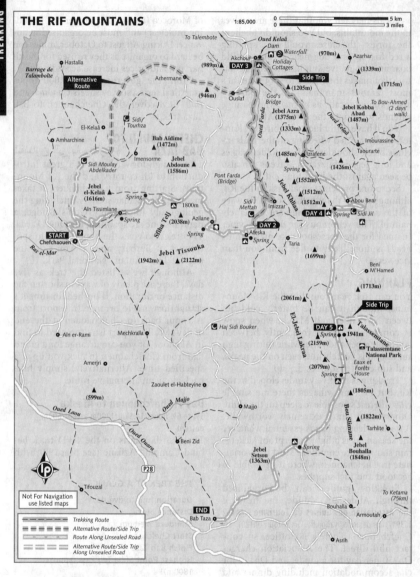

THE RIF MOUNTAINS

1:85,000

0   5 km
0   3 miles

Not For Navigation
use listed maps

Trekking Route
Alternative Route/Side Trip
Route Along Unsealed Road
Alternative Route/Side Trip
Along Unsealed Road

an initially steep ascent climbing through the trees to give great views over Chefchaouen's medina. Skirting the southern slopes of **Jebel el-Kelaâ** (1616m), the track evens out to follow the stream passing through the hamlet of **Aïn Tissimlane**, before once again rising in an arc to a high pass by the jagged limestone crags of **Sfiha Telj**. The views here are astound-ing in both directions, and on a clear day you can see the Mediterranean in the distance. There is cleared ground suitable for camping (no water source). The climb is a killer with a full pack – the hardest of the trek – so a cool early morning start is necessary.

The track turns east before descending. Stopping regularly to enjoy the fine views, take the right (southern) fork where the track splits – this takes you down in an hour or so to the village of **Azilane**, where there's a *gîte*. If you don't want to stop here, continue for another hour along a mostly level path to **Afeska**. There's a rough camp site cleared under the pines next to the football pitch.

Day 2: Afeska to Akchour
3½ to 4½ hours/10km/860m descent

From Afeska, the wide *piste* you've been following deteriorates to a smaller track. Heading north, you pass through more oak and pine woods to **Sidi Meftah**, where there's a *marabout* and spring, before leaving the woods and descending the switchbacks to **Imizzar** on the **Oued Farda**. Once beside the river, turn left (away from the village, northwest), then cross the river below some impressive overhanging cliffs and continue heading northwest. You'll join a well-worn mule track that eventually leads down to **Pont Farda**, an ancient bridge over Oued Farda.

Cross to the west bank of the river and continue north, dwarfed by the surrounding scenery. After an hour, the trails bears left away from the river towards **Ouslaf**, which is overshadowed by a giant rock buttress, but keep on the same path as it bears right, descending to rejoin the river on the outskirts of **Akchour** (398m), which sits on the **Oued Kelaâ**.

Akchour is strung out along the river. As you approach it, you first come to a small café with very welcome river-cooled soft drinks, and a dam with a deep pool that seems made for swimming, although the water temperature means short dips only! Upstream from the dam is a pleasant camping spot at the confluence of the Oued Kelaâ and Oued Farda.

Akchour has a couple of other cafés which can throw together a basic tajine, and offer even more basic rooms for the night, for a negotiable Dh50.

From Akchour, it's usually possible to get transport back to Chefchaouen – most likely one of the rugged vans or 4WDs that battle it out on the *piste*. If there's nothing going from Akchour, try **Talembote**, 2km further north, which has a market on Tuesdays with regular transport to Chefchaouen (Dh15). Most passing vehicles will stop to pick you up if they have

space – a case of paid hitchhiking. They may drop you at Dar Ackoubaa, the junction town 10km north of Chefchaouen on the P28 highway.

SIDE TRIP: GOD'S BRIDGE

With an early start from Afeska, you can reach Akchour by lunchtime, giving time for the short hike (1½ hours, 3km return) to **God's Bridge** – an unlikely geological structure that shouldn't be missed.

The path south from Akchour's dam up the Oued Farda is rough in places, but well worth any scrambling. You'll also have to cross the river twice but this is quite easy where it's not deep – if you don't mind the occasional splash. (However, if you're trekking in spring, check in Afeska that snow melt hasn't made the river impassable.) God's Bridge is about 45 minutes from Akchour. A huge red stone arch towers 25m above the river and it almost beggars belief that it was carved by nature and not by human hand. Over countless millennia, the river flowed as an underground watercourse, eroding the rock and carving a path deeper and deeper, leaving the bridge high and dry.

Day 3: Akchour to Pastures above Abou Bnar
4½ to six hours/12km/977m ascent

An early morning start sees you leaving Akchour by heading to the north, crossing the bridge over the Oued Kelaâ and then cutting right (southeast) along the track to Izrafene. It's a particularly picturesque walk as you climb up and around **Jebel Azra** (1375m). Your eyes lift from the steep gorges you've trekked through and out over the sweep of open mountains. If you're up for some scrambling, add half an hour to attain the peak, from where you can drink in further gorgeous views. For other sorts of drinking, however, you'll have done well to fill your bottles at Akchour, as there are no springs on the route until you reach Izrafene.

Having cut around the mountain, the countryside becomes gentler – rolling even – as the trail heads south. The village of **Izrafene** marks the halfway point of the day's trek. Just before the village, a track bears east at a col, tempting the adventurous to abandon the Bab Taza hike and walk to

Taourarte and on to **Bou-Ahmed** on the coast, a further two days' walk.

From Izrafene, the track turns into a 4WD *piste* – the first since Afeska. It follows a narrow valley, gradually turning east up onto a ridge with gentle views. Where it forks, turn left, and then, just 25m later, turn right onto a trail that heads southeast to **Abou Bnar** through a pretty stretch of oak wood. There's little to detain you here, so continue alongside the river (not the 4WD track) through the open, grassy country to the *marabout* of **Sidi Jil**. This is a pretty area for camping, but if you continue for another 30 minutes, you'll come to an even more beautiful spot, set in wide pasture near a spring – an idyllic place for a night's rest.

ALTERNATIVE ROUTE: RETURN TO CHEFCHAOUEN

It's possible to trek back to Chefchaouen from Akchour in a day by an alternative route. The route goes via the villages of **Ouslaf**, **Arhermane** and **El-Kelaâ**. El-Kelaâ is the site of fascinating **Mosquée Srifiyenne**, with its strange leaning tower. This route takes a quick six hours, unencumbered by any major climbs or descents.

Day 4: Pastures Above Abou Bnar to Talassemtane National Park

two to 2½ hours/6km/352m ascent
From the camp site southwest of Abou Bnar, walk back to the 4WD track. Turn left and cross the river, and walk south into the pine woodland. You'll quickly come to a T-junction, where you should keep on the right (the left goes downhill to Beni M'Hamed) where the path starts to ascend again.

Keep on the main track, ignoring further side tracks and junctions. As you rise and go through several mini-passes, the views return. To the west, the huge mass of **Jebel Lakraa** (2159m) dominates the countryside.

By late morning you'll reach the edge of **Talassemtane National Park**. A small sign indicates that you should turn left off the 4WD track to the house of the park's Eaux et Forêts *guardien*. You can camp outside his house and draw water, and he can advise on short hikes into the park.

SIDE TRIPS

The short walking day allows plenty of time to explore the area and watch wildlife.

Talassemtane National Park is where you are most likely to see Barbary apes.

Head north, back along the 4WD track above the guardian's house to a clearing and junction. Turn right and follow the track east into *mgou* country. Troops are relatively common here, although quickly retreat into the safety of the trees if you get too close. The track bends south, giving great views out across the valley to the long ridge of **Jebel Taloussisse** (2005m), before turning briefly east again. Here a trail on the right leads south over the spur of **Talassemtane** (1941m) to a football pitch – strange, but true! – on an area of flat land. From here it's possible to make a rocky traverse west, back to the camp site.

Climbing **Jebel Lakraa** is another alternative for gung-ho trekkers. The best approach is from the north of the mountain, trekking along the ridge to descend one of the stream gullies southeast of the summit. However, there's no fixed path and it's a scramble in places. Allow around 3½ hours return.

Day 5: Talassemtane National Park to Bab Taza

2½ to 3½ hours/13.5km/825m descent
The final day is a quick descent along the 4WD track to Bab Taza, where local kif cultivation is much in evidence. The trail swings through a wide pasture and on through the cork woodland of **Jebel Setsou** (1363m) before revealing the sprawl of **Bab Taza** (or so it seems after a few days in the mountains) below.

In Bab Taza, there are quite a few cafés and a couple of grotty-looking hotels strung along the main road. The main business seems to be in huge sacks of fertiliser for growing kif. Grands taxis leave regularly throughout the day for Chefchaouen (Dh12, 30 minutes) from the western end of town.

THE ANTI ATLAS
الأطلس الصغير

The last significant mountain range before the Sahara, the arid, pink-and-ochre-coloured chain of the Anti Atlas are less visited by trekkers and yet they offer some wonderful trekking opportunities. **Tafraoute** is the ideal launching point, with the quartzite massif of **Jebel Lekst** (2359m, see p396), the 'amethyst mountain', lying about 10km to the north, and the twin peaks of **Adrar Mqorn** (2344m) 10km to the southeast. Beneath the arid, jagged mass of these peaks lie lush irrigated valleys and a string of oases.

At the eastern end of the Anti Atlas, almost due south of Jebel Toubkal, **Jebel Siroua** (3305m) raises its bleak bulk above the landscape. This dramatic volcano makes an excellent centrepiece to a varied long-distance trek. See Tafraoute (p392) for more general information on this region.

AROUND TAFRAOUTE

Morocco has such a wealth of trekking options that perhaps it is not surprising that somewhere with the potential of the area around Tafraoute has not yet been fully exploited. The adventurous trekker will find here, as elsewhere in the Moroccan south, many challenging and rewarding treks because the Anti Atlas around Tafraoute has rugged, barren rocks and lush green valleys aplenty.

Jebel Lekst is the star attraction. The 'amethyst mountain' is a massive ridge that stretches away northwest of Tafraoute. In spite of the harshness of the landscape, the Berbers who live in villages such as Tagoudiche still manage to grow the mountain staples of wheat, barley, olives, figs and almonds. The latest area to be trekked in this region is around Jebel Aklim (2531m), northeast of Tafraoute. Easily reached from Taroudannt and Agadir, Jebel Aklim has the advantage of sitting in an even more remote area than Jebel Lekst, yet still surrounded by Berber villages in valleys guarded by old kasbahs. From the top of Jebel Aklim, there are great views over to the High Atlas and to Jebel Siroua.

This is a tougher region than the M'Goun or Tichka plateau and trekkers need to cope with a lack of facilities and the harsh climate. This close to the Sahara, the summers are blisteringly hot and winter sees the occasional snowfall on the high passes and peaks, so the area is best walked at the end of winter – late February is ideal. Daytime temperatures may be 20°C, but at night it can drop below freezing.

Other than the odd small store, you won't find many supplies in the area, so the great challenge is how to carry enough

food and water to keep you going. As with other remote areas in Morocco, it is often possible to stay in village houses, but you still need to be prepared to camp and to carry food and water.

The best way of doing this is by hiring a guide and mules. There is no *bureau des guides* in Taliouine, or Taroudannt for that matter, although there are guides in town – and many more *faux guides*. As ever, insist on seeing a guide's ID card before you waste your time talking through possibilities. As a rule, trained mountain guides do not tout for business in the street. Mules are not commonly used in the Anti Atlas, but you may be able to arrange this through your guide.

Jebel Lekst and the approaches from Tafraoute are covered by the 1:50,000 map sheets *Had Tahala* and *Tanalt*, while the whole area is covered by 1:100,000 sheets *Annzi, Tafrawt, Foum al-Hisn* and *Taghjijt*.

There are some twenty-six villages neatly spaced out through the Ameln Valley, the valley that runs along the south side of **Jebel Lekst**, and they make for a great walk. You would need weeks to do a full circuit, but a stunningly beautiful and suitably stretching five-day walk would start in **Oumesnate**, take in several villages, head up to the village of Tagdichte, the launching point for a day ascent of Jebel Lekst. It's a tough scramble, and the ascent is best seen as part of a gentle trek east through the valley from, say, Tirnmatmat – where there are some excellent day walks – to Oumesnate (both villages lie just off the 7148 road). This is an enchanting area to trek.

Southeast of Tafraoute the possibilities are equally exciting. The scramble up **Adrar Mqorn** is hard but worthwhile. Due south of its twin peaks are the palm-filled gorges of **Aït Mansour** and **Timguilcht**, which make up the oasis of **Afella-Ighir**. There is plenty to explore.

Jebel Aklim makes a great focal point for a four or five-day walk out of Irghem, with its copper mines. From here the route leads to the mountain, which dominates the landscape.

Transport is an issue throughout this part of the Anti Atlas. *Camionettes* provide a reliable though infrequent service to some villages and grands taxis will run on souq days, though at other times you may need to hire one to get you to the trailheads.

JEBEL SIROUA   جبل السروة

Some way south of the High Atlas, at the eastern edge of Anti Atlas, the isolated volcanic peak of **Jebel Siroua** (3304m) offers unique and exciting trekking. Isolated villages, tremendous gorges and some dramatic scenery all make this an excellent place for trekkers in search of solitude, stark beauty and a serious walk.

The ascent of Jebel Siroua is the most obvious walk to make, but, as ever in Morocco, lasting memories will be found elsewhere – in the beauty of lush valleys, in the hospitality shown in Berber homes, in the play of light on rock and the proximity of the Sahara. So if you don't fancy the climb to the summit, the mountain circuit will still make a wonderful trek.

The **Auberge Souktana** (p382), a couple of kilometres east of Taliouine on the main road, is the best place to seek advice. Owned by a Franco-Moroccan couple, it has become the trailhead – here you can arrange guides, mules and gear for the circuit. The 1:100,000 *Taliwine* and 1:50,000 *Sirwa* maps cover the route. In winter it can be fiercely cold in the region, so the best time to trek is spring. See Taliouine (p382-3) for further general information.

If you need supplies, regional markets take place at Taliouine and Aoulouz on Wednesday, Askaoun on Thursday and Tazenakht and Igli on Sunday.

Mules, as ever, can be hired at short notice (often the next day) at villages around the mountain

There's a challenging, week-long trek which allows you to walk out of Taliouine along a gentle dirt trail that heads eastward up the **Zagmouzine Valley** to **Tagmout**. It then heads northeast through **Atougha**, from where it is a six-hour trek to the summit of Jebel Siroua. Walking at a regular pace, you'll be ascending the summit on the morning of the fourth day. After descending into the gorges for the night, you'll pass the extraordinary cliff village of **Tisgui** before reaching **Tagouyamt** on the fifth day. Tagouyamt has limited supplies and, in case you can't find a room, a good place to camp in the amazing **Tislit Gorge**. From Tagouyamt, the valley continues to **Ihoukarn** from where you can either head south to the Taliouine-Ouarzazate road at Tizi n'Taghatine (you'll be able to pick up

passing transport here) or else complete the circuit by walking west back to Taliouine.

An alternative circuit that is even less trekked starts at the village of Tamlakout, where there is a classified *gîte*, and takes in Aït Tigga, the Assif Mdist and the foot of Jebel Siroua. It then ascends the mountain, continues to Aziouane and exits via the Amassines. Some of the trek is strenuous but no one day should involve more than six hours walking.

Taliouine and Anezale (for Tamlakout) are both on the main Agadir-Taroudannt-Ouarzazate road and are regularly served by grands taxis and buses.

JEBEL SARHRO   جبل صغرو

The starkly beautiful **Jebel Sarhro** range of mountains continues the line of the Anti Atlas, rising up between the High Atlas and Dadès Valley to the north, with the Sahara stretching away to the south.

Little-visited and relatively undeveloped for the tourist market, it offers a landscape of flat-topped mesas, deep gorges and twisted volcanic pinnacles softened by date palms and almond groves. This wild, arid, isolated country is inhabited by the Aït Atta tribe, great warriors famous for their last stand against the French here, on **Jebel Bou Gafer**, in 1933.

PLANNING

Jebel Sarhro throws up so many options that it can be hard to settle on a route. Wherever you go is likely to be eye-poppingly gorgeous, but be sure to choose a route that touches the heart of the range, between **Igli** and **Bab n'Ali**. The Sarhro is a winter trekking destination, although don't let that fool you: it can still freeze and snow falls as low as 1400m. But unlike some of the higher Atlas treks, it doesn't always snow in winter and even when it does, it is usually possible to trek. In spring there is still water around and night-time temperatures no longer fall well below zero. In late autumn you might see Berber clans moving their camps down from the higher mountains. Summer is scorchingly hot (above 35°C), water sources disappear, and snakes and scorpions are two a penny. Dehydration is common at any time of the year.

Jebel Sarhro has three trekking centres, the towns of **El-Kelaâ M'Gouna** (p346) and **Boumalne du Dadès** (p347) on the north side of the range, and the southern village of **N'Kob** (p344). A number of foreign tour operators (such as Explore, Exodus and Walks Worldwide) run good-value trips here, but all three of the Sarhro trekking centres have **bureau des guides** (El-Kelaâ ☎ /fax 061796101/ 062132192; Boumalne ☎ 067 593292; N'Kob ☎ 067 487 509).

Supplies should be bought beforehand in Ouarzazate or Marrakesh, although you will find tea, tinned fish, biscuits and bread in these three towns and may find eggs, dates, almonds, bread and tinned fish in some villages. In this environment, and with the amount of water that must often be carried, mules are a worthwhile investment and are usually easy to find.

The 1:100,000 *Boumalne* and *Tazzarine* maps cover the region, but the most useful trekking map is the 1:100,000 *Randonnée culturelle dans le Djebel Sarhro* by Mohamed Aït Hamza and Herbert Popp, published in Germany, written in French and available in Morocco. Expensive (Dh150), but worth the price for the history and information on the back as well as for the map.

There are minibuses that run from Boumalne du Dadès to Ikniouln (Dh20), at the northern edge of the range, departing around noon and returning to Boumalne early the next morning. Ikniouln has its market on Wednesday.

THE SARHRO LOOP

The classic Sarhro walk cuts right through the middle of the range, starting from Boumalne du Dadès or El-Kelaâ M'Gouna and following the same route to N'Kob. It is a great walk and one that many agencies, both local and international, now feature.

The Sarhro Loop is just as varied and interesting, but has one big advantage over the traverse route: it ends up on the same side of the mountains as it starts, allowing you to trek and then carry on into the Dadès gorges or to Merzouga and the dunes. You can walk it in either direction. Tents could be used, but the route offers the possibility of staying in *gîtes* or *chez l'habitant*, which

THE TREK AT A GLANCE

Duration five days
Distance 56km
Standard medium to hard
Start Boumalne
Finish El-Kelaâ M'Gouna
Highest Point Tizi n'Ouarg (approx 2300m)
Accommodation camping and *gîtes*
Public Transport yes
Summary A really good alternative to the classic Sarhro traverse, this route gives a taste of the staggering and varied beauty of the range. Some of the climbs are demanding and there are some long days walking, although there is the option of adding another night to the route.

can be very welcome in winter when you can wake in the morning to find that a metre of snow fell during the night.

Day 1: Tagdilt to the Assif Ouarg Valley
Four hours/17km/200m ascent

Tagdilt is an uninspiring village but a very useful trailhead, with three *gîtes* and the possibility of a daily *camionette* from Boumalne. The river here hasn't flowed in any meaningful way for years, but in the valley above the village there are almond, apple, fig and plum trees. For at least two and a half hours, you could follow the *piste*, used by the vans that cross the mountain to N'Kob, or the track that occasionally strays off to the side, only to rejoin the *piste* further up the slope. At **Imi n'Ouarg**, the third village above Tagdilt, the path leaves the road (which continues, along with the electric cables, to the nearby mines at Tiouit). The path turns to the right (southwest) beside the village school, which is topped with a Moroccan flag. There is a nice lunch stop, to the right of the path, just beyond the village.

The path follows the right-hand side of the winding Assif Ouarg valley, beneath the summit of **Jebel Kouaouch** (2592m). After an hour and just over 3km, above terraced fields, there is a neat farm where it is possible to stay **chez l'habitant** (☎ 061 082321; per person Dh30-50). The sons of the family can be hired as muleteers and meals may be available.

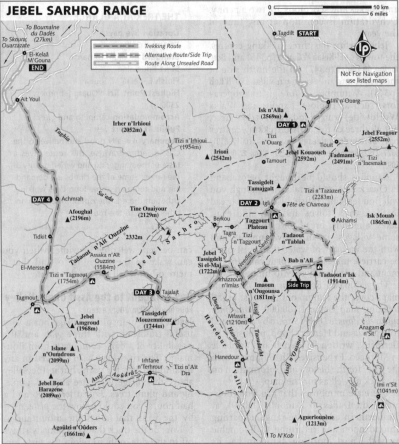

JEBEL SARHRO RANGE

| 0 | | 10 km |
| 0 | | 6 miles |

Trekking Route
Alternative Route/Side Trip
Route Along Unsealed Road

Not For Navigation
use listed maps

Day 2: Assif Ouarg Valley to Igli

Six to Seven hours/19km/620m ascent/860m descent
The most memorable and also most difficult day's walk starts with a climb, after 35 minutes, to what looks like the head of the valley, with a scattering of stone houses, and rocks ahead. Here a path leads left (south). Jebel Kouaouch dominates the landscape straight ahead, the highest of a row of peaks. The path zigzags over a stream, up towards Kouaouch and to a single, large old juniper tree – a good place for a breather. Depending on fitness and the weather, it could take another hour to slog up to the pass, at first with good views back towards Tagdilt, and then, once over the ridge, the High Atlas and most of Jebel Sarhro come into view.

From here a path drops steeply down ahead, but our track veers right (southwest) across the valley's shoulder and over another ridge, with great views south over the whole range to **N'Kob**. From here, **Igli** is more or less due south, over a series of slopes and edged in by some brilliant bare rock formations, the famous **Tête de Chameau** (Camel's Head) cliffs appearing as you walk down towards the settlement. The **gîte** (no phone; Dh30), three low buildings with sleeping room, toilet and shower with wood-fired hot water (Dh10), is basic (no mats to sleep on, no electricity), but the patron is welcoming and runs a shop selling trekkers' necessities, including mule shoes. There are breathtaking views of the mountains at sunset.

SIDE TRIP

There is an option to do a round trip to Bab n'Ali, one of the most spectacular rock formations in the Sarhro, and return to Igli for another night, or to then walk on to sleep at the Irhazzoun n'Imlas **gîte** (no phone; Dh30), making the following day's walk a little easier.

Day 3: Igli to Tajalajt
Seven to 7½ hours/24km/350m ascent/400m descent

The Camel's Head is the main feature of the first part of the walk, looming on the right-hand side, the peak of **Jebel Amlal**, sacred to the Aït Atta Berbers, some of whom meet there each August. The morning's walk is gentler than the previous day's, leading through wide, rocky valleys. After some 1½ hours, beneath a small village (Taouginte), the path curves around an Aït Atta cemetery, the graves marked with piles of stone. Beyond here, the path leads below the **Needles of Sarhro**, a long dramatic cliff that slopes down after another 1½ hours to the Amguis River. Several valleys meet in this beautiful spot, which would be a great place to camp, with palms and oleander. Half an hour southwards down the valley leads to **Ighazoun**, a small village above well-tended fields and a good lunch place beside the river.

At Ighazoun the path joins a motor *piste* which runs left to N'Kob, right towards the Dadès. Take the right track (northwest) towards a sheer cliff on the left, the rocky path leading beneath it and up to a broadening valley. The *piste* loops around the north side of Jebel Tassigdelt Si el-Haj (1722m) and then south again towards Tiguiza, where there is a basic **gîte** (☎ 071 728006; Dh 30). Before you reach Tiguiza, another *piste* leads right (west) to Akerkour village and then into a narrowing fertile valley dotted with palms and up an increasing incline to the beautifully sited village of **Tajalajt**, where it is possible to stay **chez l'habitant** (no phone; per person Dh30-40; basic meals if there is food).

Day 4: Tajalajt to Achmrah
Eight to 8½ hours/26km/200m ascent/300m descent

A long day, but another day walking in splendour, starting up the valley *piste* from Tajalajt, above the terraced fields of corn, and palm and almond groves. Under 1½ hours brings you to **Assaka n'Aït Ouzzine** (1584m), which has a large ruined kasbah just above the beautiful valley. From here the *piste* leads out of the valley into a very different landscape, a rocky steppe that might have been lifted out of Central Asia, often complete with howling wind. One and a half hours from Assaka, wedged between 2000m ridges, brings you to **Tagmout**, also sometimes called Amgroud after one of the mountains overlooking you, where there is a well-kept **gîte** (per person Dh30; breakfast Dh25) with electricity, mattresses and blankets. A simple lunch is usually available (Dh25 to Dh30).

From Tagmout the motor *piste* leads northwest to the Dadès Valley and south to N'Kob, and you may find transport moving along it to Boumalne's Wednesday souq and N'Kob's on Sunday. The trek heads due north, climbing in over an hour to the top of the Tizi n'Tagmout (1754m). There are stunning views from here to the M'Goun, Jebel Siroua and Toubkal. The track leads in another hour and more to **El-Mersse**, where there are the twin essentials of shade and a year-round spring.

The track continues due north, mostly a gentle descent, but with the occasional climb. Under 1½ hours after El Mersse, there is another camp site at **Tidkit**, set beside a river and with shade trees. There are a couple of houses here, so it may be possible to sleep *chez l'habitant*, or in **Achmrah**, another hour down the track. However, the Berbers on this side of Jebel Sarhro are semi-nomadic and may be absent. If the houses are empty, the animal shelters will be as well, a less glamorous but still effective place to sleep.

Day 5: Achmrah to the Dadès Valley
Four hours/14km/slight ascent/450m descent

The best parts of this morning walk are at the beginning and the end. The track runs north of Achmrah in a short climb that suddenly reveals more views of the M'Goun and Siroua. Less than half an hour later, it crosses a well-made motor track, which leads to an anthracite mine and should not be followed. Instead continue north, occasionally northwest, on a well-worn track that leads down a gully towards the Dadès valley. As you get closer, you will see the village of Aït Youl on your left, Aït Haroun on the right. The valley here is studded with old kasbahs. Head for Aït Haroun, where there is a bridge over the Dadès River. The Boumalne-El Kelaâ M'Gouna road is nearby.

Directory

CONTENTS

ACCOMMODATION

In this book, we have defined budget as up to Dh200 for doubles, midrange as Dh200 to Dh500 for doubles and top end as more than Dh500 for doubles. The exceptions to this are the pricier towns of Casablanca, Essaouira, Fès, Rabat and Tangier. For these towns, we have defined budget as up to Dh400, midrange as Dh400 to Dh1000 and top end as more than Dh1000. Marrakesh is another notch higher again, with budget doubles costing up to Dh500, midrange going for Dh500 to Dh1200 and top end places above Dh1200.

BOOK ACCOMMODATION ONLINE

For more accommodation reviews and rec-ommendations by Lonely Planet authors, check out the online booking service at www.lonelyplanet.com. You'll find the true, insider lowdown on the best places to stay. Reviews are thorough and independent. Best of all, you can book online.

Accommodation in Morocco ranges from friendly budget homestays or hostels to ex-pensive, top-of-the-market luxury riads (tra-ditional courtyard houses), country estates and grand converted palaces. In between are charming midrange *maisons d'hôtes* (small hotels) and riads that predominate in the larger cities such as Fès and Marrakesh. Like anywhere that caters to a European summer holiday crowd, the Moroccan coast also has its fair share of oversized tourist complexes, while budget travellers may also come across individuals' houses converted in the dead of night without the appropriate licenses.

In this book the official, government-assigned rates (including taxes) are quoted, although these are intended as a guide only. Many hotels will offer significant 'promo-tional discounts' from their advertised rates, especially in large resorts like Agadir or during the low season (May–Oct). It is always worth asking when you book.

Accommodation is often scarce during Easter week and August, when half of Spain and the whole of France seem to be on holi-day in Morocco. Another very busy time in the south, particularly in Marrakesh, is Christmas and New Year.

To make a reservation, hotels usually re-quire confirmation by fax or email plus a credit card number.

Apartments

If travelling in a small group or as a family, consider self-catering options, particularly in low season, when prices can drop sub-stantially. Agadir, El-Jadida, Asilah and the bigger tourist centres along the Mediterra-nean and Atlantic coasts have a fair number of apartments with self-catering facilities.

Camping

You can camp anywhere in Morocco if you have permission from the site's owner and there are also many official camp sites. Most of the bigger cities have camp sites, often well out of town. Some are worth the extra effort to get to, but many consist of a barren and stony area offering little shade – and are the domain of enormous campervans, to whom the basic facilities make no difference. If you're really lucky, you may have a swimming pool.

Most sites have water, electricity and, in summer, a small restaurant and grocery store. At official sites you'll pay around Dh10 to Dh20 per person, plus Dh10 to Dh20 to pitch a tent and about Dh10 to Dh15 for small vehicles (parking your campervan or caravan costs around Dh20 to Dh30, although this can go as high as

Dh45). Electricity generally costs another Dh10 to Dh15 (but can soar to Dh25) and a hot shower is about Dh5 to Dh10. As with most things, prices rise the closer you are to Marrakesh.

Gîtes d'Étape, Homestays & Refuges

Gîtes d'étape are homes or hostels, often belonging to mountain guides, which offer accommodation (often just a mattress on the floor) around popular trekking routes in the Atlas. They have basic bathrooms and sometimes hot showers. Official rates begin at Dh30 but prices do vary according to the season and location. You may also pay extra for meals (Dh30 to Dh50) and hot showers (Dh10 to Dh15) depending on the availability of facilities, such as hot-water showers and meals. You may also come across more comfortable privately owned

---

PRACTICALITIES

■ **Newspapers & Magazines** Although censorship has decreased, newspapers still practise a degree of self-censorship. Among the French-language papers, *L'Opinion* (www.lopinion.ma in French), which is attached to the opposition Istiqlal Party, airs some of the points of contention in Moroccan society. *Libération* (www.liberation.press.ma in French), the Union Socialiste des Forces Populaires' daily, is similar if less punchy. *Al-Bayane* (www.albayane.ma), another opposition French-language daily, isn't too bad for foreign news. For a full list of Moroccan newspapers online, go to www.onlinenewspapers.com/morocco.htm. A selection of European newspapers (including some British dailies) and the *International Herald Tribune* are available in most of the main cities. *Le Monde* is the most common. The British *Guardian Weekly* is also usually available, as occasionally is *USA Today*, and more commonly *Time*, *Newsweek* and the *Economist*.

■ **Radio** Moroccan radio encompasses only a handful of local AM and FM stations, the bulk of which broadcast in either Arabic or French. Midi 1 at 97.5 FM covers northern Morocco, Algeria and Tunisia, and plays reasonable contemporary music.

■ **TV** Satellite dishes are everywhere in Morocco and pick up dozens of foreign stations. There are two government-owned stations, TVM and 2M, which broadcast in Arabic and French. TV5 is a European satellite import from the Francophone world, while 2M is the primary household station.

■ **Video & DVD Systems** Morocco and France use the Secam video system, which is incompatible with both the PAL system used in Australia and most of Western Europe, and the NTSC system used in North America and Japan. Like Western Europe (but not the NTSC system of the Americas), Morocco runs on the PAL DVD system, but Moroccan DVDs share region 5 with Eastern Europe (Western Europe is region 2 while Australia is region 4), which means Moroccan DVDs may not play on all machines elsewhere.

■ **Electricity Sockets** Moroccan sockets accept the European round two-pin plugs so bring an international adaptor if your device comes from elsewhere; the electric current is 220V/50Hz but older buildings may still use 110V. Electricity is generally reliable and available nearly everywhere travellers go.

gîtes that charge as much as Dh100 for accommodation and the same for meals.

Larger than *gîtes*, mountain refuges (mostly run by the Club Alpin Français, CAF) offer Swiss chalet-style accommodation. Sleeping is in dormitories with communal showers and there is usually a lively communal dining/living room.

Similarly, if you are trekking in the High Atlas or travelling off the beaten track elsewhere, you may be offered accommodation in village homes. Many won't have running water or electricity, but you'll find them big on warmth and hospitality. You should be prepared to pay what you would in *gîtes d'étape* or mountain refuges.

Hostels
The Federation Royale Morocaine des Auberges de Jeunes (☎ 022 470952; fax 022 227677; frmaj@iam .net.ma) runs reliable youth hostels at Azrou, Casablanca, Fès, Goulmima, Marrakesh, Meknès, Plage Mehdiya, Rabat and Tangier. Some hostels have kitchens and family rooms. If you're travelling alone, they are among the cheapest places to stay (between Dh20 and Dh45 a night) but many are inconveniently located.

Hotels
You'll find cheap, unclassified (without a star rating) or one-star hotels clustered in the medinas of the bigger cities. Some are bright and spotless, others haven't seen a mop for years. Cheaper prices usually mean communal washing facilities and toilets. Occasionally there is a gas heated shower, which costs around Dh5 to Dh10. Where there is no hot water at all, head for the local public shower *(douche)* or hammam (see p442). Many cheap hotels in the south offer a mattress on the roof terrace for Dh25 to Dh30, while others also have traditional Moroccan salons, lined with banks of seats and cushions, where budget travellers can sleep for a similar price.

Midrange hotels in Morocco are generally of a high standard and range from imitation Western-style rooms, which are modern if a little soulless, to *maisons d'hôtes*, which capture the essence of Moroccan style with both comfort and character. In this price range, you should expect an ensuite room with shower. Top-end hotels are similar to midrange places but with more luxurious levels of comfort and design. Some hotels in more isolated regions offer half board *(demi-pension)* options, which means breakfast and dinner included, and can be a good deal.

You'll need to record your passport details and so on when filling in a hotel register. For registered hotels, there's a government tax (included in quoted prices throughout the book). Depending on the classification of the hotel (one-, two-, three-star etc), the tax ranges from Dh3 to Dh35 per person per day. Often it's built into the quoted room tariff.

For hotel accommodation price ranges, see p438. If you're resident in Morocco, you're entitled to a 25% discount on classified hotel rates on your third night in some establishments.

Riads & Kasbahs
The popularity of Morocco's converted riads has surged in recent years and you'll find the richest concentration in Marrakesh, Fès, Essaouira and Rabat, with other fine if solitary examples in Tangier, Meknès and Taroudannt. They are far more exotic than four- or five-star hotels, though room rates are much the same. Try to book in advance (most have only a handful of rooms), and arrange to be met outside the medina, as you'd never find the bulk of these riads on your own.

Kasbahs (old citadels), which often function as hotels, are found throughout the major tourist centres of the south. Rooms in kasbahs are small and dark, due to the nature of the building, but are lovely and cool in summer.

For an idea of properties and prices, visit the websites of these organisations:

Riads au Maroc (☎ 024 431900; fax 024 431786; www.riadomaroc.com; 1 Rue Mahjoub Rmiza, Marrakesh) A countrywide organisation with an impressive portfolio of riads and kasbahs throughout the country.

Marrakech Medina (☎ 024 442448; fax 024 391071; www.marrakech-medina.com; 102 Rue Dar el-Bacha, Marrakesh) Specialists in the Marrakesh medina, this agency has a good selection of beautifully restored riads available for weekly rental.

ACTIVITIES
Morocco is a magnificent trekking destination offering a stunning array of landscapes and treks to suit all abilities. Trekking is not

the only activity on offer, however, with bird-watching enthusiasts, golfers, cyclists, climbers, riders and spa devotees all catered for in a bewildering selection of activity holidays.

Bird-watching

Morocco is a bird-watcher's paradise. A startling array of species inhabits the country's diverse ecosystems and varied environments, especially the coastal wetlands. Around 460 species have been recorded in Morocco, many of them migrants passing through in spring and autumn when Morocco becomes a way station between sub-Saharan Africa and breeding grounds in Scandinavia, Greenland and northern Russia, while others fly to Morocco to avoid the harsh northern European winters. Early winter months at the wetlands are particularly active but the most pleasant time of year is March through May, when the weather is comfortable and the widest variety of species is usually present. For

---

MOROCCAN ADVENTURE TRAVEL

Atlas Sahara Trek (☎ 044 393901; www.atlas-sahara-trek.com; 6 bis rue Houdoud, Marrakesh) Winter camel treks to Erg Chigaga and summer hikes into the remote M'Goun valley.

Aztat Treks (☎ 068 760165; http://toubkl.guide.free.fr) Treks across the Atlas Mountains from a base in Imlil led by a fluent speaker of English, French, Berber and Spanish, who is equally at home taking a family group through the low-level M'Goun valleys or experienced trekkers and climbers up the steepest slopes.

Centre Culturel & Environmental (☎ 048 551628; 422 Derb Afferdou; ecotours@iam.net.ma) Affiliate of Naturally Morocco (www.naturallymorocco.co.uk) tours from the UK offering ecotours on botany, bird-watching, flora and fauna as well as cookery courses; they will consider arranging tours locally if they are not busy with one of their groups.

Equatorial Travel (☎ 0133 534 8770; www.equatorialtravel.co.uk; Ashbourne, Derbyshire, UK) Trekking, 4WD and camel trips off the beaten track run by a small agency based on a fair-trade concept.

Exodus (☎ 0870 240 5550; www.exodus.co.uk; London, UK) Excellent operator offering short or long treks in the High Atlas, Central Atlas, Anti Atlas and Jebel Sarhro, as well as biking and camel tours.

Explore (☎ 0870 333 4001; www.explore.co.uk; Aldershot, UK) Year-round mountain trekking and cycling trips.

Intrepid Travel (☎ 03-9473 2626; www.intrepidtravel.com; Melbourne, Australia) Small-group trekking and mountain-biking in the High Atlas and Saharan camel trekking, all with a focus on cross-cultural experiences.

KE Adventure Travel (☎ 0176 877 3966; www.keadventure.com; Keswick, Cumbria, UK) Trekking, climbing and mountain-bike specialists with treks to Toubkal, an Atlas traverse and Jebel Sarhro.

Mountain Voyage (☎ 024 421996; fax 024 421995; www.mountain-voyage.com; Imm El Batoul, 2nd fl, 5 Ave Mohammed V, Guéliz, Marrakech) The Moroccan arm of UK operator Discover, owner of the Kasbah du Toubkal. Mountain Voyage use reliable guides and equipment on tailor-made treks.

Nature Trekking Maroc (☎ 024 432477; www.maroctrekking.com; Marrakesh) Very well-organised treks by an experienced team of mountain guides.

Sahara Expédition (☎ 044 427977; www.saharaexpe.ma; Marrakesh) Camel treks in the Drâa Valley and beyond and trekking in the High Atlas.

Sherpa Expeditions (☎ 0208 577 2717; www.sherpa-walking-holidays.co.uk; Hounslow, UK) A well-respected trekking company that organises escorted and self-guided treks in the High Atlas and Jebel Sarhro.

Tribes (☎ 0172 868 5971; www.tribes.co.uk; Earl Soham, Woodbridge, UK) Highly recommended trekking, activity and cultural tours with a strong ethical and environmental basis.

Wildcat Bike Tours (☎ /fax 0178 681 6160; www.wildcat-bike-tours.co.uk; Stirling, Scotland, UK) Mountain-biking tours throughout southern Morocco.

Wilderness Travel (☎ 01-800 368 2794; www.wildernesstravel.com; Berkeley, USA) Well-established specialists offering three top-notch trekking or camel itineraries in Morocco.

Other local tour operators specialising in trekking or desert safaris can be found in Ouarzazate (p333) or Marrakesh (p295).

more information on Morocco's birdlife, see p80.

Tour companies that offer birding tours to Morocco include the following:

Birdfinders (☎ 0125 883 9066; www.birdfinders.co.uk; Westbank, Cheselbourne, Dorset DT2 7NW, UK)

Birdwatching Breaks (☎ 0138 161 0495; www .birdwatchingbreaks.com; Gordons Mill, Balblair, Ross-shire IV7 8LQ, Scotland, UK)

Naturetrek (☎ 0196 273 3051, www.naturetrek.co.uk; Cheriton Mill, Cheriton, Alresford, Hants SO24 0NG, UK)

Wildwings (☎ 0117 965 8333; www.wildwings.co.uk; 577 Fishponds Rd, Bristol BS16 3AF, UK)

Camel Treks & Desert Safaris

Exploring the Moroccan Sahara by camel is one of the country's signature activities and is one of the most rewarding wilderness experiences in the country, whether on an overnight excursion or a two-week trek. The most evocative stretches of Saharan sand include Zagora (p339) and Tinfou (p342) in the Drâa Valley; M'Hamid and the dunes of Erg Chigaga (p343), 95km further south; and the dunes of Erg Chebbi (p362) near Merzouga, southeast of Rissani.

Autumn (September to October) and winter (November to early March) are the only seasons worth considering. Prices start at around Dh300 per person per day (or DH350 for an overnight excursion), but vary depending on the number of people involved, the length of the trek and your negotiating skills. The agency will organise the bivouac, which may be a permanent camp for shorter trips, and may offer Berber music and *m'choui* (barbecued lamb).

Numerous places offer camel expeditions. Those with plenty of time can simply arrive in places like Zagora, M'Hamid and Merzouga and organise a local guide and provisions while there; this has the advantage of benefiting the local community and countering the trend towards young desert guides leaving home to look for work in the more popular tourist cities further north. If you do this, try to get recommendations from other travellers and count on spending Dh350 for an overnight excursion, although Dh300 per person per day is an average for longer trips. M'Hamid is probably the most hassle-free of the three, although the choice is wider at Zagora (which has three professional operators) and Merzouga.

If you've neither the time nor the inclination to spend time cooling your heels while you wait for negotiations to be completed, you could also organise it in advance, either through an international tour company or a local company based in Ouarzazate or Marrakesh. For more information on tour companies, see the boxed text p441, or the Zagora (p340), Ouarzazate (p333) or Marrakesh (p295) sections of the book.

Many of these agencies also offer 4WD expeditions, although it's worth remembering the environmental cost of such journeys – for more information see Environmentally Piste-Off, p84.

Hammams

Visiting a hammam (traditional bathhouse) is infinitely preferable to cursing under a cold shower in a cheap hotel. They're busy, social places where you'll find gallons of hot water and staff available to scrub you squeaky clean. They're good places to meet the locals and, especially for women, somewhere to relax for as long as you like away from the street hassle.

Every town has at least one hammam. Often there are separate hammams for men and women, while others are open to either sex at different hours or on alternate days. They can be difficult to find; some are unmarked and others simply have a picture of a man or woman stencilled on the wall outside. Local people will be happy to direct you to one. Most hammams are very welcoming, but a few (often those close to a mosque) are unwilling to accept foreign visitors.

Bring your own towels (in a waterproof bag), a plastic mat or something to sit on, and flip-flops (thongs). You'll be given a bucket and scoop – remember to use the communal bucket when filling yours with hot or cold water. Toiletries can be bought at some hammams, as can handfuls of clay mixed with herbs, dried roses and lavender (*ghassoul*).

A visit to a hammam usually costs around Dh10, with a massage costing at least an extra Dh15 or so. Most hammams also have showers. A few midrange or top-end hotels have hammams, which normally require advance notice (up to 24 hours) to heat up, and which cost up to Dh100 per person for a minimum of four or five.

> **HAMMAM KNOW-HOW**
>
> For affluent Western travellers the communal bathhouse is a cultural shock. Where do you look, where do you sit, what are you sitting too close, what do you wear? All that naked flesh appears a minefield of social disaster and embarrassment.
>
> For Muslims, however, there is nothing shameful or embarrassing about the body among your own gender, and attitudes to nakedness are a lot less prudish than those of their Western counterparts. It may seem surprising in a society where modesty on the street is so important that women will think nothing of enquiring curiously after why you don't shave your pubic hair! On a more practical level, in houses where there is often no water the hammam is the only place to get clean.
>
> Most 'good' public hammams in cities tend to be modern white-tiled and spacious affairs. Moroccans come prepared with a coarse glove (*el-kis*), black soap made from the resin of olives (stings if you get it in your eyes), henna (which is used by women) and *ghassoul*.
>
> After undressing to your underwear head straight for the hot room and stake out your area with your mat and toiletries. If in doubt, follow what everyone else is doing, which usually means covering yourself with black soap and sweating a while to soften up your skin for the pummelling it will later take. After about five minutes get a friend, or masseur/masseuse from the hammam, to scrub you down. It's by no means a tender process as rolls of dead skin peel away with the black soap. Nor is it for the modestly inclined, as arms are raised, breasts and inner thighs scrubbed and ears rinsed out with as much ceremony as a childhood bathtime.
>
> Once all the dirt has been rinsed away most people move to the tepid room to apply the reddish-brown henna (in the women's hammam only) and then *ghassoul*, which is also used to wash your hair. These products soften and smooth the skin and no self-respecting Moroccan would swap them for any fancy commercial product.
>
> Once your inhibitions have been stripped away, the hammam is a thoroughly relaxing and enjoyable experience, and it's easy to see why it is so beloved. It is intimate and friendly, a place to relax and talk about your problems and, for Moroccan women especially, a welcome break from tedious chores and difficult spouses. Afterwards you feel thoroughly wrung out and totally relaxed. You'll probably never be so clean again.

Horse Riding

The south of Morocco is popular for horse riding, be it along the southern beaches of Diabat (p148) and Agadir, through the lush valleys of the Souss and Ouirgane, in the Middle and High Atlas, or exploring the dramatic Todra Gorge and the desert landscapes of the south.

A couple of specialist foreign travel companies offer guided horse-riding trips in Morocco.

Equitours (☎ 800-545 0019, 307-455 3363; www
.equitours.com; Dubois, Wyoming, USA)

Unicorn Trails (☎ 0176 760 0606; www.unicorntrails
.com; Biggleswade, Bedfordshire, UK)

Motorbiking, Quads & Karts

The wide open spaces and stunning scenery of south-central Morocco are attracting a growing number of roadsters. The only Moroccan-based off-road biking agency is **Wilderness Wheels** (☎ 044 888128; www.wilderness
wheels.com44 Hay al-Qods, Ouarzazate). Itineraries

cover the Dadès and Drâa Valleys and even the desert as far south as Merzouga and cost Dh800/1400/3500 for a half-/full-/two-day expedition.

Quad biking and karting are also becoming popular in adventure bases such as Ouarzazate (p334), Merzouga (p363), Zagora (p341) and Erfoud (p358).

Mountain-biking

Ordinary cycling is possible in Morocco, but mountain biking opens up the options considerably. Roads are well maintained, although often very narrow. For the very fit, the vast networks of *pistes* (dirt tracks) and even the footpaths of the High Atlas offer the most rewarding biking, although the Anti Atlas, Jebel Sarhro plateau and the Drâa Valley offer some excellent trails. There are also possibilities at Oualidia (p137). A few travel agencies and midrange hotels hire out mountain bikes (Dh100 per day) but the quality isn't

DIRECTORY

really high enough for an extended trip. Serious cyclists might want to try contacting one of the adventure tour companies listed on p441.

Rock Climbing

Rock climbing is increasingly a feature of the Moroccan activities scene and there are some sublime opportunities for the vertically inclined. Anyone contemplating routes should have plenty of experience under their belt and be prepared to bring all their own equipment.

Areas in the Anti Atlas and High Atlas offer everything from bouldering to very severe mountaineering routes that shouldn't be attempted unless you have a great deal of experience. The Dadès (p348) and Todra (p352) gorges are both prime climbing territory.

It's worth contacting the following if you're keen to hook up with other climbers:

Royal Moroccan Ski & Mountaineering Federation (☎ /fax 022 474979; Le Ministère de la Jeunesse et Sport, Parc de la Ligue Arabe, PO Box 15899, Casablanca) This group runs climbing competitions in the Todra Gorge.

Cosley & Houston Alpine Guides (www.cosleyhouston.com) A well-regarded climbing agency that can put together tailor-made climbing and canyoning trips or refer you to other reliable guides.

Skiing

Although Morocco's ski stations are somewhat ramshackle in comparison with Europe's alpine offerings, skiing is a viable option from November to April.

Ski trekking (ski randonné) is increasingly popular, especially from late December to February when the Aït Bou Goumez Valley (p323) promises Morocco's prime ski trekking routes.

Oukaïmeden (p326), about 70km south of Marrakesh, is a popular downhill ski resort that boasts the highest ski lift in North Africa. You can hire equipment here. There are a few other spots dotted around the Middle Atlas.

Surfing

Morocco has thousands of kilometres of ocean coast making it a fine, if underrated, surfing destination. The beaches around Kenitra (p120) are a safe bet. Plage Mehdiya (p121), 7km to the west, has reliable year-round breaks, and there are a few other places further up the coast towards Larache.

Anchor Point in Agadir has been recommended, although it can be very inconsistent. Taghazout (p377), close by, is a laid-back spot popular with surfers, and there is a German-run surf lodge (www.surfmarokko.de) nearby at Tamraght (p376), 15km north of Agadir.

Essaouira has been singled out by some surfers, though it's a far better windsurfing destination.

Perhaps the best breaks in the country are just north of Safi. The Lalla Fatna beach (p143) is the point of access and has drawn some of the biggest names in surfing for some of the longest tubular right-handers in the world. Other beaches in the vicinity of Safi are also worth checking out. For reliable information contact **Surfland** (☎ 023 366110; Apr-mid-Nov) in Oualidia. Surfland is also a great place for beginners' lessons, which take place in the sheltered bay. For further details see p137. There's also good surf to be found around Rabat (p120) and El-Jadida (p134).

For more information contact **Oudayas Surf Club** (☎ 037 260683; fax 037 260684; Rabat). It's friendly and runs surfing courses and competitions. The Storm Rider Guide to Europe has more detailed listings.

Trekking

For the definitive guide to Morocco's world-class trekking possibilities, turn to p404.

White-Water Rafting

White-water rafting is very underdeveloped in Morocco, although the rivers in the High Atlas near Bin el-Ouidane Dam in the area around Azilal and Afourer have stunning scenery.

Only a few specialist adventure companies organise rafting trips to Morocco. Try the reputable **Water by Nature** (www.waterbynature.com), which has outlets in the UK, USA and New Zealand. Their trips cater for beginners as well as experienced kayakers.

Windsurfing & Kitesurfing

The windy conditions at Essaouira (p147) and even more so at Sidi Kaouki (p154) make them better spots for windsurfers and kitesurfers than for their wax-and-board colleagues. You can hire boards on these

---

TRAVELLING THE WAY ALLAH INTENDED

Morocco, beloved for its casual 'God-willing, now-pass-another-cup-of-tea' charm, does not provide its trekking guests with much in the way of resources for safe and responsible exploration or protection of the Moroccan environment. The following suggestions should lend a hand.

- Dress appropriately according to custom (p45).
- Use current topographical maps and run them by a local if you can: someone who lives in the area can verify water sources and indicate rivers that are now dry.
- Camp only in designated camp sites; fields are a private source of business for local families.
- Buy or collect firewood (do not chop) and use it sparingly to respect its scarcity.
- Scorpions hide under rocks and potentially in shoes and sleeping bags, so you'll want to shake these out occasionally. They will not sting unless provoked.
- Understand that laundering and bathing in rivers and streams pollutes a village's primary water source.
- Carry out rubbish to the nearest town or city.
- Be aware that some villages consider photography blasphemous and in others a camera makes you the Pied Piper. It is always inappropriate to photograph someone without permission and cameras can cause particular offence when pointed at women.
- Refrain from feeding or handling animals – even Barbary macaques, who will tease you with their charisma!
- Hitchhike at your own risk and remember: if you flag down a grand taxi then you're no longer hitchhiking – expect to pay the fare to the next town.
- Consider the impact of 4WDs before embarking on any off-*piste* adventures (see the boxed text on p84).
- Give a warm smile and some kind words to the friendly children who live in rural areas. Handing out money, candy and other gifts to kids teaches them to beg and harass tourists. If you wish to give something to children in a local community, it's better to give a donation to a local charity or school.
- Don't drink alcohol in remote villages where the practice is considered offensive.

---

beaches (Dh150 per hour for windsurfing equipment and Dh250 per hour for kitesurfing). You'll also be able to tap into a reasonable windsurfing community here year-round. The area around El-Jadida (p134) is also good while Surfland in Oualidia (see p137) runs kitesurfing classes.

BUSINESS HOURS

Although a Muslim country, for business purposes Morocco follows the Monday to Friday working week. Friday is the main prayer day, however, so many businesses take an extended lunch break on Friday afternoon. During Ramadan the rhythm of the country changes and office hours shift to around 8am to 3pm or 4pm.

For details of opening hours for shops, banks, post offices and restaurants, see the Quick Reference guide inside the front cover.

Banking hours can vary a little, with some banks closing at 11.30pm on weekdays. In the main tourist cities, *bureaux de change* (foreign-exchange bureaus) keep longer hours (often until 8pm) and open over the weekend.

Medina souqs and produce markets in the villes nouvelles (new towns) of the bigger cities tend to wind down on Thursday afternoon and are usually empty on Friday. Souqs in small villages start early and usually wind down before the onset of the afternoon heat.

Government offices open from 8.30am to noon and 2pm to 6.30pm, Monday to Thursday. On Friday, the midday break lasts from about 11.30am to 3pm.

DIRECTORY

Tourist offices are generally open from 8.30am to noon and 2.30pm to 6.30pm from Monday to Thursday and from 8.30am to 11.30am and 3pm to 6.30pm on Friday.

Téléboutiques (private telephone offices) and internet cafés are open until around 10pm.

CHILDREN

Your children have a decided advantage over the rest of us – having yet to acquire the stereotypes about Africa or the Middle East to which the rest of us are exposed, their first impression of the continent is likely to be the warmth and friendliness of the people. Indeed, many Moroccans have grown up in large families and children will help break the ice and open doors to closer contact with local people who are generally very friendly, helpful and protective towards children. The result is that travelling with children in Morocco adds a whole new dimension to your journey. Or, as one of our authors wrote: 'Travelling in Morocco with kids is a great thing to do. Done it often and loved it all'.

For more information and hints on travelling with children, Lonely Planet's *Travel with Children* by Cathy Lanigan is highly recommended.

PRACTICALITIES

Most hotels will not charge children under two years of age. For those between two and 12 years sharing the same room as their parents, it's usually 50% of the adult rate. If you want reasonable toilet and bathroom facilities, you'll need to stay in midrange hotels.

If you look hard enough, you can buy just about anything you need for young children, although you should bring any special foods required and high-factor sunscreen. Disposable nappies are a practical solution when travelling despite the environmental drawbacks. International brands are readily available and cost about Dh20 for 10.

To avoid stomach upsets, stick to purified or bottled water. UHT, pasteurised and powdered milk are also widely available. Be extra careful about choosing restaurants; steer clear of salads and stick to piping-hot tajines, couscous, soups and omelettes. Moroccan markets are full of delicious fruit and veggies, but be sure to wash or peel them.

Avoid travelling in the interior during midsummer, when temperatures rise to 40°C plus. Beware of dehydration and sunburn, even on cloudy days.

Morocco has a great rail infrastructure and travel by train may be the easiest, most enjoyable option – children can stretch their legs and the fold-down tables are handy for drawing and games. Grands taxis and buses can be a real squeeze with young children who count not as passengers in their own right but as wriggling luggage – kids have to sit on your lap. The safety record of buses and shared taxis is poor, and many roads are potholed. Hire-car companies rarely have child seats, so bring your own, and check that they clip into the seat belts.

There are few formal babysitting services but it can usually be arranged through top-end hotels or by tapping into the expat network, which is particularly active in Marrakesh. If you want an English-speaking baby-sitter, be sure to request that specifically; it's not a given.

One reader has reported that letting your kids run amok in carpet shops proved to be an excellent bargaining technique.

SIGHTS & ACTIVITIES

Successful travel with children can require a special effort. Above all, don't try to overdo things. Make sure activities include the kids (older children could help in the planning of these) and try to think of things that will capture their imagination – the latter shouldn't be difficult in Morocco.

Camel or horse rides along the beaches of Essaouira (p148) and Agadir or among the sand dunes at M'Hamid (p343) or Merzouga (p362) are sure to be a big hit, as is quad biking or karting with older children in Ouarzazate (p334). Another popular activity is the calèche (horse-drawn carriage) ride around the ramparts of cities like Marrakesh (p321) and Taroudannt (p381).

The mayhem and madness of the intricate souqs in Fès and Marrakesh is endlessly fascinating and will supply many exciting and exasperating moments. And a night round a campfire with Berber music is unforgettable.

Other organised attractions of particular interest to younger kids include Yasmina Amusement Park in Casablanca (p94); Parc Zoologique National in Rabat (p120); Surfland (p137) in Oualidia; Parque Marítimo del Mediterráneo (p180) in Ceuta; Vallée des Oiseaux (p368) in Agadir; the Atlas Film Corporation Studios (p333) in Ouarzazate; and the all-singing, all-dancing folkloric show, Reflets de Merveilles (p306), in Marrakesh.

Sights appropriate for children are covered throughout this book, with dedicated sections in Marrakesh (p306), Casablanca (p94) and Rabat (p109).

At the end of a hot day, a hotel pool may be all you need for hours of contented fun.

CLIMATE

Morocco's weather reflects its distinct geographical zones. Coastal Morocco is generally mild, but can become cool and wet in the north. Rainfall is highest in the Rif and northern Middle Atlas, where only the summer months are dry. As you go higher into the Middle and High Atlas mountains, expect bitterly cold, snowy winters and cool, fresh summers. Elsewhere, rain falls mostly between November and March but is unpredictable, and drought remains a perennial problem. Blustery winds are common along the Atlantic seaboard. The Moroccan interior can become stiflingly hot in summer, easily exceeding 40°C, with spring sandstorms (known as the sirocco, *chergui* or *irifi*) particularly uncomfortable. Fronting the desert, these plains are also subject to springtime sandstorms (usually in April).

For information on when to go to Morocco, see p18.

COURSES

Morocco has some excellent cooking and language courses.

Cooking

Marrakesh has the widest selection of courses in Moroccan cooking. Souq Cuisine (p306) and Chambres d'Amis (p306) are among the best. For the well-heeled gourmands among you, the **Rhode School of Cuisine** (www .rhodeschoolofcuisine.com) in Marrakesh is well worth considering; a comprehensive, all-inclusive, week-long programme costs about US$2395.

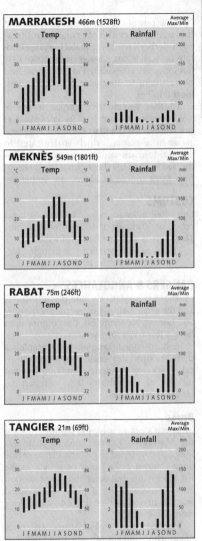

Language

There are courses in modern standard Arabic in most major towns in Morocco, with an especially high concentration in Rabat (p109), Casablanca (p94) and Tangier (p166) offering both long- and short-term programmes.

Undoubtedly the most romantic choice, however, is Fès (p227), where **DMG Arabophon** (www.arabicstudy.com; one-month intensive course

Dh3600) is one of the best language schools in the country (they also offer classes in Tamazight Berber), while the **Arabic Language Institute** (www.alif-fes.com; 3/6-week courses Dh4900/8900) has longer courses aimed at foreigners, and can assist in finding accommodation with local families.

Another imaginative choice if you're aged between 18 and 30 is in Safi (p141) at the **Jeunesse des Chantiers Marocains** (http://perso .menara.ma/youthcamps), which is dedicated to cultural tourism and ensures you'll be immersed in local life throughout the three- to four-week courses in Moroccan Arabic.

CUSTOMS

Duty-free allowances are up to 200 cigarettes; or 50 cigars; or 400g of tobacco; plus 1L of spirits and one bottle of wine.

There are no restrictions on bringing foreign currency into the country.

DANGERS & ANNOYANCES

Morocco is a relatively safe place to travel and the great majority of people are friendly and honest. Nevertheless, the country does have a few traps for the unwary.

In hard-edged Tangier and Casablanca there are some desperate people and physical attacks on foreigners are rare but not unheard of. Treat the medinas with particular caution at night.

Drugs

Morocco's era as a hippie paradise, riding the Marrakesh Express and all that, was long ago consigned to history. Plenty of fine dope (known as kif) may be grown in the Rif Mountains, but drug busts are common and Morocco is not a place where you'd want to investigate local prison conditions from the inside.

The vast majority of all Moroccan stories of extortion and rip-offs are drug related. A common ploy is to get you stoned, force you to buy a piece the size of a house brick and then turn you over to the police (or at least threaten to). Of course, once you've been tainted with a little hash, you're unlikely to call the cops, and the hustlers know it.

Associating with Tangier's lowlife is for the initiated only. New arrivals should ignore late-night offers of hashish and grass – these dealers have a sixth sense for greenness, and won't miss an opportunity to squeeze ridiculous amounts of money out of frightened people. Tetouan is another popular venue, and watch out for similar scams in Asilah, Casablanca and Marrakesh. Hashish is sometimes referred to as 'chocolate', the Spanish slang, or more often just as 'something special' or 'shit', which you will definitely be in if you get caught.

You may occasionally find someone offering you *majoun,* a kind of sticky, pasty mass (not unlike molasses) made of crushed seeds of the marijuana plant. A small ball of this can send you reeling (see Paul Bowles' *Their Heads Are Green* or *Let It Come Down* for descriptions). Anyone with a slight tendency to paranoia when smoking dope should be aware that this is a common reaction among first-time *majoun*-munchers.

Ketama and the Rif Mountains are Morocco's kif-growing heartland. Ketama in particular can be a bag-load of trouble and is best avoided unless you're accompanied by a reliable guide.

Recent legislation and a hard government line may have forced dealers to give up their more aggressive tactics, but the hassle has by no means disappeared and although locals continue to smoke as a recreational pastime, as a tourist you're rather more vulnerable. Always bear in mind that it's illegal to sell or consume hashish in Morocco, although this usually means little if you're discreet. However, smoking in public is inviting trouble. If caught, you may be looking at a fine and, in the worst case, a prison sentence of up to 5 years. See p457 for more information.

Although the police attitude in Spain is relaxed in respect to small amounts of cannabis for private use, Spanish customs will come down hard on people entering the country from Morocco if they find any and you may be done for trafficking. If you're taking a car across, the chances that it will be searched are high. *Never* carry parcels or drive vehicles across borders for other people.

Getting Lost

A minor irritation is the ever-changing street names in Moroccan cities. For years, there's been a slow process of replacing old French, Spanish and Berber names with Arabic ones. The result so far is that, depending on whom you talk to, what map you use or which part of the street you are on, you're likely to see up to three different names.

The general Arabic word for street is *sharia* (*zankat* for smaller ones). In the north you'll still find the Spanish *calle* and *avenida*, and more commonly, the French *avenue, boulevard* or *rue*.

In some cases the Arabic seems to have gained the upper hand. This is reflected in this guidebook, in which some streets appear as *sharia* or *zankat* if local usage seems to justify it.

Street names won't help much in the labyrinthine medinas, although a compass might. If you feel you're getting lost, stick to the main paths (which generally have a fair flow of people going either way) and you'll soon reach a landmark or exit.

Plumbing

Patience is required when it comes to Moroccan plumbing. In the cheap, unclassified hotels that don't have star ratings, trickling cold water only is often the norm.

Sometimes hot water is enthusiastically promised, but before you start dreaming of that powerful, steaming hot shower, remember that it may be tepid at best and is often only available at certain times of the day. In country areas, water is sometimes heated by a wood fire, but this comes at an environmental cost – wood is expensive, water is often in short supply and deforestation is a major problem in Morocco. In small towns and rural areas the hammam may be a better bet.

Scams

On some of the more popular tourist routes, in particular the road between Marrakesh and Ouarzazate, you may come across professional hitchhikers and people pretending that their cars have broken down. Once you stop to assist them various scams unfold – trying to sell you stuff, offering to take you on an amazing detour for a fee, or taking you on a wild goose chase that inevitably ends up at some friend's hotel, shop or restaurant.

Sneakier crimes are sometimes perpetrated by craft-shop owners or car-rental companies who falsify credit card vouchers (often by adding an extra '0' to the price) or who ship inferior substitute carpets to travellers.

For drug-related scams see opposite.

Smoking

Smoking is a national pastime in Morocco and nonsmoking restaurants and hotels are almost unheard of.

However, this generally affects popular places rather than top-end or exclusive restaurants and hotels, where you may find nonsmoking areas. Also, as most of the popular eateries are cafés with outdoor seating, the problem is somewhat reduced.

Only the very top-end hotels (mainly Sofitel) have a nonsmoking policy.

In Muslim countries it is generally considered unacceptable for women to smoke, and outside the big cities (and even within most of these) you'll seldom see women smokers. This is a cultural rather than religious dictate, although most religious leaders have condemned smoking, like drinking, as *haram* (forbidden). In practice, the only time the habit is seriously eschewed is during daylight hours of the holy month of Ramadan.

This shouldn't affect foreigners too much, although women may wish to refrain from smoking within local homes and be discreet elsewhere.

Theft

On the whole, theft is not a huge problem in Morocco. Travellers can minimise any risk, however, by being particularly vigilant in the major cities and by generally following a few basic precautions.

When wandering around the streets, keep the valuables you carry to a minimum and keep what you must carry around with you well hidden. Be particularly careful when withdrawing money from ATMs. External money pouches attract attention, but neck pouches or moneybelts worn under your clothes do not; that's where you should keep your money, passport and other important documents.

In some of the medinas – such as those in Marrakesh, Casablanca and Tangier, which have a particular reputation for petty theft – a common tactic is for one guy to distract you while another cleans out your pockets. There's no point walking around in a state of permanent alert, but keep your eyes open.

Other valuables such as cameras can be left with the hotel reception when you don't need them. If you prefer to keep things in your room (preferably locked inside your suitcase), nine times out of 10 you'll have no trouble. Leaving anything in a car, even out of sight, is asking for trouble.

Touts, Guides & Hustlers

The legendary hustlers of Morocco remain an unavoidable part of the Moroccan experience.

A few years ago special *brigades touristiques* (tourist police) were set up in the principal tourist centres to clamp down on Morocco's notorious *faux guides* and hustlers. Any person suspected of trying to operate as an unofficial guide could face jail and/or a huge fine.

This has greatly reduced, but not eliminated, the problem of *faux guides*. These people are often desperate to make a living, and they can be persistent and sometimes unpleasant. You'll find plenty hanging around the entrances to the big cities' medinas, and outside bus and train stations. Those disembarking (and embarking) the ferry in Tangier should expect at least some hassle from touts and hustlers (see p161). Ceuta and Melilla are far more pleasant ports of entry.

However, there's no point having a siege mentality. When arriving in a place for the first time, you might even benefit from the services of a guide – official or otherwise. *Faux guides* are not necessarily complete impostors (see the boxed text on p219). Many are very experienced and speak half a dozen languages, and sometimes their main interest is the commission gained from certain hotels or on articles sold to you in the souqs. Be sure to agree on a price before setting off and set some parameters on what you expect to see and the number of shops you're taken to. Unofficial guides charge around Dh50 to Dh100 per day (rates should always be per guide not per person); a few dirham will suffice if you want to be guided to a specific location (like a medina exit). Whatever you give, you'll often get the you-can't-possibly-be-serious look. The best reply is the I've-just-paid-you-well-over-the-odds look. Maintain your good humour and after a couple of days in a place, the hassle tends to lessen considerably.

Official guides can be engaged through tourist offices and some hotels at the fixed price of around Dh300 per day (plus tip) for a local/national guide. It's well worth taking a guide when exploring the medinas of Fès

---

GAUCHE, GREEN & GULLIBLE

Many Moroccans genuinely believe that 'Westerners', though perhaps more sophisticated than themselves, are infinitely more naive, gullible and even plain stupid. Some, including the notorious *faux guides* (unofficial guides), may try to exploit this.

Very early on in your encounter with these guides, you'll be sized up for what you're worth. Apart from the physical indications such as your watch, shoes and clothes, you'll be assessed from a series of questions: how long you've been in Morocco, whether you've visited the country before, what your job is, whether you have a family (an indication of wealth) etc. Always be suspicious of these unsolicited enquiries and pretend that you know the city or country well. A few words of Arabic will convince them of this.

Considered to be the most lucrative nationalities, in descending order, are the Japanese, Americans, Canadians, Australians, the British, northern Europeans, southern Europeans, and Middle-Eastern Arabs. Considered the least lucrative are sub-Saharan Africans and Arabs from other North African countries.

Apart from the more obvious starting point of claiming to want nothing more than friendship (such as showing you around town, taking you to a cheap shop and helping you find a hotel), other classic approaches include wanting to practise English, help with the reading or deciphering of official documents and letters from friends. If you turn them down, some will try to play on your conscience by suggesting you are racist for not liking Moroccans or Muslims.

If you feel you're being categorised, you can always cause confusion by pretending you're from some very obscure land. Sometimes it's useful just to play plain stupid and control the situation that way. Be warned, though: Moroccans have a real aptitude for languages and it could be you who looks stupid as your new friend starts spouting away in the fluent Ukrainian you claim to speak or just happens to be the brain surgeon you've claimed to be.

THANKS BUT NO THANKS

To avoid being hounded to within an inch of your life, and to help prevent nervous breakdowns and embarrassing incidents of 'medina rage', the following tips may come in handy:

■ Politely decline all offers of help and exchange a few good-humoured remarks (preferably in Arabic), but don't shake hands or get involved in lengthy conversation.

■ Give the impression that you know exactly where you're going or explain that you employed a guide on your first day and now you'd like to explore the town on your own.

■ Wear dark sunglasses and retreat to a café, restaurant or taxi if you're beginning to lose your cool. In extreme situations, use the word 'police' and look like you mean it.

and Marrakesh. Their local knowledge is extensive and they'll save you from being hassled by other would-be guides. If you don't want a shopping expedition included in your tour, make this clear beforehand.

Drivers should note that motorised hustlers operate on the approach roads to Fès and Marrakesh. These motorcycle nuisances are keen to find you a hotel, camp site and so on, and can be just as persistent as their colleagues on foot.

DISCOUNT CARDS

You can stay at most Hostelling International (HI) hostels without a membership card (usually for a few dirham extra), so it's hardly worth getting a card especially for your trip.

International student cards don't open many magic doors (eg you won't get many museum discounts) in Morocco. However, they do entitle those under 30 to discounts of up to 60% on internal travel (plus on some flights *out* of the country) with Royal Air Maroc (RAM). Student rail cards are available for train travel to Morocco and under-26 discount cards are available for internal domestic train (and air) travel (see p489).

Morocco doesn't offer any special discounts to senior travellers, although there are reductions for the over-60s on ferries to/from Spain.

EMBASSIES & CONSULATES

For details of all Moroccan embassies abroad, and for foreign embassies in Morocco, go to the Moroccan Ministry for Foreign Affairs and Cooperation website at www.maec.gov.ma.

Moroccan Embassies & Consulates

Morocco has diplomatic representation in the following countries, among others:

Australia (☎ 02-9922 4999; Suite 2, 11 West St, North Sydney, NSW 2060)

Canada (☎ 613-236 7391, www.ambassade-maroc.ottawa.on.ca; 38 Range Rd, Ottawa, Ont KIN 8J4)

Egypt (☎ 02-736 4718; morocemb@link.net; 10 Sharia Salah ad-Din, Zamalek, Cairo)

France (☎ 01 45 20 69 35; www.amb-maroc.fr; 5 Rue Le Tasse, 75016 Paris)

Germany Berlin (☎ 030-206 1240; www.maec.gov.ma/berlin; Niederwallstr 39, 10117 Berlin), Düsseldorf (☎ 211-650 4510), Frankfurt (☎ 069-955 0123)

Japan (☎ 03-3478 3271; www.morocco-emba.jp; 5-4-30 Miami Aoyama Minat 107 – 0062, Tokyo)

Mauritania (☎ 525 14 11; sifmanktt@mauritel.mr; Av du Général de Gaulle, BP 621, Nouakchott)

Netherlands (☎ 070-346 9617; www.marokkaanse-ambassade.nl; Oranjestraat 9, 2514 JB, The Hague)

Spain (☎ 91 563 1090; www.maec.gov.ma/madrid; Calle Serrano 179, 28002 Madrid)

Switzerland (☎ 31-351 0362; www.amb-maroc.ch; Helvetiastrasse 42, 3005 Berne)

Tunisia (☎ 01-782 775; sifamatunis@embmaroc.intl.tn; 39 Ave du 1er Juin, Mutuelleville 1002, Tunis)

UK (☎ 020-7581 5001; mail@sifamaldn.org; 49 Queen's Gate Gardens, London SW7 5NE)

USA Washington (☎ 202-462 7979; fmehdi@embassyofmorocco.us; 1601 21st St NW, Washington, DC 20009); New York (☎ 212-213 9644; info@moroccanconsulate.com; 24th fl, 10 E 40th St, New York, NY, 10016)

Embassies & Consulates in Morocco

Most embassies and diplomatic representation are in Rabat. Unless otherwise noted, all of the embassies are open Monday to Friday, from 9am until noon.

Algeria (☎ 037 661574; algerabat@iam.net.ma; 46-48 Ave Tariq ibn Zayid, Rabat; ☻ 8.30am-4pm Mon-Fri); Oujda (☎ 056 710452; Blvd Bir Anzarane)

Australia The Australian embassy in Paris has consular responsibility for Morocco. Consular services to Australian citizens in Morocco are provided by the Canadian embassy.

YOUR OWN EMBASSY

It's important to realise what your own embassy can and (more often) can't do to help if you get into trouble. Generally, it won't be much help in emergencies if the trouble you're in is remotely your own fault. Remember that you're bound by the laws of the country you are in. Your embassy will not be sympathetic if you end up in jail after committing a crime locally, even if such actions are legal in your own country.

In emergencies you might get some assistance, but only if other channels have been exhausted. For example, if you need to get home urgently, a free ticket home is exceedingly unlikely – the embassy would expect you to have insurance. If all your money and documents are stolen, it may assist with getting a new passport, but a loan for onward travel is out of the question.

Some embassies used to keep letters for travellers or have a small reading room with home newspapers, but these days the mail-holding service has usually been stopped and even newspapers tend to be out of date.

Belgium (☎ 037 268060; info@ambabel-rabat.org.ma; 6 Ave de Marrakesh, Rabat); Casablanca (☎ 022 223049; 9 Rue al-Farabi); Tangier (☎ /fax 039 941130; 2nd fl, 41 Blvd Mohammed V)

Canada (☎ 037 687400; fax 037 687430; 13 Rue Jaafar as-Sadiq, Agdal, Rabat; ☽ 8am-noon & 1.30-5.30pm Mon-Thu, 8am-1.30pm Fri)

France (☎ 037 689700, www.ambafrance-ma.org; 3 Rue Sahnoun, Agdal, Rabat); Consulate-general (☎ 037 268181; Rue Alla Ben Abdallah, Rabat; ☽ for visa applications 8.30-11.30am & for pick-ups 1.30-3pm Mon-Fri). Consulates-general are also in Agadir, Casablanca, Tangier, Marrakesh and Fès.

Germany (☎ 037 709662; www.amballemagne-rabat .ma; 7 Rue Madnine, Rabat)

Ireland The nearest Irish embassy is in Lisbon. Consular services to Irish citizens in Morocco are provided by the Canadian embassy.

Italy (☎ 037 706598; ambaciata@iambitalia.ma; 2 Rue Idriss el-Azhar, Rabat); Consulate-general in Casablanca (☎ 022 277558; fax 022 277139; cnr Rue Jean Jaures & Ave Hassan Souktani)

Japan (☎ 037 631782; fax 037 750078; 39 Ave Ahmed Balafrej Souissi, Rabat; ☽ 9am-1pm Mon-Fri)

Mali (☎ 037 759125; fax 037 754742; 7 Rue Thami Lamdaouar, Soussi I, Rabat; ☽ 8.30am-noon & 2.30-5.30pm Mon-Fri)

Mauritania (☎ 037 656678; ambassadeur@mauritanie .org.ma; 7 Rue Thami Lamdaouar, Soussi I, Rabat; ☽ 8.30am-3pm Mon-Thu & 8.30am-noon Fri)

New Zealand The closest embassy is in Madrid, Spain. The UK embassy provides consular support in Morocco.

Netherlands (☎ 037 219600; nlgovrab@mtds.com; 40 Rue de Tunis, Rabat)

Spain (☎ 037 633900; emb.rabat@mae.es; Rue Ain Khalouiya, Route.des Zaers, Km 5.300 Souissi, Rabat) Consulates also in Agadir, Casablanca, Nador, Rabat, Tangier & Tetouan.

Switzerland (☎ 037 268030; fax 037 268040; Place Berkane, Rabat)

Tunisia (☎ 037 730636; fax 037 730637; 6 Ave de Fès, Rabat; ☽ 9am-noon & 2pm-5.30pm Mon-Fri)

UK (☎ 037 238600; www.britain.org.ma; 17 Blvd de la Tour Hassan, Rabat; ☽ 8am-4.30pm Mon-Thu & 8am-1pm Fri, visa applications 8am-noon Mon-Fri); Consulate-general in Casablanca (☎ 022 437700; british.consulate@casanet .net.ma); Consulate in Tangier (☎ 039 936939; uktanger@ mtds.com). Staff will help citizens of some Commonwealth countries without representation in Morocco.

USA (☎ 037 762265; www.usembassy.ma; 2 Ave de Marrakesh, Rabat; ☽ 8.30am-12.30pm & 2.30-6.30pm Mon-Fri); Consulate in Casablanca (☎ 022 264550; nivcasa blanca@state.gov; 8 Blvd Moulay Youssef; ☽ 8am-6pm Mon-Fri)

FESTIVALS & EVENTS

*Moussem*s (festivals) that honour *marabout*s (local saints) pepper the Moroccan calendar. Although some are no more than an unusually lively market day, others have taken on regional and even national importance. These festivals are common among the Berbers and are usually held during the summer months.

*Moussem*s exist on the frontier where Islamic orthodoxy and local custom have met and compromised. Although the veneration of saints is frowned upon by orthodox Sunni Muslims, these festivals take their inspiration from a mix of pre-Islamic Berber tradition and Sufi mystic thought. Some of the more excessive manifestations, such as self-mutilation while in an ecstatic trance, were once a common sight at such gatherings. Today they have all but disappeared in the face of official disapproval of such 'barbarism'.

It's worth making inquiries at tourist offices to determine when *moussem*s and other such festivals are due to happen. Some of the most important festivals and events, in chronological order, are as follows.

February

Almond Blossom Festival A very pretty festival held in late February to early March in the Ameln Valley near Tafraoute when the valley is awash with blossom.

March/April

Marathon des Sables (www.saharamarathon.co.uk) A six-day footrace 243km across the desert, held in March or April. It starts and finishes in Ouarzazate.

Nomad Festival A celebration of nomadic culture in M'Hamid every March or April, with street performances, food, crafts and camel trips.

Moussem of Sidi Abdallah ibn Hassoun A procession of huge wax candle lanterns, carried by local brotherhoods to the Grand Mosque amid music and dancing. Held on the eve of Mouloud, the Prophet's birthday.

May/June

Rose Festival A colourful local festival celebrating the huge harvest of Persian roses in the valley around El Kelaâ M'Gouna, close to Ouarzazate. Dancers are showered with rose petals and children sell fragrant garlands at the roadside. Usually held in May.

Festival du Desert (www.festivaldudesert.ma) A celebration of music and dance held in May, with musicians from all across the Sahara.

Gnaoua & World Music Festival (www.festival-gnaoua .co.ma) A passionate celebration held in Essaouira on the third weekend of June, with concerts featuring international, national and local performers, and art exhibitions.

Moussem of Sidi Mohammed Ma al-Ainin Held at Tan Tan, in late May or early Jun, this is an occasion where you may see Tuareg nomads from the Sahara; it also acts as a commercial gathering of tribespeople.

Moussem of Ben Aïssa Held at Meknès' Koubba of Sidi ben Aïssa; one of the country's largest *moussems*, full of medieval pageantry with illusionists and daredevil horsemen.

Cherry Festival An annual festival held in early June lasting three days with lots of folk music and dancing. Culminates in the picturesque crowning of the Cherry Queen.

July

Festival International de Rabat Features musicians from all over Africa as well as some traditional theatre. The festival is also the venue for an annual film festival.

Moussem of Sidi Bousselham Held in Moulay Bousselham near Larache, this is another large-scale *moussem*

commemorating the local saint, in a beautiful location overlooking the sea.

Festival of World Sacred Music A huge nine day festival now attracting international attention. Concerts are held at the Dar Batha Museum, Grand Mechouar and Volubilis.

Festival of Casablanca City festival focusing on street theatre, music and cinema.

Marrakesh Popular Arts Festival (www.maghrebarts .ma in French) A hugely colourful festival held in Marrakesh, celebrating Berber music and dance, and attracting performers from all over the country.

Moussem & Camel Market A large camel-traders fair that brings Goulmime to life; it is as much a trade event as a religious get-together.

International Cultural Festival An arts festival held in Asilah celebrating contemporary art with public art demonstrations and workshops (some for children), and other theatrical and musical performances.

August

Moussem of Moulay Abdallah Held south of El-Jadida in the small village of Sidi Bouzid, this huge festival is a full-on fantasia with people gathering from all the surrounding villages.

Moussem of Sidi Ahmed Held in Tiznit, this largely religious celebration sees devotees dedicating themselves to pilgrimage and prayer.

September

Marriage Festival A three-day festival Held in late September at Imilchil, where thousands of people gather for the serious business of wedlock – women at this festival get to choose prospective husbands.

Moussem of Moulay Idriss II The largest city *moussem* in holy Fès, held in late September or early October, when thousands gather to watch the processions to the saint's tomb.

International Film Festival (www.festival-marrakech .com) A week-long festival held in September or October that showcases Arab and African cinema, as well as films from elsewhere.

October

Date Festival Held in Erfoud late in October to celebrate the date harvest, the life-blood of the oases villages. Lots of music and dancing bring this corner of the desert to life.

FOOD

In this book restaurants have been organised according to location first and then categorised into the different price ranges. In general, most midrange and top-end restaurants can be found within the ville nouvelle of large cities, with a few notable exceptions in Fès and Marrakesh. Within each section restaurants are listed in order of preference.

Eating together and communally from the same bowl has important social connotations in Morocco. Most families will rush home for the midday meal, which is shared and reinforces strong family relationships. Thus it is that the culture of eating out in restaurants is still alien for many working-class Moroccans, explaining the epic divide between the cheap popular café (frequented by Moroccans for drinks and on-the-hoof sandwiches) and the expensive fancy restaurant (usually the domain of French expatriates, wealthy Moroccans and tourists).

Sandwich bars and popular cafés can serve up sandwiches and brochettes for between Dh30 and Dh50, whereas the cheapest menus in budget restaurants and outside major cities tend to hover around Dh75 to Dh150. Sit-down meals in a mid-range restaurant within a major city will cost between Dh200 and Dh300 per person, though this usually includes wine. At the top end of the spectrum, possibilities range from palace and riad restaurants to some very fancy French establishments. Meals in one of these places will set you back around Dh400 to Dh600 per person including wine, more in Marrakesh. Wine is comparatively expensive in Morocco and will usually add an extra Dh150 to Dh250 to the bill.

A service charge may automatically be added to your bill in better restaurants; in addition to this, a TVA tax (similar to value-added tax), usually around 10%, may be charged, but generally this is built into the price of your meal.

For detailed information about Moroccan cuisine and local customs pertaining to food, see p68.

GAY & LESBIAN TRAVELLERS

Homosexual acts (including kissing) are officially illegal in Morocco – in theory you can go to jail and/or be fined. In practice, although not openly admitted or shown, male homosexuality remains relatively common and platonic affection is freely shown, more so among men than women. In most places, discretion is the key and public displays of affection should be avoided (aggression towards gay male travellers is not unheard of), advice which applies equally to homo-

sexual and heterosexual couples as a means of showing sensitivity to local feelings.

Some towns are certainly more gay-friendly than others, with Marrakesh (for more information, see the boxed text p304) winning the prize, followed by Tangier. That said, gay travellers generally follow the same itineraries as everyone else and although 'gay' bars can be found here and there, Moroccan nightlife tends to include something for everybody.

Lesbians shouldn't encounter any problems, though it's commonly believed by Moroccans that there are no lesbians in their country. Announcing that you're gay probably won't make would-be Romeos magically disappear. For Moroccan men it may simply confirm their belief that Western men don't measure up in the sexual department.

It is also worth bearing in mind that Morocco is a poor country and the pressures of poverty mean than many young men will consider having sex for money or gifts. Needless to say, exploitative relationships form an unpleasant but real dimension of the Moroccan gay scene.

Useful websites that give the lowdown on local laws and attitudes to homosexuality include the following:

Behind the Mask (www.mask.org.za/index.php?page =morocco) Detailed information for every African country.

David Tours (www.davidtours.com) US-based tour company serving the gay community.

Gay Morocco (http://gaymorocco.tripod.com) Yahoo! discussion groups for gay travellers to, and residents of, Morocco.

Gay Travel (www.gaytravel.com) Links to gay-focused tours.

Global Gayz (www.globalgayz.com) A good resource with good links on Morocco.

Kelma (www.kelma.org) Website for gays from North Africa.

Spartacus International Gay Guide (www.spartacus world.com/gayguide/) Renowned guide to gay travel around the world with information on Morocco.

HOLIDAYS

All banks, post offices and most shops shut on the main public holidays, although transport is rarely affected. Of more significance to the majority of people are the principal religious holidays, which mean interruptions and changes of time for many local bus services.

As in Europe the summer holiday period can be intensely busy along the Atlantic coast as many Moroccan families flock to the sea, especially the resorts around Asilah, El-Jadida, Oualidia, Safi and Essaouira. Over Easter and Christmas the influx of European holiday-makers also has a big impact on hotel availability – booking ahead is essential.

Public Holidays

New Year's Day 1 January
Independence Manifesto 11 January
Labour Day 1 May
Feast of the Throne 30 July – commemorates the accession to the throne of King Mohammed VI
Allegiance of Oued Eddahab 14 August – celebrates the 'return to the fatherland' of the Oued Eddahab region in the far south, a territory once claimed by Mauritania
Anniversary of the King's and People's Revolution 20 August
Young People's Day 21 August – celebrates the King's birthday
Anniversary of the Green March 6 November – commemorates the Green March 'reclaiming' the Western Sahara on November 1975
Independence Day 18 November – commemorates independence and the return of King Mohammed V

Islamic Holidays

The main Islamic holidays are celebrated countrywide and are tied to the lunar Hejira calendar. The word hejira refers to the flight of Mohammed from Mecca to Medina in AD 622, which marks the first year of the Islamic calendar. So the year AD 622 is the year 1 AH, or Anno Hegirae (Latin for 'year of the haj').

The Hejira calendar is about 11 days shorter than the Gregorian calendar, meaning that the holidays fall on different days each year. Although most business hours and aspects of daily life are organised around the Gregorian calendar, the religious rhythms of Muslim society are firmly tied to the lunar Hejira calendar. Predicting the exact day on which holidays will begin is impossible, as this depends on when the new moon is sighted – the decision rests with the religious authorities in Fès.

RAS AS-SANA

This means New Year's Day and is celebrated on the first day of the Hejira calendar year, 1 Moharram, the first month of the Muslim lunar calendar.

ASHORA

A day of public mourning observed by Shiites on 10 Moharram. Ashora commemorates the assassination of Hussein ibn Ali, the grandson of the Prophet Mohammed and pretender to the caliphate, which led to the schism between Sunnis and Shiites. However, for children it can be a joyous occasion. They receive toys and sweets and parade through the streets to the beating of drums.

MOULID AN-NABI

A lesser feast celebrating the birth of the Prophet Mohammed on 12 Rabi al-Awal, the third month of the Muslim calendar. It's also spelled Mouloud an-Nabi.

RAMADAN

Most Muslims take part in the fasting that characterises the month of Ramadan, a time when the faithful community are called upon to renew their relationship with God. Ramadan is the month in which the Quran was first revealed, and observing the fast during this month is one of the five pillars of Islam.

From dawn until dusk (defined by whether there is enough daylight to differentiate between a black thread and a white thread), Muslims are expected to refrain from eating, drinking, smoking and sex. Fasting can be a difficult discipline and only people in good health are asked to participate. Children, pregnant women, travellers, the infirm and those engaged in exacting physical work are considered exempt.

The Arabic for fasting is *sawm*. You may find yourself being asked *'Inta sa'im?'* ('Are you fasting?') and encouraged to do so if your answer is *'La, ana faatir'* ('No, I am breaking the fast'). Non-Muslims are not expected to participate, even if more pious Muslims suggest you do.

The implications of travelling during Ramadan are many.

The most obvious of these is that many restaurants close during daylight hours – for more information on eating during Ramadan, see the boxed text on p74. Equally importantly, the entire rhythm of the country changes as most offices and many shops shift to a timetable of around 8am to 3pm or 4pm and don't reopen for the evening. Public transport runs, although often on a much-reduced timetable, which is product of both supply (less drivers keen to work) and demand (with many Moroccan travellers inclined to delay travel until Ramadan ends). Most tour and trekking companies continue tours during Ramadan, but if it's a pre-booked tour, contact them in advance to make sure. If you arrive in a small village during Ramadan, you may find guides less than enthusiastic about taking to the trails, even though travellers are exempt from the dictates of the fast. Normally polite Moroccans can also become decidedly sullen during the fast and everything seems to take longer than it should; this is especially the case when Ramadan falls during the interminable daylight hours of summer.

At the same time, every evening becomes a celebration and these can be wonderfully festive occasions. *Iftar* or *ftur,* the breaking of the day's fast, is a time of animated activity when the people of the local community come together to eat and drink and to pray. If you're fortunate enough to be invited into the home of a local family for the nightly feast, you'll be embarking on a night that you'll never forget.

EID AL-FITR
The end of Ramadan – or more accurately the first days of the following month of Shawwal – mark Eid al-Fitr, the Feast of the Breaking of the Fast, also known as Eid as-Sagheer, the Small Feast. The fast is traditionally ended with a meal of *harira* (lentil soup), dates and honey cakes known as griwash. The Eid generally lasts four or five days, during which everything grinds to a halt. This is not a good time to travel, but it can be a great experience if you are invited to share in some of the festivities with a family. It is a very family-oriented feast, much in the way Christmas is for Christians.

THE HAJ & EID AL-ADHA
The fifth pillar of Islam, the sacred duty of all who can afford it, is to make the pilgrimage to Mecca – the haj. It can be done at any time, but at least once it should be accomplished in Zuul-Hijja, the 12th month of the Muslim year. The haj culminates in the ritual slaughter of a lamb, in commemoration of Ibrahim's sacrifice, and marks the beginning of Eid al-Adha, or Feast of the Sacrifice, also known as the Grand Feast or Eid al-Kabeer. Throughout the Muslim world the act of sacrifice is repeated and the streets of towns and cities seem to run with the blood of slaughtered sheep. The holiday runs from 10 to 13 Zuul-Hijja (the 12th month of the Muslim calendar).

INSURANCE
A travel-insurance policy to cover theft, loss and medical problems is highly recommended – the national health service in Morocco cannot be recommended and the few good private hospitals are expensive. Some policies offer lower and higher medical-expense options; the higher ones are chiefly for countries such as the USA, which have extremely high medical costs. Check that the policy covers ambulances or an emergency flight home and carry proof of your insurance with you; this can be vital in avoiding any delays to treatment in emergency situations.

Buy travel insurance as early as possible. Buying just before you leave home may mean that you're not covered for delays to your flight caused by strike action that began or was threatened before you took out the insurance. If you need to extend your cover on the road, do so before it expires or a more expensive premium may apply.

Paying for your airline ticket with a credit card often provides some travel accident in-

ISLAMIC HOLIDAYS				
Holiday	2007	2008	2009	2010
Ramadan begins	13 Sep	2 Sep	22 Aug	11 Aug
Eid al-Fitr	14 Oct	3 Oct	20 Sep	9 Sep
Tabaski	19 Dec	8 Dec	28 Nov	17 Nov
Moulid an-Nabi	31 Mar	20 Mar	9 Mar	27 Feb
New Year begins (year)	21 Jan (1428)	10 Jan (1429)	31 Dec (1430)	20 Dec (1431)
Eid al-Adha	21 Dec	10 Dec	30 Nov	19 Nov

surance and you may be able to reclaim the payment if the operator doesn't deliver.

Some policies specifically exclude 'dangerous activities', which can include scuba diving, motorcycling, and even trekking. A locally acquired motorcycle licence is not valid under some policies.

You may prefer a policy that pays doctors or hospitals directly rather than you having to pay on the spot and claim later. If you have to claim later, make sure you keep all documentation. Some policies ask you to call back (reverse charge) to a centre in your home country where an immediate assessment of your problem is made, so bring your insurer's emergency telephone number and keep a copy separate from your main baggage. Find out also which private medical service your insurer uses in Morocco so that you can call them direct in the event of an emergency.

Make sure that you have adequate health insurance and any relevant car insurance if you're driving (see p485). Worldwide travel insurance is available at www.lonelyplanet.com/travel_services. You can buy, extend and claim online anytime – even if you're already on the road.

INTERNET ACCESS

Very few hotels in Morocco have any kind of facility for connecting to the internet, although a limited number of the large four- and five-star hotels may have internet connection available in the rooms. Check the power-supply voltage and bring a universal adaptor. Some riads in Marrakesh offer wi-fi (p294), while other up-market *maisons d'hôtes* or riads may have a computer available for public use.

If you're travelling with a notebook or hand-held computer, your modem may not work once you leave your home country. The safest option is to buy a reputable 'global' modem before you leave home, or buy a local PC-card modem if you're spending an extended time in any one country. For more information on travelling with a portable computer, see www.teleadapt.com.

Internet access is widely available, efficient and cheap (Dh5 to Dh10 per hour) in internet cafés, although connections can be slow.

One irritant for travellers is the widespread use of French or Arabic (non-

---

> ### WHEN IS IT LEGAL TO...
>
> - **Vote** 21 years old
> - **Marry** (there is no age of consent) 16 years old
> - **Drive** 18 years old (most car rental companies require you to be 21)

---

qwerty) keyboards, which will reduce most travellers to one-finger typing and fumbled searches for hidden punctuation marks.

If you're staying in a town for a long time, it may be cheaper to buy a prepaid card for several hours' use. Internet cafés normally have a minimum charge of half an hour.

For useful internet resources see p21.

LEGAL MATTERS

Moroccan law prohibits the possession, offer, sale, purchase, distribution and transportation of cannabis and the penalty will most likely include a prison sentence ranging from three months to five years and/or a fine from Dh2400 up to Dh240,000. The UK-based **Fair Trials Abroad** (FTA; ☎ 020-8332 2800; www.fairtrialsabroad.org; London, UK) provides assistance and legal advice to nationals of EU countries imprisoned abroad.

If you get into trouble, your first call should always be to your consulate; remember that it's not unknown for the local police to be in on the scam. If you find yourself arrested by the Moroccan police, you won't have much of a legal leg to stand on and it's unlikely that any interpreter on hand will be of sufficient standard to translate an accurate statement that will, nonetheless, play a vital part in subsequent judicial proceedings. According to FTA, physical abuse while in custody is commonplace.

MAPS

Few decent maps of Morocco are available in the country itself, so get one before leaving home.

There are several reasonable maps covering all of northwestern Africa and taking in parts of Egypt and the Sudan. Kümmerley & Frey publishes *Africa, North and West* on a scale of 1:4,000,000; the Michelin map No 741 (formerly Nos 953 and 153) covers much the same area and was updated in 2003.

Michelin's No 742 (formerly No 959) map of Morocco is arguably the best. In addition to the 1:4,000,000 scale map of the whole of Morocco, including the disputed territory of Western Sahara, there is a 1:1,000,000 enlargement of Morocco and 1:600,000 enlargements of Marrakesh and the High Atlas, Middle Atlas and Meknès areas. Sites of weekly markets, kasbahs and *marabouts* (holy mausolea of local saints) are also shown. You can buy this in major Moroccan cities.

Preferred by many and with similar, often clearer, detail (and occasionally available in Morocco) is the GeoCenter World Map *Morocco,* which shows the country at a handy 1:800,000 scale. Hildebrand's *Morocco* covers the entire country at a scale of 1:900,000, includes seven small city maps and is good for the Western Sahara.

Most of these maps are available from **Stanfords** (☎ 0044 20 7836 1321; www.stanfords .co.uk), which is the world's largest map shop.

For advice on tracking down more detailed topographical maps for trekking, see p405.

It's also possible to get hold of 1:200,000 Russian survey maps and air charts of Morocco from good map shops worldwide, although these usually have to be ordered and can take up to six weeks to arrive.

MONEY

The Moroccan currency is the dirham (Dh), which is divided into 100 centimes. You will find notes in denominations up to Dh200 and coins of Dh1, Dh2, Dh5 and Dh10, as well as, less frequently, 10, 20 and 50 centimes.

The dirham is a restricted currency, meaning that it cannot be taken out of the country and is not available abroad. That said, the currency is fairly stable and there are no wild fluctuations in exchange rates. US dollars or euros are the most easily exchanged currencies.

Exchange rates are given on the inside front cover of this book and a guide to costs can be found on p19.

ATMs

ATMs (*guichets automatiques*) are a common sight and many accept Visa, MasterCard, Electron, Cirrus, Maestro and InterBank systems. BMCE (Banque Maro-

caine du Commerce Extérieur) and Crédit du Maroc ATMs are usually your best bet. Some banks will charge you every time you make a withdrawal from a foreign cash machine, and some won't. Ask your bank back home. The amount of money you can withdraw from an ATM generally depends on the conditions attached to your particular card, although the daily ATM limit on most cards is around Dh2000. ATMs sometimes run dry on weekends.

You can get cash advances on Visa and MasterCard in various banks, including the Banque Populaire, the BMCE, the Banque Marocaine pour le Commerce et l'Industrie (BMCI) and Wafa Bank.

Black Market

The easy convertibility of the dirham leaves little room for a black market, but you'll find people in the streets asking if you want to exchange money, especially in Tangier, Casablanca and on the borders of (and just inside) the enclaves of Ceuta and Melilla. Avoid these characters; there's no monetary benefit to be had from such transactions and scams are common.

Cash

Nothing beats cash for convenience…or risk. If you lose it, it's gone forever and very few travel insurers will come to the rescue. Nonetheless, you'll certainly need to carry some cash with you. Keep a handful of notes of small denomination in your wallet (never in a back pocket) for day-to-day transactions and put the rest in a moneybelt or another safe place. If you're travelling in out-of-the-way places, make sure you have enough cash to last until you get to a decent-sized town. Having a secret stash of US dollars in small denominations is also a good idea.

The endless supply of small coins may be annoying but they're handy for the payment of taxis, tips, guides and beggars.

Credit Cards

Major credit cards are widely accepted in the main tourist centres, although their use often attracts a surcharge of around 5% from Moroccan businesses.

The main credit cards are MasterCard and Visa, and if you plan to rely on plastic cards, the best bet is to take one of each.

Better still is a combination of credit cards and travellers cheques so that you have something to fall back on if an ATM swallows your card or the banks in the area are closed.

Moneychangers

The importation or exportation of Moroccan currency is prohibited, but any amount of foreign currency may be brought into the country. In the Spanish enclaves of Ceuta and Melilla the currency is the euro. Most currencies are readily exchanged in banks, but Australian, Canadian and New Zealand dollars are not recognised.

If you're arriving from, or heading for, the enclaves of Ceuta and Melilla, the Moroccan banks on the borders will exchange cash only. The banks in Melilla and Ceuta deal in dirham, but at rates inferior to those in Morocco.

Banking services inside Morocco are reasonably quick and efficient. Rates vary little from bank to bank, but it doesn't hurt to look around. Branches of BMCE and Crédit du Maroc are generally the most convenient, and often have separate *bureau de change* sections that are open on weekends. Major branches of the main banks open on Saturday morning.

You'll need your passport to change travellers cheques (plus the travellers cheque receipt in some places) and to get cash advances; some banks want to see it when you change cash, too.

As exporting Moroccan currency is illegal, wind down to nothing as you approach the end of your trip and hang on to all exchange receipts – you'll need them to convert leftover dirham at most Moroccan banks.

Tipping

Tipping is an integral part of Moroccan life. Almost any service can warrant a tip, but don't be railroaded. The judicious distribution of a few dirham for a service willingly rendered can, however, make your life a lot easier.

A tip of 10% of a restaurant bill is about right (unless the service has been poor, of course), and a couple of dirham suffices at a café. Museum guides, *gardiens de voitures* (car-park attendants), porters, baggage handlers and petrol-pump attendants

expect to be tipped (between Dh3 and Dh5, or Dh10 for overnight parking). It's worth bearing in mind that many Moroccans earn the equivalent of about US$3.25 a day.

Travellers Cheques

Travellers cheques are so old news and more travellers opt simply to withdraw money from ATMs or get cash advances on credit cards as they go. They do, however, offer some protection against theft.

Amex, Visa and Thomas Cook cheques are widely accepted and have efficient replacement policies. Keeping a record of the cheque numbers and those you have used is vital when it comes to replacing lost travellers cheques. Make sure you keep this record separate from the cheques themselves.

Almost all banks charge commission on travellers cheques (around Dh10 per cheque), though some banks charge Dh10 per transaction, so ask around before changing.

PHOTOGRAPHY & VIDEO

Morocco is a photographer's dream, but never point your camera at anything that's vaguely military or could be construed as 'strategic'. This includes airports, bridges, government buildings and members of the police or armed forces. This becomes more of an issue further south, in the Western Sahara.

It is common courtesy to ask permission before taking photographs of people. Urban Moroccans are generally easy-going about it, but in the countryside locals are not so willing to have cameras pointed at them. In particular, women and older people very often don't want to be photographed. Respect their right to privacy and don't take photos.

Memory cards and batteries for digital cameras are quite easy to find in photography shops in major cities (especially Casablanca and Marrakesh), although for a short visit there's no reason not to bring your own. Most Moroccan internet cafés can burn CDs, although, again, this can be relied upon far more in the tech-savvy cafés in larger centres than in more out-of-the-way places.

For the nondigital shooters among you, Kodak and Fuji colour negative film (35mm and APS), as well as video tapes, are readily available in bigger cities and towns, but are marginally more expensive than in Europe. Slide film is more difficult to come by. If you buy film in Morocco, be sure to check expiry dates. Professional photo labs also offer the most professional processing services.

For comprehensive advice on taking terrific photos, Lonely Planet's *Travel Photography*, *Landscape Photography* and *People Photography* have been designed to take with you on the road.

POST

Post offices are distinguished by the 'PTT' sign or the 'La Poste' logo. You can sometimes buy stamps at tabacs, the small tobacco and newspaper kiosks you see scattered about the main city centres.

The postal system is fairly reliable, if not terribly fast. It takes at least a week for letters to get to their European destinations, and two weeks to get to Australia and North America. Sending post from Rabat or Casablanca is quicker.

Express Mail & Couriers

There is usually an Express Mail Service (EMS), also known as Poste Rapide, in the same office as parcel post. In Morocco the service is run by **Chronopost** (☎ 022 202121; www.chronopost.com). A 500g package costs Dh312 to France, Dh329 to the UK, Dh417 to North America and Dh548 to Australia. Delivery takes two to three days.

Private courier companies have offices in the major cities and are faster and more expensive. One of the most reliable is **DHL** (☎ 022 972020; www.dhl.com).

Postal Rates

A postcard costs Dh7 to France, Spain or Portugal, Dh7.50 to other countries in Europe, Dh9 to North America and Dh10 to Australia. A 20g letter costs the same as a postcard to European destinations, Dh12 to North America and Dh15.50 to Australia.

A 1kg parcel costs Dh110 to Europe, Dh150 to North America and Dh195 to Australia.

Receiving Mail

Having mail addressed to 'Poste Restante, La Poste Principale' of any big town should not be a problem. However, some offices only hang on to parcels for a couple of weeks before returning them. You'll need your passport to claim mail and there may be a small charge on collection.

Possibly a more reliable way to receive mail is through Amex, which is represented by the travel agency Voyages Schwartz and has branches in Casablanca, Tangier and Marrakesh. To qualify for the client mail service, you're supposed to have Amex travellers cheques or an Amex card. In practice, you're usually asked only to produce a passport for identification and there's no charge.

Sending Mail

The parcel office, which is indicated by the sign 'colis postaux', is generally in a separate part of the post office building.

To ship your goods home, buy a box and a shipping form at the post office and take them to the shop where you bought your wares; they know the product and can wrap and pack the pieces well with newsprint and cardboard. If you've purchased carpets, the vendor should have rolled and bound them in plastic sacks; if not, return and ask them to do so. There is a 20kg limit and parcels should not be wider, longer or higher than 1.5m. Label the outside of the boxes or carpets in several places with a waterproof pen and be very clear about the destination country. Indicate the value of the contents if you like, but you may be charged taxes at the receiving end. Don't seal the box! Customs offices at the post office need to review the contents. Your packages will be weighed and you will be charged the Par Avion (air) freight rates unless you specify that that you prefer the items shipped by land (considerably less expensive but can take three months). Then, *bsmee'allah*! Your souvenirs are on their way.

Valuable specialty items such as large furniture may involve customs clearance. The shopkeeper should arrange all of this, plus shipping, for you but at your own cost; just make sure you keep copies of all documentation.

SHOPPING

An enthusiastic souvenir hunter could spend weeks trawling through the souqs of Morocco. From silver jewellery to copper and brassware, and myriad rugs and carpets, there is an enormous range.

RULES TO REMEMBER

There are three rules for shopping in Morocco's souqs: patience, patience and patience. Bargaining is an essential element in Morocco's commercial culture, and through a mix of guile, persistence and silky sales techniques, Moroccan shop owners are a world-class act. For them, bargaining is entertainment and social interaction, a game seasoned with performance and rhetoric. You'd do well to see it in the same way.

Preparation

Visiting the Ensemble Artisanal, a government-run craft shop found in most cities and where they sell quality goods at fixed prices, is ideal for discovering what constitutes a fair price before engaging the vendors of the souqs. Hotel receptionists or local friends can also give you an idea of what a local would pay. Armed with this information, set yourself an upper limit and stick to it.

Foreplay

Learn the art of wandering through the souqs and scanning your surrounds – sunglasses are the perfect aid in this devious pursuit. Once you've spotted your prey, engage the shop owner and score points with a *salam ou alekum* (peace be with you). His questions will follow: Where are you from? He will doubtless discover (what a coincidence!) that he has a brother/cousin/friend who lives in your home town. How long have you been in Morocco? Far be it for us to advocate lying, but the less time you've been here, the more the shop owner will be licking his lips. After this exchange of pleasantries you can start to browse disinterestedly – a spark of interest means the bargaining begins (though not if you're with a guide as a commission will have to factored in).

The Main Event

Whatever the vendor quotes you, offer one-third. If that's insultingly low (and even if it isn't), he'll laugh, shake his head then look pained. If you truly have insulted him, or he figures that the tour bus (filled with tourists with loads of money and little time) just around the corner is headed his way, the bargaining will end. More likely, he'll tell you that he can drop the price by a few dirhams because (a) you are his friend; (b) he likes Australian/British/American/Insert-country-here people; (c) business has been very bad and what else can he do; or (d) because you are the first/last customer of the day. Play hard to get and counter with your own sob story, tell him you've seen the same item just down the road for a fraction of the price or make him laugh and he will lower again. Perhaps give a little ground, even walk away, and if you are with someone, try the 'good cop, bad cop' routine (eg, husband wants the souvenir, cautious wife controls the purse strings). Whatever you do, don't let on how much you *really* want the piece. If it means enough to him, he won't let you leave; if not, swallow your pride and try again. But never, ever lose your temper – Dh10 probably means more to a Moroccan trader than it does to you. If you end up paying 60% of the opening price for the item you're after, you've done well.

The Aftermath

After the purchase has been sealed, other travellers will surely tell you that you paid too much, but it is worth keeping in mind that bargaining depends on a wonderfully simple concept: the price is one that both parties have accepted as fair. It doesn't matter what anybody else thinks.

And one final thing: unless you're leaving on the next bus out of town, pass by the shop on the days that follow, stopping even for a mint tea. Freed from the pressure of a looming transaction, you might even get to know the man behind the salesman, which may be worth more than money can buy..

Obviously, items of inferior quality are produced in addition to higher quality objects – it pays to take your time before buying. For more information on what to look for, see the dedicated Arts & Crafts chapter (p53).

Other popular items include herbs and spices, old-fashioned French-style tourism posters and Moroccan clothes. Many die-hard shoppers buy a large woven shopping basket as a souvenir and also use it to pack and transport souvenirs.

Always get a receipt for larger purchases, especially carpets, as you may be required to show this to customs on your departure from Morocco; otherwise you may have to pay an export tax, especially if you have more than one carpet. You may also have to pay a duty on taking carpets into your home country.

Markets

Moroccan towns and villages have weekly or twice-weekly markets (*souq hebdomadaire*) where people from the surrounding area come to sell their wares and buy goods they don't produce themselves. These markets are different from the permanent covered markets you'll find in most towns, and usually provide a lively opportunity to observe the distinctive customs and clothing of local people.

All types of markets are called souqs. These are some of the more interesting ones:

Location	Market days
Agadir	Saturday, Sunday
Azrou	Tuesday
Chefchaouen	Monday, Thursday
Figuig	Wednesday
Larache	Sunday
M'Hamid	Monday
Midelt	Sunday
Moulay Idriss	Saturday
Ouarzazate	Sunday
Ouezzane	Thursday
Oujda	Wednesday, Sunday
Sefrou	Thursday
Tafraoute	Wednesday
Taroudannt	Sunday
Tinerhir	Monday
Tinzouline	Monday
Tiznit	Wednesday
Zagora	Wednesday, Sunday

SOLO TRAVELLERS

Morocco is a great destination for solo travellers. Popular with independent travellers and backpackers, there is plenty of budget accommodation where it's easy to find a travel buddy should you be in need of one (Fès and Marrakesh are particularly good centres for this). Moroccans are also open, inquisitive and friendly, which means you will seldom be lonely. Outside the cities, the rates in many places are per person rather than per room and single occupancy of rooms is rarely a problem. However, in riads, the limited accommodation means that discounts on single occupancy are fairly minimal.

Lone female travellers to Morocco will undoubtedly find it more tiresome than solo male travellers, although the overwhelming consensus from readers is that the rewards far outweigh the hassles. Be cautious but don't be paranoid because if you close off all contact with local people you could end up missing one of Morocco's greatest rewards.

For more information on women travellers, see p466.

TELEPHONE & FAX
Telephone

Recent massive investment means that the telephone system in Morocco is excellent.

DOMESTIC DIALLING

Telephone calls in Morocco are relatively expensive, especially long-distance calls between cities.

To make a local call with a coin-operated phone you must insert a minimum of Dh1.50. Costs are worked out in units (one unit equals Dh0.90) and your initial Dh1.50 gets you about three minutes.

Long-distance domestic calls cost from Dh0.70 per minute (35km or under) to Dh2 per minute. Local and long-distance calls are half price on weekends and from 8pm to 8am weekdays. Call prices are cut by 70% on the first day of a national or religious holiday and by 50% on the second day.

INTERNATIONAL DIALLING

International calls from Morocco are fairly expensive. The cheap rate (20% off) operates on weekends and public holidays, and from 8pm to 8am weekdays.

International call rates are listed in the *Annuaire Officiel des Abonnés au Téléphone*, the standard phonebook for Morocco. You may be able to look at a copy in major post offices. Per-minute peak rates to the following countries are: Italy, France and Spain (Dh8); Germany and the UK (Dh14); Ireland, Denmark, Belgium, the Netherlands and Switzerland (Dh15); USA and Canada (Dh22.50); and Australia, New Zealand, Hong Kong and Japan (Dh35).

MOBILE PHONES

Morocco has two GSM mobile (cell) phone networks, Méditel and Maroc Telecom, which now cover most of Morocco's population centres, although most of the Atlas and Saharan Morocco remain mobile-free zones. For a map of the mobile coverage for Morocco's two carriers, click on www .cellular-news.com/coverage/morocco.php.

Ask your mobile operator about using your phone in Morocco. Bear in mind that these 'roaming' services are very expensive and rarely as user-friendly as companies make out.

A cheaper alternative may be a prepaid Moroccan mobile phone, although to buy the phone together with an initial Dh200 card will set you back about Dh500 to Dh600. You can pick up subsequent pay-as-you-go cards at any Méditel or Maroc Telecom outlet (dozens around), the local *tabac* or *téléboutique*.

Moroccan mobile numbers start with the codes ☎ 061 to ☎ 068.

PAYPHONES & PHONECARDS

A few cities and towns still have public phone offices, often next to the post office, but more common are privately run *téléboutiques*, which are found in every town and village. They are slightly more expensive than public phones but open later.

Télécartes (phonecards) for public phones are available at post offices, some *tabacs* and a few top-end hotels.

You can make local calls from hotels, but these can easily cost double the normal amount.

PHONE CODES

You must dial the local three-digit area code even if you are dialling from the same town or code area. Thus to call a number in Marrakesh from inside the city you still need to dial the code ☎ 044. Codes have been shown for all telephone numbers in this book. The domestic operator can be reached by dialling ☎ 10.

To dial the Spanish enclaves of Melilla and Ceuta you must first dial the international code (☎ 00), then the code for Spain (☎ 34) and then the nine-digit telephone number.

REVERSE CHARGES

You can make reverse-charge (collect) calls from Morocco, but it can involve painfully long waits in phone offices. If you want to do this, say 'Je voudrais téléphoner en PCV' (pronounced 'peh-seh-veh' – the French expression for this service).

Many telephone companies outside Morocco operate international services that allow you to dial a toll-free number that connects you with operators in your home country, through whom you can then request reverse-charge and credit-card calls. Ask with your phone company for the number before leaving home.

Fax

Most *téléboutiques* offer fax services, but they're often expensive. Average prices per page are local (Dh12); countrywide (Dh23); Europe and North Africa (Dh55); Scandinavia, Southern Africa, Asia, Australia, New Zealand and North America (Dh78). In some places they charge you per-minute for how long the fax takes to go through. It normally costs Dh5 to receive a fax.

TIME

Morocco is on GMT/UTC year-round, although remember that Spain and the Spanish enclaves of Ceuta and Melilla are two hours ahead in summer, which can affect plans for catching ferries and the like. For a comprehensive guide to time zones, see p526-7.

Time is something that most Moroccans seem to have plenty of and they're not in nearly as much of a hurry to get things done as Westerners. Rather than getting frustrated by this, learn to go with the flow a little. It may even lengthen your life, a sentiment reflected in the Moroccan saying, 'He who hurries has one foot in the grave'.

DIRECTORY

TOILETS

Outside the major cities, public toilets are rare and you'll need to bring paper *(papier hygiénique)*; a tip for the attendant (Dh2 to Dh3); stout-soled shoes; and very often a nose clip. Flush toilets are a luxury in a country struggling with water shortages.

Toilets are mostly of the 'squat' variety (referred to by Moroccans as 'Turkish toilets') with a tap, hose or container of water for sluicing – the idea being to wash yourself (with your left hand) after performing. There's seldom any toilet paper so keep a supply with you. Don't throw the paper into the toilet as the plumbing is often dodgy; instead discard it in the bin provided. Women who have their period will need to take along a plastic bag for disposing of used tampons and pads.

TOURIST INFORMATION
Tourist Offices in Morocco

The national tourism body, **Office National Marocain du Tourisme** (ONMT; ☎ 037 673756; visit morocco@onmt.org.ma; cnr Rue Oued El Makhazine & Rue Zalaka, Agdal; ☻ 8.30am-noon & 3-6.30pm Mon-Fri) has its head office in Rabat and offices in the main cities, which are often called Délégation Régionale du Tourisme. Regional offices, called Syndicat d'Initiative, are to be found in smaller towns and number around 20. Although there are some notable exceptions, most tourist offices inside Morocco are of limited use, offering the standard ONMT brochures and the simplest of tourist maps, along with helpless smiles. See the Information sections of the relevant city entries throughout the book.

Tourist Offices Abroad

The ONMT also has offices abroad. They generally stock brochures, some glossy maps and lists of tour operators running trips to Morocco. They include the following:

Australia (☎ 02-9957 6717; fax 9923 1053; c/o Moroccan Consulate; 11 West St, North Sydney, NSW 2060)
Canada (☎ 514-842 8111; onmt@qc.aira.com; Place Montréal Trust, 1800 Rue MacGill, Suite 2450, Montreal, Quebec H3A 3J6)
France (☎ 01 42 60 63 50; www.tourisme-marocain .com; 161 Rue Saint Honoré, Place du Théâtre Français, 75001 Paris)
Germany (☎ 0211-370551; www.tourismus-in -marokko.de; 59 Graf Adolf Strasse 4000, Düsseldorf)

Japan (☎ 03-3403 0070; Suite 303, 219 Sendagaya, Shibuya-ku, Tokyo 151)
Spain (☎ 91-542 7437; www.turismomarruecos.com; Calle Ventura Rodriguez 24, 1 Izq 28008 Madrid)
UK (☎ 020-7437 0073; mnto@morocco-tourism.org.uk; 205 Regent St, London W1R 7DE)
USA New York (☎ 212-557 2520; mntonyonmt@aol.com; Suite 1201, 20 East 46th St, New York, NY 10017); Florida (☎ 407-827 5337; fax 407-827 0146, inanmrini@aol.com; PO Box 2263, Lake Buena Vista, Orlando, Florida 32830)

TRAVELLERS WITH DISABILITIES

Morocco has few facilities for the disabled and the awkward nature of narrow medina streets and rutted pavements makes mobility even for the able-bodied something of a challenge. But that doesn't necessarily make it out of bounds for those who do have a physical disability and a sense of adventure. Not all hotels (and certainly very few of the cheaper ones) have lifts, so booking ground-floor hotel rooms ahead of time is one essential. Only a handful of the very top-end hotels have rooms designed for the disabled. Travelling by car is probably the best transport, though you'll be able to get assistance in bus and train stations (a tip will be required). Many tour operators can tailor trips to suit your requirements.

Vision- or hearing-impaired travellers are also poorly catered for with hearing loops, Braille signs and talking pedestrian crossings nonexistent.

Organisations that disseminate information, advice and assistance on world travel for the mobility impaired include the following:

Access-able Travel Source (☎ 303-232 2979; fax 239 8486; www.access-able.com; Wheatridge, CO, USA)
Accessible Travel & Leisure (☎ 0145 272 9739; www .accessibletravel.co.uk; Gloucester, UK) Claims to be the biggest UK travel agent dealing with travel for the disabled and encourages people with a disability to travel independently.
Holiday Care (☎ 0845 124 9971; www.holidaycare .org.uk; Horley, Surrey, UK) One of the largest UK travel information resources for the disabled.
Mobility International USA (☎ 541-343 1284; www .miusa.org; Eugene, Oregon, USA)
Royal Association for Disability & Rehabilitation (RADAR; ☎ 020-7250 3222; www.radar.org.uk; London, UK) Publishes a useful guide called *Holidays & Travel Abroad: A Guide for Disabled People.*
National Information Communication Awareness Network (www.nican.com.au; Australia)

VISAS

Most visitors to Morocco do not require visas and are allowed to remain in the country for 90 days on entry. Exceptions to this include nationals of Israel, South Africa and Zimbabwe. These people can apply for a three-month, single-entry visa (about US$30). They also have the option of applying for a three-month, double-entry visa (about US$50). In all cases, your passport must be valid for at least six months beyond your date of entry. Applications are normally processed in 48 hours.

In Spain, visas for nationals of Israel, South Africa and Zimbabwe are available at consulates in Madrid, Barcelona, Algeciras, and Las Palmas in the Canary Islands. In Mauritania, you can get a visa at the Moroccan embassy in Nouakchott within 48 hours.

As visa requirements change, it's a good idea to check with the Moroccan embassy in your country or a reputable travel agency before travelling.

Visa Extensions

Should the standard 90-day stay be insufficient, you can apply for an extension or even for residence, but the latter is difficult to get. Go to the nearest police headquarters (Préfecture de Police) with your passport, three photos and a letter from your embassy requesting a visa extension on your behalf. Applications can take hours or days, and different police headquarters use slightly different red tape to hold up proceedings.

Although travellers on visas are advised to go for an extension, it's probably easier to head to mainland Spain or one of the Spanish enclaves (see below) and try to re-enter after a few days. Some travellers have reported difficulties in re-entering by the same route, though this is not always the case.

Visas for Ceuta & Melilla

These two Spanish enclaves have the same visa requirements as mainland Spain. Under the 1995 Schengen agreement, one visa now covers all EU member countries except the UK, the Republic of Ireland and Denmark, and replaces those previously issued by individual nations. Australian citizens travelling to Spain as tourists, for a maximum period of three months per calendar year, do not require a Schengen visa prior to arrival in

---

VISAS FOR NEIGHBOURING COUNTRIES

Embassies for the following countries are in Rabat – see p451 for address details.

- **Algeria** Although Algeria has now emerged from over a decade of civil war, the border with Morocco remains closed due to continued tensions with Polisario, tourist abductions in the desert in 2003 and ongoing fears of Algerian-based terror groups.

- **Mali** Visas are required for everyone except French nationals and are valid for one month (Dh250), but are renewable inside Mali. Two photographs and a yellow-fever vaccination certificate are required and the visa is usually issued on the spot. Malian visas are available at Malian border posts but by no means count on that if you're crossing at a remote desert crossing.

- **Mauritania** Everyone, except nationals of Arab League countries, needs a visa, which is valid for a one-month stay (the visa lasts for three months, but that only means you have three months from the date of issue to enter the country). These can be issued the same day at the Mauritanian Embassy in Casablanca if you apply between 9am and 10am (get there by 8.30am). Visas cost Dh200 and you need two photos as well as an onward air ticket to show when you will be departing from Mauritania; in practice, many travellers get around this last requirement by buying an airline ticket in Rabat for the purpose of obtaining a visa and then sell (or refund) the ticket once the visa is issued. Officials claim that it's also possible to get a visa at Dakhla for Dh300 plus two photos and even at the border post, but don't rely on this. Good up-to-date information is available online at www.sahara-overland.com.

- **Tunisia** Citizens of EU countries, the USA and Japan can stay up to three months in Tunisia without a visa. Australians, New Zealanders and South Africans can get a three-month visa upon arrival at the airport.

Spain. On arrival their passports will be stamped with a Schengen Stamp (valid for three months) at the first port of entry.

South Africans and Israelis still need to obtain a visa before they travel to Europe.

For those who must apply for a visa, you'll need three photos, and you may also be asked for photocopies of passport details, credit cards and/or bank statements. The Spanish prefer you to apply for a visa in your country of residence – this is only rarely waived.

International Health Certificate

If you're coming to Morocco from certain parts of Asia, Africa or South America where outbreaks of yellow fever or cholera have been reported, you'll need this yellow booklet. It's a record of your recent vaccinations and is available from your physician or government health department. A yellow fever vaccination certificate is sometimes a separate document. See p490 for general information on immunisations.

WOMEN TRAVELLERS

Prior to marriage, Moroccan men have little opportunity to meet and get to know women, which is a major reason why Western women receive so much attention. Not bound by the Moroccan social structure and Islamic law, these women are seen as excitingly independent and generally available!

Around 70% of Morocco's population are under the age of 30 and by the end of their trip most women may think they've met every male in this group. The constant attention soon becomes wearing and, no matter what tactic is employed, impossible to shake off.

If it's your first time in Morocco, the first few days may be something of a shock, although you'll quickly develop a thick skin to deal with the comments and unwanted looks of men. The key to not spending the rest of your trip feeling hassled is remain wary but not paranoid – it's extremely rare for any of this low-level harassment to go any further. If it does all get too much, look for the ever-increasing number of places accustomed to having the business of single Moroccan women. The upper floor of a *salon de thé* (teahouse), many cafés and restaurants or a hotel terrace are good bets.

Hammams are good male-free zones for a relaxing reprieve.

The prevailing attitude that a Westerner is a walking visa out of a country where unemployment is rife can also impact upon the experience of women travellers. Bored youngsters (and the not so young) may have little to lose by wooing someone who can offer them an opportunity in another country. That's not to say this is the basis for all relationships of mixed nationality (of which there are many success stories), but be aware that some locals could be juggling several relationships at any one time.

Women travelling with male companions are unlikely to experience much of the hassle that solo women will inevitably encounter, although it may be better to claim to be a married couple rather than just friends – a concept usually greeted with disbelief.

If you are a Moroccan woman (or Moroccan in appearance) and you're travelling with your non-Moroccan spouse, it may be advisable to carry a copy of your marriage certificate. This is because premarital sex for Muslims is forbidden and Morocco has a real problem with prostitution. If your partner is thought to be Muslim you may meet with some uncomfortable situations at hotel reception desks, though it has to be said that in larger cities this is not really an issue.

For all the problems, there is one huge benefit of travelling as a woman in Morocco: unlike men, you'll have plenty of opportunities to meet local women and thereby enjoy a fascinating window onto one of the least-known aspects of Moroccan society. For more information on women in Morocco see p52.

Safety Precautions

Moroccans would have to be among the most hospitable people in the world. Genuinely welcoming, they are eager to help any traveller and there are times when being a woman is a distinct advantage, especially when lost or in some form of distress. Moroccans tend to be genuinely concerned for the 'weaker sex' and will offer protection and support if you feel you're in a potentially dodgy situation.

Although drugs and alcohol are having an increasing effect in Morocco, crimes against women remain extremely rare. Only slightly more common is verbal abuse from both men and women. That said, you should always take a few sensible precautions:

- Don't hitchhike.
- Be aware that some budget hotels double as brothels; any cheap hotel above a popular locals' bar is a likely contender. Don't compromise your safety for the sake of economy.
- On public transport try to sit next to a woman – especially in grands taxis where you're squeezed in far too closely for comfort, and trains where you could potentially be trapped in a compartment. In grands taxis pay for two seats and get a ride by yourself in the front. It must be said, however, that many women travel in grands taxis without the slightest problem, regardless of where they sit.
- Don't wander about alone at night as there's an attitude that all 'good women' should be at home after dark – take a taxi.
- Avoid walking alone in remote areas such as isolated beaches, forests and sand dunes.
- If you need a drink, head for a large hotel rather than a 'bunker-style', all-male preserve – any woman here is without doubt a prostitute. Then again, so are many of those in the posher places.
- Wearing dark glasses is good for avoiding eye contact, but don't spend your entire Moroccan journey hiding behind them.
- Don't react with aggression – it could be returned in kind. A good-humoured *non merci* or *la shukran* ('no thank you') is much more effective than abuse.

A wedding ring may be useful and a photo of your 'husband' and 'child' could help, although the fact that you're travelling without them will attract suspicion – counter this by saying you'll be meeting them at your next destination. It has to be said, however, that many Moroccan men aren't too concerned whether you're married or not and may still insist they're just being friendly and could even invite you home to meet their mother.

One traveller reported that the key word to use is 'respect', a concept that most Moroccans hold dear. It's worth a try, but remember the advice of one female Lonely Planet author: 'asking men to respect me did a fat lot of good in ending any unwanted attention I was getting'.

Always dress modestly and be aware that hotel and public swimming pools usually attract groups of men, whether they be swimming themselves or drinking at a poolside bar. Bikinis will always attract attention. At the other end of the scale, sporting a head scarf or even a jellaba (Moroccan-style flowing cloak) will earn you respect, particularly in the countryside, as well as a million questions as to why you're wearing it: are you Muslim? Are you Moroccan? Are you married to a Moroccan?

For further suggestions about what to wear (and what not to wear) while in Morocco, see p45.

WORK

With huge unemployment and a largely out-of-work youthful population, Morocco is not the most fruitful ground for digging up work opportunities. A good command of French is a prerequisite and some Arabic would certainly help. If you secure a position, your employer will have to help you get a work permit and arrange residency, which can be a long and involved process. There are some limited opportunities for doing volunteer work or teaching English, although this is not terribly well paid. Try the websites: www .workingabroad.com and www.idealist.org.

Teaching English

There are a few possibilities for teaching English as a foreign language in Morocco, and Rabat is one of the best places to start looking. First, you could approach the British Council (www.britishcouncil.org.ma), but you need a Royal Society of Arts (RSA) Diploma in Teaching English as a Foreign Language (TEFLA) and openings are not all that frequent. Another possibility is the American Language Center (www.aca.org .ma), which has offices around the country.

The time to try is around September to October (the beginning of the academic year) and, to a lesser extent, early January.

Volunteer Work

There are many international and local organisations that organise voluntary work on regional development projects in Morocco.

They generally pay nothing, sometimes not even lodging, and are aimed at young people looking for something different to do for a few weeks over the summer period. Sometimes these organisations are really summer camps and international exchange programmes.

A good place to start looking is the Morocco page for **Volunteer Abroad** (www .volunteerabroad.com/Morocco.cfm), which provides links to NGOs with Morocco-specific programmes. Also worth getting hold of is Lonely Planet's *The Gap Year Book,* which lists hundreds of NGOs that organise volunteer and other work and study programmes around the world. Your embassy may also be able to put you onto other projects and NGOs, but unless you have a working knowledge of Arabic or Berber, or have specific specialist skills, many will not be interested.

International or local NGOs that sometimes have Morocco placements or camps include the following:

Jeunesse des Chantiers Marocains (http://perso .menara.ma/youthcamps; internationalcamps@yahoo .com) A nonprofit group that promotes cultural exchange through three- to four-week courses in Moroccan Arabic, during which you stay with local families and take part in cultural events.

Chantiers Sociaux Marocains (☎ 037 297184; ccsm@planete.co.ma; BP 456, Rabat) A local NGO with international links.

International Cultural Youth Exchange (www.icye .org) Allows you to search for upcoming Moroccan volunteer opportunities.

United Planet (www.unitedplanet.org) Short- and long-term volunteering placements that sometimes include Morocco.

Volunteers for Peace (www.vfp.org) Membership (US$20) allows you to access a list of volunteering work camps.

Transport

GETTING THERE & AWAY

In 2006 Morocco instituted an 'open skies' policy, allowing several European budget airlines to fly into the country. At the same time, the national carrier, Royal Air Maroc (RAM), launched its own budget airlines Atlas Blue, to keep a step ahead of the competition. Other major national carriers also serve Morocco. Popular alternatives to air travel are the numerous ferry services from southern Spain and France. These offer competitive passenger prices and service the huge number of campervan tourists. Large bus companies also run an efficient

THINGS CHANGE...

The information in this chapter is particularly vulnerable to change. Check directly with the airline or a travel agent to make sure you understand how a fare (and ticket you may buy) works and be aware of the security requirements for international travel. Shop carefully. The details given in this chapter should be regarded as pointers and are not a substitute for your own careful, up-to-date research.

service via the ferries. Flights, tours and rail tickets can be booked online at www .lonelyplanet.com/travel_services.

ENTERING THE COUNTRY

When entering the country through an airport, formalities are fairly simple, but you will have to fill in an entry form stating the purpose of your visit and your profession.

Expensive electronic equipment may be entered on your passport. If you lose them during your visit, they will be assumed 'sold' unless you have police documentation to prove theft. If you don't have this documentation, you are liable to pay 100% duty. All goods on your passport should be 'cleared' when leaving to prevent problems on future trips.

Crossing the southern land border to Mauritania is straightforward if you have all the correct documentation.

If you're entering Morocco with a vehicle, you'll need a green card as proof of insurance (a requirement of Moroccan law that also applies to rental vehicles). These are obtainable from your insurer at home or at the border – see p484 for more information.

Passport

To enter Morocco, your passport must be valid for six months from the date of entry. If you need to renew your passport, allow plenty of time, as it can take up to several months.

If you lose your passport, notify the police immediately (make sure you get a statement for insurance purposes) and contact your nearest consulate.

AIR
Airports

Morocco's main international entry point is the **Mohammed V International Airport** (☎ 022 539040), 30km southeast of Casablanca. It's conveniently linked by regular shuttle trains to Casablanca and Rabat.

Passport control and customs formalities are straightforward. In the arrivals hall you'll find representatives of many international and local car-rental agencies, plus

CLIMATE CHANGE & TRAVEL

Climate change is a serious threat to the ecosystems that humans rely upon, and air travel is the fastest-growing contributor to the problem. Lonely Planet regards travel, overall, as a global benefit, but believes we all have a responsibility to limit our personal impact on global warming.

Flying & climate change

Pretty much every form of motorized travel generates CO_2 (the main cause of human-induced climate change) but planes are far and away the worst offenders, not just because of the sheer distances they allow us to travel, but because they release greenhouse gases high into the atmosphere. The statistics are frightening: two people taking a return flight between Europe and the US will contribute as much to climate change as an average household's gas and electricity consumption over a whole year.

Carbon offset schemes

Climatecare.org and other websites use 'carbon calculators' that allow travellers to offset the level of greenhouse gases they are responsible for with financial contributions to sustainable travel schemes that reduce global warming – including projects in India, Honduras, Kazakhstan and Uganda.

Lonely Planet, together with Rough Guides and other concerned partners in the travel industry, support the carbon offset scheme run by climatecare.org. Lonely Planet offsets all of its staff and author travel.

For more information check out our website: www.lonelyplanet.com.

people from some of the bigger hotels. The airport has a small **tourist information desk** (☎ 022 435858; 7am-10pm).

BMCE (Banque Marocaine du Commerce Extérieur) has a *bureau de change* (foreign exchange bureau), with ATM, in both arrivals and departures. Wafa Bank, with ATM, and Banque Populaire are also represented.

There are several cafés and newsstands dotted around the airport, plus a RAM ticket office, a *téléboutique* (privately operated telephone service) and a small newsagency selling stamps just in front of departures. The train station is down the stairs to the right, as you exit from customs.

The opening hours of all these services are timed to coincide with flight departures. After check-in you will have to find and fill in an embarkation form before going through the security check.

Marrakesh's **Ménara Airport** (☎ 044 447865) is increasingly well-served with direct flights from London, Paris (and other French cities), Brussels, Frankfurt and Geneva. RAM and other carriers now compete here with the budget airlines. Daily flights from Paris with Air France and RAM also land at **Rabat-**

Salé Airport (☎ 037 808090), 10km northeast of Rabat, while Tangier's **Boukhalef Airport** (in Ibn Batouta ☎ 039 393720), 15km southeast of the city, has direct flights to Amsterdam, Brussels, London, Madrid, Málaga and Paris. Fès's **Saïss Airport** (☎ 035 674712) has direct flights to Paris, London, Luton (UK) and Frankfurt.

Numerous charter flights arrive at the new **Al-Massira Airport** (☎ 048 839112), 22km south of Agadir. Direct flights to Paris, Zurich and Geneva are available.

There are also occasional international flights from Ouarzazate to Paris; Nador to Amsterdam, Brussels, Düsseldorf and Frankfurt; Al-Hoceima to Amsterdam and Brussels; and Oujda to Paris, Marseille, Amsterdam and Brussels.

For comprehensive information about all airports in Morocco, their facilities and customs regulations and procedures, log on to the website of **Office National des Aéroports** (www.onda.org.ma in French & Arabic).

Airlines

For flights to Morocco, the high seasons are July through to the end of August, and from mid-December to the end of December.

The lowest seasons are November to mid-December, and January to mid-February.

Direct flights are possible from cities across Europe, the Middle East, West Africa and North America, and they mostly arrive in Casablanca and Marrakesh. Morocco's national carrier, Royal Air Maroc and Air France take the lion's share of flights, with increasing competition from the budget airlines (including RAM's own subsidiary Atlas Blue).

INTERNATIONAL AIRLINES IN MOROCCO

Air Algérie (AH; ☎ 022 314181; www.airalgerie.dz)
Air Europa (UX; ☎ 902 401 501 in Spain; www.air-europa.com)
Air France (AF; ☎ 022 294040; www.airfrance.com)
Alitalia (AZ; ☎ 022 314181; www.alitalia.it)
Atlas Blue (BMM; ☎ 082 009090; www.atlas-blue.com)
British Airways (BA; ☎ 022 229464; www.britishairways.com)
EasyJet (EZY; ☎ 0870 600 0000 (UK); www.easyjet.com)
Edelweiss Air (EDW; ☎ 044 277 4100 in Switzerland; www.edelweissair.ch)
EgyptAir (MS; ☎ 022 315564; www.egyptair.com)
Gulf Air (GF; ☎ 022 491212; www.gulfairco.com)
Iberia (IB; ☎ 022 279600; www.iberia.com)
KLM-Royal Dutch Airlines (KL; ☎ 022 203222; www.klm.com)
Lufthansa Airlines (LH; ☎ 022 312371; www.lufthansa.com)
Regional Airlines (RGL; ☎ 022 536940; www.regionalmaroc.com)
Royal Air Maroc (RAM; ☎ 022 311122; www.royalairmaroc.com)
Royal Jordanian (RJ; ☎ 022 305975; www.rja.com.jo)
Ryanair (FR; ☎ 0871 246 0000 in UK; www.ryanair.com)
Thomsonfly (BY; ☎ 0870 190 0737 in UK; www.thomsonfly.com)
Tunis Air (TU; ☎ 022 293452; www.tunisair.com.tn)

Tickets

Your plane ticket is traditionally the most expensive item in your budget, but prices have tumbled if you travel with any of the European budget airlines – book as far in advance as possible to get the cheapest deals. Reputable online agencies for scheduled carriers include www.travelocity.co.uk, www.cheaptickets.com, www.expedia.com, www.travelcuts.com (in Canada) and www.travel.com.au (in Australia).

Morocco is a small market for flights, so little or no discounting takes place. This means prices offered by travel agencies will

---

> **DEPARTURE TAX**
>
> There is no departure tax upon leaving Morocco, and departure formalities are quite straightforward. You must fill in an exit card and have your passport stamped before exiting.

be much the same as the airlines. Oddly, the cheapest fares are not one-way tickets, but one-month returns. In either direction the bulk of traffic is with Royal Air Maroc.

Direct flights will cost you the most. Many airlines have code-share agreements and the cheapest deals can often entail a change of plane (and carrier) in a European city. As a rule, the cheapest fares are for flights into Casablanca. Cheaper student and under-26 tickets are sometimes available.

INTERCONTINENTAL (RTW) TICKETS

With its uncompetitive airline industry, Morocco is not an easy destination to work into a round-the-world ticket. Journeying east from Morocco, you will probably need to stop over in the UAE to get a connecting flight to Asia or Australia. Heading west to the USA, you will probably need to reroute through a European city or London. Most round-the-world tickets allow a maximum of 10 stopovers, although you can buy extras. It may be better and cheaper to buy your flights in and out of Morocco separately.

Africa

RAM has an extensive network of flights throughout North and West Africa from Casablanca, and is one of the better African carriers. Direct flights are available to and from Bamako (Mali), Nouakchott (Mauritania), Dakar (Senegal), Douala (Cameroon), Niamey (Niger), Abidjan (Ivory Coast), Libreville (Gabon) and Cotonou (Benin). North African destinations are Algiers (Algeria), Tunis (Tunisia), Tripoli (Libya) and Cairo (Egypt).

For the cheapest deals to/from Morocco to Southern Africa, you will probably have to travel via London, Paris or Amsterdam (travel time 15 hours). **Rennies Travel** (www.renniestravel.com), **STA Travel** (www.statravel.com) and **Flight Centre** (☎ 0860 400727; www.flightcentre.co.za) have offices throughout South Africa and in Nairobi, Kenya. Check their websites for branch locations.

A reliable agency in Egypt is Cairo-based **Soliman Travel** (☎ 02-6350 350; fax 02-6350 298); which also has an office in London.

Australasia

There are no direct flights between Australia or New Zealand and Morocco. All flights go via the Middle East (eg Bahrain on Gulf Air) or Europe. It can make more sense to fly to London, Paris or Madrid and make your own way down to Morocco. Prices of flights from New Zealand are comparable to those from Australia.

STA Travel is a reliable travel agency with branches around **Australia** (☎ 1300 733 035; www.statravel.com.au) and **New Zealand** (☎ 0508 782 872; www.statravel.co.nz). Flight Centre is also found throughout **Australia** (☎ 133 133; www .flightcentre.com.au) and **New Zealand** (☎ 0800 243 544; www.flightcentre.co.nz).

Continental Europe
FRANCE

There's no shortage of flights from Paris (and other French cities) to Casablanca, Agadir, Rabat, Tangier, Fès, Marrakesh, Oujda and Ouarzazate. Most travel agencies can do deals; fly-drive arrangements are an attractive option. Given the volume of traffic from France, deals here are often better than in London or Amsterdam.

Both **RAM** (☎ 08 20 82 18 21; www.royalairmaroc .com) and **Air France** (☎ 08 20 82 08 20; www.airfrance .com) operate at least three flights a day from Paris to Casablanca. RAM also has similarly priced flights to Tangier and Agadir. Between them, RAM and Air France connect Casablanca with Bordeaux, Lille, Lyon, Marseille, Nantes, Nice, Strasbourg and Toulouse, and also operate direct flights from Paris to Fès, Marrakesh, Ouarzazate and Rabat.

Budget airline **Atlas Blue** (☎ 08 20 88 78 87; www.atlas-blue.com) has flights to Marrakesh from Bordeaux, Lyon and Toulouse, and from Agadir to Strasbourg.

The student travel agency **OTU Voyages** (☎ 01 55 82 32 32; www.otu.fr in French) has a central Paris office and another 28 offices around the country and specialises in student and youth travellers. **Voyageurs du Monde** (☎ 01 73 00 81 88; www.vdm.com in French) and **Nouvelles Frontières** (☎ 08 25 00 07 47; www.nouvelles-frontieres.fr in French) are also recommended.

Online agencies include **Lastminute** (www .fr.lastminute.com in French) and **Travelprice** (http:// voyages.travelprice.com in French).

GERMANY

Royal Air Maroc offers flights from Casablanca and Nador to Frankfurt and also from Nador to Düsseldorf. Budget airline **Ryan Air** (☎ 0900 116 0500; www.ryanair.com) has daily direct flights from Frankfurt to Fès and Marrakesh. **Air Berlin** (☎ 01805 73 78 00; www.airberlin.com) flies to Agadir from Düsseldorf, Hannover, Nuremberg and Stuttgart.

STA Travel (☎ 01805-45 64 22; www.statravel.de) is an ever-reliable agency, with offices in Berlin, Frankfurt and 16 other cities across Germany. In Munich, a great source of travel information and equipment is **Darr Travel Shop** (☎ 089-28 20 32; Theresienstrasse 66). Online agencies are **Lastminute** (☎ 01805 284 366; www.lastminute.de in German) and **Expedia** (www .expedia.de in German).

NETHERLANDS

The excellent **Kilroy Travel Group** (☎ 020-524 5100; www.kilroygroups.com) offers discounted travel to people aged 16 to 33, and also has representative offices in Denmark, Sweden, Norway and Finland as well as the Netherlands.

A reliable source of discounted tickets is **My Travel** (☎ 020-638 1736; www.mytravel.nl in Dutch), with 42 branches nationwide.

RAM has direct flights to Amsterdam from Casablanca, Nador, Oujda and Tangier.

SPAIN

Given its proximity, there are plenty of flights between Morocco and Spain. From both Casablanca and Marrakesh, **RAM** (☎ 902 21 00 10; www.royalairmaroc.com) flies to Madrid and Barcelona, as well as a Tangier–Barcelona flight. You can also fly to Casablanca with **Iberia** (☎ 902-400 500; www.iberia.com) from Madrid, Barcelona and Valencia. Low-cost airline **Air Europa** (☎ 902-401-501; www.air-europa .com) flies to Marrakesh from Madrid and Barcelona. **Regional Airlines** (www.regionalmaroc .com) flies between Malaga and Casablanca, Nador and Tangier.

Some of the better travel agencies for flights include **Viajes Zeppelin** (☎ 91 542 51 54; www.viajeszeppelin.com in Spanish), **Barcelo Viajes** (☎ 902 116 226; www.barceloviajes.com in Spanish) and

TIVE (☎ 91 543 74 12; www.madrid.org/juventud/tive .htm in Spanish), the student and youth travel organisation.

It's also possible to fly to the Spanish enclaves of Ceuta and Melilla. Iberia's franchise Iberia Regional flies from Melilla to Madrid, Malaga and Granada. The fanciest way to get between mainland Spain and Ceuta is by helicopter with **Helicopteros del Sureste** (Málaga airport ☎ 95 204 870; www.helisureste.com) from Malaga.

Middle East

The Middle East is the connecting hub for travellers from Australia, New Zealand and the Far East. RAM has direct flights to Dubai and Beirut while Gulf Air offers similar prices from Abu Dhabi.

For Israel, it is best to get a flight to Europe first, though at the time of writing the **Israel Student Travel Association** (ISTA; ☎ 02-625 7257) offers student discounts and competitive fares.

UK

Discount air travel has always been big business in London, but the advent of the low-cost airlines has really slashed the price of flying to Morocco.

Of the scheduled carriers, **RAM** (☎ 020-7439 4361; www.royalairmaroc.co.uk) offers the greatest choice in number of flights and destinations, including direct flights to Tangier, Casablanca and Marrakesh from London (Heathrow). **British Airways** (☎ 0870-850 9850; www.ba.com) flies direct from London (Gatwick) to Casablanca, Fès and Marrakesh. From the UK's regional airports, it's possible to fly to Morocco with KLM, Alitalia and Air France via Amsterdam, Milan and Paris respectively.

EasyJet (☎ 0871-244 2366; www.easyjet.com) flies from London Gatwick to Marrakesh, while **Thomsonfly** (☎ 0870 1900 737; www.thomsonfly.com) flies from London and Manchester to both Marrakesh and Agadir. **Ryanair** (☎ 0871 246 0000; www.ryanair.com) flies from Luton to Fès and Marrakesh.

Trailfinders (☎ 0845-050 5891; www.trailfinders .com), **STA** (☎ 0870-160 0599; www.statravel.co.uk) and **Flight Centre** (☎ 0870-499 0040; www.flightcen tre.co.uk) all have offices throughout the UK. All are also good for discounted student flights. Other sources of discounted fares are www.cheapfares.co.uk, www.ebookers

.com and www.flynow.com. Advertisements for many further agencies appear in the travel pages of the weekend newspapers, such as the *Independent* and the *Guardian* on Saturday and the *Sunday Times*, as well as in publications such as *Time Out*.

UK VIA SPAIN

A popular and cheap way of getting to northern Morocco from the UK (and northern Europe) is by flying into Málaga in southern Spain and then catching a ferry to Tangier, Nador or the Spanish enclaves of Melilla or Ceuta (see p477).

EasyJet (in Spain ☎ 0870-600 0000, ☎ 902 29 99 92; www.easyjet.com) is the biggest operator, flying from several UK airports. Its main competitor is **Ryanair** (☎ 0818 30 30 30; www .ryanair.com), which has regular, direct flights from Dublin to Málaga. Prices vary wildly according to season and depend on how far in advance you can book them.

USA & Canada

Royal Air Maroc now flies direct from Casablanca to New York five times a week, and code-shares onward flights to Atlanta, Boston, Chicago, Dallas, Los Angeles, Miami, San Francisco, Seattle and Washington with **Delta Airlines** (www.delta.com). From Canada, there are five direct flights a week from Montréal to Casablanca with RAM. European carriers may offer a free stopover in their hub city.

A cheaper alternative is often a return flight from North America to continental Europe, and an onward ticket from there. The best connections tend to be through Paris (Orly) or London (Gatwick).

Discount travel agencies in the USA are known as consolidators. San Francisco is the ticket consolidator capital of America, although some good deals can be found in other big cities. The *New York Times*, *LA Times*, *Chicago Tribune* and *San Francisco Examiner* produce weekly travel sections containing numerous travel agencies' ads.

STA Travel (☎ 800-781 4040; www.statravel.com) is the largest student travel organisation in America, with offices nationwide including Boston, Chicago, Los Angeles, New York, Philadelphia and San Francisco. Its travel advisory number is available 24 hours, every day of the year. **Cheap Tickets** (www.cheaptickets .com) is another recommended agency.

TRANSPORT

TRANSPORT

Online travel agencies www.expedia.com and www.travelocity.com are useful and reliable, but there are plenty of others.

In Canada, **Travel CUTS** (☎ 866-246 9762; www .travelcuts.com) has offices in all major cities and is Canada's national student travel agency.

For discount and rock-bottom options to Europe from the USA it may be worth investigating stand-by and courier flights. Stand-by flights are often sold at 60% of the normal price for one-way tickets. **Courier Travel** (☎ 303 570 7586; www.couriertravel.org) is a comprehensive search engine for courier and stand-by flights. You can also check out the **International Association of Air Travel Couriers** (IAATC; ☎ 308 632 3273; www.courier.org).

LAND
Border Crossings
Despite its lengthy border with Algeria, the only open land crossing into Morocco is the Morocco–Mauritania border between Dakhla and Nouâdhibou. Once a complicated game of permits and military convoys, this crossing is now fairly straightforward and the most popular overland route to West Africa. For further details of this route, see p476.

Extensive ferry links between northern Morocco and southern Europe (mainly, but not exclusively, Spain) make entering the country 'overland' a popular option, either by bus, train or your own vehicle. For information on specific ferry connections, see p477.

Bus
The main point of entry for buses into Morocco is via the ferries from Spain. All passengers have to disembark for customs and immigration. Ad hoc public transport links exist between Dakhla and Nouâdhibou for crossing the Mauritania border.

Car & Motorcycle
Drivers will need the vehicle's registration papers, liability insurance and an international driver's permit in addition to their domestic licence. All vehicles travelling across international borders should display the nationality plate of the country of registration. A warning triangle to use in event of breakdown is also useful, and is compulsory in Europe.

Your local automobile association can provide specific details about all documentation, in particular the Green Card for insurance – see p484 for further details.

Pre-booking a rental car before leaving home will enable you to find the cheapest deals (multinational agencies are listed on p485). No matter where you hire your car, make sure you understand what is included in the price and what you liabilities are (this is particularly important if you are planning any off-*piste* driving, which probably won't be covered). Note the European hire companies do not usually permit their vehicles to be driven to Morocco.

Morocco is a country made for touring, and you'll see plenty of camper vans on the road, and pouring off the ferries in Tangier. Motorcycle touring is also becoming increasingly popular, but many bikes are unfamiliar in Morocco (particularly those with larger capacity engines), so repairs can be tricky. Some basic maintenance knowledge is essential and you should carry all necessary spares, including cables and levers, inner tubes, puncture repair kit, tyre levers, pump, fuses, chain, washable air filter, cable ties – and a good tool kit. As with a car, double-check insurance liabilities before setting off.

Morocco is well served with petrol (gas) stations, although these become few and far between south of Tan Tan towards the border of Mauritania (for more information, see Mauritania p476). Diesel is considerably cheaper than leaded fuel. If you're entering Morocco via Ceuta or Melilla, take the opportunity to fill up on duty-free fuel.

Algeria
Morocco closed its border with Algeria in the early 1990s, and despite the end of the civil war there, show no sign of being in a hurry to reopen it. Keep an eye on possible developments at **Sahara Overland** (www.sahara -overland.com), the essential online resource for Saharan travel.

Continental Europe
BUS
It's possible to get a bus ticket to destinations in Morocco from as far away as London, but journeys are long and not much cheaper than scheduled airfares. **Eurolines** (www.eurolines.co.uk) is a consortium of European coach companies that operates across Europe and to Morocco. It has offices in all major European cities. You can contact

them in your own country or via the website, which gives details of prices, passes and travel agencies where you can book tickets. In Morocco, services are run in conjunction with the Compagnie de Transports Marocains (CTM), Morocco's national line.

An alternative is the UK-based **Busabout** (☎ 020 7950 1661; www.busabout.com), which covers at least 60 west European cities and towns and offers passes of varying duration allowing you to use its hop-on, hop-off bus network. Buses run on a set route between Western European cities including Madrid, Granada, Málaga, La Línea (handy for Gibraltar) and Tarifa – but not Algeciras. The frequency of departures and the number of stops available increases between April and October. You can book onward travel and accommodation on the bus or on its website.

In addition, Busabout offers a seven- to 14-day 'overland' tour of Morocco in an open-sided truck, including a round-trip ferry link from Algeciras in southern Spain to Tangier. Passengers are issued with Busabout vouchers at their point of departure, to be exchanged for a ferry ticket at **Viajes Marruecotur** (☎ 56 65 61 85; New Ferry Terminal) in Algeciras.

For onward travel in Morocco, Busabout works in conjunction with **Marco Polo Travel** (☎ 039 944799; 72 Ave D'Espagne, Tangier), on the main drag outside the port gates.

The Moroccan bus company, **CTM** (in Casablanca ☎ 022 45 80 80; www.ctm.co.ma) operates buses from Casablanca and most other main cities to France, Belgium, Spain, Germany and Italy. Most leave from or go via Casablanca and cross to Europe at Tangier, but a few cross from Nador to Almería.

Buses to Spain leave Casablanca daily except Sunday. As it's part of the Eurolines network, you can get tickets to European cities as far afield as Paris and Brussels. Book a week in advance, or further ahead if your plans clash with major holidays in Spain or France, as the buses fill up quickly with Moroccans working abroad.

Another reliable bus service with good links from Morocco to Spanish networks is **Tramesa** (☎ 022 245274; www.tramesa.ma in French).

TRAIN

The *Thomas Cook European Timetable* has a complete listing of train schedules.

It is updated monthly and available from Thomas Cook offices worldwide or online at www.thomascookpublishing.com. The *Thomas Cook Overseas Timetable* has train, bus and ferry times for every country in Africa, including Morocco. Another useful resource for train connections is www.seat61.com.

If you just want to travel to and from Morocco, just buying normal tickets, as a rail pass is unlikely to make it any cheaper. However, if you already have a rail pass or Inter Rail card, or if you want to make other trips in France, Spain or Morocco, a rail pass may be worthwhile.

The **Inter Rail** (www.interrailnet.com) map of Europe and North Africa is divided into zones. A 22-day, two-zone pass (under/over 26 UK£205/295) allows unlimited rail travel in France, Spain and Morocco. However, you need to have lived in Europe for at least six months (take your passport along as ID).

A single zone Inter Rail pass covers Morocco and Spain, is valid for 22 days and costs under/over 26 UK£159/223. Information on prices and passes is available on the multilingual website. Cardholders get discounts on travel in the country where they purchase the ticket.

Alternatively, **Eurail** (www.eurail.com) has a pass for non-EU residents that lets you travel in 17 European countries, so will get you as far as Algeciras in Spain, but it's not valid in Morocco.

Train travel run by the **Office National des Chemins de Fer** (ONCF; www.oncf.org.ma in French) is inexpensive in Morocco, so Morocco-only Inter Rail passes are poor value. If you're planning a lot of train travel in Morocco, it's better to get a discount rail card when you arrive – either a Carte Jaune or Carte Fidelité, according to whether you're under or over 26 (see p488).

Taking a direct train from France is one option. From Paris, your best bet is to take the TGV from La Gare Montparnasse to Algeciras or Málaga via Madrid (around €162 one way with couchette, 25 hours), which can be booked through the **SNCF website** (www.voyage-sncf.com) – tickets can be posted to you across Europe, but not to North America or Australasia.

A more comfortable, and increasingly popular, alternative would be to take the

TRANSPORT

TUNNEL VISION

Mythology states that it was Hercules who first prised apart the European and African continents but his labour is now, it seems, under threat. Plans are on the table to dig a 24km-long, and 300m-deep underwater tunnel from Cap Malabata, east of Tangier, to Punta Paloma, 40km west of Gibraltar, creating a passage that backers say will reconnect Europe and Africa. The estimated €10 billion rail tunnel (original plans for a suspension bridge were dismissed as too dangerous), opens up the possibility of a train ride from London to Marrakesh.

The idea has been around since the 1970s, but it wasn't until 2004 that the two countries took serious steps towards making it a reality. Only a 500m test tunnel has been drilled so far as part of a feasibility study, with both countries so far just allocating €10 million each until engineering tests give the project the green light. Assuming the project goes ahead, the EU is expected to be asked to put its hands in its pockets for much of the funding.

If the tunnel goes ahead, it could do more than help promote trade and tourism. Relations between Spain and Morocco have been strained in recent years, with offshore territorial disputes and concerns over terrorism and immigration. It's hoped that the Herculean task of building the tunnel could literally tie the two countries closer together.

Francisco de Goya Trainhotel from Paris (Austerlitz) to Madrid. Trainhotels are a new idea in overnight train travel run by a consortium of the French and Spanish railways called **Elipsos** (www.elipsos.com). The train departs early evening and arrives in Madrid at 9am in the morning. You can book a four-berth tourist-class sleeper (one way €137) or one- and two-berth 1st-class sleepers, and there is a restaurant and a café-bar. ISIC card holders can get a 15% discount, and all tickets can be booked online.

The onward trip to Algeciras can be done in similar comfort on the **RENFE** (www.renfe.es) 'Estrella del Estrecho', which leaves from Madrid (Chamartín). Six-berth sleeping cars are available (€38 one way), or more expensive one- and two-berth rooms with bathroom. The train arrives around 9.30am in Algeciras from where you can hop straight on to a ferry.

Heading out of Morocco from Casablanca, standard one-way fares to European cities are more expensive (though sometimes only slightly more) than the coach. There are significant reductions for students and those under 26. You can book international tickets in Morocco up to a month ahead.

Mauritania
CAR & MOTORCYCLE

The trans-Saharan route via Mauritania is now the most popular route from North Africa into sub-Saharan Africa, and hundreds of adventurous souls do it every year.

The route into Mauritania from Dakhla runs south along the coast for 460km, across the border to Nouâdhibou and then south along the coast to the Mauritanian capital Nouakchott. Until recently, travel south of Dakhla had to be undertaken as part of a military convoy, but it is now possible to do this independently. Still, if driving yourself, it makes sense to travel with other vehicles and set off early in order to reach the border before dusk (particularly advisable if you are travelling in a 2WD). It's also advisable to fill up with petrol at every available station. Some stations south of Dakhla may be out of fuel, in particular the last station 50km before the border.

Moroccan border formalities are processed in the basic settlement of Guergarat. The border, about 15km from the settlement, is heavily mined, so stay on the road. The old *piste* (track, unsealed road) has now been replaced with a sealed road running all the way to Nouakchott, barring a 3km stretch in the no-man's-land between the two border posts.

Mauritanian visas can be bought without hassle at the border for €20, but border guards may sometimes add on other 'fees' to the same value (although if asked for, currency declaration forms are no longer required). Alcohol is illegal in Mauritania and vehicle searches are common. From the border it's a short drive to the first major Mauritanian town of Nouâdhibou, 50km away.

TRANSPORT

MINIBUS & JEEP

There are ad hoc transport links from Dakhla to the Mauritania border and beyond. Minibuses and 4WDs leave from the military checkpoint on the road out of Dakhla – expect to pay between Dh250 and Dh400 for a seat in a vehicle going to Nouâdhibou, or around Dh700 all the way to Nouakchott. A few grands taxis also run to the border, but you'll still need to hitch to get to the Mauritanian checkpoint, as walking across the border is forbidden.

From Nouâdhibou, bush taxis cost around UM1750 to the border, although it's worth asking around the hotels, as there are often plenty of Mauritanian businessmen travelling north who will sell you a seat in their vehicle.

For information about trans-Saharan travel, see Chris Scott's *Sahara Overland*, both a book and **website** (www.sahara-overland .com). **Horizons Unlimited's Sahara Travel Forum** (www.horizonsunlimited.com) has a useful bulletin board with regularly updated information on travel between Morocco and Mauritania.

SEA

Catching a ferry is a perennially popular way of getting to Morocco. In the summer the most popular route, from Algeciras to Tangier, is packed with both day-trippers and holiday-makers with camper-vans. Alternative crossings are to the Spanish enclaves of Ceuta and Melilla, and even a

longer voyage from Sète in France. All the port cities (and most cities in Morocco) have numerous travel agencies and ticket offices, or you can literally turn up and buy one at the dock.

If you're sailing from Europe to Morocco, discounts for students (with ISIC cards), Inter Rail or Eurail pass holders and EU pensioners are frequently advertised. They're less commonly available in Morocco, but it's still worth asking. All ferry tickets purchased in Morocco are subject to Dh20 tax.

High season for ferries is generally the European summer (June to August), Christmas and New Year. More ferries run to cope with demand – foot passengers are often safe to buy a ticket on arrival at the port, but they're worth booking in advance if you're driving a vehicle.

France
SÈTE TO TANGIER

This car-ferry service is far more luxurious than those linking Spain and Morocco. It needs to be, as the voyage takes two nights. You may be thankful for the onboard swimming pool and 'disco bar'. Sète is two hours by train from Marseilles.

Two companies are operating on this route, **Comarit** (www.comarit.com in French & Spanish) and **Comanav** (www.comanav.ma in French). Both sail around every fourth or fifth day, leaving port between 6pm and 7pm in both directions. The trip takes 36 hours.

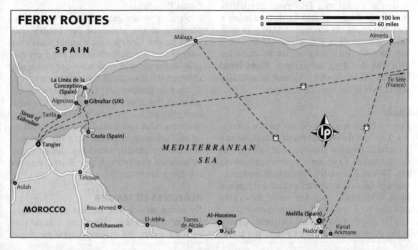

FERRY ROUTES

TRANSPORT

Fares cost around €220/410 one way/return in a four-bed cabin in high season (mid-July to mid-September), plus €5 port tax (payable twice on return journeys). Meals are included. Children aged between two and 12 travel for half-price. Low-season (November to February) fares are 50% cheaper. It costs €380 to transport a normal saloon (sedan) car. Comarit also offers chair seats for around €82, but they might be a bit of an endurance test by the end of the voyage.

Discounts of up to 20% can be had for students and those under 26, Moroccan residents abroad, and groups of four travelling together with a car.

You can book tickets for this service in the UK at **Southern Ferries** (☎ 0870 499 1305; 179 Piccadilly, London W1V 9DB) or in France at the SNCM Ferryterranée office in **Marseille** (☎ 04 91 56 32 00; fax 04 91 56 36 66; 61 Blvd des Dames, 13226) or in **Sète** (☎ 04 67 46 68 00; fax 04 67 74 93 05; 4 Quai d'Alger, 34202).

In Tangier, **Comanav** (☎ 039 940504; 43 Ave Abou al-Alâa el-Maâri) and **Comarit** (☎ 039 320032; Ave des FAR) sell tickets and have detailed timetables, as do their booths at Tangier dock.

Gibraltar

The catamaran ferry company **FRS** (www.frs .ma) claims to sail weekly between Tangier and Gibraltar (or more specifically La Línea across the border in Spain), but the service seems to be on continual hold. Should it resume, prices should be around €35/54 per passenger/car. The trip takes 90 minutes.

In the meantime, FRS runs alternative services to Algeciras and Tarifa (see below). You can check the current state of play with **FRS** (in Spain ☎ 956 68 18 30, in Tangier ☎ 039 942612; Gare Maritime), including at its main ticket office at the dock in Tangier. **Bland Travel** (☎ 77012; 81 Irish Town) in Gibraltar will also sell tickets if the service resumes.

Spain

Ferries from Spain to Morocco are plentiful. The Spanish government-run company Trasmediterránea runs regular sailings, as do Buquebus, Comanav, Comarit, EuroFerrys, FRS and Limadet. Hydrofoils and catamarans (also referred to as fast ferries) are used extensively, but are more expensive and can be disrupted by rough seas.

The most popular and frequent service is the Algeciras to Tangier route. It's tradi-

tionally been known for its hassle and hustlers, but these have largely been cleared out of the port, and entering Morocco here should no longer fill the traveller with dread (see p157). Car owners may find the Algeciras to Ceuta route to be more worthwhile because of the availability of tax-free petrol in the Spanish enclave. The other routes are Tarifa to Tangier, Almería to Melilla or Nador, and Málaga to Melilla. Heading into Morocco via Melilla (and then Nador) is easily the most hassle-free way to arrive from the Spanish mainland, though crossings can take eight hours, cost twice as much as crossing from Algeciras to Ceuta or Tangier and are much less frequent.

On most routes, more boats are scheduled in the high season (mid-June to mid-September). During August and Easter, when demand is highest, those with vehicles should book well in advance. At other times you're unlikely to have problems getting a convenient passage.

As well as in Madrid, **Trasmediterránea** (countrywide ☎ 902 45 46 45; www.trasmediterranea .es; Calle Alcalá 61) has offices at many Spanish ports, including Almería, Algeciras, Ceuta, Melilla and Málaga.

Tickets for most companies can be reserved online (see specific route details below). Alternatively **Southern Ferries** (☎ 0870 499 1305; 179 Piccadilly, London W1V 9DB), in the UK, can help with most ferry inquiries and ticket sales. In France, try **Iberrail** (☎ 01 40 82 63 63; www.iberrail.es in Spanish; 57 Rue de la Chaussé D'Antin, 75008 Paris).

Surcharges are exacted on cars not conforming to the standard 6m length and 1.8m height. Charges for camper vans also vary. Rates for motorbikes depend on engine capacity, while bicycles are normally charged the minimum motorbike rate.

Spanish passport control is quite uncomplicated but non-EU citizens should make sure they get an exit stamp before boarding the ferry. Once on board you need to fill in an embarkation form and get your passport stamped before disembarking. Customs can be slow on the Spanish side if you're coming from Morocco.

ALGECIRAS TO TANGIER

By some stretch the busiest sea crossing between Spain and Morocco, ferries run at least every 90 minutes between these ports, and hourly in the summer. Services typically run from 7am (or 6am in summer) until 10pm, but during peak demand in August 24-hour services aren't unknown. The crossing takes 80 minutes to 2½ hours, depending on the ship.

All the ferry companies operate this route: Trasmediterránea, Buquebus, Comanav, Comarit, EuroFerrys, FRS and Limadet. Competition keeps the prices uniform between them. You can expect to pay around €31 one way, standard class. Children up to four years old travel free, while children aged from four to 12 pay 50%. Cars cost between €60 and €80, and camper vans are €105. Some ferry companies offer 1st class for an extra 20%, but it's barely worth it for the short trip.

Ticket offices line up outside the ferry terminal in Tangier, so it's easy to walk between them and pick the best sailing for you. There are more ticket offices inside the terminal building itself. In Tangier itself, touts will try and guide you towards their favourite travel agency for their bit of commission, but can be safely disregarded. In Algeciras, try the **Trasmediterránea office** (☎ 956 58 34 07; Recinto del Puerto, Algeciras) or any of the ferry offices port-side.

ALGECIRAS TO CEUTA

Trasmediterránea, EuroFerrys, Buquebus and others offer over 20 high-speed ferry crossings (35 minutes) from Ceuta between 7am and 10pm, and the same number from Algeciras between 6am and 10pm. Extra services are added on demand on Sunday evening and during August.

At the time of writing, fares were €25 per person without a car (local residents pay about 50% less), and €30 per car. Children aged between two and 12 travel for half the fare, and those aged under two travel free.

In Ceuta, there are dozens of private ticket offices close to and inside the ferry terminal (Estación Marítima). The ferry companies have offices in the main building – this is often the best place to get tickets (from specific companies only) at the last minute.

ALMERÍA TO MELILLA

Melilla is a less popular destination than Tangier or Ceuta, but Trasmediterránea offers a service. In the low season there are six

ferries a week, with no sailings on Friday. Going the other way, there's a departure from Melilla every day except either Thursday or Saturday, according to the timetable. In the high season there are two crossings daily.

The trip takes six to eight hours. The base fare is €35 each way. You can also get beds in two- or four-person cabins, some with toilets, for around €85 per person. Higher-class *(preferente)* berths cost around €110 per person. Children aged from two to 12 travel for half-price (infants go free).

A normal-sized car costs €139, camper vans range from €200 to €220 depending on their length, and motorbikes are €30 to €40. Bicycles are free.

Buy your tickets at the Estación Marítima (a 10- to 15-minute walk from the train and bus stations), from travel agencies or from the **Trasmediterránea office** (☎ 956 690902; Plaza de España), in the centre of town.

Services are added on demand during the high season. Fares rise by up to 25% and fast ferries also operate at this time.

ALMERÍA TO NADOR

A Moroccan alternative to sailing to Tangier is at Nador, further east along the coast. It's much quieter, although it has poorer transport links to the rest of the country. On top of that, it's next door to Melilla, where you can fill up on duty-free fuel if you're driving (and booze if you're not).

Several companies sail from Nador's Beni Enzar port to Almería, a six or seven hour crossing. Trasmediterránea, **Ferrimaroc** (in Almería ☎ 950 27 48 00, in Morocco ☎ 036 348100; www.ferrimaroc.com), Comarit and Comanav all sail this route, in total offering two sailings a day in low season, and up to four a day in the summer. Deck fare costs €28, with other prices similar to the Melilla crossing. Fares rise by roughly 15% in high season.

MÁLAGA TO MELILLA

Trasmediterránea operates a daily service from Málaga to Melilla, which takes six to seven hours. In the high season (June to September), there is also a high-speed service, which takes four hours. Prices are around €28/416 per passenger/car.

As in Almería, you can purchase tickets most easily at the Estación Marítima, which is more or less directly south of the town centre. In Melilla, buy tickets from **Trasmediterránea** (☎ 956 690 902; Plaza de España) or at the Estación Marítima.

TARIFA TO TANGIER

Tarifa is now a regular destination for ferry crossings, with a catamaran making the trip in a nippy 35 minutes. **FRS** (www.frs.es; Tarifa port ☎ 956 68 18 30, Tangier port ☎ 039 942 612); operates the service, with two to five sailings a day according to the season (even more on Mondays).

Fares are €22 per passenger (children aged from three to 12 travel for half-price), €68 per car, €109 per caravan and €12/22 per bike/motorbike.

TOURS

Foreign tour operators running organised trips to Morocco are plentiful. The Office National Marocain Tourisme (ONMT) in your country should be able to provide you with a comprehensive list; perusing the adverts of travel magazines like **Wanderlust** (www.wanderlust.co.uk) is also a good idea.

You can find trips to match almost any activity – tours of the imperial cities, desert safaris, mountain trekking and birdwatching. Even golf.

Best of Morocco (☎ 01380-828533; www.morocco-travel.com) Over 30 years' experience with UK-based tailor-made tours and holidays including everything from camel trekking and skiing to cultural tours and beach holidays.

Bike Morocco (☎ 07940 296711; www.bikemorocco.com) Popular and nimble UK mountain-biking operator, running vehicle-supported tours in the Atlas Mountains, from weekend breaks to longer trips.

Heritage Tours (☎ 800-378 4555; www.heritagetoursonline.com) US-based customised travel with a real emphasis on culture and the arts. Good city tours and classic itineraries.

Ibertours Travel (☎ 03-9670 8388; www.ibertours.com.au) Australian Moroccan specialist, running camel treks, city tours and the like, highlighting Morocco's Andalusian links with cross-border trips to Spain.

Journeys Elite (☎ 01983-853064; www.journeyselite.com) Excellent UK-based newcomer on the block, offering tailor-made trips including riad-based city tours, desert safaris and dedicated photography tours, with fine attention to individual needs.

Marrakesh Voyage (☎ 1-888-990 2999; www.morocco-travel-agency.com) US-based company with extensive list of itineraries covering all bases, as well as special tours aimed at Morocco's various music festivals.

Morocco Made to Measure (☎ 020-7235 0123; www.clmleisure.co.uk) A comprehensive portfolio of tours and accommodation covering the entire country. It can book flights, organise car hire and arrange well thought-out touring programmes. Personalised itineraries are also available.

Naturally Morocco (☎ 0709-2343879; www.naturallymorocco.co.uk) Sustainable, ecotourism deeply involved in local communities, especially in and around Taroudannt. Special interest tours include trekking, biking, wildlife and even geology.

Yallah (☎ 044 431338; www.yallahmorocco.com) Reliable Moroccan operator, running desert safaris, city tours and trekking, either for groups or tailor-made.

GETTING AROUND

Getting around Morocco is pretty straightforward – transport networks between towns are good, and even off the beaten track there's often something going your way. Internal flights operate out of Casablanca, the rail network is excellent in linking the major cities, while large bus companies like CTM are comfortable and efficient. Local networks are more cheap and cheerful but do the job. Good sealed roads are generally the order of the day, although those in remote mountain and desert areas are often just *piste*. Car hire is comparatively expensive, but gives you the most freedom, although navigating the big cities can be stressful.

AIR

Royal Air Maroc (RAM; ☎ 022 912000 head office; www.royalairmaroc.com) dominates the Moroccan air industry, with paltry competition from one other domestic airline, **Regional Airlines** (in Casablanca ☎ 022 536940; www.regionalmaroc.com), which offers a more business-oriented (and more expensive) service. As a result, there is no real competition on fares and no choice. Both airlines use Casablanca as a hub so internal flights are routed through Mohammed V. The country is crying out for a direct Fès–Marrakesh flight. RAM's safety record is good, with tight security at airports.

Internal airports serviced by RAM are Agadir, Al-Hoceima, Casablanca, Dakhla (Ad-Dakhla), Essaouira, Fès, Laâyoune, Marrakesh, Nador, Ouarzazate, Oujda, Rabat and Tangier. The bulk of internal flights involve making a connection in Casablanca, from where Marrakesh, Tangier and Agadir are the most popular destinations (all with several daily flights). You can pick up a free timetable at most RAM offices; timetables are also online.

Domestic flights can be booked through any travel agency as well as Royal Air Maroc offices. Remember that you should always confirm flights 72 hours before departure. Student and under-26 youth discounts of 25% are available on all RAM domestic flights but only if the ticket is bought in advance from one of its offices. Children aged from two to 12 travel at half-price.

In general, flying is not really worthwhile, except for long-distance routes such as to Laâyoune or Dakhla in the Western Sahara, when it can save you a lot of time. A flight from Casablanca to Laâyoune would set you back Dh2225 (€202.50) and take just over an hour and a half (plus journey time to the airport and check-in time), compared to 19 hours by bus.

BICYCLE

If you've the energy, mountain biking can be a great way of travelling in Morocco. There are no special road rules pertaining to cyclists and they are afforded little consideration by drivers. Although surfaced roads are generally well maintained, they tend to be narrow and dusty, which can be hairy given the kamikaze drivers.

However, there's plenty of opportunity for getting off the beaten track if you choose, with thousands of kilometres of remote *pistes* to be explored. You do need to be pretty fit, though. Distances are great and you'll need to carry all supplies with you, and plenty of drinking water. Useful spares to bring include spokes, brake blocks and spare inner tubes.

Unfortunately, cyclists in remote areas have reported being besieged by gangs of stone-throwing children, so be sure to watch your back.

Bus companies are generally happy to carry bikes as luggage for an extra Dh10 or so, although it's generally only possible to transport your bike on trains if they travel in the goods wagon. Prices depend on the distance and are about 40% of the passenger fare. Most camp sites charge around Dh5 for bicycles.

There are a few external tour operators that offer organised mountain-biking trips (see p441). The UK-based **Cyclists' Touring Club** (☎ 0870 873 0060; www.ctc.org.uk) is a mine of information and has a comprehensive library of routes written up by cyclists, including Morocco.

Hire

Moroccan cities and towns are better explored on foot, though you will find bicycles for hire in the bigger places (from around Dh60 to Dh100 per day) and cycle parks where your bike can be parked and watched over for the day. Don't expect the latest model of mountain bike, as you will be sorely disappointed.

BUS

Anyone in Morocco for any length of time will undoubtedly make considerable use of the local bus networks. The cheapest and most efficient way to travel around the country, buses are generally safe, although the same can't necessarily be said for the driving. On some older buses legroom is extremely limited and long journeys can be rather an endurance test for taller travellers.

Most bus trips longer than three hours will incorporate a scheduled stop to stretch your legs and refuel your body. When travelling during the day, pay attention to where you're sitting, to avoid melting in the sun. Heading from north to south, this means sitting on the right in the morning, on the left in the afternoon. Travelling east to west, sit on the right, or on the left if going from west to east. Many buses also have rather meagre curtains. Night buses operate on many intercity routes, which can be both quicker and cooler.

There's no state bus company, but this role is fulfilled by the effective national carrier, Compagnie de Transports Marocains (CTM), which operates throughout the country. After CTM, a host of smaller local companies fight it out for custom, although outfits like Supratours and Satas are well-respected nationally.

Some Moroccan bus stations are like madhouses, with touts running around screaming out any number of destinations for buses about to depart. In most cities or towns there's a single central bus station (gare routière), but in some places CTM maintains a separate terminal. Occasionally, there are other stations for a limited number of fairly local destinations. Touts can happily guide you to the ticket booth (and take a small commission from the company), but always double-check that their recommended service really is the most comfortable, direct and convenient option.

Bus stations in the main cities have left-luggage depots (consigne), sometimes open 24 hours. Bags must be padlocked. You can transport bikes on buses, but they'll be charged as freight (around Dh10 per bike for an average journey).

Bus Operators
COMPAGNIE DE TRANSPORTS MAROCAINS
CTM (in Casablanca ☎ 022 45 80 80; www.ctm.co.ma) is the best and most reliable bus company in Morocco, and serves most destinations of interest to travellers.

On CTM buses, children aged four years and over pay full fares, which tend to be 15% to 30% more expensive than other lines, and are comparable to 2nd-class fares on normal trains. Tickets can be purchased in advance. Intercity timetables often seem to have a penchant for late-night departures.

Many CTM buses are modern and comfortable, and some 1st-class buses have videos (a mixed blessing), air conditioning and heating (they sometimes overdo both).

There is an official baggage charge on CTM buses (Dh5 per pack). Once you have bought your ticket, you get a baggage tag, which you should hang on to, as you'll need it when you arrive.

CTM also operates international buses (in conjunction with Eurolines) from all the main Moroccan cities to Spain, France, Italy and northern Europe (see p474).

SUPRATOURS
The ONCF train company runs buses through **Supratours** (☎ 037 686297; www.supratourstravel.com) to complement its train network. Thus Nador, near Melilla on the Mediterranean coast, is linked to the Oujda–Casablanca rail line by a special bus to Taourirt station.

Tetouan is linked to the main line from Tangier by bus to Tnine Sidi Lyamani. Train passengers heading further south than Marrakesh link up at Marrakesh station with buses for Essaouira, Agadir, Laâyoune and Dakhla. It's possible to buy a ticket to cover the complete trip (including the bus journey) at the railway ticket office.

Supratours services are more expensive than regular buses, but are comparable to CTM fares. They do not use the main bus stations, but depart from outside their own town-centre offices (explained in individual town sections throughout this book). Through tickets to and from connecting train stations are available (Nador through to Fès, for example), and travellers with rail tickets for connecting services have priority.

OTHER COMPANIES
Morocco's other bus companies are all privately owned and only operate regionally. The biggest of them is Satas, which covers everywhere from Casablanca and further south, and is just as good as CTM. In the north, Trans Ghazala are equally reliable. Both have modern, comfortable buses.

TRAVELLERS' CODE OF ETIQUETTE

When travelling on public transport, it's considered both selfish and bad manners to eat while those around you go without. Always buy a little extra that can be offered to your neighbours. A bag of fruit makes a great choice.

Next comes the ritual. If you have offered food, etiquette dictates that your fellow passengers should decline it. It should be offered a second time, this time a little more persuasively, but again it will be turned down. On a third more insistent offer, your neighbours are free to accept the gift if they wish to.

If, conversely, you are offered food, but you don't want it, it's good manners to accept a small piece anyway. At the same time, you should pat your stomach contentedly to indicate that you are full. In return for participating in this elaborate ritual, you should be accorded great respect, offered protection and cared for like a friend.

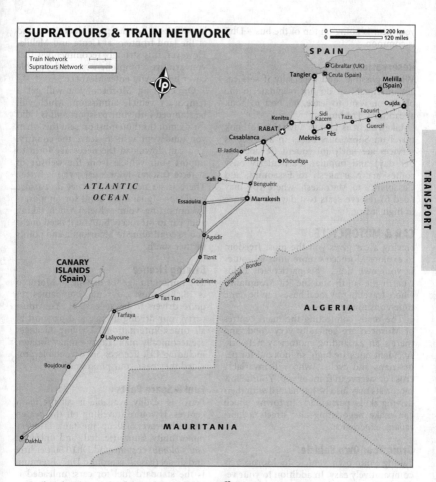

SUPRATOURS & TRAIN NETWORK

Train Network
Supratours Network

(Map of Morocco showing the Supratours and Train network connecting cities including Tangier, Ceuta (Spain), Gibraltar (UK), Melilla (Spain), Oujda, Taourirt, Kenitra, Sidi Kacem, Taza, Guercif, RABAT, Casablanca, Meknès, Fès, El-Jadida, Settat, Khouribga, Safi, Benguérir, Essaouira, Marrakesh, Agadir, Tiznit, Goulmime, Tan Tan, Tarfaya, Laâyoune, Boujdour, Dakhla; with labels for SPAIN, ATLANTIC OCEAN, CANARY ISLANDS (Spain), ALGERIA, MAURITANIA, and a Disputed Border.)

TRANSPORT

At the cheaper end of the scale, and on the shorter or local routes, there are a fair number of two-bit operations with one or two well-worn buses, so don't expect comfortable seats or any air conditioning. Unlike CTM buses, these services tend to stop an awful lot and only depart when the driver considers them sufficiently full. They're dirt cheap and good fun for shorter trips. The cheaper buses rarely have heating in winter, even when crossing the mountains, so make sure you that have plenty of warm clothing with you. If traffic is held up by snowdrifts in the mountain passes, then you'll really feel the cold. The Marrakesh to Ouarzazate road is particularly prone to this.

Classes

Some companies offer 1st- and 2nd-class, although the difference in fare and comfort is rarely great. On the secondary runs (ie, if you're not getting on the bus at the start of the route) you can often buy your tickets on the bus, but if you do, you'll probably have to stand.

Costs

Bus travel is cheap considering the distances that have to be covered. Typical fares from Casablanca to Agadir, Marrakesh, Fès and Tangier are Dh150, Dh70, Dh90 and Dh120 respectively.

More often than not you'll be charged for baggage handling by someone, especially if your gear is going on top of the bus – Dh5 is common.

Reservations

Where possible, and especially if services are infrequent or do not originate in the place you want to leave, it's best to book ahead for CTM buses.

Likewise, it is always advisable to book travel on Supratours buses in advance as services are fairly infrequent (ie one bus per day) and popular. Particularly busy routes are Marrakesh to Essaouira, and Casablanca to Marrakesh, where you may need to reserve seats two days in advance in high season.

CAR & MOTORCYCLE

Having a car gives you the most freedom to explore Morocco's more unusual routes in your own time. This particularly holds true in the south and the Rif Mountains, where travelling by local buses can be quite time-consuming.

The roads connecting the main centres of Morocco are generally very good, and there's an expanding motorway network. Accident rates are high, so look out for pedestrians and cyclists who will invariably cross or swerve in front of you. Your fellow motorists may also be haphazard with their driving skills, particularly in towns, which can make negotiating city streets a hair-raising experience.

Bring Your Own Vehicle

Taking your own vehicle to Morocco is comparatively easy. In addition to your vehicle registration document (*carte grise* in Morocco) and International Driving Permit, a Green Card (*carte verte*) is required from the car's insurer (you may be covered in your current car insurance policy, especially if you live in continental Europe, so check with your insurance company). These are relatively inexpensive (say, UK£30 per month), though often only provide third-party, fire and theft protection. Not all insurers cover Morocco.

If you cannot get a Green Card in advance, temporary insurance must be arranged at Spanish or Moroccan ferry ports; you can do this through **Assurance Frontière** (head office in Casablanca ☎ 022 470810; 28 Blvd Moulay Youssef) for around Dh800 per month. It also

has offices at Tangier port, Nador port and at the land frontiers at Ceuta and Melilla. However, it is strongly recommended that you arrange comprehensive and reliable cover before you enter Morocco.

On entering Morocco you will get a temporary vehicle admission, which will be stamped into your passport and is valid for six months. You must present this when you (and your vehicle) leave the country. You can download the necessary form to import your vehicle from the website of **Morocco Customs** (www.douane.gov.ma in French). There is no need for a *carnet de passage en douane* (guarantee bond for temporarily importing your vehicle) when taking your car to Morocco, but you'll need one if you're continuing to Mauritania and points further south.

Driving Licence

The minimum age for driving in Morocco is 18, but most car rental companies require drivers to be at least 21. You must carry your driving licence and passport at all times. International Driving Licences are technically mandatory – many foreign, including EU, licences are acceptable provided they bear your photograph.

Fuel & Spare Parts

Petrol is readily available in all the main centres. If you're travelling off the beaten track, however, fill up the tank at every opportunity. Super (leaded) and unleaded (*sans plomb*) cost around Dh10.50 per litre and diesel (*gasoil*) is around Dh7. Premium is the standard fuel for cars; unleaded is only available at larger stations, including most of the Afriquia stations.

Costs rise the further you go from the northwest of the country. The big exception is the territory of Western Sahara, where petrol is sold by the Atlas Sahara service station chain and is tax-free, so is about 30% cheaper. Keep a close eye on fuel in the southern desert and fill up wherever you get an opportunity, as stations don't always have supplies of fuel. Spare jerry cans are a good idea for emergencies.

Fuel is also very reasonably priced in the duty-free Spanish enclaves of Ceuta and Melilla, so drivers heading to Morocco and mainland Spain via the enclaves should fill up there.

Moroccan mechanics are generally extremely good and all decent-sized towns will have at least one garage (most with an extensive range of spare parts for Renaults and other French cars). If you need replacement parts and can fit them yourself, try to get a Moroccan friend to help with buying parts as this may help to keep the price closer to local levels.

Hire

Renting a car in Morocco isn't cheap, starting from Dh3500 per week or Dh500 per day for a basic car like a Renault Clio with unlimited mileage, up to Dh10,000 per week for a 4WD. Most companies demand a (returnable) cash deposit (Dh3000 to Dh5000) unless you pay by credit card, in which case an impression is made of your card (make sure you get this back later). However, some travellers using smaller, less-reputable firms have been stung after paying by credit, realising they've been charged 10 times the agreed fee after returning home.

The best cities in which to hire cars are Casablanca, Agadir, Marrakesh, Fès and Tangier, where competition is greatest. The cheapest car is the Fiat Uno, though older Renault 4s are sometimes available. If you're organised, however, it usually works out cheaper to arrange car rental in advance through the travel agent who arranges your flight. International firms such as **Hertz** (www .hertz.com), **Budget** (www.budget.com), **Europcar** (www .europcar.com), **National** (www.nationalcar.com) and **Avis** (www.avis.com) have facilities for booking from home on toll-free or cheap-rate numbers or via the internet. Rates can vary substantially between them and there is little room for bargaining. Ordering your car over the internet can get you discounts of up to 30%.

There are also numerous local agencies and many have booths beside each other at airports – this is an excellent place to haggle. Details for these are given in regional chapters.

International agencies do not necessarily offer better vehicles than local companies, but usually provide better service in the event of a breakdown or accident, as they have a network of offices around the country. Often a replacement car can be sent out to you from the nearest depot. Always check your car's condition before signing up, and make sure that the car comes with a spare tyre, tool kit and full documentation – including insurance cover, which is compulsory for all rentals.

With larger agencies you can hire the car in one place and leave it elsewhere, although this usually involves a fee if you want to leave it in a city where the company has no branch.

Note that your rental agreement will probably not cover you for off-road (*piste*) driving, so if you damage the car or break down on a *piste* you will not be covered for damages. It might be worthwhile to OK your route with the rental company before setting off.

All companies charge per hour (Dh35 to Dh100 is common) for every hour that you go over time on the return date. If you intend to drive from Morocco to the Spanish enclaves of Ceuta or Melilla, you must have a letter from the car-hire company authorising you to take the car out of the country. Europe-based hire companies do not normally permit cars to be taken to Morocco. Keep receipts for oil changes and any mechanical repairs, as these costs should be reimbursed.

Some companies offer motorcycle (Dh300 per day for a DT 125cc Yamaha) and scooter (Dh200 per day) hire. Agadir is a good place to look – you'll find a number of rental booths near the big hotels.

Insurance

Insurance must, by law, be sold along with all rental agreements. You should take out Collision Damage Waiver insurance (between Dh80 and Dh110 a day). Even with this there is often an excess of between Dh3000 and Dh5000 (depending on the company), meaning that if you have an accident that's your fault, then you are liable to pay damages up to this amount. You can opt to take out a Super Collision Damage Waiver for an extra Dh50 or so a day to get rid of this excess. It's also a good idea to take out personal insurance (around Dh30 a day). When bargaining, make sure that prices include collision damage, insurance and tax (20%).

Parking

In many towns, parking zones are watched by *gardiens de voitures* (car park attendants) in characteristic blue coats. The going rate is Dh3 for a few hours and Dh10 overnight. The parking attendants are not a guarantee of safety, but they do provide some peace of mind and will no doubt offer to wash your car for you.

In an increasing number of big city centres, parking tickets are issued from blue kerb-side machines (Dh2 per hour for a maximum stay of 2½ hours). Parking is free on Sundays.

Parking is not allowed on kerb sides painted in red and white stripes. Stopping is not allowed on green and white stripes. Fines for illegally parked cars can reach Dh1500.

Roadblocks

Police control points manned by the *Gendarmerie Royale* are common on main roads in and out of most sizable towns, although as a foreigner driving you're unlikely to be stopped. It's still a good idea to slow down and put on your best smile – you'll probably get a smile in return and be waved through. Roadblocks are more common in sensitive areas like Western Sahara, in the Rif

mountains around the cannabis-producing region of Ketama and the road to Figuig near the Algerian border. At most, you may be asked to show your passport and driving licence, the purpose of your visit, and where you're heading.

Intercity buses are usually delayed at checkpoints more than grand taxis, whose local drivers usually know the police.

Road Hazards

Driving at night is particularly hazardous: it's legal for vehicles travelling under 20km/h to drive without lights, and roads are often very busy with pedestrians (including large groups of schoolchildren), bicycles, horse and carts, donkeys and so on. Treat all as vehicles ready to veer out at inopportune moments.

Many minor roads are too narrow for normal vehicles to pass without going onto the shoulder. You'll find yourself hitting the dirt a lot in this way. Stones thrown up by oncoming vehicles present a danger for windscreens. In the *hammada* (stony desert), tar roads frequently disappear

ROAD DISTANCES (KM)

	Agadir	Al-Hoceima	Casablanca	Dakhla	Er-Rachidia	Essaouira	Fès	Figuig	Marrakesh	Meknès	Nador	Ouarzazate	Oujda	Rabat	Safi	Smara	Tan Tan	Tangier	Tarfaya	Tetouan
Agadir	---																			
Al-Hoceima	1091	---																		
Casablanca	511	536	---																	
Dakhla	1173	2264	1684	---																
Er-Rachidia	681	616	545	1854	---															
Essaouira	173	887	351	1346	745	---														
Fès	756	275	289	1920	364	640	---													
Figuig	1076	669	920	2249	395	1081	719	---												
Marrakesh	273	758	238	1448	510	176	483	905	---											
Meknès	740	335	229	1913	346	580	60	741	467	---										
Nador	1095	175	628	2260	510	979	339	516	822	399	---									
Ouarzazate	375	992	442	1548	306	380	687	701	204	652	816	---								
Oujda	1099	293	632	2272	514	983	343	326	826	403	104	820	---							
Rabat	602	445	91	1775	482	442	198	877	321	138	535	528	541	---						
Safi	294	792	256	1467	683	129	545	1078	157	486	884	361	888	347	---					
Smara	551	1642	1062	746	1232	724	1307	1627	824	1291	1646	926	1650	1153	845	---				
Tan Tan	331	1422	842	842	1012	504	1087	1407	504	1071	1426	705	1430	933	625	220	---			
Tangier	880	323	369	2053	608	720	303	988	598	287	1086	811	609	278	625	1431	1211	---		
Tarfaya	544	1635	1055	633	1225	517	1300	1620	817	1284	1639	919	1643	1146	838	331	213	1424	---	
Tetouan	892	278	385	2065	604	736	281	931	675	258	437	820	555	294	641	1443	1223	57	1436	---

without warning, replaced suddenly by stretches of sand, gravel and potholes. Take care with your speed on such roads, which are accidents waiting to happen. If a strong *chergui* (dry, easterly desert wind) is blowing and carrying a lot of dust, you'll have to wait until it eases off if you don't want to do your car considerable damage.

In contrast, driving across the mountain ranges in winter can easily involve driving through snow and ice. The High Atlas passes can often be closed altogether due to snow in the winter. Check the road signs along the routes out of Marrakesh or call the **Service des Travaux Publiques** (in Rabat ☎ 037 711717) before travelling.

Some of the *pistes* in Morocco can be negotiated by ordinary car, many are passable in a Renault 4 with its high suspension, but some are 4WD territory only. Whatever vehicle you have, the going will be slow. Many stretches of mountain *piste* will be impassable in bad weather: the Michelin No 742 map (formerly No 959) generally has these sections marked.

Whatever the season, inquire about road conditions with locals before setting off on a journey, check your tyres, take a usable spare and carry an adequate supply of water and petrol.

Road Rules

In Morocco you drive on the right, as in Continental Europe. Daylight driving is generally no problem and not too stressful, though in the bigger cities getting constantly cut off is par for the course.

In the event of a traffic accident, especially accidents involving injuries, drivers are officially required to remain at the scene and vehicles cannot be moved until the police have arrived – this may take hours.

In towns, give way to traffic entering a roundabout from the right when you're already on one. No-one seems to pay much attention to striped (zebra) crossings. The Sped limit in built-up areas is 40km/h.

Outside the towns there is a national speed limit of 100km/h, rising to 120km/h on the motorways. There are two main sections, from Tangier along the Atlantic coast to Casablanca, and from Rabat to Fès via Meknès. Plans are underway to extend the network to Marrakesh, Agadir and Oujda. Tolls apply on the motorways – for example

from Rabat to Tangier is Dh60 and Rabat to Casablanca is Dh20. You take a ticket upon entering the motorway and then pay at the end.

Yellow road signs implore drivers to follow the law and wear seat belts, but in practice no-one does, preferring instead to put their trust in Allah to reach their destination safely.

LOCAL TRANSPORT

Bus

The bigger cities, such as Casablanca, Rabat, Marrakesh, Fès and Meknès, have public bus services. They are especially good for crossing from the ville nouvelle (new town) of a city to the medina (old town). Tickets are typically Dh2 to Dh3.

Grand Taxi

The elderly Mercedes vehicles you'll see belting along Moroccan roads and gathered in great flocks near bus stations are shared taxis (*grands taxis* in French or *taxiat kebira* in Arabic). They're a big feature of Morocco's public transport system and link towns to their nearest neighbours in a kind of leapfrogging system. Taxis sometimes ply longer routes when there's demand, but these services are few and usually leave first thing in the morning. Grands taxis take six extremely cramped passengers (two in the front, four in the back) and leave when full. It can often be to your advantage to pay for two seats to get the taxi going earlier (and give yourself more space). This is particularly useful for lone women as you should get the front seat to yourself.

The fixed-rate fares (listed in individual city entries) are generally a little higher than bus fares, but are still very reasonable. When asking about fares, make it clear you want to pay for *une place* (one spot) in a *taxi collectif* (shared taxi). Another expression that helps explain that you don't want to hire a taxi for yourself is that you wish to travel *ma'a an-nas* (with other people).

Touts and taxi drivers sometimes try to bounce tourists into hiring the whole taxi. Smile and stand your ground if you're not interested, but for some routes hiring an entire grand taxi can actually be a great way to travel, especially if you're travelling with a small group – you can take your time on the road and stop whenever you want.

Before setting off, negotiate patiently for a reasonable fare (if you're hiring the whole taxi, aim for six times the fare for one place) and make sure plans for stopping en route are clear. The Ziz and Drâa Valleys, the Tizi n'Test and the Rif Mountains are particularly good to visit in a shared taxi.

Grand taxi drivers often have something of the boy-racer about them. Overtaking on blind corners can be a badge of honour, and speed limits only adhered to when there's a police roadblock in sight. Many accidents involve overworked grand taxi drivers falling asleep at the wheel, so night-time journeys are best avoided. Seat belts are a rarity – and suggesting otherwise may be taken as a slur on your driver's road skills.

Petit Taxi

Cities and bigger towns have local petits taxis, which are a different colour in every city. Petits taxis are not permitted to go beyond the city limits. They are licensed to carry up to three passengers and are usually, but not always, metered. To ask in French for the meter to be switched on say 'tourne le conteur, si'l vous plaît'. Where they are not metered, agree to a price beforehand. If the driver refuses to use the meter or won't give you a price, ask to stop and get out. Most petits taxis drivers are perfectly honest, although those in Marrakesh are notoriously greedy with tourists.

Multiple hire is the rule rather than the exception, so you can get half-full cabs if they are going your way (for the same price). From 8pm (often 9pm in summer) there is normally a 50% surcharge.

Pick-up Truck & 4WD

In more remote parts of the country, especially in the Atlas Mountains, locals get from village to village by Berber camionettes (pick-up trucks), old vans or in the back of trucks. This is a bumpy but adventurous way to get to know the country and people a little better, but can mean waiting a considerable time (even days) for the next lift. When travelling between remote towns and villages, the best time to travel is early on market days (generally once or twice a week). It's common for 4WD taxis to operate on the more remote pistes that would destroy normal taxis.

TRAIN

Morocco's excellent train network is one of Africa's best, linking most of the main centres. It is run by the **Office National des Chemins de Fer** (ONCF; www.oncf.org.ma in French). There are basically two lines that carry passengers: from Tangier in the north down to Marrakesh, and from Oujda in the northeast, also to Marrakesh, joining with the Tangier line at Sidi Kacem. Plans to extend the railway south to Agadir and on to Western Sahara never seem to get off the drawing board. Supratours runs buses linking many destinations to the rail network south and east of Marrakesh (including Essaouira and Laâyoune), and along the Mediterranean Coast (including Tetouan and Nador).

Trains are comfortable, fast and run closely to their timetables. Reasonably priced, they're far more preferable to buses where available. Drinks and snacks are available on the train. Smoking is not allowed in compartments. Stations aren't usually well signposted and announcements (in both French and Arabic) are frequently inaudible so keep an eye out for your station.

Most of the stations are located in the ville nouvelle. They usually have left-luggage depots, though these only accept luggage that can be locked.

Timetables for the whole system are posted in French at most stations, and ticket offices can print out mini-timetables to individual destinations. ONCF's French- and Arabic-language website has timetables and price information that can also download, although this website is poorly maintained and frequently offline.

Classes

There are two types of train, ordinaire (Train Navette Rapide, TNR) and rapide (Train Rapide Climatisé, TCR). Rapide trains are standard for intercity services, with ordinaire trains now reduced to a handful of late-night and local services. The main difference between the two is comfort and air conditioning, rather than speed. Prices given in the guide are for rapide trains (ordinaire trains are around 30% cheaper).

There are different 1st- and 2nd-class fares on all these trains, though there's not much difference in actual comfort – 1st-class compartments have six seats, 2nd-class have eight. Second-class is more than adequate on any journey.

Shuttle services operate regularly between Kenitra, Rabat, Casablanca and Mohammed V International Airport, and supplement the rapide services on this line. There are 12 daily services between Casablanca and the airport, running roughly between 5.15am and 8.45pm, making them a convenient way to catch most flights. For more details, see the Getting Around sections under Casablanca (p103) and Rabat (p117).

Costs

Couchettes are available on the overnight ordinaire trains between Marrakesh and Tangier, and Oujda and Casablanca. The compartments fold up into six bunks (couchettes) and they're well worth the extra Dh90. There's also a more expensive overnight rapide train from Oujda.

Sample 2nd-class fares include Casablanca to Marrakesh (Dh75.50, three hours), Rabat to Fès (Dh72, 3½ hours) and Tangier to Marrakesh (Dh188.50, 9½ hours).

Children aged under four travel free. Those aged between four and 12 years get a reduction of 10% to 50%, depending on the service.

Reservations

You are advised to buy tickets at the station, as a supplement is charged for buying tickets on the train. Tickets can be bought up to a month before travel, and are worth getting in advance for couchettes on overnight services (particularly Tangier–Marrakesh), or if you're travelling around the Eid holidays.

A ticket is technically valid for five days, so you can use it to get off at intermediate stops before reaching your final destination. You need to ask for a *bulletin d'arrêt* (proof of stop) at the intermediate stop. Always hang on to tickets, as inspectors check them on the trains and they are collected at the station on arrival.

Train Passes

Two types of rail discount cards are available in Morocco. The Carte Fidelité (Dh149) is for those aged over 26 and gives you 50% reductions on eight return or 16 one-way journeys in a 12-month period. If you're under 26, the Carte Jaune (Dh99) will give you the same discounts. To apply you need one passport-sized photo and a photocopy of your passport.

Health

CONTENTS

Prevention is the key to staying healthy while travelling in Morocco, and a little planning before departure will save you trouble later. With luck, the worst complaint you might come down with on your trip is a bad stomach; while infectious diseases can and do occur in Morocco, these are usually associated with poor living conditions and poverty, and can be avoided with a few precautions. A more common reason for travellers needing medical help is as a result of accidents – cars are not always well maintained and poorly lit roads are littered with potholes. Medical facilities can be excellent in large cities, but in remoter areas may be more basic.

BEFORE YOU GO

Health matters often get left to the last minute before travelling. A little planning is advisable, however – some vaccines don't ensure immunity for two weeks, so visit a doctor four to eight weeks before departure.

Travellers can register with the **International Association for Medical Advice to Travellers** (IAMAT; www.iamat.org). The website can help travellers find a doctor with recognised training. Those heading off to very remote areas may like to do a first-aid course (Red Cross and St John's Ambulance can help), or attend a remote medicine first-aid course such as that offered by the **Royal Geographical Society** (www.rgs.org) – a particularly good idea if you're going trekking.

Bring medications in their original, clearly labelled, containers. A signed and dated letter from your physician describing your medical conditions and medications, including generic names, is also a good idea. If carrying syringes or needles, be sure to have a physician's letter documenting their medical necessity. See your dentist before a long trip; carry a spare pair of contact lenses and glasses (and take your optical prescription with you).

INSURANCE

Adequate health insurance is vital when travelling to Morocco. Check in advance that your insurance plan will make payments directly to providers or reimburse you later for overseas health expenditures – in Morocco doctors usually expect payment on the spot. Your policy should ideally also cover emergency air evacuation home or to a hospital in a major city, which may be essential for serious problems.

RECOMMENDED VACCINATIONS

Although no specific vaccinations are required for Morocco, the World Health Organization nevertheless recommends that all travellers should be covered for diphtheria, tetanus, measles, mumps, rubella and polio, as well as hepatitis B. When making preparations to travel, ensure that all of your routine vaccination cover is complete. Ask your doctor for an International Certificate of Vaccination, which will list all the vaccinations you've received.

MEDICAL CHECKLIST

Following is a list of other items you should consider packing in your medical kit when you are travelling.

- antibiotics (if travelling off the beaten track)
- antibacterial hand gel

- antidiarrhoeal drugs (eg loperamide)
- paracetamol (eg Tylenol) or aspirin
- anti-inflammatory drugs (eg ibuprofen)
- antihistamines (for hay fever and allergic reactions)
- antibacterial ointment (eg Bactroban) for cuts and abrasions
- steroid cream or cortisone (for allergic rashes)
- bandages, gauze, gauze rolls
- adhesive or paper tape
- scissors, safety pins, tweezers
- thermometer
- pocket knife
- DEET-containing insect repellent for the skin
- permethrin-containing insect spray for clothing, tents, and bed nets
- sun block
- oral rehydration salts
- iodine tablets (for water purification)
- syringes and sterile needles (if travelling to remote areas)

INTERNET RESOURCES

There is a wealth of travel health advice on the internet. For further information, **Lonely Planet** (www.lonelyplanet.com) is a good place to start. **The World Health Organization** (www.who .int/ith/) is an excellent resource for travel health information, along with **MD Travel Health** (www.mdtravelhealth.com), which provides complete travel health recommendations for every country.

FURTHER READING

Lonely Planet's *Healthy Travel* is packed with useful information including pretrip planning, emergency first aid, immunisation and disease information and what to do if you get sick on the road. Other recommended references include *Travellers'*

Health by Dr Richard Dawood (Oxford University Press) and *The Travellers' Good Health Guide* by Ted Lankester (Sheldon Press), an especially useful health guide for volunteers and long-term expatriates working in the region.

IN TRANSIT

DEEP VEIN THROMBOSIS (DVT)

Deep vein thrombosis occurs when blood clots form in the legs during plane flights, chiefly because of prolonged immobility. The longer the flight, the greater the risk. Though most clots are reabsorbed uneventfully, some may break off and travel through the blood vessels to the lungs, where they may cause life-threatening complications.

The chief symptom of DVT is swelling or pain in the lower leg, usually but not always on just one side. When a blood clot travels to the lungs, it may cause chest pain and difficulty breathing. Travellers with any of these symptoms should immediately seek medical attention.

To prevent the development of DVT on long flights you should walk about the cabin, regularly contract your leg muscles while sitting and ensure that you drink plenty of fluids. Recent research also indicates that wearing flight socks, which gently compress the leg from the knee down, encourages blood to flow properly in the legs and reduces the risk of DVT occurring by up to 90%.

JET LAG & MOTION SICKNESS

Jet lag is common when crossing more than five time zones; it results in insomnia, fatigue or nausea. To avoid jet lag, set your watch to your destination's time zone when you board your plane, drink plenty of (non-alcoholic) fluids and eat lightly. Upon arrival, seek exposure to natural sunlight and readjust your eating and sleeping schedule as soon as possible.

Antihistamines such as dimenhydrinate (Dramamine) and meclizine (Antivert, Bonine) are usually the first choice for treating motion sickness. Their main side-effect is drowsiness. A herbal alternative is ginger, which works like a charm for some people.

TRAVEL HEALTH WEBSITES

The following government travel health websites are useful resources to consult prior to departure.

Australia (www.smartraveller.gov.au)

Canada (www.hc-sc.gc.ca/english/index.html)

UK (www.doh.gov.uk/traveladvice/)

United States (www.cdc.gov/travel/)

HEALTH

IN MOROCCO

AVAILABILITY & COST OF HEALTH CARE

Primary medical care is not always readily available outside major cities and large towns. Pharmacies are generally well stocked, however, and pharmacists can provide valuable advice (usually in French) covering common travellers' complaints, and sell over-the-counter medication, often including some drugs only available on prescription at home. They can also advise when more specialised help is needed.

If you are being treated by a doctor or at a clinic – particularly outside the major cities – you will often be expected to purchase medical supplies on the spot. This can even include sterile dressings or intravenous fluids. Your hotel may be able to locate the nearest source of medical help. In an emergency contact your embassy or consulate.

Standards of dental care are variable. Keep in mind that your travel insurance will not usually cover you for anything other than emergency dental treatment. The pliers of the street dentists around the Djemaa el-Fna in Marrakesh aren't recommended!

INFECTIOUS DISEASES

Hepatitis A

Hepatitis A is spread through contaminated food (particularly shellfish) and water. It causes jaundice, and although it is rarely fatal, can cause prolonged lethargy and delayed recovery. Symptoms include dark urine, a yellow colour to the whites of the eyes, fever and abdominal pain. Vaccination against Hepatitis A is recommended for travel to Morocco. The vaccine (Avaxim, VAQTA, Havrix) is given as an injection: a single dose will give protection for up to a year, while a booster 12 months later will provide a subsequent 10 years of protection. Hepatitis A and typhoid vaccines can also be given as a single dose vaccine (Hepatyrix or Viatim).

Hepatitis B

Infected blood, contaminated needles and sexual intercourse can all transmit hepatitis B. It can cause jaundice, and affects the liver, occasionally causing liver failure. All travellers should make this a routine vaccination (Morocco gives hepatitis B vaccination as part of routine childhood vaccination). The vaccine is given singly, or at the same time as the hepatitis A vaccine (Hepatyrix). A course will give protection for at least five years. It can be given over four weeks, or six months.

HIV

Morocco has an HIV infection rate of around 0.1% – translating to around 30,000 carriers. There is little awareness of AIDS (SIDA in French), although recent education efforts have been stepped up.

HIV is spread via infected blood and blood products and through sexual intercourse with an infected partner, so practising safe sex is essential. There is a small risk of infection through medical procedures, such as blood transfusion and improperly sterilised medical instruments.

Leishmaniasis

Spread through the bite of an infected sandfly, leishmaniasis can cause a slowly growing skin lump or ulcer. It may develop into a serious life-threatening fever usually accompanied with anaemia and weight loss. Infected dogs are also carriers of the infection. Sandfly bites should be avoided whenever possible. In Morocco, leishmaniasis may be found in rural areas in the Atlas Mountains, with sandflies more prevalent between June and October.

Rabies

Spread through bites or licks on broken skin from an infected animal, rabies is fatal and endemic to Morocco. Animal handlers should be vaccinated, as should those travelling to remote areas where a reliable source of post-bite vaccine is not available within 24 hours. Three injections are needed over a month. If you have not been vaccinated you will need a course of five injections starting within 24 hours or as soon as possible after the injury. Vaccination does not provide you with immunity, it merely buys you more time to seek appropriate medical help.

Tuberculosis

Tuberculosis (TB) is spread through close respiratory contact and occasionally through infected milk or milk products, and is guarded against by the BCG vaccine. This is more important for those visiting family or planning on a long stay, and those employed as teachers and health-care workers. TB can be asymptomatic, although symptoms can include cough, weight loss or fever months or even years after exposure. An x-ray is the best way to confirm if you have TB. BCG gives a moderate degree of protection against TB. It causes a small permanent scar at the site of injection, and is usually only given in specialised chest clinics. As it's a live vaccine, it shouldn't be given to pregnant women or immunocompromised individuals.

Typhoid

Typhoid is spread through food or water that has been contaminated by infected human faeces. Local outbreaks are unusual but well publicised by the local media. The first symptom is usually fever or a pink rash on the abdomen. Septicaemia (blood poisoning) may also occur. Typhoid vaccine (Typhim Vi, Typherix) will give protection for three years. In some countries, the oral vaccine Vivotif is also available.

Yellow Fever

There is a small risk of yellow fever, borne by mosquitos, in rural Chefchaouen province, but this is so small that the World Health Organization does not recommend vaccination.

Travellers arriving in Morocco from a yellow fever endemic area will need to show proof of vaccination before entry. This normally means if arriving directly from an infected country or if the traveller been in an infected country during the last 10 days. We would recommend, however, that travellers carry a certificate if they have been in an infected country during the previous month to avoid any possible difficulties with immigration. Note that yellow fever is endemic to Mauritania, so your documentation must be in order if entering Morocco overland from here (although anecdotal evidence disputes how rigorously the order is enforced at the land border). For a full list of these countries visit the websites of the **World Health Organization** (www.who.int/ith/en/) or the **Centers for Disease Control and Prevention** (www.cdc.gov/travel/). There is always the possibility that a traveller without a legally required, up-to-date certificate will be vaccinated and detained in isolation

at the port of arrival for up to 10 days, or possibly repatriated. The yellow fever vaccination must be given at a designated clinic and is valid for 10 years. It is a live vaccine and must not be given to immunocompromised or pregnant travellers.

TRAVELLER'S DIARRHOEA

The strains of travel – unfamiliar food, heat, long days and erratic sleeping patterns – can make your body more susceptible to upset stomachs.

To prevent diarrhoea, eat only fresh fruits or vegetables if they are cooked or if you have washed or peeled them yourself. Water is generally safe to drink in cities but elsewhere you should only drink treated water (see p495). Buffet meals, which may have been kept sitting warm for some time, can be risky – food should be piping hot. Meals freshly cooked in front of you (like much street food) or served in a busy restaurant are more likely to be safe. Be sensible, but not paranoid – the food is one of the treats of visiting Morocco, and you shouldn't miss out for fears of an upset stomach.

It's also very important to pay close attention to personal hygiene while on the road. Many Moroccan meals are eaten with the hand, so always wash before eating (even the smallest restaurant will have a sink and soap) and after using the toilet. Antibacterial hand gel, which cleans without needing water is a real travellers' friend.

If you develop diarrhoea, drink plenty of fluids, preferably an oral rehydration solution – all pharmacies stock these inexpensive *sels de réhydration orale*. Avoid fatty food and dairy products. A few loose stools don't require treatment, but if you start having more than four or five stools a day, you should start taking an antibiotic (usually a quinolone drug) and an antidiarrhoeal agent (such as loperamide). If diarrhoea is bloody, persists for more than 72 hours, is accompanied by fever, shaking chills or severe abdominal pain, you should seek medical attention.

ENVIRONMENTAL HAZARDS
Altitude Sickness

Lack of oxygen at high altitudes (over 2500m) affects most people to some extent. The effect may be mild or severe and occurs because less oxygen reaches the muscles and the brain at high altitudes, requiring the heart and lungs to compensate by working harder. Symptoms of Acute Mountain Sickness (AMS) usually (but not always) develop during the first 24 hours at altitude. Mild symptoms include headache, lethargy, dizziness, difficulty sleeping and loss of appetite. AMS may become more severe without warning and can be fatal. Severe symptoms include breathlessness, a dry, irritative cough (which may progress to the production of pink, frothy sputum), severe headache, lack of coordination, confusion, irrational behaviour, vomiting, drowsiness and unconsciousness. There is no hard-and-fast rule as to what is too high: AMS has been fatal at 3000m, although 3500m to 4500m is the usual range.

If you're trekking, build time into your schedule to acclimatise and ensure that your guide knows how to recognise and deal with altitude sickness. Morocco's most popular trek, to Jebel Toubkal, reaches the 4167m summit relatively quickly, so many people may suffer even mildly. The longer treks in the M'Goun Massif also reach heights of around 4000m. Treks in the Rif Mountains and Jebel Sarhro are considerably lower, so don't carry the same risks. See the trekking chapter (p404) for more specific information.

Treat mild symptoms by resting at the same altitude until recovery, or preferably descend – even 500m can help. Paracetamol or aspirin can be taken for headaches. If symptoms persist or become worse, however, immediate descent is necessary. Drug treatments should never be used to avoid descent or to enable further ascent.

Diamox (acetazolamide) reduces the headache of AMS and helps the body acclimatise to the lack of oxygen. It is only available on prescription, and those who are allergic to the sulfonamide antibiotics may also be allergic to Diamox.

The **British Mountaineering Council** (www .thebmc.co.uk) has an excellent series of downloadable fact sheets about altitude sickness.

Heat Illness

Morocco's sun can be fierce, so bring a hat. Heat exhaustion occurs following heavy sweating and excessive fluid loss with inadequate replacement of fluids and salt. This is particularly common when taking unaccustomed exercise before full acclimatisation. Symptoms include headache, dizziness and tiredness. Dehydration is already happening by the time you feel thirsty – aim to drink sufficient water such that you produce pale, diluted urine. The treatment of heat exhaustion involves fluid replacement with water or fruit juice or both, and cooling by cold water and fans. The treatment of the salt loss component involves consuming salty fluids such as soup or broth, and adding a little more table salt to foods than usual.

Heat stroke is much more serious. This occurs when the body's heat-regulating mechanism breaks down. Excessive rise in body temperature leads to sweating ceasing, irrational and hyperactive behaviour and eventually loss of consciousness and death. Rapid cooling by spraying the body with water and fanning is an ideal treatment. Emergency fluid and electrolyte replacement by intravenous drip is usually also required.

Insect Bites & Stings

Bites from mosquitoes and other insects are more likely to be an irritant rather than a health risk. DEET-based insect repellents will prevent bites. Bees and wasps only cause real problems to those with a severe allergy (anaphylaxis). If you have a severe allergy to bee or wasp stings, you should carry an adrenaline injection or similar. Sandflies are found around the Mediterranean beaches. They usually cause only a nasty, itchy bite but can carry a rare skin disorder called cutaneous leishmaniasis.

Scorpions are common in southern Morocco. They can cause a painful sting that is rarely life threatening.

Bedbugs are sometimes found in the cheaper hotels. They lead to very itchy lumpy bites. Spraying the mattress with an appropriate insect killer will do a good job of getting rid of them.

Scabies are also frequently found in cheap accommodation. These tiny mites live in the skin, particularly between the fingers. They cause an intensely itchy rash. Scabies is easily treated with lotion available from pharmacies; people who you come into contact with also need treating to avoid spreading scabies between asymptomatic carriers.

Snake Bites

The chances of seeing a snake in Morocco, let alone being bitten by one, are slim. Nevertheless, there are a few venomous species found in the southern desert areas, such as the horned viper. Snakes like to bask on rocks and sand, retreating during the heat of the day. Avoid walking barefoot, and the temptation to stick your hand into holes or cracks. Half of those bitten by venomous snakes are not actually injected with poison (envenomed). If bitten by a snake, do not panic. Immobilise the bitten limb with a splint (eg a stick) and apply a bandage over the site, using firm pressure, similar to a bandage over a sprain. Do not apply a tourniquet, or cut or suck the bite. Get the victim to medical help as soon as possible so that antivenin can be given if necessary.

Water

Tap water is chlorinated in Morocco's cities and generally safe to drink (and clean your teeth with). Elsewhere, stick to treated water – either filter it or use water purification tablets. Bottled water is available everywhere as an alternative, although there is a high environmental cost through the mountains of discarded (and unrecycled) plastic bottles. Off the beaten track, water drawn from wells or pumped from boreholes should be safe, but never drink water from rivers or lakes, as this may contain bacteria or viruses that can cause diarrhoea or vomiting.

TRAVELLING WITH CHILDREN

All travellers with children should know how to treat minor ailments and when to seek medical treatment. Make sure the children are up to date with routine vaccinations, and discuss possible travel vaccines well before departure as some vaccines are not suitable for children aged under a year.

Upset stomachs are always a risk for children when travelling, so take particular care with diet. If your child is vomiting or experiencing diarrhoea, lost fluid and salts must be replaced. It may be helpful to take rehydration powders for reconstituting with sterile water. Ask your doctor about this.

In Morocco's often-searing heat, sunburn, heat exhaustion and dehydration should all be guarded against.

Children should be encouraged to avoid dogs or other mammals because of the risk of rabies and other diseases – although there isn't likely to be a risk on camel rides in the desert, or with donkeys and mules working in places like Fès medina. Any bite, scratch or lick from a warm blooded, furry animal should immediately be thoroughly cleaned. If there is any possibility that the animal is infected with rabies, immediate medical assistance should be sought.

WOMEN'S HEALTH

Emotional stress, exhaustion and travelling through different time zones can all contribute to an upset in the menstrual pattern. If using oral contraceptives, remember some antibiotics, diarrhoea and vomiting can stop the pill from working and lead to the risk of pregnancy, so remember to take condoms with you just in case. Condoms should be kept in a cool dry place or they may crack and perish.

Emergency contraception is most effective if taken within 24 hours after unprotected sex. Condoms, tampons and sanitary towels are all widely available in Morocco.

Travelling during pregnancy is usually possible but there are important things to consider. Have a medical check-up before embarking on your trip. The most risky times for travel are during the first 12 weeks of pregnancy, when miscarriage is most likely, and after 30 weeks, when complications such as high blood pressure and premature delivery can occur. Most airlines will not accept a traveller after 28 to 32 weeks of pregnancy, and long-haul flights in the later stages can be very uncomfortable. Antenatal facilities vary greatly between countries in the region and you should think carefully if you're planning on getting off the beaten track. Taking written records of the pregnancy including details of your blood group, is likely to be helpful if you need medical attention while away. Ensure your insurance policy covers pregnancy, delivery and postnatal care, but remember insurance policies are only as good as the facilities available.

HEALTH

Language

CONTENTS

LANGUAGES IN MOROCCO

The official language in Morocco is Arabic, although French, the legacy of the protectorate, is still widely used in the cities (much less so among rural Berbers). Morocco's close ties to France help to explain the continued importance of French in education, business and the press.

Berber is spoken in the Rif and Atlas Mountains. Modern means of communication have left only a minority of Berbers monolingual – most speak at least some Arabic. See p502 for some Berber basics.

To a lesser extent than French, Spanish has maintained some hold in northern parts of the country, where Spain exercised administrative control until 1956. You may also come across Spanish in the territory of the former Spanish Sahara – over which Madrid relinquished control in 1975 – and the former enclave of Sidi Ifni. In towns like Tetouan, for instance, Spanish is more likely to be understood than French.

Reforms to Morocco's education system include the introduction of English into the curriculum for younger students, so it may become more widely spoken. However, English speakers will find that a smattering of French (and a little Spanish) can be a great asset. In the main cities and towns you'll find plenty of people (many of them touts that you may not necessarily want to hang around with), who speak various languages, including English, German and Italian.

MOROCCAN ARABIC

Moroccan Arabic (darija) is a dialect of the standard language, but is so different in many respects as to be virtually like another tongue. It's the everyday language that differs most from that of other Arabic-speaking peoples. More specialised or educated language tends to be much the same across the Arab world, although pronunciation varies considerably. An Arab from Jordan or Iraq will have little trouble discussing politics or literature with an educated Moroccan, but might have difficulty ordering lunch.

The influence of French is seen in some of the words that Moroccan Arabic has adopted. An example is the use of lkar for 'intercity bus', from the French word car.

The spread of radio and TV has increased Moroccans' exposure to and understanding of what is commonly known as Modern Standard Arabic (MSA). MSA, which has grown from the classical language of the Quran and poetry, is the written and spoken lingua franca (common language) of the Arab world, and in fact not so far removed from the daily language of the Arab countries of the Levant. It's the language of all media and the great majority of modern Arabic literature.

Foreign students of the language constantly face the dilemma of whether first to learn MSA (which could mean waiting some time before being able to talk with shopkeepers) and then a chosen dialect, or simply to acquire spoken competence in the latter.

If you learn even a few words and phrases, you'll discover and experience much more while travelling through the country. Just making the attempt implies a respect for

THE STANDARD ARABIC ALPHABET

Final	Medial	Initial	Alone	Transliteration	Pronunciation
ﺎ			ا	aa	as in 'father'
ﺐ	ﺒ	ﺑ	ب	b	as in 'bet'
ﺖ	ﺘ	ﺗ	ت	t	as in 'ten'
ﺚ	ﺜ	ﺛ	ث	th	as in 'thin'
ﺞ	ﺠ	ﺟ	ج	j	as in 'jet'
ﺢ	ﺤ	ﺣ	ح	H	a strongly whispered 'h', like a sigh of relief
ﺦ	ﺨ	ﺧ	خ	kh	as the 'ch' in Scottish *loch*
ﺪ			د	d	as in 'dim'
ﺬ			ذ	dh	as the 'th' in 'this'; also as **d** or **z**
ﺮ			ر	r	a rolled 'r', as in the Spanish word *caro*
ﺰ			ز	z	as in 'zip'
ﺲ	ﺴ	ﺳ	س	s	as in 'so', never as in 'wisdom'
ﺶ	ﺸ	ﺷ	ش	sh	as in 'ship'
ﺺ	ﺼ	ﺻ	ص		emphatic 's' (see below)
ﺾ	ﻀ	ﺿ	ض		emphatic 'd' (see below)
ﻂ	ﻄ	ﻃ	ط		emphatic 't' (see below)
ﻆ	ﻈ	ﻇ	ظ		emphatic 'z' (see below)
ﻊ	ﻌ	ﻋ	ع	'	the Arabic letter *'ayn*; pronounce as a glottal stop – like the closing of the throat before saying 'Oh-oh!' (see Other Sounds on p498)
ﻎ	ﻐ	ﻏ	غ	gh	a guttural sound like Parisian 'r'
ﻒ	ﻔ	ﻓ	ف	f	as in 'far'
ﻖ	ﻘ	ﻗ	ق	q	a strongly guttural 'k' sound; also often pronounced as a glottal stop
ﻚ	ﻜ	ﻛ	ك	k	as in 'king'
ﻞ	ﻠ	ﻟ	ل	l	as in 'lamb'
ﻢ	ﻤ	ﻣ	م	m	as in 'me'
ﻦ	ﻨ	ﻧ	ن	n	as in 'name'
ﻪ	ﻬ	ﻫ	ه	h	as in 'ham'
ﻮ			و	w	as in 'wet'; or
				oo	long, as in 'food'; or
				ow	as in 'how'
ﻲ	ﻴ	ﻳ	ي	y	as in 'yes'; or
				ee	as in 'beer', only softer; or
				ai/ay	as in 'aisle'/as the 'ay' in 'day'

Vowels Not all Arabic vowel sounds are represented in the alphabet. For more information on the vowel sounds used in this language guide, see Pronunciation on p498.

Emphatic Consonants To simplify the transliteration system used in this book, the emphatic consonants have not been differentiated from their non-emphatic counterparts.

LANGUAGE

local culture that Moroccans all too infrequently sense in visitors to their country.

If you'd like a more comprehensive guide to the Arabic spoken in the Maghreb, get a copy of Lonely Planet's compact and comprehensive *Moroccan Arabic Phrasebook*.

PRONUNCIATION

Pronunciation of Arabic can be tongue-tying for someone unfamiliar with the intonation and combination of sounds.

This language guide should help, but bear in mind that the myriad rules governing pronunciation and vowel use are too extensive to be covered here.

Vowels

a	as in 'had'
e	as in 'bet'
i	as in 'hit'
o	as in 'note'
u	as in 'put'

Long vowels are transliterated as double vowels.

aa	as the 'a' in 'father'
ee	as the 'e' in 'ear', only softer
oo	as the 'oo' in 'food'

Consonants

Pronunciation for all Arabic consonants is covered in the alphabet table on the preceding page. Note that when double consonants occur in transliterations, both are pronounced. For example, *hammam* (bath), is pronounced 'ham-mam'.

For those who read some Arabic, it's worth noting that written Moroccan Arabic has an extra letter. This letter is the *kaf* (**k** in transliterations) with three dots above it, which represents a hard 'g' (as in *Agadir*).

Other Sounds

Arabic has two sounds that are very tricky for non-Arabs to produce, the *'ayn* and the glottal stop. The letter *'ayn* represents a sound with no English equivalent that comes even close. It is similar to the glottal stop (which is not actually represented in the alphabet) but the muscles at the back of the throat are gagged more forcefully – it has been described as the sound of someone being strangled. In many transliteration systems *'ayn* is represented by an opening

quotation mark, and the glottal stop by a closing quotation mark.

To make the transliterations in this language guide easier to use, we haven't distinguished between the glottal stop and the 'ayn, using the closing quotation mark to represent both sounds. You should find that Arabic speakers will still understand you.

ACCOMMODATION

Where is a ...?	*feen kayn ...?*
campground	*shee mukheyyem*
hotel	*shee ootayl*
youth hostel	*daar shshabab*

I'm looking for a cheap hotel.	*kanqelleb 'ala shee ootayl rkhays*
What is the address?	*ashnoo hoowa l'unwan?*
Please write down the address.	*kteb l'unwan 'afek*
Is there a room available?	*wash kayn shee beet khaweeya?*

I'd like a room ...	*bgheet shee beet ...*
for one person	*dyal wahed*
for two people	*dyal jooj*
with a bathroom	*belhammam*

Can I see the room?	*wash yemkenlee nshoof lbeet?*
Where is the toilet?	*fin kayn lbeet lma?*
How much is a room for one day?	*bash hal kayn gbayt l wahed nhar?*
This room is too expensive.	*had lbeet bezzaf ghalee*
This room is good.	*had lbeet mezyana*
We'd like to check out now.	*bgheena nemshee daba*

air-conditioning	*kleemateezaseeyun*
bed	*namooseeya*
blanket	*bttaaneeya*
full	*'amer*
hot water	*lma skhoon*
key	*saroot*
room	*beet*
sheet	*eezar*
shower	*doosh*
toilet	*beet lma*

CONVERSATION & ESSENTIALS

When Arabic speakers meet, they often exchange more extensive and formalised greetings than Westerners are used to. Any attempt to use a couple (whether correctly or not) won't go astray.

When addressing a man the polite term more or less equivalent to 'Mr' is *aseedee* (shortened to *see* before a name); for women the polite form of address is *lalla*, followed by the first name. You may be addressed as 'Mr John' or 'Mrs Anne'. To attract the attention of someone on the street or a waiter in a cafe, the expression *shreef* is commonly used.

The abbreviations 'm/f/pl' refer to 'male/female/plural'.

SIGNS	
Entrance	مدخل
Exit	خروج
Open	مفتوح
Closed	مغلق
Prohibited	ممنوع
Information	معلومات
Hospital	مستشفى
Police	شرطة
Men's Toilet	حمام للرجال
Women's Toilet	حمام للنساء

Hi.	la bes (informal greeting)
(response)	bekheer
Hello.	es salaam alaykum ('peace upon you')
(response)	wa alaykum salaam ('and peace upon you')
Goodbye.	bessalama
Goodbye.	m'a ssalama ('with peace')
Good morning.	sbah lkheer
Good evening.	mselkheer
Please.	'afak/'afik/'afakum (to m/f/pl)
Thank you (very much).	shukran (bezzef)
You're welcome.	la shukran 'la wejb
Yes.	eeyeh/na'am (na'am can also mean 'I'm sorry, could you repeat that, please')
Yes, OK.	wakha
No.	la
No, thank you.	la shukran
Excuse me.	smeh leeya
How are you?	keef halek?
Fine, thank you.	bekheer, lhamdoo llaah
If God wills.	ensha'llaah
Go ahead/Come on!	zid!
What's your name?	asmeetek?
My name is ...	esmee ...
How old are you?	shhal f'merek?
I'm (20).	'andee ('ashreen) 'am
Where are you from?	mneen nta/nti/ntooma? (m/f/pl)
I'm/We're from ...	ana/hna men ...

DIRECTIONS

Where is (the) ...?	feen kayn ...?
beach	laplaje
mosque	jame'
museum	al-matHaf
old city	lmdeena lqdeema
palace	al-qasr
park	'arsa

How do I get to ...?	keefesh ghaadeenuwsul l ...?
How far?	bshhal b'ayd?
Go straight ahead.	seer neeshan.
Turn ...	dor ...
left/right	'al leeser/'al leemen
at the corner	felqent
at the traffic lights	fedo elhmer
here/there	hna/hunak
next to	hedda
opposite	'eks
behind	men luy
north	shamel
south	janoob
east	sherq
west	gherb

HEALTH

I'm sick.	ana mreed
It hurts here.	kaydernee henna
I'm ...	ana ...
diabetic	feeya merd ssukkar
asthmatic	feeya ddeega
I am allergic to ...	'andee lhsaseeya m'a ...
penicillin	lbeenseleen
bees	nhel
dairy products	makla llee feeha lhleeb
antibiotics	'anteebeeyoteek
asprin	aspereen
condoms	kapoot
contraceptives	dwa dyal lhmel
diarrhoea	sshal
headache	rras
medicine	ddawa
sunblock cream	lomber
tampons	fota dyal dem lheed

LANGUAGE

EMERGENCIES

Help!	'teqnee!
Help me please!	'awennee 'afak!
Call the police!	'ayyet 'la lbùlees!
Call a doctor!	'ayyet 'la shee tbeeb!
Thief!	sheffar!
I've been robbed.	tsreqt
Where's the toilet?	feen kayn lbeet lma?
Go away!	seer fhalek!
I'm lost.	tweddert
There's been an accident!	uq'at kseeda!

LANGUAGE DIFFICULTIES

Do you speak (English)?
wash kat'ref (negleezeeya)?

Does anyone here speak English?
wash kayn shee hedd henna lee kay'ref negleezeeya?

How do you say ... in Arabic?
keefash katgooloo ... bel'arabeeya?

What does this mean?
ash kat'anee hadhee?

I understand.
fhemt

I don't understand.
mafhemtsh

Please write it down for me.
ktebha leeya

Please show me on the map.
werri liya men l kharita 'afak

NUMBERS

Arabic numerals are simple enough to learn and, unlike the written language, run from left to right across the page.

Due to the fact that it was colonised by France, Morocco uses standard Western numerical systems rather than those normally associated with Arab countries.

0	sifr
1	wahed
2	jooj
3	tlata
4	reb'a
5	khamsa
6	setta
7	seb'a
8	tmenya
9	tes'ood
10	'ashra
11	hdaash
12	tnaash
13	teltaash
14	rba'taash
15	khamstaash
16	settaash
17	sbe'taash
18	tmentaash
19	tse'taash
20	'ashreen
21	wahed oo'ashreen
22	tnayn oo'ashreen
30	tlateen
40	reb'een
50	khamseen
60	setteen
70	seb'een
80	tmaneen
90	tes'een
100	mya
200	myatayn
300	teltmya
400	rba'mya
1000	alf
2000	alfayn
3000	telt alaf

first	loowel
second	tanee
third	talet
fourth	rabe'
fifth	khames

PAPERWORK

address	'unwaan'
name	smeeya
nationality	jenseeya
passport	pasbor
visa	t'sheera

I'm here on ...	jeet l lmaghreeb fe ...
business	felkhedma
holiday	fel'otla

QUESTION WORDS

Who?	shkoon?
Why?	'lash?
How?	keefash?
Which?	ashmen?
Where?	feen?
Is there ...?	wash kayn ...?
What's that?	ash dak shee?

SHOPPING & SERVICES

Where is (the) ...?	feen kayn ...?
bank	shee baanka
bookshop	shee mektaba

barber	shee hellaq
... embassy	ssifaara dyal ...
market	souk
pharmacy	farmasyan
police station	lkoomeesareeya
post office	lboostaa
restaurant	ristura/mat'am
souvenir shop	baazaar
travel agency	wekaalet el aasfaar
I want to change ...	bgheet nserref ...
some money	shee floos
travellers cheques	shek seeyahee
Can I pay by credit card?	wash nkder nkhelles bel kart kredee?
How much is it?	bshhal?
That's very expensive.	ghalee bezzaf
I'm only looking.	gheer kanshoof
I don't like it.	ma'jebatneesh
Can I look at it?	wakhkha nshoofha?
I'd like to buy ...	bgheet nshree ...
Do you have ...?	wash 'andkom ...?
stamps	ttnaber
a newspaper	jaarida
big/small	kabeer/sagheer
open	mehlool
closed	masdood
enough	kafee

TIME & DATES

What time is it?	shal fessa'a?
When?	fuqash/eemta?
today	lyoom
tomorrow	ghedda
yesterday	lbareh
morning	fessbah
afternoon	fel'sheeya
evening	'sheeya
day/night	nhar/felleel
week/month/year	l'usbu'/shshhar/l'am
after	men b'd
on time	felweqt
early	bekree
late	m'ettel
quickly	bizerba/dgheeya
slowly	beshweeya
Monday	nhar letneen
Tuesday	nhar ttlat
Wednesday	nhar larb'

Thursday	nhar lekhmees
Friday	nhar jjem'a
Saturday	nhar ssebt
Sunday	nhar lhedd
January	yanaayir
February	fibraayir
March	maaris
April	abreel
May	maayu
June	yunyu
July	yulyu
August	aghustus/ghusht
September	sibtimbir/shebtenber
October	uktoobir
November	nufimbir/nu'enbir
December	disimbir/dijenbir

TRANSPORT
Public Transport

When does the ... leave/arrive?	wufuqash kaykhrej/kaywsul ...?
boat	lbaboor
bus/intercity bus	ttubees/lkar
train	tran
plane	ttayyyaara
I'd like a ... ticket to (Casablanca).	'afak bgheet wahed lwarka l ddar lbayda (kasablanka)
return	bash nemshee oo njee
1st class	ddaraja lloola
2nd class	ddaraja ttaneeya
Where is (the) ...?	feen kayn ...?
airport	mataar
bus station	mhetta dyal ttobeesat
ticket office	maktab lwerqa
train station	lagaar
street	zenqa
city	medeena
village	qerya
bus stop	blasa dyal ttobeesat
station	mhetta
number	raqem
ticket	werqa
What's the fare?	shhal taman lwarka?
Which bus goes to ...?	ashmen kar ghaadee til ...?
Is this bus going to ...?	wash had lkar ghaadee l ...?
Please tell me when we arrive at ...	'afak eela wselna l ... goolhaleeya

I want to pay for one place only.	bgheet nkhelles blaasaawaheda
Stop here please.	wqef henna 'afak
Please wait for me.	tsennanee 'afak
Is this seat free?	wash had lblaasaa khaweeya?

Private Transport

Where can I hire a ...?	feen yimkin li nkri ...?
bicycle	bshklit
camel	jmel
car	tumubeel
donkey	hmar
horse	'awd

How do I get to ...?
keefesh ghaadee nuwsul l ...?
Where's the next petrol station?
fin kayna shi bumba dyal lisans griba?
I'd like ... litres.
bgheet ... itru 'afak

Please check the ...	'afak shuf ...
oil	zzit
water	lma

Can I park here?	wash nqder nwakef hna?
How long can I park here?	sh-hal men waket neqder nstatiun hna?
We need a mechanic.	khesna wahed lmikanisyan
The car broke down at ...	tumubeel khasra f ...
I have a flat tyre.	'ndi pyasa fruida

TRAVEL WITH CHILDREN

I need a car with a child seat.
bgheet wahed ttomobeel belkorsee dyal draree sghar?
Are there facilities for babies?
wesh kayn tsheelat dyal ddraree sghar?
I'm travelling with my family.
ana msafer m'a l'alla dyalee
Is it suitable for children?
wesh mnaseb l draree sghar?
Are there any activities for children?
wesh kayn shee tansheet dyal draree sghar?
Are children allowed?
wesh mesmuh l draree?
Is there a playground nearby?
wesh kayn shee ssaha dyal ll'eb qreeba?

BERBER

There are three main dialects commonly delineated among the speakers of Berber, which in a certain sense also serve as loose lines of ethnic demarcation.

In the north, in the area centred on the Rif, the locals speak a dialect that has been called Riffian and is spoken as far south as Figuig on the Algerian frontier. The dialect that predominates in the Middle and High Atlas and the valleys leading into the Sahara goes by various names, including Braber or Amazigh.

More settled tribes of the High Atlas, Anti Atlas, Souss Valley and southwestern oases generally speak Tashelhit or Chleuh. The following phrases are a selection from the Tashelhit dialect, the one visitors are likely to find most useful.

CONVERSATION & ESSENTIALS

Hello.	la bes darik (m)
	la bes darim (f)
Hello. (response)	la bes
Goodbye.	akayaoon arbee
Please.	barakalaufik
Thank you.	barakalaufik
Yes.	yah
No.	oho
Excuse me.	samhiy
How are you?	meneek antgeet?
Fine, thank you.	la bes, lhamdulah
Good.	eefulkee/eeshwa
Bad.	(khaib) eeghshne
See you later.	akranwes daghr
Is there ...?	ees eela ...?
big	mqorn
small	eemzee
today	(zig sbah) rass
tomorrow	(ghasad) aska
yesterday	eedgam
Do you have ...?	ees daroon ...?
a lot	bzef
a little	eemeek
food	teeremt
mule	aserdon
somewhere to sleep	kra lblast mahengane
water	arman
How much is it?	minshk aysker?
no good	oor eefulkee
too expensive	eeghla
Give me ...	fky ...
I want ...	reegh ...

NUMBERS

1	yen
2	seen
3	krad

4	*koz*
5	*smoos*
6	*sddes*
7	*sa*
8	*tem*
9	*tza*
10	*mrawet*
11	*yen d mrawet*
12	*seen d mrawet*
20	*ashreent*
21	*ashreent d yen d mrawet*
22	*ashreent d seen d mrawet*
30	*ashreent d mrawet*
40	*snet id ashreent*

50	*snet id ashreent d mrawet*
100	*smoost id ashreent/meeya*

TRANSPORT

I want to go to ...	*addowghs ...*
Where is (the) ...?	*mani gheela ...?*
village	*doorwar*
river	*aseef*
mountain	*adrar*
the pass	*tizee*
Is it near/far?	*ees eeqareb/yagoog?*
straight	*neeshan*
to the right	*fofasee*
to the left	*fozelmad*

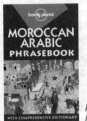

Also available from Lonely Planet:
Moroccan Arabic Phrasebook

LANGUAGE

Glossary

This glossary is a list of Arabic (A), Berber (B), French (F) and Spanish (S) terms that are used throughout this guide. For a list of trekking terms, see Words To Trek By, p410. For food-related terms see Eat Your Words, p76.

agadir (B) – fortified communal granary
'ain (A) – water source, spring
aït (B) – family (of), often precedes tribal and town names
Al-Andalus – Muslim Spain and Portugal
Alawite – hereditary dynasty that has ruled Morocco since the late 17th century
Allah (A) – God
Almohads – puritanical Muslim group (1147–1269), originally Berber, that arose in response to the corrupt Almoravid dynasty
Almoravids – Muslim group (1054–1147) that ruled Spain and the Maghreb
assif (A) – watercourse, river

bab (A) – gate
babouches (F) – traditional leather slippers
banu (A) – see *beni*
baraka (A) – divine blessing or favour
Barbary – European term used to describe the North African coast from the 16th to the 19th centuries
ben (A) – (or ibn) son of
bendir (B) – single-headed Berber drum
beni (A) – 'sons of', often precedes tribal name (also *banu*)
Berbers – indigenous inhabitants of North Africa
bidonville (F) – slum area, especially in Casablanca
borj (A) – fort (literally, 'tower')
brigade touristique (F) – tourist police
bureau de guide (F) – guides' office
burnous' (A) – warm woollen cloak with hood

caliph – successor of Mohammed; ruler of the Islamic world
calle (S) – street
camarade (F) – West-African migrant
camionette (F) – minivan or pick-up truck
capitol – main temple of Roman town, usually situated in the forum
caravanserai – large merchants' inn enclosing a courtyard, providing accommodation and a marketplace (see also *funduq*)
casa de huéspedes (S) – guesthouse
chergui (A) – dry, easterly desert wind

Compagnie de Transports Marocaine – CTM; national bus company
corniche (F) – coastal road
corsairs – 18th-century pirate bands based at Salé

dar (A) – traditional town house
Délégation Régionale du Tourisme – tourist office
douar (A) – generally used for 'village' in the High Atlas
douche (F) – public showers (see *hammam*)

Eaux et Forêts – government ministry responsible for national parks
eid (A) – feast
Ensemble Artisanal – government handicraft shop
erg (A) – sand dunes

fantasia (S) – military exercise featuring a cavalry charge, now performed for tourists
Fatimids – Muslim dynasty that rose to prominence in the 10th century
faux guides (F) – unofficial or informal guides
foum (A) – usually mouth of a river or valley (from Arabic for 'mouth')
frontera (S) – border
funduq (A) – caravanserai (often used to mean 'hotel')

gîte, gîte d'étape (F) – trekkers' hostel, sometimes a home stay
gardiens de voitures (F) – car park attendants
gare routière (F) – bus station
ghassoul (A) – type of clay mixed with herbs, dried roses and lavender used in *hammams* for removing grease and washing hair
glaoua (A) – rug with combination of flat weave and deep fluffy pile (also *zanafi*)
Gnaoua – bluesy Moroccan musical form that began with freed slaves in Marrakesh and Essaouira
grand taxi (F) – (long-distance) shared taxi

haj (A) – pilgrimage to Mecca, hence 'haji' or 'hajia', a male or female who has made the pilgrimage
halqa (A) – street theatre
hammada (A) – stony desert
hammam (A) – Turkish-style bathhouse with sauna and massage, also known by the French word *bain* (bath) or *bain maure* (Moorish bath)
hanbel (A) – see *kilim*
haram (A) – literally 'forbidden', the word is sometimes used to denote a sacred or forbidden area, such as the prayer room of a mosque

Hejira – flight of the Prophet from Mecca to Medina in AD 622; the first year of the Islamic calendar

ibn (A) – son of (see also *ben*)
Idrissids (A) – Moroccan dynasty that established a stable state in northern Morocco in the 9th century
iftar (A) – breaking of the fast at sundown during Ramadan; breakfast (also *'ftur'*)
imam (A) – Muslim cleric
Interzone – name coined by author William Burroughs for the period 1923–56, when Tangier was controlled by nine countries
irifi (A) – dry, desert wind, also called *chergui*

jami' (A) – Friday mosque (also *djemaa, jemaa* and *jamaa*)
jebel (A) – hill, mountain (sometimes *djebel* in former French possessions)
jedid (A) – new (sometimes spelled *jdid*)
jellaba (A) – popular flowing garment; men's jellabas are usually made from cotton or wool, while women's come in light synthetic fabrics

kasbah (A) – fort, citadel; often also the administrative centre (also *qasba*)
khutba – Friday sermon preached by the imam of a mosque
kif (A) – marijuana
kilim (A) – flat-woven blankets or floor coverings (also *hanbel*)
koubba (A) – sanctuary or shrine (see also *marabout*)
ksar (A) – fort or fortified stronghold (plural ksour)

Maghreb (A) – (literally 'west') area covered by Morocco, Algeria, Tunisia and Libya
maison d'hôtes (F) – guest house, often a restored traditional Moroccan house
majoun (A) – sticky paste made of crushed seeds of the marijuana plant
marabout – holy man or saint; also often used to describe the mausoleums of these men
masjid (A) – another name for a mosque, particularly in a *medersa* (see also *jami'*)
mechouar (A) – royal assembly place
medersa (A) – college for teaching theology, law, Arabic literature and grammar (also *madrassa*)
medina (A) – old city; used to describe the old Arab parts of modern towns and cities
mellah (A) – Jewish quarter of the medina
mendeel (A) – brightly coloured striped cloth
Merenids (A) – Moroccan dynasty (1269–1465), responsible for the construction of many of Morocco's *medersas*
mihrab (A) – prayer niche in the wall of a mosque indicating the direction of Mecca (the *qibla*)

minbar (A) – pulpit in mosque; the imam delivers the sermon from one of the lower steps because the Prophet preached from the top step
moulay (A) – ruler
Mouloud – Islamic festival period celebrating the birth of the Prophet
moussem (A) – pilgrimage to *marabout* tomb; festival in honour of a *marabout*
muezzin (A) – mosque official who sings the call to prayer from the minaret
muqarna (A) – decorative plasterwork
musée (F) – museum

ONMT – Office National Marocain du Tourisme, national tourist body, sometimes called Délégation Régionale du Tourisme
ordinaire (F) – less comfortable train, slightly slower than a *rapide*
oued (A) – riverbed, often dry (sometimes wad or wadi)
oulad (A) – sons (of), often precedes tribal or town name

palais de justice (F) – law court
palmeraie (F) – palm grove
pastilla – a rich, savoury-sweet chicken or pigeon pie made with fine pastry; a dish of layered pastry with cinnamon and almonds served as dessert at banquets
pasha – high official in Ottoman Empire (also *pacha*)
petit taxi (F) – local taxi
pisé (F) – building material made of sun-dried clay or mud
piste (F) – unsealed tracks, often requiring 4WD vehicles
place (F) – square, plaza
plage (F) – beach
pressing (F) – laundry
Prophet (Mohammed), the – founder of Islam, who lived between AD 570 and AD 632

qaid (A) – local chief, loose equivalent of mayor in some parts of Morocco (also *caid*)
qibla (A) – the direction of Mecca, indicated by a *mihrab*
qissaria (A) – covered market sometimes forming the commercial centre of a *medina*
Quran – sacred book of Islam

Ramadan (A) – ninth month of the Muslim year, a period of fasting
rapide (F) – type of train more comfortable and slightly faster than an *ordinaire*
Reconquista (S) – the Christian reconquest of the Iberian peninsula from the Moors
refuge (F) – mountain hut, basic hikers' shelter
riad (A) – traditional town house set around an internal garden
ribat (A) – combined monastery and fort

Saadians – Moroccan dynasty that ruled in the 16th century

sharia (A) – street

sharia'a (A) – Islamic law

shedwi (A) – flat-woven rug of black and white bands

sherif (A) – descendant of the Prophet

Shiites – one of two main Islamic sects, formed by those who believed the true imams were descended from the Prophet's son-in-law Ali (see also *Sunnis*)

sidi (A) – honorific (equivalent to 'Mr'; also *si*)

skala (A) – fortress

ski randonnée (F) – ski trekking

souq hebdomadaire (F/A) – weekly market

souq (A) – market

Sufism – mystical strand of Islam that emphasises communion with God through inner attitude

Sunnis – one of two main Islamic sects, derived from followers of the Umayyad caliphate (see also *Shiites*)

Syndicat d'Initiative (F) – government-run tourist office

tabac (F) – tobacconist and newsagency

tadelakt (A) – waterproof lime plaster mixed with pigments and polished with a stone to give it a smooth, lustrous finish, originally used for the walls of *hammams* but now a favourite of interior designers

tariq (A) – road, avenue

téléboutique (F) – privately operated telephone service

télécarte (F) – phonecard

terz Fezzi (A) – intricate geometric embroidery originating in Fès

tizi (B) – mountain pass

Tuareg – nomadic Berbers of the Sahara, also known as the Blue Men because of their indigo-dyed robes

ville nouvelle (F) – new city; town built by the French alongside existing towns

vizier – another term for a provincial governor in Ottoman Empire, or adviser to the sultan in Morocco

wali (A) – Islamic holy man or saint

Wattasids – Moroccan dynasty (mid-15th to mid-16th centuries)

zawiya (A) – religious fraternity based around a *marabout*; location of the fraternity (also *zaouia*)

zellij (A) – ceramic tilework used to decorate buildings

Behind the Scenes

THIS BOOK

This 8th edition of Morocco was researched and written by Anthony Ham (coordinating author), Alison Bing, Paul Clammer, Etain O'Carroll and Anthony Sattin. The 7th edition was the work of Paula Hardy, Mara Vorhees and Heidi Edsall, and the 6th edition was the work of Bradley Mayhew and Jan Dodd. The Health chapter of the 7th and 8th editions was based on text written by Dr Caroline Evans; it was updated for this edition by Paul Clammer.

This guidebook was commissioned in Lonely Planet's Melbourne office, and produced by the following:

Commissioning Editors Kerryn Burgess, Stefanie Di Trocchio
Coordinating Editor David Carroll
Coordinating Cartographers Joshua Geoghegan, Jacqueline Nguyen
Coordinating Layout Designer Carol Jackson
Managing Cartographer David Connolly
Assisting Editors Janice Bird, Emma Gilmour, Rowan McKinnon, Alison Ridgway, Simon Williamson
Assisting Layout Designers Clara Monitto, Wibowo Rusli
Cover Designer Rebecca Dandens
Project Manager Sarah Sloane
Managing Editor Brigitte Ellemor
Language Content Coordinator Quentin Frayne

Thanks to David Burnett, Sin Choo, Sally Darmody, Jennifer Garrett, Pablo Gastar, Mark Germanchis, Jim Hsu, Chris Lee Ack, Raphael Richards, Celia Wood

THANKS
ANTHONY HAM

A big thank you to Kerryn Burgess at Lonely Planet who is always a pleasure to work with, and to all my co-authors who made my job so easy; particular thanks to Etain for her wise suggestions for the Women Travellers section. A special thank you to Jan whose passion for Morocco carried me around my first Moroccan journey, and to Marina whose understanding of my all-night work sessions as deadlines near is one reason among countless why I thank my lucky stars I married you.

ALISON BING

Shukran bezzef to star editors Kerryn Burgess, Marg Toohey and Anthony Ham; my parents, Tony and June Bing, for the Morocco trip that started it all; and Marco Flavio Marinucci, the ultimate Rumi replacement.

PAUL CLAMMER

At Lonely Planet, thanks to Kerryn Burgess for sending me back to Morocco, and to Judy Slatyer and Stefanie Di Trocchio who were such amiable 'shadows' accompanying me on the road. Thanks to Carolyn Hunt for helpful hints. In Fès, a big glass of pomegranate juice to Jen and Sebastian. A sticky *marakchia* is due to Jillian York. Thanks also to Cezarina Jaussoin. Nick Cave's *Opium Tea* was an unlikely Moroccan inspiration. Finally, thanks and love to Jo, who got to taste a different part of Morocco this time.

THE LONELY PLANET STORY

The story begins with a classic travel adventure: Tony and Maureen Wheeler's 1972 journey across Europe and Asia to Australia. There was no useful information about the overland trail then, so Tony and Maureen published the first Lonely Planet guidebook to meet a growing need.

From a kitchen table, Lonely Planet has grown to become the largest independent travel publisher in the world, with offices in Melbourne (Australia), Oakland (USA) and London (UK). Today Lonely Planet guidebooks cover the globe. There is an ever-growing list of books and information in a variety of media. Some things haven't changed. The main aim is still to make it possible for adventurous travellers to get out there – to explore and better understand the world.

At Lonely Planet we believe travellers can make a positive contribution to the countries they visit – if they respect their host communities and spend their money wisely. Every year 5% of company profit is donated to charities around the world.

ETAIN O'CARROLL

Thanks to Mustapha and Simohamed in Casa for conversation, excellent food and a tour of Casa's hottest nightspots, to the staff at Azayla in Asilah for all their help and advice and to Bousselham Laarichi in Moulay Bousselham for the local low-down. Thanks also to Hafidia Shaiti and Nida, both in El-Jadida, and to Lisa and Séan for company and a few laughs on the last leg of the journey. Finally huge thanks to the ever-tolerant Mark who withstood the fallout from clashing deadlines and crashing computers.

ANTHONY SATTIN

As ever, many people made the travel and re-search both easier and more enjoyable, foremost among them being my partner Sylvie Franquet. In Morocco, many thanks to the directors and staff in tourist offices in Marrakech, Agadir and elsewhere, to super-guide Mohamed Aztat, Abdel Khalek Benalila and Beaubeau, Aniko Boehler, Damian Breen, Bert Fint, Kadir Guiray, Kamal Laft-imi and Laetitia Trouillet, Damien and Bénédicte Lecire and Azilal, Meryanne Loum-Martin and Gary Martin, Mike McHugo, Rosena McKeown, Lynn Perez, Catherine Rophé and Ahmed Agouni, and Regina Tongola. In the UK, thanks to Ali el Kasmi, Aziz Mnii and the staff of the Moroccan Tourist Office. Mike Wynne of Walks Worldwide and Hamish Brown of the Atlas Mountains Infor-mation Service. Thanks to all at Lonely Planet, especially commissioning editors Kerryn Burgess and Stefanie Di Trocchio, fellow authors Anthony Ham, Paul Clammer and Alison Bing, and map guru Shahara Ahmed.

OUR READERS

Many thanks to the travellers who used the last edition and wrote to us with helpful hints, useful advice and interesting anecdotes:

A Regina Abt, Samer Ali, Pranit Anard, C Elizabeth Anderson, Kathryn Anderson, Rachel Andrich, Lorna Saint Ange, Pranit Arand, Mark Aubort, Joshua Asen **B** Anne Backhaus, Simon Bagguley, Pat & Alan Barcroft, Jan, Elaine & Jandri Barnard, John Barrington, Ann Barry, Claire Beadnell, Ethan Beck, Tom Beer, Erik Berg, Landis Black, Fleur Blake, Cecile Blanchot, Florence Blondet, Brian W Boag, Tony Bostock, Andy Brabant, Lowdy Brabyn, Perdita Brown, Jane Buckler, Jacki Burgess, Lisa Butterworth **C** Lucy Campbell, Michele Campbell, Alan Cane, Roger Carland, Josh Ben Chabat, Catherine Chapdelaine, Simon Chapman, Marian Chase, Brian Chatterton, Brent Chippendale, Frances Coad, Heather Cobain, Phil Cody, Shirley Connuck, Paula Constant, Carlos Correia, Robert Cotter, Jenny Cove, Chris Coy, Joanne Crawford, David Cumming, Barbara Curchmar, Kirsty Currier **D** Ruth & Ruben Dahm, Karinna Damo, Rodriguez

Dani, Nick Daniels, Loc Dao, Chantelle Davies, Emily Davis, Kasper de Rooy, Jean-Philippe de Visscher, Annemieke Dekker, Sandro Della-Mea, Adam Dewey, Zinabe Dina, Bojan Dolinar, Graham Dowden, Justin Drerup, Heather Dunn Randall, Annette Dubois **E** Patricia Ellish, Richard Elliot, Steve Emms, Bettina Esquinazi **F** Theodor Fehr, Patrik Ferkl, Matthias Fichtenbauer, Katrin Flatscher, Jesse Fleming, Deryn Fletcher, Ellen Foucher, Fayette Fox, Rebecca Frost **G** Rebecca Gardiner, Adrian Gatton, Felix Gerl, A Gilbert, Arthur P Goldberg, Maria Gonzalez-Beato, Julien Greboval, Debbie Guest **H** Susanna Hajdu, Joanneke Heineman, Roel Heinen, Norah Henry, Tieme Hermans, Patricia Hiss, Anya Hocking, John Hodgens, Aubrey Hruby, Russell Huntington, Menno Hurenkamp **I** Lelkes Ibolya, Robert Ishida **J** Kylie Jane, Gwen Janke, Rebecca Jarvis, Ernst Johansen, Jennifer Johnson, Roopali Johri, Genevieve Jordan **K** Sebastian Kalliomaki, Barbara & Andy Kane, Julie Kawasaki, Nagesh Kelkar, Alison Kelly, Pavel Koberský, Maja Kolšek, Jon Kramer, Melanie Kramers, Neil Kreeger, Karl Krisiulevicius, Tasha Kruit, Brett Kuhnert **L** Shepherd Laughlin, Mark Le May, Rebecca Leathlean, Ruben Lelivelt, Rebecca Letven, Johann & Riana Ligthart, Andy Linderman, Jeroen Louwers, Sebastian Luning, Eric Luschen, Julian Lyne-Pirkis **M** Jeri MacDonald, Andres Mariani, Corrine Mayes, Seamus McAtee, Ali Mcgovern, Hugh Mcguire, Siobahn McIntosh, Alex Mckay, Daniel Mesnage, David Middle, Chris Morton, Margaret Moser, Ian Munro, Lisa Murray **N** Arti Nadkarni, Bernice Nair, Brigitta Negru, Diana Neuner, Stuart Newman, Allison Noffsinger **O** Christian Oberdanner, Nils Odins, Nancy Omlid, Daniele Oudinot **P** Angela Parlane, Doris Paulus, David Pavey, Liz Paxton, Jasmin Philipp, Kim Pronk **R** Jacob Rawel, Mishal Razak, Peter Reed, Kieren Reeks, Niall

---

SEND US YOUR FEEDBACK

We love to hear from travellers – your com-ments keep us on our toes and help make our books better. Our well-travelled team reads every word on what you loved or loathed about this book. Although we can-not reply individually to postal submissions, we always guarantee that your feedback goes straight to the appropriate authors, in time for the next edition. Each person who sends us information is thanked in the next edition – and the most useful submissions are rewarded with a free book.

To send us your updates – and find out about Lonely Planet events, newsletters and travel news – visit our award-winning web-site: **www.lonelyplanet.com/contact**.

Note: We may edit, reproduce and incorp-orate your comments in Lonely Planet prod-ucts such as guidebooks, websites and digital products, so let us know if you don't want your comments reproduced or your name acknowledged. For a copy of our privacy policy visit www.lonelyplanet.com/privacy.

Riddell, Dan Robertson, Laura Rosser, Wouter Rutten **S** Mauricio Santana, Robert Frank Sargent, Judy Schadt, Justus Schnellbacher, Martine Schout, Marvin & Trish Scott, Barret Sebastien, Noah Segal, Marco Simons, John Simpson,Duncan Snidal, Peter Sperling, Jonas Spriestersbach, Ken Stanton, Charlie Steel, Neil Stewart, Alice Stori, Mark Street, Barbara Streicher, Laurie Streitberg **T** Chris Taylor, David Taylor, Meg Taylor, Jane Thakker, Cora Thompson, Jerry Tilley, Mark Tissot, Alan Toal, Umberto Trinchero,Kazuhiro Tsui, David Tungate, Sibylle Tura **U** Lars Unhjem **V** Suzanne Vallance, Johan van den Heuvel,

Muriel van der Kuip, Ernst van der Pasch, Mieke & Peter van Stipdonk, Brigitte van Weele, Paulina Vegt, Manuel Villanueva, Clesio Villela, Victoria Vine, Jennifer Vivers, Jeff Vogel, Sibylle Vogel **W** Marc Wancer, Mikie Wartelle, Shenika Watlington, Lauren Weeth, Don Weimer, Ellen Weiser, Beany Wezelman, Rose Wheeler, Frances Whitaker, Rob & Ali Wilton, Lennart Wingelaar, Klaus Winterling, Thomas Wolters, John Worzencraft, Stefaan Wuyts **Y** Jillian York, Amanda Young, Andrew Youngson **Z** Daniele Zanchetta, Andreas Zellhuber, Sandra Zwollo

Index

INDEX

000 Map pages
000 Photograph pages

INDEX

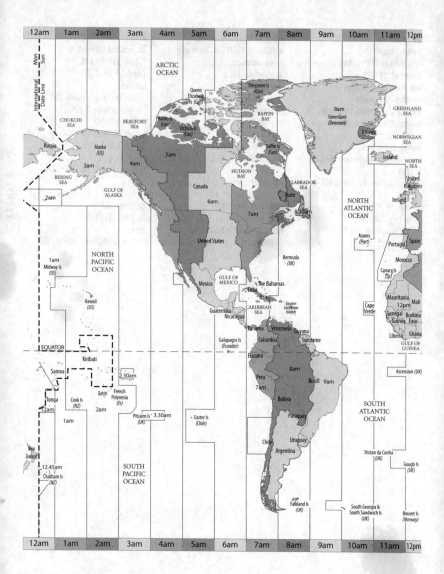

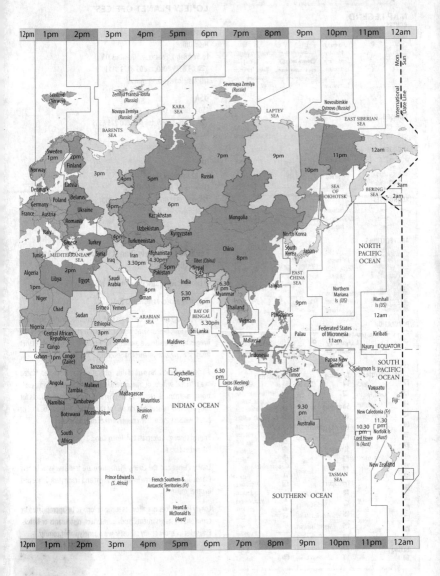

MAP LEGEND

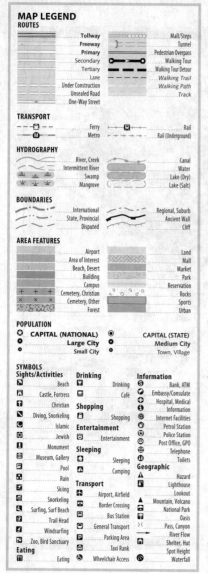

ROUTES

Tollway	Mall/Steps
Freeway	Tunnel
Primary	Pedestrian Overpass
Secondary	Walking Tour
Tertiary	Walking Tour Detour
Lane	Walking Trail
Under Construction	Walking Path
Unsealed Road	Track
One-Way Street	

TRANSPORT

Ferry	Rail
Metro	Rail (Underground)

HYDROGRAPHY

River, Creek	Canal
Intermittent River	Water
Swamp	Lake (Dry)
Mangrove	Lake (Salt)

BOUNDARIES

International	Regional, Suburb
State, Provincial	Ancient Wall
Disputed	Cliff

AREA FEATURES

Airport	Land
Area of Interest	Mall
Beach, Desert	Market
Building	Park
Campus	Reservation
Cemetery, Christian	Rocks
Cemetery, Other	Sports
Forest	Urban

POPULATION

◎ CAPITAL (NATIONAL)	◉ CAPITAL (STATE)
● Large City	● Medium City
○ Small City	○ Town, Village

SYMBOLS

Sights/Activities
- Beach
- Castle, Fortress
- Christian
- Diving, Snorkeling
- Islamic
- Jewish
- Monument
- Museum, Gallery
- Pool
- Ruin
- Skiing
- Snorkeling
- Surfing, Surf Beach
- Trail Head
- Windsurfing
- Zoo, Bird Sanctuary

Eating
- Eating

Drinking
- Drinking
- Café

Shopping
- Shopping

Entertainment
- Entertainment

Sleeping
- Sleeping
- Camping

Transport
- Airport, Airfield
- Border Crossing
- Bus Station
- General Transport
- Parking Area
- Taxi Rank
- Wheelchair Access

Information
- Bank, ATM
- Embassy/Consulate
- Hospital, Medical
- Information
- Internet Facilities
- Petrol Station
- Police Station
- Post Office, GPO
- Telephone
- Toilets

Geographic
- Hazard
- Lighthouse
- Lookout
- Mountain, Volcano
- National Park
- Oasis
- Pass, Canyon
- River Flow
- Shelter, Hut
- Spot Height
- Waterfall

LONELY PLANET OFFICES

Australia
Head Office
Locked Bag 1, Footscray, Victoria 3011
☎ 03 8379 8000, fax 03 8379 8111
talk2us@lonelyplanet.com.au

USA
150 Linden St, Oakland, CA 94607
☎ 510 893 8555, toll free 800 275 8555
fax 510 893 8572
info@lonelyplanet.com

UK
72–82 Rosebery Ave,
Clerkenwell, London EC1R 4RW
☎ 020 7841 9000, fax 020 7841 9001
go@lonelyplanet.co.uk

Published by Lonely Planet Publications Pty Ltd
ABN 36 005 607 983

© Lonely Planet Publications Pty Ltd 2007

© photographers as indicated 2007

Cover photograph by Getty Images: Morocco, Tifoultoutte, shepherd carrying lamb, barren slope behind, Sylvain Grandadam. Many of the images in this guide are available for licensing from Lonely Planet Images: www.lonelyplanetimages.com.

Printed through Colorcraft Ltd, Hong Kong.
Printed in China

Although the authors and Lonely Planet have taken all reasonable care in preparing this book, we make no warranty about the accuracy or completeness of its content and, to the maximum extent permitted, disclaim all liability arising from its use.